THE INTERACTIVE CASEBOOK SERIES™

TORTS

A Contemporary Approach

SECOND EDITION

By

Meredith J. Duncan
GEORGE BUTLER RESEARCH PROFESSOR OF LAW
UNIVERSITY OF HOUSTON LAW CENTER

and

Ronald Turner
ALUMNAE LAW CENTER PROFESSOR OF LAW
UNIVERSITY OF HOUSTON LAW CENTER

WEST®

A Thomson Reuters business

Mat #41244605

Interactive Casebook Series is a trademark registered in the U.S. Patent and Trademark Office.

© 2010 Thomson Reuters
© 2012 Thomson Reuters
  610 Opperman Drive
  St. Paul, MN 55123
  1–800–313–9378

Printed in the United States of America

ISBN: 978–0–314–28023–7

For Curtis, Graham, Schaeffer, Mom, and Dad.

MJD

For Kadi, Ron, and Mom.

RT

Acknowledgements

We are very grateful for the support of our many family members, friends, and colleagues without whose support this project would not have been possible. In particular, we thank: Hillary Valderrama (research assistant extraordinaire) as well as Ysa Rodriguez, Misty McDonald, Alexander Morningstar, Paul Kim, and Casey O'Neill for their excellent research efforts; Sandra M. Jackson, our tireless administrative assistant, and Chanquilla Gordon, Lauren Ferguson, and Ivette Rodriguez; the University of Houston Law Center and the University of Houston Law Foundation; Louis Higgins for his patience, wisdom, professionalism, and terrific advice; and the hardworking and patient staff at Red Line Editorial.

Table of Contents

Table of Cases

The principal cases are in bold type. Cases cited or discussed in the text are roman type. References are to pages. Cases cited in principal cases and within other quoted materials are not included.

Preface

This casebook is designed to facilitate the learning and teaching process of the 21st century. We hope that you will find its unique features helpful to your study of tort law.

A. Text Boxes

Throughout this text, you will notice various call-out boxes filled with useful information and set apart from the main part of the text of the book. These various boxes are designed to deepen your understanding of the materials presented throughout this casebook.

Text Box Categories

 What's That? These boxes will contain information about particular legal terms used in the main text. Where appropriate, terms will be hyperlinked to their definitions in *Black's Law Dictionary*.

 Take Note These callout boxes will seek to draw your attention to special topics of interest in the cases.

 Food for Thought Information in these boxes is designed to exercise your critical thinking skills and deepen your understanding of the materials.

 Make the Connection The information in these boxes will seek to have you connect and apply concepts from other sections of this course or from other law school courses.

 FYI These boxes will contain and inform you of interesting material.

 Practice Pointers These boxes will point out practical applications and pointers in an effort to connect what you are learning to the practice of law.

 It's Latin to Me Latin phrases will often be identified and interpreted, frequently being hyperlinked to more complete definitions in *Black's Law Dictionary*.

 Go Online Information in these boxes will direct you to various online resources with relevant or interesting information pertaining to the materials.

For More Information Information in these boxes will direct you to additional resources concerning the particular subject matter.

 See It The materials in these boxes designate visual materials such as photos, maps, diagrams, or other interesting visual materials.

 Major Themes The information in these callout boxes will assist you in connecting the broader concepts presented from chapter to chapter.

 Behind the Scenes The information in these boxes will provide background information or historical context concerning the primary cases.

B. Electronic Casebook with Hyperlinks

One of the most unique features of this casebook is that its contents are available electronically, enabling you to search throughout this casebook with ease as well as make use of the many hyperlinks and other resources electronically embedded throughout:

1. Case Names

Case names are hyperlinked to electronic versions of the cases in their entirety. Where available, clicking on the case names will lead you to the text of the case as it is available on Westlaw.

Older opinions or law review articles that do not appear on Westlaw will be linked to other electronic sources, where available.

2. Legal Terminology

Many legal terms and phrases are hyperlinked to definitions found in *Black's Law Dictionary*. When using the electronic version of this casebook, terms appearing in bold throughout the text will provide the *Black's Law Dictionary* definition when placing your cursor over the words.

3. Online Materials

Electronic versions of various online materials are hyperlinked as well.

4. Names of Jurists

Hyperlinks to names of justices and judges will lead you to biographical or other interesting information about the jurists involved in the court's decision or the law's development.

5. Court Websites

Where available, courts will be hyperlinked to their corresponding websites.

6. Internal Cross-References

These links will lead readers to additional places throughout this casebook that also address or discuss the relevant linked material.

C. Case Excerpts

As is true with most other legal casebooks, the primary cases in this text are edited. The text appearing throughout this book is excerpted from court decisions. The purpose of omitting portions of a court's opinion is to maintain your focus on the primary lessons taught by inclusion of the opinion at the point in the casebook at which it appears. Throughout this text, "[c]" indicates the omission of one citation, whereas "[Cc]" or "[cc]" indicates the omission of multiple citations. An ellipsis ("…") indicates the omission of textual material. Four periods ("….") indicates the omission of one or more full paragraphs. "[¶]" indicates the elimination of a carriage return at the beginning of a new paragraph.

Of course, the entire content of the courts' opinions are accessible elsewhere, and the hyperlink of the case names throughout this text will take you to an electronic version of the case in its entirety. In those instances where the cases are not available online at Westlaw, the hyperlink will connect you to an alternative electronic version of the case when available.

D. Discussion Points and Hypotheticals

Part of the challenge of law school and practicing law is never being presented with the same set of facts twice. It is vital to learning and practicing law that one be able to apply the law to a variety of differing factual situations. With that in mind, you will find throughout this book various points for discussion as well as hypotheticals designed to exercise your brain by applying the law that you are learning to different factual settings.

E. Perspective and Analysis

Scholarly and other commentary on subjects addressed in this casebook will be presented. Evaluate and critique the perspectives and views expressed and consider whether you agree or disagree with the posited perspective. If you disagree with the proposition or analysis, develop and be prepared to articulate the grounds and rationales supporting your disagreement.

Briefing a Case

In law school, you will likely read hundreds of cases. It is important to your study in any subject that you comprehend the purpose for which you are reading a case and the lesson(s) to be learned from its reading. The most effective way to accomplish this is to do what is commonly referred to in law school as "briefing" a case. When done diligently and properly, you will find briefing cases to be an effective way to manage the voluminous amount of material that you are required to read, a useful class time resource, and an effective study aid. Common components of a case brief include:

1. **Case Name** – the names of the parties and their alignment in the case

2. **Legally Relevant Facts** – a very brief recitation of the legally relevant facts, those facts necessary to the court's decision of the legal issues

3. **Procedural Posture** – a brief description of how the case arrived at the court authoring the opinion

4. **Issue(s)** – the precise legal issue(s) that the court is deciding that is relevant to the placement of the case in the casebook at the point that it appears

5. **Holding** – an explanation of who prevailed and the court's disposition of the case

6. **Reasoning** – a brief explanation of the court's reasoning

7. **Concurrence(s)/Dissent(s)** – reasoning of concurring or dissenting judge(s), if any

8. **Legal Lesson(s)** – the legal standards, rules, and lessons to be learned by the placement of the case in the casebook where it appears

For additional information, *see* Professor Orin S. Kerr's guide, "How to Read a Legal Opinion."

CHAPTER 1

Introduction and Overview

A. Introduction to Tort Law

1. Purpose and Sources of Tort Law

This casebook is devoted to the subject of tort law. Tort law provides a legal cause of action providing injured individuals and entities recovery for wrongs committed against them resulting in injury to their person or property. The word "**tort**" derives from the Latin word "*tortus*" meaning "twisted." Many years ago, the word "tort" was commonly used in England as a synonym for "wrong." Today, tort law provides civil redress for personal or property injuries caused by another's wrongful actions. However, not every personal or property injury sustained is compensable in tort. Likewise, not every scoundrel or person causing an injury to another or to another's property is subject to tort liability.

Tort law permits recovery for personal or property injuries resulting from civil wrongs, other than those arising from a breach of contract. Unlike contract law (which generally seeks to restore a person to the position in which he would have been if the contract been fully or properly performed), the primary purpose of tort law is to restore a wrongfully injured person to his or her pre-injury status, as much as it is possible to do so. Most often, a tort remedy is monetary, although other remedies, such as injunctive relief, may be available and appropriate.

Make the Connection

Tort law pertains to civil actions, as contrasted with criminal actions. A criminal action typically involves the government prosecuting a member of society for violating the penal laws, legislatively-enacted statutes defining criminal conduct. Criminal actions are brought by the government on behalf of the citizens of a jurisdiction. In contrast, civil actions are typically brought by individual members of society, not by the government on behalf of all citizens.

Tort law is a fertile arena of social theories, policy considerations, and reflections of current (and contested) morality. Contemporary societal, economic, and political forces and attitudes may affect tort law. Balancing the need to encourage socially useful or beneficial behavior against the need to deter harmful conduct is a complicated endeavor. When an innocent person is injured through no fault of her own, providing a system by which she can be compensated for her injuries is something our society values. However, society may want to encourage some risky behavior that in the long run benefits society overall, particularly when those engaged in the behavior can more easily pass along the cost of the injuries they cause to those who benefit most from those risks being taken. Further, society may value a system by which the moral balance may be restored between one innocently injured and one causing the injury or a system by which people can express their collective outrage against big business or the government. Simply put, in tort law policy matters and in large part drives the various contours of the law from jurisdiction to jurisdiction.

For More Information

Kenneth S. Abraham's THE FORMS AND FUNCTIONS OF TORT LAW (Foundation Press 2002) provides a wonderful exploration of many of these policy considerations.

Tort law permeates many aspects of our lives and is a fascinating area of the law. Oft-debated tort law considerations might include:

- Should a person who has been injured either intentionally or accidently be compensated by one causing the injuries?

- Must a drug manufacturer developing and producing many valuable pharmaceuticals be required to compensate for all injuries caused by the use of one of its drugs?

- Should a wrongfully injured person be permitted to recover for her mental or emotional injuries? If so, how should mental or emotional injuries be measured? Should recovery for these types of injuries be limited?

- How should the availability of insurance affect one's ability to recover in tort?

Throughout your study of tort law, remember to read critically; consider more than just what the words of a court's opinion reveal. Rather, carefully evaluate the stated – and sometimes unstated – policy driving a court's decision. After all, you are not only studying the law as a student; you are in training to be an influential participant within the legal system, one who will hopefully have an opportunity to shape the future of the law. Therefore, do not just seek to learn the "rules" of tort law or any law for that matter. Evaluate whether the law as it exists today (or existed in the past) makes sense for our society today and whether, if you could fashion the law in any way you wished, you would shape the law differently.

Perspective and Analysis

For recent exploration of these and other tort issues, *see, e.g.*, John C.P. Goldberg, *Ten Half-Truths About Tort Law*, 42 VAL. U. L. REV. 1221 (2008) (providing an exposition of conventional wisdom of tort law professors teaching tort law); Joanna M. Shepherd, *Tort Reforms' Winners and Losers: The Competing Effects of Care and Activity Levels*, 55 U.C.L.A. L. REV. 905 (2008) (analyzing relationship between medical malpractice tort reforms and death rates); Michael D. Scott, *Tort Liability for Vendors of Insecure Software: Has the Time Finally Come?*, 67 MD. L. REV. 425 (2008) (arguing for tort system sanctions as means of encouraging software vendors to produce safer product).

---

2. Brief History of Tort Law

Our tort system originated in the old **common law** writ system of England. The writ system was a scheme by which members of society who had been injured or harmed by another could seek redress.   Crime was rampant in late medieval England. Due to limited resources to deal with criminal

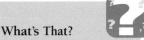

What's That?

The common law is a system by which non-statutory, non-constitutional law develops by judicial opinion.

conduct, English courts developed a system by which citizens were encouraged to deter such conduct by bringing their own private rights of action. Although criminal in origin, individuals seeking redress for wrongs committed against them by others were permitted to produce a writ, a special form identifying the specific nature of the wrongful act committed against them. Over time, these writs developed into very particular forms, requiring the injured person to allege facts fitting rigid requirements established by the royal government. If the injured person's facts did not comply with and meet the requirements of the particular writ, that person was not permitted to seek redress against the offending party.

It's Latin to Me!

The phrase *vi et armis* means "with force and arms."

One of the available writs was a writ for trespass *vi et armis*. A writ of **trespass vi et armis**, or an action in "trespass with force and arms," permitted a person to hold another responsible for directly causing an injury to another's person, land, or goods. The government's grant of this **writ of trespass** required that the victim's injuries be directly caused by the wrongdoer. This writ did not permit recovery for indirect injuries.

Dissatisfaction with the rigid requirements of the writ of trespass spurred the courts to recognize a different type of action, a writ of **trespass on the case**. A writ of trespass on the case, or "case," was a special writ permitting redress when the victim's injuries or the alleged wrongs did not fit the rigid requirements of a trespass action. An action in case could be molded *ad hoc* to fit the particular facts of the victim's situation.   As it developed over time, an action for trespass on the case permitted recovery for the indirect injuries that a writ of trespass would not.

Take Note

Where tort statutes (*i.e.*, legislature-made laws) do exist, they are often enacted to reverse or change well-established common law.

Modern tort law has its genesis in the writ of trespass and the writ of trespass on the case. Over the years, tort law has developed its own expressions, theories, and public policy priorities.

Tort law remains primarily judge-made or case law. The remaining materials in this chapter provide a brief overview of its development. The following will also introduce you to the three main categories of modern day torts covered in this casebook – intentional torts, negligence, and strict liability.

B. Overview of Tort Law

Lecture III: Torts – Trespass and Negligence

OLIVER WENDELL HOLMES, JR., THE COMMON LAW 77-80 (1881)

…The liabilities incurred by way of contract are more or less expressly fixed by the agreement of the parties concerned, but those arising from a tort are independent of any previous consent of the wrong-doer to bear the loss occasioned by his act. If A fails to pay a certain sum on a certain day, or to deliver a lecture on a certain night, after having made a binding promise to do so, the damages which he has to pay are recovered in accordance with his consent that some or all of the harms which may be caused by his failure shall fall upon him. But when A assaults or slanders his neighbor, or converts his neighbor's property, he does a harm which he has never consented to bear, and if the law makes him pay for it, the reason for doing so must be found in some general view of the conduct which every one may fairly expect and demand from every other, whether that other has agreed to it or not.

Such a general view is very hard to find. The law did not begin with a theory. It has never worked one out. The point from which it started and that at which I shall try to show that it has arrived, are on different planes. In the progress from one to the other, it is to be expected that its course should not be straight and its direction not always visible. All that can be done is to point out a tendency, and to justify it. The tendency, which is our main concern, is a matter of fact to be gathered from the cases. ...

....

The business of the law of torts is to fix the dividing lines between those cases in which a man is liable for harm which he has done, and those in which he is not. ...

....

The law of torts abounds in moral phraseology. It has much to say of wrongs, of malice, fraud, intent, and negligence. Hence it may naturally be supposed that the risk of a man's conduct is thrown upon him as the result of some moral short-coming. But while this notion has been entertained, the extreme opposite will be found to have been a far more popular opinion; – I mean the notion that a man is answerable for all the consequences of his acts, or, in other words, that he acts at his peril always, and wholly irrespective of the state of his consciousness upon the matter.

....

————————————

Points for Discussion

1. Considered by many as one of the great jurists of his time, this excerpt from soon-to-be Justice Oliver Wendell Holmes, Jr.'s treatise on the common law is a lecture concerning tort law. As explained by Justice Holmes, tort law arises by operation of law, not by any contract or agreement between the parties and has developed through the common law (judge-made law).

2. What is the common law? The common law in this country (*i.e.*, non-statutory and non-constitutional law) has primarily developed through state court opin-

ions, which interpret and apply their law. That means that each jurisdiction has developed its own tort law; jurisdictions may be similar in their development of the law or their law may vary greatly from jurisdiction to jurisdiction.

3.   What is the difference between the damages recoverable in con-tract law as compared to damages recoverable in a tort action? What is the purpose of awarding dam-ages for tortious conduct?

> **FYI**
>
> At common law, a cause of action The RESTATEMENT (SECOND) OF TORTS (1965) § 6 defines "tortious conduct" as conduct "of such a character as to subject the actor to liability under the principles of the law of Torts."

4.   Justice Holmes speaks of two differing views on assessing civil liability against an individual who has caused injury to another – liability based upon moral shortcoming or fault, and liability irrespective of fault. In your opinion, upon what basis should civil liability be based? Why? What are the benefits of defining tort liability "irrespective of the state" of one's "consciousness upon the matter"? What are the disadvantages?

5.   What is the purpose or function of tort law, as explained by Justice Holmes?

6.   Justice Holmes speaks "of wrongs, of malice, fraud, intent, and negligence." What is your understanding of the meanings of these terms?

Weaver v. Ward

King's Bench, 1616
Hobart 134, 80 Eng. Rep. 284

Weaver brought an action of trespass of assault and battery against Ward. The defendant pleaded, that he was amongst others by the commandment of the Lords of the Council a trained soldier in London ... and so was the plaintiff, and that they were skirmishing with their musquets charged with powder for their exercise *in re militari*, against another captain and his band; and as they were so skirmishing, the defendant *casualiter & per infortunium & contra voluntatem suam*, in discharging of his piece did hurt and wound the plaintiff, which is the same *&c. absque hoc*, that he was guilty *aliter sive alio modo*. And upon **demurrer** by the plaintiff, judgment was given for him; for though it were agreed, that if men tilt or turney in the pres-ence of the King, or if two masters of defence playing their prizes kill one another, that this shall be no felony; or if a lunatick kill a man, or the like, because felony must be done *animo felonico*: yet in trespass, which tends only to give damages according to hurt or loss, it is not so; and therefore if a lunatick hurt a man, he shall be answerable in trespass: and therefore no man shall be excused of a trespass (for this is the nature of an excuse, and not of a justification...) except it may be judged utterly without his fault. [¶] As if a man by force take my hand and strike you, or if here the defendant had said, that the plaintiff ran cross his piece when it was discharging, or had set forth the case with the circumstances, so as it had appeared to the Court that it had been inevitable, and that the defendant had committed no negligence to give occasion to the hurt.

> ### It's Latin to Me!
>
> The various Latin phrases mean – *in re militari* – "in a military matter"; *casualiter & per infortunium & contra voluntatem suam* – "accidentally, by misfortune, and against his will"; *absque hoc* – "without this"; *aliter sive alio modo* – "otherwise or in another manner"; *animo felonico* – "with a felonious mind"; *prout ei bene licuit* – "as is properly permitted to him." Although definitions will occasionally be provided throughout this text, it is your responsibility to understand all words and terminology used within the cases. Therefore, if there is a word or phrase that you do not understand, you should reference a legal dictionary for its definition.

Points for Discussion

1. What is the principle of law articulated by the court in *Weaver v. Ward*? Is it consistent with the common law as discussed by Justice Oliver Wendell Holmes in the previous selection from THE COMMON LAW?

2. *Weaver v. Ward* is an historically significant case because of its discussion of fault as a consideration in determining whether one should be held liable for injuries caused in tort. Prior to *Weaver*, individuals who harmed others – whether accidentally or intentionally – were responsible for the injuries caused without regard to their fault. *Weaver* is one of the first cases recognizing that a defendant might not be civilly liable for an injury he caused through no fault of his own; to be liable in tort, the defendant must have been at fault somehow. Tort liability has developed into liability based upon fault.

>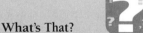
> ### What's That?
>
> The **burden of proof** is a party's obligation to prove a disputed assertion or charge at issue in the case. The burden of proof includes both the burden of production as well as the burden of persuasion. The *burden of production* requires the party upon whom the burden of proof rests to present enough evidence from which the factfinder can make an appropriate determination; the *burden of persuasion* requires the party to convince the factfinder to rule in that party's favor.

3. According to the *Weaver v. Ward* court, who has the burden of proof on the issue of fault? Do

you consider that allocation of fault described in *Weaver* to be appropriate? What, if any, is the practical significance of placing the burden of proof on one party or another?

———————————

Brown v. Kendall

60 Mass. 292 (1850)

It appeared in evidence, on the trial, which was before Wells, C. J., in the court of common pleas, that two dogs, belonging to the plaintiff and the defendant, respectively, were fighting in the presence of their masters; that the defendant took a stick about four feet long, and commenced beating the dogs in order to separate them; that the plaintiff was looking on, at the distance of about a rod, and that he advanced a step or two towards the dogs. In their struggle, the dogs approached the place where the plaintiff was standing. The defendant retreated backwards from before the dogs, striking them as he retreated; and as he approached the plaintiff, with his back towards him, in raising his stick over his shoulder, in order to strike the dogs, he accidentally hit the plaintiff in the eye, inflicting upon him a severe injury.

....

The judge...left the case to the jury under the following instructions:

"If the defendant, in beating the dogs, was doing a necessary act, or one which it was his duty under the circumstances of the case to do, and was doing it in a proper way; then he was not responsible in this action, provided he was using ordinary care at the time of the blow. If it was not a necessary act; if he was not in duty bound to attempt to part the dogs, but might with propriety interfere or not as he chose; the defendant was responsible for the consequences of the blow, unless it appeared that he was in the exercise of extraordinary care, so that the accident was inevitable, using the word inevitable not in a strict but a popular sense."

"If, however, the plaintiff, when he met with the injury, was not in the exercise of ordinary care, he cannot recover, and this rule applies, whether the interference of the defendant in the fight of the dogs was necessary or not. If the jury believe, that it was the duty of the defendant to interfere, then the burden of proving negligence on the part of the defendant, and ordinary care on the part of the plaintiff, is on the plaintiff. If the jury believe, that the act of interference in the fight was unnecessary, then the burden of proving extraordinary care on the part of the defendant, or want of ordinary care on the part of the plaintiff, is on defendant."

The jury under these instructions returned a verdict for the plaintiff; whereupon the defendant alleged **exceptions**.

Shaw, C.J.

This is an action of trespass, **vi et armis**, brought by George Brown against George K. Kendall, for an assault and battery; and the original defendant having died pending the action, his **executrix** has been summoned in. The rule of the common law, by which this action would abate by the death of either party, is reversed in this commonwealth by statute, which provides that actions of trespass for assault and battery shall survive. [C]

> **FYI**
>
> At common law, a cause of action was abated (or was extinguished) with the death of the defendant or the plaintiff. This common law rule has been reversed by survival statutes in most every jurisdiction, such as the statute cited here. Survival statutes allow a cause of action to survive the death of either party and are discussed further in Chapter 10, *infra*.

The facts set forth in the **bill of exceptions** preclude the supposition, that the blow, inflicted by the hand of the defendant upon the person of the plaintiff, was intentional. The whole case proceeds on the assumption, that the damage sustained by the plaintiff, from the stick held by the defendant, was inadvertent and unintentional; and the case involves the question how far, and under what qualifications, the party by whose unconscious act the damage was done is responsible for it. We use the term "unintentional" rather than involuntary, because in some of the cases, it is stated, that the act of holding and using a weapon or instrument, the movement of which is the immediate cause of hurt to another, is a voluntary act, although its particular effect in hitting and hurting another is not within the purpose or intention of the party doing the act.

It appears to us, that some of the confusion in the cases on this subject has grown out of the long-**vexed question**, under the rule of the common law, whether a party's remedy, where he has one, should be sought in an action of the case, or of trespass. This is very distinguishable from the question, whether in a given case, any action will lie. The result of these cases is, that if the damage complained of is the immediate effect of the act of the defendant, trespass *vi et armis* lies; if consequential only, and not immediate, case is the proper remedy. [Cc]

In these discussions, it is frequently stated by judges, that when one receives injury from the direct act of another, trespass will lie. But we think this is said in reference to the question, whether trespass and not case will lie, assuming that the facts are such, that some action will lie. These **dicta** are no authority, we think, for holding, that damage received by a direct act of force from another will be sufficient to maintain an action of trespass, whether the act was lawful or unlawful, and neither wilful, intentional, or careless. ...

Take Note

The court here is distinguishing between two different types of actions brought at common law, actions for trespass and actions for trespass on the case. At common law, a person was not permitted to bring a cause of action against another unless the alleged wrong was recognized as a legal wrong. A **writ of trespass** was available for a direct or forcible injury to a person, land, or chattel. In order to be entitled to a writ of trespass, the complained of injury must have been a direct cause of the harm or wrong. However, if a plaintiff suffered harm caused indirectly by the actions of the defendant, any remedy was available by an action for **trespass on the case** or, as this court termed it, an action on the "case". Writs of trespass alleging damages for direct injury are the legal precursors to tort actions such as battery, assault, false imprisonment, trespass to land, and trespass to chattel. Actions for trespass on the case, alleging damages for indirect injuries, are the legal precursors to tort actions such as for negligence, defamation, and nuisance, where the injuries caused are more indirect.

We think... the rule is correctly stated ... that the plaintiff must come prepared with evidence to show either that the *intention* was unlawful, or that the defendant was *in fault;* for if the injury was unavoidable, and the conduct of the defendant was free from blame, he will not be liable. [Cc] If, in the prosecution of a lawful act, a casualty purely accidental arises, no action can be supported for an injury arising therefrom. [Cc] In applying these rules to the present case, we can perceive no reason why the instructions asked for by the defendant ought not to have been given; to this effect, that if both plaintiff and defendant at the time of the blow were using ordinary care, or if at that time the defendant was using ordinary care, and the plaintiff was not, or if at that time, both the plaintiff and defendant were not using ordinary care, then the plaintiff could not recover.

In using this term, ordinary care, it may be proper to state, that what constitutes ordinary care will vary with the circumstances of cases. In general, it means that kind and degree of care, which prudent and cautious men would use, such as is required by the exigency of the case, and such as is necessary to guard against probable danger. ... To make an accident, or casualty, or as the law sometimes states it, inevitable accident, it must be such an accident as the defendant could not have avoided by the use of the kind and degree of care necessary to the exigency, and in the circumstances in which he was placed.

We are not aware of any circumstances in this case, requiring a distinction between acts which it was lawful and proper to do, and acts of legal duty. ... We can have no doubt that the act of the defendant in attempting to part the fighting dogs, one of which was his own, and for the injurious acts of which he might be responsible, was a lawful and proper act, which he might do by proper and safe means. If, then, in doing this act, using due care and all proper precautions necessary to the exigency of the case, to avoid hurt to others, in raising his stick for that purpose, he accidentally hit the plaintiff in his eye, and wounded him, this was the result of pure accident, or was involuntary and unavoidable, and therefore the action would not lie. Or if the defendant was chargeable with some negligence, and if the plaintiff was also chargeable with negligence, we think the plaintiff cannot recover without showing that the damage was caused wholly by the act of the defendant, and that the plaintiff's own negligence did not contribute as an efficient cause to produce it.

Make the Connection

The court here is referring to contributory negligence, a defense to a negligence action that may be established by proof that the plaintiff was negligent as well. Defenses to negligence actions will be covered in Chapter 6, *infra.*

The court instructed the jury, that if it was not a necessary act, and the defendant was not in duty bound to part the dogs, but might with propriety interfere or not as he chose, the defendant was responsible for the consequences of the blow, unless it appeared that he was in the exercise of extraordinary care, so that the accident was inevitable, using the word not in a strict but a popular sense. This is to be taken in connection with the charge afterwards given, that if the jury believed, that the act of interference in the fight was unnecessary (that is, as before explained, not a duty incumbent on the defendant) then the burden of proving extraordinary care on the part of the defendant, or want of ordinary care on the part of plaintiff, was on the defendant.

The court are of opinion that these directions were not conformable to law. If the act of hitting the plaintiff was unintentional, on the part of the defendant, and done in the doing of a lawful act, then the defendant was not liable, unless it was done in the want of exercise of due care adapted to the exigency of the case, and therefore such want of due care became part of the plaintiff's case, and the burden of proof was on the plaintiff to establish it. [Cc]

Perhaps the learned judge, by the use of the term extraordinary care, in the above charge, explained as it is by the context, may have intended nothing more than that increased degree of care and diligence, which the exigency of particular circumstances might require, and which men of ordinary care and prudence would use under like circumstances, to guard against danger. If such was the meaning of this part of the charge, then it does not differ from our views, as above explained. But we are of opinion, that the other part of the charge, that the burden of proof was on the defendant, was incorrect. Those facts that are essential to enable the plaintiff to recover, he takes the burden of proving. The evidence may be offered by the plaintiff or by the defendant; the question of due care, or want of care, may be essentially connected with the main facts, and arise from the same proof; but the effect of the rule, as to the burden of proof, is this, that when the proof is all in, and before the jury, from whatever side it comes, and whether directly proved, or inferred from circumstances, if it appears that the defendant was doing a lawful act, and unintentionally hit and hurt the plaintiff, then unless it also appears to the satisfaction of the jury, that the defendant is chargeable with some fault, negligence, carelessness, or want of prudence, the plaintiff fails to sustain the burden of proof, and is not entitled to recover.

Make the Connection

This discussion about evidence directly proving a fact or requiring the factfinder to infer a fact from the evidence refers to the distinction between direct evidence and circumstantial evidence. *Direct evidence* establishes the fact sought to be proved. *Circumstantial evidence* proves one fact from which the factfinder may infer the fact sought to be established. You will likely cover these distinctions more thoroughly in a course on evidence.

New trial ordered.

Points for Discussion

1. What is the distinction between an action in trespass and an action in trespass on the case? How might requiring such a distinction affect the outcome in this case?

2. Who is appealing in this case? About what are they complaining? Who prevailed on appeal?

3. The defendant complained on appeal that the trial court's instruction to the jury was erroneous. What was alleged to be wrong with the jury instruction? Why did the court here order a new trial?

4. **Intentional and Unintentional Behavior** – The court explains that in order for the plaintiff to recover in tort, the plaintiff must prove that the defendant acted either intentionally or failed to use ordinary care. What is the distinction between acting intentionally and failing to use ordinary care?

5. **Involuntary and Voluntary Acts** – The court also explains that to be liable in tort, the defendant's act must be voluntary. What is a voluntary act? What

is the difference between an intentional act and a voluntary act? What is the difference between an unintentional act and an involuntary act?

6. Upon whom does the court place the burden of proof?

7. This case is historically significant for it contains one of the earliest clear articulations that a defendant's liability in tort depends upon his or her fault. This case is also considered to be the first important negligence case, as the court discusses the difference between intentionally causing harm and unintentionally causing harm to another.

Hypo 1-1

Plaintiff was a passenger in the backseat of a car driven by Defendant, a longtime friend with whom Plaintiff had ridden many times previously and knew well. On this occasion, Defendant's wife was riding in the front passenger seat of the car when Defendant leaned toward his wife and exclaimed, "Honey, I feel sick." A moment later, Plaintiff heard Wife ask Defendant what was wrong, and immediately after that, the car careened off the road, running into an embankment. Defendant had temporarily lost consciousness, thereby causing the accident. The force of the collision caused Plaintiff to be ejected through the roof of the car and onto the ground. Defendant had never fainted before, was in good health, had eaten well that day, and was not feeling badly until the very moment of the accident. Plaintiff sustained severe physical injuries. Discuss whether Defendant should be held responsible in tort for Plaintiff's injuries. What issue(s) can you identify?

Spano v. Perini Corp.

25 N.Y.2d 11, 302 N.Y.S.2d 527 (1969)

FULD, Chief Judge.

The principal question posed on this appeal is whether a person who has sustained property damage caused by blasting on nearby property can maintain an action for damages without a showing that the blaster was negligent. Since 1893, when this court decided the case of Booth v. Rome, W. & O.T.R.R. Co., 140 N.Y. 267, 35 N.E. 592, 24 L.R.A. 105, it has been the law of this State that proof of negligence was required unless the blast was accompanied by an actual physical invasion of the damaged property – for example, by rocks or other material being cast upon the premises. We are now asked to reconsider that rule.

The plaintiff Spano is the owner of a garage in Brooklyn which was wrecked by a blast occurring on November 27, 1962. There was then in that garage, for repairs, an automobile owned by the plaintiff Davis which he also claims was damaged by the blasting. Each of the plaintiffs brought suit against the two defendants who, as joint venturers, were engaged in constructing a tunnel in the vicinity pursuant to a contract with the City of New York.[1] The two cases were tried together, without a jury, in the Civil Court of the City of New York, New York County, and judgments were rendered in favor of the plaintiffs. The judgments were reversed by the Appellate Term and the Appellate Division affirmed that order, granting leave to appeal to this court.

It is undisputed that, on the day in question …, the defendants had set off a total of 194 sticks of dynamite at a construction site which was only 125 feet away from the damaged premises. Although both plaintiffs alleged negligence in their complaints, no attempt was made to show that the defendants had failed to exercise reasonable care or to take necessary precautions when they were blasting. Instead, they chose to rely, upon the trial, solely on the principle of **absolute liability** either on a tort theory or on the basis of their being **third-party beneficiaries** of the defendants' contract with the city. At the close of the plaintiff Spano's case, when defendants' attorney moved to dismiss the action on the ground, among others, that no negligence had been proved, the trial judge expressed the view that the defendants could be held liable even though they were not shown to have been careless. The case then proceeded, with evidence being introduced solely on the question of damages and proximate cause. Following the trial, the court awarded damages of some $4,400 to Spano and of $329 to Davis.

On appeal, a divided Appellate Term reversed that judgment, declaring that it deemed itself concluded by the established rule in this State requiring proof of negligence. Justice Markowitz, who dissented, urged that the *Booth* case should no longer be considered controlling precedent.

The Appellate Division affirmed….

In our view, the time has come for this court to … declare that one who engages in blasting must assume responsibility, and be liable without fault, for any injury he causes to neighboring property.

---

1 Spano's complaint stated three causes of action: the first under the defendants' contract with the city which, it was alleged, was intended to provide recovery to neighboring property owners for any damages resulting from the job; the second, in which it was only alleged that the defendants' blasting caused damage to the plaintiff's property; and the third which contained an allegation of negligence. Davis served only a short form complaint, containing a single cause of action sounding in negligence.

The concept of absolute liability in blasting cases is hardly a novel one. The overwhelming majority of American jurisdictions have adopted such a rule. [Cc] Indeed, this court itself, several years ago, noted that a change in our law would "conform to the more widely (indeed almost universally) approved doctrine that a blaster is absolutely liable for any damages he causes, with or without trespass". (*Schlansky v. Augustus V. Riegel, Inc.*, 9 NY2d 493, 496.)

....

We need not rely solely, however, upon out-of-state decisions in order to attain our result. Not only has the rationale of the *Booth* case been overwhelmingly rejected elsewhere but it appears to be fundamentally inconsistent with earlier cases in our own court which had held, long before *Booth* was decided, that a party was absolutely liable for damages to neighboring property caused by explosions. (See, e.g., *Hay v. Cohoes Co.*, 2 N. Y. 159; [c]) In the *Hay case*, for example, the defendant was engaged in blasting an excavation for a canal and the force of the blasts caused large quantities of earth and stones to be thrown against the plaintiff's house, knocking down his stoop and part of his chimney. The court held the defendant *absolutely* liable for the damage caused, stating at pp. 160-161:

> It is an elementary principal in reference to private rights, that every individual is entitled to the undisturbed possession and lawful enjoyment of his own property. The mode of enjoyment is necessarily limited by the rights of others – otherwise it might be made destructive of their rights altogether. ... The defendants had the right to dig the canal. The plaintiff the right to the undisturbed possession of his property. If these rights conflict, the former must yield to the latter, as the more important of the two, since, upon grounds of public policy, it is better that one man should surrender a particular use of his land, than that another should be deprived of the beneficial use of his property altogether, which might be the consequence if the privilege of the former should be wholly unrestricted. The case before us illustrates this principle. For if the defendants in excavating their canal, in itself a lawful use of their land, could, in the manner mentioned by the witnesses, demolish the stoop of the plaintiff with impunity, they might, for the same purpose, on the exercise of reasonable care, demolish his house, and thus deprive him of all use of his property.

Although the court in *Booth* drew a distinction between a situation — such as was presented in the *Hay* case — where there was "a physical invasion" of, or trespass on, the plaintiff's property and one in which the damage was caused by "setting the air in motion, or in some other unexplained way" [c], it is clear that the court, in the earlier cases, was not concerned with the particular manner by which the damage was caused but by the simple fact that any explosion in a built-up area was likely to cause damage. ...

....

[T]he *intentional* setting off of explosives – that is, blasting – in an area in which it was likely to cause harm to neighboring property similarly results in absolute liability. However, the court in the *Booth* case rejected such an extension of the rule for the reason that "[t]o exclude the defendant from blasting to adapt its lot to the contemplated uses, at the instance of the plaintiff, would not be a compromise between conflicting rights, but an extinguishment of the right of the one for the benefit of the other." [C] The court expanded on this by stating, "This sacrifice, we think, the law does not exact. Public policy is sustained by the building up of towns and cities and the improvement of property. Any unnecessary restraint on freedom of action of a property owner hinders this."

This rationale cannot withstand analysis. The plaintiff in *Booth* was not seeking, as the court implied, to "exclude the defendant from blasting" and thus prevent desirable improvements to the latter's property. Rather, he was merely seeking compensation for the damage which was inflicted upon his own property as a result of that blasting. The question, in other words, was not *whether* it was lawful or proper to engage in blasting but *who* should bear the cost of any resulting damage – the person who engaged in the dangerous activity or the innocent neighbor injured thereby. Viewed in such a light, it clearly appears that *Booth* was wrongly decided and should be forthrightly overruled.

... Since blasting involves a substantial risk of harm no matter the degree of care exercised, we perceive no reason for ever permitting a person who engaged in such an activity to impose this risk upon nearby persons or property without assuming responsibility therefor.

....

There remains, then, only the matter of proof on the issue of causation. ... [T]he Appellate Division affirmed on the sole ground that no negligence had been proven against the defendants and thus had no occasion to consider the question whether, in fact, the blasting caused the damage. That being so, we must remit the case to the Appellate Division so that it may pass upon the weight of the evidence

The order appealed from should be reversed, with costs, and the matter remitted to the Appellate Division for further proceedings in accordance with this opinion.

———————

Points for Discussion

1. According to the *Spano* court, can a defendant be held liable in tort without proof of the defendant's careless or unreasonable conduct and without proof of the defendant's intent? Under what circumstances?

2. Does *Spano* impose liability without regard to fault? What is **absolute liability**?

3. What was the remedy in this case? Why?

4. Note the similarities between the *Spano* ruling and the "far more popular opinion" of the purpose of tort law articulated by Oliver Wendell Holmes in the excerpt from THE COMMON LAW.

Major Themes

As illustrated by these materials, tort law can be divided into three broad categories – intentional torts, negligence actions, and strict liability torts. Very broadly defined, (1) *intentional* torts provide a remedy for those injured by another's intentional or purposeful conduct; (2) *negligence* actions provide a remedy for injuries sustained by one's unintentional and unreasonable conduct; and (3) *strict liability* torts allow one to recover for another's abnormally or inherently dangerous activities that cause injuries. The remaining materials in this casebook are dedicated to delving more thoroughly into each of these three general categories of tort law.

For More Information

As is true for most law, tort law is in large part driven by public policy concerns. Although courts may often articulate various reasons for reaching the particular conclusion or conclusions that they do, throughout this course consider whether there is actually an underlying public policy concern that may truly be dictating the court's decision. *See generally* KENNETH S. ABRAHAM, THE FORMS AND FUNCTIONS OF TORT LAW (2d ed. 2002). You are likely to find one or more public policy concerns that may help to explain a court's conclusion, particularly when the court's explanation is less than convincing.

5. Note the importance of public policy considerations to the court's decision. The court emphasized that the question was not whether blasting was lawful but rather *who should bear the cost* if any damage ensues. The court in *Spano* explained, "The question, in other words, was not *whether* it was lawful or proper to engage in blasting, but *who* should bear the cost of any resulting damage – the person who engaged in the dangerous activity or the innocent neighbor injured thereby." What policy concerns does the court take into consideration in reaching its conclusion? Do you agree or disagree with such considerations? Upon what do you base your answer?

6.　**Perspective & Analysis –** Perhaps the preeminent authority exploring tort law is PROSSER AND KEETON ON TORTS originally published in 1941. More recent works focusing on public policy and modern tort law systems include G. EDWARD WHITE, TORT LAW IN AMERICA: AN INTELLECTUAL HISTORY (Oxford Univ. Press 2003); CARL T. BOGUS, WHY LAWSUITS ARE GOOD FOR AMERICA: DISCIPLINED DEMOCRACY, BIG BUSINESS, AND THE COMMON LAW (New York University Press 2001); and THOMAS H. KOENIG AND MICHAEL L. RUSTAD, IN DEFENSE OF TORT LAW (New York University Press 2001).

See It

As a young law student, Leroy S. Merrifield was a student in William Prosser's Torts class at the time that Professor Prosser was working on the intital publication of PROSSER AND KEETON ON TORTS. The very notes that Merrifield took during that course are now known as the Prosser Notebook. Merrifield went on to become a Torts professor and scholar. Click here to see the Prosser Notebook for yourself.

CHAPTER 2

Intentional Torts

Intentional torts are one of the three general categories of tort law. There are various types of intentional torts, each protecting a particular legally recognized interest. Although the injury required to demonstrate and prove the tort varies, the **prima facie** structure of each intentional tort is the same: intent, act, causation, and injury. As you study the following materials, remain mindful of the interest or interests protected by recognition of each tort. We begin by exploring the first element of any intentional tort, that being intent.

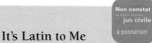

It's Latin to Me

Prima facie means "at first sight." Here, it refers to the requirement that the plaintiff produce enough evidence to allow the factfinder to rule in his or her favor.

A. Intent

Garratt v. Dailey

46 Wash.2d 197, 279 P.2d 1091 (1955)

HILL, Justice.

The liability of an infant for an alleged battery is presented to this court for the first time. Brian Dailey (age five years, nine months) was visit-
ing with Naomi Garratt, an adult and a sister of the plaintiff, Ruth Garratt, likewise an adult, in the back yard of the plaintiff's home, on July 16, 1951. It is plaintiff's contention that she

Take Note

The reference to Brian as an "infant" does not mean that he was a baby. Rather, the legal term **infant** used in this case means a person not yet of majority age.

came out into the back yard to talk with Naomi and that, as she started to sit down in a wood and canvas lawn chair, Brian deliberately pulled it out from under her. The only one of the three persons present so testifying was Naomi Garratt. (Ruth

Garratt, the plaintiff, did not testify as to how or why she fell.) The trial court, unwilling to accept this testimony, adopted instead Brian Dailey's version of what happened, and made the following findings:

'III. * * * that while Naomi Garratt and Brian Dailey were in the back yard the plaintiff, Ruth Garratt, came out of her house into the back yard. Some time subsequent thereto defendant, Brian Dailey, picked up a lightly built wood and canvas lawn chair which was then and there located in the back yard of the above described premises, moved it sideways a few feet and seated himself therein, at which time he discovered the plaintiff, Ruth Garratt, about to sit down at the place where the lawn chair had formerly been, at which time he hurriedly got up from the chair and attempted to move it toward Ruth Garratt to aid her in sitting down in the chair; that due to the defendant's small size and lack of dexterity he was unable to get the lawn chair under the plaintiff in time to prevent her from falling to the ground. That plaintiff fell to the ground and sustained a fracture of her hip, and other injuries and damages as hereinafter set forth.

'IV. That the preponderance of the evidence in this case establishes that when the defendant, Brian Dailey, moved the chair in question *he did not have any wilful or unlawful purpose* in doing so; that *he did not have any intent to injure the plaintiff, or any intent to bring about any unauthorized or offensive contact with her person* or any objects appurtenant thereto; that the circumstances which immediately preceded the fall of the plaintiff established that the defendant, *Brian Dailey, did not have purpose, intent or design to perform a prank or to effect an assault and battery upon the person of the plaintiff.*' (Italics ours, for a purpose hereinafter indicated.)

It is conceded that Ruth Garratt's fall resulted in a fractured hip and other painful and serious injuries. To obviate the necessity of a retrial in the event this court determines that she was entitled to a judgment against Brian Dailey, the amount of her damage was found to be $11,000. Plaintiff appeals from a judgment dismissing the action and asks for the entry of a judgment in that amount or a new trial.

The authorities generally, but with certain notable exceptions [C] state that when a minor has committed a tort with force he is liable to be proceeded against as any other person would be. [Cc]

In our analysis of the applicable law, we start with the basis premise that Brian, whether five or fifty-five, must have committed some wrongful act before he could be liable for appellant's injuries.

. . . .

It is urged that Brian's action in moving the chair constituted a battery. A definition (not all-inclusive but sufficient for our purpose) of a battery is the intentional infliction of a harmful bodily contact upon another. The rule that determines liability for battery is given in 1 RESTATEMENT, TORTS, 29, § 13, as:

'An act which, directly or indirectly, is the legal cause of a harmful contact with another's person makes the actor liable to the other, if
'(a) the act is done with the intention of bringing about a harmful or offensive contact or an apprehension thereof to the other or a third person, and
'(b) the contact is not consented to by the other or the other's consent thereto is procured by fraud or duress, and
'(c) the contact is not otherwise privileged.'

We have in this case no question of **consent** or **privilege**. We therefore proceed to an immediate consideration of intent and its place in the law of battery. In the comment on clause (a), the Restatement says:

'*Character of actor's intention*. In order that an act may be done with the intention of bringing about a harmful or offensive contact or an apprehension thereof to a particular person, either the other or a third person, the act must be done for the purpose of causing the contact or apprehension or with knowledge on the part of the actor that such contact or apprehension is substantially certain to be produced. [C]

We have here the conceded volitional act of Brian, *i.e.*, the moving of a chair. Had the plaintiff proved to the satisfaction of the trial court that Brian moved the chair while she was in the act of sitting down, Brian's action would patently have been for the purpose or with the intent of causing the plaintiff's bodily contact with the ground, and she would be entitled to a judgment against him for the resulting damages. [Cc]

The plaintiff based her case on that theory, and the trial court held that she failed in her proof and accepted Brian's version of the facts rather than that given by the eyewitness who testified for the plaintiff. After the trial court determined that the plaintiff had not established her theory of a battery (*i.e.*, that Brian had pulled the chair out from under the plaintiff while she was in the act of sitting down), it then became concerned with whether a battery was established under the facts as it found them to be.

In this connection, we quote another portion of the comment on the 'Character of actor's intention,' relating to clause (a) of the rule from the Restatement heretofore set forth:

'It is not enough that the act itself is intentionally done and this, even though the actor realizes or should realize that it contains a very grave risk of bringing about the contact or apprehension. Such realization may make the actor's conduct negligent or even reckless but unless he realizes that to a substantial certainty, the contact or apprehension will result, the actor has not that intention which is necessary to make him liable under the rule stated in this section.'

Take Note

Notice that the definition of "intent" can be satisfied by establishing that the defendant acted with either (1) purpose (specific intent) *or* (2) knowledge to a substantial certainty (general intent).

A battery would be established if, in addition to plaintiff's fall, it was proved that, when Brian moved the chair, he knew with substantial certainty that the plaintiff would attempt to sit down where the chair had been. If Brian had any of the intents which the trial court found, in the italicized portions of the findings of fact quoted above, that he did not have, he would of course have had the knowledge to which we have referred. The mere absence of any intent to injure the plaintiff or to play a prank on her or to embarrass her, or to commit an assault and battery on her would not absolve him from liability if in fact he had such knowledge. [C] Without such knowledge, there would be nothing wrongful about Brian's act in moving the chair and, there being no wrongful act, there would be no liability.

While a finding that Brian had no such knowledge can be inferred from the findings made, we believe that before the plaintiff's action in such a case should be dismissed there should be no question but that the trial court had passed upon that issue; hence, the case should be remanded for clarification of the findings to specifically cover the question of Brian's knowledge, because intent could be inferred therefrom. If the court finds that he had such knowledge the necessary intent will be established and the plaintiff will be entitled to recover, even though there was no purpose to injure or embarrass the plaintiff. [C] If Brian did not have such knowledge, there was no wrongful act by him and the basic premise of liability on the theory of a battery was not established.

It will be noted that the law of battery as we have discussed it is the law applicable to adults, and no significance has been attached to the fact that Brian was a child less than six years of age when the alleged battery occurred. The only circumstance where Brian's age is of any consequence is in determining what he knew, and there his experience, capacity, and understanding are of course material.

From what has been said, it is clear that we find no merit in plaintiff's contention that we can direct the entry of a judgment for $11,000 in her favor on the record now before us.

Nor do we find any error in the record that warrants a new trial.

Food for Thought

Should children be responsible for their intentional torts, just as adults are? What are the policy reasons in favor of holding children responsible for their torts? Against?

What we have said concerning intent in relation to batteries caused by the physical contact of a plaintiff with the ground or floor as the result of the removal of a chair by a defendant furnishes the basis for the answer to the contention of the plaintiff that the trial court changed its theory of the applicable law after the trial, and that she was prejudiced thereby.

It is clear to us that there was no change in theory so far as the plaintiff's case was concerned. The trial court consistently from beginning to end recognized that if the plaintiff proved what she alleged and her eyewitness testified, namely, that Brian pulled the chair out from under the plaintiff while she was in the act of sitting down and she fell to the ground in consequence thereof, a battery was established. Had she proved that state of facts, then the trial court's comments about inability to find any intent (from the connotation of motivation) to injure or embarrass the plaintiff, and the italicized portions of his findings as above set forth could have indicated a change of theory. But what must be recognized is that the trial court was trying in those comments and in the italicized findings to express the law applicable, not to the facts as the plaintiff contended they were, but to the facts as the trial court found them to be. The remand for clarification gives the plaintiff an opportunity to secure a judgment even though the trial court did not accept her version of the facts, if from all the evidence, the trial court can find that Brian knew with substantial certainty that the plaintiff intended to sit down where the chair had been before he moved it, and still without reference to motivation.

. . . .

It is argued that some courts predicate an infant's liability for tort upon the basis of the existence of an estate in the infant; hence it was error for the trial court to refuse to admit as an exhibit a policy of liability insurance as evidence that there was a source from which a judgment might be satisfied. In our opinion the liability of an infant for his tort does not depend upon the size of his estate or even upon the existence of one. That is a matter of concern only to the plaintiff who seeks to enforce a judgment against the infant.

. . . .

The cause is remanded for clarification, with instructions to make definite findings on the issue of whether Brian Dailey knew with substantial certainty that the plaintiff would attempt to sit down where the chair which he moved had been, and to change the judgment if the findings warrant it.

....

Remanded for clarification.

——————————

[On remand, the trial court found that "the defendant knew, with substantial certainty, at the time he removed the chair, that the plaintiff would attempt to sit down where the chair had been, since she was in the act of seating herself when he removed the chair. Judgment was entered for the plaintiff in the amount of eleven thousand dollars, plus costs. ...." *See Garratt v. Dailey,* 304 P.2d 681 (Wash. 1956).]

——————————

Points for Discussion

1. How could Brian be held liable for a intending a battery when he had no intent to injure or embarrass Mrs. Garratt?

2. How can one's intent – what a person is thinking at the time he or she acts – ever be proven in a court of law?

3. What are the two ways that intent can be established in support of an intentional tort action?

4. **Specific Intent and General Intent** — The court here defines intent sufficient for the intentional tort of battery as satisfied by proof of the defendant's *specific intent* – the defendant desired to bring about the harm for battery (harmful or offensive contact) – or *general intent* – the defendant had knowledge to a substantial certainty that such harm (in this case, harmful or offensive contact) would be caused by his actions. This definition of intent was adopted by the Restatement (Second) of Torts § 8A (1965) which defines intent as (1) desiring to cause the consequences of one's act or (2) believing the consequences are substantially certain to result from one's act.

5. **Liability of Minors** — This decision explains what is now a well-accepted principle of tort law: in most jurisdictions, children are responsible for their intentional torts. Public policy in support of the rationale holding children

liable includes considerations of deterrence, corrective justice, and compensation. Do you believe children can be deterred from tortious conduct by imposition of civil liability? Will holding children liable in tort prevent injured persons from engaging in self-help measures? Is the liability of children for tortious conduct justifiable because, as between the two parties, the person responsible for causing the injury should compensate the victim? Do you agree that children should

be liable for their intentional torts? Why or why not? Should there be a minimum age before children may be liable in tort? If so, what should that age be? Why?

6. That children can be civilly responsible for their torts does not make their age irrelevant. A defendant child's age may be of consequence in determining what he or she knew in light of his or her age, capacity, and understanding.

7. The trial court refused to admit into evidence proof of Brian's **liability insurance**. The court explains that such information, as well as information concerning the size of plaintiff's **estate**, is irrelevant to the battery action. Why is proof of insurance irrelevant?

Spivey v. Battaglia

258 So.2d 815 (Fla. 1972)

DEKLE, Justice.

This cause is before us on petition for **writ of certiorari** to review a decision of the District Court of Appeal, Fourth District. [C] It will be seen below that there is a misapplication and therefore conflict with McDonald v. Ford, 223 So.2d 553 (2d DCA Fla. 1969).

Petitioner (plaintiff in the trial court) and respondent (defendant) were employees of Battaglia Fruit Co. on January 21, 1965. During the lunch hour several employees of Battaglia Fruit Co., including petitioner and respondent, were seated on a work table in the plant of the company. Respondent, in an effort to tease petitioner, whom he knew to be shy, intentionally put his arm around petitioner and pulled her head toward him. Immediately after this 'friendly unsolicited hug,' petitioner suffered a sharp pain in the back of her neck and ear, and sharp pains into the base of her skull. As a result, petitioner was paralyzed on the left side of her face and mouth.

Behind the Scenes

Why is Mr. Spivey suing as well? The answer is likely that, at the time, women were not permitted to sue for their own injuries so her husband was required to sue on her behalf. He may also have been suing for his own injuries as a derivative claim based on her injuries, also known as a **loss of consortium** claim. *See infra* Chapter 8 on Damages.

An action was commenced in the Circuit Court of Orange County, Florida, wherein the petitioners, Mr. and Mrs. Spivey, brought suit against respondent for, (1) negligence, and (2) assault and battery. Respondent, Mr. Battaglia, filed his answer raising as a defense the claim that his 'friendly unsolicited hug' was an assault and battery as a matter of law and was barred by the running of the two-year statute of limitations on assault and battery. Respondent's motion for summary judgment was granted by the trial court on this basis. The district court affirmed on the authority of McDonald v. Ford, *supra*.

The question presented for our determination is whether petitioner's action could be maintained on the negligence count, or whether respondent's conduct amounted to an assault and battery as a matter of law, which would bar the suit under the two-year statute (which had run).

What's That?

A **statute of limitations** is a statute defining the time period during which a cause of action must be filed.

In *McDonald* the incident complained of occurred in the early morning hours in a home owned by the defendant. While the plaintiff was looking through some records, the defendant came up behind her, laughingly embraced her and, though she resisted, kissed her hard. As the defendant was hurting the plaintiff…, the plaintiff continued to struggle violently and the defendant continued to laugh and pursue his love-making attempts. In the process, plaintiff struck her face hard upon an object that she was unable to identify specifically. With those facts before it, the district court held that what actually occurred was an assault and battery, and not negligence. The court quoted with approval from the Court of Appeals of Ohio in Williams v. Pressman, 113 N.E.2d 395, at 396 (Ohio App.1953):

'... an assault and battery is not negligence, for such action is intentional, while negligence connotes an unintentional act.'

The intent with which such a tort liability as assault is concerned is not necessarily a hostile intent, or a desire to do harm. Where a reasonable man would believe that a particular result was substantially certain to follow, he will be held in the eyes of the law as though he had intended it.[1] It would thus be an assault (intentional). However, the knowledge and appreciation of a risk, short of substantial certainty, is not the equivalent of intent. Thus, the distinction between intent and negligence boils down to a matter of degree. 'Apparently the line has been drawn by the courts at the point where the known danger ceases to be only a foreseeable risk which a reasonable man would avoid (negligence), and becomes a substantial certainty.'[2] In the latter case, the intent is legally implied and becomes and assault rather than unintentional negligence.

Major Themes

The court here is making the distinction between two of the three general categories of torts discussed in Chapter One – intentional torts and negligence actions. An intentional tort requires a showing of the defendant's intent, whereas negligence imposes liability based upon the defendant's unintentional conduct.

The distinction between the unsolicited kisses in *McDonald* ... and the unsolicited hug in the present case turns upon this question of intent. In *McDonald*, the court, finding an assault and battery, necessarily had to find initially that the results of the defendant's acts were 'intentional.' This is a rational conclusion in view of the struggling involved there. In the instant case, the DCA must have found the same intent. But we cannot agree with that finding in these circumstances. It cannot be said that a reasonable man in this defendant's position would believe that the bizarre results herein were 'substantially certain' to follow. This is an unreasonable conclusion and is a misapplication of the rule in *McDonald*. This does not mean that he does not become liable for such unanticipated results, however. The settled law is that a defendant becomes liable for reasonably foreseeable consequences, though the exact results and damages were not contemplated. [C]

Acts that might be considered prudent in one case might be negligent in another. Negligence is a relative term and its existence must depend in each case upon the particular circumstances which surrounded the parties at the time and place of the events upon which the controversy is based.

---

1 RESTATEMENT (SECOND) OF TORTS, § 8A (1965).
2 W. PROSSER, LAW OF TORTS, p. 32 (3d ed. 1964).

The trial judge committed error when he granted summary final judgment in favor of the defendant. The cause should have been submitted to the jury with appropriate instructions regarding the elements of negligence. Accordingly, certiorari is granted; the decision of the district court is hereby **quashed** and the cause is remanded with directions to reverse the summary final judgment.

It is so ordered.

. . . .

Points for Discussion

1. Is the fact that Mrs. Spivey was paralyzed on the left side of her face and mouth legally relevant in establishing the *prima facie* case for her battery claim? That she was paralyzed will certainly impact the amount of damages she is eligible to recover if her claim is permitted, but does it affect whether the defendant is liable for a battery at all?

2. The court in *Spivey v. Battaglia* states that the defendant is not liable for the intentional torts of assault or battery because the defendant could not have intended these bizarre results. Is this the legally relevant inquiry when determining whether the defendant acted with the requisite intent? Remember that intent in support of the *prima facie* case for an intentional tort is established by proof of either specific intent or general intent. **Specific intent** is established by proof that the actor desired to bring about a result that will invade the interests of another in a way that the law forbids. **General intent** is established by proof that the actor acted with knowledge to a substantial certainty that the act would invade the interests of another in a way that the law forbids.

3. RESTATEMENT (THIRD) OF TORTS (2010) seeks to clarify what the defendant must "intend" – "In general, the intent required in order to show that the defendant's conduct is an intentional tort is the intent to bring about harm (more precisely, to bring about the type of harm that the particular tort seeks to protect against)." See RESTATEMENT (THIRD) OF TORTS: LIAB. PHYSICAL HARM § 1, cmt. *b* (2010). Thus, the court's ruling in *Spivey* clearly reaches the wrong result, if indeed the defendant intended to contact the plaintiff in an offensive manner, as that would be intent sufficient to support a finding of offensive contact battery. Why might the court have made such a patently incorrect ruling?

4. What is a statute of limitations?

5. According to the *Spivey* court, are an intentional tort action and a negligence action, arising from the same set of facts, mutually exclusive theories of recovery?

Ranson v. Kitner

31 Ill.App. 241 (3d Dist. 1888)

CONGER, J.

This was an action brought by appellee against appellants to recover the value of a dog killed by appellants, and a judgment rendered for $50.

The defense was that appellants were hunting for wolves, that appellee's dog had a striking resemblance to a wolf, that they in good faith believed it to be one, and killed it as such.

Many points are made, and a lengthy argument filed to show that error in the trial below was committed, but we are inclined to think that no material error occurred to the **prejudice** of appellants.

The jury held them liable for the value of the dog, and we do not see how they could have done otherwise under the evidence. Appellants are clearly liable for the damages caused by their mistake, notwithstanding they were acting in good faith.

We see no reason for interfering with the conclusion reached by the jury, and the judgment will be affirmed.

Judgment affirmed.

Points for Discussion

1. The issue in this case is whether a defendant's good faith or mistake might negate the intent sufficient for imposing liability for an intentional tort. Does the defendant's good faith or mistake negate intent?

2. Why is the defendant liable when he was mistaken as to the legal character of the dog? Is the defendant morally to blame for the harm caused? Does the court's decision impose liability without fault? Why is the burden of mistake placed upon the defendant rather than on the plaintiff?

Hypo 2-1

V.P. was part of a group hunting wild quail on a ranch in South Texas. Hunting dogs pointed out a covey of quail, and the birds were flushed. V.P. turned to his right and fired his shotgun at a quail heading west and toward the sun. At the exact same moment that he fired at the bird, V.P. saw another member of the hunting party, 78-year-old Friend (who was dressed in orange), standing approximately 30 yards from V.P. Birdshot from V.P.'s weapon struck Friend in his face, neck, and chest. A pellet entered Friend's heart, and he suffered a heart attack. V.P. takes full responsibility for "my accidental shooting" of Friend. Did V.P. commit an intentional tort when he shot Friend?

McGuire v. Almy

297 Mass. 323, 8 N.E.2d 760 (1937)

QUA, Justice.

This is an action of tort for assault and battery. The only question of law reported is whether the judge should have directed a verdict for the defendant.

The following facts are established by the plaintiff's own evidence: In August, 1930, the plaintiff was employed to take care of the defendant. The plaintiff was a registered nurse and was a graduate of a training school for nurses. The defendant was an insane person. Before the plaintiff was hired she learned that the defendant was a "mental case and was in good physical condition," and that for some time two nurses had been taking care of her. The plaintiff was on "24 hour duty." The plaintiff slept in the room next to the defendant's room. Except when the plaintiff was with the defendant, the plaintiff kept the defendant locked in the defendant's room. There was a wire grating over the outside of the window of that room. During the period of "fourteen months or so" while the plaintiff cared for the defendant, the defendant "had a few odd spells," when she showed some hostility to the plaintiff and said that "she would like to try and do something to her." The defendant had been violent at times and had broken dishes "and things like that," and on one or two occasions the plaintiff had to have help to subdue the defendant.

On April 19, 1932, the defendant, while locked in her room, had a violent attack. The plaintiff heard a crashing of furniture and then knew that the defendant was ugly, violent and dangerous. The defendant told the plaintiff and a Miss Maroney, "the maid," who was with the plaintiff in the adjoining room, that if they came into the defendant's room, she would kill them. The plaintiff and Miss Maroney looked into the defendant's room, "saw what the defendant had done," and "thought it best to take the broken stuff away before she did any harm to herself with it." They sent for a Mr. Emerton, the defendant's brother-in-law. When he arrived the defendant was in the middle of her room about ten feet from the door, holding upraised the leg of a low-boy as if she were going to strike. The plaintiff stepped into the room and walked toward the defendant, while Mr. Emerton and Miss Maroney remained in the doorway. As the plaintiff approached the defendant and tried to take hold of the defendant's hand which held the leg, the defendant struck the plaintiff's head with it, causing the injuries for which the action was brought.

> **FYI**
>
> A *lowboy* is a small dressing or side table, usually about three feet high.

The extent to which an **insane** person is liable for torts has not been fully defined in this Commonwealth. ... In Morain v. Devlin, 132 Mass. 87, at page 88,42 Am.Rep. 423, this court said, through Chief Justice Gray, "By the common law, as generally stated in the books, a **lunatic** is civilly liable to make compensation in damages to persons injured by his acts, although, being incapable of criminal intent, he is not liable to indictment and punishment," citing numerous cases. ...

[C]ourts in this country almost invariably say in the broadest terms that an insane person is liable for his torts. As a rule no distinction is made between those torts which would ordinarily be classed as intentional and those which would ordinarily be classed as negligent, nor do the courts discuss the effect of different kinds of insanity or of varying degrees of capacity as bearing upon the ability of the defendant to understand the particular act in question or to make a reasoned decision with respect to it, although it is sometimes said that an insane person is not liable for torts requiring **malice** of which he is incapable. Defamation and malicious prosecution are the torts more commonly mentioned in this connection. ... [Cc] These decisions are rested more upon grounds of public policy and upon what might be called a popular view of the requirements of essential justice than upon any attempt to apply logically the underlying principles of civil liability to the special instance of the mentally deranged. Thus it is said that a rule imposing liability tends to make more watchful those persons who have charge of the defendant and who may be supposed to have some interest in preserving his property; that as an insane person must pay for his support, if he is financially able, so he ought also to pay for the damage which he does; that an insane person with abundant wealth ought not to continue in unimpaired enjoyment of the comfort which it brings while his victim bears the burden unaided; and there is also a suggestion that courts are loath to introduce into the great body of civil litigation the difficulties in determining mental capacity which it has been found impossible to avoid in the criminal field.

The rule established in these cases has been criticized severely by certain eminent text writers both in this country and in England, principally on the ground that it is an archaic survival of the rigid and formal mediaeval conception of liability for acts done, without regard to fault, as opposed to what is said to be the general modern theory that liability in tort should rest upon fault. Notwithstanding these criticisms, we think that as a practical matter, there is strong force in the reasons underlying these decisions. They are consistent with the general statements found in the cases dealing with the liability of infants for torts [Cc] including a few cases in which the child was so young as to render his capacity for fault comparable to that of many insane persons [Cc]. Fault is by no means at the present day a universal prerequisite to liability, and the theory that it should be such has been obliged very recently to yield at several points to what have been thought to be paramount considerations of public good. Finally, it would be difficult not to recognize the persuasive weight of so much authority so widely extended.

But the present occasion does not require us either to accept or to reject the prevailing doctrine in its entirety. For this case it is enough to say that where an insane person by his act does intentional damage to the person or property of another he is liable for that damage in the same circumstances in which a normal person would be liable. This means that in so far as a particular intent would be necessary in order to render a normal person liable, the insane person, in order to be liable, must have been capable of entertaining that same intent and must have entertained it in fact. But the law will not inquire further into his peculiar mental condition with a view to excusing him if it should appear that delusion or other consequence of his affliction has caused him to entertain that intent or that a normal person would not have entertained it.

Food for Thought

Should the imposition of intentional tort liability on insane persons apply to negligence actions as well? How about torts predicated upon strict liability? *See* Chapter 13, *infra*.

We do not suggest that this is necessarily a logical stopping point. If public policy demands that a mentally affected person be subjection to the external standard for intentional wrongs, it may well be that public policy also demands that he should be subjected to the external standard for wrongs which are commonly classified as negligent, in accordance with what now seems to be the prevailing view. We stop here for the present, because we are not required to go further in order to decide this case, because of deference to the difficulty of the subject, because full and adequate discussion is lacking in most of the cases decided up to the present time, and because by far the greater number of those cases, however broad their statement of the principle, are in fact cases of intentional rather than of negligent injury.

Coming now to the application of the rule to the facts of this case, it is apparent that the jury could find that the defendant was capable of entertaining and that she did entertain an intent to strike and to injure the plaintiff and that she acted upon that intent. [C] We think this was enough.

The defendant further argues that she is not liable because the plaintiff, by undertaking to care for the defendant with knowledge of the defendant's condition and by walking into the room in spite of the defendant's threat under the circumstances shown, consented to the injury, or, as the defendant puts it, assumed the risk, both contractually and voluntarily. Without considering to what extent consent is in general a defence to an assault…, we think that the defendant was not entitled to a **directed verdict** on this ground. Although the plaintiff knew when she was employed that the defendant was a mental case, and despite some show of hostility and some violent and unruly conduct, there was no evidence of any previous attack o[r] even of any serious threat against anyone. The plaintiff had taken care of the defendant for "fourteen months or so." We think that the danger of actual physical injury was not, as matter of law, plain and obvious up to the time when the plaintiff entered the room on the occasion of the assault. But by that time an emergency had been created. The defendant was breaking up the furniture, and it could have been found that the plaintiff reasonably feared that the defendant would do harm to herself. Something had to be done about it. The plaintiff had assumed the duty of caring for the defendant. We think that a reasonable attempt on her part to perform that duty under the peculiar circumstances brought about by the

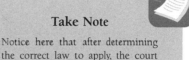

Take Note

Notice here that after determining the correct law to apply, the court then applies the law to the facts of the case. Good legal analysis requires identifying the legal issue, determining the applicable law, applying the law to the facts of the case, and after analyzing the law to the fact, reaching a conclusion.

FYI The defense of *assumption of the risk* is not traditionally available in an action for an intentional tort. Rather, as will be explained in Chapter 6, it is historically an available defense to negligence actions.

defendant's own act did not necessarily indicate a voluntary consent to be injured. Consent does not always follow from the intentional incurring of risk. ...

Judgment for the plaintiff on the verdict.

————————————

Points for Discussion

1. Does proof of the defendant's mental illness negate the intent element for an intentional tort?

2. What is the common law rule regarding the liability of mentally ill persons for their torts? Does the common law impose liability on insane persons for both intentional torts as well as negligence actions? Should the same rule apply for insane persons who are found to be liable in strict liability?

3. What are the public policy considerations in favor of holding the mentally ill responsible for their torts? What are the criticisms? Do you agree with imposing liability on the mentally ill?

4. Are the policy concerns at issue in imposing liability upon the mentally ill the same concerns the law has in determining whether to impose liability on minors? Are liability of children and liability of the mentally ill comparable considerations?

5. Does imposition of tort liability upon the mentally ill impose liability without fault?

————————————

Alteiri v. Colasso

362 A.2d 798 (Conn. 1975)

LOISELLE, Associate Justice.

This action is one for battery brought by a minor, the plaintiff Richard Alteiri, to recover for injuries he suffered, and by his mother, the named plaintiff, to recover for expenses incurred. The complaint alleges that while the minor plaintiff was playing in the back yard of a home at which he was visiting, the defendant threw a rock, stone or other missile into the yard and struck the minor plaintiff in the eye and "(a)s a result of said battery by the defendant, the plaintiff Richard Alteiri suffered severe, painful and permanent injuries."

....

Six **interrogatories** were submitted to the jury. Two interrogatories were answered in the affirmative as follows: "On April 2, 1966, did the defendant, John Colasso, throw a stone which struck the plaintiff, Richard Alteiri, in the right eye?" Answer: "Yes." "(W)as that stone thrown by John Colasso with the intent to scare any person other than Richard Alteiri?" Answer: "Yes." The jury answered "No" to four other questions concerning whether the defendant had intended to strike either the minor plaintiff or any other person and whether he had thrown the stone either negligently or wantonly and recklessly. A plaintiffs' verdict was returned. The defendant has appealed from the judgment rendered.

[The court's discussion dispensing of a statute of limitations defense is omitted.]

Error is assigned in the court's denial of the defendant's motions to set aside the verdict and for judgment notwithstanding the verdict. The defendant claims that the jury could not have reasonably and logically rendered a verdict under our law when in their answers to the interrogatories they expressly found that the defendant did not throw the stone with intent to strike either the minor plaintiff or any other person .... By their answers to the interrrogatories it is clear that the jury found that the battery to the minor plaintiff was one committed wilfully. The issue to be determined on this appeal is whether a jury upon finding that the defendant threw the stone with the intent to scare someone other than the one who was struck by the stone can legally and logically return a verdict for the plaintiffs for a wilful battery.

In Rogers v. Doody, 119 Conn. 532, 534, 178 A. 51, ... the court stated that a "wilful and malicious injury is one inflicted intentionally without just cause or excuse. It does not necessarily involve the ill will or malevolence shown in **express malice**. Nor is it sufficient to constitute such an injury that the act resulting in the injury was intentional in the sense that it was the voluntary action of the person involved. Not only the action producing the injury but the resulting injury must be intentional." The defendant claims, in reliance upon this principle, that as there was no intention either to injure the minor plaintiff or to put him in apprehension of bodily harm there could be no recovery for a wilful battery. The intention of the defendant was not only to throw the stone -- the act resulting in the injury was intentional -- but his intention was also to cause a resulting injury, that is, an apprehension of bodily harm. If the stone had struck the one whom the defendant had intended to frighten, the defendant would have been liable for a battery. The statement in *Rogers* that the "resulting injury must be intentional" would be satisfied as the injury intended was the apprehension of bodily harm and the resulting bodily harm was the direct and natural consequence of the intended act. Restatement (Second), 1 Torts § 13;[3] [Cc].

It is not essential that the precise injury which was done be the one intended. 1 Cooley, Torts (4th Ed.) § 98. An act designed to cause bodily injury to a particular person is actionable as a battery not only by the person intended by the actor to be injured but also by another who is in fact so injured.[4] Restatement (Second), 1 Torts § 13; [Cc]; Prosser, Torts (4th Ed.) § 8; [c]. This principle of "transferred intent" applies as well to the action of assault. [Cc] And where one intends merely an assault, if bodily injury results to one other than the person whom the actor intended to put in apprehension of bodily harm, it is battery actionable by the injured person. Restatement (Second), 1 Torts § 16;[5] [Cc]; Prosser, *supra*.

. . . .

It follows that the jury could logically and legally return a plaintiffs' verdict for wilful battery, and that the court in accepting that verdict and denying the defendants motions was not in error.

There is no error.

———————————

Points for Discussion

1. **Transferred Intent Doctrine** – The transferred intent doctrine originates in the old trespass actions, which permitted a plaintiff to recover only if the injury sustained was a direct consequence of the defendant's act. Trespass actions included actions for battery, assault, false imprisonment, trespass to land, and trespass to chattel. The transferred intent doctrine facilitates a plaintiff's

---

3 (Restatement (Second), 1 Torts § 13) Battery: Harmful Contact   "An actor is subject to liability to another for battery if (a) he acts intending to cause a harmful or offensive contact with the person of the other or a third person, or an imminent apprehension of such a contact, and (b) a harmful contact with the person of the other directly or indirectly results."

4 The principle of transferred intent applies to both civil and criminal cases. See [Cc]; Prosser, "Transferred Intent," 45 Tex.L.Rev. 650, for a discussion of the roots and the limits of this doctrine.

5 "(Restatement (Second), 1 Torts § 16) Character of Intent Necessary (1) If an act is done with the intention of inflicting upon another an offensive but not a harmful bodily contact, or of putting another in apprehension of either a harmful or offensive bodily contact, and such act causes a bodily contact to the other, the actor is liable to the other for a battery although the act was not done with the intention of bringing about the resulting bodily harm. (2) If an act is done with the intention of affecting a third person in the manner stated in Subsection (1), but causes a harmful bodily contact to another, the actor is liable to such other as fully as though he intended so to affect him."

task of proving intent for any one of these five intentional torts by establishing that the defendant intended to commit any one of these five intentional torts and accomplished any of those five intentional torts. The transferred intent doctrine only works within these five intentional torts; it does

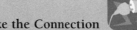

Make the Connection

The distinctions between actions in trespass and actions for trespass on the case are discussed in Chapter 1, *supra.*

not facilitate proving intent outside of these five established torts with roots in the old trespass action. For a terrific read on the history and contours of the transferred intent doctrine, *see* William L. Prosser, *Transferred Intent*, 45 TEX. L. REV. 650 (1967).

2. What are the policy considerations driving application of the transferred intent doctrine? Against?

3. The RESTATEMENT (THIRD) OF TORTS: LIABILITY FOR PHYSICAL HARM § 33 cmt. *c* (2010) describes the doctrine of transferred intent as applicable only to trespassory torts, the torts most likely to involve physical harm. The Restatement goes on to explain that "intent will be 'transferred' if the actor harms another person, even if that other person is unforeseeable."

4. Of course, proof of intent establishes only the first element of the plaintiff's *prima facie* case. Recall that the elements of all intentional torts are: (1) intent, (2) act, (3) causation, and (4) injury. The following materials consider each intentional tort in turn, with focus on the definition and purpose of each individual intentional tort action. Note that the technical injury required to satisfy the fourth element for each intentional tort differs from tort to tort as the interest sought to be protected by the law changes.

Food for Thought

Be careful in your use of legal terms. For example, section 7 of the RE-STATEMENT (SECOND) OF TORTS distinguishes between the terms "injury" and "harm." It defines *injury* as "denot[ing] the invasion of any legally protected interest of another." It defines *harm* as "denot[ing] the existence of loss or detriment in fact of any kind to a person resulting from any cause." Thus, in the context of intentional torts, "injury" refers to the technical injury required to establish commission of the tort, whereas "harm" refers to the actual damages sustained.

B. Battery

The Restatement (Second) of Torts (1965) defines two types of battery actions – *harmful contact* battery and *offensive contact* battery:

§ 13 Battery: Harmful Contact

An actor is subject to liability to another for battery if ... he acts intending to cause a harmful or offensive contact with the person of the other ... and ... a harmful contact with the person of the other directly or indirectly results.

Harmful contact is defined as bodily contact resulting in "any physical impairment of the condition of another's body, or physical pain or illness." *See* Restatement (Second) of Torts § 15.

§ 18 Battery: Offensive Contact

An actor is subject to liability to another for battery if ... he acts intending to cause a harmful or offensive contact with the person of the other ... and an offensive contact with the person of the other directly or indirectly results.

Offensive contact is defined as "bodily contact ... offend[ing] a reasonable sense of personal dignity." *See* Restatement (Second) of Torts § 19.

Wallace v. Rosen

765 N.E.2d 192 (Ind. App. 2002)

KIRSCH, Judge.

Mable Wallace appeals the jury verdict in favor of Indianapolis Public Schools (IPS) and Harriet Rosen, a teacher for IPS. On appeal, Wallace raises the following issue[]:

I. Whether the trial court erred in refusing to give her tendered jury instruction regarding battery.

....

FYI

The Restatement (Third) of Torts defers to the definitions of many intentional torts set forth in the Restatement (Second) of Torts as authoritative. *See* Restatement (Third) of Torts: Liab. for Physical Harm § 5 cmt. *c* (2010).

We affirm.

FACTS AND PROCEDURAL HISTORY

In 1994, Rosen was a teacher at Northwest High School in Indianapolis. On April 22, 1994, the high school had a fire drill while classes were in session. The drill was not previously announced to the teachers and occurred just one week after a fire was extinguished in a bathroom near Rosen's classroom.

On the day the alarm sounded, Wallace was at the high school delivering homework to her daughter Lalaya. Because Wallace was recovering from foot surgery and Lalaya's class was on the second floor, Lalaya's boyfriend Eric Fuqua accompanied Wallace up the stairs. Wallace and Fuqua were near the top of the staircase when they saw Lalaya and began to speak with her. Jamie Arnold, a student who knew Lalaya and her mother, joined the conversation. The alarm then sounded and students began filing down the stairs while Wallace took a step or two up the stairs to the second floor landing.

In response to the alarm, Rosen escorted her class to the designated stairway and noticed three or four people talking together at the top of the stairway and blocking the students' exit. Rosen did not recognize any of the individuals but approached "telling everybody to move it." ... Wallace, with her back to Rosen, was unable to hear Rosen over the noise of the alarm and Rosen had to touch her on the back to get her attention. ... Rosen then told Wallace, "you've got to get moving because this is a fire drill." ...

At trial, Wallace testified that Rosen pushed her down the stairs. ... Rosen denied pushing Wallace and testified that Wallace had not fallen, but rather had made her way down the stairs unassisted and without losing her balance. ...

At the close of the trial, Wallace tendered an instruction concerning civil battery. Over Wallace's objection, the court refused to read the instruction to the jury. ... The jury found in favor of IPS [Indianapolis Public Schools] and Rosen, and Wallace now appeals.

DISCUSSION AND DECISION

Wallace claims that the trial court erred ... in refusing to give the tendered jury instruction concerning battery.... Instruction of the jury is left to the sound discretion of the trial court. [C] Our review of a trial court's decisions is highly deferential, and we will not disturb the court's judgment absent an abuse of that discretion. [C]

....

I. Battery Instruction

Wallace first argues that it was error for the trial court to refuse to give the jury the following tendered instruction pertaining to battery:

A battery is the knowing or intentional touching of one person by another in a rude, insolent, or angry manner.

Any touching, however slight, may constitute an assault and battery.

Also, a battery may be recklessly committed where one acts in reckless disregard of the consequences, and the fact the person does not intend that the act shall result in an injury is immaterial. [C]

Wallace argues that the omission of the instruction was error because the instruction was an accurate statement of the law, was supported by the evidence, and was not covered by any other instruction read to the jury. ... Appellees respond that the instruction was properly omitted because there was no evidence presented that supported a battery instruction. ...

Practice Pointer

A pattern jury charge, also known as a model jury charge, is a form containing suggested language for a trial court to use to instruct a jury for matters arising in a typical case. In this case, the pattern jury charge provides the definition in this jurisdiction of the intentional tort of battery.

We agree with Appellees. The Indiana Pattern Jury Instruction for the intentional tort of civil battery is as follows: "A battery is the knowing or intentional touching of a person against [his] [her] will in a rude, insolent, or angry manner." 2 *Indiana Pattern Jury Instructions (Civil)* 31.03 (2d ed. Revised 2001). Battery is an intentional tort. [C] In discussing intent, Professors Prosser and Keeton made the following comments:

In a loose and general sense, the meaning of 'intent' is easy to grasp. As Holmes observed, even a dog knows the difference between being tripped over and being kicked. This is also the key distinction between two major divisions of legal liability – negligence and intentional torts....

[I]t is correct to tell the jury that, relying on circumstantial evidence, they may infer that the actor's state of mind was the same as a reasonable person's state of mind would have been. Thus, ... the defendant on a bicycle who rides down a person in full view on a sidewalk where there is ample room to pass may learn that the factfinder (judge or jury) is unwilling to credit the statement, "I didn't mean to do it."

On the other hand, the mere knowledge and appreciation of a risk – something short of substantial certainty – is not intent. The defendant who acts in the belief or consciousness that the act is causing an appreciable risk of harm to another may be negligent, and if the risk is great the conduct may be characterized as reckless or wanton, but it is not an intentional wrong. In such cases the distinction between intent and negligence obviously is a matter of degree. The line has to be drawn by the courts at the point where the known danger ceases to be only a foreseeable risk which a reasonable person would avoid, and becomes in the mind of the actor a substantial certainty.

The intent with which tort liability is concerned is not necessarily a hostile intent, or a desire to do any harm. Rather it is an intent to bring about a result which will invade the interests of another in a way that the law forbids. The defendant may be liable although intending nothing more than a good-natured practical joke, or honestly believing that the act would not injure the plaintiff, or even though seeking the plaintiff's own good.

W. Page Keeton et al., Prosser and Keeton on the Law of Torts, § 8, at 33, 36-37 (5th ed. 1984) (footnotes omitted).

Wallace, Lalaya, and Fuqua testified that Rosen touched Wallace on the back causing her to fall down the stairs and injure herself. For battery to be an appropriate instruction, the evidence had to support an inference not only that Rosen intentionally touched Wallace, but that she did so in a rude, insolent, or angry manner, i.e., that she intended to invade Wallace's interests in a way that the law forbids.

Professors Prosser and Keeton also made the following observations about the intentional tort of battery and the character of the defendant's action:

[I]n a crowded world, a certain amount of personal contact is inevitable and must be accepted. *Absent expression to the contrary, consent is assumed to all those ordinary contacts which are customary and reasonably necessary to the common intercourse of life, such as a tap on the shoulder to attract attention,* a friendly grasp of the arm, or a casual jostling to make a passage....

The time and place, and the circumstances under which the act is done, will necessarily affect its unpermitted character, and so will the relations between the parties. A stranger is not to be expected to tolerate liberties which would be allowed by an intimate friend. But unless the defendant has special reason to believe that more or less will be permitted by the individual plaintiff, the test is what would be offensive to an ordinary person not unduly sensitive as to personal dignity.

Keeton et al., § 9, at 42 (emphasis added).

During the trial, Wallace gave the following testimony concerning the manner in which Rosen touched her:

Q [Rosen] took both hands and placed them on your shoulder blades?

A Not across my shoulder. She had her finger tips [sic] and my shoulder, and turned me around like, and moving it [sic].

Q Which way did she turn you?

A She turned me – I was going up when she turned me. She turned me towards the stairwells.

Q So, you're standing here, hands come on, you're turned. Are you turned this way towards the wall? Or this way towards the open stairs?

A Towards the open stairs.

Q And, in fact, your testimony is that she took her hands, both of them, placed them on your shoulders or approximately here.

A Um-hum. (affirmative response).

Q Turned you 180 degrees around?

A She didn't force turn me. But she put her hands there, and turned me and told me to move it.

Q And she did so 180 degrees?

A Not to 180 degrees, no.

Q Half that?

A Yeah, half that.

Q Okay, about 90. So now you're like this. Now where is Ms. Rosen?

A She's still standing up there.

...

Q What happened next, Ms. Wallace?

A That's when I slipped. I turned around-when she turned me around, that's when I slipped. Because one of my-my left foot that I had the surgical [sic] on, that's when I slipped.

Practice Pointers

Most of the cases that you will read in casebooks throughout law school will be appellate decisions, issued by a court of appeals asked to make a ruling based on the record of the case developed in the trial court. This question and answer exchange between the lawyer and the witness at trial is a good reminder of how important it is for a lawyer to receive coherent verbal responses so as to build a useful record. On appeal, a court cannot read nods and gestures that are not recorded in a way that makes them part of the record.

[C]

Viewed most favorably to the trial court's decision refusing the tendered instruction, the foregoing evidence indicates that Rosen placed her fingertips on Wallace's shoulder and turned her 90° toward the exit in the midst of a fire drill. The conditions on the stairway of Northwest High School during the fire drill were an example of Professors Prosser and Keeton's "crowded world." Individuals standing in the middle of a stairway during the fire drill could expect that a certain amount of personal contact would be inevitable. Rosen had a responsibility to her students to keep them moving in an orderly fashion down the stairs and out the door. Under these circumstances, Rosen's touching of Wallace's shoulder or back with her fingertips to get her attention over the noise of the alarm cannot be said to be a rude, insolent, or angry touching. Wallace has failed to show that the trial court abused its discretion in refusing the battery instruction.

Furthermore, even if an instruction on battery was appropriate, Wallace's inclusion of language that "a battery may be recklessly committed" created an instruction that was likely to mislead or confuse the jury ....

The facts in this case can be distinguished from those cited by the Committee. Rosen's actions were clearly not intentional.... Quite the contrary, the actions that Rosen took were intended to keep the student traffic flowing out of the building and away from any potential danger. Rosen's actions are reasonably interpreted as trying to prevent danger to human life and safety that was created by Wallace's presence at the top of the stairs. ... Wallace and Rosen did not know each other before the fire drill. Any touching arose only in response to the fire drill and the attempt to facilitate a safe exit for staff and students from the building. The inclusion of the reckless instruction with the intentional tort of battery under the facts of this case would have allowed the jury to use a lesser standard to convict Rosen and IPS of battery. We find that the inclusion of the "reckless" language in the battery instruction would have been misleading and made the instructions as a whole confusing to the jury.[3]

Finally, it cannot be said that Wallace's rights were substantially and adversely affected by the court's failure to give the battery instruction. There is a well-established "'duty on the part of school personnel to exercise ordinary and reasonable care for the safety of children under their authority.'" [C] As a teacher, this duty of care fell on Rosen. A fire had been actually set in the bathroom on Rosen's floor less than a week before the fire alarm sounded. On April 22, 1994, with no prior knowledge whether the alarm signaled a drill or a fire, Rosen exercised

---

3 The inclusion of an intentional battery instruction also would have misled the jury because the court offered the instruction that **contributory negligence** was a defense to the claimed action. Wallace did not object to the inclusion of this instruction even though contributory negligence is not a defense to an intentional tort.

ordinary and reasonable care when she tried to get the students to exit as quickly as possible. Finding Wallace and three others creating a bottleneck at the top of the staircase required Rosen to take quick action. It was necessary for Rosen to both raise her voice and touch Wallace's back to get her attention. When Wallace objected to being touched and did not move, it was also reasonable for Rosen to turn Wallace toward the stairs and tell her to get moving. Failing to give the battery instruction was not error because, even if given, the facts of this case would not have supported a claim for intentional battery. ...

....

Affirmed.

SULLIVAN, J., concurs with separate opinion.

ROBB, J., concurs in part and concurs in result in part with separate opinion.

————————

Points for Discussion

1. How did the proposed jury instruction in *Wallace* differ from the law of battery as set forth in the RESTATEMENT (SECOND) OF TORTS §§ 13 & 18?

2. How does the *Wallace* court explain the distinction between intentional conduct and negligent conduct?

3. Was the plaintiff in *Wallace* suing for an offensive contact battery or a harmful contact battery? What is the difference between an offensive contact battery and a harmful contact battery?

4. What interest is sought to be protected by recognition of a battery action?

5. An action for battery protects one against contacts that are physically harmful as well as contacts that are merely offensive and insulting. Although the technical injury – a harmful or offensive touching or contact with the plaintiff's person – is essential to a battery action, actual loss or damage is not required. In other words, nominal damages as vindication of the technical right to be free from a battery are permitted. The presence of actual damages or harm may affect recovery of a monetary award, but does not affect the plaintiff's ability to prove the *prima facie* case.

6. Battery is an intentional tort and therefore requires proof of intent. In most jurisdictions, recklessness will not suffice to establish the state of mind for proof of a battery. Likewise, there is no such thing as a "negligent battery." If one does not act with the requisite intent and causes a harmful contact, a negligence action may exist. However, if one does not act with the requisite intent for a battery action and an offensive contact results, no negligence action will lie because a negligence action requires proof of actual damages. *See* RESTATEMENT (SECOND) OF TORTS § 18(2) (1965) (providing that "an act which is not done with [intent sufficient for an offensive contact battery] does not make the actor liable … for a mere offensive contact … although the act involves an unreasonable risk of inflicting it and, therefore, would be negligent or reckless if the risk threatened bodily harm").

7. Jeremy Meintsma brought charges of assault and battery against his employer and co-workers for "birthday spankings." While at work and a few days after his birthday, his co-workers grabbed Meintsma from behind, wrestled him off his stool, held him down on the concrete floor, and administered "spankings" from a paddle fashioned out of a two-by-four. The birthday spanking was so severe that Meintsma had to go to the emergency room that evening. The doctor found that he was suffering from contusions and abrasions to his back and rear end and muscle spasms caused by the spanking. Although **Worker's Compensation Acts** usually preclude an employee from suing for injuries sustained at the workplace, most recognize an exception for intentional conduct. The court held that the birthday spanking was a battery. *See Meintsma v. Loram Maint. of Way, Inc.*, 684 N.W.2d 434 (Minn. 2004).

Hypo 2-2

While Rock Band is performing at a midnight concert, Driver is getting the bus ready for the band's next big, wild adventure across the country scheduled for later tonight. While servicing the bus, Driver notices that the waste containers from the restrooms on the bus are filled almost to capacity. Because Driver is too lazy to do otherwise, Driver stops at a nearby bridge to empty the canisters into River below. As it is practically the middle of the night, he figures that no one will ever notice him emptying the 80 tons of human waste into the dingy river. However, just to be sure, before emptying the canisters, he looks carefully over the sides of the bridge to see if there is anyone below, as he figures that there is always a chance of boats traveling under a bridge.

Not being able to see too clearly in the dark, he thinks to himself "I'll just go on and chance it," as he empties the 80 tons of liquid human waste from the canisters into the dark river below.

As luck would have it, at the very moment that he empties the canisters, Love Boat, a local midnight charter boat, is stopped almost beneath the bridge. Love Boat makes several daily runs carrying young couples on peaceful, romantic river rides. However, this evening Love Boat has run out of fuel because the owner and operator of Love Boat has failed to check the gas gauge prior to steering Love Boat out of the dock. Love Boat is stranded next to the bridge, awaiting help that it has just summoned.

Romeo, 17 years old, and Juliet, 16 years old, are the only passengers aboard the Love Boat this evening. High school students and good kids, they have just left their high school's prom together and are enjoying the midnight Love Boat ride that their parents had arranged for them before heading to their respective homes. Finding it humorous that Love Boat has run out of gas, Romeo and Juliet decide to gather on deck and gaze up at the beautiful, starry night. With beverages in hand (a Diet Coke with lime and a Dr. Pepper), the couple looks up into the clear, starry night just in time to be unexpectedly drenched (and to have their drinks topped off) by the contents of the human waste canisters from Rock Band's tour bus. Discuss.

Hypo 2-3

Daugherty, an off-duty employee of a bar, is having a few drinks with the manager, who is also off-duty. The bartender, Ms. Yoder, who knows both of them well, decides to put a toothpick in Daugherty's beer as a practical joke. Unaware of the toothpick, Daugherty drinks the beer and swallows the toothpick, causing injury. Battery? Should the fact that Ms. Yoder never touched Daugherty affect any battery claim?

Fisher v. Carrousel Motor Hotel, Inc.

424 S.W.2d 627 (Tex. 1967)

GREENHILL, Justice.

What's That?

Exemplary damages, also known as punitive damages, are damages above and beyond compensatory damages and are awarded to punish the defendant. *See* Chapter 8 for further exploration of both compensatory and punitive damages issues.

This is a suit for actual and **exemplary damages** growing out of an alleged assault and battery. The plaintiff Fisher was a mathematician with the Data Processing Division of the Manned Spacecraft Center, an agency of the National Aeronautics and Space Agency, commonly called NASA, near Houston. The defendants were the Carrousel Motor Hotel, Inc., located in Houston, the Brass Ring Club, which is located in the Carrousel, and Robert W. Flynn, who as an employee of the Carrousel was the manager of the Brass Ring Club. Flynn died before the trial, and the suit proceeded as to the Carrousel and the Brass Ring. Trial was to a jury which found for the plaintiff Fisher. The trial court rendered judgment for the defendants notwithstanding the verdict. The Court of Civil Appeals affirmed. [C] The questions before this Court are whether there was evidence that an actionable battery was committed, and, if so, whether the two corporate defendants must respond in exemplary as well as actual damages for the malicious conduct of Flynn.

The plaintiff Fisher had been invited by Ampex Corporation and Defense Electronics to a one day's meeting regarding telemetry equipment at the Carrousel. The invitation included a luncheon. The guests were asked to reply by telephone whether they could attend the luncheon, and Fisher called in his acceptance. After the morning session, the group of 25 or 30 guests adjourned to the Brass Ring Club for lunch. The luncheon was buffet style, and Fisher stood in line with others and just ahead of a graduate student of Rice University who testified at the trial. As Fisher was about to be served, he was approached by Flynn, who snatched the plate from Fisher's hand and shouted that he, a Negro, could not be served in the club. Fisher testified that he was not actually touched, and did not testify that he suffered fear or apprehension of physical injury; but he did testify that he was highly embarrassed and hurt by Flynn's conduct in the presence of his associates.

The jury found that Flynn "forceably [sic] dispossessed plaintiff of his dinner plate" and "shouted in a loud and offensive manner" that Fisher could not be served there, thus subjecting Fisher to humiliation and indignity. It was stipulated that Flynn was an employee of the Carrousel Hotel and, as such, managed the Brass Ring Club. The jury also found that Flynn acted maliciously and awarded Fisher $400 actual damages for his humiliation and indignity and $500 **exemplary damages** for Flynn's malicious conduct.

The Court of Civil Appeals held that there was no assault because there was no physical contact and no evidence of fear or apprehension of physical contact. However, it has long been settled that there can be a battery without an assault, and that actual physical contact is not necessary to constitute a battery, so long as there is contact with clothing or an object closely identified with the body. 1 Harper & James, The Law of Torts 216 (1956); Restatement of Torts 2d, §§ 18 and 19. In Prosser, Law of Torts 32 (3d Ed. 1964), it is said:

> 'The interest in freedom from intentional and unpermitted contacts with the plaintiff's person is protected by an action for the tort commonly called battery. The protection extends to any part of the body, or to anything which is attached to it and practically identified with it. Thus contact with the plaintiff's clothing, or with a cane, a paper, or any other object held in his hand will be sufficient * * * The plaintiff's interest in the integrity of his person includes all those things which are in contact or connected with it.'

Under the facts of this case, we have no difficulty in holding that the intentional grabbing of plaintiff's plate constituted a battery. The intentional snatching of an object from one's hand is as clearly an offensive invasion of his person as would be an actual contact with the body. "To constitute an assault and battery, it is not necessary to touch the plaintiff's body or even his clothing; knocking or snatching anything from plaintiff's hand or touching anything connected with his person, when, done i[n] an offensive manner, is sufficient." [C]

Such holding is not unique to the jurisprudence of this State. In S. H. Kress & Co. v. Brashier, 50 S.W.2d 922 (Tex.Civ.App.1932, no writ), the defendant was held to have committed "an assault or trespass upon the person" by snatching a book from the plaintiff's hand. The jury findings in that case were that the defendant "dispossessed plaintiff of the book" and caused her to suffer "humiliation and indignity."

The rationale for holding an offensive contact with such an object to be a battery is explained in 1 Restatement of Torts 2d § 18 (Comment p. 31) as follows:

> Since the essence of the plaintiff's grievance consists in the offense to the dignity involved in the unpermitted and intentional invasion of the inviolability of his person and not in any physical harm done to his

body, it is not necessary that the plaintiff's actual body be disturbed. Unpermitted and intentional contacts with anything so connected with the body as to be customarily regarded as part of the other's person and therefore as partaking of its inviolability is actionable as an offensive contact with his person. There are some things such as clothing or a cane or, indeed, anything directly grasped by the hand which are so intimately connected with one's body as to be universally regarded as part of the person.

We hold, therefore, that the forceful dispossession of plaintiff Fisher's plate in an offensive manner was sufficient to constitute a battery, and the trial court erred in granting judgment notwithstanding the verdict on the issue of actual damages.

In Harned v. E-Z Finance Co., 151 Tex. 641, 254 S.W.2d 81 (1953), this Court refused to adopt the 'new tort' of intentional interference with peace of mind which permits recovery for mental suffering in the absence of resulting physical injury or an assault and battery. ... However, it is not necessary to adopt such a cause of action in order to sustain the verdict of the jury in this case. The *Harned* case recognized the well established rule that mental suffering is compensable in suits for willful torts "which are recognized as torts and actionable independently and separately from mental suffering or other injury." [C] Damages for mental suffering are recoverable without the necessity for showing actual physical injury in a case of willful battery because the basis of that action is the unpermitted and intentional invasion of the plaintiff's person and not the actual harm done to the plaintiff's body. RESTATEMENT OF TORTS 2D § 18. Personal indignity is the essence of an action for battery; and consequently the defendant is liable not only for contacts which do actual physical harm, but also for those which are offensive and insulting. [Cc] We hold, therefore, that plaintiff was entitled to actual damages for mental suffering due to the willful battery, even in the absence of any physical injury.

We now turn to the question of the liability of the corporations for exemplary damages. [The court's discussion regarding the appropriateness of exemplary damages is omitted.]

....

The judgments of the courts below are reversed, and judgment is here rendered for the plaintiff for $900 with interest from the date of the trial court's judgment, and for costs of this suit.

Points for Discussion

1. Battery requires that the plaintiff's body or something intimately associated with plaintiff's body be contacted in a harmful or offensive manner.

2. It is essential to the battery action that the plaintiff's body be contacted, but it is not necessary that the defendant's body touch the plaintiff. What is important is that the bodily contact be caused by an act caused by the defendant. So if A pushes B against C, knocking C down and breaking his leg, A is liable to C for battery; B is not, even though B actually came into contact with A. For example, recall that in the case of *Garratt v. Dailey*, *supra* Chapter 1, Brian never touched Mrs. Garratt.

3. The interest to be free from unpermitted harmful or offensive bodily contact is protected even if the plaintiff is not aware of the contact at the time that it takes place. So if A kisses B while B is sleeping but does not waken or harm her, A is subject to liability to B. *See* RESTATEMENT (SECOND) OF TORTS § 18 cmt. *d* (1965). A's liability is based upon A's intentional invasion of and affront to B's person. Plaintiff's conscious awareness of the invasion at the time is not required.

4. A defendant's liability extends to consequences the defendant did not intend and also to those the defendant could not have anticipated. For example, assume that A intends to offend B by kicking him on the shin so lightly that it would not usually cause physical injury. However, at the time, B is suffering from a diseased leg about which A does not know or have reason to know. The light kick aggravates B's leg so much that he now suffers from a permanent disability to his leg. Should A be liable to B for the permanent disability his leg? *See* RESTATEMENT (SECOND) OF TORTS § 16 cmt. *a* (1965). What is the rationale in support of such a rule?

5. Martha Umana was a bakery employee at a Kroger supermarket. Kroger had a policy that required employees to wear name badges. According to Umana, when she approached her supervisor at the customer service desk to discuss the possibility of a transfer to another store, he questioned whether she was wearing a name badge. In response, Umana moved the left side of her plastic apron to reveal the name badge pinned to her shirt. Umana testified that her supervisor then grabbed her and said, "You don't have it. I don't see it." He then tore her apron. There was a surveillance videotape of the incident that showed Umana's supervisor tearing the apron strap from around her neck. Battery? *See* Umana v. Kroger Texas, L.P., 239 S.W.3d 434 (Tex. Civ. App.— Dallas 2007).

6. Sandra Ponder was formerly employed by Colin Hales as a referral clerk. The atmosphere at Ponder's job was fine for the first several weeks, but then began to deteriorate when Hales began making unwanted advances toward Ponder. According to Ponder, Hales began requesting early morning meetings to discuss his personal life. She claims that at these meetings, he would hug her and "would slip a kiss in or try to." He would sit close to her on his couch, caress her hands, and put his arm underneath her arm. He would rub himself against her, and she would push away from him. Ponder claimed that this touching was uninvited and offensive to her. She claimed that this touching occurred every day until she was fired. In contrast, Hales testified that Ponder would voluntarily give him a big hug at the beginning and end of each day. He admitted kissing her on the cheek once, but denied other testimony by Ponder. Battery? *See* Ponder v. Hales, No. 09-07-411CV, 2008 WL 2129848 (Tex. Civ. App.—Beaumont May 22, 2008).

> **Make the Connection**
>
> An employee subjected to conduct such as that experienced by Ponder may also have a claim of sexual harassment under federal and state anti-discrimination statutes, a subject addressed in an employment discrimination course.

Hypo 2-4

Rachel and Jerry hire Flagstaff to cater their wedding. They instruct Flagstaff that many of the members of the wedding party will be Jewish and because of that they only want kosher food to be served at the reception. Flagstaff agrees, saying that he has experience preparing kosher food and that he will be able to handle their request. However, as the time for the reception approaches, Flagstaff finds himself short of some ingredients for the sushi plate. In a pinch, Flagstaff substitutes shrimp (a non-kosher food) for one of the types of sushi. The sushi is the only entree available for guests, with five pieces of sushi allotted per guest, and one of every five pieces of sushi is now non-kosher (because of the shrimp). Rachel and Jerry are horrified when they see the shrimp on the platter, and even more so when a rabbi brings his half-eaten sushi platter to them demanding to know what was going on. Does the rabbi have a viable cause of action against Flagstaff for an intentional tort? If so, which one(s)? Is there any additional information you might need to determine Flagstaff's tort liability to the rabbi?

C. Assault

The RESTATEMENT (SECOND) OF TORTS provides that a defendant is subject to liability for the intentional tort of assault if he acts intending to cause apprehension of an imminent harmful or offensive contact with the person of another and the person is thereby placed in such imminent apprehension. *See* RESTATEMENT (SECOND) OF TORTS § 21 (1965). Consider the next case.

Western Union Telegraph Co. v. Hill

150 So. 709 (Ala. App. 1933)

SAMFORD, Judge.

The action in this case is based upon an alleged assault on the person of plaintiff's wife by one Sapp, an agent of defendant in charge of its office in Huntsville, Ala. The assault complained of consisted of an attempt on the part of Sapp to put his hand on the person of plaintiff's wife coupled with a request that she come behind the counter in defendant's office, and that, if she would come and allow Sapp to love and pet her, he "would fix her clock."

The first question that addresses itself to us is, Was there such an assault as will justify an action for damages?

. . . .

While every battery includes an assault, an assault does not necessarily require a battery to complete it. What it does take to constitute an assault is an unlawful attempt to commit a battery, incomplete by reason of some intervening cause; or, to state it differently, to constitute an actionable assault there must be an intentional, unlawful, offer to touch the person of another in a rude or angry manner under such circumstances as to create in the mind of the party alleging the assault a well-founded fear of an imminent battery, coupled with the apparent present ability to effectuate the attempt, if not prevented. [Cc]

Food for Thought

Do you agree with the court's statement that "every battery includes an assault"?

Solicitation by a man to a woman for intercourse unaccompanied by an assault is not actionable. [Cc] Insulting words used when not accompanied by an assault are not the subject of an action for damages. [Cc]

What are the facts here? Sapp was the agent of defendant and the manager of its telegraph office in Huntsville. Defendant was under contract with plaintiff to keep in repair and regulated an electric clock in plaintiff's place of business. When the clock needed attention, that fact was to be reported to Sapp, and he in turn would report to a special man, whose duty it was to do the fixing. At 8:13 o'clock p.m. plaintiff's wife reported to Sapp over the phone that the clock needed attention, and, no one coming to attend to the clock, plaintiff's wife went to the office of defendant about 8:30 p.m. There she found Sapp in charge and behind a desk or counter, separating the public from the part of the room in which defendant's operator worked. The counter is four feet and two inches high, and so wide that, Sapp standing on the floor, leaning against the counter and stretching his arm and hand to the full length, the end of his fingers reaches just to the outer edge of the counter. The photographs in evidence show that the counter was as high as Sapp's armpits. Sapp had had two or three drinks and was "still slightly feeling the effects of whisky; I felt all right; I felt good and amiable." When plaintiff's wife came into the office, Sapp came from towards the rear of the room and asked what he could do for her. She replied: "I asked him if he understood over the phone that my clock was out of order and when he was going to fix it. He stood there and looked at me a few minutes and said: 'If you will come back here and let me love and pet you, I will fix your clock.' This he repeated and reached for me with his hand, he extended his hand toward me, he did not put it on me; I jumped back. I was in his reach as I stood there. He reached for me right along here (indicating her left shoulder and arm)." The foregoing is the evidence offered by plaintiff tending to prove an assault. Per contra, aside from the positive denial by Sapp of any effort to touch Mrs. Hill, the physical surroundings as evidenced by the photographs of the locus tend to rebut any evidence going to prove that Sapp could have touched plaintiff's wife across that counter even if he had reached his hand in her direction unless she was leaning against the counter or Sapp should have stood upon something so as to elevate him and allow him to reach beyond the counter. However, there is testimony tending to prove that, notwithstanding the width of the counter and the height of Sapp, Sapp could have reached from six to eighteen inches beyond the desk in an effort to place his hand on Mrs. Hill. The evidence as a whole presents a question for the jury. This was the view taken by the trial judge, and in the several rulings bearing on this question there is no error.

The next question is, Was the act of Sapp towards Mrs. Hill, plaintiff's wife, such as to render this defendant liable under the doctrine of **respondeat superior**? ...

It's Latin to Me!

Respondeat superior literally translated means "let the superior make answer." It is a doctrine which allows an employer to be held liable for an employee's wrongful act committed within the scope of employment. *See* Chapter 12, *infra*, Vicarious Responsibility.

… To our minds, the evidence is conclusive to the effect that, while Sapp was the agent of defendant, in the proposal and technical assault made by him on plaintiff's wife he stepped aside wholly from his master's business to pursue a matter entirely personal. Where this is so, the doctrine of respondeat superior does not apply. [Cc] The rules of law governing cases of this nature are perfectly clear and well defined. The confusion arises now and then from a failure to keep in mind the distinction between the act done by the servant within the scope of, and the act done during, his employment. The act charged in this case is clearly personal to Sapp and not referable to his employer. [C]

The rulings of the trial court with reference to this question were erroneous. The defendant was entitled to the general charge [on the issue of respondeat superior], and for the error in refusing this charge as requested the judgment is reversed and the cause is remanded.

Reversed and remanded.

———————————

Points for Discussion

1. What interest is sought to be protected by recognition of the intentional tort of assault?

2. Assault actions were the first causes of action to recognize mental injury as a harm for which the law provides a remedy. A plaintiff is entitled to recover for an assault even in the absence of physical harm.

3. Who is the defendant in the *Western Union Telegraph* case? Why is Mr. Sapp's conduct at issue in this action, even though he is not part of the lawsuit brought by the Hills?

4. The *Western Union Telegraph* court is correct in stating that "an assault does not necessarily require a battery to complete it." Consider whether the court is similarly correct in stating that "every battery includes an assault." For example, in Note 3, page 55, it was established that a person can be the victim of a battery even if unaware of the offensive contact at the time of its occurrence because she was, for example, asleep. Has that same person been assaulted? *See* RESTATEMENT (SECOND) OF TORTS § 22 (no liability for assault if victim is not aware before defendant's conduct is terminated). What if intending to frighten Sally, who is deaf, Bob discharges a pistol next to Sally's ear? Sally does not see (or hear) Bob discharge the pistol and does not discover what has happened until later. Is Bob liable for assault? *See* RESTATEMENT (SECOND) OF TORTS §22, cmt. *b*.

5. Does Mrs. Hill have a viable assault claim if it was physically impossible for Sapp to have actually touched her? Assault depends on the defendant's *apparent* ability to carry out a battery, not the defendant's *actual* ability. So if Bob points a gun at Jim threatening to shoot him, Bob is subject to liability for assault, whether the gun is loaded or not. *See* Restatement (Second) of Torts § 33.

6. Mere words, no matter how threatening, are insufficient to constitute an assault, unless they are coupled with other acts or circumstances to put the plaintiff in reasonable apprehension of imminent harmful or offensive contact. *See* Restatement (Second) of Torts § 31. Likewise, threatening future harm does not constitute an assault. So when Mr. Crip, a known member of a notoriously dangerous gang, telephones Mr. Blood and says, "The next time I see you, I will shoot you," Mr. Crip has not committed an assault, even if Mr. Crip is known to have killed in the past. However, if shortly thereafter, Mr. Blood unexpectedly encounters Mr. Crip who, without moving, says, "Your time has come," Mr. Crip has committed a civil assault. *See* Restatement (Second) of Torts § 31. But if instead Mr. Crip says, "If I had my gun, I'd shoot you dead right now," he has not committed an assault, as threats dependent upon statements contrary to fact do not constitute an assault. By informing Mr. Blood that he does not have a gun, Mr. Crip's words have negated the imminence of the bodily contact.

7. Rizzo is furious with Danny because he has told Kenickie, the love of her life, that she has been kissing another guy. Rizzo spots Danny a few yards away hanging out with his friends, the T-Birds. Rizzo picks up a stick and begins to charge toward Danny, intending to hit him with it. Danny sees Rizzo walking quickly toward him swinging the stick wildly in his direction. When Rizzo is within a few feet of him, Rizzo continues toward him with the stick still raised, threatening to strike him. Because Danny is with his fellow T-Birds, he is not afraid or fearful of Rizzo because Danny knows that his friends will interfere to prevent Rizzo from striking him, which they do. Has Rizzo assaulted Danny? *See* Restatement (Second) § 24 (apprehension and not fear is required to sustain action for assault). Assault requires *apprehension*, the belief that the defendant's act is capable of immediately inflicting contact upon the plaintiff unless something further occurs. It does not require that the plaintiff actually *fear* that the contact will ensue.

8. Allen is a very safety-conscious supervisor who works for the United States Postal Service. One day when he is making his rounds at the office, he finds Mac performing repairs to a small section of tile. Mac has a two-foot by two-foot area blocked off by safety cones and has various tools (including a hammer) spread around in his small area. Thinking that Mac is surely

releasing asbestos (a dangerous carcinogen) into his work environment, Allen becomes enraged. He screams at Mac to stop what he is doing because it constitutes a safety hazard. When Mac tells Allen to calm down, Allen picks up a safety cone and tosses it across the room and kicks Mac's tools. Mac was not seriously hurt, but Mac's fingers were smashed when Allen accidently stomped on his fingers while trying to kick the tools. Is Allen liable to Mac for battery? Assault? *See* Guirguess v. United States Postal Serv., 32 F.App'x 555 (Fed. Cir. 2002).

Hypo 2-5

Vincent is a typical fifteen-year-old high school student with no history of disciplinary problems. One day, while he is sleeping through Ms. Nadeau's dreadfully boring math class, Ms. Nadeau becomes irritated when she sees that Vincent has placed his head down on his desk. In an attempt to wake him suddenly, she slaps her open hand on the desk as hard as she can. Vincent is jolted awake by the loud noise. He was extremely traumatized by the event and awoke the next morning with bloody fluid on his pillow due to a broken eardrum. Vincent is required to have surgery on that ear to fix the eardrum and ultimately suffers a permanent partial loss to his hearing as a result. Did Ms. Nadeau batter Vincent? Did she assault him? Discuss.

D. False Imprisonment

Big Town Nursing Home, Inc. v. Newman

461 S.W.2d 195 (Tex. Civ. App. 1970)

McDONALD, Chief Justice.

This is an appeal by defendant nursing home from a judgment for plaintiff Newman for actual and exemplary damages in a false imprisonment case.

Plaintiff Newman sued defendant nursing home for actual and exemplary damages for falsely and wrongfully imprisoning him against his will from September 22, 1968 to November 11, 1968. ...

....

Plaintiff is a retired printer 67 years of age, and lives on his social security and a retirement pension from his brother's printing company. He has not worked since 1959, is single, has Parkinson's disease, arthritis, heart trouble, a voice impediment, and a hiatal hernia. He has served in the army attaining the rank of Sergeant. He has never been in a mental hospital or treated by a psychiatrist. Plaintiff was taken to defendant nursing home on September 19, 1968 by his nephew who signed the admission papers and paid one month's care in advance. Plaintiff had been arrested for drunkenness and drunk driving in times past (the last time in 1966) and had been treated twice for alcoholism. Plaintiff testified he was not intoxicated and had nothing to drink during the week prior to admission to the nursing home. The admission papers provided that patient "will not be forced to remain in the nursing home against his will for any length of time." Plaintiff was not advised he would be kept at the nursing home against his will. On September 22, 1968 plaintiff decided he wanted to leave and tried to telephone for a taxi. Defendant's employees advised plaintiff he could not use the phone, or have any visitors unless the manager knew them, and locked plaintiff's grip and clothes up. Plaintiff walked out of the home, but was caught by employees of defendant and brought back forceably [sic], and thereafter placed in Wing 3 and locked up. Defendant's Administrator testified Wing 3 contained senile patients, drug addicts, alcoholics, mentally disturbed, incorrigibles and uncontrollables, and that "they were all in the same kettle of fish." Plaintiff tried to escape from the nursing home five or six times but was caught and brought back each time against his will. He was carried back to Wing 3 and locked and taped in a "restraint chair", for more than five hours. He was put back in the chair on subsequent occasions. ... Plaintiff made every effort to leave and repeatedly asked the manager and assistant manager to be permitted to leave. ... Finally on November 11, 1968 plaintiff escaped and caught a ride into Dallas, where he called a taxi and was taken to the home of a friend. During plaintiff's ordeal he lost 30 pounds. There was never any court proceeding to confine plaintiff. Defendant's assistant manager testified that plaintiff attempted to leave the home five or six times, and on each occasion was brought back against his will.

False imprisonment is the direct restraint of one person of the physical liberty of another without adequate legal justification.

....

Defendant placed plaintiff in Wing 3 with insane persons, alcoholics and drug addicts knowing he was not in such category; punished plaintiff by locking and taping him in the restraint chair; prevented him from using the telephone for 51 days; locked up his clothes; told him he could not be released from Wing 3 until he began to obey the rules of the home; and detained him for 51 days during which period he was demanding to be released and attempting to escape.

. . . .

Defendant acted in the utter disregard of plaintiff's legal rights, knowing there was no court order for commitment, and that the admission agreement provided he was not to be kept against his will.

. . . .

However, from this record, we are of the opinion that the verdict and judgment of the trial court is excessive in the sum of $12,000, and that this cause should be reversed for that reason only. Appellee is given 10 days from this date in which to file a **remittitur** of $12,000. [Cc] If such remittitur is filed within 10 days, the judgment of the trial court will be reformed and affirmed.

What's That?

A *remittitur* is a request to the court by the defendant that the plaintiff receive less in damages than that awarded by the jury or, if that request is denied, that the defendant receive a new trial.

Reversed and Remanded.

. . . .

Points for Discussion

1. The RESTATEMENT (SECOND) OF TORTS § 35 (1965) provides that an actor may be "subject to liability for false imprisonment if

    (a) he acts intending to confine [another] within boundaries fixed by the actor, and

    (b) his act directly or indirectly results in such a confinement of the other, and

    (c) the other is conscious of the confinement or is harmed by it."

2. If there is a reasonable means of escape about which the plaintiff is aware, no false imprisonment action will lie. High School Basketball Team is showering

in the locker room after their defeat of the Local Rival Team. Jones, who takes long, deliberate showers, is still showering when Smith takes his clothes and locks all the locker room doors but for the door leading to a general waiting room where persons of both sexes are congregated. Jones is aware of the unlocked door leading to the general waiting room, but knows of no alternative route out. Has Smith committed the tort of false imprisonment? *See* RESTATEMENT (SECOND) OF TORTS § 36.

Hypo 2-6

John and Duffy are driving a car down the interstate when they see a couple of hitchhikers. They pick them up, and the hitchhikers (Ellen and Terry) continue with them until Dallas. When they reach Dallas, Ellen asks to be let out of the car. John is driving and refuses to let her out, saying they have to make it to Oklahoma by 4:00 p.m. If Ellen sues for false imprisonment, what is the likely result?

Hypo 2-7

Passenger is a customer of Airline. He has boarded one of Airline's planes late one evening on a flight that is expected to be about three hours. However, shortly after takeoff, the flight is diverted to an unexpected airport due to bad weather. When the plane arrives at its unexpected location, Passenger and his fellow cabinmates are not permitted to disembark from the airplane. Instead, the passengers are told that, given the late hour, they must stay on the plane because there are insufficient security personnel at their arrival airport to handle the large number of passengers. They are also told that it is a violation of federal law to open any of the marked emergency exits under these circumstances. The passengers wait on the airplane overnight for more than ten hours, during which time they are provided with just one beverage, no food, and are subjected to very unpleasant odors because the airplane's lavatories became out of order and began overflowing shortly after arriving at the unexpected airport. False imprisonment?

Parvi v. City of Kingston

362 N.E.2d 960 (N.Y. 1977)

Fuchsberg, J.

This appeal brings up for review the dismissal of … the plaintiff's case … aris[ing] out of … somewhat unusual … events. … The judgment of dismissal was affirmed by the Appellate Division by a vote of three to two. The issue before us … is whether a prima facie case [of false imprisonment] was made out. We believe it was.

Bearing in mind that, at the procedural point at which the case was decided, the plaintiff was entitled to the benefit of the most favorable inferences that were to be drawn from the record [C], we turn at once to the proof. In doing so, for the present we rely in the main on testimony plaintiff adduced from the defendant's own employees, especially since plaintiff's own recollection of the events was less than satisfactory.

Sometime after 9:00 P.M. on the evening of May 28, 1972, a date which occurred during the Memorial Day weekend, two police officers employed by the defendant City of Kingston responded in a radio patrol car to the rear of a commercial building in that city where they had been informed some individuals were acting in a boisterous manner. Upon their arrival, they found three men, one Raymond Dugan, his brother Dixie Dugan and the plaintiff, Donald C. Parvi. According to the police, it was the Dugan brothers who alone were then engaged in a noisy quarrel. When the two uniformed officers informed the three they would have to move on or be locked up, Raymond Dugan ran away; Dixie Dugan chased after him unsuccessfully and then returned to the scene in a minute or two; Parvi, who the police testimony shows had been trying to calm the Dugans, remained where he was.

In the course of their examinations…, the officers described all three as exhibiting, in an unspecified manner, evidence that they "had been drinking" and showed "the effects of alcohol". They went on to relate how, when Parvi and Dixie Dugan said they had no place to go, the officers ordered them into the police car and, pursuing a then prevailing police "standard operating procedure", transported the two men outside the city limits to an abandoned golf course located in an unlit and isolated area known as Coleman Hill. Thereupon the officers drove off, leaving Parvi and Dugan to "dry out". This was the first time Parvi had ever been there. En route they had asked to be left off at another place, but the police refused to do so.

No more than 350 feet from the spot where they were dropped off, one of the boundaries of the property adjoins the New York State Thruway. There were no intervening fences or barriers other than the low Thruway guardrail intended to keep vehicular traffic on the road. Before they left, it is undisputed that the police made no effort to learn whether Parvi was oriented to his whereabouts, to instruct him as to the route back to Kingston, where Parvi had then lived for 12 years, or to ascertain where he would go from there. From where the men were dropped, the "humming and buzzing" of fast-traveling, holiday-bound automobile traffic was clearly audible from the Thruway; in their befuddled state, which later left Parvi with very little memory of the events, the men lost little time in responding to its siren song. For, in an apparent effort to get back, by 10:00 P.M. Parvi and Dugan had wandered onto the Thruway, where they were struck by an automobile operated by one David R. Darling. Parvi was severely injured; Dugan was killed. (Parvi elected not to appeal from the dismissal of his cause of action against Darling, who originally had been joined as an additional defendant.)

THE CAUSE OF ACTION FOR FALSE IMPRISONMENT

With these facts before us, we ... direct our attention to Parvi's cause of action for false imprisonment. Only recently, we had occasion to set out the four elements ... where we said that "the plaintiff must show that: (1) the defendant intended to confine him, (2) the plaintiff was conscious of the confinement, (3) the plaintiff did not consent to the confinement and (4) the confinement was not otherwise privileged".

Elements (1) and (3) present no problem here. ... [¶] Element (2), consciousness of confinement, is a more subtle and more interesting subissue in this case. On that subject, we note that, while respected authorities have divided on whether awareness of confinement by one who has been falsely imprisoned should be a

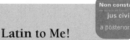

It's Latin to Me!

Sine qua non is Latin for "without which not." It refers to an indispensable condition or thing upon which something else necessarily depends.

sine qua non for making out a case[,] that question [has been laid] to rest in this State. [F]alse imprisonment, as a dignitary tort, is not suffered unless its victim knows of the dignitary invasion. Interestingly, the RESTATEMENT OF TORTS 2D (§ 42) too has taken the position that there is no liability for intentionally confining another unless the person physically restrained knows of the confinement or is harmed by it.

However, though correctly proceeding on that premise, the Appellate Division, in affirming the dismissal of the cause of action for false imprisonment, erroneously relied on the fact that Parvi, after having provided additional testimony in his own behalf on direct examination, had agreed on cross that he no longer had any *recollection* of his confinement. In so doing, that court failed to distinguish between a later recollection of consciousness and the existence of that consciousness at the time when the imprisonment itself took place. The latter, of course, is capable of being proved though one who suffers the consciousness can no longer personally describe it, whether by reason of lapse of memory, incompetency, death or other cause. Specifically, in this case, while it may well be that the alcohol Parvi had imbibed or the injuries he sustained, or both, had had the effect of wiping out his recollection of being in the police car against his will, that is a far cry from saying that he was not conscious of his confinement at the time when it was actually taking place. And, even if plaintiff's sentient state at the time of his imprisonment was something less than total sobriety, that does not mean that he had no conscious sense of what was then happening to him. To the contrary, there is much in the record to support a finding that the plaintiff indeed was aware of his arrest at the time it took place. By way of illustration, the officers described Parvi's responsiveness to their command that he get into the car, his colloquy while being driven to Coleman Hill and his request to be let off elsewhere. At the very least, then, it was for the jury, in the first instance, to weigh credibility, evaluate inconsistencies and determine whether the burden of proof had been met.

....

[U]nder plaintiff's theory, the false imprisonment count does not rest on the reasonableness of the police officers' action, but on whether the unwilling confinement of the plaintiff was the result of an arrest for a nonjustified purpose.

[T]he order of the Appellate Division should be reversed ... and a new trial ordered....

Chief Judge Breitel[, dissenting:]

I dissent. On no view of the facts should plaintiff, brought to causing his own serious injury by his voluntary intoxication, be allowed to recover from the City of Kingston for damages suffered when he wandered onto the New York State Thruway and was struck by an automobile. His attack is the familiar one on the good Samaritan, in the persons of two police officers, for not having, in retrospect, done enough.

The order of the Appellate Division should be affirmed, and the action stand dismissed.

On the night in question, the Kingston city police, responding to a complaint, found plaintiff Parvi and his companions in the midst of an uproarious argument behind a commercial establishment located on Broadway, in Kingston. Close by were railroad tracks, still in use by locomotives and freight trains. Plaintiff and his companion Dugan, both intoxicated, were asked if they had any place to go, and they said not. They were then taken to the police car, and informed that they would not be placed in jail on this holiday weekend, but, in accordance with their wishes, would instead be transported to a point out of the area where they could "sleep it off" without getting into further trouble. Dugan and Parvi repeatedly expressed their appreciation and gratitude at the option given them.

As the drive out of town proceeded, one of the men suggested a place where they might be left. The police officers, however, solicitous of the safety of their charges, declined this request, noting that the area suggested provided no shelter and, significantly, that the Thruway was "right there". As an alternative, the officers, with the consent of plaintiff and Dugan, dropped the men off at "Coleman Hill", the site of a former golf course, a spot often used by campers and equipped with several "lean-to" shelters. From the relative safety of this sheltered area, the two men, some time later, managed to wander onto the Thruway, over 350 feet away, where Dugan was killed and Parvi injured by passing automobiles.

On these facts, Parvi contends ... that he was falsely imprisoned....

In *Broughton v State of New York* (37 NY2d 451, 456, cert den 423 US 929), this court enumerated the elements necessary to sustain a false imprisonment claim: (1) intention to confine, (2) consciousness of confinement, (3) lack of consent to confinement, and (4) lack of privilege. But before those factors may even be reached, there must be evidence of a confinement. In this case, there was none, but, instead, merely an exclusion from one particular area and activity. [C]

So long as Parvi did not remain out in public, intoxicated, creating a public nuisance, and endangering his own life, the officers had no wish to interfere with Parvi's freedom of movement. Since Parvi could suggest no suitable place where the officers might take him, the officers chose another site. Apparently, Parvi and Dugan were pleased with the choice. And it should not matter that Parvi testified, although he could recall nothing else, that he was ordered into a police car "against [his] will". (On cross-examination, he said he recalled nothing that day.) Parvi's "will" was to stay where he was, intoxicated, in public. In order to deprive him of that one choice, which the officers could do without subjecting themselves to liability for false imprisonment, the officers had to transport Parvi some place else. He was given a choice as to destination. He declined it, except for his later suggestion of an unsafe place, and the officers made the choice for him. There was no confinement, and hence no false imprisonment.

Moreover, plaintiff has failed even to make out a prima facie case that he was conscious of his purported confinement, and that he failed to consent to it. His memory of the entire incident had disappeared; at trial, Parvi admitted that he no longer had any independent recollection of what happened on the day of his accident, and that as to the circumstances surrounding his entrance into the police car, he only knew what had been suggested to him by subsequent conversations. In light of this testimony, Parvi's conclusory statement that he was ordered into the car against his will is insufficient, as a matter of law, to establish a prima facie case.

. . . .

Basically, the legal issues in this case are not difficult. And the justice issues are even less so. A drunken man, a pitiable character, is found with his companions in the middle of town. Sympathetic police officers offer to take the men any where they choose, but the poor fellows have no place to go. So, rather than locking them up for a holiday weekend, the officers deposit the men in a suburban setting, where some shelter is available. The officers are thanked for their kindness. But, in the end, the efforts of the officers are to no avail, as the drunken men wander away from safety and into danger. A tragedy, certainly. A miscalculation, perhaps. But even with the aid of hindsight, the facts in this case are not the stuff on which tort liability may be premised.

Accordingly, I dissent, and vote to affirm the order of the Appellate Division.

. . . .

————————————

Points for Discussion

1. What is the area to which the plaintiff alleges he had been wrongfully confined in the *Parvi* case?

2. Contemporaneous awareness of the confinement (or harm by virtue of the confinement) is essential to the tort of false imprisonment, not recall of the confinement later. The latter may present proof problems, but does not defeat the plaintiff's *prima facie* case.

3. What legal interest is sought to be protected by recognition of the tort of false imprisonment?

4. What is the public policy consideration about which the dissenting judge is concerned? Do you agree with the dissenting judge? Should a voluntarily intoxicated person who is injured as a result be able to avail herself of the tort system and hold others responsible for her injuries?

5. The confinement for false imprisonment can be secured by actual or apparent physical barriers, by physical force or threats of physical force, or by other **duress** sufficient to make the plaintiff's consent ineffective.

Hardy v. LaBelle's Distributing Co.

661 P.2d 35 (Mont. 1983)

GULBRANDSON, Justice.

Plaintiff, Debra Jo Hardy brought this action against defendants for false imprisonment. The District Court of the Thirteenth Judicial District, Yellowstone County, issued judgment after a jury verdict in favor of defendants and plaintiff appeals.

Defendant, LaBelle's Distributing Company (LaBelle's), hired Hardy as a temporary employee on December 1, 1978. She was assigned duty as a sales clerk in the jewelry department.

On December 9, 1978, another employee for LaBelle's, Jackie Renner, thought she saw Hardy steal one of the watches that LaBelle's had in stock. Jackie Renner reported her belief to LaBelle's showroom manager that evening.

On the morning of December 10, Hardy was approached by the assistant manager of LaBelle's jewelry department and told that all new employees were given a tour of the store. He showed her into the showroom manager's office and then left, closing the door behind him.

There is conflicting testimony concerning who was present in the showroom manager's office when Hardy arrived. Hardy testified that David Kotke, the showroom manager, Steve Newsom, the store's loss prevention manager, and a uniformed policeman were present. Newsom and one of the policemen in the room testified that another policeman, instead of Kotke, was present.

Hardy was told that she had been accused of stealing a watch. Hardy denied taking the watch and agreed to take a lie detector test. According to conflicting testimony, the meeting lasted approximately from twenty to forty-five minutes.

Hardy took the lie detector test which supported her statement that she had not taken the watch. The showroom manager apologized to Hardy the next morning and told her that she was still welcome to work at LaBelle's. The employee who reported seeing Hardy take the watch also apologized. The two employees then argued briefly, and Hardy left the store.

Hardy brought this action claiming that defendants had wrongfully detained her against her will when she was questioned about the watch.

....

The two key elements of false imprisonment are the restraint of an individual against his will and the unlawfulness of such restraint. [C] The individual may be restrained by acts or merely by words which he fears to disregard. [Cc]

Here, there is ample evidence to support the jury's finding that Hardy was not unlawfully restrained against her will. While Hardy stated that she felt compelled to remain in the showroom manager's office, she also admitted that she wanted to stay and clarify the situation. She did not ask to leave. She was not told she could not leave. No threat of force or otherwise was made to compel her to stay. Although she followed the assistant manager into the office under pretense of a tour, she testified at trial that she would have followed him voluntarily if she had known the true purpose of the meeting and that two policemen were in the room. Under these circumstances, the jury could easily find that Hardy was not detained against her will. [Cc]

....

Here, the court's instructions adequately stated the law on false imprisonment. ...

....

Finding substantial evidence to support the judgment and no error in the issuance of the instructions, the District Court's judgment is affirmed.

HASWELL, C.J., and SHEA, WEBER and MORRISON, JJ., concur.

———————

Points for Discussion

1. Moral persuasion or moral pressure is insufficient to constitute force or threat of force in support of a false imprisonment action. It is essential to a false imprisonment action that the confinement be against the will of the plaintiff. A person who is free to leave but who chooses to remain does not have a viable false imprisonment action.

2. Xavier, the owner of a store, seizes and retains his customer Jacqui's purse, which contains a large sum of money. Xavier is doing so to prevent Jacqui from leaving the store, but Xavier has no privilege to do so. Has Jacqui been falsely imprisoned if she reasonably believes that she can leave the store only at the risk of losing her purse and its contents and, therefore, chooses to stay in the store? *See* RESTATEMENT (SECOND) OF TORTS § 40A (person may be falsely imprisoned by threats of force against another or valuable property).

3. For how long must one be restrained in order for a false imprisonment claim to lie? Even the briefest restraint of one's freedom may give rise to a false imprisonment claim.

Hypo 2-8

Assistant Manager at Restaurant noticed that some jewelry she had left in her office was missing. She immediately called the police and claimed that it must have been one of Restaurant's employees. When the police officer refused to perform a strip search at Assistant Manager's request and left, Assistant Manager ordered her own strip search, telling all the employees that none of them would be allowed to leave until they complied. The employees were then taken into restrooms where they were forced to remove various articles of clothing in front of Assistant Manager. Have employees been falsely imprisoned?

4. RESTATEMENT (SECOND) OF TORTS § 41 provides that a false imprisonment action may lie against one who takes "a person into custody under an asserted legal authority." A false imprisonment claim under color of law may also be termed a false arrest action. Consider the next case.

Enright v. Groves

560 P.2d 851 (Colo. App. 1977)

SMITH, Judge.

FYI An intentional infliction of emotional distress action is an intentional tort claim as well. *See* Chapter 1, Section G, *infra*.

Defendants Groves and City of Ft. Collins appeal from judgments entered against them upon jury verdicts awarding plaintiff $500 actual damages and $1,000 exemplary damages on her claim of false imprisonment .... [Plaintiff prevailed on her claims for **intentional infliction of emotional distress** ("IIED") as well as battery. The IIED and battery discussions are omitted.]

The evidence at trial disclosed that on August 25, 1974, Officer Groves, while on duty as a uniformed police officer of the City of Fort Collins, observed a dog running loose in violation of the city's 'dog leash' ordinance. He observed the animal approaching what was later identified as the residence of Mrs. Enright, the plaintiff. As Groves approached the house, he encountered Mrs. Enright's eleven-year-old son, and asked him if the dog belonged to him. The boy replied that it was his dog, and told Groves that his mother was sitting in the car parked at the curb by the house. Groves then ordered the boy to put the dog inside the house, and turned and started walking toward the Enright vehicle.

Groves testified that he was met by Mrs. Enright with whom he was not acquainted. She asked if she could help him. Groves responded by demanding her driver's license. She replied by giving him her name and address. He again demanded her driver's license, which she declined to produce. Groves thereupon advised her that she could either produce her driver's license or go to jail. Mrs. Enright responded by asking, 'Isn't this ridiculous?' Groves thereupon grabbed one of her arms, stating, 'Let's go!'

One eyewitness testified that Mrs. Enright cried out that Groves was hurting her. Her son who was just a few feet away at the time of the incident testified that his mother also screamed and tried to explain that her arm dislocated easily. Groves refused to release her arm, and Mrs. Enright struck him in the stomach with her free hand. Groves then seized both arms and threw her to the ground. With her lying on her stomach, he brought one of her arms behind her in order to handcuff her. She continued to scream in pain and asked him to stop hurting her. Groves pulled her up and propelled her to his patrol car where, for the first time, he advised her that she was under arrest.

She was taken to the police station where a complaint was signed charging her with violation of the 'dog leash' ordinance and bail was set. Mrs. Enright was released only after a friend posted bail. She was later convicted of the ordinance violation.

Unrebutted testimony by her physician at trial disclosed that she had a long history of shoulder dislocations in both arms prior to this incident, and that she had undergone surgery on both shoulders for this condition. The surgery on the left shoulder resulted in some restriction of movement and, if the arm was forced back, it was extremely painful. The surgery done on the right shoulder did not correct the dislocation problem and the evidence presented to the jury showed that if the arm was pushed back beyond a certain point that a painful dislocation would in fact then take place.

. . . .

Appellants contend that Groves had probable cause to arrest Mrs. Enright, and that she was in fact arrested for and convicted of violation of the dog-at-large ordinance. They assert, therefore, that her claim for false imprisonment or false arrest cannot lie, and that Groves use of force in arresting Mrs. Enright was permissible. We disagree.

False arrest arises when one is taken into custody by a person who claims but does not have proper legal authority. W. Prosser, Torts § 11 (4th ed.). Accordingly, a claim for false arrest will not lie if an officer has a valid warrant or probable cause to believe that an offense has been committed and that the person who was arrested committed it. Conviction of the crime for which one is specifically arrested is a complete defense to a subsequent claim of false arrest. [C]

Here, however, the evidence is clear that Groves arrested Mrs. Enright, not for violation of the dog leash ordinance, but rather for refusing to produce her driver's license. This basis for the arrest is exemplified by the fact that he specifically advised her that she would either produce the license or go to jail. We find no statute or case law in this jurisdiction which requires a citizen to show her driver's license upon demand, unless, for example, she is a driver of an automobile and such demand is made in that connection. [Cc]

. . . .

Here, there was no testimony that Groves ever even attempted to explain why he was demanding plaintiff's driver's license, and it is clear that she had already volunteered her name and address. Groves admitted that he did not ask Mrs. Enright if she had any means of identification on her person, instead he simply demanded that she give him her driver's license.

We conclude that Groves' demand for Mrs. Enright's driver's license was not a lawful order and that refusal to comply therewith was not therefore an offense in and of itself. Groves was not therefore entitled to use force in arresting Mrs. Enright. Thus Groves' defense based upon an arrest for and conviction of a specific offense must, as a matter of law, fail.

. . . .

Judgment [awarding compensatory and exemplary damages for all claims] affirmed.

Points for Discussion

1. Conviction for the crime for which one is arrested is a defense to a false arrest or false imprisonment claim. Whether the defendant's conduct was reasonable or not, a false arrest or false imprisonment action will not lie if the plaintiff actually committed the crime.

2. Plaintiff was a member and her husband was a minister of a religious sect of which Defendant was the leader. Plaintiff decided to abandon the sect and return to America. While she and her four children were awaiting passage from Jaffa on a steamer, Defendant offered her passage back to America on his yacht. He repeatedly assured her that under no circumstances would she be detained on board. However, upon arrival in port, Defendant refused to furnish her with a boat. She remained on board for nearly a month, during which time they attempted to persuade her to rejoin the sect. On several occasions, Plaintiff, always in the company of her husband, was allowed to go ashore, but she was never permitted to leave the yacht unaccompanied. She finally obtained her release with the assistance of the sheriff and a **writ of habeas**

Practice Pointer

Attorneys are not immune from liability for their intentional torts. If an arrest is made based on a warrant that an attorney sought in bad faith by intentionally misrepresenting facts to the judge or otherwise acting with malice, that attorney may be liable for any false imprisonment that ensues. Most courts recognize that an attorney is privileged for any false imprisonment as long as she was acting in good faith in seeking the warrant. However, an attorney acting in bad faith enjoys no such privilege. *See, e.g.,* Hiber v. Creditors Collection Serv. of Lincoln County, Inc., 961 P.2d 898 (Or. Ct. Ap 1998).

corpus. She sues the Defendant for false imprisonment. Does she have a valid claim? *See* Whittaker v. Sandford, 85 A. 399 (Me. 1912).

E. Trespass to Land

Dougherty v. Stepp

18 N.C. 371 (N.C. 1835)

RUFFIN, Chief Justice.

In the opinion of the Court, there is error in the instructions given to the jury. The amount of damages may depend on the acts done on the land, and the extent of injury to it therefrom. But it is an elementary principle, that every unauthorised, and therefore unlawful entry, into the **close** of another, is a trespass. From every such entry against the will of the possessor, the law infers some damage; if nothing more, the treading down the grass or the herbage, or as here, the shrubbery. Had the *locus in quo* been under cultivation or enclosed, there would have been no doubt of the plaintiff's right to recover. Now our Courts have for a long time past held, that if there be no **adverse possession**, the title makes the land the owner's close. Making the survey and marking trees, or making it without marking, differ only in the degree, and not in the nature of the injury. It is the entry that constitutes the trespass. There is no statute, nor rule of reason, that will make a wilful entry into the land of another, upon an unfounded claim of right, innocent, which one, who sat up no title to the land, could not justify or excuse. On the contrary, the pretended ownership aggravates the wrong. Let the judgment be reversed, and a new trial granted.

It's Latin to Me!

Locus in quo literally translated means "place in which." It is used here to refer to the place where the incident is alleged to have occurred.

PER CURIAM.

Judgment reversed.

Points for Discussion

1. What is a "close of another"? To have a viable trespass to land action, does one's "close" have to be fenced or otherwise marked? Does a viable tresspass to land action require proof that the defendant damaged the land?

2. In accord with *Dougherty v. Stepp* is Restatement (Second) of Torts § 158(a) (1965), which provides that "[o]ne is subject to liability to another for trespass, irrespective of whether he thereby causes harm to any legally protected interest of the other, if he intentionally "enters land in the possession of the other, or causes a thing or a third person to do so ...".

3. Trespass to land is an intentional tort. Therefore, to establish the *prima facie* case, the plaintiff must prove intent, act, causation, and harm. What must be proven regarding the defendant's intent to prevail in a trespass to land action? What act? What interest is protected by recognition of a trespass to land action?

Hypo 2-9

Mike and Deby are being pursued by a pack of ravenous wolves. In an attempt to get away from the wolves, Mike throws Deby over his shoulder and runs with her onto land possessed by Allen, but owned by Carl. Has a trespass to land been committed? By whom? Against whom?

Hypo 2-10

While riding a rollercoaster at an amusement park, a twenty-year-old man loses his hat. When the ride ends, he goes in quest of his hat as it is his favorite baseball cap. After scaling a 7-foot fence and entering an area of the amusement park marked "Restricted Area," the man is hit by the Ninja roller coaster. Has the man committed trespass to land? What if he were retrieving his five-year-old autistic child who had wandered into the restricted area instead of his favorite baseball cap?

Hypo 2-11

A seven-year-old boy scales a six-foot fence, breaking into a local zoo one evening after the zoo had closed for business. The boy wanders around the zoo for about thirty minutes, during which time he bashed three lizards in the reptile house to death with a rock. He also captures several live animals, including a turtle, a bearded dragon, and thorny devil lizards, and throws each of them over the two fences surrounding the resident 440-pound saltwater crocodile exhibit. The crocodile happily devours each of the animals. The boy is too young in the jurisdiction to be prosecuted criminally, but can he be held civilly responsible in tort?

Herrin v. Sutherland

241 P. 328 (Mont. 1925)

Action by H. J. Herrin against William Sutherland. Judgment for plaintiff, and defendant appeals. Affirmed.

....

[Plaintiff] allege[s] that on the 18th of September, 1924, the defendant, while engaged in hunting ducks and other water fowl and other migratory game birds, and while standing on the lands of another, repeatedly discharged a Winchester shotgun at water fowl in flight over plaintiff's said premises, dwelling house and over his cattle, "thereby preventing plaintiff from the quiet, undisturbed, peaceful enjoyment of his dwelling house, ranch, and property, to plaintiff's damage in the sum of $10."

....

After defendant's general demurrer ... was overruled[,] he declined to answer, and his default was entered. Upon the suggestion of counsel for plaintiff that only nominal damages would be demanded, the court rendered judgment in favor of the plaintiff for damages in the sum of $1 ..... From this judgment the defendant has appealed.

CALLAWAY, C. J. (after stating the facts as above).

....

…It must be held that when the defendant, although standing upon the land of another, fired a shotgun over plaintiff's premises, dwelling and cattle, he interfered with "the quiet, undisturbed, peaceful enjoyment" of the plaintiff, and thus committed a technical trespass at least. The plaintiff was the owner of the land. "Land," says Blackstone, "in its legal signification has an indefinite extent, upwards as well as downwards; whoever owns the land possesses all the space upwards to an indefinite extent; such is the maxim of the law." [Cc]

The Court of Appeals of New York, in Butler v. Frontier Telephone Co., 186 N. Y. 486, 79 N. E. 716, 11 L. R. A. (N. S.) 920, 116 Am. St. Rep. 563, 9 Ann. Cas. 858, had before it an **ejectment** case in which wire, unsupported by any structure resting upon plaintiff's land, was strung over the surface of the ground at a height

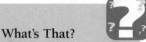

What's That?

An action in ejectment is an action by which a person wrongfully ousted from land seeks to recover damages and repossession of the land.

of from 20 to 30 feet across the entire width of plaintiff's premises. In speaking of the extent of the operation of the ancient maxim quoted above the court said:

> "The surface of the ground is a guide, but not the full measure, for within reasonable limitations land includes not only the surface but also the space above and the part beneath. … So far as the case before us is concerned, the plaintiff as the owner of the soil owned upward to an indefinite extent."

Sir Frederick Pollock, in the tenth edition of his valuable work on Torts, page 363, observes that it has been doubted whether it is a trespass to pass over land without touching the soil, as one may in a balloon, or to cause a material object, as a shot fired from a gun, to pass over it. …

> "As regards shooting it would be strange if we could object to shots being fired point blank across our land only in the event of actual injury being caused, and the passage of the foreign object in the air above our soil being thus a mere incident and a distinct trespass to person or property."

But he concludes that, when taking into account the extreme flight of projectiles fired from modern artillery which may pass thousands of feet above the land, the subject is not without difficulty. That shortly it will become one of considerable importance is indicated by the rapid approach of the airplane as an instrumentality of commerce…. However, it seems to be the consensus of the holdings of the courts in this country that the air space, at least near the ground, is almost as inviolable as the soil itself. [Cc] It is a matter of common knowledge that the shotgun is a firearm of short range. To be subjected to the danger incident to and reasonably to be anticipated from the firing of this weapon at water fowl in flight over one's dwelling house and cattle would seem to be far from inconsequential, and, while plaintiff's allegations are very general in character, it cannot be said that a cause of action is not stated for nominal damages at least.

....

The judgment is affirmed.

Affirmed.

GALEN, STARK, and MATTHEWS, JJ., concur. HOLLOWAY, J., writing separately, concurs.

....

Points for Discussion

Take Note

RESTATEMENT (SECOND) OF TORTS § 159(2) provides that "[f]light by air-craft in the air space above the land of another is a trespass if, but only if, it enters into the immediate reaches of the air space next to the land, and it interferes substantially with the other's use and enjoyment of his land." Section 159(2) is interesting because it protects the possessor's "use and enjoyment" of the land, an interest most often protected by a nuisance action rather than a trespass to land action. For further exploration of this issue, *see* Chapter 14, Nuisance, *infra*.

1. Why appeal a $1 judgment?

2. What if, when firing at the birds, the defendant had mistakenly hit the plaintiff's dog which had been on plaintiff's property at the time? Would an intentional tort have been committed? Which one? What if defendant had instead injured a person?

Rogers v. Board of Road Comm'rs for Kent County

30 N.W.2d 358 (Mich. 1947)

REID, Justice.

Plaintiff instituted this suit to recover damages because of the death of her husband, Theodore Rogers, which plaintiff claims was caused by the trespass and negligence of the defendant board of county road commissioners. Defendant filed a motion to dismiss, based on the pleadings.... The lower court granted defendant's motion and dismissed the cause. Plaintiff appeals from the judgment of dismissal of her cause.

Plaintiff claims that for two winter seasons previous to the date of the fatal injury to her husband the defendant board of road commissioners had obtained a license to place a snow fence in decedent's field parallel to the roadway past decedent's farm. Plaintiff claims in her declaration that the placing of the snow fence there was with the distinct understanding and agreement between the defendant and decedent that all of the fence together with the anchor posts should be removed by defendant at the end of each winter season when the necessity for snow fences for that season no longer existed. Plaintiff claims that such was the arrangement for the winter season of 1943-1944, that the arrangement was renewed for the winter season of 1944-1945, and that in the spring of 1945 the defendant's agents and employees removed the snow fence but did not remove a steel anchor post which protruded from 6 to 8 inches above the ground. Plaintiff further claims that the place where the post was located was a meadow where the grass grew to a considerable height, so that the anchor post was entirely hidden, and that on July 23, 1945, after decedent's husband had mowed several swaths around the field where the snow fence had been, with his mowing machine attached to his neighbor's tractor, and without any negligence or want of proper method of operation on his part, the mowing bar struck the steel stake and as a result of the impact decedent was forcibly thrown from the seat of the mowing machine to and upon the wheels of the mowing machine and upon the ground. By reason of the accident decedent received severe injuries which caused his death on October 25, 1945.

Plaintiff bases her suit upon trespass and negligence of defendant, claiming that the accident was the result of the trespass and negligence by the defendant in leaving the stake after the license to have the snow fence in place had expired, and the rest of the snow fence had been removed.

....

The court dismissed plaintiff's cause of action, ruling that the action was plainly an action based upon negligence, that there was no basis for any finding of trespass ....

Failure to remove the anchor stake upon expiration of the license to have it on defendant's land was a continuing trespass and is alleged by plaintiff to have been a proximate cause of the damage which she seeks to recover.

"§ 160. Failure to remove a thing placed on the land pursuant to a license or other privilege.

"A trespass, actionable under the rule stated in § 158, may be committed by the continued presence on the land of a structure, chattel or other thing which the actor or his predecessor in legal interest therein has placed thereon "(a) with the consent of the person then in possession of the land, if the actor fails to remove it after the consent has been effectively terminated, or

"(b) pursuant to a privilege conferred on the actor irrespective of the possessor's consent, if the actor fails to remove it after the privilege has been terminated, by the accomplishment of its purpose or otherwise." Restatement of the Law, Torts, p. 368.

....

The judgment of the court dismissing the cause of action is reversed and the cause remanded for such further proceedings as shall be found necessary. ...

....

> **FYI**
>
> The RESTATEMENT (SECOND) OF TORTS § 160 – Failure to Remove Thing Placed on Land Pursuant to License or Other Privilege, is similar to the law described in *Rogers*:
>
> A trespass may be committed by the continued presence on the land of a structure, chattel, or other thing which the actor ... has placed on the land
> (a) with the consent of the person then in possession of the land, if the actor fails to remove it after the consent has been effectively terminated, or
> (b) pursuant to a privilege conferred on the actor irrespective of the possessor's consent, if the actor fails to remove it after the privilege has been terminated, by the accomplishment of its purpose or otherwise.

Points for Discussion

1. Permission to enter one's property can be conditioned in terms of time, area, and purpose. *See* RESTATEMENT (SECOND) OF TORTS §§ 168-70.

2. For over twenty years, Jackson had threatened to bring suit against Power Company for the presence of power lines on his property, but Power Company was always able to defend successfully against any trespass action as they were protected by a **prescriptive easement** allowing their power lines to cross through Jackson's property. However, when Power Company sought to apportion its easement in order for Cable Company to lay fiber optic cables along the land, the court held that the prescriptive easement scope was limited to lines used for power, and therefore

> **What's That?**
>
> A prescriptive easement is a right to use the land created by an open, adverse, and continuous use over a statutorily defined period of time.

any attempt to apportion the easement to Cable Company did not insulate Cable Company from a trespass to land action. *See* Jackson v. City of Auburn, 971 So. 2d 696, 699 (Ala. Civ. App. 2006).

Bradley v. American Smelting and Refining Co.

709 P.2d 782 (Wash. 1985)

CALLOW, Justice.

This comes before us on a certification from the United States District Court for the Western District of Washington. Plaintiffs, landowners on Vashon Island, had sued for damages in trespass and nuisance from the deposit on their property of microscopic, airborne particles of heavy metals which came from the American Smelting and Refining Company (ASARCO) copper smelter at Ruston, Washington.

Make the Connection

The federal district court is required to apply Washington state law pursuant to the *Erie* doctrine. Washington state law was unclear on the issue presented in this case, so the federal district court certified the question to the highest court in Washington state, seeking clarification of the law. You may learn more about the *Erie* doctrine and certification of questions to state courts in your Civil Procedure course.

The issues certified for answer are as follows:

(1) Did the defendant have the requisite intent to commit intentional trespass as a matter of law?

(2) Does an intentional deposit of microscopic particulates, undetectable by the human senses, upon a person's property give rise to a cause of action for trespassory invasion of the person's right to exclusive possession of property as well as a claim of nuisance?

(3) Does the cause of action for trespassory invasion require proof of actual damages?

....

The parties have stipulated to the facts as follows: Plaintiffs Michael O. Bradley and Marie A. Bradley, husband and wife, are owners and occupiers of real property on the southern end of Vashon Island in King County, Washington. The

Bradleys purchased their property in 1978. Defendant ASARCO, a New Jersey corporation doing business in Washington, operates a primary copper smelter on real property it owns in Rushton.... On October 3, 1983, plaintiffs brought this action against defendant alleging a cause of action for intentional trespass and for nuisance.

Plaintiffs' property is located some 4 miles north of defendant's smelter. Defendant's primary copper smelter (also referred to as the Tacoma smelter), has operated in its present location since 1890. It has operated as a copper smelter since 1902, and in 1905 it was purchased and operated by a corporate entity which is now ASARCO. As a part of the industrial process of smelting copper at the Tacoma smelter, various gases such as sulfur dioxide and particulate matter, including arsenic, cadmium and other metals, are emitted. Particulate matter is composed of distinct particles of matter other than water, which cannot be detected by the human senses.

....

What's That?

A stipulation is a voluntary agreement between opposing parties about a fact or issue relevant to the proceeding.

As a part of defendant's smelting process, the Tacoma smelter emits into the atmosphere gases and particulate matter. For the purposes of resolving the certified questions, the parties stipulate that some particulate emissions of both cadmium and arsenic from the Tacoma smelter have been and are continuing to be deposited on plaintiffs' land. Defendant ASARCO has been aware since it took over operation of the Tacoma smelter in 1905 that the wind does, on occasion, cause smelter particulate emissions to blow over Vashon Island where plaintiffs' land is located.

The parties are squabbling to some extent about other "factual" assertions which are immaterial to the resolution of the issues posed by the certification. It was apparently stipulated that the record contains no proof of actual damages. ...

This case was initiated in King County Superior Court and later removed to the United States District Court. Upon the plaintiffs moving for summary judgment on the issue of liability for the claimed trespass, the stated issues were certified to this court. The issues present the conflict in an industrial society between the need of all for the production of goods and the desire of the landowner near the manufacturing plant producing those goods that his use and enjoyment of his land not be diminished by the unpleasant side effects of the manufacturing process. A reconciliation must be found between the interest of the many who are unaffected by the possible poisoning and the few who may be affected.

1.   Did the defendant have the requisite intent to commit intentional trespass as a matter of law?

The parties stipulated that as a part of the smelting process, particulate matter including arsenic and cadmium was emitted, that some of the emissions had been deposited on the plaintiffs' land and that the defendant has been aware since 1905 that the wind, on occasion, caused these emissions to be blown over the plaintiffs' land. The defendant cannot and does not deny that whenever the smelter was in operation the whim of the winds could bring these deleterious substances to the plaintiffs' premises. We are asked if the defendant, knowing what it had to know from the facts it admits, had the legal intent to commit trespass.

The Restatement (Second) of Torts § 158 (1965) states:

One is subject to liability to another for trespass, irrespective of whether he thereby causes harm to any legally protected interest of the other, if he intentionally

(a) enters land in the possession of the other, or causes a thing or a third person to do so, or

(b) remains on the land, or

(c) fails to remove from the land a thing which he is under a duty to remove.

In the comment on Clause (a) of § 158 at 278 it is stated in part:

i. Causing entry of a thing. The actor, without himself entering the land, may invade another's interest in its exclusive possession by throwing, propelling, or placing a thing, either on or beneath the surface of the land or in the air space above it. Thus, in the absence of the possessor's consent or other privilege to do so, it is an actionable trespass to throw rubbish on another's land ... In order that there may be a trespass under the rule stated in this Section, it is not necessary that the foreign matter should be thrown directly and immediately upon the other's land. It is enough that an act is done with knowledge that it will to a substantial certainty result in the entry of the foreign matter.

Addressing the definition, scope and meaning of "intent", section 8A of the Restatement (Second) of Torts says:

The word "intent" is used ... to denote that the actor desires to cause consequences of his act, or that he believes that the consequences are substantially certain to result from it.

and we find in comment *b* at 15:

Intent is not, however, limited to consequences which are desired. If the actor knows that the consequences are certain, or substantially certain, to result from his act, and still goes ahead, he is treated by the law as if he had in fact desired to produce the result.

> **Make the Connection**
>
> Notice the court's discussion of the distinction between specific intent and general intent in a trespass to land action. *See* Chapter 2, Section A, *supra*, discussing requisite intent for intentional tort actions.

The defendant has known for decades that sulfur dioxide and particulates of arsenic, cadmium and other metals were being emitted from the tall smokestack. It had to know that the solids propelled into the air by the warm gases would settle back to earth somewhere. It had to know that a purpose of the tall stack was to disperse the gas, smoke and minute solids over as large an area as possible and as far away as possible, but that while any resulting contamination would be diminished as to any one area or landowner, that nonetheless contamination, though slight, would follow. In W. Prosser, *Torts* § 8, at 31-32 (4th ed. 1971) intent is defined as follows:

The intent with which tort liability is concerned is not necessarily a hostile intent, or a desire to do any harm. Rather it is an intent to bring about a result which will invade the interests of another in a way that the law will not sanction. ...

....

This has been the reasoning of the decisions of this State. ... [omitting discussion of *Garratt v. Daily*, Chapter 2, Section A, *supra*, explaining the concept of "intent"]

It is patent that the defendant acted on its own volition and had to appreciate with substantial certainty that the law of gravity would visit the effluence upon someone, somewhere.

....

We find that the defendant had the requisite intent to commit intentional trespass as a matter of law.

2.   Does an intentional deposit of microscopic particulates, undetectable by the human senses, upon a person's property give rise to a cause of action for trespassory invasion of the person's right to exclusive possession of property as well as a claim of nuisance?

The courts have been groping for a reconciliation of the doctrines of trespass and nuisance over a long period of time and, to a great extent, have concluded that little of substance remains to any distinction between the two when air pollution is involved. *Weller v. Snoqualmie Falls Lumber Co.,* 155 Wash. 526, 285 P. 446 (1930) held that the discharge of smoke, ashes and cinders from a sawmill upon a neighboring farm was "in the nature of a continuing nuisance" and that the 2-year statute of limitations applied. The opinion also stated that an action for damages could be maintained if the injury to the premises was substantial rather than slight. [C]

We agree with the observations on the inconsequential nature of the efforts to reconcile the trappings of the concepts of trespass and nuisance in the face of industrial airborne pollution when Professor Rodgers states:

> Trespass is a theory closely related to nuisance and occasionally invoked in environmental cases. The distinction between the two originally was the difference between the old action of trespass and the action on the case: if there was a direct and immediate physical invasion of plaintiff's property, as by casting stones or water on it, it was a trespass; if the invasion was indirect, as by the seepage of water, it was a nuisance.

Today, with the abandonment of the old procedural forms, the line between trespass and nuisance has become "wavering and uncertain." The basic distinction is that trespass can be defined as any intentional invasion of the plaintiff's interest in the exclusive possession of property, whereas a nuisance requires a substantial and unreasonable interference with his use and enjoyment of it. That is to say, in trespass cases defendant's conduct typically results in an encroachment by "something" upon plaintiff's exclusive rights of possession.

The first and most important proposition about trespass and nuisance principles is that they are largely coextensive. … [¶] The principal difference in theories is that the tort of trespass is complete upon a tangible invasion of plaintiff's property, however slight, whereas a nuisance requires proof that the interference with use and enjoyment is "substantial and unreasonable." This burden of proof advantage in a trespass case is accompanied by a slight remedial advantage as well. Upon proof of a technical trespass plaintiff always is entitled to nominal damages. It is possible also that a plaintiff could get injunctive relief against a technical trespass – for example, the deposit of particles of air pollutant on his property causing no known adverse effects. The protection of the integrity of his possessory interests might justify the injunction even without proof of the substantial injury necessary to establish a nuisance. Of course absent proof of injury, or at least a reasonable suspicion of it, courts are unlikely to invoke their equitable powers to require expensive control efforts.

.....

The view recognizing a trespassory invasion where there is no "thing" which can be seen with the naked eye undoubtedly runs counter to the definition of trespass expressed in some quarters [citing the RESTATEMENT (FIRST) OF TORTS and Prosser]. It is quite possible that in an earlier day when science had not yet peered into the molecular and atomic world of small particles, the courts could not fit an invasion through unseen physical instrumentalities into the requirement that a trespass can result only from a *direct* invasion. But in this atomic age even the uneducated know the great and awful force contained in the atom and what it can do to a man's property if it is released. In fact, the now famous equation E=MC² has taught us that mass and energy are equivalents and that our concept of 'things' must be reframed. If these observations on science in relation to the law of trespass should appear theoretical and unreal in the abstract, they become very practical and real to the possessor of land when the unseen force cracks the foundation of his house. The force is just as real if it is chemical in nature and must be awakened by the intervention of another agency before it does harm.

.....

With regard to remedies, the trespass and nuisance cases are quite alike. [T]he statutes of limitation for nuisances are generally shorter than those for trespasses. The measure of damages for a permanent trespass, like a nuisance, is depreciation of market value. [Cc]

Martin v. Reynolds Metals Co., 221 Or. 86, 90-91, 101, 342 P.2d 790 (1959) was an action in trespass brought against the defendant corporation for causing gases and fluoride particulates to settle on the plaintiffs' land making it unfit for livestock. [T]he court stated:

> Trespass and private nuisance are separate fields of tort liability relating to actionable interference with the possession of land. They may be distinguished by comparing the interest invaded; and actionable invasion of a possessor's interest in the exclusive possession of land is a trespass; an actionable invasion of a possessor's interest in the use and enjoyment of his land is a nuisance. [C]

The same conduct on the part of a defendant may and often does result in the actionable invasion of both of these interests, in which case the choice between the two remedies is, in most cases, a matter of little consequence. Where the action is brought on the theory of nuisance alone the court ordinarily is not called upon to determine whether the conduct would also result in a trespassory invasion. In such cases the courts' treatment of the invasion solely in terms of the law of nuisance does not mean that the same conduct could not also be regarded as a trespass. Some of the cases relied upon by the defendant are of this type; cases in which the court holds that the interference with the plaintiff's possession through soot, dirt, smoke, cinders, ashes and similar substances constitute a nuisance, but where the court does not discuss the applicability of the law of trespass to the same set of facts.

However, there are cases which have held that the defendant's interference with plaintiff's possession resulting from the settling upon his land of effluents emanating from defendant's operations is exclusively nontrespassory. Although in such cases the separate particles which collectively cause the invasion are minute, the deposit of each of the particles constitutes a physical intrusion and, but for the size of the particle, would clearly give rise to an action of trespass. The defendant asks us to take account of the difference in size of the physical agency through which the intrusion occurs and relegate entirely to the field of nuisance law certain invasions which do not meet the dimensional test, whatever that is. In pressing this argument upon us the defendant must admit that there are cases which have held that a trespass results from the movement or deposit of rather small objects over or upon the surface of the possessor's land.

We hold that the defendant's conduct in causing chemical substances to be deposited upon the plaintiffs' land fulfilled all of the requirements under the law of trespass. [CC] We hold that theories of trespass and nuisance are not inconsistent, that the theories may apply concurrently, and that the injured party may proceed under both theories when the elements of both actions are present. The RESTATEMENT (SECOND) OF TORTS § 821D, comment *d,* at 102 (1979) states:

> For an intentional trespass, there is liability without harm; for a private nuisance, there is no liability without significant harm. In trespass an intentional invasion of the plaintiff's possession is of itself a tort, and liability follows unless the defendant can show a privilege. In private nuisance an intentional interference with the plaintiff's use or enjoyment is not of itself a tort, and unreasonableness of the interference is necessary for liability.

Comment *e* at 102 states:

> There may, however, be some overlapping of the causes of action for trespass and private nuisance. An invasion of the possession of land

normally involves some degree of interference with its use and enjoyment and this is true particularly when some harm is inflicted upon the land itself. The cause of action for trespass has traditionally included liability for incidental harms of this nature. If the interference with the use and enjoyment of the land is a significant one, sufficient in itself to amount to a private nuisance, the fact that it arises out of or is accompanied by a trespass will not prevent recovery for the nuisance, and the action may be maintained upon either basis as the plaintiff elects or both....

The two actions, trespass and private nuisance, are thus not entirely exclusive or inconsistent, and in a proper case in which the elements of both actions are fully present, the plaintiff may have his choice of one or the other, or may proceed upon both.

....

3. Does the cause of action for trespassory invasion require proof of actual damages?

When airborne particles are transitory or quickly dissipate, they do not interfere with a property owner's possessory rights and, therefore, are properly denominated as nuisances. [Cc] When, however, the particles or substance accumulates on the land and does not pass away, then a trespass has occurred. [Cc] While at common law any trespass entitled a landowner to recover nominal or punitive damages for the invasion of his property, such a rule is not appropriate under the circumstances before us. No useful purpose would be served by sanctioning actions in trespass by every landowner within a hundred miles of a manufacturing plant. Manufacturers would be harassed and the litigious few would cause the escalation of costs to the detriment of the many. The elements that we have adopted for an action in trespass ... require that a plaintiff has suffered actual and substantial damages. Since this is an element of the action, the plaintiff who cannot show that actual and substantial damages have been suffered should be subject to dismissal of his cause upon a motion for summary judgment.

....

In conclusion, we answer the certified questions as follows:

1.   The defendant had the requisite intent to commit intentional trespass.

2.   An intentional deposit of microscopic particulates, undetectable by the human senses, gives rise to a cause of action for trespass as well as a claim of nuisance.

3.   A cause of action under such circumstances requires proof of actual and substantial damages.

....

The United States District Court for the Western District of Washington shall be notified for such further action as it deems appropriate.

DOLLIVER, C.J., and UTTER, DORE, PEARSON, BRACHTENBACH, ANDERSEN, GOODLOE, and DURHAM, JJ., concur.

———————

Points for Discussion

1. How does the court distinguish between a physical trespass to land action and a non-physical trespass to land action? Are actual damages required for establishing the *prima facie* case?

2. What are the distinctions between a trespass to land action and a nuisance action? What interests are protected by recognition of each tort? Are they mutually exclusive torts or may both a trespass to land and a nuisance action inure from the same set of facts? Are nominal damages available to a nuisance action? Nuisance law is examined further in Chapter 14, *infra*.

3. What policy considerations were important to the court in reaching its decision?

4. What must be proven to establish intent sufficient for a trespass to land action? In *Bradley,* was it legally relevant to the plaintiff's case that the defendant did not know upon whose land the particulate matter would accumulate?

———————

Hypo 2-12

Defendant sprays herbicide into the air, which travels onto Plaintiff's adjoining land, killing Plaintiff's plants. Plaintiff wishes to sue Defendant in tort. Discuss.

> ### Hypo 2-13
>
> Cindy is new to the neighborhood. She loves her beautiful new home, complete with a fenced backyard so that her dog, Havana, has plenty of room to romp around. Havana is a very meticulous dog, as illustrated by Havana "taking care of her business" in only one particular area of the backyard, in the corner next to the fence. Holly lives next door to Cindy and enjoys outdoor yoga every morning in her backyard. At least she did until Cindy moved in. Now Holly cannot seem to escape the aroma from Havana's daily droppings. When she asks Cindy to make sure that her dog "does her business" in another section of the yard, Cindy laughs. After all, Havana has been relieving herself in Cindy's yard, not in Holly's yard. Holly wants to sue Cindy in tort. Discuss.

F. Trespass to Chattel and Conversion

Glidden v. Szybiak

63 A.2d 233 (N.H. 1949)

. . .

Actions at law under the provisions of R.L. c. 180, §§ 23, 24, to recover for a dog bite sustained by the plaintiff Elaine Glidden upon September 29, 2946, and for medical expenses incurred by her father, Harold Glidden. Trial by the Court, with verdicts for the plaintiffs. The plaintiff Elaine Glidden, who was four years old at the time of the occurrence here involved, left her home about noon on the day of he injury, to go to a neighborhood store for candy. On the porch of the store Elaine encountered a dog named Toby and engaged in play with him. She eventually climbed on his back and pulled his ears. The dog snapped at her and bit her nose, inflicting wounds for which a recovery is sought. She was treated by two physicians and successful result obtained. Such scars as were left are "in no way disfiguring but discernible on close view." The dog Toby was owned by the defendant Jane Szybiak … . The defendant Louis Szybiak, was found to be the head of the family at the time of the injury to Elaine Glidden. … [The trial court found further] "that Toby was in possession of the defendant Louis within the meaning of the statute." To this finding the defendant excepted as being contrary to the evidence and unsupported by the evidence. The defendants also excepted to the denial of their motions for judgment at the close of the evidence. The Court also made the following finding: "Elaine is found to have been of such tender years as to be incapable of being guilty of contributory negligence in her conduct toward the dog Toby. If she was too young to be guilty of negligence, she cannot be found to have been guilty of a trespass or a tort at the time she received her injury." To this finding the defendants duly excepted.

BRANCH, Chief Justice.

The statute under which these actions were brought reads as follows:

"23. Liability of owner. Any person to whom or to whose property damage may be occasioned by a dog not owned or kept by him shall be entitled to recover such damage of the person who owns or keeps the dog, or has it in possession, unless the damage was occasioned to him while he was engaged in the commission of a trespass or other tort."

Take Note

The parties here are pursuing a tort claim based upon a statute, not based upon judicially-created law in this jurisdiction. This statute sets forth a strict liability offense and available defenses. Strict liability offenses are explored in Chapter 13, *infra*.

It is the contention of the defendants that the plaintiff Elaine was engaged in the commission of a trespass at the time of her injury and is, therefore, barred from recovery under the statute. The law in regard to a trespass to **chattels** is thus summarized in the RESTATEMENT OF THE LAW OF TORTS, § 218:

"One who without consensual or other privilege to do so, uses or otherwise intentionally intermeddles with a chattel which is in possession of another is liable for a trespass to such person if,

(a) the chattel is impaired as to its condition, quality or value, or

(b) the possessor is deprived of the use of the chattel for a substantial time, or

(c) bodily harm is thereby caused to the possessor or harm is caused to some person or thing in which the possessor has a legally protected interest."

In comment (f) to clauses (a) and (b), it is pointed out that "the interest of a possessor of a chattel in its inviolability, unlike the similar interest of a possessor of land, is not given legal protection by an action for nominal damages for harmless intermeddlings with the chattel. ..."

No claim was advanced at the trial that the dog Toby was in any way injured by the conduct of the plaintiff Elaine. Consequently she could not be held liable for a trespass to the dog. Consequently her conduct did not constitute a trespass which will prevent her recovery under the statute here invoked.

....

... Possessor as used in the statute implies the exercise of care, custody or control of the dog by one who though not the owner assumes to act in his stead. Here the actual care, custody and control of the dog was in the owner Jane Szybiak ... and she alone was responsible for the conduct of the animal. ...

RESTATEMENT (SECOND) OF TORTS § 218 (1965) provides:
"[o]ne who commits a trespass to chattel is subject to liability to the possessor of the chattel if, but only if, he dispossesses the other of the chattel, or
the chattel is impaired as to its condition, quality, or value, or
the possessor is deprived of the use of the chattel for a substantial time, or
bodily harm is caused to the possessor, or harm is caused to some person or thing in which the possessor has a legally protected interest."

Judgment on the verdict against the defendant Jane.

....

Points for Discussion

1. Who is the plaintiff in this action? Defendant? Does the *Glidden* case involve a typical trespass to chattel cause of action? How is the quoted statute relevant to the court's analysis in this case?

2. What interest is protected by a common law trespass to chattel action?

3. Who has the right to bring a trespass to chattel action, the *owner* of the chattel or the *possessor* of the chattel? The RESTATEMENT (SECOND) OF TORTS § 216 (1965) defines the possessor of a chattel as "one who has physical control of the chattel with the intent to exercise such control on his own behalf, or on behalf of another."

4. Are nominal damages available in a trespass to chattel action? Or must an actual harm be proved to establish the plaintiff's *prima facie* case?

> ## Hypo 2-14
>
> Amy is walking her pet Chihuahua on a leash through a nearby park. Local residents have recently enacted a program using hawks to rid the neighborhood of rodents and pigeons. One of the residents is a falconer in charge of Hawk One, a highly trained bird taught to capture rodents in the area. Hawk One (who is smaller than Chihuahua) identifies Amy's Chihuahua as a rat. Hawk One swoops out of the sky, sinking its sharp talons into the dog and inflicting scratches and a serious puncture wound before horrified onlookers rush over and yank the bird off the dog. The dog survives its injuries, but Amy is completely traumatized by the event. Has Falconer committed an intentional tort? Discuss.

5. **Conversion** – Related to a trespass to chattel action is the intentional tort of conversion. The RESTATEMENT (SECOND) OF TORTS § 222A defines conversion as "an intentional exercise of dominion or control over a chattel which so seriously interferes with the right of another to control it that the actor may justly be required to pay the other the full value of the chattel." Essentially an aggravated trespass to chattel action, a conversion may be committed in a variety of ways, including but not limited to dispossessing another of a chattel, destroying or altering a chattel, misdelivering a chattel, or refusing to surrender a chattel. *See* RESTATEMENT (SECOND) OF TORTS § 223. The paramount consideration is the seriousness of the interference with another's personal property. Therefore, factors that may be helpful in determining whether property was converted include the extent and duration of the actor's exercise of dominion or control over the chattel, the actor's intent to assert a right inconsistent with the other's right of control of the chattel, the actor's good faith, the extent and duration of the resulting interference with the other's right of control, the harm done to the chattel, and the inconvenience and expense caused to the other. *See* RESTATEMENT (SECOND) OF TORTS § 222A(2) (1965). A conversion action is appropriate when one has so seriously interfered with the chattel of another in such a manner as to make it appropriate to require the converter to purchase the chattel. Hence, unlike a trespass to chattel action where the measure of damages is the *diminution in value* of the chattel, the measure of damages of a conversion action is the *full market value* of the chattel at the time of the conversion. Thus whether one pursues a trespass to chattel action or a conversion action may depend not only upon the seriousness of the defendant's interference with the chattel of another, but also upon whether the plaintiff wants to continue to possess the chattel after completion of the action. Consider the next case.

CompuServe Inc. v. Cyber Promotions, Inc.

962 F.Supp. 1015 (S.D. Ohio 1997)

GRAHAM, District Judge.

This case presents novel issues regarding the commercial use of the Internet, specifically the right of an online computer service to prevent a commercial enterprise from sending unsolicited electronic mail advertising to its subscribers.

Plaintiff CompuServe Incorporated ("CompuServe") is one of the major national commercial online computer services. It operates a computer communication service through a proprietary nationwide computer network. In addition to allowing access to the extensive content available within its own proprietary network, CompuServe also provides its subscribers with a link to the much larger resources of the Internet. This allows its subscribers to send and receive electronic messages, known as "e-mail," by the Internet. Defendants Cyber Promotions, Inc. and its president Sanford Wallace are in the business of sending unsolicited e-mail advertisements on behalf of themselves and their clients to hundreds of thousands of Internet users, many of whom are CompuServe subscribers. CompuServe has notified defendants that they are prohibited from using its computer equipment to process and store the unsolicited e-mail and has requested that they terminate the practice. Instead, defendants have sent an increasing volume of e-mail solicitations to CompuServe subscribers. CompuServe has attempted to employ technological means to block the flow of defendants' e-mail transmissions to its computer equipment, but to no avail.

This matter is before the Court on the application of CompuServe for a preliminary injunction which would extend the duration of the temporary restraining order issued by this Court on October 24, 1996 and which would in addition prevent defendants from sending unsolicited advertisements to CompuServe subscribers.

For the reasons which follow, this Court holds that where defendants engaged in a course of conduct of transmitting a substantial volume of electronic data in the form of unsolicited e-mail to plaintiff's proprietary computer equipment, where defendants continued such practice after repeated demands to cease and desist, and where defendants deliberately evaded plaintiff's affirmative efforts to protect its computer equipment from such use, plaintiff has a viable claim for trespass to personal property and is entitled to injunctive relief to protect its property. ...

The Court will begin its analysis of the issues by acknowledging, for the purpose of providing a background, certain findings of fact recently made by another district court in a case involving the Internet:

1. The Internet is not a physical or tangible entity, but rather a giant network which interconnects innumerable smaller groups of linked computer networks. It is thus a network of networks....

2. Some networks are "closed" networks, not linked to other computers or networks. Many networks, however, are connected to other networks, which are in turn connected to other networks in a manner which permits each computer in any network to communicate with computers on any other network in the system. This global Web of linked networks and computers is referred to as the Internet.

3. The nature of the Internet is such that it is very difficult, if not impossible, to determine its size at a given moment. It is indisputable, however, that the Internet has experienced extraordinary growth in recent years. … In all, reasonable estimates are that as many as 40 million people around the world can and do access the enormously flexible communication Internet medium. That figure is expected to grow to 200 million Internet users by the year 1999.

4. Some of the computers and computer networks that make up the network are owned by governmental and public institutions, some are owned by non-profit organizations, and some are privately owned. The resulting whole is a decentralized, global medium of communications- or "cyberspace"-that links people, institutions, corporations, and governments around the world....

....

11. No single entity-academic, corporate, governmental, or non-profit-administers the Internet. It exists and functions as a result of the fact that hundreds of thousands of separate operators of computers and computer networks independently decided to use common data transfer protocols to exchange communications and information with other computers (which in turn exchange communications and information with still other computers). There is no centralized storage location, control point, or communications channel for the Internet, and it would not be technically feasible for a single entity to control all of the information conveyed on the Internet.

American Civil Liberties Union v. Reno, 929 F.Supp. 824, 830-832 (E.D.Pa.1996). …

Internet users often pay a fee for Internet access. However, there is no per-message charge to send electronic messages over the Internet and such messages usually reach their destination within minutes. Thus electronic mail provides an opportunity to reach a wide audience quickly and at almost no cost to the sender. It is not surprising therefore that some companies, like defendant Cyber Promotions, Inc., have begun using the Internet to distribute advertisements by sending the same unsolicited commercial message to hundreds of thousands of Internet users at once. Defendants refer to this as "bulk e-mail," while plaintiff refers to it as "junk e-mail." In the vernacular of the Internet, unsolicited e-mail advertising is sometimes referred to pejoratively as "spam."[4]

CompuServe subscribers use CompuServe's domain name "CompuServe.com" together with their own unique alpha-numeric identifier to form a distinctive e-mail mailing address. That address may be used by the subscriber to exchange electronic mail with any one of tens of millions of other Internet users who have electronic mail capability. E-mail sent to CompuServe subscribers is processed and stored on CompuServe's proprietary computer equipment. Thereafter, it becomes accessible to CompuServe's subscribers, who can access CompuServe's equipment and electronically retrieve those messages.

Over the past several months, CompuServe has received many complaints from subscribers threatening to discontinue their subscription unless CompuServe prohibits electronic mass mailers from using its equipment to send unsolicited advertisements. CompuServe asserts that the volume of messages generated by such mass mailings places a significant burden on its equipment which has finite processing and storage capacity. CompuServe receives no payment from the mass mailers for processing their unsolicited advertising. However, CompuServe's subscribers pay for their access to CompuServe's services in increments of time and thus the process of accessing, reviewing and discarding unsolicited e-mail costs them money, which is one of the reasons for their complaints. CompuServe has notified defendants that they are prohibited from using its proprietary computer equipment to process and store unsolicited e-mail and has requested them to cease and desist from sending unsolicited e-mail to its subscribers. Nonetheless, defendants have sent an increasing volume of e-mail solicitations to CompuServe subscribers.

In an effort to shield its equipment from defendants' bulk e-mail, CompuServe has implemented software programs designed to screen out the messages and block their receipt. In response, defendants have modified their equipment and the messages they send in such a fashion as to circumvent CompuServe's screening software. Allegedly, defendants have been able to conceal the true origin of their

---

4 This term is derived from a skit performed on the British television show Monty Python's Flying Circus, in which the word "spam" is repeated to the point of absurdity in a restaurant menu.

messages by falsifying the point-of-origin information contained in the header of the electronic messages. Defendants have removed the "sender" information in the header of their messages and replaced it with another address. Also, defendants have developed the capability of configuring their computer servers to conceal their true domain name and appear on the Internet as another computer, further concealing the true origin of the messages. By manipulating this data, defendants have been able to continue sending messages to CompuServe's equipment in spite of CompuServe's protests and protective efforts.

Defendants assert that they possess the right to continue to send these communications to CompuServe subscribers. CompuServe contends that, in doing so, the defendants are trespassing upon its personal property.

....

[Plaintiff] seeks to enjoin defendants Cyber Promotions, Inc. and its president Sanford Wallace from sending any unsolicited advertisements to any electronic mail address maintained by CompuServe.

CompuServe predicates this aspect of its motion for a preliminary injunction on the common law theory of trespass to personal property or to chattels, asserting that defendants' continued transmission of electronic messages to its computer equipment constitutes an actionable tort.

Trespass to chattels has evolved from its original common law application, concerning primarily the **asportation** of another's tangible property, to include the unauthorized use of personal property:

> Its chief importance now, is that there may be recovery ... for interferences with the possession of chattels which are not sufficiently important to be classed as conversion, and so to compel the defendant to pay the full value of the thing with which he has interfered. Trespass to chattels survives today, in other words, largely as a little brother of conversion.

Prosser & Keeton, *Prosser and Keeton on Torts,* § 14, 85-86 (1984).

The scope of an action for conversion recognized in Ohio may embrace the facts in the instant case. The Supreme Court of Ohio established the definition of conversion under Ohio law in *Baltimore & O.R. Co. v. O'Donnell,* 49 Ohio St. 489, 32 N.E. 476, 478 (1892) by stating that:

> [I]n order to constitute a conversion, it was not necessary that there should have been an actual appropriation of the property by the defendant to its own use and benefit. It might arise from the exercise of a dominion

over it in exclusion of the rights of the owner, or withholding it from his possession under a claim inconsistent with his rights. If one take the property of another, for a temporary purpose only, in disregard of the owner's right, it is a conversion. Either a wrongful taking, an assumption of ownership, an illegal use or misuse, or a wrongful detention of chattels will constitute a conversion.

Id. at 497-98, 32 N.E. 476;   [Cc] While authority under Ohio law respecting an action for trespass to chattels is extremely meager, it appears to be an actionable tort.   [Cc]

Both plaintiff and defendants cite the RESTATEMENT (SECOND) OF TORTS to support their respective positions. In determining a question unanswered by state law, it is appropriate for this Court to consider such sources as the restatement of the law and decisions of other jurisdictions. [Cc]

The Restatement § 217(b) states that a trespass to chattel may be committed by intentionally using or intermeddling with the chattel in possession of another. Restatement § 217, Comment *e* defines physical "intermeddling" as follows:

> ... intentionally bringing about a physical contact with the chattel. The actor may commit a trespass by an act which brings him into an intended physical contact with a chattel in the possession of another[.]

Electronic signals generated and sent by computer have been held to be sufficiently physically tangible to support a trespass cause of action. [Cc] It is undisputed that plaintiff has a possessory interest in its computer systems. Further, defendants' contact with plaintiff's computers is clearly intentional. Although electronic messages may travel through the Internet over various routes, the messages are affirmatively directed to their destination.

Defendants, citing RESTATEMENT (SECOND) OF TORTS § 221, which defines "dispossession", assert that not every interference with the personal property of another is actionable and that physical dispossession or substantial interference with the chattel is required. Defendants then argue that they did not, in this case, physically dispossess plaintiff of its equipment or substantially interfere with it. However, the RESTATEMENT (SECOND) OF TORTS § 218 defines the circumstances under which a trespass to chattels may be actionable:

> One who commits a trespass to a chattel is subject to liability to the possessor of the chattel if, but only if,

> (a) he dispossesses the other of the chattel, or

(b) the chattel is impaired as to its condition, quality, or value, or

(c) the possessor is deprived of the use of the chattel for a substantial time, or

(d) bodily harm is caused to the possessor, or harm is caused to some person or thing in which the possessor has a legally protected interest.

Therefore, an interference resulting in physical dispossession is just one circumstance under which a defendant can be found liable. Defendants suggest that "[u]nless an alleged trespasser actually takes physical custody of the property or physically damages it, courts will not find the 'substantial interference' required to maintain a trespass to chattel claim." [C] To support this rather broad proposition, defendants cite only two cases which make any reference to the Restatement. In *Glidden v. Szybiak*, 95 N.H. 318, 63 A.2d 233 (1949), the court simply indicated that an action for trespass to chattels could not be maintained in the absence of some form of damage. The court held that where plaintiff did not contend that defendant's pulling on her pet dog's ears caused any injury, an action in tort could not be maintained. [C] In contrast, plaintiff in the present action has alleged that it has suffered several types if injury as a result of defendants' conduct. In *Koepnick v. Sears Roebuck & Co.*, 158 Ariz. 322, 762 P.2d 609 (1988) the court held that a two-minute search of an individual's truck did not amount to a "dispossession" of the truck as defined in Restatement § 221 or a deprivation of the use of the truck for a substantial time. It is clear from a reading of Restatement § 218 that an interference or intermeddling that does not fit the § 221 definition of "dispossession" can nonetheless result in defendants' liability for trespass. The *Koepnick* court did not discuss any of the other grounds for liability under Restatement § 218.

A plaintiff can sustain an action for trespass to chattels, as opposed to an action for conversion, without showing a substantial interference with its right to possession of that chattel. [Cc] Harm to the personal property or diminution of its quality, condition, or value as a result of defendants' use can also be the predicate for liability. Restatement § 218(b).

An unprivileged use or other intermeddling with a chattel which results in actual impairment of its physical condition, quality or value to the possessor makes the actor liable for the loss thus caused. In the great majority of cases, the actor's intermeddling with the chattel impairs the value of it to the possessor, as distinguished from the mere affront to his dignity as possessor, only by some impairment of the physical condition of the chattel. There may, however, be situations in which the value to the owner of a particular type of chattel may be impaired by dealing with it in a manner that does not affect its physical condition. ... In such a case, the intermeddling is actionable even though the physical condition of the chattel is not impaired.

The RESTATEMENT (SECOND) OF TORTS § 218, comment h. In the present case, any value CompuServe realizes from its computer equipment is wholly derived from the extent to which that equipment can serve its subscriber base. Michael Mangino, a software developer for CompuServe who monitors its mail processing computer equipment, states by affidavit that handling the enormous volume of mass mailings that CompuServe receives places a tremendous burden on its equipment. [C] Defendants' more recent practice of evading CompuServe's filters by disguising the origin of their messages commandeers even more computer resources because CompuServe's computers are forced to store undeliverable e-mail messages and labor in vain to return the messages to an address that does not exist. [C] To the extent that defendants' multitudinous electronic mailings demand the disk space and drain the processing power of plaintiff's computer equipment, those resources are not available to serve CompuServe subscribers. Therefore, the value of that equipment to CompuServe is diminished even though it is not physically damaged by defendants' conduct.

Next, plaintiff asserts that it has suffered injury aside from the physical impact of defendants' messages on its equipment. Restatement § 218(d) also indicates that recovery may be had for a trespass that causes harm to something in which the possessor has a legally protected interest. Plaintiff asserts that defendants' messages are largely unwanted by its subscribers, who pay incrementally to access their e-mail, read it, and discard it. Also, the receipt of a bundle of unsolicited messages at once can require the subscriber to sift through, at his expense, all of the messages in order to find the ones he wanted or expected to receive. These inconveniences decrease the utility of CompuServe's e-mail service and are the foremost subject in recent complaints from CompuServe subscribers. Patrick Hole, a customer service manager for plaintiff, states by affidavit that in November 1996 CompuServe received approximately 9,970 e-mail complaints from subscribers about junk e-mail, a figure up from approximately two hundred complaints the previous year. [C] Approximately fifty such complaints per day specifically reference defendants. [C] Defendants contend that CompuServe subscribers are provided with a simple procedure to remove themselves from the mailing list. However, the removal procedure must be performed by the e-mail recipient at his expense, and some CompuServe subscribers complain that the procedure is inadequate and ineffectual. [C]

Many subscribers have terminated their accounts specifically because of the unwanted receipt of bulk e-mail messages. [C] Defendants' intrusions into CompuServe's computer systems, insofar as they harm plaintiff's business reputation and goodwill with its customers, are actionable under Restatement § 218(d).

The reason that the tort of trespass to chattels requires some actual damage as a *prima facie* element, whereas damage is assumed where there is a trespass to real property, can be explained as follows:

> The interest of a possessor of a chattel in its inviolability, unlike the similar interest of a possessor of land, is not given legal protection by an action for nominal damages for harmless intermeddlings with the chattel. In order that an actor who interferes with another's chattel may be liable, his conduct must affect some other and more important interest of the possessor. Therefore, one who intentionally intermeddles with another's chattel is subject to liability only if his intermeddling is harmful to the possessor's materially valuable interest in the physical condition, quality, or value of the chattel, or if the possessor is deprived of the use of the chattel for a substantial time, or some other legally protected interest of the possessor is affected as stated in Clause (c). *Sufficient legal protection of the possessor's interest in the mere inviolability of his chattel is afforded by his privilege to use reasonable force to protect his possession against even harmless interference.*

RESTATEMENT (SECOND) OF TORTS § 218, Comment *e* (emphasis added). Plaintiff CompuServe has attempted to exercise this privilege to protect its computer systems. However, defendants' persistent affirmative efforts to evade plaintiff's security measures have circumvented any protection those self-help measures might have provided. In this case CompuServe has alleged and supported by affidavit that it has suffered several types of injury as a result of defendants' conduct. The foregoing discussion simply underscores that the damage sustained by plaintiff is sufficient to sustain an action for trespass to chattels. However, this Court also notes that the implementation of technological means of self-help, to the extent that reasonable measures are effective, is particularly appropriate in this type of situation and should be exhausted before legal action is proper.

Under Restatement § 252, the owner of personal property can create a privilege in the would-be trespasser by granting consent to use the property. A great portion of the utility of CompuServe's e-mail service is that it allows subscribers to receive messages from individuals and entities located anywhere on the Internet. Certainly, then, there is at least a tacit invitation for anyone on the Internet to utilize plaintiff's computer equipment to send e-mail to its subscribers. [C] However, in or around October 1995, CompuServe employee Jon Schmidt specifically told Mr. Wallace that he was "prohibited from using CompuServe's equipment to send his junk e-mail messages." [C] There is apparently some factual dispute as to this point, but it is clear from the record that Mr. Wallace became aware at about this time that plaintiff did not want to receive messages from Cyber Promotions and that plaintiff was taking steps to block receipt of those messages. [C]

Defendants argue that plaintiff made the business decision to connect to the Internet and that therefore it cannot now successfully maintain an action for trespass to chattels. Their argument is analogous to the argument that because an establishment invites the public to enter its property for business purposes, it cannot later restrict or revoke access to that property, a proposition which is erroneous under Ohio law. [Cc] On or around October 1995, CompuServe notified defendants that it no longer consented to the use of its proprietary computer equipment. Defendants' continued use thereafter was a trespass. RESTATEMENT (SECOND) OF TORTS §§ 252 and 892A(5); *see also* RESTATEMENT (SECOND) OF TORTS § 217, Comment *f* ("The actor may commit a new trespass by continuing an intermeddling which he has already begun, with or without the consent of the person in possession. Such intermeddling may persist after the other's consent, originally given, has been terminated."); RESTATEMENT (SECOND) OF TORTS § 217, Comment g.

Further, CompuServe expressly limits the consent it grants to Internet users to send e-mail to its proprietary computer systems by denying unauthorized parties the use of CompuServe equipment to send unsolicited electronic mail messages. [C] This policy statement, posted by CompuServe online, states as follows:

> Compuserve is a private online and communications services company. CompuServe does not permit its facilities to be used by unauthorized parties to process and store unsolicited e-mail. If an unauthorized party attempts to send unsolicited messages to e-mail addresses on a CompuServe service, Compuserve will take appropriate action to attempt to prevent those messages from being processed by CompuServe. Violations of CompuServe's policy prohibiting unsolicited e-mail should be reported to....

[C] Defendants Cyber Promotions, Inc. and its president Sanford Wallace have used plaintiff's equipment in a fashion that exceeds that consent. The use of personal property exceeding consent is a trespass. [Cc] It is arguable that CompuServe's policy statement, insofar as it may serve as a limitation upon the scope of its consent to the use of its computer equipment, may be insufficiently communicated to potential third-party users when it is merely posted at some location on the network. However, in the present case the record indicates that defendants were actually notified that they were using CompuServe's equipment in an unacceptable manner. To prove that a would-be trespasser acted with the intent required to support liability in tort it is crucial that defendant be placed on notice that he is trespassing.

....

Defendants' intentional use of plaintiff's proprietary computer equipment exceeds plaintiff's consent and, indeed, continued after repeated demands that defendants cease. Such use is an actionable trespass to plaintiff's chattel. …

Plaintiff has demonstrated a likelihood of success on the merits which is sufficient to warrant the issuance of the preliminary injunction it has requested.

….

Normally, a preliminary injunction is not appropriate where an ultimate award of monetary damages will suffice. [C] However, money damages are only adequate if they can be reasonably computed and collected. Plaintiff has demonstrated that defendants' intrusions into their computer systems harm plaintiff's business reputation and goodwill. This is the sort of injury that warrants the issuance of a preliminary injunction because the actual loss is impossible to compute. [Cc]

Plaintiff has shown that it will suffer irreparable harm without the grant of the preliminary injunction.

It is improbable that granting the injunction will cause substantial harm to defendant. Even with the grant of this injunction, defendants are free to disseminate their advertisements in other ways not constituting trespass to plaintiff's computer equipment. Further, defendants may continue to send electronic mail messages to the tens of millions of Internet users who are not connected through CompuServe's computer systems.

….

Based on the foregoing, plaintiff's motion for a preliminary injunction is GRANTED. The temporary restraining order filed on October 24, 1996 by this Court is hereby extended in duration until final judgment is entered in this case. Further, defendants Cyber Promotions, Inc. and its president Sanford Wallace are enjoined from sending any unsolicited advertisements to any electronic mail address maintained by plaintiff CompuServe during the pendency of this action.

It is so ORDERED.

———————————

Points for Discussion

1. What is the chattel at issue in the CompuServe case? How does the plaintiff allege that the chattel has been damaged? Why did the plaintiff not sue for conversion?

2. How does the court define "intermeddling?"

3. For what reason are nominal damages not available in a trespass to chattels action?

Practice Pointer

The ethics rules governing the conduct of lawyers in most jurisdictions prohibit attorneys from distributing payments from accounts held for clients until any dispute regarding the distribution is resolved. *See, e.g.,* MODEL RULES OF PROF'L CONDUCT R. 1.15(e) (safekeeping property). A lawyer's failure to adhere to this rule can subject a lawyer to liability for conversion. In *Grayson v. Bank of Little Rock,* 971 S.W.2d 788 (Ark. 1998), an attorney was found liable for conversion when he distributed settlement proceeds that were subject to a creditor's security interest. With knowledge of the security interest, Attorney Grayson distributed the settlement proceeds to himself to cover attorney's fees, as well as to other third parties. The Court found him liable for conversion of the entire amount, not just the amount he paid to himself to cover the attorney's fees. In a similar case, an attorney was held liable for conversion of funds when he misappropriated funds in an account held in escrow by his firm. The attorney had accepted $750,000 in an escrow account on condition that no money was to be paid until the underlying lawsuit was finalized. When the settlement agreement started to fall apart and the attorney became worried that the client would be unable to pay, the attorney disbursed $100,000 to cover his fees. Both the firm as well as the attorney in his individual capacity were found liable for conversion. *See Grand Pac. Fin. Corp. v. Brauer,* 783 N.E.2d 849 (Mass. App. Ct. 2003).

Pearson v. Dodd

410 F.2d 701 (D.C. Cir. 1969)

J. SKELLY WRIGHT, Circuit Judge:

This case arises out of the exposure of the alleged misdeeds of Senator Thomas Dodd of Connecticut by newspaper columnists Drew Pearson and Jack Anderson. The District Court has granted partial summary judgment to Senator Dodd, appellee here, finding liability on a theory of conversion. . . . We . . . reverse its grant of summary judgment for conversion.

The undisputed facts in the case were stated by the District Court as follows:

"* * * On several occasions in June and July, 1965, two former employees of the plaintiff, at times with the assistance of two members of the plaintiff's staff, entered the plaintiff's office without authority and unbeknownst to him, removed numerous documents from his files, made copies of them, replaced the originals, and turned over the copies to the defendant Anderson, who was aware of the manner in which the copies had been obtained. The defendants Pearson and Anderson thereafter published articles containing information gleaned from these documents."

. . . .

The District Court ruled that appellants' receipt and subsequent use of photocopies of documents which appellants knew had been removed from appellee's files without authorization established appellants' liability for conversion. We conclude that appellants are not guilty of conversion on the facts shown.

Dean Prosser has remarked that "conversion is the forgotten tort." That it is not entirely forgotten is attested by the case before us. History has largely defined its contours, contours which we should now follow except where they derive from clearly obsolete practices or abandoned theories.

Conversion is the substantive tort theory which underlay the ancient common law form of action for trover. A plaintiff in trover alleged that he had lost a chattel which he rightfully possessed, and that the defendant had found it and converted it to his own use. With time, the allegations of losing and finding became fictional, leaving the question of whether the defendant had "converted" the property the only operative one.

The most distinctive feature of conversion is its measure of damages, which is the value of the goods converted. The theory is that the "converting" defendant has in some way treated the goods as if they were his own, so that the plaintiff can properly ask the court to decree a forced sale of the property from the rightful possessor to the converter.

Because of this stringent measure of damages, it has long been recognized that not every wrongful interference with the personal property of another is a conversion. Where the intermeddling falls short of the complete or very substantial deprivation of possessory rights in the property, the tort committed is not conversion, but the lesser wrong of trespass to chattels.

The Second Restatement of Torts has marked the distinction by defining conversion as:

"* * * An intentional exercise of dominion or control over a chattel which so seriously interferes with the right of another to control it that the actor may justly be required to pay the other the full value of the chattel."[29]

Less serious interferences fall under the Restatement's definition of trespass.[30]

The difference is more than a semantic one. The measure of damages in trespass is not the whole value of the property interfered with, but rather the actual diminution in its value caused by the interference. More important for this case, a judgment for conversion can be obtained with only nominal damages, whereas liability for trespass to chattels exists only on a showing of actual damage to the property interfered with. Here the District Court granted partial summary judgment on the issue of liability alone, while conceding that possibly no more than nominal damages might be awarded on subsequent trial. Partial summary judgment for liability could not have been granted on a theory of trespass to chattels without an undisputed showing of actual damages to the property in question.

It is clear that on the agreed facts appellants committed no conversion of the physical documents taken from appellee's files. Those documents were removed from the files at night, photocopied, and returned to the files undamaged before office operations resumed in the morning. Insofar as the documents' value to appellee resided in their usefulness as records of the business of his office, appellee was clearly not substantially deprived of his use of them.

This of course is not an end of the matter. It has long been recognized that documents often have value above and beyond that springing from their physical possession. They may embody information or ideas whose economic value depends in part or in whole upon being kept secret. The question then arises whether the information taken by means of copying appellee's office files is of the type which the law of conversion protects. The general rule has been that ideas or information are not subject to legal protection, but the law has developed exceptions to this rule. Where information is gathered and arranged at some cost and sold as a commodity on the market, it is properly protected as property. Where ideas are formulated with labor and inventive genius, as in the case of literary works or scientific researches, they are protected. Where they constitute instruments of fair and effective commercial competition, those who develop them may gather their fruits under the protection of the law.

The question here is not whether appellee had a right to keep his files from prying eyes, but whether the information taken from those files falls under the protection of the law of property, enforceable by a suit for conversion. In our view, it does not. The information included the contents of letters to appellee

---

29 Restatement (Second) of Torts § 222A(1) (1965).
30 Id., § 217: "A trespass to a chattel may be committed by intentionally (a) dispossessing another of the chattel, or (b) using or intermeddling with a chattel in the possession of another."

from supplicants, and office records of other kinds, the nature of which is not fully revealed by the record. Insofar as we can tell, none of it amounts to literary property, to scientific invention, or to secret plans formulated by appellee for the conduct of commerce. Nor does it appear to be information held in any way for sale by appellee, analogous to the fresh news copy produced by a wire service.

Appellee complains, not of the misappropriation of property bought or created by him, but of the exposure of information either (1) injurious to his reputation or (2) revelatory of matters which he believes he has a right to keep to himself. Injuries of this type are redressed at law by suit for libel and invasion of privacy respectively, where defendants' liability for those torts can be established under the limitations created by common law and by the Constitution.

Because no conversion of the physical contents of appellee's files took place, and because the information copied from the documents in those files has not been shown to be property subject to protection by suit for conversion, the District Court's ruling that appellants are guilty of conversion must be reversed.

So ordered.

G. Intentional Infliction of Emotional Distress

State Rubbish Collectors Ass'n v. Siliznoff

240 P.2d 282 (Cal. 1952)

TRAYNOR, Justice.

On February 1, 1948, Peter Kobzeff signed a contract with the Acme Brewing Company to collect rubbish from the latter's brewery. Kobzeff had been in the rubbish business for several years and was able to secure the contract because Acme was dissatisfied with the service then being provided by another collector, one Abramoff. Although Kobzeff signed the contract,

> **FYI**
>
> Justice Roger Traynor, the author of this opinion, was instrumental in the drafting and adoption of the RESTATEMENT (SECOND) OF TORTS (1965). To read more about Justice Traynor and his tremendous impact on the development of the law, see the introduction to The Traynor Reader: A Collection of Essays by the Honorable Roger J. Traynor.

it was understood that the work should be done by John Siliznoff, Kobzeff's son-in-law, whom Kobzeff wished to assist in establishing a rubbish collection business.

Both Kobzeff and Abramoff were members of the plaintiff State Rubbish Collectors Association, but Siliznoff was not. The by-laws of the association provided that one member should not take an account from another member without paying for it. Usual prices ranged from five to ten times the monthly rate paid by the customer, and disputes were referred to the board of directors for settlement. After Abramoff lost the Acme account he complained to the association, and Kobzeff was called upon to settle the matter. Kobzeff and Siliznoff took the position that the Acme account belonged to Siliznoff, and that he was under no obligation to pay for it. After attending several meetings of plaintiff's board of directors Siliznoff finally agreed, however, to pay Abramoff $1,850 for the Acme account and join the association. The agreement provided that he should pay $500 in thirty days and $75 per month thereafter until the whole sum agreed upon was paid. Payments were to be made through the association, and Siliznoff executed a series or promissory notes totaling $1,850. None of these notes was paid, and in 1949 plaintiff association brought this action to collect the notes then payable. Defendant **cross-complained** and asked that the notes be cancelled because of duress and want of **consideration**. In addition he sought general and exemplary damages because of assaults made by plaintiff and its agents to compel him to join the association and pay Abramoff for the Acme account. The jury returned a verdict against plaintiff and for defendant on the complaint and for defendant on his cross-complaint. It awarded him $1,250 general and special damages and $7,500 exemplary damages. The trial court denied a motion for a new trial on the condition that defendant consent to a reduction of the exemplary damages to $4,000. Defendant filed the required consent, and plaintiff has appealed from the judgment.

Make the Connection

A cross-complaint is a claim asserted by a defendant in an action against another party to the action. You will likely study issues of cross-complaints in a course on civil procedure.

Plaintiff's primary contention is that the evidence is insufficient to support the judgment. Defendant testified that shortly after he secured the Acme account, the president of the association and its inspector, John Andikian, called on him and Kobzeff. They suggested that either a settlement be made with Abramoff or that the job [b]e dropped, and requested Kobzeff and defendant to attend a meeting of the association. At this meeting defendant was told that the association "ran all the rubbish from that office, all the rubbish hauling," and that if he did not pay for the job they would take it away from him. "We would take it away, even if we had to haul for nothing. … (O)ne of them mentioned that I had better pay up, or else." Thereafter, on the day when defendant finally agreed to pay for the account, Andikian visited defendant at the Rainier Brewing Company, where he was collecting rubbish. Andikian told defendant that "We will give you up till tonight to get down to the board meeting and make some kind of arrangements or agreements about the Acme Brewery, or otherwise we are going to beat you up. … He says he either would hire somebody or do it himself. And I says, 'Well, what would they do to me?' He says, well, they would physically beat me up first, cut up the truck tires or burn the truck, or otherwise put me out of business completely. He said if I didn't appear at the meeting and make some kind of an agreement that they would do that, but he says up to then they would let me alone, but if I walked out of that meeting that night they would beat me up for sure." Defendant attended the meeting and protested that he owed nothing for the Acme account and in any event could not pay the amount demanded. He was again told by the president of the association that "that table right there (the board of directors) ran all the rubbish collecting in Los Angeles and if there was any routes to be gotten that they would get them and distribute them among their members ... ." After two hours of further discussion defendant agreed to join the association and pay for the Acme account. He promised to return the next day and sign the necessary papers. He testified that the only reason "they let me go home, is that I promised that I would sign the notes the very next morning." The president "made me promise on my honor and everything else, and I was scared, and I knew I had to come back, so I believed he knew I was scared and that I would come back. That's the only reason they let me go home." Defendant also testified that because of the fright he suffered during his dispute with the association he became ill and vomited several times and had to remain away from work for a period of several days.

Plaintiff contends that the evidence does not establish an assault against defendant because the threats made all related to action that might take place in the future; that neither Andikian nor members of the board of directors threatened immediate physical harm to defendant. [Cc] We have concluded, however, that a cause of action is established when it is shown that one, in the absence of any privilege, intentionally subjects another to the mental suffering incident to serious threats to his physical well-being, whether or not the threats are made under such circumstances as to constitute a technical assault.

In the past it has frequently been stated that the interest in emotional and mental tranquility is not one that the law will protect from invasion in its own right. [Cc] [The First] Restatement of Torts took the position that "The interest in mental and emotional tranquility and, therefore, in freedom from mental and emotional disturbance is not, as a thing in itself, regarded as of sufficient importance to require others to refrain from conduct intended or recognizably likely to cause such a disturbance." RESTATEMENT, TORTS, § 46, comment *c*. The Restatement explained the rule allowing recovery for the mere apprehension of bodily harm in traditional assault cases as an historical anomaly [C] and the rule allowing recovery for insulting conduct by an employee of a common carrier as justified by the necessity of securing for the public comfortable as well as safe service. [C]

....

The view has been forcefully advocated that the law should protect emotional and mental tranquility as such against serious and intentional invasions [Cc] and there is a growing body of case law supporting this position. [Cc]   In recognition of this development the American Law Institute amended section 46 of the Restatement of Torts in 1947 to provide: "One who, without a privilege to do so, intentionally causes severe emotional distress to another is liable (a) for such emotional distress, and (b) for bodily harm resulting from it."

In explanation it stated that "The interest in freedom from severe emotional distress is regarded as of sufficient importance to require others to refrain from conduct intended to invade it. Such conduct is tortious. The injury suffered by the one whose interest is invaded is frequently far more serious to him than certain tortious invasions of the interest in bodily integrity and other legally protected interests. In the absence of a privilege, the actor's conduct has no social utility; indeed it is antisocial. No reason or policy requires such an actor to be protected from the liability which usually attaches to the wilful wrongdoer whose efforts are successful." Restatement of the Law, 1948 Supplement, Torts, § 46, comment d.

There are persuasive arguments and analogies that support the recognition of a right to be free from serious, intentional, and unprivileged invasions of mental and emotional tranquility. If a cause of action is otherwise established, it is settled that damages may be given for mental suffering naturally ensuing from the acts complained of [Cc] and in the case of many torts, such as assault, battery, false imprisonment, and defamation, mental suffering will frequently constitute the principal element of damages. [Cc] In cases where mental suffering constitutes a major element of damages it is anomalous to deny recovery because the defendant's intentional misconduct fell short of producing some physical injury.

It may be contended that to allow recovery in the absence of physical injury will open the door to unfounded claims and a flood of litigation, and that the requirement that there be physical injury is necessary to insure that serious mental suffering actually occurred. The jury is ordinarily in a better position, however, to determine whether outrageous conduct results in mental distress than whether that distress in turn results in physical injury. From their own experience jurors are aware of the extent and character of the disagreeable emotions that may result from the defendant's conduct, but a difficult medical question is presented when it must be determined if emotional distress resulted in physical injury. [C] Greater proof that mental suffering occurred is found in the defendant's conduct designed to bring it about than in physical injury that may or may not have resulted therefrom.

....

In the present case plaintiff caused defendant to suffer extreme fright. By intentionally producing such fright it endeavored to compel him either to give up the Acme account or pay for it, and it had no right or privilege to adopt such coercive methods in competing for business. In these circumstances liability is clear.

....

The judgment is affirmed.

GIBSON, C. J., and SHENK, EDMONDS, CARTER, SCHAUER, and SPENCE, JJ., concur.

———————————

Points for Discussion

1. *Siliznoff* is one of the earliest cases recognizing the tort of intentional infliction of emotional distress. Why did the court recognize a new tort rather than rely on older, established torts such as assault or false imprisonment?

2. What policy considerations does the court take into account in recognizing the new tort of intentional infliction of emotion distress?

3. Do you agree that a plaintiff should be able to recover for his or her severe mental suffering in the absence of other traditionally recognized injuries?

4. Should proof of resulting physical manifestation(s) of the severe emotional distress be required in order to establish an intentional infliction of emotional distress claim? Why or why not?

———————————

Slocum v. Food Fair Stores of Florida

100 So. 2d 396 (Fla. 1958)

DREW, Justice.

This appeal is from an order dismissing a complaint for failure to state a cause of action. Simply stated, the plaintiff sought money damages for mental suffering or emotional distress, and an ensuing heart attack and aggravation of pre-existing heart disease, allegedly caused by insulting language of the defendant's employee directed toward her while she was a customer in its store. Specifically, in reply to her inquiry as to the price of an item he was marking, he replied: "If you want to know the price, you'll have to find out the best way you can ... you stink to me."

She asserts, in the alternative, that the language was used in a malicious or grossly reckless manner, "or with intent to inflict great mental and emotional disturbance to said plaintiff."

No great difficulty is involved in the preliminary point raised as to the sufficiency of damages alleged, the only direct injury being mental or emotional with physical symptoms merely derivative therefrom. [C] While that decision would apparently allow recovery for mental suffering, even absent physical consequences, inflicted in the course of other intentional or malicious torts, it does not resolve the central problem in this case, i.e. whether the conduct here claimed to have caused the injury, the use of insulting language under the circumstances described, constituted an actionable invasion of a legally protected right. Query: does such an assertion of a deliberate disturbance of emotional equanimity state an independent cause of action in tort?

Appellant's fundamental argument is addressed to that proposition. The case is one of first impression in this jurisdiction, and she contends that this Court should recognize the existence of a new tort, an independent cause of action for intentional infliction of emotional distress.

A study of the numerous references on the subject indicates a strong current of opinion in support of such recognition, in lieu of the strained reasoning so often apparent when liability for such injury is predicated upon one or another of several traditional tort theories. [Cc]

. . . .

A most cogent statement of the doctrine covering tort liability for insult has been incorporated in the RESTATEMENT OF THE LAW OF TORTS, 1948 supplement, sec. 46, entitled "Conduct intended to cause emotional distress only." It makes a blanket provision for liability on the part of "one, who, without a privilege to do so, intentionally causes severe emotional distress to another," indicating that the requisite intention exists "when the act is done for the purpose of causing the distress or with knowledge … that severe emotional distress is substantially certain to be produced by (such) conduct." Comment (a), Sec. 46, supra. Abusive language is, of course, only one of the many means by which the tort could be committed.

However, even if we assume, without deciding, the legal propriety of that doctrine, a study of its factual applications shows that line of demarcation should be drawn between conduct likely to cause mere "emotional distress" and that causing "severe emotional distress," so as to exclude the situation at bar. [C] "So far as it is possible to generalize from the cases, the rule which seems to be emerging is that there is liability only for conduct exceeding all bounds which could be tolerated by society, of a nature especially calculated to cause mental damage of a very serious kind." [C] And the most practicable view is that the functions of court and jury are no different than in other tort actions where there is at the outset a question as to whether the conduct alleged is so legally innocuous as to present no issue for a jury. [C]

This tendency to hinge the cause of action upon the degree of the insult has led some courts to reject the doctrine **in toto**. [C] Whether or not this is desirable, it is uniformly agreed that the determination of whether words or conduct are actionable in character is to be made on an objective rather than subjective standard, from common acceptation.

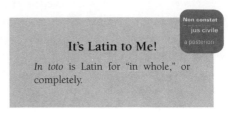

It's Latin to Me!

In toto is Latin for "in whole," or completely.

The unwarranted intrusion must be calculated to cause "severe emotional distress" to a person of ordinary sensibilities, in the absence of special knowledge or notice. There is no inclination to include all instances of mere vulgarities, obviously intended as meaningless abusive expressions. While the manner in which language is used may no doubt determine its actionable character, appellant's assertion that the statement involved in this case was made to her with gross recklessness, etc., cannot take the place of allegations showing that the words were intended to have real meaning or serious effect.

....

Affirmed.

Points for Discussion

1. RESTATEMENT (THIRD) OF TORTS: LIABILITY FOR PHYSICAL AND EMOTIONAL HARM § 45 (2010) provides that one "who by extreme and outrageous conduct intentionally or recklessly causes severe emotional disturbance to another is subject to liability for that emotional disturbance and, if the emotional disturbance causes bodily harm, also for the bodily harm." Note that the state of mind element for intentional infliction of emotional distress is satisfied by proof that the defendant acted with specific intent, general intent, or recklessness. Recklessness is established by proving that the defendant knew of the risk of causing severe emotional disturbance and was indifferent to that risk. Such indifference may be proven by showing that the defendant failed to take a precaution that would eliminate or reduce the risk even though the burden was slight relative to the magnitude of the risk. *See* RESTATEMENT (THIRD) OF TORTS: LIABILITY FOR PHYSICAL AND EMOTIONAL HARM § 45 cmt. g (2010)

2. **Extreme and Outrageous Conduct** – An intentional infliction of emotional distress claim requires that the defendant's act be both outrageous as well as sufficiently unusual to be considered extreme. The defendant will be liable "only if the conduct goes beyond the bounds of human decency and would be regarded as intolerable in a civilized community. Ordinary insults and indignities are not enough for liability to be imposed, even if the actor desires to cause emotional disturbance." RESTATEMENT (THIRD) OF TORTS: LIABILITY FOR PHYSICAL AND EMOTIONAL HARM § 45 cmt. *c* (2010). *See, e.g.,* Small v. Juniata Coll., 682 A.2d 350, 352 (Pa. Super. Ct. 1996) (coach's lawsuit for IIED failed against college and former players based on letters they wrote complaining about his coaching abilities).

3. **Severe Emotional Distress** – In an effort to ensure that the plaintiff's complained of harm is genuine, recovery for an intentional infliction of emotional distress claim is limited to injuries for severe emotional disturbance and only when a reasonable person subjected to the same extreme and outrageous conduct would suffer severe emotional disturbance as well, unless the defendant was on notice of the plaintiff's particular sensitivity. Although physical manifestation of the emotional harm is not required in most jurisdictions, the severity of the emotional injury itself affects whether the plaintiff can establish the *prima facie* case. *See, e.g.,* Harris v. Jones, 380 A.2d 611 (Md. 1977) (worsening of stutter and humiliation not severe enough to establish *prima facie* case of IIED). Thus, nominal damages are not permitted for an intentional infliction of emotional distress action.

Wilson v. Monarch Paper Co.

939 F.2d 1138 (5th Cir. 1991)

Before REYNALDO G. GARZA, JOLLY and JONES, Circuit Judges.

FYI

The ADEA, or the Age Discrimination in Employment Act of 1967, is a federal law that prohibits job discrimination based upon a person's age. The ADEA applies to all governmental entities and to businesses with more than twenty employees and protects employees forty years of age or older.

E. GRADY JOLLY, Circuit Judge:

In this employment discrimination case, Monarch Paper Company, et al., appeals a $3,400,000 jury verdict finding it liable for age discrimination and retaliation under the Age Discrimination in Employment Act (ADEA), 29 U.S.C. § 621, and for intentional infliction of emotional distress under Texas state law. Monarch challenges the sufficiency of the evidence. It also challenges the district court's denial of their motions for directed verdict, for **judgment non obstante veredicto** (JNOV), for new trial, and for remittitur. Upon review of the entire record, we affirm.

I

Because Monarch is challenging the sufficiency of the evidence, the facts are recited in the light most favorable to the jury's verdict. In 1970, at age 48, Richard E. Wilson was hired by Monarch Paper Company. Monarch is an incorporated division of Unisource Corporation, and Unisource is an incorporated group of Alco Standard Corporation. Wilson served as manager of the Corpus Christi division until November 1, 1977, when he was moved to the corporate staff in Houston to serve as "Corporate Director of Physical Distribution." During that time, he routinely received merit raises and performance bonuses. In 1980, Wilson received the additional title of "Vice President." In 1981, Wilson was given the additional title of "Assistant to John Blankenship," Monarch's President at the time.

While he was Director of Physical Distribution, Wilson received most of his assignments from Blankenship. Blankenship always seemed pleased with Wilson's performance and Wilson was never reprimanded or counseled about his performance. Blankenship provided Wilson with objective performance criteria at the beginning of each year, and Wilson's bonuses at the end of the year were based on his good performance under that objective criteria. In 1981, Wilson was placed in charge of the completion of an office warehouse building in Dallas, the largest construction project Monarch had ever undertaken. Wilson successfully completed that project within budget.

In 1981, Wilson saw a portion of Monarch's long-range plans that indicated that Monarch was presently advancing younger persons in all levels of Monarch management. Tom Davis, who was hired as Employee Relations Manager of Monarch in 1979, testified that from the time he started to work at Monarch, he heard repeated references by the division managers (including Larry Clark, who later became the Executive Vice President of Monarch) to the age of employees on the corporate staff, including Wilson.

In October 1981, Blankenship became Chairman of Monarch and Unisource brought in a new, 42-year-old president from outside the company, Hamilton Bisbee. An announcement was made that Larry Clark would be assuming expanded responsibilities in physical distribution. According to the defendants, one of Blankenship's final acts as President was to direct Clark (who was in his mid-forties at the time) to assume expanded responsibility for both the operational and physical distribution aspects of Monarch.

When Bisbee arrived at Monarch in November 1981, Wilson was still deeply involved in the Dallas construction project. Richard Gozon, who was 43 years old and the President of Unisource, outlined Blankenship's new responsibilities as Chairman of the company and requested that Blankenship, Bisbee, Wilson, and John Hartley of Unisource "continue to work very closely together on the completion of the Dallas project." Bisbee, however, refused to speak to Wilson or to "interface" with him. This "silent treatment" was apparently tactical; Bisbee later told another Monarch employee, Bill Shehan, "if I ever stop talking to you, you're dead." Shehan also testified that at a meeting in Philadelphia at about the time Bisbee became President of Monarch, Gozon told Bisbee, "I'm not telling you that you have to fire Dick Wilson. I'm telling you that he cannot make any more money."

As soon as the Dallas building project was completed, Bisbee and Gozon intensified an effort designed to get rid of Wilson. On March 8, 1982, Gozon asked for Bisbee's recommendations on how to remove Wilson from the Monarch organization. On March 9, 1982, Bisbee responded with his recommendation that Wilson be terminated, and that any salary continuance to Wilson be discontinued should Wilson elect to pursue an adversarial role toward Monarch. Gozon then asked the Unisource Employee Relations Manager, John Snelgrove, to meet with Wilson with the goal of attempting to convince Wilson to quit.

During the same time frame, Bisbee was preparing a long-range plan for Monarch, in which he made numerous references to age and expressed his desire to bring in "new blood" and to develop a "young team." This long-range plan was transmitted to Gozon, who expressed no dissatisfaction with the goals Bisbee had set out in the plan. In the meantime, Bisbee and Clark began dismantling Wilson's job by removing his responsibilities and assigning them to other employees. Clark was also seen entering Wilson's office after hours and removing files.

Blankenship was diagnosed with cancer in February 1982. In March 1982, Wilson was hospitalized for orthopedic surgery. Immediately after Blankenship's death in June 1982, Bisbee and Snelgrove gave Wilson three options: (1) he could take a sales job in Corpus Christi at half his pay; (2) he could be terminated with three months' severance pay; or (3) he could accept a job as warehouse supervisor in the Houston warehouse at the same salary but with a reduction in benefits. The benefits included participation in the management bonus plan, and the loss of the use of a company car, a company club membership, and a company expense account.

Wilson accepted the warehouse position. Wilson believed that he was being offered the position of Warehouse Manager, the only vacant position in the Houston warehouse at the time. When Wilson reported for duty at the warehouse on August 16, 1982, however, he was placed instead in the position of an entry level supervisor, a position that required no more than one year's experience in the paper business. Wilson, with his thirty years of experience in the paper business and a college degree, was vastly overqualified and overpaid for that position.

Soon after he went to the warehouse, Wilson was subjected to harassment and verbal abuse by his supervisor, Operations Manager and Acting Warehouse Manager Paul Bradley (who had previously been subordinate to Wilson). Bradley referred to Wilson as "old man" and admitted posting a sign in the warehouse that said "Wilson is old." In Bradley's absence, Wilson was placed under the supervision of a man in his twenties. Finally, Wilson was further demeaned when he was placed in charge of housekeeping but was not given any employees to assist him in the housekeeping duties. Wilson, the former vice-president and assistant to the president, was thus reduced finally to sweeping the floors and cleaning up the employees' cafeteria, duties which occupied 75 percent of his working time.

In the late fall of 1982, Wilson began suffering from respiratory problems caused by the dusty conditions in the warehouse and stress from the unrelenting harassment by his employer. On January 6, 1983, Wilson left work to see a doctor about his respiratory problems. He was advised to stay out of a dusty environment and was later advised that he had a clinically significant allergy to dust. Shortly after January 6, 1983, Wilson consulted a psychiatrist who diagnosed him as suffering from reactive depression, possibly suicidal, because of on-the-job stress. The psychiatrist also advised that Wilson should stay away from work indefinitely.

Wilson filed an age discrimination charge with the EEOC in January 1983. Although he continued being treated by a psychiatrist, his condition deteriorated to the point that in March 1983, he was involuntarily hospitalized with a psychotic manic episode. Prior to the difficulties with his employer, Wilson had no history of emotional illness.

Wilson's emotional illness was severe and long-lasting. He was diagnosed with manic-depressive illness or bipolar disorder. After his first hospitalization for a manic episode, in which he was locked in a padded cell and heavily sedated, he fell into a deep depression. The depression was unremitting for over two years and necessitated an additional hospital stay in which he was given electroconvulsive therapy (shock treatments). It was not until 1987 that Wilson's illness began remission, thus allowing him to carry on a semblance of a normal life.

II

On February 27, 1984, Wilson filed suit against the defendants, alleging age discrimination and various state law tort and contract claims. ...[T]he case was tried before a jury on Wilson's ... claims that the defendants (1) reassigned him because of his age; (2) intentionally inflicted emotional distress; and (3) terminated his long-term disability benefits in retaliation for filing charges of age discrimination under the Age Discrimination in Employment Act (ADEA).

The district court denied the defendants' motions for directed verdict. The jury returned a special verdict in favor of Wilson on his age discrimination claim, awarding him $156,000 in damages, plus an equal amount in liquidated damages. The jury also found in favor of Wilson on his claim for intentional infliction of emotional distress, awarding him past damages of $622,359.15, future damages of $225,000, and punitive damages of $2,250,000. The jury found in favor of the defendants on Wilson's retaliation claim. The district court entered judgment for $3,409,359.15 plus prejudgment interest. The district court denied the defendants' motions for judgment NOV, new trial, or, alternatively, a remittitur. The defendants appeal.

III

Monarch raises three issues, each attacking the district court's exercise of discretion in sending the case to the jury and entering judgment on its verdict. First, Monarch argues that the district court erred in denying its motions for directed verdict, JNOV, and new trial on Wilson's claim for intentional infliction of emotional distress. Second, Monarch argues that the district court erred in denying its similar motions on Wilson's age discrimination claim. Finally, Monarch argues that the district court erred in denying its motions for directed verdict, JNOV, new trial, and remittitur with respect to the amount of back pay awarded on the age discrimination claim. With respect to the emotional distress claim, neither the quantum of actual damages or the award of punitive damages are appealed.

. . . .

A

Wilson's claim for intentional infliction of emotional distress is a pendent state law claim. As such, we are bound to apply the law of Texas in determining whether the defendant's motions should have been granted. The Texas Supreme Court has not expressly recognized the tort of intentional infliction of emotional distress. [Cc] We, however, have nonetheless recognized on at least two prior occasions, [Cc] that such a cause of action exists in Texas, based on the Texas Court of Appeals' decision in Tide-

What's That?

A pendent state law claim is a state action that the federal court would ordinarily not have jurisdiction to hear, but because of the federal claim arising from the same occurrence properly before the federal court, the federal court may hear and decide the state law claim as well. In deciding the pendent claim, the federal court is required to apply state law, here, the law of Texas.

lands Auto. Club v. Walters, 699 S.W.2d 939 (Tex.App.-Beaumont 1985, writ ref'd n.r.e.). To prevail on a claim for intentional infliction of emotional distress, Texas law requires that the following four elements be established:

(1) that the defendant acted intentionally or recklessly;

(2) that the conduct was 'extreme and outrageous';

(3) that the actions of the defendant caused the plaintiff emotional distress; and

(4) that the emotional distress suffered by the plaintiff was severe.

Dean, 885 F.2d at 306 (quoting Tidelands, 699 S.W.2d at 942). The sole issue before us is whether Monarch's conduct was "extreme and outrageous."

(1)

"Extreme and outrageous conduct" is an amorphous phrase that escapes precise definition. In *Dean v. Ford Motor Credit Co., supra,* however, we stated that

[l]iability [for outrageous conduct] has been found only where the conduct has been so outrageous in character, and so extreme in degree, as to go beyond all possible bounds of decency, and to be regarded as atrocious, and utterly intolerable in a civilized community.... Generally, the case is one in which a recitation of the facts to an average member of the community would lead him to exclaim, "Outrageous."

885 F.2d at 306 (citing RESTATEMENT (SECOND) TORTS § 46, Comment d (1965)). The Restatement also provides for some limits on jury verdicts by stating that liability "does not extend to mere insults, indignities, threats, annoyances, petty oppressions, or other trivialities.... There is no occasion for the law to intervene in every case where someone's feelings are hurt." REST. (SECOND) OF TORTS § 46.

The facts of a given claim of outrageous conduct must be analyzed in context, and ours is the employment setting. We are cognizant that "the work culture in some situations may contemplate a degree of teasing and taunting that in other circumstances might be considered cruel and outrageous." KEETON, et al., PROSSER & KEETON ON TORTS (5th ed. 1984 & 1988 Supp.). We further recognize that properly to manage its business, every employer must on occasion review, criticize, demote, transfer, and discipline employees. *Id.* We also acknowledge that it is not unusual for an employer, instead of directly discharging an employee, to create unpleasant and onerous work conditions designed to force an employee to quit, i.e., "constructively" to discharge the employee. In short, although this sort of conduct often rises to the level of illegality, except in the most unusual cases it is not the sort of conduct, as deplorable as it may sometimes be, that constitutes "extreme and outrageous" conduct.

(2)

Our recent decision in *Dean v. Ford Motor Credit Co., supra*, is instructive in determining what types of conduct in the employment setting will constitute sufficiently outrageous conduct so as to legally support a jury's verdict. In *Dean*, the plaintiff presented evidence that (1) when she expressed interest in transferring to a higher paying position in the collection department, she was told that "women don't usually go into that department"; (2) she was denied a transfer to the collection department, and a lesser qualified man was selected; (3) the defendant's attitude toward the plaintiff changed after she complained about alleged discriminatory treatment; (4) management began to transfer her from desk to desk within the administrative department; (5) a coworker testified she believed management was trying to "set ... [the plaintiff] up"; (6) she was called upon to do more work than the other clerks "and subjected to unfair harassment"; and (7) management used "special" annual reviews (that only the plaintiff received) to downgrade her performance. 885 F.2d at 304-305, 306-307. Far more significant to the claim for intentional infliction of emotional distress, however, (8) the plaintiff proved that a supervisor, who had access to the employer's checks, intentionally placed checks in the plaintiff's purse in order to make it appear that she was a thief, or to put her in fear of criminal charges for theft. *Id.* We expressly held that the "check incidents" were "precisely what [took] this case beyond the realm of an ordinary employment dispute and into the realm of an outrageous one." *Id.* at 307. We concluded that without the "check incidents" the employer's conduct "would not have been outrageous." *Id.*

Wilson argues that Monarch's conduct is sufficiently outrageous to meet the *Dean* standard; in the alternative, he argues that Monarch's actions are certainly more outrageous than the conduct in *Bushell v. Dean*, 781 S.W.2d 652 (Tex.App.- Austin 1989), writ denied in part, rev'd in part on other grounds, 803 S.W.2d 711 (Tex.1991), which is a recent pronouncement by the Texas courts on the subject. Monarch contends that Wilson's evidence of outrageous conduct, that is, his reassignment to a job he did not like, his strained relationship with the company president, and isolated references to his age, is the same evidence that he used to prove his age discrimination claim. According to Monarch, unless all federal court discrimination lawsuits are to be accompanied by pendent state law claims for emotional distress, this court must make it clear that ordinary employment disputes cannot support an emotional distress claim. We agree with Monarch that more is required to prove intentional infliction of emotional distress than the usual ADEA claim. Accord *Dean, supra.*

(3)

In *Dean*, we found that the "check incidents" took the case beyond an ordinary discrimination case and supported the claim of infliction of emotional distress. Wilson contends that Monarch's conduct was equally outrageous as the "check incidents" in Dean. Generally, Wilson argues that an average member of the community would exclaim "Outrageous! " upon hearing that a 60-year-old man, with 30 years of experience in his industry, was subjected to a year-long campaign of harassment and abuse because his company wanted to force him out of his job as part of its expressed written goal of getting rid of older employees and moving younger people into management. More precisely, Wilson argues that substantial evidence of outrageous conduct supports the jury's verdict, including: (1) his duties in physical distribution were assigned to a younger person; (2) Bisbee deliberately refused to speak to him in the hallways of Monarch in order to harass him; (3) certain portions of Monarch's long-range plans expressed a desire to move younger persons into sales and management positions; (4) Bisbee wanted to replace Wilson with a younger person; (5) other managers within Monarch would not work with Wilson, and he did not receive his work directly from Bisbee; (6) he was not offered a fully guaranteed salary to transfer to Corpus Christi; (7) he was assigned to Monarch's Houston warehouse as a supervisor, which was "demeaning"; (8) Paul Bradley, the Warehouse Manager, and other Monarch managers, referred to Wilson as old; (9) Bradley prepared a sign stating "Wilson is old" and, subsequently, "Wilson is a Goldbrick"; and (10) Monarch filed a counterclaim against Wilson in this action. We are not in full agreement.

Most of Monarch's conduct is similar in degree to conduct in *Dean* that failed to reach the level of outrageousness. We hold that all of this conduct, except as explicated below, is within the "realm of an ordinary employment dispute," *Dean*, 885 F.2d at 307, and, in the context of the employment milieu, is not so extreme and outrageous as to be properly addressed outside of Wilson's ADEA claim.

(4)

Wilson argues, however, that what takes this case out of the realm of an ordinary employment dispute is the degrading and humiliating way that he was stripped of his duties and demoted from an executive manager to an entry level warehouse supervisor with menial and demeaning duties. We agree. Wilson, a college graduate with thirty years experience in the paper field, had been a long-time executive at Monarch. His title was Corporate Director of Physical Distribution, with the added title of Vice-President and Assistant to the President. He had been responsible for the largest project in the company's history, and had completed the project on time and under budget. Yet, when transferred to the warehouse, Wilson's primary duty became housekeeping chores around the warehouse's shipping and receiving area. Because Monarch did not give Wilson any employees to supervise or assist him, Wilson was frequently required to sweep the warehouse. In addition, Wilson also was reduced to cleaning up after the employees in the warehouse cafeteria after their lunch hour. Wilson spent 75 percent of his time performing these menial, janitorial duties.

Monarch argues that assigning an executive with a college education and thirty years experience to janitorial duties is not extreme and outrageous conduct. The jury did not agree and neither do we. We find it difficult to conceive a workplace scenario more painful and embarrassing than an executive, indeed a vice-president and the assistant to the president, being subjected before his fellow employees to the most menial janitorial services and duties of cleaning up after entry level employees: the steep downhill push to total humiliation was complete. The evidence, considered as a whole, will fully support the view, which the jury apparently held, that Monarch, unwilling to fire Wilson outright, intentionally and systematically set out to humiliate him in the hopes that he would quit.[5] A reasonable jury could have found that this employer conduct was intentional and mean spirited, so severe that it resulted in institutional confinement and treatment for someone with no history of mental problems. Finally, the evidence supports the conclusion that this conduct was, indeed, so outrageous that civilized society should not tolerate it. [C] Accordingly, the judgment of the district court in denying Monarch's motions for directed verdict, JNOV and a new trial on this claim is affirmed.

. . . .

[The court's discussions affirming the age discrimination claim and award of back pay are omitted.]

IV

In conclusion, we express real concern about the consequences of applying the cause of action of intentional infliction of emotional distress to the workplace. This concern is, however, primarily a concern for the State of Texas, its courts and its legislature. Although the award in this case is astonishingly high, neither the quantum of damages, nor the applicability of punitive damages has been appealed.

For the reasons set forth above, the district court's denial of the motions for direct verdict, new trial and JNOV with respect to the intentional infliction of

---

5 Nevertheless, we are not unaware of the irony in this case: if Monarch had chosen only to fire Wilson outright, leaving him without a salary, a job, insurance, etc., it would not be liable for intentional infliction of emotional distress. There is some suggestion in the record, however, that Monarch was unwilling to fire Wilson outright because it had no grounds and perhaps feared a lawsuit. Although Monarch was willing to accept Wilson's resignation, Wilson was unwilling to resign. Once he was unwilling to resign, the evidence supports the inference that Monarch's efforts intensified to force his resignation.

emotional distress verdict is AFFIRMED. The denial of Monarch's motions with respect to the age discrimination and back pay is also AFFIRMED.

AFFIRMED.

——————————

Points for Discussion

1. Is the intentional infliction of emotional distress claim at issue in *Wilson* a federal claim? Why is a federal court deciding this state common law action?

2. Is the court in *Wilson* right to be concerned about the wisdom of recognizing an intentional infliction of emotional distress claim in the workplace? What competing policy considerations are at issue?

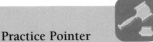

> **Practice Pointer**
>
> As is true for other intentional torts, lawyers are not immune from liability from intentional infliction of emotional distress claims for conduct they engage in while representing a client. *See, e.g.,* Kunau v. Pillers, Pillers, & Pillers, P.C., 404 N.W.2d 573, 577 (Iowa Ct. App. 1987) (discussing existence of IIED claims in attorney-client context).

3. In *Pleasant Glade Assembly of God v. Schubert*, the plaintiff sued her church for numerous intentional torts, including intentional infliction of emotional distress, false imprisonment, assault, and battery, after her youth pastor and other members of the church "laid hands" on her to expel evil demons. On two occasions within one week, the plaintiff was forcibly held down at the sanctuary while the youth pastor and others prayed over her, resulting in bruises, carpet burns, scrapes, and a later diagnosis of post-traumatic stress disorder. The jury found in favor of the plaintiff and awarded $300,000 in damages. In an interesting twist, the state supreme court held that the practice of "laying hands" and the church's belief about demon possession were so "intertwined with [the plaintiff's] tort claims" that imposing liability against the church would unconstitutionally burden the church's free exercise of religion. The state supreme court dismissed the case over a very strong dissent that argued such a ruling was a grant of complete impunity to religious organizations to commit intentional torts against their members as long as they occur during religious activities. *See* Pleasant Glade Assembly of God v. Schubert, 264 S.W.3d 1 (Tex. 2008).

——————————

Taylor v. Vallelunga

339 P.2d 910 (Ca. Ct. App. 1959)

O'DONNELL, Justice pro tem.

The complaint in this action contains three counts. We are concerned here, however, only with the allegations of the first two counts. In the first count, plaintiff Clifford Gerlach alleges that on December 25, 1956, defendants struck and beat him causing him bodily injury for which he seeks damages. In the second count, plaintiff and appellant Gail E. Taylor incorporates by reference the charging allegations of the first count and proceeds to allege that she is the daughter of plaintiff Clifford Gerlach, that she was present at and witnessed the beating inflicted upon her father by defendants, and that as a result thereof, she suffered severe fright and emotional distress. She seeks damages for the distress so suffered. It is not alleged that any physical disability or injury resulted from the mental distress. A general demurrer to the second count of the complaint was interposed by defendants. The demurrer was sustained and appellant was granted ten days leave to amend. Appellant failed to amend and judgment of dismissal of the second count was entered. The appeal is from the judgment of dismissal.

> **FYI**
>
> A justice *pro tem* is one who has been appointed to the bench temporarily. *"Pro tem"* is an abbreviation for the Latin term *pro tempore*, meaning "for the time being."

The California cases have for some time past allowed recovery of damages where physical injury resulted from intentionally subjecting the plaintiff to serious mental distress. See cases cited in State Rubbish Collectors Ass'n v. Siliznoff, 38 Cal.2d 330, 337, 240 P.2d 282. In the Siliznoff case the Supreme Court extended the right of recovery to situations where no physical injury follows the suffering of mental distress, saying that "a cause of action is established when it is shown that one, in the absence of any privilege, intentionally subjects another to the mental suffering incident to serious threats to his physical well-being, whether or not the threats are made under such circumstances as to constitute a technical assault." [C] In arriving at this result the court relied in substantial part upon the development of the law in this field of torts as traced by the American Law Institute, and it quotes with approval ... section 46, as amended, of the RESTATEMENT OF TORTS ... which reads: "One who, without a privilege to do so, intentionally causes severe emotional distress to another is liable (a) for such emotional distress, and (b) for bodily harm resulting from it." In explanation of the meaning of the term "intentionally" as it is employed in said section 46, the Reporter says in subdivision (a) of that section: "An intention to cause severe emotional distress exists when the act is done for the purpose of causing the distress or with knowledge on the part of the actor that severe emotional distress is substantially certain to be produced by his conduct. See Illustration 3." Illustration 3 referred to reads as follows: "A is sitting on her front porch watching her husband B, who is standing on the sidewalk. C, who hates B and is friendly to A, *whose presence is known to him*, stabs B, killing him. C is liable to A for the mental anguish, grief and horror he causes." (Emphasis added.)

The failure of the second count of the complaint in the case at bar to meet the requirements of section 46 of the RESTATEMENT OF TORTS is at once apparent. There is no allegation that defendants knew that appellant was present and witnessed the beating that was administered to her father; nor is there any allegation that the beating was administered for the purpose of causing her to suffer emotional distress, or, in the alternative, that defendants knew that severe emotional distress was substantially certain to be produced by their conduct.

. . . .

Appellant argues that the intent to cause her severe emotional distress or knowledge that such distress was substantially certain to be produced might be proved upon the trial. Her complaint failed to allege such facts and since she was granted leave to amend and failed to do so, we are limited on appeal to a determination of whether the complaint states a cause of action, not whether it might be amended to do so. [C]

Judgment affirmed.

———————

Points for Discussion

1. The intentional infliction of emotional defense action brought by the daughter fails here for lack of sufficient proof of the defendant's intent. Proof of the defendant's specific or general intent or reckless state of mind requires knowledge of the plaintiff's presence. The defendant cannot be held liable for intentional infliction of emotional distress if the defendant is unaware of the plaintiff's presence at the time.

2. Why did the plaintiff not use the transferred intent doctrine to establish intent in this case?

3. In order to prevail in bringing an intentional infliction of emotional defense action, the plaintiff must have contemporaneously witnessed the defendant's extreme and outrageous conduct.

Hypo 2-15

One evening, Mary is driving her sports utility vehicle ("SUV") across town to deliver dinner to her husband, who is working late. With her are their four children – an 11-year-old daughter, a 9-year-old daughter, and two 6-month-old twin boys. Unknown to Mary, she is being followed by Repo Man who is following her because she and her husband are currently delinquent in payments on the SUV. Repo Man has been instructed by his boss to seize the SUV if given the opportunity. When Mary pulls up at her husband's office, she quickly jumps out of the car to run dinner into him. Both of their daughters are awake and playing with the twins, so she leaves them in the car for the quick minute it will take her to run into her husband's office. As soon as she leaves the car, Repo Man jumps into the driver's seat of the SUV. Seeing the four kids in the back seat of the car, he drives off in the SUV. Mary and her husband immediately see that their car has been driven off with their four kids in the back. They understandably become emotionally distraught, running after the car and calling the police on their cell phones to report the incident. Once on the road, Repo Man calls his boss, stating that, although he would like to keep his job, he does not want anything to do with taking the kids. Moments later, Repo Man decides to abandon the SUV, leaving the car running and the terrified girls in the back (the young twin boys do not appear to be upset at all). Within an hour, the police discover the kids and the SUV on the side of a road. The kids are physically unharmed, but the girls are emotionally traumatized by the event. The twins are sound asleep. Mary and her husband are likewise emotionally traumatized by the event. Do any of the family members have an actionable and valid intentional tort claim? Discuss.

CHAPTER 3

Defenses to Intentional Torts

There are several ways that a defendant can avoid tort liability. The defendant may attack the plaintiff's ***prima facie*** case. In an intentional tort action, this may be done, for example, by putting on evidence disputing intent, the first element of the plaintiff's *prima facie* case. A defendant may also avoid liability by establishing that she was privileged to commit the tort. To do so, the defendant does not defeat an element of the plaintiff's *prima facie* case, but rather avoids liability by providing an independent reason that the plaintiff should not be permitted to recover. Such avoidance is what is known as an **affirmative defense**. An affirmative defense provides an independent reason why the plaintiff should not recover even though the plaintiff may be able to prove the *prima facie* claim. Affirmative defenses are typically required to be pleaded and proven by the defendant. This chapter will focus on affirmative defenses to intentional tort actions.

Make the Connection

In *Garratt v. Dailey, see* Chapter 2, *supra,* the defendant Brian Dailey sought to avoid liability by proving that he did not act with the requisite intent, thereby defeating the first element of the plaintiff's battery claim. If he had been successful, it would be a successful defense, but not by proof of a privilege. Rather, the plaintiff would not have been able to prove her *prima facie* case.

A. Consent

A plaintiff may not recover for an intentional tort if it is established that the plaintiff was willing for the conduct or result to occur or when the plaintiff has manifested apparent consent. In other words, a defendant is privileged to commit an intentional tort that the plaintiff was willing to have occur. This affirmative defense of consent, explored in the next case, is set forth in the RESTATEMENT (SECOND) OF TORTS § 892A: "[o]ne who effectively consents to conduct of another intended to invade his interests cannot recover in an action of tort for the conduct or for harm resulting from it."

Koffman v. Garnett

574 S.E.2d 258 (Va. 2003)

Opinion by Justice ELIZABETH B. LACY.

In this case we consider whether the trial court properly dismissed the plaintiffs' second amended motion for judgment for failure to state causes of action for … assault … and battery. [The plaintiff alleged gross negligence as well. The court's discussion reinstating the gross negligence claim is omitted.]

Because this case was decided on **demurrer**, we take as true all material facts properly pleaded in the motion for judgment and all inferences properly drawn from those facts. [C]

In the fall of 2000, Andrew W. Koffman, a 13-year old middle school student at a public school in Botetourt County, began participating on the school's football team. It was Andy's first season playing organized football, and he was positioned as a third-string defensive player. James Garnett was employed by the Botetourt County School Board as an assistant coach for the football team and was responsible for the supervision, training, and instruction of the team's defensive players.

The team lost its first game of the season. Garnett was upset by the defensive players' inadequate tackling in that game and became further displeased by what he perceived as inadequate tackling during the first practice following the loss.

Food for Thought

Even though the focus of this chapter is affirmative defenses to intentional torts, as you read the following opinions, consider whether the facts provided by the court establish the *prima facie* case for the intentional tort at issue.

Garnett ordered Andy to hold a football and "stand upright and motionless" so that Garnett could explain the proper tackling technique to the defensive players. Then Garnett, without further warning, thrust his arms around Andy's body, lifted him "off his feet by two feet or more," and "slamm[ed]" him to the ground. Andy weighed 144 pounds, while Garnett weighed approximately 260 pounds. The force of the tackle broke the humerus bone in Andy's left arm. During prior practices, no coach had used physical force to instruct players on rules or techniques of playing football.

In his second amended motion for judgment, Andy, by his father and next friend, Richard Koffman, and Andy's parents, Richard and Rebecca Koffman, individually, (collectively "the Koffmans") alleged that Andy was injured as a result of Garnett's … intentional acts of assault and battery. Garnett filed a demurrer and plea of **sovereign immunity**, asserting that the second amended motion for judgment did not allege sufficient facts to support a lack of consent to the tackling demonstration and, therefore, did not plead causes of action for either … assault … or battery. The trial court dismissed the action, finding that … the facts alleged were insufficient to state causes of action for … assault … or battery because the instruction and playing of football are "inherently dangerous and always potentially violent."

What's That?

Sovereign immunity essentially means that a governmental entity cannot be sued in tort in its own courts without its consent. *See* Chapter II, Immunities, *infra*, for further exploration of immunities issues.

In this appeal, the Koffmans do not challenge the trial court's ruling on Garnett's plea of sovereign immunity but do assert that they pled sufficient facts in their second amended motion for judgment to sustain their claims of … assault … and battery.

….

The trial court held that the second amended motion for judgment was insufficient as a matter of law to establish causes of action for the torts of assault and battery. We begin by identifying the elements of these two independent torts. [C] The tort of assault consists of an act intended to cause either harmful or offensive contact with another person or apprehension of such contact, and that creates in that other person's mind a reasonable apprehension of an imminent battery. RESTATEMENT (SECOND) OF TORTS § 21 (1965); [Cc].

The tort of battery is an unwanted touching which is neither consented to, excused, nor justified. [C] Although these two torts "go together like ham and eggs," the difference between them is "that between physical contact and the mere apprehension of it. One may exist without the other." [Cc]

The Koffmans' second amended motion for judgment does not include an allegation that Andy had any apprehension of an immediate battery. This allegation cannot be supplied by inference because any inference of Andy's apprehension is discredited by the affirmative allegations that Andy had no warning of an imminent forceful tackle by Garnett. The Koffmans argue that a reasonable inference of apprehension can be found "in the very short period of time that it took the coach to lift Andy into the air and throw him violently to the ground." At this point, however, the battery alleged by the Koffmans was in progress. Accordingly, we find that the pleadings were insufficient as a matter of law to establish a cause of action for civil assault.

The second amended motion for judgment is sufficient, however, to establish a cause of action for the tort of battery. The Koffmans pled that Andy consented to physical contact with players "of like age and experience" and that neither Andy nor his parents expected or consented to his "participation in aggressive contact tackling by the adult coaches." Further, the Koffmans pled that, in the past, coaches had not tackled players as a method of instruction. Garnett asserts that, by consenting to play football, Andy consented to be tackled, by either other football players or by the coaches.

Whether Andy consented to be tackled by Garnett in the manner alleged was a matter of fact. Based on the allegations in the Koffmans' second amended motion for judgment, reasonable persons could disagree on whether Andy gave such consent. Thus, we find that the trial court erred in holding that the Koffmans' second amended motion for judgment was insufficient as a matter of law to establish a claim for battery.

For the above reasons, we will reverse the trial court's judgment that the Koffmans' second amended motion for judgment was insufficient as a matter of law to establish the causes of actions for gross negligence and battery and remand the case for further proceedings consistent with this opinion.[1]

Reversed and remanded.

Justice KINSER, concurring in part and dissenting in part.

I agree with the majority opinion except with regard to the issue of consent as it pertains to the intentional tort of battery. In my view, the second amended motion for judgment filed by the plaintiffs, Andrew W. Koffman, by his father and next friend, and Richard Koffman and Rebecca Koffman, individually, was insufficient as a matter of law to state a claim for battery.

Absent fraud, consent is generally a defense to an alleged battery. [Cc]; RESTATEMENT (SECOND) OF TORTS § 13, cmt. d (1965). In the context of this case, "[t]aking part in a game manifests a willingness to submit to such bodily contacts or restrictions of liberty as are permitted by its rules or usages." RESTATEMENT (SECOND) OF TORTS § 50, cmt. b (1965) [Cc]. However, participating in a particular sport "does not manifest consent to contacts which are prohibited by rules or usages of the game if such rules or usages are designed to protect the participants and not merely to secure the better playing of the game as a test of skill." RESTATEMENT (SECOND) OF TORTS § 50, cmt. b (1965); [Cc].

---

1 Because we have concluded that a cause of action for an intentional tort was sufficiently pled, on remand, the Koffmans may pursue their claim for **punitive damages**.

The thrust of the plaintiffs' allegations is that they did not consent to "Andy's participation in aggressive contact tackling by the adult coaches" but that they consented only to Andy's engaging "in a contact sport with other children of like age and experience." They further alleged that the coaches had not previously tackled the players when instructing them about the rules and techniques of football.

It is notable, in my opinion, that the plaintiffs admitted in their pleading that Andy's coach was "responsible ... for the supervision, training and instruction of the defensive players." It cannot be disputed that one responsibility of a football coach is to minimize the possibility that players will sustain "something more than slight injury" while playing the sport. [C] A football coach cannot be expected "to extract from the game the body clashes that cause bruises, jolts and hard falls." [C] Instead, a coach should ensure that players are able to "withstand the shocks, blows and other rough treatment with which they would meet in actual play" by making certain that players are in "sound physical condition," are issued proper protective equipment, and are "taught and shown how to handle [themselves] while in play." [C] The instruction on how to handle themselves during a game should include demonstrations of proper tackling techniques. [C] By voluntarily participating in football, Andy and his parents necessarily consented to instruction by the coach on such techniques. The alleged battery occurred during that instruction.

The plaintiffs alleged that they were not aware that Andy's coach would use physical force to instruct on the rules and techniques of football since neither he nor the other coaches had done so in the past. Surely, the plaintiffs are not claiming that the scope of their consent changed from day to day depending on the coaches' instruction methods during prior practices. Moreover, they did not allege that they were told that the coaches would not use physical demonstrations to instruct the players.

Additionally, the plaintiffs did not allege that the tackle itself violated any rule or usage of the sport of football. Nor did they plead that Andy could not have been tackled by a larger, physically stronger, and more experienced player either during a game or practice. Tackling and instruction on proper tackling techniques are aspects of the sport of football to which a player consents when making a decision to participate in the sport.

In sum, I conclude that the plaintiffs did not sufficiently plead a claim for battery. We must remember that acts that might give rise to a battery on a city street will not do so in the context of the sport of football. [C] …

For these reasons, I respectfully concur, in part, and dissent, in part, and would affirm the judgment of the circuit court sustaining the demurrer with regard to the claim for battery.

Points for Discussion

1. Do you agree with that part of the *Koffman* court's decision holding that the defendant did not assault Andy? Why or why not?

2. Consent is an affirmative defense to an intentional tort and requires proof that the plaintiff was in fact willing for the tortious conduct to occur. Thus, words or conduct reasonably understood to be consent may provide effective consent. *See* RESTATEMENT (SECOND) OF TORTS § 892(2); *see also* O'Brien v. Cunard S.S. Co., 28 N.E 266 (Mass. Ct. App. 1891) (plaintiff's apparent willingness to be vaccinated through her actions, even when not verbally communicated to defendant, amounted to valid consent).

3. As indicated by the court's discussion in *Koffman,* consent is often an issue of fact. Consent may be express or implied by conduct. Likewise, culture and social mores may inform whether the plaintiff impliedly consented to the conduct at issue. Consent also may be assumed based on local custom in the absence of any notification to the contrary.

Hypo 3-1

Lynne is traveling in New York for the very first time, having lived her entire life on the west coast. Her friend introduces her to LuAnn, who warmly embraces Lynne and kisses her on both cheeks. Battery? If so, has Lynne consented?

4. As discussed in the principal case, a participant in a sporting activity impliedly consents to conduct permitted by the rules of the game. However, a player does not consent to conduct prohibited by the rules if those rules are designed for the safety of the players rather than just the enjoyment of the game. *See* Hackbart v. Cincinnati Bengals, Inc., 601 F.2d 516 (1979) (ruling in battery action against one professional football player against another that players of sport do not consent to intentional striking of players in face or from rear).

5. The rematch in June 1997 between boxing heavyweights Evander Holyfield and Mike Tyson is one of the most memorable boxing matches ever, but not for the typical reasons. Rather, this fight is infamous because in the third round of the rematch, while losing miserably and holding Holyfield in a clinch, Tyson spat out his own mouthpiece and bit off a chunk of Holyfield's right ear. After Tyson spat the piece of Holyfield's ear onto the ground, the match was temporarily

halted in order for the official to instruct Tyson as to the inappropriateness of his conduct, as biting off an opponent's ear during a boxing match is outside of the rules of boxing. Moments later, the match resumed, only to be stopped for good and Holyfield declared the victor, after Tyson unbelievably bit off an even larger piece of flesh from Holyfield's *other* ear. Holyfield had to undergo plastic surgery immediately following the match to have his ears surgically repaired (fortunately for Holyfield, a bystander saved a one-inch piece of his right ear). Boxing is a violent sport, but might Holyfield have had a viable tort action against Tyson?

For More Information

The Tyson-Holyfield match has been selected by ESPN as one of the most memorable moments in sports history. Click here to read further about this incredible boxing match.

Hypo 3-2

Friends Graham and Trey, 22 years old each, are playing a game of touch football one sunny, fall weekend day at the neighborhood park. Graham is playing at wide receiver, and Trey is a defensive back for the opposing team. The quarterback for Graham's team throws a perfect spiral in Graham's direction. As the ball has been thrown a little high (so as to make it catchable only by Graham and not any of the defenders), both Graham and Trey leap in the air, simultaneously attempting to catch the ball, all the while knowing that doing so would result in bumping into the other. (The rules of football allow for both the receiver and the defender to attempt to catch the ball in the way that Graham and Trey did on this day.) The two collide and fall to the ground. Graham gets up, ball in hand. Trey gets up, cradling one of his arms in his other hand. His forearm has two fractures that require surgery, complete with four pins and a metal plate. Trey wishes to sue Graham for battery. Discuss.

Mohr v. Williams

104 N.W. 12 (Minn. 1905)

BROWN, J.

Defendant is a physician and surgeon of standing and character, making disorders of the ear a specialty, and having an extensive practice in the city of St. Paul. He was consulted by plaintiff, who complained to him of trouble with her right ear, and, at her request, made an examination of that organ for the purpose of ascertaining its condition. He also at the same time examined her left ear, but, owing to foreign substances therein, was unable to make a full and complete diagnosis at that time. The examination of her right ear disclosed a large perforation in the lower portion of the drum membrane, and a large polyp in the middle ear, which indicated that some of the small bones of the middle ear (ossicles) were probably diseased. He informed plaintiff of the result of his examination, and advised an operation for the purpose of removing the polyp and diseased ossicles. After consultation with her family physician, and one or two further consultations with defendant, plaintiff decided to submit to the proposed operation. She was not informed that her left ear was in any way diseased, and understood that the necessity for an operation applied to her right ear only. She repaired to the hospital, and was placed under the influence of anesthetics; and, after being made unconscious, defendant made a thorough examination of her left ear, and found it in a more serious condition than her right one. A small perforation was discovered high up in the drum membrane, hooded, and with granulated edges, and the bone of the inner wall of the middle ear was diseased and dead. He called this discovery to the attention of Dr. Davis -- plaintiff's family physician, who attended the operation at her request -- who also examined the ear, and confirmed defendant in his diagnosis. Defendant also further examined the right ear, and found its condition less serious than expected, and finally concluded that the left, instead of the right, should be operated upon; devoting to the right ear other treatment. He then performed the operation of ossiculectomy on plaintiff's left ear; removing a portion of the drum membrane, and scraping away the diseased portion of the inner wall of the ear. The operation was in every way successful and skillfully performed. It is claimed by plaintiff that the operation greatly impaired her hearing, seriously injured her person, and, not having been consented to by her, was wrongful and unlawful, constituting an assault and battery; and she brought this action to recover damages therefor. The trial in the court below resulted in a verdict for plaintiff for $14,322.50. Defendant thereafter moved the court for judgment notwithstanding the verdict, on the ground that, on the evidence presented, plaintiff was not entitled to recover, or, if that relief was denied, for a new trial on the ground, among others, that the verdict was excessive; appearing to have been given under the influence of passion and prejudice. The trial court denied the motion for judgment, but granted a new trial on the ground, as stated in the order, that the damages were excessive. Defendant appealed from the order denying the motion for judgment, and plaintiff appealed from the order granting a new trial.

....

2. We come then to a consideration of the questions presented by defendant's appeal from the order denying his motion for judgment notwithstanding the verdict. It is contended that final judgment should be ordered in his favor for the following reasons: (a) That it appears from the evidence received on the trial that plaintiff consented to the operation on her left ear. (b) If the court shall find that no such consent was given, that, under the circumstances disclosed by the record, no consent was necessary. (c) That, under the facts disclosed, an action for assault and battery will not lie; it appearing conclusively, as counsel urge, that there is a total lack of evidence showing or tending to show malice or an evil intent on the part of defendant, or that the operation was negligently performed.

We shall consider first the question whether, under the circumstances shown in the record, the consent of plaintiff to the operation was necessary. If, under the particular facts of this case, such consent was unnecessary, no recovery can be had, for the evidence fairly shows that the operation complained of was skillfully performed and of a generally beneficial nature. But if the consent of plaintiff was necessary, then the further questions presented become important. ... We have given it very deliberate consideration, and are unable to concur with counsel for defendant in their contention that the consent of plaintiff was unnecessary. The evidence tends to show that, upon the first examination of plaintiff, defendant pronounced the left ear in good condition, and that, at the time plaintiff repaired to the hospital to submit to the operation on her right ear, she was under the impression that no difficulty existed as to the left. In fact, she testified that she had not previously experienced any trouble with that organ. It cannot be doubted that ordinarily the patient must be consulted, and his consent given, before a physician may operate upon him. ... "The patient must be the final arbiter as to whether he will take his chances with the operation, or take his chances of living without it. Such is the natural right of the individual, which the law recognizes as a legal one[.] Consent, therefore, of an individual, must be either expressly or impliedly given before a surgeon may have the right to operate." [C] ... No reason occurs to us why the same rule should not apply between physician and patient. If the physician advises his patient to submit to a particular operation, and the patient weighs the dangers and risks incident to its performance, and finally consents, he

What's That?

The **informed consent doctrine** is a topic that also arises in medical malpractice actions, a subject explored more thoroughly in the materials on negligence. *See* Chapter 4, Negligence, *infra*.

thereby, in effect, enters into a contract authorizing his physician to operate to the extent of the consent given, but no further. It is not, however, contended by defendant that under ordinary circumstances consent is unnecessary, but that, under the particular circumstances of this case, consent was implied; that it was an emergency case, such as to authorize the operation without express consent or permission. ... The physician impliedly contracts that he possesses, and will exercise in the treatment of patients, skill and learning, and that he will exercise reasonable care and exert his best judgment to bring about favorable results. The methods of treatment are committed almost exclusively to his judgment, but we are aware of no rule or principle of law which would extend to him free license respecting surgical operations. Reasonable latitude must, however, be allowed the physician in a particular case; and we would not lay down any rule which would unreasonably interfere with the exercise of his discretion, or prevent him from taking such measures as his judgment dictated for the welfare of the patient in a case of emergency. If a person should be injured to the extent of rendering him unconscious, and his injuries were of such a nature as to require prompt surgical attention, a physician called to attend him would be justified in applying such medical or surgical treatment as might reasonably be necessary for the preservation of his life or limb, and consent on the part of the injured person would be implied. And again, if, in the course of an operation to which the patient consented, the physician should discover conditions not anticipated before the operation was commenced, and which, if not removed, would endanger the life or health of the patient, he would, though no express consent was obtained or given, be justified in extending the operation to remove and overcome them. But such is not the case at bar. The diseased condition of plaintiff's left ear was not discovered in the course of an operation on the right, which was authorized, but upon an independent examination of that organ, made after the authorized operation was found unnecessary. Nor is the evidence such as to justify the court in holding, as a matter of law, that it was such an affection as would result immediately in the serious injury of plaintiff, or such an emergency as to justify proceeding without her consent. She had experienced no particular difficulty with that ear, and the questions as to when its diseased condition would become alarming or fatal, and whether there was an immediate necessity for an operation, were, under the evidence, questions of fact for the jury.

3. The contention of defendant that the operation was consented to by plaintiff is not sustained by the evidence. At least, the evidence was such as to take the question to the jury. This contention is based upon the fact that she was represented on the occasion in question by her family physician; that the condition of her left ear was made known to him, and the propriety of an operation thereon suggested, to which he made no objection. It is urged that by his conduct he assented to it, and that plaintiff was bound thereby. It is not claimed that he gave his express consent. It is not disputed but that the family physician of plaintiff

was present on the occasion of the operation, and at her request. But the purpose of his presence was not that he might participate in the operation, nor does it appear that he was authorized to consent to any change in the one originally proposed to be made. Plaintiff was naturally nervous and fearful of the consequences of being placed under the influence of anaesthetics, and the presence of her family physician was requested under the impression that it would allay and calm her fears. The evidence made the question one of fact for the jury to determine.

4. The last contention of defendant is that the act complained of did not amount to an assault and battery. This is based upon the theory that, as plaintiff's left ear was in fact diseased, in a condition dangerous and threatening to her health, the operation was necessary, and, having been skillfully performed at a time when plaintiff had requested a like operation on the other ear, the charge of assault and battery cannot be sustained; that, in view of these conditions, and the claim that there was no negligence on the part of defendant, and an entire absence of any evidence tending to show an evil intent, the court should say, as a matter of law, that no assault and battery was committed, even though she did not consent to the operation. In other words, that the absence of a showing that defendant was actuated by a wrongful intent, or guilty of negligence, relieves the act of defendant from the charge of an unlawful assault and battery. We are unable to reach that conclusion, though the contention is not without merit. It would seem to follow from what has been said on the other features of the case that the act of defendant amounted at least to a technical assault and battery. If the operation was performed without plaintiff's consent, and the circumstances were not such as to justify its performance without, it was wrongful; and, if it was wrongful, it was unlawful. [E]very person has a right to complete immunity of his person from physical interference of others, except in so far as contact may be necessary under the general doctrine of privilege; and any unlawful or unauthorized touching of the person of another, except it be in the spirit of pleasantry, constitutes an assault and battery.

In the case at bar, as we have already seen, the question whether defendant's act in performing the operation upon plaintiff was authorized was a question for the jury to determine. If it was unauthorized, then it was, within what we have said, unlawful. It was a violent assault, not a mere pleasantry; and, even though no negligence is shown, it was wrongful and unlawful. ...

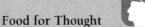

Food for Thought

Is the court correct here that "any unlawful or unauthorized touching ... of another ... constitutes an assault and battery"? Was the plaintiff in *Mohr* assaulted?

The amount of plaintiff's recovery, if she is entitled to recover at all, must depend upon the character and extent of the injury inflicted upon her, in determining which the nature of the malady intended to be healed and the beneficial nature of the operation should be taken into consideration, as well as the good faith of the defendant.

Order affirmed.

————————————

Points for Discussion

1. The plaintiff's family physician was present at the surgery, and the court discusses whether he may have consented on behalf of the plaintiff while she was unconscious. Who has authority to consent on behalf of another? In order to be able to consent, the plaintiff must have the capacity to consent or must be capable of appreciating the nature, extent, and probable consequences of the conduct consented to. *See* RESTATEMENT (SECOND) OF TORTS § 892A (1965). To be effective, consent must be made by the individual or by a person empowered to consent on his or her behalf. Similarly, consent must be provided by one having the capacity to do so or by one authorized to consent for the person. Infancy, intoxication, or mental incompetence normally vitiates effective consent. Minors may not provide valid consent to medical procedures. Consent of their parent or legal guardian is ordinarily required. If a parent refuses to provide consent based on the parent's religious beliefs, the hospital or medical provider may be liable for any intentional tort if treatment is provided, unless the treatment is life threatening.

2. Patricia Saucier is a mentally disabled young woman who has required special attention since a young age when she contracted spinal meningitis and was left with diminished mental capacity. *Saucier v. McDonald's Rests. of Mont., Inc.*, 179 P.3d 481 (Mont. 2008). After living most of her life in state facilities, she eventually was able to move into an apartment of her own with limited supervision and work at a local McDonald's Restaurant. After working there for four months, she became sexually involved with the married manager of the restaurant. The manager was aware of Patricia's diminished capacity and had convinced Patricia that he was in love with her and she with him. On Patricia's behalf, her sister brought battery charges against the manager and McDonald's, arguing that because of Patricia's diminished capacity, she was not able to provide effective consent to the sexual contact. Should Patricia be able to consent to such contact? *See id.*

3. Why was the plaintiff in the principal case not permitted to pursue a negligence action against the doctor? Why did she have to rely on the intentional tort of battery?

4. As illustrated by the principal case, when consent is an asserted defense to a battery action, the fact that the battery was beneficial does not negate the battery action itself. Rather, the beneficial quality of the battery may inform as to the appropriateness of any damages award; it does not shield the defendant from liability for the technical battery itself. For example, upon a new trial in the principal case, the jury awarded the plaintiff just $39, a paltry sum even at that time.

5. As discussed in the principal case, consent may be implied when an injured person is unconscious and suffering from injuries requiring prompt medical attention as long as there is not time to wait for consent. If a patient is unable to provide consent, for whatever reason, and there is a reasonable risk of serious bodily harm if treatment is delayed, consent may similarly be implied as long as the defendant has no reason to believe that the plaintiff would not consent and a reasonable person would consent under the circumstances. What if a person in need of life saving medical treatment is conscious and otherwise able to consent, but refuses to do so?

Hypo 3-3

Tennis Star, a well-known professional tennis player, is playing in an important tennis match. Physically imposing at 5'9" tall and 150 pounds, Tennis Star is unquestionably a tremendous athlete. It is well known that she is a physically strong person, often serving the ball at her opponents at speeds in excess of 100 miles per hour. At a critical point in this particular match, an official officiating the match, Line Judge, makes a controversial call that may put Tennis Star's chance of prevailing at the match in jeopardy. (When officiating, Line Judge sits in a chair approximately thirty feet away from the player who is serving.) Tennis Star becomes furious. With a tennis ball in one hand and her tennis racket in the other, Tennis Star begins walking quickly toward Line Judge, and pointing at Line Judge with her racket as she screams, "If I could, I would take this [expletive deleted] ball and shove it down your [expletive deleted] throat! I should kill you!" During her tirade, Tennis Star gets no closer than six feet away from Judge. Star then returns to the court to complete the match. However, Tennis Star has allowed herself to become so upset that when she attempts to hit the next serve toward her opponent, it misfires terribly, ricochets off the far wall, and whizzes right by Line Judge with enough force to knock her hat right off her head. The hat falls to the ground. Although she didn't mean to hit Line Judge with the serve, Tennis Star is not upset that it has happened. She thinks to herself, "Karma," and continues playing. The match continues without incident, but Tennis Star loses. (More karma.)

As a result of this episode, Line Judge is traumatized. She tells her friends that she thought that Tennis Star was going to kill her, right there on national TV for everyone to see! Line Judge ends up suffering from nightmares and nausea for weeks following this event. In fact, it upsets her so much that she is unable to return to her job as a tennis official. Her husband suggests that she speak to you, a lawyer, to discuss possible tort actions against Tennis Star. Discuss.

De May v. Roberts

9 N.W. 146 (Mich. 1881)

MARSTON, C.J.

The declaration in this case in the first count sets forth that the plaintiff was at a time and place named a poor married woman, and being confined in child-bed and a stranger, employed in a professional capacity defendant De May who was a physician; that defendant visited the plaintiff as such, and against her desire and intending to deceive her wrongfully, etc., introduced and caused to be present at the house and lying-in room of the plaintiff and while she was in the pains of parturition the defendant Scattergood, who intruded upon the privacy of the plaintiff, indecently, wrongfully and unlawfully laid hands upon and assaulted her, the said Scattergood, which was well known to defendant De May, being a young unmarried man, a stranger to the plaintiff and utterly ignorant of the practice of medicine, while the plaintiff believed that he was an assistant physician, a competent and proper person to be present and to aid her in her extremity.

    ....

The evidence on the part of the plaintiff tended to prove the allegations of the declaration. On the part of the defendants evidence was given tending to prove that Scattergood very reluctantly accompanied Dr. De May at the urgent request of the latter; that the night was a dark and stormy one, the roads over which they had to travel in getting to the house of the plaintiff were so bad that a horse could not be rode or driven over them; that the doctor was sick and very much fatigued from overwork, and therefore asked the defendant Scattergood to accompany and assist him in carrying a lantern, umbrella and certain articles deemed necessary upon such occasions; that upon arriving at the house of the plaintiff the doctor knocked, and when the door was opened by the husband of the plaintiff, De May said to him, "that I had fetched a friend along to help carry my things;" he, plaintiff's husband, said all right, and seemed to be perfectly satisfied. They were bid to enter, treated kindly and no objection whatever made to the presence of defendant Scattergood. That while there Scattergood, at Dr. De May's request, took hold of plaintiff's hand and held her during a paroxysm of pain, and that both of the defendants in all respects throughout acted in a proper and becoming manner actuated by a sense of duty and kindness.

Some preliminary questions were raised during the progress of the trial which may first be considered. The plaintiff when examined as a witness was asked, what idea she entertained in reference to Scattergood's character and right to be in the house during the time he was there, and answered that she thought he was a student or a physician. To this there could be no good legal objection. It was not only important to know the character in which Scattergood went there, but to learn what knowledge the plaintiff had upon that subject. It was not claimed that the plaintiff or her husband, who were strangers in that vicinity, had ever met Scattergood before this time or had any knowledge or information concerning him beyond what they obtained on that evening, and it was claimed by the defendant that both the plaintiff and her husband must have known, from certain ambiguous expressions used, that he was not a physician.

We are of opinion that the plaintiff and her husband had a right to presume that a practicing physician would not, upon an occasion of that character, take with him and introduce into the house, a young man in no way, either by education or otherwise, connected with the medical profession; and that something more clear and certain as to his non-professional character would be required to put the plaintiff and her husband upon their guard, or remove such presumption, than the remark made by De May that he had brought a friend along to help carry his things. ...

....

It yet remains to consider the principal questions raised in the case. They relate to the sufficiency of the declaration, to which the general issue was pleaded, and further that admitting the facts to be true as claimed by the plaintiff she was not entitled to recover....

....

Dr. De May therefore took an unprofessional young unmarried man with him, introduced and permitted him to remain in the house of the plaintiff, when it was apparent that he could hear at least, if not see all that was said and done, and as the jury must have found, under the instructions given, without either the plaintiff or her husband having any knowledge or reason to believe the true character of such third party. It would be shocking to our sense of right, justice and propriety to doubt even but that for such an act the law would afford an ample remedy. To the plaintiff the occasion was a most sacred one and no one had a right to intrude unless invited or because of some real and pressing necessity which it is not pretended existed in this case. The plaintiff had a legal right to the privacy of her apartment at such a time, and the law secures to her this right by requiring others to observe it, and to abstain from its violation. The fact that at the time, she consented to the presence of Scattergood supposing him to be a physician, does not preclude her from maintaining an action and recovering substantial damages upon afterwards ascertaining his true character. In obtaining admission at such a time and under such circumstances without fully disclosing his true character, both parties were guilty of deceit, and the wrong thus done entitles the injured party to recover the damages afterwards sustained, from shame and mortification upon discovering the true character of the defendants.

Where a wrong has been done another, the law gives a remedy, and although the full extent and character of the injury done may not be ascertained or known until long after, yet in an action brought damages therefor may be fully awarded. … The charge of the court upon the duty and liability of the defendants and the rights of the plaintiff was full and clear, and meets with our full approval.

It follows therefore that the judgment must be affirmed with costs.

(The other justices concurred.)

————————

Points for Discussion

1. One of the first **privacy** cases, *De May v. Roberts* demonstrates that consent procured by **fraud** is invalid. The Restatement (Second) of Torts § 892B(2) (1965) provides that "[i]f the person consenting … is induced to consent by a substantial mistake concerning the nature of the invasion of his interests or the extent of the harm to be expected from it and the mistake is known to the other or is induced by the other's misrepresentation, the consent is not effective…."

2. In order to invalidate consent, the fraud must go to the essential character of conduct to which the plaintiff consented, not merely to a collateral matter. A *collateral* matter is one that accompanies, but is secondary or subordinate to, the essential matter at issue.

Hypo 3-4

Defendant deliberately exposes seventeen women to HIV, the virus that causes AIDS, by having unprotected sex with them over a course of several months. On separate occasions, each of the seventeen women had individually agreed to have sexual intercourse with Defendant, but did not know at the time that he was infected with HIV. Appearing to be kidding around with several of his friends, Defendant has told them that if he ever developed HIV he would give it to as many people as he could. Five of the seventeen women that Defendant exposed tested positive for HIV and sue Defendant for battery. Will Defendant have a viable affirmative defense of consent? Discuss.

---

3. Should one be able to consent to criminal conduct? What if a man dies during a street fight in which he was a willing participant, but in a jurisdiction that criminalizes such conduct? What about a sixteen-year-old girl who willingly has sex with a 21-year-old man in a jurisdiction which criminalizes such conduct as **statutory rape**? The general tort rule is that a plaintiff's consent to criminal conduct is valid, unless the defendant's conduct violates a criminal statute designed to protect a class of persons to which the plaintiff belongs. *See* RESTATEMENT (SECOND) OF TORTS § 892C (1965).

Hypo 3-5

The penal code in this jurisdiction makes committing suicide, as well as assisting in the commission of suicide, crimes. Alpha provides Beta with a large number of sleeping pills, knowing that Beta intends to use them to kill herself. Beta uses them to commit suicide. Beta's family seeks your guidance as to whether they can hold Alpha liable in tort. Discuss.

B. Defense of Self and Others

Poliak v. Adcock

2002 WL 31109737 (Tenn. Ct. App. 2002)

WILLIAM C. KOCH, JR., J.

This appeal involves a dispute between a father and his adult daughter's live-in boyfriend. The boyfriend filed a personal injury suit against his girlfriend's father in the Circuit Court for Davidson County after the father assaulted him with a piece of two-by-four. The father admitted that he had assaulted his daughter's boyfriend but asserted the defenses of self-defense ... and defense of property. In response to the boyfriend's motion for partial summary judgment, the trial court

> **FYI**
>
> The court's discussion addressing the defense of property is excerpted later in this chapter. *See*, Section C, *infra* (exploring affirmative defense of Defense of Real Property). The plaintiff also asserted the affirmative defense of **provocation**, a partial defense recognized in Tennessee to mitigate damages. The court's discussion of the provocation defense has been omitted.

determined that the father had failed to produce evidence to substantiate any of these defenses. ... We have determined that the trial court was correct when it determined that the father's evidence regarding the circumstances surrounding the assault could not, as a matter of law, support his **affirmative defenses**. Accordingly, we affirm the trial court.

OPINION

I.

James M. Adcock and his wife own a house in Nashville. Their adult daughter, Anna Michelle Adcock-Butler, and her two children live with them. Ms. Adcock-Butler's boyfriend, Matthew Poliak was a frequent visitor in the Adcock home. Despite at least one run-in with Mr. Adcock in early 1998, Mr. Poliak moved his clothing and other personal effects into Mr. Adcock's house several months later and apparently began spending significant amounts of time there. Even though Mr. Adcock was not pleased with Mr. Poliak's actions, he never directly opposed or protested Mr. Poliak's presence in his house after Mr. Poliak moved back in.

By mid-1998 Mr. Adcock decided he could not permit Mr. Poliak to live in his house any longer. On the afternoon of July 11, 1998, armed with a piece of two-by-four, Mr. Adcock entered his daughter's bedroom where he found Mr.

Poliak lying alone on the bed. As Mr. Poliak began to arise from the bed, Mr. Adcock, without warning, struck him with the two-by four. He told Mr. Poliak that he was going to leave the house for a while and that he would kill Mr. Poliak if he was still there when he returned. Mr. Poliak sustained severe injuries and was taken by ambulance to the hospital.

In July 1999, Mr. Poliak sued Mr. Adcock for assault and battery in the Circuit Court for Davidson County, seeking $150,000 in compensatory damages and $150,000 in punitive damages. Mr. Adcock responded by admitting that he had struck Mr. Poliak with a two-by-four. He also asserted that he had been provoked and that he was acting in self-defense because Mr. Poliak was a younger and larger man. After taking Mr. Adcock's **discovery** deposition, Mr. Poliak moved for a partial summary judgment seeking dismissal of Mr. Adcock's affirmative defenses of provocation, self-defense, and protection of property. The trial court granted Mr. Poliak's motion because Mr. Adcock had failed to demonstrate that he would be able to provide material evidence to support his affirmative defenses. Mr. Adcock has now appealed.

II.

STANDARD OF REVIEW

The standards for reviewing an order granting a **summary judgment** are well-settled. A summary judgment is proper in virtually any civil case where the moving party demonstrates that no genuine issues of material fact exist and that it is entitled to a judgment as a matter of law. [Cc] ...

... In this process, we must consider the evidence in the light most favorable to the nonmoving party and resolve all inferences in the nonmoving party's favor. [Cc]

....

III.

Mr. Adcock does not dispute that he assaulted Mr. Poliak with a two-by-four. However, he has undertaken to deflect liability for Mr. Poliak's injuries by asserting ... ... self-defense. ...

Self-defense is a complete defense to a civil action for battery. [C] Thus, persons who can prove that they were acting in self-defense when they assaulted another person will be absolved from liability for the injuries they may have caused.

The elements of the defense are essentially the same in civil and criminal cases. [C], RESTATEMENT (SECOND) OF TORTS § 63 (1965). The defense reflects the principle that persons are entitled to defend themselves when they reasonably believe they are about to be seriously injured. RESTATEMENT (SECOND) OF TORTS §§ 63, 65 (1965); [C]. However, persons are entitled to use force to defend themselves only as long as the threat of injury continues, [C], and may use only as much force as is necessary to defend themselves. [Cc]

The Restatement provides fact-finders with factors for determining whether the amount of force used by a person acting in self-defense was reasonable. These factors include: (1) the amount of force the defender exerted, (2) the means or the object by which the defender applied the force, (3) the manner or method used by the defender to apply the force, and (4) the surrounding circumstances under which the defender applied the force. RESTATEMENT (SECOND) OF TORTS § 70 cmt. b. ...

According to Mr. Adcock, he and Mr. Poliak had at least one previous confrontation. However, even though Mr. Poliak is the younger and larger man, there is no evidence in the record that Mr. Poliak had ever attempted to intimidate or harm Mr. Adcock. Nonetheless, Mr. Adcock armed himself with a two-by-four and entered the room where Mr. Poliak was sleeping with the settled intention to strike Mr. Poliak over the head to dissuade him from resisting Mr. Adcock's ultimatum to leave his house. When Mr. Adcock entered the room cursing at Mr. Poliak, Mr. Poliak's only actions before Mr. Adcock struck him were to mumble something and to begin to get out of bed. Viewing Mr. Adcock's own testimony in a light most favorable to him, the only conclusions that a reasonable person can draw are that on the afternoon of July 11, 1998, Mr. Adcock had no reasonable basis to fear that Mr. Poliak was about to injure him seriously and that Mr. Adcock's attack on Mr. Poliak was clearly disproportionate to Mr. Poliak's conduct. Accordingly, the trial court correctly held that Mr. Poliak was entitled to a summary judgment striking Mr. Adcock's defense of self-defense because Mr. Adcock had failed to demonstrate that he would be able to substantiate this defense at trial.

....

We affirm the partial summary judgment foreclosing Mr. Adcock's affirmative defenses as a matter of law and remand the case to the trial court for further proceedings consistent with this opinion. ...

——————————

Points for Discussion

1. The principal case provides a terrific discussion of the contours of the affirmative defense of self-defense. That defense provides a person with a privilege to use reasonable force to defend against a threatened battery. In the majority of jurisdictions, the privilege is based on the actor's reasonable belief that the use of force is necessary. The actor need not be correct in his belief, as long as his belief is a reasonable one. The privilege of self-defense ends when the threat of battery stops. Retaliation is not permitted. Thus, when the battery stops or is no longer threatened, the privilege terminates.

2. A defendant loses the privilege to use force in self-defense when the plaintiff is him- or herself privileged to commit the battery upon the defendant or when the defendant uses excessive force to defend himself or herself. Words alone are insufficient provocation to give rise to a claim of self-defense. In order to be able to rely on self-defense, abusive words must be accompanied by an actual threat of a battery. Plaintiff Purvis Touchet was a sales manager at Hampton Mitsubishi, a car dealership owned by defendant Mark Hampton. Touchet's employment was terminated during the summer of 2002. A few months later, Touchet called Hampton to make fun of the dealership, which had been suffering since he left. Touchet cursed him, threatened him, and told him that he knew where Hampton lived. On other separate occasions, Touchet left Hampton several threatening messages. Hampton went to Touchet's new place of employment to tell Touchet to stop harassing him. When Touchet saw Hampton there, he turned around in his chair and yelled, "F--- you, Hampton." Hampton then entered the office and hit him several times. Hampton claimed that it appeared as if Touchet was about to hit him. Self-defense? *See* Touchet v. Hampton, 950 So.2d 895 (La. Ct. App. 2007).

3. A defendant may not defend on the basis of self-defense if the defendant was the initial aggressor. The **aggressor doctrine** completely bars a plaintiff from recovery in tort for battery if the plaintiff's own actions were sufficient to provoke a reasonable person to use physical force for protection. However, a person who was initially the aggressor regains the right to self-defense once he has retreated and otherwise has communicated clearly his intent to abandon the altercation. The right of an aggressor to use force is also permitted if the defendant uses excessive force to protect herself. Plaintiff Byron Landry stopped at a local bar for a drink. Defendant Luke Bellanger was also at the bar. Landry and Bellanger were former high school classmates. They talked and drank for a while. Bellanger then left the bar and returned later with his friend, Lonnie Bell. When Bellanger returned, Landry began talking to him in a loud voice and became belligerent toward Bellanger. Bellanger continually asked Landry to calm down and leave him alone, but Landry continued,

becoming louder and more aggressive. At no time did Bellanger physically threaten Landry or say anything threatening to him. Bellanger then asked Landry to step outside so they could talk. Once the two were outside, Landry pushed Bellanger and kept moving toward him. According to Bellanger, he then struck Landry in the head with a partially closed fist. Landry fell backwards and hit his head on the cement. Landry sues for battery. Should he prevail? *See* Landry v. Bellanger, 851 So.2d 943 (La. 2003); *see also* State Farm Fire and Casualty Co. v. Totarella, 2003 WL 22236027 (Ohio Ct. App. 2003) (defendant violated duty to retreat when he became aggressor and chased plaintiff off his property and restrained him).

4. The use of force in self-defense must be necessary at the time the defendant uses the force and in proportion to the force threatened or used. The allowable force is limited to force reasonably necessary for protection against the threatened battery. Plaintiff Clifford Kilbourne and defendant Dale Kilbourne are brothers who formed a **partnership** in order to undertake several construction projects. Soon after, their partnership went sour, and there was a dispute during the **dissolution** and winding up of the partnership's affairs. A verbal fight between the brothers broke out near the end of the partnership, and Clifford claimed Dale became angry during the fight and shoved him. Clifford reacted by punching Dale twice. Dale fell to the floor, but then stood up and left the house disoriented with an injury to his eye and a headache. Dale missed several weeks of work after the fight. A doctor initially did not find any eye injury and told Dale his headache and blurred vision should improve. However, when Dale returned to his doctor a few months later, his doctor found he was missing the bottom left corner of his vision. Dale also continued to suffer from light sensitivity, watering of the left eye, and headaches. Clifford claimed he was acting in self-defense because Dale shoved him first; Dale claims that Clifford could have walked away. Do either of the brothers have a viable claim of self-defense? *See* Kilbourne v. Kilbourne, 2003 WL 21977234 (Mich. Ct. App. 2003).

5. **Deadly Force** – force creating a substantial risk of causing death or serious bodily harm – may be used in self-defense, but only if necessary and proportionate. Ronnie Clark was riding a motorcycle at a high rate of speed (approximately 120 mph) on a Louisiana highway. The State Troopers pursuing him spotted a handgun tucked into the back of his belt and attempted to pull him over. Clark refused to stop and continued to travel at a high rate of speed down the interstate, forcing motorists off the road. Lt. Sunseri and Sgt. Dorris heard the broadcast of Clark's chase and teamed up to construct a roadblock. Clark saw the roadblock and began driving on the shoulder to avoid it. Sunseri and Dorris stepped onto the shoulder and began waving their arms and shouting for Clark to stop. Clark did not stop. He crouched down and attempted to continue on

past the roadblock. It was at this point that both troopers fired at Clark hitting him several times and causing serious injuries. Sunseri and Dorris believed that Clark was making an attempt to kill them. They fired at Clark because they feared for their lives. Clark sued for battery. The appellate court held that Sunseri and Clark were justified in using deadly force to protect themselves and each other. *See* Clark v. Department of Public Safety and Corrections, 861 So.2d 603 (La. Ct. App. 2003).

6.   At common law, before employing *deadly* force in self-defense, one was required to "retreat to the wall," meaning that one was required to retreat to a place of complete safety, if able to do so. *See* Restatement (Second) of Torts § 65(3). Currently, the majority of jurisdictions provide that one is privileged to stand one's ground and use deadly force, if necessary at the time and in proportion to the threat with which one is faced; retreat is not required.

Hypo 3-6

Gene and Laura Graves do not have a good relationship with their neighbors, Ron and Katrina Parker. One morning, Mr. Graves is on his land shooting dogs that are attacking his sheep. Graves believes the dogs belong to the Parkers. Although Graves remains on his land, at one point he is close to the fence line separating his and the Parkers' land. The Parkers suddenly emerge from their house, and Mr. Parker fires a pistol shot. Graves returns fire toward Mr. Parker, killing him. The bullet passes through Mr. Parker and strikes Mrs. Parker, leaving her seriously and permanently injured. Mrs. Parker, on behalf of herself and her deceased husband's estate, sues for battery. Was Graves privileged to use deadly force?

C. Defense of Others

The privilege of defense of others mirrors the privilege of defense of self. One is privileged to use force for the protection of another human being when the defendant reasonably believes that the other person would be privileged to use force in self-defense and one's intervention is necessary at the time. Most jurisdictions provide that one steps into the shoes of the person whom she is defending; if she would be liable for using force in self-defense, then the person using the force in defense of her is liable for doing so. Other jurisdictions provide that as long as the defendant's mistake regarding the need to use force in protection of the other is reasonable, the defendant may still successfully assert the affirmative defense of defense of others. James Armstrong drove his girlfriend J.M.S. to her uncle's house to pick up her car, which the uncle was repairing. At the time, the uncle was high on drugs or alcohol. When J.M.S. discovered that her uncle had not finished the repairs, she told him that she would not pay him for the work, as they had previously agreed, until the work was completed. The two began to argue, and the uncle struck the windshield of J.M.S.'s car with his hand. The uncle, who was 5'10" and 230 pounds, then retrieved a large monkey wrench while J.M.S., who was pregnant at the time, walked to Armstrong's car to get a hammer. She walked back to her own car with the hammer and stood between her uncle and her car. Her uncle grabbed J.M.S., shook her, and demanded money from her. Armstrong, 5'6" and 135 lbs., then exited his vehicle and shouted at the uncle to stop. The uncle moved toward Armstrong, monkey wrench in hand. Armstrong struck the uncle in the head at least twice with an aluminum baseball bat, while J.M.S. also struck her uncle with the hammer. They both stopped when the uncle was immobilized. The uncle suffered multiple skull fractures and a broken arm. Do either J.M.S. or Armstrong have a viable self-defense claim? *See* Armstrong v. Commissioner of Human Services, 2009 WL 66347 (Minn. Ct. App. 2009).

———————

D. Defense of Real Property

In a portion of the *Poliak* decision not included in the excerpt beginning at p. 144, the court explains the basics of the affirmative defense of defense of property:

> "Property owners may use as much force as is reasonably necessary to prevent another from unlawfully coming onto their property or to remove another who is trespassing on their property. [Cc] To raise the defense of property defense, a property owner must prove (1) that the plaintiff was trespassing on his or her property, (2) that he or she reasonably believed that the force used on the trespasser was necessary to get the trespasser off or to keep the trespasser off his or her property, and (3) that he or she first asked the trespasser to leave and that the trespasser refused or that he or she reasonably believed that any such attempt would have been useless or would have caused substantial harm. RESTATEMENT (SECOND) OF TORTS § 77 (1965). Property owners can never use force that endangers human life or inflicts serious bodily harm. [Cc]

> "Mr. Adcock's testimony in his deposition fails to substantiate any of the ingredients of a defense of property defense. Mr. Poliak was not

an uninvited guest in Mr. Adcock's house. He was living there at the invitation of Mr. Adcock's adult daughter, who was a resident of the home. After his daughter invited Mr. Poliak to live with her, Mr. Adcock did not express dissatisfaction about Mr. Poliak's presence. His silence over a period of months, as a matter of law, must reasonably be construed as permission for Mr. Poliak to remain in the house. RESTATEMENT (SECOND) OF TORTS § 892 (1965) (stating that inaction can be construed as consent if the circumstances would make a reasonable person believe that he or she had consent to be on the property).

"Similarly, Mr. Adcock's testimony does not demonstrate that striking Mr. Poliak with a two-by-four was immediately necessary to prevent or terminate Mr. Poliak's trespass or that the assault did not cause serious bodily harm. Months earlier, Mr. Adcock had ordered Mr. Poliak out of the house when he discovered Mr. Poliak in bed with his daughter and granddaughter. Mr. Poliak had complied with this demand making further force or threats of force unnecessary. Accordingly, the record provides no basis for concluding that Mr. Adcock was required to resort to violence on July 11, 1998 to remove Mr. Poliak from his house. There is certainly no factual justification for seriously injuring Mr. Poliak. If Mr. Adcock wanted Mr. Poliak to leave his house on July 11, 1998, he should have asked him to leave. The circumstances as described by Mr. Adcock do not provide a justification for using force to defend his house. Accordingly, the trial court properly concluded that Mr. Adcock would have been unable to substantiate a defense of property defense had this case gone to trial."

Poliak v. Adcock, 2002 WL 31109737 (Tenn. Ct. App. 2002).

Whether one is ever privileged to use *deadly* force to defend real property is the subject of the next case.

Katko v. Briney

183 N.W.2d 657 (1971)

MOORE, Chief Justice.

The primary issue presented here is whether an owner may protect personal property in an unoccupied boarded-up farm house against trespassers and thieves by a spring gun capable of inflicting death or serious injury.

We are not here concerned with a man's right to protect his home and members of his family. Defendants' home was several miles from the scene of the incident to which we refer **infra**.

Plaintiff's action is for damages resulting from serious injury caused by a shot from a 20-gauge spring shotgun set by defendants in a bedroom of an old farm house which had been uninhabited for several years. Plaintiff and his companion, Marvin McDonough, had broken and entered the house to find and steal old bottles and dated fruit jars which they considered antiques.

At defendants' request plaintiff's action was tried to a jury consisting of residents of the community where defendants' property was located. The jury returned a verdict for plaintiff and against defendants for $20,000 actual and $10,000 punitive damages.

After careful consideration of defendants' motions for judgment notwithstanding the verdict and for new trial, the experienced and capable trial judge overruled them and entered judgment on the verdict. Thus we have this appeal by defendants.

I. In this action our review of the record as made by the parties in the lower court is for the correction of errors at law. We do not review actions at law **de novo**. [C] Findings of fact by the jury are binding upon this court if supported by substantial evidence. [C]

> **It's Latin to Me!**
>
> Non constat jus civile a posteriori
>
> *De novo* means "anew." The court here is referring to the standard of review on appeal. Review *de novo* means that the appellate court makes a fresh determination and is not bound by the determinations of the trial court.

II. Most of the facts are not disputed. In 1957 defendant Bertha L. Briney inherited her parents' farm land in Mahaska and Monroe Counties. Included was an 80-acre tract in southwest Mahaska County where her grandparents and parents had lived. No one occupied the house thereafter. Her husband, Edward, attempted to care for the land. He kept no farm machinery thereon. The outbuildings became dilapidated.

For about 10 years, 1957 to 1967, there occurred a series of trespassing and housebreaking events with loss of some household items, the breaking of windows and 'messing up of the property in general'. The latest occurred June 8, 1967, prior to the event on July 16, 1967 herein involved.

Defendants through the years boarded up the windows and doors in an attempt to stop the intrusions. They had posted 'no trespass' signs on the land several years before 1967. The nearest one was 35 feet from the house. On June 11, 1967 defendants set 'a shotgun trap' in the north bedroom. After Mr. Briney cleaned and oiled his 20-gauge shotgun, the power of which he was well aware, defendants took it to the old house where they secured it to an iron bed with the barrel pointed at the bedroom door. It was rigged with wire from the doorknob to the gun's trigger so it would fire when the door was opened. Briney first pointed the gun so an intruder would be hit in the stomach but at Mrs. Briney's suggestion it was lowered to hit the legs. He admitted he did so 'because I was mad and tired of being tormented' but 'he did not intend to injure anyone'. He gave no explanation of why he used a loaded shell and set it to hit a person already in the house. Tin was nailed over the bedroom window. The spring gun could not be seen from the outside. No warning of its presence was posted.

Plaintiff lived with his wife and worked regularly as a gasoline station attendant in Eddyville, seven miles from the old house. He had observed it for several years while hunting in the area and considered it as being abandoned. He knew it had long been uninhabited. In 1967 the area around the house was covered with high weeds. Prior to July 16, 1967 plaintiff and McDonough had been to the premises and found several old bottles and fruit jars which they took and added to their collection of antiques. On the latter date about 9:30 p.m. they made a second trip to the Briney property. They entered the old house by removing a board from a porch window which was without glass. While McDonough was looking around the kitchen area plaintiff went to another part of the house. As he started to open the north bedroom door the shotgun went off striking him in the right leg above the ankle bone. Much of his leg, including part of the tibia, was blown away. Only by McDonough's assistance was plaintiff able to get out of the house and after crawling some distance was put in his vehicle and rushed to a doctor and then to a hospital. He remained in the hospital 40 days.

Plaintiff's doctor testified he seriously considered amputation but eventually the healing process was successful. Some weeks after his release from the hospital plaintiff returned to work on crutches. He was required to keep the injured leg in a cast for approximately a year and wear a special brace for another year. He continued to suffer pain during this period.

There was undenied medical testimony plaintiff had a permanent deformity, a loss of tissue, and a shortening of the leg.

The record discloses plaintiff to trial time had incurred $710 medical expense, $2056.85 for hospital service, $61.80 for orthopedic service and $750 as loss of earnings. In addition thereto the trial court submitted to the jury the question of damages for pain and suffering and for future disability.

III. Plaintiff testified he knew he had no right to break and enter the house with intent to steal bottles and fruit jars therefrom. He further testified he had entered a plea of guilty to **larceny** in the nighttime of property of less than $20 value from a private building. He stated he had been fined $50 and costs and paroled during good behavior from a 60-day jail sentence. Other than minor traffic charges this was plaintiff's first brush with the law. On this civil case appeal it is not our prerogative to review the disposition made of the criminal charge against him.

IV. The main thrust of defendants' defense in the trial court and on this appeal is that 'the law permits use of a spring gun in a dwelling or warehouse for the purpose of preventing the unlawful entry of a burglar or thief'. They repeated this contention in their exceptions to the trial court's instructions ....

....

Instruction 5 stated: 'You are hereby instructed that one may use reasonable force in the protection of his property, but such right is subject to the qualification that one may not use such means of force as will take human life or inflict great bodily injury. Such is the rule even though the injured party is a trespasser and is in violation of the law himself.'

Instruction 6 stated: 'An owner of premises is prohibited from willfully or intentionally injuring a trespasser by means of force that either takes life or inflicts great bodily injury; and therefore a person owning a premise is prohibited from setting out 'spring guns' and like dangerous devices which will likely take life or inflict great bodily injury, for the purpose of harming trespassers. The fact that the trespasser may be acting in violation of the law does not change the rule. The only time when such conduct of setting a 'spring gun' or a like dangerous device is justified would be when the trespasser was committing a felony of violence or a felony punishable by death, or where the trespasser was endangering human life by his act.'

....

The overwhelming weight of authority, both textbook and case law, supports the trial court's statement of the applicable principles of law.

Prosser on Torts, Third Edition, pages 116-118, states:

> '* * * the law has always placed a higher value upon human safety than upon mere rights in property, it is the accepted rule that there is no privilege to use any force calculated to cause death or serious bodily injury to repel the threat to land or chattels, unless there is also such a threat to the defendant's personal safety as to justify a self-defense. * * * spring guns and other mankilling devices are not justifiable against a mere trespasser, or even a petty thief. They are privileged only against

those upon whom the landowner, if he were present in person would be free to inflict injury of the same kind.'

RESTATEMENT OF TORTS, section 85, page 180, states:

'The value of human life and limb, not only to the individual concerned but also to society, so outweighs the interest of a possessor of land in excluding from it those whom he is not willing to admit thereto that a possessor of land has, as is stated in § 79, no privilege to use force intended or likely to cause death or serious harm against another whom the possessor sees about to enter his premises or meddle with his chattel, unless the intrusion threatens death or serious bodily harm to the occupiers or users of the premises. * * * A possessor of land cannot do indirectly and by a mechanical device that which, were he present, he could not do immediately and in person. Therefore, he cannot gain a privilege to install, for the purpose of protecting his land from intrusions harmless to the lives and limbs of the occupiers or users of it, a mechanical device whose only purpose is to inflict death or serious harm upon such as may intrude, by giving notice of his intention to inflict, by mechanical means and indirectly, harm which he could not, even after request, inflict directly were he present.'

....

Similar statements are found in [other authorities].

....

In addition to civil liability many jurisdictions hold a land owner criminally liable for serious injuries or homicide caused by spring guns or other set devices.

....

In Wisconsin, Oregon and England the use of spring guns and similar devices is specifically made unlawful by statute. [C]

The legal principles stated by the trial court ... are well established and supported by the authorities cited and quoted **supra**. There is no merit in defendants' objections and exceptions thereto. Defendants' various motions based on the same reasons stated in exceptions to instructions were properly overruled.

....

Study and careful consideration of defendants' contentions on appeal reveal no reversible error.

Affirmed.

All Justices concur except LARSON, J., who dissents.

[Dissent of Justice Larson, omitted.]

————————

Points for Discussion

1. The majority of jurisdictions are in accord with the principal case – use of deadly force to protect real property is an excessive, non-proportionate use of force and not permitted. One is not privileged to use force intended or likely to cause death or serious bodily harm unless the intrusion threatens death or serious bodily harm to a person who is actually present at the time. *See, e.g.,* Allison v. Fiscus, 156 Ohio St. 120, 100 N.E.2d 237, 44 A.L.R.2d 369 (1951) (plaintiff permitted to recover for injuries received when he feloniously broke door latch and started to enter defendant's warehouse with intent to steal, when trap of two sticks of dynamite buried under the doorway by defendant-owner exploded); Starkey v. Dameron, 96 Colo. 459, 45 P.2d 172 (1935) (plaintiff permitted to recover compensatory and punitive damages for injuries received from spring gun which defendant filling station operator had concealed in automatic gasoline pump as protection against thieves); Weis v. Allen, 35 P.2d 478 (Or. 1934); Wilder v. Gardner, 39 Ga.App. 608, 147 S.E. 911 (1929) (plaintiff permitted to recover for injuries received from spring gun which defendant had set); Phelps v. Hamlett, 207 S.W. 425 (Tex. Civ.App. 1918) ("While the law authorizes an owner to protect his property by such reasonable means as he may find to be necessary, yet considerations of humanity preclude him from setting out, even on his own property, traps and devices dangerous to the life and limb of those whose appearance and presence may be reasonably anticipated, even though they may be trespassers.").

2. Plaintiff and her husband owned a Labrador Retriever puppy named "Jackie." Defendant lived across the street from the couple. One day, Jackie was playing on defendant's property, which defendant did not like. When defendant shooed the puppy away, Jackie jumped on defendant's right shoulder in a playful manner and defendant backhanded him. Jackie yelped, barked, and growled, but never charged or tried to attack defendant. Although defendant could have just closed the door to protect himself from the dog, he decided

instead to get his .22 caliber rifle and shoot Jackie. After he shot the dog, defendant moved Jackie's body to a ditch where she was eventually discovered by plaintiff's husband. May defendant successfully defend against any tort claim on defense of property grounds? *See* Meyers v. Sparrow, 2009 WL 533057 (Ohio Ct. App. 2009).

3. What if a landowner keeps a vicious watchdog who may inflict serious bodily injury or death in the landowner's absence? Is a dangerous dog a deadly weapon?

4   Gene Davidson owned a barn from which thieves one night stole various items. Davidson's home was located approximately one hundred feet from the barn. Three days later, around midnight, Davidson's wife spotted one or two men standing by the barn. Davidson called the police and retrieved his .38 caliber firearm from his bedroom. He opened the kitchen window and yelled at the men, who began running away. Davidson continued yelling at the men and fired four shots in their direction. He stated that he fired "warning shots" over their heads, attempting to get the men to stop so they could be arrested. Officers later found the body of one of the men lying near the barn. He had been fatally wounded by a bullet. Was Davidson privileged to use such force? *See* Goldfuss v. Davidson, 679 N.E.2d 1099 (Ohio 1997).

Hypo 3-7

Graduate Student returned home one evening to find that his home had been broken into and that two laptops and a video-game console had been taken. The neighborhood in which he lived had recently been victimized by more than a half-dozen **burglaries.** Later that same evening, well past midnight, Graduate Student hears a noise coming from his garage out back. Graduate Student grabs his samurai sword, a 3- to 5-foot long razor sharp weapon, to investigate the noise. (Graduate Student has no advanced training in sword use.) As he approaches the garage and notices that the door has been pried open, Intruder lunges at him from inside the garage. Sword in hand, Graduate Student strikes at Intruder, nearly severing one of his hands and inflicting a severe sword laceration. Intruder dies from the injuries. Defense of property? Defense of self? Discuss.

E. Defense and Recovery of Personal Property

Hodgeden v. Hubbard

18 Vt. 504 (1846)

REDFIELD, J., presiding.

On trial the plaintiff gave evidence, tending to prove, that, on the nineteenth day of September, 1842, he purchased at the Tyson ware house, in Montpelier, a stove, and gave his promissory note therefor, payable in six months; that the agent, who had charge of the warehouse, was absent at the times, and the sale was made by the defendant Hubbard, who was clerk for the agent, as was also the defendant Ayres; that on the same day, and soon after the sale, the defendants learned, that the plaintiff was irresponsible as to property, and started in pursuit of him, and overtook him about two miles from Montpelier and took the stove from him by force; but it did not appear, how much force was used, or its character; but it did appear, that, in the attempt to dispossess the plaintiff of the stove, he drew his knife, and that he was then forcibly held by one of the defendants, while the other took possession of the stove; and the testimony tended to prove, that the resistance of the plaintiff was such, that the defendants used violence and applied force to his person with great rudeness and outrage.

The defendants then gave evidence, tending to prove that the purchase of the stove by the plaintiff was effected by means of his false and fraudulent representations as to his ability to pay, and as to the amount of his property; that, among other things, the plaintiff represented, that he owned a farm in Cabot and considerable stock upon it, that he owned the team that he then had with him, and that he carried on a large business manufacturing butter firkins, &c.; that it was only by means of these representations, and others of like character, that Hubbard was induced to sell the stove to the plaintiff on credit; that soon after the delivery of the stove, on the same day, Hubbard learned, upon inquiry, from a person whom he saw from Cabot, that the plaintiff was entirely irresponsible, and that his representations as to his property were wholly false; and that the defendants immediately followed the plaintiff, and took the stove from him, and told him that he could have the note by calling for it.

The defendants requested the court to instruct the jury, that, if they should find, that the purchase of the stove on credit was effected only by means of the false and fraudulent representations of the plaintiff, as above specified, the title to the stove did not vest in the plaintiff, and the defendants, as servants of the agent of the Tyson warehouse, were justified in pursuing the plaintiff and taking the stove from him by force, and that, if they used no more force, than was absolutely necessary to effect this object, the plaintiff could not recover upon his count for an assault and battery.

But the court charged the jury, that, although the plaintiff was guilty of mis-representation and fraud, in obtaining the stove, in the manner attempted to be proved by the defendants, yet this would not justify the defendants in forcibly taking the property from him; that the property in the stove would not be changed by the purchase, and the defendants might take it peaceably, wherever they could find it; but that the defendants, having delivered the stove to the plaintiff, could not justify taking it from him by blows inflicted upon his person, or by holding him, but should resort to redress by legal process; and that, if they should find, that the property in the stove was not changed, for the reason stated, and that the defendants took it by violence, in the manner attempted to be shown by the plaintiff, although they used no more force than was necessary to accomplish that object under the resistance of the plaintiff, they would still be liable in this action; but the court, in that case, recommended to the jury to give small damages.

Verdict for plaintiff for one dollar damages. **Exceptions** by defendants.

....

The opinion of the court was delivered by WILLIAMS, Ch. J.

It is admitted, in this case, that the property in the stove did not pass to the plaintiff, that, though the plaintiff obtained possession of the stove, yet it was by such means of falsehood and fraud, criminal in the eye of the law, as made the possession unlawful, and that, although the consent of the owner was apparently obtained to the delivery of the possession to the plaintiff, yet, as it respects the plaintiff, and so far as the right of property was concerned, no such consent was given. ...

In the present case the defendants had clearly a right to retake the property, thus fraudulently obtained from them, if it could be done without unnecessary violence to the person, or without breach of the peace. It is admitted by the counsel for the plaintiff, that a right to re-capture existed in the defendants, if it could be done without violence, or breach of the peace. And how far this qualification of the right to retake property, thus taken, was intended for the security, or benefit, of the fraudulent possessor may admit of some doubt. Whoever is guilty of a breach of the peace, or of doing unnecessary violence to the person of another, although it may be in the assertion of an unquestioned and undoubted right, is liable to be prosecuted therefor. But the fraudulent possessor is not the protector of the public interest.

In the case before us it is stated, that it did not appear "how much force was used, or its character," before the defendants were assaulted by the plaintiff.

To obtain possession of the property in question no violence to the person of the plaintiff was necessary, or required, unless from his resistance. It was not like property carried about the person, as a watch, or money, nor did it require a number of people to effect the object. The plaintiff had no lawful possession, nor any right to resist the attempt of the defendants to regain the property, of which he had unlawfully and fraudulently obtained the possession. By drawing his knife he became the aggressor, inasmuch as he had no right thus to protect his fraudulent attempt to acquire the stove, and the possession of the same, and it was the right of the defendants to hold him by force, and, if they made use of no unnecessary violence, they were justified; if they were guilty of more, they were liable.

Under the view of the evidence, as considered and claimed by the defendants, they were entitled to the charge requested. The refusal of the court so to charge was erroneous; and although the court stated to the jury correctly, that the defendants could not justify retaking the property by blows inflicted on the person of the plaintiff, yet this was not meeting the request; and the charge was evidently erroneous, when the jury were told, that the defendants would be liable, although they used no more force than was necessary to accomplish the object of retaking the property, under the resistance of the plaintiff. The resistance of the plaintiff was unlawful, in regard to the particular species of property, which was then the subject of controversy, under the facts claimed by the defendants, and which must have been found to the satisfaction of the jury, as would seem from their verdict.

On the second count in the declaration the plaintiff could have no claim whatever. The defendants were the agents of the true owner; the plaintiff was the wrong doer, and acquired no right, against the defendants, to either property, or possession, if the facts were as stated in the case.

The judgment of the county court is reversed.

Bonkowski v. Arlan's Department Store

162 N.W.2d 347 (Mich. Ct. App. 1968)

NEAL E. FITZGERALD, Judge.

This appeal from a jury verdict for **false arrest** and **slander**, rendered against the defendant store whose agent stopped and questioned the plaintiff whom he suspected of **larceny**, surprisingly presents questions that are novel to the appellate courts of this jurisdiction.

The plaintiff, Mrs. Marion Bonkowski, accompanied by her husband, had left the defendant's Saginaw, Michigan store about 10:00 p.m. on the night of

December 18, 1962 after making several purchases, when Earl Reinhardt, a private policeman on duty that night in the defendant's store, called to her to stop as she was walking to her car about 30 feet away in the adjacent parking lot. Reinhardt motioned to the plaintiff to return toward the store, and when she had done so, Reinhardt said that someone in the store had told him the plaintiff had put three pieces of costume jewelry into her purse without having paid for them. Mrs. Bonkowski denied she had taken anything unlawfully, but Reinhardt told her he wanted to see the contents of her purse. On a cement step in front of the store, plaintiff emptied the contents of her purse into her husband's hands. The plaintiff produced sales slips for the items she had purchased, and Reinhardt, satisfied that she had not committed larceny, returned to the store.

Plaintiff brought this action against Earl Reinhardt and Arlan's Department Store, seeking damages on several counts. She complains that as a result of defendant's tortious acts she has suffered numerous psychosomatic symptoms, including headaches, nervousness, and depression. ... On the counts of false arrest and slander the case went to the jury, who returned a verdict of $43,750. The defendant's motions for judgment notwithstanding the verdict, remittitur, and new trial were denied by the trial court.

Numerous errors are alleged on appeal; we consider those necessary to the disposition of the case.

We conclude the plaintiff established a case entitling her to go to the jury on a charge of false arrest.[1] ... Therefore, there must be a new trial.

....

Defendant contends the charge of false arrest was erroneously allowed to go to the jury.

....

To the common-law tort of false arrest, privilege is a common-law defense, and we recognize as applicable here a privilege similar to that recognized by the American Law Institute in the Restatement of Torts, 2d. In section 120A, the Institute recognizes a privilege in favor of a merchant to detain for reasonable investigation a person whom he reasonably believes to have taken a chattel unlawfully. We adopt the concept embodied in section 120A, and we state the rule for this action as follows: if defendant Arlan's agent, Earl Reinhardt, reasonably believed the plaintiff had unlawfully taken goods held for sale in the defendant's

---

1 Although the distinctions are not always clearly set out in the authorities, false arrest, or unlawful arrest, is a species of the common-law action for false imprisonment. See 1 Restatement of Torts, 2d, § 35, comment A. ...

store, then he enjoyed a privilege to detain her for a reasonable investigation of the facts.

The Commissioners' comment states the strong reason behind recognizing such a privilege:

'The privilege stated in this section is necessary for the protection of a shopkeeper against the dilemma in which he would otherwise find himself when he reasonably believes that a shoplifter has taken goods from his counter. If there were no such privilege, he must either permit the suspected person to walk out of the premises and disappear, or must arrest him, at the risk of liability for false arrest if the theft could not be proved.' 1 Restatement of Torts, 2d, page 202.

That the problem of shoplifting, faced by merchants, has reached serious dimensions is common knowledge, and we find compelling reason to recognize such a privilege, similar to that recognized in other jurisdictions. [C]

....

The privilege we recognize here goes beyond that set forth in the Restatement, for the Commissioners there stated a caveat that 'the Institute expresses no opinion as to whether there may be circumstances under which this privilege may extend to the detention of one who has left the premises but is in their immediate vicinity.' [C]

In their comment, the Commissioners state that, by their caveat, in the absence of express authority, they intended to leave the question open. [C] We think the privilege should be so extended here because we think it entirely reasonable to apply it to the circumstances of the case at bar, for the reason that a merchant may not be able to form the reasonable belief justifying a detention for a reasonable investigation before a suspected person has left the premises. ...

On remand on the cause for false arrest, therefore, it will be the duty of the jury to determine in accordance with the rule we have set down, whether or not the defendant's agent, Earl Reinhardt, reasonably believed the plaintiff had unlawfully taken any goods held for sale at the defendant's store. If the jury finds the defendant's agent did so reasonably believe, then it must further determine whether the investigation that followed was reasonable under all the circumstances. If the jury finds the defendant does not come within this privilege, then from the facts as discussed above, it could find a false arrest.

....

Reversed and remanded for new trial in accordance with this opinion. The award of costs to await final determination of the cause.

Points for Discussion

1. A person wrongfully deprived of **chattel** is privileged to use reasonable force to recover the chattel immediately after its dispossession. This privilege to recover personal property permits the defendant to reclaim the chattel only when it can be done without unnecessary violence or breach of the peace.

2. The privilege to recover personal property is subject to several limitations. For instance, a *demand for return* of the chattel must be made prior to employing force, unless it reasonably appears that such a request would be futile or dangerous. Additionally, the privilege to use force to recover personal property is limited to *prompt discovery* of the dispossession and a prompt and persistent effort to recover it. Any unnecessary time lag during which pursuit does not take place or is suspended eliminates the privilege.

3. **Shoplifting** is a problem of large magnitude. The shopkeeper's privilege discussed in *Bonkowski* stems from the recovery of property privilege and allows shop owners the privilege to commit an intentional tort, if their reason for so doing is to investigate a reasonable suspicion of theft. Thus, as discussed in the principal case, a shopkeeper is privileged to detain a person for reasonable investigation whom he reasonably suspects to have taken chattel unlawfully. Of course, the basis of the suspicion must be reasonable, as well as the means and length of the detention. *See* Restatement (Second) of Torts § 120A (1965) (providing that request to stay must be made if practicable prior to using reasonable force); Davis v. Dillard's Department Store, 2008 WL 1903794 (Tex. Civ. App.—Eastland, 2008); *see also* Messer v. Robinson, 250 S.W.3d 344 (Ky. Ct. App. 2008) (woman suspected of child abuse sues and loses based on statutory shopkeeper's privilege); Cruz v. HomeBase, 83 Cal. App.4th 160 (Cal.Ct.App. 2000) (store not liable when plaintiff, shopping at defendant Homebase's store, is accused of stealing sheet of plywood and loss prevention supervisor refuses to let him produce receipt).

> ### Hypo 3-8
>
> Ashanti and Ashley Davis are shopping at Department Store when Manager and Security Guard ask both to follow them to the rear of the store, as they suspect Ashanti and Ashley of shoplifting. The manager takes their pictures, and they are escorted out of the store. The Davis's wish to sue Department Store. For what tort(s) might Ashanti and Ashley sue, if any. What defense(s), if any, might Department Store successfully assert in response?

F. Necessity

Surocco v. Geary

3 Cal. 69 (1853)

MURRAY, Chief Justice, delivered the opinion of the Court—

HEYDENFELDT, Justice, concurred.

This was an action, commenced in the court below, to recover damages for blowing up and destroying the plaintiffs' house and property, during the fire of the 24th of December, 1849.

Geary, at that time **Alcalde** of San Francisco, justified, on the ground that he had the authority, by virtue of his office, to destroy said building, and also that it had been blown up by him to stop the progress of the conflagration then raging.

It was in proof, that the fire passed over and burned beyond the building of the plaintiffs', and that at the time said building was destroyed, they were engaged in removing their property, and could, had they not been prevented, have succeeded in removing more, if not all of their goods.

The cause was tried by the court sitting as a jury, and a verdict rendered for the plaintiffs, from which the defendant prosecutes this appeal....

The only question for our consideration is, whether the person who tears down or destroys the house of another, in good faith, and under apparent necessity, during the time of a conflagration, for the purpose of saving the buildings adjacent, and stopping its progress, can be held personally liable in an action by the owner of the property destroyed.

This point has been so well settled in the courts of New York and New Jersey, that a reference to those authorities is all that is necessary to determine the present case.

The right to destroy property, to prevent the spread of a conflagration, has been traced to the highest law of necessity, and the natural rights of man, independent of society or civil government. "It is referred by moralists and jurists to the same great principle which justifies the exclusive appropriation of a plank in a shipwreck, though the life of another be sacrificed; with the throwing overboard goods in a tempest, for the safety of a vessel; with the trespassing upon the lands of another, to escape death by an enemy. It rests upon the maxim, ***Necessitas inducit privilegium quod jura privata.***"

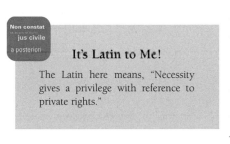

It's Latin to Me!

The Latin here means, "Necessity gives a privilege with reference to private rights."

The common law adopts the principles of the natural law, and places the justification of an act otherwise tortious precisely on the same ground of necessity. [C]

[T]he instances of tearing down houses to prevent a conflagration, or to raise bulwarks for the defence of a city, are made use of as illustrations, rather than as abstract cases, in which its exercise is permitted. At such times, the individual rights of property give way to the higher laws of impending necessity.

A house on fire, or those in its immediate vicinity, which serve to communicate the flames, becomes a nuisance, which it is lawful to abate, and the private rights of the individual yield to the considerations of general convenience, and the interests of society. Were it otherwise, one stubborn person might involve a whole city in ruin, by refusing to allow the destruction of a building which would cut off the flames and check the progress of the fire, and that, too, when it was perfectly evident that his building must be consumed.

The respondent has invoked the aid of the constitutional provision which prohibits the taking of private property for public use, without just compensation being made therefor. This is not "a taking of private property for public use," within the meaning of the Constitution.

The right of taking individual property for public purposes belongs to the State, by virtue of her right of **eminent domain**, and is said to be justified on the ground of state necessity; but this is not a taking or a destruction for a public purpose, but a destruction for the benefit of the individual or the city, but not properly of the State.

The counsel for the respondent has asked, who is to judge of the necessity of the destruction of property?

This must, in some instances, be a difficult matter to determine. The necessity of blowing up a house may not exist, or be as apparent to the owner, whose judgment is clouded by interest, and the hope of saving his property, as to others. In all such cases the conduct of the individual must be regulated by his own judgment as to the exigencies of the case. If a building should be torn down without apparent or actual necessity, the parties concerned would undoubtedly be liable in an action of trespass. But in every case the necessity must be clearly shown. It is true, many cases of hardship may grow out of this rule, and property may often in such cases be destroyed, without necessity, by irresponsible persons, but this difficulty would not be obviated by making the parties responsible in every case, whether the necessity existed or not.

The legislature of the State possess the power to regulate this subject by providing the manner in which buildings may be destroyed, and the mode in which compensation shall be made; and it is to be hoped that something will be done to obviate the difficulty, and prevent the happening of such events as those supposed by the respondent's counsel.

In the absence of any legislation on the subject, we are compelled to fall back upon the rules of the common law.

The evidence in this case clearly establishes the fact, that the blowing up of the house was necessary, as it would have been consumed had it been left standing. The plaintiffs cannot recover for the value of the goods which they might have saved; they were as much subject to the necessities of the occasion as the house in which they were situate; and if in such cases a party was held liable, it would too frequently happen, that the delay caused by the removal of the goods would render the destruction of the house useless.

The court below clearly erred as to the law applicable to the facts of this case. The testimony will not warrant a verdict against the defendant.

Judgment reversed.

———————————

Points for Discussion

1. What is an alcalde? Is the fact that the defendant was Alcalde of San Francisco legally relevant to the successful assertion of public necessity as an affirmative defense?

2. The affirmative defense of **public necessity** permits the defendant, acting as the champion of the public, to destroy, damage, or use the real or personal property of another as long as the defendant reasonably believes that doing so is necessary to avert an imminent public disaster. If the defendant commits an intentional tort to protect the public from a danger affecting the entire community, the defendant enjoys a complete privilege for the commission of the intentional tort, as long as his belief of the necessity of his actions is reasonable. One is privileged to commit an intentional tort based on public necessity when that person seeks to prevent a threatened injury or harm from some force of nature or some other independent cause not connected with the plaintiff.

Vincent v. Lake Erie Transp. Co.

124 N.W. 221 (Minn. 1910)

O'BRIEN, J.

The steamship Reynolds, owned by the defendant, was for the purpose of discharging her cargo on November 27, 1905, moored to plaintiff's dock in Duluth. While the unloading of the boat was taking place a storm from the northeast developed, which at about 10 o'clock p. m., when the unloading was completed, had so grown in violence that the wind was then moving at 50 miles per hour and continued to increase during the night. There is some evidence that one, and perhaps two, boats were able to enter the harbor that night, but it is plain that navigation was practically suspended from the hour mentioned until the morning of the 29th, when the storm abated, and during that time no master would have been justified in attempting to navigate his vessel, if he could avoid doing so. After the discharge of the cargo the Reynolds signaled for a tug to tow her from the dock, but none could be obtained because of the severity of the storm. If the lines holding the ship to the dock had been cast off, she would doubtless have drifted away; but, instead, the lines were kept fast, and as soon as one parted or chafed it was replaced, sometimes with a larger one. The vessel lay upon the outside of the dock, her bow to the east, the wind and waves striking her starboard quarter with such force that she was constantly being lifted and thrown against the dock, resulting in its damage, as found by the jury, to the amount of $500.

We are satisfied that the character of the storm was such that it would have been highly imprudent for the master of the Reynolds to have attempted to leave the dock or to have permitted his vessel to drift a way from it. One witness testified upon the trial that the vessel could have been warped into a slip, and that, if the attempt to bring the ship into the slip had failed, the worst that could have happened would be that the vessel would have been blown ashore upon a soft and muddy bank. The witness was not present in Duluth at the time of the storm, and, while he may have been right in his conclusions, those in charge of the dock and the vessel at the time of the storm were not required to use the highest human intelligence, nor were they required to resort to every possible experiment which could be suggested for the preservation of their property. Nothing more was demanded of them than ordinary prudence and care, and the record in this case fully sustains the contention of the appellant that, in holding the vessel fast to the dock, those in charge of her exercised good judgment and prudent seamanship.

It is claimed by the respondent that it was negligence to moor the boat at an exposed part of the wharf, and to continue in that position after it became apparent that the storm was to be more than usually severe. We do not agree with this position. The part of the wharf where the vessel was moored appears to have been commonly used for that purpose. It was situated within the harbor at Duluth, and must, we think, be considered a proper and safe place, and would undoubtedly have been such during what would be considered a very severe storm. The storm which made it unsafe was one which surpassed in violence any which might have reasonably been anticipated.

The appellant contends by ample assignments of error that, because its conduct during the storm was rendered necessary by prudence and good seamanship under conditions over which it had no control, it cannot be held liable for any injury resulting to the property of others, and claims that the jury should have been so instructed. An analysis of the charge given by the trial court is not necessary, as in our opinion the only question for the jury was the amount of damages which the plaintiffs were entitled to recover, and no complaint is made upon that score.

The situation was one in which the ordinary rules regulating properly rights were suspended by forces beyond human control, and if, without the direct intervention of some act by the one sought to be held liable, the property of another was injured, such injury must be attributed to the act of God, and not to the wrongful act of the person sought to be charged. If during the storm the Reynolds had entered the harbor, and while there had become disabled and been thrown against the plaintiffs' dock, the plaintiffs could not have recovered. Again, if which attempting to hold fast to the dock the lines had parted, without any negligence, and the vessel carried against some other boat or dock in the harbor, there would be no liability upon her owner. But here those in charge of the vessel deliberately and by their direct efforts held her in such a position that the damage to the dock resulted, and, having thus preserved the ship at the expense of the dock, it seems to us that her owners are responsible to the dock owners to the extent of the injury inflicted.

....

Theologians hold that a starving man may, without moral guilt, take what is necessary to sustain life; but it could hardly be said that the obligation would not be upon such person to pay the value of the property so taken when he became able to do so. And so public necessity, in times of war or peace, may require the taking of private property for public purposes; but under our system of jurisprudence compensation must be made.

Let us imagine in this case that for the better mooring of the vessel those in charge of her had appropriated a valuable cable lying upon the dock. No matter how justifiable such appropriation might have been, it would not be claimed that, because of the overwhelming necessity of the situation, the owner of the cable could not recover its value.

This is not a case where life or property was menaced by any object or thing belonging to the plaintiff, the destruction of which became necessary to prevent the threatened disaster. Nor is it a case where, because of the act of God, or unavoidable accident, the infliction of the injury was beyond the control of the defendant, but is one where the defendant prudently and advisedly availed itself of the plaintiffs' property for the purpose of preserving its own more valuable property, and the plaintiffs are entitled to compensation for the injury done.

Order affirmed.

LEWIS, J. [, dissenting:]

I dissent. It was assumed on the trial before the lower court that appellant's liability depended on whether the master of the ship might, in the exercise of reasonable care, have sought a place of safety before the storm made it impossible to leave the dock. The majority opinion assumes that the evidence is conclusive that appellant moored its boat at respondent's dock pursuant to contract, and that the vessel was lawfully in position at the time the additional cables were fastened to the dock, and the reasoning of the opinion is that, because appellant made use of the stronger cables to hold the boat in position, it became liable under the rule that it had voluntarily made use of the property of another for the purpose of saving its own.

In my judgment, if the boat was lawfully in position at the time the storm broke, and the master could not, in the exercise of due care, have left that position without subjecting his vessel to the hazards of the storm, then the damage to the dock, caused by the pounding of the boat, was the result of an inevitable accident. If the master was in the exercise of due care, he was not at fault. The reasoning of the opinion admits that if the ropes, or cables, first attached to the dock had not parted, or if, in the first instance, the master had used the stronger cables, there would be no liability. If the master could not, in the exercise of reasonable care, have anticipated the severity of the storm and sought a place of safety before it became impossible, why should he be required to anticipate the severity of the storm, and, in the first instance, use the stronger cables?

I am of the opinion that one who constructs a dock to the navigable line of waters, and enters into contractual relations with the owner of a vessel to moor at the same, takes the risk of damage to his dock by a boat caught there by a storm, which event could not have been avoided in the exercise of due care, and further, that the legal status of the parties in such a case is not changed by renewal of cables to keep the boat from being cast adrift at the mercy of the tempest.

————————————

Points for Discussion

1. A defendant enjoys an incomplete privilege to commit an intentional tort when doing so out of **private necessity**. Unlike public necessity, a private necessity is one personal to the defendant rather than for the public good. Private necessity is an incomplete or partial privilege because it allows for the defendant to commit the intentional tort; the defendant is required to pay for any actual damages he causes in doing so. Thus, when a defendant is acting to protect his own interests and not those of the public, his privilege is limited. Defendant is relieved for commission of the technical tort itself, but is required to compensate the plaintiff for any actual damages he has caused. *See, e.g.,* Depue v. Flateau, 100 Minn. 299, 111 N. W. 1 (1907) (when plaintiff, while lawfully in defendants' house, became so ill he was incapable of traveling with safety, defendants held responsible for compelling him to leave premises, thereby resulting in his injuries).

2. What result if the plaintiff in *Vincent* had cut the rope causing damage to the defendant's boat? If a defendant enjoys the privilege of private necessity, the plaintiff is not permitted to resist or prevent commission of the tort. If the plaintiff does so, he is liable for the commission of the tort itself. *See, e.g.,* Ploof v. Putnam, 71 Atl. 188 (Vt. 1908) (where under stress of weather, vessel was without permission moored to private dock at island owned by defendant, plaintiff was not liable for trespass and defendant was responsible in damages because defendant unmoored the vessel, permitting it to drift upon the shore, with resultant injuries to it).

3. Should a person be privileged to inflict serious bodily injury or death upon another when acting out of private necessity? Say for example that a group of four people is visiting an alligator park when all of the sudden, one of the

alligators takes out in pursuit of them. Realizing that he might not be able to outrun the alligator, one of the people in the fleeing group intentionally trips another member, causing her to stumble. She is devoured by the alligator. The estate of the devoured woman sues the man for battery. The man asserts private necessity as a defense. He was acting out of private necessity to prevent a threatened injury from some force of nature independent of him. Should he be relieved of the technical tort of battery and permitted to pay only for any actual damage caused by his battery?

Hypo 3-9

Defendant destroys Farmer's herd of cattle because Defendant reasonably believes the entire herd to have been exposed to Mad Cow's disease, a fatal, neurodegenerative disease in cattle that can be passed to human beings with deadly consequences. In fact, Farmer's herd was not infected with Mad Cow's disease. Farmer wishes to sue Defendant in tort for the loss of his cattle. Discuss.

G. Justification

In a portion of the opinion omitted from *Parvi v. City of Kingston,* Chapter 2, *supra,* the court discusses the affirmative defense of **justification**:

> "…[S]ince the alleged imprisonment here was without a warrant and therefore an extrajudicial act, the burden not only of proving, but of pleading legal justification was on the city, whose failure to have done so precluded it from introducing such evidence under its general denial. [Cc]

> ….

> "In *Sindle v New York City Tr. Auth.* (33 NY2d 293), we reflected on the scope of the privileges which constitute justification. We there said [c], '[G]enerally, restraint or detention, reasonable under the circumstances and in time and manner, imposed for the purpose of preventing another from inflicting personal injuries or interfering with or damaging real or personal property in one's lawful possession or custody is not unlawful'. Consequently, it may be that taking a person who is in a state of intoxication to a position of greater safety would constitute justification. But it is clearly not privileged to arrest such a person for

the sole purpose of running him out of town, or, as further proof at the trial here established, once having arrested such a person, to follow a practice of running him out of town to avoid guardhouse chores for the police whenever there were no other prisoners in the local jail. Such acts cannot be sanctioned with the mantle of the privilege of justification. A person who has had too much to drink is not a chattel to be transported from one locus to another at the whim or convenience of police officers.

"The Restatement of Torts 2d (§ 10, Comment *d*) states it well: 'Where the privilege is based upon the value attached to the interest to be protected or advanced by its exercise, the privilege protects the actor from liability only if the acts are done for the purpose of protecting or advancing the interest in question. Such privileges are often called conditional, because the act is privileged only on condition that it is done for the purpose of protecting or advancing the particular interest. They are sometimes called "defeasible", to indicate the fact that the privilege is destroyed if the act is done for any purpose other than the protection or advancement of the interest in question.' It follows that, if the conduct of the officers indeed is found to have been motivated by the desire to run the plaintiff out of town, the action for false imprisonment would not have been rebutted by the defense of legal justification. For, under plaintiff's theory, the false imprisonment count does not rest on the reasonableness of the police officers' action, but on whether the unwilling confinement of the plaintiff was the result of an arrest for a nonjustified purpose."

Hypo 3-10

Alpha is a famous chef and cookbook author. For the last several months, she has been working on her much-anticipated cookbook. She is so excited that her new cookbook is finally slated to come out that she invites her close friend and colleague, Beta, to her personal kitchen to "see what's cooking." Beta is impressed, so much so that a couple of days later, she decides to break into Alpha's kitchen in the middle of the night to snoop around. When she arrives, she is pleased to find that she does not really have to "break into" Alpha's kitchen at all because the door is unlocked. White Beta is inside, Alpha comes along and, not knowing that Beta is inside, locks the door from the outside as she does every night. Realizing that she is trapped inside the kitchen until someone returns in the morning, Beta entertains herself by rummaging around. She eventually finds several copies of Alpha's newest recipes on a counter and stuffs them into her knapsack. Janitor arrives early the next morning and unlocks the door, freeing Beta. (Janitor never realizes that Beta was inside the kitchen.) Beta leaves the kitchen unnoticed.

After returning home exhausted from her all-night escapade, Beta commences with her daily ritual of updating her blog on which she discloses the contents of Alpha's recipes that she had taken the night before.

When Alpha enters her kitchen that morning, she notices that her recipes have vanished! A short time later, she discovers the very recipes that are missing have been revealed on Beta's blog. Alpha is furious. She visits Beta, confronting her about the blog. Beta tells Alpha that she can have her stinking recipes back, returning the copies of the recipes to Alpha. However, Beta refuses to remove the blog entries, even after Alpha begs her to do so.

Three days after her confrontation with Alpha, Beta travels to her hometown to escort her mother to the annual family reunion and cookout. As Beta and her mother enter the park where the reunion will be held, Beta notices that her uncle, Omega, has already arrived. Beta remembers that at the previous year's reunion she and Omega had a heated argument, which escalated into a face-to-face shouting match over an unpaid $5,000 loan Omega had made to Beta and that Omega had said to Beta, "If you don't have my money the next time I see you I'm going to hurt you. Hurt you bad." Seeing Omega again for the first time since last year's reunion, and knowing that she had not paid off the loan, Beta vividly remembers what Omega told her would happen the next time he saw her. Beta picks up a bottle of ketchup from a nearby picnic table, approaches Omega, who is standing with his back to her, and strikes him in the back of the head with the bottle. Stunned, Omega falls to the ground (it is later determined that he suffered a slight concussion from the blow to the head).

Identify and discuss any and all intentional torts committed by Alpha, Beta, Omega, or Janitor and any defenses thereto.

CHAPTER 4

Negligence

When, and under what circumstances, can a plaintiff seek and obtain a legal remedy for harms caused by the negligence of other persons and entities? Consider the following scenarios:

1. Late for work again and heeding his employer's warning that further tardiness would result in his termination, Driver jumps into his car and speeds from his home to the office. While en route he drives at a speed of 50 miles per hour through two school zones with posted 20 mile per hour speed limits and runs two red lights at intersections busy with morning and rush hour traffic. Approaching a last intersection one mile from his destination, Driver decides to run yet another red light. In the middle of the intersection his car slams into the side of a crossing vehicle traveling with a green light.

2. Same facts as the preceding scenario with the following change: As Driver approaches the last intersection one mile from his destination the cell phone in the front pocket of his suit coat begins to ring. Driver removes the phone from his pocket, looks at the caller ID, and sees that his boss is calling. Driver, terrified, stares at the number. As he brings the phone up to his ear, he turns his attention back to the road, only to discover that in front of him is a car stopped at the red light. Unable to stop in time, Driver slams into the rear of that vehicle.

3. While eating a salad she purchased from the restaurant of a large fast-food chain, Customer discovers a cockroach in the bowl.

Did Driver or the restaurant or both engage in negligent conduct? Do the drivers of the vehicles struck by Driver's car and Customer have viable causes of action for negligence against Driver and the restaurant? What are the legal and operative definitions of "negligence" in these and other instances? What should a plaintiff have to prove in order to win her case?

A. Elements of a Negligence Action

A plaintiff alleging and seeking to prevail in a cause of action for negligence must prove and establish the following five elements:

1. The defendant had and owed a **duty** to the plaintiff to use reasonable and due care. As noted in the RESTATEMENT (THIRD) OF TORTS, "[a]n actor ordinarily has a duty to exercise reasonable care when the actor's conduct creates a risk of physical harm." RESTATEMENT (THIRD) OF TORTS: LIABILITY FOR PHYSICAL HARM § 7 (2010).

2. The defendant failed to meet and therefore committed a **breach** of the duty and standard of care.

3. The defendant's negligent conduct (*i.e.*, breach of duty) injured the plaintiff. To establish **causation** the plaintiff must prove that the defendant's negligence was both the **cause-in-fact** (the **but-for cause**) and the **legal cause** or **proximate cause** of the plaintiff's injury.

4. The plaintiff suffered **actual damages**. Note that **nominal damages** cannot be recovered in negligence.

This chapter will address and focus on the first two elements of a negligence claim—duty and breach—and the legal determination of a defendant's compliance with or failure to meet the standard of care. The following chapter will then turn to the issue of causation.

B. Negligence: Formulation and Factors

RESTATEMENT (SECOND) OF TORTS (1965)

§ 290. What Actor is Required to Know

For the purpose of determining whether the actor should recognize that his conduct involves a risk, he is required to know

(a) the qualities and habits of human beings and animals and the qualities, characteristics, and capacities of things and forces in so far as they are matters of common knowledge at the time and in the community; and

(b) the common law, legislative enactments, and general customs in so far as they are likely to affect the conduct of the other or third persons.

§ 291. Unreasonableness; How Determined; Magnitude of Risk and Utility of Conduct

Where an act is one which a reasonable [person] would recognize as involving a risk of harm to another, the risk is unreasonable and the act is negligent if the risk is of such magnitude as to outweigh what the law regards as the utility of the act or of the particular manner in which it is done.

§ 292. Factors Considered in Determining Utility of Actor's Conduct

In determining what the law regards as the utility of the actor's conduct for the purpose of determining whether the actor is negligent, the following factors are important:

(a) the social value which the law attaches to the interest which is to be advanced or protected by the conduct;

(b) the extent of the chance that this interest will be advanced or protected by the particular course of conduct;

(c) the extent of the chance that such interest can be adequately advanced or protected by another and less dangerous course of conduct.

§ 293. Factors Considered in Determining Magnitude of Risk

In determining the magnitude of risk for the purposes of determining whether the actor is negligent, the following factors are important:

(a) the social value which the law attaches to the interests which are imperiled;

(b) the extent of the chance that the actor's conduct will cause an invasion of any interest of the other or of one of a class of which the other is a member;

(c) the extent of the harm likely to be caused to the interests imperiled;

(d) the number of persons whose interests are likely to be invaded if the risk takes effect in harm.

Lubitz v. Wells

19 Conn. Supp. 322, 113 A.2d 147 (1955)

TROLAND, Judge.

> The American Law Institute, an influential organization comprised of more than 4,000 lawyers, judges, and law professors, publishes Restatements of the Law (including the law of torts), model statutes, and other materials. For more on the ALI, go to www.ali.org. In addition, the ALI has published *A Concise Restatement of Torts* (compiled by Kenneth S. Abraham, 2000).

The complaint alleges that James Wells was the owner of a golf club and that he left it for some time lying on the ground in the backyard of his home. That thereafter his son, the defendant James Wells, Jr., aged eleven years, while playing in the yard with the plaintiff, Judith Lubitz, aged nine years, picked up the golf club and proceeded to swing at a stone lying on the ground. In swinging the golf club, James Wells, Jr., caused the club to strike the plaintiff about the jaw and chin.

Negligence alleged against the young Wells boy is that he failed to warn his little playmate of his intention to swing the club and that he did swing the club when he knew she was in a position of danger.

In an attempt to hold the boy's father, James Wells, liable for his son's action, it is alleged that James Wells was negligent because although he knew the golf club was on the ground in his backyard and that his children would play with it, and that although he knew or 'should have known' that the negligent use of the golf club by children would cause injury to a child, he neglected to remove the golf club from the backyard or to caution James Wells, Jr., against the use of the same.

The **demurrer** challenges the sufficiency of the allegations of the complaint to state a cause of action or to support a judgment against the father, James Wells.

It would hardly be good sense to hold that this golf club is so obviously and intrinsically dangerous that it is negligence to leave it lying on the ground in the yard. The father cannot be held liable on the allegations of this complaint. [Cc]

The demurrer is sustained.

Points for Discussion

1. Do you agree with the court's decision?

2. Why did the lawsuit focus on the parent's and not the child's negligence?

3. Suppose that this is the second time in which the defendant's son struck another child with a golf club left lying on the ground at the defendant's home. Same result? Why or why not?

4. The court concluded that a golf club was not "obviously and intrinsically dangerous." Consider whether the following items or materials fall into that category: a baseball bat; a hockey stick; a ten-pound dumbbell; a gardening hoe; a shovel; a hammer; a child's BB gun.

Chicago, B. & Q. R. Co. v. Krayenbuhl

65 Neb. 889, 91 N.W. 880 (1902)

ALBERT, C.

This action was brought on behalf of Leo Krayenbuhl, whom we shall hereafter call the plaintiff, by his **next friend**, against the Chicago, Burlington & Quincy Railroad Company to recover for personal injuries received by the plaintiff while playing on a turntable belonging to the defendant.

It sufficiently appears from the evidence that on and prior to the 20th day of October, 1895, the defendant operated a line of railroad, which extended through the village of Palmer, at which point it maintained a passenger depot, roundhouse, coalhouse, water tank, and turntable. A few rods northwest of the depot the road branched, one branch taking a westerly and the other a northwesterly course. The turntable was situated between those two branches, at a point about 1,600 feet from the depot, and about 100 feet from each branch, and a track extended to it from the point of divergence of the two branches. A path or footway, beginning some distance northwest of the turntable, extended in a southeasterly direction, passed within about 70 feet of it, and crossed the track at the south. This path was in common use, not only by the members of the family to which the plaintiff belonged, but by the public generally, and there was no fence between it and the turntable. The turntable was provided with a movable bolt, which by means of a lever could be thrown into a socket in the surrounding framework, thus holding the turntable in position. Provision was also made for locking it with a padlock. The rules of the defendant in force at the time required the foreman of the roundhouse, or in his absence the station agent, to keep the

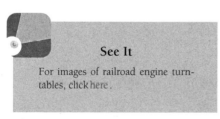

See It

For images of railroad engine turntables, click here.

turntable locked when not in use; but there is considerable evidence to the effect that this rule was frequently disregarded, and that, owing to the looseness of one of the staples used in connection with the lock, even when thus fastened, it could be unfastened by young children without much difficulty. . . . There is evidence tending to show that it was the common practice for the children of the family and other children in the neighborhood to resort to the coalhouse, roundhouse, and turntable, and to amuse themselves by revolving the turntable, and riding on it while it was in motion, and that this practice was known to the defendant, who permitted it without protest.

. . . .

It is true, as said in Loomis v. Terry, 17 Wend. 497, 31 Am. Dec. 306, "the business of life must go forward"; the means by which it is carried forward cannot be rendered absolutely safe. Ordinarily, it can be best carried forward by the unrestricted use of private property by the owner; therefore the law favors such use to the fullest extent consistent with the main purpose for which, from a social standpoint, such business is carried forward, namely, the public good. Hence, in order to determine the extent to which such use may be enjoyed, its bearing on such main purpose must be taken into account, and a balance struck between its advantages and disadvantages. If, on the whole, such use defeats, rather than promotes, the main purpose, it should not be permitted; on the other hand, if the restrictions proposed would so operate, they should not be imposed. The business of life is better carried forward by the use of dangerous machinery; hence the public good demands its use, although occasionally such use results in the loss of life or limb. It does so because the danger is insignificant, when weighed against the benefits resulting from the use of such machinery, and for the same reason demands its reasonable, most effective, and unrestricted use, up to the point where the benefits resulting from such use no longer outweigh the danger to be anticipated from it. At that point the public good demands restrictions. For example, a turntable is a dangerous contrivance, which facilitates railroading; the general benefits resulting from its use outweigh the occasional injuries inflicted by it; hence the public good demands its use. We may conceive of means by which it might be rendered absolutely safe, but such means would so interfere with its beneficial use that the danger to be anticipated would not justify their adoption; therefore the public good demands its use without them. But the danger incident to its use may be lessened by the use of a lock which would prevent children, attracted to it, from moving it; the interference with the proper use of the turntable occasioned by the use of such lock is so slight that it is outweighed by the danger to be anticipated from an omission to use it; therefore the public good, we think, demands the use of the lock. The public good would not require the owner of a vacant lot on which there is a pond to fill up the pond or inclose the lot with an impassable wall to insure the safety of children resorting to it, because the burden of doing so is out of proportion to the danger to be anticipated from leaving it undone. [C] But where there is an open well on a vacant lot, which is frequented by children, of which the owner of the lot has knowledge, he is liable for injuries sustained by children falling into the well, because the danger to be anticipated from the open well, under the circumstances, outweighs the slight expense or inconvenience that would be entailed in making it safe. [C]

. . . .

For the reasons stated in the foregoing opinion, the **judgment** of the district court is **reversed**, and the cause **remanded** for further proceedings according to law.

Points for Discussion

1. Note that the court engaged in a balancing analysis, weighing the public goods and benefits resulting from the use of dangerous machinery against the machinery's danger to life and limb. How should the respective benefits and dangers at issue be determined and weighed? What factors would you consider on both sides of the balance?

2. Do you agree with the court that the owner of a vacant lot with a pond has no duty to insure the safety of children who come to the pond, but would be liable for injuries sustained by children who fall into an open well on the owner's property? Why might the court have distinguished between a pond and an open well?

United States v. Carroll Towing Co.

159 F.2d 169 (2d Cir. 1947)

L. HAND, Circuit Judge.

These appeals concern the sinking of the barge, 'Anna C,' on January 4, 1944, off Pier 51, North River. The Conners Marine Co., Inc., was the owner of the barge, which the Pennsylvania Railroad Company had chartered; the Grace Line, Inc., was the charterer of the tug, 'Carroll,' of which the Carroll Towing Co., Inc., was the owner. . . .

The facts, as the judge found them, were as follows. On June 20, 1943, the Conners Company chartered the barge, 'Anna C.' to the Pennsylvania Railroad Company at a stated hire per diem, by a charter of the kind usual in the Harbor, which included the services of a bargee, apparently limited to the hours 8 A.M. to 4 P.M. On January 2, 1944, the barge, which had lifted the cargo of flour, was made fast off the end of Pier 58 on the Manhattan side of the North River, whence she was later shifted to Pier 52. At some time not disclosed, five other barges were moored outside her, extending into the river; her lines to the pier were not then strengthened. At the end of the next pier north (called the Public Pier), lay four barges; and a line had been made fast from the outermost of these to the fourth barge of the tier hanging to Pier 52. The purpose of this line is not entirely apparent, and in any event it obstructed entrance into the slip between the two piers of barges. The Grace Line, which had chartered the tug, 'Carroll,' sent her down to the **locus in quo** to 'drill' out one of the barges which lay at the end of the Public Pier; and in order to do so it was necessary to throw off the line between the two tiers. On board the 'Carroll' at the time were not only her master, but a 'harbormaster' employed by the Grace Line. Before throwing off the line between the two tiers, the 'Carroll'

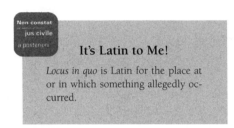

It's Latin to Me!

Locus in quo is Latin for the place at or in which something allegedly occurred.

nosed up against the outer barge of the tier lying off Pier 52, ran a line from her own stem to the middle bit of that barge, and kept working her engines 'slow ahead' against the ebb tide which was making at that time. The captain of the 'Carroll' put a deckhand and the 'harbormaster' on the barges, told them to throw off the line which barred the entrance to the slip; but, before doing so, to make sure that the tier on Pier 52 was safely moored, as there was a strong northerly wind blowing down the river. The 'harbormaster' and the deckhand went aboard the barges and readjusted all the fasts to their satisfaction, including those from the 'Anna C.' to the pier.

After doing so, they threw off the line between the two tiers and again boarded the 'Carroll,' which backed away from the outside barge, preparatory to 'drilling' out the barge she was after in the tier off the Public Pier. She had only got about seventy-five feet away when the tier off Pier 52 broke adrift because the fasts from the 'Anna C,' either rendered, or carried away. The tide and wind carried down the six barges, still holding together, until the 'Anna C' fetched up against a tanker, lying on the north side of the pier below- Pier 51- whose propeller broke a hole in her at or near her bottom. Shortly thereafter: i.e., at about 2:15 P.M., she careened, dumped her cargo of flour and sank. The tug, 'Grace,' owned by the Grace Line, and the 'Carroll,' came to the help of the flotilla after it broke loose; and, as both had syphon pumps on board, they could have kept the 'Anna C' afloat, had they learned of her condition; but the bargee had left her on the evening before, and nobody was on board to observe that she was leaking. . . .

It appears . . . that there is no general rule to determine when the absence of a bargee or other attendant will make the owner of the barge liable for injuries to other vessels if she breaks away from her moorings. However, in any cases where he would be so liable for injuries to others obviously he must reduce his damages proportionately, if the injury is to his own barge. It becomes apparent why there can be no such general rule, when we consider the grounds for such a liability. Since there are occasions when every vessel will break from her moorings, and since, if she does, she becomes a menace to those about her; the owner's duty, as in other similar situations, to provide against resulting injuries is a function of three variables: (1) The probability that she will break away; (2) the gravity of the resulting injury, if she does; (3) the burden of adequate precautions. Possibly it serves to bring this notion into relief to state it in algebraic terms: if the probability be called P; the injury, L; and the burden, B; liability depends upon whether B is less than L multiplied by P: i.e., whether B less than PL. Applied to the situation at bar, the likelihood that a barge will break from her fasts and the damage she will do, vary with the place and time; for example, if a storm threatens, the danger is greater; so it is, if she is in a crowded harbor where moored barges are constantly being shifted about. On the other hand, the barge must not be the bargee's prison, even though he lives aboard; he must go ashore at times. We need not say whether, even in such crowded waters as New York Harbor a bargee must be aboard at night at all; it may be that the custom is otherwise . . . and that, if so, the situation is one where custom should control. We leave that question open; but we hold that it is not in all cases a sufficient answer to a bargee's absence without excuse, during working hours, that he has properly made fast his barge to a pier, when he leaves her. In the case at bar the bargee left at five o'clock in the afternoon of January 3rd, and the flotilla broke away at about two o'clock in the afternoon of the following day, twenty-one hours afterwards. The bargee had been away all the time, and we hold that his fabricated story was affirmative evidence that he had no excuse for his absence. At the locus in quo- especially during the short January days and in the full tide of war activity- barges were being constantly 'drilled' in and out. Certainly it was not beyond reasonable expectation that, with the inevitable haste and bustle, the work might not be done with adequate care. In such circumstances we **hold**- and it is all that we do hold- that it was a fair requirement that the Conners Company should have a bargee aboard (unless he had some excuse for his absence), during the working hours of daylight.

. . . .

Decrees reversed and cause remanded for further proceedings in accordance with the foregoing.

For More Information

Students interested in learning more about *Carroll Towing* may consult the following resource: Stephen G. Gilles, United States v. Carroll Towing Co.: *The Hand Formula's Home Port*, in TORTS STORIES 11-39 (Robert L. Rabin & Stephen D. Sugarman eds., 2003).

Conway v. O'Brien

111 F.2d 611 (2d Cir. 1940)

L. HAND, Circuit Judge.

This is an appeal from a judgment entered upon a verdict, holding the defendant, O'Brien, liable for a collision between a motor car which he was driving and another car, driven by one Wilson, upon a little travelled country road in Vermont. The plaintiff was a passenger in O'Brien's car, and her right of action for injuries depends upon the 'Guest-Occupant' law of Vermont (Public Laws of Vermont Sec. 5113), by which the operator of a motor is not liable for injuries to 'any occupant of the same' unless the operator receives pay for carrying the occupant, 'or unless such injuries are caused by the gross or wilful negligence of the operator'. The only point we shall consider is whether the evidence of the defendant's 'gross * * * negligence' was enough to support a verdict. The collision happened just south of a covered bridge crossing a small river running east and west; O'Brien was going north, Wilson south, and the cars came together about twenty feet beyond the south end of the bridge. The jury was justified in finding that O'Brien had been clear over on the west side of the road, until he saw Wilson's car come out from the bridge. Coming from the south the road runs almost east for some distance, and then turns on a radius of about sixty feet through an angle of about 70 degrees to enter the bridge. The road is seventeen feet wide at the widest part of the turn and fourteen or fifteen elsewhere, and is protected by a fence because the ground slopes off sharply to the east. There is a down grade of about nine degrees approaching the bridge from the south, and the view to the left is somewhat obstructed until one gets fairly on the turn. O'Brien's car was going at only fifteen miles an hour (as to this there was curiously enough no dispute) but he did not blow his horn, or do anything to avoid collision until he saw Wilson emerge, when he swung sharply to the right so that the collision was between the left fore wheels of each car. Wilson swore that he was moving at two miles an hour, and that he blew a horn before entering the bridge. Any such speed is of course incredible, but the issue is not important, as his speed does not count in determining O'Brien's negligence. Only five or six families lived on the road, and the wheel tracks at the turn showed that it had been the custom to take it on the left side in order to make the turn more easily.

The degree of care demanded of a person by an occasion is the resultant of three factors: the likelihood that his conduct will injure others, taken with the

> **FYI**
>
> A guest-occupant law or a guest statute is one that typically bars passengers in a non-commercial vehicle from suing the driver for injuries caused by the driver's ordinary negligence.

seriousness of the injury if it happens, and balanced against the interest which he must sacrifice to avoid the risk. All these are practically not susceptible of any quantitative estimate, and the second two are generally not so, even theoretically. For this reason a solution always involves some preference, or choice between . . . incommensurables, and it is consigned to a jury because their decision is thought most likely to accord with commonly accepted standards, real or fancied. A statute like that before us presupposes that the answer to the general question has been against the defendant (that is, that his conduct has been inexcusable) but it imposes upon his liability a condition which cannot even be described in quantitative terms; not only must the interest which he would have had to sacrifice be less than the risk to which he subjects others, but it must so far fail to match that risk that some opprobrium or reproach attaches to him. . . .

It is of course always careless to drive on the wrong side of the road on a curve, where one cannot see ahead; it is careless to do so even at low a speed as fifteen miles; another car may be coming fast, and a collision may be inescapable. But few who have driven a motor, do not at times take the chance, when going slowly on a back country road; most of us rely more than we should upon our alertness to become aware of, and our deftness to avert, oncoming danger; we should not, but we do; and in the hierarchy of guilt such carelessness does not stand high. O'Brien conceded that he knew the spot well and that it ought to be taken at a 'snail's pace' if another car was coming; what he did was to **assume the risk**, and it was not a great one. Nor was he so totally without excuse as in other situations which themselves would be border-line- a car climbing a hill on the wrong side, for example, which has no reason not to keep to the right; O'Brien was in a position where it saved him trouble to cut the curve. Had he been driving twice as fast, or on a much travelled highway, we might think otherwise; but on that road and at that speed it seems to us that his fault was only a routine dereliction, not grave enough to fall within the statute. It is plain from the Vermont decisions that we cannot properly devolve the entire responsibility for a decision upon a jury.

. . . .

Judgment reversed; complaint dismissed.

Points for Discussion

1. In *Carroll Towing,* Judge Learned Hand reasoned that the owner's duty depended on whether (1) the burden of adequate precautions was less than (2) the probability of the vessel breaking away from her moorings multiplied by (3) the gravity of the resulting injury. Stated algebraically, the owner's liability depended upon whether B<PL.

2. Discussing Judge Hand's negligence formula, Judge Richard A. Posner commented that "Hand was adumbrating, perhaps unwittingly, an economic meaning of negligence. Discounting (multiplying) the cost of an accident if it occurs by the probability of occurrence yields a measure of the economic benefit to be anticipated from incurring the costs necessary to prevent the accident." Richard A. Posner, *A Theory of Negligence*, 1 JOURNAL OF LEGAL STUDIES 29, 32 (1972).

3. In *Conway*, decided seven years before *Carroll Towing*, Judge Hand stated that the degree of care demanded of a person is measured by (1) the likelihood that others would be injured by his conduct and (2) the seriousness of injury if the conduct occurs (3) balanced against the interest the person would have to sacrifice to avoid the risk. Note that in *Conway* Judge Hand comments that these factors "are practically not susceptible of any quantitative estimate, and the second two are generally not so, even theoretically." Is this aspect of *Conway* consistent with Judge Hand's algebraic approach in *Carroll Towing*? Which explanation of when a duty of care arises in negligence is most helpful?

Hypo 4-1

A is the owner of a strip mine. Part of the strip mine area includes a water-filled quarry (known to many as "the pit") and for a number of years many persons have come from surrounding areas to dive into and swim in the quarry's 35 to 55 feet deep water. Although A knew that the pit was being used in this manner, no signs prohibiting trespassing or warning of the dangers of diving or swimming have ever been posted, nor have any barricades ever been placed around or near the pit. A did consider erecting a six-foot high steel chain-link fence with steel posts set in concrete, at a cost of $15,000 to $20,000. Although he was informed and concluded that the fence would have effectively barred persons from using the pit, A decided against building the fence.

A few weeks after A decided that the fence would not be built, B, a 14-year-old teenager, dove into the pit. His head struck the pit's sand bottom and B's neck was broken; he is now a quadriplegic.

Apply Judge Hand's *Carroll Towing* negligence formula to the foregoing facts. Is B<PL? Did A breach his duty of care (*i.e.*, did A act negligently)? What factors are legally relevant in determining whether A breached the standard of care?

C. Determining a Standard of Care

There are four ways that the standard of care can be established in a negligence action: (1) by determining the conduct of the reasonable prudent person under the facts of the case; (2) by applying a rule of law previously formulated by a binding court; (3) by applying a non-tort specific legislative enactment or administrative regulation; or (4) by applying a legislative enactment or administrative regulation that expressly defines the standard of care in a negligence action. *See* RESTATEMENT (SECOND) OF TORTS § 285 (1965) (How Standard of Conduct is Determined). The materials that follow consider each of these methods in turn.

1. Establishing the Standard of Care by Case Law

> **RESTATEMENT (SECOND) OF TORTS § 285(d) (1965)**
>
> The standard of conduct of a reasonable [person] may be . . . applied to the facts of the case by the trial judge or the jury, if there is no [legislative] enactment, regulation, or [judicial] decision.

a. The Reasonable Prudent Person

Vaughan v. Menlove

Court of Common Pleas
3 Bing. (N.C.) 468, 132 Eng. Rep. 490 (1837)

[The defendant was "possessed of a certain close near to" cottages owned by the plaintiff and also possessed "a certain rick or stack of hay before then heaped, stacked, or put together, and then standing, and being in and upon the said close" of the defendant.]

At the trial it appeared that the rick in question had been made by the Defendant near the boundary of his own premises; that the hay was in such a state when put together, as to give rise to discussions on the probability of fire; that though there were conflicting opinions on the subject, yet during a period of five weeks, the Defendant was repeatedly warned of his peril; that his stock was insured; and that upon one occasion, being advised to take the rick down to avoid all danger, he said "he would chance it." He made an aperture or chimney through the rick; but in spite, or perhaps in consequence of this precaution, the rick at length burst into flames from the spontaneous heating of the materials; the flames communicated to the Defendant's barn and stables, and then to the Plaintiff's cottages, which were entirely destroyed.

A verdict having been found for the Plaintiff, a rule **nisi** for a new trial was obtained, on the ground that the jury should have been directed to consider, not whether the Defendant has been guilty of **gross negligence** with reference to the standard of ordinary prudence, a standard too uncertain to afford any criterion; but whether he had acted **bona fide** to the best of his judgment; if he had, he ought not to be responsible for the misfortune of not possessing the highest order of intelligence. The action under such circumstances, was of the **first impression**.

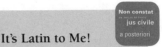

It's Latin to Me!

Nisi is Latin for "unless"; a rule *nisi* is issued when the party adversely affected by a court's ruling has shown cause requiring the withdrawal of the ruling or judgment.

What's That?

Primae impressionis: Latin for "of the first impression." A case of first impression is one presenting a court with a legal issue not previously decided in that jurisdiction.

TINDAL C.J.   I agree that this is a case primae impressionis; but I feel no difficulty in applying to it the principles of law as laid down in other cases of a similar kind. Undoubtedly this is not a case of contract, such as a **bailment** or the like where the **bailee** is responsible in consequence of the remuneration he is to receive: but there is a rule of law which says you must so enjoy your own property as not to injure that of another; and according to that rule the Defendant is liable for the consequence of his own neglect: and though the Defendant did not himself light the fire, yet mediately, he is as much the cause of it as if he had himself put a candle to the rick; for it is well known that hay will ferment and take fire if it be not carefully stacked. It has been decided that if an occupier burns weeds so near the boundary of his own land that damage ensues to the property of his neighbour, he is liable to an action for the amount of injury done, unless the accident were occasioned by a sudden blast which he could not foresee. [C] But put the case of a chemist making experiments with ingredients, singly innocent, but when combined, liable to ignite; if he leaves them together, and injury is thereby occasioned to the property of his neighbour, can any one doubt that an action on the case would lie?

It is contended, however, that the learned Judge was wrong in leaving this to the jury as a case of gross negligence, and that the question of negligence was so mixed up with reference to what would be the conduct of a man of ordinary prudence that the jury might have thought the latter rule by which they were to decide; that such a rule would be too uncertain to act upon; and that the question ought to have been whether the Defendant had acted honestly and bona fide to the best of his own judgment. That, however, would leave so vague a line as afford no rule at all, the degree of judgment belonging to each defendant being infinitely various: and though it has been urged that the care which a prudent man would take, is not an intelligible proposition as a rule of law, yet such has always been the rule adopted in cases of bailment . . . . The care taken by a prudent man has always been the rule laid down; and as to the supposed difficulty of applying it, a jury has always been able to say, whether, taking that rule as their guide, there has been negligence on the occasion in question.

Instead, therefore, of saying that the liability for negligence should be co-extensive with the judgment of each individual, which would be as variable as the length of the foot of each individual, we ought rather to adhere to the rule which requires in all cases a regard to caution such as a man of ordinary prudence would observe. That was in substance the criterion presented to the jury in this case, and therefore the present rule must be discharged.

PARK J. I entirely concur in what has fallen from his Lordship. . . .

. . . Under the circumstances of the case it was proper to leave it to the jury whether with reference to the caution which would have been observed by a man of ordinary prudence, the Defendant has not been guilty of gross negligence. After he had been warned repeatedly during five weeks as to the consequences likely to happen, there is no colour for altering the verdict, unless it were to increase the damages.

GASLEE J. concurred in discharging the rule.

VAUGHAN J. The principle on which this action proceeds, is by no means new. It has been urged that the Defendant in such a case takes no duty on himself; but I do not agree with that position: every one takes upon himself the duty of so dealing with his own property as not to injure the property of others. It was, if any thing, too favourable to the Defendant to leave it to the jury whether he had been guilty of gross negligence; for when the Defendant upon being warned of the consequences likely to ensue from the condition of the rick said, "he would chance it" . . . Here, there was not a single witness whose testimony did not go to establish gross negligence in the Defendant. He had repeated warnings of what was likely to occur, and the whole calamity was occasioned by his procrastination.

Points for Discussion

1. What err by the trial court was corrected by the Court of Common Pleas?

2. How would you explain the legal meaning and significance of a prudent or reasonable man or person to a client sued for allegedly negligent conduct, or to a judge or jury?

3. Who is a, or the, prudent and reasonable person? Consider the following: "In determining what a reasonable and prudent man would do under the circumstances, you will remember that presumably a jury is composed of such reasonable and prudent persons, and you may each ask yourself, Did the defendants do, or fail to do, anything which, under the circumstances, I would not have done or would have done." *Freeman v. Adams*, 63 Cal.App. 225, 218 P. 600 (1923). Do you agree with the court's approach?

4. Is it legally relevant to the negligence action that the defendant had been warned of the consequences of not stacking one's hay properly?

————————————

Restatement (Second) of Torts § 295A (1965)
Custom

In determining whether conduct is negligent, the customs of the community, or of others under like circumstances, are factors to be taken into account, but are not controlling where a reasonable [person] would not follow them.

Restatement (Third) of Torts:
Liability for Physical Harm § 13 (2010)
Custom

(a) An actor's compliance with the custom of the community, or of others in like circumstances, is evidence that the actor's conduct is not negligent but does not preclude a finding of negligence.

(b) An actor's departure from the custom of the community, or of others in like circumstances, in a way that increases risk is evidence of the actor's negligence but does not require a finding of negligence.

Sears, Roebuck and Co. v. Midcap

893 A.2d 542 (Del. 2006)

. . . .

On April 8, 1999, a gas explosion occurred at the Midcap home in Dover, Delaware. Terry Midcap died as a result of that explosion, which demolished the family home and left "a mere hole in the ground." The explosion resulted from a propane leak that originated from a kitchen range that the Midcaps had purchased from Sears in November 1995. Southern States, which was the Midcaps' gas supplier, owned the propane cylinders and the regulator components of the Midcaps' propane system.

FYI

Where two or more causes of action involve the same parties or legal issue, a court may consolidate those actions into one case for purposes of trial and judgment.

Terry Midcap's Estate; Maria Midcap, his widow; and the Midcaps' three daughters, Carla, Sharon and Natalia, filed a survival and wrongful death action in the Superior Court against Sears and Southern States. Allstate Insurance Company, the Midcaps' insurance carrier, also brought a separate **subrogation** action against the defendants. Those actions were consolidated for trial.

The plaintiffs' claim against Southern States was that Southern States had not exercised due care in inspecting the Midcaps' propane supply system. The plaintiffs urged that if such an inspection had occurred, Southern States would have discovered the deficiencies in the Midcaps' system, and specifically, the improper fittings that connected the kitchen range to the propane system. The plaintiffs offered the expert testimony of Alan Bullerdiek to support its negligence claim. The trial court permitted Mr. Bullerdiek to testify, but precluded him from opining that the "GAS Check" program, which was a voluntary inspection program, constituted the relevant standard of care in the propane supply industry.

. . . .

The **standard of care** required of defendants in tort actions is that of a "reasonably prudent" person. The inquiry in all cases is what a reasonable person would have done under the circumstances--a determination that necessarily will depend on the particular facts of each case. The **custom** or practice in a particular industry is **probative** of what conduct is reasonable under the circumstances. In the context of a natural gas company, this Court has previously held that:

The defendant is liable for injuries from gas caused by its negligence, but is not an **insurer**. It is presumed to know the inherent danger presented by gas and is required to exercise a degree of care commensurate with the danger. It is bound to guard against any contingency, combination of circumstances, or accidents which a person of ordinary intelligence would have foreseen as probable to happen. The extent of its duty and the standard of care it must conform to are measured in terms of the **foreseeability** of injury from the situation created by it. Each case is to be decided in the light of its own facts, with due regard to the surrounding circumstances, and whether or not the subsequent act was normal and expectable. But negligence cannot be predicated upon a failure to anticipate extraordinary and unprecedented acts of others.

Here, the plaintiffs urge, the evidence showed that the GAS Check program was a safety procedure that was uniformly accepted and recommended in the gas supply industry, and that therefore, a reasonably prudent propane supplier would have complied with the GAS Check program and conducted periodic checks of the Midcaps' propane system. We conclude that the Superior Court correctly held that Mr. Bullerdiek's opinion that the GAS Check program constituted a standard of care was not admissible, because there was no evidence that that program was a standard adopted by the gas supply industry as a whole.

GAS Check is designed to provide a limited inspection of certain components of a residential gas system, including its connected appliances. The information in the brief submitted by the *amici curiae,* Propane Education and Research Council ("PERC"), shows that GAS Check is a voluntary program that no state or federal agency has yet adopted as mandatory. Moreover, and importantly, the Gas Check program does not specifically recommend when and under what conditions an inspection should be conducted. It is difficult to conclude, therefore, that the program constitutes a "standard" of care in the industry where the suppliers who use the program have implemented it voluntarily and in a variety of different ways. For example, some suppliers (including Southern States) conduct a check when a new customer is added to their service, or when a customer smells a propane odor. Other suppliers offer the inspection as an additional service that a customer may request, sometimes for an additional fee.

Those facts also show that it is not clear how the argued-for "standard" could be defined. How often, for example, should periodic checks occur? The GAS Check program is not standardized. Rather, it is a recommended inspection procedure that suppliers are free to adopt-and modify-as needed. For that reason as well, neither Mr. Bullerdiek nor anyone else could reliably testify that the GAS Check program constitutes a gas supply industry standard. We conclude, therefore, that the Superior Court did not err in excluding his testimony on that issue.

Guaman v. Industry City Management

40 A.D.3d 698, 835 N.Y.S.2d 680 (N.Y.App.Ct. 2007)

In an action to recover damages for personal injuries, the plaintiff appeals, as limited by her brief, from so much of an order of the Supreme Court, Kings County (Bayne, J.), dated December 3, 2005, as granted the motion of the defendant Planned Building Services, Inc., pursuant to CPLR 4401, made at the close of evidence, for **judgment as a matter of law** dismissing the complaint insofar as asserted against it and,

What's That?

A judgment as a matter of law is rendered against a party in a case tried to a jury before or after the jury reaches a verdict on the ground. The judgment is entered by the court where a jury has no legally sufficient basis to find in favor of that party.

in effect, denied that branch of her motion which was for judgment as a matter of law on the issue of liability.

ORDERED that the order is modified, on the law, by deleting the provision thereof granting the motion of the defendant Planned Building Services, Inc., pursuant to CPLR 4401 for judgment as a matter of law dismissing the complaint insofar as asserted against it and substituting therefor a provision denying that motion; as so modified, the order is affirmed insofar as appealed from, with costs to the plaintiff, and the matter is remitted to the Supreme Court, Kings County, for a new trial on the issue of liability as to that defendant.

To be entitled to judgment as a matter of law pursuant to CPLR 4401, a defendant has the burden of showing that there is no rational process by which the jury could find in favor of the plaintiff and against the moving defendant . . . [Cc] The plaintiff's evidence must be accepted as true, and the plaintiff is entitled to every favorable inference which can reasonably be drawn from the evidence presented at trial . . . [C] Here, viewing the evidence in the light most favorable to the plaintiff, and resolving all issues of credibility in her favor, [c] a reasonable juror could have concluded that the defendant Planned Building Services, Inc. (hereinafter PBS), the operator of the subject freight elevator wherein the plaintiff's accident occurred, breached its common-law duty to operate the elevator in a safe manner . . . [C]

Additionally, "[p]roof of a generally accepted practice, custom or usage within a particular trade or industry is admissible as tending to establish a standard of care, and proof of a departure from that general custom or usage may constitute evidence of negligence" . . . [Cc] The plaintiff presented evidence that PBS's use of a freight elevator to transport passengers departed from the generally accepted custom in the elevator industry. Accordingly, the Supreme Court erred in granting

PBS's motion pursuant to CPLR 4401 for judgment as a matter of law dismissing the complaint insofar as asserted against it.

. . . .

Points for Discussion

1. What evidentiary and adjudicatory role should industry custom or practice play in evaluating the reasonableness of a defendant's conduct? Should custom be determinative on the issue of whether the defendant met the standard of care? What positions do the RESTATEMENT (SECOND) and (THIRD) OF TORTS take on this issue?

2. Suppose that an established industry custom is itself unsafe and careless, that a defendant operating within that industry acts in acting in accordance with custom, and that a plaintiff alleges that she has been injured by the defendant's custom-conforming conduct. Can the defendant validly contend that its conduct satisfied the requisite standard of care? How would you analyze and answer that question?

3. In *The T.J. Hooper*, 60 F.2d 737 (2d Cir. 1932), Judge Learned Hand gave this answer to the preceding question: "[I]n most cases reasonable prudence is in fact common prudence; but strictly it is never its measure; a whole calling may have unduly lagged in the adoption of new and available devices. It may never set its own tests, however persuasive be its usages. Courts must in the end say what is required; there are precautions so imperative that even their universal disregard will not excuse their omission."

Cordas v. Peerless Transportation Co.

27 N.Y.S.2d 198 (City Court of New York 1941)

CARLIN, Justice.

This case presents the ordinary man--that problem child of the law--in a most bizarre setting. As a lowly chauffeur in defendant's employ he became in a trice the protagonist in a breach-bating drama with a denouement almost tragic. It appears that a man, whose identity it would be indelicate to divulge was feloniously relieved of his portable goods by two nondescript highwaymen in an alley near 26th Street and Third Avenue, Manhattan; they induced him to relinquish his possessions by a strong argument ad hominem couched in the convincing cant of the criminal and pressed at the point of a most persuasive pistol. Laden with their loot, but not thereby impeded, they took an abrupt departure and he, shuffling off the coil of that discretion which enmeshed him in the alley, quickly gave chase through 26th Street toward 2d Avenue, whither they were resorting 'with expedition swift as thought' for most obvious reasons. Somewhere on that thoroughfare of escape they indulged the stratagem of separation ostensibly to disconcert their pursuer and allay the ardor of his pursuit. He then centered on for capture the man with the pistol whom he saw board defendant's taxicab, which quickly veered south toward 25th Street on 2d Avenue where he saw the chauffeur jump out while the cab, still in motion, continued toward 24th Street; after the chauffeur relieved himself of the cumbersome burden of his fare the latter also is said to have similarly departed from the cab before it reached 24th Street.

The chauffeur's story is substantially the same except that he states that his uninvited guest boarded the cab at 25th Street while it was at a standstill waiting for a less colorful fare; that his 'passenger' immediately advised him 'to stand not upon the order of his going but to go at once' and added finality to his command by an appropriate gesture with a pistol addressed to his sacro iliac. The chauffeur in reluctant acquiescence proceeded about fifteen feet, when his hair, like unto the quills of the fretful porcupine, was made to stand on end by the hue and cry of the man despoiled accompanied by a clamourous concourse of the law-abiding which paced him as he ran; the concatenation of 'stop thief', to which the patter of persistent feet did maddingly beat time, rang in his ears as the pursuing posse all the while gained on the receding cab with its quarry therein contained. The hold-up man sensing his insecurity suggested to the chauffeur that in the event there was the slightest lapse in obedience to his curt command that he, the chauffeur, would suffer the loss of his brains, a prospect as horrible to an humble chauffeur as it undoubtedly would be to one of the intelligentsia. The chauffeur apprehensive of certain dissolution from either Scylla, the pursuers, or Charybdis, the pursued, quickly threw his car out of first speed in which he was proceeding, pulled on the emergency, jammed on his brakes and, although he thinks the motor was still running, swung open the door to his left and jumped out of his car. He confesses that the only act that smacked of intelligence was that by which he jammed the brakes in order to throw off balance the hold-up man who was half-standing and half-sitting with his pistol menacingly poised. Thus abandoning his car and passenger the chauffeur sped toward 26th Street and then turned to look; he saw the cab proceeding south toward 24th Street where it mounted the sidewalk. The plaintiff-mother and her two infant children were there injured by the cab which, at the time, appeared to be also minus its passenger who, it appears, was apprehended in the cellar of a local hospital where he was pointed out to a police officer by a remnant of the posse, hereinbefore mentioned. He did not appear at the trial. The three aforesaid plaintiffs and the husband-father sue the defendant for damages predicating their respective causes of action upon the contention that the chauffeur was negligent in abandoning the cab under the aforesaid circumstances. Fortunately the injuries sustained were comparatively slight.

Negligence has been variously defined but the common legal acceptation is the failure to exercise that care and caution which a reasonable and prudent person ordinarily would exercise under like conditions or circumstances. It has been most authoritatively held that 'negligence in the abstract, apart from things related, is surely not a tort, if indeed it is understandable at all.' Cardozo, C. J., in Palsgraf v. Long Island Railroad Co., 248 N.Y. 339, 345, 162 N.E. 99, 101, 59 A.L.R. 1253. In Steinbrenner v. M. W. Forney Co., 143 App.Div. 73, 127 N.Y.S. 620, 622 it is said, 'The test of actionable negligence is what reasonably prudent men would have done under the same circumstances'; Connell v. New York Central & Hudson River Railroad Co., 144 App.Div. 664, 129 N.Y.S. 666, 669, holds that actionable negligence must be predicated upon 'a breach of duty to the plaintiff. Negligence is 'not absolute or intrinsic,' but 'is always relevant to some circumstances of time, place or person." In slight paraphrase of the world's first bard it may be truly observed that the expedition of the chauffeur's violent love of his own security outran the pauser, reason, when he was suddenly confronted with unusual emergency which 'took his reason prisoner'. The learned attorney for the plaintiffs concedes that the chauffeur acted in an emergency but claims a right to recovery upon the following proposition taken verbatim from his brief: 'It is respectfully submitted that the value of the interests of the public at large to be immune from being injured by a dangerous instrumentality such as a car unattended while in motion is very superior to the right of a driver of a motor vehicle to abandon same while it is in motion even when acting under the belief that his life is in danger and by abandoning same he will save his life'.

To hold thus under the facts adduced herein would be tantamount to a repeal by implication of the primal law of nature written in indelible characters upon the fleshy tablets of sentient creation by the Almighty Law-giver, 'the supernal Judge who sits on high'. There are those who stem the turbulent current for bubble fame, or who bridge the yawning chasm with a leap for the leap's sake or who 'outstare the sternest eyes that look outbrave the heart most daring on the earth, pluck the young sucking cubs from the she-bear, yea, mock the lion when he roars for prey' to win a fair lady and these are the admiration of the generality of men; but they are made of sterner stuff than the ordinary man upon whom the law places no duty of emulation. The law would indeed be fond if it imposed upon the ordinary man the obligation to so demean himself when suddenly confronted with a danger, not of his creation, disregarding the likelihood that such a contingency may darken the intellect and palsy the will of the common legion of the earth, the fraternity of ordinary men,-whose acts or omissions under certain conditions or circumstances make the yardstick by which the law measures culpability or innocense, negligence or care. If a person is placed in a sudden peril from which death might ensue, the law does not impel another to the rescue of the person endangered nor does it condemn him for his unmoral failure to rescue when he can; this is in recognition of the immutable law written in frail flesh.

Returning to our chauffeur. If the philosophic Horatio and the martial companions of his watch were 'distilled almost to jelly with the act of fear' when they beheld 'in the dead vast and middle of the night' the disembodied spirit of Hamlet's father stalk majestically by 'with a countenance more in sorrow than in anger' was not the chauffeur, though unacquainted with the example of these eminent men-at-arms, more amply justified in his fearsome reactions when he was more palpably confronted by a thing of flesh and blood bearing in its hand an engine of destruction which depended for its lethal purpose upon the quiver of a hair? When Macbeth was cross-examined by Macduff as to any reason he could advance for his sudden despatch of Duncan's grooms he said in plausible answer 'Who can be wise, amazed, temperate and furious, loyal and neutral, in a moment? No man'. . . .

Kolanka v. Erie Railroad Co., 215 App.Div. 82, 86, 212 N.Y.S. 714, 717, says: 'The law in this state does not hold one in an emergency to the exercise of that mature judgment required of him under circumstances where he has an opportunity for deliberate action. He is not required to exercise unerring judgment, which would be expected of him, were he not confronted with an emergency requiring prompt action'. The circumstances provide the foil by which the act is brought into relief to determine whether it is or is not negligent. If under normal circumstances an act is done which might be considered negligent it does not follow as a corollary that a similar act is negligent if performed by a person acting under an emergency, not of his own making, in which he suddenly is faced with a patent danger with a moment left to adopt a means of extrication.

The chauffeur--the ordinary man in this case--acted in a split second in a most harrowing experience. To call him negligent would be to brand him coward; the court does not do so in spite of what those swaggering heroes, 'whose valor plucks dead lions by the beard', may bluster to the contrary. The court is loathe to see the plaintiffs go without recovery even though their damages were slight, but cannot hold the defendant liable upon the facts adduced at the trial. Motions, upon which decision was reserved, to dismiss the complaint are granted with **exceptions** to plaintiffs. Judgment for defendant against plaintiffs dismissing their complaint upon the merits.

Points for Discussion

1. Do you agree with the court's judgment dismissing the plaintiffs' complaint?

2. What standard of care is expected and required of a person faced with a sudden emergency? As noted in the *Cordas* court's decision, *Kolanka v. Erie Railroad* instructed that the law in New York did "not hold one in an emergency to the exercise of that mature judgment required of him under circumstances where he has an opportunity for deliberate action."

3. For an interesting discussion and application of the **sudden emergency doctrine**, *see* Cook v. Thomas, 25 Wis.2d 467 (1964).

Roberts v. State of Louisiana

396 So.2d 566 (La. Ct. App. 1981)

LABORDE, Judge.

In this tort suit, William C. Roberts sued to recover damages for injuries he sustained in an accident in the lobby of the U. S. Post Office Building in Alexandria, Louisiana. Roberts fell after being bumped into by Mike Burson, the blind operator of the concession stand located in the building.

Plaintiff sued the State of Louisiana, through the Louisiana Health and Human Resources Administration, advancing two theories of liability: respondeat superior and negligent failure by the State to properly supervise and oversee the safe operation of the concession stand. The stand's blind operator, Mike Burson, is not a party to this suit although he is charged with negligence.

> **It's Latin to Me!**
>
> Non constat
> jus civile
> a posteriori
>
> *Respondeat superior*: Latin for "let the superior make answer." In the employment context the term refers to an employer's responsibility and liability for the wrongful actions of its employees acting within the scope of their employment.

The trial court [dismissed] plaintiff's suit . . . holding that there is no respondeat superior liability without an employer-employee relationship and that there is no negligence liability without a cause in fact showing.

We affirm the trial court's decision for the reasons which follow.

On September 1, 1977, at about 12:45 in the afternoon, operator Mike Burson left his concession stand to go to the men's bathroom located in the building. As he was walking down the hall, he bumped into plaintiff who fell to the floor and injured his hip. Plaintiff was 75 years old, stood 5'6 and weighed approximately 100 pounds. Burson, on the other hand, was 25 to 26 years old, stood approximately 6' and weighed 165 pounds.

At the time of the incident, Burson was not using a cane nor was he utilizing the technique of walking with his arm or hand in front of him.

Even though Burson was not joined as a defendant, his negligence or lack thereof is crucial to a determination of the State's liability. Because of its importance, we begin with it.

Plaintiff contends that operator Mike Burson traversed the area from his concession stand to the men's bathroom in a negligent manner. To be more specific, he focuses on the operator's failure to use his cane even though he had it with him in his concession stand.

In determining an actor's negligence, various courts have imposed differing standards of care to which handicapped persons are expected to perform. Professor William L. Prosser expresses one generally recognized modern standard of care as follows:

> "As to his physical characteristics, the reasonable man may be said to be identical with the actor. The man who is blind ... is entitled to live in the world and to have allowance made by others for his disability, and he cannot be required to do the impossible by conforming to physical standards which he cannot meet ... At the same time, the conduct of the handicapped individual must be reasonable in the light of his knowledge of his infirmity, which is treated merely as one of the circumstances under which he acts ... It is sometimes said that a blind man must use a greater degree of care than one who can see; but it is now generally agreed that as a fixed rule this is inaccurate, and that the correct statement is merely that he must take the precautions, be they more or less, which the ordinary reasonable man would take if he were blind." W. Prosser, The Law of Torts, Section 32, at Page 151-52 (4th ed. 1971).

A careful review of the record in this instance reveals that Burson was acting as a reasonably prudent blind person would under these particular circumstances.

Mike Burson is totally blind. Since 1974, he has operated the concession stand located in the lobby of the post office building. It is one of twenty-three vending stands operated by blind persons under a program funded by the federal government and implemented by the State through the Blind Services Division of the Department of Health and Human Resources. Burson hired no employees, choosing instead to operate his stand on his own.

Prior to running the vending stand in Alexandria, Burson attended Arkansas Enterprises for the blind where he received mobility training. In 1972, he took a refresher course in mobility followed by a course on vending stand training. In that same year, he operated a concession stand in Shreveport, his first under the vending stand program. He later operated a stand at Centenary before going to Alexandria in 1974 to take up operations there.

On the date of the incident in question, Mike Burson testified that he left his concession stand and was on his way to the men's bathroom when he bumped into plaintiff. He, without hesitancy, admitted that at the time he was not using his cane, explaining that he relies on his facial sense which he feels is an adequate technique for short trips inside the familiar building. Burson testified that he does use a cane to get to and from work.

Plaintiff makes much of Burson's failure to use a cane when traversing the halls of the post office building. Yet, our review of the testimony received at trial indicates that it is not uncommon for blind people to rely on other techniques when moving around in a familiar setting. For example George Marzloff, the director of the Division of Blind Services, testified that he can recommend to the blind operators that they should use a cane but he knows that when they are in a setting in which they are comfortable, he would say that nine out of ten will not use a cane and in his personal opinion, if the operator is in a relatively busy area, the cane can be more of a hazard than an asset. Mr. Marzloff further testified that he felt a reasonably functioning blind person would learn his way around his work setting as he does around his home so that he could get around without a cane. Mr. Marzloff added that he has several blind people working in his office, none of whom use a cane inside that facility.

Mr. Marzloff's testimony is similar to testimony received from Guy DiCharry, a blind business enterprise counselor with the Blind Services Division. As part of his responsibilities Mr. DiCharry supervised the Alexandria vending stand providing him with an opportunity to observe Mike Burson in a work setting. He testified that Burson knew his way around the building pretty well and that like most of his other blind operators, he did not use a cane on short trips within the building. He added that he discussed the use of a cane on such short trips as these with some of his other blind operators but they took offense to his suggestions, explaining that it was their choice.

The only testimony in the record that suggests that Burson traversed the halls in a negligent manner was that elicited from plaintiff's expert witness, William

Henry Jacobson. Jacobson is an instructor in peripathology, which he explained as the science of movement within the surroundings by visually impaired individuals. Jacobson, admitting that he conducted no study or examination of Mike Burson's mobility skills and that he was unfamiliar with the State's vending program, nonetheless testified that he would require a blind person to use a cane in traversing the areas outside the concession stand. He added that a totally blind individual probably should use a cane under any situation where there in an unfamiliar environment or where a familiar environment involves a change, whether it be people moving through that environment or strangers moving through that environment or just a heavy traffic within that environment.

When cross examined however, Jacobson testified:

"Q. Now, do you, in instructing blind people on their mobility skills, do you tell them to use their own judgment in which type of mobility assistance technique they're to employ?

A. Yes I do.

Q. Do you think that three (3) years is a long enough period for a person to become acquainted with an environment that he might be working with?

A. Yes I do.

Q. So you think that after a period of three (3) years an individual would probably, if he is normal ... has normal mobility skills for a blind person, would have enough adjustment time to be ... to call that environment familiar?

A. Yes.

Q. That's not including the fact that there may be people in and out of the building?

A. Right.

Q. Now is it possible that if he's familiar with the sounds of the people inside a building that he may even at some point in time become so familiar with the people in an area, regular customers or what not that you could say that the environment was familiar, including the fact that there are people there, is that possible?

A. Uh ... I would hesitate to say that, in a public facility where we could not ... uh ... control strangers coming in.

Q. Well, let's say that a business has a particular group of clients that are always there, perhaps on a daily or weekly basis. Now you've stated that a blind person sharpens his auditory skills in order to help him articulate in an area?

A. With instruction, yes.

Q. Right. Isn't is possible that if he can rely on a fixed travel of a fixed type and number of persons that it's possible that that is a familiar environment even though there are people there?

A. Only if they were the same people all the time and they know him, yes."

Upon our review of the record, we feel that plaintiff has failed to show that Burson was negligent. Burson testified that he was very familiar with his surroundings, having worked there for three and a half years. He had special mobility training and his reports introduced into evidence indicate good mobility skills. He explained his decision to rely on his facial sense instead of his cane for these short trips in a manner which convinces us that it was a reasoned decision. Not only was Burson's explanation adequate, there was additional testimony from other persons indicating that such a decision is not an unreasonable one. Also important is the total lack of any evidence in the record showing that at the time of the incident, Burson engaged in any acts which may be characterized as negligence on his part. For example, there is nothing showing that Burson was walking too fast, not paying attention, et cetera. Under all of these circumstances, we conclude that Mike Burson was not negligent.

. . . .

For the above and foregoing reasons, the judgment of the trial court dismissing plaintiff's claims against defendant is affirmed and all costs of this appeal are assessed against the plaintiff-appellant.

AFFIRMED.

Points for Discussion

1. The court concludes that Mike Burson acted as the reasonably blind person would act under similar circumstances. Do you agree?

2. How did the court evaluate the testimony of the plaintiff's expert witness?

3. The Restatement provides that where an "actor is ill or otherwise physically disabled, the standard of conduct to which he must conform to avoid being negligent is that of a reasonable man under like disability." RESTATEMENT (SECOND) OF TORTS § 283C (1965). Do you agree or disagree with this approach?

4. Describe the standard of care and reasonable formulation for a person who is: deaf; narcoleptic; epileptic; an alcoholic; a narcotic user; a narcotic addict.

5. Is the principle of law applied in *Roberts* inconsistent with the decision in *Vaughan v. Menlove, supra*? How can *Roberts* and *Vaughan* be reconciled, if at all?

Breunig v. American Family Insurance Company

45 Wis.2d 536, 173 N.W.2d 619 (1970)

This is an action by Phillip A. Breunig to recover damages for personal injuries which he received when his truck was struck by an automobile driven by Erma Veith and insured by the defendant American Family Insurance Company (Insurance Company). The accident happened about 7:00 o'clock in the morning of January 28, 1966, on highway 19 a mile west of Sun Prairie, while Mrs. Veith was returning home from taking her husband to work. Mrs. Veith's car was proceeding west in the eastbound lane and struck the left side of the plaintiff's car near its rear end while Breunig was attempting to get off the road to his right and avoid a head-on collision.

The Insurance Company alleged Erma Veith was not negligent because just prior to the collision she suddenly and without warning was seized with a mental aberration or delusion which rendered her unable to operate the automobile with her conscious mind.

The jury returned a verdict finding her causally negligent on the theory she had knowledge or forewarning of her mental delusions or disability. The jury also found Breunig's damages to be $10,000. The court, on motions after verdict, reduced the amount of damages to $7,000, approved the verdict's finding of negligence, and gave Breunig the option of a new trial or the lower amount of damages. Breunig elected to accept the lower amount and judgment was accordingly entered. The defendant insurance company appeals.

. . . .

HALLOWS, Chief Justice.

There is no question that Erma Veith was subject at the time of the accident to an insane delusion which directly affected her ability to operate her car in an ordinarily prudent manner and caused the accident. The specific question considered by the jury under the negligence inquiry was whether she had such foreknowledge of her susceptibility to such a mental aberration, delusion or hallucination as to make her negligent in driving a car at all under such conditions.

At the trial Erma Veith testified she could not remember all the circumstances of the accident and this was confirmed by her psychiatrist who testified this loss of memory was due to his treatment of Erma Veith for her mental illness. This expert also testified to what Erma Veith had told him but could no longer recall. The evidence established that Mrs. Veith, while returning home after taking her husband to work, saw a white light on the back of a car ahead of her. She followed this light for three or four blocks. Mrs. Veith did not remember anything else except landing in a field, lying on the side of the road and people talking. She recalled awaking in the hospital.

The psychiatrist testified Mrs. Veith told him she was driving on a road when she believed that God was taking ahold of the steering wheel and was directing her car. She saw the truck coming and stepped on the gas in order to become air-borne because she knew she could fly because Batman does it. To her surprise she was not air-borne before striking the truck but after the impact she was flying.

Actually, Mrs. Veith's car continued west on highway 19 for about a mile. The road was straight for this distance and then made a gradual turn to the right. At this turn her car left the road in a straight line, negotiated a deep ditch and came to rest in a cornfield. When a traffic officer came to the car to investigate the accident, he found Mrs. Veith sitting behind the wheel looking off into space. He could not get a statement of any kind from her. She was taken to the Methodist Hospital and later transferred to the psychiatric ward of the Madison General Hospital.

The psychiatrist testified Erma Veith was suffering from 'schizophrenic reaction, paranoid type, acute.'[1] He stated that from the time Mrs. Veith commenced following the car with the white light and ending with the stopping of her vehicle

---

1 In layman's language, the doctor explained: "The schizophrenic reaction is a thinking disorder of a severe type usually implying disorientation with the world. Usually implying a break with reality. The paranoid type is a subdivision of the thinking disorder in which one perceives oneself either as very powerful or being persecuted or being attacked by other people. And acute implies that the rapidity of the onset of the illness, the speed of onset is meant by acute."

in the cornfield, she was not able to operate the vehicle with her conscious mind and that she had no knowledge or forewarning that such illness or disability would likely occur.

The Insurance Company argues Erma Veith was not negligent as a matter of law because there is no evidence upon which the jury could find that she had knowledge or warning or should have reasonably foreseen that she might be subject to a mental delusion which would suddenly cause her to lose control of the car. Plaintiff argues there was such evidence of forewarning and also suggests Erma Veith should be liable because **insanity** should not be a defense in negligence cases.

> **FYI**
>
> The issue of insanity as a defense to a crime committed by a defendant is addressed in the criminal law course

The case was tried on the theory that some forms of insanity are a defense to and preclude liability for negligence under the doctrine of Theisen v. Milwaukee Automobile Mut. Ins. Co. (1962), 18 Wis.2d 91, 118 N.W.2d 140, 119 N.W.2d 393. We agree. Not all types of insanity vitiate responsibility for a negligent tort. The question of liability in every case must depend upon the kind and nature of the insanity. The effect of the mental illness or mental hallucinations or disorder must be such as to affect the person's ability to understand and appreciate the duty which rests upon him to drive his car with ordinary care, or if the insanity does not affect such understanding and appreciation, it must affect his ability to control his car in an ordinarily prudent manner. And in addition, there must be an absence of notice of forewarning to the person that he may be suddenly subject to such a type of insanity or mental illness.

In *Theisen* we recognized one was not negligent if he was unable to conform his conduct through no fault of his own but held a sleeping driver negligent as a matter of law because one is always given conscious warnings of drowsiness and if a person does not heed such warnings and continues to drive his car, he is negligent for continuing to drive under such conditions. But we distinguished those exceptional cases of loss of consciousness resulting from injury inflicted by an outside force, or fainting, or heart attack, or epileptic seizure, or other illness which suddenly incapacitates the driver of an automobile when the occurrence of such disability is not attended with sufficient warning or should not have been reasonably foreseen.

. . . .

The policy basis of holding a permanently insane person liable for his tort is: (1) Where one of two innocent persons must suffer a loss it should be borne by the one who occasioned it; (2) to induce those interested in the estate of the insane person (if he has one) to restrain and control him; and (3) the fear an insanity defense would lead to false claims of insanity to avoid liability. . . .

. . . .

. . . The cases holding an insane person liable for his torts have generally dealt with pre-existing insanity of a permanent nature and the question here presented was neither discussed nor decided. The plaintiff cites Sforza v. Green Bus Lines (1934), 150 Misc. 180, 268 N.Y.S. 446; Shapiro v. Tchernowitz (1956), 3 Misc.2d 617, 115 N.Y.S.2d 1011; Johnson v. Lombotte (1961), 147 Colo. 203, 363 P.2d 165, for holding insanity is not a defense in negligence cases. *Sforza* and *Shapiro* are New York trial court decisions which do not discuss the question here presented and are unconvincing. In *Johnson*, the defendant was under observation by order of the county court and was being treated in a hospital for 'chronic schizophrenic state of paranoid type.' On the day in question, she wanted to leave the hospital and escaped therefrom and found an automobile standing on a street with its motor running a few blocks from the hospital. She got into the car and drove off, having little or no control of the car. She soon collided with the plaintiff. Later she was adjudged mentally incompetent and committed to a state hospital. Johnson is not a case of sudden mental seizure with no forewarning. The defendant knew she was being treated for a mental disorder and hence would not have come under the nonliability rule herein stated.

We think the statement that insanity is no defense is too broad when it is applied to a negligence case where the driver is suddenly overcome without forewarning by a mental disability or disorder which incapacitates him from conforming his conduct to the standards of a reasonable man under like circumstances. These are rare cases indeed, but their rarity is no reason for overlooking their existence and the justification which is the basis of the whole doctrine of liability for negligence, i.e., that it is unjust to hold a man responsible for his conduct which he is incapable of avoiding and which incapability was unknown to him prior to the accident.

. . . All we hold is that a sudden mental incapacity equivalent in its effect to such physical causes as a sudden heart attack, epileptic seizure, stroke, or fainting should be treated alike and not under the general rule of insanity.

An interesting case holding this view in Canada is Buckley & Toronto Transp. Comm'n v. Smith Transport, Ltd., 1946 Ont.Rep. 798, 4 Dom.L.Rep. 721, which is almost identical on the facts with the case at bar. There, the court found no negligence when a truck driver was overcome by a sudden insane delusion that his truck was being operated by remote control of his employer and as a result he was in fact helpless to avert a collision.

The Insurance Company argues that since the psychiatrist was the only **expert witness** who testified concerning the mental disability of Mrs. Veith and the lack of forewarning that as a matter of law there was no forewarning and she could not be held negligent; and the trial court should have so held. While there was testimony of friends indicating she was normal for some months prior to the accident, the psychiatrist testifies the origin of her mental illness appeared in August, 1965, prior to the accident. In that month Mrs. Veith visited the Necedah Shrine where she was told the Blessed Virgin had sent her to the shrine. She was told to pray for survival. Since that time she felt it had been revealed to her the end of the world was coming and that she was picked by God to survive. Later she had visions of God judging people and sentencing them to Heaven or Hell; she thought Batman was good and was trying to help save the world and her husband was possessed of the devil. Mrs. Veith told her daughter about her visions.

The question is whether she had warning or knowledge which would reasonably lead her to believe that hallucinations would occur and be such as to affect her driving an automobile. Even though the doctor's testimony is uncontradicted, it need not be accepted by the jury. It is an expert's opinion but it is not conclusive. It is for the jury to decide whether the facts underpinning an expert opinion are true. [Cc] The jury could find that a woman, who believed she had a special relationship to God and was the chosen one to survive the end of the world, could believe that God would take over the direction of her life to the extent of driving her car. Since these mental aberrations were not constant, the jury could infer she had knowledge of her condition and the likelihood of a hallucination just as one who has knowledge of a heart condition knows the possibility of an attack. While the evidence may not be strong upon which to base an inference, especially in view of the fact that two jurors dissented on this verdict and expressly stated they could find no evidence of forewarning, nevertheless, the evidence to sustain the verdict of the jury need not constitute the great weight and clear preponderance.

. . . .

Judgment affirmed.

Points for Discussion

1. What did the court hold?

2. The Restatement provides that an individual's "insanity or other mental deficiency does not relieve the actor from liability for conduct which does not conform to the standard of a reasonable man under like circumstances." RESTATEMENT (SECOND) OF TORTS § 283B (1965).

3. Why hold persons who are insane or who have mental deficiencies to the same standard as all other persons? What legal and social policies are furthered by this approach? Consider the following: "Is a victim any less entitled to compensation for his loss because of the mental deficiencies of his tortfeasor? We believe that the answer is no, and the tort law as it stands has long served to accommodate that principle. This view does not penalize the mentally incompetent; it merely places them on a par with the rest of society in terms of responsibility for their wrongful acts." Goff v. Taylor, 708 S.W.2d 113 (1986). Your reaction?

Gould v. American Family Mutual Insurance Co.

198 Wis.2d 450, 543 N.W.2d 282 (1996)

BRADLEY, Justice.

Both the plaintiffs, Sheri and Scott Gould, and the defendant, American Family Mutual Insurance Company, seek review of a court of appeals' decision which reversed and remanded a judgment of the Circuit Court of St. Croix County, Eric J. Lundell, Judge. The judgment imposed liability against American Family for personal injuries caused by its insured, Roland Monicken, who was institutionalized suffering from Alzheimer's disease. The Goulds assert that the court of appeals erred by abandoning the objective reasonable person standard and adopting a subjective mental incapacity defense in negligence cases. American Family challenges the need for a remand.

While we affirm the court of appeals' reversal of the judgment, we do so on other grounds. We hold that an individual institutionalized, as here, with a mental disability, and who does not have the capacity to control or appreciate his or her conduct cannot be liable for injuries caused to caretakers who are employed for financial compensation. Because the Goulds, in essence, admit that it would be impossible to rebut the evidence of Monicken's incapacity, we reverse the part of the court of appeals' decision remanding the case to the trial court for a determination of Monicken's capacity.

Monicken was diagnosed with Alzheimer's disease after displaying bizarre and irrational behavior. As a result of his deteriorating condition, his family was later forced to admit him to the St. Croix Health Care Center. Sheri Gould was the head nurse of the center's dementia unit and took care of him on several occasions.

Monicken's records from St. Croix indicate that he was often disoriented, resistant to care, and occasionally combative. When not physically restrained, he often went into other patients' rooms and sometimes resisted being removed by staff. On one such occasion, Gould attempted to redirect Monicken to his own room by touching him on the elbow. She sustained personal injuries when Monicken responded by knocking her to the floor.

Gould and her husband brought suit against Monicken and his insurer, American Family. American Family admitted coverage and filed a motion for **summary judgment**, arguing that Monicken was incapable of negligence as a matter of law due to his lack of mental capacity. An affidavit of Monicken's treating psychiatrist filed in

What's That?

A summary judgment for either the plaintiff or the defendant is granted when there is no genuine issue of material fact to submit to the fact-finder.

support of the motion stated that Monicken was unable to appreciate the consequences of his acts or to control his behavior. The trial court denied American Family's summary judgment motion and the liability portion of the bifurcated trial was tried to a jury.

FYI

Birfucated trials are separated into two phases or stages. In the first phase, the question whether the defendant is liable is answered. If that question is answered in the affirmative, the proceedings move to the next stage in which the amount of damages is determined.

After presenting its case, American Family proposed giving instructions and a special verdict that directed the jury to decide, as a threshold question of law, whether Monicken had the mental capacity to understand and appreciate the duty to act with reasonable care at the time of the incident based on his Alzheimer's disease. The trial court denied this request. Pursuant to Wis JI-Civil 1021, the court instructed the jury to disregard any evidence related to Monicken's mental condition and to determine his negligence under the objective reasonable person standard. The jury found Monicken totally negligent and a judgment of liability was entered against American Family.

The court of appeals granted American Family's interlocutory appeal and reversed the judgment, holding that "a person may not be held civilly liable where a mental condition deprives that person of the ability to control his or her conduct." [C] The court remanded the case "for a determination of whether there is a disputed issue of material fact as to whether Monicken's mental condition prevented him from controlling or appreciating the consequences of his conduct." [C]

Both the Goulds and American Family petitioned this court for review. The Goulds argue that the court of appeals abandoned clear, long-standing precedent in determining that mental disability may constitute a defense to negligence. American Family agrees with the court of appeals' holding, but petitioned for cross review to reverse the court's remand mandate. American Family asserts that a remand is unnecessary because Monicken's mental incapacity was virtually conceded at trial.

It is a widely accepted rule in most American jurisdictions that mentally disabled adults are held responsible for the torts they commit regardless of their capacity to comprehend their actions; they are held to an objective reasonable person standard. *See generally,* RESTATEMENT (SECOND) OF TORTS § 283B (1965); W. Page Keeton et al., *Prosser and Keeton on the Law of Torts,* § 135 (1984). Legal scholars trace the origins of this rule to an English trespass case decided in 1616, at a time when **strict liability** controlled. [C]

When fault-based liability replaced strict liability, American courts in **common law** jurisdictions identified this as a question of public policy and maintained the rule imposing liability on the mentally disabled. Although early case law suggested that Wisconsin followed this trend, this court specifically adopted the common law rule and the public policy justifications behind it in *German Mut. Fire Ins. Soc'y v. Meyer,* 218 Wis. 381, 385, 261 N.W. 211 (1935).

In *Meyer,* the defendant was criminally charged with arson to a barn but was committed to a mental hospital after he was found to be insane. In the civil claim filed by the insurer who covered the loss, the defendant pled his insanity as a defense. [C] The court primarily relied on cases from other jurisdictions to conclude that insanity was not a defense for tort liability. [C]

In doing so the court quoted with approval the following statement of the general rule and public policy rationale behind it:

It is the well settled rule that a person *non compos mentis* is liable in damages to one injured by reason of a tort committed by him unless evil intent or express malice constitutes an essential

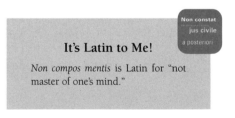

It's Latin to Me!

Non compos mentis is Latin for "not master of one's mind."

element in the plaintiff's recovery. This rule is usually considered to be based on the principle that where a loss must be borne by one of two innocent persons, it shall be borne by him who occasioned it, and it has also been held that public policy requires the enforcement of the liability in order that those interested in the estate of the insane person, as relatives or otherwise, may be under inducement to restrain him and that tort-feasors may not simulate or pretend insanity to defend their wrongful acts causing damage to others....

[C]

This court did not have occasion to address the issue again until *Breunig v. American Family Ins. Co.,* 45 Wis.2d 536, 173 N.W.2d 619 (1970). In *Breunig,* Erma Veith was overcome with a mental delusion while driving and crossed the center line of a roadway, striking the plaintiff's vehicle. The plaintiff sued Veith's automobile liability insurer, and a jury returned a verdict finding her causally negligent on the theory that she had knowledge or forewarning of her mental delusions. [C]

On appeal, the insurer argued that Veith could not be negligent as a matter of law because she was unable to drive with a conscious mind based on the sudden mental delusion. This court created a limited exception to the common law rule, holding that insanity could be a defense in the rare case "where the [person] is suddenly overcome without forewarning by a mental disability or disorder which incapacitates him from conforming his conduct to the standards of a reasonable man under like circumstances." [C] However, because this court concluded that there was sufficient evidence for the jury to find that Veith had forewarning of the mental delusions, she was not entitled to use her condition as a defense. [C]

> **FYI**
> *Dicta,* also sometimes termed as *gratis dicta* or *obiter dicta,* means something said in passing and usually refers to a court's remarks that are unnecessary to the legal question presented or a court stating a legal principle more broadly than necessary.

The court of appeals in the present case relied on expansive **dicta** in *Breunig* to hold that *Breunig* overruled *Meyer.* It interpreted *Breunig* as a turning point in the law. [C] We disagree. In contrast to the broad dicta found in *Breunig,* the actual holding was very limited:

> All we hold is that a sudden mental incapacity equivalent in its effect to such physical causes as a sudden heart attack, epileptic seizure, stroke, or fainting should be treated alike and not under the general rule of insanity.

[C] *Breunig* was not a turning point in the development of the common law, but rather it was a limited exception to the *Meyer* rule based on sudden mental disability.

The court of appeals erroneously perceived the underlying premise of *Breunig* to be that a person should not be held negligent where a mental disability prevents that person from controlling his or her conduct. [C] By limiting its holding to cases of sudden mental disability, the *Breunig* court chose not to adopt that broad premise. We also decline to do so.

We are concerned that the adoption of the premise, as set forth by the court of appeals, would entail serious administrative difficulties. Mental impairments and emotional disorders come in infinite types and degrees. As the American Law Institute recognized in its Restatement of Torts, a legitimate concern in formulating a test for mentally disabled persons in negligence cases is "[t]he difficulty of drawing any satisfactory line between mental deficiency and those variations of temperament, intellect and emotional balance which cannot, as a practical matter, be taken into account in imposing liability for damage done." Restatement (Second) of Torts, § 283B, cmt. b.1.

The difficulties encountered by the trier of fact in determining the existence, nature, degree, and effect of a mental disability may introduce into the civil law some of the issues that currently exist in the insanity defense in criminal law. We are wary of establishing a defense to negligence based on indeterminate standards of mental disability given the complexities of the various mental illnesses and the increasing rate at which new illnesses are discovered to explain behavior. [C]

Further, while the traditional public policy rationale relied on by this court in *Meyer* in support of the common law rule are subject to criticism, we remain hesitant to abandon the long-standing rule in favor of a broad rule adopting the subjective standard for all mentally disabled persons. Generally, the public policy rationale, in varying degrees, remain legitimate concerns. Accordingly, we turn our discussion to how those rationale apply to the facts before us.

American Family does not dispute that Monicken committed an act that was a substantial factor in causing Gould's injury. Rather, it asserts that Monicken cannot be held liable for his alleged negligence as a matter of law based on his lack of mental capacity.

Even though the jury determined that Monicken was negligent and that his negligence was a cause of the plaintiff's injuries, liability does not necessarily follow. Public policy considerations may preclude liability. [Cc] Whether public policy considerations should preclude liability in this instance is a question of law which we review *de novo*. [C]

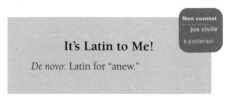

It's Latin to Me!

De novo: Latin for "anew."

One recognized public policy reason for not imposing liability despite a finding of negligence is that allowance of recovery would place an unreasonable burden on the negligent tortfeasor. [C] As explained in detail below, this court concludes that the circumstances of this case totally negate the rationale behind the *Meyer* rule imposing liability on the mentally disabled, and therefore application of the rule would place an unreasonable burden on the institutionalized mentally disabled tortfeasor.

The first rationale set forth in *Meyer* is that "where a loss must be borne by one of two innocent persons, it shall be borne by him who occasioned it." [C] The record reveals that Gould was not an innocent member of the public unable to anticipate or safeguard against the harm when encountered. Rather, she was employed as a caretaker specifically for dementia patients and knowingly encountered the dangers associated with such employment. It is undisputed that Gould, as head nurse of the dementia unit, knew Monicken was diagnosed with Alzheimer's disease and was aware of his disorientation and his potential for violent outbursts. Her own notes indicate that Monicken was angry and resisted being removed from another patient's room on the day of her injury.

By analogy, this court in *Hass v. Chicago & N.W. Ry.*, 48 Wis.2d 321, 326-27, 179 N.W.2d 885 (1970), relied on public policy considerations to exonerate negligent fire-starters or homeowners from liability for injuries suffered by the firefighters called to extinguish the fire. This court held that to make one who negligently starts a fire respond in damages to a firefighter who is injured placed too great a burden on the homeowner because the hazardous situation is the very reason the fireman's aid was enlisted. [C]

What's That?

The firefighter's rule prohibits emergency personnel from holding a person liable for injuries suffered when responding to a situation created or caused by that person.

Likewise, Gould, as the head nurse in the secured dementia unit and Monicken's caretaker, had express knowledge of the potential danger inherent in dealing with Alzheimer's patients in general and Monicken in particular. Holding Monicken negligent under these circumstances places too great a burden on him because his disorientation and potential for violence is the very reason he was institutionalized and needed the aid of employed caretakers. Accordingly, we conclude that the first *Meyer* rationale does not apply in this case.

The second rationale used to justify the rule is that "those interested in the estate of the insane person, as relatives or otherwise, may be under inducement to restrain him...." [C] This rationale also has little application to the present case. Monicken's relatives did everything they could to restrain him when they placed him in a secured dementia unit of a restricted health care center. When a mentally disabled person is placed in a nursing home, long-term care facility, health care center, or similar restrictive institution for the mentally disabled, those "interested in the estate" of that person are not likely in need of such further inducement.

The third reason for the common law rule set forth in *Meyer* is to prevent tortfeasors from "simulat[ing] or pretend[ing] insanity to defend their wrongful acts...." [C] This rationale is likewise inapplicable under the facts of this case. To suggest that Mr. Monicken would "simulate or pretend" the symptoms of Alzheimer's disease over a period of years in order to avoid a future tort liability is incredible. It is likewise difficult to imagine circumstances under which persons would feign the symptoms of a mental disability and subject themselves to commitment in an institution in order to avoid some future civil liability.

In sum, we agree with the Goulds that ordinarily a mentally disabled person is responsible for his or her torts. However, we conclude that this rule does not apply in this case because the circumstances totally negate the rationale behind the rule and would place an unreasonable burden on the negligent institutionalized mentally disabled. When a mentally disabled person injures an employed caretaker, the injured party can reasonably foresee the danger and is not "innocent" of the risk involved. By placing a mentally disabled person in an institution or similar restrictive setting, "those interested in the estate" of that person are not likely to be in need of an inducement for greater restraint. It is incredible to assert that a tortfeasor would "simulate or pretend insanity" over a prolonged period of time and even be institutionalized in order to avoid being held liable for damages for some future civil act. Therefore, we hold that a person institutionalized, as here, with a mental disability, and who does not have the capacity to control or appreciate his or her conduct cannot be liable for injuries caused to caretakers who are employed for financial compensation.

We next address American Family's challenge to the need for a remand. The court of appeals here remanded the case to the trial court to determine whether there is a disputed issue of fact regarding whether Monicken's mental capacity prevented him from controlling or appreciating the consequences of his conduct. [C] American Family alleges that Monicken's total incapacity was virtually conceded at trial and therefore a remand is not necessary. Although the Goulds request a remand, in their brief they admit, in essence, that upon remand it would be impossible to rebut the evidence of Monicken's incapacity. Based on our review of the record, we reach a similar conclusion.

Accordingly, we reverse that part of the decision of the court of appeals remanding the case to the trial court for a determination on the issue of Monicken's mental capacity. We remand to the trial court with directions to enter judgment for American Family in accordance with this decision.

The decision of the court of appeals is affirmed in part and reversed in part; the cause is remanded to the circuit court with directions to enter judgment in accordance with this decision.

————————

Points for Discussion

1. What did the Wisconsin Supreme Court hold? What rationale(s) did it proffer in support of its decision?

2. How did the court view and apply its prior decision in *Breunig*?

3. Is Alzheimer's disease a physical condition or a mental illness? How would you analyze the standard of care issue if the disease was the former? The latter?

4. Why did the plaintiff not sue for an intentional tort? If the plaintiff had, would the result have been the same?

Dellwo v. Pearson

259 Minn. 452, 107 N.W.2d 859 (1961)

LOEVINGER, Justice.

This case arises out of a personal injury to Jeanette E. Dellwo, one of the plaintiffs. She and her husband, the other plaintiff, were fishing on one of Minnesota's numerous and beautiful lakes by trolling at a low speed with about 40 to 50 feet of line trailing behind the boat. Defendant, a 12-year-old boy, operating a boat with an outboard motor, crossed behind plaintiffs' boat. Just at this time Mrs. Dellwo felt a jerk on her line which suddenly was pulled out very rapidly. The line was knotted to the spool of the reel so that when it had run out the fishing rod was pulled downward, the reel hit the side of the boat, the reel came apart, and part of it flew through the lens of Mrs. Dellwo's glasses and injured her eye. Both parties then proceeded to a dock where inspection of defendant's motor disclosed 2 to 3 feet of fishing line wound about the propeller.

The case was fully tried to the court and jury and submitted to the jury upon instructions which, in so far as relevant here, instructed the jury that: . . . In considering the matter of negligence the duty to which defendant is held is modified because he is a child, a child not being held to the same standard of conduct as an adult and being required to exercise only that degree of care which ordinarily is exercised by children of like age, mental capacity, and experience under the same or similar circumstances . . . Several hours after the jury retired it returned and asked for additional instructions with respect to 'foreseeable responsibility' and 'the responsibility of a youngster compared to a more mature person.' The court there-upon repeated the instructions relating to negligence, [and] the standard of care . . .

. . . .

A more important point involves the instruction that defendant was to be judged by the standard of care of a child of similar age rather than of a reasonable man. There is no doubt that the instruction given substantially reflects the language of numerous decisions in this and other courts. However, the great majority of these cases involve the issue of contributory negligence and the standard of care that may properly be required of a child in protecting himself against some hazard. The standard of care stated is proper and appropriate for such situations.

However, this court has previously recognized that there may be a difference between the standard of care that is required of a child in protecting himself against hazards and the standard that may be applicable when his activities expose others to hazards. Certainly in the circumstances of modern life, where vehicles moved by powerful motors are readily available and frequently operated by immature individuals, we should be skeptical of a rule that would allow motor vehicles to be operated to the hazard of the public with less than the normal minimum degree of care and competence.

To give legal sanction to the operation of automobiles by teen-agers with less than ordinary care for the safety of others is impractical today, to say the least. We may take **judicial notice** of the hazards of automobile traffic, the frequency of accidents, the often catastrophic results of accidents, and the fact that immature individuals are no less prone to accidents than adults. While minors are entitled to be judged by standards commensurate with age, experience, and wisdom when engaged in activities appropriate to their age, experience, and wisdom, it would be unfair to the public to permit a minor in the operation of a motor vehicle to observe any other standards of care and conduct than those expected of all others. A person observing children at play with toys, throwing balls, operating tricycles or velocipedes, or engaged in other childhood activities may anticipate conduct that does not reach an adult standard of care or prudence. However, one cannot know whether the operator of an approaching automobile, airplane, or power-boat is a minor or an adult, and usually cannot protect himself against youthful imprudence even if warned. Accordingly, we hold that in the operation of an automobile, airplane, or powerboat, a minor is to be held to the same standard of care as an adult.

Undoubtedly there are problems attendant upon such a view. However, there are problems in any rule that may be adopted applicable to this matter. They will have to be solved as they may present themselves in the setting of future cases.

The latest tentative revision of the Restatement of Torts proposes an even broader rule that would hold a child to adult standards whenever he engages 'in an activity which is normally undertaken only by adults, and for which adult qualifications are required.' However, it is unnecessary to this case to adopt a rule in such broad form, and, therefore, we expressly leave open the question whether or not that rule should be adopted in this state. For the present it is sufficient to say that no reasonable grounds for differentiating between automobiles, airplanes, and powerboats appears, and that a rule requiring a single standard of care in the operation of such vehicles, regardless of the age of the operator, appears to us to be required by the circumstances of contemporary life.

Reversed and remanded for a new trial.

Points for Discussion

1. The court noted the proposed rule of the then-tentative RESTATEMENT OF TORTS. Section 283A of the subsequently issued RESTATEMENT (SECOND) OF TORTS provided that "the standard of conduct to which" a child "must conform to avoid being negligent is that of a reasonable person of like age, intelligence, and experience under like circumstances." Comment *c* to § 283A states that an exception to this rule "may arise when the child engages in an activity which is normally undertaken only by adults, and for which adult qualifications are required." In those situations the child "may be held to the standard of adult skill, knowledge, and competence, and no allowance may be made for his immaturity." Thus, the age and inexperience of a fourteen-year-old attempting to fly an airplane or drive a car would not insulate the minor from liability for any negligent flying or driving.

2. In Robinson v. Lindsay, 92 Wash.2d 410 (1979), the court held that a minor operating a snowmobile should be held to the standard of care and conduct expected of an adult. Noting that in the past it had "compared a child's conduct to that expected of a reasonably careful child of the same age, intelligence, maturity, training, and experience," the court reasoned a child engaging in inherently dangerous activity "should be held to an adult standard of care."

3. Should the adult standard of care apply to child hunters, golfers, skiers, and drivers of automobiles and tractors?

b. The Reasonable Prudent Professional

Heath v. Swift Wings, Inc.

40 N.C. App. 158, 252 S.E.2d 526 (1979)

On 3 August 1975 a Piper 180 Arrow airplane crashed immediately after takeoff from the Boone-Blowing Rock Airport. Killed in the crash was the pilot, Fred Heath; his wife, Jonna; their son, Karl; and a family friend, Vance Smathers. Valerie Heath, a daughter of Fred and Jonna Heath, and sister of Karl, became the sole survivor of the Heath family. This action was instituted by Richard E. Heath as **ancillary administrator** of the estates of Jonna and Karl Heath against (1) Swift Wings, Inc., the corporate owner of the aircraft, on the grounds of agency; (2) the four shareholders of Swift Wings, Inc. Fred Heath, Frank Kish, Richard Kish, and Kermit Rockett alleging they actually constituted a de facto partnership, and (3) The Bank of Virginia Trust Company, **Executor** of the Estate of Frederick B. Heath, Jr.

The plaintiff's complaint alleged several grounds of negligence: (1) operation of the aircraft in an overloaded condition beyond its performance capabilities, (2) failure to follow the operating manual with regard to takeoff distance for short and soft field takeoffs, (3) failure to take into account specific runway and weather conditions, (4) failure to take appropriate emergency steps including aborting takeoff, (5) flying below safe speed, (6) improper control after takeoff, and (7) violation of federal aircraft safety regulations.

Defendants answered, generally denying negligence, the existence of agency, and a de facto partnership.

Plaintiff's evidence, except to the extent it is quoted from the record, is briefly summarized as follows: Mary Payne Smathers Curry, widow of Vance Smathers, observed the takeoff of the Piper aircraft shortly after 5:00 o'clock on 3 August 1975. She observed Fred Heath load and reload the passengers and luggage, apparently in an effort to improve the balance of the aircraft. He also "walked around (the airplane) and looked at everything . . . She remembers seeing him and thinking that he's doublechecking it to be sure no one has slashed the tires." The airplane engine started promptly and the plane was taxied to the end of the runway where it paused for approximately five minutes before takeoff. The airplane came very close to the end of the runway before takeoff. However "(t)he engine sounded good the entire time, and she did not recall hearing the engine miss or pop or backfire." After takeoff, the airplane "gained altitude but it didn't go up very high" and then "leveled off pretty low".

. . . .

Robert Bumgardner, a representative of the local electric membership corporation, testified that at the point where they were apparently struck by the plane, the power lines were close to 30 feet above the ground. One pole had been broken some distance above the ground, the cross arm on another had been broken, and one of four power lines had been snapped.

Richard G. Rodriquez, an investigator for the National Transportation Safety Board, testified that his investigation indicated that the grass runway was firm and essentially level. The landing gear was apparently down and locked at the time of the crash. The flaps were up. He testified that the fuel was flowing to all four cylinder injectors and that a test of each magneto indicated that they were functioning properly. He concluded, "Yes, my testimony would be that we found no evidence of preimpact malfunction."

William B. Gough, Jr., a free-lance mechanical engineering consultant and pilot, testified concerning the operation and flight performance of the Piper 180 Arrow. He testified concerning the many factors affecting the takeoff capabilities of the Piper and the calculations to be made by the pilot before takeoff, utilizing flight performance charts. He testified that in his opinion, according to his calculations, the pilot should have used flaps to aid in the takeoff. Furthermore, he stated that in his opinion the reasonably prudent pilot should have made a controlled landing in the corn field shortly after takeoff if he were experiencing difficulty attaining flight speed, and that if he had done so Jonna Heath and Karl Heath would have survived.

. . . .

After the customary motions at the conclusion of all the evidence, the case was submitted to the jury upon voluminous instructions by the trial court. The jury returned a verdict answering the following issue as indicated: "1. Was Fred Heath, Jr., negligent in the operation of PA-28R 'Arrow' airplane on August 3, 1975 as alleged in the complaint?" Answer: "No". Plaintiff appeals assigning error to the exclusion of certain evidence and to the charge to the jury. . . .

MORRIS, Chief Judge.

. . . .

Assignment of error No. 4 is directed to the trial court's **charge** concerning the definition of negligence and the applicable standard of care:

> "Negligence, ladies and gentlemen of the jury, is the failure of someone to act as a reasonably and careful and prudent person would under the same or similar circumstances. Obviously, this could be the doing of

something or the failure to do something, depending on the circumstances. With respect to aviation negligence could be more specifically defined as the failure to exercise that degree of ordinary care and caution, which an ordinary prudent pilot having the same training and experience as Fred Heath, would have used in the same or similar circumstances."

It is a familiar rule of law that the standard of care required of an individual, unless altered by statute, is the conduct of the reasonably prudent man under the same or similar circumstances. [Cc] While the standard of care of the reasonably prudent man remains constant, the quantity or degree of care required varies significantly with the attendant circumstances. [Cc]

The trial court improperly introduced a **subjective standard** of care into the definition of negligence by referring to the "ordinary care and caution, which an ordinary prudent pilot having the same training and experience as Fred Heath, would have used in the same or similar circumstances." . . . We are aware of the authorities which support the application of a greater standard of care than that of the ordinary prudent man for persons shown to possess special skill in a particular endeavor. [C] Indeed, our courts have long recognized that one who engages in a business, occupation, or profession must exercise the requisite degree of learning, skill, and ability of that calling with reasonable and ordinary care. See e. g., Insurance Co. v. Sprinkler Co., 266 N.C. 134, 146 S.E.2d 53 (1966) (fire sprinkler contractor); Service Co. v. Sales Co., 261 N.C. 660, 136 S.E.2d 56 (1964) (industrial designer); Hunt v. Bradshaw, 242 N.C. 517, 88 S.E.2d 762 (1955) (physician); Hodges v. Carter, 239 N.C. 517, 80 S.E.2d 144 (1954) (attorney). Furthermore, the specialist within a profession may be held to a standard of care greater than that required of the general practitioner. [C] Nevertheless, the professional standard remains an **objective standard**. . . .

Such objective standards avoid the evil of imposing a different standard of care upon each individual. The instructions in this case concerning the pilot's standard of care are misleading at best, and a misapplication of the law. They permit the jury to consider Fred Heath's own particular experience and training, whether outstanding or inferior, in determining the requisite standard of conduct, rather than applying a minimum standard generally applicable to all pilots. The plaintiff is entitled to an instruction holding Fred Heath to the objective minimum standard of care applicable to all pilots.

. . . .

This matter was well tried by both counsel for plaintiff and counsel for defendants, and several days were consumed in its trial. Nevertheless, for **prejudicial errors** in the charge, there must be a

New trial.

Points for Discussion

1. What was the flaw in the trial court's charge concerning the applicable standard of care?

2. What is the difference between an objective and a subjective standard of care?

3. What is the standard of care for persons in particular occupations, professions, or businesses? For specialists?

4. What is a "professional"?

Hypo 4-2

You are an appellate court judge. A trial court judge in a case before you on appeal instructed the jury that "the standard of care is the knowledge, training and skill or ability of the average member of the profession." Assess the validity of that instruction.

Wolski v. Wandel

275 Neb. 266, 746 N.W.2d 143 (2008)

STEPHAN, J.

This is a professional negligence action brought by Stanley Wolski, Jr., against attorney Josephine Walsh Wandel. Wolski appeals from an order of the district court for Douglas County granting Wandel's motion for summary judgment and dismissing the action. The question presented is whether there is a genuine issue of material fact with respect to Wolski's allegation that Wandel was negligent in representing him in a prior action which was concluded by a settlement. We conclude that there is not and affirm the judgment of the district court.

BACKGROUND

UNDERLYING CASE

In June 2000, Wolski retained Wandel to represent him in a dispute with his sister, Rosemary Parriott, regarding ownership of real property located in Cass County, Nebraska. The controversy arose from the conveyance of two tracts of farmland totaling 119 acres. On December 30, 1974, and January 9, 1975, Wolski's parents conveyed the two tracts by **warranty deed** to Wolski. Another warranty deed, dated January 14, 1975, transferred the same 119 acres from Wolski to Parriott as "Trustee." This deed did not identify the **trust**, name a **beneficiary**, or describe the trust in any other way. Wolski had a longstanding dispute with Parriott regarding income from the property, and in 2000, he retained Wandel to "break" any trust and secure **fee simple** title in the 119 acres purportedly held in trust. Wandel filed a **petition for declaratory judgment** for Wolski in Cass County District Court, naming Parriott as the sole defendant. The petition sought to set aside any trust agreement and the warranty deed from Wolski to Parriott. It also requested that Parriott be ordered to give an accounting with respect to funds generated by the property.

Parriott testified that the original trust was amended on May 29, 1982, by a document entitled "Amendments of Trust Agreement." The amendment was signed by Wolski as **grantor** and Parriott as trustee and provides that the trust would be irrevocable, that Wolski would have a life estate in the real property, and that the remainder would pass to Parriott or her lineal heirs. The signatures on this document were not notarized.

Discovery in the case also disclosed that Wolski was married in 1982, several months after the date of the amendment. On September 8, 1987, Parriott was appointed guardian and **conservator** for Wolski. In that capacity, she brought a successful action to annul his marriage. The record reflects that the conservatorship was terminated in 1995 and that the guardianship was terminated in 1997.

During the pendency of the underlying suit against Parriott, Wandel filed a motion for the appointment of a guardian ad litem for Wolski, alleging that his mother, who had previously acted as his "natural Guardian," was unable to attend trial or assist him due to deterioration of her health. Attached to the motion were medical records showing

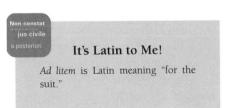

It's Latin to Me!

Ad litem is Latin meaning "for the suit."

that Wolski had certain disabilities affecting his mental capacity and speech. The court sustained the motion and appointed attorney Thomas Harmon as guardian ad litem for Wolski on August 21, 2001. Upon his appointment, Harmon conducted an investigation which included interviews with Wolski, Parriott, various members of their family, and attorneys who had represented the parties in the past. According to Harmon, Wolski told him that he wanted to ensure that he always had a place to live and that he would have money for living expenses.

[After extensive discovery at] a November 2, 2001 hearing, the parties advised the court that they had settled the case. . . .

. . . [T]he court approved the settlement agreement and awarded Wolski a **life estate** in the real property and awarded the remainder interest to Parriott and her **lineal heirs**, subject to the condition that mineral lease payments and condemnation awards with respect to the property were to be divided equally between the parties. Parriott deeded the property to Harmon, as Wolski's conservator. Through his current attorney, Wolski unsuccessfully sought to vacate the order approving the settlement.

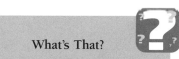

What's That?

A lineal heir is a deceased person's ancestor or descendant, for example, a child or parent.

. . . .

ANALYSIS

A client who has agreed to the settlement of an action is not barred from recovering against his or her attorney for **malpractice** if the client can establish that the settlement agreement was the product of the attorney's negligence. Wolski claims that Wandel was negligent in recommending settlement of the litigation against Parriott instead of proceeding to trial. In a civil action for legal malpractice, a plaintiff alleging professional negligence on the part of an attorney must prove three elements: (1) the attorney's employment; (2) the attorney's neglect of a reasonable duty; and (3) that such negligence resulted in and was the proximate cause of loss (damages) to the client.

In this case, we focus on the second element: neglect of a reasonable duty. The general rule regarding an attorney's duty to his or her client is that the attorney, by accepting employment to give legal advice or to render other legal services, impliedly agrees to use such skill, prudence, and diligence as lawyers of ordinary skill and capacity commonly possess and exercise in the performance of the tasks which they undertake. Although this general standard is established by law, the question of what an attorney's specific conduct should be in a particular case and whether an attorney's conduct fell below that specific standard is a question of fact. Expert testimony is generally required to establish an attorney's standard of conduct in a particular circumstance and that the attorney's conduct was not in conformity therewith. This is so because a jury cannot rationally apply a general statement of the standard of care unless it is made aware of what a reasonable attorney would have done in similar circumstances. An exception to this general rule is that where the evidence and circumstances are such that recognition of the alleged negligence may be presumed to be within the comprehension of laypersons, no expert testimony is required.

Once the party moving for summary judgment makes a **prima facie** case, as Wandel did here, the burden to produce evidence showing the existence of a material issue of fact that prevents judgment as a matter of law shifts to the party opposing the motion. This case does not fall within the exception to the general rule requiring expert testimony to prove that an attorney was negligent, in that a layperson could not be expected to know, without the assistance of expert testimony, whether an attorney was negligent in counseling a client to settle litigation of the type involved here. Thus, in order to defeat Wandel's motion for summary judgment, Wolski was required to present an expert's opinion contradicting Jones' opinion that Wandel's performance had met the standard of care.

There is evidence from three attorneys concerning Wandel's representation of Wolski. Ronald E. Reagan, a practicing attorney and retired district judge, was retained by Wolski's attorney to review documents and "formulate some opinions as to whether or not ... Wandel had breached any particular duty or standard of care." His deposition was taken by Wandel's attorney prior to the date of Jones' affidavit, and thus his testimony is not directly responsive to Jones' opinions. Reagan testified that Wandel owed the same duty to Wolski and to Harmon as Wolski's guardian ad litem. He criticized Wandel for not providing certain "relevant information" about the underlying litigation to Harmon and opined that if Harmon had

Take Note

A lawsuit for professional negligence against an attorney is typically referred to as a legal malpractice action.

been given this information, he would not have concluded that the settlement was in Wolski's best interests. Reagan testified that, in his opinion, the underlying case should have been tried and that Wolski would have prevailed. Reagan did not specifically express an opinion that Wandel breached the applicable standard of care.

Harmon testified by deposition, taken prior to that of Reagan, and also by an affidavit sworn after Reagan's deposition. In the affidavit, Harmon stated that after his appointment as guardian ad litem, he had a meeting with Wolski and Wandel and two other meetings with Wolski, to discuss the pending case and Wolski's desires concerning its outcome. He stated that despite Wolski's speech impediment, Harmon was able to "communicate with him sufficiently to understand his desires, wishes and position on the issues we discussed." Harmon further stated that he conducted several interviews and reviewed court records before reaching an independent determination that the settlement was in Wolski's best interests. Harmon stated that he had reviewed Reagan's deposition and that Reagan was incorrect regarding the information he possessed at the time of the settlement. Harmon stated that he had all of the information which Reagan said should have been provided to him, either as a result of his own investigation or from conversations with Wandel, with the exception of one document. Harmon stated that after reviewing this document, which was attached to Reagan's deposition, he would not have considered it relevant to the case or the proposed settlement. He concluded: "I therefore believe I was aware of all the relevant matters ... Reagan erroneously assumed [what] I did not know and needed to be advised of by ... Wandel." Harmon did not express an opinion that Wandel breached the applicable standard of care.

The record also includes Wandel's deposition, in which she responded to questions concerning her representation of Wolski. The deposition does not include any admissions of professional negligence.

We conclude that Wolski did not meet his burden of demonstrating the existence of a genuine issue of material fact. Reagan's testimony falls short of this objective. Although Reagan expressed criticism of certain aspects of Wandel's representation, he did not specifically opine that her performance deviated from the applicable standard of care. In a medical malpractice case, we have held that an expert's testimony that a surgical procedure should have been performed in a different manner did not constitute evidence that the defendant had departed from the applicable standard of care in performing the surgery in the way that he did. We noted that if the expert believed that there had been a deviation from the standard of care, "it would have been a simple matter ... to have said exactly that." Reagan's "criticism" of Wandel was similarly insufficient as evidence of professional negligence. At most, Reagan's testimony establishes that his evaluation of the underlying case differed from that of Wandel. It is not uncommon for lawyers to have differing views about the merits of a contested case, and such a difference of opinion between lawyers does not necessarily mean that one of them has been negligent in evaluating the case. Reagan's testimony does not establish that Wandel's professional performance fell below that expected of lawyers of ordinary skill and capacity under similar circumstances.

For More Information

Most every jurisdiction has adopted some form of the ABA's Model Rules of Professional Conduct, ethics rules which govern the conduct of lawyers.

The decision to settle a controversy is the client's. In order to meaningfully make that decision, a client must have the information necessary to assess the risks and benefits of either settling or proceeding to trial. A lawyer should exert his or her best efforts to ensure that the decisions of a client are made only after the client has been informed of relevant considerations. Under the Code of Professional Responsibility which governed lawyers' conduct at the time of Wandel's representation, Wandel was required to look to Harmon, as guardian ad litem, to make decisions concerning settlement on behalf of Wolski. The record includes an expert's opinion that Wandel complied with the standard of care in advising Harmon with regard to the settlement, and Wolski has presented no expert opinion to the contrary. There is no genuine issue of material fact as to the allegations of professional negligence.

CONCLUSION

FYI

A lawyer's responsibilities and obligations are the subject of professional responsibility and legal ethics courses.

For the reasons discussed, we conclude that the district court did not err in granting Wandel's motion for summary judgment and dismissing this action. We affirm the judgment of the district court.

AFFIRMED.

Points for Discussion

1. What elements did the plaintiff have to prove in order to prevail in an action alleging attorney malpractice?

2. Why require expert testimony in professional malpractice cases?

3. Within the attorney-client relationship, who makes the decision to settle a lawsuit—the client or the attorney?

4. Do you agree that the district court correctly granted summary judgment and dismissed the plaintiff's case?

5. "Attorneys are liable to their clients for damages in malpractice actions only when they fail to exercise a reasonable degree of care and skill." *Barth v. Reagan*, 139 Ill.2d 399, 564 N.E.2d 1196 (1990).

6. An attorney "may be held liable for damages incurred by a client based on the attorney's failure to act with a reasonable degree of care, skill, and dispatch. . . . Good faith tactical decisions or decisions made on a fairly debatable point of law are generally not actionable under the rule of judgmental immunity." Crosby v. Jones, 705 So.2d 1356 (Fla. 1998).

7. Note the importance of the *Wolski* court's discussion of the "underlying case." Legal malpractice plaintiffs are required—as part of proof of the causation element in the negligence action—to prove, what is known as, the "case-within-the-case." The causation component of negligence actions will be explored more thoroughly, *infra*.

Hypo 4-3

Attorney is handling two cases.

Case 1 is subject to and must be filed prior to the expiration of a one-year **statute of limitations**. Attorney has not filed the suit and the limitations period has now expired.

In Case 2 Attorney submitted a brief to the state supreme court in which she argued that that court's *Smith v. Jones* decision governs and warrants a reversal of a lower court judgment against her client. Five days prior to the submission of the brief, and unbeknownst to Attorney, the state supreme court overruled *Smith v. Jones* and announced a new legal rule declining to recognize the very same cause of action at issue in Case 2. The appeal to the supreme court is pending.

You are an attorney specializing in legal malpractice cases. The clients involved in Cases 1 and 2 have contacted you and seek your legal opinion with regard to Attorney's conduct and actions. What advice would you give? What questions would you ask, and what additional legal and factual inquiries would you need to make?

Morrison v. MacNamara

407 A.2d 555 (D.C. 1979)

NEWMAN, Chief Judge:

Appellant Morrison, a plaintiff in a **medical malpractice** action in the trial court, challenges a judgment in favor of appellees, a nationally certified medical laboratory and a medical technician. He contends that the trial court erred in denying his requested jury instruction that the standard of care to which appellees should be held is a national standard as opposed to a local one. We agree with appellant . . . and reverse.

. . . .

The facts at trial were basically undisputed. They indicated that upon orders of his personal physician, appellant went to appellee Oscar B. Hunter Memorial Laboratories, Inc., a nationally certified clinical medical laboratory located in the District of Columbia, for the performance of a urethral smear test. The test was administered by appellee Tom MacNamara, a clinical technician, who at that time had been employed by appellee Hunter Laboratories for approximately seven months. According to the technician, he administered the test by inserting a cotton swab about a quarter-inch into the penis with appellant in a standing position. Following the completion of the first test, appellant complained of feeling faint. The technician instructed appellant to sit down and rest, and to place his head between his legs. The technician did not attempt to examine appellant or seek medical assistance so that the source and extent of appellant's complaints could be ascertained.

Approximately two to three minutes later, the technician asked appellant "if it was okay to go ahead" with a second test and appellant replied "yes." The technician then proceeded to perform the test a second time, again with appellant in a standing position. While the test was being administered a second time, appellant fainted, striking his head on a metal blood pressure stand and on the tile covered floor. Subsequently, he was taken to George Washington University Hospital where he was admitted as a neurosurgery patient. As a result of this incident, appellant sustained a number of injuries including a permanent loss of his sense of smell and a partial loss of his sense of taste. Appellant brought an action against appellees charging them with professional malpractice in the manner in which they conducted the test and for proceeding with the test despite the fact that appellant had complained of feeling faint.

At the close of all the evidence, appellant submitted several jury instructions which were based on the national standard of care. Appellant maintained that in view of the national certification of the laboratory, the laboratory was under a duty to adhere to nationally accepted standards for administering the urethral smear test, and that the jury should be so instructed. Appellees argued that the laboratory owed only the duty to adhere to that standard of medical care recognized in the Washington, D.C. metropolitan area. The trial court agreed with appellees and instructed the jury as follows:

> You are instructed that a medical laboratory and its personnel are required to exercise such care and skill as is exercised by other medical laboratories and their employees in good standing in the same community. That the degree of care and skill required is not the highest degree of care and skill known to the profession, but that which is exercised by ordinary and reasonably competent laboratory personnel in the treatment of patients under the same or similar circumstances. . . .

THE STANDARD OF CARE IN MEDICAL MALPRACTICE

A. General Principles

The elements which govern ordinary negligence actions are also applicable in actions for professional negligence. The plaintiff bears the burden of presenting evidence "which establishes the applicable standard of care, demonstrates that this standard has been violated, and develops a causal relationship between the violation and the harm complained of." Kosberg v. Washington Hospital Center, Inc., 129 U.S.App.D.C. 322, 324, 394 F.2d 947, 949 (1968) . . . In negligence actions the standard of care by which the defendant's conduct is measured is often stated as "that degree of care which a reasonably prudent person would have exercised under the same or similar circumstances." Washington Hospital Center v. Butler, 127 U.S.App.D.C. 379, 383, 384 F.2d 331, 335 (1967); [cc]. Accordingly, this standard of care, which evaluates a defendant's conduct against that conduct which is reasonable under the circumstances, is also applicable in the law of professional negligence. The law of negligence generally does not acknowledge differing standards or categories of care, but requires an adherence to a uniform standard of conduct: that of reasonable care under the circumstances. [Cc]

. . . .

In **medical malpractice**, a term referring to ordinary negligence concepts in the area of medical diagnosis, treatment, and the like, the duty of care is generally formulated as that degree of reasonable care and skill expected of members of the medical profession under the same or similar circumstances. [Cc] Thus, whether health care professionals be physicians, [c] radiologists, [cc] or hospitals, [cc] their conduct must comport with that degree of care reasonably expected of other medical professionals with similar skills acting under the same or similar circumstances, i. e., they must adhere to the standard of reasonable care.

B. Geographic Limitations on the Standard of Care

The **locality rule** states that the conduct of members of the medical profession is to be measured solely by the standard of conduct expected of other members of the medical profession in the same locality or the same community. [Cc] This doctrine is indigenous to American jurisprudence and appears to have developed in the late nineteenth century. [Cc] The rule was designed to protect doctors in rural areas who, because of inadequate training and experience, and the lack of effective means of transportation and communication, could not be expected to exhibit the skill and care of urban doctors. [Cc] . . . .

In addition, it was argued that in view of the ability of urban areas to attract the most talented doctors, a rule which would hold rural doctors to urban standards of care would precipitate the departure of doctors from rural areas and thereby leave rural communities without sufficient medical care. [Cc] In sum, the locality rule was premised on the notion that the disparity in education and access to advances in medical science between rural and urban doctors required that they be held to different standards of care.

The cases in this jurisdiction exhibit a lack of uniformity on the issue of the geographic area in which the conduct of members of the medical profession is to be measured. For example, a number of cases state that members of the medical profession are held to the skill and learning exercised by members of their profession in the District of Columbia. [Cc] In other cases, the standard is referred to as that degree of care exercised by other members of the medical profession in the District or a similar locality. [Cc] Finally, a number of cases have articulated the medical standard of care without referring to any geographic limitation whatsoever. [Cc] Since courts in this jurisdiction were never directly presented with this issue, the empirical validity of the assumptions behind the locality rule has not previously been examined.

Even a cursory analysis of the policy behind the locality doctrine reveals that whatever relevance it has to the practice of medicine in remote rural communities, it has no relevance to medical practice in the District of Columbia. Clearly the nation's capital is not a community isolated from recent advances in the quality of care and treatment of patients. Rather, it is one of the leading medical centers in quality health care. The medical schools in the nation's capital rate as some of the most outstanding schools in the nation. The hospitals in the District not only possess some of the most recent medical technology, but also attract some of the best medical talent from all over the country. Moreover, medical journals from all over the country are available to health care professionals in the District of Columbia, serving to keep practitioners abreast of developments in other communities. In short, the locality rule was designed to protect medical practitioners in rural communities, not practitioners in leading metropolitan centers such as the District of Columbia.

Moreover, any purported disparity between the skills of practitioners in various urban centers has for the most part been eliminated. Unlike the diversified and often limited training that was available a hundred years ago, medical education has been standardized throughout the nation through a system of national accreditation. [C] Moreover, the significant improvements in transportation and communication over the past hundred years cast further doubt on continued vitality of the doctrine. . . .

Quite apart from the locality rule's irrelevance to contemporary medical practice, the doctrine is also objectionable because it tends to immunize doctors from communities where medical practice is generally below that which exists in other communities from malpractice liability. [Cc] Rather than encouraging medical practitioners to elevate the quality of care and treatment of patients to that existing in other communities, the doctrine may serve to foster substandard care, by testing the conduct of medical professionals by the conduct of other medical professionals in the same community.

The locality rule is peculiar to medical malpractice. Architects are not held to a standard of conduct exercised by other architects in the District or a similar locality. [Cc] Moreover, the conduct of lawyers is not measured solely by the conduct of other lawyers in the District or a similar community. [Cc]

Despite these criticisms, the locality rule is still followed in several jurisdictions. [Cc] The majority of jurisdictions, however, have abandoned the locality rule. [Cc]

Courts which have abandoned the locality rule have taken different approaches in defining the geographical boundary within which the conduct of a medical practitioner is to be measured. For example, a number of courts have modified the locality rule by extending the geographical reference group of the standard of care to include that of "the same or similar localities." [Cc]

This approach has been criticized because of the difficulty in determining whether two communities are similar. [Cc] In addition, the similar locality formulation has been criticized for containing the same deficiencies as the traditional locality rule, i. e., if the standard of conduct in a similar community is substandard, the similar locality rule would immunize those medical professionals whose conduct conforms to the substandard medical practice in a similar community. [Cc]

Other courts, noting that medical standards have been nationalized largely through a system of national board certification, have adopted a national standard of care, and accordingly have eliminated any reference to a geographically defined area in their formulation of the standard of care applicable to medical professionals. [Cc] The import of these decisions is that health care professionals who are trained according to national standards and who hold themselves out to the public as such, should be held to a national standard of care.

We are in general agreement with those courts which have adopted a national standard of care. Varying geographical standards of care are no longer valid in view of the uniform standards of proficiency established by national board certification. Moreover, the tremendous resources available in the District for medical professionals keep them abreast of advances in the care and treatment of patients that occur in all parts of the country. More importantly, residents of the District desirous of medical treatment do not rely upon a medical professional's conforming to the standard of care practiced in the District or in a similar locality. Rather, they rely upon his training, certification, and proficiency. "Negligence cannot be excused on the ground that others in the same (or similar locality) practice the same kind of negligence." [C] Substandard practice is substandard whether it is followed in the same or in a similar community.

Although we have found no cases which address the issue of the standard of care applicable to a clinical laboratory, the same reasons which justify the application of a national standard of care to physicians and hospitals appear to apply with equal validity to medical laboratories. Medical laboratories are often staffed and operated by doctors who undergo the same rigorous training as other physicians. The opportunities for keeping abreast of medical advances that are available to doctors are equally available to clinical laboratories. Indeed medical laboratories are often an integral part of a hospital. [C] Moreover, clinical laboratories generally conduct many of the routine tests that would normally be performed by physicians and hospitals. Accordingly, they owe similar duties in their care and treatment of patients. [C]

Thus we hold that at least as to board certified physicians, hospitals, medical laboratories, and other health care providers, the standard of care is to be measured by the national standard. It follows that an instruction which compares a nationally certified medical professional's conduct exclusively with the standard of care in the District or a similar community is erroneous.

In the present case, appellees concede that they are a nationally certified medical laboratory and that they hold themselves out to the public as such. Appellant's expert witness testified at trial that the proper procedure to be employed in conducting a urethral smear test, according to national standards, is with the patient in a sitting or prone position. Appellees' expert witnesses who were all from the Washington metropolitan area testified that they were not aware of any national standards for conducting the test and that they always conducted the test with the patient in a standing position. However, the trial court instructed the jury that the appellees' conduct is to be compared solely with the standard of care prevailing in Washington, D.C. Thus, in effect the jury was instructed to ignore the testimony of appellant's expert witness on the standard of care. This instruction was error. The conflict in expert testimony was for the jury to resolve. Accordingly, we vacate the judgment in favor of appellees and order a new trial.

. . . .

Reversed.

Points for Discussion

1. What was the general formulation of the duty of care to which the court referred?

2. Describe, distinguish, and consider the advantages and disadvantages of the following rules: the locality rule; the same or similar localities rule; the national standard of care rule. (Note—it appears that the same or similar locality or community rule is no longer recognized in most jurisdictions.)

3. Which geographical standard of care rule did the *Morrison* court adopt in the context of a clinical laboratory? Do you agree with the court's decision?

Helling v. Carey

83 Wash.2d 514, 519 P.2d 981 (1974)

HUNTER, Associate Justice.

This case arises from a malpractice action instituted by the plaintiff (petitioner), Barbara Helling.

The plaintiff suffers from primary open angle glaucoma. Primary open angle glaucoma is essentially a condition of the eye in which there is an interference in the ease with which the nourishing fluids can flow out of the eye. Such a condition results in pressure gradually rising above the normal level to such an extent that damage is produced to the optic nerve and its fibers with resultant loss in vision. The first loss usually occurs in the periphery of the field of vision. The disease usually has few symptoms and, in the absence of a pressure test, is often undetected until the damage has become extensive and irreversible.

The defendants (respondents), Dr. Thomas F. Carey and Dr. Robert C. Laughlin, are partners who practice the medical specialty of ophthalmology. Ophthalmology involves the diagnosis and treatment of defects and diseases of the eye.

The plaintiff first consulted the defendants for myopia, nearsightedness, in 1959. At that time she was fitted with contact lenses. She next consulted the defendants in September, 1963, concerning irritation caused by the contact lenses. Additional consultations occurred in October, 1963; February, 1967; September, 1967; October, 1967; May, 1968; July, 1968; August, 1968; September, 1968; and October, 1968. Until the October 1968 consultation, the defendants considered the plaintiff's visual problems to be related solely to complications associated with her contact lenses. On that occasion, the defendant, Dr. Carey, tested the plaintiff's eye pressure and field of vision for the first time. This test indicated that the plaintiff had glaucoma. The plaintiff, who was then 32 years of age, had essentially lost her peripheral vision and her central vision was reduced to approximately 5 degrees vertical by 10 degrees horizontal.

Thereafter, in August of 1969, after consulting other physicians, the plaintiff filed a complaint against the defendants alleging, among other things, that she sustained severe and permanent damage to her eyes as a proximate result of the defendants' negligence. During trial, the testimony of the medical experts for both the plaintiff and the defendants established that the standards of the profession for that specialty in the same or similar circumstances do not require routine pressure tests for glaucoma upon patients under 40 years of age. The reason the pressure test for glaucoma is not given as a regular practice to patients under the age of 40 is that the disease rarely occurs in this age group. Testimony indicated, however, that the standards of the profession do require pressure tests if the patient's complaints and symptoms reveal to the physician that glaucoma should be suspected.

. . . .

We find this to be a unique case. The testimony of the medical experts is undisputed concerning the standards of the profession for the specialty of ophthalmology. It is not a question in this case of the defendants having any greater special ability, knowledge and information than other ophthalmologists which would require the defendants to comply with a higher duty of care than that 'degree of care and skill which is expected of the average practitioner in the class to which he belongs, acting in the same or similar circumstances.' [C] The issue is whether the defendants' compliance with the standard of the profession of ophthalmology, which does not require the giving of a routine pressure test to persons under 40 years of age, should insulate them from liability under the facts in this case where the plaintiff has lost a substantial amount of her vision due to the failure of the defendants to timely give the pressure test to the plaintiff.

The defendants argue that the standard of the profession, which does not require the giving of a routine pressure test to persons under the age of 40, is adequate to insulate the defendants from liability for negligence because the risk of glaucoma is so rare in this age group. The testimony of the defendant, Dr. Carey, however, is revealing as follows:

Q. Now, when was it, actually, the first time any complaint was made to you by her of any field or visual field problem? A. Really, the first time that she really complained of a visual field problem was the August 30th date. (1968) Q. And how soon before the diagnosis was that? A. That was 30 days. We made it on October 1st. Q. And in your opinion, how long, as you nor have the whole history and analysis and the diagnosis, how long had she had this glaucoma? A. I would think she probably had it ten years or longer. Q. Now, Doctor, there's been some reference to the matter of taking pressure checks of persons over 40. What is the incidence of glaucoma, the statistics, with persons under 40? A. In the instance of glaucoma under the age of 40, is less than 100 to one per cent. The younger you get, the less the incidence. It is thought to be in the neighborhood of one in 25,000 people or less. Q. How about the incidence of glaucoma in people over 40? A. Incidence of glaucoma over 40 gets into the two to three per cent category, and hence, that's where there is this great big difference and that's why the standards around the world has been to check pressures from 40 on.

The incidence of glaucoma in one out of 25,000 persons under the age of 40 may appear quite minimal. However, that one person, the plaintiff in this instance, is entitled to the same protection, as afforded persons over 40, essential for timely detection of the evidence of glaucoma where it can be arrested to avoid the grave and devastating result of this disease. The test is a simple pressure test, relatively inexpensive. There is no judgment factor involved, and there is no doubt that by giving the test the evidence of glaucoma can be detected. The giving of the test is harmless if the physical condition of the eye permits. The testimony indicates that although the condition of the plaintiff's eyes might have at times prevented the defendants from administering the pressure test, there is an absence of evidence in the record that the test could not have been timely given.

. . . .

Under the facts of this case reasonable prudence required the timely giving of the pressure test to this plaintiff. The precaution of giving this test to detect the incidence of glaucoma to patients under 40 years of age is so imperative that irrespective of its disregard by the standards of the opthalmology profession, it is the duty of the courts to say what is required to protect patients under 40 from the damaging results of glaucoma.

We therefore hold, as a matter of law, that the reasonable standard that should have been followed under the undisputed facts of this case was the timely giving of this simple, harmless pressure test to this plaintiff and that, in failing to do so, the defendants were negligent, which proximately resulted in the blindness sustained by the plaintiff for which the defendants are liable.

There are no disputed facts to submit to the jury on the issue of the defendants' liability. Hence, a discussion of the plaintiff's proposed instructions would be inconsequential in view of our disposition of the case.

The judgment of the trial court and the decision of the Court of Appeals is reversed, and the case is remanded for a new trial on the issue of damages only.

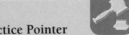

> **Practice Pointer**
>
> Parties may submit to the judge written requests for proposed jury instructions they want the court to give, and disputes as to the proper instructions may arise. The court will determine what instructions will be given, and the parties must timely object to the court's instruction or failure to give an instruction.

. . . .

UTTER, Associate Justice (concurring).

I concur in the result reached by the majority. I believe a greater duty of care could be imposed on the defendants than was established by their profession. The duty could be imposed when a disease, such as glaucoma, can be detected by a simple, well-known harmless test whose results are definitive and the disease can be successfully arrested by early detection, but where the effects of the disease are irreversible if undetected over a substantial period of time.

The difficulty with this approach [adopted today by the court] is that we as judges, by using a negligence analysis, seem to be imposing a stigma of moral blame upon the doctors who, in this case, used all the precautions commonly prescribed by their profession in diagnosis and treatment. Lacking their training in this highly sophisticated profession, it seems illogical for this court to say they failed to exercise a reasonable standard of care. It seem to me we are, in reality, imposing liability, because, in choosing between an innocent plaintiff and a doctor, who acted reasonably according to his specialty but who could have prevented the full effects of this disease by administering a simple, harmless test and treatment, the plaintiff should not have to bear the risk of loss. As such, imposition of liability approaches that of strict liability.

. . . .

Although the incidence of glaucoma in the age range of the plaintiff is approximately one in 25,000, this alone should not be enough to deny her a claim. Where its presence can be detected by a simple, well-known harmless test, where the results of the test are definitive, where the disease can be successfully arrested by early detection and where its effects are irreversible if undetected over a substantial period of time, liability should be imposed upon defendants even though they did not violate the standard existing within the profession of ophthalmology.

. . . .

Points for Discussion

1. Given the incidence of glaucoma in persons under the age of 40, did the defendants reasonably and understandably follow the standard of the profession of ophthalmology which did not require routine pressure tests for glaucoma on patients under 40 years of age?

2. Recall Judge Learned Hand's negligence formula, B<PL. Can you apply that formula to the facts of this case?

3. What concerns were expressed by Justice Utter in his concurring opinion? What point did he make about the judiciary's institutional competency to determine the applicable standard of care?

Scott v. Bradford

606 P.2d 554 (Okla. 1979)

DOOLIN, Justice:

This appeal is taken by plaintiffs in trial below, from a judgment in favor of defendant rendered on a jury verdict in a medical malpractice action.

Mrs. Scott's physician advised her she had several fibroid tumors on her uterus. He referred her to defendant surgeon. Defendant admitted her to the hospital where she signed a routine consent form prior to defendant's performing a hysterectomy. After surgery, Mrs. Scott experienced problems with incontinence.

She visited another physician who discovered she had a vesico-vaginal fistula which permitted urine to leak from her bladder into the vagina. This physician referred her to an urologist who, after three surgeries, succeeded in correcting her problems.

Mrs. Scott, joined by her husband, filed the present action alleging medical malpractice, claiming defendant failed to advise her of the risks involved or of available alternatives to surgery. She further maintained had she been properly informed she would have refused the surgery.

The case was submitted to the jury with instructions to which plaintiffs objected. The jury found for defendant and plaintiffs appeal.

. . . .

The issue involved is whether Oklahoma adheres to the doctrine of **informed consent** as the basis of an action for medical malpractice, and if so did the present instructions adequately advise the jury of defendant's duty.

Anglo-American law starts with the premise of thoroughgoing self-determination, each man considered to be his own master. This law does not permit a physician to substitute his judgment for that of the patient by any form of artifice. The doctrine of informed consent arises out of this premise.

Consent to medical treatment, to be effective, should stem from an understanding decision based on adequate information about the treatment, the available alternatives, and the collateral risks. This requirement, labeled "informed consent," is, legally speaking, as essential as a physician's care and skill in the Performance of the therapy. The doctrine imposes a duty on a physician or surgeon to inform a patient of his options and their attendant risks. If a physician breaches this duty, patient's consent is defective, and physician is responsible for the consequences.

If treatment is completely unauthorized and performed without any consent at all, there has been a **battery**. However, if the physician obtains a patient's consent but has breached his duty to inform, the patient has a cause of action sounding in negligence for failure to inform the patient of his options, regardless of the due care exercised at treatment, assuming there is injury.

. . . .

The first buds of court decisions heralding this new medical duty are found in Salgo v. Leland Stanford, Jr., University Board of Trustees, 154 Cal.App.2d 560, 317 P.2d 170 (1957). That court grounded the disclosure requirement in negligence law holding a physician violates a duty to his patient and subjects himself to liability if he withholds any facts which are necessary to form the basis of an intelligent consent by the patient to the proposed treatment. The court strongly suggested a physician is obligated not only to disclose *what* he intends to do, but to supply information which addresses the question of *whether* he should do it. This view was a marked divergence from the general rule of "professional standard of care" in determining what must be disclosed. Under that standard, earlier decisions seemed to perpetuate medical paternalism by giving the profession sweeping authority to decide unilaterally what is in the patient's best interests. Under the "professional standard of care" a physician needed only to inform a patient in conformance with the prevailing medical practice in the community.

More recently, in perhaps one of the most influential informed consent decisions, Canterbury v. Spence, 150 U.S.App.D.C. 263, 464 F.2d 772 (D.C.Cir.1972), cert. den. 409 U.S. 1064, 93 S.Ct. 560, 34 L.Ed.2d 518, the doctrine received perdurable impetus. Judge Robinson observed that suits charging failure by a physician adequately to disclose risks and alternatives of proposed treatment were not innovative in American law. He emphasized the fundamental concept in American jurisprudence that every human being of adult years and sound mind has a right to determine what shall be done with his own body. True consent to what happens to one's self is the informed exercise of a choice. This entails an opportunity to evaluate knowledgeably the options available and the risks attendant upon each. It is the prerogative of every patient to chart his own course and determine which direction he will take.

The decision in *Canterbury* recognized the tendency of some jurisdictions to turn this duty on whether it is the custom of physicians practicing in the community to make the particular disclosure to the patient. That court rejected this standard and held the standard measuring performance of the duty of disclosure is conduct which is reasonable under the circumstances: "(We can not) ignore the fact that to bind disclosure obligations to medical usage is to arrogate the decision on revelation to the physician alone." We agree. A patient's right to make up his mind whether to undergo treatment should not be delegated to the local medical group. What is reasonable disclosure in one instance may not be reasonable in another. We decline to adopt a standard based on the professional standard. We, therefore, hold the scope of a physician's communications must be measured by his patient's need to know enough to enable him to make an intelligent choice. In other words, full disclosure of all material risks incident to treatment must be made. There is no bright line separating the material from the immaterial; it is a question of fact. A risk is material if it would be likely to affect patient's decision. When non-disclosure of a particular risk is open to debate, the issue is for the finder of facts.

This duty to disclose is the first element of the cause of action in negligence based on lack of informed consent. However, there are exceptions creating a privilege of a physician not to disclose. There is no need to disclose risks that either ought to be known by everyone or are already known to the patient. Further, the primary duty of a physician is to do what is best for his patient and where full disclosure would be detrimental to a patient's total care and best interests a physician may withhold such disclosure, for example, where disclosure would alarm an emotionally upset or apprehensive patient. Certainly too, where there is an emergency and the patient is in no condition to determine for himself whether treatment should be administered, the privilege may be invoked.

The patient has the burden of going forward with evidence tending to establish prima facie the essential elements of the cause of action. The burden of proving an exception to his duty and thus a privilege not to disclose, rests upon the physician as an affirmative defense.

The cause of action, based on lack of informed consent, is divided into three elements: the duty to inform being the first, the second is causation, and the third is injury. The second element, that of causation, requires that plaintiff patient would have chosen no treatment or a different course of treatment had the alternatives and material risks of each been made known to him. If the patient would have elected to proceed with treatment had he been duly informed of its risks, then the element of causation is missing. In other words, a causal connection exists between physician's breach of the duty to disclose and patient's injury when and only when disclosure of material risks incidental to treatment would have resulted in a decision against it. A patient obviously has no complaint if he would have submitted to the treatment if the physician had complied with his duty and informed him of the risks. This fact decision raises the difficult question of the correct standard on which to instruct the jury.

The court in *Canterbury v. Spence, supra,* although emphasizing principles of self-determination permits liability only if non-disclosure would have affected the decision of a fictitious "reasonable patient," even though actual patient testifies he would have elected to forego therapy had he been fully informed.

Decisions discussing informed consent have emphasized the disclosure element but paid scant attention to the consent element of the concept, although this is the root of causation. Language in some decisions suggest the standard to be applied is a subjective one, i. e., whether that particular patient would still have consented to the treatment, reasonable choice or otherwise. [Cc]

Although the *Canterbury* rule is probably that of the majority, its "reasonable man" approach has been criticized by some commentators as backtracking on its own theory of self-determination. The *Canterbury* view certainly severely limits the protection granted an injured patient. To the extent the plaintiff, given an adequate disclosure, would have declined the proposed treatment, and a reasonable person in similar circumstances would have consented, a patient's right of self-determination is irrevocably lost. This basic right to know and decide is the reason for the full-disclosure rule. Accordingly, we decline to jeopardize this right by the imposition of the "reasonable man" standard.

If a plaintiff testifies he would have continued with the proposed treatment had he been adequately informed, the trial is over under either the subjective or objective approach. If he testifies he would not, then the causation problem must be resolved by examining the credibility of plaintiff's testimony. The jury must be instructed that it must find plaintiff would have refused the treatment if he is to prevail.

Although it might be said this approach places a physician at the mercy of a patient's hindsight, a careful practitioner can always protect himself by insuring that he has adequately informed each patient he treats. If he does not breach this duty, a causation problem will not arise.

The final element of this cause of action is that of injury. The risk must actually materialize and plaintiff must have been injured as a result of submitting to the treatment. Absent occurrence of the undisclosed risk, a physician's failure to reveal its possibility is not actionable.

In summary, in a medical malpractice action a patient suing under the theory of informed consent must allege and prove:

1) defendant physician failed to inform him adequately of a material risk before securing his consent to the proposed treatment;

2) if he had been informed of the risks he would not have consented to the treatment;

3) the adverse consequences that were not made known did in fact occur and he was injured as a result of submitting to the treatment.

As a defense, a physician may plead and prove plaintiff knew of the risks, full disclosure would be detrimental to patient's best interests or that an emergency existed requiring prompt treatment and patient was in no condition to decide for himself.

Because we are imposing a new duty on physicians, we hereby make this opinion prospective only, affecting those causes of action arising after the date this opinion is promulgated.

The trial court in the case at bar gave rather broad instructions upon the duty of a physician to disclose. The instructions objected to did instruct that defendant should have disclosed material risks of the hysterectomy and feasibility of alternatives. Instructions are sufficient when considered as a whole they present the law applicable to the issues. Jury found for defendant. We find no basis for reversal.

AFFIRMED.

LAVENDER, C. J., and HODGES, HARGRAVE and OPALA, JJ., concur.

BARNES, Justice, concurring in part, dissenting in part:

I concur with the majority opinion in all respects except I would adopt the reasonable man test set out in Canterbury v. Spence, 150 U.S.App.D.C. 263, 464 F.2d 772 (D.C.Cir.1972), cert. den. 409 U.S. 1064, 93 S.Ct. 560, 34 L.Ed.2d 518.

———

Points for Discussion

1. What is the difference between the doctrine of informed consent and medical treatment constituting a battery?

2. Declining to adopt the professional standard of care, the court instead recognized what standard governing the analysis of informed consent cases?

3. According to the *Scott* court, what must a plaintiff allege and prove in an action alleging medical malpractice under the informed consent theory?

4. What defenses are available to a physician-defendant, if any?

5. Note that the court applied its decision prospectively. Why did the court depart from the usual practice of applying decisions retroactively to all causes of action pending at the time of its decision?

6. What is a "material" risk? Is a one percent possibility of a serious and adverse consequence of a particular medical treatment "material"? Three percent? Ten percent?

Ashe v. Radiation Oncology Associates

9 S.W.3d 119 (Tenn. 1999)

HOLDER, J.

We granted this appeal to address the appropriate standard to be employed when assessing the issue of causation in a medical malpractice informed consent case. We find that the objective standard as set forth in this opinion best balances a patient's right to self-determination with the need for a realistic framework for rational resolution of the issue of causation. We hold that the standard to be applied in informed consent cases is whether a reasonable person in the patient's position would have consented to the procedure or treatment in question if adequately informed of all significant perils. The decision of the Court of Appeals is affirmed, and the case is remanded to the trial court for a new trial.

BACKGROUND

The plaintiff, Patricia P. Ashe, was diagnosed with breast cancer in 1988. She ultimately underwent a double mastectomy and chemotherapy as treatment for her breast cancer. In 1993, she began experiencing problems with a cough and a fever. She returned to her oncologist, Dr. Michael Kuzu, where she presented symptoms of fever, cough, pain in the abdomen, weight loss, decreased appetite, and irritability. A chest x-ray and a CT scan revealed the presence of a mass in the medial left apex of her left lung.

The record indicates that the lung tumor could possibly have been metastatic cancer from the breast. Ms. Ashe underwent surgery, and the upper portion of her left lung was removed. She underwent chemotherapy and was referred to the defendant, Dr. Steven L. Stroup, for consideration of radiation therapy. Dr. Stroup testified that chemotherapy alone would be indicated if the lung tumor were metastasized breast cancer. He, however, opined that radiation therapy would be indicated if the lung cancer were primary as opposed to secondary cancer.

Dr. Stroup prescribed radiation treatment for Ms. Ashe. She received a daily dose of 200 centigray for twenty-five days. He described the dose as a "midplane dose." Ms. Ashe sustained "radiation myelitis" caused by a permanent radiation injury to her spinal cord. She is now a paraplegic.

Dr. Stroup did not inform Ms. Ashe that the radiation treatment might result in a permanent injury to her spinal cord. According to Dr. Stroup, the risk that she would sustain a spinal cord injury was less than one percent. Mrs. Ashe proffered the testimony of her expert, Dr. Carlos Perez. Dr. Perez opined that the risk of spinal cord injury was one to two percent. Dr. Perez testified that the applicable standard of care required physicians to warn patients about the risk of radiation injury to the spinal cord.

Ms. Ashe filed the present action alleging claims for medical malpractice and lack of informed consent. At trial, she testified that she would not have consented to the radiation therapy had she been informed of the risk of paralysis. Defense counsel on cross-examination pointed out that the plaintiff did equivocate in her deposition on the issue of consent. Her deposition testimony indicated that she did not know what she would have done had she been warned about the risk of spinal cord injury. She then testified on redirect examination as follows:

> True, but the risk of being paralyzed and put in a wheelchair for the rest of your life was not one of the items, if there was any discussed, because had he said that within a six-month period-which they said that would be the time frame for it to happen-had he said, 'Patty, if you do this there is a risk that you will be in a wheelchair six months from now,' I would have told him, 'I will take my chances.' I would not have it done.

The trial court found that the plaintiff's trial testimony conflicted with her deposition testimony regarding whether she would have consented to the procedure had she been warned of the risk of spinal cord injury. The trial court, therefore, struck the trial testimony and granted the defendant a **directed verdict** on the informed consent claim. The plaintiff's malpractice claim went to the jury. The jury was unable to reach a verdict, and a mistrial was declared.

The plaintiff appealed to the Court of Appeals. The Court of Appeals held that as part of the plaintiff's informed consent claim she was required to prove that a reasonable person knowing of the risk for spinal cord injury would have decided not to have had the procedure performed. The Court held that the discrepancy between the trial testimony and deposition testimony went to the issue of credibility and that the trial testimony should not have been stricken. The Court of Appeals reversed the trial court's grant of a directed verdict on the informed consent claim and remanded the case for a new trial.

ANALYSIS

The burden of proof on the standard of care element in medical malpractice informed consent cases is controlled by Tenn.Code Ann. § 29-26-118. Pursuant to § 29-26-118, a plaintiff must prove by expert testimony that

> the defendant did not supply appropriate information to the patient in obtaining his informed consent to the procedure out of which plaintiff's claim allegedly arose in accordance with the recognized standard of acceptable professional practice in the profession and in the specialty, if

any, that the defendant practices in the community in which he practices or in similar communities.

. . . In addition, Tenn.Code Ann. § 29-26-115 requires that the plaintiff prove the recognized standard of acceptable professional practice, that the defendant acted with less than ordinary and reasonable care in accordance with that standard, and that the plaintiff sustained injuries as a result of the defendant's negligent act or omission. Accordingly, the plaintiff in an informed consent medical malpractice case has the burden of proving: (1) what a reasonable medical practitioner in the same or similar community would have disclosed to the patient about the risk posed by the proposed procedure or treatment; and (2) that the defendant departed from the norm. [C]

. . . .

The case now before us is not a medical battery case. Ms. Ashe had authorized the radiation treatment. Ms. Ashe, however, contends that she was not apprised of certain risks inherent in the treatment. Her claim, therefore, is premised on the lack of informed consent.

The issue with which we are now confronted is whether an objective, subjective, or a hybrid subjective/objective test shall be employed when assessing causation in medical malpractice informed consent cases. The issue is one of first impression in Tennessee. The majority of jurisdictions having addressed this issue follow an objective standard. A minority of jurisdictions having addressed the issue follow the subjective approach. One jurisdiction, Hawaii, employed a "modified objective standard" for informed consent cases for approximately ten years. Hawaii has now abandoned the modified approach in favor of the objective standard. We shall now examine the various approaches and the rationales behind these approaches.

Subjective Standard

The plaintiff urges this Court to follow the minority rule or adopt a subjective standard when evaluating causation in an informed consent case. **Causation** under the subjective standard is established solely by patient testimony. Patients must testify and prove that they would not have consented to the procedures had they been advised of the particular risk in question. *See e.g., Scott v. Bradford,* 606 P.2d 554 (Okla.1979); [c]. Accordingly, resolution of causation under a subjective standard is premised exclusively on the credibility of a patient's testimony.

The subjective standard engages in an abstract analysis. The abstract analysis not only poses a purely hypothetical question but seeks to answer the hypothetical question. One commentator has framed this hypothetical question as follows: "Viewed from the point at which [the patient] had to decide, would the patient have decided differently had he known something he did not know?" Canterbury v. Spence, 464 F.2d 772, 790 (D.C.Cir.1972) *quoting* Waltz & Scheuneman, *Informed Consent to Therapy,* 64 Nw.U.L.Rev. 628, 647 (1970).

Proponents of the subjective test argue that a patient should have the right to make medical determinations regardless of whether the determination is rational or reasonable. [C] Opponents, however, focus on the unfairness of allowing the issue of causation to turn on the credibility of the hindsight of a person seeking recovery after experiencing a most undesirable result. [C] "Patients cannot divorce their re-created decision process from hindsight." [C] Accordingly, the subjective test potentially places the physician in jeopardy of the patient's hindsight and bitterness. [C] Moreover, the adoption of a subjective standard could preclude recovery in an informed consent case in which the patient died as a result of an unforewarned collateral consequence. . . .

Objective Standard

The majority approach or the so-called objective standard emanates from the seminal decision in *Canterbury v. Spence,* 464 F.2d 772 (D.C.Cir.1972). In *Canterbury,* the court held that causation in informed consent cases is better resolved on an objective basis "in terms of what a prudent person in the patient's position would have decided if suitably informed of all perils bearing significance." [C] The objective view recognizes that neither the plaintiff nor the fact-finder can provide a definitive answer as to what the patient would have done had the patient known of the particular risk prior to consenting to the procedure or treatment. [C] Accordingly, the patient's testimony is relevant under an objective approach, but the testimony is not controlling. [C]

Modified Objective Standard

The modified objective standard was first recognized in *Leyson v. Steuermann,* 5 Haw.App. 504, 705 P.2d 37 (1985). In *Leyson,* the Hawaii Court of Appeals attempted to balance patient's right to self-determination with the concerns espoused in *Canterbury* of subjecting a physician to a patient's bitterness or hindsight following an undesirable result. The resulting test determined causation "from the viewpoint of the actual patient acting rationally and reasonably." [C]

Approximately ten years after the inception of the modified approach, the approach was declared to be onerous in application. In *Bernard v. Char,* 79 Hawai'i 362, 903 P.2d 667 (1995), the Hawaii Supreme Court elaborated that:

> In its effort to achieve the desired result of combining the objective and subjective standards, the modified objective standard injects at least one extra level of complexity into the causation analysis. Under the objective

standard, the factfinder must suspend his or her own viewpoint and step into the viewpoint of a reasonable person to objectively assess the plaintiff-patient's decision to undergo treatment. Under the subjective standard, the factfinder must simply assess the credibility of the plaintiff-patient when he or she invariably asserts that he or she would have declined treatment with proper disclosure. Under the "modified objective standard," however, the factfinder must first suspend his or her viewpoint, then place himself or herself in the mind of the actual patient, and, then, while maintaining the viewpoint of the actual patient, try to determine what the actual patient would have decided about the proposed medical treatment or procedure, if the actual patient were acting rationally and reasonably.

[C] Accordingly, the modified approach was abandoned in favor of the objective standard. . . .

The Court held: (1) that the objective standard provided "a better, simpler, and more equitable analytical process;" and (2) that the objective standard ultimately addressed the concerns which prompted the creation of the modified test.

CONCLUSION

We agree with the majority of jurisdictions having addressed this issue and hold that the objective approach is the better approach. The objective approach circumvents the need to place the fact-finder in a position of deciding whether a speculative and perhaps emotional answer to a purely hypothetical question shall dictate the outcome of the litigation. The objective standard is consistent with the prevailing standard in negligence cases which measures the conduct of the person in question with that of a reasonable person in like circumstances. RESTATEMENT (SECOND) OF TORTS § 283, p. 12 (1965); [cc]. The objective test provides a realistic framework for rational resolution of the issue of causation. We, therefore, believe that causation may best be assessed in informed consent cases by the finder of fact determining how nondisclosure would affect a reasonable person in the plaintiff's position.

We also are of the opinion that the objective test appropriately respects a patient's right to self-determination. The finder of fact may consider and give weight to the patient's testimony as to whether the patient would have consented to the procedure upon full disclosure of the risks. When applying the objective standard, the finder of fact may also take into account the characteristics of the plaintiff including the plaintiff's idiosyncrasies, fears, age, medical condition, and religious beliefs. [Cc] Accordingly, the objective standard affords the ease of applying a uniform standard and yet maintains the flexibility of allowing the finder of fact to make appropriate adjustments to accommodate the individual characteristics and idiosyncrasies of an individual patient. We, therefore, hold that the standard to be applied in informed consent cases is whether a reasonable person in the patient's position would have consented to the procedure or treatment in question if adequately informed of all significant perils.

In applying the objective standard to the facts of this case, we agree with the Court of Appeals that the jury should not have been precluded from deciding the issue of informed consent. Under the objective analysis, the plaintiff's testimony is only a factor when determining the issue of informed consent. The dispositive issue is not whether Ms. Ashe would herself have chosen a different course of treatment. The issue is whether a reasonable patient in Ms. Ashe's position would have chosen a different course of treatment. The jury, therefore, should have been allowed to decide whether a reasonable person in Ms. Ashe's position would have consented to the radiation therapy had the risk of paralysis been disclosed.

The judgment of the Court of Appeals reversing the trial court is affirmed. The case is remanded for a new trial consistent with this opinion. . . .

———————————

Points for Discussion

1. According to the court, which party bears the burden of proof in medical malpractice informed consent cases?

2. How does the court frame and distinguish the subjective, objective, and modified objective standards of informed consent?

3. Why does the court adopt, and how does it apply, the objective standard?

4. Imagine that you were a member of the *Ashe* court. Would you have joined the court's opinion? If not, why not?

———————————

Moore v. The Regents of the University of California

51 Cal.3d 120, 793 P.2d 479, 271 Cal.Rptr. 146 (1990)

PANELLI, J.

I. Introduction

We granted review in this case to determine whether plaintiff has stated a cause of action against his physician and other defendants for using his cells in potentially lucrative medical research without his permission. Plaintiff alleges that his physician failed to disclose preexisting research and economic interests in the cells before obtaining consent to the medical procedures by which they were extracted. The superior court sustained all defendants' demurrers to the third amended complaint, and the Court of Appeal reversed. We hold that the complaint states a cause of action for breach of the physician's disclosure obligations, but not for **conversion**.

II. Facts

. . . .

The plaintiff is John Moore (Moore), who underwent treatment for hairy-cell leukemia at the Medical Center of the University of California at Los Angeles (UCLA Medical Center). The five defendants are: (1) Dr. David W. Golde (Golde), a physician who attended Moore at UCLA Medical Center; (2) the Regents of the University of California (Regents), who own and operate the university; (3) Shirley G. Quan, a researcher employed by the Regents; (4) Genetics Institute, Inc. (Genetics Institute); and (5) Sandoz Pharmaceuticals Corporation and related entities (collectively Sandoz).

Moore first visited UCLA Medical Center on October 5, 1976, shortly after he learned that he had hairy-cell leukemia. After hospitalizing Moore and "withdr[awing] extensive amounts of blood, bone marrow aspirate, and other bodily substances," Golde confirmed that diagnosis. At this time all defendants, including Golde, were aware that "certain blood products and blood components were of great value in a number of commercial and scientific efforts" and that access to a patient whose blood contained these substances would provide "competitive, commercial, and scientific advantages."

On October 8, 1976, Golde recommended that Moore's spleen be removed. Golde informed Moore "that he had reason to fear for his life, and that the proposed splenectomy operation ... was necessary to slow down the progress of his disease." Based upon Golde's representations, Moore signed a written consent form authorizing the splenectomy.

Before the operation, Golde and Quan "formed the intent and made arrangements to obtain portions of [Moore's] spleen following its removal" and to take them to a separate research unit. Golde gave written instructions to this effect on October 18 and 19, 1976. These research activities "were not intended to have ... any relation to [Moore's] medical ... care." However, neither Golde nor Quan informed Moore of their plans to conduct this research or requested his permission. Surgeons at UCLA Medical Center, whom the complaint does not name as defendants, removed Moore's spleen on October 20, 1976.

Moore returned to the UCLA Medical Center several times between November 1976 and September 1983. He did so at Golde's direction and based upon representations "that such visits were necessary and required for his health and well-being, and based upon the trust inherent in and by virtue of the physician-patient relationship ...." On each of these visits Golde withdrew additional samples of "blood, blood serum, skin, bone marrow aspirate, and sperm." On each occasion Moore travelled to the UCLA Medical Center from his home in Seattle because he had been told that the procedures were to be performed only there and only under Golde's direction.

"In fact, [however,] throughout the period of time that [Moore] was under [Golde's] care and treatment, ... the defendants were actively involved in a number of activities which they concealed from [Moore] ...." Specifically, defendants were conducting research on Moore's cells and planned to "benefit financially and competitively ... [by exploiting the cells] and [their] exclusive access to [the cells] by virtue of [Golde's] ongoing physician-patient relationship ...."

Sometime before August 1979, Golde established a cell line from Moore's T-lymphocytes. On January 30, 1981, the Regents applied for a patent on the cell line, listing Golde and Quan as inventors. . . . "[B]y virtue of an established policy ..., [the] Regents, Golde, and Quan would share in any royalties or profits ... arising out of [the] patent." The patent issued on March 20, 1984, naming Golde and Quan as the inventors of the cell line and the Regents as the assignee of the patent. . . .

. . . .

With the Regents' assistance, Golde negotiated agreements for commercial development of the cell line and products to be derived from it. . . .

Based upon these allegations, Moore attempted to state 13 causes of action. Each defendant demurred to each purported cause of action. The superior court, however, expressly considered the validity of only the first cause of action, conversion. Reasoning that the remaining causes of action incorporated the earlier, defective allegations, the superior court sustained a general demurrer to the entire complaint with leave to amend. In a subsequent proceeding, the superior court sustained Genetics Institute's and Sandoz's demurrers without leave to amend on the grounds that Moore had not stated a cause of action for conversion and that the complaint's allegations about the entities' secondary liability were too conclusory. In accordance with its earlier ruling that the defective allegations about conversion rendered the entire complaint insufficient, the superior court took the remaining demurrers off its calendar.

With one justice dissenting, the Court of Appeal reversed, holding that the complaint did state a cause of action for conversion. The Court of Appeal agreed with the superior court that the allegations against Genetics Institute and Sandoz were insufficient, but directed the superior court to give Moore leave to amend. The Court of Appeal also directed the superior court to decide "the remaining causes of action, which [had] never been expressly ruled upon."

III. Discussion

A. *Breach of Fiduciary Duty and Lack of Informed Consent*

Moore repeatedly alleges that Golde failed to disclose the extent of his research and economic interests in Moore's cells before obtaining consent to the medical procedures by which the cells were extracted. These allegations, in our view, state a cause of action against Golde for invading a legally protected interest of his patient. This cause of action can properly be characterized either as the breach of a **fiduciary duty** to disclose facts **material** to the patient's consent or, alternatively, as the performance of medical procedures without first having obtained the patient's informed consent.

What's That?

A *fiduciary* is one who is required to act for the benefit of another person on all matters within the scope of their relationship. Lawyers and physicians are examples of fiduciaries.

Our analysis begins with three well-established principles. First, "a person of adult years and in sound mind has the right, in the exercise of control over his own body, to determine whether or not to submit to lawful medical treatment." [Cc] Second, "the patient's consent to treatment, to be effective, must be an informed consent." [C] Third, in soliciting the patient's consent, a physician has a fiduciary duty to disclose all information material to the patient's decision. [Cc]

These principles lead to the following conclusions: (1) a physician must disclose personal interests unrelated to the patient's health, whether research or economic, that may affect the physician's professional judgment; and (2) a physician's failure to disclose such interests may give rise to a cause of action for performing medical procedures without informed consent or breach of fiduciary duty.

To be sure, questions about the validity of a patient's consent to a procedure typically arise when the patient alleges that the physician failed to disclose medical risks, as in malpractice cases, and not when the patient alleges that the physician had a personal interest, as in this case. The concept of informed consent, however, is broad enough to encompass the latter. "The scope of the physician's communication to the patient ... must be measured by the patient's need, and that need is whatever information is material to the decision." [C]

Indeed, the law already recognizes that a reasonable patient would want to know whether a physician has an economic interest that might affect the physician's professional judgment. As the Court of Appeal has said, "[c]ertainly a sick patient deserves to be free of any reasonable suspicion that his doctor's judgment is influenced by a profit motive." [C] The desire to protect patients from possible conflicts of interest has also motivated legislative enactments. . . .

It is important to note that no law prohibits a physician from conducting research in the same area in which he practices. Progress in medicine often depends upon physicians, such as those practicing at the university hospital where Moore received treatment, who conduct research while caring for their patients.

Yet a physician who treats a patient in whom he also has a research interest has potentially conflicting loyalties. This is because medical treatment decisions are made on the basis of proportionality - weighing the benefits *to the patient* against the risks *to the patient*. As another court has said, "the determination as to whether the burdens of treatment are worth enduring for any individual patient depends upon the facts unique in each case," and "the patient's interests and desires are the key ingredients of the decision-making process." [C] A physician who adds his own research interests to this balance may be tempted to order a scientifically useful procedure or test that offers marginal, or no, benefits to the patient. The possibility that an interest extraneous to the patient's health has affected the physician's judgment is something that a reasonable patient would want to know in deciding whether to consent to a proposed course of treatment. It is material to the patient's decision and, thus, a prerequisite to informed consent. [C]

Golde argues that the scientific use of cells that have already been removed cannot possibly affect the patient's medical interests. The argument is correct in one instance but not in another. If a physician has no plans to conduct research on a patient's cells at the time he recommends the medical procedure by which they are taken, then the patient's medical interests have not been impaired. In that instance the argument is correct. On the other hand, a physician who does have a preexisting research interest might, consciously or unconsciously, take that into consideration in recommending the procedure. In that instance the argument is incorrect: the physician's extraneous motivation may affect his judgment and is, thus, material to the patient's consent.

We acknowledge that there is a competing consideration. To require disclosure of research and economic interests may corrupt the patient's own judgment by distracting him from the requirements of his health. But California law does not grant physicians unlimited discretion to decide what to disclose. Instead, "it is the prerogative of the patient, not the physician, to determine for himself the direction in which he believes his interests lie." [C] "Unlimited discretion in the physician is irreconcilable with the basic right of the patient to make the ultimate informed decision ...." [C]

Accordingly, we hold that a physician who is seeking a patient's consent for a medical procedure must, in order to satisfy his fiduciary duty and to obtain the patient's informed consent, disclose personal interests unrelated to the patient's health, whether research or economic, that may affect his medical judgment.

. . . .

Points for Discussion

1. The court concluded that Moore's claim could properly be characterized as what type(s) of cause(s) of action?

2. The *Moore* court applies a reasonable patient standard to establish duty for informed consent cases. In the context of the case brought by Moore, is that standard preferable to a reasonable physician standard? Why or why not?

3. Doctor Golde argued that a patient's medical interests could not be affected by the scientific use of cells that are already removed from the patient's body. How did the court respond to that argument?

4. Could the court's analysis and ruling hinder and adversely affect medical research? Should the court be concerned about the consequences of its decision? If so, how does a judge discern and measure those consequences?

5. The *Moore* court held that the plaintiff's complaint did not state a cause of action for conversion. "Since Moore clearly did not expect to retain possession of his cells following their removal, to sue for their conversion he must have retained an ownership interest in them." The court doubted that any such interest had been retained. "First, no reported judicial decision supports Moore's claim, either directly or by close analogy. Second, California statutory law drastically limits any continuing interest of a patient in excised cells. Third, the subject matters of the Regents' patent—the patented cell line and the products derived from it—cannot be Moore's property." Regarding the third conclusion, the court opined:

    > "This is because the patented cell line is both factually and legally distinct from the cells taken from Moore's body. Federal law permits the patenting of organisms that represent the product of 'human

ingenuity,' but not naturally occurring organisms. . . . Human cell lines are patentable because '[l]ong-term adaptation and growth of human tissues and cells in culture is difficult—often considered an art . . .', and the probability of success is low. . . . It is this *inventive effort* that patent law rewards, not the discovery of naturally occurring raw materials. Thus, Moore's allegations that he owns the cell line and the products derived from it are inconsistent with the patent, which constitutes an authoritative determination that the cell line is the product of invention. . . ."

While the court did "not purport to hold that excised cells can never be property for any purpose whatsoever," it set forth three reasons supporting its conclusion that imposing liability for conversion based upon the allegations of Moore's complaint was inappropriate. "First, a fair balancing of the relevant policy considerations counsels against extending the tort. Second, problems in this area are better suited to legislative resolution. Third, the tort of conversion is not necessary to protect patients' rights. For these reasons, we conclude that the use of excised human cells in medical research does not amount to a conversion."

6. In 1951, Henrietta Lacks, a poor, black tobacco farmer, died from cervical cancer. Prior to her death, a surgeon took samples from her tumor. Lacks' cells were and continue to be used by scientists and were critical to the development of the polio vaccine, advances in *in vitro* fertilization, gene mapping, and other scientific advances. Lacks' story is chronicled in Rebecca Skloot, The Immortal Life of Henrietta Lacks (Crown Publishers, 2010).

Hypo 4-4

Two surgeons employed by Hospital are preparing to operate on patients. Surgeon 1 has just completed a six-month stay in an in-patient rehabilitation program where she was treated for a longstanding addiction to alcohol and prescription painkillers. Surgeon 2 has just learned that he is infected with the human immunodeficiency virus (HIV). Should the surgeons be legally obligated to inform their patients of these facts? Why or why not?

c. Aggravated Negligence

Archibald v. Kemble

971 A.2d 513 (Pa. Super. 2009)

OPINION BY CLELAND, J.:

¶ 1 Appellants, Robert and Krista Archibald (Archibald or Archibalds), appeal the December 6, 2007 Order granting Appellee Cody Kemble's (Kemble) Motion for Summary Judgment. The crux of this case is the standard of care to be applied when a player in an adult "no-check" ice hockey league checks and injures another player in violation of the league rules. Because we conclude the applicable standard of care is **recklessness** and because the Archibalds were not required to specifically plead recklessness in their Complaint and because they produced evidence of recklessness in their discovery, we vacate and remand.

¶ 2 Archibalds' Complaint alleges:

. . . .

3. The events hereinafter took place on or about June 2, 2003 at the Twin Ponds East skating facility in Lower Paxton Township, Dauphin County, Pennsylvania.

4. At the aforementioned time and place, the Plaintiff, Robert Archibald, and Defendant were participating in an adult non-checking ice hockey league game.

5. At the aforementioned time and place, the Plaintiff, Robert Archibald, was playing the position of right wing and in a corner of the ice rink and playing the puck when he was, without provocation or warning, checked by the Defendant into the boards of the ice hockey rink.

6. The check into the boards resulted in ... Robert Archibald's body hitting the side of the ice rink, causing injuries set forth below.

7. At the aforesaid time and place, the Plaintiff, Robert Archibald, was exercising due care at all times and participating in the non-checking adult ice hockey league.

8. As a result of the aforesaid check into the boards, the Plaintiff, Robert Archibald, suffered serious and what may be permanent injuries . . .

9. The Plaintiff, Robert Archibald is advised and therefore avers that the injuries may be progressing, and permanent in nature and effect.

....

11. The Defendant, Cody Kemble's negligence consisted of the following:

a. failing to assure that Robert Archibald was aware and/or warned that the check was going to be attempted before checking him into the boards;

b. failing to assure that Robert Archibald was willing to be checked;

c. checking Robert Archibald when not safe to do so;

d. failing to understand and learn the rules, prohibition and limitation on any checking prior to participating in the non-checking league and game.

. . . .

¶ 3 Robert Archibald testified the hockey league is a nonchecking league. . . . He further testified that nonchecking means "no bodily contact" other than incidental contact. . . . Archibald explained the league rules set forth that checking is not permitted and that the league rules are posted on bulletin boards and in the league's brochures. . . . The game in issue was a "spirited" game because "playoff positions were at stake." . . . He explained Kemble, who was "the best player on the ice that night," got into a verbal altercation with one of Archibald's teammates before Archibald's injury. . . . In describing Kemble's approach, Archibald testified, "[M]y head was down, and I saw him pick up his right skate and jamb [sic] it into my left skate as we skated side by side." . . . When asked whether he actually saw Kemble's skate come into contact with his skate, he answered, "Absolutely.... I saw the skate lift up and I saw the skate come down.... My left skate, he pulls up, lifts his right skate and jambs [sic] it this way into my skate." . . . Archibald described this act as "proactive physical contact." . . . As a result of Kemble's check, Archibald explained he "crashed into the boards, hip first." . . . He was transported from the hockey rink to the hospital by ambulance. . . . Archibald suffered severe pain. . . . His femur was "completely shattered" and the bone is "gone." He now has two rods "down the length of his thigh." He also suffered from significant blood loss and infection. He has a twelve-inch incision on his leg. . . . He can no longer jog or play hockey. . . . His leg is permanently injured. His medical bills are approximately $35,000.00. . . .

¶ 4 Hockey expert Patrick Quinn testified that if the incident occurred as Archibald described, the action is called "slew-foot." . . . Based on Archibald's version of the facts, Quinn testified: "And Mr. Archibald was piled into the rink, into the boards at the end of the rink, in a very dangerous manner, dangerous enough to cause some serious injury." . . . He further explained, "A slew-foot basically is taking your own foot, and from behind usually it happens where you just kick the foot. Generally the foot is planted ... as you're skating, and you kick that foot out from behind with the intention of knocking the player off his feet." Quinn explained slew footing is not accepted at the professional level and definitely not expected in a no-contact league. Quinn continued, "[I]t's a very deliberate action." . . . In evaluating whether the act as described by Archibald was intentional, Quinn explained, "[Kemble] knows the rules. He knows how the game is played. He knows what contact is. And if he, indeed, slew-footed this guy, that was intentional." . . .

¶ 5 Cody Kemble testified he had been playing hockey since he was four years old. . . . He was eighteen years old at the time of the incident. Kemble testified the league was a nonchecking hockey league. (The parties stipulated the league was a nonchecking league. Kemble testified nonchecking means "no hitting ... no ... slamming your body into another person to knock them over and off the puck." He explained slew footing would be in violation of league rules. Kemble asserts he did not recall any bodily contact with Archibald. Kemble explained he did, however, attempt to lift Archibald's hockey stick and take the puck from underneath.

¶ 6 We first turn to the standard of care to be applied when a player in an adult "no-check" ice hockey league checks and injures another player in violation of the league rules. There is no Pennsylvania appellate authority on point.

¶ 7 After thorough review of the law of other jurisdictions, we hold that a hockey player must have engaged in reckless conduct to be subject to liability for injuries received by another player in a no-check league. The trial court determined recklessness or intentional conduct must be shown.

¶ 8 Any analysis must begin with the recognition that "reckless" and "intentional" conduct are not synonymous.

¶ 9 The Restatement (Second) of Torts explains the distinction:

> Reckless misconduct differs from intentional wrongdoing in a very important particular. While an act to be reckless must be intended by the actor, the actor does not intend to cause the harm which results from it. It is enough that he realizes or, from the facts which he knows, should realize that there is a strong probability that harm may result, even though

he hopes or even expects that his conduct will prove harmless. However, a strong probability is a different thing from the substantial certainty without which cannot be said to intend the harm in which his act results.

Restatement (Second) of Torts § 500 cmt. *f* (1965).

. . . .

¶ 11 Several other jurisdictions have applied the standard of recklessness in factually similar sports situations. Of those jurisdictions that have decided cases of this nature, a majority apply the standard of recklessness. [C]

¶ 12 Vigorous participation in athletic competition is a public policy to be encouraged. *See Hackbart v. Cincinnati Bengals, Inc. and Charles "Booby" Clark,* 601 F.2d 516 (10th Cir.1979); [cc]. "Fear of civil liability stemming from negligent acts occurring in an athletic event could curtail the proper fervor with which the game should be played." [C]

¶ 13 However, we also recognize that "organized, athletic competition does not exist in a vacuum." [C] Where, as in the present case, the participants are engaged in an adult competition governed by a set of rules, and when the participants know or should know the rules and understand the rules serve to protect the participants, then each player has a duty to the next to comply with those rules. "A reckless disregard for the safety of other players cannot be excused." [C]

¶ 14 We are also mindful that adopting a mere negligence standard could lead to an overabundance of litigation. In a sport, such as hockey, where some risk of injury is inherent in the nature of the game, litigation should not potentially follow every time a participant negligently causes injury. "If simple negligence were to be adopted as the standard of care, every punter with whom contact is made, every midfielder high sticked, every basketball player fouled, every batter struck by a pitch, and every hockey player tripped would have ingredients for a lawsuit if injury resulted." [C]

¶ 15 The majority of jurisdictions that have dealt with this issue have adopted the Restatement's standard for recklessness and we do so as well under the facts of this case.

¶ 16 The Restatement provides:

> The actor's conduct is in reckless disregard of the safety of another if he does an act or intentionally fails to do an act which it is his duty to the other to do, knowing or having reason to know of facts which would lead a reasonable man to realize, not only that his conduct creates an unreasonable risk of

physical harm to another, but also that such risk is substantially greater than that which is necessary to make his conduct negligent.

....

Special Note: The conduct described in this Section is often called "wanton or wilful misconduct" both in statutes and judicial opinions. On the other hand, this phrase is sometimes used by courts to refer to conduct intended to cause harm to another.

Restatement (Second) of Torts § 500 (1965).

¶ 17 Recklessness, or willfulness, or wantonness refers to a degree of care Prosser describes as "aggravated negligence." Nevertheless, "[t]hey apply to conduct which is still, at essence, negligent, rather than actually intended to do harm, but which is so far from a proper state of mind that it is to be treated in many respects as if it were so intended." W. PAGE KEETON ET AL., PROSSER AND KEETON ON TORTS § 34 (5th ed. 1984). In this case, even though we hold Archibald must prove Kemble acted recklessly, the cause of action remains sounding in negligence. [C] Therefore, merely determining the degree of care is recklessness does not give rise to a separate tort that must have been pled within the applicable statute of limitations. The trial judge was correct in ruling the degree of care is recklessness. . . .

. . . .

¶ 20 Factors to be considered in determining whether a player's conduct was reckless and gives rise to liability include:

The specific game involved, the ages and physical attributes of the participants, their respective skills at the game and their knowledge of its rules and customs, their status as amateurs or professionals, the type of risks which inhere in the game and those which are outside the realm of reasonable anticipation, the presence or absence of protective uniforms or equipment, the degree of zest with which the game is being played, and doubtless others.

[C]

¶ 21 Having determined the standard of care is recklessness, we now examine the record to evaluate whether the Archibalds came forward with evidence to support each element of their cause of action.

¶ 22 Archibald has produced evidence that he and Kemble played in a league where Kemble knew he had a responsibility to Archibald not to engage in certain conduct including checking. Thus, Archibald has produced evidence that Kemble owed a duty of care to Archibald.

¶ 23 Archibald described the action as being intentional. Hockey expert Quinn explained if the incident occurred as Archibald explained that it was a "deliberate action." Quinn explained Kemble's action could cause serious injury. Kemble explained he had been skating for fourteen years, that he understood the term "check" to mean knocking a person down, and that he understood slew-footing was prohibited by league rules. Thus, Archibald has produced evidence that Kemble breached his duty of care by acting recklessly.

. . . .

¶ 26 The issue before the trial court was whether or not to grant Kemble's Motion for Summary Judgment. Summary judgment could only have been granted in favor of Kemble if Archibald had failed to present evidence to support each element of the cause of action. As we have determined, it is clear from the record there is evidence that Kemble owed a duty of care to Archibald, [and] that he breached the duty by acting recklessly . . .

¶ 27 The trial court's Order of December 7, 2007 granting the Motion for Summary Judgment is **vacated** and the matter is remanded. Jurisdiction relinquished.

Parret v. UNICCO Serv. Co.

127 P.3d 572 (Okla. 2005)

[In this case the court addressed the United States District Court for the Western District of Oklahoma's certified questions of state law, including the issue of the tiers of negligence.]

What's That?

A federal court posing a certified question to the highest court of a state asks the state court for its views, position, and guidance on an issue of state law arising in the lawsuit before the federal court.

. . . .

¶ 3 On July 20, 1999, Glenn Parret, an employee of UNICCO Service Company (UNICCO), was electrocuted while replacing emergency lights at the Dayton Tire Plant owned by defendant Bridgestone/Firestone, Inc. (Bridgestone) in Oklahoma City, Oklahoma. He died as a result of his injuries two days later . . .

. . . .

TORT LIABILITY CONTINUUM

¶ 12 In *Graham v. Keuchel,* 1993 OK 6, 847 P.2d 342, 362, this Court explained that the common law divides *"actionable tortious conduct* into (1) *negligence,* and (2) *willful acts that result in intended or unintended harm."* In the lower tier of tortious conduct lie three levels of negligence. [C] These are defined by statute in Oklahoma as slight negligence, ordinary negligence, and gross negligence. *See* OKLA. STAT. tit. 25, §§ 5 & 6 (2001). In the higher tier lie two distinct levels: (1) wilful and wanton misconduct and (2) intentional misconduct. [C]

¶ 13 The level termed "wilful and wanton" misconduct, according to Professor Prosser, occupies "a penumbra of what has been called 'quasi intent'" lying between gross negligence and intentional conduct. William L. Prosser, Handbook of the Law of Torts § 34, at 184 (4th ed.1971). As *Graham* explained:

> [t]he intent in *wilful and wanton misconduct* is *not* an *intent to cause the injury;* it is an *intent to do an act*-or the failure to do an act-in reckless disregard of the consequences and *under such circumstances that a reasonable man would know,* or have reason to know, *that such conduct would be likely to result in substantial harm to another.*

[C] *Graham* noted that "[w]hile 'ordinary' and 'gross' negligence differ in *degree,* 'negligence' and 'willful and wanton misconduct' differ in *kind."* [C] . . . ("[W]hile ordinary negligence of the plaintiff may be used as a defense against gross negligence, it may not be considered as a defense against any form of conduct found to be willful and wanton or intentional.").

¶ 14 The Oklahoma Uniform Jury Instruction, which was derived from the *Graham* decision, explains:

> The conduct of [Defendant] was willful and wanton if [Defendant] was either aware, or did not care, that there was a substantial and unnecessary risk that [his/her/its] conduct would cause serious injury to others. In order for the conduct to be willful and wanton, it must have been unreasonable under the circumstances, and also there must have been a high probability that the conduct would cause serious harm to another person.

Oklahoma Uniform Jury Instructions (OUJI) (civil), No. 9.17. The instruction goes on to describe a higher level of misconduct explaining that a "[Defendant]'s conduct was intentional if he/she desired to cause injury to [Plaintiff] or knew that such injury was substantially certain to result from [his/her] conduct."

¶ 15 The analysis in *Graham* and the definitions derived therefrom and articulated in OUJI formulate a continuum of tort liability which may be outlined as follows:

    I. Negligence

        A. Slight Negligence-want of great care and diligence.

        B. Ordinary Negligence-want of ordinary care and diligence.

        C. Gross Negligence-want of slight care and diligence. [1]

    . . . .

Points for Discussion

1. Why does the *Archibald* court allow the case to proceed as one in which the defendant breached his duty of care to the plaintiff where the defendant's conduct was assertedly intentional and deliberate? Why do you think that the plaintiff framed his claim as one involving a negligent and not an intentional tort?

2. As the *Archibald* court notes, reckless, willful, or wanton conduct has been described as "aggravated negligence."

3. In an early English case a judge noted three different types and degrees of negligence—slight, ordinary, and gross. *See* Coggs v. Bernard, 92 Eng. Rep. 107 (1703). In *Parret* the Oklahoma Supreme Court discussed the slight-ordinary-gross negligence continuum. Can you define and distinguish between the different degrees of negligence?

---

1 Section 5 of title 25 provides: "There are three degrees of negligence, namely, slight, ordinary and gross. The latter includes the former." Section 6 of title 25 provides: " Slight negligence consists in the want of great care and diligence; ordinary negligence in the want of ordinary care and diligence; and gross negligence in the want of slight care and diligence."

Perspective & Analysis

Consider the views of one scholar on this tripartite division of the standard of care:

"It is not easy to believe that there are three and only three degrees of fault, since risks imposed by the defendant's conduct range in virtually infinite gradations. But in the great mass of cases there is no occasion at all to distinguish among any degrees of fault . . . In most cases, a defendant is subject to liability for negligence whether his negligence is great or small. He is liable for damages that will compensate the plaintiff for the plaintiff's actual harm, but that liability is not diminished if the defendant's negligence is slight, nor is it increased if the defendant's negligence is gross."

Dan B. Dodds, The Law of Torts 349 (2000).

2. Establishing a Standard of Care by Applying a Rule of Law

Restatement (Second) of Torts § 285(c) (1965)

The standard of conduct of a reasonable [person] may be . . . established by judicial decision.

Baltimore & O. R. Co. v. Goodman

275 U.S. 66 (1927)

Mr. Justice HOLMES delivered the opinion of the Court.

This is a suit brought by the widow and administratrix of Nathan Goodman against the petitioner for causing his death by running him down at a grade crossing. The defence is that Goodman's own negligence caused the death. At the trial the defendant asked

Take Note

A "plaintiff's contributory negligence bars recovery against a defendant whose negligent conduct would otherwise make him liable to the plaintiff for the harm sustained by him." Restatement (Second) of Torts § 467 (1965).

the Court to direct a verdict for it, but the request and others looking to the same direction were refused, and the plaintiff got a verdict and a judgment which was affirmed by the Circuit Court of Appeals. [C].

Goodman was driving an automobile truck in an easterly direction and was killed by a train running southwesterly across the road at a rate of not less than 60 miles an hour. The line was straight but it is said by the respondent that Goodman 'had no practical view' beyond a section house 243 feet north of the crossing until he was about 20 feet from the first rail, or, as the respondent argues, 12 feet from danger, and that then the engine was still obscured by the section house. He had been driving at the rate of 10 or 12 miles an hour but had cut down his rate to 5 or 6 miles at about 40 feet from the crossing. It is thought that there was an emergency in which, so far as appears, Goodman did all that he could.

We do not go into further details as to Goodman's precise situation, beyond mentioning that it was daylight and that he was familiar with the crossing, for it appears to us plain that nothing is suggested by the evidence to relieve Goodman from responsibility for his own death. When a man goes upon a railroad track he knows that he goes to a place where he will be killed if a train comes upon him before he is clear of the track. He knows that he must stop for the train not the train stop for him. In such circumstances it seems to us that if a driver cannot be sure otherwise whether a train is dangerously near he must stop and get out of his vehicle, although obviously he will not often be required to do more than to stop and look. It seems to us that if he relies upon not hearing the train or any signal and takes no further precaution he does so at his own risk. If at the last moment Goodman found himself in an emergency it was his own fault that he did not reduce his speed earlier or come to a stop. It is true as said in Flannelly v. Delaware & Hudson Co., 225 U. S. 597, 603, 32 S. Ct. 783, 56 L. Ed. 1221, 44 L. R. A. (N. S.) 154, that the question of due care very generally is left to the jury. But we are dealing with a standard of conduct, and when the standard is clear it should be laid down once for all by the Courts. See Southern Pacific Co. v. Berkshire, 254 U. S. 415, 417, 419, 41 S. Ct. 162, 65 L. Ed. 335.

Judgment reversed.

———————————

Points for Discussion

1. According to Justice Holmes, when is the driver of an automobile who is approaching a railroad track required to "stop and look"?

2. The Court concluded that questions of due care are generally left for juries and that "clear" standards of conduct "should be laid down once for all by the Courts." Do you agree with this understanding of the respective roles and functions of juries and judges? How does a judge determine that a standard is or is not "clear"?

Pokora v. Wabash Railway Co.

292 U.S. 98 (1934)

Mr. Justice CARDOZO delivered the opinion of the Court.

John Pokora, driving his truck across a railway grade crossing in the city of Springfield, Ill., was struck by a train and injured. Upon the trial of his suit for damages, the District Court held that he had been guilty of contributory negligence, and directed a verdict for the defendant. The Circuit Court of Appeals (one judge dissenting) affirmed, [cc] resting its judgment on the opinion of this court in B. & O.R. Co. v. Goodman, 275 U.S. 66, 48 S.Ct. 24, 25, 72 L.Ed. 167, 56 A.L.R. 645. A writ of **certiorari** brings the case here.

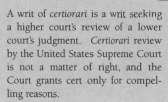

What's That?

A writ of *certiorari* is a writ seeking a higher court's review of a lower court's judgment. *Certiorari* review by the United States Supreme Court is not a matter of right, and the Court grants cert only for compelling reasons.

It's Latin to Me!

Certiorari is Latin for "to be more fully informed."

Pokora was an ice dealer, and had come to the crossing to load his truck with ice. The tracks of the Wabash Railway are laid along Tenth street, which runs north and south. There is a crossing at Edwards street running east and west. Two ice depots are on opposite corners of Tenth and Edward streets; one at the northeast corner, the other at the southwest. Pokora, driving west along Edwards street, stopped at the first of these corners to get his load of ice, but found so many trucks ahead of him that he decided to try the depot on the other side of the way. In this crossing of the railway, the accident occurred.

The defendant has four tracks on Tenth street; a switch track on the east, then the main track, and then two switches. Pokora, as he left the northeast corner where his truck had been stopped, looked to the north for approaching trains. He did this at a point about ten or fifteen feet east of the switch ahead of him. A string of box cars standing on the switch, about five to ten feet from the north line of Edwards street, cut off his view of the tracks beyond him to the north. At the same time he listened. There was neither bell nor whistle. Still listening, he crossed the switch, and reaching the main track was struck by a passenger train coming from the north at a speed of twenty-five to thirty miles an hour.

. . . .

The argument is made, however, that our decision in *B. & O. R. Co. v. Goodman*, *supra*, is a barrier in the plaintiff's path, irrespective of the conclusion that might commend itself if the question were at large. There is no doubt that the opinion in that case is correct in its result. Goodman, the driver, traveling only five or six miles an hour, had, before reaching the track, a clear space of eighteen feet within which the train was plainly visible. With that opportunity, he fell short of the legal standard of duty established for a traveler when he failed to look and see. This was decisive of the case. But the court did not stop there. It added a remark, unnecessary upon the facts before it, which has been a fertile source of controversy. 'In such circumstances it seems to us that if a driver cannot be sure otherwise whether a train is dangerously near he must stop and get out of his vehicle, although obviously he will not often be required to do more than to stop and look.'

There is need at this stage to clear the ground of brushwood that may obscure the point at issue. We do not now inquire into the existence of a duty to stop, disconnected from a duty to get out and reconnoitre. The inquiry, if pursued, would lead us into the thickets of conflicting judgments. Some courts apply what is often spoken of as the Pennsylvania rule, and impose an unyielding duty to stop, as well as to look and listen, no matter how clear the crossing or the tracks on either side. [Cc] Other courts, the majority, adopt the rule that the traveler must look and listen, but that the existence of a duty to stop depends upon the circumstances, and hence generally, even if not invariably, upon the judgment of the jury. [Cc] The subject has been less considered in this court, but in none of its opinions is there a suggestion that at any and every crossing the duty to stop is absolute, irrespective of the danger. Not even in *B. & O. R. Co. v. Goodman*, *supra*, which goes farther than the earlier cases, is there support for such a rule. To the contrary, the opinion makes it clear that the duty is conditioned upon the presence of impediments whereby sight and hearing become inadequate for the traveler's protection. [Cc]

Choice between these diversities of doctrine is unnecessary for the decision of the case at hand. Here the fact is not disputed that the plaintiff did stop before he started to cross the tracks. If we assume that by reason of the box cars, there was a duty to stop again when the obstructions had been cleared, that duty did not arise unless a stop could be made safely after the point of clearance had been reached.

[Cc] For reasons already stated, the testimony permits the inference that the truck was in the zone of danger by the time the field of vision was enlarged. No stop would then have helped the plaintiff if he remained seated on his truck, or so the triers of the facts might find. His case was for the jury, unless as a matter of law he was subject to a duty to get out of the vehicle before it crossed the switch, walk forward to the front, and then, afoot, survey the scene. We must say whether his failure to do this was negligence so obvious and certain that one conclusion and one only is permissible for rational and candid minds. [Cc]

Standards of prudent conduct are declared at times by courts, but they are taken over from the facts of life. To get out of a vehicle and reconnoitre is an uncommon precaution, as everyday experience informs us. Besides being uncommon, it is very likely to be futile, and sometimes even dangerous. If the driver leaves his vehicle when he nears a cut or curve, he will learn nothing by getting out about the perils that lurk beyond. By the time he regains his seat and sets his car in motion, the hidden train may be upon him. [Cc] Often the added safeguard will be dubious though the track happens to be straight, as it seems that this one was, at all events as far as the station, about five blocks to the north. A train traveling at a speed of thirty miles an hour will cover a quarter of a mile in the space of thirty seconds. It may thus emerge out of obscurity as the driver turns his back to regain the waiting car, and may then descend upon him suddenly when his car is on the track. Instead of helping himself by getting out, he might do better to press forward with all his faculties alert. So a train at a neighboring station, apparently at rest and harmless, may be transformed in a few seconds into an instrument of destruction. At times the course of safety may be different. One can figure to oneself a roadbed so level and unbroken that getting out will be a gain. Even then the balance of advantage depends on many circumstances and can be easily disturbed. Where was Pokora to leave his truck after getting out to reconnoitre? If he was to leave it on the switch, there was the possibility that the box cars would be shunted down upon him before he could regain his seat. The defendant did not show whether there was a locomotive at the forward end, or whether the cars were so few that a locomotive could be seen. If he was to leave his vehicle near the curb, there was even stronger reason to believe that the space to be covered in going back and forth would make his observations worthless. One must remember that while the traveler turns his eyes in one direction, a train or a loose engine may be approaching from the other.

Illustrations such as these bear witness to the need for caution in framing standards of behavior that amount to rules of law. The need is the more urgent when there is no background of experience out of which the standards have emerged. They are then, not the natural flowerings of behavior in its customary forms, but rules artificially developed, and imposed from without. Extraordinary situations may not wisely or fairly be subjected to tests or regulations that are fitting for the commonplace or normal. In default of the guide of customary conduct, what is suitable for the traveler caught in a mesh where the ordinary safeguards fail him is for the judgment of a jury. [Cc] The opinion in Goodman's Case has been a source of confusion in the federal courts to the extent that it imposes a standard for application by the judge, and has had only wavering support in the courts of the states. We limit it accordingly.

The judgment should be reversed, and the cause remanded for further proceedings in accordance with this opinion.

It is so ordered.

————————

Points for Discussion

1. What is the "Pennsylvania rule"? The majority rule? Did the Court adopt one of these rules in deciding the case?

2. Justice Cardozo expressed "the need for caution in framing standards of behavior that amount to rules of law." What is the difference between a standard and a rule? Suppose that the speed of automobiles on a highway is subject to and regulated by (1) a "don't drive too fast" standard or (2) a 60 miles per hour speed limit. Is the standard or the rule preferable? Enforcement of the "don't drive too fast" standard will require the consideration of matters not explicitly set forth therein (for example, weather conditions, traffic, straight versus curving road, etc.). Enforcement of the rule only requires an answer to the question whether the speed of the automobile did or did not exceed 60 miles per hour. In the context of regulating the speed of automobiles, what is preferable—a standard or a rule? More generally, what are the advantages and disadvantages of establishing legally mandated behaviors by standards or, instead, by rules?

3. The Court concluded that its decision in the *Goodman* case resulted in confusion in the federal courts and had limited support in state courts. Why did the Court so conclude? Did the *Pokora* Court overrule *Goodman*?

4. Why did the Court not apply the *Erie* doctrine?

————————

3. Establishing a Standard of Care by Using a Non-Tort Statute

> RESTATEMENT (SECOND) OF TORTS § 285(b) (1965)
>
> The standard of conduct of a reasonable [person] may be . . . adopted by a court from a legislative enactment or an administrative regulation which does not so provide .

Osborne v. McMasters

40 Minn. 103, 41 N.W. 543 (1889)

MITCHELL, J.

Upon the record in this case it must be taken as the facts that defendant's clerk in his drug-store, in the course of his employment as such, sold to plaintiff's intestate a deadly poison without labeling it "Poison," as required by statute; that she, in ignorance of its deadly qualities, partook of the poison which caused her death. Except for the ability of counsel and the earnestness with which they have argued the case, we would not have supposed that there could be any serious doubt of defendant's liability on this state of facts. . . . It is now well settled, certainly in this state, that where a statute or municipal ordinance imposes upon any person a specific duty for the protection or benefit of others, if he neglects to perform that duty he is liable to those for whose protection or benefit it was imposed for any injuries of the character which the statute or ordinance was designed to prevent, and which were proximately produced by such neglect. [C] Defendant contends that this is only true where a right of action for the alleged negligent act existed at common law; that no liability existed at common law for selling poison without labeling it, and therefore none exists under this statute, no right of civil action being given by it. Without stopping to consider the correctness of the assumption that selling poison without labeling it might not be actionable negligence at common law, it is sufficient to say that, in our opinion, defendant's contention proceeds upon an entire misapprehension of the nature and gist of a cause of action of this kind. The common law gives a right of action to every one sustaining injuries caused proximately by the negligence of another. The present is a common-law action, the gist of which is defendant's negligence, resulting in the death of plaintiff's intestate. Negligence is the breach of legal duty. It is immaterial whether the duty is one imposed by the rule of common law requiring the exercise of ordinary care not to injure another, or is imposed by a statute designed for the protection of others. In either case the failure to perform the duty constitutes negligence, and renders the party liable for injuries resulting from it. The only difference is that in the one case the measure of legal duty is to be determined upon common-law principles, while in the other the statute fixes it, so that the violation of the statute constitutes conclusive evidence of negligence, or, in other words, **negligence per se**. The action in the latter case is not a statutory one, nor does the statute give the right of action in any other sense, except that it makes an act negligent which otherwise might not be such, or at least only evidence of negligence. All that the statute does is to establish a fixed standard by which the fact of negligence may be determined. The gist of the action is still negligence, or the non-performance of a legal duty to the person injured. . . . Judgment affirmed.

Points for Discussion

1. What statute did the clerk violate when he sold the poison later ingested by and causing the death of the customer?

2. Is the lawsuit before the court a common-law or a statutory action?

3. Define "negligence per se."

4. What is the significance of the poison-labeling statute in determining the negligence issue?

5. Agree or disagree with the following proposition: In negligence actions, courts should not fashion standards of care from criminal statutes, civil statutes, ordinances, or regulations.

---

a. When a Statute May Be Used to Establish the Standard of Care

Sanchez v. Wal-Mart Stores, Inc.

221 P.3d 1276 (Nev. 2009)

By the Court, HARDESTY, C.J.:

This appeal raises issues concerning whether a pharmacy owes a duty of care to unidentified third parties who were injured by a pharmacy customer who was driving while under the influence of controlled prescription drugs. In addressing this appeal, we consider . . . whether Nevada's pharmacy statutory and regulatory laws allow third parties to maintain a negligence per se claim for alleged violations concerning dispensation of prescription drugs and maintenance of customers' records.

The underlying matter arose after a pharmacy customer, while driving under the influence of prescription drugs, allegedly caused an automobile accident resulting in one person's death and severe injuries to another. Appellants filed a **wrongful death** and personal injury complaint against, among others, respondent pharmacies that filled multiple prescriptions for the woman driving the car. The appellants claimed that because the pharmacies had knowledge of the woman's prescription-filling activities, the pharmacies owed appellants a duty of care to not fill the woman's prescriptions. The pharmacies filed a motion to dismiss the action, which the district court granted after finding that the pharmacies did not owe appellants a statutory duty of care, and thus, that appellants' claims failed to state a valid cause of action.

We conclude that . . . Nevada's pharmacy statutes and regulations concerning prescription drug dispensation and customer recordkeeping maintenance are not intended to protect the general public from the type of injury sustained in this case, and thus, do not support the appellants' negligence per se claim. We therefore affirm.

. . . .

Appellants assert that the district court erred in dismissing their negligence per se claim against the pharmacies because the pharmacies violated a number of Nevada statutes and regulations enacted to protect the general public, of whom the appellants are members, from the unlawful distribution of controlled substances.[5] The pharmacies counter that the statutes and regulations relied on by appellants do not mandate that a pharmacist must refuse to fill a valid prescription for the general public's protection.

A negligence per se claim arises when a duty is created by statute. [C] A civil statute's violation establishes the duty and breach elements of negligence when the injured party is in the class of persons whom the statute is intended to protect and the injury is of the type against which the statute is intended to protect.

---

5 Appellants cite to the following statutes and regulations to support their negligence per se claim: NRS 453.1545 (creating computerized program to track prescriptions for controlled substances); NRS 453.256 (outlining requirements for dispensing specific controlled substances); NRS 453.257 (prohibiting the filing of second or subsequent prescriptions for certain controlled substances "unless the frequency of prescriptions is in conformity with the directions for use" and the increased amount is verified by the practitioner personally by telephone or in writing); NRS 639.2392 (establishing requirements for maintaining patient records); NRS 639.2393 (establishing limitations on filling controlled substance prescriptions); NAC 639.485 (concerning the maintenance of records for controlled substances); NAC 639.742 (discussing the duties and authority of a dispensing practitioner to dispense controlled substances); NAC 639.926 (regarding dispensing controlled substances to certain individuals and maintaining records).

[Cc] But a statute that regulates the communication of information regarding the administration of drugs does not impose a duty on a pharmacy that runs to an unidentifiable third party. [C]

The statutes and regulatory provisions the appellants rely on to assert a negligence per se claim against the pharmacies are not intended for the general public's protection or to protect against any injury that the third-party appellants may have sustained. The duty owed under these statutes or regulations is to the person for whom the prescription was written, the pharmacy's customer, if anyone, and not for the general public's protection. And although various statutory and regulatory provisions may express standards of care for the practice of pharmacology, under the circumstances of this case, those standards of care do not extend to unidentified third parties. Therefore, we conclude that the district court properly dismissed appellants' negligence per se claims asserted against the pharmacies.

. . . .

CHERRY, J., with whom SAITTA, J., agrees, dissenting:

I differ with my colleagues as to their resolution of this appeal. In particular, I conclude that the district court erred when it granted the pharmacies' motions to dismiss because the appellants have sufficiently stated common-law negligence and negligence per se claims that preclude dismissal. I therefore dissent.

. . . .

The majority concludes that a negligence per se claim is unavailable to appellants because the statutes and regulations relied on by appellants were not intended for the general public's protection or to protect against any injury that third parties may sustain. I disagree.

A negligence per se claim is available when a defendant violates a statute that is designed to protect others against the type of injury that was incurred. [C] The Legislature has recognized that pharmacology affects public safety and welfare. NRS 639.213. Consequently, the Legislature regulates the profession, including in what manner and when controlled substances may be dispensed. *See* NRS 639.2171; NRS 639.0124; NRS 453.381. To that end, the Legislature directed the Board of Pharmacy to adopt regulations "as are necessary for the protection of the public, appertaining to the practice of pharmacy." NRS 639.070(1)(a).

Nevada law requires pharmacists to review customers' records before filling prescriptions to determine prescriptions' therapeutic appropriateness. NAC 639.707(4). Pharmacists must ensure that the substance is being dispensed solely for medically necessary purposes and in accordance with prevailing professional standards of care. NAC 639.742(3)(h).

Based on the enactment of these statutory and regulatory provisions, it is apparent to me that the Legislature intended to prevent pharmacy shopping and the overfilling of certain controlled substances, and ultimately, to protect the general public from prescription-drug abuse and its effects. The abuse of either hydrocodone or SOMA can impair one's driving ability. In my opinion, motorists, like appellants, who are injured by an individual who is driving under the influence of prescription drugs are in the class of persons that the Legislature intended to protect and the injury is a type that the statutes and regulations intended to prevent. Having reached this conclusion, I would reverse the district court's dismissal of appellants' negligence per se claim and remand this matter to the district court for additional proceedings.

. . . .

Points for Discussion

1. Do you agree with the *Sanchez* court's decision, in particular its ruling that the cited statutes and regulations were not intended to protect the general public from the illegal distribution of controlled substances? If not the general public, who is protected?

2. The dissent, disagreeing with the majority's dismissal of the negligence per se claim, argues that the Nevada legislature recognized that pharmacology affects the safety and welfare of the public and that state law specifically directed the board of pharmacy to adopt regulations "as are necessary for the protection of the public, appertaining to the practice of pharmacy." Do you agree or disagree that the state legislature intended to protect the general public from the harms of the abuse of prescription drugs?

3. In negligence per se cases, would you favor a default rule requiring a broad and generous reading of statutory provisions and regulations providing more protection of the general public from prohibited activities?

Stachniewicz v. Mar-Cam Corp.

259 Ore. 583, 488 P.2d 436 (1971)

HOLMAN, Justice.

The patron of a drinking establishment seeks to recover against the operator for personal injuries allegedly inflicted by other customers during a barroom brawl. The jury returned a verdict for defendant. Plaintiff appealed.

From the evidence introduced, the jury could find as follows:

A fight erupted in a bar between a group of persons of American Indian ancestry, who were sitting in a booth, and other customers who were at an adjacent table with plaintiff. One of plaintiff's friends had refused to allow a patron from the booth to dance with the friend's wife because the stranger was intoxicated. Thereafter, such threats as, 'Hey, Whitey, how big are you?' were shouted from the booth at plaintiff and his companions. One of the persons at the table, after complaining to the bartender, was warned by him, 'Don't start trouble with those guys.' Soon thereafter, those individuals who had been sitting in the booth approached the table and one of them knocked down a person who was talking to a member of plaintiff's party. With that, the brawl commenced.

After a short melee, someone shouted 'Fuzz!' and those persons who had been sitting in the booth ran out a door and into the parking lot, with one of plaintiff's friends in hot pursuit. Upon reaching the door, the friend discovered plaintiff lying just outside with his feet wedging the door open.

Plaintiff suffered retrograde amnesia and could remember nothing of the events of the evening. No one could testify to plaintiff's whereabouts at the time the band in the booth went on the warpath or to the cause of the vicious head injuries which plaintiff displayed when the brawl was ended.

The customers in the booth had been drinking in defendant's place of business for approximately two and one-half hours before the affray commenced.

The principal issue is whether, as plaintiff contends, violations of ORS 471.410(3) and of Oregon Liquor Control Regulation No. 10-065(2) constitute negligence as a matter of law. The portion of the statute relied on by plaintiff reads as follows:

'(3) No person shall give or otherwise make available any alcoholic liquor to a person visibly intoxicated * * *.'

The portion of the regulation to which plaintiff points provides:

'(2) No **licensee** shall permit or suffer any loud, noisy, disorderly or boisterous conduct, or any profane or abusive language, in or upon his licensed premises, or permit any visibly intoxicated person to enter or remain upon his licensed premises.'

The trial court held that a violation of either the statute or the regulation did not constitute negligence per se. It refused requested instructions and withdrew allegations of negligence which were based on their violation.

A violation of a statute or regulation constitutes negligence as a matter of law when the violation results in injury to a member of the class of persons intended to be protected by the legislation and when the harm is of the kind which the statute or regulation was enacted to prevent. [Cc] The reason behind the rule is that when a legislative body has generalized a standard from the experience of the community and prohibits conduct that is likely to cause harm, the court accepts the formulation. . . .

However, in addition, it is proper for the court to examine preliminarily the appropriateness of the standard as a measure of care for civil litigation under the circumstances presented. [Cc] The statute in question prevents making available alcohol to a person who is already visibly intoxicated. This makes the standard particularly inappropriate for the awarding of civil damages because of the extreme difficulty, if not impossibility, of determining whether a third party's injuries would have been caused, in any event, by the already inebriated person. Unless we are prepared to say that an alcoholic drink given after visible intoxication is the cause of a third party's injuries as a matter of law, a concept not advanced by anyone, the standard would be one almost impossible of application by a factfinder in most circumstances.

. . . .

The regulation promulgated by the commission is an altogether different matter. The regulation requires certain conduct of licensees in the operation of bars. The regulation was issued under ORS 471.730(5) which provides:

'The function, duties and powers of the commission include the following:

'* * *.

'(5) To adopt such regulations as are necessary and feasible for carrying out the provisions of this chapter and to amend or repeal such regulations.

When such regulations are adopted they shall have the full force and effect of law.'

ORS 471.030, entitled 'Purpose of Liquor Control Act,' provides, in part, as follows:

'(1) The Liquor Control Act shall be liberally construed so as:

'(a) To prevent the recurrence of abuses associated with saloons or resorts for the consumption of alcoholic beverages.

'* * *.'

An examination of the regulation discloses that it concerns matters having a direct relation to the creation of physical disturbances in bars which would, in turn, create a likelihood of injury to customers. A common feature of our western past, now preserved in story and reproduced on the screen hundreds of times, was the carnage of the barroom brawl. No citation of authority is needed to establish that the 'abuses associated with saloons,' which the Liquor Control Act seeks to prevent, included permitting on the premises profane, abusive conduct and drunken clientele (now prohibited by the regulation) which results in serious personal injuries to customers in breach of the bar owner's duty to protect his patrons from harm. We find it reasonable to assume that the commission, in promulgating the regulation, intended to prevent these abuses, and that they had in mind the safety of patrons of bars as well as the general peace and quietude of the community. In view of the quoted purpose of the Act and of the history of injury to innocent patrons of saloons, we cannot assume otherwise.

In addition, we see no reason why the standard is not an appropriate one for use in the awarding of civil damages. Because plaintiff was within the class of persons intended to be protected by the regulation and the harm caused to him was the kind the statute was intended to prevent, we hold that the trial court erred in not treating the alleged violations of the regulation as negligence as a matter of law.

. . . We believe it would be fair for the jury to infer, in the circumstances set forth in the statement of the facts, that plaintiff was injured by one of the persons in the booth who had created the disturbance and that the injuries would not have occurred except for defendant's violation of the commission's regulation, as alleged.

The judgment of the trial court is reversed and the case is remanded for a new trial.

———————————

Points for Discussion

1. What is the legally relevant inquiry in determining whether a legislative enactment may be applied to establish a standard of care in a negligence action?

2. Why does the *Mar-Cam* court note the "group of persons of American Indian ancestry"? How do you react to the court's statement that "the band in the booth went on the warpath"?

3. *Mar-Cam* concluded that the relevant statute did not establish the appropriate standard applicable to civil litigation of the case before it. What reasoning was offered by the court in support of this conclusion?

4. Do you agree that the plaintiff was a member of the class of individuals intended to be protected by the regulation?

5. Although the plaintiff suffered from retrograde amnesia and had no memory of the events on the evening of the fight, the court concluded that "it would be fair for the jury to infer" that the plaintiff had been injured by one of the persons sitting in the booth at the bar. Why and how would such an inference be "fair"? At the new trial of the case, what argument should the defendant's counsel make in response to Oregon Supreme Court's fair inference observation?

Perry v. S.N. and S.N.

973 S.W.2d 301 (Tex. 1998)

PHILLIPS, Chief Justice, delivered the opinion of the Court.

. . . .

This is a suit for injuries arising out of the abuse of children at a day care center. Plaintiffs filed suit individually and as next friends of their two children, alleging that defendants witnessed the abuse and failed to report it to the police or child welfare officials. The sole issue before us is whether plaintiffs may maintain a cause of action for negligence per se based on the Family Code, which requires any person having cause to believe a child is being abused to report the abuse to state authorities and makes the knowing failure to do so a misdemeanor. *See* TEX. FAM.CODE §§ 261.101(a), 261.109 . . . The trial court granted summary judgment for defendants, but the court of appeals reversed and remanded plaintiffs' negligence per se and gross negligence claims for trial. [C] We reverse the judgment of the court of appeals and render judgment that plaintiffs take nothing. Because plaintiffs did not preserve their common law negligence claims, we do not decide whether there should be a common law duty to report child abuse in some circumstances.

B.N. and K.N. attended a day care center operated by Francis Keller and her husband Daniel Keller from March 25, 1991, to August 28, 1991. Their parents, S.N. and S.N., allege that during that period, Daniel Keller regularly abused B.N. and K.N. and other children at the center both physically and sexually. Mr. and Mrs. N. brought suit against the Kellers and three of the Kellers' friends, Douglas Perry, Janise White, and Raul Quintero. Plaintiffs claim that Francis Keller confided in White at an unspecified time that Daniel Keller had "abusive habits toward children." They further allege that on one occasion in August 1991, while visiting the Kellers, defendants Perry, White, and Quintero all saw Daniel Keller bring a number of children out of the day care center into the Kellers' adjoining home and sexually abuse them. The record does not indicate whether B.N. and K.N. were among these children. According to plaintiffs, Perry, White, and Quintero did not attempt to stop Daniel Keller from abusing the children or report his crimes to the police or child welfare authorities.

. . . .

. . . Mr. and Mrs. N. alleged only that Perry, White, and Quintero were negligent per se because they violated a statute requiring any person who "has cause to believe that a child's physical or mental health or welfare has been or may be adversely affected by abuse" to file a report with the police or the Department of Protective and Regulatory Services. [C] Plaintiffs also asserted gross negligence and common law negligence claims. They claimed that Perry, White, and Quintero's failure to report the abuse proximately caused them harm by permitting the day care center to remain open, thus enabling Daniel Keller to continue abusing the children at the center. They sought damages for pain, mental anguish, and medical expenses, as well as loss of income when they could not work outside the home because of B.N. and K.N.'s injuries.

Perry, White, and Quintero moved for summary judgment on the sole ground that plaintiffs failed to state a cause of action. None of the parties presented any summary judgment evidence. . . .

The trial court granted Perry, White, and Quintero's motions for summary judgment and severed plaintiffs' claims against those three defendants from their suit against the Kellers, which is not before us. Because defendants' motions for summary judgment argued only that plaintiffs failed to state a cognizable claim, the trial court's judgment can be upheld, if at all, only on that ground. [C] When the ground for the trial court's decision is that plaintiffs failed to state a cause of action, we must take the allegations in the pleadings as true in determining whether a cause of action exists. [C]

The court of appeals affirmed the summary judgment on plaintiffs' common law negligence claims but reversed and remanded for trial on the issues of negligence per se and gross negligence, holding that a violation of the Family Code's child abuse reporting requirement is negligence per se. [C] Mr. and Mrs. N. have not appealed the court of appeals' judgment affirming the summary judgment against them on common law negligence. Therefore, the question of whether Texas should impose a new common law duty to report child abuse on the facts of this case is not before us. [Cc] . . .

"It is fundamental that the existence of a legally cognizable duty is a prerequisite to all tort liability." [C] The court of appeals found a duty in the following mandatory child abuse reporting provisions of the Texas Family Code:

> A person having cause to believe that a child's physical or mental health or welfare has been adversely affected by abuse or neglect by any person shall immediately make a report as provided by this subchapter.

TEX. FAM.CODE § 261.101(a).

> (a) A person commits an offense if the person has cause to believe that a child's physical or mental health or welfare has been or may be adversely affected by abuse or neglect and knowingly fails to report as provided in this chapter.
>
> (b) An offense under this section is a Class B misdemeanor.

Id. § 261.109.

The court concluded that these provisions create a "statutory duty" to report child abuse, and that a violation of this duty is negligence per se. [C]

All persons have a duty to obey the criminal law in the sense that they may be prosecuted for not doing so, but this is not equivalent to a duty in tort. [C] "It is well-established that the mere fact that the Legislature adopts a criminal statute does not mean that this court must accept it as a standard for civil liability." [C] "The considerations which warrant imposing tort liability are not identical with those which warrant criminal conviction," [cc] and we will not apply the doctrine of negligence per se if the criminal statute does not provide an appropriate basis for civil liability. [Cc]

Before we begin our analysis of whether section 261.109 of the Family Code is an appropriate basis for tort liability, we emphasize that we must look beyond the facts of this particular case to consider the full reach of the statute. We do not decide today whether a statute criminalizing only the type of egregious behavior with which these defendants are charged- the failure of eyewitnesses to report the sexual molestation of preschool children-would be an appropriate basis for a tort action. That is not the

Food for Thought

The court emphasizes that its analysis was not limited to and would go beyond the specific facts of the case. Why does the court approach the case in this way? Is such an approach appropriate? Can this approach advantage or disadvantage parties seeking appellate review of lower court decisions?

statute the Legislature passed. Rather, the issue before us is whether it is appropriate to impose tort liability on any and every person who "has cause to believe that a child's physical or mental health or welfare has been or may be adversely affected by abuse or neglect and knowingly fails to report." TEX. FAM.CODE § 261.109(a). *Cf.* Leonard, *The Application of Criminal Legislation to Negligence Cases: A Reexamination,* 23 SANTA CLARA L.REV. 427, 457-66 (1983) (contrasting the rigidity of statutory standards with the flexibility of case-by-case common law determinations of duty and breach).

The threshold questions in every negligence per se case are whether the plaintiff belongs to the class that the statute was intended to protect and whether the plaintiff's injury is of a type that the statute was designed to prevent. [Cc] Texas's first mandatory child abuse reporting statute, from which Family Code section 261.101(a) is derived, stated that "[t]he purpose of this Act is to protect children who [ ] ... are adversely affected by abuse or neglect." Act of May 24, 1971, 62d Leg., R.S., ch. 902, § 1, 1971 Tex. Gen. Laws 2790. Similarly, the current Family Code provision governing the investigation of reports of child abuse states that "[t]he primary purpose of the investigation shall be the protection of the child." TEX. FAM.CODE § 261.301(d).

B.N. and K.N. are within the class of persons whom the child abuse reporting statute was meant to protect, and they suffered the kind of injury that the Legislature intended the statute to prevent. But this does not end our inquiry. [C] The Court must still determine whether it is appropriate to impose tort liability for violations of the statute. [C] This determination is informed by a number of factors, some discussed by the court of appeals in this case and others derived from past negligence per se decisions of Texas courts and from scholarly analyses. These factors are not necessarily exclusive, nor is the issue properly resolved by merely counting how many factors lean each way. Rather, we set out these considerations as guides to assist a court in answering the ultimate question of whether imposing tort liability for violations of a criminal statute is fair, workable, and wise.

We first consider the fact that, absent a change in the common law, a negligence per se cause of action against these defendants would derive the element of duty solely from the Family Code. At common law there is generally no duty to protect another from the criminal acts of a third party or to come to the aid of another in distress. [Cc] Although there are exceptions to this no-duty rule, [cc] this case does not fall within any of the established exceptions, and Mr. and Mrs. N. have not asked this Court to impose on persons who are aware of child abuse a new common law duty to report it or take other protective action.

In contrast, the defendant in most negligence per se cases already owes the plaintiff a pre-existing common law duty to act as a reasonably prudent person, so that the statute's role is merely to define more precisely what conduct breaches that duty. [Cc] For example, the overwhelming majority of this Court's negligence per se cases have involved violations of traffic statutes by drivers and train operators-actors who already owed a common law duty to exercise reasonable care toward others on the road or track. [Cc]

When a statute criminalizes conduct that is also governed by a common law duty, as in the case of a traffic regulation, applying negligence per se causes no great change in the law because violating the statutory standard of conduct would usually also be negligence under a common law reasonableness standard. [Cc] But recognizing a new, purely statutory duty "can have an extreme effect upon the common law of negligence" when it allows a cause of action where the common law would not. [C] In such a situation, applying negligence per se "bring[s] into existence a new type of tort liability." *Burnette v. Wahl,* 284 Or. 705, 588 P.2d 1105, 1109 (1978). The change tends to be especially great when, as here, the statute criminalizes inaction rather than action. [Cc]

. . . .

The court of appeals in this case listed several factors to consider in deciding whether to apply negligence per se. [C] According to the court of appeals, the principal factors favoring negligence per se are that the Legislature has determined that compliance with criminal statutes is practicable and desirable and that criminal statutes give citizens notice of what conduct is required of them. As considerations against negligence per se, the court of appeals cautioned that some penal statutes may be too obscure to put the public on notice, may impose liability without fault, or may lead to ruinous monetary liability for relatively minor offenses. The first of these factors is not helpful because it points the same way in every case: the very existence of a criminal statute implies a legislative judgment that its requirements are practicable and desirable. The court of appeals' remaining factors, however, are pertinent to our analysis.

On the question of notice, this Court has held that one consideration bearing on whether to apply negligence per se is whether the statute clearly defines the prohibited or required conduct. [Cc] The Family Code's reporting requirement is triggered when a person "has cause to believe that a child's physical or mental health or welfare has been or may be adversely affected by abuse or neglect." TEX. FAM.CODE § 261.109(a). In this case, defendants allegedly were eyewitnesses to sexual abuse. Under these facts, there is no question that they had cause to believe abuse was occurring, and thus that the statute required them to make a report. In many other cases, however, a person may become aware of a possible case of child abuse only through second-hand reports or ambiguous physical symptoms, and it is unclear whether these circumstances are "cause to believe" that such conduct "may be" taking place. [C] A statute that conditions the requirement to report on these difficult judgment calls does not clearly define what conduct is required in many conceivable situations.

The next factor the court of appeals considered was whether applying negligence per se to the reporting statute would create liability without fault. [C] We agree with the court of appeals that it would not, because the statute criminalizes only the "knowing[ ]" failure to report. [Cc] This characteristic of the statute weighs in favor of imposing civil liability.

Our next consideration is whether negligence per se would impose ruinous liability disproportionate to the seriousness of the defendant's conduct. In analyzing this factor, the court of appeals treated child abuse as the relevant conduct. [C] The conduct criminalized by section 261.109, however, is not child abuse but the failure to report child abuse. Through its penal laws, the Legislature has expressed a judgment that abuse and nonreporting deserve very different legal consequences. The abuser in this case committed the offense of aggravated sexual assault on a child under the age of fourteen, a first degree felony carrying a penalty of five to ninety-nine years in prison and a fine of up to $10,000. See TEX. PEN.CODE §§ 22.021, 12.32. Almost all of the other acts of abuse and neglect covered by the reporting requirement, see TEX. FAM.CODE § 261.001(1), (4) (defining "abuse" and "neglect"), are also felonies. See TEX. PEN.CODE § 22.04 (injury to a child); id. § 22.041 (abandoning or endangering child); id. § 22.011(a)(2), (f) (statutory rape). Even the lowest level of felony is punishable by 180 days to two years in jail and a $10,000 fine, see id. § 12.35, and automatically deprives the offender of certain civil rights such as the franchise, [c] eligibility for public office, [c] and the right to own a firearm, [c]. By contrast, failure to report abuse or neglect, no matter how serious the underlying crime, is a class B misdemeanor punishable by no more than six months in jail and a $2,000 fine. *See* TEX. FAM.CODE § 261.109(b); TEX. PEN.CODE § 12.22. This evidence of legislative intent to penalize nonreporters far less severely than abusers weighs against holding a person who fails to report suspected abuse civilly liable for the enormous damages that the abuser subsequently inflicts. The specter of disproportionate liability is particularly troubling when, as in the case of the reporting statute, it is combined with the likelihood of "broad and wide-ranging liability" by collateral wrongdoers . . .

Finally, in addition to the factors discussed by the court of appeals, we have also looked to whether the injury resulted directly or indirectly from the violation of the statute. [C] In *Carter v. William Sommerville & Son, Inc.,* we refused to apply negligence per se liability to a provision of the Texas Motor Carrier Act making it a misdemeanor to aid and abet any violation of the Act. *See Carter,* 584 S.W.2d at 278-79. We concluded that the aiding and abetting section was "too far removed to be adopted as a standard" for civil liability, in part because "[i]t is only by first finding a violation of some other section of the Act that the court may then find a violation" of that provision. [C] Like the aiding and abetting provision in *Carter,* Family Code section 261.109 defines the misdemeanor of failure to report child abuse in terms of the wrongful act of a third party. Under *Carter*'s reasoning, the indirect relationship between violation of such a statute and the plaintiff's ultimate injury is a factor against imposing tort liability.

. . . .

We conclude by noting that for a variety of reasons, including many of those we have discussed, most other states with mandatory reporting statutes similar to Texas's have concluded that the failure to report child abuse is not negligence per se. . . .

In summary, we have considered the following factors regarding the application of negligence per se to the Family Code's child abuse reporting provision: (1) whether the statute is the sole source of any tort duty from the defendant to the plaintiff or merely supplies a standard of conduct for an existing common law duty; (2) whether the statute puts the public on notice by clearly defining the required conduct; (3) whether the statute would impose liability without fault; (4) whether negligence per se would result in ruinous damages disproportionate to the seriousness of the statutory violation, particularly if the liability would fall on a broad and wide range of collateral wrongdoers; and (5) whether the plaintiff's injury is a direct or indirect result of the violation of the statute. Because a decision to impose negligence per se could not be limited to cases charging serious misconduct like the one at bar, but rather would impose immense potential liability under an ill-defined standard on a broad class of individuals whose relationship to the abuse was extremely indirect, we hold that it is not appropriate to adopt Family Code section 261.109(a) as establishing a duty and standard of conduct in tort. Therefore, Mr. and Mrs. N. and their children may not maintain a claim for negligence per se or gross negligence based on defendants' violation of the child abuse reporting statute. Because plaintiffs did not appeal the court of appeals' adverse decision on their common law negligence claims, we do not consider whether Texas should impose a common law duty to report or prevent child abuse.

For the foregoing reasons, we reverse the judgment of the court of appeals and render judgment that plaintiffs take nothing.

────────

Points for Discussion

1. Note that the *Perry* court opined that a person's duty to obey criminal laws is not equivalent to a duty in tort and a standard for civil liability, and that the doctrine of negligence per se would not be applied where a criminal statute did not provide an appropriate basis for civil liability.

2. Were the plaintiffs within the class of persons protected by the child abuse reporting provisions of the Texas Family Code? Were they injured in a manner the Texas legislature sought to prevent?

3. What factors did the court consider in deciding whether tort liability could be imposed for violations of the child abuse reporting statute? How did the court apply those factors?

4. The plaintiffs did not preserve or pursue their common law negligence claims, and the Texas Supreme Court did not decide whether the state should impose a common law duty requiring the reporting and prevention of child abuse. Would you be for or against the imposition of such a duty?

────────

b. The Effect of Proof When a Statute is Applied to Establish the Standard of Care

RESTATEMENT (SECOND) OF TORTS § 288A (1965)

Excused Violations

(1) An excused violation of a legislative enactment or an administrative regulation is not negligence.

(2) Unless such enactment or regulation is construed not to permit such excuse, its violation is excused when
   (a) the violation is reasonable because of the actor's incapacity;
   (b) he neither knows nor should know of the occasion for compliance;
   (c) he is unable after reasonable diligence or care to comply;
   (d) he is confronted by an emergency not due to his own misconduct;
   (e) compliance would involve a greater risk of harm to the actor or to others.

Zeni v. Anderson

397 Mich. 117, 243 N.W.2d 270 (1976)

WILLIAMS, Justice.

. . . We hold that violation of a statute by plaintiff or defendant creates a prima facie case from which a jury may draw an inference of negligence. The jury may also consider whether a legally sufficient excuse has been presented to refute this inference. . . .

I-FACTS

The accident which precipitated this action occurred one snowy morning, March 7, 1969, when the temperature was 11° F, the sky was clear and the average snow depth was 21 inches. Plaintiff Eleanor Zeni, then a 56-year-old registered nurse, was walking to her work at the Northern Michigan University Health Center in Marquette. Instead of using the snow-covered sidewalk, which in any event would have required her to walk across the street twice to get to her job, she traveled along a well-used pedestrian snowpath, with her back to oncoming traffic.

Defendant Karen Anderson, a college student, was driving within the speed limit in a steady stream of traffic on the same street. Ms. Anderson testified that she had turned on the defroster in the car and her passenger said she had scraped the windshield. An eyewitness whose deposition was read at trial, however, testified that defendant's windshield was clouded and he doubted that the occupants could see out. He also testified that the car was traveling too close to the curb and that he could tell plaintiff was going to be hit.

Defendant's car struck the plaintiff on the driver's right side. Ms. Anderson testified she first saw the plaintiff between a car parked on the right-hand side of the road and defendant's car, and that she did not hear nor feel her car strike Ms. Zeni. The eyewitness reported seeing plaintiff flip over the fender and hood. He said when he went over to help her his knees were on or inside the white line delineating a parking space. A security officer observed blood stains on the pavement approximately 13 feet from the curb.

Ms. Zeni's injuries were serious and included an intra-cerebral subdural hematoma which required neurosurgery. She has retrograde amnesia and therefore, because she does not remember anything from the time she began walking that morning until sometime after the impact, there is no way to determine whether she knew defendant was behind her. Following an extended period of convalescence, plaintiff, still suffering permanent disability, could return to work on only a part-time basis.

Testimony at trial indicated that it was common for nurses to use the roadway to reach the Health Center, and a security officer testified that in the wintertime it was safer to walk there than on the one sidewalk. Apparently, several days before the accident, Ms. Zeni had indeed fallen on the sidewalk. Although she was not hurt when she fell, the Director of University Security was hospitalized when he fell on the walk.

Defendant, however, maintained that plaintiff's failure to use that sidewalk constituted **contributory negligence** because, she said, it violated M.C.L.A. § 257.655; M.S.A. § 9.2355, which requires:

> 'Where sidewalks are provided, it shall be unlawful for pedestrians to walk upon the main traveled portion of the highway. Where sidewalks are not provided, pedestrians shall, when practicable, walk on the left side of the highway facing traffic which passes nearest.'

. . . .

The jury found defendant 'guilty of subsequent negligence' and awarded plaintiff damages of $30,000.

. . . .

We granted leave to appeal . . .

II-EFFECT OF VIOLATION OF STATUTE

An analysis of the Michigan cases indicates that the real Michigan rule as to the effect of violation of a penal statute in a negligence action is that such violation creates only a prima facie case from which the jury may draw an inference of negligence. It is true that a number of passages in cases speak of negligence per se almost in terms of **strict liability**, but closer examination of the application of the rule reveals that Michigan does not subscribe to such a harsh dogma.

A. Violation of Statute as Rebuttable Presumption

In a growing number of states, the rule concerning the proper role of a **penal statute** in a civil action for damages is that violation of the statute which has been found to apply to a particular set of facts establishes only a prima facie case of negligence, a presumption which may be rebutted by a showing on the part of the party violating the statute of an adequate excuse under the facts and circumstances of the case. The excuses may not necessarily be applicable in a criminal action, since, in the absence of legislatively-mandated civil penalties, acceptance of the criminal statute itself as a standard of care in a civil action is purely discretionary. See Comment and Illustrations, 2 RESTATEMENT TORTS, 2D, § 288A, pp. 33-37.

Michigan cases have in effect followed this rule. For example, over a 65 year period, cases concerning the effect in a negligence action of violation of the statute requiring vehicles to keep to the right side of the road have almost consistently adopted a **rebuttable presumption** approach, even though the language of the statute is not written in terms of a presumption.

. . . .

We think the test of the applicable law was well stated by our brother Justice Fitzgerald when he was a judge on the Court of Appeals. In Lucas v. Carson, 38 Mich.App. 552, 196 N.W.2d 819 (1972), he analyzed a case where, in spite of defendant's precautions, her vehicle 'inexplicably slid into the rear of plaintiff's stopped car' where plaintiff was waiting at a traffic signal. . . .

First, in analyzing whether the presumption of negligence attributed to a rear-end collision had been rebutted in the case before them, the Court of Appeals acknowledged that the usual grounds for rebuttal, sudden emergency, did not appear in this case. In effect accepting defendant's contention that the doctrine of sudden emergency was not the sole basis for rebutting a presumption of negligence, the Court held:

'The general rule appears to be that evidence required to rebut this presumption as a matter of law should be positive, unequivocal, strong, and credible. In the case at bar, defendant driver contended that she was at all times driving in a reasonable and prudent manner. * * * (T)here was sufficient evidence at least to generate a jury question regarding rebutting of the presumption.' [C]

As to the other alleged statutory violations, Justice Fitzgerald observed:

"Whereas, at one time, the application of the statute (assured clear distance) was strictly construed and applied as evidenced by the rule in the case of Lewis v. Yund, 339 Mich. 441, 64 N.W.2d 696 (1954), recent cases indicate that the statute must be reasonably construed and exceptions to the statutory edict have been created to accomplish justice, including bringing the assured clear distance rule to qualification by the test of due or ordinary care, exercised in the light of the attending conditions. [Cc]

. . . .

This is the approach we follow today. For one, it recognizes that the Legislature has spoken in a particular area . . .

Particularly in the area of health and safety regulations, we find ourselves attempting 'to further the ultimate policy for the protection of individuals which they find underlying the statute.' [C] Then, too, it is felt that 'the reasonably prudent man usually tries to comply' with the criminal law. [C]

Another attraction of this approach is that it is fair. 'If there is sufficient excuse or justification, there is ordinarily no violation of a statute and the statutory standard is inapplicable.' [C] It would be unreasonable to adhere to an automatic rule of negligence 'where observance would subject a person to danger which might be avoided by disregard of the general rule.' [C]

The approach is logical. Liability without fault is not truly negligence, and in the absence of a clear legislative mandate to so extend liability, the courts should be hesitant to do so on their own. Because these are, after all, criminal statutes, a court is limited in how far it may go in plucking a statute from its criminal milieu and inserting it into the civil arena. The rule of rebuttable presumption has arisen in part in response to this concern, and in part because of the reluctance to go to the other extreme and in effect, discard or disregard the legislative standard.

B. Violation of Statute as Negligence Per Se

While some Michigan cases seem to speak of negligence per se as a kind of strict liability, [c], an examination indicates that there are a number of conditions that attempt to create a more reasonable approach than would result from an automatic application of a per se rule.

The first such condition is that the penal standard does not have to be applied in the civil action. Absent explicit legislative language creating civil liability for violation of a criminal statute, a court is free to exercise its discretion and either adopt the legislative standard, or retain the common law reasonable person standard of care. [Cc] By its interpretation of the statutory purpose a court may in effect excuse an individual from the consequences of violating a statute. For example, the court may find the statute's purpose was not to protect the person allegedly injured, or, even if it was, that the harm suffered was not what the Legislature designed the statute to do.

> **FYI**
>
> The questions of when and whether certain negligent conduct constitutes the proximate cause of injury is discussed in Chapter 5.

Once this threshold is crossed and the court determines that the statute is applicable to the facts in the case before it, [c] liability still does not attach unless the finder of fact determines that the violation of the statute is the proximate cause of the injury. [Cc] . . .

Despite such limitations, the judge-made rule of negligence per se has still proved to be too inflexible and mechanical to satisfy thoughtful commentators and judges. It is forcefully argued that no matter how a court may attempt to confine the negligence per se doctrine, if defendant is liable despite the exercise of due care and the availability of a reasonable excuse, this is really strict liability, and not negligence. PROSSER, THE LAW OF TORTS (4th ed), § 36, p. 197. Since it is always possible that the Legislature's failure to deal specifically with the question of private rights was not accidental, and that there might have been no legislative intent to change the law of torts, such treatment of the statute may well be a gross perversion of the legislative will. It is troublesome, too, that 'potentially ruinous civil liability' may follow from a 'minor infraction of petty criminal regulations', [c] or may, in a jurisdiction burdened by contributory negligence, serve to deprive an otherwise deserving plaintiff of a much-needed recovery.

The rule, too, may have unfortunate effects on the administration of justice. Justice Talbot Smith suggests that adoption of the statutory standard improperly takes from the jury its function of setting the standard of care. Richardson v. Grezeszak, 358 Mich. 206, 235, 99 N.W.2d 648 (1959) (for affirmance). He also suggests that in order to avoid what may be an unfair result, courts may attempt to distort one of the negligence per se conditions, and create instead a negligence per se loophole. . . .

Similar judicial liberties may be taken with the meaning of statutory terms, in order to avoid the results from literal interpretation. Surely, the prevalence of such devices, combined with the increasing dominance of the rebuttable presumption standard, indicate the negligence per se approach just does not work.

C. Violation of Statute as Evidence of Negligence

Just as the rebuttable presumption approach to statutory violations in a negligence context apparently arose, at least in part, from dissatisfaction with the result of a mechanical application of the per se rule, a parallel development in our state with respect to infractions of ordinances and of administrative regulations, has been that violations of these amount to only evidence of negligence. [Cc]

We have not, however, chosen to join that small minority which has decreed that violation of a statute is only evidence of negligence. In view of the fairness and ease with which the rebuttable presumption standard has been and can be administered, we believe the litigants are thereby well served and the Legislature is given appropriate respect.

D. Application of Statutory Standard to This Case

We have seen, therefore, that while some of our Michigan cases seem to present negligence per se as an unqualified rule, the fact of the matter is that there are a number of qualifications which make application of this rule not really a per se approach at all. Not only must the statutory purpose doctrine and the requirement of proximate cause be satisfied, but the alleged wrongdoer has an opportunity to come forward with evidence rebutting the presumption of negligence.

An accurate statement of our law is that when a court adopts a penal statute as the standard of care in an action for negligence, violation of that statute establishes a prima facie case of negligence, with the determination to be made by the finder of fact whether the party accused of violating the statute has established a legally sufficient excuse. If the finder of fact determines such an excuse exists, the appropriate standard of care then becomes that established by the common law. Such excuses shall include, but shall not be limited to, these suggested by the SECOND RESTATEMENT OF TORTS, § 288A, and shall be determined by the circumstances of each case.

In the case at bar, moreover, the statute itself provides a guideline for the jury, for a violation will not occur when it is impracticable to use the sidewalk or to walk on the left side of a highway. This is ordinarily a question for the finder of fact, [c] and thus the statute itself provides not only a legislative standard of care which may be accepted by the court, but a legislatively mandated excuse as well.

. . . .

[W]e find the jury was adequately instructed as to the effect of the violation of this particular statute on plaintiff's case.

. . . The Court of Appeals is reversed and the trial court is affirmed. . . .

Points for Discussion

1. The court's opinion discusses the following approaches concerning the role and function of a penal statute in a civil suit for damages: (1) a statutory violation as a *prima facie* and rebuttable presumption of negligence; (2) a violation of a statute as negligence per se; and (3) a violation of a statute as only evidence of negligence. What is your understanding of each of these approaches and their differences? As a matter of law and policy, do you have a preference as to the best or better approach?

2. Which of the foregoing approaches does the *Zeni* court adopt, and why? How does the court utilize § 288A of the Restatement?

3. Who decides whether or not it was practicable for the plaintiff to use the sidewalk or walk on the left side of the street—judge or the jury?

    The court decides questions of law. The factfinder—usually the jury—determines questions of fact.

4. In its opinion the court uses the terms "fair" and "unfair"? Should a judge resort to and employ a fairness analysis in the adjudication of a negligence claim? What factors can and should be evaluated in making a fairness determination?

Teply v. Lincoln

125 Idaho 773, 874 P.2d 584 (Ct. App. 1994)

WALTERS, Chief Judge.

This is an appeal from a judgment entered on a jury verdict finding a motorist not liable for injuries and property damage sustained when his automobile slid across the highway and collided with an oncoming vehicle. The dispositive issue is whether a driver is legally excused from compliance with the safety statues relating to driving on the right-hand side of the highway, where icy road conditions unexpectedly cause him to lose control of his vehicle and slide across the centerline of the highway. Adhering to the decision of the Idaho Supreme Court in *Haakonstad v. Hoff,* 94 Idaho 300, 486 P.2d 1013 (1971), we hold the driver is not excused, and that the jury's verdict representing a contrary finding in this case must therefore be set aside.

Facts and Procedural Background

For purposes of this appeal the following facts are not disputed. While driving southbound on Highway 55 during an October snowfall, Douglas Lincoln lost control of his pickup truck as it slid across the centerline of the highway and collided with a northbound vehicle that was occupied by Louis Teply, his wife Vonda Teply, and their daughter Sondra Bryant (hereinafter referred to collectively as "the Teplys"). The Teplys brought this negligence action against Lincoln, seeking recovery for personal injuries and for the damage to their automobile.

At trial, Lincoln testified that on the morning of the accident he left Lewiston, Idaho, travelling south. His two-wheel drive pickup had new tires, was in excellent condition, and had its bed weighted down. The roads from Lewiston to New Meadows had been fairly clear. At New Meadows, Lincoln turned onto Highway 55 and proceeded south at a constant speed of between forty and fifty miles per hour. Suddenly and without warning, the back-end of his pickup slid left, toward the centerline. Lincoln did not brake but tried, unsuccessfully, to steer into the slide and to keep the direction of his pickup straight on the road ahead of him. However, the pickup slid at an angle, crossed the centerline, and collided with the Teplys' vehicle. Witnesses at the scene later testified that a light snow had fallen and the road beneath was slick. There was no evidence of negligence on the part of anyone in the Teplys' vehicle.

At the close of the evidence, the trial court instructed the jury on the relevant highway safety statutes, including the statutes requiring that vehicles be driven upon the right-hand side of the highway, I.C. § 49-630, and that drivers approaching from opposite directions pass each other to the right, I.C. § 49-631. Over the Teplys' objection, the court additionally instructed the jury as follows:

> A violation of a statute is negligence unless compliance with the statute was impossible or something over which the party had no control placed him in a position of violation of a statute or an emergency not of the party's own making caused him to fail to obey a statute.

Following its deliberations, the jury returned a verdict finding Lincoln not negligent. . . . The Teplys appealed . . .

. . . .

Negligence Per Se

In civil actions for damages, where injury occurs as a proximate result of a violation of a statute enacted for the protection of motorists, such violation is negligence as a matter of law, and not merely prima facie evidence of negligence. [C] Thus, one "cannot excuse himself from compliance [with a safety statute] by showing that he did or attempted to do what any reasonably prudent person would have done under similar circumstances." [C] Rather, the question of liability under the negligence *per se* theory turns not upon whether the defendant has demonstrated his freedom from common-law negligence, but on whether he has established a "legal excuse" for his violation of the statute. [Cc]

The Idaho Supreme Court has recognized four limited categories of excusing circumstances: (1) anything that would make compliance with the statute impossible; (2) anything over which the driver has no control which places his vehicle in a position violative of the statute; (3) an emergency not of the driver's own making by reason of which he fails to obey the statute; and (4) an excuse specifically provided by statute. [Cc]

In this case, undisputed evidence established that Lincoln had violated the highway statutes requiring that he operate his vehicle on the right side of the highway and that he pass oncoming vehicles on the right. The jury was not at liberty to disregard such evidence. [C]   It is also clear that I.C. §§ 49-630 and 49-631 are safety statutes, enacted for the protection of motorists and other persons using Idaho's roads and highways. [C] Accordingly, Lincoln was negligent as a matter of law unless his violations were found to have been excused. [C]

The only evidence offered at trial to explain or justify Lincoln's violations was the testimony concerning the icy conditions of the road. Thus, the dispositive issue is whether the fact of icy road conditions, alone, was sufficient to excuse Lincoln's violations of the highway safety statutes. The answer to this question is provided by the Idaho Supreme Court's decision in *Haakonstad v. Hoff,* 94 Idaho 300, 486 P.2d 1013 (1971).

Haakonstad involved an automobile collision at an intersection. The plaintiff in that case alleged that the accident was caused by the defendant's failure to yield the right of way, in violation of a highway safety statute. Sitting as the trier of fact, the trial court found that the defendant had in fact failed to yield, but that the "extreme icy conditions of the road" had caused, and therefore excused, the defendant's violation. Reversing the trial court, the Idaho Supreme Court held that a finding that the icy road conditions had caused the defendant to slide could *not* serve to excuse him from liability.

Although the rule stated in *Haakonstad* seems to be embraced by only a small minority of jurisdictions, it has not been overruled in Idaho and therefore controls in this case. Thus constrained, we hold that the evidence of icy roads in this case was insufficient, as a matter of law, to excuse Lincoln's statutory violations. It follows that the jury was incorrectly instructed otherwise. Because we set aside the jury's liability determination, a new trial is required on the issue of damages. Accordingly, we need not discuss further the trial court's denial of Teplys' motion for a new trial.

Conclusion

We conclude that the jury verdict must be set aside and that the Teplys are entitled to a judgment n.o.v. on the issue of Lincoln's negligence. Accordingly, the judgment entered in favor of Lincoln is vacated. The case is remanded for further proceedings to determine the amount of Teplys' damages which were proximately caused by Lincoln's negligence.

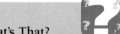

What's That?

Judgment n.o.v. is an abbreviation for judgment *non obstante veredicto,* or judgment notwithstanding the verdict. Such a judgment is entered by the court for a party after and even though a jury has rendered a verdict for the opposing party.

Points for Discussion

1. How and why did the defendant violate state law?

2. Do you agree with the court's analysis and holding? Given the facts of the case, was the defendant really at fault?

3. What circumstances and events might fall within the limited categories of excusing circumstances recognized by the Idaho Supreme Court? A toddler walking in traffic on the right side of the road? Swerving to avoid hitting a deer? A blown tire that causes the vehicle to swerve into the left lane?

---

4. Establishing a Standard of Care By Applying a Tort-Specific Statute

> ### RESTATEMENT (SECOND) OF TORTS § 285(a) (1965)
> #### Excused Violations
>
> The standard of conduct of a reasonable [person] may be established by a legislative enactment or administrative regulation which so provides.

A common example of establishing a standard of care via a "legislative enact-ment . . . which so provides" is a **dram shop** act. Dram shop acts generally govern the conduct of providers of intoxicating liquors and beverages. For example, one such statute provides that a drinking establishment that "knowingly sells, furnishes, or serves alcoholic beverages to a person who is in a state of noticeable intoxication, knowing that such person will soon be driving a motor vehicle, may become liable for injury or damage caused by or resulting from the intoxication of such . . . person when the sale, furnishing, or serving is the **proximate cause** of such injury or damage." GA. CODE ANN. § 51-1-40(b) (2009). *See also* OHIO R.C. § 4399.18 (2010) (a person has a cause of action against a liquor permit holder or the permit holder's employee "for personal injury, death, or property damage caused by the negligent actions of an intoxicated person" upon a showing that the permit holder or employee "knowingly sold an intoxicating beverage" to a "noticeably intoxicated person").

As there are substantive and material differences in the scope and require-ments of dram shop acts, research concerning the applicable and governing law in a specific jurisdiction is essential. For a listing of such acts, see 4 Drinking/Driving

Litigation: Criminal and Civil § 29:1. For recent decisions addressing dram shop act liability claims, see Shin v. Estate of Camacho, 302 Ga. App. 243, 690 S.E.2d 444 (2010) (host of party not liable under Dram Shop Act for death of motorist and motorist's son); Bauer v. Nesbitt, 969 A.2d 1122 (N.J. 2009) (exclusivity provision of New Jersey Dram Shop Act barred plaintiff's common-law negligence claim against drinking establishment).

D. Proving Negligence

1. Direct and Circumstantial Evidence

Goddard v. Boston & Maine R.R. Co.

179 Mass. 52, 60 N.E. 486 (1901)

Action by Wilfred H. Goddard against the Boston & Maine Railroad Company for personal injuries received by falling upon a banana skin lying upon the platform at defendant's station at Boston. The evidence showed that plaintiff was a passenger who had just arrived, and was about the length of the car from where he alighted when he slipped and fell. There was evidence that there were many passengers on the platform. Verdict directed for defendant, and plaintiff excepts.

HOLMES, C. J.

The banana skin upon which the plaintiff stepped and which caused him to slip may have been dropped within a minute by one of the persons who was leaving the train. It is unnecessary to go further to decide the case.

Exceptions overruled.

Anjou v. Boston Elevated Railway Co.

208 Mass. 273, 94 N.E. 386 (1911)

RUGG, J.

The plaintiff arrived on one of defendant's cars on the upper level of the Dudley Street terminal; other passengers arrived on same car, but it does not appear how many. She waited until the crowd had left the platform, when she inquired of one of defendant's uniformed employés the direction to another car. He walked along a narrow platform, and she, following a few feet behind him toward the stairway he had indicated, was injured by slipping upon a banana peel. It was described by several who examined it in these terms: It 'felt dry, gritty, as if there were dirt upon it,' as if 'trampled over a good deal,' as 'flattened down, and black in color,' 'every bit of it was black, there wasn't a particle of yellow,' and as 'black, flattened out and gritty.' It was one of the duties of employés of the defendant, of whom there was one at this station all the time, to observe and remove whatever was upon the platform to interfere with the safety of travelers. These might have been found to be the facts.

The **inference** might have been drawn from the appearance and condition of the banana peel that it had been upon the platform a considerable period of time, in such position that it would have been seen and removed by the employés of the defendant if they had been reasonably careful in performing their duty. Therefore there is something on which to base a conclusion that it was not dropped a moment before by a passenger, and Goddard v. Boston & Maine R. R., 179 Mass. 52, 60 N. E. 486, and Lyons v. Boston Elevated Railway Co., 204 Mass. 227, 90 N. E. 419, are plainly distinguishable. The obligation rested upon the defendant to keep its station reasonably safe for its passengers. It might have been found that the platform was suffered to remain in such condition as to be a menace to those rightfully walking upon it. Hence there was evidence of negligence on the part of the defendant, which should have been submitted to the jury. [Cc]

In accordance with the terms of the report, let the entry be:

Judgment for the plaintiff for $1,250 with costs.

Points for Discussion

1. Compare and contrast the Massachusetts Supreme Judicial Court's decisions in *Goddard* and *Anjou*.

2. In the *Anjou* court's view, what evidence of the defendant's negligence should have been submitted to the jury?

3. What is direct evidence? What is circumstantial evidence? "The conventional distinction is that direct evidence is testimony by a witness about a matter within his personal knowledge and so does not require drawing an inference from the evidence (his testimony) to the proposition that it is offered to establish, whereas circumstantial evidence does require drawing inferences." The probative value of direct and circumstantial evidence is "the same in principle." *Sylvester v. SOS Children's Villages Illinois, Inc.*, 453 F.3d 900,

904 (7th Cir. 2006). What was the direct evidence of defendant's alleged negligence in *Goddard*? In *Anjou*? What was the circumstantial evidence in each case?

———————

Wal-Mart Stores, Inc. v. Rosa

52 S.W.3d 842 (Tex. Ct. App. 2001)

OPINION ON APPELLEE'S AMENDED MOTION
FOR REHEARING EN BANC

Opinion by: SARAH B. DUNCAN, Justice.

Wal-Mart Stores, Inc. appeals the trial court's judgment against it in Petra Rosa's premise defect suit. The court has reconsidered the case en banc and with-draws the panel opinion and judgment dated October 31, 2000. We hold there is no evidence from which it can be inferred that Wal-Mart had actual knowledge or constructive notice of the premise defect for so long that it should have been discovered and removed. We therefore reverse the trial court's judgment and render judgment in Wal-Mart's favor.

> **FYI**
> A motion for rehearing *en banc* seeks the rehearing of a case by all judges of a court. In this case, the court withdrew the ruling by a panel of judges and issued this decision of the *en banc* bench.

. . .

After paying for her groceries, Petra Rosa slipped and fell on a piece of banana. She later sued Wal-Mart for negligence. After a jury trial, the trial court rendered judgment in Rosa's favor. Wal-Mart appeals.

. . .

To recover in a slip-and-fall case, a plaintiff must establish:

(1) Actual or constructive knowledge of some condition on the premises by the owner/operator;

(2) That the condition posed an unreasonable risk of harm;

(3) That the owner/operator did not exercise reasonable care to reduce or eliminate the risk; and

(4) That the owner/operator's failure to use such care proximately caused the plaintiff's injuries.

Keetch v. Kroger Co., 845 S.W.2d 262, 264 (Tex.1992). "[W]hen circumstantial evidence is relied upon to prove constructive notice, the evidence must establish that it is more likely than not that the dangerous condition existed long enough to give the proprietor a reasonable opportunity to discover the condition." *Wal-Mart Stores, Inc. v. Gonzalez,* 968 S.W.2d 934, 936 (Tex.1998).

There is no evidence any Wal-Mart employee had actual knowledge of the piece of banana upon which Rosa fell. To meet the **circumstantial evidence** standard, Rosa points to the testimony of her daughter-in-law, Melissa Rosa. She testified the piece of banana was "brown," and when her children dropped pieces of banana, it took at least forty-five minutes to one hour for the banana to turn brown. However, this testimony is no evidence that the banana had been on the floor long enough to charge Wal-Mart with constructive notice. [C]

Melissa Rosa also testified the piece of banana looked to her to have been there a while. Again, however, this is not evidence from which constructive notice may be inferred. [C]

Rosa also points to the number and proximity of Wal-Mart employees near where she fell, as well as a 3-inch wide-angled mirror on the wall behind her, as evidence that Wal-Mart should have discovered the piece of banana. . . . However, this evidence does not tend to prove the piece of banana had been on the floor long enough to charge Wal-Mart with constructive notice. *See Gonzalez,* 968 S.W.2d at 938 ("Gonzalez had to demonstrate that it was *more likely than not* that the macaroni salad had been there for a long time.").

CONCLUSION

As in *Gonzalez,* "the circumstantial evidence ... supports only the *possibility* that the dangerous condition existed long enough to give Wal-Mart a reasonable opportunity to discover it." *Gonzalez,* 968 S.W.2d at 936. We therefore reverse the trial court's judgment and render judgment in Wal-Mart's favor.

Justice RICKHOFF concurring.

Generally, concurrence writing is wasted effort. However, this is another case, determined not by the facts, law, or analysis, but by the predisposition of judges.

The result is a refined tort reform analysis that largely eliminates both the equity power of jury judgments and another cause of action—the slip and fall. If as *Wal-Mart Stores, Inc. v. Gonzalez,* 968 S.W.2d 934, 938 (Tex.1998), says, Rosa must demonstrate "that it was more likely than not" that discolored macaroni salad or a banana "had been there for a long time" most slip and fall cases will be exceedingly hard to prove. I concur, but I am very uncomfortable with the trend that makes us senior jurors.

> **FYI**
>
> Tort reform refers generally to legislative efforts and measures to limit the causes of action and damages available to tort plaintiffs. For discussion and analysis of tort reform, *see* Andrew F. Popper, TORT REFORM—COMMENTARY AND OTHER MATERIALS (West 2010).

I see a distinction between our case and the Supreme Court's guidance in *Gonzalez.* In both, the central issue was whether the store had constructive knowledge of the spill and, in each, meager evidence (age of a fallen banana estimated from discoloration/age of fallen macaroni from dirt and cart tire tracks) supported "equally plausible but appropriate inferences." The distinction is that on the day of the accident here, the Wal-Mart staff acquiesced in letting a baby transverse the store dangling a peeled banana. . . .

. . . .

The inescapable conclusion is that, if you allow children to eat bananas in your store, customers will slip, fall, and injure themselves. . . .

Here, the jury was asked whether "the negligence of any person or entity ... proximately cause[d] the occurrence or injury in question?" The jury was instructed that Wal-Mart was negligent if, among things, it "knew or reasonably should have known of the danger[.]" The jury found Wal-Mart negligent. I would leave it to the jury if I were free to do so.

Chief Justice HARDBERGER joined by Justice LÓPEZ and Justice STONE, dissenting.

HARDBERGER, Chief Justice, dissenting.

. . . .

Two Wal-Mart employees testified that the customer in line ahead of Rosa was holding a baby that was eating a banana. The employees stated that their attention became focused on this fact when the cashier who was checking out that customer asked one of the Wal-Mart employees, who was a manager, for guidance as to how the customer should be charged for the banana. The employee was uncertain as to how the banana should be charged because customers are normally charged for a banana based on its weight, but the baby had consumed part of the banana. The manager told the employee not to charge the customer. The other employee admitted that it should be a concern of Wal-Mart to ensure that the baby did not create a mess when eating the banana.

At the time the banana was dropped, three Wal-Mart employees were aware that the baby was eating a banana. At least one of those employees was aware of the potential for the baby to create a mess by dropping the banana. None of those employees took the time to check and determine whether the baby had in fact dropped the banana.

Under these circumstances, the length of time that Wal-Mart needed to have a reasonable opportunity to discover the condition was significantly reduced. Three Wal-Mart employees were in the immediate vicinity and were aware of the potential for a dangerous condition to develop. They knew of the exact dangerous condition that developed. In fact, they knew what every parent knows from common experience: that there is a good chance when a baby is eating a banana that as much of the banana will wind up on the floor as in the baby's stomach. [C] That was the concern. But no one did anything about it. None of those employees checked to ensure that the condition did not develop within the few minutes it took to complete the customer's transaction. *See Wal-Mart Stores, Inc. v. Garcia,* 30 S.W.3d 19, 23 (Tex.App.-San Antonio 2000, no pet.) (taking into consideration close proximity of personnel to site of hazardous condition). The cashier even chose not to check the floor when moving the customer's cart to the end of the check-out stand despite the fact that each Wal-Mart employee carries a paper towel in their pocket to wipe spills.

Wal-Mart asserts that the evidence as to the source of the dangerous condition is not refuted. The condition was caused by the baby eating the banana. The same baby who was the focus of at least three Wal-Mart employees' attention, and the same baby that one Wal-Mart employee thought might create the very condition that caused Rosa to slip. Given those circumstances, a jury could reasonably infer that it was more likely than not that Wal-Mart had a reasonable opportunity to discover that the baby had dropped the banana and created the dangerous condition. That was the jury's finding, and there was sufficient evidence to support that finding.

Wallace v. Wal-Mart Stores, Inc.

272 Ga. App. 343, 612 S.E.2d 528 (2005)

MIKELL, Judge.

In this slip and fall action, Karen and James Wallace appeal the trial court's grant of summary judgment to Wal-Mart Stores, Inc. ("Wal-Mart"), contending that genuine issues of material fact remain. For the reasons set forth below, we affirm.

. . . .

Viewed most favorably to the plaintiffs, the evidence shows that Mrs. Wallace and her husband visited a Wal-Mart store in Valdosta to purchase some frozen okra and butterbeans. While Mrs. Wallace was walking from the frozen foods section to the produce department, she slipped and fell, breaking her hip and injuring her back. Mrs. Wallace was not looking at the floor and did not notice anything on the floor that might have caused her to fall. She testified in her deposition that she did not notice any employees in the area before her fall.

Mr. Wallace, who had been walking behind his wife, was the first to arrive on the scene, followed by Heather Rountree, a produce department employee, and then Johnny Stephens, co-manager of the store. According to Stephens's deposition testimony, Mr. Wallace stated that his wife "stepped on a grape." Stephens recalled seeing a grape in the area. Stephens filled out an incident report and photographed a mashed grape. According to Stephens, no one saw Mrs. Wallace fall. Rountree and Daren Fleming, another produce department employee, told Stephens that they had "been through the area" 15 to 20 minutes before the fall and did not notice a grape on the floor.

While Mrs. Wallace was in the hospital later that evening, she overheard someone say that she slipped on a grape. Mrs. Wallace did not actually see the grape and did not know how long it had been on the floor. Mr. Wallace testified that just after Stephens arrived on the scene, he noticed a female employee walk over "and put her foot over [a] grape that was laying on the floor. She had her heel down and her toes up, the grape underneath." Mr. Wallace told the unidentified woman to "get her damn foot off that thing." Stephens did not recall anyone putting their foot over the grape, but he recalled Mr. Wallace mentioning that someone was trying to cover up the grape.

Rountree testified in her deposition that she and Fleming were both working in the produce section on the evening in question, and that she was stocking produce by herself in the salad section when she heard someone call for help. Rountree did not notice the grape on the floor until after an ambulance arrived to transport Mrs. Wallace to the hospital. Rountree denied putting her foot over the grape.

Fleming averred that prior to Mrs. Wallace's fall, he and Rountree were in the back of the store loading boxes of bananas onto a rolling cart to take to a display tree located outside of the produce department. Fleming pushed the cart out of the back area of the store while Rountree walked beside him behind the cart. According to Fleming,

> [w]e walked in this position over the area of the floor where Ms. Wallace fell. It took us about three to five minutes to cross the store to the banana tree. It took us approximately five to ten minutes to arrange the bananas on the [display]. We then left the [display] to return to the produce department. I was pushing the cart with the empty boxes. [Rountree] walked ahead of me. As I approached the produce department, I heard a Code White called. I saw Ms. Wallace lying on the ground. She was complaining of her hip area and said she slipped on some grapes. I saw a grape peel smeared on the floor and moisture from the grape on the floor.

As best we can discern from their single enumeration of error, appellants contend that the trial court erred in granting summary judgment to Wal-Mart for two reasons: (1) Rountree's testimony creates questions of fact, and (2) there is no evidence of reasonable inspection procedures. We disagree.

To recover for injuries sustained in a slip and fall, appellants must prove (1) that Wal-Mart had actual or constructive knowledge of the hazard; and (2) that appellants lacked knowledge of the hazard, despite exercising ordinary care, due to actions or conditions within Wal-Mart's control. The crux of this case is whether Wal-Mart had actual or constructive knowledge of the hazard. Since appellants raise the question of reasonable inspection procedures and do not point to any evidence of actual knowledge, we will assume that appellants are attempting to show that Wal-Mart had constructive knowledge of the hazard. Constructive knowledge may be demonstrated in two ways: (1) by showing that a store employee was present in the immediate area and could easily have seen the substance and removed it, or (2) by showing that the substance had been on the floor for such a time that it would have been discovered and removed had the proprietor exercised reasonable care in inspecting the premises.

Appellants seem to contend that Fleming's affidavit coupled with Rountree's conflicting testimony proves that Wal-Mart had constructive knowledge. This argument fails for several reasons. First, Rountree's affidavit, though referenced in Wal-Mart's motion for summary judgment, is not included in the record. Accordingly, we are unable to consider any references to it or determine if Rountree's affidavit and deposition testimony are conflicting. Second, Rountree testified in her deposition that she did not notice a grape on the floor until after the ambulance arrived. Third, Mrs. Wallace testified that she did not notice an employee in the immediate area prior to her fall. Fourth, regardless of whether Rountree was stocking produce in the salad section or helping Fleming with the banana display, the evidence shows that neither Rountree nor Fleming was in the immediate area when Mrs. Wallace fell and, therefore, could not have removed the grape before the fall. Wal-Mart's constructive knowledge cannot be established through the testimony of Mrs. Wallace, Rountree, or Fleming.

Moreover, Mr. Wallace's testimony that an unidentified employee tried to cover the grape with her foot after Stephens arrived on the scene is not enough to raise a genuine issue of material fact, as Wal-Mart does not dispute that Mrs. Wallace slipped on a grape.

Appellants next contend that Wal-Mart had constructive knowledge of the hazard because it failed to employ reasonable inspection procedures. Specifically, appellants contend that the testimony of Rountree and Stephens proves that there is no evidence that employees performed a "zone defense" or inspection of the area on the day of the accident.

. . . .

With respect to Wal-Mart's inspection procedures, Rountree testified that employees are given a copy of "The Wal-Mart Manual," which requires them to clean and check the floors every hour. Additionally, employees are supposed to inspect and clean the floor

> as you go along, as you work. As you put things up, you are supposed to check the floor. When you go in, you check underneath the tables. If there's apples that rolled underneath the tables, you are supposed to get them. If they are out on wet section, if it's wet, you are supposed to clean it up. If you see one little pea or something, you are supposed to pick it up.

When questioned about who checked the floor and how often, Stephens explained that "[a] zone defense is called usually about every hour, but a zone defense is done continuously. A zone defense is a where you're continuously checking your area for any kind of obstructions or paper or anything anybody could get hurt on." According to Stephens, a "zone defense" is called approximately every hour, but employees are trained to look continuously for hazards. Stephens testified that the store did not keep a log of when or how often "zone defenses" were called, but that the produce department "practice[s] zone defense all the time."

Regardless of whether or not a "zone defense" was called on the day of the accident, the unrefuted evidence shows that Rountree and Fleming had "been through the area" 15 to 20 minutes before the fall and did not notice a grape on the floor. "In cases where a proprietor has shown that an inspection occurred within a brief period prior to an invitee's fall, we have held that the inspection procedure was adequate as a matter of law." Since appellants have failed to establish either actual or constructive knowledge in this case, the trial court did not err in granting summary judgment to Wal-Mart.

Judgment affirmed.

Points for Discussion

1. Wal-Mart prevailed in both *Rosa* and *Wallace*. Do you agree with the outcome in either or both cases? Why or why not?

2. What were the grounds of disagreement among the judges in the *Rosa* majority, concurring, and dissenting opinions? Were you most persuaded by the majority or by the dissent? Did the majority properly reverse the jury's findings and the trial court's judgment in favor of the plaintiff?

3. In *Wallace* the court concluded that the plaintiffs failed to establish that the defendant had either **actual** or **constructive knowledge** of a grape on the floor. The court determined that the uncontradicted evidence showed that two employees had "been through the area" 15-20 minutes before the plaintiff fell and did not notice a grape on the floor; that evidence, not refuted by the plaintiff, warranted summary judgment for the defendant.

4. Can it be anticipated that a plaintiff will not have information or evidence concerning the length of time that a grape or banana or other substance was on the floor prior to a slip-and-fall? Where the plaintiff bears the burden of pleading and proving negligence, the absence of such evidence can be outcome-determinative in the defendant's favor. *Rosa* and *Wallace* are exemplars of the general view that the plaintiff bears the burden of proving the defendant's actual or constructive knowledge and failure to exercise reasonable care under the circumstances. For a different approach, see *Lanier v. Wal-Mart Stores, Inc.*, 99 S.W.3d 431 (Ky. 2003), wherein the court concluded that it is unreasonable to require a customer to prove a foreign substance was caused to be on the floor or how long it was there. Accordingly, the court placed upon the defendant the burden of proving the absence of negligence.

---

2. *Res Ipsa Loquitur*

Byrne v. Boadle

Court of Exchequer
2 H. & C. 722. 159 Eng. Rep. 299
(1863)

Declaration. For that the defendant, by his servants, so negligently and unskillfully managed and lowered certain barrels of flour by means of a certain jigger-hoist and machinery attached to the shop of the defendant, situated in a certain highway, along which the plaintiff was then passing, that by and through the negligence of the defendant, by his said servants, one of the said barrels of flour fell upon and struck against the plaintiff, whereby the plaintiff was thrown down, wounded, lamed, and permanently injured, and was prevented from attending to his business for a long time, to wit, thence hitherto, and incurred great expense for medical attendance, and suffered great pain and anguish, and was otherwise damnified.

> **Non constat**
> **jus civile**
> a posteriori
>
> **It's Latin to Me!**
>
> *Res ipsa loquitur* is Latin for "the thing speaks for itself."

Plea. Not guilty.

> **FYI**
>
> The Court of Exchequer was an English superior court responsible for the adjudication of legal disputes involving public revenue matters and collections.

At the trial before the learned Assessor of the Court of Passage at Liverpool . . . [a] witness named Critchley said: "On the 18th of July, I was in Scotland Road, on the right side going north, defendant's shop is on that side. When I was opposite to his shop, a barrel of flour fell from a window in the defendant's house and shop, and knocked the plaintiff down." He was carried into an adjoining shop. . . . The plaintiff said: "On approaching Scotland Place and defendant's shop, I lost all recollection. I felt no blow. I saw nothing to warn me of danger. I was taken home in a cab. I was helpless for a fortnight." . . . Another witness said: "I saw a barrel falling. I don't know how, but from defendant's." The only other witness was a surgeon, who described the injury which the plaintiff had received. It was admitted that the defendant was a dealer in flour.

It was submitted on the part of the defendant, that there was no evidence of negligence for the jury. The learned Assessor was of that opinion, and **nonsuited** the plaintiff, reserving leave to him to move the Court of Exchequer to enter the verdict for him with 50*l.* damages, the amount assessed by the jury.

. . . .

> **FYI**
>
> The verdict of "50*l*" is one for 50 pounds. After the Norman Conquest in 1066 and prior to 1971, the British pound was divided into 20 shillings or 240 pennies.

POLLOCK, C.B. We are all of opinion that the rule must be absolute to enter the verdict for the plaintiff. The learned counsel was quite right in saying that there are many accidents from which no presumption of negligence can arise, but I think it would be wrong to lay down as a rule that in no case can presumption of negligence arise from the fact of an accident. Suppose in this case the barrel had rolled out of the warehouse and fallen on the plaintiff, how could he possibly ascertain from what cause it occurred? It is the duty of persons who keep barrels in a warehouse to take care that they do not roll out, and I think that such a case would, beyond all doubt, afford prima facie evidence of negligence. A barrel could not roll out of a warehouse without some negligence, and to say that a plaintiff who is injured by it must call witnesses from the warehouse to prove negligence seems to me preposterous. So in the building or repairing a house, or putting pots on the chimneys, if a person passing along the road is injured by something falling upon him, I think the accident alone would be prima facie evidence of negligence. Or if an article calculated to cause damage is put in the wrong place and does mischief, I think that those whose duty it was to put it in the right place are prima facie responsible, and if there is any state of facts to rebut the presumption of negligence, they must prove them. The present case upon the evidence comes to this, a man is passing in front of the premises of a dealer in flour, and there falls down upon him a barrel of flour. I think it apparent that the barrel was in the custody of the defendants who occupied the premises, and who is responsible for the acts of his servants who had the controul of it, and in my opinion the facts of its falling is prima facie evidence of negligence, and the plaintiff who was injured by it is not bound to shew that it could not fall without negligence, but if there are any facts inconsistent with negligence it is for the defendant to prove them.

[Concurring opinion omitted]

Points for Discussion

1. Byrne is the fount of the ***res ipsa loquitur*** doctrine. What is the legally relevant inquiry in determining whether *res ipsa loquitur* applies?

2. Did the plaintiff, struck by the barrel of flour falling from the defendant's shop, have any evidence that the defendant had engaged in any negligent conduct? In the absence of such proof, can you understand why the Assessor nonsuited the plaintiff?

3. Do you agree with Chief Baron Pollock that a barrel does not roll out of a warehouse without some negligence?

4. Who is in the best or better position to explain how and why the barrel fell from the defendant's window, the plaintiff or the defendant?

5. Chief Baron Pollock's opinion places what evidentiary burden on the defendant?

6. In your opinion, is it appropriate to hold a defendant liable in tort for negligence in the absence of proof that she breached the duty of care? Why or why not?

———————

RESTATEMENT (SECOND) OF TORTS § 328D (1965)
Res Ipsa Loquitur

(1) It may be inferred that harm suffered by the plaintiff is caused by negligence of the defendant when

    (a) the event is of a kind which ordinarily does not occur in the absence of negligence;

    (b) other responsible causes, including the conduct of the plaintiff and third persons, are sufficiently eliminated by the evidence; and

    (c) the indicated negligence is within the scope of the defendant's duty to the plaintiff.

(2) It is the function of the court to determine whether the inference may reasonably be drawn by the jury, or whether it must necessarily be drawn.

(3) It is the function of the jury to determine whether the inference is to be drawn in any case where different conclusions may reasonably be reached.

See also RESTATEMENT (THIRD) OF TORTS: LIABILITY FOR PHYSICAL HARM § 17 (2010): in *res ipsa loquitur* cases the "factfinder may infer that the defendant has been negligent when the accident causing the plaintiff's harm is a type of accident that ordinarily happens as a result of the negligence of a class of actors of which the defendant is the relevant member."

Safeco Insur. Co. v. Mobile Power and Light Co., Inc.

810 So.2d 756 (Ala. 2001)

MOORE, Chief Justice.

Safeco Insurance Company ("Safeco") had issued a homeowner's policy to Audrey Loyd and Brenda Loyd, husband and wife. The Loyds, along with Safeco . . . sued Mobile Power and Light Company, Inc. ("Mobile Power"), claiming that negligence on the part of Mobile Power had caused a fire in 1996 that destroyed the Loyds' home. The trial court entered a summary judgment for Mobile Power. Safeco appealed. The Court of Civil Appeals reversed. [C] We granted Mobile Power's petition for certiorari review. We reverse and remand.

On August 20, 1996, a fire consumed Audrey and Brenda Loyd's home. This was the third fire the Loyds had suffered at the same home in a two-year period. In 1994, a fire heavily damaged their home. In 1996, a second fire erupted in the Loyds' panel box "only a few months prior to the [August 1996] fire." The Loyds hired Mobile Power, a private company, to repair their electrical system after the 1994 fire. In his deposition, George Casellas, an expert technical consultant hired by Safeco to investigate the third fire, stated that a "fused disconnect" had been replaced after a second fire. Mobile Power was not involved in the second repair.

After the third fire, Safeco apparently paid the Loyds' claim under their homeowner's insurance policy and was subrogated to their interest. As **subrogee**, Safeco sued Mobile Power, alleging that Mobile Power had negligently repaired the electrical wiring in the Loyds' home and that its negligence had caused the August 1996 fire.

Mobile Power moved for a summary judgment. The trial court initially denied its motion. Later, the court granted it. Safeco appealed from the summary judgment. [The Court of Civil Appeals,] with Judges Crawley and Thompson dissenting, reversed the summary judgment and remanded for further proceedings. We granted certiorari to consider Mobile Power's claim that the decision of the Court of Civil Appeals conflicted with *Bell v. Colony Apartments Co., Ltd.,* 568 So.2d 805 (Ala.1990), on which the Court of Civil Appeals had relied.

The Mobile County Building Inspection Department issued Mobile Power all three of the permits required for its work on the Loyds' home after the 1994 fire. Ted Blunt, a licensed master electrician and an inspector for the Inspection Department for 18 years, personally conducted the "rough-in" and "service-release" inspections. At the rough-in phase, Blunt approved the overall plans, the type and size of the wire to be used, and the installation methods to be used. At the service-release phase, Blunt tested the circuits and authorized the activation of power to the Loyds' residence. John Freil, another inspector for the Department, conducted the final inspection. Blunt testified that all of the work conformed to the National Electrical Code, which he said had been adopted by Mobile County. Blunt further testified that Mobile Power's work did not breach any applicable standard of care. Mobile Power performed no other work for the Loyds after their house passed the Department's final inspection in December 1994.

Safeco hired George Casellas, an expert technical consultant, to conduct an investigation into the cause and origin of the third fire. Casellas reported that the third fire began in the circuit breaker/disconnect panel of the ventilation closet. At his pretrial deposition, he testified that the heating that caused this third fire might have developed over a period ranging from two hours to a couple of weeks, but he could not determine with any certainty "what happened there." Casellas attributed the last fire to one of three possible defects: (1) improper lug torque during installation, (2) mechanical failure of the screwed lug, or (3) thermal shrinkage of the conductor inside the lug. Casellas gave an affidavit that stated that "a previous electrical fire [the second fire] had taken place [in the Loyds' panel box] only a few months prior to the subject fire occurrence."

. . . .

In *Bell,* . . . Amy Bell sued the owner of her apartment complex for damages, based on a fire that had occurred 30 minutes after 2 employees of the complex had made electrical repairs inside her apartment. The defendant moved for a summary judgment, and the trial court granted its motion. This Court reversed the summary judgment and remanded the case, holding that the circumstantial evidence presented by Bell was sufficient to create a genuine issue of material fact. This Court stated:

> "Findings of fact cannot be based upon mere conjecture, of course, but it
> is also clear that direct evidence is not necessary to prove negligence on

the part of a defendant and that proof of negligence may be established completely through circumstantial evidence."

Bell, 568 So.2d at 810. The Court of Civil Appeals apparently premised its opinion in this present case on the doctrine of res ipsa loquitur.

"The elements of res ipsa loquitur are generally stated as:

"(1) [T]he defendant must have had full management and control of the instrumentality which caused the injury; (2) the circumstances must be such that according to common knowledge and the experience of mankind the accident could not have happened if those having control of the management had not been negligent; (3) the plaintiff's injury must have resulted from the accident."

Khirieh v. State Farm Mut. Auto. Ins. Co., 594 So.2d 1220, 1223 (Ala.1992) (citations omitted).

We disagree with the Court of Civil Appeals' reliance on *Bell*. First, the defendant in *Bell* had performed electrical work for Bell 30 minutes before the fire began. Here, the defendant had performed electrical work for the Loyds approximately two years before the fire. Second, the defendant in *Bell* had had exclusive management and control of the electrical panel box just before the fire began. In the Loyds' case, an unidentified third party had repaired the Loyds' electrical panel box in 1996 by replacing the "fused disconnect"-after the second fire and before the third one. Mobile Power did not perform this work. Proof of that intervening work, as well as the intervening two-year period, established that Mobile Power lacked the exclusive management and control required for Safeco to successfully invoke the doctrine of res ipsa loquitur. ...

. . . .

REVERSED AND REMANDED.

———————

Points for Discussion

1. What is the Alabama Supreme Court's formulation of the elements of a *res ipsa loquitur* claim?

2. Do you agree with the court's analysis of the *res ipsa loquitur* issue and the court's decision?

Hypo 4-5

Which of the following are or are not examples of *res ipsa loquitur*?

1. Two trains traveling on the same track, one headed north and the other south, collide. Defendant is the railroad.

2. A plane takes off from Paris, France heading to its destination in New York City. The plane never arrives in New York. The defendant is the airline.

3. A 500-pound gorilla escapes from its enclosure in a zoo and attacks and injures five people. Defendant is the zoo.

4. The automatic door at a shopping center slams shut on a customer entering the store, spraining his wrist. The defendant is the store.

5. A descending escalator in the same shopping center jolts to a halt, causing several customers to fall. Defendant is the shopping center.

6. A surgeon amputates the wrong leg of the patient. The defendant is the surgeon.

7. A guest in a hotel is scalded and injured by hot water while taking a shower. The defendant is the hotel.

Ybarra v. Spangard

25 Cal.2d 486, 154 P.2d 687 (1944)

GIBSON, Chief Justice.

This is an action for damages for personal injuries alleged to have been inflicted on plaintiff by defendants during the course of a surgical operation. The trial court entered judgments of **nonsuit** as to all defendants and plaintiff appealed.

On October 28, 1939, plaintiff consulted defendant Dr. Tilley, who diagnosed his ailment as appendicitis, and made arrangements for an appendectomy to be performed by defendant Dr. Spangard at a hospital owned and managed by defendant Dr. Swift. Plaintiff entered the hospital, was given a hypodermic injection, slept, and later was awakened by Drs. Tilley and Spangard and wheeled into the operating room by a nurse whom he believed to be defendant Gisler, an employee of Dr. Swift. Defendant Dr. Reser, the anesthetist, also an employee of Dr. Swift, adjusted plaintiff for the operation, pulling his body to the head of the operating table and, according to plaintiff's testimony, laying him back against two hard objects at the top of his shoulders, about an inch below his neck. Dr. Reser then administered the anesthetic and plaintiff lost consciousness. When he awoke early the following morning he was in his hospital room attended by defendant Thompson, the special nurse, and another nurse who was not made a defendant.

Plaintiff testified that prior to the operation he had never had any pain in, or injury to, his right arm or shoulder, but that when he awakened he felt a sharp pain about half way between the neck and the point of the right shoulder. He complained to the nurse, and then to Dr. Tilley, who gave him diathermy treatments while he remained in the hospital. The pain did not cease but spread down to the lower part of his arm, and after his release from the hospital the condition grew worse. He was unable to rotate or lift his arm, and developed paralysis and atrophy of the muscles around the shoulder. He received further treatments from Dr. Tilley until March, 1940, and then returned to work, wearing his arm in a splint on the advice of Dr. Spangard.

Plaintiff also consulted Dr. Wilfred Sterling Clark, who had X-ray pictures taken which showed an area of diminished sensation below the shoulder and atrophy and wasting away of the muscles around the shoulder. In the opinion of Dr. Clark. plaintiff's condition was due to trauma or injury by pressure or strain applied between his right shoulder and neck.

Plaintiff was also examined by Dr. Fernando Garduno, who expressed the opinion that plaintiff's injury was a paralysis of traumatic origin, not arising from pathological causes, and not systemic, and that the injury resulted in atrophy, loss of use and restriction of motion of the right arm and shoulder.

Plaintiff's theory is that the foregoing evidence presents a proper case for the application of the doctrine of res ipsa loquitur, and that the inference of negligence arising therefrom makes the granting of as nonsuit improper. Defendants take the position that, assuming that plaintiff's condition was in fact the result of an injury, there is no showing that the act of any particular defendant, nor any particular instrumentality, was the cause thereof. They attack plaintiff's action as an attempt to fix liability 'en masse' on various defendants, some of whom were not responsible for the acts of others; and they further point to the failure to show which defendants had control of the instrumentalities that may have been involved. Their main defense may be briefly stated in two propositions: (1) that where there are several defendants, and there is a division of responsibility in the use of an instrumentality causing the injury, and the injury might have resulted from the separate act of either one of two or more persons, the rule of res ipsa loquitur cannot be invoked against any one of them; and (2) that where there are several instrumentalities, and no showing is made as to which caused the injury or as to the particular defendant in control of it, the doctrine cannot apply. We are satisfied, however, that these objections are not well taken in the circumstances of this case.

The doctrine of res ipsa loquitur has three conditions: '(1) the accident must be of a kind which ordinarily does not occur in the absence of someone's negligence; (2) it must be caused by an agency or instrumentality within the exclusive control of the defendant; (3) it must not have been due to any voluntary action or contribution on the part of the plaintiff.' PROSSER, TORTS, p. 295. It is applied in a wide variety of situations, including cases of medical or dental treatment and hospital care. [Cc]

There is, however, some uncertainty as to the extent to which res ipsa loquitur may be invoked in cases of injury from medical treatment. This is in part due to the tendency, in some decisions, to lay undue emphasis on the limitations of the doctrine, and to give too little attention to its basic underlying purpose. The result has been that a simple, understandable rule of circumstantial evidence, with a sound background of common sense and human experience, has occasionally been transformed into a rigid legal formula, which arbitrarily precludes its application in many cases where it is most important that it should be applied. If the doctrine is to continue to serve a useful purpose, we should not forget that 'the particular force and justice of the rule, regarded as a presumption throwing upon the party charged the duty of producing evidence, consists in the circumstance that the chief evidence of the true cause, whether culpable or innocent, is practically accessible to him but inaccessible to the injured person.' 9 WIGMORE, EVIDENCE, 3d Ed., § 2509, p. 382; [cc].

The present case is of a type which comes within the reason and spirit of the doctrine more fully perhaps than any other. The passenger sitting awake in a railroad car at the time of a collision, the pedestrian walking along the street and struck by a falling object or the debris of an explosion, are surely not more entitled to an explanation than the unconscious patient on the operating table. Viewed from this aspect, it is difficult to see how the doctrine can, with any justification, be so restricted in its statement as to become inapplicable to a patient who submits himself to the care and custody of doctors and nurses, is rendered unconscious, and receives some injury from instrumentalities used in his treatment.

Without the aid of the doctrine a patient who received permanent injuries of a serious character, obviously the result of some one's negligence, would be entirely unable to recover unless the doctors and nurses in attendance voluntarily chose to disclose the identity of the negligent person and the facts establishing liability. [C] If this were the state of the law of negligence, the courts, to avoid gross injustice, would be forced to invoke the principles of absolute liability, irrespective of negligence, in actions by persons suffering injuries during the course of treatment under anesthesia. But we think this juncture has not yet been reached, and that the doctrine of res ipsa loquitur is properly applicable to the case before us.

The condition that the injury must not have been due to the plaintiff's voluntary action is of course fully satisfied under the evidence produced herein; and the same is true of the condition that the accident must be one which ordinarily does not occur unless some one was negligent. We have here no problem of negligence in treatment, but of distinct injury to a healthy part of the body not the subject of treatment, nor within the area covered by the operation. The decisions in this state make it clear that such circumstances raise the inference of negligence and call upon the defendant to explain the unusual result. [Cc]

The argument of defendants is simply that plaintiff has not shown an injury caused by an instrumentality under a defendant's control, because he has not shown which of the several instrumentalities that he came in contact with while in the hospital caused the injury; and he has not shown that any one defendant or his servants had exclusive control over any particular instrumentality. Defendants assert that some of them were not the employees of other defendants, that some did not stand in any permanent relationship from which liability in tort would follow, and that in view of the nature of the injury, the number of defendants and the different functions performed by each, they could not all be liable for the wrong, if any.

We have no doubt that in a modern hospital a patient is quite likely to come under the care of a number of persons in different types of contractual and other relationships with each other. For example, in the present case it appears that Drs. Smith, Spangard and Tilley were physicians or surgeons commonly placed in the legal category of **independent contractors**; and Dr. Reser, the anesthetist, and defendant Thompson, the special nurse, were employees of Dr. Swift and not of the other doctors. But we do not believe that either the number or relationship of the defendants alone determines whether the doctrine of res ipsa loquitur applies. Every defendant in whose custody the plaintiff was placed for any period was bound to exercise ordinary care to see that no unnecessary harm came to him and each would be liable for failure in this regard. Any defendant who negligently injured him, and any defendant charged with his care who so neglected him as to allow injury to occur, would be liable. The defendant employers would be liable for the neglect of their employees; and the doctor in charge of the operation would be liable for the negligence of those who became his temporary servants for the purpose of assisting in the operation.

In this connection, it should be noted that while the assisting physicians and nurses may be employed by the hospital, or engaged by the patient, they normally become the temporary servants or agents of the surgeon in charge while the operation is in progress, and liability may be imposed upon him for their negligent acts under the doctrine of respondeat superior. Thus a surgeon has been held liable for the negligence of an assisting nurse who leaves a sponge or other object inside a patient, and the fact that the duty of seeing that such mistakes do not occur is delegated to others does not absolve the doctor from responsibility for their negligence. [Cc]

It may appear at the trial that, consistent with the principles outlined above, one or more defendants will be found liable and others absolved, but this should not preclude the application of the rule of res ipsa loquitur. The control at one time or another, of one or more of the various agencies or instrumentalities which might have harmed the plaintiff was in the hands of every defendant or of his employees or temporary servants. This, we think, places upon them the burden of initial explanation. Plaintiff was rendered unconscious for the purpose of undergoing surgical treatment by the defendants; it is manifestly unreasonable for them to insist that he identify any one of them as the person who did the alleged negligent act.

The other aspect of the case which defendants so strongly emphasize is that plaintiff has not identified the instrumentality any more than he has the particular guilty defendant. Here, again, there is a misconception which, if carried to the extreme for which defendants contend, would unreasonably limit the application of the res ipsa loquitur rule. It should be enough that the plaintiff can show an injury resulting from an external force applied while he lay unconscious in the hospital; this is as clear a case of identification of the instrumentality as the plaintiff may ever be able to make.

An examination of the recent cases, particularly in this state, discloses that the test of actual exclusive control of an instrumentality has not been strictly followed, but exceptions have been recognized where the purpose of the doctrine of res ipsa loquitur would otherwise be defeated. Thus, the test has become one of right of control rather than actual control. [C] In the bursting bottle cases where the bottler has delivered the instrumentality to a retailer and thus has given up actual control, he will nevertheless be subject to the doctrine where it is shown that no change in the condition of the bottle occurred after it left the bottler's possession, and it can accordingly be said that he was in constructive control. Escola v. Coca

Bottling Co., 24 Cal.2d , 150 P.2d 436. Moreover, this court departed from the single instrumentality theory in the colliding vehicle cases, where two defendants were involved, each in control of a separate vehicle. [Cc] Finally, it has been suggested that the hospital cases may properly be considered exceptional, and that the doctrine of res ipsa loquitur 'should apply with equal force in cases wherein medical and nursing staffs take the place of machinery and may, through carelessness or lack of skill, inflict, or permit the infliction of injury upon a patient who is thereafter in no position to say how he received his injuries.' [C]

In the face of these examples of liberalization of the tests for res ipsa loquitur, there can be no justification for the rejection of the doctrine in the instant case. As pointed out above, if we accept the contention of defendants herein, there will rarely be any compensation for patients injured while unconscious. A hospital today conducts a highly integrated system of activities, with many persons contributing their efforts. There may be, e.g., preparation for surgery by nurses and internes who are employees of the hospital; administering of an anesthetic by a doctor who may be an employee of the hospital, an employee of the operating surgeon, or an independent contractor; performance of an operation by a surgeon and assistants who may be his employees, employees of the hospital, or independent contractors; and post surgical care by the surgeon, a hospital physician, and nurses. The number of those in whose care the patient is placed is not a good reason for denying him all reasonable opportunity to recover for negligent harm. It is rather a good reason for re-examination of the statement of legal theories which supposedly compel such a shocking result.

We do not at this time undertake to state the extent to which the reasoning of this case may be applied to other situations in which the doctrine of res ipsa loquitur is invoked. We merely hold that where a plaintiff receives unusual injuries while unconscious and in the course of medical treatment, all those defendants who had any control over his body or the instrumentalities which might have caused the injuries may properly be called upon to meet the inference of negligence by giving an explanation of their conduct.

The judgment is reversed.

Points for Discussion

1.   Do you agree with the court's conclusion that this is a *res ipsa loquitur* case?

2.   According to the *Ybarra* court, what are the elements of a plaintiff's *res ipsa loquitur* claim?

3. What is the procedural effect and impact of a plaintiff's showing of *res ipsa loquitur* on the plaintiff's and defendant's evidentiary and adjudicatory burdens?

4. The defendants argued that the plaintiff did not show that his injury was caused by an instrumentality under a particular defendant's control. What was the court's response to this argument?

5. What is the court's holding in *Ybarra*?

6. The court concluded that the plaintiff's successful invocation of the doctrine of *res ipsa loquitur* established an inference of negligence. While most courts have adopted this position, in some jurisdictions *res ipsa loquitur* establishes a rebuttable presumption of negligence, and the burden of proof shifts to and must be met by the defendant.

7. **The Procedural Effects of *Res Ipsa Loquitur*—**The *res ipsa loquitur* doctrine allows a plaintiff's lawsuit to proceed in the absence of factual evidence on the issues of duty and breach. The procedural effect of a plaintiff's successful invocation of the *res ipsa loquitur* doctrine in most jurisdictions is that the plaintiff can survive a no-evidence procedural challenge brought by the defendant, and an inference of a defendant's negligence can be argued to the factfinder where it may be accepted or rejected. *See e.g. McLaughlin Freight Lines, Inc. v. Gentrup*, 281 Neb. 725, 798 N.W.2d 386 (2011); *Aguilar v. Morales*, 162 S.W.3d 825 (Tex. App. 2005).

————————

CHAPTER 5

Causation

The preceding chapter considered the first two elements of a cause of action for negligence: **duty** and **breach**. This chapter turns to the next stage of the analysis and the requirement that the plaintiff prove that the defendant's negligence (breach of duty) caused the plaintiff's injury. To establish causation the plaintiff must show that the defendant's negligence was (1) the **cause-in-fact** (the **but-for cause**) *and* (2) the legal or **proximate cause** of the injuries for which the plaintiff seeks compensation.

A. Causation-In-Fact

1. *Sine Qua Non*

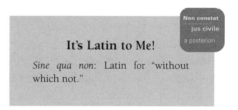

It's Latin to Me!

Sine qua non: Latin for "without which not."

Non constat
jus civile
a posteriori

Perkins v. Texas and New Orleans Ry. Co.

243 La. 829, 147 So.2d 646 (1962)

SANDERS, Justice.

This is a tort action. Plaintiff, the 67-year-old widow of Tanner Perkins, seeks damages for the death of her husband in the collision of an automobile, in which he was riding, with a train of the defendant railroad. The district court awarded damages. The Court of Appeal affirmed. We granted certiorari to review the judgment of the Court of Appeal.

The tragic accident which gave rise to this litigation occurred at the intersection of Eddy Street and The Texas and New Orleans Railroad Company track in the town of Vinton, Louisiana, at approximately 6:02 a.m., after daylight, on September 28, 1959. At this crossing Eddy Street runs north and south, and the railroad track, east and west. Involved was a 113-car freight train pulled by four diesel engines traveling east and a Dodge automobile driven by Joe Foreman in a southerly direction on Eddy Street. Tanner Perkins, a guest passenger, was riding in the front seat of the automobile with the driver.

Located in the northwest quadrant of the intersection of the railroad track and Eddy Street was a warehouse five hundred feet long. A 'house track' paralleled the main track on the north to serve the warehouse. This warehouse obstructed the view to the west of an automobile driver approaching the railroad crossing from the north on Eddy Street. It likewise obstructed the view to the north of trainmen approaching the crossing from the west. Having previously served on this route, the engineer and brakeman were aware of this obstruction.

To warn the public of the approach of trains, the defendant railroad had installed at the crossing an automatic signal device consisting of a swinging red light and a bell. At the time of the accident, this signal was operating. A standard Louisiana railroad stop sign and an intersection stop sign were also located at the crossing.

Proceeding east, the train approached the intersection with its headlight burning, its bell ringing, and its whistle blowing.

The engineer, brakeman, and fireman were stationed in the forward engine of the train. The engineer was seated on the right or south side, where he was unable to observe an automobile approaching from the left of the engine. The brakeman and fireman, who were seated on the left or north side of the engine, were looking forward as the train approached the intersection. These two crewmen saw the automobile emerge from behind the warehouse. At that time the front wheels of the automobile were on or across the north rail of the house track. The fireman estimated that the train was approximately 60 feet from the crossing when the automobile emerged from behind the warehouse. The brakeman, however, estimated that the train was 30 to 40 feet from the crossing at the time the automobile came into view. Both crewmen immediately shouted a warning to the engineer, who applied the emergency brakes. The train struck the right side of the automobile and carried it approximately 1250 feet. The two occupants were inside the automobile when it came to rest. Both were killed.

The speed of the automobile in which Tanner Perkins was riding was variously estimated from 3-4 miles per hour to 20-25 miles per hour.

The plaintiff and defendant railroad concede in their pleadings that Joe Foreman, the driver of the automobile, was negligent in driving upon the track in front of the train and that his negligence was a proximate cause of the death of Tanner Perkins.

It is conceded that the railroad's safety regulations imposed a speed limit of 25 miles per hour on trains in the town of Vinton. The plaintiff has conceded in this Court that this self-imposed speed limit was a safe speed at the crossing. The train was in fact traveling at a speed of 37 miles per hour.

Applicable here is the rule that the violation by trainmen of the railroad's own speed regulations adopted in the interest of safety is evidence of negligence. The rule has special force in the instant case because of the unusually hazardous nature of the crossing. We find, as did the Court of Appeal, that the trainmen were negligent in operating the train 12 miles per hour in excess of the speed limit.

As one of several defenses, the defendant railroad strenuously contends that the excessive speed of the train was not a **proximate cause** of the collision for the reason that the accident would not have been averted even had the train been traveling at the prescribed speed of 25 miles per hour. Contrariwise, the plaintiff contends that the speed of the train constituted a 'proximate, direct and contributing cause' of the accident.

Thus presented, the prime issue in this case is whether the excessive speed of the train was a **cause in fact** of the fatal collision.

It is fundamental that negligence is not actionable unless it is a cause in fact of the harm for which recovery is sought. It need not, of course, be the sole cause. Negligence is a cause in fact of the harm to another if it was a **substantial factor** in bringing about that harm. Under the circumstances of the instant case, the excessive speed was undoubtedly a substantial factor in bringing about the collision if the collision would not have occurred without it. On the other hand, if the collision would have occurred irrespective of such negligence, then it was not a substantial factor.

The burden of proving this causal link is upon the plaintiff. Recognizing that the fact of causation is not susceptible of proof to a mathematical certainty, the law requires only that the evidence show that it is more probable than not that the harm was caused by the tortious conduct of the defendant. Stated differently, it must appear that it is more likely than not that the harm would have been averted but for the negligence of the defendant.

In the instant case the train engineer testified that at a speed of 25 miles per hour he would have been unable to stop the train in time to avoid the accident. Other facts of record support his testimony in this regard. With efficient brakes, the mile-long train required 1250 feet to stop at a speed of 37 miles per hour. It is clear, then, that even at the concededly safe speed of 25 miles per hour, the momentum of the train would have, under the circumstances, carried it well beyond the crossing. This finding, of course, does not fully determine whether the collision would have been averted at the slower speed. The automobile was also in motion during the crucial period. This necessitates the further inquiry of whether the automobile would have cleared the track and evaded the impact had the train been moving at a proper speed at the time the trainmen observed the automobile emerge from behind the warehouse. Basic to this inquiry are the speed of the automobile and the driving distance between it and a position of safety.

The testimony of the witnesses is in hopeless conflict as to the speed of the automobile at the time of the collision. The estimates range from a low of 3 miles per hour to a high of 25 miles per hour. Both the district court and Court of Appeal concluded that the speed of the automobile had not been definitely established. Each of these courts found only that the automobile was proceeding at 'a slow speed.' In her brief the plaintiff states: 'The speed of the automobile cannot be determined, at least by the testimony.' We conclude that the evidence fails to establish the speed of the automobile with reasonable certainty.

Although the record discloses that the train struck the automobile broadside, it does not reflect the driving distance required to propel the vehicle from the danger zone.

Finally, we also note that the defendant railroad produced testimony, which is the only testimony of record on this point, that the deceased made no attempt to leave the moving automobile. That he was in the vehicle when it came to rest is undisputed. Moreover, the record fails to reflect the distance required for the deceased to scramble past the diesel engine to a place of safety, had he succeeded in getting out of the automobile.

Despite these deficiencies in the evidence, the plaintiff argues that had the train been traveling at a proper speed the driver of the automobile would 'conceivably' have had some additional time to take measures to avert disaster and the deceased would have had some additional time to extricate himself from danger. Hence, the plaintiff reasons, the collision and loss of life 'might not' have occurred.

On the facts of this case, we must reject the escape theory advanced in this argument. Because of the deficiencies in the evidence which we have already noted, it is devoid of evidentiary support. The record contains no probative facts from which the Court can draw a reasonable inference of causation under this theory. In essence, the argument is pure conjecture.

Based upon the evidence of record, it appears almost certain that the fatal accident would have occurred irrespective of the excessive speed of the train. It follows that this speed was not a substantial factor in bringing about the accident.

We conclude that the plaintiff has failed to discharge the burden of proving that the negligence of the defendant was a cause in fact of the tragic death. The judgment in favor of plaintiff is **manifestly erroneous**.

For the reasons assigned, the judgment of the Court of Appeal is reversed, and the plaintiff's suit is dismissed at her cost.

———————————

Points for Discussion

1. In addressing the question whether the excessive speed of the train was the cause-in-fact of the collision, the court stated that "[n]egligence is a cause in fact of the harm to another if it was a substantial factor in bringing about that harm." How would you describe or define "substantial factor"?

2. The RESTATEMENT (SECOND) OF TORTS provides that an "actor's negligent conduct is a legal cause of harm to another if . . . his conduct is a substantial factor in bringing about that harm . . ." RESTATEMENT (SECOND) OF TORTS § 431 (1965). "The word 'substantial' is used to denote the fact that the defendant's conduct has such an effect in producing the harm as to lead reasonable men to regard it as a cause, using that word in the popular sense, in which there always lurks the idea of responsibility, rather than in the so-called 'philosophic sense,' which includes every one of the great number of events without which any happening would not have occurred." RESTATEMENT (SECOND) OF TORTS § 431 comment *a* (1965).

3. Addressing the issue of "factual cause," the RESTATEMENT (THIRD) OF TORTS provides: "Tortious conduct must be a factual cause of physical harm for liability to be imposed. Conduct is a factual cause of harm when the harm would not have occurred absent the conduct. . . ." RESTATEMENT (THIRD) OF TORTS: LIABILITY FOR PHYSICAL HARM § 26 (2010).

Riley v. Salley

874 So.2d 874 (La. App. 2004)

Judge DENNIS R. BAGNERIS SR.

Coleen Salley ("Salley") and her insurer, State Farm Mutual Automobile Insurance ("State Farm Mutual") seek to reverse the trial court's judgment rendered in favor of the plaintiff Octavia Riley ("Riley") for damages she sustained as a result of an automobile accident. We affirm.

. . . .

On October 1, 1999, Riley was involved in a two-vehicle accident at the intersection of Chartes Street and Esplanade Avenue in New Orleans, Louisiana. Riley was struck by another vehicle driven by Salley while she traveling southbound on Esplanade Avenue. Salley ran a stop sign and struck Riley's vehicle. Riley sustained injuries as a result on the accident.

Riley filed a lawsuit against Salley and her insurer, State Farm Mutual for damages for negligence. Prior to trial, all parties stipulated to liability on the part of Salley in causing the October 1, 1999 accident. The trial court rendered judgment in favor of Riley and against Salley and State Farm Mutual in the amount of $137,652.60. Salley and State Farm Mutual appeal.

. . . .

On appeal, Salley and State Farm Mutual contends the trial court erred in finding that Riley's neck injury and [t]he resulting surgery was caused by the October 1, 1999 automobile accident. Salley and State Farm Mutual argues that Riley failed to present any evidence to support the trial court's finding of liability on the part of Salley and State Farm Mutual for causing Riley's injuries. Further, that Riley failed to present evidence to sustain her burden of proof on the issue of medical causation thus the trial court's judgment should be reduced. We disagree.

Salley and State Farm Mutual contends that in order for Riley to prevail she had to establish a causal relationship between October 1, 1999, accident and the injury of her herniated disc at C4-5 she claimed she sustained as a result of the accident. We disagree. Further, they argue that Riley had to produce medical testimony at trial to meet her burden. Specifically, they argue she had to prove through medical testimony that it was more probable than not that the accident caused that injury or aggravated a previous injury to the extent that she required surgery. We find that the medical testimony during the trial proved it was more probable than not that the accident caused Mrs. Riley's injury or aggravated her previous injury to the extent that she needed surgery.

In Louisiana tort cases and other ordinary civil actions, the plaintiff, in general, has the burden of proving every essential element of his case, including the cause-in-fact of damage, by a preponderance of the evidence, not by some artificially created greater standard. [Cc] Proof by direct or circumstantial evidence is sufficient to constitute a preponderance, when, taking the evidence as a whole, such proof shows that the fact or causation sought to be proved is more probable than not. [Cc]

The defendant's liability for damages is not mitigated by the fact that the plaintiff's pre-existing physical infirmity was responsible in part for the consequences of the plaintiff's injury by the defendant. It is clear that a defendant takes his victim as he finds him and is responsible for all natural and probable consequences of his tortious conduct. [Cc] The defendant is liable for the harm it causes even though under the same circumstances a normal person would not have suffered that illness or injury. When the defendant's tortious conduct aggravates a **pre-existing condition**, the defendant must compensate the victim for the full extent of the aggravation. [Cc]

. . . .

In the instant case, our review of the record reveals that Riley met her burden of proving that he[r] physical injuries were caused by the accident. Riley had previously received physical therapy for a pre-existing condition. After the October 1, 1999 accident she experienced increased cervical pain, loss of sensation in her C-6 dermatome pattern and weakness in her right arm. Riley's treating physician conducted a myelogram, which indicated she had spinal cord compression on the right side of her cervical spine. Accordingly, we find that Riley is entitled to recover damages for her physical injuries and aggravation of her preexisting condition.

. . . .

Affirmed.

Points for Discussion

1. Do you agree with the court's analysis and decision?

2. What was the plaintiff required to prove in order to prevail, and what was her burden of proof?

3. The court notes that a defendant can be held liable when his or her conduct aggravates a plaintiff's pre-existing condition. Do you agree? If not, what rule would you prefer, and why?

4. *Riley v. Salley* involves application of a widely accepted principle in tort law commonly referred to as the eggshell skull plaintiff rule. The **eggshell skull plaintiff** rule provides that, in tort, a defendant takes his plaintiff as he finds her and is responsible for the full extent of the injuries caused by his negligence, even if unforeseeable or uncommon, and even if they are injuries that would not have been suffered by others.

---

2. Proof of Causation-In-Fact

Reynolds v. Texas & Pacific Ry. Co.

37 La.Ann. 694 (La. App. 1885)

The opinion of the Court was delivered by Fenner, J.

The plaintiff and his wife claim damages of the defendant company for injuries suffered [b]y the wife and caused by the alleged negligence of the company.

Mr. Reynolds, with his wife, sister-in-law, three small children and two colored attendants, had purchased tickets as passengers on the defendant [rail]road, and were at the depot at Morrogh Station for the purpose of boarding the eastbound train, which was due at that station at about midnight, but, being behind time, did not reach there till about two o'clock in the morning.

Between the depot and the regular track on which the passenger train arrived there was a switch-track, which, on the night in question, was occupied by a freight train, and, by uncoupling the latter, a passage way was opened to the passenger cars.

The mode of getting from the depot to the cars was as follows: passengers went down a stairway of several steps, which ran parallel to the track and led to a lower platform; on reaching which they turned squarely to the right and passed between the uncoupled cars to the train. These steps were unprotected by railing, and on the left of them there was a ditch. The platform at the bottom extended five feet towards the front, and beyond it there was a slope running to the bottom of a ditch. If, in descending, the passenger went too far to the left, he tumbled into a ditch; if he did not turn promptly to the right on reaching the bottom and went too far forward, he fell down the slope in front; and if he stumbled in going down the stairs his impetus was likely to carry him over the narrow platform in front and down the slope beyond.

It is obvious that, while such a passage might fulfill all customary and reasonable requirements of safety in the daytime, or when well lighted, yet at night, and when not sufficiently lighted up, it undoubtedly exposed passengers unfamiliar with it to danger of fall and injury. Although both the east and west-bound trains customarily stopped at this station in the night-time, no stationary lights were provided for the depot platform or the steps. There was no moon on this night. The lights of the engine and passenger coaches were intercepted by the intervening freight cars, except such as might have passed through the opening above referred to, which we are satisfied was of no value. The lights in the rooms of the station could have shed no light on the bottom of the steps. There is much conflict of testimony touching the presence and position of a conductor and brakeman with lanterns, which we need not discuss. After an attentive study of the evidence, we clearly concur in the conclusion of the district judge that there was no sufficient light; that its absence rendered this passage from the depot to the train insecure, and constituted negligence in the company and a failure to perform its duty of providing safe modes of **ingress** and **egress** between its depots and its trains. We are impressed by the judicious comments of the judge on the conflicts in the evidence, **viz**: "There are here, as there will always be, contradictions and discrepancies amongst witnesses in all such cases, so long as stationary lights are not provided, and so long as this mode of providing lights for passengers boarding or leaving the cars is adhered to. What is sufficient for purposes of ingress and egress from cars, until stationary fixed lights are provided, will ever be a matter dependent on the discretion of conductors, brakemen and other employees, liable to be varied by every change made in these employees. * * * Even granting there were lanterns or lamps held by employees, a change of position of a few feet, even a step or two, would suffice to leave positions in darkness one minute which were in light the next, and *vice versa*."

> **It's Latin to Me!**
>
> *"Viz."* is an abbreviation for the Latin term *Videlicet* which means "namely" or "that is to say."

The train was behind time. Several witnesses testify that passengers were warned to "hurry up." Mrs. Reynolds, a corpulent woman, weighing two hundred and fifty pounds, emerging from the bright light of the sitting-room, which naturally exaggerated the outside darkness, and hastening down these unlighted steps, made a misstep in some way and was precipitated beyond the narrow platform in front and down the slope beyond, incurring the serious injuries complained of. [The trial court entered judgment for the plaintiffs and awarded $2,000 in damages, and the defendant appealed.]

. . . .

[The defendant] contends that, even conceding the negligence of the company in the above respect, it does not follow that the accident to plaintiff was necessarily caused thereby, but that she might well have made the misstep and fallen even had it been broad daylight. We concede that this is possible, and recognize the distinction between *post hoc* and *propter hoc*. But where the negligence of the defendant greatly multiplies the chances of accident to the plaintiff, and is of a character naturally leading to its occurrence, the mere possibility that it might have happened without the negligence is not

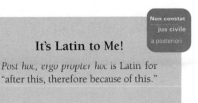

> **It's Latin to Me!**
>
> *Post hoc, ergo propter hoc* is Latin for "after this, therefore because of this."

sufficient to break the chain of cause and effect between the negligence and the injury. Courts, in such matters, consider the natural and ordinary course of events, and do not indulge in fanciful suppositions. The whole tendency of the evidence connects the accident with the negligence.

Judgment affirmed.

———————————

Points for Discussion

1. What point did the court make in distinguishing between *post hoc* and *propter hoc*?

2. What constitutes "the natural and ordinary course of events" for purposes of making the cause-in-fact determination? Who should make that determination and on what basis or bases?

3. Is it legally relevant that Mrs. Reynolds was a "corpulent woman"?

———————————

Hypo 5-1

A deck hand employed on a barge fell into the water as the barge approached the pier. Two other deck hands on the barge, hearing the cries of their coworker (who could not swim), threw two heaving lines (used to tie the barge to the pier) in the direction of the cries for help. Both lines came within two feet of the spot of the deck hand in the water; when he did not grab the lines the deck hands on the barge pulled in and again threw out the lines. The screaming deck hand did not grab either of the lines and his body was carried away from the pier by the outgoing tide. He drowned and his body was recovered the next day. At the time of this incident, several life preservers were on a rack located near the front of the barge. The preservers remained in the rack and were not used.

Sued by the deceased deck hand's family for negligence, the barge's owner argues that the failure to use the life preservers was not the cause-in-fact (or "but-for") cause of the drowning of the deceased. Is the owner correct? What counterargument(s) would you make?

Hypo 5-2

Don is visiting New Orleans on an overnight business trip. The evening that Don arrives, he visits Bar located in the famous French Quarter, two blocks south of Hotel. The Bar is on Bourbon Street in an area of New Orleans well known for its party-like atmosphere. Don and his friends have a grand time, and as many visitors to New Orleans do, they consume a large quantity of alcohol that evening. At about 2:00 a.m., they decide it is time to return to their respective hotels. Don is the only one from his group staying at Hotel, so he begins the short walk to Hotel. However, Don is so inebriated that instead of walking two blocks north in the direction of Hotel, he heads south. Don ends up wandering onto a two-foot wide walkway bordering the Mississippi River. The walkway is located three blocks from the French Quarter, is not lit, and has no railing or barrier bordering the river. Don missteps, falling into the Mississippi River and drowns. What is the cause-in-fact of Don's death?

Kramer Service, Inc. v. Wilkins

184 Miss. 483, 186 So. 625 (1939)

GRIFFITH, Justice.

Appellant was and is the owner and operator of a large hotel. About 5:30 o'clock P. M. on January 15, 1935, one Clockey registered as a guest and was given a room, to which he was conducted by a bellboy. Mr. Clockey was the district sales representative of an oil company, and appellee was the local representative. The business which brought Clockey to the hotel was to have a conference with appellee. It was the long established custom of the hotel that a guest should have the privilege of inviting to his room any person whom the guest wished to see on business. It was the purpose of Clockey to telephone appellee of his arrival, and expected that a telephone would be in his room.

Soon after entering the room, Clockey discovered that there was no telephone therein, and that the windows could not be raised nor the transom lowered so as to give ventilation. The reason that the guest could not undertake to lower the transom was that there was a break in the glass thereof, the break being described by this witness as cone-shaped and about twenty inches in length at the base, the broken portion clinging nevertheless in the transom.

Clockey was obliged to go to the hotel office in order to telephone appellee, his business associate, which he did in about twenty minutes after he had registered.

While on this mission Clockey informed the hotel clerk of the objectionable condition of the room, including a reference to the condition of the transom. The clerk explained that there was a convention in session at the hotel, and that the room assigned was the only one left, but that a better room could be given on the next day.

About two hours later appellee came to Clockey's room in response to the telephone message, and when the business conference was concluded appellee was in the act of leaving the room. When he opened the door, which was done in an ordinary manner, without any violence, the broken piece of the transom fell striking appellee upon the head. Three wounds were thus made upon appellee's head, one of which was a jagged abrasion on the temple.

The foregoing statement of the facts is supported by competent evidence which in the light of the verdict of the jury must be accepted as true. There is further competent evidence to the effect that the condition of unrepair which resulted in the fall of the broken transom glass had existed for a sufficient length of time to charge appellant with responsible notice thereof, and that the condition was such that a reasonably prudent and careful operator should have foreseen the fall of the broken glass and an injury thereby as a likelihood of appreciable weight and moment. [C]

. . . The wound on the temple did not heal, and some months after the injury appellee was advised by his local physician to visit a specialist in skin diseases, which he did in January, 1937, about two years after the injury, and it was then found that at the point where the injury occurred to appellee's temple, a skin cancer had developed, of which a cure had not been fully effected at the time of the trial, some three years after the injury first mentioned.

Appellee sued for a large sum in damages, averring and contending that the cancer resulted from the stated injury; and the jury evidently accepted that contention, since there was an award by the verdict in the sum of twenty thousand dollars. Appellant requested an instruction to the effect that the cancer or any prolongation of the trouble on account thereof should not be taken into consideration by the jury, but this instruction was refused.

Two physicians or medical experts, and only two, were introduced as witnesses, and both were specialists in skin diseases and dermal traumatisms. One testified that it was possible that a trauma such as appellee suffered upon his temple, could or would cause a skin cancer at the point of injury, but that the chances that such a result would ensue from such a cause would be only one out of one hundred cases. The other testified that there is no causal connection whatever between trauma and cancer, and went on to illustrate that if there were such a connection nearly every person of mature age would be suffering with cancer. Further reference to the medical testimony will be made later herein.

. . . .

There is one heresy in the judicial forum which appears to be Hydra-headed, and although cut off again and again, has the characteristic of an endless renewal. That heresy is that proof that a past event possibly happened, or that a certain result was possibly caused by a past event, is sufficient in probative force to take the question to a jury. Such was never the law in this state, and we are in accord with almost all of the other common-law states. Nearly a half century ago, when our Court stood forth in point of ability never excelled, and when the principles of the jurisprudence of this state were being put into a more definite form than ever before, Chief Justice Campbell said in Railroad v. Cathey, 70 Miss. 332, 337, 12 So. 253: "It is not enough that negligence of the employer and injury to the employe coexisted, but the injury must have been caused by the negligence. *** 'Post hoc ergo propter hoc' is not sound as evidence or argument. Nor is it sufficient for a plaintiff seeking recovery for alleged negligence by an employer towards an employe to show a possibility that the injury complained of was caused by negligence. Possibilities will not sustain a verdict. It must have a better foundation."

. . . .

Taking the medical testimony in this case in the strongest light in which it could be reasonably interpreted in behalf of the plaintiff, this testimony is that as a **possibility** a skin cancer could be caused by an injury such as here happened, but as a probability the physicians were in agreement that there was or is no such a probability.

Take Note

The court notes the difference between a possibility and a probability. A *possibility* is an event that may or may not happen ("anything's possible"), while a *probability* is an event or effect that more likely than not will follow a supposed cause.

And the medical testimony is conclusive on both judge and jury in this case. That testimony is undisputed that after long and anxious years of research the exact cause of cancer remains unknown-- there is no dependably known origin to which it can be definitely traced or ascribed. If, then, the cause be unknown to all those who have devoted their lives to a study of the subject, it is wholly beyond the range of the common experience and observation of judges and jurors, and in such a case medical testimony when undisputed, as here, must be accepted and acted upon in the same manner as is other undisputed evidence; otherwise the jury would be allowed to resort to and act upon nothing else than the proposition post hoc ergo propter hoc, which, as already mentioned, this Court has long ago rejected as unsound, whether as evidence or as argument.

In all other than the exceptional cases . . . the testimony of medical experts, or other experts, is advisory only; but we repeat that where the issue is one which lies wholly beyond the range of the experience or observation of laymen and of which they can have no appreciable knowledge, courts and juries must of necessity depend upon and accept the undisputed testimony of reputable specialists, else there would be no substantial foundation upon which to rest a conclusion. [Cc]

Affirmed as to liability; reversed and remanded on the issue of the amount of the damages.

——————————

Points for Discussion

1. The court noted that one of the physicians testified that "it was possible that a trauma such as appellee suffered upon his temple, could or would cause a skin cancer at the point of injury, but that the chances that such a result would ensue from such a cause would be only one out of one hundred cases." What can and should be made of the fact that, as the cancer did not occur at any other spot on the plaintiff's body, the cancer developed at the exact spot of the cut caused by the falling glass from the transom? Can a persuasive argument be made that the chances were greater than one in a hundred?

2. The court concluded that the medical testimony proffered in the case was conclusive on both judge and jury and that the exact cause of cancer was unknown to those who had devoted their lives to studying that subject. If this is the correct legal analysis of the causation issue, could a plaintiff ever recover in a case similar to the plaintiff in *Kramer Service*?

——————————

Herskovits v. Group Health Cooperative of Puget Sound

99 Wash.2d 609, 664 P.2d 474 (1983)

DORE, Justice.

This appeal raises the issue of whether an estate can maintain an action for professional negligence as a result of failure to timely diagnose lung cancer, where the estate can show probable reduction in statistical chance for survival but cannot show and/or prove that with timely diagnosis and treatment, decedent probably would have lived to normal life expectancy.

Both counsel advised that for the purpose of this appeal we are to *assume* that the **respondent** Group Health Cooperative of Puget Sound and Dr. William Spencer negligently failed to diagnose Herskovits' cancer on his first visit to the hospital and *proximately* caused at 14 percent reduction in his chances of survival. It is undisputed that Herskovits had less than a 50 percent chance of survival at all times herein.

The main issue we will address in this opinion is whether a patient, with less than a 50 percent chance of survival, has a cause of action against the hospital and its employees if they are negligent in diagnosing a lung cancer which reduces his chances of survival by 14 percent.

. . . .

The ultimate question raised here is whether the relationship between the increased risk of harm and Herskovits' death is sufficient to hold Group Health responsible. Is a 36 percent (from 39 percent to 25 percent) reduction in the decedent's chance for survival sufficient evidence of causation to allow the jury to consider the possibility that the physician's failure to timely diagnose the illness was the proximate cause of his death? We answer in the affirmative. To decide otherwise would be a blanket release from liability for doctors and hospitals any time there was less than a 50 percent chance of survival, regardless of how flagrant the negligence.

. . . .

We are persuaded by the reasoning of the Pennsylvania Supreme Court in *Hamil v. Bashline,* [481 Pa. 256, 392 A.2d 1280 (1978)]. While *Hamil* involved an original survival chance of greater than 50 percent, we find the rationale used by the *Hamil* court to apply equally to cases such as the present one, where the original survival chance is less than 50 percent. The plaintiff's decedent was suffering from severe chest pains. His wife transported him to the hospital where he was negligently treated in the emergency unit. The wife, because of the lack of help, took her husband to a private physician's office, where he died. In an action brought under the **wrongful death** and **survivorship** statutes, the main medical witness testified that if the hospital had employed proper treatment, the decedent would have had a substantial chance of surviving the attack. The medical expert expressed his opinion in terms of a 75 percent chance of survival. It was also the doctor's opinion that the substantial loss of a chance of recovery was the result of the defendant hospital's failure to provide prompt treatment. The defendant's expert witness testified that the patient would have died regardless of any treatment provided by the defendant hospital.

. . . .

The *Hamil* court distinguished the facts of that case from the general tort case in which a plaintiff alleges that a defendant's act or **omission** set in motion a force which resulted in harm. In the typical tort case, the "but for" test, requiring proof that damages or death probably would not have occurred "but for" the negligent conduct of the defendant, is appropriate. In *Hamil* and the instant case, however, the defendant's act or omission failed in a *duty* to protect against harm from *another source*. Thus, as the *Hamil* court noted, the fact finder is put in the position of having to consider not only what *did* occur, but also what *might have* occurred. . . . [C] The *Hamil* court held that once a plaintiff has demonstrated that the defendant's acts or omissions have increased the risk of harm to another, such evidence furnishes a basis for the jury to make a determination as to whether such increased risk was in turn a substantial factor in bringing about the resultant harm.

. . . .

Where percentage probabilities and decreased probabilities are submitted into evidence, there is simply no danger of speculation on the part of the jury. More speculation is involved in requiring the medical expert to testify as to what would have happened had the defendant not been negligent. [C]

. . . .

Both counsel have agreed for the purpose of arguing this summary judgment, that the defendants were negligent in failing to make a diagnosis of cancer on Herskovits' initial visit in December 1974, and that such negligence was the proximate cause of reducing his chances of survival by 14 percent. It is undisputed that Herskovits had less than a 50 percent chance of survival at that time. Based on this agreement and Dr. Ostrow's deposition and affidavit, a prima facie case is shown. We reject Group Health's argument that plaintiffs *must show* that Herskovits "probably" would have had a 51 percent chance of survival if the hospital had not been negligent. We hold that medical testimony of a reduction of chance of survival from 39 percent to 25 percent is sufficient evidence to allow the proximate cause issue to go to the jury.

Causing reduction of the opportunity to recover (loss of chance) by one's negligence, however, does not necessitate a total recovery against the negligent party for all damages caused by the victim's death. Damages should be awarded to the injured party or his family based only on damages caused directly by premature death, such as lost earnings and additional medical expenses, etc.

We reverse the trial court and reinstate the cause of action.

. . . .

DOLLIVER, Justice (dissenting).

This is apparently a case of **first impression**. As is usually true in such instances, the court is called upon to make a policy decision. The issue before us is whether, when the chance of survival is less than a probability, *i.e.,* less than 50 percent, proof that the chance of survival--not the probability of survival--is reduced is sufficient to take the case to the jury.

The majority answer in the affirmative cites several cases in support of this view and adopts the reasoning of *Hamil v. Bashline,* 481 Pa. 256, 392 A.2d 1280 (1978). . . .

The majority states the variations from 39 percent to 25 percent in the decedent's chance for survival are sufficient evidence to "consider the possibility" that the failure of the physician to diagnose the illness in a timely manner was the "proximate cause of his death." This reasoning is flawed. Whether the chances were 25 percent or 39 percent decedent would have survived for 5 years, in both cases, it was more probable than not he would have died. . . . "'It is legally and logically impossible for it to be probable that a fact exists, and at the same time probable that it does not exist.'" [C] It would be pure speculation, given these figures, for an expert, a jury, or anyone else to conclude the decedent would live more or less time within the 5-year period with or without the proper diagnosis.

. . . .

[The *Herskovitz* court ruled in favor of the plaintiff by a vote of 6-3. Justice Dore's opinion was joined by Justice Rosellini. A concurring opinion by Justice Pearson (not included in your readings), joined by Justices Williams, Utter, and Stafford, agreed with the reversal of the trial court and the reinstatement of the action but found a 14% reduction in the plaintiff's chance of survival as the relevant measure and not the 36% reduction set out in Justice Dore's lead opinion. The concurring justices also argued that the lost chance of survival analysis should have focused on, and the calculations of damages should have been based on, the plaintiff's injury and not his death. Justice Dolliver's dissent is excerpted above, and Justice Brachtenbach, joined by Justice Dimmick, filed a separate dissent. It has been noted that most courts and scholars have agreed that 14% was the correct figure for purposes of determining the chance-of-survival reduction. *See* Lars Noah, *An Inventory of Mathematical Blunders in Applying the Loss-of-a-Chance Doctrine,* 24 Rev. Litig. 369 (2005).]

Smith v. Parrott

833 A.2d 843 (Vt. 2003)

¶ 1. ALLEN, C.J. (Ret.), Specially Assigned.

Stephen L. Smith, plaintiff in this medical malpractice action, appeals from a summary judgment of the Windsor Superior Court in favor of defendant Thomas Parrott, M.D. Plaintiff contends the trial court erred in . . . rejecting plaintiff's theory of recovery based on a showing that Dr. Parrott's negligence had reduced plaintiff's chances of recovery, even if it was not the probable cause of his injuries. We affirm.

¶ 2. The undisputed material facts may be briefly summarized. On July 31, 1995, plaintiff awoke to find that he had no motor control over the use of his left foot. That afternoon he went to see Dr. Parrott, a family practitioner in White River Junction. Dr. Parrott noted that plaintiff had had two prior back surgeries, and described plaintiff's condition as a "[d]ramatic foot drop on the left side." Foot-drop is a neurological condition in which the motor functions of the foot and lower leg are diminished or terminated. Dr. Parrott referred plaintiff to a neurosurgeon.

¶ 3. Eleven days later, plaintiff was examined by Dr. Joseph Phillips, a neurosurgeon at Dartmouth-Hitchcock Medical Center. Dr. Phillips concluded that plaintiff's condition was complete or permanent, and that there was no possibility of any functional recovery. Plaintiff underwent surgery in early September to alleviate pain. His motor functions did not improve.

¶ 4. Plaintiff filed a **medical malpractice** action against Dr. Parrott, alleging that his failure to advise plaintiff of the need for an immediate neurological examination, and his failure to arrange such an examination, had resulted in the deterioration of plaintiff's condition to the point of permanence by the time he saw Dr. Phillips. Following extensive **discovery**, Dr. Parrott moved for summary judgment . . . The motion cited Dr. Phillips' **deposition** testimony that plaintiff's foot-drop was complete two to three weeks before his neurological examination on August 11, and therefore that the delay in surgery had no impact on plaintiff's chances of recovery. Dr. Parrott also relied on the deposition testimony of plaintiff's expert witness, Dr. Donald Myers, who had initially opined that an earlier consultation with a neurosurgeon could have yielded a "50-50 chance" of "some recovery," but later amended his opinion to state that, in light of plaintiff's history of back surgery, the chance of some recovery was "a little bit" less than fifty percent.

. . . .

¶ 8. The **loss of chance doctrine** has received substantial support among academic commentators and has been accepted--in one form or another--in a growing number of jurisdictions, particularly in medical malpractice cases. See generally *Crosby v. United States,* 48 F.Supp.2d 924, 926-28 (D.Alaska 1999) (providing comprehensive review of cases accepting and rejecting loss of chance doctrine); D. Fischer, *Tort Recovery For Loss of a Chance,* 36 WAKE FOREST L. REV. 605, 607 (2001) (comparing applications in Great Britain and the United States); . . . Note, *Loss of a Chance as a Cause of Action in Medical Malpractice Cases,* 59 Mo. L. REV. 969, 973 n. 29 (1994) (listing cases allowing recovery for loss of chance); see also Annotation, *Medical Malpractice: Measure and Elements of Damages in Actions Based on Loss of Chance,* 81 A.L.R.4th 485 (1990); Annotation, *Medical Malpractice: "Loss of Chance" Causality,* 54 A.L.R.4th 10 (1987). Supporters cite a number of policy arguments in favor of the doctrine, most notably the harshness of the traditional rule in denying recovery even in cases where a doctor's negligence may have significantly reduced the plaintiff's chances of recovery; the inherent worth of a chance of recovery, no matter how small, as a compensable interest; and the deterrent value in penalizing a poor prognosis, even if it reduced the plaintiff's chances of recovery by less than fifty percent. See, e.g., *Crosby,* 48 F.Supp.2d at 928;*Wendland v. Sparks,* 574 N.W.2d 327, 330 (Iowa 1998); *Delaney v. Cade,* 255 Kan. 199, 873 P.2d 175, 180-83 (1994); *Lord v. Lovett,* 146 N.H. 232, 770 A.2d 1103, 1106 (2001); *Jorgenson v. Vener,* 2000 SD 87, 616 N.W.2d 366, 369; Note, *supra,* 59 Mo. L. REV. at 984-85.

¶ 9. These cases and commentators notwithstanding, the traditional causation standard in medical malpractice--as in tort law generally--"still commands substantial support." [C] Indeed, a significant number of jurisdictions have expressly rejected invitations to adopt the loss of chance doctrine to allow recovery where--as here-the defendant's negligence was not shown to have been the likely cause of injury. See, e.g., *Crosby,* 48 F.Supp.2d at 930-32 (applying Alaska law); *Williams v. Spring Hill Mem'l Hosp.,* 646 So.2d 1373, 1374-75 (Ala.1994); *Grant v. Am. Nat'l Red Cross,* 745 A.2d 316, 322-23 (D.C.Ct.App.2000); *Gooding v. Univ. Hosp. Bldg., Inc.,* 445 So.2d 1015, 1020-21 (Fla.1984); *Manning v. Twin Falls Clinic & Hosp., Inc.,* 122 Idaho 47, 830 P.2d 1185, 1189-90 (1992); *Fennell v. S. Md. Hosp. Ctr., Inc.,* 320 Md. 776, 580 A.2d 206, 211 (1990); *Fabio v. Bellomo,* 504 N.W.2d 758, 762-63 (Minn.1993); *Jones v. Owings,* 318 S.C. 72, 456 S.E.2d 371, 374 (1995); *Kilpatrick v. Bryant,* 868 S.W.2d 594, 602 (Tenn. 1993); *Kramer v. Lewisville Mem'l Hosp.,* 858 S.W.2d 397, 407 (Tex.1993). Opposition to the loss of chance doctrine is generally based on several policy arguments, including the anomaly and unfairness of applying a lower causation standard to health care providers than other professionals; the risk of increasing the number of successful claims and thereby elevating the price of malpractice insurance and

Food for Thought

As can be seen, policy concerns can be part of the analytical and adjudicative calculus.

health care costs in general, as doctors are forced to practice "defensive" medicine; and the illusion of deterrence where it cannot be shown that the defendant in fact caused the injury. [Cc]

. . . .

¶ 11. The requirements for establishing medical malpractice in Vermont are set forth in 12 V.S.A. § 1908, which provides that the plaintiff shall have the burden of proving: (1) "[t]he degree of knowledge or skill possessed or the degree of care ordinarily exercised by" a prudent health care professional in a similar practice under similar circumstances; (2) that the defendant "lacked this degree of knowledge or skill or failed to exercise this degree of care"; and (3) "[t]hat as a proximate result of this lack of knowledge or skill or the failure to exercise this degree of care the plaintiff suffered injuries that would not otherwise have been incurred." We have observed that, apart from substituting a national for a community standard of care, the statute essentially codifies "[t]he common law elements of a medical malpractice action." [C] Those elements have traditionally included a requirement that the plaintiff adduce evidence of a "reasonable probability or reasonable degree of medical certainty" that the defendant's conduct caused the injury. [Cc]

¶ 12. The loss of chance theory of recovery is thus fundamentally at odds with the settled common law standard, codified in 12 V.S.A. § 1908(3), for establishing a causal link between the plaintiff's injury and the defendant's tortious conduct. Where--as in Vermont--the plaintiff must prove that as a result of the defendant's conduct the injuries "would not otherwise have been incurred," 12 V.S.A. § 1908(3), an act or omission of the defendant *cannot* be considered a cause of the plaintiff's injury if the injury would probably have occurred without it. This was precisely the state of the record evidence here. Accordingly, the summary judgment in favor of defendant was sound under the law.

¶ 13. . . . Although some of the arguments in favor of the loss of chance doctrine are appealing, we are mindful that it represents a significant departure from the traditional meaning of causation in tort law. Implicated in such a departure are fundamental questions about its potential impact on not only the cost, but the very practice of medicine in Vermont; about its effect on causation standards applicable to other professions and the principles--if any--which might justify its application to medicine but not other fields such as law, architecture, or accounting; and ultimately about the overall societal costs which may result from awarding damages to an entirely new class of plaintiffs who formerly had no claim under the common law in this state. [Cc]

¶ 14. In short, we are persuaded that the decision to expand the definition of causation and thus the potential liability of the medical profession in Vermont "involves significant and far-reaching policy concerns" more properly left to the

Legislature, where hearings may be held, data collected, and competing interests heard before a wise decision is reached. [Cc] Accordingly, we hold that the trial court correctly rejected plaintiff's claim for recovery under the loss of chance doctrine, and properly entered judgment for defendant.

Affirmed.

Points for Discussion

1. What is the "traditional causation standard" to which the *Smith v. Parrott* court refers? How is the traditional causation standard altered by application of the loss of chance doctrine?

2. What questions were asked and answered in *Herskovitz* and in *Parrott*? Do you agree with Justice Dore's opinion in the former case or with the majority opinion in the latter decision?

3. In *Herskovitz*, Justice Dore stated that the case before the court was not the typical tort case in which the "but for" test was appropriate, and that in *Herskovitz* the finder of fact had to consider what did occur and what might have occurred. Does placing on the jury the function of finding of "what might have occurred" run the risk of jury speculation with respect to the cause-in-fact or substantial factor question?

4. *Parrott* concluded that the "loss of chance theory is . . . fundamentally at odds with the settled common law standard . . . for establishing a causal link between the plaintiff's injury and the defendant's tortious conduct." What rationales and reasoning supported the court's conclusion? Do you agree with the court that the issue of the adoption of the theory should be left to state legislature?

5. Does the loss of chance doctrine require application of a different causation-in-fact standard, or might the problems with which courts such as *Herskovitz* and *Parrott* were presented be more easily resolved by recharacterizing the harm for which the plaintiff seeks recovery, as suggested by the concurring justices in *Herskovitz*? *See also* Columbia Rio Grande Healthcare, LP v. Hawley, 284 S.W.3d 851 (Tex. 2009) (rejecting loss of chance in medical malpractice claims).

6. **Expert Testimony Regarding Causation-in-Fact in the Federal Courts**—In *Daubert v. Merrell Dow Pharmaceuticals, Inc.*, 509 U.S. 579, 113 S.Ct. 2786

(1993), the United States Supreme Court held that the Federal Rules of Evidence, and not the "general acceptance" test formulated in *Frye v. United States*, 293 F. 1013 (1923), provide the standard for the admission of expert scientific testimony in a federal trial. Federal Rule of Evidence 702 provides that where "scientific, technical, or other specialized knowledge will assist the trier of fact to understand the evidence or to determine a fact in issue [*i.e.*, causation], a witness qualified as an expert by knowledge, skill, experience, training, or education, may testify thereto in the form of an opinion or otherwise." The Court instructed that "the Rules of Evidence—especially Rule 702—do assign to the trial judge the task of ensuring that an expert's testimony both rests on a reliable foundation and is relevant to the task at hand. Pertinent evidence based on scientifically valid principles will satisfy those demands." A more recent decision, *Kuhmo Tire Company, Ltd. v. Carmichael*, 526 U.S. 137, 119 S.Ct. 1167 (1999), makes clear that the *Daubert* "gatekeeping" requirement applies not only to "scientific" testimony but to all expert testimony.

> ### Make the Connection
>
> A negligence action requires proof of *harm*. Contrast this proof with the study of intentional torts, in which a prima facie case requires proof of *injury*. *See* Chapter 2, *supra*, distinguishing harm from injury.

3. Problems in Proving Causation-In-Fact

> ### RESTATEMENT (SECOND) OF TORTS § 432 (1965)
> #### Negligent Conduct as Necessary Antecedent of Harm
>
> (1) Except as stated in Subsection 2, the actor's negligent conduct is not a substantial factor in bringing about harm to another if the harm would have been sustained even if the actor had not been negligent.
>
> (2) If two forces are actively operating, one because of the actor's negligence, the other not because of any misconduct on his part, and each of itself is sufficient to bring about the harm to another, the actor's negligence may be found to be a substantial factor in bringing it about.

> **RESTATEMENT (THIRD) OF TORTS:**
> **LIABILITY FOR PHYSICAL HARM § 27 (2010)**
> **Multiple Sufficient Causes**
>
> If multiple acts exist, each of which alone would have been a factual cause . . . of the physical harm at the same time, each act is regarded as a factual cause of the harm.

Anderson v. Minneapolis, St. P. & S. St. M. R. Ry. Co.

146 Minn. 430, 179 N.W. 45 (1920)

LEES, C.

This is a fire case, brought against the defendant railway company and the Director General of Railroads. For convenience, we shall refer to the railway company, throughout this opinion, as the defendant. Plaintiff had a verdict. The appeal is from an order denying a motion in the alternative for judgment notwithstanding the verdict or for a new trial.

The complaint alleged that early in August, 1918, sparks from one of defendant's locomotive engines set a fire on or near the right of way, and that this fire spread until it finally reached plaintiff's land, where it destroyed some of his property. The answer was a general denial, followed by an allegation that, if plaintiff was damaged by fire, the fire was not due to any act of defendant, was of unknown origin, and, by reason of extraordinary weather conditions, became a huge conflagration. The reply put these allegations in issue.

Plaintiff's **case in chief** was directed to proving that in August, 1918, one of defendant's engines started a fire in a bog near the west side of plaintiff's land; that it smoldered there until October 12, 1918, when it flared up and burned his property, shortly before it was reached by one of the great fires which swept through Northeastern Minnesota at the close of that day. Defendant introduced evidence to show that on and prior to October 12th fires were burning west and northwest of, and were swept by the wind towards, plaintiff's premises. It did not show how such fires originated, neither did it clearly and certainly trace the destruction of plaintiff's property to them. By cross-examination of defendant's witnesses and by his rebuttal evidence plaintiff made a showing which would have justified the jury in finding that the fires proved by defendant were started by its locomotive on or near its right of way in the vicinity of Kettle River.

. . . .

Numerous special instructions were requested. . . . In instructing the jury, the court said in part:

> 'If the plaintiff was burned out by some fire other than the bog fire, which other fire was not set by one of defendant's engines, then, of course, defendant is not liable. If plaintiff was burned out by fire set by one of defendant's engines in combination with some other fire not set by one of its engines, then it is liable. * * *

> 'If you find that other fires not set by one of defendant's engines mingled with one that was set by one of defendant's engines, there may be difficulty in determining whether you should find that the fire set by the engine was a material or substantial element in causing plaintiff's damage. If it was, the defendant is liable; otherwise, it is not. * * *

> 'If you find that bog fire was set by defendant's engine, and that some greater fire swept over it before it reached plaintiff's land, then it will be for you to determine whether the bog fire * * * was a material or substantial factor in causing plaintiff's damage. If it was, defendant was liable. If it was not, defendant was not liable. . . .'

. . . .

The following proposition is stated in defendant's brief and relied on for a reversal:

> 'If plaintiff's property was damaged by a number of fires combining, one being the fire pleaded, and the others being of no responsible origin, but of such sufficient or superior force that they would have produced the damage to plaintiff's property, regardless of the fire pleaded, then defendant was not liable.'

This proposition is based upon Cook v. M., St. P. & S. S. M. Ry. Co., 98 Wis. 624, 74 N. W. 561, 40 L. R. A. 457, 67 Am. St. Rep. 830. . . . If the Cook Case merely decides that one who negligently sets a fire is not liable if another's property is damaged, unless it is made to appear that the fire was a material element in the destruction of the property, there can be no question about the soundness of the decision. But if it decides that if such fire combines with another of no responsible origin, and after the union of the two fires they destroy the property and either fire independently of the other would have destroyed it, then, irrespective of whether the first fire was or was not a material factor in the destruction of the property, there is no liability, we are not prepared to adopt the doctrine as the law of this state. If a fire set by the engine of one railroad company unites with a fire set by the engine of another company, there is **joint and several liability**, even though either fire would have destroyed plaintiff's property. But if the doctrine of the Cook Case is applied, and one of the fires is of unknown origin, there is no liability. . . . We therefore hold that the trial court did not err in refusing to instruct the jury in accordance with the rule laid down in the Cook Case. . . .

. . . .

We find no error requiring a reversal, and hence the order appealed from is affirmed.

Trevino v. Hirsch

492 P.2d 899 (Colo. App. 1971)

ENOCH, Judge.

This is a personal injury case in which plaintiff Margo Ann Trevino, a minor, by her parents, Cruz and Yolanda Trevino, sued John C. Hirsch for damages resulting from third degree burns caused by a gasoline fire. Trial was to a jury. At the close of plaintiff's case, the trial court granted defendant's motion for a **directed verdict**. The issue on appeal is whether the evidence presented by the plaintiff was sufficient to establish a prima facie case of negligence against the defendant. We affirm the judgment of the trial court.

Plaintiff's evidence established that on August 1, 1967, Yolanda Trevino and her two children, Margo (2) and Tony (5), were visiting Mrs. Trevino's parents, Cosme and Ramona Torrez, on a farm the Torrezes operated for defendant Hirsch. A number of children lived on the farm. The Torrezes had three small children and another daughter of Yolanda Trevino living with them, and defendant's lessor had two, including a thirteen year-old son, David. Following the Trevino's arrival that day, the children, with the permission of Mrs. Torrez and Mrs. Trevino, decided to resume their morning activity of roasting marshmallows. After experiencing some difficulty in starting the fire David went over to a gasoline storage tank and drained a small quantity of gasoline out of its hose into a tin can. David warned the other children to stand back as he poured the gasoline on the damp wood which he had experienced difficulty in igniting. The gasoline in the can was ignited by a spark from the wood and David dropped the can into a nearby bucket of water. Margo was splashed with the burning gasoline and suffered extensive burns as a result.

The gasoline tank from which David obtained the gasoline was used as a fuel supply for the farm and was located in the farm yard adjacent to one of the utility buildings. The gasoline was drawn from the tank by means of a hose which, when not in use, was hung on the tank in a receptacle constructed so that it could be padlocked. A padlock was not used, but the switch to the pumping mechanism was located in a locked building. After the pump was shut off and the hose returned to its receptacle, a small quantity of gasoline remained in the bottom loop of the hose. It was this residue which David obtained to start the fire.

. . . .

Both parties rely on the case of Burley v. McDowell, 133 Colo. 566, 298 P.2d 399, as authority for their respective positions. In that case the plaintiff, a nine-year-old, who was found to be a trespasser, obtained some gasoline from an unlocked storage room on the premises of the defendant. The child had been instructed to stay out of the storage room. In that case the court held that under the facts as presented, the land owner was not negligent in keeping gasoline on his premises for a lawful and reasonable purpose. The court there recognized, however, that under a different set of facts, there could be liability. The holding of that case tends to support the defendant in the case at hand and the plaintiff interprets the **dictum** therein to be supportive of her position. We do not find the *Burley* case to be that decisive of the issues at hand.

. . . .

Assuming arguendo, that defendant was shown to have been negligent in not providing a lock for the hose or in failing to instruct the tenant to drain the hose after use, liability does not follow unless it is also shown that such negligence was a substantial factor in producing the injuries. Where, as here, several events may have brought about the harm to plaintiff, and an event other than the defendant's negligence appears predominant, the alleged negligence cannot be considered a substantial factor. [C]

> **Non constat**
> **jus civile**
> **a posteriori**
>
> ### It's Latin to Me!
>
> *Arguendo* is Latin for "arguing" and is used here as "for the sake of argument."

There are several factors present which appear as the predominant or more substantial causes of the injury than defendant's failure to lock or drain the hose, such as the parents' allowing the children to build a fire unsupervised, David's obtaining the gasoline which the plaintiff could not have done on her own, and David's dropping the burning can of gasoline in a bucket of water causing the burning gas to splash on the plaintiff. Under these circumstances the defendant's alleged negligence was insignificant and not a substantial factor in causing plaintiff's injury.

Judgment affirmed.

Points for Discussion

1. Do you agree with the results reached by the *Anderson* and *Trevino* courts?

2. Consider and apply RESTATEMENT (SECOND) OF TORTS § 432 and RESTATEMENT (THIRD) OF TORTS § 27 to the facts of *Anderson* and *Trevino*. Do you reach the same results as the courts did in those two decisions?

3. What should be the rule governing causation-in-fact in negligence actions involving concurrent causes?

RESTATEMENT (SECOND) OF TORTS § 433B (1965)
Burden of Proof

(1) Except as stated in Subsections (2) and (3), the burden of proof that the tortious conduct of the defendant has caused the harm to the plaintiff is upon the plaintiff.

(2) Where the tortious conduct of two or more actors has combined to bring about harm to the plaintiff, and one or more of the actors seeks to limit his liability on the ground that the harm is capable of apportionment among them, the burden of proof as to the apportionment is upon each such actor.

(3) Where the conduct of two or more actors is tortious, and it is proved that harm has been caused to the plaintiff by only one of them, but there is uncertainty as to which one has caused it, the burden is upon each such actor to prove that he has not caused the harm.

> **RESTATEMENT (THIRD) OF TORTS:**
> **LIABILITY FOR PHYSICAL HARM § 28 (2010)**
> **Burden of Proof**
>
> (a) Subject to Subsection (b), the plaintiff has the burden to prove that the defendant's tortious conduct was a factual cause of the plaintiff's physical harm.
>
> (b) When the plaintiff sues all of multiple actors and proves that each engaged in tortious conduct that exposed the plaintiff to a risk of physical harm and that the tortious conduct of one or more of them caused the plaintiff's harm but the plaintiff cannot reasonably be expected to prove which actor caused the harm, the burden of proof, including both production and persuasion, on factual causation is shifted to the defendants.

Summers v. Tice

33 Cal.2d 80, 199 P.2d 1 (1948)

CARTER, Justice.

Each of the two defendants appeals from a judgment against them in an action for personal injuries. Pursuant to **stipulation** the appeals have been **consolidated**.

Plaintiff's action was against both defendants for an injury to his right eye and face as the result of bring struck by bird shot discharged from a shotgun. The case was tried by the court without a jury and the court found that on November 20, 1945, plaintiff and the two defendants were hunting quail on the open range. Each of the defendants was armed with a 12 gauge shotgun loaded with shells containing 7 1/2 size shot. Prior to going hunting plaintiff discussed the hunting procedure with defendants, indicating that they were to exercise care when shooting and to 'keep in line.' In the course of hunting plaintiff proceeded up a hill, thus placing the hunters at the points of a triangle. The view of defendants with reference to plaintiff was unobstructed and they knew his location. Defendant Tice flushed a quail which rose in flight to a ten foot elevation and flew between plaintiff and defendants. Both defendants shot at the quail, shooting in plaintiff's direction. At that time defendants were 75 yards from plaintiff. One shot struck plaintiff in his eye and another in his upper lip. Finally it was found by the court that as the direct result of the shooting by defendants the shots struck plaintiff as above mentioned and that defendants were negligent in so shooting . . .

First, on the subject of negligence, defendant Simonson contends that the evidence is insufficient to sustain the finding on that score, but he does not point out wherein it is lacking. There is evidence that both defendants, at about the same time or one immediately after the other, shot at a quail and in so doing shot toward plaintiff who was uphill from them, and that they knew his location. That is sufficient from which the trial court could conclude that they acted with respect to plaintiff other than as persons of ordinary prudence. . . .

. . . .

The problem presented in this case is whether the judgment against both defendants may stand. It is argued by defendants that they are not **joint tortfeasors**, and thus **jointly and severally liable**, as they were not acting in concert, and that there is not sufficient evidence to show which defendant was guilty of the negligence which caused the injuries the shooting by Tice or that by Simonson. Tice argues that there is evidence to show that the shot which struck plaintiff came from Simonson's gun because of admissions allegedly made by him to third persons and no evidence that they came from his gun. Further in connection with the latter contention, the court failed to find on plaintiff's allegation in his complaint that he did not know which one was at fault did not find which defendant was guilty of the negligence which caused the injuries to plaintiff.

Considering the last argument first, we believe it is clear that the court sufficiently found on the issue that defendants were **jointly liable** and that thus the negligence of both was the cause of the injury or to that legal effect. It found that both defendants were negligent and 'That as a direct and proximate result of the shots fired by defendants, and each of them, a birdshot pellet was caused to and did lodge in plaintiff's right eye and that another birdshot pellet was caused to and did lodge in plaintiff's upper lip.' In so doing the court evidently did not give credence to the admissions of Simonson to third persons that he fired the shots, which it was justified in doing. It thus determined that the negligence of both defendants was the legal cause of the injury or that both were responsible. Implicit in such finding is the assumption that the court was unable to ascertain whether the shots were from the gun of one defendant or the other or one shot from each of them. The one shot that entered plaintiff's eye was the major factor in assessing damages and that shot could not have come from the gun of both defendants. It was from one or the other only.

It has been held that where a group of persons are on a hunting party, or otherwise engaged in the use of firearms, and two of them are negligent in firing in the direction of a third person who is injured thereby, both of those so firing are liable for the injury suffered by the third person, although the negligence of only one of them could have caused the injury. [Cc] . . . These cases speak of the action of defendants as being in concert as the ground of decision, yet it would seem they are straining that concept and the more reasonable basis appears in Oliver v. Miles, [144 Miss. 852, 110 So. 666]. There two persons were hunting together. Both shot at some partridges and in so doing shot across the highway injuring plaintiff who was travelling on it. The court stated they were acting in concert and thus both were liable. The court then stated [c] 'We think that * * * each is liable for the resulting injury to the boy, although no one can say definitely who actually shot him. *To hold otherwise would be to exonerate both from liability, although each was negligent, and the injury resulted from such negligence.*' [C]

. . . .

When we consider the relative position of the parties and the results that would flow if plaintiff was required to pin the injury on one of the defendants only, a requirement that the burden of proof on that subject be shifted to defendants becomes manifest. They are both wrongdoers both negligent toward plaintiff. They brought about a situation where the negligence of one of them injured the plaintiff, hence it should rest with them each to absolve himself if he can. The injured party has been placed by defendants in the unfair position of pointing to which defendant caused the harm. If one can escape the other may also and plaintiff is remediless. Ordinarily defendants are in a far better position to offer evidence to determine which one caused the injury. This reasoning has recently found favor in this Court. In a quite analogous situation this Court held that a patient injured while unconscious on an operating table in a hospital could hold all or any of the persons who had any connection with the operation even though he could not select the particular acts by the particular person which led to his disability. Ybarra v. Spangard, 25 Cal.2d 486, 154 P.2d 687, 162 A.L.R. 1258. There the Court was considering whether the patient could avail himself of **res ipsa loquitur**, rather than where the burden of proof lay, yet the effect of the decision is that plaintiff has made out a case when he has produced evidence which gives rise to an inference of negligence . . . Similarly in the instant case plaintiff is not able to establish which of defendants caused his injury.

Take Note

Ybarra v. Spangard and the *res ipsa loquitur* doctrine are considered in Chapter 4, *supra.*

. . . .

[T]he same reasons of policy and justice shift the burden to each of defendants to absolve himself if he can relieving the wronged person of the duty of apportioning the injury to a particular defendant, apply here where we are concerned with whether plaintiff is required to supply evidence for the apportionment of damages. If defendants are independent tortfeasors and thus each liable for the damage caused by him alone, and, at least, where the matter of apportionment is incapable of proof, the innocent wronged party should not be deprived of his right to redress. The wrongdoers should be left to work out between themselves any apportionment. [C]

. . . .

The judgment is affirmed.

Points for Discussion

1. Why did the *Summers* court place the burden of proof on the defendants?

2. Do you agree with the court that both defendants are wrongdoers even though the plaintiff was struck by one and only one shot?

3. You are counsel for one of the defendants. Given the court's ruling, how would you (can you successfully) defend your client?

4. Suppose that ten hunters fired in the direction of the plaintiff and that plaintiff was struck by one shot? Same analysis? Same result?

Hellums v. Raber

853 N.E.2d 143 (Ind. App. 2006)

CRONE, Judge.

Charles D. Hellums appeals the trial court's grant of Alan Raber's motion for summary judgment. We reverse and remand.

. . . .

On November 15, 2003, a partly sunny day with no precipitation, Alan was hunting deer with William Nugent and his cousin, Ernest Raber. Hellums was with a separate party hunting deer on the same property. Alan had seen another truck parked on the property with a "kid" standing next to it and had assumed that there were other people hunting there. . . . As they were walking through a field, Alan's party spotted a deer, and each member of his party shot at the deer. Alan claims that he fired four rapid shots at the deer. Alan's party moved forward to determine whether they had hit the deer. About five to ten seconds later, a second deer came into view, running in approximately the same direction as the first. Ernest fired multiple shots at this deer, and one of his bullets struck Hellums. According to Nugent, Alan might have also shot at this deer. However, all parties acknowledge that the bullet that struck Hellums did not come from Alan's gun.

Hellums's party had spotted Alan's party before they began shooting at the first deer. Hellums estimates that they were about 175 to 200 yards to the east of Alan's party. Hellums and his father were both wearing orange hats. Hellums waved his hat at Alan's party, hoping to get their attention. When the second deer came into view, Hellums and his father began shouting as well, but unfortunately did not get the attention of Alan's party in time.

On September 22, 2004, Hellums filed suit against Alan, Ernest, and Nugent, alleging that they had been negligent in failing to ascertain the presence of other hunters before shooting. . . . On November 17, 2005, Alan moved for summary judgment on the basis that Hellums was not hit by a bullet from his gun, and that he therefore had not proximately caused Hellums's injuries. The trial court granted Alan's motion on December 12, 2005.

. . . .

The parties agree that Hellums was not injured by a bullet from Alan's gun. Hellums alleges, however, that Alan shot his gun negligently and that this encouraged Ernest to shoot negligently as well. He argues that multiple hunters may be held liable for a plaintiff's injuries even when it is possible to determine which one shot the plaintiff. As there is no Indiana case law directly on point, Hellums urges us to adopt the position of the Restatement (Second) of Torts. Section 876 of the Restatement states:

> For harm resulting to a third person from the tortious conduct of another, one is subject to liability if he (a) does a tortious act in concert with the other or pursuant to a common design with him, or (b) knows that the other's conduct constitutes a breach of duty and gives substantial assistance or encouragement to the other so to conduct himself, or (c) gives substantial assistance to the other in accomplishing a tortious result and his own conduct, separately considered, constitutes a breach of duty to the third person.

Hellums argues that this case falls under clause (b). The Restatement's comments to clause (b) contain the following example: "A and B are members of a hunting party. Each of them in the presence of the other shoots across a public road at an animal, which is negligent toward persons on the road. A hits the animal. B's bullet strikes C, a traveler on the road. A is subject to liability to C." . . .[1]

. . . We agree with Hellums's assertion that it is possible that Alan's shooting in Hellums's direction may have encouraged Ernest to shoot or believe it was safe to shoot in that direction, and therefore, there is a genuine issue of material fact . . . [and] Hellums should have the opportunity to further develop the case factually.

. . . .

Reversed and remanded.

Points for Discussion

1. Is this case relevantly different from *Summers v. Tice*?

2. In remanding the case, the court notes that it is "possible" that one hunter's shooting in the direction of the plaintiff may have encouraged the other hunter to either shoot or believe that it was safe to discharge his weapon in that same direction. You are Hellums' legal counsel. What facts and evidence must you develop in order to place the case before a jury?

Sindell v. Abbott Laboratories

26 Cal.3d 588, 607 P.2d 924 (1980)

MOSK, Justice.

This case involves a complex problem both timely and significant: may a plaintiff, injured as the result of a drug administered to her mother during pregnancy, who knows the type of drug involved but cannot identify the manufacturer of the precise product, hold liable for her injuries a maker of a drug produced from an identical formula?

---

1 We note that [the courts' findings of liability in] these cases are often justified on the basis that the defendants were acting in concert. However, it is not necessary for Hellums to prove that Alan and Ernest were acting in concert in order for joint liability to attach. Joint liability may be premised upon independent acts that combine to produce an injury. [C]

Plaintiff Judith Sindell brought an action against eleven drug companies and Does 1 through 100, on behalf of herself and other women similarly situated. The complaint alleges as follows:

Between 1941 and 1971, defendants were engaged in the business of manufacturing, promoting, and marketing diethylstilbesterol (DES), a drug which is a synthetic compound of the female hormone estrogen. The drug was administered to plaintiff's mother and the mothers of the class she represents, for the purpose of preventing miscarriage.

> **Practice Pointer**
>
> The fictitious name "Doe" is used to refer to a party in a legal proceeding when the true identity of a party is not known or the real name of a party is withheld.

In 1947, the Food and Drug Administration authorized the marketing of DES as a miscarriage preventative, but only on an experimental basis, with a requirement that the drug contain a warning label to that effect.

> **Make the Connection**
>
> The Food and Drug Administration, a division of the United States Department of Health and Human Services, enforces the Food, Drug, and Cosmetic Act of 1938. FDA regulation is covered in a Food and Drug Law course.

DES may cause cancerous vaginal and cervical growths in the daughters exposed to it before birth, because their mothers took the drug during pregnancy. The form of cancer from which these daughters suffer is known as adenocarcinoma, and it manifests itself after a minimum latent period of 10 or 12 years. It is a fast-spreading and deadly disease, and radical surgery is required to prevent it from spreading. DES also causes adenosis, precancerous vaginal and cervical growths which may spread to other areas of the body. The treatment for adenosis is cauterization, surgery, or cryosurgery. Women who suffer from this condition must be monitored by biopsy or colposcopic examination twice a year, a painful and expensive procedure. Thousands of women whose mothers received DES during pregnancy are unaware of the effects of the drug.

In 1971, the Food and Drug Administration ordered defendants to cease marketing and promoting DES for the purpose of preventing miscarriages, and to warn physicians and the public that the drug should not be used by pregnant women because of the danger to their unborn children.

During the period defendants marketed DES, they knew or should have known that it was a carcinogenic substance, that there was a grave danger after varying periods of latency it would cause cancerous and precancerous growths in the daughters of the mothers who took it, and that it was ineffective to prevent miscarriage. Nevertheless, defendants continued to advertise and market the drug as a miscarriage preventative. They failed to test DES for efficacy and safety; the tests performed by others, upon which they relied, indicated that it was not safe or effective. In violation of the authorization of the Food and Drug Administration, defendants marketed DES on an unlimited basis rather than as an experimental drug, and they failed to warn of its potential danger.

Because of defendants' advertised assurances that DES was safe and effective to prevent miscarriage, plaintiff was exposed to the drug prior to her birth. She became aware of the danger from such exposure within one year of the time she filed her complaint. As a result of the DES ingested by her mother, plaintiff developed a malignant bladder tumor which was removed by surgery. She suffers from adenosis and must constantly be monitored by biopsy or colposcopy to insure early warning of further malignancy.

The first cause of action alleges that defendants were jointly and individually negligent in that they manufactured, marketed and promoted DES as a safe and efficacious drug to prevent miscarriage, without adequate testing or warning, and without monitoring or reporting its effects.

A separate cause of action alleges that defendants are jointly liable regardless of which particular brand of DES was ingested by plaintiff's mother because defendants collaborated in marketing, promoting and testing the drug, relied upon each other's tests, and adhered to an industry-wide safety standard. DES was produced from a common and mutually agreed upon formula as a fungible drug interchangeable with other brands of the same product; defendants knew or should have known that it was customary for doctors to prescribe the drug by its generic rather than its brand name and that pharmacists filled prescriptions from whatever brand of the drug happened to be in stock.

. . . .

Plaintiff seeks **compensatory damages** of $1 million and **punitive damages** of $10 million for herself. For the members of her class, she prays for equitable relief in the form of an order that defendants warn physicians and others of the danger of DES and the necessity of performing certain tests to determine the presence of disease caused by the drug, and that they establish free clinics in California to perform such tests.

Defendants demurred to the complaint. While the complaint did not expressly allege that plaintiff could not identify the manufacturer of the precise drug ingested by her mother, she stated in her points and authorities in opposition to the **demurrers** filed by some of the defendants that she was unable to make the identification, and the trial court sustained the demurrers of these defendants without leave to amend on the ground that plaintiff did not and stated she could not identify which defendant had manufactured the drug responsible for her injuries. Thereupon, the court dismissed the action. This appeal involves only five of ten defendants named in the complaint.

This case is but one of a number filed throughout the country seeking to hold drug manufacturers liable for injuries allegedly resulting from DES prescribed to the plaintiffs' mothers since 1947. According to a note in the Fordham Law Review, estimates of the number of women who took the drug during pregnancy range from 1 ½ million to 3 million. Hundreds, perhaps thousands, of the daughters of these women suffer from adenocarcinoma, and the incidence of vaginal adenosis among them is 30 to 90 percent. (Comment, *DES and a Proposed Theory of Enterprise Liability* (1978) 46 FORDHAM L.REV. 963, 964-967 [hereafter Fordham Comment].) Most of the cases are still pending. With two exceptions, those that have been decided resulted in judgments in favor of the drug company defendants because of the failure of the plaintiffs to identify the manufacturer of the DES prescribed to their mothers. . . . The present action is another attempt to overcome this obstacle to recovery.

Take Note

Interestingly, the court refers to and relies on a student-authored law review note.

We begin with the proposition that, as a general rule, the imposition of liability depends upon a showing by the plaintiff that his or her injuries were caused by the act of the defendant or by an instrumentality under the defendant's control. The rule applies whether the injury resulted from an accidental event [c] or from the use of a defective product. [Cc]

There are, however, exceptions to this rule. Plaintiff's complaint suggests several bases upon which defendants may be held liable for her injuries even though she cannot demonstrate the name of the manufacturer which produced the DES actually taken by her mother. The first of these theories, classically illustrated by Summers v. Tice (1948) 33 Cal.2d 80, 199 P.2d 1, places the burden of proof of causation upon tortious defendants in certain circumstances. The second basis of liability emerging from the complaint is that defendants acted in concert to cause injury to plaintiff. There is a third and novel approach to the problem, sometimes called the theory of "**enterprise liability**," but which we prefer to designate by the more accurate term of "industry-wide" liability, which might obviate the necessity for identifying the manufacturer of the injury-causing drug. We shall conclude that these doctrines, as previously interpreted, may not be applied to hold defendants liable under the allegations of this complaint. However, we shall propose and adopt a fourth basis for permitting the action to be tried, grounded upon an extension of the *Summers* doctrine.

I

Plaintiff places primary reliance upon cases which hold that if a party cannot identify which of two or more defendants caused an injury, the burden of proof may shift to the defendants to show that they were not responsible for the harm. This principle is sometimes referred to as the "**alternative liability**" theory.

The celebrated case of *Summers v. Tice, supra,* . . . a unanimous opinion of this court, best exemplifies the rule. In *Summers,* the plaintiff was injured when two hunters negligently shot in his direction. It could not be determined which of them had fired the shot which actually caused the injury to the plaintiff's eye, but both defendants were nevertheless held jointly and severally liable for the whole of the damages. We reasoned that both were wrongdoers, both were negligent toward the plaintiff, and that it would be unfair to require plaintiff to isolate the defendant responsible, because if the one pointed out were to escape liability, the other might also, and the plaintiff-victim would be shorn of any remedy. In these circumstances, we held, the burden of proof shifted to the defendants, "each to absolve himself if he can." [C] We stated that under these or similar circumstances a defendant is ordinarily in a "far better position" to offer evidence to determine whether he or another defendant caused the injury.

. . . .

The rule developed in *Summers* has been embodied in the Restatement of Torts. (Rest.2d Torts, § 433B, subsec. (3).)[11] . . .

Defendants assert that these principles are inapplicable here. First, they insist that a predicate to shifting the burden of proof under *Summers-Ybarra* is that the defendants must have greater access to information regarding the cause of the injuries than the plaintiff, whereas in the present case the reverse appears.

Plaintiff does not claim that defendants are in a better position than she to identify the manufacturer of the drug taken by her mother or, indeed, that they have the ability to do so at all, but argues, rather, that *Summers* does not impose such a requirement as a condition to the shifting of the burden of proof. In this respect we believe plaintiff is correct.

---

11 Section 433B, subsection (3) of the Restatement provides: "Where the conduct of two or more actors is tortious, and it is proved that harm has been caused to the plaintiff by only one of them, but there is uncertainty as to which one has caused it, the burden is upon each such actor to prove that he has not caused the harm." The reason underlying the rule is "the injustice of permitting proved wrongdoers, who among them have inflicted an injury upon the entirely innocent plaintiff, to escape liability merely because the nature of their conduct and the resulting harm has made it difficult or impossible to prove which of them has caused the harm." (Rest.2d Torts, § 433B, com. f, p. 446.)

In *Summers*, the circumstances of the accident themselves precluded an explanation of its cause. To be sure, *Summers* states that defendants are "(o)rdinarily . . . in a far better position to offer evidence to determine which one caused the injury" than a plaintiff [c], but the decision does not determine that this "ordinary" situation was present. Neither the facts nor the language of the opinion indicate that the two defendants, simultaneously shooting in the same direction, were in a better position than the plaintiff to ascertain whose shot caused the injury. As the opinion acknowledges, it was impossible for the trial court to determine whether the shot which entered the plaintiff's eye came from the gun of one defendant or the other. Nevertheless, burden of proof was shifted to the defendants.

Here, as in *Summers*, the circumstances of the injury appear to render identification of the manufacturer of the drug ingested by plaintiff's mother impossible by either plaintiff or defendants, and it cannot reasonably be said that one is in a better position than the other to make the identification. Because many years elapsed between the time the drug was taken and the manifestation of plaintiff's injuries she, and many other daughters of mothers who took DES, are unable to make such identification. Certainly there can be no implication that plaintiff is at fault in failing to do so the event occurred while plaintiff was in utero, a generation ago.[13]

On the other hand, it cannot be said with assurance that defendants have the means to make the identification. In this connection, they point out that drug manufacturers ordinarily have no direct contact with the patients who take a drug prescribed by their doctors. Defendants sell to wholesalers, who in turn supply the product to physicians and pharmacies. Manufacturers do not maintain records of the persons who take the drugs they produce, and the selection of the medication is made by the physician rather than the manufacturer. Nor do we conclude that the absence of evidence on this subject is due to the fault of defendants. While it is alleged that they produced a defective product with delayed effects and without adequate warnings, the difficulty or impossibility of identification results primarily from the passage of time rather than from their allegedly negligent acts of failing to provide adequate warnings. . . .

It is important to observe, however, that while defendants do not have means superior to plaintiff to identify the maker of the precise drug taken by her mother, they may in some instances be able to prove that they did not manufacture the injury-causing substance. In the present case, for example, one of the original defendants was dismissed from the action upon proof that it did not manufacture DES until after plaintiff was born.

---

13 Defendants maintain that plaintiff is in a better position than they are to identify the manufacturer because her mother might recall the name of the prescribing physician or the hospital or pharmacy where the drug originated, and might know the brand and strength of dosage, the appearance of the medication, or other details from which the manufacturer might be identified, whereas they possess none of this information. As we point out in footnote 12, we assume for purposes of this appeal that plaintiff cannot point to any particular manufacturer as the producer of the DES taken by her mother.

Thus we conclude that the fact defendants do not have greater access to information which might establish the identity of the manufacturer of the DES which injured plaintiff does not per se prevent application of the Summers rule.

Nevertheless, plaintiff may not prevail in her claim that the Summers rationale should be employed to fix the whole liability for her injuries upon defendants, at least as those principles have previously been applied. There is an important difference between the situation involved in *Summers* and the present case. There, all the parties who were or could have been responsible for the harm to the plaintiff were joined as defendants. Here, by contrast, there are approximately 200 drug companies which made DES, any of which might have manufactured the injury-producing drug.

Defendants maintain that, while in *Summers* there was a 50 percent chance that one of the two defendants was responsible for the plaintiff's injuries, here since any one of 200 companies which manufactured DES might have made the product which harmed plaintiff, there is no rational basis upon which to infer that any defendant in this action caused plaintiff's injuries, nor even a reasonable possibility that they were responsible.

These arguments are persuasive if we measure the chance that any one of the defendants supplied the injury-causing drug by the number of possible tortfeasors. In such a context, the possibility that any of the five defendants supplied the DES to plaintiff's mother is so remote that it would be unfair to require each defendant to exonerate itself. There may be a substantial likelihood that none of the five defendants joined in the action made the DES which caused the injury, and that the offending producer not named would escape liability altogether. While we propose, *infra*, an adaptation of the rule in *Summers* which will substantially overcome these difficulties, defendants appear to be correct that the rule, as previously applied, cannot relieve plaintiff of the burden of proving the identity of the manufacturer which made the drug causing her injuries.

II

The second principle upon which plaintiff relies is the so-called "**concert of action**" theory. Preliminarily, we briefly describe the procedure a drug manufacturer must follow before placing a drug on the market. Under federal law as it read prior to 1962, a new drug was defined as one "not generally recognized as . . . safe." (§ 102, 76 Stat. 781 (Oct. 10, 1962).) Such a substance could be marketed only if a new drug application had been filed with the Food and Drug Administration and had become "effective." If the agency determined that a product was no longer a "new drug," i. e., that it was "generally recognized as . . . safe," (21 U.S.C.A. § 321, subd. (p) (1)) it could be manufactured by any drug company without submitting an application to the agency. According to defendants, 123 new drug applications for DES had been approved by 1952, and in that year DES was declared not to be a "new drug," thus allowing any manufacturer to produce it without prior testing and without submitting a new drug application to the Food and Drug Administration.

With this background we consider whether the complaint states a claim based upon "concert of action" among defendants. The elements of this doctrine are prescribed in section 876 of the Restatement of Torts. The section provides, "For harm resulting to a third person from the tortious conduct of another, one is subject to liability if he (a) does a tortious act in concert with the other or pursuant to a common design with him, or (b) knows that the other's conduct constitutes a breach of duty and gives substantial assistance or encouragement to the other so to conduct himself, or (c) gives substantial assistance to the other in accomplishing a tortious result and his own conduct, separately considered, constitutes a breach of duty to the third person." With respect to this doctrine, Prosser states that "those who, in pursuance of a common plan or design to commit a tortious act, actively take part in it, or further it by cooperation or request, or who lend aid or encouragement to the wrongdoer, or ratify and adopt his acts done for their benefit, are equally liable with him. Express agreement is not necessary, and all that is required is that there be a tacit understanding . . . ." (PROSSER, LAW OF TORTS (4th ed. 1971), sec. 46, p. 292.)

. . . .

. . . The **gravamen** of the charge of concert is that defendants failed to adequately test the drug or to give sufficient warning of its dangers and that they relied upon the tests performed by one another and took advantage of each others' promotional and marketing techniques. These allegations do not amount to a charge that there was a tacit understanding or a common plan among defendants to fail to conduct adequate tests or give sufficient warnings, and that they substantially aided and encouraged one another in these omissions.

The complaint charges also that defendants produced DES from a "common and mutually agreed upon formula," allowing pharmacists to treat the drug as a "fungible commodity" and to fill prescriptions from whatever brand of DES they had on hand at the time. It is difficult to understand how these allegations can form the basis of a cause of action for wrongful conduct by defendants, acting in concert. The formula for DES is a scientific constant. It is set forth in the United States Pharmacopeia, and any manufacturer producing that

FYI The U.S. Pharmacopeia is a non-governmental, official public standards-setting authority for prescription and over-the-counter medicines and other healthcare products.

drug must, with exceptions not relevant here, utilize the formula set forth in that compendium. [C]

What the complaint appears to charge is defendants' parallel or imitative conduct in that they relied upon each others' testing and promotion methods. But such conduct describes a common practice in industry: a producer avails himself of the experience and methods of others making the same or similar products. Application of the concept of concert of action to this situation would expand the doctrine far beyond its intended scope and would render virtually any manufacturer liable for the defective products of an entire industry, even if it could be demonstrated that the product which caused the injury was not made by the defendant.

None of the cases cited by plaintiff supports a conclusion that defendants may be held liable for concerted tortious acts. They involve conduct by a small number of individuals whose actions resulted in a tort against a single plaintiff, usually over a short span of time, and the defendant held liable was either a direct participant in the acts which caused damage, or encouraged and assisted the person who directly caused the injuries by participating in a joint activity.

Orser v. George (1967) 252 Cal.App.2d 660, 60 Cal.Rptr. 708 upon which plaintiff primarily relies, is also distinguishable. There, three hunters negligently shot at a mudhen in decedent's direction. Two of them shot alternately with the gun which released the bullet resulting in the fatal wound, and the third, using a different gun, fired alternately at the same target, shooting in the same line of fire, perhaps acting tortiously. It was held that there was a possibility the third hunter knew the conduct of the others was tortious toward the decedent and gave them substantial assistance and encouragement, and that it was also possible his conduct, separately considered, was a breach of duty toward decedent. Thus, the granting of summary judgment was reversed as to the third hunter.

The situation in *Orser* is similar to Agovino v. Kunze, *supra,* 181 Cal.App.2d 591, 5 Cal.Rptr. 534, in which liability was imposed upon a participant in a drag race, rather than to the facts alleged in the present case. There is no allegation here that each defendant knew the other defendants' conduct was tortious toward plaintiff, and that they assisted and encouraged one another to inadequately test DES and to provide inadequate warnings. Indeed, it seems dubious whether liability on the concert of action theory can be predicated upon substantial assistance and encouragement given by one alleged tortfeasor to another pursuant to a tacit understanding to fail to perform an act. Thus, there was no concert of action among defendants within the meaning of that doctrine.

III

A third theory upon which plaintiff relies is the concept of industry-wide liability, or according to the terminology of the parties, **"enterprise liability."** This theory was suggested in Hall v. E. I. Du Pont de Nemours & Co., Inc. (E.D.N.Y.1972) 345 F.Supp. 353. In that case, plaintiffs were 13 children injured by the explosion of blasting caps in 12 separate incidents which occurred in 10 different states between 1955 and 1959. The defendants were six blasting cap manufacturers, comprising virtually the entire blasting cap industry in the United States, and their trade association. There were, however, a number of Canadian blasting cap manufacturers which could have supplied the caps. The gravamen of the complaint was that the practice of the industry of omitting a warning on individual blasting caps and of failing to take other safety measures created an unreasonable risk of harm, resulting in the plaintiffs' injuries. The complaint did not identify a particular manufacturer of a cap which caused a particular injury.

The court reasoned as follows: there was evidence that defendants, acting independently, had adhered to an industry-wide standard with regard to the safety features of blasting caps, that they had in effect delegated some functions of safety investigation and design, such as labelling, to their trade association, and that there was industry-wide cooperation in the manufacture and design of blasting caps. In these circumstances, the evidence supported a conclusion that all the defendants jointly controlled the risk. Thus, if plaintiffs could establish by a preponderance of the evidence that the caps were manufactured by one of the defendants, the burden of proof as to causation would shift to all the defendants. The court noted that this theory of liability applied to industries composed of a small number of units, and that what would be fair and reasonable with regard to an industry of five or ten producers might be manifestly unreasonable if applied to a decentralized industry composed of countless small producers.

Plaintiff attempts to state a cause of action under the rationale of *Hall*. She alleges joint enterprise and collaboration among defendants in the production, marketing, promotion and testing of DES, and "concerted promulgation and adherence to industry-wide testing, safety, warning and efficacy standards" for the drug. We have concluded above that allegations that defendants relied upon one another's testing and promotion methods do not state a cause of action for concerted conduct to commit a tortious act. Under the theory of industry-wide liability, however, each manufacturer could be liable for all injuries caused by DES by virtue of adherence to an industry-wide standard of safety.

In the Fordham Comment, the industry-wide theory of liability is discussed and refined in the context of its applicability to actions alleging injuries resulting from DES. The author explains causation under that theory as follows, ". . . (T)he industrywide standard becomes itself the cause of plaintiff's injury, just as defendants' joint plan is the cause of injury in the traditional concert of action plea. Each defendant's adherence perpetuates this standard, which results in the manufacture of the particular, unidentifiable injury-producing product. Therefore, each industry member has contributed to plaintiff's injury." [C]

The Comment proposes seven requirements for a cause of action based upon industry-wide liability,[24] and suggests that if a plaintiff proves these elements, the burden of proof of causation should be shifted to the defendants, who may exonerate themselves only by showing that their product could not have caused the injury.

We decline to apply this theory in the present case. At least 200 manufacturers produced DES; *Hall*, which involved 6 manufacturers representing the entire blasting cap industry in the United States, cautioned against application of the doctrine espoused therein to a large number of producers. [C] Moreover, in *Hall*, the conclusion that the defendants jointly controlled the risk was based upon allegations that they had delegated some functions relating to safety to a trade association. There are no such allegations here, and we have concluded above that plaintiff has failed to allege liability on a concert of action theory.

Equally important, the drug industry is closely regulated by the Food and Drug Administration, which actively controls the testing and manufacture of drugs and the method by which they are marketed, including the contents of warning labels. To a considerable degree, therefore, the standards followed by drug manufacturers are suggested or compelled by the government. Adherence to those standards cannot, of course, absolve a manufacturer of liability to which it would otherwise be subject. [C] But since the government plays such a pervasive role in formulating the criteria for the testing and marketing of drugs, it would be unfair to impose upon a manufacturer liability for injuries resulting from the use of a drug which it did not supply simply because it followed the standards of the industry.

IV

If we were confined to the theories of *Summers* and *Hall*, we would be constrained to hold that the judgment must be sustained. Should we require that plain-

---

24 The suggested requirements are as follows:
   1. There existed an insufficient, industry-wide standard of safety as to the manufacture of the product.
   2. Plaintiff is not at fault for the absence of evidence identifying the causative agent but, rather, this absence of proof is due to defendant's conduct.
   3. A generically similar defective product was manufactured by all the defendants.
   4. Plaintiff's injury was caused by this defect.
   5. Defendants owed a duty to the class of which plaintiff was a member.
   6. There is clear and convincing evidence that plaintiff's injury was caused by a product made by one of the defendants. For example, the joined defendants accounted for a high percentage of such defective products on the market at the time of plaintiff's injury.
   7. All defendants were tortfeasors.

tiff identify the manufacturer which supplied the DES used by her mother or that all DES manufacturers be joined in the action, she would effectively be precluded from any recovery. As defendants candidly admit, there is little likelihood that all the manufacturers who made DES at the time in question are still in business or that they are subject to the jurisdiction of the California courts. There are, however, forceful arguments in favor of holding that plaintiff has a cause of action.

In our contemporary complex industrialized society, advances in science and technology create fungible goods which may harm consumers and which cannot be traced to any specific producer. The response of the courts can be either to adhere rigidly to prior doctrine, denying recovery to those injured by such products, or to fashion remedies to meet these changing needs. . . . [W]e acknowledge that some adaptation of the rules of causation and liability may be appropriate in these recurring circumstances. The Restatement comments that modification of the *Summers* rule may be necessary in a situation like that before us. [C]

The most persuasive reason for finding plaintiff states a cause of action is that advanced in *Summers*: as between an innocent plaintiff and negligent defendants, the latter should bear the cost of the injury. Here, as in Summers, plaintiff is not at fault in failing to provide evidence of causation, and although the absence of such evidence is not attributable to the defendants either, their conduct in marketing a drug the effects of which are delayed for many years played a significant role in creating the unavailability of proof.

From a broader policy standpoint, defendants are better able to bear the cost of injury resulting from the manufacture of a defective product. As was said by Justice Traynor in *Escola*, "(t)he cost of an injury and the loss of time or health may be an overwhelming misfortune to the person injured, and a needless one, for the risk of injury can be insured by the manufacturer and distributed among the public as a cost of doing business." (24 Cal.2d p. 462, 150 P.2d p. 441; see also REST.2d TORTS, § 402A, com. c, pp. 349-350.) The manufacturer is in the best position to discover and guard against defects in its products and to warn of harmful effects; thus, holding it liable for defects and failure to warn of harmful effects will provide an incentive to product safety. [Cc] These considerations are particularly significant where medication is involved, for the consumer is virtually helpless to protect himself from serious, sometimes permanent, sometimes fatal, injuries caused by deleterious drugs.

Where, as here, all defendants produced a drug from an identical formula and the manufacturer of the DES which caused plaintiff's injuries cannot be identified through no fault of plaintiff, a modification of the rule of *Summers* is warranted. As we have seen, an undiluted *Summers* rationale is inappropriate to shift the burden of proof of causation to defendants because if we measure the chance that any particular manufacturer supplied the injury-causing product by the number of producers of DES, there is a possibility that none of the five defendants in this case produced the offending substance and that the responsible manufacturer, not named in the action, will escape liability.

But we approach the issue of causation from a different perspective: we hold it to be reasonable in the present context to measure the likelihood that any of the defendants supplied the product which allegedly injured plaintiff by the percentage which the DES sold by each of them for the purpose of preventing miscarriage bears to the entire production of the drug sold by all for that purpose. Plaintiff asserts in her briefs that Eli Lilly and Company and 5 or 6 other companies produced 90 percent of the DES marketed. If at trial this is established to be the fact, then there is a corresponding likelihood that this comparative handful of producers manufactured the DES which caused plaintiff's injuries, and only a 10 percent likelihood that the offending producer would escape liability.[28]

If plaintiff joins in the action the manufacturers of a substantial share of the DES which her mother might have taken, the injustice of shifting the burden of proof to defendants to demonstrate that they could not have made the substance which injured plaintiff is significantly diminished. While 75 to 80 percent of the market is suggested as the requirement by the Fordham Comment [c], we hold only that a substantial percentage is required.

The presence in the action of a substantial share of the appropriate market also provides a ready means to apportion damages among the defendants. Each defendant will be held liable for the proportion of the judgment represented by its share of that market unless it demonstrates that it could not have made the product which caused plaintiff's injuries. In the present case, as we have see, one DES manufacturer was dismissed from the action upon filing a declaration that it had not manufactured DES until after plaintiff was born.

Once plaintiff has met her burden of joining the required defendants, they in turn may **cross-complaint** against other DES manufacturers, not joined in the action, which they can allege might have supplied the injury-causing product.

Make the Connection

A defendant's cross-claim against other defendants is a concept and practice covered in a Civil Procedure course.

---

28 The Fordham Comment explains the connection between percentage of market share and liability as follows: "(I)f X Manufacturer sold one-fifth of all the DES prescribed for pregnancy and identification could be made in all cases, X would be the sole defendant in approximately one-fifth of all cases and liable for all the damages in those cases. Under alternative liability, X would be joined in all cases in which identification could not be made, but liable for only one-fifth of the total damages in these cases. X would pay the same amount either way. Although the correlation is not, in practice, perfect (footnote omitted), it is close enough so that defendants' objections on the ground of fairness lose their value." (Fordham Comment, *supra*, at p. 94.)

Under this approach, each manufacturer's liability would approximate its responsibility for the injuries caused by its own products. Some minor discrepancy in the correlation between market share and liability is inevitable; therefore, a defendant may be held liable for a somewhat different percentage of the damage than its share of the appropriate market would justify. It is probably impossible, with the passage of time, to determine market share with mathematical exactitude. But just as a jury cannot be expected to determine the precise relationship between fault and liability in applying the doctrine of comparative fault [c] or partial indemnity [c] the difficulty of apportioning damages among the defendant producers in exact relation to their market share does not seriously militate against the rule we adopt. As we said in *Summers* with regard to the liability of independent tortfeasors, where a correct division of liability cannot be made "the trier of fact may make it the best it can." [C]

We are not unmindful of the practical problems involved in defining the market and determining **market share**,[29] but these are largely matters of proof which properly cannot be determined at the pleading stage of these proceedings. Defendants urge that it would be both unfair and contrary to public policy to hold them liable for plaintiff's injuries in the absence of proof that one of them supplied the drug responsible for the damage. Most of their arguments, however, are based upon the assumption that one manufacturer would be held responsible for the products of another or for those of all other manufacturers if plaintiff ultimately prevails. But under the rule we adopt, each manufacturer's liability for an injury would be approximately equivalent to the damages caused by the DES it manufactured.

The judgments are reversed.

———————————

Points for Discussion

1. Describe and distinguish the "alternative liability," "concert of action," and "enterprise liability" theories.

2. On what grounds did the *Sindell* court distinguish the case before it from its earlier decision in *Summers v. Tice*?

———————————

29 Defendants assert that there are no figures available to determine market share, that DES was provided for a number of uses other than to prevent miscarriage and it would be difficult to ascertain what proportion of the drug was used as a miscarriage preventative, and that the establishment of a time frame and area for market share would pose problems.

3. Did the court apply or decline to apply the industry-wide liability suggested in *Hall v. E. I. du Pont de Nemours & Co., Inc.*? Do you agree with its decision on this issue?

4. The court notes that the "injustice of shifting the burden of proof to the defendants to demonstrate that they could not have made the substance which injured plaintiff is significantly diminished" where a plaintiff joins those companies which manufactured "a substantial share of the DES which the mother might have taken." Is this burden shift unjust? If you agree that it is unjust, did the court err in placing the burden on the defendants in DES cases?

5. For cases and jurisdictions adopting the market share liability theory or a version thereof in DES cases, *see Brown v. Superior Court,* 44 Cal.3d 1049, 751 P.2d 470, 245 Cal.Rptr. 412 (1988) (plaintiffs must sue defendants with substantial share of market, with a defendant dismissed if it proves that it did not manufacture the drug ingested by plaintiff's mother; remaining defendants are **severally** liable for portion of damages reflecting that defendant's market share); *Hymowitz v. Eli Lilly and Co.,* 73 N.Y.2d 487, 539 N.E.2d 1069 (1989) (defendants severally liable for that part of plaintiff's damages corresponding to its share of national market and defendant cannot exculpate itself by proving that it did not manufacture pill that injured plaintiff); *Martin v. Abbott Labs.,* 102 Wash.2d 581, 689 P.2d 368 (1984) (defendant who establishes that it did not manufacture the drug at-issue is dismissed from case; it is presumed that remaining defendants have equal share of market and each defendant must prove its actual market share, with shares of defendants unable to prove actual market share increased to reflect one hundred percent of market); *Conley v. Boyle Drug Co.,* 570 So.2d 275 (Fla. 1990) (same); *Collins v. Eli Lilly Co.,* 342 N.W.2d 37 (Wis. 1984) (risk contribution theory; plaintiff must sue one defendant and that defendant impleads other defendants; defendant who proves that it did not manufacture drug taken by mother of plaintiff is dismissed and jury assigns risk contributed by defendants under comparative negligence principles).

6. Michigan has adopted the *Summers v. Tice* "alternative liability" theory in DES cases. *See* Abel v. Eli Lilly & Co., 418 Mich. 311, 343 N.W.2d 164 (1984).

7. For cases rejecting the DES market share liability approach, *see Sutowski v. Eli Lilly & Co.,* 696 N.E.2d 187 (Ohio 1998); *Smith v. Eli Lilly & Co.,* 137 Ill.2d 222, 560 N.E.2d 324 (1990); *Mulcahy v. Eli Lilly & Co.,* 386 N.W.2d 67 (Iowa 1986); *Zafft v. Eli Lilly & Co.,* 676 S.W.2d 241 (Mo. 1984).

B. Legal or Proximate Causation

Atlantic Coast Line R. Co. v. Daniels

8 Ga.App. 775, 70 S.E. 203 (1911)

POWELL, J.

. . . .

Cause and effect find their beginning and end in the limitless and unknowable. Therefore courts, in their finitude, do not attempt to deal with cause and effect in any absolute degree, but only in such a limited way as is practical and as is within the scope of ordinary human understanding. Hence arbitrary limits have been set, and such qualifying words as "proximate" and "natural" have come into use as setting the limits beyond which the courts will not look in the attempt to trace the connection between a given cause and a given effect. A plaintiff comes into court alleging, as an effect, some injury that has been done to his person or to his property. He shows that **antecedent** to the injury a wrongful act of another person occurred, and that, if this wrongful act had not occurred, the injury complained of would not (as human probabilities go) have occurred. We then say, in common speech, that the wrong was a cause of the injury. But to make such a standard (that, if the cause had not existed, the effect would not have occurred) the basis of legal responsibility would soon prove very unsatisfactory; for a *reduction ad absurdum* may be promptly established by calling to mind, that, if the injured person had never been born, the injury would not have happened. So the courts ask another question: Was the wrongful act the proximate cause?

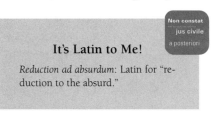

It's Latin to Me!

Reduction ad absurdum: Latin for "reduction to the absurd."

All the past is a part of the cause of every present effect. The courts can deal with that great body of cause only as it relates to human activity; and a particular court dealing with a particular case must as a practical necessity isolate the activities near by to the effect in question, and from these must make the juridic determination of responsibility. Now, as activities are viewed by the courts in administering the law, they divide themselves into two classes--proper or non-negligent activities, and wrongful or negligent activities. The word "activity" is here used in a sense broad enough to include both **omission** and **commission**. The normal course of things which the law seeks to establish, and for a violation of which the law professes to give redress, is for all men to regulate their activities properly--that is to say, nonnegligently--and whether a man has so regulated his activities is usually determined by comparing what he did under the circumstances with what an ordinary man of common prudence would have done under the same circumstances. If hurt comes to a person and, by looking back through the nearby causes which concentrated and became effectual in the hurtful thing, it appears that all those whose activities were concerned acted lawfully and as ordinarily prudent men would have acted, we say that the person so hurt has suffered an accident, and no legal responsibility can be asserted against any one. But if, in examining the causes which joined in producing the effect, we find that one or more of them consisted in somebody's having violated the standard and having done something which an ordinarily prudent man would not have done, the first step toward the declaration of legal responsibility is established. We then say that the injury was the result of negligence (or sometimes of willful tort, which, for the sake of brevity, we are here classing under the general term "negligence").

Though negligence is discovered in relation to one of the causes which have preceded the injurious effect, it does not follow that the author of the negligence is to be held legally responsible for the injury. In the first place, to judge the transaction according to the natural probabilities which men's minds take as the basis for passing judgment upon the course of human affairs, it may appear that causes other than the negligent one referred to so preponderated in bringing about the result as to lead us to say, from a human point of view, that the injury was just as likely to have ensued (with only its details somewhat varied, perhaps) if the negligent thing had not occurred. In such cases we exempt the author of the negligence from liability.

. . . .

Now, call one other thing to mind . . . In every case where a personal injury is complained of, the activities of the injured person are, of necessity, a part of the general conditions attendant upon the particular effect asserted. If his conduct at the time of the injury and precedent thereto has conformed to the normal standard of prudence, his activities are considered as merely a part of the ordinary flow of human activity. If he has been guilty of negligence, then, in determining the proximate cause of the injury, his negligence counts just as if it were anybody else's. It may itself be the proximate cause. It may so intervene between prior negligence of some other person and the injurious effect as to break the line of causal connection. It may concur with the negligence of another person.

. . . .

Points for Discussion

1. Recall the elements of a negligence action: duty, breach, causation (cause-in-fact and proximate cause) and actual damages. Where a defendant has breached her duty owed to plaintiff, and that breach is the cause-in-fact of the plaintiff's injury, the causal chain and connection between the negligent conduct and injury will be broken in the absence of proximate causation, and the defendant cannot be held liable.

2. Consider the following discussion of the difference between cause-in-fact and proximate cause: "The distinction between cause in fact and proximate, or legal, cause is not merely an exercise in semantics. The terms are not interchangeable. Although both cause in fact and proximate, or legal, cause are elements of negligence that the plaintiff must prove, they are very different concepts. Cause in fact refers to the cause and effect relationship between the defendant's tortious conduct and the plaintiff's injury or loss. Thus, cause in fact deals with the 'but for' consequences of an act. The defendant's conduct is a cause of the event if the event would not have occurred but for that conduct. In contrast proximate cause, or legal cause, concerns a determination of whether legal liability should be imposed where cause in fact has been established. Proximate or legal cause is a policy decision made by the legislature or the courts to deny liability for otherwise actionable conduct based on considerations of logic, common sense, policy, precedent and 'our more or less inadequately expressed ideas of what justice demands or of what is administratively possible and convenient'." Snyder v. LTG Lufttechnische GmbH, 955 S.W.2d 252 (Tenn. 1997).

RESTATEMENT (SECOND) OF TORTS § 431 (1965)

What Constitutes Legal Cause

The actor's negligent conduct is a legal cause of harm to another if

(a) his conduct is a substantial factor in bringing about the harm, and

(b) there is no rule of law relieving the actor from liability because of the manner in which his negligence has resulted in the harm.

RESTATEMENT (THIRD) OF TORTS: LIABILITY FOR
PHYSICAL HARM § 29 (2010)
Limitations on Liability for Tortious Conduct

An actor's liability is limited to those physical harms that result from
the risks that made the actor's conduct tortious.

1. Unforeseeable Consequences

Ryan v. New York Central R.R. Co.

35 N.Y. 210 (1866)

HUNT, J.

On the 15th day of July, 1854, in the city of Syracuse, the defendant, by the
careless management, or through the insufficient condition, of one of its engines,
set fire to its woodshed, and a large quantity of wood therein. The plaintiff's house,
situated at a distance of one hundred and thirty feet from the shed, soon took fire
from the heat and sparks, and was entirely consumed, notwithstanding diligent
efforts were made to save it. A number of other houses were also burned by the
spreading of the fire. The plaintiff brings this action to recover from the railroad
company the value of his building thus destroyed. The judge at the Circuit **nonsuited** the plaintiff, and the General Term of the fifth district affirmed the judgment.

The question may be thus stated: A house in a populous city takes fire,
through the negligence of the owner or his servant; the flames extend to and
destroy an adjacent building: Is the owner of the first building liable to the second
owner for the damage sustained by such burning?

It is a general principle that every person is liable for the consequences of
his own acts. He is thus liable in damages for the proximate results of his own
acts, but not for remote damages. It is not easy at all times to determine what are
proximate and what are remote damages. . . . So if an engineer upon a steamboat
or locomotive, in passing the house of A., so carelessly manages its machinery
that the coals and sparks from its fires fall upon and consume the house of A., the
railroad company or the steamboat proprietors are liable to pay the value of the
property thus destroyed. [C] Thus far the law is settled and the principle is apparent. If, however, the fire communicates from the house of A. to that of B., and that

is destroyed, is the negligent party liable for his loss? And if it spreads thence to the house of C., and thence to the house of D., and thence consecutively through the other houses, until it reaches and consumes the house of Z., is the party liable to pay the damages sustained by these twenty-four sufferers? The counsel for the plaintiff does not distinctly claim this, and I think it would not be seriously insisted that the sufferers could recover in such case. Where, then, is the principle upon which A. recovers and Z. fails?

It has been suggested that an important element exists in the difference between an intentional firing and a negligent firing merely; that when a party designedly fires his own house or his own fallow land, not intending, however, to do any injury to his neighbor, but a damage actually results, that he may be liable for more extended damages than where the fire originated in accident or negligence. It is true that the most of the cases where the liability was held to exist, were cases of an intentional firing. The case, however, of *Vaughn v. Menlove* (32 Eng. C. L., 613) was that of a spontaneous combustion of a hay-rick. The rick was burned, the owner's buildings were destroyed, and thence the fire spread to the plaintiff's cottage, which was also consumed. The defendant was held liable. Without deciding upon the importance of this distinction, I prefer to place my opinion upon the ground that, in the one case, to wit, the destruction of the building upon which the sparks were thrown by the negligent act of the party sought to be charged, the result was to have been anticipated the moment the fire was communicated to the building; that its destruction was the ordinary and natural result of its being fired. In the second, third or twenty-fourth case, as supposed, the destruction of the building was not a natural and expected result of the first firing. That a building upon which sparks and cinders fall should be destroyed or seriously injured must be expected, but that the fire should spread and other buildings be consumed, is not a necessary or an usual result. That it is possible, and that it is not unfrequent, cannot be denied. The result, however, depends, not upon any necessity of a further communication of the fire, but upon a concurrence of accidental circumstances, such as the degree of the heat, the state of the atmosphere, the condition and materials of the adjoining structures and the direction of the wind. These are accidental and varying circumstances. The party has no control over them, and is not responsible for their effects.

My opinion, therefore, is, that this action cannot be sustained, for the reason that the damages incurred are not the immediate but the remote result of the negligence of the defendants. The immediate result was the destruction of their own wood and sheds; beyond that, it was remote.

. . . .

To sustain such a claim as the present, and to follow the same to its legitimate consequences, would subject to a liability against which no prudence could guard, and to meet which no private fortune would be adequate. Nearly all fires are caused by negligence, in its extended sense. In a country where wood, coal, gas and oils are universally used, where men are crowded into cities and villages, where servants are employed, and where children find their home in all houses, it is impossible that the most vigilant prudence should guard against the occurrence of accidental or negligent fires. A man may insure his own house or his own furniture, but he cannot insure his neighbor's building or furniture, for the reason that he has no interest in them. To hold that the owner must not only meet his own loss by fire, but that he must guarantee the security of his neighbors on both sides, and to an unlimited extent, would be to create a liability which would be the destruction of all civilized society. No community could long exist, under the operation of such a principle. In a commercial country, each man, to some extent, runs the hazard of his neighbor's conduct, and each, by insurance against such hazards, is enabled to obtain a reasonable security against loss. To neglect such precaution, and to call upon his neighbor, on whose premises a fire originated, to **indemnify** him instead, would be to award a punishment quite beyond the offense committed. It is to be considered, also, that if the negligent party is liable to the owner of a remote building thus consumed, he would also be liable to the insurance companies who should pay losses to such remote owners. The principle of **subrogation** would entitle the companies to the benefit of every claim held by the party to whom a loss should be paid.

. . . .

The remoteness of the damage, in my judgment, forms the true rule on which the question should be decided, and which prohibits a recovery by the plaintiff in this case.

Judgment should be affirmed.

Points for Discussion

1. Note the following statement by the court: "It is a general principle that every person is liable for the consequences of his own acts. He is thus liable in damages for the proximate results of his own acts, but not for remote damages." What constitutes, and how would you discern, define, and separate "proximate damages" and "remote damages"?

2. Consider the court's discussion of a fire spreading from the house of A. to the house of B. to the house of C. and so on. If that fire is the result of the defendant's negligence, should the law of torts hold the defendant liable for all the harmful consequences of that negligence, including W., X., Y., and Z.

who lost their homes to the fire as well? If you answered that question in the negative, what is and what should be the dividing line between those houses for which the defendant is, and those houses for which the defendant is not, liable?

3. What role did the availability of insurance play in the court's analysis and decision? What role *should* the availability of insurance play in assessing tort liability?

4. In later cases the Court of Appeals of New York permitted recovery for the owner of immediately adjacent premises, Webb v. Rome W. & O. R.R. Co., 49 N.Y. 420 (1872), and for the owner of the first but not adjacent property set afire by sparks from a railroad's engine. Homac Corp. v. Sun Oil Co., 258 N.Y. 462, 180 N.E. 172 (1932).

Atchison, T. & S.F.R. Co. v. Stanford

12 Kan. 354 (1874)

VALENTINE, J.

This was an action for damages caused by fire originating from sparks emitted from one of the locomotive engines of the plaintiff in error, defendant below. . . .

. . . .

There is [a] very important question in this case. It is whether or not the injury to the plaintiff is not too remote to constitute the basis of a cause of action. The plaintiff in error claims that under the maxim, *causa proxima, non remota spectatur,* that it is. The fire from the defendant's engine did not fall upon the plaintiff's property. Two fires were kindled by sparks emitted from the defendant's engine, but each was kindled on land not belonging to the plaintiff, and each was kindled on land belonging to a different owner. These two fires spread, finally uniting, and

> **Non constat**
> no testimony or figures
> **jus civile**
> a posteriori
>
> ### It's Latin to Me!
>
> *Causa proxima, non remota spectatur* is Latin for "the proximate and not the remote cause must be looked into."

then passed northwardly over the property of several other landed proprietors, and finally reached the plaintiff's property, about three and one-half or four miles distant from the railroad track, and there did the damage of which the plaintiff complains. After a careful examination of this question we are satisfied, both upon reason and authority, that the damage is not too remote to be recovered. We have already decided that where the fire runs thirty rods from the place where it is first kindled, and there does the damage, the plaintiff may recover. St. Joseph & D. C. R. Co. v. Chase, 11 Kan. 47. Now, if the plaintiff may recover when the fire has run thirty rods, why may he not recover when the fire has run forty rods, or a mile, or four miles? Will it be claimed that the ownership of the property over which the fire runs can make any difference? If a rick of hay should be stacked thirty rods from a railroad track, on the land of A., and if another rick should be stacked just ten rods further, on the land of B., and the fire should spread from the railroad track and first burn the rick of A., and then pass on and burn the rick of B., why should not B. recover as well as A.? And why should not C., and D., and E., still beyond, also recover? While A. recovers for his loss, must B., and C., and others, set their loss down to a remote cause, and suffer in uncomplaining silence? If A. should own a field of forty acres, and the whole of it should be overrun by fire, we suppose he could recover for the whole loss; then why should not B. recover for a part of the same loss provided he, instead of A., owned the furthest twenty acres from the railroad track, and the twenty acres last overrun by the fire? In the popular and ordinary sense the fire, however far it may go, is one continuous fire,--the same fire,--and is the proximate cause of all the injuries it may produce in its destructive march, whether it go one rod, or four miles. This may not be strictly the case in the philosophical sense. A spark drops and sets fire to the grass, an inch in circumference; this to another inch; this to another, and so on, *ad infinitum*. The spark is the cause of the burning of the first inch, the first inch of the second, the second of the third, and so on, *ad infinitum*. The spark falling within a rod of the railroad track is not, philosophically speaking, the proximate cause of the burning of the hay-rick thirty rods distant. It is the proximate cause of the burning of the first inch of grass only, and the remote cause of the burning of the hay-rick. A spark could not burn a hayrick at such a great distance. In this sense the spark is an infinitely remote cause of the burning of the hay-rick. In this sense the spark could not be the proximate cause, unless it fell upon the hay-rick and directly set it on fire. Falling one rod, one yard, or even one foot from the hay-rick, would not answer.

What's That?

A rod is a unit of measure equaling 5-½ yards.

It's Latin to Me!

Ad infinitum: Latin for "without limit."

But this sense of proximate and remote causes and effects is not the one adopted and used by the courts. The courts use the terms in a broader and more comprehensive sense. The courts really use the terms in their ordinary and popular sense. The spark negligently allowed to escape from the engine of the defendant is, in law as well as popularly, the proximate cause of the burning of the hay-rick thirty rods, or four miles, away. The first efficient and adequate cause, as well as every intermediate cause necessarily following from the first cause, is always held in law to be the proximate cause, unless some new cause, independent of the first cause, shall intervene between the first cause and the final injurious result. This is equally true where the successive events are separated by clearer and better defined outlines than they are in the burning of prairie grass, or a stubble field. . . . In law, proximate and remote causes and effects do not have reference to time, nor distance, nor merely to a succession of events, or to a succession of causes and effects. A wrongdoer is not merely responsible for the first result of his wrongful act, but he is also responsible for every succeeding injurious result which could have been foreseen, by the exercise of reasonable diligence, as the reasonable, natural, and probable consequence of his wrongful act. He is responsible for any number of injurious results consecutively produced by impulsion, one upon another, and constituting distinct and seperate events, provided they all necessarily follow from the first wrongful cause. Any number of causes and effects may intervene between the first wrongful cause and the final injurious consequence; and if they are such as might, with **reasonable diligence**, have been foreseen, the last result, as well as the first, and every intermediate result, is to be considered in law as the proximate result of the first wrongful cause. But whenever a new cause intervenes which is not a consequence of the first wrongful cause, which is not under the control of the wrong-doer, which could not have been foreseen by the exercise of reasonable diligence by the wrong-doer, and except for which the final injurious consequence could not have happened, then such injurious consequence must be deemed to be too remote to constitute the basis of a cause of action.

. . . . Why should not every person, whether far away or near, recover for losses sustained by reason of the wrongful acts of another? Even if it should bankrupt the wrong-doer, would that be any reason for not compensating an innocent sufferer? As a question of ethics and morals, as well as of law, where a great loss is to be borne by somebody, who should bear it,--the innocent, or the guilty? Would it be better, more equitable, and just, to distribute it among a hundred innocent victims than to visit it wholly upon the wrong-doer who caused it? Possibly, if the loss were distributed among the innocent sufferers, it would bankrupt many of them. Would that be more equitable and just than to bankrupt the guilty wrong-doer? . . .

The views that we have expressed upon the question of proximate and remote causes and effects may not be in harmony with the following decisions, to-wit: *Pennsylvania R. Co. v. Kerr*, 62 Pa. St. 353; *Ryan v. New York Cent. R. Co.*, 35 N. Y. 210; *Macon R. Co. v. McConnell*, 27 Ga. 481. And yet there may be enough to distinguish this case from the last two cases cited, and possibly from the first. But we think our views upon this question are in entire harmony with reason, and with the great weight of authority both in this country and in England. [Cc]

. . . .

The judgment of the court below is affirmed.

Points for Discussion

1. The court determined "that the damage is not too remote to be recovered." Do you agree?

2. Compare and contrast the court's view, understanding, and analysis of "proximate cause" with that expressed in *Ryan v. New York Central R.R. Co.*

3. How do you answer the court's question: "Why should not every person, whether far away or near, recover for losses sustained by reason of the wrongful acts of another?"

4. The court asked whether it would more equitable and just to bankrupt "the innocent" instead of the "guilty wrong-doer." Is that an appropriate and relevant inquiry? What should a judge or a court resort to and examine in answering that query?

5. The plaintiff in *Atchison* owned a farm located four miles from the defendant railroad's tracks in a state containing a large amount of grain not covered by insurance. Might this have impacted the *Atchison* court's decision?

In re Arbitration Between Polemis and Furness, Withy & Co., Ltd.

Court of Appeal, [1921] 3 K.B. 560

APPEAL from the judgment of Sankey J. on an award in the form of a special case.

The owners of the Greek steamship *Thrasyvoulos* claimed to recover damages for the total loss of the steamship by fire.

. . . .

The vessel by the directions of the charterers or their agents in or about the months of June and July, 1917, loaded at Nantes a part cargo of cement and general cargo for Casablanca, Morocco. She then proceeded to Lisbon and was loaded with further cargo, consisting of cases of benzine and/or petrol and iron for Casablanca and other ports on the Morocco coast. She arrived at Casablanca on July 17, and there discharged a portion of her cargo. The cargo was discharged by Arab workmen and winchmen from the shore supplied and sent on board by the charterers' agents. The cargo in No. 1 hold included a considerable quantity of cases of benzine or petrol which had suffered somewhat by handling and/or by rough weather on the voyage, so that there had been some leakage from the tins in the cases into the hold. On July 21 it had become necessary to shift from No. 1 lower hold a number of the cases of benzine which were required to be taken on by the ship to Safi, and for this purpose the native **stevedores** had placed heavy planks across the forward end of the hatchway in the 'tween decks, using it as a platform in the process of transferring the cases from the lower hold to the 'tween decks. There were four or five of the Arab shore labourers in the lower hold filling the slings which, when filled, were hove up by means of the winch situated on the upper deck to the 'tween decks level of the platform on which some of the Arabs in the 'tween decks were working. In consequence of the breakage of the cases there was a considerable amount of petrol vapour in the hold. In the course of heaving a sling of the cases from the hold the rope by which the sling was being raised or the sling itself came into contact with the boards placed across the forward end of the hatch, causing one of the boards to fall into the lower hold, and the fall was instantaneously followed by a rush of flames from the lower hold, and this resulted eventually in the total destruction of the ship.

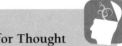

Food for Thought

Why does the court refer to "Arab" workers? Is this a fact that is legally relevant to the court's determination?

The owners contended (so far as material) that the charterers were liable for the loss of the ship; that fire caused by negligence was not an excepted peril; and that the ship was in fact lost by the negligence of the stevedores, who were the charterers' servants, in letting the sling strike the board, knocking it into the hold, and thereby causing a spark which set fire to the petrol vapour and destroyed the ship.

The charterers contended that fire however caused was an excepted peril; that there was no negligence for which the charterers were responsible, inasmuch as to let a board fall into the hold of the ship could do no harm to the ship and therefore was not negligence towards the owners; and that the danger and/or damage were too remote—i.e., no reasonable man would have foreseen danger and/or damage of this kind resulting from the fall of the board.

The three **arbitrators** made the following findings of fact:—

"(a) That the ship was lost by fire.

"(b) That the fire arose from a spark igniting petrol vapour in the hold.

"(c) That the spark was caused by the falling board coming into contact with some substance in the hold.

"(d) That the fall of the board was caused by the negligence of the Arabs (other than the winchman) engaged in the work of discharging.

"(e) That the said Arabs were employed by the charterers or their agents the Cie. Transatlantique on behalf of the charterers, and that the said Arabs were the servants of the charterers.

"(f) That the causing of the spark could not reasonably have been anticipated from the falling of the board, though some damage to the ship might reasonably have been anticipated.

"(g) There was no evidence before us that the Arabs chosen were known or likely to be negligent.

"(h) That the damages sustained by the owners through the said accident amount to the sum of 196,165*l*. 1*s*. 11*d*. as shown in the second column of the schedule hereto."

Subject to the opinion of the Court on any questions of law arising the arbitrators awarded that the owners were entitled to recover from the charterers the before-mentioned sum.

If the Court should be of opinion that the above award was wrong, then the arbitrators awarded that the owners should recover nothing from the charterers

Sankey J. affirmed the award. The charterers appealed.

. . . .

BANKES L.J.

By a time **charterparty** dated February 21, 1917, the respondents chartered their vessel to the appellants. . . . The vessel was employed by the charterers to carry a cargo to Casablanca in Morocco. The cargo included a quantity of benzine or petrol in cases. While discharging at Casablanca a heavy plank fell into the hold in which the petrol was stowed, and caused an explosion, which set fire to the vessel and completely destroyed her. The owners claimed the value of the vessel from the charterers, alleging that the loss of the vessel was due to the negligence of the charterers' servants. The charterers contended that the damages claimed were too remote. The claim was referred to **arbitration**, and the arbitrators stated a special case for the opinion of the Court. . . .

> An arbitration is a dispute resolution procedure in which nonjudicial adjudicators, usually selected by the parties, render binding decisions.

. . . .

In the present case the arbitrators have found as a fact that the falling of the plank was due to the negligence of the defendants' servants. The fire appears to me to have been directly caused by the falling of the plank. Under these circumstances I consider that it is immaterial that the causing of the spark by the falling of the plank could not have been reasonably anticipated. The appellants' junior counsel sought to draw a distinction between the anticipation of the extent of damage resulting from a negligent act, and the anticipation of the type of damage resulting from such an act. He admitted that it could not lie in the mouth of a person whose negligent act had caused damage to say that he could not reasonably have foreseen the extent of the damage, but he contended that the negligent person was entitled to rely upon the fact that he could not reasonably have anticipated the type of damage which resulted from his negligent act. I do not think that the distinction can be admitted. Given the breach of duty which constitutes the negligence, and given the damage as a direct result of that negligence, the anticipations of the person whose negligent act has produced the damage appear to me to be irrelevant. I consider that the damages claimed are not too remote.

. . . .

For these reasons I think that the appeal fails, and must be dismissed with costs.

WARRINGTON L.J.

. . . .

The only question for the Court is whether on the findings of the arbitrators as to facts they were justified in law in making an award in favour of the respondents. Sankey J. has held that they were so justified. The charterers appeal.

. . . .

The result may be summarised as follows: The presence or absence of reasonable anticipation of damage determines the legal quality of the act as negligent or innocent. If it be thus determined to be negligent, then the question whether particular damages are recoverable depends only on the answer to the question whether they are the direct consequence of the act. . . .

On the whole in my opinion the appeal fails and must be dismissed with costs.

SCRUTTON L.J.

The steamship *Thrasyvoulos* was lost by fire while being discharged by workmen employed by the charterers. Experienced arbitrators, by whose findings of fact we are bound, have decided that the fire was caused by a spark igniting petrol vapour in the hold, the vapour coming from leaks from cargo shipped by the charterers, and that the spark was caused by the Arab workmen employed by the charterers negligently knocking a plank out of a temporary staging erected in the hold, so that the plank fell into the hold, and in its fall by striking something made the spark which ignited the petrol vapour.

On these findings the charterers contend that they are not liable for two reasons: first, that they are protected by an exception of "fire" which in the charter is "mutually excepted"; secondly, that as the arbitrators have found that it could not be reasonably anticipated that the falling of the board would make a spark, the actual damage is too remote to be the subject of a claim. In my opinion both these grounds of defence fail.

. . . .

The second defence is that the damage is too remote from the negligence, as it could not be reasonably foreseen as a consequence. On this head we were referred to a number of well known cases in which vague language, which I cannot think to be really helpful, has been used in an attempt to define the point at which damage becomes too remote from, or not sufficiently directly caused by, the breach of duty, which is the original cause of action, to be recoverable. For instance, I cannot think it useful to say the damage must be the natural and probable result. This suggests that there are results which are natural but not probable, and other results which are probable but not natural. I am not sure what either adjective means in this connection; if they mean the same thing, two need not be used; if they mean different things, the difference between them should be defined. And as to many cases of fact in which the distinction has been drawn, it is difficult to see why one case should be decided one way and one another. . . . To determine whether an act is negligent, it is relevant to determine whether any reasonable person would foresee that the act would cause damage; if he would not, the act is not negligent. But if the act would or might probably cause damage, the fact that the damage it in fact causes is not the exact kind of damage one would expect is immaterial, so long as the damage is in fact directly traceable to the negligent act, and not due to the operation of independent causes having no connection with the negligent act, except that they could not avoid its results. Once the act is negligent, the fact that its exact operation was not foreseen is immaterial. . . . In the present case it was negligent in discharging cargo to knock down the planks of the temporary staging, for they might easily cause some damage either to workmen, or cargo, or the ship. The fact that they did directly produce an unexpected result, a spark in an atmosphere of petrol vapour which caused a fire, does not relieve the person who was negligent from the damage which his negligent act directly caused.

For these reasons the experienced arbitrators and the judge appealed from came, in my opinion, to a correct decision, and the appeal must be dismissed with costs.

Appeal dismissed.

———————————

Points for Discussion

1. Each of the three justices of the King's Bench concluded that the fire that destroyed the ship was directly caused by the falling of the plank due to the negligence of the defendants' workers. Given the rule announced and applied by the court, it was legally irrelevant that the type of damage caused by the negligent act was not anticipated or reasonably foreseeable. As Justice Scrutton stated, "the fact that the damage [caused by negligent conduct] is not the exact kind of damage one would expect is immaterial, so long as the damage is in fact directly traceable to the negligent act, and not due to the operation of independent causes having no connection with the negligent act, except that they could not avoid its results."

2. What policies and purposes of tort law are advanced by the *Polemis* rule and approach?

———————————

Palsgraf v. Long Island R.R. Co.

248 N.Y. 339, 162 N.E. 99 (1928)

CARDOZO, Ch. J. Plaintiff was standing on a platform of defendant's railroad after buying a ticket to go to Rockaway Beach. A train stopped at the station, bound for another place. Two men ran forward to catch it. One of the men reached the platform of the car without mishap, though the train was already moving. The other man, carrying a package, jumped aboard the car, but seemed unsteady as if about to fall. A guard on the car, who had held the door open, reached forward to help him in, and another guard on the platform pushed him from behind. In this act, the package was dislodged, and fell upon the rails. It was a package of small size, about fifteen inches long, and was covered by a newspaper. In fact it contained fireworks, but there was nothing in its appearance to give notice of its contents. The fireworks when they fell exploded. The shock of the explosion threw down some scales at the other end of the platform, many feet away. The scales struck the plaintiff, causing injuries for which she sues.

The conduct of the defendant's guard, if a wrong in its relation to the holder of the package, was not a wrong in its relation to the plaintiff, standing far away. Relatively to her it was not negligence at all. Nothing in the situation gave notice that the falling package had in it the potency of peril to persons thus removed. Negligence is not actionable unless it involves the invasion of a legally protected interest, the violation of a right. "Proof of negligence in the air, so to speak, will not do" (Pollock, Torts [11th ed.], p. 455; [cc]. "Negligence is the absence of care, according to the circumstances." [Cc] The plaintiff as she stood upon the platform of the station might claim to be protected against intentional invasion of her bodily security. Such invasion is not charged. She might claim to be protected against unintentional invasion by conduct involving in the thought of reasonable men an unreasonable hazard that such invasion would ensue. These, from the point of view of the law, were the bounds of her immunity, with perhaps some rare exceptions, survivals for the most part of ancient forms of liability, where conduct is held to be at the peril of the actor. [C] If no hazard was apparent to the eye of ordinary vigilance, an act innocent and harmless, at least to outward seeming, with reference to her, did not take to itself the quality of a tort because it happened to be a wrong, though apparently not one involving the risk of bodily insecurity, with reference to some one else. "In every instance, before negligence can be predicated of a given act, back of the act must be sought and found a duty to the individual complaining, the observance of which would have averted or avoided the injury." [Cc] "The ideas of negligence and duty are strictly correlative." [C] The plaintiff sues in her own right for a wrong personal to her, and not as the vicarious beneficiary of a breach of duty to another.

A different conclusion will involve us, and swiftly too, in a maze of contradictions. A guard stumbles over a package which has been left upon a platform. It seems to be a bundle of newspapers. It turns out to be a can of dynamite. To the eye of ordinary vigilance, the bundle is abandoned waste, which may be kicked or trod on with impunity. Is a passenger at the other end of the platform protected by the law against the unsuspected hazard concealed beneath the waste? If not, is the result to be any different, so far as the distant passenger is concerned, when the guard stumbles over a valise which a truckman or a porter has left upon the walk? The passenger far away, if the victim of a wrong at all, has a cause of action, not derivative, but original and primary. His claim to be protected against invasion of his bodily security is neither greater nor less because the act resulting in the invasion is a wrong to another far removed. In this case, the rights that are said to have been violated, the interests said to have been invaded, are not even of the same order. The man was not injured in his person nor even put in danger. The purpose of the act, as well as its effect, was to make his person safe. If there was a wrong to him at all, which may very well be doubted, it was a wrong to a property interest only, the safety of his package. Out of this wrong to property, which threatened injury to nothing else, there has passed, we are told, to the plaintiff by derivation or succession a right of action for the invasion of an interest of another order, the right to bodily security. The diversity of interests emphasizes the futility of the effort to build the plaintiff's right upon the basis of a wrong to some one else. The gain is one of emphasis, for a like result would follow if the interests were the same. Even then, the orbit of the danger as disclosed to the eye of reasonable vigilance would be the orbit of the duty. One who jostles one's neighbor in a crowd does not invade the rights of others standing at the outer fringe when the unintended contact casts a bomb upon the ground. The wrongdoer as to them is the man who carries the bomb, not the one who explodes it without suspicion of the danger. Life will have to be made over, and human nature transformed, before prevision so extravagant can be accepted as the norm of conduct, the customary standard to which behavior must conform.

The argument for the plaintiff is built upon the shifting meanings of such words as "wrong" and "wrongful," and shares their instability. What the plaintiff must show is "a wrong" to herself, *i. e.*, a violation of her own right, and not merely a wrong to some one else, nor conduct "wrongful" because unsocial, but not "a wrong" to any one. We are told that one who drives at reckless speed through a crowded city street is guilty of a negligent act and, therefore, of a wrongful one irrespective of the consequences. Negligent the act is, and wrongful in the sense that it is unsocial, but wrongful and unsocial in relation to other travelers, only because the eye of vigilance perceives the risk of damage. If the same act were to be committed on a speedway or a race course, it would lose its wrongful quality. The risk reasonably to be perceived defines the duty to be obeyed, and risk imports relation; it is risk to another or to others within the range of apprehension.

[Cc] This does not mean, of course, that one who launches a destructive force is always relieved of liability if the force, though known to be destructive, pursues an unexpected path. "It was not necessary that the defendant should have had notice of the particular method in which an accident would occur, if the possibility of an accident was clear to the ordinarily prudent eye" (*Munsey v. Webb*, 231 U. S. 150, 156; [cc].) Some acts, such as shooting, are so imminently dangerous to any one who may come within reach of the missile, however unexpectedly, as to impose a duty of prevision not far from that of an insurer. Even today, and much oftener in earlier stages of the law, one acts sometimes at one's peril. [Cc] Under this head, it may be, fall certain cases of what is known as transferred intent, an act willfully dangerous to A resulting by misadventure in injury to B (*Talmage v. Smith,* 101 Mich. 370, 374). These cases aside, wrong is defined in terms of the natural or probable, at least when unintentional. [C] The range of reasonable apprehension is at times a question for the court, and at times, if varying inferences are possible, a question for the jury. Here, by concession, there was nothing in the situation to suggest to the most cautious mind that the parcel wrapped in newspaper would spread wreckage through the station. If the guard had thrown it down knowingly and willfully, he would not have threatened the plaintiff's safety, so far as appearances could warn him. His conduct would not have involved, even then, an unreasonable probability of invasion of her bodily security. Liability can be no greater where the act is inadvertent.

Negligence, like risk, is thus a term of relation. Negligence in the abstract, apart from things related, is surely not a tort, if indeed it is understandable at all. [C] Negligence is not a tort unless it results in the commission of a wrong, and the commission of a wrong imports the violation of a right, in this case, we are told, the right to be protected against interference with one's bodily security. But bodily security is protected, not against all forms of interference or aggression, but only against some. One who seeks redress at law does not make out a cause of action by showing without more that there has been damage to his person. If the harm was not willful, he must show that the act as to him had possibilities of danger so many and apparent as to entitle him to be protected against the doing of it though the harm was unintended. Affront to personality is still the keynote of the wrong. Confirmation of this view will be found in the history and development of the action on the case. Negligence as a basis of civil liability was unknown to mediaeval law. [Cc] For damage to the person, the sole remedy was **trespass**, and trespass did not lie in the absence of aggression, and that direct and personal. [Cc] Liability for other damage, as where a servant without orders from the master does or omits something to the damage of another, is a plant of later growth. [Cc] When it emerged out of the legal soil, it was thought of as a variant of trespass, an offshoot of the parent stock. This appears in the form of action, which was known as **trespass on the case**. [Cc] The victim does not sue derivatively, or by right of subrogation, to vindicate an interest invaded in the person of another. Thus to view his cause of action is to ignore the fundamental difference between tort and crime. [C] He sues for breach of a duty owing to himself.

The law of causation, remote or proximate, is thus foreign to the case before us. The question of liability is always anterior to the question of the measure of the consequences that go with liability. If there is no tort to be redressed, there is no occasion to consider what damage might be recovered if there were a finding of a tort. We may assume, without deciding, that negligence, not at large or in the abstract, but in relation to the plaintiff, would entail liability for any and all consequences, however novel or extraordinary. [Cc]; cf. *Matter of Polemis*, L. R. 1921, 3 K. B. 560; [c]. There is room for argument that a distinction is to be drawn according to the diversity of interests invaded by the act, as where conduct negligent in that it threatens an insignificant invasion of an interest in property results in an unforseeable invasion of an interest of another order, as, *e. g.*, one of bodily security. Perhaps other distinctions may be necessary. We do not go into the question now. The consequences to be followed must first be rooted in a wrong.

FYI

Judge John Noonan has noted that Cardozo imposed costs on Mrs. Palsgraf. JOHN T. NOONAN, JR., PERSONS AND MASKS OF THE LAW 144 (1976), and Mrs. Palsgraf complained that the $559 in costs were "so large a sum to me that I have been and will be unable to pay it, except at great sacrifice after a long time." William H. Manz, *Palsgraf: Cardozo's Urban Legend?*, 107 DICKINSON L. REV. 785, 786 n.6 (2003).

The judgment of the Appellate Division and that of the Trial Term should be reversed, and the complaint dismissed, with costs in all courts.

ANDREWS, J. (dissenting).

Assisting a passenger to board a train, the defendant's servant negligently knocked a package from his arms. It fell between the platform and the cars. Of its contents the servant knew and could know nothing. A violent explosion followed. The concussion broke some scales standing a considerable distance away. In falling they injured the plaintiff, an intending passenger.

Upon these facts may she recover the damages she has suffered in an action brought against the master? The result we shall reach depends upon our theory as to the nature of negligence. Is it a relative concept-the breach of some duty owing to a particular person or to particular persons? Or where there is an act which unreasonably threatens the safety of others, is the doer liable for all its proximate consequences, even where they result in injury to one who would generally be thought to be outside the radius of danger? This is not a mere dispute as to words. We might not believe that to the average mind the dropping of the bundle would seem to involve the probability of harm to the plaintiff standing many feet away whatever might be the case as to the owner or to one so near as to be likely to be struck by its fall. If, however, we adopt the second hypothesis we have to inquire only as to the relation between cause and effect. We deal in terms of proximate cause, not of negligence.

Negligence may be defined roughly as an act or omission which unreasonably does or may affect the rights of others, or which unreasonably fails to protect oneself from the dangers resulting from such acts. Here I confine myself to the first branch of the definition. Nor do I comment on the word "unreasonable." For present purposes it sufficiently describes that average of conduct that society requires of its members.

There must be both the act or the omission, and the right. It is the act itself, not the intent of the actor, that is important. [Cc] In criminal law both the intent and the result are to be considered. Intent again is material in tort actions, where punitive damages are sought, dependent on actual malice- not on merely reckless conduct. But here neither insanity nor infancy lessens responsibility. [C]

As has been said, except in cases of **contributory negligence**, there must be rights which are or may be affected. Often though injury has occurred, no rights of him who suffers have been touched. A licensee or trespasser upon my land has no claim to affirmative care on my part that the land be made safe. [C] Where a railroad is required to fence its tracks against cattle, no man's rights are injured should he wander upon the road because such fence is absent. [C] An unborn child may not demand immunity from personal harm. [C]

But we are told that "there is no negligence unless there is in the particular case a legal duty to take care, and this duty must be one which is owed to the plaintiff himself and not merely to others." [C] This, I think too narrow a conception. Where there is the unreasonable act, and some right that may be affected there is negligence whether damage does or does not result. That is immaterial. Should we drive down Broadway at a reckless speed, we are negligent whether we strike an approaching car or miss it by an inch. The act itself is wrongful. It is a wrong not only to those who happen to be within the radius of danger but to all who might have been there- a wrong to the public at large. Such is the language of the street. Such the language of the courts when speaking of contributory negligence. Such again and again their language in speaking of the duty of some defendant and discussing proximate cause in cases where such a discussion is wholly irrelevant on any other theory. [C] As was said by Mr. Justice HOLMES many years ago, "the measure of the defendant's duty in determining whether a wrong has been committed is one thing, the measure of liability when a wrong has been committed is another." [C] Due care is a duty imposed on each one of us to protect society from unnecessary danger, not to protect A, B or C alone.

It may well be that there is no such thing as negligence in the abstract. "Proof of negligence in the air, so to speak, will not do." In an empty world negligence would not exist. It does involve a relationship between man and his fellows. But not merely a relationship between man and those whom he might reasonably expect his act would injure. Rather, a relationship between him and those whom he does in fact injure. If his act has a tendency to harm some one, it harms him a mile away as surely as it does those on the scene. We now permit children to recover for the negligent killing of the father. It was never prevented on the theory that no duty was owing to them. A husband may be compensated for the loss of his wife's services. To say that the wrongdoer was negligent as to the husband as well as to the wife is merely an attempt to fit facts to theory. An insurance company paying a fire loss recovers its payment of the negligent incendiary. We speak of subrogation-of suing in the right of the insured. Behind the cloud of words is the fact they hide, that the act, wrongful as to the insured, has also injured the company. Even if it be true that the fault of father, wife or insured will prevent recovery, it is because we consider the original negligence not the proximate cause of the injury. [C]

In the well-known *Polemis Case* (1921, 3 K. B. 560), SCRUTTON, L. J., said that the dropping of a plank was negligent for it might injure "workman or cargo or ship." Because of either possibility the owner of the vessel was to be made good for his loss. The act being wrongful the doer was liable for its proximate results. Criticized and explained as this statement may have been, I think it states the law as it should be and as it is. [Cc]

The proposition is this. Every one owes to the world at large the duty of refraining from those acts that may unreasonably threaten the safety of others. Such an act occurs. Not only is he wronged to whom harm might reasonably be expected to result, but he also who is in fact injured, even if he be outside what would generally be thought the danger zone. There needs be duty due the one complaining but this is not a duty to a particular individual because as to him harm might be expected. Harm to some one being the natural result of the act, not only that one alone, but all those in fact injured may complain. We have never, I think, held otherwise. Indeed in the *Di Caprio* case we said that a breach of a general ordinance defining the degree of care to be exercised in one's calling is evidence of negligence as to every one. We did not limit this statement to those who might be expected to be exposed to danger. Unreasonable risk being taken, its consequences are not confined to those who might probably be hurt.

If this be so, we do not have a plaintiff suing by "derivation or succession." Her action is original and primary. Her claim is for a breach of duty to herself-not that she is subrogated to any right of action of the owner of the parcel or of a passenger standing at the scene of the explosion.

The right to recover damages rests on additional considerations. The plaintiff's rights must be injured, and this injury must be caused by the negligence. We build a dam, but are negligent as to its foundations. Breaking, it injures property down stream. We are not liable if all this happened because of some reason other than the insecure foundation. But when injuries do result from our unlawful act we are liable for the consequences. It does not matter that they are unusual, unexpected, unforeseen and unforeseeable. But there is one limitation. The damages must be so connected with the negligence that the latter may be said to be the proximate cause of the former.

These two words have never been given an inclusive definition. What is a cause in a legal sense, still more what is a proximate cause, depend in each case upon many considerations, as does the existence of negligence itself. Any philosophical doctrine of causation does not help us. A boy throws a stone into a pond. The ripples spread. The water level rises. The history of that pond is altered to all eternity. It will be altered by other causes also. Yet it will be forever the resultant of all causes combined. Each one will have an influence. How great only omniscience can say. You may speak of a chain, or if you please, a net. An analogy is of little aid. Each cause brings about future events. Without each the future would not be the same. Each is proximate in the sense it is essential. But that is not what we mean by the word. Nor on the other hand do we mean sole cause. There is no such thing.

Should analogy be thought helpful, however, I prefer that of a stream. The spring, starting on its journey, is joined by tributary after tributary. The river, reaching the ocean, comes from a hundred sources. No man may say whence any drop of water is derived. Yet for a time distinction may be possible. Into the clear creek, brown swamp water flows from the left. Later, from the right comes water stained by its clay bed. The three may remain for a space, sharply divided. But at last, inevitably no trace of separation remains. They are so commingled that all distinction is lost.

As we have said, we cannot trace the effect of an act to the end, if end there is. Again, however, we may trace it part of the way. A murder at Serajevo may be the necessary antecedent to an assassination in London twenty years hence. An overturned lantern may burn all Chicago. We may follow the fire from the shed to the last building. We rightly say the fire started by the lantern caused its destruction.

A cause, but not the proximate cause. What we do mean by the word "proximate" is, that because of convenience, of public policy, of a rough sense of justice, the law arbitrarily declines to trace a series of events beyond a certain point. This is not logic. It is practical politics. Take our rule as to fires. Sparks from my burning haystack set on fire my house and my neighbor's. I may recover from a negligent railroad. He may not. Yet the wrongful act as directly harmed the one as the other. We may regret that the line was drawn just where it was, but drawn somewhere it had to be. We said the act of the railroad was not the proximate cause of our neighbor's fire. Cause it surely was. The words we used were simply indicative of our notions of public policy. Other courts think differently. But somewhere they reach the point where they cannot say the stream comes from any one source.

Take the illustration given in an unpublished manuscript by a distinguished and helpful writer on the law of torts. A chauffeur negligently collides with another car which is filled with dynamite, although he could not know it. An explosion follows. A, walking on the sidewalk nearby, is killed. B, sitting in a window of a building opposite, is cut by flying glass. C, likewise sitting in a window a block away, is similarly injured. And a further illustration. A nursemaid, ten blocks away, startled by the noise, involuntarily drops a baby from her arms to the walk. We are told that C may not recover while A may. As to B it is a question for court or jury. We will all agree that the baby might not. Because, we are again told, the chauffeur had no reason to believe his conduct involved any risk of injuring either C or the baby. As to them he was not negligent.

But the chauffeur, being negligent in risking the collision, his belief that the scope of the harm he might do would be limited is immaterial. His act unreasonably jeopardized the safety of any one who might be affected by it. C's injury and that of the baby were directly traceable to the collision. Without that, the injury would not have happened. C had the right to sit in his office, secure from such dangers. The baby was entitled to use the sidewalk with reasonable safety.

The true theory is, it seems to me, that the injury to C, if in truth he is to be denied recovery, and the injury to the baby is that their several injuries were not the proximate result of the negligence. And here not what the chauffeur had reason to believe would be the result of his conduct, but what the prudent would foresee, may have a bearing. May have some bearing, for the problem of proximate cause is not to be solved by any one consideration.

It is all a question of expediency. There are no fixed rules to govern our judgment. There are simply matters of which we may take account. We have in a somewhat different connection spoken of "the stream of events." We have asked whether that stream was deflected-whether it was forced into new and unexpected channels. [C] This is rather rhetoric than law. There is in truth little to guide us other than common sense.

There are some hints that may help us. The proximate cause, involved as it may be with many other causes, must be, at the least, something without which the event would not happen. The court must ask itself whether there was a natural and continuous sequence between cause and effect. Was the one a substantial factor in producing the other? Was there a direct connection between them, without too many intervening causes? Is the effect of cause on result not too attentuated?

Is the cause likely, in the usual judgment of mankind, to produce the result? Or by the exercise of prudent foresight could the result be foreseen? Is the result too remote from the cause, and here we consider remoteness in time and space. [C] Clearly we must so consider, for the greater the distance either in time or space, the more surely do other causes intervene to affect the result. When a lantern is overturned the firing of a shed is a fairly direct consequence. Many things contribute to the spread of the conflagration—the force of the wind, the direction and width of streets, the character of intervening structures, other factors. We draw an uncertain and wavering line, but draw it we must as best we can.

Once again, it is all a question of fair judgment, always keeping in mind the fact that we endeavor to make a rule in each case that will be practical and in keeping with the general understanding of mankind.

Here another question must be answered. In the case supposed it is said, and said correctly, that the chauffeur is liable for the direct effect of the explosion although he had no reason to suppose it would follow a collision. "The fact that the injury occurred in a different manner than that which might have been expected does not prevent the chauffeur's negligence from being in law the cause of the injury." But the natural results of a negligent act—the results which a prudent man would or should foresee—do have a bearing upon the decision as to proximate cause. We have said so repeatedly. What should be foreseen? No human foresight would suggest that a collision itself might injure one a block away. On the contrary, given an explosion, such a possibility might be reasonably expected. I think the direct connection, the foresight of which the courts speak, assumes prevision of the explosion, for the immediate results of which, at least, the chauffeur is responsible.

It may be said this is unjust. Why? In fairness he should make good every injury flowing from his negligence. Not because of tenderness toward him we say he need not answer for all that follows his wrong. We look back to the catastrophe, the fire kindled by the spark, or the explosion. We trace the consequences—not indefinitely, but to a certain point. And to aid us in fixing that point we ask what might ordinarily be expected to follow the fire or the explosion.

This last suggestion is the factor which must determine the case before us. The act upon which defendant's liability rests is knocking an apparently harmless package onto the platform. The act was negligent. For its proximate consequences the defendant is liable. If its contents were broken, to the owner; if it fell upon and crushed a passenger's foot, then to him. If it exploded and injured one in the immediate vicinity, to him also as to A in the illustration. Mrs. Palsgraf was standing some distance away. How far cannot be told from the record—apparently twenty-five or thirty feet. Perhaps less. Except for the explosion, she would not have been injured. We are told by the appellant in his brief "it cannot be denied that the explosion was the direct cause of the plaintiff's injuries." So it was a substantial factor in producing the result—there was here a natural and continuous sequence—direct connection. The only intervening cause was that instead of blowing her to the ground the concussion smashed the weighing machine which in turn fell upon her. There was no remoteness in time, little in space. And surely, given such an explosion as here it needed no great foresight to predict that the natural result would be to injure one on the platform at no greater distance from its scene than was the plaintiff. Just how no one might be able to predict. Whether by flying fragments, by broken glass, by wreckage of machines or structures no one could say. But injury in some form was most probable.

Under these circumstances I cannot say as a matter of law that the plaintiff's injuries were not the proximate result of the negligence. That is all we have before us. The court refused to so charge. No request was made to submit the matter to the jury as a question of fact, even would that have been proper upon the record before us.

The judgment appealed from should be affirmed, with costs.

POUND, LEHMAN and KELLOGG, JJ., concur with CARDOZO, Ch. J.

ANDREWS, J., dissents in opinion in which CRANE and O'BRIEN, JJ., concur.

Judgment reversed, etc.

────────────

Points for Discussion

1. What is the holding of *Palsgraf*? In answering this question consider the following. Cardozo: "The law of causation, remote or proximate, is thus foreign to the case before us." Andrews: "We deal in terms of proximate cause, not of negligene."

2. Cardozo argues that "no hazard [to the plaintiff] was apparent to the eye of ordinary vigilance," and that "[t]he risk reasonably to be perceived defines the duty to be obeyed and risk imports relation; it is risk to another or to others within the range of apprehension." Discussing the jostling of a person in the crowd unintentionally causing a bomb to fall onto the ground, he opines: "The wrongdoer . . . is the man who carries the bomb, not the one who explodes it without suspicion of the danger. Life will have to be made over, and human nature transformed, before prevision so extravagant can be accepted as the norm of conduct, the customary standard to which behavior

must conform." Is Cardozo referring to the issue of the defendant's duty or the breach thereof or both duty and breach?

3. In Cardozo's view, if the defendant's conduct in relation to Mrs. Palsgraf had constituted actionable negligence, would the defendant have been liable for her injuries?

4. In dissent, Andrews argues that "[e]very one owes to the world at large the duty of refraining from those acts that may unreasonably threaten the safety of others." As for proximate cause, he opined: "What we do mean by the word 'proximate' is, that because of convenience, of public policy, of a rough sense of justice, the law arbitrarily declines to trace a series of events beyond a certain point. This is not logic. It is practical politics." Is this a useful approach to the proximate causation issue? What is "practical politics"? And what rule would Andrews have applied with respect to a defendant's liability for negligent conduct?

5. Note that Cardozo states that, at the time of the explosion of the fireworks, Mrs. Palsgraf was standing "at the other end of the platform, many feet away." The dissenting Andrews wrote that "Mrs. Palsgraf was standing some distance away. How far cannot be told from the record—apparently 25 or 30 feet, perhaps less." Any disagreement as to the distance between the source of the explosion and where Mrs. Palsgraf was actually standing on the platform did not change the court's view of the proper resolution of the case. Denying a motion for reargument, the court stated, "If we assume that the plaintiff was nearer the scene of the explosion than the prevailing opinion would suggest, she was not so near that the injury from a falling package, not known to contain explosives, would be within the range of reasonable prevision." Palsgraf v. Long Island R.R. Co., 164 N.E. 564 (N.Y. 1928) (per curiam).

6. See Restatement (Second) of Torts § 281 (1965): an "actor is liable for an invasion of an interest of another" if "the interest invaded is protected against unintentional invasion" and "the conduct of the actor is negligent with respect to the other, or a class of persons within which he is included. . . ." See also Restatement (Third) of Torts: Liability for Physical Harm § 29 (2010) ("An actor's liability is limited to those physical harms that result from the risks that made the actor's conduct tortious.") and comment *d* ("[A]n actor should be held liable only for harm that was among the potential harms—the risks—that made the actor's conduct tortious. . . . This limit on liability serves the purpose of avoiding what might be unjustified or enormous liability by confining liability's scope to the reasons for holding the actor liable in the first place.").

Overseas Tankship (U.K.) Ltd. v. Morts Dock & Engineering Co. Ltd. (Wagon Mound No. 1)

[1961] A.C. 388

Appeal . . . from an order of the Full Court of the Supreme Court of New South Wales . . . dismissing an appeal by the appellants, Overseas Tankship (U.K.) Lrd., from a judgment of Kinsella, J. . . .

The following facts are taken from the judgmen of the Judicial Committee: In the action the respondents sought to recover from the appellants compensation for the damage which is the property known as the Sheerlegs Wharf, in Sydney Harbour, and the equipment thereon had suffered by reason of fire which broke out on November 1, 1951. For that damage they claimed that the appellants were in law responsible.

. . . .

The respondents at the relevant time carried on the business of ship-building, ship-repairing and general engineering at Morts Bay, Balmain, in the Port of Sydney. They owned and used for their business the Sheerlegs Wharf, a timber wharf about 400 feet in length and 40 feet wide, where there was a quantity of tools and equipment. In October and November, 1951, a vessel known as the *Corrimel* was moored alongside the wharf and was being refitted by the respondents. Her mast was lying on the wharf and a number of the respondents' employees were working both upon it and upon the vessel itself, using for that purpose electric and oxy-acetylene welding equipment.

At the same time the appellants were charterers by demise of the *S.S. Wagon Mound*, an oil-burning vessel, which was moored at the Caltex Wharf on the northern shore of the harbour at a distance of about 600 feet from the Sheerlegs Wharf. She was there from about 9 a.m. on October 29 until 11 a.m. on October 30, 1951, for the purpose of discharging gasoline products and taking in bunkering oil.

During the early hours of October 30, 1951, a large quantity of bunkering oil was, through the carelessness of the appellants' servants, allowed to spill into the bay, and by 10:30 on the morning of that day it had spread over a considerable part of the bay, being thickly concentrated in some places and particularly along the foreshore near the respondents' property. The appellants made no attempt to disperse the oil. The *Wagon Mound* unberthed and set sail very shortly after.

When the respondents' work manager became aware of the condition of things in the vicinity of the wharf he instructed their workmen that no welding or burning was to be carried on until further orders. He inquired of the manager of the Caltex

Oil Company, at whose wharf the *Wagon Mound* was then still berthed, whether they could safely continue their operations on the wharf or upon the *Corrimal*. The results of the inquiry coupled with his own belief as to the inflammability of furnace oil in the open led him to think that the respondents could safely carry on their operations. He gave instructions accordingly, but directed that all safety precautions should be taken to prevent inflammable material falling off the wharf into the oil.

For the remainder of October 30 and until about 2 p.m. on November 1 work was carried on as usual, the condition and congestion of the oil remaining substantially unaltered. But at about that time the oil under or near the wharf was ignited and a fire, fed initially by the oil, spread rapidly and burned with great intensity. The wharf and the *Corrimal* caught fire and considerable damage was done to the wharf and the equipment upon it.

The outbreak of the fire was due, as the judge found, to the fact that there was floating in the oil underneath the wharf a piece of debris on which lay some smouldering cotton waste or rag which had been set on fire by molten metal falling from the wharf: that the cotton waste or rag burst into flames: that the flames from the cotton waste set the floating oil afire either directly or by first setting fire to a wooden pile coated with oil, and that after the floating oil became ignited the flames spread rapidly over the surface of the oil and quickly developed into a conflagration which severely damages the wharf.

1961. January 18. The judgment of their Lordships was delivered by Viscount Simonds, who stated the facts set out above and continued: The trial judge also made the all-important finding, which must be set out in his own words: "The raison d'être of furnace oil is, of course, that it shall burn, but I find the defendant did not know and could not be reasonably be expected to have known that it was capable for being set afire when spread on water." This finding was reached after a wealth of evidence . . .

One other finding must be mentioned. The judge held that apart from damage by fire the respondents had suffered some damage from the spillage of the oil in that it had got upon their slipways and congealed upon them and interfered with their use of the slips. He said: "The evidence of this damage is slight and no claim for compensation is made in respect of it. Nevertheless it does establish some damage, which may be insignificant in comparison with the magnitude of the damage by fire, but which nevertheless is damage which, beyond question, was a direct result of the escape of the oil." It is upon this footing that their Lordships will consider the question whether the appellants are liable for the fire damage. . . .

It is inevitable that first consideration should be given to the case of *In Re Polemis and Furness, Withy & Co., Ltd.* . . . For it was avowedly in deference to that decision and to decisions of the Court of Appeal that followed it that the Full

Court was constrained to decide the present case in favour of the respondents. In doing so Manning J., after a full examination of that case, said: "To say that the problems, doubts and difficulties which I have expressed above render it difficult for me to apply the decision in *In re Polemis* with any degree of confidence to a particular set of facts would be a grave understatement. I can only express the hope that, if not in this case, then in some other case in the near future, the subject will be pronounced upon by the House of Lords or the Privy Council in terms which, if even beyond my capacity fully to understand, will facilitate, for those placed as I am, its everyday application to current problems." This cri de coeur would in any case be irresistible, but in the years that have passed since its decision *Polemis* has been so much discussed and qualified that it cannot claim, as counsel for the respondents urged for it, the status of a decision of such long standing that it should not be reviewed.

. . . .

There can be no doubt that the decision of the Court of Appeal in *Polemis* plainly asserts that, if the defendant is guilty of negligence, he is responsible for all the consequences whether reasonably foreseeable or not. The generality of the proposition is perhaps qualified by the fact that each of the Lords Justices refers to the outbreak of fire as the direct result of the negligent act. There is thus introduced the conception that the negligent actor is not responsible for consequences which are not "direct," whatever that may mean. It has to be asked, then, why this conclusion should have been reached. The answer appears to be that it was reached upon a consideration of certain authorities, comparatively few in number, that were cited to the court. . . .

. . . .

. . . The impression that may well be left upon the reader of the scores of cases in which liability for negligence has been discussed is that the courts were feeling their way to a coherent body of doctrine and were at times in grave danger of being led astray by scholastic theories of causation and their ugly and barely intelligible jargon.

. . . .

Enough has been said to show that the authority of *Polemis* has been severely shaken though lip-service has from time to time been paid to it. In their Lordships' opinion it should no longer be regarded as good law. It is not probable that many cases will for that reason have a different result, though it is hoped that the law will be thereby simplified, and that in some cases, at least, palpable injustice will be avoided. For it does not seem consonant with current ideas of justice or morality that for an act of negligence, however slight or venial, which results in some trivial foreseeable damage the actor should be liable for all consequences however unforeseeable and however grave, so long as they can be said to be "direct." It is a principle of civil liability, subject only to qualifications which have no present relevance, that a man must be considered to be responsible for the probable consequences of his act. To demand more of him is too harsh a rule, to demand less is to ignore that civilized order requires the observance of a minimum standard of behaviour.

This concept applied to the slowly developing law of negligence has led to a great variety of expressions which can, as it appears to their Lordships, be harmonized with little difficulty with the single exception of the so-called rule in *Polemis*. For, if it is asked why a man should be responsible for the natural or necessary or probable consequences of his act (or any other similar description of them) the answer is that it is not because they are natural or necessary or probable, but because, since they have this quality, it is judged by the standard of the reasonable man that he ought to have foreseen them. Thus it is that over and over again it has happened that in different judgments in the same case, and sometimes in a single judgment, liability for a consequence has been imposed on the ground that it was reasonably foreseeable or, alternatively, on the ground that it was natural or necessary or probable. The two grounds have been treated as coterminous, and so they largely are. But, where they are not, the question arises as to which the wrong answer was given in *Polemis*. For, if some limitation must be imposed upon the consequences for which the negligent actor is to be held responsible—and all are agreed that some limitation there must be—why should that test (reasonable foreseeability) be rejected which, since he is judged by what the reasonable man ought to foresee, corresponds with the common conscience of mankind, and a test (the "direct" consequence) be substituted which leads to nowhere but the never-ending and insoluble problems of causation. "The lawyer," said Sir Frederick Pollock, "cannot afford to adventure himself with philosophers in the logical and metaphysical controversies that beset the idea of cause." Yet this is just what he has most unfortunately done and must continue to do if the rule in *Polemis* is to prevail. A conspicuous example occurs when the actor seeks to escape liability on the ground that the "chain of causation" is broken by a "nova causa" or "novus actus interveniens."

> **It's Latin to Me!**
>
> Non constat
> jus civile
> a posteriori
>
> *Nova causa* or *novus actus interveniens* are Latin for an intervening cause, a subject discussed below in section B.2.

. . . .

In the same connection may be mentioned the conclusion to which the Full Court finally came in the present case. Applying the rule in *Polemis* and holding therefore that the unforeseeability of the damage by fire afforded no defence, they went on to consider the remaining question. Was it a "direct" consequence? Upon this Manning J. said: "Notwithstanding that, if regard is had separately to each individual occurrence in the chain of events that led to this fire, each occurrence was improbable and, in one sense, improbability was heaped upon improbability. I cannot escape from the conclusion that if the ordinary man in the street had been asked, as a matter of common sense, without any detailed analysis of the circumstances, to state the cause of the fire at Mort's Dock, he would unhesitatingly have assigned such cause to spillage of oil by the appellant's employees." Perhaps he would, and probably he would have added: "I never should have thought it possible." But with great respect to the Full Court this is surely irrelevant, or, if it is relevant, only serves to show that the *Polemis* rule works in a very strange way. After the event even a fool is wise. But it is not the hindsight of a fool; it is the foresight of the reasonable man which alone can determine responsibility. The *Polemis* rule by substituting "direct" for "reasonably foreseesable" consequence leads to a conclusion equally illogical and unjust.

. . . .

It is, no doubt, proper when considering tortious liability for negligence to analyse its elements and to say that the plaintiff must prove a duty owed to him by the defendant, a breach of that duty by the defendant, and consequent damage. But there can be no liability until the damage has been done. It is not the act but the consequences on which tortious liability is founded. Just as (as it has been said) there is no such thing as negligence in the air, so there is no such thing as liability in the air. Suppose an action brought by A for damage caused by the carelessness (a neutral word) of B, for example, a fire caused by the careless spillage of oil. It may, of course, become relevant to know what duty B owed to A, but the only liability that is in question is the liability for damage by fire. It is vain to isolate the liability from its context and to say that B is or is not liable, and then to ask for what damage he is liable. For his liability is in respect of that damage and no other. If, as admittedly it is, B's liability (culpability) depends on the reasonable foreseeability of the consequent damage, how is that to be determined except by the foreseeability of the damage which in fact happened—the damage in suit? And, if that damage is unforeseeable so as to displace liability at large, how can the liability be restored so as to make compensation payable?

But, it is said, a different position arises if B's careless act has been shown to be negligent and has caused some foreseeable damage to A. Their Lordships have already observed that to hold B liable for consequences however unforeseeable of a careless act, if, but only if, he is at the same time liable for some other damage however trivial appears to be neither logical nor just. This becomes more clear if it is supposed that similar unforeseeable damage is suffered by A and C but other foreseeable damage, for which B is liable, by A only. A system of law which would hold B liable to A but not to C for similar damage suffered by each of them could not easily be defended. Fortunately, the attempt is not necessary. For the same fallacy is at the root of the proposition. It is irrelevant to the question whether B is liable for unforeseeable damage that he is liable for foreseeable damage, as irrelevant as would the fact that he trespassed on Whiteacre be to the question whether he had trespassed on Blackacre. Again, suppose a claim by A for damage by fire by the careless act of B. Of what relevance is it to that claim that he has another claim arising out of the same careless act? It would surely not prejudice his claim if that other claim failed: it cannot assist it if it succeeds. Each of them rests on its own bottom, and will fail if it can be established that the damage could not reasonably be foreseen. . . .

Their Lordships conclude this part of the case with some general observations. They have been concerned primarily to displace the proposition that unforesesability is irrelevant if damage is "direct." In doing so they have inevitably insisted that the essential factor in determining liability is whether the damage is of such a kind as the reasonable man should have foreseen. This accords with the general view stated by Lord Atkin in *Donoghue v. Stevenson:* "The liability for negligence, whether you style it such or treat it as in other systems as a species of 'culpa,' is no doubt based upon a general public sentiment of moral wrongdoing for which the offender must pay." [1932] A.C. 562, 580. It is a departure from this sovereign principle if liability is made to depend solely on the damage being the "direct" or "natural" consequence of the precedent act. Who knows or can be assumed to know all the processes of nature? But if it would be wrong that a man should be held liable for damage unpredictable by a reasonable man because it was "direct" or "natural," equally it would be wrong that he should escape liability, however "indirect" the damage, if he foresaw or could reasonably foresee the intervening events which led to its being done. [C] Thus, foreseeability becomes the effective test. . . .

. . . .

Their Lordships will humbly advise Her Majesty that this appeal should be allowed, and the respondents' action so far as it related to damage caused by the negligence of the appellants be dismissed with costs, but that the action so far as it related to damage caused by nuisance should be remitted to the Full Court to be dealt with as that court may think fit. . . .

Overseas Tankship (U.K.) Ltd. v. Miller Steamship Co. (Wagon Mound No. 2)

[1967] 1 A.C. 617

1966. May 25.

The judgment of the Board was delivered by LORD REID.

This is an appeal from a judgment of Walsh J. dated October 10, 1963, in the Supreme Court of New South Wales in commercial cases by which he awarded to the respondents sums of £80,000 and £1,000 in respect of damage from fire sustained by their vessels *Corrimal* and *Audrey D* on November 1, 1951. These vessels were then at Sheerlegs Wharf, Morts Bay, in Sydney Harbour undergoing repairs. The appellant was charterer by demise of a vessel, the *Wagon Mound*, which in the early hours of October 30, 1951, had been taking in bunkering oil from Caltex Wharf not far from Sheerlegs Wharf. By reason of carelessness of the *Wagon Mound* engineers a large quantity of this oil overflowed from the *Wagon Mound* onto the surface of the water. Some hours later much of the oil had drifted to and accumulated round Sheerlegs Wharf and the respondents' vessels. About 2 p.m. on November 1 this oil was set alight: the fire spread rapidly and caused extensive damage to the wharf and to the respondents' vessels.

An action was raised against the present appellant by the owners of Sheerlegs Wharf on the ground of negligence. On appeal to the Board it was held that the plaintiffs were not entitled to recover on the ground that it was not foreseeable that such oil on the surface of the water could be set alight: The issue of nuisance was also raised but their Lordships did not deal with it: they remitted this issue to the Supreme Court and their Lordships now understand that the matter was not pursued there in that case.

In the present case the respondents sue alternatively in nuisance and negligence. Walsh J. had found in their favour in nuisance but against them in negligence. Before their Lordships the appellant appeals against his decision on nuisance and the respondents appeal against his decision on negligence.

Their Lordships are indebted to that learned judge for the full and careful survey of the evidence which is set out in his judgment. Few of his findings of fact have been attacked, and their Lordships do not find it necessary to set out or deal with the evidence at any length. But it is desirable to give some explanation of how the fire started before setting out the learned judge's findings.

In the course of repairing the respondents' vessels the Morts Dock Co., the owners of Sheerlegs Wharf, were carrying out oxyacetylene welding and cutting. This work was apt to cause pieces or drops of hot metal to fly off and fall in the sea. So when their manager arrived on the morning of October 30 and saw the thick scum of oil round the wharf he was apprehensive of fire danger and he stopped the work while he took advice. He consulted the manager of Caltex wharf and after some further consultation he was assured that he was safe to proceed: so he did so, and the repair work was carried on normally until the fire broke out on November 1. Oil of this character with a flash point of 170°F. is extremely difficult to ignite in the open. But we now know that that is not impossible. There is no certainty about how this oil was set alight, but the most probable explanation, accepted by Walsh J., is that there was floating in the oil covered water some object supporting a piece of inflammable material, and that a hot piece of metal fell on it when it burned for a sufficient time to ignite the surrounding oil.

The findings of the learned trial judge are as follows:

"(1) Reasonable people in the position of the officers of the *Wagon Mound* would regard the furnace oil as very difficult to ignite upon water. (2) Their personal experience would probably have been that this had very rarely happened. (3) If they had given attention to the risk of fire from the spillage, they would have regarded it as a possibility, but one which could become an actuality only in very exceptional circumstances. (4) They would have considered the chances of the required exceptional circumstances happening whilst the oil remained spread on the harbour waters as being remote. (5) I find that the occurrence of damage to the plaintiff's property as a result of the spillage was not reasonably foreseeable by those for whose acts the defendant would be responsible. (6) I find that the spillage of oil was brought about by the careless conduct of persons for whose acts the defendant would be responsible. (7) I find that the spillage of oil was a cause of damage to the property of each of the plaintiffs. (8) Having regard to those findings, and because of finding (5), I hold that the claim of each of the plaintiffs, framed in negligence, fails."

. . . .

. . . In their Lordships' judgment the similarities between nuisance and other forms of tort to which *The Wagon Mound (No. 1)* applies far outweigh any differences, and they must therefore hold that the judgment appealed from is wrong on this branch of the case. It is not sufficient that the injury suffered by respondents' vessels was the direct result of the nuisance if that injury was in the relevant sense unforeseeable.

It is now necessary to turn to the respondents' submission that the trial judge was wrong in holding that damage from fire was not reasonably foreseeable. In *The Wagon Mound (No. 1)* the finding on which the Board proceeded was that of the trial judge: "the defendant did not know and could not reasonably be expected to have known that [the oil] was capable of being set afire when spread on water." In the present case the evidence led was substantially different from the evidence led in and the findings of Walsh J. are significantly different. That is not due to there having been any failure by the plaintiffs in *The Wagon Mound (No. 1)* in preparing and presenting their case. The plaintiffs there were no doubt embarrassed by a difficulty which does not affect the present plaintiffs. The outbreak of the fire was consequent on the act of the manager of the plaintiffs in *The Wagon Mound (No. 1)* in resuming oxy-acetylene welding and cutting while the wharf was surrounded by this oil. So if the plaintiffs in the former case had set out to prove that it was foreseeable by the engineers of the *Wagon Mound* that this oil could be set alight, they might have had difficulty in parrying the reply that this must also have been foreseeable by their manager. Then there would have been contributory negligence and at that time contributory negligence was a complete defence in New South Wales.

The crucial finding of Walsh J. in this case is in finding (5): that the damage was "not reasonably foreseeable by those for whose acts the defendant would be responsible." That is not a primary finding of fact but an inference from the other findings, and it is clear from the learned judge's judgment that in drawing this inference he was to a large extent influenced by his view of the law. The vital parts of the findings of fact which have already been set out in full are (1) that the officers of the *Wagon Mound* "would regard furnace oil as very difficult to ignite upon water" - not that they would regard this as impossible; (2) that their experience would probably have been "that this had very rarely happened" - not that they would never have heard of a case where it had happened, and (3) that they would have regarded it as a "possibility, but one which could become an actuality only in very exceptional circumstances" - not, as in , that they could not reasonably be expected to have known that this oil was capable of being set afire when spread on water. The question which must now be determined is whether these differences between the findings in the two cases do or do not lead to different results in law.

In *The Wagon Mound (No. 1)* the Board were not concerned with degrees of foreseeability because the finding was that the fire was not foreseeable at all. So Lord Simonds had no cause to amplify the statement that the "essential factor in determining liability is whether the damage is of such a kind as the reasonable man should have foreseen." But here the findings show that some risk of fire would have been present to the mind of a reasonable man in the shoes of the ship's chief engineer. So the first question must be what is the precise meaning to be attached in this context to the words "foreseeable" and "reasonably foreseeable."

Before *Bolton v. Stone* [(1932 146 L.T. 391] the cases had fallen into two classes: (1) those where, before the event, the risk of its happening would have been regarded as unreal either because the event would have been thought to be physically impossible or because the possibility of its happening would have been regarded as so fantastic or farfetched that no reasonable man would have paid any attention to it—"a mere possibility which would never occur to the mind of a reasonable man". . . or (2) those where there was a real and substantial risk or chance that something like the event which happens might occur, and then the reasonable man would have taken the steps necessary to eliminate the risk.

Bolton v. Stone posed a new problem. There a member of a visiting team drove a cricket ball out of the ground onto an unfrequented adjacent public road and it struck and severely injured a lady who happened to be standing in the road. That it might happen that a ball would be driven onto this road could not have been said to be a fantastic or far-fetched possibility: according to the evidence it had happened about six times in 28 years. And it could not have been said to be a far-fetched or fantastic possibility that such a ball would strike someone in the road: people did pass along the road from time to time. So it could not have been said that, on any ordinary meaning of the words, the fact that a ball might strike a person in the road was not foreseeable or reasonably foreseeable—it was plainly foreseeable. But the chance of its happening in the foreseeable future was infinitesimal. A mathematician given the data could have worked out that it was only likely to happen once in so many thousand years. The House of Lords held that the risk was so small that in the circumstances a reasonable man would have been justified in disregarding it and taking no steps to eliminate it.

But it does not follow that, no matter what the circumstances may be, it is justifiable to neglect a risk of such a small magnitude. A reasonable man would only neglect such a risk if he had some valid reason for doing so, e.g., that it would involve considerable expense to eliminate the risk. He would weigh the risk against the difficulty of eliminating it. If the activity which caused the injury to Miss Stone had been an unlawful activity, there can be little doubt but that would have been decided differently. In their Lordships' judgment *Bolton v. Stone* did not alter the general principle that a person must be regarded as negligent if he does not take steps to eliminate a risk which he knows or ought to know is a real risk and not a mere possibility which would never influence the mind of a reasonable man. What that decision did was to recognise and give effect to the qualification that it is justifiable not to take steps to eliminate a real risk if it is small and if the circumstances are such that a reasonable man, careful of the safety of his neighbour, would think it right to neglect it.

In the present case there was no justification whatever for discharging the oil into Sydney Harbour. Not only was it an offence to do so, but it involved considerable loss financially. If the ship's engineer had thought about the matter, there could have been no question of balancing the advantages and disadvantages. From every point of view it was both his duty and his interest to stop the discharge immediately.

It follows that in their Lordships' view the only question is whether a reasonable man having the knowledge and experience to be expected of the chief engineer of the *Wagon Mound* would have known that there was a real risk of the oil on the water catching fire in some way: if it did, serious damage to ships or other property was not only foreseeable but very likely. Their Lordships do not dissent from the view of the trial judge that the possibilities of damage "must be significant enough in a practical sense to require a reasonable man to guard against them" but they think that he may have misdirected himself in saying

> "there does seem to be a real practical difficulty, assuming that some risk of fire damage was foreseeable, but not a high one, in making a factual judgment as to whether this risk was sufficient to attract liability if damage should occur."

In this difficult chapter of the law decisions are not infrequently taken to apply to circumstances far removed from the facts which gave rise to them and it would seem that here too much reliance has been placed on some observations in *Bolton v. Stone* and similar observations in other cases.

In their Lordships' view a properly qualified and alert chief engineer would have realised there was a real risk here and they do not understand Walsh J. to deny that. But he appears to have held that if a real risk can properly be described as remote it must then be held to be not reasonably foreseeable. That is a possible interpretation of some of the authorities. But this is still an open question and on principle their Lordships cannot accept this view. If a real risk is one which would occur to the mind of a reasonable man in the position of the defendant's servant and which he would not brush aside as far-fetched, and if the criterion is to be what that reasonable man would have done in the circumstances, then surely he would not neglect such a risk if action to eliminate it presented no difficulty, involved no disadvantage, and required no expense.

In the present case the evidence shows that the discharge of so much oil onto the water must have taken a considerable time, and a vigilant ship's engineer would have noticed the discharge at an early stage. The findings show that he ought to have known that it is possible to ignite this kind of oil on water, and that the ship's engineer probably ought to have known that this had in fact happened before. The most that can be said to justify inaction is that he would have known that this could only happen in very exceptional circumstances. But that does not mean that a reasonable man would dismiss such a risk from his mind and do nothing when it was so easy to prevent it. If it is clear that the reasonable man would have realised or foreseen and prevented the risk, then it must follow that the appellant is liable in damages. The learned judge found this a difficult case: he says that this matter is "one upon which different minds would come to different conclusions." Taking a rather different view of the law from that of the judge, their Lordships must hold that the respondents are entitled to succeed on this issue.

The judgment appealed from is in the form of a verdict in favour of the respondents upon the claim based upon nuisance, a verdict in favour of the appellant on the claim based upon negligence, and a direction that judgment be entered for the respondents in the sums of £80,000 and £1,000 respectively. The result of their Lordships' findings is that the direction that judgment be entered for the respondents must stand but that the appeal against the verdict in favour of the respondents and the cross-appeal against the verdict in favour of the appellant must both be allowed.

Accordingly, their Lordships will humbly advise Her Majesty that the appeal and the cross-appeal should be allowed and that the judgment for the respondents in the sums of £80,000 and £1,000 should be affirmed. The appellant must pay two-thirds of the respondents' costs in the appeal and cross-appeal.

Points for Discussion

1. *Wagon Mound No. 1*, questioning and moving away from "the so-called rule in *Polemis*," "displace[d] the proposition that unforeseeability is irrelevant if damage is 'direct'" and held that foreseeability is the "effective test." Is this the same rule that the court announced in *Wagon Mound No. 2*? What explains the different results, if any, reached in *Wagon Mound No. 1* and *Wagon Mound No. 2*?

2. In *Wagon Mound No. 2* the court stated that a "reasonable man would only neglect [a risk of small magnitude] if he had some valid reason for doing so, *e.g.*, that it would involve considerable expense to eliminate the risk." Does this sound familiar? *See* United States v. Carroll Towing Co., 159 F.2d 169 (2d Cir. 1947).

In re Kinsman Transit Co.

338 F.2d 708 (2d Cir. 1964)

FRIENDLY, Circuit Judge:

. . . .

The Buffalo River flows through Buffalo from east to west, with many turns and bends, until it empties into Lake Erie. Its navigable western portion is lined with docks, grain elevators, and industrial installations; during the winter, lake vessels tie up there pending resumption of navigation on the Great Lakes, without power and with only a shipkeeper aboard. About a mile from the mouth, the City of Buffalo maintains a lift bridge at Michigan Avenue. Thaws and rain frequently cause freshets to develop in the upper part of the river and its tributary, Cazenovia Creek; currents then range up to fifteen miles an hour and propel broken ice down the river, which sometimes overflows its banks.

On January 21, 1959, rain and thaw followed a period of freezing weather. The United States Weather Bureau issued appropriate warnings which were published and broadcast. Around 6 P.M. an ice jam that had formed in Cazenovia Creek disintegrated. Another ice jam formed just west of the junction of the creek and the river; it broke loose around 9 P.M.

The MacGilvray Shiras, owned by The Kinsman Transit Company, was moored at the dock of the Concrete Elevator, operated by Continental Grain Company, on the south side of the river about three miles upstream of the Michigan Avenue Bridge. She was loaded with grain owned by Continental. The berth, east of the main portion of the dock, was exposed in the sense that about 150' of the Shiras' forward end, pointing upstream, and 70' of her stern—a total of over half her length—projected beyond the dock. This left between her stem and the bank a space of water seventy-five feet wide where the ice and other debris could float in and accumulate. The position was the more hazardous in that the berth was just below a bend in the river, and the Shiras was on the inner bank. None of her anchors had been put out. From about 10 P.M. large chunks of ice and debris began to pile up between the Shiras' starboard bow and the bank; the pressure exerted by this mass on her starboard bow was augmented by the force of the current and of floating ice against her port quarter. The mooring lines began to part, and a 'deadman,' to which the No. 1 mooring cable had been attached, pulled out of the ground—the judge finding that it had not been properly constructed or inspected. About 10:40 P.M. the stern lines parted, and the Shiras drifted into the current. During the previous forty minutes, the shipkeeper took no action to ready the anchors by releasing the devil's claws; when he sought to drop them after the Shiras broke loose, he released the compressors with the claws still hooked in the chain so that the anchors jammed and could no longer be dropped. The trial judge reasonably found that if the anchors had dropped at that time, the Shiras would probably have fetched up at the hairpin bend just below the Concrete Elevator, and that in any case they would considerably have slowed her progress, the significance of which will shortly appear.

Careening stern first down the S-shaped river, the Shiras, at about 11 P.M., struck the bow of the Michael K. Tewksbury, owned by Midland Steamship Line, Inc. The Tewksbury was moored in a relatively protected area flush against the face of a dock on the outer bank just below a hairpin bend so that no opportunity was afforded for ice to build up between her port bow and the dock. Her ship-keeper had left around 5 P.M. and spent the evening watching television with a girl friend and her family. The collision caused the Tewksbury's mooring lines to part; she too drifted stern first down the river, followed by the Shiras. The collision caused damage to the Steamer Druckenmiller which was moored opposite the Tewksbury.

Thus far there was no substantial conflict in the testimony; as to what followed there was. Judge Burke found, and we accept his findings as soundly based, that at about 10:43 P.M., Goetz, the superintendent of the Concrete Elevator, telephoned Kruptavich, another employee of Continental, that the Shiras was adrift; Kruptavich called the Coast Guard, which called the city fire station on the river, which in turn warned the crew on the Michigan Avenue Bridge, this last call being made about 10:48 P.M. Not quite twenty minutes later the watchman at the elevator where the Tewksbury had been moored phoned the bridge crew to raise the bridge. Although not more than two minutes and ten seconds were needed to elevate the bridge to full height after traffic was stopped, assuming that the motor started promptly, the bridge was just being raised when, at 11:17 P.M., the Tewksbury crashed into its center. The bridge crew consisted of an operator and two tenders; a change of shift was scheduled for 11 P.M. The inference is rather strong, despite contrary testimony, that the operator on the earlier shift had not yet returned from a tavern when the telephone call from the fire station was received; that the operator on the second shift did not arrive until shortly before the call from the elevator where the Tewksbury had been moored; and that in consequence the bridge was not raised until too late.

The first crash was followed by a second, when the south tower of the bridge fell. The Tewksbury grounded and stopped in the wreckage with her forward end resting against the stern of the Steamer Farr, which was moored on the south side of the river just above the bridge. The Shiras ended her journey with her stern against the Tewksbury and her bow against the north side of the river. So wedged, the two vessels substantially dammed the flow, causing water and ice to back up and flood installations on the banks with consequent damage as far as the Concrete Elevator, nearly three miles upstream. Two of the bridge crew suffered injuries. Later the north tower of the bridge collapsed, damaging adjacent property.

[The owners of flooded and otherwise damaged property brought suit against Kinsman, Continental, the City of Buffalo, and others.]

Judge Burke concluded that Continental and the Shiras had committed various faults discussed below; that the faults of the Shiras were without the **privity** or knowledge of her owner, thus entitling Kinsman to limit its liability, 46 U.S.C. § 183; that the Tewksbury and her owner were entitled to exoneration; and that the City of Buffalo was at fault for failing to raise the Michigan Avenue Bridge. The City was not faulted for the manner in which it had constructed and maintained flood improvements on the river and on Cazenovia Creek, or for failing to dynamite the ice jams. For the damages sustained by the Tewksbury and the Druckenmiller in the collisions at the Standard Elevator dock, Judge Burke allowed those vessels to recover equally from Continental and from Kinsman, jointly and severally, subject however, to the latter's right to limit liability. He held the City, Continental and Kinsman equally liable jointly and severally (again subject to Kinsman's limitation of liability) for damages to persons and property sustained by all others as a result of the disaster at the bridge. But, on the basis of the **last clear chance rule**, he held the City solely liable for damages sustained by the other tort-feasors, to wit, the Shiras and Continental as operator of the Concrete Elevator, and refused to allow recovery by the City against them.

. . . .

We thus come to what we consider the most serious issues: (I) Whether the City of Buffalo was at fault for failing to raise the bridge on learning of the prospective advent of the Shiras and the Tewksbury; (II) the consequences of the time relation of the City's failure to the prior faults of the Shiras and Continental; and (III) the effect of the allegedly unexpectable character of the events leading to much of the damage- and here of the *Palsgraf* case, infra.

I. The City's failure to raise the bridge.

If this were a run of the mine negligence case, the City's argument against liability for not promptly raising the Michigan Avenue Bridge would be impressive: All the vessels moored in the harbor were known to be without power and incapable of controlled movement save with the aid of tugs. The tugs had quit at 4 P.M.; they were not docked in the river, and would not undertake after quitting time to tow a vessel into or out of the inner harbor. Since the breaking loose of a ship was not to be anticipated, it would have been consistent with prudence for the City to relieve the bridge crews of their duties. Neglect by the crews ought not subject the City to liability merely because, out of abundance of caution, it had ordered them to be present when prudence did not so require. The case is unlike those in which a railway or a city, having undertaken to give warning signals at a crossing although under no duty to do so, is held liable to a plaintiff who relied on the absence of warning when it failed to continue its practice. See Prosser, Torts, 187, and fn. 87 (1955). It would be nonsense to suppose that Continental and the Shiras did what they did, and didn't what they didn't, in reliance on the bridge operators being sufficiently alert to avert disaster if the Shiras should break loose.

Buffalo's adversaries answer with 4 of the Bridge Act of 1906, 33 U.S.C. § 494, which requires, inter alia, that if a bridge over a navigable stream 'shall be constructed with a draw, then the draw shall be opened promptly by the persons owning or operating such bridge upon reasonable signal for the passage of boats and other water craft.' Buffalo replies that this general language cannot reasonably be construed to require that all drawbridges over all navigable streams in all fifty states shall be tended at all times of day or night, summer or winter, despite the near certainty that no traffic will approach. Alternatively it is arguable that a signal given when no traffic was to be expected would not be a 'reasonable signal' unless this gave the bridge owner reasonable time to get someone down to the bridge to open it. However, an older statute, 28 Stat. 362 (1894), as amended, 33 U.S.C. § 499, makes it 'the duty of all persons owning, operating, and tending the drawbridges * * * across the navigable rivers and other waters of the United States, to open, or cause to be opened, the draws of such bridges under such rules and regulations as in the opinion of the Secretary of the Army the public interests require to govern the opening of drawbridges for the passage of vessels and other watercrafts, and such rules and regulations, when so made and published, shall have the force of law. * * *' The section goes on to authorize the promulgation of such regulations by the Secretary of the Army and to make it a misdemeanor to delay unreasonably the opening of a draw after reasonable signal. Pursuant to this authority, the Corps of Engineers promulgated 33 C.F.R. § 203.707, as follows:

'(a) The Michigan Avenue bridges across Buffalo River and Buffalo Ship Canal will not be required to open for the passage of vessels from 7:00 to 7:30 a.m., 8:00 to 8:30 a.m., 3:45 to 4:30 p.m., and 5:15 to 6:00 p.m.

'(d) The closed periods prescribed in this section shall not be effective on Sundays and on New Year's day * * * (and other holidays).

'(e) The draws of these bridges shall be opened promptly on signal for the passage of any vessel at all times during the day or night except as otherwise provided in this section.' (None of the unquoted subsections provide otherwise.)

It is possible to read this statute and the regulations thereunder as creating by implication a cause of action, irrespective of negligence, for any person, or at least for any ship, injured by their breach. . . .

. . . The effect of the Corps of Engineers' regulation was to withdraw decision as to when the bridge might be left untended from what would otherwise have been a permissible area for exercise of the City's prudent judgment. [C] Indeed, Buffalo exercised no judgment contrary to the regulation; the fault lay in its employees' failure to carry out the United States' commands and those of their employer.

II. The time relation of the City's failure to the prior faults of the Shiras and Continental.

All three parties held liable complain of the effect which the judge gave to the failure of the City to raise the bridge. Kinsman and Continental contend that the City's failure insulates them from liability for damages to others resulting from the collision at the bridge; the City objects to the imposition of sole liability for damage to the Shiras and to Continental and to the exoneration of these parties from liability for destruction of the bridge.

We speedily overrule the objections of Kinsman and Continental. Save for exceptions which are not here pertinent, an actor whose negligence has set a dangerous force in motion is not saved from liability for harm it has caused to innocent persons solely because another has negligently failed to take action that would have avoided this. [Cc] As against third persons, one negligent actor cannot defend on the basis that the other had 'the last clear chance.' [Cc] The contrary argument grows out of the discredited notion that only the last wrongful act can be a cause- a notion as faulty in logic as it is wanting in fairness. The established principle is especially appealing in **admiralty** which will divide the damages among the negligent actors or non-actors.

On the other hand, we disagree with the judge's holding that because the City had 'the **last clear chance**,' Kinsman and Continental as plaintiffs against it are absolved of their negligence and the City as plaintiff is left without recourse against them. Here, as in the case of the injuries to persons not at fault, the damages should be divided. . . .

. . . .

None of the cases in which this Court has applied the last clear chance rule to impose sole liability in admiralty is at all analogous to this one; indeed we doubt whether this case would come within the principle as generally applied at common law. . . .

. . . .

III. The allegedly unexpectable character of the events leading to much of the damage.

The very statement of the case suggests the need for considering Palsgraf v. Long Island RR., 248 N.Y. 339, 162 N.E. 99, 59 A.L.R. 1253 (1928), and the closely related problem of liability for unforeseeable consequences.

In Sinram v. Pennsylvania R.R., 61 F.2d 767, 770 (2 Cir. 1932), which received Palsgraf into the admiralty, Judge Learned Hand characterized the issue in that case as 'whether, if A. omitted to perform a positive duty to B., C., who had been damaged in consequence, might invoke the breach, though otherwise A. owed him no duty; in short, whether A. was chargeable for the results to others of his breach of duty to B.' Thus stated, the query rather answers itself; Hohfeld's analysis tells us that once it is concluded that A. had no duty to C., it is simply a correlative that C. has no right against A. The important question is what was the basis for Chief Judge Cardozo's conclusion that the Long Island Railroad owed no 'duty' to Mrs. Palsgraf under the circumstances.

Certainly there is no general principle that a railroad owes no duty to persons on station platforms not in immediate proximity to the tracks, as would have been quickly demonstrated if Mrs. Palsgraf had been injured by the fall of improperly loaded objects from a passing train. [C] Neither is there any principle that railroad guards who jostle a package-carrying passenger owe a duty only to him; if the package had contained bottles, the Long Island would surely have been liable for injury caused to close bystanders by flying glass or spurting liquid. The reason why the Long Island was thought to owe no duty to Mrs. Palsgraf was the lack of any notice that the package contained a substance demanding the exercise of any care toward anyone so far away; Mrs. Palsgraf was not considered to be within the area of apparent hazard created by whatever lack of care the guard had displayed to the anonymous carrier of the unknown fireworks.[5] . . .

We see little similarity between the *Palsgraf* case and the situation before us. The point of *Palsgraf* was that the appearance of the newspaper-wrapped package gave no notice that its dislodgement could do any harm save to itself and those nearby, and this by impact, perhaps with consequent breakage, and not by explosion. In contrast, a ship insecurely moored in a fast flowing river is a known danger not only to herself but to the owners of all other ships and structures down-river, and to persons upon them. No one would dream of saying that a

---

5 There was exceedingly little evidence of negligence of any sort. The only lack of care suggested by the majority in the Appellate Division was that instead of endeavoring to assist the passenger, the guards 'might better have discouraged and warned him not to board the moving train.' [C] Chief Judge Cardozo said: 'The man was not injured in his person nor even put in danger. The purpose of the act, as well as its effect, was to make his person safe. If there was a wrong to him at all, which may very well be doubted, it was a wrong to a property interest only, the safety of his package.' [C] Judge Andrews' dissent said the Long Island had been negligent, [c], but did not state in what respect.

How much ink would have been saved over the years if the Court of Appeals had reversed Mrs Palsgraf's judgment on the basis that there was no evidence of negligence at all.

shipowner who 'knowingly and wilfully' failed to secure his ship at a pier on such a river 'would not have threatened' persons and owners of property downstream in some manner.   The shipowner and the wharfinger in this case having thus owed a duty of care to all within the reach of the ship's known destructive power, the impossibility of advance identification of the particular person who would be hurt is without legal consequence. [Cc] Similarly the foreseeable consequences of the City's failure to raise the bridge were not limited to the Shiras and the Tewksbury. Collision plainly created a danger that the bridge towers might fall onto adjoining property, and the crash of two uncontrolled lake vessels, one 425 feet and the other 525 feet long, into a bridge over a swift ice-ridden stream, with a channel only 177 feet wide, could well result in a partial damming that would flood property upstream. As to the City also, it is useful to consider, by way of contrast, Chief Judge Cardozo's statement that the Long Island would not have been liable to Mrs. Palsgraf had the guard wilfully thrown the package down. If the City had deliberately kept the bridge closed in the face of the onrushing vessels, taking the risk that they might not come so far, no one would give house-room to a claim that it 'owed no duty' to those who later suffered from the flooding. Unlike Mrs. Palsgraf, they were within the area of hazard.

. . . .

Since all the claimants here met the *Palsgraf* requirement of being persons to whom the actors owed a 'duty of care,' we are not obliged to reconsider whether that case furnishes as useful a standard for determining the boundaries of liability in admiralty for negligent conduct as was thought in *Sinram*, when *Palsgraf* was still in its infancy. But this does not dispose of the alternative argument that the manner in which several of the claimants were harmed, particularly by flood damage, was unforeseeable and that recovery for this may not be had- whether the argument is put in the forthright form that unforeseeable damages are not recoverable or is concealed under a formula of lack of 'proximate cause.'[8]

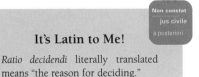

It's Latin to Me!

Ratio decidendi literally translated means "the reason for deciding."

So far as concerns the City, the argument lacks factual support. Although the obvious risks from not raising the bridge were damage to itself and to the vessels, the danger of a fall of the bridge and of flooding would not have been unforeseeable under the circumstances to anyone who gave them thought. And the same can be said as to the failure of Kinsman's shipkeeper to ready the anchors after the danger had become apparent. The

---

8 It is worth underscoring that the **ratio decidendi** in *Palsgraf* was that the Long Island was not required to use any care with respect to the package vis-a-vis Mrs. Palsgraf; Chief Judge Cardozo did not reach the issue of 'proximate cause' for which the case is often cited. [C]

exhibits indicate that the width of the channel between the Concrete Elevator and the bridge is at most points less than two hundred fifty feet. If the Shiras caught up on a dock or vessel moored along the shore, the current might well swing her bow across the channel so as to block the ice floes, as indeed could easily have occurred at the Standard Elevator dock where the stern of the Shiras struck the Tewksbury's bow. At this point the channel scarcely exceeds two hundred feet, and this was further narrowed by the presence of the Druckenmiller moored on the opposite bank. Had the Tewksbury's mooring held, it is thus by no means unlikely that these three ships would have dammed the river. Nor was it unforeseeable that the drawbridge would not be raised since, apart from any other reason, there was no assurance of timely warning. What may have been less foreseeable was that the Shiras would get that far down the twisting river, but this is somewhat negated both by the known speed of the current when freshets developed and by the evidence that, on learning of the Shiras' departure, Continental's employees and those they informed foresaw precisely that.

Continental's position on the facts is stronger. It was indeed foreseeable that the improper construction and lack of inspection of the 'deadman' might cause a ship to break loose and damage persons and property on or near the river- that was what made Continental's conduct negligent. With the aid of hindsight one can also say that a prudent man, carefully pondering the problem, would have realized that the danger of this would be greatest under such water conditions as developed during the night of January 21, 1959, and that if a vessel should break loose under those circumstances, events might transpire as they did. But such post hoc step by step analysis would render 'foreseeable' almost anything that has in fact occurred; if the argument relied upon has legal validity, it ought not be circumvented by characterizing as foreseeable what almost no one would in fact have foreseen at the time.

The effect of unforeseeability of damage upon liability for negligence has recently been considered by the Judicial Committee of the Privy Council, *Overseas Tankship (U.K.) Ltd. v. Morts Dock & Engineering Co. (The Wagon Mound)*. [c] The Committee there disapproved the proposition, thought to be supported by *Re Polemis and Furness, Withy & Co. Ltd.*, [c] 'that unforeseeability is irrelevant if damage is 'direct." We have no difficulty with the result of *The Wagon Mound*, in view of the finding, [c] that the appellant had no reason to believe that the floating furnace oil would burn. [C] On that view the decision simply applies the principle which excludes liability where the injury sprang from a hazard different from that which was improperly risked . . . Although some language in the judgment goes beyond this, we would find it difficult to understand why one who had failed to use the care required to protect others in the light of expectable forces should be exonerated when the very risks that rendered his conduct negligent produced other and more serious consequences to such persons than were fairly foreseeable when he fell short of what the law demanded. Foreseeability of danger is necessary to render conduct negligent; where as here the damage was caused by just those forces whose existence required the exercise of greater care than was taken- the current, the ice, and the physical mass of the Shiras, the incurring of consequences other and greater than foreseen does not make the conduct less culpable or provide a reasoned basis for insulation. [C] The oft encountered argument that failure to limit liability to foreseeable consequences may subject the defendant to a loss wholly out of proportion to his fault seems scarcely consistent with the universally accepted rule that the defendant takes the plaintiff as he finds him and will be responsible for the full extent of the injury even though a latent susceptibility of the plaintiff renders this far more serious than could reasonably have been anticipated. [C]

Take Note

The court here refers to and recognizes the eggshell-skull plaintiff rule and a defendant's liability for a plaintiff's unforeseeable and uncommon reaction to a defendant's negligent conduct or intentional act.

The weight of authority in this country rejects the limitation of damages to consequences foreseeable at the time of the negligent conduct when the consequences are 'direct,' and the damage, although other and greater than expectable, is of the same general sort that was risked. [Cc] Other American courts, purporting to apply a test of foreseeability to damages, extend that concept to such unforeseen lengths as to raise serious doubt whether the concept is meaningful; indeed, we wonder whether the British courts are not finding it necessary to limit the language of *The Wagon Mound* as we have indicated.

We see no reason why an actor engaging in conduct which entails a large risk of small damage and a small risk of other and greater damage, of the same general sort, from the same forces, and to the same class of persons, should be relieved of responsibility for the latter simply because the chance of its occurrence, if viewed alone, may not have been large enough to require the exercise of care. By hypothesis, the risk of the lesser harm was sufficient to render his disregard of it actionable; the existence of a less likely additional risk that the very forces against whose action he was required to guard would produce other and greater damage than could have been reasonably anticipated should inculpate him further rather than limit his liability. This does not mean that the careless actor will always be held for all damages for which the forces that he risked were a cause in fact. Somewhere a point will be reached when courts will agree that the link has become too tenuous- that what is claimed to be consequence is only fortuity. Thus, if the destruction of the Michigan Avenue Bridge had delayed the arrival of a doctor, with consequent loss of a patient's life, few judges would impose liability on any of the parties here, although the agreement in result might not be paralleled by similar unanimity in reasoning; perhaps in the long run one returns to Judge Andrews' statement in *Palsgraf.* 'It is all a question of expediency, * * * of fair judgment, always keeping in mind the fact that we endeavor to make a rule in each case that will be practical and in keeping with the general understanding of mankind.' It would be pleasant if greater certainty were possible, see Prosser, Torts, 262, but the many efforts that have been made at defining the locus of the 'uncertain and wavering line,' [c] are not very promising; what courts do in such cases makes better sense than what they, or others, say. Where the line will be drawn will vary from age to age; as society has come to rely increasingly on insurance and other methods of loss-sharing, the point may lie further off than a century ago. Here it is surely more equitable that the losses from the operators' negligent failure to raise the Michigan Avenue Bridge should be ratably borne by Buffalo's taxpayers than left with the innocent victims of the flooding; yet the mind is also repelled by a solution that would impose liability solely on the City and exonerate the persons whose negligent acts of commission and omission were the precipitating force of the collision with the bridge and its sequelae. We go only so far as to hold that where, as here, the damages resulted from the same physical forces whose existence required the exercise of greater care than was displayed and were of the same general sort that was expectable, unforeseeability of the exact developments and of the extent of the loss will not limit liability. Other fact situations can be dealt with when they arise.

MOORE, Circuit Judge (concurring and dissenting):

I do not hesitate to concur with Judge Friendly's well-reasoned and well-expressed opinion as to limitation of Kinsman's liability, the extent of the liability of the City of Buffalo, Continental and Kinsman for the damages suffered by the City, the Shiras, the Tewksbury, the Druckenmiller and the Farr and the division of damages.

I cannot agree, however, merely because 'society has come to rely increasingly on insurance and other methods of loss-sharing' that the courts should, or have the power to, create a vast judicial insurance company which will adequately compensate all who have suffered damages. Equally disturbing is the suggestion that 'Here it is surely more equitable that the losses from the operators' negligent failure to raise the Michigan Avenue Bridge should be ratably borne by Buffalo's taxpayers than left with the innocent victims of the flooding.' Under any such principle, negligence suits would become further simplified by requiring a claimant to establish only his own innocence and then offer, in addition to his financial statement, proof of the financial condition of the respective defendants. Judgment would be entered against the defendant which court or jury decided was best able to pay. Nor am I convinced that it should be the responsibility of the Buffalo taxpayers to reimburse the 'innocent victims' in their community for damages sustained. In my opinion, before financial liability is imposed, there should be some showing of legal liability.

Unfortunate though it was for Buffalo to have had its fine vehicular bridge demolished in a most unexpected manner, I accept the finding of liability for normal consequences because the City had plenty of time to raise the bridge after notice was given. Bridges, however, serve two purposes. They permit vehicles to cross the river when they are down; they permit vessels to travel on the river when they are up. But no bridge builder or bridge operator would envision a bridge as a dam or as a dam potential.

See It

Rube Goldberg was a cartoonist who drew comically involved, complicated devices that were contrived to perform very simple tasks. To see some of his artwork, click here.

By an extraordinary concatenation of even more extraordinary events, not unlike the humorous and almost-beyond-all-imagination sequences depicted by the famous cartoonist, Rube Goldberg, the Shiras with its companions which it picked up en route did combine with the bridge demolition to create a very effective dam across the Buffalo River. Without specification of the nature of the damages, claims in favor of some twenty persons and companies were allowed (Finding of Fact #33, Interlocutory Decree, par. 11) resulting from the various collisions and from 'the damming of the river at the bridge, the backing up of the water and ice upstream, and the overflowing of the banks of the river and flooding of industrial installations along the river banks.' (Sup. Finding of Fact #26a.)

My dissent is limited to that portion of the opinion which approves the awarding of damages suffered as a result of the flooding of various properties upstream. I am not satisfied with reliance on hindsight or on the assumption that since flooding occurred, therefore, it must have been foreseeable. In fact, the majority hold that the danger 'of flooding would not have been unforeseeable under the circumstances to anyone who gave them thought.' But believing that 'anyone' might be too broad, they resort to that most famous of all legal mythological characters, the reasonably 'prudent man.' Even he, however, 'carefully pondering the problem,' is not to be relied upon because they permit him to become prudent 'With the aid of hindsight.'

The majority, in effect, would remove from the law of negligence the concept of foreseeability because, as they say, "The weight of authority in this country rejects the limitation of damages to consequences foreseeable at the time of the negligent conduct when the consequences are 'direct.'" Yet lingering thoughts of recognized legal principles create for them lingering doubts because they say: 'This does not mean that the careless actor will always be held for all damages for which the forces that he risked were a cause in fact. Somewhere a point will be reached when courts will agree that the link has become too tenuous—that what is claimed to be consequence is only fortuity.' The very example given, namely, the patient who dies because the doctor is delayed by the destruction of the bridge, certainly presents a direct consequence as a factual matter yet the majority opinion states that 'few judges would impose liability on any of the parties here,' under these circumstances.

In final analysis the answers to the questions when the link is 'too tenuous' and when 'consequence is only fortuity' are dependent solely on the particular point of view of the particular judge under the particular circumstances. In differing with my colleagues, I must be giving 'unconscious recognition of the harshness of holding a man for what he could not conceivably have guarded against, because human foresight could not go so far.' (L. Hand, C.J., in Sinram v. Pennsylvania R. Co., 61 F.2d 767, 770, 2 Cir., 1932.) If 'foreseeability' be the test, I can foresee the likelihood that a vessel negligently allowed to break its moorings and to drift uncontrolled in a rapidly flowing river may well strike other ships, piers and bridges. Liability would also result on the 'direct consequence' theory. However, to me the fortuitous circumstance of the vessels so arranging themselves as to create a dam is much 'too tenuous.'

The decisions bearing on the foreseeability question have been so completely collected in three English cases[1] that no repetition of the reasoning pro and con of this principle need be made here. To these cases may be added the many American cases cited in the majority opinion which to me push the doctrine of foreseeability to ridiculous lengths- ridiculous, I suppose, only to the judge whose 'human foresight' is restricted to finite limits but not to the judge who can say: It happened; ergo, it must have been foreseeable. The line of demarcation will always be 'uncertain and wavering,' Palsgraf v. Long Island R.R., 248 N.Y. 339, 354, 162 N.E. 99, 59 A.L.R. 1253 (1928), but if, concededly, a line exists, there must be areas on each side. The flood claimants are much too far on the non-liability side of the line. As to them, I would not award any recovery even if the taxpayers of Buffalo are better able to bear the loss.

Points for Discussion

1. What did Judge Friendly look to and rely upon in his consideration of the problem of liability for unforeseeable consequences?

---

1 In re Polemis and Furness, Withy & Co., (1921) 3 K.B. 560 (C.A.); Overseas Tankship (U.K.), Ltd. v. Morts Dock & Engineering Co., Ltd. (The Wagon Mound), (1961) 1 All E.R. 404; Miller Steamship Company, Pty., Ltd. v. Overseas Tankship (U.K.) Ltd., (1963) 1 Lloyd's Law List Rep. 402 (Sup.Ct., New South Wales).

2. Judge Friendly: "The weight of authority in this country rejects the limitation of damages to consequences foreseeable at the time of the negligent conduct when the consequences are 'direct' and the damage, although other and greater than expectable, is of the same general sort that was risked." Judge Moore's concurrence/dissent argued that this position would remove the foreseeability concept from the law of negligence. Are you persuaded by Judge Moore's argument? Did Judge Friendly resurrect the *Polemis* direct consequence test?

3. Judge Friendly: "We see no reason why an actor engaging in conduct which entails a risk of small damage and a small risk of other and greater damage, of the same general sort, from the same forces, and to the same class of persons, should be relieved of responsibility for the latter simply because the chance of its occurrence, if viewed alone, may not have been large enough to require the exercise of care." On this view, a defendant who has and breaches a duty of care in the form of precautionary measures protecting plaintiffs against particular kinds of harm may also be held liable for other kinds of harm caused by the negligence. Does this view square with your understanding of foreseeability?

4. Referencing and quoting Judge Andrews' *Palsgraf* dissent, Judge Friendly reasons that the proximate cause determination takes into account expediency, "fair judgment," and practical rules made "in each case that will be practical and in keeping with the general understanding of mankind." Noting increasing societal reliance on insurance and loss-sharing methods, Friendly posits that "it is surely more equitable that the losses from the operators' negligent failure to raise the Michigan Avenue Bridge should be ratably borne by Buffalo's taxpayers than left with the innocent victims of the flooding . . ."

5. In In re *Kinsman Transit Co. (Kinsman No. 2)*, 388 F.2d 821 (2d Cir. 1968), the court concluded that the defendants held liable in the 1964 *Kinsman* decision were not liable for the economic losses suffered by carriers who were unable to unload wheat stored on their ships. The court, in an opinion by Judge Kaufman, held that the "injuries . . . were too 'remote' or 'indirect' a consequence of defendant's negligence."

6. Consider RESTATEMENT (SECOND) OF TORTS § 435(2) (1965): "The actor's conduct may be held not to be a legal cause of harm where after the event and looking back from the harm to the actor's negligent conduct, it appears to the court highly extraordinary that it should have brought about the harm." Does this section provide any useful guidance on the issue of the foreseeability or manner of harm?

Hypo 5-3

James drives a bus, and the route regularly takes the bus across train tracks. One day while approaching the tracks, James does not look for any oncoming train as the crossing gates are not down. Just as the bus crosses the tracks, Christopher, the operator of the crossing gates, realizes a train is coming and closes the gates, trapping the bus on the tracks. The bus passengers realize a train is coming and stampede toward the two exits of the bus. Everyone makes it out of the bus safely, but Darla (one of the passengers) is trampled by other panicked passengers and sustains permanent injuries. At trial, James and Christopher both dispute that their negligence caused Darla's harm. What result and why?

Hypo 5-4

Jennifer is negligently driving her car when she collides with another car driven by Dan, who was also driving negligently at the time. Immediately after the collision, Jane runs a red light and plows into the two cars. Jennifer's passenger, Nancy, dies from internal bleeding caused by the collision. Nancy's estate seeks to bring a negligence action against Jennifer, Dan, and Jane. Discuss.

Wilke v. Woodhouse Ford, Inc.

278 Neb. 800, 774 N.W.2d 370 (2009)

McCORMACK, J.

I. NATURE OF CASE

Elizabeth A. Wilke and her husband, Mark Wilke, purchased a van from Woodhouse Ford, Inc. (Woodhouse). That same day, Elizabeth was injured when their 3-year-old daughter allegedly pulled the gearshift out of park, allowing the van to roll over Elizabeth's foot and leg, causing her to fall and hit her head on a concrete driveway. The Wilkes testified that the key was out of the ignition at the time of the accident. The van was purchased that day from Woodhouse. Woodhouse sold the van to the Wilkes "as is" . . . The Wilkes brought suit against Woodhouse alleging . . . negligence . . . The district court entered summary judgment in favor of Woodhouse, and the Wilkes appealed. . . ..

. . . .

The Wilkes . . . alleged a theory of recovery based on negligence. . . . [A] negligence claim focuses on the seller's conduct. A common-law duty exists to use due care so as not to negligently injure another person. . . ..

The Wilkes alleged that Woodhouse was negligent because it failed to reasonably inspect the van for safety defects prior to its sale and that but for such negligence, Elizabeth would not have sustained her injuries by being run over by the van.

Ordinary negligence is defined as the doing of something that a reasonably careful person would not do under similar circumstances, or the failing to do something that a reasonably careful person would do under similar circumstances. In order to prevail in a negligence action, there must be a legal duty on the part of the defendant to protect the plaintiff from injury, a failure to discharge that duty, and damage proximately caused by the failure to discharge that duty.

. . . .

Woodhouse first maintains that it had no duty to inspect the van prior to its sale. In negligence cases, a duty may be defined as an obligation, to which the law will give recognition and effect, to conform to a particular standard of conduct toward another. When determining whether a legal duty exists, a court employs a risk-utility test concerning (1) the magnitude of the risk, (2) the relationship of the parties, (3) the nature of the attendant risk, (4) the opportunity and ability to exercise care, (5) the foreseeability of the harm, and (6) the policy interest in the proposed solution.

The existence of a duty and the identification of the applicable standard of care are questions of law, but the ultimate determination of whether a party deviated from the standard of care and was therefore negligent is a question of fact. To resolve the issue, a finder of fact must determine what conduct the standard of care would require under the particular circumstances presented by the evidence and whether the conduct of the alleged tort-feasor conformed with the standard.

We have never before addressed whether a used-car dealer has a duty to its customers to inspect vehicles for safety defects before they are sold. Most courts which have considered the issue have recognized a limited duty on the part of the dealer to inspect for patent safety defects existing at the time of sale. . . .

But courts which have recognized a duty on the part of used-car dealers to inspect for safety defects prior to sale have also emphasized that the duty is limited. . . .

Applying our risk-utility test for the existence of a legal duty to use reasonable care, we conclude that there is a relatively great magnitude of risk of injury in the circumstance where an unknowing buyer drives off the dealer's lot in a used vehicle which has a patent safety defect, such as defective brakes or steering. The dealer is better equipped than the purchaser to perceive such a defect before it causes harm. The nature of the risk is such that personal injury or death could result not only with respect to the purchaser of the defective vehicle, but to other members of the motoring public. The dealer has the earliest opportunity to discover and repair a patent safety defect in a used vehicle. An unknown safety defect existing at the time of sale poses foreseeable harm to the purchaser and the general public, and there exists a policy interest in requiring reasonable conduct on the part of the dealer to prevent such harm.

We, therefore, hold that a commercial dealer of used vehicles intended for use on public streets and highways has a duty to conduct a reasonable inspection of the vehicle prior to sale in order to determine whether there are any patent defects existing at the time of sale which would make the vehicle unsafe for ordinary operation and, upon discovery of such a defect, to either repair it or warn a prospective purchaser of its existence. The dealer has no duty to disassemble the vehicle to discover latent defects or to anticipate the future development of safety defects which do not exist at the time of sale. . . .

That being the case, whether or not the court properly entered summary judgment in favor of Woodhouse depends upon whether Woodhouse breached this duty. It is undisputed that Woodhouse did not inspect the van prior to selling it. However, that alone does not rise to the level of a breach of the applicable standard of care, because its duty extends only to patent, not to latent, defects. Thus, a breach of duty occurred if a reasonable inspection would have revealed the alleged defect in the gearshift. This is a question of fact that must be decided by the fact finder. . . . The record presents conflicting testimony as to whether the gearshift malfunctioned occasionally or regularly. . . . As such, there is a genuine issue of material fact whether a reasonable inspection of the van would have revealed any alleged defect.

. . . .

Woodhouse argues that even if there is a duty that was breached, there is no material issue of fact that Woodhouse was not the proximate cause of the accident. Rather, Woodhouse asserts that Mark and the child were the proximate cause of the accident.

Determination of causation is, ordinarily, a matter for the trier of fact. To establish proximate cause, the plaintiff must meet three basic requirements: (1) Without the negligent action, the injury would not have occurred, commonly known as the "but for" rule; (2) the injury was a natural and probable result of the negligence; and (3) there was no efficient intervening cause.

Assuming that Woodhouse breached its duty to reasonably inspect, Woodhouse proximately caused the vehicle to be placed into the hands of the Wilkes with a defect that could have been discovered by a reasonable inspection. This defect undoubtedly existed at the time of sale. And it is undisputed that the van was not altered in any way prior to the incident. . . .

We conclude . . . that commercial dealers of used vehicles have a duty to exercise reasonable care to discover any existing safety defects that are patent or discoverable in the exercise of reasonable care or through reasonable inspection. Because there are genuine issues of material fact . . . we conclude that the district court incorrectly granted summary judgment in favor of Woodhouse on the Wilkes' negligence claim. . . .

AFFIRMED IN PART, AND IN PART REVERSED.

—————————

Points for Discussion

1. Do you agree with the court's evaluation of and answer to the proximate cause question?

2. Is the proximate (or legal) cause determination ordinarily one of law or fact?

3. What arguments can Woodhouse make at trial in support of its position that the proximate cause of the accident was the actions of the plaintiffs' 3-year old daughter?

—————————

2. Intervening Causes

Derdiarian v. Felix Contracting Corp.

51 N.Y.2d 308, 414 N.E.2d 666 (1980)

OPINION OF THE COURT

Chief Judge Cooke

The operator of a motor vehicle, who failed timely to ingest a dosage of medication, suffered an epileptic seizure and his vehicle careened into an excavation site where a gas main was being installed beneath the street surface. The automobile crashed through a single wooden horse-type barricade put in place by the contractor and struck an employee of a subcontractor, who was propelled into the air. Upon landing the employee was splattered by boiling liquid enamel from a kettle also struck by the vehicle. Principally at issue on this appeal is whether plaintiffs, the employee and his wife, failed to establish as a matter of law that the contractor's inadequate safety precautions on the work site were the proximate cause of the accident.

. . . .

During the fall of 1973 defendant Felix Contracting Corporation was performing a contract to install an underground gas main in the City of Mount Vernon for defendant Con Edison. Bayside Pipe Coaters, plaintiff Harold Derdiarian's employer, was engaged as a subcontractor to seal the gas main.

On the afternoon of November 21, 1973, defendant James Dickens suffered an epileptic seizure and lost consciousness, allowing his vehicle to careen into the work site and strike plaintiff with such force as to throw him into the air. When plaintiff landed, he was splattered over his face, head and body with 400 degree boiling hot liquid enamel from a kettle struck by the automobile. The enamel was used in connection with sealing the gas main. Although plaintiff's body ignited into a fire ball, he miraculously survived the incident.

At trial, plaintiff's theory was that defendant Felix had negligently failed to take adequate measures to insure the safety of workers on the excavation site. Plaintiff's evidence indicates that the accident occurred on Oak Street, a two-lane, east-west roadway. The excavation was located in the east-bound lane, and ran from approximately one foot south of the center line to within 2 or 3 feet of the curb. When plaintiff arrived on the site, he was instructed by Felix' foreman to park his truck on the west side of the excavation, parallel to the curb. As a result, there was a gap of some 7 1/2 feet between the side of the truck and the curb line.

Derdiarian testified that he made a request to park his truck on the east side of the hole, so he could set up the kettle away from the oncoming eastbound traffic. The Felix foreman instructed him to leave his truck where it was, and plaintiff then put the kettle near the curb, on the west side of the excavation.

James Dickens was driving eastbound on Oak Street when he suffered a seizure and lost consciousness. Dickens was under treatment for epilepsy and had neglected to take his medication at the proper time. His car crashed through a single wooden horse-type barricade that was set up on the west side of the excavation site. As it passed through the site, the vehicle struck the kettle containing the enamel, as well as the plaintiff, resulting in plaintiff's injuries.

To support his claim of an unsafe work site, plaintiff called as a witness Lawrence Lawton, an expert in traffic safety. According to Lawton, the usual and accepted method of safeguarding the workers is to erect a barrier around the excavation. Such a barrier, consisting of a truck, a piece of heavy equipment or a pile of dirt, would keep a car out of the excavation and protect workers from oncoming traffic. The expert testified that the barrier should cover the entire width of the excavation. He also stated that there should have been two flagmen present, rather than one, and that warning signs should have been posted advising motorists that there was only one lane of traffic and that there was a flagman ahead.

. . . .

The concept of proximate cause, or more appropriately legal cause, has proven to be an elusive one, incapable of being precisely defined to cover all situations (see, e.g., Pagan v. Goldberger, 51 A.D.2d 508, 509 [Hopkins, Acting P. J.]; Prosser, Law of Torts [4th ed], § 42, p 249; see, also, 1 Shearman & Redfield, Negligence, § 35). This is, in part, because the concept stems from policy considerations that serve to place manageable limits upon the liability that flows from negligent conduct (e.g., Ventricelli v. Kinney System Rent A Car, 45 N.Y.2d 950, 952; Palsgraf v. Long Is. R. R. Co., 248 N.Y. 339, 352 [Andrews, J., dissenting]). Depending upon the nature of the case, a variety of factors may be relevant in assessing legal cause. Given the unique nature of the inquiry in each case, it is for the finder of fact to determine legal cause, once the court has been satisfied that a prima facie case has been established (see, e.g., Nallan v Helmsley-Spear, Inc., 50 N.Y.2d 507, 520, 521; Sheehan v. City of New York, 40 N.Y.2d 496, 502, 503; Kingsland v Erie County Agric. Soc., 298 N.Y. 409, 424, 427). To carry the burden of proving a prima facie case, the plaintiff must generally show that the defendant's negligence was a substantial cause of the events which produced the injury (Nallan v. Helmsley-Spear, Inc., supra, at p 520; RESTATEMENT, TORTS 2d, § 431). Plaintiff need not demonstrate, however, that the precise manner in which the accident happened, or the extent of injuries, was foreseeable (RESTATEMENT, TORTS 2d, § 435, subd 2).

Where the acts of a third person intervene between the defendant's conduct and the plaintiff's injury, the causal connection is not automatically severed. In such a case, liability turns upon whether the **intervening act** is a normal or foreseeable consequence of the situation created by the defendant's negligence (see Parvi v. City of Kingston, 41 N.Y.2d 553, 560; RESTATEMENT, TORTS 2d, §§ 443, 449; Prosser, Law of Torts, § 44). If the intervening act is extraordinary under the circumstances, not foreseeable in the normal course of events, or independent of or far removed from the defendant's conduct, it may well be a superseding act which breaks the causal nexus (see, e.g., Martinez v. Lazaroff, 48 N.Y.2d 819, 820; Ventricelli v. Kinney System Rent A Car, 45 N.Y.2d 950, 952, supra; Rivera v. City of New York, 11 N.Y.2d 856). Because questions concerning what is foreseeable and what is normal may be the subject of varying inferences, as is the question of negligence itself, these issues generally are for the fact finder to resolve.

There are certain instances, to be sure, where only one conclusion may be drawn from the established facts and where the question of legal cause may be decided as a matter of law. Those cases generally involve independent intervening acts which operate upon but do not flow from the original negligence. . . .

[I]n the present case, we cannot say as a matter of law that defendant Dickens' negligence was a **superseding cause** which interrupted the link between Felix' negligence and plaintiff's injuries. From the evidence in the record, the jury could have found that Felix negligently failed to safeguard the excavation site. A prime hazard associated with such dereliction is the possibility that a driver will negligently enter the work site and cause injury to a worker. That the driver was negligent, or even reckless, does not insulate Felix from liability . . . [Cc]. Nor is it decisive that the driver lost control of the vehicle through a negligent failure to take medication, rather than a driving mistake. [C] The precise manner of the event need not be anticipated. The finder of fact could have concluded that the foreseeable, normal and natural result of the risk created by Felix was the injury of a worker by a car entering the improperly protected work area. An intervening act may not serve as a superseding cause, and relieve an actor of responsibility, where the risk of the intervening act occurring is the very same risk which renders the actor negligent.

In a similar vein, plaintiff's act of placing the kettle on the west side of the excavation does not, as a matter of law, absolve defendant Felix of responsibility. Serious injury, or even death, was a foreseeable consequence of a vehicle crashing through the work area. The injury could have occurred in numerous ways, ranging from a worker being directly struck by the car to the car hitting an object that injures the worker. Placement of the kettle, or any object in the work area, could affect how the accident occurs and the extent of injuries. That defendant could not anticipate the precise manner of the accident or the exact extent of injuries, however, does not preclude liability as a matter of law where the general risk and character of injuries are foreseeable.

. . . .

For the foregoing reasons, the order of the Appellate Division should be affirmed, with costs. . . .

Watson v. Kentucky & Indiana Bridge & R.R. Co.

137 Ky. 619, 126 S.W. 146 (1910)

SETTLE, J.

This action was instituted by the appellant, John Watson, in the court below against the appellees, Kentucky & Indiana Bridge & Railroad Company, hereinafter called the Bridge & Railroad Company, the Southern Railway Company, the Southern Railway Company in Kentucky, and the Union Tank Line Company, to recover $20,000 damages for injuries sustained to his person on the night of June 14, 1907, from an explosion of gas caused, as alleged, by the negligence of the appellees. It was, in substance, alleged in the petition as amended that while a tank car, owned by the appellee Union Tank Line Company, and filled with a highly explosive substance known as gasoline, was being transported through a populous section of the city of Louisville over the roadbed of the appellee Bridge & Railroad Company, it was derailed and its valve broken, thereby causing all the gasoline to escape and flow in large quantities on the street and into the gutters; that from the gasoline thus flowing and standing in pools upon the street and gutters there arose and spread over the neighborhood of the place of derailment and into the houses of the residents thereof, great quantities of highly explosive and combustible gas which, three hours after the derailment of the tank car, exploded with force from contact with a lighted match thrown on the street by one Chas. Duerr, who claimed to have used it in igniting a cigar; that the explosion threw appellant from his bed and almost demolished his house, from the ruins of which he was taken unconscious and bleeding with a fractured jaw and one cheek nearly torn from his face. . . . At the conclusion of appellant's evidence, the appellees Bridge & Railroad Company and Union Tank Line Company moved the court peremptorily to instruct the jury to find for them. The motion was overruled . . . and the jury . . . returned a verdict in behalf of appellees, upon which judgment was entered in their favor for costs. Appellant being dissatisfied with that judgment and the refusal of the circuit court to grant him a new trial, has appealed.

. . . .

There is no contrariety of proof as to the fact that Charles Duerr lighted the match that caused the explosion. Indeed, the act was admitted by him, but he testified that when it was done he and Miller, a companion, were standing on

Madison street in front of the Warner residence a square from the derailed car, talking with the two Warner girls, the four having just returned from Shawnee Park; that he took a cigar and match from his pockets, struck a light from the match, and ignited the cigar; that the explosion followed before the match reached the ground; and that he was knocked down by the explosion. He further testified that at the time of lighting the match he had just returned from Shawnee Park and knew nothing of the derailment of the tank car, or of the existence of the gas arising from the escaping gasoline, and that he did not intend to cause the explosion, nor did he know that the lighting of the match would cause it. Duerr was corroborated by Miller and one of the Warner girls . . .

Appellees were permitted to prove that Duerr, who had been a telegraph operator in the employ of the appellee Bridge & Railroad Company, was on the morning of the day of the explosion discharged from its service, and that 20 minutes before the explosion Duerr remarked to his companion, in the hearing of Giacometti and Darnall, "Let us go and set the damn thing on fire." . . .

There was, as previously indicated, evidence from which the jury might have found the appellee Bridge & Railroad Company guilty of negligence in failing to keep in proper repair and condition its roadbed and track at the place where the tank car was derailed, and that such failure caused the derailment resulting in the escape from the tank of the gasoline, contact of the gas from which with the match lighted by Duerr caused the explosion. . . .

The lighting of the match by Duerr having resulted in the explosion, the question is, was that act merely a contributing cause, or the efficient and, therefore, proximate cause of appellant's injuries? The question of proximate cause is a question for the jury. In holding that Duerr in lighting or throwing the match acted maliciously or with intent to cause the explosion, the trial court invaded the province of the jury. There was, it is true, evidence tending to prove that the act was wanton or malicious, but also evidence conducing to prove that it was inadvertently or negligently done by Duerr. It was therefore for the jury and not the court to determine from all the evidence whether the lighting of the match was done by Duerr inadvertently or negligently, or whether it was a wanton and malicious act. . . .

If the presence on Madison street in the city of Louisville of the great volume of loose gas that arose from the escaping gasoline was caused by the negligence of the appellee Bridge & Railroad Company, it seems to us that the probable consequences of its coming in contact with fire and causing an explosion was too plain a proposition to admit of doubt. Indeed, it was most probable that some one would strike a match to light a cigar or for other purposes in the midst of the gas. In our opinion, therefore, the act of one lighting and throwing a match under such circumstances cannot be said to be the efficient cause of the explosion. It did not of itself produce the explosion, nor could it have done so without the assistance and contribution resulting from the primary negligence, if there was such negligence, on the part of the appellee Bridge & Railroad Company in furnishing the presence of the gas in the street. This conclusion, however, rests upon the theory that Duerr inadvertently or negligently lighted and threw the match in the gas. . . .

If, however, the act of Duerr in lighting the match and throwing it into the vapor or gas arising from the gasoline was malicious, and done for the purpose of causing the explosion, we do not think appellees would be responsible, for while the appellee Bridge & Railroad Company's negligence may have been the efficient cause of the presence of the gas in the street, and it should have understood enough of the consequences thereof to have foreseen that an explosion was likely to result from the inadvertent or negligent lighting of a match by some person who was ignorant of the presence of the gas or of the effect of lighting or throwing a match in it, it could not have foreseen or deemed it probable that one would maliciously or wantonly do such an act for the evil purpose of producing the explosion. Therefore, if the act of Duerr was malicious, we quite agree with the trial court that it was one which the appellees could not reasonably have anticipated or guarded against, and in such case the act of Duerr, and not the primary negligence of the appellee Bridge & Railroad Company, in any of the particulars charged, was the efficient or proximate cause of appellant's injuries. The mere fact that the concurrent cause or intervening act was unforeseen will not relieve the defendant guilty of the primary negligence from liability, but if the intervening agency is something so unexpected or extraordinary as that he could not or ought not to have anticipated it, he will not be liable, and certainly he is not bound to anticipate the criminal acts of others by which damage is inflicted and hence is not liable therefor. [Cc]

. . . .

For the reasons indicated, the judgment is . . . reversed as to the Bridge & Railroad Company, and the cause remanded for a new trial consistent with the opinion.

———————————

Points for Discussion

1. "An intervening force is one which actively operates in producing harm to another after the actor's negligent act or omission has been committed." RESTATEMENT (SECOND) OF TORTS § 441 (1965). "A superseding act is an act of a third person or other force which by its intervention prevents the actor from being liable for harm to another which his antecedent negligence is a substantial factor in bringing about." RESTATEMENT (SECOND) OF TORTS § 440. For a listing of factors considered in determining whether an intervening force is a superseding cause, see RESTATEMENT (SECOND) OF TORTS § 442.

2. The RESTATEMENT (THIRD) OF TORTS contains the following section on intervening acts and superseding causes: "When a force of nature or an independent act is also a factual cause of physical harm, an actor's liability is limited to those harms that result from the risks that made the actor's conduct tortious." RESTATEMENT (THIRD) OF TORTS: LIABILITY FOR PHYSICAL HARM § 34 (2010).

3. The *Watson* court opined that a tortfeasor "is not to anticipate the criminal acts of others by which damage is inflicted and hence is not liable therefor." Do you agree with this view? Consider the following hypothetical illustration set forth in the RESTATEMENT (THIRD) OF TORTS:

Hypo 5-5

"Laurie was a guest at the Rogers Motor Inn, which was located in a neighborhood where significant violent crime existed. After Laurie returned to her room, David was able to gain entrance to Laurie's room because the lock on the door was of the simple residential type that could easily be defeated with a credit card. After gaining entrance to Laurie's room, David sexually assaulted her. Laurie sues Rogers claiming negligence in providing inadequate locks for guest rooms."

Is David's criminal act a superseding cause? See RESTATEMENT (THIRD) OF TORTS: LIABILITY FOR PHYSICAL HARM § 34 Illustration 1 (2010).

Fuller v. Preis

35 N.Y.2d 425, 322 N.E.2d 263 (1974)

OPINION OF THE COURT

Chief Judge Breitel.

Plaintiff executor, in a wrongful death action, recovered a jury verdict for $200,000. The Appellate Division set aside the verdict and judgment in favor of plaintiff executor and dismissed the complaint. In doing so, that court noted that even if it were not to dismiss the complaint, it would set the verdict aside as contrary to the weight of the credible evidence. Plaintiff executor appeals.

Decedent, Dr. Lewis, committed suicide some seven months after an automobile accident from which he had walked away believing he was uninjured. In fact he had suffered head injuries with consequences to be detailed later. The theory of the case was that defendants, owner and operator of the vehicle which struck decedent's automobile, were responsible in tort for the suicide as a matter of proximate cause and effect. The issue is whether plaintiff's evidence of cause of the suicide was sufficient to withstand dismissal of the complaint.

There should be a reversal of the order of the Appellate Division and a new trial ordered. Regardless of how the evidence might be viewed by those entitled to weigh it for its probative effect, there was enough to establish plaintiff's right to have his evidence assessed by a trial jury, and it was unwarranted to dismiss the complaint. In so concluding, it is emphasized that reasonable men might, would, and do differ on how the jury as fact-finders, should have resolved the issue of fact. . . .

. . . .

On December 2, 1966, decedent Dr. Lewis, a 43-year-old surgeon, was involved in an intersection collision. Upon impact, the left side of his head struck the frame and window of his automobile. Suffering no evident injuries, he declined aid and drove himself home. Early the next day he experienced an episode of vomiting. An examination later that day at his hospital was inconclusive.

Two days after the accident, Dr. Lewis had a seizure followed by others. After a four- or five-day stay in the hospital as a patient he was diagnosed as having had a subdural contusion and cerebral concussion. Medication was prescribed.

He sustained recurring seizures, was hospitalized again, was further tested, and after five days, was discharged with diagnosis of "post traumatic focal seizures". Then ensued a period of deterioration and gradual contraction of his professional and private activities. Meanwhile, his wife, partially paralyzed as a result of an old poliomyelitis, suffered "nervous exhaustion" and his mother became ill with cancer.

On July 7, 1967, the day he learned of his mother's illness, decedent executed his will. On July 9, after experiencing three seizures that day, he went to the bathroom of his home, closed the door and shot himself in the head. He died the following day. Just before the gunshot, his wife heard him say to himself, "I must do it, I must do it", or words to that effect.

Two suicide notes, both dated July 9, 1967, were found next to the body. One, addressed to his wife, professed his love. The other, addressed to the family, contained information about a bank account and the location of his will and requested discreet disposition of certain personal property. He warned that the note "must never be seen by anyone except the three of you as it would alter the outcome of the 'case'--i.e., it's worth a million dollars to you all." And he went on to say that "I am perfectly sane in mind" and "I know exactly what I am doing". Alluding to the accident, the loss of his office and practice, his mother's and his wife's illnesses, the imposition caused thereby to his children, and his mounting responsibilities, he professed inability to continue.

Precedent of long standing establishes that public policy permits negligent tort-feasors to be held liable for the suicide of persons who, as the result of their negligence, suffer mental disturbance destroying the will to survive (e.g., *Koch v. Fox,* 71 App. Div. 288, 298-299; Liability for Suicide, Ann., 11 ALR 2d 751,esp. 758-762; cf. *Gioia v. State of New York,* 16 A D 2d 354, 357-359 [Halpern, J.]; *McMahon v. City of New York,* 16 Misc 2d 143, 144 [Christ, J.]; *Cauverien v. De Metz,* 20 Misc 2d 144, 148 [Nathan, J.]). . . .

. . . .

Hence, the act of suicide, as a matter of law, is not a superseding cause in negligence law precluding liability. An initial tort-feasor may be liable for the wrongful acts of a third party if foreseeable (see RESTATEMENT, 2D, TORTS, § 442A). Thus a tort-feasor may be liable for the ensuing malpractice of a physician treating the victim for the tortiously caused injuries (see, e.g., *Milks v. McIver,* 264 N. Y. 267, 269). No different rule applies when death results from an "involuntary" suicidal act of the victim as a direct consequence of the wrongful conduct.

That suicide may be encouraged by allowing recovery for suicide, a highly doubtful proposition in occidental society, is unpersuasive to preclude recovery for the suicide of a mentally deranged person. The remote possibility of fraudulent claims connecting a suicide with mental derangement affords no basis for barring recovery. [Cc] The obvious difficulty in proving or disproving causal relation should not bar recovery. [C]

. . . .

Dr. Lewis was physically and mentally healthy immediately prior to the automobile accident in which he struck his head against the interior of his own vehicle. After the accident he suffered several epileptic seizures, often with unconsciousness. Before the accident he had never suffered a seizure. For seven months between the accident and his death, Dr. Lewis experienced no fewer than 38 separate seizures. The neurologist who treated him testified that as the result of the blow on the head he sustained a cerebral contusion which caused seizures and underlying hemorrhaging in the brain covering, destroying part of the brain. According to the neurologist, brain hemorrhage causes scarring which distorts impulses, producing further seizures, further scarring, cell atrophy, and wasting, in a deadly cycle. On the day of his death Dr. Lewis had three seizures.

The truncated description of the testimony demonstrates, and it is not seriously disputed, that there was sufficient evidence from which a reasonable person might conclude that the accident caused traumatic organic brain damage.

The only authentic issue is whether the suicide was an "irresistible impulse" caused by traumatic organic brain damage. The issue is limited on this appeal because of the theory of the case based on the traditional but not entirely satisfactory concept of the "irresistible impulse". Medical and legal lore have developed an incisive critique of that concept but its evolution or clarification must await another day and another case. It has been cogently argued that it ought to be sufficient to accept mental illness, traumatic in origin, as a substantial cause of particular behavior, including suicide. [C]

The brain damage and the seizures compelled Dr. Lewis to give up his surgical practice and many other activities. The seizures were acceleratedly and progressively severe and uncontrolled by drugs. The treating neurologist testified that the brain cells in the area where he struck his head are concerned with the emotions and motor activity. After the accident, in addition to the accelerated severe seizures, decedent showed symptoms never before observed. He was constantly depressed, unsteady on his feet, irritable, complained of headaches, and walked askew.

. . . .

That Dr. Lewis believed himself sane should, of course, not control. Most insane people are certain of their sanity. Sanity is never established by a self-serving certification. He was not mentally retarded and his belief that his death might secure a large amount of money is hardly surprising.

In tort law, as contrasted with criminal law, there is recognition that one may retain the power to intend, to know, and yet to have an irresistible impulse to act and therefore be incapable of voluntary conduct. . . . The issue in this case was, precisely, whether Dr. Lewis, who obviously knew what he was doing and intended to do what he did, nevertheless, was, because of mental derangement, incapable of resisting the impulse to destroy himself. Precedents and modern knowledge say that that could have been. The jury found that it was so.

No doubt Dr. Lewis at some conscious level desired to take his life. This is demonstrated by the acquisition of the gun, his changing his will two days before his death, and the suicide notes. A suicide note, moreover, does not preclude, as a matter of law, a finding that the writer was unable to control his suicidal act. [Cc] An irresistible impulse does not necessarily mean a "sudden" impulse. [C] The evidence supports a finding that the insane "irresistible impulse" that caused decedent to take his life also impelled the acquisition of the gun and the writing of the suicide notes.

. . . .

Of course, there may be and undoubtedly have been cases where the causal nexus becomes too tenuous to permit a jury to "speculate" as to the proximate cause of the suicide. And the tenuous link is not strengthened or made more real by however strong a verbalization of cause. [C]

A suicide is a strange act and no rationalistic approach can fit the act into neat categories of rationality or irrationality. When the suicide is preceded by a history of trauma, brain damage, epileptic seizures, aberrational conduct, depression and despair, it is at the very least a fair issue of fact whether the suicide was the rational act of a sound mind or the irrational act or irresistible impulse of a deranged mind evidenced by a physically damaged brain. It would be illogical to conclude otherwise. Consequently, although the Appellate Division in exercise of its supervisory power to review the facts could set the jury verdict aside, it was impermissible for it to dismiss the complaint.

Since the Appellate Division, in reversing, stated that in any event it would have set the verdict aside as contrary to the weight of the evidence, the verdict in favor of plaintiff may not be reinstated and a new trial is required.

Accordingly, the order of the Appellate Division should be reversed, with costs, and a new trial directed.

La Quinta Inns, Inc. v. Leech

289 Ga.App. 812, 658 S.E.2d 637 (2008)

ELLINGTON, Judge.

On May 21, 2004, John Leech jumped or fell to his death from the window of a seventh-floor room at a La Quinta Inn. Carol Leech, Mr. Leech's surviving spouse and the representative of his estate, brought this **wrongful death** action against La Quinta Inns, Inc., LQ Management, LLC, La Quinta Corporation (collectively "La Quinta"), and Linda Cotton. The trial court denied in part the motion for summary judgment filed by La Quinta and Cotton, and we granted their application for **interlocutory appeal**. Mrs. Leech filed a cross-appeal from the trial court's ruling that the evidence of record demands a finding that Mr. Leech committed suicide. For the reasons that follow, we affirm in part and reverse in part.

. . . .

Viewed in the light most favorable to Mrs. Leech, the record shows the following undisputed facts. Before his death, Mr. Leech had lived in Room 322 of the hotel for about six months while separated from his wife. On May 20, 2004, Mr. Leech had dinner with his girlfriend, his adult son, James Leech ("James"), and his long-time friend, John Rivera; James and Rivera were both in town to attend the high school graduation of Mr. and Mrs. Leech's daughter, Ashley Leech ("Ashley"). After dinner, the group decided to go to a nearby bar. Ashley and her boyfriend met up with the group in the bar's parking lot. When Ashley saw her father with his girlfriend, she became upset and confronted her father about his affair.

Mr. Leech returned to the hotel shortly after midnight and had a brief conversation with Cotton, who was managing the front desk that night. Cotton was the only hotel employee on duty at the time and the only hotel employee with whom Mr. Leech interacted that day. About ten minutes later, Mr. Leech returned to the front desk to book a room for Rivera. Because he specifically requested a smoking room, Cotton gave him a room on the seventh floor, where all of the hotel's smoking rooms were located. During this transaction, Mr. Leech and Cotton had a friendly conversation about Ashley's graduation the next day and his friend's visit. According to Cotton, Mr. Leech was calm and cheerful when he left the front desk.

James and Rivera also went to the hotel after they left the bar. They arrived at approximately 1:05 a.m. and asked Cotton for Mr. Leech's room number. Cotton advised them that she could not give out room numbers but would call Mr. Leech's room and inform him of their presence. She tried to contact him at Room 322, but there was no answer, so she then called him at Room 721, the room that he had just engaged. Mr. Leech answered the phone, instructed Cotton not to give out his room numbers, and told her that he would call his son on his cell phone.

Mr. Leech called James on his cell phone at approximately 1:10 a.m. Mr. Leech invited his son up to his room, but James declined, saying that he and Rivera had other plans for the night. James testified that at approximately 1:13 a.m., after a few minutes of "normal" conversation, his "father began talking strangely and [James] became concerned that [Mr. Leech] was threatening to harm himself." Specifically, Mr. Leech told James "he was sorry for some of the things that had happened" and asked James to "tell the family he was sorry." James told him he could do that himself, and Mr. Leech responded that "he wouldn't be here." At that point, James covered his cell phone and told Rivera to get help because his father was talking about harming himself. Rivera demanded that Cotton give them Mr. Leech's room number, summon hotel security, and call 911 because he was threatening to harm himself.

For the next several minutes, James continued his conversation with Mr. Leech, in an effort to keep him on the telephone until help arrived. James testified that his father was calm, that he joked with him, and that he talked excitedly about Ashley's graduation party, his grandchildren, and his plans to move to Florida. Believing that Cotton was "dragging her feet," James yelled at her to "Stop f-ing around and get us the room number or get help." Mr. Leech overheard James' demand and told his son, "it would be over before [he] got [there]," and then the call ended.

Cotton called 911 at 1:27 a.m. At 1:34 a.m., two police officers arrived at the hotel. When they arrived, the officers asked Cotton where Mr. Leech was. Cotton was on the telephone and did not respond immediately. After that delay, Cotton told the officers that Mr. Leech stayed in Room 322, that he had just rented Room 721, and that she did not know which room he was in. She did not mention that, when she had last spoken with Mr. Leech, he was in Room 721. The officers and Rivera went to Room 322; James went alone to Room 721. As James approached Room 721 at 1:38 a.m., he heard his father talking on the phone. James knocked on the door, and, after getting no response, he kicked the door open. No one was in the room. James looked through the open window and saw his father's body on the ground below. There is no direct evidence regarding whether Mr. Leech jumped or fell to his death.

According to Mr. Leech's wife, his son, and his daughter, Mr. Leech had no history of depression or threats of suicide. The hotel staff knew Mr. Leech well from his long residence there. The record contains no evidence that any employee at La Quinta observed any unusual or suicidal behavior on the part of Mr. Leech at any time, including the night he died. No witness testified that they thought Mr.

Leech was intoxicated, under the influence of drugs, incapacitated, or depressed on the evening of May 20-21. The first indication that Mr. Leech was upset came 14 minutes before Cotton called 911, when Mr. Leech told James that he was sorry.

The window opening through which Mr. Leech jumped or fell was 56 inches in height, and the sill was 24 inches above the floor. An HVAC unit was installed directly below the window and protruded 10 to 12 inches into the room. The window could be opened to a width of 26 inches. La Quinta required window stops to prevent guest windows from being opened wider than six inches, unless the stops were disengaged by an adult. The window in Room 721 lacked window stops.

In her complaint, Mrs. Leech alleges . . . that Cotton, acting as La Quinta's agent, negligently failed to timely intervene to prevent Mr. Leech from jumping to his death and that La Quinta failed to provide adequate staffing, safety standards, and training in responding to emergencies. The trial court denied La Quinta's motion for summary judgment, in part, to the extent Mrs. Leech travels under [the negligence] theory of liability. . . .

. . . .

"Generally, suicide is an unforeseeable intervening cause of death which absolves the tortfeasor of liability." *Dry Storage Corp. v. Piscopo,* 249 Ga.App. 898, 900, 550 S.E.2d 419 (2001).[2] In this case, assuming that Mr. Leech intentionally jumped from the window, and pretermitting whether La Quinta and/or Cotton owed Mr. Leech a duty to act to prevent his suicide and breached that duty, there was an intervening act of someone other than La Quinta or Cotton sufficient of itself to cause his death. There is no evidence that Mr. Leech's suicide was triggered by anything La Quinta or Cotton did or failed to do. Furthermore, although Mrs. Leech claims that Mr. Leech's suicide could have been prevented if help had reached him sooner, the undisputed evidence establishes that Mr. Leech jumped out the window only *after* help arrived. In short, Mrs. Leech's theory that La Quinta and Cotton could have prevented Mr. Leech from jumping to his death if Cotton had responded differently to the crisis is pure speculation.

---

2 *Cf. Thomas v. Williams,* 105 Ga.App. 321, 326-329(3), 124 S.E.2d 409 (1962) (where the police chief in charge of the city jail left a very drunk prisoner in a small cell with matches, and a detainee died after setting his mattress on fire, the officer was not entitled to dismissal because every person is charged with the knowledge that "a man staggering drunk is incapable of exercising ordinary care for his own safety"); *Emory Univ. v. Shadburn,* 47 Ga.App. 643(1), 171 S.E. 192 (1933) aff'd, 180 Ga. 595, 180 S.E. 137 (1935) (where a hospital patient later jumped out of a window, the hospital was not entitled to summary judgment because the hospital was on notice that the patient was delirious when it left the patient unsupervised).

Because the evidence demands a finding that Mr. Leech's act of suicide was the sole proximate cause of his death, the trial court erred in denying La Quinta's and Cotton's motion for summary judgment, to the extent Mrs. Leech alleges that they negligently failed to prevent Mr. Leech's suicide. [Cc].[5]

. . . .

Judgment affirmed in part and reversed in part.

Points for Discussion

1. Agree or disagree with the following proposition: Suicide is a superseding event breaking the chain of causation in a negligence action.

2. How does the *Fuller* court define and apply the "irresistible impulse" concept? Were the actions of Dr. Lewis preceding his suicide, including the changing of his will and preparation of a suicide note, evidence of an "irresistible impulse"?

3. The *La Quinta* court concluded that Mr. Leech's suicide was the sole proximate cause of his death. Note that there can be more than one proximate cause of an injury and that a plaintiff pursuing a negligence cause of action may be able to recover from more than one defendant in a particular case.

---

5 Cf. *Sneider v. Hyatt Corp.,* 390 F.Supp. 976 (N.D.Ga.1975) (where there was evidence that the hotel was on notice that its multistory atrium had become an attractive location for suicides, that a guest who later committed suicide had suicidal tendencies, was noticeably inebriated when she checked in without luggage, and was wandering around the twenty-first floor in a confused state, and that a family member had repeatedly called the hotel for help in finding the guest, the hotel was not entitled to summary judgment on a wrongful death claim) (applying Georgia law).

Hypo 5-6

Father, a police officer, came home after completing his shift. Taking off his holster belt containing his firearm, Father placed the holster on the kitchen table. Daughter, age 16, approached Father, told him that there was no milk in the refrigerator, and asked if he would go to the store for her. Father went to the store and purchased the milk. Returning home, he noticed that his firearm was missing from its holster. Going into Daughter's room, Father found Daughter dead in the shower from an apparent gunshot wound to her head.

Six months prior to her death, Daughter had attempted suicide by taking a large number of sleeping pills; she survived that attempt when her brother found her and took her to the hospital for treatment. Daughter received counseling after that incident and, according to her counselor, was no longer having suicidal thoughts.

The personal representative of Daughter's estate sued Father, alleging that he was negligent in leaving his firearm unattended. Is Daughter's suicide a superseding cause that broke the causal chain of Father's negligence, if any?

---

3. Public Policy

Kelly v. Gwinnell

96 N.J. 538, 476 A.2d 1219 (1984)

WILENTZ, C.J.

This case raises the issue of whether a social host who enables an adult guest at his home to become drunk is liable to the victim of an automobile accident caused by the drunken driving of the guest. Here the host served liquor to the guest beyond the point at which the guest was visibly intoxicated. We hold the host may be liable under the circumstances of this case.

At the trial level, the case was disposed of, insofar as the issue before us is concerned, by summary judgment in favor of the social host. The record on which the summary judgment was based (pleadings, depositions, and certifications) discloses that defendant Donald Gwinnell, after driving defendant Joseph Zak home, spent an hour or two at Zak's home before leaving to return to his own home. During that time, according to Gwinnell, Zak, and Zak's wife, Gwinnell consumed two or three drinks of scotch on the rocks. Zak accompanied Gwinnell outside to his car, chatted with him, and watched as Gwinnell then drove off to go home. About twenty-five minutes later Zak telephoned Gwinnell's home to make sure Gwinnell had arrived there safely. The phone was answered by Mrs. Gwinnell, who advised Zak that Gwinnell had been involved in a head-on collision. The collision was with an automobile operated by plaintiff, Marie Kelly, who was seriously injured as a result.

After the accident Gwinnell was subjected to a blood test, which indicated a blood alcohol concentration of 0.286 percent.[1] Kelly's expert concluded from that reading that Gwinnell had consumed not two or three scotches but the equivalent of thirteen drinks; that while at Zak's home Gwinnell must have been showing unmistakable signs of intoxication; and that in fact he was severely intoxicated while at Zak's residence and at the time of the accident.

Kelly sued Gwinnell and his employer; those defendants sued the Zaks in a third party action; and thereafter plaintiff amended her complaint to include Mr. and Mrs. Zak as direct defendants. The Zaks moved for summary judgment, contending that as a matter of law a host is not liable for the negligence of an adult social guest who has become intoxicated while at the host's home. The trial court granted the motion on that basis. . . . The Appellate Division affirmed, *Kelly v. Gwinnell,* 190 N.J.Super. 320, 463 A.2d 387 (1983). It noted, correctly, that New Jersey has no **Dram Shop Act** imposing liability on the provider of alcoholic beverages, and that while our decisional law had imposed such liability on licensees, common-law liability had been extended to a social host only where the guest was a minor. [Cc] It explicitly declined to expand that liability where, as here, the social guest was an adult. [C]

What's That?

A number of states have enacted **dram-shop acts** which, in addition to criminal penalties, provide a civil cause of action against commercial sellers of alcohol for injuries caused by a customer's intoxication. See Chapter 4, *infra.*

The Appellate Division's determination was based on the apparent absence of decisions in this country imposing such liability (except for those that were

[1] Under present law, a person who drives with a blood alcohol concentration of 0.10 percent or more violates *N.J.S.A.* 39:4-50 as amended by *L.* 1983, c. 129, the statute concerning driving while under the influence of intoxicating liquor.

promptly overruled by the Legislature).[2] [C] The absence of such determinations is said to reflect a broad consensus that the imposition of liability arising from these social relations is unwise. Certainly this immunization of hosts is not the inevitable result of the law of negligence, for conventional negligence analysis points strongly in exactly the opposite direction. "Negligence is tested by whether the reasonably prudent person at the time and place should recognize and foresee an unreasonable risk or likelihood of harm or danger to others." [Cc] When negligent conduct creates such a risk, setting off foreseeable consequences that lead to plaintiff's injury, the conduct is deemed the proximate cause of the injury. "[A] tortfeasor is generally held answerable for the injuries which result in the ordinary course of events from his negligence and it is generally sufficient if his negligent conduct was a substantial factor in bringing about the injuries." [Cc]

Under the facts here defendant provided his guest with liquor, knowing that thereafter the guest would have to drive in order to get home. Viewing the facts most favorably to plaintiff (as we must, since the complaint was dismissed on a motion for summary judgment), one could reasonably conclude that the Zaks must have known that their provision of liquor was causing Gwinnell to become drunk, yet they continued to serve him even after he was visibly intoxicated. By the time he left, Gwinnell was in fact severely intoxicated. A reasonable person in Zak's position could foresee quite clearly that this continued provision of alcohol to Gwinnell was making it more and more likely that Gwinnell would not be able to operate his car carefully. Zak could foresee that unless he stopped providing drinks to Gwinnell, Gwinnell was likely to injure someone as a result of the negligent operation of his car. The usual elements of a cause of action for negligence are clearly present: an action by defendant creating an unreasonable risk of harm to plaintiff, a risk that was clearly foreseeable, and a risk that resulted in an injury equally foreseeable. Under those circumstances the only question remaining is whether a duty exists to prevent such risk or, realistically, whether this Court should impose such a duty.

---

2 The Appellate Division noted that several state court decisions imposing liability against social hosts under circumstances similar to those in this case were abrogated by later legislative action. We note that legislation enacted in Oregon did not abrogate the state court's holding in *Wiener v. Gamma Phi Chapter of Alpha Tau Omega Fraternity,* 258 *Or.* 632, 485 *P.*2d 18 (1971). The court found that a host directly serving liquor to a guest has a duty to refuse to serve the guest when it would be unreasonable under the circumstances to permit the guest to drink. Eight years later the legislature enacted *Or.Rev. Stat.* § 30.955, limiting a cause of action against a private host for damages incurred or caused by an intoxicated social guest to when the host "has served or provided alcoholic beverages to a social guest when such guest was visibly intoxicated." The legislature did not, therefore, preclude liability of private hosts under a negligence theory but instead decided that the social guest must be visibly intoxicated before the host will be held accountable for injuries caused by the guest's intoxicated conduct.

Nevertheless, we acknowledge that many jurisdictions have declined to extend liability to social hosts in circumstances similar to those present in this case. See, *e.g., Klein v. Raysinger,* --- *Pa.* ---, 470 A.2d 507, 510 (1983), and collected cases cited therein.

. . . .

When the court determines that a duty exists and liability will be extended, it draws judicial lines based on fairness and policy. In a society where thousands of deaths are caused each year by drunken drivers, where the damage caused by such deaths is regarded increasingly as intolerable, where liquor licensees are prohibited from serving intoxicated adults, and where long-standing criminal sanctions against drunken driving have recently been significantly strengthened to the point where the Governor notes that they are regarded as the toughest in the nation, see Governor's Annual Message to the N.J. State Legislature, Jan. 10, 1984, the imposition of such a duty by the judiciary seems both fair and fully in accord with the State's policy. Unlike those cases in which the definition of desirable policy is the subject of intense controversy, here the imposition of a duty is both consistent with and supportive of a social goal-the reduction of drunken driving-that is practically unanimously accepted by society.

. . . .

We therefore hold that a host who serves liquor to an adult social guest, knowing both that the guest is intoxicated and will thereafter be operating a motor vehicle, is liable for injuries inflicted on a third party as a result of the negligent operation of a motor vehicle by the adult guest when such negligence is caused by the intoxication. We impose this duty on the host to the third party because we believe that the policy considerations served by its imposition far outweigh those asserted in opposition. While we recognize the concern that our ruling will interfere with accepted standards of social behavior; will intrude on and somewhat diminish the enjoyment, relaxation, and camaraderie that accompany social gatherings at which alcohol is served; and that such gatherings and social relationships are not simply tangential benefits of a civilized society but are regarded by many as important, we believe that the added assurance of just compensation to the victims of drunken driving as well as the added deterrent effect of the rule on such driving outweigh the importance of those other values. Indeed, we believe that given society's extreme concern about drunken driving, any change in social behavior resulting from the rule will be regarded ultimately as neutral at the very least, and not as a change for the worse; but that in any event if there be a loss, it is well worth the gain.

The liability we impose here is analogous to that traditionally imposed on owners of vehicles who lend their cars to persons they know to be intoxicated. *Knight v. Gosselin,* 124 Cal.App. 290, 12 P.2d 454 (Dist.Ct.App.1932); *Harris v. Smith,* 119 Ga.App. 306, 167 S.E.2d 198 (Ct.App.1969); *Pennington v. Davis-Child Motor Co.,* 143 Kan. 753, 57 P.2d 428 (1936); *Deck v. Sherlock,* 162 Neb. 86, 75 N.W.2d 99 (1956); *Mitchell v. Churches,* 119 Wash. 547, 206 P. 6 (1922). If, by lending a car to a drunk, a host becomes liable to third parties injured by the drunken driver's negligence, the same liability should extend to a host who furnishes liquor to a visibly drunken guest who he knows will thereafter drive away.

Some fear has been expressed that the extent of the potential liability may be disproportionate to the fault of the host. A social judgment is therein implied to the effect that society does not regard as particularly serious the host's actions in causing his guests to become drunk, even though he knows they will thereafter be driving their cars. We seriously question that value judgment; indeed, we do not believe that the liability is disproportionate when the host's actions, so relatively easily corrected, may result in serious injury or death. The other aspect of this argument is that the host's insurance protection will be insufficient. While acknowledging that homeowners' insurance will cover such liability, this argument notes the risk that both the host and spouse will be jointly liable. The point made is not that the level of insurance will be lower in relation to the injuries than in the case of other torts, but rather that the joint liability of the spouses may result in the loss of their home and other property to the extent that the policy limits are inadequate. If only one spouse were liable, then even though the policy limits did not cover the liability, the couple need not lose their home because the creditor might not reach the interest of the spouse who was not liable. [Cc] . . .

Given the lack of precedent anywhere else in the country, however, we believe it would be unfair to impose this liability retroactively. [Cc] Homeowners who are social hosts may desire to increase their policy limits; apartment dwellers may want to obtain liability insurance of this kind where perhaps they now have none. The imposition of retroactive liability could be considered unexpected and its imposition unfair. We therefore have determined that the liability imposed by this case on social hosts shall be prospective, applicable only to events that occur after the date of this decision. We will, however, apply the doctrine to the parties before us on the usual theory that to do otherwise would not only deprive the plaintiff of any benefit resulting from her own efforts but would also make it less likely that, in the future, individuals will be willing to claim rights, not yet established, that they believe are just.

The goal we seek to achieve here is the fair compensation of victims who are injured as a result of drunken driving. The imposition of the duty certainly will make such fair compensation more likely. While the rule in this case will tend also to deter drunken driving, there is no assurance that it will have any significant effect. The lack of such assurance has not prevented us in the past from imposing liability on licensees. Indeed, it has been only recently that the sanction of the *criminal* law was credited with having some significant impact on drunken driving. We need not, however, condition the imposition of a duty on scientific proof that it will result in the behavior that is one of its goals. No one has suggested that the common-law duty to drive carefully should be abolished because it has apparently not diminished the mayhem that occurs regularly on our highways. We believe the rule will make it more likely that hosts will take greater care in serving alcoholic beverages at social gatherings so as to avoid not only the moral responsibility but the economic liability that would occur if the guest were to injure someone as a result of his drunken driving.

We do not agree that the issue addressed in this case is appropriate only for legislative resolution. Determinations of the scope of duty in negligence cases has traditionally been a function of the judiciary. The history of the cases cited above evidences a continuing judicial involvement in these matters. Without the benefit of any Dram Shop Act imposing liability on licensees, legislation that is quite common in other states, this Court determined that such liability nevertheless existed. We did so in 1959 and have continued to expand that concept since then. We know of no legislative activity during that entire period from 1959 to date suggesting that our involvement in these matters was deemed inappropriate . . . The subject matter is not abstruse, and it can safely be assumed that the Legislature is in fact aware of our decisions in this area. Absent such adverse reaction, we assume that our decisions are found to be consonant with the strong legislative policy against drunken driving.

. . . .

This Court senses that there may be a substantial change occurring in social attitudes and customs concerning drinking, whether at home or in taverns. We believe that this change may be taking place right now in New Jersey and perhaps elsewhere. It is the upheaval of prior norms by a society that has finally recognized that it must change its habits and do whatever is required, whether it means but a small change or a significant one, in order to stop the senseless loss inflicted by drunken drivers. We did not cause that movement, but we believe this decision is in step with it.

. . . We hold only that where a host provides liquor directly to a social guest and continues to do so even beyond the point at which the host knows the guest is intoxicated, and does this knowing that the guest will shortly thereafter be operating a motor vehicle, that host is liable for the foreseeable consequences to third parties that result from the guest's drunken driving. We hold further that the host and guest are liable to the third party as joint tortfeasors . . . [cc]

. . . .

We therefore reverse the judgment in favor of the defendants Zak and remand the case to the Law Division for proceedings consistent with this opinion.

GARIBALDI, J., dissenting.

Today, this Court holds that a social host who knowingly enables an adult guest to become intoxicated knowing that the guest will operate a motor vehicle is liable for damages to a third party caused by the intoxicated guest. The imposition of this liability on a social host places upon every citizen of New Jersey who pours a drink for a friend a heavy burden to monitor and regulate guests. It subjects the host to substantial potential financial liability that may be far beyond the host's resources.

. . . .

Prior to today's decision, this Court had imposed liability only on those providers of alcoholic beverages who were licensed by the State. *See Rappaport v. Nichols,* 31 N.J. 188, 156 A.2d 201 (1959). The Appellate Division also had expanded the liability to a social host who served liquor to a minor. *Lind v. Rand,* 140 N.J.Super. 212, 356 A.2d 15 (App.Div.1976). Although both of these cases were based on common-law negligence, the courts deemed the regulations restricting the service of alcohol to minors significant enough evidence of legislative policy to impart knowledge of foreseeable risk on the provider of the alcohol and to fashion a civil remedy for negligently creating that risk.

Many other states have considered the problem before us today but no judicial decision establishing a cause of action against a social host for serving liquor to an adult social guest is currently in force. Any prior judicial attempts to establish such a cause of action have been abrogated or restricted by subsequent legislative action. *See, e.g., Cal.Civ.Code* § 1714 (as amended Stats.1978, ch. 929, § 2, p. 2904); *Or.Rev.Stat.* § 30.955 (1979).

State courts have found that imposition of this new form of liability on social hosts is such a radical departure from prior law, with such extraordinary effects on the average citizen, that the issue is best left to a legislative determination. *See Kowal v. Hofher,* 181 Conn. 355, 436 A.2d 1 (1980); *Miller v. Moran,* 96 Ill.App.3d 596, 52 Ill.Dec. 183, 421 N.E.2d 1046 (1981); *Behnke v. Pierson,* 21 Mich.App. 219, 175 N.W.2d 303 (1970); *Cole v. City of Spring Lake Park,* 314 N.W.2d 836 (Minn.1982); *Runge v. Watts,* 180 Mont. 91, 589 P.2d 145 (1979); *Hamm v. Carson City Nugget, Inc.,* 85 Nev. 99, 450 P.2d 358 (1969); *Schirmer v. Yost,* 60 A.D.2d 789, 400 N.Y.S.2d 655 (1977); *Edgar v. Kajet,* 84 Misc.2d 100, 375 N.Y.S.2d 548 (Sup.Ct.1975), aff'd, 55 A.D.2d 597, 389 N.Y.S.2d 631 (1976); *Klein v. Raysinger, supra,* 504 Pa. 141, 470 A.2d 507; *Halvorson v. Birchfield Boiler, Inc.,* 76 Wash.2d 759, 458 P.2d 897 (1969).

. . . .

My reluctance to join the majority is not based on any exaggerated notion of judicial deference to the Legislature. Rather, it is based on my belief that before this Court plunges into this broad area of liability and imposes high duties of care on social hosts, it should carefully consider the ramifications of its actions. The Court acts today with seemingly scant knowledge and little care for the possible negative consequences of its decision.

. . . .

The Legislature of this state has enacted a comprehensive auto insurance program to guarantee that those injured on our highways have remedies. Even in cases in which the drunk driver is insolvent and has no insurance, the victim's own automobile insurance policy is required by law, *N.J.S.A.* 17:28-1.1, to include coverage for all or part of the sums that the insured "shall be legally entitled to recover as damages from owners or operators of uninsured automobiles * * *." Furthermore, all motorists must have uninsured motorist coverage. *N.J.S.A.* 39:6A-14. If the drunk driver hits an uninsured pedestrian, the pedestrian, after obtaining a judgment, and unsuccessfully attempting to satisfy it, could satisfy the judgment out of the Unsatisfied Claim and Judgment Fund. *N.J.S.A.* 39:6-73. Thus, only in the situation in which a victim of a drunk driver is himself an uninsured motorist at the time of the injury will the victim have no remedy under our insurance laws. There, the victim, having broken the law by driving without insurance, is not entitled to collect from the Unsatisfied Claim and Judgment Fund.

I do not know whether the Legislature's insurance scheme provides adequate protection for victims of drunk drivers and whether further relief may be necessary. I have seen no statistics to indicate the extent of this problem. However, the Legislature can collect information indicating the number of victims of drunk drivers who have not been adequately compensated. These statistics would be significant factors in ascertaining the scope of the problem and in creating solutions that would protect the injured party without excessively burdening the average citizen.

. . . .

The majority holds that a host will be liable only if he serves alcohol to a guest knowing both that the guest is intoxicated and that the guest will drive. [C] Although this standard calls for a subjective determination of the extent of the host's knowledge, a close reading of the opinion makes clear that the majority actually is relying on objective evidence. The majority takes the results of Gwinnell's blood alcohol concentration test and concludes from that test that "the Zaks must have known that their provision of liquor was causing Gwinnell to become drunk * * *." [C]

Whether a guest is or is not intoxicated is not a simple issue. Alcohol affects everyone differently. "[T]he precise effects of a particular concentration of alcohol in the blood varies from person to person depending upon a host of other factors. [Cc] One individual can consume many drinks without exhibiting any signs of intoxication. Alcohol also takes some time to get into the bloodstream and show its outward effects. Experts estimate that it takes alcohol twenty to thirty minutes to reach its highest level in the bloodstream. See *American Medical Association, Alcohol and the Impaired Driver* (1968). Thus, a blood alcohol concentration test demonstrating an elevated blood alcohol level after an accident may not mean that the subject was obviously intoxicated when he left the party some time earlier. "Moreover, a state of obvious intoxication is a condition that is very susceptible to after the fact interpretations, *i.e.,* objective review of a subjective decision. These factors combine to make the determination that an individual is obviously intoxicated not so obvious after all." [C] Accordingly, to impose on average citizens a duty to comprehend a person's level of intoxication and the effect another drink would ultimately have on such person is to place a very heavy burden on them.

The nature of home entertaining compounds the social host's difficulty in determining whether a guest is obviously intoxicated before serving the next drink. In a commercial establishment, there is greater control over the liquor; a bartender or waitress must serve the patron a drink. Not so in a home when entertaining a guest. At a social gathering, for example, guests frequently serve themselves or guests may serve other guests. Normally, the host is so busy entertaining he does not have time to analyze the state of intoxication of the guests. Without constant face-to-face contact it is difficult for a social host to avoid serving alcohol to a person on the brink of intoxication. Furthermore, the commercial bartender usually does not drink on the job. The social host often drinks with the guest, as the Zaks did here. The more the host drinks, the less able he will be to determine when a guest is intoxicated. It would be anomalous to create a rule of liability that social hosts can deliberately avoid by becoming drunk themselves.

. . . .

Further, it is not clear from the Court's opinion to what lengths a social host must go to avoid liability. Is the host obligated to use physical force to restrain an intoxicated guest from drinking and then from driving? Or is the host limited to delay and subterfuge tactics short of physical force? What is the result when the host tries to restrain the guest but fails? Is the host still liable? The majority opinion is silent on the extent to which we must police our guests.

. . .

The most significant difference between a social host and a commercial licensee, however, is the social host's inability to spread the cost of liability. The commercial establishment spreads the cost of insurance against liability among its customers. The social host must bear the entire cost alone. . . .

. . . .

. . . I believe that an in depth review of this problem by the Legislature will result in a solution that will further the goals of reducing injuries related to drunk driving and adequately compensating the injured party, while imposing a more limited liability on the social host. Imaginative legislative drafting could include: funding a remedy for the injured party by contributions from the parties most responsible for the harm caused, the intoxicated motorists; making the social host secondarily liable by requiring a judgment against the drunken driver as a prerequisite to suit against the host; limiting the amount that could be recovered from a social host; and requiring a finding of wanton and reckless conduct before holding the social host liable.

I do not propose to fashion a legislative solution. That is for the Legislature. I merely wish to point out that the Legislature has a variety of alternatives to this Court's imposition of unlimited liability on every New Jersey adult. Perhaps, after investigating all the options, the Legislature will determine that the most effective course is to impose the same civil liability on social hosts that the majority has imposed today. I would have no qualms about that legislative decision so long as it was reached after a thorough investigation of its impact on average citizens of New Jersey.

Points for Discussion

1. In 1987 the New Jersey legislature passed a law limiting the duty imposed by *Kelly* on a social host. "No social host shall be held liable to a person who has attained the legal age to purchase and consume alcoholic beverages for damages suffered as a result of the social host's negligent provision of alcoholic beverages to that person." N.J.S.A. 2A:15-5.7. This statute "applies only to social hosts, and appears to be a response to, among other things, the court's recognition in *Kelly* . . . that the decision would interfere with accepted standards of social behavior including the enjoyment, relaxation and camaraderie that accompany social gatherings where alcohol is served." Wagner v. Schlue, 255 N.J. Super. 391, 605 A.2d 294 (1992). *See also* Graff v. Beard, 858 S.W.2d 918 (Tex. 1993) (social host has no legal responsibility to supervise drinking of adult guests).

2. Is a social host required to monitor the drinking of minors? *See* Biscan v. Brown, 160 S.W.3d 462 (Tenn. 2005); Smith v. Merritt, 940 S.W.2d 602 (Tex. 1997).

3. "At common law a tavern owner who furnishes alcoholic beverages to another is not civilly liable for a third person's injuries that are caused by the acts of an intoxicated person. Such a rule is principally based upon concepts of causation that, as a matter of law, it is not the sale of liquor by the tavern owner, but the voluntary consumption by the intoxicated person, which is the proximate cause of resulting injuries, so that the tavern owner is therefore not liable for negligence in selling the liquor." Brigance v. Velvet Dove Restaurant, Inc., 725 P.2d 300 (Okla. 1986). Do you agree or disagree?

———————

Enright v. Eli Lilly & Co.

77 N.Y.2d 377, 570 N.E.2d 198 (1991)

Chief Judge Wachtler.

The question in this case is whether the liability of manufacturers of the drug diethylstilbestrol (DES) should extend to a so-called "third generation" plaintiff, the granddaughter of a woman who ingested the drug. According to the allegations of the complaint, the infant plaintiff's injuries were caused by her premature birth, which in turn resulted from damage to her mother's reproductive system caused by the mother's in utero exposure to DES. We hold, in accord with our decision in *Albala v. City of New York* (54 N.Y.2d 269), that in these circumstances no cause of action accrues in favor of the infant plaintiff against the drug manufacturers.

I.

The plaintiffs in this case are Karen Enright, born August 9, 1981, and her parents, Patricia and Earl Enright. According to their complaint, the events underlying this action began more than 30 years ago, when Karen Enright's maternal grandmother ingested DES during a pregnancy which resulted in the birth of plaintiff Patricia Enright on January 29, 1960. Plaintiffs allege that because of her in utero exposure to DES, Patricia Enright developed a variety of abnormalities and deformities in her reproductive system. As a result, several of her pregnancies terminated in spontaneous abortions and another resulted in the premature birth of Karen Enright. Karen suffers from cerebral palsy and other disabilities that plaintiffs attribute to her premature birth and, ultimately, to her grandmother's ingestion of DES.

This action was commenced by Patricia and Earl Enright individually and on behalf of their daughter against several manufacturers of DES. After issue was joined, the defendants sought summary judgment dismissing the complaint. Defendants contended that the actions were barred by . . . plaintiffs' inability to identify the manufacturer of the drug ingested by Karen's grandmother. In addition, defendants argued that Karen's claims of a preconception tort presented no cognizable cause of action.

Supreme Court, relying principally on *Albala v. City of New York* (54 N.Y.2d 269, *supra*), agreed with defendants that those claims stemming from Karen's injuries were not legally cognizable and dismissed all four causes of action [for negligence, **breach of warranty**, **fraud**, and **strict liability**] brought on her behalf and those asserted by her parents for their emotional injuries resulting from Karen's birth. Defendants' motions were otherwise denied, however, leaving intact Patricia Enright's claims relating to her own physical injuries and Earl Enright's derivative claim based upon his wife's injuries.

On cross appeals, the Appellate Division modified by reinstating the third cause of action in the complaint--that cause of action brought on behalf of Karen Enright based upon strict products liability. The Appellate Division agreed with Supreme Court that *Albala* foreclosed preconception tort liability based upon negligence, but held that public policy in favor of providing a remedy for DES victims justified recognizing a strict products liability cause of action.

. . . .

II.

The tragic DES tale is well documented in this Court's decisions and need not be recounted here. [Cc] It is sufficient to note that between 1947 and 1971, the drug, a synthetic estrogen-like substance produced by approximately 300 manufacturers, was prescribed for use and ingested by millions of pregnant women to prevent miscarriages. In 1971, the Food and Drug Administration banned the drug's use for the treatment of problems of pregnancy after studies established a link between in utero exposure to DES and the occurrence in teen-age women of a rare form of vaginal and cervical cancer. Plaintiffs allege that in utero exposure to DES has since been linked to other genital tract aberrations in DES daughters, including malformations or immaturity of the uterus, cervical abnormalities, misshapen Fallopian tubes and abnormal cell and tissue growth, all of which has caused in this population a marked increase in the incidence of infertility, miscarriages, premature births and ectopic pregnancies.

The Legislature and this Court have both expressed concern for the victims of this tragedy by removing legal barriers to their tort recovery--barriers which may have had their place in other contexts, but which in DES litigation worked a peculiar injustice because of the ways in which DES was developed, marketed and sold and because of the insidious nature of its harm.

. . . .

More recently, this Court responded to the fact that--for a variety of reasons unique to the DES litigation context--a DES plaintiff generally finds it impossible to identify the manufacturer of the drug that caused her injuries. We held that liability could be imposed upon DES manufacturers in accordance with their share of the national DES market, notwithstanding the plaintiff's inability to identify the manufacturer particularly at fault for her injuries. [C]

III.

In the present case, we are asked to do something significantly different. We are asked, not to remove some barrier to recovery that presents unique problems in DES cases, but to recognize a cause of action not available in other contexts simply (or at least largely) because this is a DES case.

In *Albala v City of New York* (54 NY2d 269, 271, *supra*), we were presented with the question "whether a cause of action lies in favor of a child for injuries suffered as a result of a preconception tort committed against the mother". There, the mother suffered a perforated uterus during the course of an abortion. Four years later, she gave birth to a brain-damaged child, whose injuries were allegedly attributable to the defendants' negligence in perforating the mother's uterus. We declined, as a matter of policy, to recognize a cause of action on behalf of the child, believing that to do so would "require the extension of traditional tort concepts beyond manageable bounds" [c]. Among other things, we were concerned with "the staggering implications of any proposition which would honor claims assuming the breach of an identifiable duty for less than a perfect birth" and the difficulty, if such a cause of action were recognized, of confining liability by other than artificial and arbitrary boundaries [c].

The case now before us differs from *Albala* only in that the mother's injuries in this case were caused by exposure to DES instead of by medical malpractice. A different rule is justified, therefore, only if that distinction alters the policy balance we struck in *Albala.*

The primary thrust of plaintiffs' argument and the Appellate Division's decision is that DES itself alters that balance. From the Legislature's actions in modifying the applicable Statute of Limitations and reviving time-barred DES cases and from our adoption of a **market-share liability** theory in *Hymowitz,* plaintiffs perceive a public policy favoring a remedy for DES-caused injuries sufficient to overcome the countervailing policy considerations we identified in *Albala*. The implication, of course, is that the public interest in providing a remedy for those injured by DES is stronger than the public interest in providing a remedy for those injured by other means--medical malpractice, for example. We do not believe that such a preference has been established.

To be sure, recent developments demonstrate legislative and judicial solicitude for the victims of DES, but they do not establish DES plaintiffs as a favored class for whose benefit all traditional limitations on tort liability must give way. To the extent that special rules have been fashioned, they are a response to unique procedural barriers and problems of proof peculiar to DES litigation.

. . . .

In the present case . . . neither plaintiffs, the Appellate Division, nor the dissent has identified any unique feature of DES litigation that justifies the novel proposition they advance--recognition of a multigenerational cause of action that we have refused to recognize in any other context. The fact that this is a DES case does not by itself justify a departure from the *Albala* rule.

Closer to the mark, though still falling short, is plaintiffs' second argument. They note that *Albala* was a negligence case and that we left open the question whether a different result might obtain under a strict products liability theory, because of the potentially different policy considerations in such a case [c]. Having now examined the question in the context of this particular strict products liability claim, we find no basis for reaching a different conclusion than we did in *Albala*.

. . . .

. . . To begin, the concerns we identified in *Albala* are present in equal measure here. The nature of the plaintiffs' injuries in both cases--birth defects--and their cause--harm to the mothers' reproductive systems before the children were conceived--are indistinguishable for these purposes. They raise the same vexing questions with the same "staggering implications" (*Albala v City of New York, supra,* at 273). As in *Albala,* the cause of action plaintiffs ask us to recognize here could not be confined without the drawing of artificial and arbitrary boundaries. For all we know, the rippling effects of DES exposure may extend for generations. It is our duty to confine liability within manageable limits [cc]. Limiting liability to those who ingested the drug or were exposed to it in utero serves this purpose.

At the same time, limiting liability in this fashion does not unduly impair the deterrent purposes of tort liability. The manufacturers remain amenable to suit by all those injured by exposure to their product, a class whose size is commensurate with the risk created. In addition, we note that the tort system is not the only means of encouraging prescription drug safety; the Federal Food and Drug Administration has primary responsibility for that task [c]. We do not suggest, as some have [c], that for this reason the judicial system should abandon its traditional role. But in light of the FDA's responsibility in this area, the need for the tort system to promote prescription drug safety is at least diminished.

That the product involved here is a prescription drug raises other considerations as well. First, as in most prescription drug cases [c], liability here is predicated on a failure to warn of dangers of which the manufacturers knew or with adequate testing should have known. Such a claim, though it may be couched in terms of strict liability, is indistinguishable from a negligence claim [c]. Concepts of reasonable care and foreseeability are not divorced from this theory of liability, as they may be under other strict products liability predicates. Thus, the effort to distinguish this case from *Albala* is strained.

More important, however, is recognition that public policy favors the availability of prescription drugs even though most carry some risks [cc] That is not to say that drug manufacturers should enjoy immunity from liability stemming from their failure to conduct adequate research and testing prior to the marketing of their products. They do not enjoy such immunity, as evidenced by our recognition of liability in favor of those who have been injured by ingestion or in utero exposure to DES. But we are aware of the dangers of overdeterrence--the possibility that research will be discouraged or beneficial drugs withheld from the market. These dangers are magnified in this context, where we are asked to recognize a legal duty toward generations not yet conceived.

The dissent would have us believe that this case involves nothing but application of straightforward strict products liability doctrine. But this case is fundamentally different in the same way that *Albala* was fundamentally different from other negligence cases. In neither this case nor *Albala* was the infant plaintiff exposed to the defendants' dangerous product or negligent conduct; rather, both were injured as a consequence of injuries to the reproductive systems of their mothers.

. . . .

In sum, the distinctions between this case and *Albala* provide no basis for a departure from the rule that an injury to a mother which results in injuries to a later-conceived child does not establish a cause of action in favor of the child against the original tort-feasor. For this reason, we decline to recognize a cause of action on behalf of plaintiff Karen Enright. . . .

Grover v. Eli Lilly & Co.

63 Ohio St. 3d 756, 591 N.E.2d 696 (1992)

WRIGHT, Justice.

The United States District Court for the Northern District of Ohio has **certified** the following question to us:

"Does Ohio recognize a cause of action on behalf of a child born prematurely, and with severe birth defects, if it can be established that such injuries were proximately caused by defects in the child's mother's reproductive system, those defects in turn being proximately caused by the child's grandmother ingesting a defective drug (DES) during her pregnancy with the child's mother?"

For purposes of this question, we are required to assume that Charles Grover can prove that his injuries were proximately caused by his mother's exposure to DES. We are not evaluating the facts of this case, but determining, as a matter of law, whether Charles Grover has a legally cognizable cause of action.

DES was prescribed to pregnant women during the 1940s, 1950s and 1960s to prevent miscarriage. The FDA banned its use by pregnant women in 1971 after medical studies discovered that female children exposed to the drug *in utero* had a high incidence of a rare type of vaginal cancer. See 36 Fed.Reg. 21,537 (1971). Candy Grover was exposed to DES as a fetus. Her son, Charles Grover, claims that his mother's DES-induced injuries were the cause of his premature birth and resulting injuries.

Because the mother and the child whose injury results from her injury are uniquely interrelated, and because it is possible that the mother may not discover the extent of her own injury until she experiences difficulties during pregnancy, the facts of this case pose a novel issue. Courts and commentators refer to the child's potential cause of action in such cases as a "preconception tort." [C] The terminology stems from the fact that a child is pursuing liability against a party for a second injury that flows from an initial injury to the mother that occurred before the child was conceived.

. . . .

. . . The cause of action certified to us involves the scope of liability for the manufacture of a prescription drug that allegedly had devastating side effects on the original patient's female fetus. However, this case is not about the devastating side effects of DES on the women who were exposed to it, which have indeed been well documented in medical studies and court opinions. [C] This case is concerned with the rippling effects of that exposure on yet another generation, when that female child reaches sexual maturity and bears a child. Because a plaintiff in Charles Grover's position cannot be injured until the original patient's child bears children, the second injury will typically have occurred more than sixteen years after the ingestion of the drug.

Several courts have addressed a fact pattern virtually identical to the facts of the case currently before this court. The New York Court of Appeals held that a child does not have a cause of action, in negligence or strict liability, against a prescription drug company based on the manufacture of DES if the child was never exposed to the drug *in utero. Enright v. Eli Lilly & Co.* (1991), 77 N.Y.2d 377, 568 N.Y.S.2d 550, 570 N.E.2d 198, certiorari denied (1991), 502 U.S. 868, 112 S.Ct. 197, 116 L.Ed.2d 157. The court relied in part on its earlier opinion in *Albala v. New York,* [54 N.Y.2d 269, 445 N.Y.S.2d 108, 429 N.E.2d 786 (1981).] In both cases, the court was concerned with the "staggering implications of any proposition which would honor claims assuming the breach of an identifiable duty for less than a perfect birth and by what standard and the difficulty in establishing a standard or definition of perfection. * * *" *Id.,* 54 N.Y.2d at 273, 445 N.Y.S.2d at 109, 429 N.E.2d at 788. See *Enright v. Eli Lilly & Co., supra,* 77 N.Y.2d at 384, 568 N.Y.S.2d at 553, 570 N.E.2d at 201. The court was troubled by the possibility that doctors would forgo certain treatments of great benefit to persons already in existence out of fear of possible effects on future children. *Albala, supra,* 54 N.Y.2d at 274, 445 N.Y.S.2d at 110, 429 N.E.2d at 788-789. In *Enright,* the court noted that "the cause of action plaintiffs ask us to recognize here could not be confined without the drawing of artificial and arbitrary boundaries. For all we know, the rippling effects of DES exposure may extend for generations. It is our duty to confine liability within manageable limits * * *. Limiting liability to those who ingested the drug or were exposed to it in utero serves this purpose." *Id.,* 77 N.Y.2d at 387, 568 N.Y.S.2d at 555, 570 N.E.2d at 203. See, also, *Loerch v. Eli Lilly & Co.* (Minn.1989), 445 N.W.2d 560 (the evenly divided Supreme Court of Minnesota affirmed, without opinion, a lower court's decision that a child who was not exposed to DES has no cause of action).

One court has held that a plaintiff situated similarly to Charles Grover has a cause of action. The United States Court of Appeals for the Seventh District reversed a lower court's directed verdict on the issue of a pharmaceutical company's liability to a child for injuries caused by a premature birth. *McMahon v. Eli Lilly & Co.* (C.A.7, 1985), 774 F.2d 830. The court concluded that under Illinois law the company could be liable for failing to warn of the dangerous propensities of the drug, and need not have anticipated a particular side effect. [C]

We find the reasoning applied by the New York Court of Appeals persuasive on the issue currently before us. As an initial matter, we note that the pharmaceutical companies' conduct must be evaluated based on whether they knew or should have known of a particular risk through the exercise of ordinary care. The marketing of prescription drugs differs significantly from other consumer goods. Each drug is tested and approved for use by the Food and Drug Administration and is selected for use by a physician, who then prescribes the drug to the ultimate user. As a result, the drug manufacturer's primary responsibility is to provide adequate warnings to the physician. [C] The manufacturer does not breach its duty to warn—in negligence, in strict liability for breach of warranty, or in strict liability in tort—until the company knew or should have known of a particular risk through the exercise of ordinary care. [C]

It is on this point that Ohio law differs from Illinois law as construed in *McMahon v. Eli Lilly & Co., supra,* 774 F.2d at 834-835. The Seventh Circuit held that knowledge of the general dangerous propensities of the drug was sufficient to subject the company to liability for failure to warn. . . . Even if knowledge of the drug's "dangerous propensities" is sufficient to create liability to the women exposed to the drug *in utero,* this same knowledge does not automatically justify the extension of liability to those women's children. It is one thing to say that knowledge of a propensity to harm the reproductive organs is sufficient to impose liability for a variety of different injuries to the reproductive organs. It is yet another thing to say that this generalized knowledge is sufficient to impose liability for injuries to a third party that occur twenty-eight years later.

Knowledge of a risk to one class of plaintiffs does not necessarily extend an actor's liability to every potential plaintiff. While we must assume that DES was the proximate cause of Charles Grover's injuries, an actor is not liable for every harm that may result from his actions. " * * *

When a pharmaceutical company prescribes drugs to a woman, the company, under ordinary circumstances, does not have a duty to her daughter's infant who will be conceived twenty-eight years later. Charles Grover's injuries are not the result of his own exposure to the drug, but are allegedly caused by his mother's injuries from her *in utero* exposure to the drug. Because of the remoteness in time and causation, we hold that Charles Grover does not have an independent cause of action, and answer the district court's question in the negative. A pharmaceutical company's liability for the distribution or manufacture of a defective prescription drug does not extend to persons who were never exposed to the drug, either directly or *in utero.*

Judgment accordingly.

ALICE ROBIE RESNICK, Justice, dissenting.

I dissent from the result reached in this case, but more importantly from the superficial treatment of the issue which was certified to this court, in light of its complexity. . . .

. . . .

In the present case, June Rose ingested DES during her pregnancy in 1952 and 1953. June gave birth to Candace Grover on March 30, 1953. Petitioners maintain that as a result of her mother's ingestion of DES, Candace was born with an incompetent cervix. Candace gave birth, prematurely, to Charles Grover, who was born with cerebral palsy. Petitioners assert Charles' disabilities are directly and proximately attributable to his premature birth, which in turn was caused by his mother's DES-induced incompetent cervix.

. . . .

I discern no sound basis, in law or public policy, for holding that there is no duty owed to persons in Charles Grover's position. We are dealing with a drug which was widely prescribed for many years to virtually millions of pregnant women. It was a drug which had FDA approval but, perhaps, was not adequately tested in view of a considerable body of scientific and medical literature that raised serious questions concerning the safety of DES to the developing fetus and its efficacy for treatment of pregnancy complications. Petitioners aver that, despite warnings from independent researchers dating back to the 1930s that DES caused reproductive tract abnormalities and cancer in exposed animal offspring, that drug companies, including Eli Lilly, performed no tests as to the effects of DES on the developing fetus, either in animals or humans. Petitioners also assert that by 1947 there were twenty-one studies which supported these findings; that recent medical studies have established a significant link between DES exposure and various uterine and cervical abnormalities in DES daughters; and that these studies have demonstrated that mature DES daughters have a significantly higher risk of miscarriage, infertility and premature deliveries.

In light of the foregoing there can be no question that pharmaceutical companies should have known the dangers of this drug. If in the 1930s and 1940s the manufacturers of DES knew or should have known of the reproductive system defects in the animal fetus exposed to DES, how then is it not foreseeable that this might mean abnormalities in the human fetus' reproductive system? In other words, it would appear that DES manufacturers knew or should have known that the human fetus exposed *in utero* might have a defect in the female reproductive system. Additionally, is it not then foreseeable that that female fetus would at some point seek to employ the defective reproductive system? The answer must be a resounding "yes." Hence, there can be no logic to the holding of the majority that "[b]ecause of the remoteness in time and causation, * * * Charles Grover does not have an independent cause of action." What could have a more direct causal connection than a premature birth by a woman who was known to have an incompetent cervix? From this it becomes readily apparent that DES grand-children were a foreseeable group of plaintiffs. It can hardly be argued that there is no duty owed to a *foreseeable* plaintiff. In the landmark case of *Palsgraf v. Long Island RR. Co.* (1928), 248 N.Y. 339, 162 N.E. 99, the court held that an actor has a duty to all plaintiffs within the actor's "range of apprehension." [C] Indeed, a federal court of appeals had recently stated: "There was sufficient evidence from which a jury could reasonably have found that in 1955 Lilly knew or should have known that DES might cause reproductive abnormalities, such as prematurity, in the female offspring of women exposed to DES during pregnancy." *McMahon v. Eli Lilly & Co.* (C.A.7, 1985), 774 F.2d 830, 835-836.

. . . .

DES continues to create difficult legal and social problems nationwide. The majority has failed to consider the uniqueness of DES. Instead, it has simply applied an arbitrary "blanket no-duty rule." Today's holding will have profound and devastating effects. To hold under these circumstances that Charles Grover's injuries were not foreseeable is to ignore an entire body of scientific information which was available or could have easily become available with a measure of care concerning the effects of DES on subsequent generations.

. . . I would conclude that individuals such as Charles Grover properly have a cause of action for their injuries. This in no way opens the floodgates because litigation can easily be concluded with Charles Grover's generation. Moreover, the majority completely disregards the fact that the petitioners still bear the burden of proving proximate cause. I strenuously dissent.

SWEENEY and DOUGLAS, JJ., concur in the foregoing dissenting opinion.

Points for Discussion

1. Were you persuaded by Justice Resnick's dissent in *Grover*?

2. Proposition: Courts should recognize intergenerational or preconception negligence actions seeking compensation for injuries allegedly caused by a grandmother's ingestion of DES. Do you agree or disagree?

3. What role does and should public policy favoring the availability of prescription drugs play in the litigation and adjudication of DES cases?

———————

CHAPTER 6

Defenses (and Partial Defenses) to Negligence Actions

When a plaintiff satisfies the duty, breach, causation, and harm elements of a negligence claim, a defendant can assert and seek to establish certain affirmative defenses which can defeat or reduce its tort liability. This chapter focuses on the following menu available to those individuals and entities facing a negligence action: contributory negligence; comparative negligence; assumption of the risk; statutes of limitations; and statutes of repose.

A. Contributory Negligence

Butterfield v. Forrester

11 East 59, 103 Eng. Rep. 926 (K.B. 1809)

This was an action on the case for obstructing a highway, by means of which obstruction the plaintiff, who was riding along the road, was thrown down with his horse, and injured, & c. At the trial before Bayley J. at Derby, it appeared that the defendant, for the purpose of making some repairs to his house, which was close by the road side at one end of the town, had put up a pole across this part of the road, a free passage being left by another branch or street in the same direction. That the plaintiff left a public house not far distant from the place in question at 8 o'clock in the evening in August, when they were just beginning to light candles, but while there was light enough left to discern the obstruction at 100 yards distance: and the witness, who proved this, said that if the plaintiff had not been riding very hard he might have observed and avoided it: the plaintiff however, who was riding violently, did not observe it, but rode against it, and fell with his horse and was much hurt in consequence of the accident; and there was no evidence of his being intoxicated at the time. On this evidence Bayley J. directed the jury, that if a person riding with **reasonable and ordinary care** could have seen and avoided the obstruction; and if they were satisfied that the plaintiff was riding along the street extremely hard, and without ordinary care, they should find a verdict for the defendant: which they accordingly did.

Vaughan Serjt. now objected to this direction, on moving for a new trial; and referred to Buller's Ni.Pri. 26(*a*), where the rule is laid down, that "if a man lay logs of wood across a highway; though a person may with care ride safely by, yet if by means thereof my horse stumble and fling me, I may bring an action."

BAYLEY J. The plaintiff was proved to be riding as fast as his horse could go, and this was through the streets of Derby. If he had used ordinary care he must have seen the obstruction; so that the accident appeared to happen entirely from his own fault.

LORD ELLENBOROUGH C.J. A party is not to cast himself upon an obstruction which has been made by the fault of another, and avail himself of it, if he do not himself use common and ordinary caution to be in the right. In cases of persons riding upon what is considered to be the wrong side of the road, that would not authorize another purposefully to ride up against them. One person being in fault will not dispense with another's using ordinary care for himself. Two things must concur to support this action, an obstruction in the road by the fault of the defendant, and no want of ordinary care to avoid it on the part of the plaintiff.

PER CURIAM. RULE REFUSED.

————————

Points for Discussion

1. Do you agree with the court's ruling and analysis? Why should a plaintiff ever be denied a recovery where a defendant has engaged in negligent conduct?

2. In determining whether the plaintiff's conduct constitutes contributory negligence, the plaintiff's acts or omissions must be a substantial factor in the result or accident.

3. The defendant bears the burden of pleading and producing evidence concerning, and persuading the factfinder of, the plaintiff's contributory negligence. *See* RESTATEMENT (THIRD) OF TORTS: APPORTIONMENT OF LIABILITY § 4 (2000).

————————

Davies v. Mann

10 M. & W. 546, 152 Eng. Rep. (1842)

At the trial, before Erskine, J., at the last Summer Assizes for the county of Worcester, it appeared that the plaintiff, having fettered the fore feet of an ass belonging to him, turned it into a public highway, and at the time in question the ass was grazing off the side of a road about eight yards wide, when the defendant's waggon, with a team of three horses, coming down a slight descent, at what the witness termed a smartish pace, ran against the ass, knocked it down, and the wheels passing over it, it died soon after. The ass was fettered at the time, and it was proved that the driver of the waggon was some little distance behind the horses. The learned Judge told the jury, that though the act of the plaintiff, in leaving the donkey on the highway so fettered as to prevent his getting out of the way of carriages travelling along it, might be illegal, still, if the **proximate cause** of the injury was attributable to the want of proper conduct on the part of the driver of the waggon, the action was maintainable against the defendant; and his Lordship directed them, if they thought that the accident might have been avoided by the exercise of ordinary care on the part of the driver, to find for the plaintiff. The jury found their verdict for the plaintiff, damages 40s.

Godson now moved for a new trial, on the ground of **misdirection**. . . .

LORD ABINGER, C.B. I am of opinion that there ought to be no rule in this case. The defendant has not denied that the ass was lawfully in the highway, and therefore we must assume it to have been lawfully there; but even were it otherwise, it would have made no difference, for as the defendant might, by proper care, have avoided injuring the animal, and did not, he is liable for the consequences of his negligence, though the animal may have been improperly there.

PARKE, B. . . . [N]egligence which is to preclude a plaintiff from recovering in an action of this nature, must be such as that he could, by ordinary care, have avoided the consequences of the defendant's negligence. . . . I believe . . . that "the rule of law is laid down with perfect correctness in the case of *Butterfield v. Forrester*, that, although there may have been negligence on the part of the plaintiff, yet unless he might, by the exercise of ordinary care, have avoided the consequences of the defendant's negligence, he is entitled to recover; if by ordinary care he might have avoided them, he is the author of his own wrong." . . . [A]lthough the ass may have been wrongfully there, still the defendant was bound to go along the road at such a pace as would be likely

Make the Connection

Recall that the doctrine of last clear chance was discussed in *In re Kinsman*, Chapter 5, *supra*.

to prevent mischief. Were this not so, a man might justify the driving over goods left on a public highway, or even over a man lying asleep there, or the purposely running against a carriage on the wrong side of the road.

. . . .

RULE REFUSED.

—————————

Points for Discussion

1. What did the *Davies* court hold? If the defendant proves contributory negligence on the part of the plaintiff, is the defendant liable? If so, what may the plaintiff recover?

2. Note that the *Davies* court opined that a plaintiff who may have engaged in negligent conduct could still prevail and recover where the defendant, exercising ordinary care, could have avoided (had the last clear chance to avoid) the accident. Consider the following discussion of the "**last clear chance doctrine**:"

> "No very satisfactory reasons for the rule ever has been suggested. The first explanation given, and the one which still is most often stated, is that if the defendant has the last clear opportunity to avoid the harm, the plaintiff's negligence is not a 'proximate cause' of the result. While this coincides rather well with the attempt made in an older day to fix liability upon the 'last human wrongdoer,' it is quite out of line with the evolving ideas of proximate cause. In such a case the negligence of the plaintiff undoubtedly has been a cause, and a substantial and important one, of his own damage, and it cannot be said that injury through the defendant's negligence was not fully within the risk which the plaintiff has created. . . .

> "The real explanation would seem to be a fundamental dislike for the harshness of the contributory negligence defense."

PROSSER AND KEETON ON TORTS 463, 464 (5th ed. 1984).

3. For more on the last clear chance doctrine, see RESTATEMENT (SECOND) OF TORTS §§ 479, 480 (1965).

—————————

Burleson v. RSR Group Florida, Inc.

981 So.2d 1109 (Ala. 2007)

BOLIN, Justice.

Terry Wayne Burleson and Donna B. Montgomery, as co-administrators of the estate of Stanley Duane Burleson ("the plaintiffs"), sued Sportarms of Florida, Inc., Donna J. Newton, and certain fictitiously named parties ("the defendants"), on May 21, 2001, alleging claims under the Alabama Extended Manufacturer's Liability Doctrine ("the AEMLD"). Specifically, the plaintiffs alleged that the defendants defectively designed and manufactured a firearm that proximately caused the death of Stanley Duane Burleson. On August 24, 2001, the plaintiffs amended their complaint to assert their AEMLD claims against RSR Group Florida, Inc. RSR answered the complaint and raised certain affirmative defenses, including **assumption of the risk** and **contributory negligence**. Thereafter, the plaintiffs amended their complaint a second time to add as a defendant Mack Brown d/b/a The Trading Post, from whom Stanley purchased the firearm.

On March 28, 2005, RSR moved the trial court for a summary judgment, arguing that . . . RSR is not liable for Stanley's death because, RSR argued, Stanley was . . . contributorily negligent. On May 23, 2005, the plaintiffs responded to RSR's summary-judgment motion. Following a hearing, the trial court, on November 15, 2005, entered a summary judgment in favor of RSR. . . .

. . . .

The evidence viewed in a light most favorable to the plaintiffs indicates the following: The firearm that killed Stanley is a Herbert Schmidt brand, model 21S, .22 caliber, single-action revolver manufactured in Germany. The revolver was imported into the United States by Sportarms of Florida. On May 25, 1984, Sportarms of Florida sold the revolver to RSR Wholesale Guns Dallas, Inc., from which RSR acquired the revolver on December 21, 1984. On January 8, 1985, RSR sold the revolver to Mack Brown d/b/a The Trading Post, a federally licensed retail firearms dealer located in Hamilton, Alabama. On April 26, 1985, Stanley was completed a federally mandated Firearms Transaction Record and purchased the revolver from The Trading Post.

The revolver holds six cartridges in its cylinder; it is a single-action revolver, which means that the hammer must be manually placed in the "full cock" position and the trigger pulled before the revolver will fire. The hammer is in the "full cock" position when it is at the farthest point from the firing pin. Once the trigger is pulled, the hammer is released and falls forward, striking the firing pin, which in turn strikes the cartridge primer, discharging the revolver.

The hammer may be lowered to the "half cock" position by placing one's thumb on the hammer and pulling the trigger until the hammer is released. The finger is then removed from the trigger and the hammer is slowly lowered to the "half cock" position. The "half cock" position is midway between the "full cock" position and the firing pin. The "half cock" position allows the cylinder to spin and facilitates loading and unloading the revolver.

The hammer may also be lowered to the "safety cock" position in the same manner in which it is lowered from the "full cock" position to the "half cock" position. The hammer is full forward in the "safety cock" position with its face resting on the head of the firing pin. If the trigger is pulled while the hammer is in the "safety cock" position, the revolver will not fire.

The revolver is also equipped with a manual safety that, when engaged by the operator, imposes a mechanism between the face of the hammer and the firing pin that blocks the fall of the hammer and prevents it from contacting the firing pin. If the manual safety is engaged, the revolver will not discharge under any foreseeable circumstance, including pulling the trigger or dropping the revolver. The owner's manual for the revolver recommends that those who "care much about safety" load the revolver with only five cartridges, leaving empty the chamber aligned with the hammer.

John T. Butters, the plaintiffs' expert, testified that the revolver could be discharged in only two ways; in both ways, the manual safety must be disengaged. He described the normal mode of discharge as pulling the trigger when the hammer is in the "full cock" position while a cartridge is in a chamber in line with the hammer and the firing pin. He described the second manner of discharge as occurring when force is applied to the back of the hammer when the hammer is in the "safety cock" position and resting on the head of the firing pin while a cartridge is in a chamber in line with the hammer and the firing pin.

On April 2, 2000, Stanley was hanging the revolver in its holster on a gun rack in his home when the revolver fell from the holster; it struck a desk and discharged. Stanley was struck in the abdomen by the discharged round and died as a result of the wound. Stanley was 51 years old at the time of his death. Stanley's wife, Bernice, testified that Stanley had a "rule" that all firearms he kept in the house be stored unloaded. Bernice further stated that Stanley had not had any firearm-related accidents before the one that killed him. Terry, Stanley's son, testified that Stanley was "safety conscious" and had taught him the importance of never keeping a live round chambered in line with the hammer and the firing pin.

The plaintiffs contend that . . . Stanley was contributorily negligent because he failed to engage the manual safety and he was putting the revolver away with a cartridge chambered directly in line with the hammer and the firing pin. . . . [W]e conclude that Stanley's own contributory negligence bars recovery in this case.

This Court has stated:

"In *Hannah v. Gregg, Bland & Berry, Inc.,* 840 So.2d 839 (Ala.2002), this Court stated the following principles concerning the application of contributory negligence at the summary-judgment stage of an action:

"'A plaintiff cannot recover in a negligence action where the plaintiff's own negligence is shown to have proximately contributed to his damage, notwithstanding a showing of negligence on the part of the defendant. Likewise, a plaintiff's contributory negligence will preclude recovery in an AEMLD action. The question of contributory negligence is

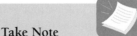

Take Note

As the court notes, the answer to the question whether a plaintiff has engaged in contributory negligence is normally provided by the jury and may be provided by the judge where all reasonable persons would reach the same conclusion on the facts presented.

normally one for the jury. However, where the facts are such that all reasonable persons must reach the same conclusion, contributory negligence may be found as a matter of law.

"'To establish contributory negligence as a matter of law, a defendant seeking a summary judgment must show that the plaintiff put himself in danger's way and that the plaintiff had a conscious appreciation of the danger at the moment the incident occurred. The proof required for establishing contributory negligence as a matter of law should be distinguished from an instruction given to a jury when determining whether a plaintiff has been guilty of contributory negligence. A jury determining whether a plaintiff has been guilty of contributory negligence must decide only whether the plaintiff failed to exercise reasonable care. We protect against the inappropriate use of a summary judgment to establish contributory negligence as a matter of law by requiring the defendant on such a motion to establish by undisputed evidence a plaintiff's conscious appreciation of danger.' "

Tell v. Terex Corp., 962 So.2d 174, 177 (Ala.2007).

The evidence is undisputed that the manual safety on the revolver was disengaged when Stanley was placing the holstered revolver on the gun rack. The evidence indicates that if the manual safety is engaged, the revolver could not fire under any foreseeable conditions, including a pull of the trigger or an accidental drop. The evidence is further undisputed that Stanley had a chambered cartridge in line with the hammer and the firing pin when the revolver was being placed on the gun rack. Obviously, the revolver could not discharge if a cartridge was not chambered in line with the hammer and the firing pin. The owner's manual accompanying the revolver recommends that those who "care much about safety" leave empty the chamber aligned with the hammer and the firing pin. Terry testified that Stanley was "safety conscious" and that Stanley had taught him the importance of never keeping a live round chambered in line with the hammer and the firing pin. Bernice testified that Stanley had a "rule" that all firearms stored in the house be unloaded. Butters testified that storing the revolver fully loaded, unless it was anticipated that the revolver would be needed for rapid deployment, was an unsafe firearm-handling practice.

. . . .

[T]he danger of handling a firearm with a live cartridge chambered in line with the hammer and the firing pin without having first engaged the manual safety is self-evident, especially to an experienced and safety-conscious gun owner like Stanley, so that reasonable people would have to logically conclude that he *should have* at least appreciated the danger associated with doing so.

We conclude that Stanley placed himself in danger's way by handling the revolver with the manual safety disengaged and with a cartridge chambered in line with the hammer and the firing pin. [C] Further, as evidenced by Stanley's awareness of the importance of never storing a loaded firearm, much less one with a cartridge chambered in line with the hammer and the firing pin, we conclude that he should have had a conscious awareness of the danger in which he placed himself. [C] Accordingly, Stanley's own contributory negligence bars the plaintiffs' recovery in this case.

AFFIRMED.

COBB, Chief Justice (dissenting).

I respectfully dissent. Nothing in the record or the materials before this Court, even taking the facts as presented by RSR Group Florida, Inc., one of the defendants below, shows that the decedent knew that a cartridge was under the hammer of the revolver or that the manual safety was not engaged. However, it is readily inferable from the facts in this case that the decedent believed that there was no cartridge under the hammer, in light of the evidence that he had instructed his son that a revolver should not be stored loaded that way because of safety concerns.

Generally, questions of contributory negligence . . . are questions for the jury. *Halsey v. A.B. Chance Co.,* 695 So.2d 607 (Ala.1997), and *Hicks v. Commercial Union Ins. Co.,* 652 So.2d 211 (Ala.1994). In *Hannah v. Gregg, Bland & Berry, Inc.,* 840 So.2d 839 (Ala.2002), this Court addressed the plaintiff's wrongful-death claim based on the Alabama Extended Manufacturer's Liability Doctrine ("the AEMLD") arising from her husband's death in an industrial accident, again noting the legal principle that questions of contributory negligence are usually questions of fact for the jury. The decedent in *Hannah* was crushed to death between two large industrial machines. With respect to the decedent's appreciation of the danger when standing between the machines and his use of a safety device, the Court said:

> "Based upon Hannah's evidence, a jury could conclude that at the time of his accident, Jerry Hannah was standing *in what he may have believed to be a safe position,* on the outer edge of the recoiler and that he did not appreciate the danger posed by the belt wrapper. A jury could also conclude that Hannah may have inserted the safety pin, believing that it was set, but that the bend in the pin did not allow it to properly lock. Either way, we cannot say that the facts are such that all reasonable persons must reach the same conclusion regarding whether Hannah was contributorily negligent. Whether Hannah was contributorily negligent is a question that must be left to the finder of fact to determine."

840 So.2d at 861-62 (emphasis added).

In *Horn v. Fadal Machining Centers, LLC,* 972 So.2d 63 (Ala.2007), a case similar to *Hannah* in which the decedent was killed in an accident involving a milling machine, and his personal representative brought an AEMLD claim, the Court discussed the requirements for . . . contributory negligence . . . in the context of AEMLD claims:

. . . .

> " 'To establish *contributory negligence* as a matter of law . . . a defendant seeking a summary judgment must show that the plaintiff put [herself] in danger's way and that the plaintiff had a *conscious appreciation* of the danger *at the moment the incident occurred.* See *H.R.H. Metals, Inc. v. Miller,* 833 So.2d 18 (Ala.2002); see also *Hicks v. Commercial Union Ins. Co.,* 652 So.2d 211, 219 (Ala.1994). The proof required for establishing contributory negligence as a matter of law should be distinguished from an instruction given to a jury when determining whether a plaintiff has been guilty of contributory negligence. A *jury* determining whether a plaintiff has been guilty of contributory negligence must decide only

whether the plaintiff failed to exercise reasonable care. *We protect against the inappropriate use of a summary judgment to establish contributory negligence as a matter of law by requiring the defendant on such a motion to establish by undisputed evidence a plaintiff's conscious appreciation of danger. H.R.H. Metals,* supra.'

"*Hannah v. Gregg, Bland & Berry, Inc.,* 840 So.2d 839, 860-61 (Ala.2002) (emphasis added). . . ." [C]

Thus, our caselaw makes clear that a summary judgment for the defendant in an AEMLD case must be based upon evidence of the *plaintiff's awareness of the dangerous condition.* There is no evidence in this case that the decedent had a "conscious appreciation," i.e., that he *actually knew,* that the revolver was loaded with a cartridge under the hammer or that the manual safety was not engaged. . . . .[T]here is no evidence in this case that it would have been immediately evident to the decedent from his observation of the holstered revolver that a bullet was chambered under the hammer or that the manual safety was disengaged. The fact remains that the record contains no evidence to support an inference that the decedent actually knew that a bullet was chambered under the hammer or that the manual safety was not engaged. Under our law as noted above, I do not believe that the Court can properly conclude that there is no genuine issue of material fact about contributory negligence . . . so that RSR is entitled to a judgment as a matter of law. Accordingly, I dissent.

————————

Points for Discussion

1. Explain the court's reasoning in support of its finding of contributory negligence.

2. Is the question of contributory negligence one of fact or law?

3. Do you agree with the Alabama Supreme Court's affirmance of the trial court's summary judgment in favor of defendant RSR?

4. What is the principal argument of the dissent? Were you persuaded by the dissent's position? Did the decedent have a conscious appreciation of the fact that the revolver was loaded and that the safety was not engaged?

————————

B. Comparative Fault

McIntyre v. Balentine

833 S.W.2d 52 (Tenn. 1992)

DROWOTA, Justice.

In this personal injury action, we granted Plaintiff's application for permission to appeal in order to decide whether to adopt a system of comparative fault in Tennessee. . . . We now replace the common law defense of contributory negligence with a system of **comparative fault**. . . .

In the early morning darkness of November 2, 1986, Plaintiff Harry Douglas McIntyre and Defendant Clifford Balentine were involved in a motor vehicle accident resulting in severe injuries to Plaintiff. The accident occurred in the vicinity of Smith's Truck Stop in Savannah, Tennessee. As Defendant Balentine was traveling south on Highway 69, Plaintiff entered the highway (also traveling south) from the truck stop parking lot. Shortly after Plaintiff entered the highway, his pickup truck was struck by Defendant's Peterbilt tractor. At trial, the parties disputed the exact chronology of events immediately preceding the accident.

Both men had consumed alcohol the evening of the accident. After the accident, Plaintiff's blood alcohol level was measured at .17 percent by weight. Testimony suggested that Defendant was traveling in excess of the posted speed limit.

Plaintiff brought a negligence action against Defendant Balentine and Defendant East-West Motor Freight, Inc.[1] Defendants answered that Plaintiff was contributorially negligent, in part due to operating his vehicle while intoxicated. After trial, the jury returned a verdict stating: "We, the jury, find the plaintiff and the defendant equally at fault in this accident; therefore, we rule in favor of the defendant."

After judgment was entered for Defendants, Plaintiff brought an appeal alleging the trial court erred by . . . refusing to instruct the jury regarding the doctrine of comparative negligence . . . The Court of Appeals affirmed, holding that . . . **comparative negligence** is not the law in Tennessee . . .

I.

The common law contributory negligence doctrine has traditionally been traced to Lord Ellenborough's opinion in *Butterfield v. Forrester,* 11 East 60, 103

---

1 Defendant East-West Motor Freight, Inc. is a party to this action as **lessee** of the Peterbilt tractor Defendant-Balentine was operating at the time of the accident. Defendant-Balentine is the owner-**lessor** of the tractor.

Eng.Rep. 926 (1809). There, plaintiff, "riding as fast as his horse would go," was injured after running into an obstruction defendant had placed in the road. Stating as the rule that "[o]ne person being in fault will not dispense with another's using ordinary care," plaintiff was denied recovery on the basis that he did not use ordinary care to avoid the obstruction. [C]

The contributory negligence bar was soon brought to America as part of the common law, *see Smith v. Smith,* 19 Mass. 621, 624 (1824), and proceeded to spread throughout the states. *See* H.W. Woods, The Negligence Case: Comparative Fault § 1:4 (1978). This strict bar may have been a direct outgrowth of the common law system of issue pleading; issue pleading posed questions to be answered "yes" or "no," leaving common law courts, the theory goes, no choice but to award all or nothing. *See* J.W. Wade, W.K. Crawford, Jr., and J.L. Ryder, *Comparative Fault In Tennessee Tort Actions: Past, Present and Future,* 41 Tenn.L.Rev. 423, 424-25 (1974). A number of other rationalizations have been advanced in the attempt to justify the harshness of the "all-or-nothing" bar. Among these: the plaintiff should be penalized for his misconduct; the plaintiff should be deterred from injuring himself; and the plaintiff's negligence supersedes the defendant's so as to render defendant's negligence no longer proximate. *See* W. Keeton, *Prosser and Keeton On The Law Of Torts,* § 65, at 452 (5th ed. 1984); J.W. Wade, *supra,* at 424.

In Tennessee, the rule as initially stated was that "if a party, by his own gross negligence, brings an injury upon himself, or contributes to such injury, he cannot recover;" for, in such cases, the party "must be regarded as the author of his own misfortune." *Whirley v. Whiteman,* 38 Tenn. 610, 619 (1858). In subsequent decisions, we have continued to follow the general rule that a plaintiff's contributory negligence completely bars recovery. *See, e.g., Hudson v. Gaitan,* 675 S.W.2d 699, 704 (Tenn.1984); *Talbot v. Taylor,* 184 Tenn. 428, 432, 201 S.W.2d 1, 3 (1935); *Nashville Ry. v. Norman,* 108 Tenn. 324, 333, 67 S.W. 479, 481 (1902); *Railroad v. Pugh,* 97 Tenn. 624, 627, 37 S.W. 555, 557 (1896); *Postal Telegraph-Cable Co. v. Zopfi,* 93 Tenn. 369, 373, 24 S.W. 633, 634 (1894); *East Tennessee V. & G.R.R. v. Conner,* 83 Tenn. 254, 258 (1885); *Louisville & N.R.R. v. Robertson,* 56 Tenn. 276, 282 (1872); *Nashville & C.R.R. v. Carroll,* 53 Tenn. 347, 366-67 (1871); *Cogdell v. Yett,* 41 Tenn. 230, 232 (1860).

Equally entrenched in Tennessee jurisprudence are exceptions to the general all-or-nothing rule: contributory negligence does not absolutely bar recovery where defendant's conduct was intentional, *see, e.g., Stagner v. Craig,* 159 Tenn. 511, 514, 19 S.W.2d 234, 234-35 (1929); *Memphis St. Ry. v. Roe,* 118 Tenn. 601, 612-13, 102 S.W. 343, 346 (1907); where defendant's conduct was "grossly" negligent, *see, e.g., Ellithorpe v. Ford Motor Co.,* 503 S.W.2d 516, 522 (Tenn.1973); *Carroll,* 53 Tenn. at 366-67; where defendant had the "**last clear chance**" with which, through the exercise of ordinary care, to avoid plaintiff's injury, *see, e.g., Roseberry v. Lippner,* 574 S.W.2d 726, 728 (Tenn.1978); *Kansas City, M. & B.R.R. v. Wil-*

liford, 115 Tenn. 108, 120-21, 88 S.W. 178, 181-82 (1905); *Davies v. Mann,* 152 Eng.Rep. 588 (1842); or where plaintiff's negligence may be classified as "remote." *See, e.g., Arnold v. Hayslett,* 655 S.W.2d 941, 945 (Tenn.1983); *Street v. Calvert,* 541 S.W.2d 576, 585 (Tenn.1976); *Norman,* 108 Tenn. at 333, 67 S.W. at 481; *East Tennessee, V & G. Ry. v. Hull,* 88 Tenn. 33, 36, 12 S.W. 419, 419-20 (1889).

Take Note

Generally, the contributory negligence bar to a plaintiff's recovery is not available in cases of intentional torts, gross negligence, and cases in which a defendant exercising due and ordinary care could have avoided (had the last clear chance to avoid) the injury to the plaintiff.

In contrast, comparative fault has long been the federal rule in cases involving injured employees of interstate railroad carriers, *see* Federal Employers' Liability Act, ch. 149, § 3, 35 Stat. 66 (1908) (codified at 45 U.S.C. § 53 (1988)), and injured seamen. *See* Death On The High Seas Act, ch. 111, § 6, 41 Stat. 537 (1920) (codified at 46 U.S.C. § 766 (1988)); Jones Act, ch. 250, § 33, 41 Stat. 1007 (1920) (codified as amended at 46 U.S.C. § 688 (1988)). *See generally* V. Schwartz, *Comparative Negligence* § 1.4(A) (2d ed. 1986).

Similarly, by the early 1900s, many states, including Tennessee, had statutes providing for the apportionment of damages in railroad injury cases. [C] While Tennessee's railroad statute did not expressly sanction damage apportionment, it was soon given that judicial construction. In 1856, the statute was passed in an effort to prevent railroad accidents; it imposed certain obligations and liabilities on railroads "for all damages accruing or resulting from a failure to perform said dut[ies]." Act of Feb. 28, 1856, ch. 94, § 9, 1855-56 Tenn. Acts 104. [C] Apparently this **strict liability** was deemed necessary because "the consequences of carelessness and want of due skill [in the operation of railroads at speeds previously unknown] ... are so frightful and appalling that the most strict and rigid rules of accountability must be applied." *See East Tennessee & G.R.R. v. St. John,* 37 Tenn. 524, 527 (1858); Note, *Railroads-Precautions Act-Effect of 1959 Amendment,* 28 Tenn.L.Rev. 437, 439 (1961). The statute was then judicially construed to permit the jury to consider "[n]egligence of the person injured, which caused, or contributed to cause the accident ... in determining the amount of damages proper to be given for the injury." *Louisville & N.R.R. v. Burke,* 46 Tenn. 45, 51-52 (1868). This system of comparative fault was utilized for almost a century until 1959 when, trains no longer unique in their "astonishing speeds," the statute was overhauled, its strict liability provision being replaced by negligence per se and the common law contributory negligence bar. *See* Act of Mar. 10, 1959, ch. 130, § 2, 1959 Tenn.Pub. Acts 419; [c].[3]

Strict liability is discussed in Chapter 13.

Between 1920 and 1969, a few states began utilizing the principles of comparative fault in all tort litigation. *See* C. Mutter, *Moving to Comparative Negligence in an Era of Tort Reform: Decisions for Tennessee,* 57 Tenn.L.Rev. 199, 227 n. 127 (1990). Then, between 1969 and 1984, comparative fault replaced contributory negligence in 37 additional states. [C] In 1991, South Carolina became the 45th state to adopt comparative fault, *see Nelson v. Concrete Supply Co.,* 303 S.C. 243, 399 S.E.2d 783 (1991), leaving Alabama, Maryland, North Carolina, Virginia, and Tennessee as the only remaining common law contributory negligence jurisdictions.

Eleven states have judicially adopted comparative fault.[3] Thirty-four states have legislatively adopted comparative fault.[4]

---

3 In the order of their adoption, these states are Florida, California, Alaska, Michigan, West Virginia, New Mexico, Illinois, Iowa, Missouri, Kentucky, and South Carolina.

Nine courts adopted pure comparative fault: *See Hoffman v. Jones,* 280 So.2d 431 (Fla.1973); *Li v. Yellow Cab Co.,* 13 Cal.3d 804, 532 P.2d 1226, 119 Cal.Rptr. 858 (1975); *Kaatz v. State,* 540 P.2d 1037 (Alaska 1975); *Placek v. City of Sterling Heights,* 405 Mich. 638, 275 N.W.2d 511 (1979); *Scott v. Rizzo,* 96 N.M. 682, 634 P.2d 1234 (1981); *Alvis v. Ribar,* 85 Ill.2d 1, 52 Ill.Dec. 23, 421 N.E.2d 886 (1981); *Goetzman v. Wichern,* 327 N.W.2d 742 (Iowa 1982); *Gustafson v. Benda,* 661 S.W.2d 11 (Mo.1983); *Hilen v. Hays,* 673 S.W.2d 713 (Ky.1984). In two of these states, legislatures subsequently enacted a modified form. *See* Ill.Ann.Stat. ch. 110, para. 2-1116 (Supp.1991); Iowa Code Ann. § 668.3 (West 1987).

Two courts adopted a modified form of comparative fault. *See Bradley v. Appalachian Power Co.,* 163 W.Va. 332, 256 S.E.2d 879 (1979) (plaintiff may recover if his negligence is less than defendants'); *Nelson v. Concrete Supply Co.,* 303 S.C. 243, 399 S.E.2d 783 (1991) (plaintiff may recover if his negligence is not greater than defendants').

4 Six states have legislatively adopted pure comparative fault: Mississippi, Rhode Island, Washington, New York, Louisiana, and Arizona; Eight legislatures have enacted the modified "49 percent" rule (plaintiff may recover if plaintiff's negligence *is less than* defendant's): Georgia, Arkansas, Maine, Colorado, Idaho, North Dakota, Utah, and Kansas; Eighteen legislatures have enacted the modified "50 percent" rule (plaintiff may recover so long as plaintiff's negligence *is not greater than* defendant's): Wisconsin, Hawaii, Massachusetts, Minnesota, New Hampshire, Vermont, Oregon, Connecticut, Nevada, New Jersey, Oklahoma, Texas, Wyoming, Montana, Pennsylvania, Ohio, Indiana, and Delaware; Two legislatures have enacted statutes that allow a plaintiff to recover if plaintiff's negligence is slight when compared to defendant's gross negligence: Nebraska and South Dakota. *See* V. Schwartz, *supra,* at § 2.1.

Following is a list of statutes for those states who have codified their comparative fault systems, including the statutes of those states where comparative fault was initially adopted by judicial action:

See Alaska Stat. § 09.17.060 (Supp.1991); Ariz.Rev.Stat.Ann. § 12-2505(A) (Supp.1991); Ark.Stat.Ann. § 16-64-122 (Supp.1991); Colo.Rev.Stat. § 13-21-111 (1987); Conn.Gen.Stat.Ann. § 52-572h (1991); Del.Code Ann. tit. 10, § 8132 (Supp.1990); Fla.Stat.Ann. § 768.81 (West Supp.1992); Ga.Code Ann. § 105-603 (Harrison 1984); Haw.Rev.Stat. § 663-31 (1985); Idaho Code § 6-801 (1990); Ill.Ann.Stat. ch. 110, para. 2-1116 (Smith-Hurd Supp.1991); Ind.Code Ann. § 34-4-33-3, 4 (West Supp.1991); Iowa Code Ann. § 668.3 (West 1987); Kan.Stat.Ann. § 60-258a (Supp.1991); La.Civ.Code Ann. art. 2323 (West Supp.1992); Me.Rev.Stat.Ann. tit. 14, § 156 (1980); Mass.Gen.Laws Ann. ch. 231 § 85 (West 1985); Minn.Stat.Ann. § 604.01(1) (West Supp.1992); Miss.Code Ann. § 11-7-15 (1972); Mont.Code Ann. § 27-1-702 (1991); Neb.Rev.Stat. § 25-21, 185.01 to .06 (Supp.1991); Nev.Rev.Stat. § 41.141 (1991); N.H.Rev.Stat.Ann. § 507; 7-d (Supp.1991); N.J.Stat.Ann. § 2A: 15-5.1 (West 1987); N.Y.Civ. Prac.L. & R. 1411 (McKinney 1976); N.D.Cent.Code § 32-03.2-01 to -03 (Supp.1991); Ohio Rev.Code Ann. § 2315.19 (Anderson 1991); Okla.Stat.Ann. tit. 23, §§ 13, 14 (West 1987); Or.Rev.Stat. § 18.470 (1988); 42 Pa.Cons.Stat.Ann. § 7102 Purdon (1982 & Supp.1991); R.I.Gen.Laws § 9-20-4 (1985); S.D. Codified Laws Ann. § 20-9-2 (1987); Tex.Civ.Prac. & Rem.Code Ann. §§ 33.001, 33.012 (Vernon Supp.1992); Utah Code Ann. § 78-27-38 (1992); Vt.Stat.Ann. tit. 12, § 1036 (Supp.1991); Wash.Rev. Code Ann. § 4.22.005 (1988); Wis.Stat.Ann. § 895.045 (West 1983); Wyo.Stat. § 1-1-109 (1988).

. . . .

II.

Over 15 years ago, we stated, when asked to adopt a system of comparative fault:

We do not deem it appropriate to consider making such a change unless and until a case reaches us wherein the pleadings and proof present an issue of contributory negligence accompanied by advocacy that the ends of justice will be served by adopting the rule of comparative negligence.

Street v. Calvert, 541 S.W.2d at 586. Such a case is now before us. After exhaustive deliberation that was facilitated by extensive briefing and argument by the parties, amicus curiae, and Tennessee's scholastic community, we conclude that it is time to abandon

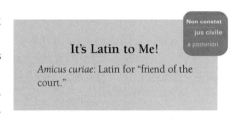

It's Latin to Me!

Amicus curiae: Latin for "friend of the court."

the outmoded and unjust common law doctrine of contributory negligence and adopt in its place a system of comparative fault. Justice simply will not permit our continued adherence to a rule that, in the face of a judicial determination that others bear primary responsibility, nevertheless completely denies injured litigants recompense for their damages.

We recognize that this action could be taken by our General Assembly. However, legislative inaction has never prevented judicial abolition of obsolete common law doctrines, especially those, such as contributory negligence, conceived in the judicial womb. [C] Indeed, our abstinence would sanction "a mutual state of inaction in which the court awaits action by the legislature and the legislature awaits guidance from the court," [c] thereby prejudicing the equitable resolution of legal conflicts.

It's Latin to Me!

Stare decisis is Latin for "to stand by things decided" and refers to the doctrine of precedent under which a court applies and follows previous decisions addressing the same legal issues in the case before it.

Nor do we today abandon our commitment to *stare decisis.* While "[c]onfidence in our courts is to a great extent dependent on the uniformity and consistency engendered by allegiance to *stare decisis,* ... mindless obedience to this precept can confound the truth and foster an attitude of contempt." [C]

III.

Two basic forms of comparative fault are utilized by 45 of our sister jurisdictions, these variants being commonly referred to as either "pure" or "modified." In the "pure" form[5], a plaintiff's damages are reduced in proportion to the percentage negligence attributed to him; for example, a plaintiff responsible for 90 percent of the negligence that caused his injuries nevertheless may recover 10 percent of his damages. In the "modified" form[6], plaintiffs recover as in pure jurisdictions, but only if the plaintiff's negligence either (1) does not exceed ("50 percent" jurisdictions) or (2) is less than ("49 percent" jurisdictions) the defendant's negligence. *See generally* V. Schwartz, *supra,* at §§ 3.2, 3.5.

Although we conclude that the all-or-nothing rule of contributory negligence must be replaced, we nevertheless decline to abandon totally our fault-based tort system. We do not agree that a party should necessarily be able to recover in tort even though he may be 80, 90, or 95 percent at fault. We therefore reject the pure form of comparative fault.

We recognize that modified comparative fault systems have been criticized as merely shifting the arbitrary contributory negligence bar to a new ground. *See, e.g., Li v. Yellow Cab Co.,* 13 Cal.3d 804, 532 P.2d 1226, 119 Cal.Rptr. 858 (1975). However, we feel the "49 percent rule" ameliorates the harshness of the common law rule while remaining compatible with a fault-based tort system. *Accord Bradley v. Appalachian Power Co.,* 163 W.Va. 332, 256 S.E.2d 879, 887 (1979). We therefore hold that so long as a plaintiff's negligence remains less than the defendant's negligence the plaintiff may recover; in such a case, plaintiff's damages are to be reduced in proportion to the percentage of the total negligence attributable to the plaintiff.

In all trials where the issue of comparative fault is before a jury, the trial court shall instruct the jury on the effect of the jury's finding as to the percentage of negligence as between the plaintiff or plaintiffs and the defendant or defendants. *Accord* Colo.Rev.Stat. § 13-21-111.5(5) (1987). The attorneys for each party shall be allowed to argue how this instruction affects a plaintiff's ability to recover.

---

5 The 13 states utilizing pure comparative fault are Alaska, Arizona, California, Florida, Kentucky, Louisiana, Mississippi, Missouri, Michigan, New Mexico, New York, Rhode Island, and Washington. *See* V. Schwartz, *supra,* at § 2.1.

6 The 21 states using the "50 percent" modified form: Connecticut, Delaware, Hawaii, Illinois, Indiana, Iowa, Massachusetts, Minnesota, Montana, Nevada, New Hampshire, New Jersey, Ohio, Oklahoma, Oregon, Pennsylvania, South Carolina, Texas, Vermont, Wisconsin, and Wyoming. The 9 states using the "49 percent" form: Arkansas, Colorado, Georgia, Idaho, Kansas, Maine, North Dakota, Utah, and West Virginia. Two states, Nebraska and South Dakota, use a slight-gross system of comparative fault. *See* V. Schwartz, *supra,* at § 2.1.

IV.

Turning to the case at bar, the jury found that "the plaintiff and defendant [were] equally at fault." Because the jury, without the benefit of proper instructions by the trial court, made a gratuitous apportionment of fault, we find that their "equal" apportionment is not sufficiently trustworthy to form the basis of a final determination between these parties. Therefore, the case is remanded for a new trial in accordance with the dictates of this opinion.

Food for Thought

The court determines that the jury's "equal" apportionment of fault was "gratuitous." Should courts be concerned about such "equal" apportionments in negligence cases?

V.

We recognize that today's decision affects numerous legal principles surrounding tort litigation. For the most part, harmonizing these principles with comparative fault must await another day. However, we feel compelled to provide some guidance to the trial courts charged with implementing this new system.

First, and most obviously, the new rule makes the doctrines of remote contributory negligence and last clear chance obsolete. The circumstances formerly taken into account by those two doctrines will henceforth be addressed when assessing relative degrees of fault.

Second, in cases of multiple tortfeasors, plaintiff will be entitled to recover so long as plaintiff's fault is less than the combined fault of all tortfeasors.

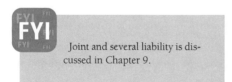

Joint and several liability is discussed in Chapter 9.

Third, today's holding renders the doctrine of **joint and several liability** obsolete. Our adoption of comparative fault is due largely to considerations of fairness: the contributory negligence doctrine unjustly allowed the entire loss to be borne by a negligent plaintiff, notwithstanding that the plaintiff's fault was minor in comparison to defendant's. Having thus adopted a rule more closely linking liability and fault, it would be inconsistent to simultaneously retain a rule, joint and several liability, which may fortuitously impose a degree of liability that is out of all proportion to fault.[7]

---

7 Numerous other comparative fault jurisdictions have eliminated joint and several liability. *See, e.g.,* Alaska Stat. § 09.17.080(d) (Supp.1991); Colo.Rev.Stat. § 13-21-111.5(1) (1987); Kan.Stat. Ann. § 60-258a(d) (Supp.1991); N.M.Stat.Ann. § 41-3A-1 (1989); N.D.Cent.Code § 32-03.2-02 (Supp.1991); Utah Code Ann. § 78-27-38, -40 (1992); Wyo.Stat.Ann. § 1-1-109(d) (1988).

Further, because a particular defendant will henceforth be liable only for the percentage of a plaintiff's damages occasioned by that defendant's negligence, situations where a defendant has paid more than his "share" of a judgment will no longer arise, and therefore the Uniform Contribution Among Tortfeasors Act, T.C.A. §§ 29-11-101 to 106 (1980), will no longer determine the apportionment of liability between codefendants.

Fourth, fairness and efficiency require that defendants called upon to answer allegations in negligence be permitted to allege, as an affirmative defense, that a nonparty caused or contributed to the injury or damage for which recovery is sought. In cases where such a defense is raised, the trial court shall instruct the jury to assign this nonparty the percentage of the total negligence for which he is responsible. However, in order for a plaintiff to recover a judgment against such additional person, the plaintiff must have made a timely amendment to his complaint and caused process to be served on such additional person. Thereafter, the additional party will be required to answer the amended complaint. The procedures shall be in accordance with the Tennessee Rules of Civil Procedure.

Fifth, until such time as the Tennessee Judicial Conference Committee on Civil Pattern Jury Instructions promulgates new standard jury instructions, we direct trial courts' attention to the suggested instructions and special verdict form set forth in the appendix to this opinion.

VI.

The principles set forth today apply to (1) all cases tried or retried after the date of this opinion, and (2) all cases on appeal in which the comparative fault issue has been raised at an appropriate stage in the litigation.

. . . .

For the foregoing reasons, the judgment of the Court of Appeals is reversed in part and affirmed in part, and the case is remanded to the trial court for a new trial in accordance with the dictates of this opinion. The costs of this appeal are taxed equally to the parties.

APPENDIX

The following instructions may be used in cases where the negligence of the plaintiff is at issue. These instructions are intended for two-party litigation. Appropriate modifications would be necessary for more complex litigation.

Suggested Jury Instructions

[The following instructions should be preceded by instructions on negligence, proximate cause, damages, etc.:]

1. If you find that defendant was not negligent or that defendant's negligence was not a proximate cause of plaintiff's injury, you will find for defendant.

2. If you find that defendant was negligent and that defendant's negligence was a proximate cause of plaintiff's injury, you must then determine whether plaintiff was also negligent and whether plaintiff's negligence was a proximate cause of his/her injury.

3. In this state, negligence on the part of a plaintiff has an impact on a plaintiff's right to recover damages. Accordingly, if you find that each party was negligent and that the negligence of each party was a proximate cause of plaintiff's damages, then you must determine the degree of such negligence, expressed as a percentage, attributable to each party.

4. If you find from all the evidence that the percentage of negligence attributable to plaintiff was equal to, or greater than, the percentage of negligence attributable to defendant, then you are instructed that plaintiff will not be entitled to recover any damages for his/her injuries. If, on the other hand, you determine from the evidence that the percentage of negligence attributable to plaintiff was less than the percentage of negligence attributable to defendant, then plaintiff will be entitled to recover that portion of his/her damages not caused by plaintiff's own negligence.

5. The court will provide you with a special verdict form that will assist you in your duties. This is the form on which you will record, if appropriate, the percentage of negligence assigned to each party and plaintiff's total damages. The court will then take your findings and either (1) enter judgment for defendant if you have found that defendant was not negligent or that plaintiff's own negligence accounted for 50 percent or more of the total negligence proximately causing his/her injuries or (2) enter judgment against defendant in accordance with defendant's percentage of negligence.

SPECIAL VERDICT FORM

We, the jury, make the following answers to the questions submitted by the court:

1. Was the defendant negligent?

Answer: _____ (Yes or No)

(If your answer is "No," do not answer any further questions. Sign this form and return it to the court.)

2. Was the defendant's negligence a proximate cause of injury or damage to the plaintiff?

Answer: _____ (Yes or No)

(If your answer is "No," do not answer any further questions. Sign this form and return it to the court.)

3. Did the plaintiff's own negligence account for 50 percent or more of the total negligence that proximately caused his/her injuries or damages?

Answer: _____ (Yes or No)

(If your answer is "Yes," do not answer any any further questions. Sign this form and return it to the court.)

4. What is the total amount of plaintiff's damages, determined without reference to the amount of plaintiff's negligence?

Amount in dollars: $_____

5. Using 100 percent as the total combined negligence which proximately caused the injuries or damages to the plaintiff, what are the percentages of such negligence to be allocated to the plaintiff and defendant?

Plaintiff_____%

Defendant_____%

(Total must equal 100%)

———————————————

Signature of Foreman

Points for Discussion

1. What explanation does the *McIntyre* court provide for the move from contributory to comparative negligence?

2. Describe and explain the difference between (a) "pure" comparative fault and (b) "modified" comparative fault.

3. In jurisdictions adopting a "modified" comparative fault regime, describe and explain the difference between the "plaintiff not greater than" and the "plaintiff not as great as" forms. What is the significance of either approach for cases in which juries apportion 50 percent of the fault to the defendant and 50 percent of the fault to the plaintiff?

4. Would the court permit the jury to determine and assign to a nonparty a percentage of the negligence for which the nonparty is responsible? What are the advantages and disadvantages of considering nonparty fault in the litigation of a particular case?

5. The Tennessee Supreme Court abolished joint and several liability and the last clear chance doctrine. Why? Note that other jurisdictions have not necessarily eliminated these doctrines. See RESTATEMENT (THIRD) OF TORTS: APPORTIONMENT OF LIABILITY § 3, comment *b* (2000).

6. South Dakota has enacted the following comparative negligence statute:

    > In all actions brought to recover damages for injuries to a person or to that person's property caused by the negligence of another, the fact that the plaintiff may have been guilty of contributory negligence does not bar a recovery when the contributory negligence of the plaintiff is slight in comparison with the negligence of the defendant, but in such case, the damages shall be reduced in proportion to the amount of plaintiff's contributory negligence.

    SDCL § 20-9-2. For a recent decision of the South Dakota Supreme Court applying this provision, *see* Gettysburg School District 53-1 v. Helms and Associates, 751 N.W.2d 266 (2008).

——————————

Hypo 6-1

Suppose that a plaintiff sues three defendants as multiple tortfeasors in a negligence action. The jury determines that the plaintiff is 25 percent at fault, and that each of the defendants is also 25 percent at fault, respectively. Is the plaintiff entitled to recover?

Hockema v. J.S.

832 N.E.2d 537 (Ind. App. 2005)

VAIDIK, Judge.

Case Summary

Seventeen-year-old Anne Hockema and her father Stanley Hockema appeal the trial court's grant of **additur** after the jury found Jacob Secrest to be 66.75% at fault and awarded $0 damages. Because under our comparative fault scheme Jacob was barred from recovering for his damages and his parents' claim for medical expenses are derivative claims, we conclude that the trial court erred by allowing the parents to recover 33.25% of Jacob's stipulated medical expenses. Consequently, we reverse and remand with instructions to reinstate the jury's verdict.

Facts and Procedural History

In September 2001, Anne was driving along Hanawalt Road in White County, Indiana. As she was driving, eight-year-old Jacob Secrest darted out into the road and collided with Hockema's vehicle. Jacob's nine-year-old sister, Erica Secrest, witnessed the collision, and Jacob's mother, Merri Secrest, came running out of her parents' house to assist Jacob immediately after the collision. Jacob's father, Eric Secrest, was not present at the scene of the accident. Jacob was transported to the hospital by ambulance with his mother accompanying him. As a result of the impact, Jacob broke his right elbow and collarbone, which required him to undergo surgery and attend physical therapy.

The Secrests filed a complaint for damages against Anne and Stanley (collectively, "the Hockemas"), which sought recovery for medical expenses; permanent injuries; emotional distress; loss of services; and pain and suffering. A jury trial ensued during which the parties stipulated that Jacob's medical expenses totaled $38,708.44. Following the presentation of evidence, the parties argued final jury instructions to the judge. Included among the final instructions were the following verdict instructions and verdict form:

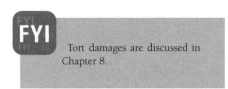

Tort damages are discussed in Chapter 8.

VERDICT INSTRUCTIONS

If you find the Defendant is not at fault, then your verdict must be for the Defendants, and no further deliberation of the jury is necessary. (*Use Verdict Form A-1.*)

If however you find there is fault on behalf of the Defendant, Anne Hockema, you are required to apportion the fault on a percentage basis between Jacob Secrest and Anne Hockema to determine whether the Plaintiffs are entitled to recover damages, and if so, the amount of such recovery. You may not apportion fault to any other person or entity.

You will therefore determine the comparative fault issues in this case as follows:

First, you must determine the percentage of fault, if any, of Jacob Secrest and of Anne Hockema in the proximate causation of the Plaintiffs' injuries and damages. These percentages must total 100 percent.

[I]f you find Anne Hockema is at fault and Jacob Secrest's fault is greater than 50 percent, then you must return your verdict for the Defendants and against Jacob Secrest. No further deliberation is required as to Jacob Secrest. . . .

However, if you find that Jacob Secrest's fault is 50 percent or less, then you must determine the total amount of damages Jacob Secrest is entitled to recover, if any, without regard to fault. Then you must multiply Jacob Secrest's total damages by Anne Hockema's percentage of fault and return your verdict for Jacob Secrest and against the Defendants in the amount of the product of that multiplication. . . .

If you find that Anne Hockema is at fault *at all,* [then] you must also determine the total amount of damages Eric Secrest, Merri Secrest, and Erica Secrest are each entitled to recover, if any, without regard to fault.

Then you must multiply Eric Secrest, Merri Secrest, and Erica Secrest's total damages by Anne Hockema's percentage of fault and return your verdicts for each of Eric Secrest, Merri Secrest, and Erica Secrest and against the Defendants in the amount of the product of that multiplication. (*Use Verdict Form B-2.*)

The verdict forms provided to you by the Court will help guide you through this process.

. . . .

Verdict Form B-2

VERDICT FOR PLAINTIFF ERIC SECREST

We, the Jury, find for Plaintiff, Eric Secrest, and we assess the percentages of fault as follows:

Plaintiff Jacob Secrest	_____	%
Defendant Anne Hockema	_____	%
TOTAL	100	%

We, further find that the total amounts of damages which the Plaintiff, Eric Secrest, is entitled to recover, disregarding fault, is the sum of $_____. (*Enter this amount below as Total Damages.*)

We, the Jury, now find for the Plaintiff, Eric Secrest, and against the Defendants, Anne Hockema and Stanley Hockema, in the sum of:

Total Damages	$	_____
Defendants' percentage of fault	x	_____
Verdict Amount	$	_____

[C] The Hockemas objected to the Verdict Instructions and Verdict Form B-2:

We ... object to the Verdict Instructions and Verdict Form for the reason that ... as written the verdict instructions and the verdict form allows [sic] for purely **derivative** claims of ... Eric, Merri, and Eri[c]a Secrest, to survive, even though the jury ... determine[s] that ... Jacob Secrest was ... fifty one percent [or] more at fault. And for that reason we think it's an inaccurate ... statement of the law and would result in an improper, an incorrect ... verdict.

[C] The trial court overruled the objection.

The jury returned a defense verdict. In particular, the jury found Jacob to be 66.75% at fault, Anne to be 33.25% at fault, and awarded the Secrests $0 in damages.

The Secrests filed a motion to correct errors seeking additur or a new trial, in which it claimed that the jury erred by not awarding Jacob's parents damages for a percentage of the stipulated medical expenses. The Hockemas responded by asserting that the Secrests "failed to take into account the expenses and damage claims made by the family members were *derivative* to Jacob's primary cause of action," [c], and consequently, "the 'parent' plaintiffs *cannot* prevail if a jury decides against the 'child's' claim." [C] Following a hearing on the motion, the trial court entered judgment in favor of the Secrests for $12,780.56, which is 33.25% of the stipulated amount of medical expenses. In its Order, the trial court stated:

> The Court instructed the Jury that there was a stipulation as to the medical expenses incurred by the parents in the sum of Thirty-eight Thousand Seven Hundred Eight Dollars Forty-four Cents ($38,708.44), and that the Jury in this matter found that the Defendant, Ann[c] Hockema, was thirty-three point two-five percent (33.25%) negligent in the action.

> The Court had previously instructed the Jury that the parent's right of recovery for their medical expenses was not contingent on the child's right of recovery for his injuries.

> Therefore, the Court finds that the parents should be entitled to their stipulated expenses of thirty-three point two-five percent (33.25%) of Thirty-eight Thousand Seven Hundred Eight Dollars Forty-four Cents ($38,708.44).

> The Court directs that the jury verdict be modified in this matter that the Court now orders a judgment entered against the Defendant, Anne Hockema, in the sum of Twelve Thousand Eight Hundred Seventy Dollars Fifty-six Cents ($12,870.56).

[C] The Hockemas now appeal.

Discussion and Decision

The Hockemas argue that the trial court erred by granting the Secrests' request for additur following the jury's award of $0 damages to the Secrests. . . .

The Hockemas claim that the trial court abused its discretion when it granted the Secrests' motion to correct error pursuant to Indiana Trial Rule 59(J)(5) and awarded $12,870.56 to the Secrests notwithstanding the jury's verdict of $0. . . .

Trial courts must afford juries great latitude in making damage award determinations. [C] A verdict must be upheld if the award determination falls within the bounds of the evidence. [C] Additionally, a trial court may only reverse a jury's award determination "when it is apparent from a review of the evidence that the amount of damages awarded by the jury is so small or so great as to clearly indicate that the jury was motivated by prejudice, passion, partiality, corruption or that it considered an improper element." [C]

Curiously, the issue with which we are faced today—namely, whether a parent is precluded from recovering necessary medical expenses paid by them on behalf of an injured child whose comparative negligence exceeds the negligence of the tortfeasor—is an issue of **first impression** in Indiana. The Comparative Fault Act, now codified at Indiana Code 34-51-2, was adopted in Indiana in 1983 and went into effect in 1985. *Control Techniques, Inc. v. Johnson,* 762 N.E.2d 104, 107 (Ind.2002). By adopting the Comparative Fault Act, the General Assembly rejected the common law doctrine of contributory negligence as a complete bar to recovery in negligence cases,[5] thereby bringing this state in line with the vast majority of states that adhere to some form of a comparative fault law. *Walters v. Dean,* 497 N.E.2d 247, 250 (Ind.Ct.App.1986).

There are two basic forms of comparative fault laws, which are designated as "pure" or "modified." Under the "pure" form, a plaintiff may recover a percentage of his damages even though his fault exceeds that of the defendant. [C] Under "modified" comparative fault statutes, a plaintiff normally may recover a reduced amount of his damages so long as his negligence either does not equal ("modified forty-nine percent") or exceed that of the defendant ("modified fifty percent"). [C]; I Matthew Bender, Comparative Negligence §§ 1.20, 1.30 (Richard E. Kaye ed.2004). The Indiana statute is a type of modified fifty percent comparative fault law that requires, in some cases, consideration of the degree of fault of non-parties to the action as well as the fault of the parties. *See* Ind.Code §§ 34-51-2-6; 34-51-2-7; 34-52-2-14. Thus, if a claimant is deemed to be more than fifty percent at fault, then the claimant is barred from recovery. *See* I.C. § 34-51-2-6 ("In an action based on fault that is brought against ... one (1) defendant or ... two (2) or

---

5 Indiana has retained the common law concept of contributory negligence in claims brought under the Indiana Medical Malpractice Act and the Indiana Tort Claims Act. *See* Ind.Code § 34-51-2-1(b) ("This [comparative fault] chapter does not apply to an action: (1) brought against a qualified health care provider under IC 16-9.5 (before its repeal), IC 27-12 (before its repeal), or IC 34-18 for medical malpractice."); Ind.Code § 34-51-2-2 ("This [comparative fault] chapter does not apply in any manner to tort claims against governmental entities or public employees under IC 34-13-3 (or IC 34-4-16.5 before its repeal).").

more defendants who may be treated as a single party; the claimant is barred from recovery if the claimant's contributory fault is greater than the fault of all persons whose fault proximately contributed to the claimant's damages.").

The jury found Jacob Secrest to be 66.75% at fault for the accident. Thus, under Indiana's comparative fault scheme, Jacob is barred from recovering any damages from Hockema. Nonetheless, Eric and Merri Secrest argue that they should be able to recover a percentage of the stipulated medical expenses, and therefore the trial court did not err by granting their request for additur. We disagree.

Eric and Merri Secrest, as the parents of Jacob, are responsible for the costs of the medical attention furnished to Jacob by the various providers. *See, e.g., Scott County Sch. Dist. 1 v. Asher,* 263 Ind. 17, 51-52, 324 N.E.2d 496, 499 (1975) ("The parent also is liable because of his common law and, in some instances, statutory duty to support and maintain his child.... This parental duty includes the provision of necessary medical care."). The obligation to pay medical expenses is not a damage inflicted directly on the parents; rather, the parents' debt arises only because, as parents, they are obligated to contract for necessary medical care for their minor child. If the child was not a minor, the medical expenses would be his own, and the parents would not be obligated to pay them. The right of the parents to recover the child's medical expenses, hence, rests upon the child's right to recover and therefore may be appropriately categorized as a derivative right. Accordingly, when a child is injured, the parent has a cause of action against the tortfeasor to recover compensation for the necessary medical treatment arising from the tortious conduct. [C] Because of the derivative nature of this right, however, the right is not absolute. Instead, the right to recover medical expenses may be barred by the child's comparative negligence if it exceeds the negligence of the tortfeasor.

This result is consistent with the approach taken by our courts under the common law doctrine of contributory negligence. For example, in *Brown v. Slentz,* 237 Ind. 497, 147 N.E.2d 239 (Ind.1958), a father brought a lawsuit for loss of services and medical expenses he paid on behalf of his minor son for injuries the son sustained as a result of an automobile collision. The son was driving his father's car when he was involved in a collision with another driver who was allegedly operating his vehicle negligently. Following a trial on the matter, a jury returned a verdict in favor of the alleged tortfeasor, presumably based on the theory that the minor's negligence was imputable to the father. On appeal, our supreme court held that "the contributory negligence of the minor child ... is imputable to the parent ...." *Brown,* 237 Ind. at 500, 147 N.E.2d at 240. The parties advance no valid reason why we should not follow a similar approach here. Thus, although Indiana has abandoned contributory negligence in cases such as the one with which we are faced today, the concept of **imputation** is still viable under our comparative fault scheme. This means that if a child's comparative fault is less than fifty percent, then a parent may recover the appropriate percentage of the medical expenses paid on behalf of the child from the tortfeasors. If, however, the child's comparative fault exceeds fifty percent, the parents are barred from recovering medical expenses.

As mentioned above, the jury determined that Jacob was 66.75% at fault and that Anne was 33.25% at fault. By seeking to recover a percentage of the stipulated medical expenses in spite of Jacob's negligence exceeding that of Anne's, the Secrests essentially are requesting that we abandon the concept of modified comparative fault in favor of a pure comparative fault scheme with regard to medical expenses. The Indiana General Assembly has chosen to adopt a modified comparative fault system. It is not our province to override the legislature's clear intent of barring recovery when a claimant is more than fifty percent at fault. Consequently, the trial court erred by granting additur, and we reverse and remand with instructions that the jury verdict be reinstated.

Reversed and remanded.

———————————

Points for Discussion

1. What form of comparative fault law is recognized in Indiana and applied by the *Hockema* court?

2. Describe the jury's percentage apportionment of fault between Jacob and Anne. On the facts presented, is this apportionment correct or at least defensible? May a child be comparatively negligent? Should he or she be?

3. What is an additur? On what bases did the trial judge grant and the appeals court reject the Secrests' additur motion?

4. Do you agree with the appeals court's view that it was not the court's "province to override the legislature's clear intent of barring recovery when a claimant is more than fifty percent at fault"? What is a court's role or function in the interpretation and application of a statutory scheme? When, if ever, should a court depart from or add to a legislative enactment in furtherance of "fairness" or "justice"?

———————————

C. Assumption of the Risk

1. Express Assumption of Risk

McCune v. Myrtle Beach Indoor Shooting Range, Inc.

364 S.C. 242, 612 S.E.2d 462 (2005)

BEATTY, J.:

Christine McCune brought an action for negligence and strict liability against the Myrtle Beach Indoor Shooting Range (the Range) for injuries sustained while she was participating in a paintball game. McCune appeals from the trial court's grant of summary judgment to the Range. We affirm.

FACTS

The Range offers paintball games and allows participants to rent protective equipment, including face masks, provided by the Range. McCune participated in a paintball match with her husband and friends. She utilized a mask provided by the Range. Prior to being allowed to participate, McCune signed a general **waiver**. The waiver released the Range from liability from all known or unknown dangers for any reason with the exception of **gross negligence** on the part of the Range.

During her play, the mask was loose and ill fitting. She attempted to have the mask tightened or replaced on several occasions and an employee of the Range attempted to properly fit the mask for McCune. While playing in a match, McCune caught the mask on the branch of a tree. The tree was obscured from her field of vision by the top of the mask. The mask was raised off her face because it was loose, and provided no protection against an incoming paintball pellet. The pellet struck McCune in the eye, rendering her legally blind in the eye.

McCune brought suit, alleging causes of action for negligence and strict liability based on the failure of the mask to properly be fitted and protect her during play. The Range filed an answer asserting the waiver released them from all liability as a result of the paintball striking McCune. Additionally, it asserted McCune's comparative negligence barred recovery.

Subsequently, the Range filed a motion for summary judgment, again alleging the waiver and McCune's comparative negligence barred recovery. The court granted the Range's motion, finding the waiver was sufficient to show McCune expressly assumed the risks associated with playing paintball. Additionally, the court found her overwhelming comparative fault barred recovery. The trial court subsequently denied McCune's motion for reconsideration. This appeal followed.

. . . .

Discussion

McCune maintains the trial court erred in granting summary judgment to the Range on the basis of the exculpatory language in the **release** of liability signed by McCune. McCune asserts she did not anticipate the harm that was inflicted or the manner in which it occurred. Additionally, she contends the failure of the equipment was unexpected and she could not have voluntarily assumed such a risk. We disagree.

As an initial matter, we must determine whether this is a case involving express assumption or **implied assumption of the risk**. Express assumption of the risk sounds in contract and occurs when the parties agree beforehand, "either in writing or orally, that the plaintiff will relieve the defendant of his or her legal duty toward the plaintiff." *Davenport v. Cotton Hope Plantation Horizontal Prop. Regime,* 333 S.C. 71, 79-80, 508 S.E.2d 565, 569-70 (1998).

Take Note

A plaintiff's express and contractual assumption of risk may result from and come in the form of a written or oral agreement.

"Express assumption of risk is contrasted with implied assumption of risk which arises when the plaintiff implicitly, rather than expressly, assumes known risks. As noted above, implied assumption of risk is characterized as either primary or secondary." *Id.* at 80-81, 508 S.E.2d at 570. "**[P]rimary implied assumption of risk** is but another way of stating the conclusion that a plaintiff has failed to establish a prima facie case [of negligence] by failing to establish that a duty exists." *Id.* at 81, 508 S.E.2d at 570 (quoting *Perez v. McConkey,* 872 S.W.2d 897, 902 (Tenn.1994)). "**Secondary implied assumption of risk**, on the other hand, arises when the plaintiff knowingly encounters a risk created by the defendant's negligence." *Id.* at 82, 508 S.E.2d 565, 508 S.E.2d at 571.

In the instant case, we are confronted with a defense based upon McCune's express assumption of the risk. She signed a **release** from liability prior to participating in the paintball match. As acknowledged by *Davenport,* the courts of South Carolina have analyzed express assumption of the risk cases in terms of exculpatory contracts. *Id.* at 80, 508 S.E.2d at 570.

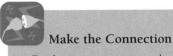

Make the Connection

Exculpatory contracts may be addressed in a Contracts course.

Exculpatory contracts, such as the one in this case, have previously been upheld by the courts of this state. *See Huckaby v. Confederate Motor Speedway, Inc.,* 276 S.C. 629, 630, 281 S.E.2d 223, 224 (1981) (finding plaintiff's action against speedway for injuries sustained during a race was barred by "waiver and release" voluntarily signed by plaintiff prior to entering the race track); *Pride v. Southern Bell Tel. & Tel. Co.,* 244 S.C. 615, 619-22, 138 S.E.2d 155, 157-58 (1964) (holding it was not violative of public policy for telephone company to legally limit its liability by contract for negligence in the publication of a paid advertisement in the yellow pages of its telephone directory). "However, notwithstanding the general acceptance of exculpatory contracts, '[s]ince such provisions tend to induce a want of care, they are not favored by the law and will be strictly construed against the party relying thereon.' " *Fisher v. Stevens,* 355 S.C. 290, 295, 584 S.E.2d 149, 152 (Ct.App.2003) (quoting *Pride,* 244 S.C. at 619, 138 S.E.2d at 157). This court has explained:

> Common sense and good faith are the leading touchstones of the construction of a contract and contracts are to be so construed as to avoid an absurd result. Where one construction would make a contract unusual or extraordinary and another, equally consistent, would make the contract reasonable, fair and just, the latter construction will prevail.

Georgetown Mfg. & Warehouse Co. v. South Carolina Dep't of Agric., 301 S.C. 514, 518, 392 S.E.2d 801, 804 (Ct.App.1990) (citing *C.A.N. Enters., Inc. v. South Carolina Health & Human Servs. Fin. Comm'n,* 296 S.C. 373, 373 S.E.2d 584 (1988)).

Contracts that seek to exculpate a party from liability for the party's own negligence are not favored by the law. *Pride,* 244 S.C. at 619, 138 S.E.2d at 157. An exculpatory clause, our supreme court has held, is to be strictly construed against the party relying thereon. *Id.* An exculpatory clause will never be construed to exempt a party from liability for his own negligence " 'in the absence of explicit language clearly indicating that such was the intent of the parties.' " *South Carolina Elec. & Gas Co. v. Combustion Eng'g, Inc.,* 283 S.C. 182, 191, 322 S.E.2d 453, 458 (Ct.App.1984) (quoting *Hill v. Carolina Freight Carriers Corp.,* 235 N.C. 705, 71 S.E.2d 133, 137 (1952)).

The release in the instant case explicitly and unambiguously limited the Range's liability. Specifically, McCune signed the release, thereby acknowledging the following pertinent clauses:

1.   The risk of injury from the activity and weaponry involved in paintball is significant, including the potential for permanent disability and death, and while particular protective equipment and personal discipline will minimize this risk, the risk of serious injury does exist;

2.   I KNOWINGLY AND FREELY ASSUME ALL SUCH RISKS, both known and unknown, EVEN IF ARISING FROM THE NEGLIGENCE of those persons released from liability below, and assume full responsibility for my participation; and,

...

4.   I, for myself and on behalf of my heirs ... HEREBY RELEASE AND HOLD HARMLESS THE AMERICAN PAINTBALL LEAGUE (APL), THE APL CERTIFIED MEMBER FIELD, the owners and lessors of premises used to conduct the paintball activities, their officers, officials, agents, and/or employees ("Releasees"), WITH RESPECT TO ANY AND ALL INJURY, DISABILITY, DEATH, or loss or damage to person or property, WHETHER CAUSED BY THE NEGLIGENCE OF THE RELEASEES OR OTHERWISE, except that which is the result of gross negligence and/or wanton misconduct.

...

I HAVE READ THIS RELEASE OF LIABILITY AND ASSUMPTION OF RISK AGREEMENT, FULLY UNDERSTANDING ITS TERMS, UNDERSTAND THAT I HAVE GIVEN UP SUBSTANTIAL RIGHTS BY SIGNING IT, AND SIGN IT FREELY AND VOLUNTARILY WITHOUT ANY INDUCEMENT.

The agreement is then signed by McCune and dated the date of the incident.

The above agreement is sufficient to limit the liability of the Range to McCune. The agreement was voluntarily signed and specifically stated: (1) she assumed the risks, whether known or unknown; and (2) she released the Range from liability, even from injuries sustained because of the Range's own negligence. It is clear McCune voluntarily entered into the release in exchange for being allowed to participate in the paintball match.

Additionally, she expressly assumed the risk for all known and unknown risks while participating and cannot now complain because she did not fully appreciate the exact risk she faced. "*Except where he expressly so agrees,* a plaintiff does not assume a risk of harm arising from the defendant's conduct unless he then knows of the existence of the risk and appreciates its unreasonable character." *Restatement (Second) of Torts* 496D (1965) (emphasis added).

We find the release entered into by the parties does not contravene public policy. In *Huckaby,* the plaintiff signed a waiver similar to the one above, which was required before he could participate in a sanctioned automobile race. He maintained his injuries were caused by the speedway's faulty installation and maintenance of a guardrail. *Huckaby,* 276 S.C. at 630, 281 S.E.2d at 223. As was found in *Huckaby,* participation in a paintball match is voluntary. " 'If these agreements, voluntarily entered into, were not upheld, the effect would be to increase the liability of those organizing or sponsoring such events to such an extent that no one would be willing to undertake to sponsor a sporting event. Clearly, this would not be in the public interest.' " *Huckaby,* 276 S.C. at 631, 281 S.E.2d at 224 (quoting *Gore v. Tri-County Raceway, Inc.,* 407 F.Supp. 489, 492 (M.D.Ala.1974)).

Furthermore, we find the instant case to be distinguishable from this court's decision in *Fisher v. Stevens,* 355 S.C. 290, 584 S.E.2d 149 (Ct.App.2003). In *Fisher,* the plaintiff worked on a wrecker crew at the Speedway of South Carolina. In order to work at the Speedway, Fisher was required to sign a release and waiver of liability. During a race, the wrecker on which Fisher was working responded to a crash. While the wrecker was moving towards one of the vehicles, Fisher, who was riding on the back of the wrecker, fell off and suffered severe head injuries. Through a guardian, Fisher brought suit alleging negligence, gross negligence, and recklessness against the driver and the owner of the wrecker as well as the Speedway. The defendants raised the Release as an **affirmative defense**. All parties filed cross-motions for summary judgment, alleging the Release acted as a complete bar to Fisher's claims. The circuit court judge granted partial summary judgment to Fisher against the driver and the owner of the wrecker on the ground the Release, as a matter of law, did not bar Fisher's claims. Additionally, the court denied summary judgment to the Speedway. The court found an issue of material fact existed as to whether Fisher was an employee of the Speedway.

On appeal, the driver and the owner of the wrecker argued the circuit court erred in finding the Release was inapplicable to them. Specifically, they contended they were released from liability given the Release encompassed "VEHICLE OWNERS, DRIVERS, [and] ... ANY PERSONS IN ANY RESTRICTED AREA." *Id.* at 294, 584 S.E.2d at 151-52. In analyzing this issue, we found the Release, an exculpatory contract, was ambiguous because the terms, "driver" and "vehicle owner" were "terms of art [which were] not used to identify *any* owner or driver of *any* vehicle." *Id.* at 295, 584 S.E.2d at 152. Additionally, we agreed with the circuit court that the phrase "ANY PERSONS IN ANY RESTRICTED AREA" did not relieve the driver and the owner of the wrecker of liability on the ground it was overly broad and, thus, in contravention of public policy. Because the contract "did not clearly inform Fisher he would be waiving all claims due to the [driver's and vehicle owner's negligence]," we held the driver and the vehicle owner could not be released from liability "based on the broad 'catch-all' phrase." *Id.* at 298, 584 S.E.2d at 153.

In contrast, the release in the case at bar is neither ambiguous nor overbroad. In fact, McCune in her deposition characterized the release as a "standard waiver." Although our research reveals no South Carolina case that deals specifically with a release for paintball, other jurisdictions have found similarly worded releases to be unambiguous. *See Taylor v. Hesser,* 991 P.2d 35, 38 (Okla.Civ.App.1998) (affirming grant of summary judgment to operators of paintball facility and shooter where plaintiff, who was injured during the paintball game, signed a release prior to participating); *Kaltenbach v. Splatball, Inc.,* No. C7-99-235, 1999 WL 690191, at *2 (Minn.Ct.App.1999) (finding paintball participant was precluded from recovering against owner of a paintball facility for injuries where participant signed a release of owner's liability).

We would also note that unlike the release in *Fisher,* the release signed by McCune did not preclude recovery for a cause of action involving gross negligence. Thus, this opinion should not be construed as creating an indefensible position for all injuries sustained during inherently dangerous recreational activities. *Cf. Adams v. Roark,* 686 S.W.2d 73, 75-76 (Tenn.1985) (recognizing, in an action to recover for injuries sustained by a motorcyclist at a drag way, that an agreement to contract against liability for gross negligence is unenforceable); *Murphy v. N. Am. River Runners, Inc.,* 186 W.Va. 310, 412 S.E.2d 504, 510 (1991) (stating, in an action to recover for injuries sustained during a whitewater rafting accident, "a general clause in a pre-injury exculpatory agreement or anticipatory release purporting to exempt a defendant from all liability for any future loss or damage will not be construed to include the loss or damage resulting from the defendant's intentional or reckless misconduct or gross negligence, unless the circumstances clearly indicate that such was the plaintiff's intention").

Take Note

The court makes clear that the at-issue release did not bar a plaintiff's recovery in cases involving gross negligence or certain inherently dangerous activities.

Accordingly, we hold the trial court properly determined the release signed by McCune was sufficient to release the Range from all liability in this incident. Therefore, the decision of the trial court is

AFFIRMED.

Points for Discussion

1. Describe and explain the differences between (a) an express assumption of risk and (b) an implied assumption of risk. With respect to an implied assumption of risk, what is the difference between the primary and secondary categories of this defense?

2. How does assumption of the risk differ from consent, if at all?

3. Do you agree with the court's reading of the release signed by McCune?

4. The court emphasizes that exculpatory contracts are not favored by the law and are to be strictly construed against the party relying thereon. What is the practical significance of and policy reflected in this approach to such contracts?

5. Can and should a general release preclude a plaintiff's recovery for gross negligence, inherently dangerous recreational activities, or a defendant's intentional or reckless misconduct? In *Jones v. Dressel*, 623 P.2d 370 (Colo. 1981), the court stated that an exculpatory agreement does not and cannot provide a shield against a plaintiff's claim alleging willful and wanton negligence by a defendant.

Hypo 6-2

Joining Fitness Club on a one-month trial basis, Plaintiff signed a Participation Agreement which contained the following clause: "I, the undersigned applicant, agree and understand that I must report any and all injuries immediately to Fitness Club's staff. It is further agreed that all exercises shall be undertaken by me at my sole risk and that Fitness Club shall not be liable to me for any claims, demands, injuries, damages, action, or courses or causes of action whatsoever, to my person or property arising out of or in connection with the use of the services and facilities of Fitness Club by me. Furthermore, I do expressly hereby forever release and discharge Fitness Club from all claims, demands, injuries, damages, actions, or courses or causes of action, and from all acts of active or passive negligence on the part of Fitness Club, its servants, agents, or employees."

> A few days after signing the aforementioned agreement, Plaintiff came to Fitness Club for a scheduled initial evaluation. While using an upper torso weight machine as directed by a Fitness Club trainer, Plaintiff heard a loud pop in her shoulder and experienced a great deal of pain. Examined by her physician that same day, Plaintiff was advised to have and subsequently had surgery to repair torn tissue and other structural damage in her shoulder (which the doctor attributed to Plaintiff's use of the weight machine).
>
> Plaintiff has filed a negligence action against Fitness Club, alleging that Fitness Club is liable for the actions of the employee who conducted Plaintiff's evaluation and for the company's negligence in failing to train and supervise the employee properly. Fitness Club has filed a motion to dismiss on the ground that the exculpatory clause contained in the Participation Agreement signed by Plaintiff was valid and enforceable and released Fitness Club from liability for the acts alleged by Plaintiff. You are a trial court judge. Consider and rule on Fitness Club's motion.

2. Implied Assumption of Risk

Wirtz v. Gillogly

152 Wash. App. 1, 216 P.3d 416 (2009)

HUNT, J.

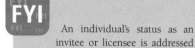

An individual's status as an invitee or licensee is addressed in Chapter 7.

¶ 1 Robert L. Wirtz appeals the trial court's summary judgment dismissal of his negligence claims against Dennis and David Gillogly and their marital communities. He argues that the trial court erred in (1) concluding that Wirtz assumed the risk of injury associated with felling trees on David Gillogly's property and (2) failing to distinguish between Wirtz's status on the property as an **invitee** rather than a **licensee**. Holding that Wirtz knowingly and voluntarily consented to participate in the tree-felling project and, thus, assumed the risks involved, we affirm the trial court's grant of summary judgment in the Gillogly's favor. Accordingly, we need not reach Wirtz's second argument about his legal status.

Facts

I. Tree-Felling Accident

¶ 2 In February 2003, Dennis Gillogly (Dennis) asked longtime friend Robert Wirtz to help with a tree-felling project on Dennis's father's (David Gillogly) Longview property to prevent interference with nearby cable television lines. Wirtz agreed to assist the Gilloglys as a favor; he neither requested nor received anything of value in exchange for his help. Dennis had some experience felling trees as a seasonal firefighter for the forest service, from which he had received a tree-felling certificate. Wirtz, however, had no tree-felling experience.

¶ 3 On the first day of the tree-felling project, Dennis offered Wirtz a hardhat, but Wirtz refused to wear it. During the first few days of work, Wirtz helped by stacking wood with David after Dennis cut the logs into rounds, but he (Wirtz) did not cut the wood or assist in felling the trees. David also monitored the work.

¶ 4 After several days, Dennis asked Wirtz to help him fell a tree that stood close to the property's cable television lines. To avoid hitting the lines, (1) David and Dennis decided to set a cable around the tree's trunk to ensure that it would fall uphill; and (2) Dennis notched the tree with his chainsaw to make it fall uphill. Wirtz wrapped a cable around the tree's trunk, 20-30 feet above the ground; David secured the cable, using a "come along ratchet" to tighten the lines so they would not drag. Both Dennis and David had used this method to fell trees in the past.

¶ 5 The men decided that Dennis would cut the tree with a chainsaw while Wirtz operated the ratchet to keep the cable lines taut. David stood at the driveway, and Wirtz waited for his signal to begin operating the ratchet. As Dennis cut the tree, David intermittently signaled to Wirtz to use the ratchet to tighten the cables. During the felling process, the tree's trunk split; Dennis stopped sawing to discuss how to proceed.

¶ 6 David and Dennis determined what to do, they informed Wirtz, and Wirtz and Dennis resumed felling the tree. Moments later, the tree split from the point where Dennis had applied the chainsaw; the splitting tree broke at the cable line. Wirtz tried to move out of the way, but the broken part of the tree hit him in the head, knocking him unconscious. When he awoke, he was bleeding from one ear; Dennis and David were standing over him. David and Dennis then took Wirtz to the hospital.

II. Procedure

A. Wirtz's Negligence Complaint

¶ 7 On February 27, 2006, Wirtz filed a personal injury action for damages against David and Diana Gillogly, individually and as a marital community, and Dennis and Melinda Gillogly, individually and as a marital community. Wirtz alleged that the Gilloglys were negligent in (1) letting Wirtz remove trees without safety equipment; (2) failing to provide him with safety equipment, including a hardhat; (3) creating/maintaining dangerous conditions on their property; (4) failing to exercise ordinary care for him; and (5) failing to provide him with appropriate training for felling trees on their property. Wirtz further alleged that as a result of the defendants' negligence, he suffered economic damages and personal injuries in an amount to be determined at trial. Wirtz also broadly requested actual, special, general, compensatory, and noneconomic damages, plus costs and disbursements.

. . . .

ANALYSIS

¶ 15 The **dispositive** issue is whether Wirtz assumed the risk of injury from a falling tree when he participated in the Gilloglys' tree-removal project. We agree with the trial court and answer, "Yes."

I. Wirtz's Assumption of Risk

. . . .

¶ 18 Washington courts have held that assumption of risk traditionally has four facets: (1) express assumption of risk, (2) implied primary assumption of risk, (3) implied reasonable assumption of risk, and (4) implied unreasonable assumption of risk. *Erie v. White,* 92 Wash.App. 297, 302, 966 P.2d 342 (1998), *review denied,* 137 Wash.2d 1022, 980 P.2d 1280 (1999). The parties agree that the theory at issue here is "implied primary assumption of risk." Implied primary assumption of risk arises when (1) the plaintiff impliedly consents to relieve the defendant of a duty to him (plaintiff) about specific, known, and appreciated risks, *Scott v. Pac. W. Mountain Resort,* 119 Wash.2d 484, 497, 834 P.2d 6 (1992); and (2) the plaintiff engages in conduct, from which consent is implied. *Erie,* 92 Wash.App. at 303, 966 P.2d 342 (citing *Alston v. Blythe,* 88 Wash.App. 26, 33, 943 P.2d 692 (1997)). To prove that the plaintiff assumed the risk, the defendant must show that the plaintiff knowingly and voluntarily chose to encounter it. *Erie,* 92 Wash.App. at 303, 966 P.2d 342 (citing Restatement (Second) of Torts § 496G (1965)). Knowledge and voluntariness are questions of fact for the jury, except when reasonable minds could not differ. *Id.* at 303, 966 P.2d 342 (citing *Alston,* 88 Wash.App. at 33, 943 P.2d 692).

. . . .

¶ 22 [R]easonable minds could not differ about whether Wirtz knowingly and voluntarily assumed the risk inherent in felling trees. We address both *Erie* factors in turn.

1. Knowledge

¶ 23 We first examine the knowledge component. As the Gilloglys correctly argue, Wirtz consented to operate the ratchet and cable system to cause the tree to fall in his direction, knowing that the tree could strike him. The record further demonstrates that despite his inexperience, Wirtz (1) observed the tree-felling process for several days before actually participating in it; (2) discussed the tree-felling and ratcheting processes with the Gilloglys; (3) recognized that using the ratchet and cable system would guide the falling tree uphill, toward where he was standing; and (4) planned an escape route to avoid the falling tree because he knew that it could hit him.

¶ 24 Moreover, as Wirtz himself testified, he had observed Dennis wearing a hardhat while felling trees. Although Dennis and David had repeatedly offered Wirtz a hardhat, Wirtz had repeatedly refused to wear one, apparently, because he did not think that he needed one. Accordingly, under *Erie,* we hold that because Wirtz appreciated the risk involved in the tree-felling process, no reasonable juror could conclude that he acted without knowledge of the associated risks.

2. Voluntariness

¶ 25 We next examine the voluntariness component. As the Gilloglys note in their briefing, there is no evidence that they compelled Wirtz to assist them with the work. The Gilloglys did not offer to pay or otherwise to compensate Wirtz for his assistance; nor did they pressure him to participate. Wirtz could have simply refused to help at any step in the process if he felt uncomfortable with the work; but he voiced no concerns about the project nor refused to participate.

¶ 26 If Wirtz had felt uncomfortable with the tree-felling process or concerned for his safety, he could have refused to assist in that activity and limited his involvement to stacking wood. After the tree split, David specifically advised Wirtz that he could stop the process if he felt uncomfortable continuing. But in spite of his own observations and David's warnings, Wirtz chose to continue participating in the tree-felling process—without wearing a hardhat. Consequently, as in *Erie,* because Wirtz had reasonable alternative courses of action available to him but elected to continue felling the tree, no reasonable juror could conclude that his acts were involuntary.

¶ 27 Wirtz emphasizes that he and the Gilloglys proceeded with the felling process even after the trunk had split; but there is no evidence that the split in the tree trunk materially altered the risk that Wirtz had already assumed. Wirtz knew that he was participating in tree-felling, had observed the others doing it, had volunteered to do it, and persisted even after the tree split and David again offered him an opportunity to opt out. Therefore, reasonable minds could not differ that Wirtz assumed the risk of participating in the tree-felling activity, thus relieving the Gilloglys of liability for his injury. Reviewing the trial court's ruling **de novo** and viewing the record in the light most favorable to Wirtz, we affirm the trial court's summary judgment dismissal of his complaint.

. . . .

¶ 29 We affirm.

————————

Points for Discussion

1. The parties agreed, and the court concluded, that the theory at issue in the case before it was the plaintiff's implied assumption of risk. What were the elements of that form of assumption of risk, and what burden did the defendant bear in establishing that Wirtz assumed the risk of injury?

2. Did Wirtz appreciate the risk involved in participating in the tree-felling project? Did he voluntarily assume that risk? If you were Wirtz's attorney, would you have pursued this lawsuit?

3. Distinguish (a) assumption of the risk and (b) contributory negligence.

————————

Turner v. Mandalay Sports Entertainment, LLC

180 P.3d 1172 (Nev. 2008)

BEFORE THE COURT EN BANC.

OPINION

By the Court, PARRAGUIRRE, J.:

In this appeal, we address whether baseball stadium owners and operators have a duty to protect spectators against injuries caused by foul balls that are errantly projected into the stands. We conclude that stadium owners and operators have a limited duty to protect against such injuries and that respondent satisfied its duty as a matter of law under the facts presented in this case. Accordingly, we affirm the district court's judgment in respondent's favor.

FACTUAL AND PROCEDURAL BACKGROUND

At all times relevant to this appeal, respondent Mandalay Sports Entertainment, LLC, owned and operated the Las Vegas 51s, a minor league baseball team that plays its home games at Cashman Field in Clark County. From 2000 to 2002, appellants Kathleen and Michael Turner owned season tickets for home games played by the 51s.

Like most professional baseball teams, the 51s include a **disclaimer** on their tickets informing fans that the team is not responsible for injuries caused by foul balls.[1] In addition, the public address announcer at Cashman Field warns the crowd about the danger of foul balls hit into the stands before each 51s home game. The 51s also post warning signs at every Cashman Field entry gate, cautioning fans to stay alert because of the risks posed by foul balls. The Turners acknowledge that they were aware of these warnings.

On May 4, 2002, while attending a 51s game at Cashman Field, Mr. and Mrs. Turner left their assigned seats and walked to the "Beer Garden," a concessions area located in the upper concourse level above the stands. The Beer Garden-which is several hundred feet from the playing field-contains tables and chairs where patrons can eat and drink but also has a railing where patrons can stand and continue to watch the game. Unlike other concession areas at Cashman Field, the Beer Garden has no protective screen surrounding it.

While at the Beer Garden, Mr. Turner purchased a beverage for himself and a sandwich for his wife. Mr. Turner then stood at the railing so that he could continue to watch the game. Mrs. Turner, on the other hand, took her sandwich and sat at one of the available tables. According to Mrs. Turner, she was unable to see any part of the field from her table.

As Mrs. Turner sat in the Beer Garden, a foul ball struck her in the face. The force of the ball's impact rendered her unconscious, broke her nose, and lacerated her face. According to Mrs. Turner, she never saw the ball coming and had no opportunity to get out of the way.

---

1 Specifically, this notice provides that the "Holder assumes all danger incidental to the game whether occurring before, during or after the game, including the dangers of being injured by thrown bats or thrown or batted balls, and agrees that the TEAMS, their agents, and players are not liable for resulting injuries."

The Turners subsequently filed a complaint in district court against the Las Vegas 51s, alleging three causes of action: negligence, **loss of consortium**, and **negligent infliction of emotional distress** (NIED). While the negligence action pertained to Mrs. Turner's alleged injuries, the loss of consortium and NIED claims pertained to Mr. Turner's alleged injuries.

In response to the Turners' complaint, the 51s filed a motion for summary judgment, which the Turners opposed. After considering the parties' arguments, the district court granted the 51s' motion, concluding that the team "did not breach any duty of care to Plaintiffs to protect them from harm [and] ... even if there were any such duty, the [foul] ball [was] a known and obvious risk." This appeal followed.

DISCUSSION

. . . .

Mrs. Turner's negligence claim

The district court concluded that Mrs. Turner's negligence claim failed because the Las Vegas 51s did not owe a duty to protect her from the foul ball in question. For the following reasons, we agree with the district court's conclusion.

A claim for negligence in Nevada requires that the plaintiff satisfy four elements: (1) an existing duty of care, (2) breach, (3) legal causation, and (4) damages. At issue in this case is whether the 51s owed a duty to protect Mrs. Turner from foul balls hit into the area where she was sitting. Although we have previously recognized that "a proprietor owes a general duty to use reasonable care to keep the premises in a reasonably safe condition for use," we have never specifically defined the scope of that duty as it pertains to baseball stadium owners and operators.

. . . .

Here, the record establishes that foul balls occasionally fly into the Beer Garden, some parts of which have an obstructed view of the field. The risk of an occasional foul ball, however, does not amount to "an unduly high risk of injury." Indeed, Mrs. Turner has conspicuously failed to demonstrate that any other spectator suffered injuries as a result of errant balls landing in the Beer Garden. Thus, we conclude that she failed to establish a genuine issue of material fact as to the 51s' negligence, and the 51s were entitled to judgment as a matter of law.

Clarification of Mizushima v. Sunset Ranch and the implied assumption of risk doctrine

Separately, . . . we take this opportunity to clarify certain strained language from this court's decision in *Mizushima v. Sunset Ranch.*[19] In *Mizushima,* the court addressed the viability of the assumption of risk doctrine as a defense to negligence actions in Nevada. According to the court, although express assumption of risk remained a viable defense (in part because it stemmed from a contractual undertaking expressly relieving the potential defendant from liability), the implied assumption of risk doctrine failed to survive the enactment of Nevada's comparative negligence statute. Because this conclusion was based on an incorrect understanding of primary implied assumption of risk, however, we now readdress the issue.

The implied assumption of risk doctrine generally is divided into two subcategories: "primary" and "secondary." Of these subcategories, only "primary" implied assumption of risk is at issue here. As commonly understood, this form of assumption of risk arises when "the plaintiff impliedly assumes those risks that are *inherent* in a particular activity."

In *Mizushima,* this court described the doctrine of primary implied assumption of risk as "a relationship voluntarily accepted with an imputed understanding that the other party has *no duty* to the injured plaintiff." After making this statement, however, the court mischaracterized duty as a factor "left to the jury ... in the comparative negligence analysis."

We have clearly and consistently stated-since at least 2001-that whether a duty exists is actually a question of law to be determined solely by the courts. Several other courts that have recognized duty as a legal question also have recognized that the primary implied assumption of risk doctrine merely "goes to the initial determination of whether the defendant's legal duty encompasses the risk encountered by the plaintiff." These courts treat the doctrine as a part of the initial duty analysis, rather than as an affirmative defense to be decided by a jury. In our opinion, this is a better application of the doctrine, and one that makes it compatible with our comparative negligence statute. Accordingly, we overrule *Mizushima* to the extent that it held that the primary implied assumption of risk doctrine was abolished by our comparative negligence statute. Whether that doctrine bars a plaintiff's claim should be incorporated into the district court's initial duty analysis, and therefore it should not be treated as an affirmative defense to be decided by a jury.

. . . .

————————————

19 103 Nev. 259, 737 P.2d 1158 (1987).

Points for Discussion

1.   Proposition: The court erroneously affirmed the district court's judgment in favor of the baseball team. Agree or disagree.

2.   Are there and should there be limits on or exceptions to disclaimers on tickets informing fans that a sports team is not responsible for dangers incidental to the game?

3.   Why did the court overrule its prior decision in *Mizushima v. Sunset Ranch*?

———————————

Hypo 6-3

Golfer 1 was on her favorite golf course playing in a foursome. Golfer 2 was playing in another foursome immediately behind Golfer 1's group. Having teed off from the fifth tee, Golfer 2 was waiting in the fairway for Golfer 1's group to clear the fifth hole before continuing to play. Golfer 2 was 175 yards away from the hole when he hit his approach shot to the fifth hole green. His shot hit the right side of the fairway, bounced into the rough and again on the dirt area. It then bounced onto the cart path and headed toward a golf cart in which Golfer 1 was seated. The ball struck Golfer 1 in the left eye as her golf cart emerged from behind a restroom building. As a result of the incident, Golfer 1 was rushed to the hospital for emergency medical treatment and has allegedly sustained serious injuries to her left eye, including the permanent loss of peripheral vision, permanent pupil dilation, and blurred vision.

Golfer 1 contends that she heard no warning before she was hit by the golf ball, and Golfer 2 admits that he never yelled "fore" or gave any other warning to Golfer 1 or anyone else before or after hitting the errant shot.

Golfer 1 has brought a negligence action against Golfer 2 for his failure to yell "fore" and give warning of the errant shot and against the owner of the golf course for negligently failing to place warning signs or safety netting to minimize the risks that golfers would be hit by golf balls. Both defendants contend that Golfer 1's implied assumption of risk bars her negligence claims. Discuss.

D. Statutes of Limitations

Genrich v. OHIC Insurance Company

318 Wis.2d 553, 769 N.W.2d 481 (2009)

PATIENCE DRAKE ROGGENSACK, J.

¶ 1 We review an unpublished decision of the court of appeals that affirmed a decision of the circuit court granting summary judgment in favor of OHIC Insurance Company and other defendants (collectively, OHIC). Our review requires us to address . . . whether the claim of the Estate of Robert V. Genrich (the estate) for "injury" to Robert Genrich (Robert) that resulted in his death and allegedly was caused by medical negligence is precluded by Wis. Stat. § 893.55(1m)(a) (2005-06) as untimely-filed . . . .

¶ 2 Because we conclude that Robert suffered an "injury" for purposes of Wis. Stat. § 893.55(1m)(a) when he experienced a "physical injurious change," and that the "physical injurious change" occurred more than three years prior to the filing of the estate's claim, we conclude that the estate's claim is time-barred by § 893.55(1m)(a). . . . Accordingly, we affirm the decision of the court of appeals that affirmed the circuit court's decision granting summary judgment in favor of OHIC.

I. BACKGROUND

¶ 3 On July 23-24, 2003, Robert underwent surgery to have an ulcer repaired. The surgery appeared to have been successfully completed. However, Robert soon developed a fever and his white blood cell count became elevated, suggesting an infection. On August 8, 2003, it was determined that a sponge had been left inside Robert's abdominal cavity at the conclusion of the surgery on July 24, 2003, and that the sponge probably was the source of the infection. That same day, a second surgery was performed and the sponge was removed. Unfortunately, in the days following the second surgery, Robert's health did not improve, and on August 11, 2003, he died from sepsis allegedly associated with the retained sponge.

¶ 4 On August 9, 2006, the estate and Kathy filed suit against the doctors and support staff involved in Robert's surgery, as well as OHIC Insurance Company and others. The estate alleged medical negligence in Robert's care and treatment, and made claims for damages. . . . OHIC moved for summary judgment, arguing that . . . the estate's . . . [claim was] barred by the medical negligence **statute of limitations**, Wis. Stat. § 893.55(1m)(a). Section 893.55(1m) provides:

[A]n action to recover damages for injury arising from any treatment or operation performed by, or from any omission by, a person who is a health care provider, regardless of the theory on which the action is based, shall be commenced within the later of:

(a) Three years from the date of the injury, or

(b) One year from the date the injury was discovered or, in the exercise of reasonable diligence should have been discovered, except that an action may not be commenced under this paragraph more than 5 years from the date of the act or omission.

. . . .

¶ 6 The circuit court granted OHIC's motion, concluding that, under *Fojut v. Stafl,* 212 Wis.2d 827, 569 N.W.2d 737 (Ct.App.1997), Robert suffered an "injury" triggering the statute of limitations no later than August 8, 2003, when the second surgery to remove the sponge occurred. As a result, the circuit court dismissed the estate's claim, filed on August 9, 2006, as untimely under Wis. Stat. § 893.55(1m)(a).

. . . .

¶ 9 We granted review and now affirm.

II. DISCUSSION

. . . .

B. Medical Negligence

¶ 11 The estate's **survival action** is a claim for medical negligence asserted on Robert's behalf. The parties do not dispute, and we agree, that Wis. Stat. § 893.55(1m)(a) is the applicable statute of limitations for this claim, and that the claim **accrued** on the date that Robert sustained an "injury" as that term is used in the statute. Where the parties differ is with respect to the meaning of the term "injury."

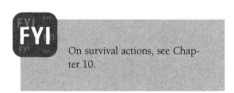

On survival actions, see Chapter 10.

¶ 12 The statute does not define "injury." . . .

....

¶ 15 OHIC contends that Robert suffered an injury on July 24, 2003, when the sponge was left in his abdominal cavity and he developed an infection. This was a "physical injurious change" to Robert's body . . . . In the alternative, OHIC asserts that any "physical injurious change" could have occurred no later than August 8, 2003, when Robert underwent the second surgery to remove the sponge. As a result, because the claims were filed on August 9, 2006, and more than three years had passed, the estate's and Kathy's claims are time-barred by Wis. Stat. § 893.55(1m)(a).

. . . .

¶ 18 . . . [W]e conclude that Robert's "injury" that triggered the three-year limitations period in Wis. Stat. § 893.55(1m)(a) occurred on July 24, 2003. It was on that date that an infection-producing sponge was left in Robert's abdomen, which eventually caused his death. The second surgery performed on August 8, 2003, while it may have inflicted an additional injury on Robert because he was subjected to more surgery, mainly confirmed Robert's injury from the first surgery.

¶ 19 It was the negligence during the first surgery that resulted in an infection-producing sponge being present in Robert's abdomen. Stated otherwise, by leaving the sponge inside of Robert, the doctors "cause[d] a greater harm than existed at the time of the [negligent act]." [C] Robert suffered an injury when the doctors left an infection-producing sponge in his abdominal cavity, and the sponge was not there prior to the doctors' negligent conduct.

¶ 20 Accordingly, the presence of an infection-producing sponge in Robert's abdominal cavity is [a] "physical injurious change" . . . When the doctors negligently left a sponge inside of Robert, which caused the sepsis that resulted in his death, he sustained an "injury" that triggered Wis. Stat. § 893.55(1m)(a)'s three-year limitations period. Because this injury occurred more than three years prior to August 9, 2006, when the claim was filed, we conclude that the estate's claim is time-barred by § 893.55(1m)(a).

¶ 21 Furthermore, accepting the estate's and Kathy's definition of "injury" would contradict the maxim that " '[a] later injury from the same tortious act does not restart the running of the statute' of limitations." [C] That is, even though an infection-producing sponge was present inside of Robert's abdomen as a result of the first surgery, the estate and Kathy urge us to restart the statute of limitations by concluding that Robert sustained an injury only when his condition became irreversible. We decline to do so.

¶ 22 Were we to conclude as the estate and Kathy suggest, it would logically follow that Robert could not have filed a medical negligence action once the infection-producing sponge was present inside of his abdomen, even if that injury led only to a protracted recovery course, rather than to death. However, many claims of medical negligence are not grounded in untreatable injuries. . . . Because all injuries that result from medical negligence do not lead to death or to an irreversible medical course, it is not reasonable to interpret the word "injury" as the estate and Kathy suggest. As we also have explained, "once a claimant has sustained an injury and has an enforceable claim, that claimant cannot sit on that claim until all consequential damages have come to fruition." [C]. Accordingly, we conclude that the estate's claim for medical negligence accrued more than three years before the estate filed suit. Therefore, it is untimely under Wis. Stat. § 893.55(1m)(a).

. . . .

III. CONCLUSION

¶ 49 Because we conclude that Robert suffered an "injury" for purposes of Wis. Stat. § 893.55(1m)(a) when he experienced a "physical injurious change," and that the "physical injurious change" occurred more than three years prior to the filing of the estate's claim, we conclude that the estate's claim is time-barred by § 893.55(1m)(a). . . . Accordingly, we affirm the decision of the court of appeals that affirmed the circuit court's decision granting summary judgment in favor of OHIC.

The decision of the court of appeals is affirmed.

————————————

Points for Discussion

1. Under the applicable Wisconsin statute of limitations, the plaintiff was required to file suit before the expiration of what time period?

2. On what date did the plaintiff's injury accrue? Do you agree with the court's treatment of the limitations issue?

3. As illustrated in *Genrich*, the failure to file a lawsuit within the applicable statute of limitations serves as a complete bar to the plaintiff's action and will result in the dismissal of untimely filed suits with no consideration or adjudication of the merits. Lawyers must always be conscious of and must research and discern the governing statute of limitations; failure to do so can extinguish a client's case and subject the lawyer to a malpractice claim. In addition, the running of the statute of limitations can be **tolled** (*i.e.*, the statute does not run for a period of time) in certain circumstances, for example, where a defendant has fraudulently concealed its injury-causing

negligence from a plaintiff, or for a period of time before a minor reaches the age of majority.

4. "A cause of action for a tort may be barred through lapse of time because of the provisions of a statute of limitations." RESTATEMENT (SECOND) OF TORTS § 899 (1965). The Restatement provides that a "cause of action for negligently harming a person or a thing is complete when the harm occurs," § 899 comment *c*. Thus, under an **accrual rule** the limitations period begins to run when a plaintiff is harmed by the defendant's negligence. The Restatement also notes a different approach in court decisions "holding that the statute must be construed as not intended to start to run until the plaintiff has in fact discovered the fact that he has suffered injury or by the exercise of reasonable diligence should have discovered it." § 899 comment *e*. Unlike an accrual rule, a **discovery rule** does not start the running of the statute of limitations clock until (1) the plaintiff knows, has reason to know, or should have known of the injury, and (2) that the injury was caused by a specific defendant's conduct or product.

E. Statutes of Repose

Orlak v. Loyola University Health System

228 Ill.2d 1, 885 N.E.2d 999, 319 Ill. Dec. 319 (2007)

OPINION

Justice GARMAN delivered the judgment of the court, with opinion:

In July 2002, plaintiff, Diane Orlak, sued defendant Loyola University Health System (Loyola) in the circuit court of Cook County, alleging that Loyola was liable to her for an alleged failure to notify her in a timely manner that she may have contracted hepatitis C (HCV) from a blood transfusion that she received in 1989 during hospitalization for injuries sustained in an accident. The circuit court granted Loyola's motion to dismiss, finding that plaintiff's action was barred by the **statute of repose** contained in section 13-212(a) of the Code of Civil Procedure (Code) (735 ILCS 5/13-212(a) (West 2002)). The appellate court affirmed (No. 1-04-0401 (unpublished order under Supreme Court Rule 23)) and we granted plaintiff's petition for leave to appeal (210 Ill.2d R. 315).

BACKGROUND

Plaintiff was hospitalized at Foster G. McGaw Hospital in Maywood, Illinois, in April and May 1989, for burns suffered during a work-related accident. During the course of her hospitalization, plaintiff was given a blood transfusion. Because plaintiff was unconscious at the time, her mother signed a consent form for the transfusion. That form stated in part, " In making such request and in giving such consent, I hereby acknowledge that I have been informed that there is no known definitive test for the determination of the existence or non-existence of viral hepatitis in blood and that I fully understand that the transfusion or administration of blood or blood components to me may result in viral hepatitis or other untoward reactions." Sometime in 1990, Loyola advised plaintiff to be tested for the presence of the human immunodeficiency virus (HIV). Plaintiff underwent testing and tested negative for the presence of the virus. In August 2000, Loyola notified plaintiff by letter that she should be tested for HCV because her blood donor had recently tested positive for the virus. After being tested, plaintiff learned that the test was positive for HCV.

In her third amended complaint, plaintiff alleged that following Loyola's advice to her in 1990 to be tested for HIV, she reasonably believed that, after testing negative for that virus, the blood she had received was safe and free from deadly disease. She also took issue with Loyola's statement in its August 2000 letter that at the time she received her blood transfusion, no reliable tests for HCV were available. She alleged that in 1996, the Food and Drug Administration (FDA) issued a memorandum to hospitals advising them to notify patients who received blood transfusions prior to 1992 to be tested for the presence of HCV. Plaintiff also alleged that in 1997 the National Institutes of Health (NIH) published a "Consensus Development Conference Statement," which found that HCV progresses at a slow rate with no symptoms in the majority of patients during the first 20 years after infection. The NIH also found that HCV patients who consume alcoholic beverages are at greater risk of rapidly developing cirrhosis of the liver and end-stage liver disease. The NIH recommended that individuals who had received blood transfusions prior to 1990 should be tested for HCV. According to plaintiff, the NIH report was posted on the Internet in April 1997 and was published in the Journal of Hepatology in September 1997.

FYI

The federal Food and Drug Administration is a division of the Department of Health and Human Services' ("HHS") Public Health Service and administers and enforces the Food, Drug, and Cosmetic Act of 1938, 29 USC § 301 et seq. The National Institutes of Health, also part of the HHS, is the principal federal agency for conducting and supporting medical research.

Plaintiff's complaint contained counts alleging **constructive fraud**, medical negligence, medical battery, and ordinary negligence. In count I, for constructive fraud, plaintiff alleged that Loyola's failure to inform her of the need to be tested for HCV at the time it advised her to be tested for HIV lulled her into a false sense of security that the blood she had received was free of disease. She alleged that her reliance in that regard was justifiable and reasonable. In count IV, for ordinary negligence, plaintiff alleged that in 1996 and 1997 Loyola knew or should have known of the need for plaintiff to be tested for HCV and that, beginning in 1996, or at the latest in March 1997, Loyola owed plaintiff a duty of reasonable care to notify her that she had potentially contracted HCV through her blood transfusion and that she needed to be tested. Plaintiff also alleged that for every day thereafter that the duty existed, Loyola continued to breach its duty of care by failing to notify plaintiff of the potential for infection and the need to be tested.

Loyola filed a motion to dismiss all counts (735 ILCS 5/2-619(a)(5) (West 2002)) on the ground that plaintiff's action was time-barred. Loyola argued that plaintiff's cause of action arose out of patient care stemming from her 1989 hospitalization and blood transfusion. Thus, the medical malpractice statute of repose (735 ILCS 5/13-212(a) (West 2002)) was applicable. Loyola argued that this applied as well to plaintiff's claims for constructive fraud and ordinary negligence. The circuit court agreed and dismissed plaintiff's complaint with prejudice.

The appellate court affirmed. With respect to plaintiff's ordinary negligence claim, the court rejected her argument that because she was no longer a patient and she challenged only the failure to timely give notice of the need for testing, her cause of action did not arise out of patient care. The appellate court also rejected plaintiff's constructive fraud and **equitable estoppel** claims. No. 1-04-0401 (unpublished order under Supreme Court Rule 23).

ANALYSIS

. . . .

Plaintiff argues that the circuit and appellate courts erred in holding that the four-year medical malpractice statute of repose applies to bar her claim for ordinary negligence. That statute provides in part:

> "Except as provided in Section 13-215 of this Act, no action for damages for injury or death against any physician, dentist, registered nurse or hospital duly licensed under the laws of this State, whether based upon tort, or breach of contract, or otherwise, *arising out of patient care* shall be brought more than 2 years after the date on which the claimant knew, or through the use of reasonable diligence should have known,

or received notice in writing of the existence of the injury or death for which damages are sought in the action, whichever of such date occurs first, but in no event shall such action be brought more than 4 years after the date on which occurred the act or omission or occurrence alleged in such action to have been the cause of such injury or death." (Emphasis added.) 735 ILCS 5/13-212(a) (West 2002).

This statute contains both a two-year period of limitations and a four-year period of repose. The two-year limitations period is triggered by the plaintiff's discovery of the injury; in contrast, the four-year repose period is triggered by the occurrence of the act or omission that caused the injury. The only exception to the four-year statute of repose is the fraudulent-concealment exception contained in section 13-215 of the Code (735 ILCS 5/13-215 (West 2002)). The statute of repose sometimes bars actions even before the plaintiff has discovered the injury. While this may result in harsh consequences, the legislature enacted the statute of repose for the specific purpose of curtailing the "long tail" exposure to medical malpractice claims brought about by the advent of the discovery rule. *Anderson v. Wagner,* 79 Ill.2d 295, 312, 37 Ill.Dec. 558, 402 N.E.2d 560 (1979).

Only claims "arising out of patient care" are affected by the medical malpractice statute of repose. Our analysis of this issue is governed by familiar principles of statutory construction. The cardinal rule of statutory construction is to ascertain and give effect to the intent of the legislature. *Murray v. Chicago Youth Center,* 224 Ill.2d 213, 235, 309 Ill.Dec. 310, 864 N.E.2d 176 (2007). That intent is best gleaned from the words of the statute itself, and where the statutory language is clear and unambiguous, it must be given effect. *General Motors Corp. v. State of Illinois Motor Vehicle Review Board,* 224 Ill.2d 1, 13, 308 Ill.Dec. 611, 862 N.E.2d 209 (2007). A court should interpret a statute, where possible, according to the plain and ordinary meaning of the language used. *Paris v. Feder,* 179 Ill.2d 173, 177, 227 Ill.Dec. 800, 688 N.E.2d 137 (1997). In determining the plain meaning of a statute's terms, we consider the statute in its entirety, keeping in mind the subject it addresses, and the apparent intent of the legislature in enacting the statute. *People v. Perry,* 224 Ill.2d 312, 323, 309 Ill.Dec. 330, 864 N.E.2d 196 (2007). Issues of statutory construction are reviewed *de novo. Paris,* 179 Ill.2d at 177-78, 227 Ill.Dec. 800, 688 N.E.2d 137.

Make the Connection

Judicial interpretation and construction of statutes is examined in legislation and statutory interpretation courses.

Plaintiff argues that the question in this case is whether the injury she has alleged arose from patient care or from an administrative decision by Loyola not to send notice of the need to be tested for HCV. She argues that, under the appellate court's construction of the statute, once a person becomes a patient of a medical provider, virtually any subsequent interaction between the patient and the provider is governed by the statute of repose. According to plaintiff, such a construction would impermissibly expand the scope of the statute beyond its plain language. She points out that her "patient care" ended in 1989 and that she has not alleged any wrongdoing by Loyola during the time she was hospitalized. Plaintiff believes that by using the phrase "arising out of patient care," the legislature intended the statute of repose to govern claims based on events that involve actual patient care.

Loyola, on the other hand, argues that plaintiff's interpretation of the phrase "arising out of patient care" is much too narrow. That plaintiff's hospitalization ended long ago is not determinative; it is the nature of the conduct, not the timing thereof, that determines whether a claim arises out of patient care. Loyola argues that accepting plaintiff's interpretation would eviscerate the statute of repose because plaintiffs could avoid the statute by casting their claims as based on a failure to provide follow-up care at a later date. According to Loyola, plaintiff's contention that Loyola breached only an administrative duty by its failure to notify her in 1996 and 1997 would impose a duty with no temporal bounds on Loyola and other health-care providers.

Plaintiff cites several Illinois and foreign cases in support of her argument. *Cammon v. West Suburban Hospital Medical Center,* 301 Ill.App.3d 939, 235 Ill. Dec. 158, 704 N.E.2d 731 (1998), dealt, in relevant part, with a claim against the defendant hospital for spoliation of evidence. One ground upon which the circuit court dismissed the claim was that the action was filed outside the statute of repose. The appellate court disagreed, noting that a negligence action for spoliation of evidence is predicated on a breach of the duty to preserve evidence. It does not involve patient care. Thus, the claim was not governed by the medical malpractice statute of repose. *Cammon,* 301 Ill.App.3d at 950, 235 Ill.Dec. 158, 704 N.E.2d 731. Contrary to plaintiff's argument, *Cammon* is not applicable to this case. The duty there had nothing whatever to do with patient care. It dealt with a duty imposed on a party to the litigation to preserve evidence relevant to the case. *Cammon* stands only for the unremarkable proposition that not all negligence actions against physicians or hospitals involve patient care.

Plaintiff also cites a Tennessee case, *Estate of Doe v. Vanderbilt University, Inc.,* 958 S.W.2d 117 (Tenn.App.1997). There, the plaintiff's decedent received a blood transfusion in 1984 in connection with surgery. The donor blood was not tested for the presence of HIV. The decedent was not informed that she had received the transfusion, nor was she advised that she was at risk of having been infected with HIV. She later married and became pregnant. It was only when she gave birth to a daughter who had become infected with the virus *in utero* that the decedent learned of her condition. The infant died of acquired immune deficiency syndrome (AIDS) shortly after her birth and the decedent died of AIDS subsequent to the initiation of a lawsuit against Vanderbilt based on Vanderbilt's failure to notify the decedent in 1987 and 1988 that the blood she received in the transfusion had not been tested for HIV. Vanderbilt admitted that it did not search its records to provide notice to transfusion recipients. The circuit court found that the case was governed by the Tennessee medical malpractice statute and that absent expert testimony that Vanderbilt had deviated from the recognized standard of care for hospitals in the area, no genuine issue of material fact existed and that summary judgment was appropriate. The court of appeals phrased the issue as whether Vanderbilt's failure to notify decedent and other patients was a medical decision subject to the medical malpractice statute. The court determined that it was not. Extensive evidence had been taken in the circuit court in connection with Vanderbilt's summary judgment motion. That evidence convinced the court of appeals that the decision not to notify was not a medical one. *Doe,* 958 S.W.2d at 121.

Doe is inapplicable to the instant case. We are not concerned with whether Loyola's failure to notify in 1996 and 1997 involved the exercise of medical judgment or some other type of judgment. The only inquiry is whether plaintiff's cause of action arose from patient care. This is a completely different standard from the one involved in *Doe.*

Plaintiff also cites a Georgia case, *Canas v. Al-Jabi,* 282 Ga.App. 764, 639 S.E.2d 494 (2006). The plaintiff in that case had received blood transfusions in 1985 while a pediatric patient at a hospital. The blood was not tested for the presence of HIV. The plaintiff developed AIDS, which was not diagnosed until he was a teenager. The hospital considered implementing a notification program, but decided not to do so based on concerns about the expense, logistical complexity, and legal implications of such a program. The relevant inquiry as framed by the Georgia court of appeals was whether the case involved a "medical question," which the court defined as requiring highly specialized expert knowledge with respect to which a layperson can have no knowledge at all. The court contrasted acts involving such medical questions with administrative, clerical, or routine acts demanding no special expertise. Those acts, the court stated, fall into the realm of ordinary negligence. *Canas,* 282 Ga.App. at 787-88, 639 S.E.2d at 517. The court noted that the record showed the decision not to notify the plaintiff and others like him of the risk of HIV infection was not based on medical expertise but, rather, was based on administrative concerns. Thus, the court concluded that the plaintiff's claim was based on ordinary negligence and was not subject to the medical malpractice statutes of limitation and repose. *Canas,* 282 Ga.App. at 790, 639 S.E.2d at 518.

As with *Doe,* the *Canas* case does not support plaintiff's argument. The statute of repose in *Canas* stated that an "action for medical malpractice" may not be brought more than five years after the date on which the negligent act or omission occurred. *Canas,* 282 Ga.App. at 770, 639 S.E.2d at 505-06. In contrast, the Illinois statute of repose encompasses any action for damages arising out of patient care, regardless of whether it arises from a tort, a contract, or from some other source. Indeed, this court has held that the reach of the statute is not limited to actions at law. In *Hayes v. Mercy Hospital & Medical Center,* 136 Ill.2d 450, 458, 145 Ill.Dec. 894, 557 N.E.2d 873 (1990), we held that the legislature intended the phrase "or otherwise" in the statute of repose to be all-inclusive and we concluded that the phrase includes actions for contribution against a physician for injuries arising out of patient care.

. . . .

It is clear that the legislature intended the statute of repose to operate in a very broad manner and it has been interpreted in that manner by courts addressing the issue. The question is not whether the plaintiff has alleged medical negligence or ordinary negligence. Rather, the sole issue is whether the plaintiff's claim arose from patient care. The word "**arise**" is defined in Black's Law Dictionary as "[t]o originate; to stem (from)," or "to result (from)." Black's Law Dictionary 115 (8th ed. 2004). "Arise" is also defined elsewhere as "to originate from a source." Merriam-Webster's Collegiate Dictionary 66 (11th ed. 2006).

. . . .

The question remains whether plaintiff here has alleged an injury arising out of patient care. In addressing this question, plaintiff focuses on Loyola's failure to notify her and argues that this omission did not involve the provision of medical care. However, the omission itself cannot be viewed in a vacuum. Plaintiff's allegations of a duty to notify her and Loyola's alleged violation of that duty flows from the blood transfusion she received during her 1989 hospitalization. This case is unlike the situation in *Cammon* (claim against hospital for spoliation of evidence was unrelated to any patient care). It is apparent here that there is a causal connection between plaintiff's 1989 hospitalization and blood transfusion and her current claim against Loyola. Accordingly, her claim arises out of patient care.

Our decision is in keeping with the purpose behind the statute of repose. Were we to endorse plaintiff's position, we would be opening the door to potentially open-ended liability for health-care providers anytime new medical tests were developed that might suggest the need for a notification program for present and former patients. This obligation might even include patients with whom a hospital may have had no contact for many years. Such a result would undermine the purpose behind the enactment of the medical malpractice statute of repose. That statute was part of the legislative response to a medical malpractice insurance crisis;

the purpose was to reduce the cost of medical malpractice insurance and to assure its continued availability to medical practitioners. [C] The crisis was thought to stem from the advent of the "discovery rule" in the late 1960s, in which a cause of action accrued only when a person learned of an injury or reasonably should have learned of it. Because the application of the discovery rule in malpractice actions created a "long tail" of liability, the ability of malpractice insurance companies to predict future liabilities was reduced. [C] It was in response to this problem that the General Assembly enacted the statute of repose. Allowing plaintiff's action to go forward would be contrary to that purpose. Therefore, we conclude that plaintiff's claim arises out of patient care and is thus subject to the four-year statute of repose contained in section 13-212(a). Since plaintiff brought this action some 13 years after her claim arose, the trial court properly dismissed her lawsuit.

Plaintiff argues that, even if her claims against Loyola are barred by the statute of repose contained in section 13-212, Loyola fraudulently concealed the grounds for her cause of action. In the alternative, plaintiff also argues that Loyola should be equitably estopped from asserting the statute of repose as a defense to her action.

Section 13-212 explicitly recognizes that **fraudulent concealment** tolls the running of the statute of limitations/repose. Section 13-215 of the Code (735 ILCS 5/13-215 (West 2002)) provides that when a cause of action is fraudulently concealed, the plaintiff may bring an action within five years of the discovery of the cause of action.

In count I of her third amended complaint, plaintiff alleged a cause of action for constructive fraud. She alleged that because Loyola advised her to be tested for HIV, but did not advise her prior to 2000 to be tested for HCV, she was falsely led to believe that, following her negative test for HIV, the blood she had received in the transfusion was free of all life-threatening viruses. She alleged that her reliance was reasonable, given that she was not a medical professional and that Loyola advised her to be tested for one risk known to the medical community, but not another risk.

The concealment contemplated by section 13-215 must consist of affirmative acts or representations calculated to lull or induce a claimant into delaying filing of his or her claim, or to prevent a claimant from discovering a claim. Mere silence on the part of the defendant is insufficient. *Smith v. Cook County Hospital,* 164 Ill. App.3d 857, 862, 115 Ill.Dec. 811, 518 N.E.2d 336 (1987). A plaintiff must plead and prove that the defendant made misrepresentations or performed acts which were known to be false, with the intent to deceive the plaintiff, and upon which the plaintiff detrimentally relied. *Foster v. Plaut,* 252 Ill.App.3d 692, 699, 192 Ill.Dec. 238, 625 N.E.2d 198 (1993).

Plaintiff points to no affirmative acts by Loyola that were calculated to conceal a cause of action. The mere act of notifying plaintiff that she should be tested for HIV cannot be transformed into an affirmative act of concealment of the need for HCV testing. Recognizing the absence of affirmative acts or misrepresentations on Loyola's part, plaintiff argues that the general rule requiring affirmative acts of concealment does not apply where the parties have a fiduciary or confidential relationship. In such situations, plaintiff argues, the mere failure to disclose material information, standing alone, is sufficient to toll the statute of repose.

. . . .

Plaintiff was discharged from Loyola in 1989. Thus, there was no confidential or fiduciary relationship between plaintiff and Loyola in 1996 and 1997, the time plaintiff alleges Loyola should have notified her of the need for HCV testing.

. . . .

Loyola notified plaintiff of the need to be tested for HCV once it had notice that plaintiff was at risk for HCV due to her blood donor's positive HCV test. We reject plaintiff's argument that Loyola's silence in 1996 or 1997, without more, constitutes a fraudulent concealment of a cause of action.

Plaintiff also argues that Loyola should be equitably estopped from relying on the statute of repose because Loyola's notification to plaintiff in 1990 that she should be tested for HIV lulled her into a false sense of security that she was not at risk for any other diseases stemming from her 1989 blood transfusion. This court has set forth the requirements for equitable estoppel as follows:

> "A party claiming estoppel must demonstrate that: (1) the other person misrepresented or concealed material facts; (2) the other person knew at the time he or she made the representations that they were untrue; (3) the party claiming estoppel did not know that the representations were untrue when they were made and when that party decided to act, or not, upon the representations; (4) the other person intended or reasonably expected that the party claiming estoppel would determine whether to act, or not, based upon the representations; (5) the party claiming estoppel reasonably relied upon the representations in good faith to his or her detriment; and (6) the party claiming estoppel would be prejudiced by his or her reliance on the representations if the other person is permitted to deny the truth thereof." *DeLuna v. Burciaga,* 223 Ill.2d 49, 82-83, 306 Ill.Dec. 136, 857 N.E.2d 229 (2006).

It is not necessary that the defendant intentionally mislead or deceive the plaintiff. All that is required is that the plaintiff reasonably relied on the defendant's conduct or representations in delaying suit. *DeLuna,* 223 Ill.2d at 83, 306 Ill.Dec. 136, 857 N.E.2d 229.

In the instant case, plaintiff relies on Loyola's notification to her of the need to be tested for HIV and Loyola's silence with regard to the need for HCV testing in 1996 and 1997 as somehow misleading plaintiff into believing that the blood she received in the transfusion was free from other diseases. . . .

Loyola's conduct does not meet the requirements of equitable estoppel. That plaintiff was notified to be tested for HIV does not suggest that she was entitled to assume the donated blood was safe from all other risks. Plaintiff points out that it was reasonable for her to conclude that if there was a need for further testing, Loyola would notify her of that fact. However, Loyola did notify plaintiff to be tested for HCV when it learned that she was at risk for that virus. We therefore reject plaintiff's fraudulent concealment and equitable estoppel arguments.

CONCLUSION

We hold that plaintiff's claim arises from patient care and that the statute of repose contained in section 13-212(a) of the Code applies to bar her action. We also reject plaintiff's allegations of fraudulent concealment and equitable estoppel. Accordingly, we affirm the judgment of the appellate court.

Appellate court judgment affirmed.

————————————

Points for Discussion

1. The *Orlak* court opines that the issue before it was not whether the plaintiff alleged medical negligence or ordinary negligence; rather, "the sole issue is whether the plaintiff's claim arose from patient care." Why does the court frame the inquiry in this way?

2. What was the legislature's purpose in enacting the medical malpractice statute of repose?

3. According to the *Orlak* court, in what time period must a plaintiff bring a lawsuit when a cause of action is fraudulently concealed?

4. How does the court respond to the plaintiff's equitable estoppel argument?

5. Explain the difference between a statute of limitations and a statute of repose. Consider the following: the "statute of limitations eliminates stale claims, and

the statute of repose provides immunity for claims." O'Neill v. Dunham, 41 Kan.App.2d 540, 203 P.3d 68 (2009). Does this statement accurately define the distinction between the two?

6. Note that statutes of repose are typically longer than statutes of limitations and are usually not subject to tolling. *See, e.g.,* Albrecht v. General Motors Corp., 648 N.W.2d 87 (Iowa 2002). A statute of limitations provides a time by which a plaintiff's cause of action must be *filed*. Statutes of limitations are procedural rules, as contrasted with statutes of repose, which define the time period during which a case must *arise* and are substantive rules rather than procedural.

CHAPTER 7

Advanced Topics in Negligence Actions

This chapter more deeply explores the complex issues that may arise in negligence actions. For example, should negligence law require the existence of a previous relationship between the plaintiff and the defendant upon which to base a cause of action? Must one affirmatively act in order to owe another a duty of care? Should one be able to recover in negligence for a purely economic injury? Should a plaintiff be able to recover in negligence for a mental or emotional injury if no other injury was sustained? What duty of care does one owe to the unborn? These and other topics are considered in the materials that follow.

A. Privity of Contract

Should a defendant owe a duty of care in negligence to a plaintiff injured as the result of the defendant's non-performance of services required by the defendant's contractual relationship with another individual or entity? "In a number of cases, the defendant may undertake a service to A under circumstances that make it foreseeable that B may be injured if the service is not performed." DAN B. DODDS, THE LAW OF TORTS 869 (2000).

In *Winterbottom v. Wright,* 152 Eng. Rep. 402 (1842), the court was presented with the following case: "A. [Wright] contracted with the Postmaster-General to provide a mail-coach to convey the mail bags along a certain line of road; and B. and others also contracted to house the coach along the same line. B and his co-contractors hired C. [Winterbottom] to drive the coach;--Held, that C. could not maintain an action against A. for an injury sustained by him while driving the coach, by its breaking down from latent defects in its construction." Winterbottom was "lamed for life" by his injuries sustained after the collapse of a wheel on the coach he was driving. Having no contractual relationship with Wright or with the Postmaster-General, Winterbottom could not sue Wright.

As explained by the Chief Baron, Lord Abinger, Wright did not have, and therefore did not breach, any duty of care owed to Winterbottom:

Here the action is brought simply because the defendant was a contractor with a third person; and it is contended that thereupon he became liable to every body who might use the carriage. . . .

. . . There is no **privity of contract** between these parties; and if the plaintiff can sue, every passenger, or even any person passing along the road, who was injured by the upsetting of the coach, might bring a similar action. Unless we confine the operation of such contracts as this to the parties who entered into them, the most absurd and outrageous consequences, to which I can see no limit, would ensue. . . . The plaintiff in this case could not have brought an action on the contract; if he could have done so, what would have been the situation, supposing the Postmaster-General had released the defendant? That would, at all events, have defeated his claim altogether. By permitting this action, we should be working this injustice, that after the defendant had done everything to the satisfaction of his employer, and after all matters between them had been adjusted, and all accounts settled on the footing of their contract, we should subject them to be ripped open by this action of tort being brought against him.

Baron Alderson concurred: "If we were to hold that the plaintiff could sue in such a case, there is no point at which such actions would stop. The only safe rule is to confine the right to recover to those who enter into the contract . . ." And Baron Rolfe opined that the "breach of the defendant's duty . . . is his omission to keep the carriage in a safe condition . . . to wit, under and by virtue of his said contract, to keep and maintain the said mail-coach in a fit, proper, safe, and secure state and condition." The duty "shewn to have arisen solely from the contract" was a duty to the Postmaster-General and not to Winterbottom. "This is one of those unfortunate cases in which there certainly has been *damnum*, but it is ***damnum absque injuria*** . . . Hard cases, it has frequently been observed, are apt to introduce bad law."

It's Latin to Me!

Damnum absque injuria is Latin for a loss or damage without injury. One injured by the conduct of another has no remedy in law.

Compare *Winterbottom* with the Court of Appeals of New York's approach to and analysis of the privity issue in the following important case.

MacPherson v. Buick Motor Co.

217 N.Y. 382, 111 N.E. 1050 (1916)

CARDOZO, J.

The defendant is a manufacturer of automobiles. It sold an automobile to a retail dealer. The retail dealer resold to the plaintiff. While the plaintiff was in the car, it suddenly collapsed. He was thrown out and injured. One of the wheels was made of **defective** wood, and its spokes crumbled into fragments. The wheel was not made by the defendant; it was bought from another manufacturer. There is evidence, however, that its defects could have been discovered by reasonable inspection, and that inspection was omitted. There is no claim that the defendant knew of the defect and willfully concealed it. . . . The charge is one, not of **fraud**, but of **negligence**. The question to be determined is whether the defendant owed a duty of care and vigilance to any one but the immediate purchaser.

The foundations of this branch of the law, at least in this state, were laid in *Thomas v. Winchester* (6 N. Y. 397). A poison was falsely labeled. The sale was made to a druggist, who in turn sold to a customer. The customer recovered damages from the seller who affixed the label. 'The defendant's negligence,' it was said, 'put human life in imminent danger.' A poison falsely labeled is likely to injure any one who gets it. Because the danger is to be foreseen, there is a duty to avoid the injury. Cases were cited by way of illustration in which manufacturers were not subject to any duty irrespective of contract. The distinction was said to be that their conduct, though negligent, was not likely to result in injury to any one except the purchaser. We are not required to say whether the chance of injury was always as remote as the distinction assumes. Some of the illustrations might be rejected to-day. The *principle* of the distinction is for present purposes the important thing.

Thomas v. Winchester became quickly a landmark of the law. In the application of its principle there may at times have been uncertainty or even error. There has never in this state been doubt or disavowal of the principle itself. The chief cases are well known, yet to recall some of them will be helpful. *Loop v. Litchfield* (42 N. Y. 351) is the earliest. It was the case of a defect in a small balance wheel used on a circular saw. The manufacturer pointed out the defect to the buyer, who wished a cheap article and was ready to assume the risk. The risk can hardly have been an imminent one, for the wheel lasted five years before it broke. In the meanwhile the buyer had made a lease of the machinery. It was held that the manufacturer was not answerable to the lessee. *Loop v. Litchfield* was followed in *Losee v. Clute* (51 N. Y. 494), the case of the explosion of a steam boiler. That decision has been criticised (Thompson on Negligence, 233; Shearman & Redfield on Negligence [6th ed.], § 117); but it must be confined to its special facts. It was put upon the ground that the risk of injury was too remote. The buyer in that case had not only accepted the boiler, but had tested it. The manufacturer knew that his own test was not the final one. The finality of the test has a bearing on the measure of diligence owing to persons other than the purchaser. [Cc]

These early cases suggest a narrow construction of the rule. Later cases, however, evince a more liberal spirit. First in importance is *Devlin v. Smith* (89 N. Y. 470). The defendant, a contractor, built a scaffold for a painter. The painter's servants were injured. The contractor was held liable. He knew that the scaffold, if improperly constructed, was a most dangerous trap. He knew that it was to be used by the workmen. He was building it for that very purpose. Building it for their use, he owed them a duty, irrespective of his **contract** with their **master**, to build it with care.

From *Devlin v. Smith* we pass over intermediate cases and turn to the latest case in this court in which *Thomas v. Winchester* was followed. That case is *Statler v. Ray Mfg. Co.* (195 N. Y. 478, 480). The defendant manufactured a large coffee urn. It was installed in a restaurant. When heated, the urn exploded and injured the plaintiff. We held that the manufacturer was liable. We said that the urn 'was of such a character inherently that, when applied to the purposes for which it was designed, it was liable to become a source of great danger to many people if not carefully and properly constructed.'

It may be that *Devlin v. Smith* and *Statler v. Ray Mfg. Co.* have extended the rule of *Thomas v. Winchester.* If so, this court is committed to the extension. The defendant argues that things imminently dangerous to life are poisons, explosives, deadly weapons--things whose normal function it is to injure or destroy. But whatever the rule in *Thomas v. Winchester* may once have been, it has no longer that restricted meaning. A scaffold (*Devlin v. Smith, supra*) is not inherently a destructive instrument. It becomes destructive only if imperfectly constructed. A large coffee urn (*Statler v. Ray Mfg. Co., supra*) may have within itself, if negligently made, the potency of danger, yet no one thinks of it as an implement whose normal function is destruction. What is true of the coffee urn is equally true of bottles of aerated water (*Torgesen v. Schultz,* 192 N. Y. 156). We have mentioned only cases in this court. But the rule has received a like extension in our courts of intermediate appeal. In *Burke v. Ireland* (26 App. Div. 487), in an opinion by CULLEN, J., it was applied to a builder who constructed a defective building; in *Kahner v. Otis Elevator Co.* (96 App. Div. 169) to the manufacturer of an elevator; in *Davies v. Pelham Hod Elevating Co.* (65 Hun, 573; affirmed in this court without opinion, 146 N. Y. 363) to a contractor who furnished a defective rope with knowledge of the purpose for which the rope was to be used. We are not required at this time either to approve or to disapprove the application of the rule that was made in these cases. It is enough that they help to characterize the trend of judicial thought.

Devlin v. Smith was decided in 1882. A year later a very similar case came before the Court of Appeal in England (*Heaven v. Pender,* L. R. [11 Q. B. D.] 503). We find in the opinion of BRETT, M. R., afterwards Lord ESHER (p. 510), the same conception of a duty, irrespective of contract, imposed upon the manufacturer by the law itself: 'Whenever one person supplies goods, or machinery, or the like, for the purpose of their being used by another person under such circumstances that every one of ordinary sense would, if he thought, recognize at once that unless he used ordinary care and skill with regard to the condition of the thing supplied or the mode of supplying it, there will be danger of injury to the person or property of him for whose use the thing is supplied, and who is to use it, a duty arises to use ordinary care and skill as to the condition or manner of supplying such thing.' He then points out that for a neglect of such ordinary care or skill whereby injury happens, the appropriate remedy is an action for negligence. The right to enforce this liability is not to be confined to the immediate buyer. The right, he says, extends to the persons or class of persons for whose use the thing is supplied. It is enough that the goods 'would in all probability be used at once * * * before a reasonable opportunity for discovering any defect which might exist,' and that the thing supplied is of such a nature 'that a neglect of ordinary care or skill as to its condition or the manner of supplying it would probably cause danger to the person or property of the person for whose use it was supplied, and who was about to use it.' On the other hand, he would exclude a case 'in which the goods are supplied under circumstances in which it would be a chance by whom they would be used or whether they would be used or not, or whether they would be used before there would probably be means of observing any defect,' or where the goods are of such a nature that 'a want of care or skill as to their condition or the manner of supplying them would not probably produce danger of injury to person or property.' What was said by Lord ESHER in that case did not command the full assent of his associates. His opinion has been criticised 'as requiring every man to take affirmative precautions to protect his neighbors as well as to refrain from injuring them' (Bohlen, Affirmative Obligations in the Law of Torts, 44 Am. Law Reg. [N. S.] 341). It may not be an accurate exposition of the law of England. Perhaps it may need some qualification even in our own state. Like most attempts at comprehensive definition, it may involve errors of inclusion and of exclusion. But its tests and standards, at least in their underlying principles, with whatever qualification may be called for as they are applied to varying conditions, are the tests and standards of our law.

We hold, then, that the principle of *Thomas v. Winchester* is not limited to poisons, explosives, and things of like nature, to things which in their normal operation are implements of destruction. If the nature of a thing is such that it is reasonably certain to place life and limb in peril when negligently made, it is then a thing of danger. Its nature gives warning of the consequences to be expected. If to the element of danger there is added knowledge that the thing will be used by persons other than the purchaser, and used without new tests, then, irrespective of contract, the manufacturer of this thing of danger is under a duty to make it carefully. That is as far as we are required to go for the decision of this case. There must be knowledge of a danger, not merely possible, but probable. It is *possible* to use almost anything in a way that will make it dangerous if defective. That is not enough to charge the manufacturer with a duty independent of his contract. Whether a given thing is dangerous may be sometimes a question for the court and sometimes a question for the jury. There must also be knowledge that in the usual course of events the danger will be shared by others than the buyer. Such knowledge may often be inferred from the nature of the transaction. But it is possible that even knowledge of the danger and of the use will not always be enough. The proximity or remoteness of the relation is a factor to be considered. We are dealing now with the liability of the manufacturer of the finished product, who puts it on the market to be used without inspection by his customers. If he is negligent, where danger is to be foreseen, a liability will follow. We are not required at this time to say that it is legitimate to go back of the manufacturer of the finished product and hold the manufacturers of the component parts [liable]. To make their negligence a cause of imminent danger, an independent cause must often intervene; the manufacturer of the finished product must also fail in *his* duty of inspection. It may be that in those circumstances the negligence of the earlier members of the series is too remote to constitute, as to the ultimate user, an actionable wrong. [Cc] We leave that question open. We shall have to deal with it when it arises. The difficulty which it suggests is not present in this case. There is here no break in the chain of cause and effect. In such circumstances, the presence of a known danger, attendant upon a known use, makes vigilance a duty. We have put aside the notion that the duty to safeguard life and limb, when the consequences of negligence may be foreseen, grows out of contract and nothing else. We have put the source of the obligation where it ought to be. We have put its source in the law.

From this survey of the decisions, there thus emerges a definition of the duty of a manufacturer which enables us to measure this defendant's liability. Beyond all question, the nature of an automobile gives warning of probable danger if its construction is defective. This automobile was designed to go fifty miles an hour. Unless its wheels were sound and strong, injury was almost certain. It was as much a thing of danger as a defective engine for a railroad. The defendant knew the danger. It knew also that the car would be used by persons other than the buyer. This was apparent from its size; there were seats for three persons. It was apparent also from the fact that the buyer was a dealer in cars, who bought to resell. The maker of this car supplied it for the use of purchasers from the dealer just as plainly as the contractor in *Devlin v. Smith* supplied the scaffold for use by the servants of the owner. The dealer was indeed the one person of whom it might be said with some approach to certainty that by him the car would not be used. Yet the defendant would have us say that he was the one person whom it was under a legal duty to protect. The law does not lead us to so inconsequent a conclusion. Precedents drawn from the days of travel by stage coach do not fit the conditions of travel to-day. The principle that the danger must be imminent does not change, but the things subject to the principle do change. They are whatever the needs of life in a developing civilization require them to be.

Food for Thought

The court argues that precedents from another time and era may not bind future courts applying laws and principles to different and changed circumstances. Do you agree?

. . . .

In England the limits of the rule are still unsettled. *Winterbottom v. Wright* (10 M. & W. 109) is often cited. The defendant undertook to provide a mail coach to carry the mail bags. The coach broke down from latent defects in its construction. The defendant, however, was not the manufacturer. The court held that he was not liable for injuries to a passenger. The case was decided on a demurrer to the declaration. Lord ESHER points out in *Heaven v. Pender* (*supra,* at p. 513) that the form of the declaration was subject to criticism. It did not fairly suggest the existence of a duty aside from the special contract which was the plaintiff's main reliance. (See the criticism of *Winterbottom v. Wright,* in Bohlen, *supra,* at pp. 281, 283). At all events, in *Heaven v. Pender* (*supra*) the defendant, a dock owner, who put up a staging outside a ship, was held liable to the servants of the shipowner. In *Elliott v. Hall* (15 Q. B. D. 315) the defendant sent out a defective truck laden with goods which he had sold. The buyer's servants unloaded it, and were injured because of the defects. It was held that the defendant was under a duty 'not to be guilty of negligence with regard to the state and condition of the truck.' There seems to have been a return to the doctrine of *Winterbottom v. Wright* in *Earl v. Lubbock* (L. R. [1905] 1 K. B. 253). In that case, however, as in the earlier one, the defendant was not the manufacturer. He had merely made a contract to keep the van in repair. A later case (*White v. Steadman,* L. R. [1913], 3 K. B. 340, 348) emphasizes that element. A livery stable keeper who sent out a vicious horse was held liable not merely to his customer but also to another occupant of the carriage, and *Thomas v. Winchester* was cited and followed (*White v. Steadman, supra,* at pp. 348, 349). It was again cited and followed in *Dominion Natural Gas Co. v. Collins* (L. R. [1909] A. C. 640, 646). From these cases a consistent principle is with difficulty extracted. The English courts, however, agree with ours in holding that one who invites another to make use of an appliance is bound to the exercise of reasonable care (*Caledonian Ry. Co. v. Mulholland,* L. R. [1898] A. C. 216, 227; *Indermaur v. Dames,* L. R. [1 C. P.] 274). That at bottom is the underlying principle of *Devlin v. Smith.* The contractor who builds the scaffold invites the owner's workmen to use it. The manufacturer who sells the automobile to the retail dealer invites the dealer's customers to use it. The invitation is addressed in the one case to determinate persons and in the other to an indeterminate class, but in each case it is equally plain, and in each its consequences must be the same.

There is nothing anomalous in a rule which imposes upon A, who has contracted with B, a duty to C and D and others according as he knows or does not know that the subject-matter of the contract is intended for their use. We may find an analogy in the law which measures the liability of **landlords**. If A leases to B a tumbledown house he is not liable, in the absence of fraud, to B's guests who enter it and are injured. This is because B is then under the duty to repair it, the **lessor** has the right to suppose that he will fulfill that duty, and, if he omits to do so, his guests must look to him. [C] But if A leases a building to be used by the **lessee** at once as a place of public entertainment, the rule is different. There injury to persons other than the lessee is to be foreseen, and foresight of the consequences involves the creation of a duty (*Junkermann v. Tilyou R. Co.*, 213 N. Y. 404, and cases there cited).

. . . Subtle distinctions are drawn by the defendant between things **inherently dangerous** and things **imminently dangerous**, but the case does not turn upon these verbal niceties. If danger was to be expected as reasonably certain, there was a duty of vigilance, and this whether you call the danger inherent or imminent. In varying forms that thought was put before the jury. We do not say that the court would not have been justified in ruling as a matter of law that the car was a dangerous thing. If there was any error, it was none of which the defendant can complain.

We think the defendant was not absolved from a duty of inspection because it bought the wheels from a reputable manufacturer. It was not merely a dealer in automobiles. It was a manufacturer of automobiles. It was responsible for the finished product. It was not at liberty to put the finished product on the market without subjecting the component parts to ordinary and simple tests. [C] . . . The obligation to inspect must vary with the nature of the thing to be inspected. The more probable the danger, the greater the need of caution. . . .

. . . .

The judgment should be affirmed with costs.

WILLARD BARTLETT, Ch. J. (dissenting).

. . . .

. . . . It has heretofore been held in this state that the liability of the vendor of a manufactured article for negligence arising out of the existence of defects therein does not extend to strangers injured in consequence of such defects but is confined to the immediate vendee. The exceptions to this general rule which have thus far been recognized in New York are cases in which the article sold was of such a character that danger to life or limb was involved in the ordinary use thereof; in other words, where the article sold was inherently dangerous. As has already been pointed out, the learned trial judge instructed the jury that an automobile is not an inherently dangerous vehicle.

. . . .

The doctrine of [*Winterbottom*] was recognized as the law of this state by the leading New York case of *Thomas v. Winchester* (6 N. Y. 397, 408), which, however, involved an exception to the general rule. . . . Chief Judge RUGGLES, who delivered the opinion of the court, distinguished between an act of negligence imminently dangerous to the lives of others and one that is not so, saying: 'If A. builds a wagon and sell it to B., who sells it to C. and C. hires it to D., who in consequence of the gross negligence of A. in building the wagon is overturned and injured, D. cannot recover damages against A., the builder. A.'s obligation to build the wagon faithfully, arises solely out of his contract with B. The public have nothing to do with it. * * *'

. . . .

I do not see how we can uphold the judgment in the present case without overruling what has been so often said by this court and other courts of like authority in reference to the absence of any liability for negligence on the part of the original vendor of an ordinary carriage to any one except his immediate **vendee**. The absence of such liability was the very point actually decided in the English case of *Winterbottom v. Wright (supra),* and the illustration quoted from the opinion of Chief Judge RUGGLES in *Thomas v. Winchester (supra)* assumes that the law on the subject was so plain that the statement would be accepted almost as a matter of course. In the case at bar the defective wheel on an automobile moving only eight miles an hour was not any more dangerous to the occupants of the car than a similarly defective wheel would be to the occupants of a carriage drawn by a horse at the same speed; and yet unless the courts have been all wrong on this question up to the present time there would be no liability to strangers to the original sale in the case of the horse-drawn carriage.

. . . .

Points for Discussion

1. The court notes that the case before it involves the liability of a manufacturer of a finished product placed on the market for use, without inspection, by

customers. "If he is negligent, where danger is foreseen, a liability will follow." In addition, the court makes clear that the inspection obligation "must vary with the nature of the thing to be inspected." What types of product should be subject to inspection, and what kind of inspection must be performed?

2.   In rejecting the view that "the duty to safeguard life and limb . . . grows out of contract and nothing else," the court states: "We have put the source of the obligation where it ought to be. We have put its source in law." How do you interpret this passage?

3.   What is the *MacPherson* court's understanding of *Winterbottom v. Wright* and *Thomas v. Winchester*? Why is the court's discussion of these cases important to its decision?

4.   Were you persuaded by Chief Judge Bartlett's dissent?

———————

Clagett v. Dacy

47 Md.App. 23, 420 A.2d 1285 (Md. Ct. Spec. App. 1980)

WILNER, Judge.

Appellants were the high bidders at a **foreclosure** sale, but because the attorneys conducting the sale failed to follow the proper procedures, the sale was set aside. This occurred twice. Ultimately, the debtor discharged the loan, thus "redeeming" his land, and appellants lost the opportunity to acquire the property and make a profit on its resale. They sued the attorneys in the Circuit Court for Prince George's County to recover their loss, alleging that the attorneys in question owed them, as bidders, a duty to use care and diligence and to conduct the sale "properly and carefully." By sustaining the attorneys' demurrer without leave to amend, the court concluded that no such duty existed—at least not one from which an action for damages will arise; and, by affirming that order, we shall indicate our concurrence with the court's conclusion.

. . . .

The traditional rule, in Maryland and elsewhere, is that an attorney's duty of diligence and care flows only to his direct client/employer, and that, whether in an action of contract or tort, only that client/employer can recover against him for a breach of that duty. The Court of Appeals adopted that view in Wlodarek v. Thrift,

178 Md. 453, 13 A.2d 774 (1940), an action for breach of contract, and in Kendall v. Rogers, 181 Md. 606, 31 A.2d 312 (1943), an action based on negligence.

. . . .

Although [Prescott v. Coppage, 266 Md. 562, 296 A.2d 150 (1972)] has a most unusual factual setting, it does seem to suggest a modest relaxation of the strict privity requirement to the extent of allowing a true **third party beneficiary** to sue an attorney as he could sue any other defaulting or tortious party to a contract made for his benefit. This extension is not unique to Maryland. [C]

It is, however, a limited one with a special utility. It is most often seen and applied in actions based on drafting errors in wills and other such documents or on erroneous title reports—errors that, by their very nature, will likely have a long or delayed effect and will most probably impact upon persons other than the attorney's immediate employer [cc] although it has been applied in other contexts as well. See Donald v. Garry, 19 Cal.App.3d 769, 97 Cal.Rptr. 191 (1971) (creditor who assigned claim to collection agency for collection allowed to sue agency's attorney for negligence in prosecuting his claim).

The Coppage Court made clear that only those persons who qualify under the normal rules for determining third party beneficiaries will be afforded the privileged status vis a vis attorney defendants; i.e., creditor beneficiaries. [C] This would seem to limit the extension to actions based upon contract, to which the third party beneficiary theory is peculiarly applicable, and would not supply a basis for permitting third parties to sue attorneys on a pure negligence theory—violation of some general duty arising in the absence of an underlying contractual **attorney-client relationship**.

In *Donald v. Garry*, supra, the California court utilized the concept expressed in Restatement of Torts 2d, § 324A, to support a third party action, concluding that "(a)n attorney may be liable for damage caused by his negligence to a person intended to be benefited by his performance irrespective of any lack of privity of contract between the attorney and the party to be benefited." (Emphasis supplied.) The context of this, as noted above, was an action by the true creditor against the collection agency attorney, and the court was careful to mention that "the transaction in which the respondent's negligence occurred was intended primarily for the benefit of (the creditor). Respondent was retained to collect an account due him."

. . . .

It will, moreover, take more than general conclusory allegations to satisfy that requirement. Attorneys are not quite the free agents as some others are in the world of commerce. There are well-recognized limitations, judicially imposed and enforced, upon how they may conduct themselves, and who they may, and may not, represent in certain situations. Except in very limited circumstances, they may not represent or act for conflicting interests in a transaction; their manifest **duty of loyalty** to their employer/client forbids it. See, for example, Code of Professional Responsibility, Canon 5, EC5-14, 5-15, 5-16, 5-19, 5-22; DR5-105.

> An attorney's obligation to identify representational conflicts are examined in professional responsibility and legal ethics courses.

These limitations, predominant but not necessarily exclusive with attorneys, must, of necessity, be taken into account when dealing with actions founded upon an implied duty owed by an attorney to a person who is not his direct employer/client, or upon an employment relationship alleged to arise by implication rather than by express agreement. Thus, the duties or obligations inherent in an attorney-client relationship will not be presumed to flow to a third party and will not be presumed to arise by implication when the effect of such a presumption would be tantamount to a prohibited or improbable employment, absent the clearest exposition of facts from which such an employment may be fairly and rationally inferred.

When judged against these principles, it becomes clear that the Declaration at issue here has failed to state a cause of action. It does not sufficiently allege a proper standing on the part of appellants to sue the appellee attorneys; nor, from what is alleged, could it do so. Appellees were engaged to represent the mortgagee (**deed of trust** beneficiary), not the bidders, whose interest would likely be in conflict with that of the **mortgagee**. The mortgagee's economic interest, and legal obligation, is to secure the highest possible price for the property, whereas the bidders' goal is to pay as little as possible. It is evident, in that circumstance, that an attorney could not lawfully represent both the mortgagee and the bidder in the transaction; and it will not be lightly presumed or inferred that appellees did so.

Nor may the prohibited employment be inferred from an allegation that appellees' fees would ultimately be paid from the proceeds of sale. The mere fact that those fees, along with the other costs of the proceeding, may be taken from the purchase price paid by the successful bidder does not mean that the purchaser is actually paying the fees. Quite the contrary. The **debtor/mortgagor** ultimately pays the fees and all other costs, for he gets only the net surplus (if any) available after all such fees and costs are discharged. The bidder pays only for the property, not the cost of selling it; and he is not, therefore, the client (express or implied) of the attorney engaged to sell the property.

JUDGMENT AFFIRMED; APPELLANTS TO PAY THE COSTS.

———————

Points for Discussion

1. Proposition: The attorney-client relationship should be subject to a strict privity requirement such that third parties cannot sue and recover from attorneys in contract or tort actions. Do you agree or disagree with this proposition? Why or why not?

2. In addition to attorneys, what other jobs, professions, or services should be subject to the third-person liability approach?

3. Consider § 324A of the RESTATEMENT (SECOND) OF TORTS, which provides that one who gratuitously or for consideration renders services to another "which he should recognize as necessary for the protection of a third person or his things, is subject to liability to the third person for physical harm resulting from his failure to exercise reasonable care for his undertaking" where (1) the failure to exercise such care "increases the risk of such harm," or (2) "he has undertaken to perform a duty owed by the other to the third person," or (3) the "harm is suffered because of reliance of the other or the third person upon the undertaking."

Hypo 7-1

Office Building ("OB") contracts with Elevator Inspectors, Inc. ("EI") to inspect the elevators of one of its commercial properties. EI negligently inspects an elevator. As a result of that flawed inspection, the elevator comes to a sudden stop while descending from a top floor, injuring a person in the elevator who falls and fractures his wrist. Is EI subject to liability to the injured person? Is OB subject to liability?

B. Failure To Act

Hegel v. Langsam

29 Ohio Misc. 147, 55 Ohio Ops.2d 476, 273 N.E.2d 351 (1971)

BETTMAN, Judge.

This matter is before the Court on defendant's motion for judgment on the pleadings. The **gravamen** of plaintiff's position is that the defendants permitted the **minor** plaintiff, a seventeen year old female student from Chicago, Illinois, enrolled at the University, to become associated with criminals, to be seduced, to become a drug user and further allowed her to be absent from her dormitory and failed to return her to her parents' custody on demand.

On our opinion plaintiffs completely misconstrue the duties and functions of a university. A university is an institution for the advancement of knowledge and learning. It is neither a nursery school, a boarding school nor a prison. No one is required to attend. Persons who meet the required qualifications and who abide by the university's rules and regulations are permitted to attend and must be presumed to have sufficient maturity to conduct their own personal affairs.

We know of no requirement of the law and none has been cited to us placing on a university or its employees any duty to regulate the private lives of their students, to control their comings and goings and to supervise their associations.

We do not believe that O.R.C. 3345.21 requiring a university to maintain 'law and order' on campus, nor O.R.C. 2151.41, making it a crime to contribute to the **delinquency** of a **child**, have any bearing on the fact situation before us.

For these reasons we hold that plaintiffs have failed to state a cause of action and defendants' motion for judgment on the pleadings should be granted.

Having so determined it is not necessary to consider the defense that the University and its employees are immune from suit.

. . . .

J.S. and M.S. v. R.T.H.

155 N.J. 330, 714 A.2d 924 (1998)

HANDLER, J.

In this case, two young girls, ages 12 and 15, spent substantial periods of recreational time with their neighbor at his horse barn, riding and caring for his horses. Betraying the trust this relationship established, the neighbor, an older man, sexually abused both girls for a period of more than a year. Following the man's conviction and imprisonment for these sexual offenses, the girls, along with their parents, brought this action against the man and his wife for damages, contending that the wife's negligence rendered her, as well as her husband, liable for their injuries. The man conceded liability for both the intentional and negligent injuries that he inflicted on the girls by his sexual abuse. His wife, however, denied that, under the circumstances, she could be found negligent for the girls' injuries.

This case presents the issue of whether a wife who suspects or should suspect her husband of actual or prospective sexual abuse of their neighbors' children has any duty of care to prevent such abuse. And, if there is such a duty, does a breach of that duty constitute a proximate cause of the harm that results from sexual abuse.

I

Defendants R.T.H. and R.G.H., husband and wife (called "John" and "Mary" for purposes of this litigation), moved into a house in Vineland, New Jersey, and became next door neighbors of plaintiffs, J.S. and M.S. and their two daughters, C.S. and M.S.

John, 64 years old, was charged with sexually assaulting the two sisters over a period of more than a year. He pled guilty to endangering the welfare of minors and was sentenced to eighteen months in state prison. Plaintiffs, as the natural parents and **guardians** *ad litem* of their two daughters, filed a complaint against John alleging intentional, reckless, and/or negligent acts of sexual assault against each of the two girls. In an amended complaint, plaintiffs added Mary as a defendant, alleging that she "was negligent in that she knew and/or should have known of her husband's proclivities/propensities" and that as a result of her negligence the two girls suffered physical and emotional injury.

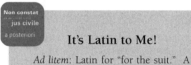

It's Latin to Me!

Ad litem: Latin for "for the suit." A guardian *ad litem* is appointed by a court to represent a party who is a minor or is incompetent.

Defendants filed a joint answer in which they denied plaintiffs' allegations. In an amended answer, Mary offered the defenses that she owed no duty to plaintiffs, that any alleged negligence on her part was not the proximate cause of any injuries or damages sustained by plaintiffs, and that any damages sustained by plaintiffs were the result of actions by a third party over whom she exercised no control. Mary also filed a crossclaim for **contribution** and **indemnification** against John, alleging that even if plaintiffs' allegations were proven, John was the primary, active, and sole culpable cause of any injuries to the plaintiffs.

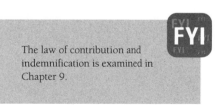

The law of contribution and indemnification is examined in Chapter 9.

Mary filed a motion for summary judgment, contending that there was no legal basis for finding her negligent. In opposition, plaintiffs submitted the certifications of the two minor plaintiffs.

Plaintiffs also argued that the summary judgment motion was premature, in that they had not yet had the opportunity to depose John, who was still incarcerated, nor had they completed other discovery.

The trial court entered summary judgment on behalf of Mary. On appeal, the Appellate Division reversed the order and remanded for entry of an order granting plaintiffs extended discovery. [C]

This Court granted defendant's petition for certification. [C]

. . . .

II

A.

In determining whether a duty is to be imposed, courts must engage in a rather complex analysis that weighs and balances several, related factors, including the nature of the underlying risk of harm, that is, its foreseeability and severity, the opportunity and ability to exercise care to prevent the harm, the comparative interests of, and the relationships between or among, the parties, and, ultimately, based on considerations of public policy and fairness, the societal interest in the proposed solution. [C]

Foreseeability of the risk of harm is the foundational element in the determination of whether a duty exists. [C] The "[a]bility to foresee injury to a potential plaintiff" is "crucial" in determining whether a duty should be imposed. [C]

Foreseeability as a component of a duty to exercise due care is based on the defendant's knowledge of the risk of injury and is susceptible to objective analysis. [C] That knowledge may be an actual awareness of risk. [C] Such knowledge may also be constructive; the defendant may be charged with knowledge if she is "in a position" to "discover the risk of harm." [C] In some cases where the nature of the risk or the extent of harm is difficult to ascertain, foreseeability may require that the defendant have a "special reason to know" that a "particular plaintiff" or "identifiable class of plaintiffs" would likely suffer a "particular type" of injury. [C] Further, when the risk of harm is that posed by third persons, a plaintiff may be required to prove that defendant was in a position to "know or have reason to know, from past experience, that there [was] a likelihood of conduct on the part of [a] third person[ ]" that was "likely to endanger the safety" of another. [C]

"[T]he question whether there is a 'duty' merely begs the more fundamental question whether the plaintiff's interests are entitled to legal protection against the defendant's conduct." [C] The imposition of a duty thus requires an evaluation and a balancing of the conflicting interests of the respective parties. [C] That assessment necessarily includes an examination of the relationships between and among the parties. Also implicated in this analysis is an assessment of the defendant's "responsibility for conditions creating the risk of harm" and an analysis of whether the defendant had sufficient control, opportunity, and ability to have avoided the risk of harm. [Cc]

Ultimately, the determination of the existence of a duty is a question of fairness and public policy. [C] In fixing the limits of liability as a matter of public policy, courts must draw on "notions of fairness, common sense, and morality." [C] Public policy must be determined in the context of contemporary circumstances and considerations. *See, e.g., Kelly v. Gwinnell,* 96 N.J. 538, 544-45, 476 A.2d 1219 (1984) (noting that in a society growing increasingly intolerant of drunken driving, the imposition of a duty on social hosts "seems both fair and fully in accord with the State's policy"). Thus, " '[d]uty' is not a rigid formalism" that remains static through time, but rather is a malleable concept that "must of necessity adjust to the changing social relations and exigencies and man's relation to his fellows." [C]

The Court, in its determination whether to impose a duty, must also consider the scope or boundaries of that duty. [C] The scope of a duty is determined under "the totality of the circumstances," [c] and must be "reasonable" under those circumstances. [C] Factors to be taken into consideration include the risk of harm involved and the practicality of preventing it. [Cc] When the defendant's actions are "relatively easily corrected" and the harm sought to be prevented is "serious," it is fair to impose a duty. [C] In the final analysis, the "reasonableness of action" that constitutes such a duty is "an essentially objective determination to be made on the basis of the material facts" of each case. [C]

B.

Here, a man criminally sexually assaulted unrelated, adolescent children whom he had befriended. The defendant is the spouse of the wrongdoer. The abuse occurred on her own property over an extended period of time. The tortious, assaultive conduct is of a type that is extremely difficult to identify, anticipate, and predict. While these considerations bear on all of the factors that are relevant in determining whether a duty of care should be recognized and imposed on the spouse, they bear materially on the primary element of foreseeability.

Although conduct involving sexual abuse is often secretive, clandestine, and furtive, a number of factors are relevant when determining whether or not it is foreseeable to a wife that her husband would sexually abuse a child. These include whether the husband had previously committed sexual offenses against children;

the number, date, and nature of those prior offenses; the gender of prior victims; the age of prior victims; where the prior offenses occurred; whether the prior offense was against a stranger or a victim known to the husband; the husband's therapeutic history and regimen; the extent to which the wife encouraged or facilitated her husband's unsupervised contact with the current victim; the presence of physical evidence such as pornographic materials depicting children and the unexplained appearance of children's apparel in the marital home; and the extent to which the victims made inappropriate sexual comments or engaged in age-inappropriate behavior in the husband and wife's presence. [Cc]

Moreover, there is some empirical support for the conclusion that sexual abuse of a child, while extremely difficult to detect or anticipate, is a risk that can be foreseen by a spouse. This evidence indicates that an extremely high percentage of child sexual molesters are men, many of whom are married. U.S. Dept. of Justice, Bureau of Justice Statistics, *Child Victimizers: Violent Offenders and Their Victims* 5 (March 1996). The vast majority of child victims are female and many child victims fall prey to an immediate relative or a family acquaintance; most of these sexual assaults are committed either in the offender's home or the victim's home. [C] Given those factors, the wife of a sexual abuser of children is in a unique position to observe firsthand telltale signs of sexual abuse. A wife may well be the only person with the kind of knowledge or opportunity to know that a particular person or particular class of persons is being sexually abused or is likely to be abused by her husband. [Cc]

These considerations warrant a standard of foreseeability in this case that is based on "particular knowledge" or "special reason to know" that a "[p]articular plaintiff" or "identifiable class of plaintiffs" would suffer a "particular type" of injury. [Cc] "Particularized foreseeability" in this kind of case will conform the standard of foreseeability to the **empirical** evidence and common experience that indicate a wife may often have actual knowledge or special reason to know that her husband is abusing or is likely to abuse an identifiable victim and will accommodate the concerns over the inherent difficulties in predicting such furtive behavior. That test of foreseeability will also ensure that the wife is not subject to a broad duty that may expose her to liability to every child whom her husband may threaten and harm. Foreseeability under that definitional standard is neither unrealistic nor unfair.

The nature of the parties' interests bears on the need to recognize a duty of care. "There can be no doubt about the strong policy of this State to protect children from sexual abuse and to require reporting of suspected child abuse." [C] That policy is so obvious and so powerful that it can draw little argument. It is an interest that is massively documented.

The Legislature has dealt comprehensively with the subject of child abuse and has enacted a plethora of statutes designed to prevent the sexual abuse of children. For example, *N.J.S.A.* 9:6-8.10 requires any person having reasonable cause to believe that a child has been subject to abuse to report the abuse immediately to the Division of Youth and Family Services. The duty to report is not limited to professionals, such as doctors, psychologists, and teachers, but is required of every citizen. *State v. Hill,* 232 N.J.Super. 353, 356, 556 A.2d 1325 (Law Div.1989). Indeed, friends or neighbors are often in the best position to fulfill this statutory duty because they are the people "who frequently hear or observe acts of child abuse." [C] The purpose of the sexual abuse reporting statute is

> to provide for the protection of children under 18 years of age who have had serious injury inflicted upon them by other than accidental means. It is the intent of this legislation to assure that the lives of innocent children are immediately safeguarded from further injury and possible death and that the legal rights of such children are fully protected.

[*N.J.S.A.* 9:6-8.8.]

. . . .

"**Megan's Law,**" *N.J.S.A.* 2C:7-1 to -11, provides yet more evidence of the State's intolerance of sexual abuse of children. In affirming the constitutionality of the community notification and registration requirements of Megan's Law for convicted sex offenders, this Court recognized the enormous public interest in protecting society from the threat of potential molestation, rape, or murder of women and children. [C]

FYI

New Jersey's "Megan's Law" was named after Megan Kanka, a 7-year-old girl raped and brutally murdered by a twice-convicted sex offender who was the Kankas' next door neighbor. All fifty states have enacted some type of sex offender registry legislation.

While the interest in protecting children from sexual abuse is great, this Court must also take into consideration defendants' interests in a stable marital relationship and in marital privacy. [C] That interest traditionally found expression in the common-law doctrine of interspousal immunity wherein one spouse could not sue or be sued by another, [cc] and the testimonial disqualification wherein one spouse was not permitted to testify for or against the other. [Cc] Both courts and scholars, however, increasingly questioned whether the doctrine

Make the Connection

Interspousal and other immunities are discussed in Chapter 11.

of marital immunity actually succeeded in promoting the marital tranquility and privacy it was designed to serve. [C] The testimonial disqualification has also been criticized. *See* 8 *Wigmore, supra,* § 2228 at 221 (terming the spousal testimonial privilege "the merest anachronism in legal theory and an indefensible obstruction to truth in practice"); [cc].

Moreover, the societal interest in enhancing marital relationships cannot outweigh the societal interest in protecting children from sexual abuse. The child-abuse reporting statute itself has mandated that balance-it applies to every citizen, including a spouse. [C] As the Appellate Division here described, "the Legislature's adoption of that statute [*i.e.,* "Megan's Law"] is an expression of New Jersey's strong public policy favoring protection of children over the privacy of an offending adult." [C] . . .

Considerations of fairness and public policy also govern whether the imposition of a duty is warranted.[C] Public policy considerations based in large measure on the comparative interests of the parties support overwhelmingly the recognition of a duty of care in these circumstances. This Court has recognized that the sexual abuse of children not only traumatizes the victims, but also exacts a heavy toll on society . . .

. . . .

Considerations of fairness implicate the scope as well as the existence of a duty. In defining the duty to be imposed, the court must weigh the ability and opportunity of the defendant to exercise reasonable care. [C] Defendant contends that the imposition of a duty to prevent her husband from engaging in sexual abuse of another person would be unfair. She argues that sexual offenses are extremely difficult to combat and that she did not necessarily have the power, the ability, or the opportunity to control her husband and should not be expected or required to police his conduct continuously. However, fairness concerns in these circumstances can be accommodated by a flexible duty of care that requires a spouse, when there is particularized foreseeability of harm of sexual abuse to a child, to take reasonable steps to prevent or warn of the harm. [Cc]

C.

Considerations of foreseeability, the comparative interests and relationships of the parties, and public policy and fairness support the recognition of a duty of care. Based in large measure on the strong public policy of protecting children from sexual abuse, we conclude that there is a sound, indeed, compelling basis for the imposition of a duty on a wife whose husband poses the threat of sexually victimizing young children.

Make the Connection

See Chapter 5 for analysis of proximate causation.

Closely-related to the recognition of a duty, however, is the issue of **proximate causation**, which must also be considered in determining whether any liability may be allowed for the breach of such a duty. Proximate causation is "that combination of 'logic, common sense, justice, policy and precedent' that fixes a point in the chain of events, some foreseeable and some unforeseeable, beyond which the law will bar recovery." [Cc]

. . . .

It does not seem highly extraordinary that a wife's failure to prevent or warn of her husband's sexual abuse or his propensity for sexual abuse would result in the occurrence or the continuation of such abuse. The harm from the wife's breach of duty is both direct and predictable. There is little question, here, that the physical and emotional injuries allegedly suffered by the girls are hardly an extraordinary result of John's acts of molestation and that their victimization is not an extraordinary consequence of Mary's own negligence. Mary's negligence could be found to be a proximate cause of plaintiffs' injuries. [C]

Accordingly, we hold that when a spouse has actual knowledge or special reason to know of the likelihood of his or her spouse engaging in sexually abusive behavior against a particular person or persons, a spouse has a duty of care to take reasonable steps to prevent or warn of the harm. Further, we hold that a breach of such a duty constitutes a proximate cause of the resultant injury, the sexual abuse of the victim.

III

In determining how the standards for duty, negligence, and proximate cause should be applied in this case, we view the facts in the light most favorable to plaintiffs. [C]

It may be found that the relationship between the next-door neighbors' in this case had been close. Mary knew that the neighbors' adolescent girls were visiting at her home nearly every day and that they spent considerable amounts of time there alone with her husband. Moreover, she never "confronted" her husband about the unsupervised time he was spending with the girls. At both the trial level and on appeal, Mary conceded for the purposes of argument that "at all relevant times" she "knew or should have known of her husband's proclivities/propensities." Thus, it may be determined that it was particularly foreseeable that John was abusing the young girls. Further, the evidence at trial could support a finding of negligence on Mary's part. It is inferable, as explained by the Appellate

Division, that Mary could have discharged her duty by confronting her husband and warning him, by insisting or seeing that the girls were not invited to ride or care for the horses, by keeping a watchful eye when she knew the girls to be visiting with her husband, by asking the girls' parents to ensure that the children not visit when she was not present, or by warning the girls or their parents of the risk she perceived. [C] Finally, the evidence may be found sufficient to support the determination that the harm suffered by the girls was not a highly extraordinary result of the breach of that duty.

. . . .

We affirm the judgment of the Appellate Division.

—————————

Points for Discussion

1. Do you agree with the *Hegel* court that the university had no duty to supervise the plaintiff's associations and private life? If you do not agree, what should the rule be governing a university's responsibility for a plaintiff such as the one in *Hegel* and other students in the same or similar circumstances?

2. What is the holding in the *J.S.* decision? In your opinion, was the case correctly decided?

3. The *J.S.* court argued that the public policy relative to determining duty and establishing liability limits must draw on fairness as well as common sense and morality. Is this a workable and useful approach? How should judges (and how would you) define fairness? Morality?

4. Imagine that you represent the wife in *J.S.* Given her concession that she knew or should have known of her husband's proclivities, how would you advise her to proceed on remand?.

—————————

Hypo 7-2

Sean, 16 years of age, and five of his friends were in his second floor bedroom. His father was in the basement of the home watching television. At some point during the evening Sean produced an unloaded revolver and ammunition and asked if anyone had ever played Russian Roulette, a lethal "game" of chance where participants place a single bullet into a revolver, spin the chamber, place the muzzle to their heads, and pull the trigger. One of his friends told the group that someone he knew had died playing Russian Roulette. Sean, smiling, stated that he wanted to "try the game" and put a bullet into the revolver, pointed it at his head, and pulled the trigger three times. While everyone in the room watched Sean play the game, no one said anything. He then put the gun down, picked it up again, checked the cylinder before spinning it, and pulled the trigger two times. The gun went off on the second pull, killing Sean.

Sean's parents have brought a wrongful death action against the five friends who were in Sean's room at the time their son shot himself. The parents' principal argument: Sean's friends should have taken the gun from Sean or should have informed his father that his son was playing Russian Roulette.

Can and should the friends be held civilly liable to the parents?

Tarasoff v. Regents of University of California

17 Cal.3d 425, 551 P.2d 334, 131 Cal.Rptr. 14 (1976)

TOBRINER, J.

On October 27, 1969, Prosenjit Poddar killed Tatiana Tarasoff.[1] Plaintiffs, Tatiana's parents, allege that two months earlier Poddar confided his intention to kill Tatiana to Dr. Lawrence Moore, a psychologist employed by the Cowell Memorial Hospital at the University of California at Berkeley. They allege that on Moore's request, the campus police briefly detained Poddar, but released him when he appeared rational. They further claim that Dr. Harvey Powelson, Moore's superior, then directed that no further action be taken to detain Poddar. No one warned plaintiffs of Tatiana's peril.

Concluding that these facts set forth causes of action against neither therapists and policemen involved, nor against the Regents of the University of California as their employer, the superior court sustained defendants' demurrers to plaintiffs' second amended complaints without leave to amend.[2] This appeal ensued.

---

1 The criminal prosecution stemming from this crime is reported in *People v. Poddar,* (1974) 10 Cal.3d 750 [111 Cal.Rptr. 910, 518 P.2d 342].

2 The therapist defendants include Dr. Moore, the psychologist who examined Poddar and decided that Poddar should be committed; Dr. Gold and Dr. Yandell, psychiatrists at Cowell Memorial Hospital who concurred in Moore's decision; and Dr. Powelson, chief of the department of psychiatry, who countermanded Moore's decision and directed that the staff take no action to confine Poddar. The police defendants include Officers Atkinson, Brownrigg and Halleran, who detained Poddar briefly but released him; Chief Beall, who received Moore's letter recommending that Poddar be confined; and Officer Teel, who, along with Officer Atkinson, received Moore's oral communication requesting detention of Poddar.

Plaintiffs' complaints predicate liability on two grounds: defendants' failure to warn plaintiffs of the impending danger and their failure to bring about Poddar's confinement pursuant to the Lanterman-Petris-Short Act (Welf. & Inst. Code, § 5000ff.) Defendants, in turn, assert that they owed no duty of reasonable care to Tatiana and that they are immune from suit under the California Tort Claims Act of 1963 (Gov. Code, § 810ff.).

We shall explain that defendant therapists cannot escape liability merely because Tatiana herself was not their patient. When a therapist determines, or pursuant to the standards of his profession should determine, that his patient presents a serious danger of violence to another, he incurs an obligation to use reasonable care to protect the intended victim against such danger. The discharge of this duty may require the therapist to take one or more of various steps, depending upon the nature of the case. Thus it may call for him to warn the intended victim or others likely to apprise the victim of the danger, to notify the police, or to take whatever other steps are reasonably necessary under the circumstances.

In the case at bar, plaintiffs admit that defendant therapists notified the police, but argue on appeal that the therapists failed to exercise reasonable care to protect Tatiana in that they did not confine Poddar and did not warn Tatiana or others likely to apprise her of the danger. Defendant therapists, however, are public employees. Consequently, to the extent that plaintiffs seek to predicate liability upon the therapists' failure to bring about Poddar's confinement, the therapists can claim immunity under Government Code section 856. No specific statutory provision, however, shields them from liability based upon failure to warn Tatiana or others likely to apprise her of the danger, and Government Code section 820.2 does not protect such failure as an exercise of discretion.

Plaintiffs therefore can amend their complaints to allege that, regardless of the therapists' unsuccessful attempt to confine Poddar, since they knew that Poddar was at large and dangerous, their failure to warn Tatiana or others likely to apprise her of the danger constituted a breach of the therapists' duty to exercise reasonable care to protect Tatiana.

Plaintiffs, however, plead no relationship between Poddar and the police defendants which would impose upon them any duty to Tatiana, and plaintiffs suggest no other basis for such a duty. Plaintiffs have, therefore, failed to show that the trial court erred in sustaining the demurrer of the police defendants without leave to amend.

. . . .

The second cause of action can be amended to allege that Tatiana's death proximately resulted from defendants' negligent failure to warn Tatiana or others likely to apprise her of her danger. Plaintiffs contend that as amended, such allegations of negligence and proximate causation, with resulting damages, establish a cause of action. Defendants, however, contend that in the circumstances of the present case they owed no duty of care to Tatiana or her parents and that, in the absence of such duty, they were free to act in careless disregard of Tatiana's life and safety.

. . . .

Although . . . under the common law, as a general rule, one person owed no duty to control the conduct of another,[5] [cc] nor to warn those endangered by such conduct, the courts have carved out an exception to this rule in cases in which the defendant stands in some **special relationship** to either the person whose conduct needs to be controlled or in a relationship to the foreseeable victim of that conduct. [C].. . .

Although plaintiffs' pleadings assert no special relation between Tatiana and defendant therapists, they establish as between Poddar and defendant therapists the special relation that arises between a patient and his doctor or psychotherapist. Such a relationship may support affirmative duties for the benefit of third persons. Thus, for example, a hospital must exercise reasonable care to control the behavior of a patient which may endanger other persons. A doctor must also warn a patient if the patient's condition or medication renders certain conduct, such as driving a car, dangerous to others.

Although the California decisions that recognize this duty have involved cases in which the defendant stood in a special relationship *both* to the victim and to the person whose conduct created the danger, we do not think that the duty should logically be constricted to such situations. Decisions of other jurisdictions hold that the single relationship of a doctor to his patient is sufficient to support the duty to exercise reasonable care to protect others against dangers emanating from the patient's illness. The courts hold that a doctor is liable to persons infected by his patient if he negligently fails to

---

5 This rule derives from the common law's distinction between **misfeasance** and **nonfeasance**, and its reluctance to impose liability for the latter. [C] Morally questionable, the rule owes its survival to "the difficulties of setting any standards of unselfish service to fellow men, and of making any workable rule to cover possible situations where fifty people might fail to rescue ...." (Prosser, Torts (4th ed. 1971) § 56, p. 341.) Because of these practical difficulties, the courts have increased the number of instances in which affirmative duties are imposed not by direct rejection of the common law rule, but by expanding the list of special relationships which will justify departure from that rule. [C]

What's That?

Misfeasance refers to active misconduct and a lawful act performed in a wrongful way; *nonfeasance* is a failure to act by one who is obligated to act in a manner not to harm another.

diagnose a contagious disease, [c] or, having diagnosed the illness, fails to warn members of the patient's family. [Cc]

. . . .

Defendants contend, however, that imposition of a duty to exercise reasonable care to protect third persons is unworkable because therapists cannot accurately predict whether or not a patient will resort to violence. In support of this argument amicus representing the American Psychiatric Association and other professional societies cites numerous articles which indicate that therapists, in the present state of the art, are unable reliably to predict violent acts; their forecasts, **amicus** claims, tend consistently to overpredict violence, and indeed are more often wrong than right. Since predictions of violence are often erroneous, amicus concludes, the courts should not render rulings that predicate the liability of therapists upon the validity of such predictions.

> **FYI**
> The American Psychiatric Association is an international organization comprised of medical specialists who are qualified psychiatrists. See the association's website at www.psych.org.

The role of the psychiatrist, who is indeed a practitioner of medicine, and that of the psychologist who performs an allied function, are like that of the physician who must conform to the standards of the profession and who must often make diagnoses and predictions based upon such evaluations. Thus the judgment of the therapist in diagnosing emotional disorders and in predicting whether a patient presents a serious danger of violence is comparable to the judgment which doctors and professionals must regularly render under accepted rules of responsibility.

We recognize the difficulty that a therapist encounters in attempting to forecast whether a patient presents a serious danger of violence. Obviously, we do not require that the therapist, in making that determination, render a perfect performance; the therapist need only exercise "that reasonable degree of skill, knowledge, and care ordinarily possessed and exercised by members of [that professional specialty] under similar circumstances." [Cc] Within the broad range of reasonable practice and treatment in which professional opinion and judgment may differ, the therapist is free to exercise his or her own best judgment without liability; proof, aided by hindsight, that he or she judged wrongly is insufficient to establish negligence.

In the instant case, however, the pleadings do not raise any question as to failure of defendant therapists to predict that Poddar presented a serious danger of violence. On the contrary, the present complaints allege that defendant therapists did in fact predict that Poddar would kill, but were negligent in failing to warn.

Amicus contends, however, that even when a therapist does in fact predict that a patient poses a serious danger of violence to others, the therapist should be absolved of any responsibility for failing to act to protect the potential victim. In our view, however, once a therapist does in fact determine, or under applicable professional standards reasonably should have determined, that a patient poses a serious danger of violence to others, he bears a duty to exercise reasonable care to protect the foreseeable victim of that danger. While the discharge of this duty of due care will necessarily vary with the facts of each case, in each instance the adequacy of the therapist's conduct must be measured against the traditional negligence standard of the rendition of reasonable care under the circumstances. [C] . . .

. . . .

The risk that unnecessary warnings may be given is a reasonable price to pay for the lives of possible victims that may be saved. We would hesitate to hold that the therapist who is aware that his patient expects to attempt to assassinate the President of the United States would not be obligated to warn the authorities because the therapist cannot predict with accuracy that his patient will commit the crime.

Defendants further argue that free and open communication is essential to psychotherapy [c]; that "Unless a patient … is assured that … information [revealed by him] can and will be held in utmost confidence, he will be reluctant to make the full disclosure upon which diagnosis and treatment … depends." (Sen. Com. on Judiciary, comment on Evid. Code, § 1014.) The giving of a warning, defendants contend, constitutes a breach of trust which entails the revelation of confidential communications.

We recognize the public interest in supporting effective treatment of mental illness and in protecting the rights of patients to privacy, [c] and the consequent public importance of safeguarding the confidential character of psychotherapeutic communication. Against this interest, however, we must weigh the public interest in safety from violent assault. The Legislature has undertaken the difficult task of balancing the countervailing concerns. In Evidence Code section 1014, it established a broad rule of privilege to protect confidential communications between patient and psychotherapist. In Evidence Code section 1024, the Legislature created a specific and limited exception to the psychotherapist-patient privilege: "There is no privilege … if the psychotherapist has reasonable cause to believe that the patient is in such mental or emotional condition as to be dangerous to himself or to the person or property of another and that disclosure of the communication is necessary to prevent the threatened danger."

We realize that the open and confidential character of psychotherapeutic dialogue encourages patients to express threats of violence, few of which are ever executed. Certainly a therapist should not be encouraged routinely to reveal such threats; such disclosures could seriously disrupt the patient's relationship with his therapist and with the persons threatened. To the contrary, the therapist's obligations to his patient require that he not disclose a confidence unless such disclosure is necessary to avert danger to others, and even then that he do so discreetly, and in a fashion that would preserve the privacy of his patient to the fullest extent compatible with the prevention of the threatened danger. [C]

The revelation of a communication under the above circumstances is not a **breach of trust** or a violation of professional ethics; as stated in the Principles of Medical Ethics of the American Medical Association (1957), section 9: "A physician may not reveal the confidence entrusted to him in the course of medical attendance ... *unless he is required to do so by law or unless it becomes necessary in order to protect the welfare of the individual or of the community.*" (Italics added.) We conclude that the public policy favoring protection of the confidential character of patient-psychotherapist communications must yield to the extent to which disclosure is essential to avert danger to others. The protective privilege ends where the public peril begins.

Our current crowded and computerized society compels the interdependence of its members. In this risk-infested society we can hardly tolerate the further exposure to danger that would result from a concealed knowledge of the therapist that his patient was lethal. If the exercise of reasonable care to protect the threatened victim requires the therapist to warn the endangered party or those who can reasonably be expected to notify him, we see no sufficient societal interest that would protect and justify concealment. The containment of such risks lies in the public interest. For the foregoing reasons, we find that plaintiffs' complaints can be amended to state a cause of action against defendants Moore, Powelson, Gold, and Yandell and against the Regents as their employer, for breach of a duty to exercise reasonable care to protect Tatiana.

. . . .

Turning now to the police defendants, we conclude that they do not have any such special relationship to either Tatiana or to Poddar sufficient to impose upon such defendants a duty to warn respecting Poddar's violent intentions. [Cc] Plaintiffs suggest no theory, and plead no facts that give rise to any duty to warn on the part of the police defendants absent such a special relationship. They have thus failed to demonstrate that the trial court erred in denying leave to amend as to the police defendants. [Cc]

. . . .

For the reasons stated, we conclude that plaintiffs can amend their complaints to state a cause of action against defendant therapists by asserting that the therapists in fact determined that Poddar presented a serious danger of violence to Tatiana, or pursuant to the standards of their profession should have so determined, but nevertheless failed to exercise reasonable care to protect her from that danger. . . . . Further, as to the police defendants we conclude that plaintiffs have failed to show that the trial court erred in sustaining their demurrer without leave to amend.

. . . .

Mosk, J., Concurring and Dissenting.

I concur in the result in this instance only because the complaints allege that defendant therapists did in fact predict that Poddar would kill and were therefore negligent in failing to warn of that danger. Thus the issue here is very narrow: we are not concerned with whether the therapists, pursuant to the standards of their profession, "should have" predicted potential violence; they allegedly did so in actuality. Under these limited circumstances I agree that a cause of action can be stated.

Whether plaintiffs can ultimately prevail is problematical at best. As the complaints admit, the therapists *did* notify the police that Poddar was planning to kill a girl identifiable as Tatiana. While I doubt that more should be required, this issue may be raised in defense and its determination is a question of fact.

I cannot concur, however, in the majority's rule that a therapist may be held liable for failing to predict his patient's tendency to violence if other practitioners, pursuant to the "standards of the profession," would have done so. The question is, what standards? Defendants and a responsible amicus curiae . . . demonstrate that psychiatric predictions of violence are inherently unreliable.

. . . .

I would restructure the rule designed by the majority to eliminate all reference to conformity to standards of the profession in predicting violence. If a psychiatrist does in fact predict violence, then a duty to warn arises. The majority's expansion of that rule will take us from the world of reality into the wonderland of clairvoyance.

Clark, J.

Until today's majority opinion, both legal and medical authorities have agreed that confidentiality is essential to effectively treat the mentally ill, and that imposing a duty on doctors to disclose patient threats to potential victims would greatly impair treatment. Further, recognizing that effective treatment and society's safety are necessarily intertwined, the Legislature has already decided effective and confidential treatment is preferred over imposition of a duty to warn.

The issue whether effective treatment for the mentally ill should be sacrificed to a system of warnings is, in my opinion, properly one for the Legislature, and we are bound by its judgment. Moreover, even in the absence of clear legislative direction, we must reach the same conclusion because imposing the majority's new duty is certain to result in a net increase in violence.

. . . .

Generally, a person owes no duty to control the conduct of another. [Cc] Exceptions are recognized only in limited situations where (1) a special relationship exists between the defendant and injured party, or (2) a special relationship exists between defendant and the active wrongdoer, imposing a duty on defendant to control the wrongdoer's conduct. The majority does not contend the first exception is appropriate to this case.

Policy generally determines duty. [C] Principal policy considerations include foreseeability of harm, certainty of the plaintiff's injury, proximity of the defendant's conduct to the plaintiff's injury, moral blame attributable to defendant's conduct, prevention of future harm, burden on the defendant, and consequences to the community. [C]

Overwhelming policy considerations weigh against imposing a duty on psychotherapists to warn a potential victim against harm. While offering virtually no benefit to society, such a duty will frustrate psychiatric treatment, invade fundamental patient rights and increase violence.

The importance of psychiatric treatment and its need for confidentiality have been recognized by this court. . . .

Assurance of confidentiality is important for three reasons.

Deterrence From Treatment

First, without substantial assurance of confidentiality, those requiring treatment will be deterred from seeking assistance. [Cc] It remains an unfortunate fact in our society that people seeking psychiatric guidance tend to become stigmatized. Apprehension of such stigma--apparently increased by the propensity of people considering treatment to see themselves in the worst possible light--creates a well-recognized reluctance to seek aid. [Cc] This reluctance is alleviated by the psychiatrist's assurance of confidentiality.

Full Disclosure

Second, the guarantee of confidentiality is essential in eliciting the full disclosure necessary for effective treatment. [Cc] The psychiatric patient approaches treatment with conscious and unconscious inhibitions against revealing his innermost thoughts. "Every person, however well-motivated, has to overcome resistances to therapeutic exploration. These resistances seek support from every possible source and the possibility of disclosure would easily be employed in the service of resistance." [Cc] Until a patient can trust his psychiatrist not to violate their confidential relationship, "the unconscious psychological control mechanism of repression will prevent the recall of past experiences." [C]

Successful Treatment

Third, even if the patient fully discloses his thoughts, assurance that the confidential relationship will not be breached is necessary to maintain his trust in his psychiatrist - the very means by which treatment is effected. "[T]he essence of much psychotherapy is the contribution of trust in the external world and ultimately in the self, modelled upon the trusting relationship established during therapy." [C] Patients will be helped only if they can form a trusting relationship with the psychiatrist. [Cc] All authorities appear to agree that if the trust relationship cannot be developed because of collusive communication between the psychiatrist and others, treatment will be frustrated. [Cc]

Given the importance of confidentiality to the practice of psychiatry, it becomes clear the duty to warn imposed by the majority will cripple the use and effectiveness of psychiatry. Many people, potentially violent--yet susceptible to treatment--will be deterred from seeking it; those seeking it will be inhibited from making revelations necessary to effective treatment; and, forcing the psychiatrist to violate the patient's trust will destroy the interpersonal relationship by which treatment is effected.

Violence and Civil Commitment

By imposing a duty to warn, the majority contributes to the danger to society of violence by the mentally ill and greatly increases the risk of civil commitment--the total deprivation of liberty--of those who should not be confined. The impairment of treatment and risk of improper commitment resulting from the new duty to warn will not be limited to a few patients but will extend to a large number of the mentally ill. Although under existing psychiatric procedures only a relatively few receiving treatment will ever present a risk of violence, the number making threats is huge, and it is the latter group--not just the former--whose treatment will be impaired and whose risk of commitment will be increased.

Both the legal and psychiatric communities recognize that the process of determining potential violence in a patient is far from exact, being fraught with complexity and uncertainty. [Cc] In fact, precision has not even been attained in predicting who of those having already committed violent acts will again become violent, a task recognized to be of much simpler proportions. [C]

This predictive uncertainty means that the number of disclosures will necessarily be large. As noted above, psychiatric patients are encouraged to discuss all thoughts of violence, and they often express such thoughts. However, unlike this court, the psychiatrist does not enjoy the benefit of overwhelming hindsight in seeing which few, if any, of his patients will ultimately become violent. Now, confronted by the majority's new duty, the psychiatrist must instantaneously calculate potential violence from each patient on each visit. The difficulties researchers have encountered in accurately predicting violence will be heightened for the practicing psychiatrist dealing for brief periods in his office with heretofore nonviolent patients. And, given the decision not to warn or commit must always be made at the psychiatrist's civil peril, one can expect most doubts will be resolved in favor of the psychiatrist protecting himself.

Neither alternative open to the psychiatrist seeking to protect himself is in the public interest. The warning itself is an impairment of the psychiatrist's ability to treat, depriving many patients of adequate treatment. It is to be expected that after disclosing their threats, a significant number of patients, who would not become violent if treated according to existing practices, will engage in violent conduct as a result of unsuccessful treatment. In short, the majority's duty to warn will not only impair treatment of many who would never become violent but worse, will result in a net increase in violence.

The second alternative open to the psychiatrist is to commit his patient rather than to warn. Even in the absence of threat of civil liability, the doubts of psychiatrists as to the seriousness of patient threats have led psychiatrists to overcommit to mental institutions. This overcommitment has been authoritatively documented in both legal and psychiatric studies. [Cc] This practice is so prevalent that it has been estimated that "as many as twenty harmless persons are incarcerated for every one who will commit a violent act." [C]

Given the incentive to commit created by the majority's duty, this already serious situation will be worsened . . .

. . . .

The judgment should be affirmed.

————————————

Points for Discussion

1. The court recognizes the difficulty therapists face in forecasting whether a patient presents a serious danger of violence. Does the court place therapists

and their patients in an untenable position? Are courts competent to weigh the risks of unnecessary warnings against the benefits of warning others? Did the court give sufficient weight to patient-therapist and doctor-patient confidentiality?

2. Justice Mosk agreed with the result reached by the court given the allegations that the therapists in fact predicted that Poddar would kill Tatiana Tarasoff. Why should a duty to warn *not* be required in a case where such a prediction is made? In those circumstances should not the therapists err on the side of warning a third party?

3. A dissenting Justice Clark argues that a failure-to-warn system should be established by the legislature and not the courts; predicts a "net increase in violence" as a consequence of the court's decision; and states that the duty to warn imposed by the court "will cripple the use and effectiveness of psychiatry." Are you persuaded?

4. In *Thompson v. County of Alameda*, 27 Cal.3d 741, 614 P.2d 728, 167 Cal. Rptr. 70 (1980), the California Supreme Court concluded that the affirmative duty to warn depends on and arises from the existence of a prior threat to a specific identifiable victim and does not apply to threats made to a large and amorphous public group.

5. Should an attorney have a duty to warn of a client whom she knows to be dangerous?

Thapar v. Zezulka

994 S.W.2d 635 (Tex. 1999)

Justice ENOCH delivered the opinion for a unanimous court.

The primary issue in this case is whether a mental-health professional can be liable in negligence for failing to warn the appropriate third parties when a patient makes specific threats of harm toward a readily identifiable person. In reversing the trial court's summary judgment, the court of appeals recognized such a cause of action. Because the Legislature has established a policy against such a common-law cause of action, we refrain from imposing on mental-health professionals a duty to warn third parties of a patient's threats. Accordingly, we reverse the court of appeals' judgment and render judgment that Zezulka take nothing.

Because this is an appeal from summary judgment, we take as true evidence favorable to Lyndall Zezulka, the nonmovant. Freddy Ray Lilly had a history of mental-health problems and psychiatric treatment. Dr. Renu K. Thapar, a psychiatrist, first treated Lilly in 1985, when Lilly was brought to Southwest Memorial Hospital's emergency room. Thapar diagnosed Lilly as suffering from moderate to severe post-traumatic stress disorder, alcohol abuse, and paranoid and delusional beliefs concerning his stepfather, Henry Zezulka, and people of certain ethnic backgrounds. Thapar treated Lilly with a combination of psychotherapy and drug therapy over the next three years.

For the majority of their relationship, Thapar treated Lilly on an outpatient basis. But on at least six occasions Lilly was admitted to Southwest Memorial Hospital, or another facility, in response to urgent treatment needs. Often the urgency involved Lilly's problems in maintaining amicable relationships with those with whom he lived. Lilly was also admitted on one occasion after threatening to kill himself. In August 1988, Lilly agreed to be admitted to Southwest Memorial Hospital. Thapar's notes from August 23, 1988, state that Lilly "feels like killing" Henry Zezulka. These records also state, however, that Lilly "has decided not to do it but that is how he feels." After hospitalization and treatment for seven days, Lilly was discharged. Within a month Lilly shot and killed Henry Zezulka.

Despite the fact that Lilly's treatment records indicate that he sometimes felt homicidal, Thapar never warned any family member or any law enforcement agency of Lilly's threats against his stepfather. Nor did Thapar inform any family member or any law enforcement agency of Lilly's discharge from Southwest Memorial Hospital.

Lyndall Zezulka, Henry's wife and Lilly's mother, sued Thapar for negligence resulting in her husband's wrongful death. Zezulka alleged that Thapar was negligent in diagnosing and treating Lilly and negligent in failing to warn of Lilly's threats toward Henry Zezulka. It is undisputed that Thapar had no **physician-patient relationship** with either Lyndall or Henry Zezulka. Based on this fact, Thapar moved for summary judgment on the ground that Zezulka had not stated a claim for medical negligence because Thapar owed no duty to Zezulka in the absence of a doctor-patient relationship. The trial court overruled Thapar's motion.

. . . .

To decide this case we must determine the duties a mental-health professional owes to a nonpatient third party. Zezulka stated her claims against Thapar in negligence. Liability in negligence is premised on duty, a breach of which proximately causes injuries, and damages resulting from that breach. Whether a legal duty exists is a threshold question of law for the court to decide from the facts surrounding the occurrence in question. If there is no duty, there cannot be negligence liability.

In her second amended petition Zezulka lists seventeen particulars by which she alleges Thapar was negligent. But each allegation is based on one of two proposed underlying duties: (1) a duty to not negligently diagnose or treat a patient that runs from a psychiatrist to nonpatient third parties; or (2) a duty to warn third parties of a patient's threats. In her motion for summary judgment Thapar asserted that she owed Zezulka no duty. Thus, we must determine if Thapar owed Zezulka either of these proposed duties.

NEGLIGENT DIAGNOSIS AND TREATMENT

First, we consider Zezulka's allegations that Thapar was negligent in her diagnosis and treatment of Lilly's psychiatric problems. Among other claims, Zezulka alleged that Thapar was negligent in releasing Lilly from the hospital in August 1988, in failing to take steps to have Lilly involuntarily committed, and in failing to monitor Lilly after his release to ensure that he was taking his medication. All of these claims are based on Thapar's medical diagnosis of Lilly's condition, which dictated the treatment Lilly should have received and the corresponding actions Thapar should have taken. The underlying duty question here is whether the absence of a doctor-patient relationship precludes Zezulka from maintaining medical negligence claims against Thapar based on her diagnosis and treatment of Lilly.

[W]e [hold] that no duty runs from a psychologist to a third party to not negligently misdiagnose a patient's condition. . . . Thapar owes no duty to Zezulka, a third party nonpatient, for negligent misdiagnosis or negligent treatment of Lilly. Accordingly, Thapar was entitled to summary judgment on all of the claims premised on Zezulka's first duty theory.

FAILURE TO WARN

Second, we consider Zezulka's allegations that Thapar was negligent for failing to warn either the Zezulkas or law enforcement personnel of Lilly's threats. We are not faced here with the question of whether a doctor owes a duty to third parties to warn a patient of risks from treatment which may endanger third parties. Instead, we are asked whether a mental-health professional owes a duty to directly warn third parties of a patient's threats.

The California Supreme Court first recognized a mental-health professional's duty to warn third parties of a patient's threats in the seminal case *Tarasoff v. Regents of University of California*. The court of appeals here cited *Tarasoff* in recognizing a cause of action for Thapar's failure to warn of her patient's threats. But we have never recognized the only underlying duty upon which such a cause of action could be based-a mental-health professional's duty to warn third parties of a patient's threats. Without considering the effect of differences in the development of California and Texas jurisprudence on the outcome of this issue, we decline to adopt a duty to warn now because the confidentiality statute governing mental-health professionals in Texas makes it unwise to recognize such common-law duty.

The Legislature has chosen to closely guard a patient's communications with a mental-health professional. In 1979, three years after *Tarasoff* issued, the Legislature enacted a statute governing the disclosure of communications during the course of mental-health treatment.[16] The statute classifies communications between mental-health "professional[s]" and their "patient[s]/client[s]" as confidential and prohibits mental-health professionals from disclosing them to third parties unless an exception applies.

Zezulka complains that Thapar was negligent in not warning members of the Zezulka family about Lilly's threats. But a disclosure by Thapar to one of the Zezulkas would have violated the confidentiality statute because no exception in the statute provides for disclosure to third parties threatened by the patient. We considered a similar situation in *Santa Rosa Health Care Corp. v. Garcia*,[19] in which we concluded there is no duty to disclose confidential information when disclosure would violate the confidentiality statute. The same reasoning applies here. Under the applicable statute, Thapar was prohibited from warning one of his patient's potential victims and therefore had no duty to warn the Zezulka family of Lilly's threats.

. . . .

We consider legislative enactments that evidence the adoption of a particular public policy significant in determining whether to recognize a new common-law duty. For example, in recognizing the existence of a common-law duty to guard children from sexual abuse, we found persuasive the Legislature's strongly avowed policy to protect children from abuse. The statute expressing this policy, however, makes the reporting of sexual abuse mandatory[25] and makes failure to report child abuse a crime.[26] Further, under the statute, those who report child abuse in good faith are immune from civil and criminal liability.[27] Thus, imposing a common law duty to report was consistent with the legislative scheme governing child abuse.

---

16 *See* Act of May 9, 1979, 66th Leg., R.S., ch. 239, 1979 Tex. Gen. Laws 512 (amended 1991) (current version at TEX. HEALTH & SAFETY CODE § 611.002 (1996)).

19 964 S.W.2d 940, 941 (Tex.1998) (involving disclosure of HIV test under TEX.REV.CIV. STAT. art. 4419b-1, § 9.03).

25 TEX. FAM.CODE § 261.101(a) states:

> A person having cause to believe that a child's physical or mental health or welfare has been adversely affected by abuse or neglect by any person *shall* immediately make a report as provided by this subchapter. (emphasis added).

26 *See* TEX. FAM.CODE § 261.109.

27 *See* TEX. FAM.CODE § 261.106.

The same is not true here. The confidentiality statute here does not make disclosure of threats mandatory nor does it penalize mental-health professionals for not disclosing threats. And, perhaps most significantly, the statute does not shield mental-health professionals from civil liability for disclosing threats in good faith. On the contrary, mental-health professionals make disclosures at their peril.

FYI

A "Catch 22" refers to a no-win situation and is the title of Joseph Heller's 1955 satirical novel set in the closing months of World War II.

Thus, if a common-law duty to warn is imposed, mental-health professionals face a Catch-22. They either disclose a confidential communication that later proves to be an idle threat and incur liability to the patient, or they fail to disclose a confidential communication that later proves to be a truthful threat and incur liability to the victim and the victim's family.

The confidentiality statute here evidences an intent to leave the decision of whether to disclose confidential information in the hands of the mental-health professional. In the past, we have declined to impose a common-law duty to disclose when disclosing confidential information by a physician has been made permissible by statute but not mandatory. We have also declined to impose a common-law duty after determining that such a duty would conflict with the Legislature's policy and enactments concerning the employment-at-will doctrine. Our analysis today is consistent with the approach in those cases.

Because of the Legislature's stated policy, we decline to impose a common law duty on mental-health professionals to warn third parties of their patient's threats. Accordingly, we conclude that Thapar was entitled to summary judgment because she owed no duty to Zezulka, a third-party nonpatient. We reverse the court of appeals' judgment and render judgment that Zezulka take nothing.

Points for Discussion

1. *Thapar* concludes that there is no duty to warn a patient's potential victim where doing so would violate a confidentiality statute containing no express exception for disclosure to third parties threatened by a patient. Do you agree that the statute prohibits such disclosure and that mental-health professionals would face a Catch-22 if the courts imposed a common-law duty to disclose?

2. Which is the best or preferred approach: *Tarasoff's* duty-to-warn requirement and analysis, or *Thapar's* no-duty rule? Why?

3. Which institution is best suited to determine whether a mental-health professional must warn a third party of threats of harms made by a patient: legislatures or courts?

Hypo 7-3

Attorney received a phone call from Client after Client was released from prison after serving a four-year sentence for drug possession and distribution. Advising Attorney that the trial resulting in her conviction was a "**kangaroo court**" and that she wanted to bring a civil action against the state, Client told Attorney that the district attorney, public defender, and judge involved in her case had conspired to send her to prison. During that telephone conversation, Attorney told Client that he would represent her. After the call ended, Attorney thought about Client's conspiracy theory and decided that he did not want to represent Client.

The following day Attorney telephoned Client and informed her that he was not sure that he wanted to represent her. Client became upset. "You're the fifth lawyer I've talked to and no one will help me! What am I going to do? I'll tell you what I need to do. I'm going to get a gun and blow them all away--the prosecutor, the judge, and the D.A." At that point Attorney told Client he would not represent her and ended the telephone conversation.

Attorney immediately called the district attorney (who also happened to be Attorney's lifelong best friend) and described his conversation with Client. The district attorney informed Attorney that Judge Smith had presided over Client's case. Attorney telephoned Judge Smith and discussed with her what had taken place and told her about what he referred to as Client's "serious threat." The judge and the district attorney reported the matter to the police department. After a brief investigation, Client was arrested and charged with the crime of intimidating a judge. Client was subsequently convicted and sentenced to 24 months in prison.

Pursuant to the applicable Rules of Professional Responsibility, "A lawyer may reveal confidences or secrets to the extent that the lawyer reasonably believes necessary to prevent the client from committing a crime that the lawyer believes is likely to result in imminent death or substantial bodily harm." Was Client's "blow them all away" statement protected by his duty of confidentiality? Did Attorney have an affirmative duty in tort to warn Judge Smith of Client's threat?

C. Pure Economic Loss

Aikens v. Debow

541 S.E.2d 576 (W. Va. 2000)

SCOTT, Justice.

This case arises upon certified question from the Circuit Court of Berkeley County and presents the issue of entitlement to recovery in tort of economic loss not accompanied by bodily injury or property damage, a matter not previously resolved with precision by this Court.

. . . .

Plaintiff Richard Aikens operates a motel and restaurant known as the Martinsburg Econo-Lodge ("Econo-Lodge"), which is located on Route 901 and can be accessed by exiting from Interstate 81 at the Spring Mills Road exit. While the Route 901 overpass bridge permits the shortest, most-convenient means of accessing the Econo-Lodge for south-bound travelers traveling on I-81, the establishment can still be accessed through alternate routing. On September 18, 1996, Defendant Robert Debow, a truck driver and employee of Defendant Craig Paving, Inc., was driving a flatbed truck north on I-81 carrying a trackhoe. Because the trackhoe was too high to pass safely under the Route 901 overpass, an accident resulted which caused substantial damage to the bridge. It was closed for nineteen days to make the necessary repairs.

Plaintiff instituted the underlying cause of action on May 28, 1997, seeking recovery for the decreased revenues he experienced due to closure of the Route 901 overpass. Asserting that his reduced revenues were proximately caused by the accident, Plaintiff seeks recovery of $9,000 in lost income.

Arguing that as a matter of law Plaintiff could not recover for his economic losses in the absence of direct bodily injury or property damage, Defendants moved for summary judgment. The circuit court denied Defendants' motion for summary judgment, ruling that "there are factual issues in this case pertaining to causation and foreseeability which remain appropriate for jury determination." . . .

Following the circuit court's denial of Defendants' motion for summary judgment, the parties requested and the circuit court agreed to certification of the following issue:

Whether a claimant who has sustained no physical damage to his person or property may maintain an action against another for negligent injury to another's property which results consequentially in purely **economic loss** to the claimant.

It's Latin to Me!

Sub judice is Latin for "under a judge" and refers to the case before a judge or court for consideration and ruling.

The circuit court answered this question in the affirmative. . . . Recognizing that this Court, in addressing certified questions, has "retained the right to address them with some flexibility[,]" we reframe the question presented in the case sub judice to more thoroughly encompass the full breadth of the question to be answered. [C] The question, as reformulated, is consequently as follows:

> May a claimant who has sustained purely economic loss as a result of an interruption in commerce caused by negligent injury to the property of a third person recover damages absent either privity of contract or some other special relationship with the alleged tortfeasor?

We answer this question in the negative.

. . . .

The resolution of any question of tort liability must be premised upon fundamental concepts of the duty owed by the tortfeasor.

> "In order to establish a *prima facie* case of negligence in West Virginia, it must be shown that the defendant has been guilty of some act or omission in violation of a duty owed to the plaintiff. No action for negligence will lie without a duty broken." . . . *Parsley v. General Motors Acceptance Corp.,* 167 W.Va. 866, 280 S.E.2d 703 (1981).

[C] Importantly, the determination of whether a defendant in a particular case owes a duty to the plaintiff is not a factual question for the jury; rather, "[t]he determination of whether a plaintiff is owed a duty of care by the defendant must be rendered as a matter of law by the court." [C] . . .

. . . .

We recognized in *Robertson v. LeMaster,* 171 W.Va. 607, 301 S.E.2d 563 (1983), that while foreseeability of risk is a primary consideration in determining the scope of a duty an actor owes to another, "[b]eyond the question of foreseeability, the existence of duty also involves policy considerations underlying the core issue of the scope of the legal system's protection[.]" [C] "Such considerations include the likelihood of injury, the magnitude of the burden of guarding against it, and the consequences of placing that burden on the defendant." [C]

. . . .

Emphasizing the relationship between foreseeability and duty, we explained in . . . *Sewell v. Gregory,* 179 W.Va. 585, 371 S.E.2d 82 (1988):

The ultimate test of the existence of a duty to use care is found in the foreseeability that harm may result if it is not exercised. The test is, would the ordinary man in the defendant's position, knowing what he knew or should have known, anticipate that harm of the general nature of that suffered was likely to result?

Commentators have similarly evaluated the critical element of duty:

[T]he obligation to refrain from particular conduct is owed only to those who are foreseeably endangered by the conduct and only with respect to those risks or hazards whose likelihood made the conduct unreasonably dangerous. Duty, in other words, is measured by the scope of the risk which negligent conduct foreseeably entails.

2 F. Harper & F. James, *The Law of Torts* § 18.2 (1956) footnote omitted.

. . . .

The appropriate application of these fundamental tort principles has served as a source of great controversy. Justice Benjamin Cardozo, in *Ultramares Corp. v. Touche,* 255 N.Y. 170, 174 N.E. 441 (1931), expressed the danger of expanding the concept of duty in tort to include economic interests and consequent exposure of defendants "to a liability in an indeterminate amount for an indeterminate time to an indeterminate class. The hazards of a business conducted on these terms are so extreme as to enkindle doubt whether a flaw may not exist in the implicating of a duty that exposes to these consequences." [C] The ascertainment of a universal and inviolate formula for defining the parameters of duty in the abstract has proven evasive.

Perhaps the most acclaimed declaration of the concept of duty was announced by Justice Cardozo in *Palsgraf v. Long Island Railroad Co.,* 248 N.Y. 339, 162 N.E.

99 (1928), three years prior to the decision quoted above. In *Palsgraf,* Justice Cardozo succinctly observed: "The risk reasonably to be perceived defines the duty to be obeyed." [C] The frequently cited reasoning of *Palsgraf* was premised upon the following factual scenario: An individual carrying a package of fireworks was pushed by a Long Island Railroad employee while

Make the Connection

Cardozo's *Palsgraf* decision can be found in Chapter 4.

attempting to board the train. The individual dropped the package of fireworks, and the resulting shock of the explosion caused some of the scales at the other end of the platform to fall, striking the plaintiff. [C] The court concluded that the plaintiff could not recover against the railroad because the employee's conduct did not involve any foreseeable risk of harm to the plaintiff. [C] The fact that the conduct was unjustifiably risky toward the individual carrying the fireworks was deemed irrelevant. Justice Cardozo reasoned the "risk imports relation; it is the risk to another or to others within the range of apprehension." [C] "*What we do mean by the word 'proximate' [in causation] is that, because of convenience, of public policy, of a rough sense of justice, the law arbitrarily declines to trace a series of events beyond a certain point. This is not logic. It is practical politics.*" [C]

. . . .

The need to restrict the spatial concept of duty to something less than the limits of logical connection was cogently stated as follows in *In re Exxon Valdez,* No. A89-0095-CV, 1994 WL 182856 (D.Alaska March 23, 1994):

> There is no question but that the Exxon Valdez grounding impacted, in one fashion or another, far more people than will ever recover anything in these proceedings. There is an understandable public perception that if one suffers harm which is perceived to be a result of the conduct of another, the harmed person should be compensated. That perception does not always square up with the institutional guidelines (statutes and case law) under which the court must operate. It is the function of both Congress and the courts (principally the courts of appeal and supreme courts) to determine the extent to which public expectations with respect to financial responsibility are to be realized. Legal liability does not always extend to all of the foreseeable consequences of an accident. In the area of harm to one's body, the reach of what is recoverable is very great. Where one's property is injured, the extent of legal liability is considerable, but not to the same extent as with bodily injury. Where pure economic loss is at issue—not connected with any injury to one's body or property, and especially where that economic loss occurs in a

marine setting—the reach of legal liability is quite limited except as to commercial fishermen.[2]

....

Were it otherwise, we would have a form of organized anarchy in which no one could count on what rule would apply at any given time or in any given situation.

[C]

While the holding of the majority in *Harris* [*v. R.A. Martin, Inc.*, 204 W.Va. 397, 513 S.E.2d 170 (1998)] is not in conflict with our decision in the present case, we underscore the reasoning of Justice Maynard in his insightful dissent in *Harris*. Justice Maynard cautioned against the limitless expansion of the element of duty, postulating that the majority had "so expand[ed] the element of duty, that its existence now becomes almost a given in any tort case. If a party is injured by the conduct of another, there must have been a duty to avoid such conduct." [C] In his dissent, Justice Maynard quoted, with approval, the following language from 57A Am.Jur.2d *Negligence* § 87:

> A line must be drawn between the competing policy considerations of providing a remedy to everyone who is injured and of extending exposure to tort liability almost without limit. It is always tempting to impose new duties and, concomitantly, liabilities, regardless of the economic and social burden. Thus, the *courts have generally recognized that public policy and social considerations, as well as foreseeability, are important factors in determining whether a duty will be held to exist in a particular situation.*

[C]

The obvious question: Who draws the line demarcating tort liability? Who, in our society, has the burden of defining the existence and extent of the element of "duty" in tort actions? It necessarily falls to the courts to consider all relevant claims of the competing parties; to determine where and upon whom the burden

---

2 The Ninth Circuit, in *Union Oil Co. v. Oppen*, 501 F.2d 558 (9th Cir.1974), found that the routine reliance by commercial fishermen upon an ability to fish in unpolluted waters satisfied the foreseeability requirement and justified an award of economic damages as an exception to the general rule. The Ninth Circuit emphasized that offshore oil producers have a duty to commercial fishermen to conduct their operations in a reasonably prudent manner designed to avoid any diminution in marine life. [Cc] The rationale for this limited exception for commercial fishermen was explained in *Burgess v. M/V Tamano*, 370 F.Supp. 247 (D.Me.1973), *aff'd per curiam*, 559 F.2d 1200 (1st Cir.1977). In *Tamano*, the court reasoned that while fishermen and clammers have no individual property rights to the aquatic life harmed by oil pollution, the fishermen could sue for tortious invasion of a public right, having suffered damages greater in degree than the general public. [C] The court recognized the oil spill as an interference with the "direct exercise of the public right to fish and to dig clams" which was, in fact, a special interest different from that of the general public. [C]

of carrying the risk of injury will fall; and to draw the line, to declare the existence or absence of "duty," in every case, as a matter of law. The temptation is to accede to the arguments of logical connection in every instance of resulting harm while, in fact, the consequences of pure logic would be socially and economically ruinous.

. . . .

The sole issue presented for our resolution is whether economic loss from an interruption in commerce in the absence of damage to a plaintiff's person or property is recoverable in a tort action. While this Court has never directly addressed this issue, other jurisdictions, almost without exception, have concluded that economic loss alone will not warrant recovery in the absence of some special relationship between the plaintiff and the tortfeasor. In the seminal decision of *Robins Dry Dock & Repair Co. v. Flint,* 275 U.S. 303, 48 S.Ct. 134, 72 L.Ed. 290 (1927), the United States Supreme Court refused to permit recovery from the dry dock owner when plaintiffs were denied use of a vessel for two weeks because of a third party's act of negligence during the ship's refurbishing. In establishing this long-standing rule of denying recovery in tort for indirect economic injury, Justice Holmes articulated the rationale, based upon English and American precedent, that continues to justify the nonexistence of a legally cognizable or compensable claim for such attenuated injuries even today: "The law does not spread its protection so far." [C] In writing *Robins Dry Dock,* Justice Holmes relied upon the reasoning of the English case of *Elliott Steam Tug Co. v. The Shipping Controller,* 1 K.B. 127 (1922), in which recovery was refused for negligent interference with contractual rights. . . . [C]

Where the factual scenario involves a plaintiff's contractual right to use property damaged by a tortfeasor, courts have invoked the Restatement of Torts as a basis for denying causes of action limited to economic damages. In *Philip Morris, Inc. v. Emerson,* 235 Va. 380, 368 S.E.2d 268 (1988), the plaintiff sought recovery of **lost profits** to his campground business due to the negligent release of gases from the defendant's property. Citing the well-recognized principle in the Restatement of Torts which recognizes that interference with the ability to contract with third persons is too remote to permit recovery, the court refused to permit recovery of the profits plaintiffs allegedly sustained from his inability to contract with campers for overnight stays. [C]

In denying economic damages in the absence of physical impact, courts frequently refer to this element of remoteness between the injury and the act of negligence that is the source of such injury. In *Rickards v. Sun Oil Co.,* 23 N.J. Misc. 89, 41 A.2d 267 (N.J.Sup.1945), a case remarkably similar to the one under scrutiny by this Court, plaintiff business owners sought to recover "losses from expectant gains" from a defendant whose barge negligently damaged a drawbridge which served as the only means of access to the island on which plaintiffs' business premises were situated. [C] In granting the defendant's motions to strike the complaints, the court held that "[defendant's] negligent action may be a cause of injury to the plaintiffs, but it is not the natural and proximate effect of such negligence and therefore [is] not actionable." [C] The court observed:

> The entire doctrine assumes the defendant is not necessarily to be held for all consequences of his acts. Professor McLaughlin, Article 39 Harvard Law Review (Dec.1925) 149 at 155. It is fundamental that there must be some reasonable limitation of liability for the commission of the tort. The **wrongdoer** is not liable in the eyes of the law for all possible consequences. He is thus responsible in damages only for the natural and probable consequence of his negligent act.

[C] The court recognized that "[n]o rule embraces within its scope all the resulting consequences of the given act. The effect would be to impose a liability entirely disproportionate to the act committed or to the failure to perform the duty assumed." [C]

. . . .

The recognized necessity of imposing a line of demarcation on actionable theories of recovery serves as another rationale for the denial of purely economic damages. In *Stevenson v. East Ohio Gas. Co.,* 73 N.E.2d 200 (Ohio Ct.App.1946), the Ohio court held that employees of a neighboring company could not recover lost wages incurred after they were evacuated due to an explosion and fire allegedly caused by the defendant's negligence. The *Stevenson* court reasoned as follows:

> While the reason usually given for the refusal to permit recovery in this class of cases is that the damages are "indirect" or are "too remote" it is our opinion that the principal reason that has motivated the courts in denying recovery in this class of cases is that *to permit recovery of damages in such cases would open the door to a mass of litigation which might very well overwhelm the courts so that in the long run while injustice might result in special cases, the ends of justice are conserved. ...*

[C]

In similar fashion, the Seventh Circuit, in affirming the district court's dismissal of an action seeking economic damages arising from a bridge closing, reasoned that extension of liability in the absence of harm to a plaintiff's person or property would thrust courts into "a field with no sensible or just stopping point." *Leadfree Enterprises, Inc. v. United States Steel Corp.,* 711 F.2d 805, 808 (7th Cir.1983) (citing *Hass v. Chicago & North Western Ry. Co.,* 48 Wis.2d 321, 179 N.W.2d 885, 888 (1970))

. . . .

A few jurisdictions have permitted recovery of economic damages without damage to person or property under certain limited circumstances. The New Jersey Supreme Court's approach to this concept is recognized as the leading authority for the minority view and represents a departure from a substantial collection of American and British cases. In *People Express Airlines, Inc. v. Consolidated Rail Corp.,* 100 N.J. 246, 495 A.2d 107 (1985), the New Jersey court permitted economic recovery where a leak of toxic chemicals from a railway car forced a twelve-hour evacuation of a commercial airline office building adjacent to the site of the leak. [C] The plaintiff sought to recover expenses incurred for flight cancellations, lost bookings and revenue, and certain operating expenses. In permitting the action, the court applied a special foreseeability rule, reasoning that the defendant would be liable only for damages proximately caused and requiring that the defendant must have "knowledge or special reason to know of the consequences of the tortious conduct in terms of the persons likely to be victimized and the nature of the damages likely to be suffered...." [C]

Narrowly crafting its decision to apply to a limited and particularized group, the New Jersey court held:

> that a defendant owes a duty of care to take reasonable measures to avoid the risk of causing economic damages, aside from physical injury, to particular plaintiffs or plaintiffs comprising an identifiable class with respect to whom defendant knows or has reason to know are likely to suffer such damages from its conduct. A defendant failing to adhere to this duty of care may be found liable for such economic damages proximately caused by its breach of duty.

[C] In further explaining its rationale for departure from established doctrine, the New Jersey court noted:

> the close proximity of the North Terminal and People Express Airlines to the Conrail freight yard; the obvious nature of the plaintiff's operations and particular foreseeability of economic losses resulting from an accident and evacuation; the defendants' actual or constructive knowledge of the volatile properties of ethylene oxide; and the existence of an emergency response plan prepared by some of the defendants (alluded to in the course of oral argument), which apparently called for the nearby area to be evacuated to avoid the risk of harm in case of an explosion.

[C] In fashioning its test, the court in *People Express* determined that liability and foreseeability "stand in direct proportion to one another[:] The more particular is the foreseeability that economic loss will be suffered by the plaintiff as a result of defendant's negligence, the more just is it that liability be imposed and recovery allowed." [C]

An analysis of the facts involved in the *People Express* decision supports the conclusion that the New Jersey court traversed a logical path more closely akin to that navigated in cases involving physical damage to property. Subsequent to the Three Mile Island nuclear incident, plaintiffs similarly asserted claims of temporary loss of use of property and "damage to property" as a result of the intrusion of radioactive materials through the ambient air. In resolving their claims in *Commonwealth of Pennsylvania v. General Public Utilities Corp.,* 710 F.2d 117 (3rd Cir.1983), the United States Court of Appeals for the Third Circuit acknowledged that the complaints did not contain any claim of damages for direct physical damage to any of the plaintiffs' property. [C] While the lower court had concluded that the losses claimed were purely economic in nature and unrecoverable, the plaintiffs contended that "increased radioactivity and radioactive materials emitted during the nuclear incident permeated the entire area, and this rendered the public buildings unsafe for a temporary period of time, and constituted a physical intrusion upon the plaintiffs' properties." [C] The plaintiffs maintained that the gaseous intrusion satisfied the requirement of physical harm to justify the recovery of damages in tort. The Third Circuit found that the plaintiffs' contentions were sufficient to defeat a motion for summary judgment, permitting the plaintiffs an opportunity to prove that an invasion by an invisible substance may still constitute a physical damage warranting recovery of economic loss. Similar to the inhabitability problems experienced by the Three Mile Island plaintiffs, the plaintiff's building in *People Express* was rendered uninhabitable by the negligent release of toxic gases. Thus, in *People Express,* the New Jersey court could have reached its decision by reasoning that to render a building uninhabitable by releasing poison gas against it constitutes a direct physical damage to that building.

. . . .

In another case typically referenced as supportive of a minority position on this issue, a California court applied the "special relationship" exception and permitted a restaurant owner to sue for lost profits allegedly caused by a contractor's failure to promptly install and maintain an air conditioner. *J'Aire Corp. v. Gregory,* 24 Cal.3d 799, 157 Cal.Rptr. 407, 598 P.2d 60 (1979). The plaintiff introduced evidence that the reliance upon the air conditioning function was repeatedly brought to the defendant's attention. In concluding that such action could be maintained, the court explained that "a contractor owes a duty of care to the tenant of a building undergoing construction work to prosecute that work in a manner which does not cause undue injury to the tenant's business, where such injury is reasonably foreseeable." [C] The court's decision to permit recovery was expressly predicated on the existence of a special relationship: "Where a special relationship exists between the parties, a plaintiff may recover for loss of expected economic advantage through the negligent performance of a contract although the parties were not in contractual privity." [C]

In another case frequently cited as support for the minority position, an employer sought recovery for economic loss sustained as a result of tortious injuries to his employees. *Mattingly v. Sheldon Jackson College,* 743 P.2d 356 (Alaska 1987). Plaintiff's employees were injured when a trench dug by Sheldon Jackson College employees collapsed, which prevented them from cleaning a drainpipe. Plaintiff sought recovery of economic damages as a result of the loss of services of his employees. Pivotal to the Alaska Supreme court's decision to permit economic recovery in this case was its determination that the plaintiff was a "foreseeable and particularized plaintiff." [C] Although recovery of economic damages was permitted, the court made clear that such recovery is only permitted where it can be established that the defendant owed a duty to "particular plaintiffs or plaintiffs comprising an identifiable class with respect to whom defendant knows or has reason to know are likely to suffer such damages from its conduct." [C]

. . . .

After thoroughly considering the intricacies of a potential rule permitting the recovery of economic damages absent physical or personal injury, we conclude that an individual who sustains purely economic loss from an interruption in commerce caused by another's negligence may not recover damages in the absence of physical harm to that individual's person or property, a contractual relationship with the alleged tortfeasor, or some other special relationship between the alleged tortfeasor and the individual who sustains purely economic damages sufficient to compel the conclusion that the tortfeasor had a duty to the particular plaintiff and that the injury complained of was clearly foreseeable to the tortfeasor. The existence of a special relationship will be determined largely by the extent to which the particular plaintiff is affected differently from society in general. It may be evident from the defendant's knowledge or specific reason to know of the potential consequences of the wrongdoing, the persons likely to be injured, and the damages likely to be suffered. Such special relationship may be proven through evidence of foreseeability of the nature of the harm to be suffered by the particular plaintiff or an identifiable class and can arise from contractual privity or other close nexus. . . . Any attempt by this Court to more specifically define the parameters of circumstances which may be held to establish a "special relationship" would create more confusion than clarity.

We base our holding upon our analysis of the complexities of this area of tort law, demonstrated through both historical evolvement and current concerns, and our belief that a hybrid approach must be fabricated to authorize recovery of meritorious claims while simultaneously providing a barrier against limitless liability. The common thread which permeates the analysis of potential economic recovery in the absence of physical harm is the recognition of the underlying concept of duty. Absent some special relationship, the confines of which will differ depending upon the facts of each relationship, there simply is no duty. A thorough examination of the cases comprising what has been referenced as the minority view reveals reasoning similar to ours, which provides the opportunity for recovery only upon a showing of a special relationship between the plaintiff and alleged tortfeasor and narrowly tailors the recovery to conform to the facts of the case under scrutiny.

Our decision under the limited factual scenario presented in this certified question has no impact upon our prior rulings permitting recovery of purely economic damages in negligence actions where a special relationship exists between the plaintiff and the alleged tortfeasor. Our holding in the case sub judice is, in fact, consistent with the rationale underlying such rulings, and we affirm our previous recognition that where a special and narrowly defined relationship can be established between the tortfeasor and a plaintiff who was deprived of an economic benefit, the tortfeasor can be held liable. In cases of that nature, the duty exists because of the special relationship. The special class of plaintiffs involved in those cases were particularly foreseeable to the tortfeasor, and the economic losses were proximately caused by the tortfeasor's negligence.

For example, auditors[8] have been held liable to plaintiffs who bought stock in reliance upon a financial statement negligently prepared for a corporation; surveyors[9] and termite inspectors[10] liable to remote purchasers of property; engineers[11] and architects[12] liable to contractors who relied upon plans negligently

---

8 *See H. Rosenblum, Inc. v. Adler,* 93 N.J. 324, 461 A.2d 138 (1983) (finding independent auditor whose negligence resulted in an inaccurate public financial statement held liable to plaintiff who bought stock in company; stock subsequently proved to be worthless).

9 *See Capper v. Gates,* 193 W.Va. 9, 454 S.E.2d 54 (1994) (holding evidence supported finding that defendant surveyor was negligent in connection with unsuccessful subdivision project.); *Rozny v. Marnul,* 43 Ill.2d 54, 250 N.E.2d 656 (1969) (finding surveyor whose negligence resulted in error in depicting boundary of lot held liable to remote purchaser).

10 *See Stemple v. Dobson,* 184 W.Va. 317, 400 S.E.2d 561 (1990) (inspectors charged with negligence in failing to discover termite infestation during termite inspection.); *Hardy v. Carmichael,* 207 Cal. App.2d 218, 24 Cal.Rptr. 475 (Cal.Ct.App.1962) (termite inspectors whose negligence resulted in purchase of infested home liable to out-of-privity home buyers).

11 *See National Sand, Inc. v. Nagel Constr., Inc.,* 182 Mich.App. 327, 451 N.W.2d 618 (1990) (subcontractor could recover additional contract costs from engineering firm which negligently prepared plans).

12 *See Board of Educ. v. Van Buren and Firestone, Architects, Inc.,* 165 W.Va. 140, 267 S.E.2d 440 (1980) (permitting board of education maintained action against contractor, engineer, and bonding company for alleged negligence in site preparation for school project); *Donnelly Constr. Co. v. Obera/Hunt/ Gilleland,* 139 Ariz. 184, 677 P.2d 1292, 1295 (1984) (holding architect, hired by county, liable to contractor for increased cost of construction due to errors in plans and specifications).

prepared for property owners who later hired the contractors; attorneys[13] and notaries public[14] liable to beneficiaries of negligently prepare wills; real estate brokers for failure to disclose defects; and telegraph companies[15] liable to individuals who failed to secure a contract due to the negligent transmission of a message.

. . . .

The resolution of this matter of restrictions on tort liability is ultimately a matter of "practical politics." *Palsgraf,* 162 N.E. at 103 (Andrews, J., dissenting). The "law arbitrarily declines to trace a series of events beyond a certain point." [C] In other words, it is a question of public policy. The purely economic damages sought by a plaintiff may be indistinguishable in terms of societal entitlement from those damages incurred by the restaurant owner in the next block, the antique dealer in the next town, and all the ripple-effect "losses" experienced by each employer and each resident of every town and village surrounding the location of the initial act of negligence. In crafting a rule to address the issue of economic damages, we have attempted to avoid the expression of a judicial definition of duty which would permit the maintenance of a class action as a result of almost every car wreck and other inconvenience that results to our state's citizenry.

In determining questions of duty and extension of duty to particular plaintiffs, the court in *Stevenson* echoed widespread speculation concerning the ripple effects of a negligence claim based upon pure economic loss and observed:

> Cases might well occur where a manufacturer would be obliged to close down his factory because of the inability of his supplier due to a fire loss to make prompt deliveries; the power company with a contract to supply a factory with electricity would be deprived of the profit which it would have made if the operation of the factory had not been interrupted by reason of fire damage; a man who had a contract to paint a building

---

13 *See Keister v. Talbott,* 182 W.Va. 745, 391 S.E.2d 895 (1990) (examining attorney's negligence in certifying or examining title to real estate); *Lucas v. Hamm,* 56 Cal.2d 583, 15 Cal.Rptr. 821, 364 P.2d 685 (1961), cert. denied 368 U.S. 987, 82 S.Ct. 603, 7 L.Ed.2d 525 (1962) (finding attorney whose negligence deprived intended beneficiary of proceeds of the will was liable to beneficiary); *Heyer v. Flaig,* 70 Cal.2d 223, 74 Cal.Rptr. 225, 449 P.2d 161 (1969) (attorney held liable for failing to inform plaintiff-beneficiary's mother of the testamentary consequences of a planned remarriage, reducing beneficiary's share of estate).

14 *See Galloway v. Cinello,* 188 W.Va. 266, 423 S.E.2d 875 (1992) (based upon West Virginia Code § 29C-6-101(1999), a notary public is liable to persons involved for all damages proximately caused by notary's official misconduct); *Biakanja v. Irving,* 49 Cal.2d 647, 320 P.2d 16 (1958) (notary public who failed to secure valid witnesses to signature of will held liable to intended beneficiary who was deprived of proceeds of will).

15 *See Western Union Tel. Co. v. Tatum,* 35 Ala.App. 478, 49 So.2d 673 (1950), *cert. denied,* 35 Ala.App. 478, 49 So.2d 673 (1950) (telegraph company could be held liable for delayed delivery of telegram containing a contract offer, thereby causing plaintiff to not obtain a contract); *Bluefield Milling Co. v. Western Union Tel. Co.,* 104 W.Va. 150, 139 S.E. 638 (1927) (proof of an unreasonable delay in the transmission of message creates a presumption of negligence on part of telegraph company).

may not be able to proceed with his work; a salesman who would have sold the products of the factory may be deprived of his commissions; the neighborhood restaurant which relies on the trade of the factory employees may suffer a substantial loss. The claims of workmen for loss of wages who were employed in such a factory and cannot continue to work there because of a fire, represent only a small fraction of the claims which would arise if recovery is allowed in this class of cases.

[C]

. . . .

Tort law is essentially a recognition of limitations expressing finite boundaries of recovery. Using the absurdity of these chain-of-reaction but purely logical examples, courts and commentators have expressed disdain for limitless liability and have also cautioned against the potential injustices which might result. This Court's obligation is to draw a line beyond which the law will not extend its protection in tort, and to declare, as a matter of law, that no duty exists beyond that court-created line. It is not a matter of protection of a certain class of defendants; nor is it a matter of championing the causes of a certain class of plaintiffs. It is a question of public policy. Each segment of society will suffer injustice, whether situated as plaintiff or defendant, if there are no finite boundaries to liability and no confines within which the rights of plaintiffs and defendants can be determined. We accept the wise admonition expressed over a century ago, in language both simple and eloquent, proven by the passage of time and the lessons of experience: "There would be no bounds to actions and litigious intricacies, if the ill effects of the negligences of men could be followed down the chain of results to the final effect." [C]

Certified Question Answered.

[Concurring opinions omitted]

Points for Discussion

1. For additional decisions addressing the issue of recovery for economic loss caused by unintentional maritime torts, *see* Robins Dry Dock & Repair Co. v. Flint, 275 U.S. 303 (1927), (cited by *Aikens*) and State of Louisiana ex rel. Guste v. M/V TESTBANK, 752 F.2d 1019 (5th Cir. 1986).

2. *Aikens* follows the majority rule. For a contrary approach and conclusion, *see* People Express Airlines, Inc. v. Consolidated Rail Corp., 100 N.J. 246, 495 A.2d 107 (1985), in which a railroad tank car accident required the

evacuation of the plaintiff's Newark, New Jersey airport offices. Noting what it perceived as "the hopeless artificiality of the *per se* rule against recovery for purely economic losses," the court concluded that "a defendant who has breached his duty of care to avoid the risk of economic injury to particularly foreseeable plaintiffs may be held liable for actual economic losses that are proximately caused by its breach of duty."

———————

D. Negligent Infliction of Emotional Distress

Daley v. LaCroix

384 Mich. 4, 179 N.W.2d 390 (1970)

T. M. KAVANAGH, Judge.

This appeal presents as a threshold question . . . viz., whether the **'impact' rule** in **emotional distress** has any continued vitality in the Michigan civil jurisprudence.

On July 16, 1963, about 10:00 p.m., defendant was traveling west on 15 Mile Road near plaintiffs' farm in Macomb county. Defendant's vehicle left the highway, traveled 63 feet in the air and 209 feet beyond the edge of the road and, in the process, sheared off a utility pole. A number of high voltage lines snapped, striking the electrical lines leading into plaintiffs' house and caused a great electrical explosion resulting in considerable property damage.

Plaintiffs claimed, in addition to property damage, that Estelle Daley suffered traumatic neurosis, emotional disturbance and nervous upset, and that Timothy Daley suffered emotional disturbance and nervousness as a result of the explosion and the attendant circumstances.

The case was tried to a jury in Macomb county circuit court. At the conclusion of plaintiffs' proofs, on motion of defendant, the trial judge directed a verdict against Timothy Daley in that no proper evidence of a personal injury to him had been presented, and against Estelle Daley in that she had failed to prove a causal relationship between the accident and her claimed personal injury. In the Leonard H. Daley action he directed the jury to disregard any proof of hospital expenses paid by plaintiff on behalf of Timothy and Estelle. The jury returned a judgment in favor of Leonard H. Daley for property damage in the amount of $2,015.20.

The Court of Appeals [c] affirmed the trial court's grant of a directed verdict upon the ground that Michigan law denies recovery for negligently caused emotional disturbance absent a showing of physical impact . . .

. . . .

Recovery for mental disturbance caused by defendant's negligence, but without accompanying physical injury or physical consequences or any independent basis for tort liability, has been generally denied with the notable exception of the *sui generis* cases involving telegraphic companies and negligent mishandling of corpses. [Cc]

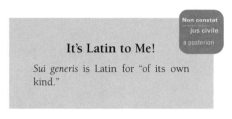

It's Latin to Me!

Sui generis is Latin for "of its own kind."

On the other hand the law had always permitted recovery in closely analogous situations notwithstanding the fact that plaintiff's mental or emotional reactions were a necessary element in the chain of causation. [C] Also, compensation for a purely mental component of damages where defendant negligently inflicts an immediate physical injury has always been awarded as 'parasitic damages.' [Cc]

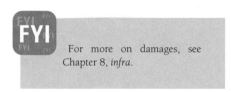

For more on damages, see Chapter 8, *infra*.

Where, however, a mental disturbance results immediately in physical injury, the authorities divide.[2] . . .

"The same objections against allowing recovery have been advanced: it is said that mental disturbance cannot be measured in terms of money, and so cannot serve in itself as a basis for the action; that its physical consequences are too remote, and so not 'proximately caused;' that there is a lack of precedent, and that a vast increase in litigation would follow." (Prosser, Torts (3d Ed.), § 55, p. 346)

. . . The final bastion against allowing recovery is the requirement of some impact upon the person of the plaintiff. It is this doctrine and its continued vitality in our State which we must now consider.

---

2 The state of case law in this field is excellently summarized in 64 A.L.R.2d 100, at p. 103:

"The case law in the field here treated is in an almost unparalleled state of confusion and any attempt at a consistent exegesis of the authorities is likely to break down in embarrassed perplexity. Early attempts by the courts to deal with the questions were complicated by the lack of any adequate body of legal authorities as well as by the inadequacy of the factual or scientific information available."

In the landmark decision of *Victorian Railways Commissioners v. Coultas* (1888), 13 A.C. 222, recovery for a much disputed damage to plaintiff's nervous system caused by defendant's oncoming train was denied upon the ground that:

> "Damages arising from mere sudden terror unaccompanied by any actual physical injury, but occasioning a nervous or mental shock, cannot under such circumstances, their Lordships think, be considered a consequence which, in the ordinary course of things, would flow from the negligence of the gate-keeper. If it were held that they can, it appears to their Lordships that it would be extending the liability for negligence much beyond what that liability has hitherto been held to be. Not only in such a case as the present, but in every case where an accident caused by negligence had given a person a serious nervous shock, there might be a claim for damages on account of mental injury. The difficulty which now often exists in case of alleged physical injuries of determining whether they were caused by the negligent act would be greatly increased, and a wide field opened for imaginary claims."

As a further hedge against fraudulent or fancied claims and the feared flood of litigation, a large number of American courts in adopting the *Victorian Railways Commissioners* rule superimposed the additional requirement of a contemporaneous physical impact. The leading American authority of Mitchell v. Rochester Ry. Co. (1896), 151 N.Y. 107, 45 N.E. 354, with 'remorseless logic' stated the position as follows [c]:

> "Assuming that fright cannot form the basis of an action, it is obvious that no recovery can be had for injuries resulting therefrom. That the result may be nervous disease, blindness, insanity, or even a miscarriage, in no way changes the principle. These results merely show the degree of fright, or the extent of the damages. * * * Therefore the logical result of the respondent's concession would seem to be, not only that no recovery can be had for mere fright, but also that none can be had for injuries which are the direct consequences of it. * * * These considerations lead to the conclusion that no recovery can be had for injuries sustained by fright occasioned by the negligence of another, where there is no immediate personal injury."

. . . .

The life of the law, however, has not been logic but experience. Bowing to the onslaught of exceptions[9] and the growing irreconcilability between legal fact and and **decretal** fiction, a rapidly increasing majority of courts have repudiated the 'requirement of impact' and have regarded the physical consequences themselves or the circumstances of the accident as sufficient guarantee.

Pertinently, the New York Court of Appeals in Battalla v. State (1961), 10 N.Y.2d 237, 219 N.Y.S.2d 34, 176 N.E.2d 729, expressly overruled its Mitchell v. Rochester Ry. Co., decision, supra, observing [c]:

"Before passing to a resume of the evolution of the doctrine in this State, it is well to note that it has been thoroughly repudiated by the English courts which initiated it, rejected by a majority of American jurisdictions, abandoned by many which originally adopted it, and diluted, through numerous exceptions, in the minority which retained it. Moreover, it is the opinion of the scholars that the right to bring an action should be enforced."

Based upon close scrutiny of our precedential cases and the authority upon which they rested and cognizant of the changed circumstances relating to the factual and scientific information available, we conclude that the 'impact' requirement of the common law should not have a continuing effect in Michigan and we therefore overrule the principle to the contrary contained in our previous cases.

We hold that where a definite and objective physical injury is produced as a result of emotional distress proximately caused by defendant's negligent conduct, the plaintiff in a properly pleaded and proved action may recover in damages for such physical consequences to himself notwithstanding the absence of any physical impact upon plaintiff at the time of the mental shock.

The rule we adopt today is, of course, subject to familiar limitations.

Generally, defendant's standard of conduct is measured by reactions to be expected of normal persons. Absent specific knowledge of plaintiff's unusual sen-

---

9 The divergent approaches of the courts to find an exception to the *Rochester Ry. Co.* rule is excellently summarized by Prosser, Torts (3d Ed.), pp. 350, 351:

"Apart from some quite untenable notions of causal connection, the theory seems to be that the 'impact' affords the desired guarantee that the mental disturbance is genuine. But the same courts have found 'impact' in minor contacts with the person which play no part in causing the real harm, and in themselves can have no importance whatever. 'Impact' has meant a slight blow, a trifling burn or electric shock, a trivial jolt or jar, a forcible seating on the floor, dust in the eye, or the inhalation of smoke. The requirement has even been satisfied by a fall brought about by a faint after a collision, or the plaintiff's own wrenching of her shoulder in reaction to the fright. 'The magic formula 'impact' is pronounced; the door opens to the full joy of a complete recovery.' A Georgia circus case has reduced the whole matter to a complete absurdity by finding 'impact' where the defendant's horse 'evacuated his bowels' into the plaintiff's lap."

sitivity, there should be no recovery for hypersensitive mental disturbance where a normal individual would not be affected under the circumstances. [Cc] . . .

Further, plaintiff has the burden of proof that the physical harm or illness is the natural result of the fright proximately caused by defendant's conduct. In other words, men of ordinary experience and judgment must be able to conclude, after sufficient testimony has been given to enable them to form an intelligent opinion, that the physical harm complained of is a natural consequence of the alleged emotional disturbance which in turn is proximately caused by defendant's conduct.

. . . .

In view of the above holding it becomes necessary to discuss another issue raised by plaintiffs-whether, considering the evidence in the light most favorable to plaintiffs, sufficient evidence was presented to create a jury question. Denying plaintiffs' motion for a new trial which sought to set aside the directed verdict against plaintiffs Timothy and Estelle Daley, the trial court reasoned:

> "There was no expert or medical testimony offered on behalf of the minor, Timothy. Extremely vague lay testimony was offered to the effect he was nervous. It was so vague and uncertain it did not, in the court's opinion, reach the dignity of possessing any evidentiary value whatever. It afforded the jury nothing into which the jury could put its 'damage-assessment teeth'.   Vachon v. Todorovich, 356 Mich. 182 (97 N.W.2d 122).

> "On behalf of Estelle Daley, Dr. Goldin, a psychiatrist, testified. Direct and cross examination were extensive. He testified clearly that she had been neurotic since childhood and the incident complained of did not cause her neurosis. Dr. Goldin indicated the incident could have broken down her 'balances' somewhat although she did not consult him until a year after the accident.

> "The lay testimony was of the same type as was given in Timothy's claim. It was vague and uncertain and indefinite."

From an examination of the evidence presented on behalf of Timothy Daley, we believe that, even though the question is a close one, on favorable view, he presented facts from which under our new rule, as announced in this case, a jury could reasonably find or infer a causal relation between defendant's alleged negligence and the injuries alleged. We conclude that Timothy Daley should be given an opportunity to prove his alleged cause of action, if he can do so, at a new trial.

Plaintiff Estelle Daley's claim that she suffered physical consequences naturally arising from the fright proximately caused by defendant's conduct is amply supported by the record. Her sudden loss of weight, her inability to perform ordinary household duties, her extreme nervousness and irritability, repeatedly testified to by plaintiffs, are facts from which a jury could find or infer a compensable physical injury.

The plaintiffs' testimony is also supported by the medical expert witness, who diagnosed plaintiff Estelle Daley as 'a chronic psychoneurotic * * * in partial remission,' and who attributed this state or condition to the explosion directly caused by defendant's acts:

"Q. I want to ask one more question, from everything that you know about this case, Doctor, do you feel there is a causal relationship between the explosion of July, 1963 and the symptoms that she has shown that you have reported?

"A. Yes, the trauma is the triggering point for her breaking the balance in her.

"Q. By trauma?

"A. Any trauma, may be emotional trauma or physical trauma, in this case having this explosive sound that she heard and the fears that were attendant with the explosive sounds."

We hold . . . that this record presents sufficient facts from which a jury could reasonably find, or infer therefrom, a causal relationship between the fright occasioned by defendant's negligence and the injuries alleged in plaintiffs' complaint. The trial court erred in taking plaintiff Estelle Daley's case from the jury. [Cc] It follows that the trial court also erred in striking plaintiff Leonard H. Daley's claim for **medical expenses**.

The order of the trial court granting directed verdicts against plaintiffs Estelle Daley and Timothy Daley and the Court of Appeals' affirmance thereof are reversed and the causes remanded for new trials. The judgment in favor of plaintiff Leonard H. Daley for property damage and the Court of Appeals' affirmance thereof are reversed and the cause remanded for a new trial to include the claimed medical expenses.

Costs shall abide the final result.

DETHMERS, T. G. KAVANAGH, ADAMS and BLACK, JJ., concurred with T. M. KAVANAGH.

. . . .

BRENNAN, Chief Justice (dissenting).

If this were a case where a definite and objective physical injury was produced without impact by the negligent act of the defendant, it might be appropriate to adopt the rule set forth in the [RESTATEMENT (SECOND) OF TORTS § 436(2)].

This is not such a case. Plaintiffs did not suffer definite and objective physical injury. Plaintiffs suffered, if anything, indefinite and subjective injury. Traumatic neurosis, emotional disturbance and nervous upset are the very type of complaints which ought to be eliminated by restricting 'no impact' cases to those in which a definite and objective physical injury occurs.

I would affirm the trial court's grant of directed verdict.

KELLY, J., concurred with BRENNAN, C.J.

———————

Points for Discussion

1. What must a plaintiff prove in order to prevail under the rule adopted by the *Daley* court?

2. Consider policy reasons for and against the impact rule, a rule not adopted in most jurisdictions.

3. Chief Justice Brennan argues that the plaintiffs suffered "indefinite and subjective injury." Do you agree with that view and characterization of the plaintiffs' injuries? If so, what legal and policy implications follow?

4. RESTATEMENT (SECOND) OF TORTS § 436(2), referenced by the court, provides that "[i]f the actor's conduct is negligent as creating an unreasonable risk of causing bodily harm to another otherwise than by subjecting him to fright, shock, or other similar and immediate emotional disturbance, the fact that such harm results solely from the internal operation of fright or other emotional disturbance does not protect the actor from liability."

———————

Hedgepeth v. Whitman Walker Clinic

980 A.2d 1229 (D.C. 2009)

PER CURIAM:

This appeal presents the court with a question we have addressed before, although not in the context of facts as stark as in this case, namely, whether a patient may recover damages for acute emotional distress resulting from a negligent misdiagnosis of Human Immunodeficiency Virus ("HIV"), where the misdiagnosis did not directly place the patient in physical danger.

There is no dispute that appellant, Terry Hedgepeth, never was HIV-positive, and, indeed, that laboratory test reports made available to appellees indicated that he was not. Nevertheless, because of a series of errors within Whitman Walker Clinic ("WWC"), appellant was misdiagnosed and misinformed that he was HIV-positive. The Superior Court granted summary judgment against appellant and dismissed his complaint, concluding that it was bound by our precedent requiring that a claimant be exposed to a "zone of physical danger" in order to claim **negligent infliction of emotional distress**. [C] Because as a division we are bound by prior decisions of this court, we too must affirm. [C]

I. Facts and Procedural Background

. . . [A]fter learning that his girlfriend was being treated for HIV, appellant went to WWC and requested an HIV test on December 13, 2000. At WWC, appellant told an intake worker that he "thought [he] had HIV" because he "found out that [his] girlfriend was HIV-positive." Relying at least in part on appellant's self-report, the intake worker made a notation in his file that he was HIV-positive. Appellant then underwent a blood test. Blood was drawn at WWC and sent to American Medical Laboratories, Inc. ("AML") for testing. The test administered by AML, an HIV-1/HIV-2 Antibodies ELISA test, was "non-reactive," meaning that appellant was not HIV-positive. WWC admits that because of an erroneous interpretation of the negative test report, a "Client Lab Results" form showed appellant as testing positive for HIV. The Client Lab Results form showing appellant as HIV-positive and the negative AML test results were made available to Dr. Mary Fanning, M.D. at WWC. When Dr. Fanning met with appellant, however, she misinformed appellant that he was HIV-positive, and noted in his patient file that he was HIV-positive, but asymptomatic and with a "normal" viral load.

After telling appellant that he was HIV-positive, WWC filed medical forms that made appellant's treatment at WWC eligible for funding under the Ryan White program. WWC personnel also signed off on an AIDS Drug Assistance Program form to apply for public assistance to pay for HIV medication for appellant. This form indicated that appellant's drug regimen required Combivir and Crixivan. This too was in error, as appellant was never prescribed either one of these drugs by WWC doctors and he never took any HIV medications.

Appellant continued to believe he was HIV-positive for five years, when another blood test revealed he is not positive for HIV. During that time, appellant suffered severe emotional distress. Appellant became depressed, which in turn affected all aspects of his life, including his relationship with his twelve-year-old daughter. Appellant's depression (as well as a knee injury) also eventually led him to lose his job as a restaurant manager. Following his misdiagnosis for HIV, appellant began to have suicidal thoughts, and he was committed to psychiatric wards on two occasions, first at George Washington University Hospital in January of 2001, and, later, at Sibley Hospital in 2002. He was prescribed medications for his depression . . . Despair over the misdiagnosis led appellant to "heavy" use of illegal drugs, to suffer from an eating disorder, and to become isolated from his relatives because of the shame he experienced from being HIV-positive. Appellant also began to have sexual intercourse with a woman he knew to be HIV-positive "[b]ecause [he] was diagnosed with HIV and there was no reason for [him] to live."

In mid-2005, appellant visited a different medical clinic, the Abundant Life Clinic, which ran an ELISA test to confirm his HIV status. The test revealed instead that he was not HIV-positive, and appellant was informed that he was HIV-negative.

II. Analysis

. . . .

In *Williams v. Baker,* 572 A.2d 1062, 1067 (D.C.1990) (en banc), we abandoned our longstanding rule that negligently inflicted mental distress was compensable only where it resulted from a direct physical impact. We maintained, however, a requirement that there be evidence that the plaintiff was in physical danger before she could recover damages for mental or emotional distress. [C] We held that "if the plaintiff was in the zone of physical danger and was caused by defendant's negligence to fear for his or her own safety, the plaintiff may recover for negligent infliction of serious emotional distress...." [C]

Since *Williams,* we have described the "zone of physical danger" test as a "strict" one and have reiterated that it "is the sole means for assessing a claim for damages for negligently inflicted emotional distress." *Washington v. John T. Rhines Co.,* 646 A.2d 345, 348 (D.C.1994). Moreover, we have insisted on this requirement not only in cases where the claimant has been a **bystander**, as in *Williams,* [cc] but also in cases where claimants had a direct relationship with the negligent actor. [Cc]

Although appellant presented evidence that supports that he suffered genuine and severe emotional distress during the years he believed he was infected with

HIV, he was never within a "zone of physical danger"--as defined by *Williams* and it progeny--as a result of appellees' HIV misdiagnosis. Because we, as a division, are bound by *Williams,* we conclude, as did the trial court, that even if appellant were otherwise able to prove his case, he cannot recover as a matter of law. As noted, appellant did not take medication and was not otherwise medically treated for the purported HIV-positive condition. Appellant does not argue-nor do we think our cases would support-that the needle pricks he underwent for blood tests satisfy the zone of physical danger requirement that has been enunciated in our cases.

Accordingly, the order of the Superior Court granting summary judgment is hereby

Affirmed.

RUIZ, Associate Judge, concurring:

This is a case in which no one disputes that appellant was owed a duty by appellees, and he has presented evidence that as a result of their breach of the standard of care, he suffered severe and verifiable emotional distress. Thus, but for the rule set out in *Williams,* as it has been applied in subsequent cases, appellant would be entitled to present his case to the jury. I write separately because I believe that this case warrants reconsideration by the full court of the applicability of the *Williams* "zone of physical danger" requirement to cases where foreseeable and severe emotional distress is inflicted on a patient as a result of breach of the standard of care. When dealing with common law, as we do here, courts should revisit and reconsider rules when subsequent legal or other developments so warrant.

In abandoning the "impact rule" and adopting the "**zone of danger**" doctrine in *Williams,* we meant to expand the reach of tort law, recognizing that "[t]he tortfeasor owes a duty of care to all persons who are physically endangered by the tortfeasor's negligent act, regardless of whether actual impact occurs." [C] In reaching this conclusion, we cited advances in medical research and improved diagnostic techniques that can objectively verify and assess emotional distress such as grief, anxiety and anger, which mitigated the concerns that had led to the requirement that, to recover for emotional distress, a plaintiff must have received an actual physical impact. [C] Unwilling to eliminate all limitations, *Williams* held that so long as the plaintiff is in the "zone of physical danger," she may recover for negligent infliction of emotional distress. [C]

Appellant presents compelling arguments as to why, just as we held in *Williams* that the requirement of physical impact should not be interposed to defeat otherwise meritorious claims, it is similarly unnecessary to require that a plaintiff be in the "zone of physical danger" as a condition of recovery in certain extreme situations. He points, specifically, to the circumstances of this case, where there was a direct doctor-patient relationship and the emotional harm caused by the negligent misdiagnosis of a potentially life-threatening condition is so severe, and so foreseeable, that it provides assurance that a claim to recover for negligent infliction of emotional distress is genuine, and is unlikely to subject doctors and other healthcare providers to spurious claims.

According to appellant, the concerns we expressed in *Williams*--the need to safeguard against fraudulent claims, the difficulty of establishing the nature and extent of emotional distress injury, and the fear of opening the floodgates of litigation, [c] are not present where the emotional injury is as serious and clearly caused by the negligent conduct as can be shown in this case. [C] . . .

Other jurisdictions have noted that there should be an exception to the "zone of physical" danger requirement for cases where there exists "an especial likelihood of genuine and serious mental distress, arising from the special circumstances, which serves as a guarantee that the claim is not spurious." *Johnson v. State,* 37 N.Y.2d 378, 372 N.Y.S.2d 638, 334 N.E.2d 590, 592 (1975) (citation omitted).[11] In *Baker v. Dorfman,* 239 F.3d 415, 422 (2d Cir.2000), the Second Circuit applied the *Johnson* rule to a case where the plaintiff sued to recover for emotional distress resulting from a clinic's negligence in informing him of an erroneous HIV-positive test. And, in some jurisdictions, the "zone of physical danger" requirement is applied only to claimants who are bystanders. *See Corgan v. Muehling,* 143 Ill.2d 296, 158 Ill.Dec. 489, 574 N.E.2d 602, 606 (1991) (noting that "the zone-of-physical-danger rule is patently inapplicable to direct victims"); *Johnson v. Commodore Cruise Lines, Ltd.,* 897 F.Supp. 740, 745 (S.D.N.Y.1995) ("The 'zone of danger' rule has to do with situations where plaintiff has witnessed or has otherwise been affected by a traumatic injury to a third person.").

This issue can present difficult choices and imprecise line-drawing. But it is an important one. I write separately because I believe that, if asked to do so, this may be an opportune case for the full court to revisit the question.

Hypo 7-4

Defendant Hospital calls the wrong telephone number and negligently informs Plaintiff, who had taken an AIDS test, that she is HIV-positive. Plaintiff, terrified by the phone call, cannot sleep or work and suffers from severe depression. Her husband believes that Plaintiff "cheated on me" and is threatening to file for divorce. Does (should) Plaintiff have a claim for negligent infliction of emotional distress?

---

11 In *Johnson,* the hospital negligently misinformed kin that a patient, who was very much alive, had died. [C]

> ## Hypo 7-5
>
> Defendant Hospital negligently diagnosed a three-year-old child with chlamydia, a sexually transmitted disease, and reported possible sexual abuse of the child to the authorities. The erroneous diagnosis is discovered two weeks later, after the child was removed from the home and the parents were interrogated by the police and child welfare authorities. As a result of the negligent diagnosis, the child's mother experienced and was prescribed medication for panic attacks, and the child's father developed an ulcer as his weight fell from 190 to 171 pounds. Do (should) the parents have a claim against Hospital for negligent infliction of emotional distress?

Thing v. La Chusa

48 Cal.3d 644, 771 P.2d 814, 257 Cal.Rptr. 865 (1989)

EAGLESON, J.

The narrow issue presented by the parties in this case is whether the Court of Appeal correctly held that a mother who did not witness an accident in which an automobile struck and injured her child may recover damages from the negligent driver for the emotional distress she suffered when she arrived at the accident scene. The more important question this issue poses for the court, however, is whether the "guidelines" enunciated by this court in *Dillon v. Legg* (1968) 68 Cal.2d 728 [69 Cal.Rptr. 72, 441 P.2d 912, 29 A.L.R.3d 1316] are adequate, or if they should be refined to create greater certainty in this area of the law.

Although terms of convenience identify the cause of action here as one for negligent infliction of emotional distress (NIED) and the plaintiff as a "**bystander**" rather than a "direct victim," the common law tort giving rise to plaintiff's claim is negligence. [Cc] It is in that context that we consider the appropriate application of the concept of "duty" in an area that has long divided this court--recognition of the right of persons, whose only injury is emotional distress, to recover damages when that distress is caused by knowledge of the injury to a third person caused by the defendant's negligence. Although we again find ourselves divided, we shall resolve some of the uncertainty over the parameters of the NIED action, uncertainty that has troubled lower courts, litigants, and, of course, insurers.

. . . .

On December 8, 1980, John Thing, a minor, was injured when struck by an automobile operated by defendant James V. La Chusa. His mother, plaintiff Maria Thing, was nearby, but neither saw nor heard the accident. She became aware of the injury to her son when told by a daughter that John had been struck by a car. She rushed to the scene where she saw her bloody and unconscious child, who she believed was dead, lying in the roadway. Maria sued defendants, alleging that she suffered great emotional disturbance, shock, and injury to her nervous system as a result of these events, and that the injury to John and emotional distress she suffered were proximately caused by defendants' negligence.

The trial court granted defendants' motion for summary judgment, ruling that, as a matter of law, Maria could not establish a claim for negligent infliction of emotional distress because she did not contemporaneously and sensorily perceive the accident. . ...

. . . .

[N]egligence cases permitting recovery of damages for emotional distress had developed in California at the time [*State Rubbish Collectors Assn. v. Siliznoff,* (1952) 38 Cal.2d 330, [240 P.2d 282]] was decided. Initially, however, in negligence cases the right to recover for emotional distress had been limited to circumstances in

Make the Connection

The *Siliznoff* case, recognizing one of the first intentional infliction of emotional distress actions, is discussed in Chapter 3, *supra.*

which the victim was himself injured and emotional distress was a "parasitic" item of damages, or if a plaintiff who had been in the "zone of danger" did not suffer injury from impact, but did suffer physical injury as a result of the emotional trauma. [Cc]

Where the conduct was negligent, emotional distress caused solely by fear for a third person's safety or apprehension of injury to the third person, was first recognized as an injury for which damages could be sought in *Dillon v. Legg, supra,* 68 Cal.2d 728.

But shortly before *Dillon,* in *Amaya v. Home Ice, Fuel & Supply Co.,* [59 Cal.2d 295, 29 Cal.Rptr. 33, 379 P.2d 513 (1963)], the court had declined the opportunity to broaden the right to recover for emotional distress. *Amaya,* after confirming that the "impact rule" making a contemporaneous physical impact a prerequisite to recovery for negligently induced fright or shock was not applicable in California, held damages could not be recovered by persons outside the zone of danger created by the defendant's negligence even when that shock was reflected in physiological symptoms. . . .

The court explained the restriction on the right to recover damages for emotional distress in negligence actions on the ground that the defendant had not breached a legal duty to the plaintiff. The court concluded that existence of a duty could not be defined, or left to the jury to find, on the basis of whether the injury was foreseeable. Rather the existence and scope of the defendant's duty in this context was one for the court.

. . . .

The *Amaya* view was short lived, however. Only five years later, the decision was overruled in *Dillon v. Legg, supra*, 68 Cal.2d 728. . . .

In *Dillon* itself, the issue was limited. The mother and sister of a deceased infant each sought damages for "great emotional disturbance and shock and injury to her nervous system" which had caused them great mental pain and suffering. Allegedly these injuries were caused by witnessing the defendant's negligently operated vehicle collide with and roll over the infant as she lawfully crossed a street. The mother was not herself endangered by the defendant's conduct. The sister may have been. The trial court had therefore granted the defendant's motion for judgment on the pleadings as to the mother, but had denied it with respect to the sister of the decedent. Faced with the incongruous result demanded by the "zone of danger" rule which denied recovery for emotional distress and consequent physical injury unless the plaintiff himself had been threatened with injury, the court overruled *Amaya*.

. . . .

The difficulty in defining the limits on recovery anticipated by the *Amaya* court was rejected as a basis for denying recovery, but the court did recognize that "to limit the otherwise potentially infinite liability which would follow every negligent act, the law of torts holds defendant amenable only for injuries to others which to defendant at the time were reasonably foreseeable." (*Dillon, supra*, 68 Cal.2d at p. 739.) Thus, while the court indicated that foreseeability of the injury was to be the primary consideration in finding duty, it simultaneously recognized that policy considerations mandated that infinite liability be avoided by restrictions that would somehow narrow the class of potential plaintiffs. But the test limiting liability was itself amorphous.

In adopting foreseeability of the injury as the basis of a negligent actor's duty, the *Dillon* court identified the risks that could give rise to that duty as both physical impact and emotional disturbance brought on by the conduct. Having done so, the *Dillon* court conceded: "We cannot now predetermine defendant's obligation in every situation by a fixed category; no immutable rule can establish the extent of that obligation for every circumstance of the future." [C] . . .

. . . .

The expectation of the *Dillon* majority that the parameters of the tort would be further defined in future cases has not been fulfilled. Instead, subsequent decisions of the Courts of Appeal and this court, have created more uncertainty. And, just as the "zone of danger" limitation was abandoned in *Dillon* as an arbitrary restriction on recovery, the *Dillon* guidelines have been relaxed on grounds that they, too, created arbitrary limitations on recovery. Little consideration has been given in post-*Dillon* decisions to the importance of avoiding the limitless exposure to liability that the pure foreseeability test of "duty" would create and towards which these decisions have moved.

. . . .

Both the physical harm and accident or sudden occurrence elements were eliminated, however, in *Molien v. Kaiser Foundation Hospitals, supra,* 27 Cal.3d 916, at least as to those plaintiffs who could claim to be "direct victims" of the defendant's negligence. The court held in *Molien* that a defendant hospital and doctor owed a duty directly to the husband of a patient who had been diagnosed erroneously as having syphilis, and had been told to so advise the husband in order that he could receive testing and, if necessary, treatment.

In finding the existence of a duty to the husband of the patient, the court reasoned that the risk of harm to the husband was reasonably foreseeable, and that the tortious conduct was directed to him as well as the patient. [C] The status of the plaintiff mother in *Dillon* was distinguished as she suffered her injury solely as a "percipient witness" to the infliction of injury on another. She was therefore a "bystander" rather than a "direct victim."

. . . .

The subtleties in the distinction between the right to recover as a "bystander" and as a "direct victim" created what one Court of Appeal has described as an "amorphous nether realm" [cc] and have contributed in some measure to the present difficulty in defining the scope of an NIED action. In *Andalon v. Superior Court, supra,* 162 Cal.App.3d 600, the court found that a physician's duty arose out of contract, after it had abandoned the effort to resolve the "direct" or "bystander" dilemma: "The problem which arises from this cryptic explanation is: how are we to distinguish between 'direct victim' cases and 'bystander' cases? An impression is given that the foreseeability of the particular injury to the husband alone explains the result. The inference suggested is that a 'direct victim' is a person whose emotional distress is a reasonably foreseeable consequence of the conduct of the defendant. This does not provide criteria which delimit what counts as reasonable foreseeability. It leads into the quagmire of novel claims which the Supreme Court foresaw as an unacceptable consequence of a 'pure' foreseeability analysis ...." [C]

"[F]oreseeability," the court noted later in *Newton v. Kaiser Foundation Hospitals, supra*, 184 Cal.App.3d 386, 391, "is endless because foreseeability, like light, travels indefinitely in a vacuum." *Molien, supra*, [c], thus, left to future cases the "unenviable tasks of distinguishing bystander from direct victim cases and establishing limits for the latter ... with a 'foreseeable' diversity of results." [C]

. . . .

. . . In order to avoid limitless liability out of all proportion to the degree of a defendant's negligence, and against which it is impossible to insure without imposing unacceptable costs on those among whom the risk is spread, the right to recover for negligently caused emotional distress must be limited.

We acknowledged and addressed one aspect of this problem in *Elden v. Sheldon* (1988) 46 Cal.3d 267 [250 Cal.Rptr. 254, 758 P.2d 582], holding that cohabitation, without formal marriage, did not constitute the close relationship contemplated by the *Dillon* guidelines and that foreseeability of injury alone does not justify imposition of liability for negligently caused emotional distress. In so doing, we again recognized that policy considerations justify restrictions on recovery for emotional distress notwithstanding the sometimes arbitrary result, and that the court has an obligation to establish those restrictions. *Elden* confirmed that those policy considerations include both the burden on the courts in applying vaguely defined criteria and the importance of limiting the scope of liability for negligence. If the consequences of a negligent act are not limited an intolerable burden is placed on society. A "bright line in this area of the law is essential." [C]

The issue resolved in *Elden* was too narrow to create that "bright line" for all NIED actions. This case, however, presents a broader question and thus affords the court a better opportunity to meet its obligation to create a clear rule under which liability may be determined. In so doing we balance the impact of arbitrary lines which deny recovery to some victims whose injury is very real against that of imposing liability out of proportion to culpability for negligent acts. We also weigh in the balance the importance to the administration of justice of clear guidelines under which litigants and trial courts may resolve disputes. . . .

. . . .

. . . The impact of personally observing the injury-producing event in most, although concededly not all, cases distinguishes the plaintiff's resultant emotional distress from the emotion felt when one learns of the injury or death of a loved one from another, or observes pain and suffering but not the traumatic cause of the injury. Greater certainty and a more reasonable limit on the exposure to liability for negligent conduct is possible by limiting the right to recover for negligently caused emotional distress to plaintiffs who personally and contemporaneously perceive the injury-producing event and its traumatic consequences.

Similar reasoning justifies limiting recovery to persons closely related by blood or marriage since, in common experience, it is more likely that they will suffer a greater degree of emotional distress than a disinterested witness to negligently caused pain and suffering or death. Such limitations are indisputably arbitrary since it is foreseeable that in some cases unrelated persons have a relationship to the victim or are so affected by the traumatic event that they suffer equivalent emotional distress. As we have observed, however, drawing arbitrary lines is unavoidable if we are to limit liability and establish meaningful rules for application by litigants and lower courts.

No policy supports extension of the right to recover for NIED to a larger class of plaintiffs. Emotional distress is an intangible condition experienced by most persons, even absent negligence, at some time during their lives. Close relatives suffer serious, even debilitating, emotional reactions to the injury, death, serious illness, and evident suffering of loved ones. These reactions occur regardless of the cause of the loved one's illness, injury, or death. That relatives will have severe emotional distress is an unavoidable aspect of the "human condition." The emotional distress for which monetary damages may be recovered, however, ought not to be that form of acute emotional distress or the transient emotional reaction to the occasional gruesome or horrible incident to which every person may potentially be exposed in an industrial and sometimes violent society. Regardless of the depth of feeling or the resultant physical or mental illness that results from witnessing violent events, persons unrelated to those injured or killed may not now recover for such emotional upheaval even if negligently caused. Close relatives who witness the accidental injury or death of a loved one and suffer emotional trauma may not recover when the loved one's conduct was the cause of that emotional trauma. The overwhelming majority of "emotional distress" which we endure, therefore, is not compensable.

Unlike an award of damages for intentionally caused emotional distress which is punitive, the award for NIED simply reflects society's belief that a negligent actor bears some responsibility for the effect of his conduct on persons other than those who suffer physical injury. In identifying those persons and the circumstances in which the defendant will be held to redress the injury, it is appropriate to restrict recovery to those persons who will suffer an emotional impact beyond the impact that can be anticipated whenever one learns that a relative is injured, or dies, or the emotion felt by a "disinterested" witness. The class of potential plaintiffs should be limited to those who because of their relationship suffer the greatest emotional distress. When the right to recover is limited in this manner, the liability bears a reasonable relationship to the culpability of the negligent defendant.

The elements which justify and simultaneously limit an award of damages for emotional distress caused by awareness of the negligent infliction of injury to a close relative are those noted in *Ochoa*—the traumatic emotional effect on the plaintiff who contemporaneously observes both the event or conduct that causes serious injury to a close relative and the injury itself. Even if it is "foreseeable" that persons other than closely related percipient witnesses may suffer emotional distress, this fact does not justify the imposition of what threatens to become unlimited liability for emotional distress on a defendant whose conduct is simply negligent. Nor does such abstract "foreseeability" warrant continued reliance on the assumption that the limits of liability will become any clearer if lower courts are permitted to continue approaching the issue on a "case-to-case" basis some 20 years after *Dillon*.

We conclude, therefore, that a plaintiff may recover damages for emotional distress caused by observing the negligently inflicted injury of a third person if, but only if, said plaintiff: (1) is closely related to the injury victim;[10] (2) is present at the scene of the injury-producing event at the time it occurs and is then aware that it is causing injury to the victim; and (3) as a result suffers serious emotional distress - a reaction beyond that which would be anticipated in a disinterested witness and which is not an abnormal response to the circumstances.[12] These factors were present in *Ochoa* and each of this court's prior decisions upholding recovery for NIED.

. . . .

The undisputed facts establish that plaintiff was not present at the scene of the accident in which her son was injured. She did not observe defendant's conduct and was not aware that her son was being injured. She could not, therefore, establish a right to recover for the emotional distress she suffered when she subsequently learned of the accident and observed its consequences. The order granting summary judgment was proper.

The judgment of the Court of Appeal is reversed.

Each party shall bear its own costs on appeal.

---

10 In most cases no justification exists for permitting recovery for NIED by persons who are only distantly related to the injury victim. Absent exceptional circumstances, recovery should be limited to relatives residing in the same household, or parents, siblings, children, and grandparents of the victim.

12 As explained by the Hawaii Supreme Court, "serious mental distress may be found where a reasonable [person] normally constituted, would be unable to adequately cope with the mental distress engendered by the circumstances of the case." (*Rodrigues v. State* (1970) 52 Hawaii 156, 173 [472 P.2d 509, 519-520].)

Points for Discussion

1. What distinguishes the "bystander" from the "direct victim"? What approaches have courts adopted in dealing with the liability issue in this category of cases?

2. Is it foreseeable that a mother, father, husband, or wife may suffer emotional distress as the result of a negligent act harming, say, a child or spouse even though they did not directly and contemporaneously witness the injury-causing event?

3. Who should be included in the court's "closely related to the injury victim" test? The relationships noted in the preceding question? A fiancé or fiancée? A lifelong best friend? Cousins? Nephews and nieces?

4. Define "serious emotional distress."

Hypo 7-6

A mother and her eleven-year-old son are out for an afternoon walk. As they near their home, the mother tells the son to go ahead to the house as she stops to talk to a neighbor. The son turns the corner and continues the walk home. A few seconds later, the mother hears the screeching of tires and a loud thump. Running around the corner, she is stunned to see her son lying in the middle of the street, bleeding and apparently unconscious, in front of an automobile. It is later determined that the driver of the car was intoxicated and had run a stop sign before striking the child. Mother becomes emotionally distraught.

Assume that the applicable law is the three-prong test of *Thing v. La Chusa*. Discuss.

Jaynes v. Strong-Thorne Mortuary, Inc.

124 N.M. 613, 954 P.2d 45 (1997)

FRANCHINI, Chief Justice.

1 Kiro Arthur Jaynes died in February of 1994. His brother, William Jaynes, and his son Arthur Jaynes, arranged for the burial with Strong-Thorne Mortuary,

doing business as Fairview Memorial Park. The Jaynes family owned a family plot at Fairview Memorial Gardens. In preparing the grave for Kiro, Strong-Thorne disturbed the grave of Vondaine Jaynes, William's mother. The surviving children of Vondaine Jaynes: William Jaynes, his brother, Robert Jaynes, and sisters, Linda Gray, and Carolyn Salter, sued Strong-Thorne Mortuary on claims of breach of contract, intentional infliction of emotional distress, negligent infliction of emotional distress, and prima facie tort.

2 Strong-Thorne moved for summary judgment on all the claims, and the district court granted the motion. . . . We affirm.

. . . .

21 *Negligent infliction of emotional distress.* . . . "[T]here exists in New Mexico no recognized cause of action for negligent infliction of emotional distress except for bystander liability." [C] Appellants, citing *Acosta v. Castle Constr.,* 117 N.M. 28, 868 P.2d 673 (Ct.App.1994), argue that it is not always necessary to show a visual observation of the wrongful conduct to establish bystander liability, and, that they had a contemporary sensory perception of the events giving rise to the claim sufficient to qualify as bystanders. It is correct that a person may be considered a bystander for the purpose of negligent infliction of emotional distress without a visual observation. In *Acosta* our Court of Appeals held that "visual observance of the accident is merely one of the ways in which the required 'sensory perception' may occur." [C] In that case the decedent's brother did not see him electrocuted. However, he heard screams, took no more than 18 seconds to run 322 feet from his office to the scene, and observed his brother's mouth and nostrils smoking, as a result of his electrocution. [C] The Court set aside the trial court's grant of summary judgment finding that a genuine issue of material fact existed "whether [Acosta] satisfied the 'contemporaneous sensory perception' requirement." [C]

22 The facts in this case are very different from those in *Acosta.* Although learning that their mother's grave had been disturbed and that her remains were exposed must have been painful for William Jaynes, his brother, and sisters, they did not learn about the desecration through any of their senses. They did not observe their mother's remains nor see her grave in a disturbed state. Although they did observe pieces of her casket on a truck or trailer in the vicinity of Kiro's grave this is not enough to satisfy the "contemporary sensory perception" requirement.

23 In *Flores* we explained that "[n]egligent services may give rise to claims for relief in both ordinary negligence and breach of contract." [C] Following *Flores,* family members may claim relief for ordinary negligence when the contract for funeral services is breached, because in a contract for funeral services the provider

of these services "assume[s] contract obligations to use reasonable skill and care to avoid severe mental distress to the family members of the deceased."[C]

24 It is the severity requirement which Appellants in this case have failed to allege. . . . In this case, neither William Jaynes nor his brother or sisters allege severe mental distress. . . . We hold that the district court properly granted summary judgment on the issue of negligent infliction of emotional distress.

25 Appellants urge us to consider adopting a tort for a funeral director's negligent infliction of emotional distress. Jurisdictions which recognize this cause of action do not require that a person seeking recovery for negligent infliction of emotional distress have a contemporaneous sensory perception of the negligent act. *Christensen v. Superior Court,* 54 Cal.3d 868, 876, 2 Cal.Rptr.2d 79, 820 P.2d 181, 189 (1991). In *Christensen* the mortuary harvested body parts from decedent's remains and sold them to a biological supply company, and otherwise mishandled human remains. *Christensen v. Superior Court,* 271 Cal.Rptr. 360 (1990) (cited for facts only). The facts of this case do not warrant our reaching the question of whether to recognize a cause of action in tort for a funeral director's negligent infliction of emotional distress. We are not persuaded that even jurisdictions which have adopted this cause of action would extend it to a case such as this one.

. . . .

28 *Conclusion.* We affirm the district court's grant of summary judgment for breach of contract, intentional infliction of emotional distress, negligent infliction of emotional distress and prima facie tort.

29 IT IS SO ORDERED.

——————————

Points for Discussion

1. The Jaynes' family did not actually see or perceive "through any of their senses" that their mother's grave had been desecrated. How did this fact affect the analysis and outcome of the case?

2. If you had been a member of the *Jaynes* court, would you have voted in favor of providing a tort cause of action and recovery for a funeral director's negligent infliction of emotional distress? Why or why not?

3. Emotional harm recoveries have been recognized in a number of jurisdictions where the defendant negligently transmitted an erroneous telegram informing

the recipient of an individual's death. *See, e.g.*, Camper v. Minor, 915 S.W.2d 437 (Tenn. 1996); Johnson v. State, 37 N.Y.2d 378, 334 N.E.2d 590 (1975).

4. The mishandling and negligent treatment and handling of dead bodies can also result in liability. *See, e.g.*, Mokry v. University of Texas Health Science Center, 529 S.W.2d 802 (Tex.Civ.App. 1975); Contreraz v. Michelotti-Sawyers, 271 Mont. 300, 896 P.2d 1118 (1995). *But see* Audia v. Rossi Brothers Funeral Home, Inc., 140 Ohio App.3d 589, 748 N.E.2d 587 (2000) (funeral home not liable for negligent infliction of emotional distress when husband and daughter of deceased woman discovered, during calling hours, that woman's body had been switched with body of another deceased woman).

———

E. Wrongful Life and Wrongful Birth

Clark v. Children's Memorial Hospital

391 Ill.App.3d 321, 907 N.E.2d 49, 329 Ill.Dec. 730 (2009)

Presiding Justice SHEILA M. O'BRIEN delivered the opinion of the court:

Plaintiffs, Amy and Jeff Clark, appeal the dismissal of their 16-count third-amended complaint alleging negligence against defendants, Children's Memorial Hospital and Doctor Barbara K. Burton, in connection with their son's birth with Angelman Syndrome. The primary issue on appeal is whether plaintiffs may recover in a so-called "**wrongful birth**" action for their damages for the extraordinary costs of caring for their unemancipated, disabled son beyond the age of **majority**. We hold that such damages are recoverable and affirm in part, reverse in part, and remand for further proceedings.

. . . .

Plaintiffs' first son, Brandon, was born July 13, 1997. At about 15 months of age, Brandon began to demonstrate certain developmental problems, including poor head growth and the inability to walk or talk.

On or about February 6, 2001, Amy Clark sought genetic testing and counseling from Doctor Burton to determine whether Brandon suffered from a condition known as Angelman Syndrome . . . a genetic disorder that can be caused by abnormal function of the gene UBE3A, located within a small region on chromosome No. 15. In about 80% of individuals with Angelman Syndrome, this region is deleted from the maternally derived chromosome due to a UBE3A truncating mutation. Individuals with Angelman Syndrome suffer from seizures, gait and movement disorders, hyperactivity, sleep disturbances, behavorial disorders, inappropriate happy demeanor, and mental retardation.

On February 6, 2001, Doctor Burton informed Amy that all known genetic mechanisms for Angelman Syndrome in Brandon had been ruled out. This information was incorrect, as Baylor College of Medicine previously had performed a UBE3A sequence analysis of Brandon's DNA and had issued a report on November 8, 2000, indicating that Brandon suffered from Angelman Syndrome due to a UBE3A truncating mutation. The siblings of a child with a mutation of the UBE3A gene have a 50% risk of being born with Angelman Syndrome.

Doctor Burton never obtained the results of the Baylor College of Medicine UBE3A sequence analysis and never informed Amy that the sequence analysis confirmed that Brandon suffered from Angelman Syndrome due to a UBE3A truncating mutation. Because Doctor Burton informed Amy that all known genetic mechanisms for Angelman Syndrome in Brandon had been ruled out, Amy planned to conceive another child.

On or about March 27, 2002, Amy gave birth to a son, Timothy. In June 2002, Amy noticed that Timothy experienced jerky and unpredictable motor movements, was inappropriately happy, and suffered from a flat occiput. In September 2002, Amy contacted Doctor Soma Das at the University of Chicago Hospitals to discuss Timothy's symptoms. Doctor Das informed Amy that Timothy and Brandon should be entered into a study of Angelman Syndrome, but that the boys could not enter the study without a complete set of Brandon's medical records.

On or about September 30, 2002, Amy contacted Baylor College of Medicine by phone to obtain a copy of Brandon's UBE3A sequence analysis. On or about September 30, 2002, Amy learned for the first time, from an employee of the Baylor College of Medicine, that the result of Brandon's UBE3A sequence analysis was "not normal." Subsequently, Timothy was diagnosed with Angelman Syndrome.

. . . .

The trial court determined plaintiffs could only recover damages for the extraordinary costs of caring for Timothy during his minority and could not recover damages for the extraordinary costs of caring for Timothy during his majority. . . .

Plaintiffs filed this timely appeal of the order dismissing all claims in their third-amended complaint for extraordinary expenses of caring for Timothy during his majority, damages for emotional distress, and damages for lost wages.

. . . .

First, plaintiffs contend the trial court erred in determining plaintiffs could not recover damages in their wrongful birth case for the extraordinary expenses of caring for Timothy during his majority. We begin our analysis by discussing *Siemieniec v. Lutheran General Hospital,* 117 Ill.2d 230, 111 Ill.Dec. 302, 512 N.E.2d 691 (1987), in which our supreme court recognized a claim for "wrongful birth."

In *Siemieniec,* Janice Siemieniec became pregnant in February 1980 and was concerned about the possibility that her baby might be born with hemophilia because two of her cousins were afflicted with that disease. [C] She sought genetic counseling at Lutheran General Hospital, where Doctor Carol Booth informed her of the availability of prenatal genetic diagnostic tests to determine the risk of the baby being born with hemophilia. [C] Mrs. Siemieniec purportedly told Doctor Booth of her desire to abort the pregnancy if there was a substantial risk of her bearing a hemophilic child. [C]

Doctor Booth referred Mrs. Siemieniec to Doctor Juan Chediak at Michael Reese Hospital. Doctor Chediak gave Mrs. Siemieniec the same advice regarding testing, and he promised to check on whether her cousins were registered hemophiliacs and to examine her deceased cousin's death certificate. [C] Two weeks later, Doctor Chediak sent a letter to Doctor Booth stating that Mrs. Siemieniec had a very low risk of being a carrier of classic hemophilia. [C] Doctor Booth sent a copy of the letter to Mrs. Siemieniec. [C] Based on this information, the Siemieniecs proceeded with the pregnancy. [C] Adam Siemieniec was born in October 1980 and later diagnosed with hemophilia. [C]

The Siemieniecs filed a complaint against Doctor Booth, Doctor Chediak, Lutheran General Hospital, and Michael Reese Hospital. [C] The complaint alleged that, as a proximate result of defendants' negligent diagnosis and failure to accurately advise Mrs. Siemieniec of the risk of the child being born a hemophiliac, Adam Siemieniec was not aborted, to his personal injury and to the financial injury of his parents. [C]

The trial court denied defendants' motions to dismiss, and the case eventually was appealed to the supreme court. [C] The pertinent issues before the supreme court were whether the child has a cause of action on his own behalf for extraordinary medical expenses during the age of majority and whether the parents have a cause of action for the extraordinary medical expenses of the hemophilic child during his minority. [C]

The supreme court began its analysis by examining whether actions for **"wrongful life"** and "wrongful birth" should be recognized in Illinois. With regard to "wrongful birth," the court stated:

" ' Wrongful birth' refers to the claim for relief of parents who allege they would have avoided conception or terminated the pregnancy by abortion but for the negligence of those charged with prenatal testing, genetic prognosticating, or counseling parents as to the likelihood of giving birth to a physically or mentally impaired child. The underlying premise is that prudent medical care would have detected the risk of a congenital or hereditary genetic disorder either prior to conception or during pregnancy. As a proximate result of this negligently performed or omitted genetic counseling or prenatal testing, the parents were foreclosed from making an informed decision whether to conceive a potentially handicapped child or, in the event of a pregnancy, to terminate the same." *Siemieniec,* 117 Ill.2d at 235, 111 Ill.Dec. 302, 512 N.E.2d 691.

With regard to "wrongful life," the supreme court stated:

"The corresponding action by or on behalf of an infant who suffers from a genetic or congenital disorder is denominated one for 'wrongful life.' The child claims that the physician or other health-care provider: (1) failed to accurately perform genetic screening tests prior to conception or to correctly inform the prospective parents of the hereditary nature of certain genetic disorders; (2) failed to accurately advise, counsel, or test his parents during pregnancy concerning genetic or teratogenic risks associated with childbirth suggested by maternal age, physical condition, family medical history, or other circumstances particular to the parents; or (3) failed to perform a surgical procedure intended to prevent the birth of a congenitally or genetically defective child. * * * The essence of the child's claim is that the medical professional's breach of the applicable standard of care precluded an informed parental decision to avoid his conception or birth. But for this negligence, the child allegedly would not have been born to experience the pain and suffering attributable to his affliction." *Siemieniec,* 117 Ill.2d at 236, 111 Ill.Dec. 302, 512 N.E.2d 691.

The supreme court refused to recognize a cause of action for "wrongful life," as it was unwilling to hold either that a child can recover damages for achieving life or that a child has suffered a legally cognizable injury by being born with a congenital or genetic impairment as opposed to not being born at all. [C] The supreme court further held "the public policy of this State to protect and to preserve the sanctity of all human life, as expressed in section 1 of the Illinois Abortion Law of 1975, militates against the judgment that an individual life is so wretched that one would have been better off not to exist." [C]

The supreme court next considered the Siemieniecs' claim for "wrongful birth," in which they alleged that they were tortiously injured because Mrs.

Siemieniec was deprived of the option of making an informed decision either to abort the fetus or give birth to a potentially genetically defective child. [C] The supreme court noted that the courts which have considered such wrongful birth claims have been "almost unanimous" in recognizing such a cause of action. [C] The supreme court further noted that judicial acceptance of wrongful birth claims has been premised on a number of rationales, including: the theory that wrongful birth claims are "a logical and necessary extension of existing principles of tort law"; that wrongful birth claims "vindicate[ ] the societal interest in reducing and preventing the incidence of [genetic] defects"; that to refuse to recognize wrongful birth claims would "frustrate" the policies of tort law to compensate the victim, deter negligence, and encourage due care; and to refuse to recognize wrongful birth claims would "impermissibly burden the constitutional rights involved in conception, procreation, and other familial decisions." [C]

The supreme court held, the "great weight of authority * * * forces [it] to agree with the majority of the courts and the legal commentators and to hold that an action for the wrongful birth of a genetically or congenitally defective child may be maintained by the parents of such child." [C]

The supreme court next considered the element of damages that may be recovered by the parents. The supreme court noted that most courts that have recognized a cause of action for wrongful birth have limited damages to the extraordinary expenses attendant to the care and treatment of the disabled child and have not included expenses associated with the raising of a healthy child. [C] The supreme court held that it aligned itself "with the majority of jurisdictions which have limited the parents' recovery of damages to the extraordinary expenses—medical, hospital, institutional, educational and otherwise—which are necessary to properly manage and treat the congenital or genetic disorder." [C]

Importantly for the purposes of the present case, the supreme court emphasized that the Siemieniecs sought to recover "only those extraordinary expenses that will be incurred *prior* to the child's reaching his majority." (Emphasis in original.) [C] Thus, the supreme court did not address the pertinent issue here, specifically, whether plaintiffs may recover damages in a wrongful birth action for the extraordinary costs of caring for their unemancipated, disabled son beyond the age of majority.

In the absence of any case law addressing whether plaintiffs may recover damages in a wrongful birth action for the extraordinary costs of caring for their unemancipated, disabled son beyond the age of majority, the parties look to Illinois statutory law for guidance. Plaintiffs cite section 15(a)(1) of the Rights of Married Persons Act, commonly referred to as the family expense statute, which states:

"The expenses of the family and of the education of the children shall be chargeable upon the property of both husband and wife, or of either of them, in favor of creditors therefor, and in relation thereto they may be sued jointly or separately." 750 ILCS 65/15(a)(1) (West 2006).

Plaintiffs contend they will be obligated to provide for the extraordinary costs of Timothy's postmajority medical care under the family expense statute, and they should be allowed to recover said costs from defendants.

Defendants counter that the family expense statute does not obligate parents to support their children after they reach the age of majority. Defendants contend that since plaintiffs have no legal liability for Timothy's postmajority costs under the family expense statute, recovery for such costs is not allowable. . . .

Defendants further argue that no Illinois statute requires parents to support their children after they reach the age of majority, even if the children are disabled and unemancipated. Defendants contend that in the absence of any statutory obligation to provide for Timothy's extraordinary, post-majority medical expenses, any payment by plaintiffs for such expenses are a voluntary assumption of financial responsibility for which defendants may not be held liable.

However, plaintiffs correctly respond that parents properly may be ordered to provide support of an unemancipated, disabled adult child pursuant to section 513(a)(1) of the Illinois Marriage and Dissolution of Marriage Act. Section 513(a)(1) states:

"(a) The court may award sums of money out of the property and income of either or both parties or the estate of a deceased parent, as equity may require, for the support of the child or children of the parties who have attained majority in the following instances:

"(1) When the child is mentally or physically disabled and not otherwise emancipated, an application for support may be made before or after the child has attained majority." 750 ILCS 5/513(a)(1) (West 2006)."

Thus, in section 513(a)(1), the legislature refused to foreclose all parental support for an unemancipated, disabled child after the age of majority, but instead allowed the trial court to determine "as equity may require" whether to award sums of money from the parties in a dissolution proceeding for the support of the disabled child. 750 ILCS 5/513(a)(1) (West 2006). Section 513(a)(1) reflects the legislative intent that the trial court consider the unique challenges and needs of mentally and physically disabled children on a case-by-case basis in determining whether to award moneys for the support thereof into their majority.

Although the present case is not a dissolution proceeding, section 513(a)(1) is relevant here in that it demonstrates the legislature's reluctance to draw an **arbitrary** line at the age of majority in determining when support obligations for unemancipated, disabled children must cease; rather, as discussed, the legislature determined that support obligations for an unemancipated, disabled child over the age of majority must be made on a case-by-case basis.

We see no cause why a different set of rules should apply here, in a nondissolution proceeding, and instead follow the lead of the General Assembly in refusing to automatically foreclose damages in a wrongful birth case for the extraordinary costs of caring and supporting an unemancipated, disabled child beyond the age of majority.

. . . .

. . . [W]e are *not* holding that parents always "own" the obligation for adult care of their disabled child, nor are we holding that medical providers have a cause of action against the parents of disabled children over the age of majority. Rather, our holding here is limited to answering "yes" to the question of whether plaintiffs may plead a cause of action for wrongful birth against a tortfeasor to recover damages for the extraordinary costs of caring for their unemancipated, disabled child beyond the age of majority.

Defendants contend plaintiffs should not be allowed to recover in wrongful birth the damages that Timothy is precluded from recovering in wrongful life. As discussed above, the supreme court refused to recognize a cause of action for wrongful life because it was unwilling to hold that a child can recover damages for achieving life or that a child has suffered a legally cognizable injury by being born with an impairment as opposed to not being born at all. [C] These principles are not implicated by an award in a wrongful birth case for the extraordinary costs of caring for an unemancipated, disabled child beyond the age of majority. Such an award does not constitute damages for achieving life, nor does it constitute a recognition or admission the child would have been better off never having been born; rather, the damages rightfully compensate the parents for the costs they will incur for caring for their disabled child.

Accordingly, we reverse the order of the circuit court . . . and remand for further proceedings.

This case presents perplexing issues over which many will differ, as we have differed from the able and learned trial judge here. We are mindful of the gravity of our words and this holding and we are eager for our supreme court and General Assembly to address these issues.

Affirmed in part and reversed in part; cause remanded.

STEELE, J. concurs.

GALLAGHER, J., specially concurring:

> **Take Note**
>
> The court expresses its hope that the state high court or legislature will address the matters decided by the appellate court. As asked earlier in this chapter, which institution—the judiciary or the legislature—should, and is best equipped to, fashion the legal rules such as those governing wrongful birth or wrongful life claims?

I write to concur with the majority and to make one succinct point: We believe very simply that it is the public policy of this State to allow parents of a permanently disabled child to allege and prove damages for the costs of caring for the child after reaching majority. The parents have a right to allege and seek to prove an action against tortfeasors, rather than have to assume personally the costs of providing for the child's lifelong needs. Moreover, we believe it is preferable for the alleged **tortfeasors** to pay these costs if found liable, than for the taxpayers to be required to assist in paying them.

In short, if there is a tortfeasor, that person should bear the burden he, she or it caused rather than the parents or society. If we are incorrect about our assumption regarding the State's public policy, it will be remedied through the legal or political process. Before that occurs, we think the approach we have chosen is a rational one.

———————————

Points for Discussion

1. What does the *Clark* court hold?

2. Define and distinguish actions for (a) "wrongful birth" and (b) "wrongful life."

3. Do you agree with Judge Gallagher that "if there is a tortfeasor, that person should bear the burden . . . rather than the parents or society"?

4. Does a mother owe a duty of care to her unborn fetus? *See* Remy v. MacDonald, 440 Mass. 675, 801 N.E.2d 260 (2004) (answering the question in the negative); Chenault v. Huie, 989 S.W.2d 474 (Tex. App. 1999) (same). In *Leighton v. City of New York*, 39 A.D.3d 84, 830 N.Y.S.2d 749 (2007), the

court held that an infant injured in utero when her then-four-month pregnant mother fell because of a defective toilet seat had a cause of action and could recover damages for her injuries.

5. RESTATEMENT (SECOND) OF TORTS § 869 (1979): "One who tortiously causes harm to an unborn child is subject to liability to the child for the harm if the child is born alive." There is no liability "[i]f the child is not born alive" unless recovery may be sought under a wrongful death statute.

6. Note that most states recognize a civil claim for an unborn child's wrongful death.

7. In *Endresz v. Friedberg*, 24 N.Y.2d 478, 248 N.E.2d 901 (1969), the court observed: "Even if, as science and theology teach, the child begins a separate 'life' from the moment of conception, it is clear that, except in so far as is necessary to protect the child's own rights . . . the law has never considered the unborn foetus as having a separate juridical existence . . . or a legal personality or identity until it sees the light of day." (Quotations marks and citations omitted). And: "It is argued that it is arbitrary and illogical to draw the line at birth, with the result that the distributees of an injured foetus which survives birth by a few minutes may have a recovery while those of a stillborn foetus may not. However, such difficulties are always present where a line must be drawn." Your reaction?

Procanik by Procanik v. Cillo

97 N.J. 339, 478 A.2d 755 (1984)

POLLOCK, J.

The primary issue on this appeal is the propriety of a grant of a partial summary judgment dismissing a "wrongful life" claim brought by an infant plaintiff through his mother and guardian *ad litem*. That judgment, which was granted on the pleadings, dismissed the claim because it failed to state a cause of action upon which relief may be granted. [C]

The infant plaintiff, Peter Procanik, alleges that the defendant doctors . . . negligently failed to diagnose that his mother, Rosemary Procanik, had contracted German measles in the first trimester of her pregnancy. As a result, Peter was born with congenital rubella syndrome. Alleging that the doctors negligently deprived his parents of the choice of terminating the pregnancy, he seeks general damages for his **pain and suffering** and for "his parents' impaired capacity to cope with his problems." He also seeks **special damages** attributable to the extraordinary expenses he will incur for medical, nursing, and other health care. The Law Division granted defendants' motion to dismiss, and the Appellate Division affirmed in an unreported opinion.

We granted certification [C]. We now conclude that an infant plaintiff may recover as special damages the extraordinary medical expenses attributable to his affliction, but that he may not recover **general damages** for emotional distress or for an impaired childhood. Consequently, we affirm in part and reverse in part the judgment of the Appellate Division, and remand the matter to the Law Division.

I

. . . .

. . . On June 9, 1977, during the first trimester of her pregnancy with Peter, Mrs. Procanik consulted the defendant doctors and informed Dr. Cillo "that she had recently been diagnosed as having measles but did not know if it was German measles." Dr. Cillo examined Mrs. Procanik and ordered "tests for German measles, known as Rubella Titer Test." The results "were 'indicative of past infection of Rubella.' " Instead of ordering further tests, Dr. Cillo negligently interpreted the results and told Mrs. Procanik that she "had nothing to worry about because she had become immune to German measles as a child." In fact, the "past infection" disclosed by the tests was the German measles that had prompted Mrs. Procanik to consult the defendant doctors.

Ignorant of what an accurate diagnosis would have disclosed, Mrs. Procanik allowed her pregnancy to continue, and Peter was born on December 26, 1977. Shortly thereafter, on January 16, 1978, he was diagnosed as suffering from congenital rubella syndrome. As a result of the doctors' negligence, Mr. and Mrs. Procanik were deprived of the choice of terminating the pregnancy, and Peter was "born with multiple birth defects," including eye lesions, heart disease, and auditory defects. The infant plaintiff states further that "he has suffered because of his parents' impaired capacity to cope with his problems," and seeks damages for his pain and suffering and for his "impaired childhood."

In April 1983, while this matter was pending in the Appellate Division, Peter moved to amend the first count to assert a claim to recover, as special damages, the expenses he will incur as an adult for medical, nursing, and related health care services. In its opinion, the Appellate Division denied without prejudice leave to amend. Although this claim was not raised before the trial court and not considered by the Appellate Division, fairness, justice, and judicial efficiency persuade us to consider the claim for special damages.

. . . .

II

In this case we survey again the changing landscape of family torts. [C] Originally that landscape presented a bleak prospect both to children born with birth defects and to their parents. If a doctor negligently diagnosed or treated a pregnant woman who was suffering from a condition that might cause her to give birth to a defective child, neither the parents nor the child could maintain a cause of action against the negligent doctor. *Gleitman v. Cosgrove,* 49 N.J. 22, 227 A.2d 689 (1967).

Like the present case, *Gleitman* involved a doctor who negligently treated a pregnant woman who had contracted German measles in the first trimester of her pregnancy. Reasoning from the premise that the doctor did not cause the infant plaintiff's birth defects, the *Gleitman* Court found it impossible to compare the infant's condition if the defendant doctor had not been negligent with the infant's impaired condition as a result of the negligence. Measurement of "the value of life with impairments against the nonexistence of life itself" was, the Court declared, a logical impossibility. [C] Consequently, the Court rejected the infant's claim.

The Court denied the parents' claim for emotional distress and the costs of caring for the infant, because of the impossibility of weighing the intangible benefits of parenthood against the emotional and monetary injuries sustained by them. Prevailing policy considerations, which included a reluctance to acknowledge the availability of abortions and the mother's right to choose to terminate her pregnancy, prevented the Court from awarding damages to a woman for not having an abortion. Another consideration was the Court's belief that "[i]t is basic to the human condition to seek life and hold on to it however heavily burdened." [C]

In the seventeen years that have elapsed since the *Gleitman* decision, both this Court and the United States Supreme Court have reappraised, albeit in different contexts, the rights of pregnant women and their children. The United States Supreme Court has recognized that women have a constitutional right to choose to terminate a pregnancy. *Roe v. Wade,* 410 U.S. 113, 93 S.Ct. 705, 35 L.Ed.2d 147 (1973). Recognition of that right by the high court subsequently influenced this Court in *Berman v. Allan, supra,* 80 N.J. 421, 404 A.2d 8 [1979].

In *Berman,* the parents sought to recover for their emotional distress and for the expenses of raising a child born with Down's Syndrome. Relying on *Roe v. Wade* . . . the Court found that public policy now supports the right of a woman to choose to terminate a pregnancy. [C] That finding eliminated one of the supports for the *Gleitman* decision-i.e., that public policy prohibited an award for depriving a woman of the right to choose whether to have an abortion. Finding that a trier of fact could place a dollar value on the parents' emotional suffering, the *Berman*

Court concluded "that the monetary equivalent of this distress is an appropriate measure of the harm suffered by the parents." [C]

Nonetheless, the Court rejected the parents' claim for "medical and other expenses that will be incurred in order to properly raise, educate and supervise the child." [C] The Court reasoned that the parents wanted to retain "all the benefits inhering in the birth of the child—i.e., the love and joy they will experience as parents-while saddling defendants with enormous expenses attendant upon her rearing." [C] Such an award would be disproportionate to the negligence of the defendants and constitute a **windfall** to the parents. [C]

The *Berman* Court also declined to recognize a cause of action in an infant born with birth defects. Writing for the Court, Justice Pashman reasoned that even a life with serious defects is more valuable than non-existence, the alternative for the infant plaintiff if his mother chose to have an abortion. [C]

More recently we advanced the parents' right to compensation by permitting recovery of the extraordinary expenses of raising a child born with cystic fibrosis, including medical, hospital, and pharmaceutical expenses. *Schroeder v. Perkel*, 87 N.J. 53, 432 A.2d 834 (1981)]. No claim on behalf of the infant was raised in that case, [c] and we elected to defer consideration of such a claim until another day. [C] That day is now upon us, and we must reconsider the right of a infant in a "wrongful life" claim to recover general damages for diminished childhood and pain and suffering, as well as special damages for medical care and the like.

III

The terms "wrongful birth" and "wrongful life" are but shorthand phrases that describe the causes of action of parents and children when negligent medical treatment deprives parents of the option to terminate a pregnancy to avoid the birth of a defective child. [C]In the present context, "wrongful life" refers to a cause of action brought by or on behalf of a defective child who claims that but for the defendant doctor's negligent advice to or treatment of its parents, the child would not have been born. "Wrongful birth" applies to the cause of action of parents who claim that the negligent advice or treatment deprived them of the choice of avoiding conception or, as here, of terminating the pregnancy. [Cc]

Both causes of action are distinguishable from the situation where negligent injury to a fetus causes an otherwise normal child to be born in an impaired condition. [Cc] In the present case, the plaintiffs do not allege that the negligence of the defendant doctors caused the congenital rubella syndrome from which the infant plaintiff suffers. Neither do plaintiffs claim that the infant ever had a chance to be a normal child. The essence of the infant's claim is that the defendant doctors wrongfully deprived his mother of information that would have prevented his birth.

Analysis of the infant's cause of action begins with the determination whether the defendant doctors owed a duty to him. The defendant doctors do not deny they owed a duty to the infant plaintiff, and we find such a duty exists. [Cc] In evaluating the infant's cause of action, we assume, furthermore, that the defendant doctors were negligent in treating the mother. Moreover, we assume that their negligence deprived the parents of the choice of terminating the pregnancy and of preventing the birth of the infant plaintiff.

Notwithstanding recognition of the existence of a duty and its breach, policy considerations have led this Court in the past to decline to recognize any cause of action in an infant for his wrongful life. The threshold problem has been the assertion by infant plaintiffs not that they should not have been born without defects, but that they should not have been born at all. [C] The essence of the infant's cause of action is that its very life is wrongful. [C] Resting on the belief that life, no matter how burdened, is preferable to non-existence, the *Berman* Court stated that the infant "has not suffered any damage cognizable at law by being brought into existence." [C] Although the premise for this part of the *Berman* decision was the absence of cognizable damages, the Court continued to be troubled, as it was in *Gleitman*, by the problem of ascertaining the measure of damages. [C]

The courts of other jurisdictions have also struggled with the issues of injury and damages when faced with suits for wrongful life. Although two intermediate appellate courts in New York and California recognized an infant's claim for general damages, those decisions were rejected by the courts of last resort in both jurisdictions. . . .

Other courts have uniformly found that the problems posed by the damage issues in wrongful life claims are insurmountable and have refused to allow the action on behalf of the infant. [Cc]

Even when this Court declined to recognize a cause of action for wrongful life in *Gleitman* and *Berman,* dissenting members urged recognition of that claim. . . .

Recently we recognized that extraordinary medical expenses incurred by parents on behalf of a birth-defective child were predictable, certain, and recoverable. *Schroeder v. Perkel, supra,* 87 N.J. at 68-69, 432 A.2d 834. In reaching that conclusion, we discussed the interdependence of the interests of parents and children in a family tort:

> The foreseeability of injury to members of a family other than one immediately injured by the wrongdoing of another must be viewed in light of the legal relationships among family members. A family is woven of the fibers of life; if one strand is damaged, the whole structure may suffer. The filaments of family life, although individually spun, create a web of interconnected legal interests. This Court has recognized that a

wrongdoer who causes a direct injury to one member of the family may indirectly damage another. [C]

When a child requires extraordinary medical care, the financial impact is felt not just by the parents, but also by the injured child. As a practical matter, the impact may extend beyond the injured child to his brothers or sisters. Money that is spent for the health care of one child is not available for the clothes, food, or college education of another child.

Recovery of the cost of extraordinary medical expenses by either the parents or the infant, but not both, is consistent with the principle that the doctor's negligence vitally affects the entire family. [C] . . .

Law is more than an exercise in logic, and logical analysis, although essential to a system of ordered justice, should not become a instrument of injustice. Whatever logic inheres in permitting parents to recover for the cost of extraordinary medical care incurred by a birth-defective child, but in denying the child's own right to recover those expenses, must yield to the inherent injustice of that result. The right to recover the often crushing burden of extraordinary expenses visited by an act of medical malpractice should not depend on the "wholly fortuitous circumstance of whether the parents are available to sue." [C]

The present case proves the point. Here, the parents' claim is barred by the statute of limitations. Does this mean that Peter must forego medical treatment for his blindness, deafness, and retardation? We think not. His claim for the medical expenses attributable to his birth defects is reasonably certain, readily calculable, and of a kind daily determined by judges and juries. We hold that a child or his parents may recover special damages for extraordinary medical expenses incurred during infancy, and that the infant may recover those expenses during his majority.

. . . .

In restricting the infant's claim to one for special damages, we recognize that our colleagues, Justice Schreiber and Justice Handler, disagree with us and with each other. From the premise that "man does not know whether non-life would have been preferable to an impaired life," . . . Justice Schreiber concludes that a child does not have a cause of action for wrongful life and, therefore, that is "unfair and unjust to charge the doctors with the infant's medical expenses." [C] Justice Handler reaches a diametrically opposite conclusion. He would allow the infant to recover not only his medical expenses, but also general damages for his pain and suffering and for his impaired childhood.

We find, however, that the infant's claim for pain and suffering and for a diminished childhood presents insurmountable problems. The philosophical problem of finding that such a defective life is worth less than no life at all has perplexed not only Justice Schreiber, but such other distinguished members of this Court as Chief Justice Weintraub, [c] Justice Proctor, [c] and Justice Pashman. [c] We need not become preoccupied, however, with these metaphysical considerations. Our decision to allow the recovery of extraordinary medical expenses is not premised on the concept that non-life is preferable to an impaired life, but is predicated on the needs of the living. We seek only to respond to the call of the living for help in bearing the burden of their affliction.

Sound reasons exist not to recognize a claim for general damages. Our analysis begins with the sad but true fact that the infant plaintiff never had a chance of being born as a normal, healthy child. For him, the only options were non-existence or an impaired life. Tragically, his only choice was a life burdened with his handicaps or no life at all. The congenital rubella syndrome that plagues him was not caused by the negligence of the defendant doctors; the only proximate result of their negligence was the child's birth.

The crux of the problem is that there is no rational way to measure non-existence or to compare non-existence with the pain and suffering of his impaired existence. Whatever theoretical appeal one might find in recognizing a claim for pain and suffering is outweighed by the essentially irrational and unpredictable nature of that claim. Although damages in a personal injury action need not be calculated with mathematical precision, they require at their base some modicum of rationality.

Underlying our conclusion is an evaluation of the capability of the judicial system, often proceeding in these cases through trial by jury, to appraise such a claim. Also at work is an appraisal of the role of tort law in compensating injured parties, involving as that role does, not only reason, but also fairness, predictability, and even deterrence of future wrongful acts. In brief, the ultimate decision is a policy choice summoning the most sensitive and careful judgment.

From that perspective it is simply too speculative to permit an infant plaintiff to recover for emotional distress attendant on birth defects when that plaintiff claims he would be better off if he had not been born. Such a claim would stir the passions of jurors about the nature and value of life, the fear of non-existence, and about abortion. That mix is more than the judicial system can digest. We believe that the interests of fairness and justice are better served through more predictably measured damages-the cost of the extraordinary medical expenses necessitated by the infant plaintiff's handicaps. Damages so measured are not subject to the same wild swings as a claim for pain and suffering and will carry a sufficient sting to deter future acts of medical malpractice.

As speculative and uncertain as is a comparison of the value of an impaired life with non-existence, even more problematic is the evaluation of a claim for diminished childhood. The essential proof in such a claim is that the doctor's negligence deprives the parents of the knowledge of the condition of the fetus. The deprivation of that information precludes the choice of terminating the pregnancy by abortion and leaves the parents unprepared for the birth of a defective child, a birth that causes them emotional harm. The argument proceeds that the parents are less able to love and care for the child, who thereby suffers an impaired childhood. [Cc]

Several considerations lead us to decline to recognize a cause of action for impaired childhood. At the outset, we note the flaw in such a claim in those instances in which the parents assert not that the information would have prepared them for the birth of the defective child, but that they would have used the information to prevent that birth. Furthermore, even its advocates recognize that a claim for "the kind of injury suffered by the child in this context may not be readily divisible from that suffered by her wronged parents." [C] We believe the award of the cost of the extraordinary medical care to the child or the parents, when combined with the right of the parents to assert a claim for their own emotional distress, comes closer to filling the dual objectives of a tort system: the compensation of injured parties and the deterrence of future wrongful conduct.

. . . .

The judgment of the Appellate Division is affirmed in part, reversed in part, and the matter is remanded to the Law Division. The infant plaintiff shall have leave to file an amended complaint asserting a claim for extraordinary medical, hospital, and other health care expenses.

[Concurring and dissenting opinions are omitted.]

Smith v. Cote

128 N.H. 231, 513 A.2d 341 (1986)

BATCHELDER, Justice.

In this interlocutory transfer of questions arising in a medical malpractice case, we address for the first time two difficult and troubling areas of the law of prenatal torts: wrongful birth and wrongful life.

The transferred record discloses the following facts. Plaintiff Linda J. Smith became pregnant early in 1979. During the course of her pregnancy Linda was under the care of the defendants, physicians who specialize in obstetrics and gynecology. Linda consulted the defendants on April 8, 1979, complaining of nausea, abdominal pain and a late menstrual period. The defendants prescribed

Keflex, an antibiotic, and recommended that Linda undergo a pregnancy test if her menstrual period did not begin. Two days later, Linda again consulted the defendants, complaining of an itchy rash and a slight fever. The defendants diagnosed Linda's condition as an allergic reaction to Keflex. Some time thereafter, the defendants determined that she was pregnant.

On August 3, 1979, nearly four months after the April visits, Linda underwent a rubella titre test at the direction of the defendants. The test indicated that Linda had been exposed to rubella. At the time the test was performed, Linda was in the second trimester of pregnancy.

Linda brought her pregnancy to full term. On January 1, 1980, she gave birth to a daughter, Heather B. Smith, who is also a plaintiff in this action. Heather was born a victim of congenital rubella syndrome. Today, at age six, Heather suffers from bilateral cataracts, multiple congenital heart defects, motor retardation, and a significant hearing impairment. She is legally blind, and has undergone surgery for her cataracts and heart condition.

In March 1984 the plaintiffs began this negligence action. They allege that Linda contracted rubella early in her pregnancy and that, while she was under the defendants' care, the defendants negligently failed to test for and discover in a timely manner her exposure to the disease. The plaintiffs further contend that the defendants negligently failed to advise Linda of the potential for birth defects in a fetus exposed to rubella, thereby depriving her of the knowledge necessary to an informed decision as to whether to give birth to a potentially impaired child. . . .

The plaintiffs do not allege that the defendants caused Linda to conceive her child or to contract rubella, or that the defendants could have prevented the effects of the disease on the fetus. Rather, the plaintiffs contend that if Linda had known of the risks involved she would have obtained a eugenic abortion.

. . . .

The defendants moved to dismiss . . . contending that the plaintiffs had failed to state a claim for which relief could be granted, and that New Hampshire law does not recognize the plaintiffs' asserted causes of action. Without ruling on the motion, the Superior Court (*Wyman,* J.) transferred [the case] to us . . .

. . . .

At the outset we emphasize that in deciding this case we express no opinion as to whether the plaintiffs ultimately should prevail in this action.

. . . .

I. *Wrongful Birth: Cause of Action*

We first must decide whether New Hampshire law recognizes a cause of action for wrongful birth. Although we have never expressly recognized this cause of action, we have considered a similar claim, one for "**wrongful conception**." In *Kingsbury v. Smith,* 122 N.H. 237, 442 A.2d 1003 (1982), the plaintiffs, a married couple, had had three children and wanted no more. In an attempt to prevent the conception of additional offspring, Mrs. Kingsbury underwent a tubal ligation. The operation failed, however, and Mrs. Kingsbury later gave birth to a fourth child, a normal, healthy infant. The plaintiffs sued the physicians who had performed the operation, alleging that in giving birth to an unwanted child they had sustained an injury caused by the defendants' negligence.

We held that the common law of New Hampshire permitted a claim for wrongful conception, an action "for damages arising from the birth of a child to which a negligently performed sterilization procedure or a negligently filled birth control prescription which fails to prevent conception was a contributing factor." [C] We reasoned that failure to recognize a cause of action for wrongful conception would leave "a void in the area of recovery for medical malpractice" that would dilute the standard of professional conduct in the area of family planning. [C]

In this case, the mother contends that her wrongful birth claim fits comfortably within the framework established in *Kingsbury* and is consistent with well established tort principles. The defendants argue that tort principles cannot be extended so as to accommodate wrongful birth, asserting that they did not cause the injury alleged here, and that in any case damages cannot be fairly and accurately ascertained.

. . . .

[W]e turn to the first issue before us: whether New Hampshire recognizes a cause of action for wrongful birth. In general, at common law, one who suffers an injury to his person or property because of the negligent act of another has a right of action in tort. [C] In order to sustain an action for negligence, the plaintiff must establish the existence of a duty, the breach of which proximately causes injury to the plaintiff. [C]

The first two elements of a negligence action, duty and breach, present no conceptual difficulties here. If the plaintiff establishes that a physician-patient relationship with respect to the pregnancy existed between the defendants and her, it follows that the defendants assumed a duty to use reasonable care in attending and treating her. [C] Given the decision in *Roe v. Wade,* we recognize that the "due care" standard, [c] may have required the defendants to ensure that Linda had an opportunity to make an informed decision regarding the procreative options available to her. [C] It is a question of fact whether this standard required the defendants, at an appropriate stage of Linda's pregnancy, to test for, diagnose, and disclose her exposure to rubella. The standard is defined by reference to the standards and recommended practices and procedures of the medical profession, the training, experience and professed degree of skill of the average medical practitioner, and all other relevant circumstances. [C]. We note that this standard does not require a physician to identify and disclose every chance, no matter how remote, of the occurrence of every possible birth "defect," no matter how insignificant. [C] If (1) the applicable standard of care required the defendants to test for and diagnose Linda's rubella infection in a timely manner, and to inform her of the possible effects of the virus on her child's health; and (2) the defendants failed to fulfill this obligation; then the defendants breached their duty of due care.

The third element, causation, is only slightly more troublesome. The defendants point out that proof that they caused the alleged injury depends on a finding that Linda would have chosen to terminate her pregnancy if she had been fully apprised of the risks of birth defects. The defendants argue that this hypothetical chain of events is too remote to provide the basis for a finding of causation.

We do not agree. No logical obstacle precludes proof of causation in the instant case. Such proof is furnished if the plaintiff can show that, but for the defendants' negligent failure to inform her of the risks of bearing a child with birth defects, she would have obtained an abortion. [Cc] To be sure, establishment of causation will depend on proof of a counterfactual, *i.e.*, had Linda been properly informed, she would have chosen to terminate her pregnancy. This circumstance, however, does not entail inability to establish such proof; it is present in every informed consent case involving a subjective standard of causation. [C]

We turn to the final element of a negligence action, injury. Linda contends that, in bearing a defective child after being deprived of the opportunity to make an informed procreative decision, she sustained an injury. The defendants argue that, because both benefits (the joys of parenthood) and harms (the alleged emotional and **pecuniary damages**) have resulted from Heather's birth, damages cannot accurately be measured, and no injury to Linda can be proved. The defendants in effect assert that the birth of a child can never constitute an injury to its parents; hence, when an actor's negligence causes a child to be born, that actor cannot be held liable in tort.

We do not agree. We recognize, as we did in *Kingsbury,* that in some circumstances parents may be injured by the imposition on them of extraordinary liabilities following the birth of a child. Under *Roe,* prospective parents may have constitutionally cognizable reasons for avoiding the emotional and pecuniary burdens that may attend the birth of a child suffering from birth defects. Scientific advances in prenatal health care provide the basis upon which parents may make the informed decisions that *Roe* protects. We see no reason to hold that as a matter of law those who act negligently in providing such care cannot cause harm, and hence are immune from suit. Such a holding would "leave[ ] a void in the area of recovery for medical malpractice and dilute[ ] the standard of professional conduct" in a growing and increasingly important professional field. [C]

. . . .

We hold that New Hampshire recognizes a cause of action for wrongful birth. Notwithstanding the disparate views within society on the controversial practice of abortion, we are bound by the law that protects a woman's right to choose to terminate her pregnancy. Our holding today neither encourages nor discourages this practice, [c] nor does it rest upon a judgment that, in some absolute sense, Heather Smith should never have been born. [C] We cannot (and need not, for purposes of this action) make such a judgment. We must, however, do our best to effectuate the first principles of our law of negligence: to deter negligent conduct, and to compensate the victims of those who act unreasonably.

II. *Wrongful Birth: Damages*

We next must decide what elements of damages may be recovered in a wrongful birth action. The wrongful birth cause of action is unique. Although it involves an allegation of medical malpractice, it is not (as are most medical malpractice cases) a claim arising from physical injury. It is instead based on a negligent invasion of the parental right to decide whether to avoid the birth of a child with congenital defects. When parents are denied the opportunity to make this decision, important personal interests may be impaired, including an interest in avoiding the special expenses necessitated by the condition of a child born with defects, an interest in preventing the sorrow and anguish that may befall the parents of such a child, and an interest in preserving personal autonomy, which may include the making of informed reproductive choices. [C] The task of assessing and quantifying the **tangible** and **intangible** harms that result when these interests are impaired presents a formidable challenge.

. . . .

A. Tangible Losses

The usual rule of compensatory damages in tort cases requires that the person wronged receive a sum of money that will restore him as nearly as possible to the position he would have been in if the wrong had not been committed. *Emery v. Caledonia Sand & Gravel Co.,* 117 N.H. 441, 447, 374 A.2d 929, 933 (1977). In the present case, if the defendants' failure to advise Linda of the risks of birth defects amounted to negligence, then the reasonably foreseeable result of that negligence was that Linda would incur the expenses involved in raising her daughter. According to the usual rule of damages, then, Linda should recover the entire cost of raising Heather, including both ordinary child-rearing costs and the extraordinary costs attributable to Heather's condition.

. . . .

The extraordinary costs rule ensures that the parents of a deformed child will recover the medical and educational costs attributable to the child's impairment. At the same time it establishes a necessary and clearly defined boundary to liability in this area. [C] Accordingly, we hold that a plaintiff in a wrongful birth case may recover the extraordinary medical and educational costs attributable to the child's deformities, but may not recover ordinary child-raising costs.

Three points stand in need of clarification. First, parents may recover extraordinary costs incurred both before and after their child attains majority. Some courts do not permit recovery of post-majority expenses, on the theory that the parents' obligation of support terminates when the child reaches twenty-one. . . .

Second, recovery should include compensation for the extraordinary maternal care that has been and will be provided to the child. Linda alleges that her parental obligations and duties, which include feeding, bathing, and exercising Heather, substantially exceed those of parents of a normal child. . . . We see no reason . . . to treat as noncompensable the burdens imposed on a parent who must devote extraordinary time and effort to caring for a child with birth defects. [Cc] . . .

. . . .

Third, to the extent that the parent's alleged emotional distress results in tangible pecuniary losses, such as medical expenses or counseling fees, such losses are recoverable. [Cc]

B. Intangible Losses

Existing damages principles do not resolve the issue whether recovery for emotional distress should be permitted in wrongful birth cases. Emotional distress damages are not uniformly recoverable once a protected interest is shown to have been invaded. [Cc]

. . . .

This case arises from a child's birth, not a child's injury or death. . . . [I]n wrongful birth cases the defendant's conduct results, not in injuries or death, but in the birth of an unavoidably impaired child. . . .

. . . We already have held that a wrongful birth defendant is liable for the pecuniary losses incurred by the parents. Were we additionally to impose liability for parents' emotional distress, we would run the risk of penalizing and overdeterring merely negligent conduct.

We hold that damages for emotional distress are not recoverable in wrongful birth actions. [Cc]

III. *Wrongful Life*

The theory of Heather's wrongful life action is as follows: during Linda's pregnancy the defendants owed a duty of care to both Linda and Heather. The defendants breached this duty when they failed to discover Linda's exposure to rubella and failed to advise her of the possible effects of that exposure on her child's health. Had Linda been properly informed, she would have undergone an abortion, and Heather would not have been born. Because Linda was not so informed, Heather must bear the burden of her afflictions for the rest of her life. The defendant's conduct is thus the proximate cause of injury to Heather.

This theory presents a crucial problem, however: the question of injury. It is axiomatic that there is no cause of action for negligence unless and until there has been an injury. [C] . . . In the present case Heather claims to have had an interest in avoiding "the lifetime of suffering inflicted on [her] by [her] condition." [C] In order to recognize Heather's wrongful life action, then, we must determine that the fetal Heather had an interest in avoiding her own birth, that it would have been best *for Heather* if she had not been born.

This premise of the wrongful life action—that the plaintiff's own birth and suffering constitute legal injury—has caused many courts to decline to recognize the claim. [C] According to the Supreme Court of Texas, the perplexities involved in comparing the relative benefits of life and nonexistence render it "impossible" to decide the question of injury. *Nelson v. Krusen,* 678 S.W.2d 918, 925 (Tex.1984). The notion that nonexistence may be preferable to life with severe birth defects appears to contravene the policy favoring "the preciousness and sanctity of human life." [C] . . .

Moreover, compelling policy reasons militate against recognition of wrongful life claims. The first such reason is our conviction that the courts of this State should not become involved in deciding whether a given person's life is or is not worthwhile. As one commentator has written, "[i]f plaintiff prevails, the result is a formal judicial declaration that it would have been better if plaintiff had not been born." [C] The right to life, and the principle that all are equal under the law, are basic to our constitutional order. N.H. CONST. pt. I, arts. 1, 2. To presume to decide that Heather's life is not worth living would be to forsake these ideals.

. . . .

The same cannot be said of wrongful life cases. At issue is not protection of the impaired child's right to choose nonexistence over life, but whether legal injury has occurred as a result of the defendant's conduct. The necessary inquiry is objective, not subjective; the court cannot avoid assessing the "worth" of the child's life. Simply put, the judiciary has an important role to play in protecting the privacy rights of the dying. It has no business declaring that among the living are people who never should have been born.

. . . .

. . . [W]e perceive no anomaly in permitting the parents but not the child to recover the medical and educational expenses attributable to the child's impairments. This result obtains because the loss at issue is the parents', not the child's. A parent is liable for a minor's medical expenses when the minor is living with or supported by the parents. Hence the parent, and not the child, may recover the medical expenses of a minor child injured by another. [C] If the parent has sustained an ascertainable injury, the right of recovery is properly hers. [A rule] permitting a child to recover for her parents' injury . . . contravenes the principle that "negligence as a legal source of liability gives rise only to an obligation to compensate the person immediately injured." [C]

. . . .

We decline to recognize a cause of action for wrongful life.

IV. *Conclusion*

. . . .

A. New Hampshire recognizes a cause of action for wrongful birth.

B. The damages that may be recovered are the extraordinary medical and educational costs of raising the impaired child. Such damages should reflect costs that will be incurred both before and after the child attains majority, and should include compensation for extraordinary parental care. In addition, the mother may recover her tangible losses attributable to her emotional distress.

C. New Hampshire does not recognize a cause of action for wrongful life.

. . . .

Remanded.

SOUTER, Justice, concurring:

I concur in the majority opinion and add this further word, not because

> **FYI**
>
> The concurring New Hampshire Supreme Court Justice David H. Souter was later appointed to and served for 19 years on the United States Supreme Court.

that opinion fails to respond to the questions transferred to us, but because those questions fail to raise a significant issue in the area of malpractice litigation that we address today. The trial court did not ask whether, or how, a physician with conscientious scruples against abortion, and the testing and counselling that may inform an abortion decision, can discharge his professional obligation without engaging in procedures that his religious or moral principles condemn. To say nothing about this issue could lead to misunderstanding.

In response to the questions transferred, the court holds that a sphere of medical practice necessarily permitted under *Roe v. Wade,* 410 U.S. 113, 93 S.Ct. 705, 35 L.Ed.2d 147 (1973), is not exempt from standards of reasonable medical competence. Consequently we hold that the plaintiff alleges a violation of the physician's duty when she claims, in the circumstances of the case, that prevailing standards of medical practice called for testing and advice, which the defendants failed to provide.

It does not follow, however, and I do not understand the court to hold, that a physician can discharge the obligation of due care in such circumstances only by personally ordering such tests and rendering such advice. The court does not hold that some or all physicians must make a choice between rendering services that they morally condemn and leaving their profession in order to escape malpractice exposure. The defensive significance, for example, of timely disclosure of professional limits based on religious or moral scruples, combined with timely referral to other physicians who are not so constrained, is a question open for consideration in any case in which it may be raised. [Cc]

Food for Thought

Why does Justice Souter focus on and leave open the question of the professional obligation of a physician who has conscientious scruples against or religious or moral objections to abortion? Is a pharmacist who is morally opposed to Plan B, the "morning after" pill, required to fill a prescription even though doing so is contrary to the pharmacist's religious views?

Points for Discussion

1. Compare and contrast *Procanik* and *Cote*. *Cote* recognizes wrongful birth but not wrongful life claims. What explanation does the court give for its recognition of the former but not the latter claims (one recognized in only a few jurisdictions)?

2. What duty, if any, is owed to an infant in a wrongful birth or a wrongful life

case? What duty is owed to the parents?

3. What are special damages? General damages?

4. The *Procanik* court stated that the "passion of jurors" would be stirred "about the nature and value of life, the fear of non-existence, and about abortion. That mix is more than the judicial system can digest." Do you agree with this view? Should there also be concern that the "passion of judges" will be stirred?

5. In *Chamberland v. Physicians for Women's Health, LLC*, 2006 WL 437553 (Conn. Super. 2006), the court upheld a jury verdict for the plaintiffs of a child born with spina bifida who alleged that the physicians' group negligently failed to inform the pregnant mother of a blood test to determine the risk of the birth defect. The jury awarded $5 million for economic damages and $7 million for non-economic damages.

6. For more on the wrongful life claim, *see* Philip G. Peters, Jr., *Rethinking Wrongful Life: Bridging the Boundary Between Tort and Family Law*, 67 Tul. L. Rev. 397 (1992).

Hypo 7-7

Patient sees Doctor, a gynecologist, complaining of abdominal pain. Doctor diagnoses Patient as suffering from an ovarian cyst on her right ovary. After informing Patient of the material risks and alternative available treatments, Patient agrees, at Doctor's suggestion, to undergo surgery for removal of the cyst. The express consent form that Patient executes with Doctor provides that Patient has consented to surgery to remove the cyst on Patient's right ovary only. However, while Patient is under anesthesia, Doctor makes the decision to remove the entire ovary rather than just the cyst. It is only after he does so that he examines Patient's left side and discovers that Patient has no left ovary or fallopian tube. The removal of the entire right ovary has rendered Patient infertile. After the surgery, Patient sues Doctor in negligence, alleging Doctor failed to obtain informed consent. Patient and Husband have three children, but wanted to have more. Discuss.

F. Owners and Occupiers of Land

1. Trespassers

Sheehan v. St. Paul & Duluth Ry. Co.

76 Fed. 201 (7th Cir. 1896)

[While walking on the defendant's railroad track, the plaintiff's foot was caught between a cattle guard and the rail. As the defendant's train approached, with the crew of the train not able to see the plaintiff until it was not possible to stop the train, the plaintiff was not able to free his foot or remove or untie his shoe, and the train ran over his foot. The trial court directed a verdict for the defendant, stating that the plaintiff's "injury did not occur through any wrongful action upon the part of the defendant." The plaintiff's appeal was considered in the following opinion.]

SEAMAN, District Judge, after stating the case as above, delivered the opinion of the court.

. . . .

The plaintiff, at the time of his injury, was neither in the relation of passenger, nor of one in a public crossing or place in which the public were licensed to travel, but, upon the undisputed facts, was a mere intruder on the tracks of the defendant,--technically, a **trespasser**; and this record excludes any of the elements of implied license or invitation to such use which have given rise to much discussion and diversity of views in the courts. Therefore the inquiry is here squarely presented: What is the duty which a railway company owes to a trespasser on its tracks, and how and when does the duty arise? The decisions upon this subject uniformly recognize that the trespasser cannot be treated as an outlaw; and, at the least, that, if **wantonly** injured in the operation of the railroad, the company is answerable in damages. Clearly, then, an obligation is placed upon the company to exercise some degree of care when the danger becomes apparent. Is it, however, bound to foresee or assume that rational beings will thus enter as trespassers in a place of danger, and to exercise in the running of its trains the constant vigilance in view of the probability which is imposed for public crossings? There are cases which would seem to hold this strict requirement [cc]; but by the great preponderance of authority, in this country, and in England, the more reasonable doctrine is pronounced, in effect, as follows: That the railroad company has the right to a free track in such places; that it is not bound to any act or service in anticipation of trespassers thereon; and that the trespasser who ventures to enter upon a track for any purpose of his own assumes all risks of the conditions which may be found there, including the operation of engines and cars. [Cc]

. . . .

The well-established and just rule which holds the railroad company to the exercise of constant and strict care against injury through its means is applicable only to the relation on which it is founded, of an existing duty or obligation. This active or positive duty arises in favor of the public at a street crossing or other place at which it is presumable that persons or teams may be met. It is not material, so far as concerns this inequity, whether the place is one for which a lawful right of passage exists, as it is the fact of notice to the company, arising out of its existence and the probability of its use, which imposes the positive duty to exercise care; the requirement of an extreme degree of care being superadded because of the hazards which attend the operations of the company. The case of a trespasser on the track, in a place not open to travel, is clearly distinguishable in the absence of this notice to the company. There is no **constructive notice** upon which to base the obligation of constant lookout for his presence there, and no actual notice up to the moment the trainmen have discovered the fact of his peril. As that peril comes wholly from his unauthorized act and temerity, the risk, and all positive duty of care for his safety, rests with the trespasser. The obligation of the company and its operatives is not, then, pre-existing, but arises at the moment of discovery, and is negative in its nature,--a duty, which is common to human conduct, to make all reasonable effort to avert injury to others from means which can be controlled. This is the issue presented here. It excludes all inquiry respecting the character of the roadbed, cattle guard, locomotive, brake appliances, or other means of operation, or of the speed or manner of running the train up to the moment of notice, because no breach of positive duty is involved. It is confined to the evidence relating to the discovery by the engineer and fireman of the plaintiff's peril, and to the efforts then made to avert the injury, and, out of that, to ascertain whether, in any view which may justly be taken, it is shown that these men, or the engineer, in disregard of the duty which then confronted them, neglected to employ with reasonable promptness the means at hand for stopping the train. . . .

. . . .

The court was clearly justified in directing a verdict for the defendant, and the judgment is affirmed.

Points for Discussion

1. Explain the court's decision and rationale. Is the court's decision and rule fair? Just? Harsh?

2. What rule should govern in negligence cases involving a trespasser injured by the acts or omissions of an individual or entity? Consider the wisdom or lack thereof of the following rule regarding trespassers: (a) No liability to trespassers. (b) Defendants are only liable to trespassers for **willful** and **wanton** conduct (the rule in some states). (c) Upon discovery of a trespasser, the defendant owes the trespasser the duty of ordinary care and avoidance of injury (the rule in most states).

3. For an interesting case on a homeowner's liability to a trespasser, *see Estate of Cilley v. Lane*, 985 A.2d 481 (Me. 2009) (because defendant's former boyfriend was a trespasser in her home, the defendant's only duty to him was to refrain from wanton, willful, or **reckless** behavior).

———————————

2. Licensees

Barmore v. Elmore

83 Ill.App.3d 1056, 403 N.E.2d 1355, 38 Ill.Dec. 751 (1980)

LINDBERG, Justice:

Plaintiff, Leon Barmore ("plaintiff"), appeals from an order of the Circuit Court of Winnebago County directing a verdict in favor of defendants, Thomas Elmore, Sr., and Esther Elmore ("defendants").

On August 8, 1977, at approximately 5:30 or 6:00 p.m., plaintiff came to the defendants' home. Both plaintiff and Thomas Elmore, Sr. ("Thomas, Sr.") were officers of a Masonic Lodge and plaintiff's purpose in making the visit was to discuss lodge business. During the course of plaintiff's visit, codefendant, Thomas Elmore, Jr., ("Thomas, Jr."), the defendants' 47-year old son, entered the living room with a steak knife. Thomas, Jr. said "You've been talking about me," and advanced toward plaintiff. Thomas, Sr. tried to restrain his son while plaintiff left the house. However, Thomas, Jr. was able to get away from his father, and he followed plaintiff out of the house where he stabbed the plaintiff several times in the chest area. Thomas, Sr. followed his son out of the house and, when he saw that plaintiff had been injured, he summoned help.

Based on this incident, plaintiff filed suit against Thomas Elmore, Sr., Esther Elmore, and Thomas Elmore, Jr. . . . .

. . . .

. . . [P]laintiff's basic contention is that defendants, as **landowners**, were negligent in failing to protect him from a dangerous condition upon their premises namely their son who had a history of mental illness. The extent of defendants' duty in this regard is based in part on whether the plaintiff had the status of an **invitee** or of a **licensee** at the time he visited the premises of the defendants. . . .

A person is an invitee on the land of another if "(1) he enters by invitation, express or implied, (2) his entry is connected with the owner's business or with an activity (that) the owner conducts or permits to be conducted on his land and (3) there is a mutuality of benefit or a benefit to the owner." [C] In order for a person to be classified as an invitee it is sufficient that he go on the land in furtherance of the owner's business. It is not necessary that the invited person gain an advantage by his entry on the land. [C] A **social guest** is considered a licensee and has been defined as one who enters the premises of the owner by permission, but for the licensee's own purposes. Therefore, a social guest is a person who goes on another's property for companionship, diversion, or entertainment. [C]

The duty owed by the owner of premises towards an invitee is greater than that owed towards a licensee. [C] A social guest as a licensee, generally must take the **premises** of his host as he finds them. However, the owner of the premises has a duty to warn the licensee of any hidden dangers which are unknown to his guest, of which he, the owner, has knowledge, and to refrain from injuring his guest willfully or wantonly. [Cc] Towards an invitee, the owner of the premises has a duty to exercise reasonable care in keeping the premises reasonably safe for use by the invitee. [C] There may be circumstances by which this duty is extended to include the responsibility to protect the invitee from criminal attacks by third parties. [C]

Plaintiff asserts that sufficient evidence was presented at trial to establish his status as an invitee at the time of the incident. Specifically, plaintiff argues that Illinois courts have recognized that the transaction of business of a fraternal organization carries with it such a status. . . .

There is no question that defendants failed to warn plaintiff of the danger that their son might attack a house guest before the attack was underway. Thus the issue becomes whether under the facts of this case defendants had a duty to do so. Plaintiff contends that he presented sufficient evidence by which a jury could have concluded that the defendants had knowledge of previous incidents which would charge them with a duty to anticipate the criminal acts of their son toward the plaintiff. We disagree.

Both defendants testified at trial that they knew that their son was going to the Janet Wattles Mental Health Center as an outpatient and that he was supposed to be taking medication for his emotional problems. Thomas, Jr. testified that in 1967 he had smashed the car window of his parents' next door neighbor with a hoe. He further testified that his parents knew about the incident after it had happened. Thomas, Jr. also told of another incident in which he had been involved where he had gotten into a "fricass" (sic) with his brother-in-law. This incident with the brother-in-law did not occur in his parents' home and there is no evidence that the defendants knew of this incident, although they testified that they knew that their son had been hospitalized on several occasions. Thomas, Jr. was hospitalized as a result of the incident with his brother-in-law. Another witness, Robert Johnson, testified that he had once gone to the defendants' home to pay lodge dues and was "tackled" by Thomas, Jr. While Johnson was not injured as a result of this incident, his eyeglasses were slightly damaged. Johnson was uncertain as to the exact time of the occurrence. On the basis of the plaintiff's testimony of when Johnson reported this attack to plaintiff, the trial court found that this incident occurred in 1968. In our view this finding is not against the manifest weight of the evidence. Moreover, there is no evidence that Esther Elmore knew of this incident. Thomas, Sr. testified that he did not see the incident when it occurred but that he heard about it afterwards from Johnson.

The previous incidents in which Thomas, Jr. was involved all had occurred almost ten years before the present attack. In the intervening years, Thomas, Jr. became employed at a Chrysler plant as an assembly worker. He worked there for approximately six and one-half years, until the early part of 1977. From 1973 to 1977, he lived away from home in a house that he was purchasing by himself. In approximately February, 1977, Thomas, Jr. moved back with his parents after he left his job at the Chrysler plant and became unable to pay his bills. During the period from February to August, 1977, Thomas, Jr. received several collection letters and calls regarding debts that he owed. His parents were aware that the receipt of these requests at times upset him, and that he was under stress during this time. However, there was no evidence that Thomas, Jr. had ever threatened or effected violence on anyone during this time. Indeed, plaintiff testified that he had been alone with Thomas, Jr. on one occasion and had had a friendly conversation about a ball game.

Verdicts should be directed and **judgments n. o. v.** entered "only in those cases in which all of the evidence, when viewed in its aspect most favorable to the opponent, so overwhelmingly favors movant that no contrary verdict based on that evidence could ever stand." [C] In our view, the evidence so overwhelmingly established that the defendants did not know or have reason to know of the possibility that Thomas, Jr. would commit a criminal act toward plaintiff that no contrary verdict could ever stand. Although they did know that their son had a history of mental problems and had been hospitalized several times, and also that approximately ten years before the present incident their son had been involved in what could be characterized as two or three violent incidents, the length of time which had passed would not give them reason to know that their son would engage in violent behavior in August, 1977. This conclusion is buttressed by the fact that plaintiff had previous contact with Thomas, Jr. without incident.

Accordingly, the judgment of the Circuit Court of Winnebago County is affirmed.

AFFIRMED.

Evans v. Hodge

2 So.3d 683 (Miss. App. 2008)

BARNES, J., for the Court.

¶ 1. Diane Evans sued Bonnie Hodge for negligence in the Circuit Court of Hinds County, Mississippi. Evans slipped and fell on Hodge's doorstep. The trial court granted Hodge's motion for summary judgment and dismissed the case with prejudice. Evans now appeals.

. . . .

¶ 2. On the evening of January 2, 2001, Evans traveled to Hodge's home in Pocahontas, Mississippi. Evans was delivering mail to Hodge's sister, Betty Russell, who was temporarily living with Hodge because Russell's house in Jackson had recently burned down. Russell and Hodge were college friends of Evans. Russell, who does not drive due to her impaired vision, made arrangements with Evans, her next door neighbor in Jackson, to pick up her mail approximately one time a week. Usually, Hodge drove to Jackson and retrieved Russell's mail from Evans. On the day at issue, however, for the first time, Evans drove to Hodge's home to deliver the mail to Russell; Evans believed Russell had received mail she was expecting from an insurance company. Presumably, the mail contained a check to pay for damages arising from the fire. Evans testified in her **deposition** that Russell, therefore, asked Evans to deliver her mail to Hodge's home in Pocahontas, and Evans agreed. After giving Russell her mail, Evans chatted with her for a little while, and then Evans left. During Evans's visit, Hodge was in the front den watching television. Hodge did not get up to let Evans out. As Evans was exiting Hodge's home, she slipped and fell on a doormat covered with ice and snow located at the entrance to Hodge's home.

¶ 3. In July 2001, Evans sued Hodge for negligence, claiming she was an invitee of Hodge. . . .

. . . .

5. Evans raises one issue: whether the trial court committed reversible error in granting summary judgment in favor of Hodge. . . . In a **premises liability** case such as this, the analysis proceeds in three steps. [C] First, the legal status of the injured person must be decided, as the duty of care owed the plaintiff is contingent on this status at the time of injury-that is, whether the injured person is an invitee, licensee, or trespasser. Second, the appropriate duty of care must be determined. Finally, it must be determined whether the landowner breached the duty. [C]

¶ 6. The distinction between the legal status at issue here, an invitee and a licensee, has been described by the supreme court as follows:

> [A]n invitee is a person who goes upon the premises of another in answer to the express or implied invitation of the owner or occupant for their mutual advantage. A licensee is one who enters upon the property of another for his own convenience, pleasure, or benefit pursuant to the license or implied permission of the owner....

[C] Social guests are licensees. [C] **Business visitors** are invitees. [C] The level of the duty of care Hodge, the property owner, owed Evans, the injured party, is dependent on Evans's legal status. A landowner owes the licensee the mere duty to refrain from willful or wanton injury to the licensee. [C] A landowner owes an invitee the higher standard of keeping "the premises reasonably safe and when not reasonably safe to warn only where there is hidden danger or peril that is not plain and open to view." [C]

¶ 7. Evans maintains that there is a genuine issue of material fact regarding whether she was an invitee or a licensee at the time of the accident. She also argues that there was a genuine issue of material fact regarding whether Hodge breached her duty to Evans to warn her about the icy doormat. After carefully examining the record pursuant to our **de novo** standard of review, we find there is a genuine issue of material fact regarding Evans's legal status based on the possible legal status of Russell in relation to her living arrangement with Hodge. Specifically, if Russell is found to be an invitee of Hodge, this determination will impact Evans's legal status in relation to Hodge. However, the evidence presented in the record is insufficient to determine the legal status of Russell in relation to Hodge; consequently, we find summary judgment inappropriate at this stage. Further, until Russell's legal status is determined, and hence Evans's legal status, the issue of whether Hodge breached the duty of care she owed to Evans cannot be determined.

It's Latin to Me!

De novo: Latin for "anew." An appellate court applying the *de novo* standard of review does not defer to the lower court's findings or legal analysis.

¶ 8. Evans's and Russell's legal statuses are determined by whether a "mutual advantage" was present and between whom. [C] The supreme court has held that a visitor may be considered an invitee if she comes to the home of another not for business, but for the occupant's benefit. [Cc] Regarding Evans, the record indicates she was not invited by Hodge-the homeowner and named defendant in this action-but by the third party, Russell, who was temporarily living at Hodge's residence while her own home was being repaired.

¶ 9. Although not addressed by either party, we find that Russell could not be an "**occupant**" of the home so as to be able to confer invitee status upon Evans within the meaning of *Pinnell.* According to Black's Law Dictionary, an "occupant" is the "[p]erson in possession"; "[p]erson having possessory rights, who can control what goes on on premises." *See* Black's Law Dictionary, 1078 (6th ed.1990). This definition is in keeping with the Restatement (Second) of Torts which imposes premises liability upon the "possessor of land"--"possessor" meaning a person in occupation of the land "with the intent to control it." Restatement (Second) of Torts § 328(E) (1965). Therefore, an "occupant" is not merely the person residing on the premises, but one with some type of control over it. The record indicates Russell did not have control over Hodge's property.

¶ 10. Regarding how Russell's status impacts Evans's status, the Restatement (Second) of Torts explains that the visitor does not have to be upon the property for the sole purpose of the possessor's business to be considered an "invitee," but "[t]he visit may be for the convenience or arise out of the necessities of others who are themselves upon the land for such a purpose." Restatement (Second) of Torts § 332 cmt. (g) (1965).[2] Additionally, while members of the possessor's family are usually deemed licensees, they will be considered invitees if they pay board or give other valuable consideration for their stay on the possessor's land. Restatement (Second) of Torts § 332 cmt. (i) (1965). We find these comments could be applicable to the instant case. Analyzing the two restatement comments together, Russell could be conferred invitee status due to a possible business relationship with the possessor/landowner, such as if she were paying rent during her stay with Hodge. Thus, any interactions Russell had with Evans for Russell's convenience or necessity could confer this same invitee status upon Evans. Neither party has argued this point,[3] but we find, based on our de novo review, it determinative regarding the propriety of the grant of the motion for summary judgment.

2 The Restatement cites as an example those "who go to a hotel to pay social calls upon the guests ... are business visitors, since it is part of the business of the hotelkeeper ... to afford the guest ... such conveniences." Restatement (Second) of Torts § 332 cmt. (g) (1965). [C]

3 The parties argued whether there was an advantage to Hodge by virtue of the delivery of the mail by Evans. Specifically, Evans argued that Hodge was an unintended beneficiary who derived an indirect benefit from Evans's mail delivery because Hodge, therefore, did not have to drive to Jackson to retrieve Russell's mail from Evans. However, Hodge was under no legal duty to perform this service for her sister, and if benefit to Hodge were the only way invitee status could be conferred upon Evans, we would affirm.

. . . .

¶ 12. For the above reasons, we find the trial court erred in granting Hodge's motion for summary judgment. Therefore, we reverse and remand for further proceedings consistent with this opinion.

. . . .

———————————

Points for Discussion

1. What questions must one ask in determining a land owner's legal responsibility in a premises liability case? What is the legally relevant inquiry in determining whether one is a trespasser? A licensee? An invitee?

2. What duty does an owner of premises owe to an invitee? A licensee? Do you agree with the characterization of social guests as licensees rather than invitees?

3. How did the Restatement inform the court's analysis? *See also* RESTATEMENT (SECOND) OF TORTS § 342 (1965).

———————————

3. Invitees

Campbell v. Weathers

153 Kan. 316, 111 P.2d 72 (1941)

WEDELL, Justice.

This was an action against three defendants to recover damages for personal injury. The demurrers of the defendants to plaintiff's evidence were sustained and those rulings constitute the sole basis of appeal.

The defendants were the lessee of a building, who operated a cigar and lunch business, the owner of the building and the owner's manager of the building.

The building was located in the business section of the city of Wichita, and at the southeast corner of an intersection. The building faced north. It had an entrance at the west front corner and from the north near the northeast corner. A counter was located near the front and across the building east and west. Between the east end of the counter and the east wall of the building was an opening which led to a hallway along the east side of the building. The hallway led to a toilet which was located toward the west end of the hall. The toilet was west of the hallway. Immediately to the south of the portion of the building occupied by the defendant lessee another tenant operated a shoeshine parlor. There was an entrance to the shoeshine parlor from the west. There was access from the shoeshine parlor to the toilet and hallway by means of a door into the toilet. There was a trap door in the floor of the hallway approximately half way between the lunch counter of the defendant lessee and the toilet room. The hallway was 29 or 31 inches in width. Plaintiff had been a customer of the defendant lessee for a number of years. On Sunday morning, June 4, 1939, between 8:30 and nine o'clock, plaintiff entered the place of business operated by the defendant lessee, as a cigar and lunch business. He spent probably fifteen or twenty minutes in the front part of the building and then started for the toilet. He stepped into the open trap door in the floor of the hallway, broke his right arm and sustained some other injuries.

. . . .

The first issue to be determined is the relationship between plaintiff and the lessee. Was plaintiff a trespasser, a lessee or an invitee? The answer must be found in the evidence. A part of the answer is contained in the nature of the business the lessee conducted. It is conceded lessee operated a business which was open to the public. Lessee's business was that of selling cigars and lunches to the public. It was conceded in oral argument, although the abstract does not reflect it, that the lessee also operated a bar for the sale of beer but that beer was not being sold on Sunday, the day of the accident. Plaintiff had been a customer of the lessee for a number of years. He resided in the city of Wichita. He was a switchman for one of the railroads. He stopped at the lessee's place of business whenever he was in town. He had used the hallway and toilet on numerous occasions, whenever he was in town, and had never been advised the toilet was not intended for public use. When he entered lessee's place of business the lessee and three of his employees were present. He thought he had stated he was going back to use the toilet but he was not certain he had so stated. None of the persons present heard the remark. He saw no signs which warned him not to use the hallway or toilet. The hallway was the direct route to the toilet. One of lessee's employees testified he had never been told by the lessee or anyone else that the toilet was a private toilet. On that point the examination of one of lessee's employees discloses the following:

> "Q. Mr. Hodges, do you know or were you ever told by Mr. Weathers or by Mr. Black or anybody who purported to be the manager of that building that that toilet was a private toilet? A. No, sir.

"Q. Do you know whether or not it was used by people other than the employees and the lessees and lessors of that building? A. Yes, sir.

"Q. Well, was it used? A. Yes, it was used by everybody, used by the public."

Appellant insists the evidence discloses he was an invitee. Appellee counters with the contention appellant was not an invitee for the purpose of using the toilet. Appellee also urges the evidence does not disclose appellant purchased anything on this particular day and hence was not a customer on this occasion.

The evidence disclosed appellant had been a regular customer of the lessee for a number of years and that he had used the hallway and toilet about every day he had been in town. He had never seen any signs not to use the toilet and had never been forbidden to use it. That the public had a general invitation to be or to become lessee's customers cannot be doubted. . . . Was a specific invitation or permission necessary in this case? That lessee was operating a lunch counter is conceded. No valid reason is advanced by appellee for his contention that lessee was not conducting a restaurant business within the ordinary acceptation of that term. We think it would constitute undue and unwarranted nicety of discrimination to say that a person who operates a public lunch counter is not engaged in the restaurant business. This appellee, a restaurant operator in the city of Wichita, was required by statute to provide a water closet for the accommodation of his guests. . . . The word "toilet" might refer to either a water closet or washroom. [C] Appellant was an invitee not only while in the front part of the place of business where the lunch counter was located but while he was on his way to the toilet. He was an invitee, at all times. [C] Appellant had been a regular customer of the lessee, for a number of years. We think it is clear appellant, in view of the evidence in the instant case, was an invitee to use the toilet. . . .

Can we say as a matter of law, in view of the record in this particular case, appellant had no implied invitation to use the toilet simply because he had not made an actual purchase before he was injured? . . .

The evidence of lessee's own employee was that the toilet was not regarded as a private toilet. The evidence is that it was not used only by the lessor, the lessee, or by lessee's employees. Did the evidence disclose that in addition to the lessor, the lessee and his employees, it was to be used only by customers of the lessee? It did not. . . . In a densely populated business district such a privilege may have constituted a distinct inducement to bring not only old customers like appellant, but prospective customers into lessee's place of business. It is not our province to say the lessee could not provide such facilities or hold out such inducement. The jury may ultimately determine that toilet facilities were not provided by the lessee for the use of everybody. Such a negative finding, however, would be directly contrary to the evidence before us now. The evidence before us now is the only evidence with which we are now concerned.

For this court to say everybody, including appellant, was invited to use the toilet facilities does not even require that we indulge in any inference in appellant's favor, it simply requires that, on demurrer, we do not ignore the plain, direct and unqualified testimony of lessee's own employee. But we need not rest our conclusion that appellant was an invitee upon the fact that, according to the unqualified evidence, not only customers but everybody was permitted to use the toilet.

The writer cannot subscribe to the theory that a regular customer of long standing is not an invitee to use toilet facilities required by law to be provided by the operator of a restaurant, simply because the customer had not actually made a purchase on the particular occasion of his injury, prior to his injury. It would seem doubtful whether such a doctrine could be applied justly to regular customers of a business which the law does not specifically require to be supplied with toilet facilities, but which does so for the convenience or accommodation of its guests. Women do a great deal of shopping. They sometimes shop all day in their favorite stores and sometimes fail to make a single purchase. Shall courts say, as a matter of law, they were not invitees of the business simply because on a particular occasion they had not yet made a purchase? No business concern would contend they were not invitees unless perchance an injury had occurred. Men frequently, during spare moments, step into a place of business, which they patronize regularly, where drinks, cigars and lunches are sold. They may not have intended definitely to presently make a purchase. They may, nevertheless, become interested, for example, in a new brand of cigars on display which they may purchase then or on some future occasion. Would the owner or operator of the business contend they were not invitees? We do not think so. Then why should courts arbitrarily say so, as a matter of law? It is common knowledge that business concerns invest huge sums of money in newspaper, radio and other mediums of advertising in order to induce regular and prospective customers to frequent their place of business and to examine their stocks of merchandise. They do not contemplate a sale to every invitee. They do hope to interest regular customers and cultivate prospective customers. It is common knowledge that an open door of a business place, without special invitation by advertisement or otherwise, constitutes an invitation to the public generally, to enter. Shall courts say, as a matter of law, that such guests are not invitees until they actually make a purchase? We think the mere statement of the question compels a negative answer. Manifestly this does not imply that a trespasser or that a mere licensee who enters the premises on a personal errand for the advancement of his own interest or benefit is entitled to the protection due an invitee. . . .

. . . .

It is true, in the instant case, there was no direct evidence of appellant's intention to make a purchase on this particular occasion. We cannot, however, well ignore the pertinent fact that this appellant had been a customer of lessee of long standing. He had patronized lessee's business for a number of years and had done so whenever he was in town. In view of this record, we think it unreasonable to say, as a matter of law, appellant lost his status as an invitee, simply because he had not actually made a purchase prior to his injury on this single occasion, or because the record did not affirmatively disclose he actually intended to make a specific purchase presently or in the future. . . .

. . . .

The order sustaining the demurrer of the lessee is reversed.

————————————

Foss v. Kincade

766 N.W.2d 317 (Minn. 2009)

ANDERSON, PAUL H., Justice.

On October 15, 2003, three-year-old David Foss, Jr., was seriously injured by a falling bookcase while he was a guest in the home of respondents Stephanie and Jeremy Kincade. David Foss, Sr., on behalf of himself and his son, brought this action against the Kincades alleging that the Kincades' negligent failure to secure the bookcase to a wall was the cause of David's injuries. The Rice County District Court granted summary judgment in favor of the Kincades, and the Minnesota Court of Appeals affirmed. We conclude that the Kincades did not owe a legal duty to affix a typical household object because the harm that occurred was not foreseeable. Therefore, we affirm.

On the afternoon of October 15, 2003, Peggy Foss, David's mother and Stephanie Kincade's longtime friend, had taken David and his nine-year-old sister on a visit to the Kincade home. The Kincade family had moved into the Foss's neighborhood a few weeks earlier and, as a result of the move, there were boxes around the house and some of the rooms were relatively empty of furniture. On that afternoon, the two women were visiting as their children played. While talking in the dining room, Peggy Foss and Stephanie Kincade heard a loud bang. They proceeded quickly to discover the source of the noise. The two women went to where they believed the sound had originated--a small spare bedroom located a few steps from the dining room. Upon entering the room, the women saw that a bookshelf, approximately six feet tall by three feet wide, had fallen over onto the carpeted floor.

Peggy Foss and Stephanie Kincade promptly lifted the bookcase and discovered three-year-old David underneath it. According to his mother, David was bleeding and turning blue. Stephanie Kincade quickly called 911, and an ambulance arrived to take David to the hospital. Because of the accident, David suffered serious injuries to his head, was hospitalized, and underwent several invasive surgical procedures. David's injuries caused permanent disfigurement to the left side of his face and possible future eye complications.

David's father, David Foss, Sr. (Foss), commenced this action against Jeremy and Stephanie Kincade in September 2005, claiming the Kincades' negligence caused David's injuries. Specifically, Foss claims that the Kincades were negligent in failing to secure the empty bookcase to the wall to prevent it from tipping over.

Peggy Foss gave deposition testimony that she had seen David climb shelves and furniture in her own home before the accident and had warned David not to do so. Peggy Foss said she was unaware of the bookcase in the Kincades' spare bedroom, but admitted she had probably been in the room at some point. While Peggy Foss acknowledges that she never specifically told the Kincades that David climbed furniture, she claims they were aware that David was a very active child.

The Kincades gave deposition testimony acknowledging that a bookcase could tip over, but said they did not consider the bookcase in the spare bedroom to be a hazard to their own children. After the accident, the Kincades remodeled the spare bedroom, and moved the bookcase to the garage. Although the Kincades were contacted by an insurance representative about possible claims on David's behalf, the Kincades threw the bookcase away in the spring of 2004.

The Kincades moved for summary judgment. The district court granted the motion, concluding that the Kincades owed no duty to David because the accident was not foreseeable. The court of appeals affirmed the district court, holding that because of the presence of Peggy Foss, the harm that occurred was not foreseeable, and therefore, the Kincades did not owe David a duty as matter of law. [C] . . . Foss appealed to our court, arguing that a landowner owes a duty of care to children invited on the premises and that the presence of the child's parent does not eliminate the duty owed by the landowner. . . .

. . . .

Foss argues that the Kincades' negligence was the cause of the injuries David sustained at the Kincades' residence. In order to establish a prima facie case of negligence, Foss must show the following elements: (1) that the Kincades owed a duty to David; (2) that the Kincades breached that duty; (3) that the breach of duty was the proximate cause of David's injury; and (4) that David did in fact suffer an injury. [C] The Kincades are entitled to summary judgment if the record reflects a complete lack of proof on any of the four elements of a prima facie case. [C]

Analyzing an action brought against a landowner alleging negligence begins "with an inquiry into whether the landowner owed the entrant a duty." [C] Historically in landowner cases, the duty owed to an entrant varied depending on the entrant's status on the land. [C] A landowner owed a greater duty to a licensee than a trespasser and an even greater duty to a business invitee than to a licensee. [C] But in *Peterson v. Balach*, [294 Minn. 161, 199 N.W.2d 639 (1972)] we "abolish[ed] the traditional distinctions governing licensees and invitees" in determining a landowner's duty. [C]

Peterson arose from the death of a child who, while an overnight guest in the defendant's cabin, was killed by carbon monoxide poisoning from a faulty propane refrigerator. [C] As part of our analysis in *Peterson*, we held that a landowner owed a duty "to use reasonable care for the safety of all such persons invited upon the premises, regardless of the status of the individuals." [C] Under the rule announced in *Peterson*, "the extent of the duty of the owner to inspect, repair, or warn those who come upon the land as licensees or invitees will be decided by the test of reasonable care." [C] According to *Peterson*, among the factors that might be considered in determining liability are "the circumstances under which the entrant enters the land (licensee or invitee); foreseeability or possibility of harm; duty to inspect, repair, or warn; reasonableness of inspection or repair; and opportunity and ease of repair or correction." [C]

Foss argues for application of the child trespasser standard as the minimum standard of care of this case. Before *Peterson*, landowner negligence cases involving injuries to children were decided using the standard on child trespassers, regardless of "whether the child is an invitee, licensee, or trespasser." [C] Cases decided after *Peterson* clarified that the child trespasser standard is the minimum standard of care and that child licensees and invitees have greater protection than a trespasser. [C] Therefore, although the child trespasser standard may set the minimum standard of care, the standard of care applicable to a child injured on a landowner's premises is the general duty of reasonable care. [C]

The result of this approach, as in any premises liability negligence case, is that the "landowner's duty of reasonable care is modified according to the expected use of the land." [C] Here, we must determine whether the harm to David implicated the Kincades' duty "to use reasonable care for the safety of all such persons invited upon the premises, regardless of the status of the individuals." [C]

. . . .

. . . [W]e . . . conclude that the harm to David was not reasonably foreseeable. When determining whether a danger is foreseeable, we "look at whether the specific danger was objectively reasonable to expect, not simply whether it was within the realm of any conceivable possibility." [C] A harm which is not objectively reasonable to expect is too remote to create liability. [C] Although in most cases the question of foreseeability is an issue for the jury, the foreseeability of harm can be decided by the court as a matter of law when the issue is clear. [C]

Foss argues that because the Kincades, in their deposition testimony, admitted to being aware that a bookcase that is not secured to the wall could fall, the harm that occurred was sufficiently foreseeable to create an issue of fact for the jury. We disagree. When dealing with a three-year-old child, the realm of possible harm is much larger than the realm of reasonably foreseeable harm. It is not difficult to make a laundry list of common household items with which a three-year-old could conceivably injure himself, but negligence law does not require a homeowner to take every precaution to guard against every possible eventuality. For example, we would not expect homeowners to bolt down their table lamps before inviting a three-year-old into their house, even though it is possible that such a child could be injured by pulling the lamp onto himself.

Here, David was injured by a similar common household item-a freestanding bookcase. Such bookcases are a common feature in homes, yet homeowners do not expect their guests to climb on them. The Kincades' admission that it is within the "realm of conceivable possibility" that a bookcase could tip over, therefore, does not create an issue of fact. It is not objectively reasonable to expect a homeowner to foresee that a guest-even a child-will climb on a bookcase nor is it objectively reasonable to expect the homeowner to guard against that possibility.

Foss argues that the harm to David was foreseeable because the Kincades' bookcase was not secured to the wall, on a carpeted floor, and left empty. It is not difficult to imagine a different set of facts in which a jury question as to foreseeability would arise. For example, if the Kincades had actual knowledge that David had a tendency to climb bookcases, the Kincades may have had a duty to secure the bookcase or at least to warn Peggy Foss of its unsecured condition. But those are not the facts before us. Here, the mere fact that the Kincades' bookcase was in a condition that made it more prone to tipping if climbed is unpersuasive because it was simply not reasonably foreseeable that David would try to climb on the bookcase.

. . . .

Affirmed.

PAGE, Justice (dissenting).

I respectfully dissent. I disagree with the court's determination that the Kincades had no duty to young David Foss because "it was simply not reasonably foreseeable that David would try to climb on the bookcase."

Other courts have noted "the known 'propensity' of children to roam and climb and play." [Cc] As one court put it, "Surely anyone familiar with young children, especially two-year-olds, is aware of their propensity to climb...." *Amos v. Alpha Prop. Mgmt.,* 73 Cal.App.4th 895, 87 Cal.Rptr.2d 34, 39 (Cal.Ct.App.1999). As a father and now a grandfather, I must agree with these courts. In addition to courts that have recognized children's propensity to climb, any number of Internet websites discuss child safety and the propensity for children to climb. *See, e.g.,* Household Safety: Preventing Injuries From Falling, Climbing, and Grabbing, http://kidshealth.org/parent/firstaid_safe/home/safety_falls.html (last visited May 7, 2009). Given the known propensity of young children to climb, the court is simply wrong in holding that it was not "reasonably foreseeable that David would try to climb on the bookcase."

I would hold that it is reasonably foreseeable as a matter of law that David might attempt to climb the bookcase, and I would reverse the lower courts and remand this matter to the district court for further proceedings.

. . . .

————————

Points for Discussion

1. Do you agree or disagree with the holdings and analyses of *Campbell* and *Foss*?

2. The *Campbell* court states that women "do a great deal of shopping" and "sometimes shop all day in their favorite stores and sometimes fail to make a single purchase." The court then opines that men frequently stop into places of business "during spare moments." Why might the court have made such references to female and male shoppers? Does this part of the court's opinion reveal a sexist judical worldview?

3. In his dissenting opinion in *Foss,* Justice Page argued that it was reasonably foreseeable that the child might attempt to climb the bookcase. Do you agree? Justice Page also noted that he is a father and a grandfather. Should a judge refer to his personal views, status, and experiences in determining legal questions?

————————

Hypo 7-8

Plaintiff is meeting her book club at The Book Cafe, a popular bookstore in town. The members of her book club never purchase their books from The Book Cafe. Instead they purchase all of their books online. They meet monthly at The Book Cafe because they enjoy the atmosphere of the well-read crowd and the comfortable, overstuffed armchairs. They bring their own drinks and snacks with them, as they prefer to keep the costs of their book club low. This evening, while entering The Book Cafe, Plaintiff (literally) runs into Delivery Guy, a vendor of The Book Cafe who is there to replenish the soda machines in the back of the store and who is not paying careful attention to where he is going. What duty of care, if any, does The Book Cafe owe to Plaintiff? To Delivery Guy?

4. Other Categories

a. Children and Attractive Nuisances

Pinegar v. Harris

20 So.3d 1081 (La. App. 2009)

GAIDRY, J.

The mother of a minor child appeals a summary judgment dismissing her cause of action for damages against the owner of a residence where her child was accidentally injured. . . .For the following reasons, we affirm the trial court's summary judgment but reverse the judgment sustaining the **exception**, and **remand** this matter for further proceedings.

. . . .

Brooklynn Pinegar is the minor daughter of the plaintiff, Jamie Pinegar Springman, and the defendant, Bradley Harris. . . .

Brooklynn was four years old when the accident forming the basis of this action occurred. On November 4, 2006, Brooklynn accompanied her father on a social visit to Michael Cas-

Food for Thought

What if Pinegar were suing the dad on behalf of Brooklyn? Should a child ever be permitted to sue a parent for injuries resulting from that parent's negligence? For further exploration of this issue, *see* Chapter 11, Immunities, *infra*.

cio's home in Baton Rouge. . . . On that day, Mr. Cascio, Mr. Harris, Mr. Cascio's brother, and another friend intended to watch a football game on television. . . .

After arriving at Mr. Cascio's home, Mr. Harris and Brooklynn played for a time. Neither Mr. Harris nor Mr. Cascio had consumed any alcoholic beverages. Shortly before the game began, Brooklynn became hungry and wanted something to eat. Mr. Harris took her into the kitchen and dining room, where he gave her a snack and positioned a dining table chair so that Brooklynn could watch cartoons on a small television in that room. The television, an older model, was securely placed on top of a small table or stand near the dining room table. On top of that television was a glass bowl (the turtle bowl) measuring about a foot wide and six inches tall, the home of a small pet turtle named "Vinnie." In that position, the turtle bowl was approximately four to five feet from the floor, and Brooklynn could not have reached it either standing on the floor or sitting in the chair. The bowl had a volume or capacity of about a gallon and a flat bottom, and was filled with water to about a third of its capacity. A rock or similar object was also placed within it.

After seating his daughter in the dining room, Mr. Harris walked into the living room to a point about ten steps from where she was seated, from which he had a clear view of her if looking in that direction. He stood there and began to watch the football game when he heard a crash. Mr. Harris estimated that only about ten seconds had elapsed from the time he left his daughter's side to the time he heard the crash. Mr. Harris ran to his daughter, who was on the floor with the broken turtle bowl. Brooklynn was bleeding from two lacerations to her face, over and under her right eye, and was immediately taken to the emergency room of Our Lady of the Lake Hospital in Baton Rouge.

Ms. Springman filed a petition for damages on March 8, 2007, naming Mr. Harris and Mr. Cascio as defendants. She alleged that Brooklynn's injuries were caused by the negligence of Mr. Harris and Mr. Cascio in failing to supervise Brooklynn on the date of the accident. She subsequently amended her petition to add Farmers Insurance Exchange (Farmers), Mr. Cascio's liability insurer, as a defendant.

. . . .

Mr. Cascio and Farmers answered the petition, denying liability, alleging that Brooklynn was under the control and supervision of Mr. Harris at the time of the accident, that the accident was the fault of either Brooklynn or Mr. Harris, and that Mr. Cascio had no responsibility to supervise Brooklynn.

On January 25, 2008, Mr. Cascio and Farmers filed a motion for summary judgment, seeking the dismissal of Ms. Springman's claims against them. . . .

. . . .

The motion for summary judgment and the **dilatory exception** of prematurity were heard by the trial court . . . Following argument by counsel . . . the trial court issued its ruling, granting the motion and sustaining the exception. In its oral reasons for judgment, the trial court determined that . . . the **doctrine of attractive nuisance** . . . was [not] applicable under the facts shown. The trial court further found that the placement of the turtle bowl was not unreasonably dangerous, and that Mr. Cascio did not breach any duty to Brooklynn under the circumstances. . . . Ms. Springer [sic] appeals both judgments.

. . . .

We reject the application of the doctrine of attractive nuisance to the factual circumstances of this matter. Unless a hidden trap or inherently dangerous instrumentality peculiarly attractive to children exists, there can be no application of the doctrine. [C] Generally, the doctrine of attractive nuisance is to be accorded limited application and employed by the courts only with caution. The instrumentality or condition must be of a nature likely to incite the curiosity of a child and fraught with such danger as to reasonably require precaution to prevent children from making improper use of it. [C] The evidence put forth by Mr. Cascio and Farmers demonstrates that while the presence of "Vinnie" within the turtle bowl might be expected to attract the attention and curiosity of a child, neither the object itself, a glass bowl serving as an aquarium or terrarium, nor its placement atop the television was inherently or unreasonably dangerous.

Brooklynn had no known behavioral problems, and had never broken anything at Mr. Cascio's home on any prior visit. The deposition testimony of Ms. Springman indicates that Brooklynn advised the emergency room physician that she pulled the chair in which she was sitting closer to the television and stood on it to get a closer look at the turtle bowl. That testimony also suggests that Brooklynn either struck the television accidentally or attempted to lift the turtle bowl. However, the undisputed testimony of Mr. Harris demonstrated that any such actions on the part of Brooklynn took place within the very brief interval (about ten seconds) from when he left her sitting on the chair, walked about ten steps away to the living room, and briefly directed his attention to the football game. The evidence further confirms that Mr. Cascio had no reason to believe that Brooklynn was not being adequately supervised by her father nor that Brooklynn would attempt to stand on the chair in an attempt to obtain an object out of her normal reach, and that Mr. Cascio had not been asked to assist in her supervision.

We must agree with the trial court's conclusion that the turtle bowl was not unreasonably dangerous and that Mr. Cascio did not breach a specific legal duty to Brooklynn under the circumstances shown. Life is full of risk, but not every risk is unreasonable and actionable. [C]

. . . .

The summary judgment of the trial court dismissing with prejudice the cause of action of the plaintiff, Jamie Pinegar Springer, against the defendants, Michael Cascio and Farmers Insurance Exchange, is affirmed. . . . The costs of this appeal are assessed in equal proportions to the plaintiff and the defendant, Bradley Harris.

————

Points for Discussion

1. What condition constitutes an "attractive nuisance"? *See, e.g.,* Cruzen v. Sports Auth., 369 F.Supp.2d 1003 (S.D. Ill. 2005) (pogo stick not an attractive nuisance); Norberg v. Labor Ready, Inc., 384 F.Supp.2d 1328, 1333 (S.D. Iowa 2005) (box of toys not an attractive nuisance); Butler v. Newark Country Club, Inc., 2005 WL 2158637 (August 29, 2005) (iced over irrigation pond on golf course not attractive nuisance); *but see* Dilley v. S & R Holdings, LLC, 137 Wash. App. 774, 154 P.3d 955 (Wash. Ct. App. 2007) (pit on defendant's land ruled attractive nuisance).

2. Is it foreseeable that a 4-year-old child could be attracted and drawn to a turtle in a glass bowl? If your answer is yes, is *Pinegar* wrongly decided?

3. The court notes that the child, Brooklyn, had no known behavioral problems and had not broken anything on prior visits to the Cascio home. Why are these facts significant?

4. An attractive nuisance need be neither attractive nor a nuisance. The condition of the premises need not be that which attracted the child or children to the premises. Likewise, whether the condition constitutes a nuisance is not relevant to the defendant's lability. *See, e.g.* Norberg v. Labor Ready, Inc., 384 F.Supp.2d 1328, 1333 (S.D. Iowa 2005) ("The so-called attractive nuisance doctrine was merely another attempt to ameliorate the harsh result of … trespasser status when applied to children. … Most jurisdictions now agree the element of 'attraction' is important only insofar as it may mean the presence of a child is to be anticipated, and that the basis of liability is merely the foreseeability of harm to the child."). *See also* Chapter 14, *infra*, exploring the tort of nuisance.

————

b. Public Employees or Officials

Rivas v. Oxon Hill Joint Venture

130 Md.App. 101, 744 A.2d 1076 (2000)

BYRNES, Judge.

The Circuit Court for Prince George's County granted summary judgment in favor of Oxon Hill Joint Venture ("Oxon Hill") and Southern Management Corporation ("Southern"), appellees, in a **slip and fall** tort action brought against them by Jaime Rivas, appellant. On review, Rivas poses the following question, which we have rephrased:

> Did the circuit court err as a matter of law in ruling that the duty of care owed to him was that owed to a licensee, not that owed to an invitee?

. . . .

On the evening of February 15, 1995, Jaime Rivas, a deputy sheriff for Prince George's County, was going to an apartment in the Oxon Hill Village Apartments to serve a witness in a district court landlord-tenant case with a subpoena. Rivas parked his car on the apartment complex parking lot, near the unit in which the witness lived. He got out of his car and started to walk across a stretch of asphalt ten to fifteen feet from the sidewalk of the apartment complex. As he did so, he slipped and fell on a patch of ice, sustaining serious personal injuries.

Rivas filed a negligence action in the Circuit Court for Prince George's County against Oxon Hill, the owner of the apartment complex, and Southern, Oxon Hill's managing agent. He alleged that he had been an invitee on the premises, that Oxon Hill and Southern had breached their duty to keep the premises reasonably safe, and that their breach of duty had been the proximate cause of his injuries. . . .

Upon the completion of discovery, Oxon Hill and Southern filed a joint motion for summary judgment. They argued that, as a law enforcement officer, Rivas had assumed the risk of his injury as a matter of law, under the common law Fireman's Rule, and that his claim thus was barred as a matter of public policy. They also argued that Rivas had been a **bare licensee** on the premises, that he therefore had been owed the limited duty to refrain from willful injury or entrapment, and that the undisputed facts could not support a finding that they had breached such a duty. . . .

The lower court held a hearing on the motion for summary judgment and, at the conclusion of argument of counsel, granted it. . . .

. . . .

The legal question presented by this case can be broken down into two sub-issues: 1) Whether the "Fireman's Rule" precluded Rivas from recovering in tort; and if not, 2) whether Rivas was owed a duty of ordinary care or a duty only to refrain from willful and wanton misconduct or entrapment.

Maryland has long recognized the common law "**Fireman's Rule**," which in some circumstances operates to preclude firefighters and police officers from tort recovery for injuries sustained in the course of their employment. Until 1987, when the Court of Appeals decided *Flowers v. Rock Creek Terrace,* 308 Md. 432, 520 A.2d 361 (1987), the Fireman's Rule had been explained in terms of the firefighter or policeman being a bare licensee on the premises to whom was owed the limited duty to "abstain from willful or wanton misconduct or entrapment ... [which] encompasses a duty to warn of hidden dangers, where there was knowledge of such danger and an opportunity to warn." *Flowers,* 308 Md. at 443, 520 A.2d 361. In *Flowers,* the Court of Appeals held that the Fireman's Rule is best explained by public policy, and not by application of the law of premises liability. The Court took a causation oriented approach to the Fireman's Rule, focusing upon the roles of fire fighters and police officers in society. It explained:

> [I]t is the nature of the firefighting occupation that limits a fireman's ability to recover in tort for work-related injuries. Instead of continuing to use a rationale based on the law of premises liability, we hold that, as a matter of public policy, firemen and police officers generally cannot recover for injuries attributable to the negligence that requires their assistance. This public policy is based on a relationship between firemen and policemen and the public that calls on these safety officers specifically to confront certain hazards on behalf of the public. A fireman or police officer may not recover if injured by the negligently created risk that was the very reason for his presence on the scene in his occupational capacity. Someone who negligently creates the need for a public safety officer will not be liable to a fireman or policeman for injuries caused by this negligence.

[C]

. . . .

Non constat
jus civile
a posteriori

It's Latin to Me!

Sub judice is Latin for "under judgment" and refers to the case before the court.

In the case *sub judice* . . . the Fireman's Rule did not apply. To be sure, as a deputy sheriff for Prince George's County, Rivas was a law enforcement officer, [c] and his duties as such required him to confront certain risks on behalf of the public. Under the Fireman's Rule, he was deemed to have accepted the risks inherent in those duties by accepting the position of deputy sheriff and the compensation of his office. The purpose for Rivas's visit to the Oxon Hill Apartments was to perform the duty of serving a **subpoena**. The negligence that allegedly caused his injury, however, was unrelated to the situation that required his services. Rivas was injured on account of an allegedly defective condition of the **common area** parking lot of the apartment complex, across which he walked on his approach to the apartment unit in which he intended to serve the subpoena. He was not in the process of serving the subpoena when he was injured and his injuries were not brought about by the activity of subpoena serving. Because Rivas's injuries did not arise out of the very occasion for his employment, i.e., the serving of the subpoena, the Fireman's Rule was inapplicable.

The second sub-issue in this case . . . concerns the standard of care that was owed by Oxon Hill and Southern to Rivas, given the inapplicability of the Fireman's Rule. In Maryland, it is well-established premises liability law that the duty of care that is owed by the owner of property to one who enters on the property depends upon the entrant's legal status. [C] Ordinarily, one entering onto the property of another will occupy the status of invitee, **licensee by invitation**, bare licensee, or trespasser. [C] "An invitee is a person 'on the property for a purpose related to the possessor's business.' " [C] He is owed a duty of ordinary care to keep the property safe. A licensee by invitation is a social guest to whom is owed the "duty to exercise reasonable care to warn ... of dangerous conditions that are known to the possessor but not easily discoverable." [C] A bare licensee is one who enters the property of another with the possessor's knowledge and consent, but for the licensee's own purpose or interest. [C] He is owed a duty to refrain from willfully or wantonly injuring him "and from creating 'new and undisclosed sources of danger without warning'" him. [C] Finally, "a trespasser is one who intentionally and without consent or privilege enters another's property." [C] He is owed the most limited duty: to refrain from willfully or wantonly injuring or entrapping. [C]

[P]ublic officials and employees who enter upon land pursuant to a privilege do not fit easily into this matrix of classifications. Because they are privileged to enter the property, they are not trespassers. Yet, because they generally do not receive an invitation from the possessor to enter onto the property, they are "not literally either an invitee or licensee." [C] Usually, public employees such as postal workers, sanitary and building inspectors, garbage men, and tax collectors are considered invitees who are owed a duty of due care. [Cc] Their invitee status is explained on the ground that they enter onto private property for reasons related to the possessor's business, either to confer a direct benefit on the possessor (e.g., trash removal or mail delivery) or to enable the possessor to legally conduct business (e.g., the various types of inspectors and revenue officers). [C]

In this case, Rivas did not enter upon Oxon Hill's and Southern's property to provide a direct benefit to them or to any of the residents of their apartment complex; nor did he do so to advance a particular business purpose they might have had. Oxon Hill and Southern maintain that, for these reasons, the trial court correctly categorized Rivas as a bare licensee on the premises, to whom no duty of ordinary care was owed. We disagree.

Although the specific task that Rivas entered upon the grounds of the apartment complex to perform on the evening in question may not have been for the direct benefit of Oxon Hill and Southern, as business entities, or any of the apartment dwellers; as individuals, the overall public safety benefit conferred by law enforcement officers upon business owners and individuals enured to the benefit of Oxon Hill and Southern, their **tenants**, and their tenant's visitors. Indeed, it is because they confer a public safety benefit that law enforcement officers and firefighters are privileged to enter upon private property to begin with.

. . . .

It is well-settled in Maryland that a landlord who leases a portion of his property to tenants and reserves another portion of the property for the common use of the tenants must exercise ordinary care to keep the common area reasonably safe. [Cc] "[L]andlord liability in common areas is generally premised on the control a landlord maintains over the common areas. This duty stems in part 'from the responsibility engendered in the Landlord by his having extended an invitation, express or implied, to use the portion of the property retained by him.' " [C] The landlord's duty to exercise reasonable care to keep common areas safe extends not only to his tenants but also to his tenants' guests. [Cc]

In the case *sub judice,* the parking lot over which Rivas was walking when he slipped and fell was a common area of the apartment complex retained by Oxon Hill and Southern for the use of tenants and their guests and over which Oxon Hill and Southern maintained control. Thus, Oxon Hill and Southern already owed to their tenants and their tenants' guests a duty of ordinary care to keep the parking lot reasonably safe. It was undisputed that the parking lot was accessible to and used by tenants and their guests at all hours of the day and night. There was no evidence that the law enforcement purpose for Rivas's entry upon the parking lot caused him to come upon it at a time or in a manner implicating risks above and beyond those the tenants and guests of tenants entering upon the property might encounter. As we see it, therefore, neither public policy nor premises liability law justifies drawing a distinction between the duty owed by Oxon Hill and Southern to tenants and their guests entering upon the common area parking lot by express or implied invitation and the duty owed by them to Rivas, who entered upon the same property by privilege.

Because Rivas was owed a duty of ordinary care, liability in this case was a jury question.

JUDGMENT REVERSED. CASE REMANDED FOR FURTHER PROCEED-INGS CONSISTENT WITH THIS OPINION.

COSTS TO BE PAID BY APPELLEES.

Points for Discussion

1. What is, and what is the rationale for, the "Fireman's Rule"?

2. What is a "bare licensee"?

3. The *Rivas* court concludes that the duty owed to the deputy sheriff was the same as the duty owed to the tenants of the apartment complex and their guests. Do you agree with that positon? Would you favor a higher of duty of care owed to police officers, firefighters, and other public employees? Why or why not?

---

5. Merging or Rejecting the Categories

Koenig v. Koenig

766 N.W.2d 635 (Iowa 2009)

APPEL, Justice.

The question of whether Iowa should retain the traditional common-law distinction between an invitee and a licensee in premises liability cases has sharply divided this court in recent years. In this case, we hold that the common-law distinction between an invitee and a licensee no longer makes sound policy, unnecessarily complicates our law, and should be abandoned.

. . . .

Valerie Koenig visited the home of her son, Marc Koenig, when he was ill in order to care for him and help with household chores. After doing laundry, she fell on a carpet cleaner hose while carrying clothes to a bedroom. As a result of the fall, Valerie was injured and required medical care, including the placement of a plate in her leg.

Valerie filed a petition alleging that Marc's negligent conduct caused her permanent injuries, pain and suffering, loss of function, and substantial medical costs. Marc generally denied her claim and further asserted that Valerie was negligent in connection with the occurrence and that she failed to mitigate her damages.

At trial, Valerie offered evidence that Marc was aware that the carpet cleaner hose was broken but did not warn her of the defect. Valerie further offered evidence that the color of the hose blended in with the color of the carpet, thereby making it difficult to see, and that one of two lights in the hallway near where she fell was not working, which lessened the light available to detect the hazard. Marc offered evidence that the broken hose was an open and obvious hazard and that Valerie did not turn on the light which was functioning in the hallway area.

At the close of trial, Valerie sought a general negligence instruction rather than the uniform jury instruction on the duty of care owed to a licensee. The district court found that the law in Iowa on the proper instruction in a premises liability case was unsettled, declined to give the general negligence instruction sought by Valerie, and instead used the uniform jury instruction for licensees.

The jury returned a verdict in favor of Marc. After the district court entered judgment, Valerie filed a motion for a new trial based on the district court's failure to use her proposed general negligence instruction. Although the district court stated that it did not necessarily disagree with Valerie's position, it denied the motion. The district court noted that "Iowa appellate courts have not yet ruled that continued use of the stock instructions for premises liability cases constitutes error." . . .

. . . .

. . . The premises liability trichotomy, which distinguishes between invitees, licensees, and trespassers, finds its roots in the English common law. John Ketchum, Note, *Missouri Declines an Invitation to Join the Twentieth Century: Preservation of the Licensee-Invitee Distinction in Carter v. Kinney,* 64 UMKC L.Rev. 393, 395 (1995). "The distinctions which the common law draws between licensee and invitee were inherited from a culture deeply rooted to the land, a culture which traced many of its standards to a heritage of feudalism." *Kermarec v. Compagnie Generale Transatlantique,* 358 U.S. 625, 630, 79 S.Ct. 406, 410, 3 L.Ed.2d 550, 554 (1959). The trichotomy emerged in an era where land ownership was paramount and the primary source of power, wealth, and dominance. *Nelson v. Freeland,* 349 N.C. 615, 507 S.E.2d 882, 887 (1998). At the core of the trichotomy was the presumption that landowners generally were free to act as they pleased within the confines of their own property. Robert S. Driscoll, Note, *The Law of Premises Liability in America: Its Past, Present, and Some Considerations for Its Future,* 82 Notre Dame L.Rev. 881, 893 (2006).

These common-law classifications arose from reluctance "to leave the determination of liability to a jury 'composed mainly of potential land entrants.' " Michael Sears, Comment, *Abrogation of the Traditional Common Law of Premises Liability,* 44 U. Kan. L.Rev. 175, 176 (1995) (quoting Norman S. Marsh, *The History and Comparative Law of Invitees, Licensees and Trespassers,* 69 L.Q. Rev. 182, 184 (1953)). The distinctions, therefore, were

> created to disgorge the jury of some of its power by either allowing the judge to take the case from the jury based on legal rulings or by forcing the jury to apply the mechanical rules of the trichotomy instead of considering the pertinent issue of whether the landowner acted reasonably in maintaining his land.

[C].

The trichotomy emerged in a time of tort law far different from our own. When the trichotomy was developing, "the principle that a man should be held responsible for foreseeable damages" was only reluctantly recognized in a limited number of cases. [C] Today, the situation has changed dramatically as the concept of negligence is a predominant concept in our tort law.

The emergence of negligence law almost immediately conflicted with the common-law system. Kathryn E. Eriksen, Comment, *Premises Liability in Texas—Time for a "Reasonable" Change,* 17 St. Mary's L.J. 417, 422 (1986). "Common-law courts, however, decided not to replace the trichotomy with modern principles of negligence law, as they did in almost all other tort areas, but rather 'superimposed the new [negligence] principles upon the existing framework of entrant categories.'" [C]

Modern courts that have retained the trichotomy have largely set forth the traditional justifications: (1) the continued fear of jury abuse; (2) the fear that by "substituting the negligence standard of care for the common-law categories, landowners will be forced to bear" the financial burden of taking precautions such as maintaining adequate insurance policies, and (3) the need to promote stability and predictability in the law. [C]

. . . The first American blow to the trichotomy was hurled by the United States Supreme Court. In [*Kermarec v. Compagnie Generale Transatlantique,* 358 U.S. 625 (1959)] the Court refused to extend the common-law distinctions to admiralty law. The Court heavily criticized the doctrine, noting:

> In an effort to do justice in an industrialized urban society, with its complex economic and individual relationships, modern common-law courts have found it necessary to formulate increasingly subtle verbal refinements, to create subclassifications among traditional common-law categories, and to delineate fine gradations in the standards of care

which the landowner owes to each. Yet even within a single jurisdiction, the classifications and subclassifications bred by the common law have produced confusion and conflict. As new distinctions have been spawned, older ones have become obscured. Through this semantic morass the common law has moved, unevenly and with hesitation, towards "imposing on owners and occupiers a single duty of reasonable care in all the circumstances."

[C]

After *Kermarec,* the movement away from the common-law distinctions received a major boost in 1968 with the California Supreme Court's decision in *Rowland v. Christian,* 69 Cal.2d 108, 70 Cal.Rptr. 97, 443 P.2d 561 (1968), *abrogated in part by statute as stated in Calvillo-Silva v. Home Grocery,* 19 Cal.4th 714, 80 Cal.Rptr.2d 506, 968 P.2d 65, 72 (1998). In rejecting application of the common-law formulation, the *Rowland* court noted,

> [W]e are satisfied that continued adherence to the common law distinctions can only lead to injustice or, if we are to avoid injustice, further fictions with the resulting complexity and confusion. We decline to follow and perpetuate such rigid classifications ... although the plaintiff's status as a trespasser, licensee, or invitee may in the light of the facts giving rise to such status have some bearing on the question of liability, the status is not determinative.

[C] Following *Rowland,* numerous courts abandoned the common-law system. *See Smith v. Arbaugh's Rest., Inc.,* 469 F.2d 97, 107 (D.C.Cir.1972); *Webb v. City & Borough of Sitka,* 561 P.2d 731, 734 (Alaska 1977), *abrogated in part by statute as stated in Univ. of Alaska v. Shanti,* 835 P.2d 1225, 1228 n. 5 (Alaska 1992); *Mile High Fence Co. v. Radovich,* 175 Colo. 537, 489 P.2d 308, 314-15 (1971), *abrogated by statute as stated in Bath Excavating & Constr. Co. v. Wills,* 847 P.2d 1141, 1145 (Colo.1993); *Pickard v. City & County of Honolulu,* 51 Haw. 134, 452 P.2d 445, 446 (1969); *Cates v. Beauregard Elec. Coop., Inc.,* 328 So.2d 367, 370-71 (La.1976); *Limberhand v. Big Ditch Co.,* 218 Mont. 132, 706 P.2d 491, 496 (1985); *Moody v. Manny's Auto Repair,* 110 Nev. 320, 871 P.2d 935, 942 (1994), *superseded by statute as stated in Wiley v. Redd,* 110 Nev. 1310, 885 P.2d 592, 595 (1994); *Ouellette v. Blanchard,* 116 N.H. 552, 364 A.2d 631, 634 (1976); *Basso v. Miller,* 40 N.Y.2d 233, 386 N.Y.S.2d 564, 352 N.E.2d 868, 872 (1976); *Mariorenzi v. Joseph DiPonte, Inc.,* 114 R.I. 294, 333 A.2d 127, 131-32 (1975), *overruled in part by Tantimonico v. Allendale Mut. Ins. Co.,* 637 A.2d 1056, 1057 (R.I.1994); *see also* Vitauts M. Gulbis, Annotation, *Modern Status of Rules Conditioning Landowner's Liability Upon Status of Injured Party as Invitee, Licensee, or Trespasser,* 22 A.L.R.4th 294 (2008).

After *Rowland,* however, a second, more moderate trend began to emerge in the case law. Instead of abandoning the trichotomy entirely, some courts began to abandon the distinction between invitees and licensees, while retaining the trespasser classification. *See Wood v. Camp,* 284 So.2d 691, 695 (Fla.1973); *Jones v. Hansen,* 254 Kan. 499, 867 P.2d 303, 310 (1994); *Poulin v. Colby Coll.,* 402 A.2d 846, 851 n. 5 (Me.1979); *Mounsey v. Ellard,* 363 Mass. 693, 297 N.E.2d 43, 51-52 & n. 7 (1973); *Peterson v. Balach,* 294 Minn. 161, 199 N.W.2d 639, 642 (1972); *Heins v. Webster County,* 250 Neb. 750, 552 N.W.2d 51, 57 (1996); *Ford v. Bd. of County Comm'rs,* 118 N.M. 134, 879 P.2d 766, 770 (1994); *Nelson,* 507 S.E.2d at 892; *O'Leary v. Coenen,* 251 N.W.2d 746, 751 (N.D.1977); *Hudson v. Gaitan,* 675 S.W.2d 699, 703 (Tenn.1984), *overruled in part on other grounds by McIntyre v. Balentine,* 833 S.W.2d 52, 54 (Tenn.1992); *Mallet v. Pickens,* 206 W.Va. 145, 522 S.E.2d 436, 446 (1999); *Antoniewicz v. Reszcynski,* 70 Wis.2d 836, 236 N.W.2d 1, 11 (1975); *Clarke v. Beckwith,* 858 P.2d 293, 296 (Wyo.1993).

Still other states, including Iowa, limited the common law system by refusing to apply the doctrine to child entrants. *See Cope v. Doe,* 102 Ill.2d 278, 80 Ill.Dec. 40, 464 N.E.2d 1023, 1028 (1984); *Rosenau v. City of Estherville,* 199 N.W.2d 125, 136 (Iowa 1972). Some courts and the Restatement drew another exception-imposing a duty of reasonable care upon landowners to warn a "discovered" or "foreseeable" trespasser of any dangerous condition which is known by the landowner but not by the trespasser. *See* 2 Restatement (Second) of Torts § 337 cmt. b (1979); *Appling v. Stuck,* 164 N.W.2d 810, 814-15 (Iowa 1969); *Latimer v. City of Clovis,* 83 N.M. 610, 495 P.2d 788, 792 (1972) (reversing summary judgment because there was a genuine issue of material fact as to whether decedent was a discovered or ordinary trespasser).

Although a bare majority of states have now departed from the original trichotomy in some fashion, a number of courts have declined to abandon the common-law system. *See McMullan v. Butler,* 346 So.2d 950, 952 (Ala.1977); *Nicoletti v. Westcor, Inc.,* 131 Ariz. 140, 639 P.2d 330, 332 (1982); *Bailey v. Pennington,* 406 A.2d 44, 47-48 (Del.1979); *Mooney v. Robinson,* 93 Idaho 676, 471 P.2d 63, 65 (1970); *Kirschner ex rel. Kirschner v. Louisville Gas & Elec. Co.,* 743 S.W.2d 840, 844 (Ky.1988); *Sherman v. Suburban Trust Co.,* 282 Md. 238, 384 A.2d 76, 83 (1978); *Little ex rel. Little v. Bell,* 719 So.2d 757, 764 (Miss.1998); *Vega ex rel. Muniz v. Piedilato,* 154 N.J. 496, 713 A.2d 442, 448-49 (1998); *Sutherland v. Saint Francis Hosp., Inc.,* 595 P.2d 780, 782 (Okla.1979); *Di Gildo v. Caponi,* 18 Ohio St.2d 125, 247 N.E.2d 732, 736 (1969); *Musch v. H-D Elec. Coop., Inc.,* 460 N.W.2d 149, 156-57 (S.D.1990); *Buchholz v. Steitz,* 463 S.W.2d 451, 454 (Tex.Civ. App.1971); *Tjas v. Proctor,* 591 P.2d 438, 441 (Utah 1979).

In total, the jurisdictions are now split, with a majority of states departing from the common-law classifications in some manner, and a substantial minority either rejecting abolition or not taking a recent position.

. . . Almost four decades ago this court noted, "The application of rigid common-law rules (which turn the liability of the land possessor on the status of the person harmed) in the context of our complex, industrialized and heavily populated society has come under increasing criticism." [C] Despite this observation, this court has not yet expressly rejected use of the common-law system in the intervening years. [Cc]

. . . .

. . . Taking into consideration the wealth of case law in our sister jurisdictions, academic commentary, and the history of the common-law distinctions, we now conclude that the advantages of abolishing the distinction between invitees and licensees outweigh the value of its retention.

The primary advantage of abolishing the invitee-licensee distinction is to avoid confusion. While there is no issue in this case as to Valerie's status, properly categorizing an entrant's status has proven a dubious task in other cases. . . .

Not only does this confusion provide ample grounds for appeal, it also prevents the development of an easily applicable standard for future cases. As a result, retention of the common-law system has not fulfilled its goal of predictability, but rather has "produced confusion and conflict." [Cc]

The difficulty in distinguishing between invitees and licensees underscores another disadvantage of the classification-people do not alter their behavior based on an entrant's status as an invitee or licensee. . . . The fungible and unpredictable nature of the classifications makes it impossible for landowners to conform their behavior to current community standards. [C] It also makes it impossible for entrants to understand to what level of danger or risk they are being exposed.

In addition, abandonment of the common-law distinction between invitees and licensees is consistent with modern notions of tort law and liability. When this distinction was adopted in the nineteenth century by American courts, our tort law was replete with special rules and arguably arbitrary common-law distinctions. Since that time, these doctrines, such as **contributory negligence**, which often yielded inequitable results, have fallen by the wayside in favor of **comparative fault**. "The use of a general standard of reasonable care under all the circumstances ... will bring this area of the law into conformity with modern tort principles by allowing increased jury participation and the use of contemporary standards." [C] Contrary to courts that have upheld the trichotomy, there is nothing to fear about jury involvement. . . .

Moreover, both logic and almost forty years of practice suggest that there is no reason to question a jury's ability to perform in the area of premises liability as opposed to any other area of tort law. [C] The fear of a runaway, standardless jury has not been substantiated in the jurisdictions that have abolished the common-law distinction between invitees and licensees. *See generally* Carl S. Hawkins, *Premises Liability After Repudiation of Status Categories: Allocation of Judge and Jury Functions,* 1981 Utah L.Rev. 15 (concluding ordinary negligence principles have constrained jury discretion in premises liability cases in jurisdictions that abolished the classification system).

Finally, abandonment of this common-law distinction recognizes a higher valuation of public safety over property rights. . . .

. . . .

In place of the common-law formulation, we adopt the multifactor approach advanced by the Nebraska Supreme Court and adopted by the . . . court in [*Sheets v. Ritt, Ritt & Ritt, Inc.,* 581 N.W.2d 602 (Iowa 1998)]:

> "We impose upon owners and occupiers only the duty to exercise reasonable care in the maintenance of their premises for the protection of lawful visitors. Among the factors to be considered in evaluating whether a landowner or occupier has exercised reasonable care for the protection of lawful visitors will be: (1) the foreseeability or possibility of harm; (2) the purpose for which the entrant entered the premises; (3) the time, manner, and circumstances under which the entrant entered the premises; (4) the use to which the premises are put or are expected to be put; (5) the reasonableness of the inspection, repair, or warning; (6) the opportunity and ease of repair or correction or giving of the warning; and (7) the burden on the land occupier and/or community in terms of inconvenience or cost in providing adequate protection."

[C]

This multifactored approach will ensure that the interests of land owners and injured parties are properly balanced. It further allows the jury to take into consideration common sense notions of reasonable care in assessing liability. By adopting this test, we eliminate an arcane and difficult-to-understand distinction from our law and make it simpler and more easily understood.

As a result of our holding abandoning the distinction between invitees and licensees in premises liability cases, it follows that the instruction given by the district court in this case was erroneous.

. . . .

On remand, the district court should develop a more direct, simple instruction consistent with our adoption of the multipronged test to guide the jury in its deliberations.

. . . .

The district court's ruling on the motion for new trial is reversed, the judgment vacated, and the matter remanded for a new trial using a general negligence instruction to define the scope of duty owed by the defendant in this case.

REVERSED.

————————————

Points for Discussion

1. What is the holding of *Koenig v. Koenig*?

2. What is the premises liability trichotomy? How has that trichotomy been critiqued by courts?

3. Why does the *Koenig* court abolish the invitee-licensee distinction? What approach does the court adopt in determining the duty of owners and occupiers of land?

4. The court reasons that its approach will ensure the proper balancing of the interests of land owners and injured parties. How might a juror make that determination? What should the jury consider?

————————————

6. Lessors and Lessees

Kline v. 1500 Massachusetts Ave. Apartment Corp.

439 F.2d 477, 141 U.S.App.D.C. 370 (1970)

WILKEY, Circuit Judge:

The appellee apartment corporation states that there is 'only one issue presented for review * * * whether a duty should be placed on a landlord to take steps to protect tenants from foreseeable criminal acts committed by third parties.'

The District Court as a matter of law held that there is no such duty. We find that there is, and that in the circumstances here the applicable standard of care was breached. We therefore reverse and remand to the District Court for the determination of damages for the appellant.

. . . .

The appellant, Sarah B. Kline, sustained serious injuries when she was criminally assaulted and robbed at approximately 10:15 in the evening by an intruder in the common hallway of an apartment house at 1500 Massachusetts Avenue. This facility, into which the appellant Kline moved in October 1959, is a large apartment building with approximately 585 individual apartment units. It has a main entrance on Massachusetts Avenue, with side entrances on both 15th and 16th Streets. At the time the appellant first signed a lease a doorman was on duty at the main entrance twenty-four hours a day, and at least one employee at all times manned a desk in the lobby from which all persons using the elevators could be observed.[1] The 15th Street door adjoined the entrance to a parking garage used by both the tenants and the public. Two garage attendants were stationed at this dual entranceway; the duties of each being arranged so that one of them always was in position to observe those entering either the apartment building or the garage. The 16th Street entrance was unattended during the day but was locked after 9:00 P.M.

By mid-1966, however, the main entrance had no doorman, the desk in the lobby was left unattended much of the time, the 15th Street entrance was generally unguarded due to a decrease in garage personnel, and the 16th Street entrance was often left unlocked all night. The entrances were allowed to be thus unguarded in the face of an increasing number of assaults, larcenies, and robberies being perpetrated against the tenants in and from the common hallways of the apartment building. These facts were undisputed, and were supported by a detailed chronological listing of offenses admitted into evidence. The landlord had notice of these crimes and had in fact been urged by appellant Kline herself prior to the events leading to the instant appeal to take steps to secure the building.

Shortly after 10:00 P.M. on November 17, 1966, Miss Kline was assaulted and robbed just outside her apartment on the first floor above the street level of this 585 unit apartment building. This occurred only two months after Leona Sullivan, another female tenant, had been similarly attacked in the same commonway.

. . . .

In this jurisdiction, certain duties have been assigned to the landlord because of his control of common hallways, lobbies, stairwells, etc., used by all tenants in

---

1 Miss Kline testified that she had initially moved into the building not only because of its central location, but also because she was interested in security, and had been impressed by the precautions taken at the main entrance.

multiple dwelling units. This Court in Levine v. Katz, 132 U.S.App.D.C. 173, 174, 407 F.2d 303, 304 (1968), pointed out that:

> It has long been well settled in this jurisdiction that, where a landlord leases separate portions of property and reserves under his own control the halls, stairs, or other parts of the property for use in common by all tenants, he has a duty to all those on the premises of legal right to use ordinary care and diligence to maintain the retained parts in a reasonably safe condition.

While Levine v. Katz dealt with a physical defect in the building leading to plaintiff's injury, the rationale as applied to predictable criminal acts by third parties is the same. The duty is the landlord's because by his control of the areas of common use and common danger he is the only party who has the power to make the necessary repairs or to provide the necessary protection.

As a general rule, a private person does not have a duty to protect another from a criminal attack by a third person. We recognize that this rule has sometimes in the past been applied in **landlord-tenant** law, even by this court. Among the reasons for the application of this rule to landlords are: judicial reluctance to tamper with the traditional common law concept of the landlord tenant relationship; the notion that the act of a third person in committing an intentional tort or crime is a superseding cause of the harm to another resulting therefrom; the oftentimes difficult problem of determining foreseeability of criminal acts; the vagueness of the standard which the landlord must meet; the economic consequences of the imposition of the duty; and conflict with the public policy allocating the duty of protecting citizens from criminal acts to the government rather than the private sector.

But the rationale of this very broad general rule falters when it is applied to the conditions of modern day urban apartment living, particularly in the circumstances of this case. The rationale of the general rule exonerating a third party from any duty to protect another from a criminal attack has no applicability to the landlord-tenant relationship in multiple dwelling houses. The landlord is no insurer of his tenants' safety, but he certainly is no bystander. And where, as here, the landlord has notice of repeated criminal assaults and robberies, has notice that these crimes occurred in the portion of the premises exclusively within his control, has every reason to expect like crimes to happen again, and has the exclusive power to take preventive action, it does not seem unfair to place upon the landlord a duty to take those steps which are within his power to minimize the predictable risk to his tenants.

. . . .

[I]nnkeepers have been held liable for **assaults** which have been committed upon their guests by third parties, if they have breached a duty which is imposed by reason of the innkeeper-**guest** relationship. By this duty, the innkeeper is generally bound to exercise reasonable care to protect the guest from abuse or molestation from third parties, be they innkeeper's employees, fellow guests, or intruders, if the attack could, or in the exercise of reasonable care, should have been anticipated.

Liability in the innkeeper-guest relationship is based as a matter of law either upon the innkeeper's supervision, care, or control of the premises, or by reason of a contract which some courts have implied from the entrustment by the guest of his personal comfort and safety to the innkeeper. In the latter analysis, the contract is held to give the guest the right to except a standard of treatment at the hands of the innkeeper which includes an obligation on the part of the latter to exercise reasonable care in protecting the guest.

Other relationships in which similar duties have been imposed include land-owner-invitee, businessman-patron, employer-employee, school district-pupil, hospital-patient, and carrier-passenger. In all, the theory of liability is essentially the same; that since the ability of one of the parties to provide for his own protection has been limited in some way by his submission to the control of the other, a duty should be imposed upon the one possessing control (and thus the power to act) to take reasonable precautions to protect the other one from assaults by third parties which, at least, could reasonably have been anticipated. However, there is no liability normally imposed upon the one having the power to act if the violence is sudden and unexpected provided that the source of the violence is not an employee of the one in control.

. . . .

As between tenant and landlord, the landlord is the only one in the position to take the necessary acts of protection required. He is not an **insurer**, but he is obligated to minimize the risk to his tenants. Not only as between landlord and tenant is the landlord best equipped to guard against the predictable risk of intruders, but even as between landlord and the police power of government, the landlord is in the best position to take the necessary protective measures. Municipal police cannot patrol the entryways and the hallways, the garages and the basements of private multiple unit apartment dwellings. They are neither equipped, manned, nor empowered to do so. In the area of the predictable risk which materialized in this case, only the landlord could have taken measures which might have prevented the injuries suffered by appellant.

. . . .

We . . . hold in this case that the applicable standard of care in providing protection for the tenant is that standard which this landlord himself was employing in October 1959 when the appellant became a resident on the premises at 1500

Massachusetts Avenue. The tenant was led to expect that she could rely upon this degree of protection. While we do not say that the precise measures for security which were then in vogue should have been kept up (e.g., the number of people at the main entrances might have been reduced if a tenant-controlled intercom-automatic latch system had been installed in the common entryways), we do hold that the same relative degree of security should have been maintained.

. . . .

Having said this, it would be well to state what is not said by this decision. We do not hold that the landlord is by any means an insurer of the safety of his tenants. His duty is to take those measures of protection which are within his power and capacity to take, and which can reasonably be expected to mitigate the risk of intruders assaulting and robbing tenants. The landlord is not expected to provide protection commonly owed by a municipal police department; but as illustrated in this case, he is obligated to protect those parts of his premises which are not usually subject to periodic patrol and inspection by the municipal police. We do not say that every multiple unit apartment house in the District of Columbia should have those same measures of protection which 1500 Massachusetts Avenue enjoyed in 1959, nor do we say that 1500 Massachusetts Avenue should have precisely those same measures in effect at the present time. Alternative and more up-to-date methods may be equally or even more effective.

. . . .

The landlord is entirely justified in passing on the cost of increased protective measures to his tenants, but the rationale of compelling the landlord to do it in the first place is that he is the only one who is in a position to take the necessary protective measures for overall protection of the premises, which he owns in whole and rents in part to individual tenants.

Reversed and remanded to the District Court for the determination of damages.

———————————

Points for Discussion

1. What did the *Kline* court hold? Did the court hold that a landlord is an insurer of a tenant's safety? What is the scope of the landlord's obligations?

2. Kline moved into the apartment house in 1959; she was assaulted and robbed in 1966. Do you agree that the landlord's standard of care owed to Kline was the standard applicable in 1959 when Kline became a resident of the premises? Is Kline only entitled to the degree of protection available in 1959

throughout her entire residency at the apartments, even if she were to reside there for ten or twenty years?

3. What responsibility, if any, does a tenant have for her own safety when she moves into an apartment building or continues to reside there in the face of a growing crime rate?

Batra v. Clark

110 S.W.3d 126 (Tex. Ct. App. 2003)

TIM TAFT, Justice.

Appellant, Dinesh Batra, appeals a verdict finding him negligent and awarding damages to appellee, Tammy Clark, individually and as **next friend** of Clarissa Ewell. We determine whether Batra, an out-of-possession landlord who retained no control over the premises of the rental property, owed a duty to Ewell, a third party who was injured on the property. We reverse and render judgment that Clark take nothing from Batra.

. . . .

Ewell, a nine-year-old girl, was attacked by a pit bull at a house located in Baytown, Texas. Batra was the owner and landlord of the rental house, and Martha Torres was the tenant. The pit bull belonged to Torres' son, who was not a resident of the rental property, but Torres sometimes kept the dog at the house. The lease agreement signed by Batra and Torres contained a clause prohibiting pets on the premises of the rental property without the written consent of Batra. The clause also provided that Batra could remove any unauthorized animal and give custody of the animal to local authorities.

Ewell went over to the Torres' house to play with Torres' daughter, Georgina. The house was surrounded by a fence, with gate openings in the front and on the back side. Although the dog was typically chained on the side of the house, it was not chained on the day Ewell was attacked. As Ewell stood on the sidewalk outside the fence of the Torres' house, she was told by Georgina to "agitate" the dog to distract it so that Georgina could leave the house and exit through the gate at the back side of the house. Ewell distracted the dog by running back and forth up and down the fence line. The dog broke through the fence and attacked Ewell, biting her numerous times on the legs. Ewell required medical treatment and stitches as a result of the attack.

Clark sued Batra and Torres for negligence. During trial, Batra moved for a **directed verdict**, arguing that he owed no duty to Ewell because he was an out-of-possession landlord who had no control over the dog or the rental property. After a bench trial, the trial court found Batra and Torres each 50% liable for Ewell's injuries. Batra moved for a new trial under the same grounds as his motion for directed verdict.

. . . .

In his first point of error, Batra contends that the trial court erred by overruling his motion for directed verdict and motion for new trial because he did not owe a duty to Ewell. Batra argues that, as an out-of-possession landlord who allegedly did not retain any control of the premises, he had no duty to exercise reasonable care to prevent the attack of the dog owned by the son of his tenant. Clark responds with the argument that Batra owed Ewell a duty of care because Batra (1) had actual knowledge that the dog was on the premises of the rental property and imputed knowledge of the dog's dangerous propensities, (2) retained the ability to control the rental property because of the lease provisions allowing him to access the leased premises at any time, and (3) retained the ability to control the dog because of the lease provisions prohibiting pets on the property without his written consent and giving him the right to remove any unauthorized pet.

. . . .

Both parties cite *Baker v. Pennoak Props., Ltd.* to support their arguments. *See id.*, 874 S.W.2d 274, 277 (Tex.App.–Houston [14th Dist.] 1994, no writ). In *Baker,* the court held that a landlord retaining control over premises used in common by different occupants of his property has a duty to protect tenants from dog attacks in the common areas of his property and will be held liable if (1) the injury occurred in a common area under the control of the landlord and (2) the landlord had actual or imputed knowledge of the dog's vicious propensities. [C] *Baker* is distinguishable because it involved a landlord in possession with control over the common areas, whereas this case involves a landlord out of possession with arguably no, or limited, control over the premises. [Cc] Moreover, the *Baker* court expressly refused to decide the issue of whether an out-of-possession landlord may be liable for harm caused by a tenant's dog to third parties. [C] Thus, we are faced with an issue of first impression.

Several other jurisdictions have imposed liability on out-of-possession landlords for dog attacks against third parties on the landlords' single-dwelling premises. *See* Danny R. Veilleux, Annotation, *Landlord's Liability to Third Person for*

Injury Resulting from Attack on Leased Premises by Dangerous or Vicious Animal Kept by Tenant, 87 A.L.R.4th 1004, 1012-13 (1991). The majority of cases have held that a landlord will be liable for injuries caused by the attack of a tenant's dog only when the landlord (1) had actual knowledge of the dog's presence on the leased premises, actual knowledge of the dog's dangerous propensities, and the ability to control the leased premises, either by the terms of the lease or by trailer park or subdivision regulations; and (2) failed to exercise that ability to control. *See Uccello v. Laudenslayer,* 44 Cal.App.3d 504, 118 Cal.Rptr. 741, 746-47 (1975) (holding duty of care arises when landlord has actual knowledge of presence of dangerous animal and of its dangerous propensities and right to remove animal by retaking possession of premises); *McCullough v. Bozarth,* 232 Neb. 714, 724-25, 442 N.W.2d 201, 208 (1989) (ruling that landlord is liable for injuries caused by attack of tenant's dog only when landlord had actual knowledge of dangerous propensities of dog and, by terms of lease, had power to control dog and neglected to exercise that power); *Strunk v. Zoltanski,* 62 N.Y.2d 572, 479 N.Y.S.2d 175, 468 N.E.2d 13, 16 (1984) (stating that landlord may be liable who, with knowledge that prospective tenant has vicious dog which will be kept on premises, leases premises to tenant without taking reasonable measures, by provisions in lease or otherwise, to prevent attacks by dog); *Vigil v. Payne,* 725 P.2d 1155, 1157 (Colo.Ct.App.1986) (holding that landlord who has actual knowledge that tenant owns animal with vicious propensities has duty to take reasonable precautions to prevent attacks by animal); *Palermo v. Nails,* 334 Pa.Super. 544, 483 A.2d 871, 873 (1984) (finding landlord liable for injuries by animals owned by his tenant when landlord had knowledge of presence of dangerous animal and right to control or remove animal by retaking possession of premises). *Cf. Royer v. Pryor,* 427 N.E.2d 1112, 1119 (Ind.Ct.App.1981) (refusing to hold landlord liable when he did not know of vicious propensities of tenant's dog and did not retain or exercise control over portion of premises on which attack occurred); *Roy v. Neibauer,* 191 Mont. 224, 623 P.2d 555, 556 (1981) (affirming summary judgment in favor of landlord when tenant agreed, pursuant to lease, that he would not maintain or permit to be maintained on premises dog with dangerous propensities); *Parker v. Sutton,* 72 Ohio App.3d 296, 594 N.E.2d 659, 661-62 (1991) (holding that landlord with knowledge of presence of vicious animal on premises may not be held liable if he had reasonable belief that dog was removed from property or if insufficient time has passed for landlord to take legal steps to abate hazard); *but see Vasques v. Lopez,* 509 So.2d 1241, 1242 (Fla.Dist. Ct.App.1987) (finding liable landlord who had imputed knowledge of vicious dog's presence and ability to control premises); *Merwin v. McCann,* 129 A.D.2d 925, 926, 514 N.Y.S.2d 566 (N.Y.App.Div.1987) (reversing summary judgment and remanding to trial court to determine whether landlord had actual or imputed knowledge that vicious dogs were kept on premises); *Bessent v. Matthews,* 543 So.2d 438, 439 (Fla.Dist.Ct.App.1989) (affirming judgment when there was no evidence that landlord knew or had reason to know that his tenant's dog was vicious); *Clemmons v. Fidler,* 58 Wash.App. 32, 791 P.2d 257, 259 (1990) (holding that landlord cannot be liable for injuries caused by tenant's vicious dog even if landlord has actual or implied knowledge of dog's presence on property and vicious tendencies).

We agree with the majority of cases that liability should be imposed on an out-of-possession landlord only when he has **actual knowledge**, rather than **imputed knowledge**, of the presence of a vicious animal on the leased premises. We hold that, if a landlord has actual knowledge of an animal's dangerous propensities and presence on the leased property, and has the ability to control the premises, he owes a duty of ordinary care to third parties who are injured by this animal.

. . . .

Cynthia Taplin, Torres' neighbor, testified at trial that she saw Batra fixing the roof of the rental house at some time before the dog attacked Ewell, that the dog was chained up on the side of the house, and that the dog was barking the entire time Batra fixed the roof. In factual finding number nine, the trial court found that Batra had actual knowledge of the dog's presence on the premises before Ewell was attacked, which finding Taplin's testimony supports. In conclusion of law number three, the trial court decided that Batra had control over the leased premises and imputed knowledge of the dog's vicious propensities.

Here, although the trial court found that Batra had actual knowledge of the dog's presence on the property and that Batra had control over the leased property, the trial court did not make any conclusion that Batra had actual knowledge of the dog's vicious propensities. Instead, the trial court found only that Batra had imputed knowledge of the dog's vicious propensities. We have already determined that actual knowledge, as opposed to imputed knowledge, of a dog's vicious propensities is necessary to establish a duty to Ewell. Further, the evidence at trial does not support a conclusion that Batra actually knew that the particular dog that attacked Ewell had vicious propensities. Although Taplin testified that Batra was on the property when the dog was barking, there is no evidence showing that Batra either saw the dog and knew that it was a potentially vicious animal or identified the dog's bark as the bark of a potentially vicious animal. Thus, there is no evidence showing that Batra owed Ewell a duty of ordinary care.

We hold that the trial court erred by overruling Batra's motion for directed verdict and motion for new trial. [C]

. . . .

We reverse that portion of the judgment allocating 50% of the liability for the damages to Batra and order that Clark take nothing from Batra.

————————————————

Points for Discussion

1. What is, and what should be, the rule or standard governing a landlord's responsibility to protect tenants from dog attacks?

2. Did the *Batra* court conclude that the landlord had actual knowledge of the pit bull's vicious propensities?

3. Should a landlord's duty to protect tenants from dog attacks in common areas of a property be greater depending upon the breed of dog, such as pit bulls?

———————

CHAPTER 8

Strict Liability

Strict liability is liability imposed without regard to a defendant's intent or breach of the duty to use reasonable care. Historically imposed for injuries caused by wild animals and abnormally dangerous activities, **strict liability** is often mischaracterized as synonymous with **absolute liability**. However, equating strict liability with absolute liability is misguided, as *absolute liability* connotes the imposition of liability without limitation whatsoever. *Strict liability* is in fact subject to several limitations, as discussed in the cases that follow.

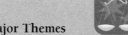

Major Themes

The study of strict liability completes the trilogy of tort law– intentional torts, negligence, and strict liability.

A. Animals

Irvine v. Rare Feline Breeding Ctr.

685 N.E.2d 120 (Ind. Ct. App. 1997)

CHEZEM, Judge.

Appellant-Plaintiff, Scott Irvine ("Irvine"), appeals an order denying his motion for partial summary judgment. We affirm.

....

Facts and Procedural History

For the past thirty years, Mosella Schaffer ("Schaffer") has lived on a fifty acre farm in Hamilton County, Indiana where she has raised and maintained exotic animals. These animals have included zebras, llamas, camels, kangaroos, and, beginning in 1970, Siberian tigers. Although her original intent was to breed and sell the animals, she soon found it difficult to part with many of them.

In 1993, Scott Bullington ("Bullington") was renting a room in the garage area of Schaffer's house. Aware of his friend Irvine's interest in wild animals, Bullington informed Irvine of Schaffer's farm and the animals she kept there. Irvine, then in his late twenties, began to stop by and see the animals as per Schaffer's open invitation. Over the next two years, Irvine visited Schaffer's farm several dozen times. During these visits, people would occasionally pet the tigers through a fence.

On the afternoon of December 2, 1995, Irvine arrived at Schaffer's home to see Bullington. The two men drank alcohol and watched television until early evening when Bullington announced that he had to leave to attend his employer's Christmas party. Because Irvine had consumed a substantial amount of alcohol, Bullington told Irvine he could stay over night on the couch. Some time after Bullington had left, Irvine exited Bullington's apartment, walked to the front of Schaffer's property and visited with the llamas and zebras. As he was doing so, Schaffer drove up, stopped her car, had a brief, friendly conversation with Irvine, and went into her house.

Around 8:00 p.m., Irvine decided to visit the tigers before going to sleep. Thus, he went through Schaffer's garage, proceeded through the utility room, continued through the sun room, and ended up in the back yard. Irvine then approached the wire caging, as he and others had done in the past, placed a couple fingers inside the enclosure, and attempted to pet a male tiger. As he was scratching the male tiger, a female tiger made some commotion, which caused Irvine to look away from the male tiger. At that moment, the male tiger pulled Irvine's arm through the two inch by six inch opening of the wire fence.

Upon hearing Irvine's shouts, Schaffer came out of her house, banged an object against the fence, and freed Irvine. Schaffer immediately drove Irvine to the hospital. Irvine was treated and admitted to the hospital. Later, he was transferred to another hospital, and underwent six surgeries during a thirteen day hospital stay. Further surgeries are indicated though Irvine is uninsured.

On May 30, 1996, Irvine filed a complaint against Schaffer containing four counts: negligence, strict liability, nuisance, and punitives. On September 6, 1996, Irvine filed his motion for partial summary judgment on the basis that **incurred risk** and assumption of risk are not valid defenses to a strict liability wild animal claim, on the basis that assumption of risk is not available in a non-contract case, and on the basis that the defense of open and obvious is not available in an animal liability case. Schaffer filed a response on January 14, 1997. Irvine filed a reply on January 21, 1997. The trial court denied Irvine's motion for summary judgment on the strict liability count, denied summary judgment on the issue of assumption of risk, and granted summary judgment on the issue of open and obvious. The trial court granted Irvine's petition to certify three issues for **interlocutory appeal**: 1) whether incurred risk or other defenses are available in a strict liability animal case; 2) whether Irvine was an invitee as a matter of law; and 3) whether the defense of assumption of risk is available .... We accepted jurisdiction of the interlocutory appeal.

What's That?

An interlocutory appeal is an appeal that is permitted to be considered prior to the trial court's final ruling on the entire case.

Discussion and Decision

Irvine first argues that Indiana has historically adhered to strict tort liability in wild animal cases. He further argues that when the Indiana Comparative Fault Act (Ind.Code § 34-4-33-1 *et seq.,* the

Make the Connection

The statute at issue here was Indiana's adaptation of a comparative fault scheme. *See* Chapter 6 on comparative fault as a (sometimes partial) defense to tort actions.

"Act") was adopted, it did not change the law in wild animal cases. Moreover, he claims that no exceptions to strict liability in wild animal cases have ever been applied in Indiana. He also argues that even if his status is somehow relevant, he was clearly an **invitee**. Thus, he asserts that the trial court should not have denied his summary judgment on the strict liability issue. In contrast, Schaffer argues that Indiana has not adopted, and should not adopt, strict liability in wild animal cases. In the alternative, Schaffer asserts that if strict liability is the general rule, an exception should apply here.

Upon review of the grant or denial of a **summary judgment** motion, we apply the same legal standard as the trial court: summary judgment is appropriate only when there are no genuine issues of material fact and the moving party is entitled to judgment as a matter of law. ...

I. Liability in a Wild Animal Case

We first address whether strict liability is the common law rule for wild animal cases in Indiana. The parties have not cited and we have not found a case specifically applying strict liability to a true wild animal case in Indiana. However, the basic rule has been frequently stated in various contexts. *Holt v. Myers,* 47 Ind.App. 118, 93 N.E. 31 (1910) (mentioning wild animal strict liability rule although case dealt with vicious dog); *Gordan v. Kaufman,* 44 Ind.App. 603, 89 N.E. 898 (1909); *Bostock-Ferari Amusement Co. v. Brocksmith,* 34 Ind.App. 566, 73 N.E. 281 (1904) (setting out wild animal rule and its rationale, but not applying it because bear's inherent dangerousness was not cause of harm); [c]. Accordingly, we have little difficulty concluding that Indiana's common law recognized the strict liability rule for wild animal cases—despite the fact that previously, Indiana courts have not had the opportunity to apply the rule.

[The court's discussion, finding that the comparative fault statute did not change the common law rule of strict liability in wild animal cases, is omitted.]

II. Exceptions or Defenses

[W]e next address Irvine's contention that no exceptions to strict liability in wild animal cases have ever been applied in this state. … As this is an issue of **first impression**, we look to the reason behind the strict liability wild animal rule and consult other sources as necessary.

We have previously set out the rationale for imposing strict liability against owners for injuries caused by an attack by a naturally ferocious or dangerous animal. [C] Strict liability is appropriately placed:

> upon those who, even with proper care, expose the community to the risk of a very dangerous thing…. The kind of "dangerous animal" that will subject the keeper to strict liability … must pose some kind of an abnormal risk to the particular community where the animal is kept; hence, the keeper is engaged in an activity that subjects those in the vicinity, including those who come onto his property, to an abnormal risk … The possessor of a wild animal is strictly liable for physical harm done to the person of another … if that harm results from a dangerous propensity that is characteristic of wild animals of that class. Thus, strict liability has been imposed on keepers of lions and tigers, bears, elephants, wolves, monkeys, and other similar animals. No member of such a species, however domesticated, can ever be regarded as safe, and liability does not rest upon any experience with the particular animal.

W. Page Keeton et al., Prosser and Keeton on the Law of Torts § 76, at 541-42 (5th ed. 1984). … [In a recent case,] Judge Posner concisely set out the rationale for the wild animal strict liability rule using the following hypothetical:

> [k]eeping a tiger in one's backyard would be an example of an abnormally hazardous activity. The hazard is such, relative to the value of the activity, that we desire not just that the owner take all due care that the tiger not escape, but that he consider seriously the possibility of getting rid of the tiger altogether; and we give him an incentive to consider this course of action by declining to make the exercise of due care a defense to a suit based on an injury caused by the tiger--in other words, by making him strictly liable for any such injury.

G.J. Leasing Co. v. Union Electric Co., 54 F.3d 379, 386 (7th Cir.1995).

With the[se] rationale[s] for the rule in mind, we analyze whether any exceptions or defenses to the strict liability wild animal rule are appropriate. [T]he *Restatement* provides:

> (1) A possessor of a wild animal is subject to liability to another for harm done by the animal to the other, his person, land or chattels, although the possessor has exercised the utmost care to confine the animal, or otherwise prevent it from doing harm.

> (2) This liability is limited to harm that results from a dangerous propensity that is characteristic of wild animals of the particular class, or of which the possessor knows or has reason to know.

Restatement (Second) of Torts § 507 (1977). However, because the general rule in § 507 is "subject to a number of exceptions and qualifications, which are too numerous to state in a single Section," § 507 should be read together with § 508, § 510, § 511, § 512, § 515, and § 517. *Restatement, supra* cmt. a, § 507. Thus, we look to those other sections to help flesh out the *Restatement's* rule.

Section 510(a) provides: "The possessor of a wild animal ... is subject to strict liability for the resulting harm, although it would not have occurred but for the unexpectable ... innocent, negligent or reckless conduct of a third person." However, "[a] possessor of land is not subject to strict liability to one who intentionally or negligently trespasses upon the land, for harm done to him by a wild animal ... that the possessor keeps on the land, even though the **trespasser** has no reason to know that the animal is kept there." *Restatement, supra* § 511. **Invitees** and **licensees** are dealt with in § 513, which states: "The possessor of a wild animal ... who keeps it upon land in his possession, is subject to strict liability to persons coming upon the land in the exercise of a privilege whether derived from his consent to their entry or otherwise." Yet, if the invitee or licensee "knows that the dangerous animal is permitted to run at large or has escaped from control they may be barred from recovery if they choose to act upon the possessor's consent or to exercise any other privilege and thus expose themselves to the risk of being harmed by the animal. (See § 515)." *Restatement, supra* cmt. a, § 513.

Section 515(2), in turn, provides: "The plaintiff's **contributory negligence** in knowingly and unreasonably subjecting himself to the risk that a wild animal ... will do harm to his person ... is a defense to the strict liability." Comment c. to § 515(2) explains:

> Although one harmed by a wild ... animal that has escaped from control of its possessor or harborer is not barred from recovery because he has not exercised ordinary care to observe the presence of the animal or to

escape from its attack, he is barred if he intentionally and unreasonably subjects himself to the risk of harm by the animal. Thus *one who without any necessity for so doing that is commensurate with the risk involved knowingly puts himself in reach of an animal that is effectively chained or otherwise confined cannot recover against the possessor or harborer of the animal.* So, too, although a licensee or an invitee upon land of another upon which he knows that wild ... animals are kept under the possessor's control does not take the risk that they will escape and harm him, he does nonetheless take the risk of harm by the animals that he knows are roaming at large, so that he will to a reasonable certainty encounter them if he avails himself of the invitation or permission held out to him by the possessor of the land. (Emphasis added).

Comment d. to § 515(2) states: "This kind of contributory negligence, which consists of voluntarily and unreasonably encountering a known danger, is frequently called either contributory negligence or assumption of risk, or both."

Section 515(3) provides: "The plaintiff's **assumption of the risk** of harm from the animal is a defense to the strict liability." The comment to § 515(3) states that "one employed as a lion tamer in a circus may be barred from recovery by his assumption of the risk when he is clawed by a lion. In the same manner, *one who* voluntarily teases and provokes a chained bear, or *goes within reach of a vicious dog,* is barred from recovery if he does so with knowledge of the danger." (Emphases added).

As indicated by the extensive quotations above, the *Restatement* clearly recognizes exceptions or defenses to wild animal strict liability. ... "[C]ontributory negligence by way of knowingly and unreasonably subjecting oneself to a risk of harm from an abnormally dangerous animal will constitute a defense" to a strict liability claim. [C] "Thus, a plaintiff who voluntarily and unreasonably comes within reach of an animal which he knows to be dangerous, ... has no cause of action when it attacks him." [C]; *see also Opelt v. Al. G. Barnes Co.,* (1918), 41 Cal.App. 776, 183 P. 241 (crawling under rope near leopard's cage); *Heidemann v. Wheaton,* (1948), 72 S.D. 375, 34 N.W.2d 492 (going within reach of bear).

Food for Thought

The court here downplays any distinction between contributory negligence, comparative fault, and assumption of the risk, concepts all discussed in Chapter 6, Defenses (and Partial Defenses) to Negligence Actions. Is the court correct to downplay the distinctions between these defenses? What are the differences (in definition and effect) between each?

Because we agree with the rationale of the exceptions and/or defenses set out in the *Restatement,* and because we find it to be in keeping with Indiana's recent policy regarding allocation of fault, we adopt the *Restatement's* approach in wild animal cases.

III. Genuine Issues of Material Fact

Finally, we address whether any genuine issues of material fact exist which would support the trial court's partial denial of summary judgment.

A. Irvine's Status

In view of our adoption of the *Restatement's* strict liability wild animal rule along with its exceptions and defenses, Irvine's status becomes important. In some circumstances, a party's status (as either an invitee, licensee, or trespasser) is a question of fact not determinable at the summary judgment level. ... [T]here is some conflicting evidence regarding Irvine's status, thus precluding summary judgment on this issue.

B. Defenses

In adopting the Restatement's view that incurred risk/assumed risk may be a defense to a strict liability wild animal claim, we must next examine whether genuine issues of material fact exist regarding a defense in Irvine's case. ...

Here, the parties designated conflicting evidence regarding whether Irvine knowingly and unreasonably put himself within reach of a wild animal that was effectively chained or otherwise confined. ... In view of the conflicting evidence and inferences, summary judgment was properly denied on the issue of whether a defense was appropriate in this case.

Affirmed.

Points for Discussion

1. The *Irvine* court's decision states the current majority law regarding the imposition of strict liability for injuries caused by wild animals – the possessor of a wild animal is strictly liable for physical harm done to the person or property of another if that harm results from a dangerous propensity that is characteristic of wild animals of that class. In such circumstances, liability is imposed against the defendant without regard to due care used

2. What are considerations supporting the imposition of strict liability for injuries caused by wild animals? Do you agree with strict liability as a regime to control injuries by wild animals?

3. According to the *Irvine* court, what are the exceptions or limitations to the imposition of strict liability for harm caused by wild animals? May trespassers hold a defendant liable for injuries caused by a wild animal on the land owner's property? Is a plaintiff's contributory or comparative negligence a defense to a strict liability action? Might a plaintiff's assumption of the risk constitute a viable defense?

4. How might the legal status of Irvine as a **trespasser**, **invitee**, or **licensee** impact Irvine's ability to recover from the defendant in strict liability?

Make the Connection

The distinctions between definitions of and the respective duties owed to trespassers, licensees, and invitees are explored in Chapter 7 (Advanced Topics in Negligence Actions).

5. **Wild Animals –** The *Irvine* court explains that a defendant possessing a vicious dog may have a defense to a strict liability claim if the plaintiff has voluntarily gone in reach of the animal. How is the court's discussion of strict liability against owners of ***wild animals*** related to a defendant's possession of a ***domestic animal***, such as a dog? The answer is that if an owner of a domestic animal knows or has reason to know of the animal's **vicious propensities**, the animal is classified as a wild animal for purposes of tort law. Injuries caused by domestic animals without known vicious propensities may still be recoverable in tort, but the plaintiff would need to pursue an intentional tort or negligence action rather than one based on strict liability. *See, e.g.,* Belhumeur v. Zilm, 157 N.H. 233 (2008) (recognizing negligence action for injuries caused by defendant's bees); Poznanski v. Horvath, 788 N.E.2d 1255 (Ind. 2003) (mixed-breed sheep dog is domestic animal given owner's lack of knowledge of dog's vicious propensities and therefore negligence, not strict liability, governs); *see also* Zinter v. Oswskey, 247 Wis.2d 497 (Ct. App. 2001) (whether rabbit was domestic or wild is question of fact); Tipton v. Tabor, 567 N.W.2d 351 (S.D. 1997) (evaluating whether a wolf-German Shepherd hybrid, which was 95% wolf, was wild or domestic); Harper v. Robinson, 263 Ga.App. 727 (Ct. App. 2004) (evidence of animal's direct pedigree as dog sufficient to show it was domestic animal and therefore owner not subject to strict liability).

FYI

In law, wild animals are also referred to as *ferae naturae,* Latin for "of a wild nature."

6. Owners or possessors of wild animals are subject to strict liability, even if they have no knowledge or reason to believe that their animal is dangerous. *See, e.g.,* Whitefield v. Stewart, 577 P.2d 1295 (Okla. 1978) (strict liability allowable against owner of pet monkey even though monkey had played with over 100 children without harming any of them).

7. To be strictly liable, the defendant must own, possess, control, or harbor the animal. *See, e.g.,* Nichols v. Lowe's Home Ctr., Inc., 407 F.Supp.2d 979 (S.D. Ill. 2006) (no strict liability permitted where plaintiff, walking through outside gardening area of defendant's home improvement store, was struck in back of head by bird, as defendant did not own or possess bird); Briley v. Mitchell, 238 La. 551 (1959) (defendant strictly liable when deer he caught and held temporarily, intending to release, attacked an officer called to defendant's house where deer was chained in front yard).

8. **Dog Statutes** – Many jurisdictions have modified the common law imposition of strict liability for dogs by statute. *See, e.g.,* Pepper v. Triplet and Allstate Ins. Co, 864 So.2d 181 (La. 2004) (statute provides for strict liability of dog owner "for injuries to persons or property caused by the dog and which the owner could have prevented and which did not result from the injured person's provocation of the dog"); Cook v. Whitsell-Sherman, 796 N.E.2d 271 (Ind. 2003) (dog owners strictly liable for dog bites of public servants without provocation, but may only be held liable in negligence for dog bites to non-public servants).

9. Should owners of particular breeds of dogs be subject to strict liability, even if the owner did not know and had no reason to know of the specific dog's vicious propensities? *Compare* Carter v. Metro North Assoc., 255 A.D.2d 251 (N.Y. App. Div. 1998) (ruling no strict liability for pit bull attack absent owner's knowledge or reason to know of animal's vicious propensities) *with* Tucker v. Duke, 873 N.E.2d 664 (Ind. Ct. App. 2007) (ruling pit bull is dangerous breed which puts owner on notice of animal's vicious propensities).

10. **Plaintiff's Fault as a Defense to Strict Liability** – Historically, a plaintiff's assumption of the risk was a defense to a strict liability claim in most jurisdictions, but the plaintiff's contributory negligence was not. In one well-known case, plaintiff turned his mare and colt out in the pasture of a neighbor. Other horses occupied the pasture during the season, including the defendant's three-year old colt, which plaintiff knew to be vicious. When plaintiff went to the pasture to grain his mare, he was kicked by the defendant's horse, sustaining serious injuries. What result? *See* Sandy v. Bushey, 128 A. 513 (Me. Sup. J. Ct 1925) (explaining that if plaintiff assumed the risk, his con-

duct would bar any recovery in strict liability); *see also* Marshall v. Ranne, 511 S.W.2d 255 (Tex. 1974) (ruling in action for injuries caused by neighbor's wild boar that contributory negligence was not valid defense to strict liability claim, but assumption of the risk was).

11. What of jurisdictions that have adopted a comparative fault scheme, particularly where assumption of the risk has been subsumed into the comparative fault scheme? *See* Chapter 6 (exploring comparative fault issues). Should a plaintiff's fault be compared against a defendant subject to strict liability? *See* Mills v. Smith, 9 Kan.App.2d 80 (Ct. App. 1983) (in strict liability action against owner of lion for injuries to 21-month-old child, comparative fault principles operated to compare plaintiff's fault to defendant's fault).

————————

Hypo 8-1

Bourassa, a zookeeper, sued for an injury sustained in performing a simulated blood draw on Busch Gardens' lion, Max. Busch Gardens had developed a method of drawing blood from Max by bringing him into a smaller cage and drawing blood from his tail while another zookeeper gave him positive reinforcement in the form of food. This had been the practice for years without injury. One day when Bourassa's family came to visit the park, she asked to be permitted to perform the blood draw and to be the one to feed Max. Unfortunately, Bourassa got a little too close to the big cat, and the full-grown male lion pulled her arm into the cage, severing it at the elbow. Bourassa sued her employer in strict liability. Busch Gardens moved for summary judgment. Assume that in this jurisdiction, an employer is not immune from strict liability in an action by its employees for work-related injuries. How should the court rule on defendant's motion?

Hypo 8-2

Sandra has owned her beloved chimpanzee, Travis, for many years. Sandra and Travis, who is full-grown at 200 pounds, are well known in City. They are often seen walking together hand in hand throughout City and have even been known to picnic with one another in public places, despite the fact that there is a City ordinance prohibiting the presence of wild animals in public places. One day, Travis is feeling a bit more combative than usual, and he has escaped from the locked bedroom in which he spends most of his time.

Sandra calls her friend Mary to help her lure Travis back into the house. Mary and Travis know one another well. Mary has taken care of Travis in the past for Sandra, but over the years, she has been less excited to do so as she has developed a healthy and well-founded fear of Travis. Travis has previously bitten Mary on the hand and has become increasingly more difficult to control. Mary fears that Travis has become too large and strong and that it is just a matter of time before he gravely injures someone. She believes that he is fully capable of grievously injuring a human being at any moment if he makes up his mind to do so.

When Mary arrives to help Sandra, she finds Travis wandering wildly in the street in front of Sandra's house. Noticing Mary, Travis immediately runs toward her and attacks, inflicting life-threatening injuries. As a result of the attack, Mary nearly dies and is hospitalized for months. Mary seeks to hold Sandra responsible in tort for the injuries inflicted by Travis. Discuss.

B. Activities

Rylands v. Fletcher

[1868] UKHL 1 (17 July 1868)

THE LORD CHANCELLOR (Lord *Cairns*): My Lords, in this case the Plaintiff ... is the occupier of a mine and works under a **close** of land. The Defendants are the owners of a mill in his neighbourhood, and they proposed to make a reservoir for the purpose of keeping and storing water to be used about their mill upon another close of land, which, for the purposes of this case, may be taken as being adjoining to the close of the Plaintiff.... Underneath the close of land of the Defendants on which they proposed to construct their reservoir there were certain old and disused mining passages and works. There were five vertical shafts, and some horizontal shafts communicating with them. The vertical shafts had been filled up with soil and rubbish, and it does not appear that any person was aware of the existence either of the vertical shafts or of the horizontal works communicating with them. In the course of the working by the Plaintiff of his mine, he had gradually worked through the seams of coal underneath the close, and had come into contact with the old and disused works underneath the close of the Defendants.

In that state of things the reservoir of the Defendants was constructed. It was constructed by them through the agency and inspection of an engineer and contractor. Personally, the Defendants appear to have taken no part in the works, or to have been aware of any want of security connected with them. As regards the engineer and the contractor, we must take it from the case that they did not exercise, as far as they were concerned, that reasonable care and caution which they might have exercised, taking notice, as they appear to have taken notice, of the vertical shafts filled up in the manner which I have mentioned. However, my Lords, when the reservoir was constructed, and filled, or partly filled, with water, the weight of the water bearing upon the disused and imperfectly filled-up vertical shafts, broke through those shafts. The water passed down them and into the horizontal workings, and from the horizontal workings under the close of the Defendants it passed on into the workings under the close of the Plaintiff, and flooded his mine, causing considerable damage, for which this action was brought.

The **Court of Exchequer**, when the special case stating the facts to which I have referred, was argued, was of opinion that the Plaintiff had established no cause of action. The **Court of Exchequer Chamber**, before which an appeal from this judgment was argued, was of a contrary opinion, and the Judges there unanimously arrived at the conclusion that there was a cause of action, and that the Plaintiff was entitled to damages.

My Lords, the principles on which this case must be determined appear to me to be extremely simple. The Defendants, treating them as the owners or occupiers of the close on which the reservoir was constructed, might lawfully have used that close for any purpose for which it might in the ordinary course of the enjoyment of land be used; and if, in what I may term the natural use of that land, there had been any accumulation of water, either on the surface or underground, and if, by the operation of the laws of nature, that accumulation of water had passed off into the close occupied by the Plaintiff, the Plaintiff could not have complained that that result had taken place. If he had desired to guard himself against it, it would have lain upon him to have done so, by leaving, or by interposing, some barrier between his close and the close of the Defendants in order to have prevented that operation of the laws of nature. ...

On the other hand if the Defendants, not stopping at the natural use of their close, had desired to use it for any purpose which I may term a non-natural use, for the purpose of introducing into the close that which in its natural condition was not in or upon it, for the purpose of introducing water either above or below ground in quantities and in a manner not the result of any work or operation on or under the land, - and if in consequence of their doing so, or in consequence of any imperfection in the mode of their doing so, the water came to escape and to pass off into the close of the Plaintiff, then it appears to me that that which the Defendants were doing they were doing at their own peril; and, if in the course of their doing it, the evil arose to which I have referred, the evil, namely, of the escape of the water and its passing away to the close of the Plaintiff and injuring the Plaintiff, then for the consequence of that, in my opinion, the Defendants would be liable. ...

My Lords, these simple principles, if they are well founded, as it appears to me they are, really dispose of this case.

The same result is arrived at on the principles referred to by Mr. Justice *Blackburn* in his judgment, in the Court of Exchequer Chamber, where he states the opinion of that Court as to the law in these words:

"We think that the true rule of law is, that the person who, for his own purposes, brings on his land and collects and keeps there anything likely to do mischief if it escapes, must keep it in at his peril; and if he does not do so, is *primâ facie* answerable for all the damage which is the natural consequence of its escape. He can excuse himself by shewing that the escape was owing to the Plaintiff's default; or, perhaps, that the escape was the consequence of **vis major**, or the act of God; but as nothing of this sort exists here, it is unnecessary to inquire what excuse would be sufficient. The general rule, as above stated, seems on principle just. The person whose grass or corn is eaten down by the escaping cattle of his neighbour, or whose mine is flooded by the water from his neighbour's reservoir, or whose cellar is invaded by the filth of his neighbour's privy, or whose habitation is made unhealthy by the fumes and noisome vapours of his neighbour's alkali works, is damnified without any fault of his own; and it seems but reasonable and just that the neighbour who has brought something on his own property (which was not naturally there), harmless to others so long as it is confined to his own property, but which he knows will be mischievous if it gets on his neighbour's, should be obliged to make good the damage which ensues if he does not succeed in confining it to his own property. But for his act in bringing it there no mischief could have accrued, and it seems but just that he should at his peril keep it there, so that no mischief may accrue, or answer for the natural and anticipated consequence. And upon authority this we think is established to be the law, whether the things so brought be beasts, or water, or filth, or stenches."

My Lords, in that opinion, I must say I entirely concur. Therefore, I have to move your Lordships that the judgment of the Court of Exchequer Chamber be affirmed, and that the present appeal be dismissed with costs.

[Concurrence of Lord Cransworth omitted.]

Points for Discussion

1.   What types of activities are subject to strict liability?

2.   *Rylands v. Fletcher* is one of the first cases to apply strict liability to activities. Why did the plaintiffs need to rely on a theory of recovery other than negligence against the defendants in this case? Why not hold the defendants vicariously liable for the carelessness of the engineer or contractor? Why not hold them liable in negligence?

3.   What was the ruling in the Exchequer Chamber? What is the ruling from the House of Lords? Are the rulings the same or does the ruling in the House of Lords limit the ruling of the Exchequer Chamber?

4.   What are the policy justifications for imposition of strict liability for activities?

5.   **Limitations on Strict Liability –** Remember that strict liability does not equate with absolute liability; limitations may be placed on a plaintiff's ability to recover in strict liability. So, for example, when a plaintiff sought to hold a company, which was blasting dynamite, strictly liable when the vibrations from the blasting operations frightened the plaintiff's female mink, causing the mink to kill her kittens, the court refused to impose liability. Although the defendants were engaged in an activity routinely subject to strict liability and the death of the kittens was causally linked to that activity, the court ruled that the defendants were not responsible for the plaintiff's injuries. "[T]he risk of causing harm of the kind here experi-

For More Information

Fowler V. Harper's article "Liability Without Fault and Proximate Cause," 30 Mɪᴄʜ. L. Rᴇᴠ. 1001 (1932) provides a good historical account of strict liability law in the United States.

enced ... is not the kind of risk which makes the activity of blasting ultrahazardous." *See* Foster v. Preston Mill Co., 268 P.2d 645 (Wash. 1954).

6. Courts have also placed limitations on a plaintiff's ability to recover in the event of a **vis major** or unforeseeable Act of God. So in a case where the defendants owned a hydroelectric plant that was hit by an unexpected hurricane, releasing

Food for Thought

Might limitations on strict liability actions be alternatively termed proximate cause determinations, inasmuch as they limit as a defendant's strict liability only to certain consequences? *Cf.* Chapter 5 (considering proximate causation in negligence actions).

water that caused property damage to the plaintiff, the court denied the plaintiff recovery, explaining that "the flood, as disclosed by the evidence, was plainly beyond the capacity of any one to anticipate, and was clearly an act of God. For this reason ... the defendants cannot be held liable for injury caused by the flood waters." *See* Golden v. Amory, 109 N.E.2d 131 (Mass. Sup. J. Ct. 1952); *see also* Scorza v. Martinez & Worldwide Primates, Inc., 683 So.2d 1115 (Fla. Dist. Ct. App. 1996) (monkey left outside during hurricane).

Non constat jus civile a posteriori

It's Latin to Me!

A *vis major* is Latin for "a superior force." It is sometimes also referred to as a *force majeure*.

7. The Restatement (First) of Torts used the term "ultrahazardous" to define activity subject to strict liability. Ultrahazardous activities are those that necessarily involve a risk of serious harm, which cannot be eliminated by the exercise of care and is not a matter of common usage. *See* Restatement (First) of Torts § 520. In determining whether an activity is ultrahazardous, the focus is on the activity itself. Contrast that with the approach taken by the Restatement (Second) of Torts, which adopted the term "abnormally dangerous." Restatement (Second) of Torts § 520 shifted the focus away from the dangerousness of the activity itself to considering the appropriateness of the activity in the place and surrounding in which the activity takes place. The following case provides a good discussion of important factors and policy considerations in determining whether a particular activity is appropriately subject to strict liability.

Take Note

Court sometimes (mistakenly) use the terms "ultrahazardous" and "abnormally dangerous" as if they are interchangeable. *See, e.g.,* Miller v. Civil Constructors, Inc., 651 N.E.2d 239 (Ill. Ct. App. 1995). How do the two terms differ, if at all?

Indiana Harbor Belt R.R. Co. v. American Cyanamid Co.

916 F.2d 1174 (7th Cir. 1990)

Before POSNER, MANION and KANNE, Circuit Judges.

POSNER, Circuit Judge.

American Cyanamid Company, the defendant in this **diversity** tort suit governed by Illinois law, is a major manufacturer of chemicals, including acrylonitrile, a chemical used in large quantities in making acrylic fibers, plastics, dyes, pharmaceutical chemicals, and other intermediate and final goods. On January 2, 1979, at its manufacturing plant in Louisiana, Cyanamid loaded 20,000 gallons of liquid acrylonitrile into a railroad tank car that it had leased from the North American Car Corporation.

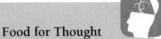

Food for Thought

Why is this federal court applying Illinois state law?

The next day, a train of the Missouri Pacific Railroad picked up the car at Cyanamid's siding. The car's ultimate destination was a Cyanamid plant in New Jersey served by Conrail rather than by Missouri Pacific. The Missouri Pacific train carried the car north to the Blue Island railroad yard of Indiana Harbor Belt Railroad, the plaintiff in this case, a small switching line that has a contract with Conrail to switch cars from other lines to Conrail, in this case for travel east. The Blue Island yard is in the Village of Riverdale, which is just south of Chicago and part of the Chicago metropolitan area.

The car arrived in the Blue Island yard on the morning of January 9, 1979. Several hours after it arrived, employees of the switching line noticed fluid gushing from the bottom outlet of the car. The lid on the outlet was broken. After two hours, the line's supervisor of equipment was able to stop the leak by closing a shut-off valve controlled from the top of the car. No one was sure at the time just how much of the contents of the car had leaked, but it was feared that all 20,000 gallons had, and since acrylonitrile is flammable at a temperature of 30° Fahrenheit or above, highly toxic, and possibly carcinogenic ..., the local authorities ordered the homes near the yard evacuated. The evacuation lasted only a few hours, until the car was moved to a remote part of the yard and it was discovered that only about a quarter of the acrylonitrile had leaked. Concerned nevertheless that there had been some contamination of soil and water, the Illinois Department of Environmental Protection ordered the switching line to take decontamination measures that cost the line $981,022.75, which it sought to recover by this suit.

One count of the two-count complaint charges Cyanamid with having maintained the leased tank car negligently. The other count asserts that the transportation of acrylonitrile in bulk through the Chicago metropolitan area is an abnormally dangerous activity, for the consequences of which the shipper (Cyanamid) is strictly liable to the switching line, which bore the financial brunt of those consequences because of the decontamination measures that it was forced to take. ... [T]he district judge denied Cyanamid's motion to dismiss the strict liability count, 517 F.Supp. 314 (N.D.Ill.1981)[; t]he switching line moved for summary judgment on that count—and won. 662 F.Supp. 635 (N.D.Ill.1987). ... The district judge then, over the switching line's objection, dismissed the negligence claim with prejudice, thus terminating proceedings in the district court and clearing the way for Cyanamid to file an appeal of which we would have jurisdiction. ... The switching line has cross-appealed, challenging the dismissal of the negligence count.

The question whether the shipper of a hazardous chemical by rail should be strictly liable for the consequences of a spill or other accident to the shipment en route is a novel one in Illinois ....

The parties agree that the question whether placing acrylonitrile in a rail shipment that will pass through a metropolitan area subjects the shipper to strict liability is, as recommended in Restatement (Second) of Torts § 520, comment *l* (1977), a question of law.... They also agree ... that the Supreme Court of Illinois would treat as authoritative the provisions of the Restatement governing abnormally dangerous activities. The key provision is section 520, which sets forth six factors to be considered in deciding whether an activity is abnormally dangerous and the actor therefore strictly liable.

The roots of section 520 are in nineteenth-century cases. The most famous one is *Rylands v. Fletcher*, 1 Ex. 265, aff'd, L.R. 3 H.L. 300 (1868), but a more illuminating one in the present context is *Guille v. Swan*, 19 Johns. (N.Y.) 381 (1822). A man took off in a hot-air balloon and landed, without intending to, in a vegetable garden in New York City. A crowd that had been anxiously watching his involuntary descent trampled the vegetables in their endeavor to rescue him when he landed. The owner of the garden sued the balloonist for the resulting damage, and won. Yet the balloonist had not been careless. In the then state of ballooning it was impossible to make a pinpoint landing.

Guille is a paradigmatic case for strict liability. (a) The risk (probability) of harm was great, and (b) the harm that would ensue if the risk materialized could be, although luckily was not, great (the balloonist could have crashed into the crowd rather than into the vegetables). The confluence of these two factors established the urgency of seeking to prevent such accidents. (c) Yet such accidents could not be prevented by the exercise of due care; the technology of care in ballooning was insufficiently developed. (d) The activity was not a matter of common usage, so there was no presumption that it was a highly valuable activity despite its unavoidable riskiness. (e) The activity was inappropriate to the place in which it took place-densely populated New York City. The risk of serious harm to others (other than the balloonist himself, that is) could have been reduced by shifting the activity to the sparsely inhabited areas that surrounded the city in those days. (f) Reinforcing (d), the value to the community of the activity of recreational ballooning did not appear to be great enough to offset its unavoidable risks.

These are, of course, the six factors in section 520. They are related to each other in that each is a different facet of a common quest for a proper legal regime to govern accidents that negligence liability cannot adequately control. The interrelations might be more perspicuous if the six factors were reordered. One might for example start with (c), inability to eliminate the risk of accident by the exercise of due care. [C] The baseline common law regime of tort liability is negligence. When it is a workable regime, because the hazards of an activity can be avoided by being careful (which is to say, nonnegligent), there is no need to switch to strict liability. Sometimes, however, a particular type of accident cannot be prevented by taking care but can be avoided, or its consequences minimized, by shifting the activity in which the accident occurs to another locale, where the risk or harm of an accident will be less ((e)), or by reducing the scale of the activity in order to minimize the number of accidents caused by it ((f)). [Cc] By making the actor strictly liable—by denying him in other words an excuse based on his inability to avoid accidents by being more careful—we give him an incentive, missing in a negligence regime, to experiment with methods of preventing accidents that involve not greater exertions of care, assumed to be futile, but instead relocating, changing, or reducing (perhaps to the vanishing point) the activity giving rise to the accident. [C] The greater the risk of an accident ((a)) and the costs of an accident if one occurs ((b)), the more we want the actor to consider the possibility of making accident-reducing activity changes; the stronger, therefore, is the case for strict liability. Finally, if an activity is extremely common ((d)), like driving an automobile, it is unlikely either that its hazards are perceived as great or that there is no technology of care available to minimize them; so the case for strict liability is weakened.

The largest class of cases in which strict liability has been imposed under the standard codified in the Second Restatement of Torts involves the use of dynamite and other explosives for demolition in residential or urban areas. Restatement, *supra,* § 519, comment d; [c]. Explosives are dangerous even when handled carefully, and we therefore want blasters to choose the location of the activity with care and also to explore the feasibility of using safer substitutes (such as a wrecking ball), as well as to be careful in the blasting itself. Blasting is not a commonplace activity like driving a car, or so superior to substitute methods of demolition that the imposition of liability is unlikely to have any effect except to raise the activity's costs.

Against this background we turn to the particulars of acrylonitrile. Acrylonitrile is one of a large number of chemicals that are hazardous in the sense of being flammable, toxic, or both; acrylonitrile is both, as are many others. A table in the record ... contains a list of the 125 hazardous materials that are shipped in highest volume on the nation's railroads. Acrylonitrile is the fifty-third most hazardous on the list. Number 1 is phosphorus (white or yellow), and among the other materials that rank higher than acrylonitrile on the hazard scale are anhydrous ammonia, liquified petroleum gas, vinyl chloride, gasoline, crude petroleum, motor fuel antiknock compound, methyl and ethyl chloride, sulphuric acid, sodium metal, and chloroform. The plaintiff's lawyer acknowledged at argument that the logic of the district court's opinion dictated strict liability for all 52 materials that rank higher than acrylonitrile on the list, and quite possibly for the 72 that rank lower as well, since all are hazardous if spilled in quantity while being shipped by rail. Every shipper of any of these materials would therefore be strictly liable for the consequences of a spill or other accident that occurred while the material was being shipped through a metropolitan area. The plaintiff's lawyer further acknowledged the irrelevance, on her view of the case, of the fact that Cyanamid had leased and filled the car that spilled the acrylonitrile; all she thought important is that Cyanamid introduced the product into the stream of commerce that happened to pass through the Chicago metropolitan area. Her concession may have been incautious. One might want to distinguish between the shipper who merely places his goods on his loading dock to be picked up by the carrier and the shipper who, as in this case, participates actively in the transportation. But the concession is illustrative of the potential scope of the district court's decision.

    ....

[W]e can get little help from precedent, and might as well apply section 520 to the acrylonitrile problem from the ground up. To begin with, we have been given no reason ... for believing that a negligence regime is not perfectly adequate to remedy and deter, at reasonable cost, the accidental spillage of acrylonitrile from rail cars ... Acrylonitrile could explode and destroy evidence, but of course did not here, making imposition of strict liability ... premature. More important, although acrylonitrile is flammable even at relatively low temperatures, and toxic, it is not so corrosive or otherwise destructive that it will eat through or otherwise damage or weaken a tank car's valves although they are maintained with due (which essentially means, with average) care. No one suggests, therefore, that the leak in this case was caused by the *inherent* properties of acrylonitrile. It was caused by carelessness-whether that of the North American Car Corporation in failing to maintain or inspect the car properly, or that of Cyanamid in failing to maintain or inspect it, or that of the Missouri Pacific when it had custody of the car, or that of the switching line itself in failing to notice the ruptured lid, or some combination of these possible failures of care. Accidents that are due to a lack of care can be prevented by taking care; and when a lack of care can … be shown in court, such accidents are adequately deterred by the threat of liability for negligence.

It is true that the district court purported to find as a fact that there is an inevitable risk of derailment or other calamity in transporting "large quantities of anything." [C] This is not a finding of fact, but a truism: anything can happen. The question is, how likely is this type of accident if the actor uses due care? For all that appears from the record of the case or any other sources of information that we have found, if a tank car is carefully maintained the danger of a spill of acrylonitrile is negligible. If this is right, there is no compelling reason to move to a regime of strict liability, especially one that might embrace all other hazardous materials shipped by rail as well. This also means, however, that the **amici curiae** who have filed briefs in support of Cyanamid cry wolf in predicting "devastating" effects on the chemical industry if the district court's decision is affirmed. If the vast majority of chemical spills by railroads are preventable by due care, the imposition of strict liability should cause only a slight, not as they argue a substantial, rise in liability insurance rates, because the incremental liability should be slight. The amici have momentarily lost sight of the fact that the feasibility of avoiding accidents simply by being careful is an argument *against* strict liability.

It's Latin to Me!

Literally translated to "friend of the court," *amici curiae* is a person who is not a party to the lawsuit but who has petitioned the court or filed a brief in the case because of a strong interest in its subject matter.

....

The district judge and the plaintiff's lawyer make much of the fact that the spill occurred in a densely inhabited metropolitan area. Only 4,000 gallons spilled; what if all 20,000 had done so? Isn't the risk that this might happen even if everybody were careful sufficient to warrant giving the shipper an incentive to explore alternative routes? Strict liability would supply that incentive. But this argument overlooks the fact that, like other transportation networks, the railroad network is a hub-and-spoke system. And the hubs are in metropolitan areas. Chicago is one of the nation's largest railroad hubs. In 1983, the latest year for which we have figures, Chicago's railroad yards handled the third highest volume of hazardous-material shipments in the nation. East St. Louis, which is also in Illinois, handled the second highest volume. … With most hazardous chemicals (by volume of shipments) being at least as hazardous as acrylonitrile, it is unlikely—and certainly not demonstrated by the plaintiff—that they can be rerouted around all the metropolitan areas in the country, except at prohibitive cost. Even if it were feasible to reroute them one would hardly expect shippers, as distinct from carriers, to be the firms best situated to do the rerouting. Granted, the usual view is that **common carriers** are not subject to strict liability for the carriage of materials that make the transportation of them abnormally dangerous, because a common carrier cannot refuse service to a shipper of a lawful commodity. *Restatement, supra,* § 521. ...

> **What's That?**
>
> A common carrier is a commercial enterprise holding itself out to the public as offering to transport freight or passengers for a fee. Common carriers are generally required to transport freight or passengers as long as the approved fee is paid.

The difference between shipper and carrier points to a deep flaw in the plaintiff's case. Unlike *Guille* ... and unlike the storage cases, beginning with *Rylands* itself, here it is not the actors—that is, the transporters of acrylonitrile and other chemicals—but the manufacturers, who are sought to be held strictly liable. ... It is easy to see how the accident in this case might have been prevented at reasonable cost by greater care on the part of those who handled the tank car of acrylonitrile. It is difficult to see how it might have been prevented at reasonable cost by a change in the activity of transporting the chemical. This is therefore not an apt case for strict liability.

....

In emphasizing the flammability and toxicity of acrylonitrile rather than the hazards of transporting it, as in failing to distinguish between the active and the passive shipper, the plaintiff overlooks the fact that ultrahazardousness or abnormal dangerousness is, in the contemplation of the law at least, a property not of substances, but of activities: not of acrylonitrile, but of the transportation of acrylonitrile by rail through populated areas. [C] Natural gas is both flammable and poisonous, but the operation of a natural gas well is not an ultrahazardous activity. [C] Whatever the situation under products liability law (section 402A of the Restatement), the manufacturer of a product is not considered to be engaged in an abnormally dangerous activity merely because the product becomes dangerous when it is handled or used in some way after it leaves his premises, even if the danger is foreseeable. [Cc] ...

The relevant activity is transportation, not manufacturing and shipping. This essential distinction the plaintiff ignores. But even if the defendant is treated as a transporter and not merely a shipper, the plaintiff has not shown that the transportation of acrylonitrile in bulk by rail through populated areas is so hazardous an activity, even when due care is exercised, that the law should seek to create—perhaps quixotically-incentives to relocate the activity to nonpopulated areas, or to reduce the scale of the activity, or to switch to transporting acrylonitrile by road rather than by rail.... It is no more realistic to propose to reroute the shipment of all hazardous materials around Chicago than it is to propose the relocation of homes adjacent to the Blue Island switching yard to more distant suburbs. It may be less realistic. Brutal though it may seem to say it, the inappropriate use to which land is being put in the Blue Island yard and neighborhood may be, not the transportation of hazardous chemicals, but residential living. The analogy is to building your home between the runways at O'Hare.

The briefs hew closely to the Restatement, whose approach to the issue of strict liability is mainly *allocative* rather than *distributive*. By this we mean that the emphasis is on picking a liability regime (negligence or strict liability) that will control the particular class of accidents in question most effectively, rather than on finding the deepest pocket and placing liability there. At argument, however, the plaintiff's lawyer invoked distributive considerations by pointing out that Cyanamid is a huge firm and the Indiana Harbor Belt Railroad a fifty-mile-long switching line that almost went broke in the winter of 1979, when the accident occurred. Well, so what? A corporation is not a living person but a set of contracts the terms of which determine who will bear the brunt of liability. Tracing the incidence of a cost is a complex undertaking which the plaintiff sensibly has made no effort to assume, since its legal relevance would be dubious. We add only that however small the plaintiff may be, it has mighty parents: it is a jointly owned subsidiary of Conrail and the Soo line.

The case for strict liability has not been made. Not in this suit in any event. We need not speculate on the possibility of imposing strict liability on shippers of more hazardous materials ... any more than we need differentiate (given how the plaintiff has shaped its case) between active and passive shippers. We noted earlier that acrylonitrile is far from being the most hazardous among hazardous materials shipped by rail in highest volume. Or among materials shipped, period. The Department of Transportation has classified transported materials into sixteen separate classes by the degree to which transporting them is hazardous. Class number 1 is radioactive material. Class number 2 is poisons. Class 3 is flammable gas and 4 is nonflammable gas. Acrylonitrile is in Class 5. [C]

Ordinarily when summary judgment is denied, the movant's rights are not extinguished; the case is simply set down for trial. If this approach were followed here, it would require remanding the case for a trial on whether Cyanamid should be held strictly liable. Yet that would be a mistake. The parties have agreed that the question whether the transportation of acrylonitrile through densely populated areas is abnormally dangerous is one of law rather than of fact; and trials are to determine facts, not law. ... An evidentiary hearing would be of no use in the present case, however, because the plaintiff has not indicated any facts that it wants to develop through such a hearing.

....

...[T]he plaintiff had an alternative theory of liability[, so this lawsuit] is not over now. But with damages having been fixed at a relatively modest level by the district court and not challenged by the plaintiff, and a voluminous record having been compiled in the summary judgment proceedings, we trust the parties will find it possible now to settle the case. Even the Trojan War lasted only ten years.

The judgment is reversed (with no award of costs in this court) and the case remanded for further proceedings, consistent with this opinion, on the plaintiff's claim for negligence.

REVERSED AND REMANDED, WITH DIRECTIONS.

Points for Discussion

1. Why does the court not permit the plaintiff to pursue strict liability as a theory of recovery in this case? What does the *Indiana Harbor* court define as the relevant legal inquiry in determining whether strict liability is the proper legal regime to control a defendant's activity?

2. What are the policy concerns driving imposition of strict liability? What does Judge Posner mean when he states that strict liability is "*allocative* rather than *distributive*" (emphasis in original)?

3. According to the court, is the determination of whether an activity is ultrahazardous or abnormally dangerous a question of law or fact?

4. Is the purpose for which the chemical was being used legally relevant to the court's quest for the appropriate legal regime?

5. Note that the plaintiffs in *Indiana Harbor* brought both a strict liability action as well as a negligence action. Strict liability and negligence are not mutually exclusive theories of recovery. A plaintiff can successfully sue under both theories in the same lawsuit. Can you think of reasons why plaintiffs would pursue one theory over the other? Or why a plaintiff may choose to pursue both theories of recovery?

6. How, if at all, is the determination of an abnormally dangerous activity pursuant to RESTATEMENT (SECOND) OF TORTS § 520 similar to Judge Learned Hand's negligence formula? How does it differ?

Make the Connection

See Chapter 5 for exploration of Judge Learned Hand's negligence formula, B < PL.

7. As Judge Posner explains in *Indiana Harbor,* courts are reluctant to extend strict liability as a theory of recovery in tort. Why might that be?

8. What result when a plaintiff seeks to hold the owners of a firing range strictly liable for injuries caused by police officers discharging their weapons? Plaintiff was injured when a ricocheting bullet fired during police training struck him. Plaintiff alleged that the owners of the firing range, which was located at a rock quarry, and others should be strictly liable because firing a firearm is an "ultrahazardous, highly dangerous activity." Applying the factors in RESTATEMENT (SECOND) OF TORTS § 520, the court held as a matter of law that the discharge of firearms is not an activity that would support plaintiff's strict liability claims. *See* Miller v. Civil Constructors, Inc., 651 N.E.2d 239 (Ill. Ct. App. 1995). The court held that although firing a gun was a dangerous activity, its risks could be controlled by exercising due care and therefore strict liability was an inappropriate regime to apply against the defendants. Do you agree?

9. The drafters of the RESTATEMENT (THIRD) OF TORTS adopted the following provision to succeed § 520 RESTATEMENT (SECOND) OF TORTS, streamlining the definition of an abnormally dangerous activity:

> **RESTATEMENT (THIRD) OF TORTS: LIABILITY FOR PHYSICAL HARM §
> 20 (2010)**
> **Abnormally Dangerous Activities**
>
> (a) An actor who carries on an abnormally dangerous activity is subject to strict liability for physical harm resulting from the activity.
>
> (b) An activity is abnormally dangerous if:
>
>   1. the activity creates a foreseeable and highly significant risk of physical harm even when reasonable care is exercised by all actors; and
>
>   2. the activity is not one of common usage.

10. How does RESTATEMENT (THIRD) OF TORTS § 20 differ from RESTATEMENT (FIRST) and RESTATEMENT (SECOND) OF TORTS § 520? How does the RESTATEMENT (THIRD) OF TORTS § 20 differ from Judge Posner's discussion in *Indiana Harbor*? In your opinion, which is the preferable analysis?

11. All traditional tort damages are available in a strict liability action, including damages for mental injuries. *See* Chapter 8 (Damages).

12. Although the sphere of activities governed by strict liability is infrequently expanded, strict liability has played an important role in the ever-emerging field of **products liability**. Liability for unreasonably dangerous products has been recognized under various theories of recovery, including strict liability and negligence. Products liability is a dynamic area of tort law, where all tort policy concerns and theories of recovery converge.

Hypo 8-3

James drives his car while under the influence of alcohol, causing property damage to Linda. Linda sues James in strict liability. Discuss.

Hypo 8-4

Chris has sexual intercourse with Julie, knowing that he is infected with a sexually transmitted disease. Julie, who contracts the disease, sues Chris in strict liability. Discuss.

Hypo 8-5

Bill decides to commit suicide by carbon monoxide poisoning. He lives in a duplex with an attached garage. He pulls his car into the garage, puts the garage door down, and lets the car engine run. Bill eventually succumbs to the carbon monoxide. Unfortunately, the exhaust fumes also leak out of Bill's closed garage into the duplex apartment next door, killing Neighbor. Neighbor's estate sues Bill's estate, seeking to recover in strict liability. Discuss.

CHAPTER 9

Tort Damages

Tort damages seek to restore a plaintiff, as much as possible, to one's pre-tort condition. In tort, the primary means of restoring one to that condition is by awarding money. Tort damages may also be used to deter a defendant (and others like it) from engaging in similarly tortious conduct in the future – **specific deterrence** and **general deterrence**, respectively. To those ends, there are three primary types of damages available in tort – nominal, compensatory, and punitive damages.

Make the Connection

Damage awards in other areas of the law may differ. For instance, the purpose of contract damages is typically to place the plaintiff in the position that the plaintiff would have been in if the contract had been properly performed.

Nominal Damages – Nominal damages are awarded when a tort has been committed against a plaintiff, but the plaintiff has suffered no substantial loss or injury. An award of nominal damages is a trivial amount of money – for example, $1 – in recognition that the plaintiff's legal interests were invaded or violated, despite the fact that no real loss has been suffered.

Compensatory Damages – The primary means by which tort law restores a plaintiff to pre-tort status is permitting the recovery of compensatory damages. Compensatory damages are typically comprised of economic losses and non-economic losses. Economic losses, sometimes referred to as **special damages**, are losses that are readily subject to objective measurement. Special damages, or "specials," typically include such **pecuniary losses** as:

- *lost earnings* – income, including wages or salary, that the plaintiff was unable to earn in the past because of the tortious injury;

- *loss or impairment of future earning capacity* – income, including wages or salary, that the plaintiff would have earned in the future if the plaintiff had not been tortiously injured; and

- *past and future medical expenses* – expenses for medical treatment or healthcare.

Non-economic losses, or **general damages**, compensate one for injuries not easily reduced to a dollar figure. Examples of non-economic damages typically include:

- *past and future physical pain and suffering* – physical pain and suffering about which the plaintiff is aware as a result of the plaintiff's physical injuries;

- *past and future mental pain* – emotional distress caused by the plaintiff's injuries; and

- *permanent disability and disfigurement* – injuries that will indefinitely prevent a plaintiff from performing some or all of the duties that could be performed before the injury or physical disfigurement caused by tortious conduct.

Punitive Damages – Punitive damages are damages that are awarded above and beyond compensatory damages for the distinct purpose of punishing a defendant for engaging in particularly egregious conduct. Sometimes termed "**exemplary**" or "**vindictive**" **damages**, a court's ability to award punitive damages is often constrained by constitutional considerations.

As you consider the following materials, keep in mind that one purpose of tort law is to protect one from personal or property injuries. The primary tool for restoring one to his or her pre-tort status is money. Therefore, all losses, whether past, present, or future, must be reduced to the one-time monetary award to which the plaintiff is entitled, as the plaintiff will not be permitted to return to court later to collect for more damages that may arise. Most jurisdictions require this one-time lump sum award to be reduced to **present value**.

Courts continuously wrestle with the composition of a compensatory damage award as well as the general or non-economic components of such an award. Whether a plaintiff can ever be made whole again, particularly by a money award, is subject to debate, as indicated by the following case.

A. Compensatory Damages

McGee v. AC and S, Inc.

933 So.2d 770 (La. 2006)

KIMBALL, Justice.

> **FYI**
>
> A jury verdict form is a form submitted to the jury to ascertain the jury's findings. The specific rules governing the contents of a jury form vary by jurisdiction. For example, some jurisdictions mandate that the jury answer a general verdict form requiring the jury to apply the law to the facts and find in favor of either the plaintiff or the defendant. Other jurisdictions mandate submission of a special jury form requiring the jury to make specific findings of the facts. The judge then applies the factual findings to the applicable law in order to determine which party or parties prevail. This subject is typically covered more extensively in a civil procedure course.

The issue presented in this case is whether loss of enjoyment of life is recoverable as a separate element of general damages that may be included as a separate item on a jury verdict form. For the reasons that follow, we hold that loss of enjoyment of life is recoverable as a separate element of general damages that may be included as a separate item on a jury verdict form and find that the court of appeal erred in holding that a separate award for loss of enjoyment of life is erroneous as a matter of law. Therefore, we reverse the court of appeal's ruling granting the **motion *in limine*** and reinstate the district court's ruling denying the motion *in limine*.

FACTS AND PROCEDURAL HISTORY

Plaintiffs, the widow and children of James Edward McGee, filed the instant wrongful death and survival actions against many defendants, including James Edward McGee's former employers and manufacturers of asbestos-containing products used during his employment (collectively "defendants"), seeking to recover damages for injuries sustained as a result of James Edward McGee's exposure to asbestos, from which he died on January 28, 2000.

>
>
> **Take Note**
>
> An entire chapter of this casebook is dedicated to the study of wrongful death and survival actions. *See* Chapter 10, *infra*.

In their petition, plaintiffs sought damages for, among other things, James Edward McGee's loss of enjoyment of life. Thereafter, defendants filed a motion *in limine* seeking to preclude plaintiffs from asserting a claim for loss of enjoyment of life. At the hearing on the motion, counsel for plaintiffs stated that plaintiffs were entitled to put on evidence and to have the jury give them an award for loss of enjoyment of life. Defense counsel stated that loss of enjoyment of life was a part of the general damage award and was not its own separate category of damages, but counsel for plaintiffs rebutted that loss of enjoyment of life was a separate item of damages. The district court remarked that it had allowed a separate category for loss of enjoyment of life in previous cases and denied defendants' motion *in limine*.

Defendants applied for **supervisory writs,** which the Fourth Circuit Court of Appeal granted. In reviewing the district court's ruling, the court of appeal stated that a separate award for loss of enjoyment of life was erroneous as a matter of law and stated that expert testimony concerning loss of enjoyment of life was inadmissible…. Accordingly, the court of appeal reversed the district court and granted defendants' motion *in limine* to prohibit plaintiffs from asserting a claim for loss of enjoyment of life. From that decision, plaintiffs applied for supervisory writs to this court, stating that the court of appeal erred in reversing the district court and holding that a separate award for loss of enjoyment of life is erroneous as a matter of law. We granted plaintiffs' writ application to determine whether loss of enjoyment of life is recoverable as a separate element of general damages that may be reflected as a line item on a jury verdict form.

What's That?

A *supervisory writ* is a writ issued by a court to correct an error made by a lower court in that jurisdiction where there is no appeal and a gross injustice is threatened as a result of the erroneous ruling.

DISCUSSION

Loss of enjoyment of life, sometimes known as **hedonic damages**, refers to the detrimental alterations of a person's life or lifestyle or a person's inability to participate in the activities or pleasures of life that were formerly enjoyed. [C]

In Louisiana, **delictual** actions are governed by La. C.C. art. 2315, which states that "[e]very act of man that causes damage to another obliges him by whose fault it happened to repair it." Thus, under La. C.C. art. 2315, a tortfeasor must compensate a tort victim for all of the damages occasioned by his act. The term "damages" refers to "pecuniary compensation, recom-

FYI

Unlike other American jurisdictions, Louisiana tort law is based on French law, rather than the common law of England. As a result, Louisiana law often employs different terminology, such as use of the term "delict" rather than "tort."

pense, or **satisfaction** for an injury sustained." [C] In the delictual context, La. C.C. art. 2315 authorizes compensatory damages. Compensatory damages encompass those damages "designed to place the plaintiff in the position in which he would have been if the tort had not been committed." [C]

Compensatory damages are further divided into the broad categories of special damages and general damages. Special damages are those which have a "ready market value," such that the amount of the damages theoretically may be determined with relative certainty, including medical expenses and lost wages, while general damages are inherently speculative and cannot be calculated with mathematical certainty. [C]

This court has previously defined general damages as "those which may not be fixed with any degree of **pecuniary** exactitude but which, instead, involve mental or physical pain or suffering, inconvenience, the loss of gratification of intellectual or physical enjoyment, or other losses of life or life-style which cannot really be measured definitively in terms of money." *Duncan v. Kansas City S. R.R.,* 00-0066, p. 1(La.10/30/00), 773 So.2d 670, 682. [Cc]

Loss of enjoyment of life falls within the definition of general damages because it involves the quality of a person's life, which is inherently speculative and cannot be measured definitively in terms of money. "The loss of gratification of intellectual or physical enjoyment" included in the definition of general damages directly results from a person's "inability to participate in the activities or pleasures of life that a person formerly enjoyed" as set forth in the definition of loss of enjoyment of life. Similarly, "the loss of life or life-style" included in the definition of general damages is substantially similar to the "detrimental alteration of a person's life or lifestyle" as included in the definition of loss of enjoyment of life. Thus, loss of enjoyment of life is clearly encompassed within "the loss of gratification of intellectual or physical enjoyment, or other losses of life or life-style" component of this court's existing definition of general damages.

La. C.C. art. 2315 authorizes a tort victim to be compensated for the damage sustained as a result of the **delict**, including those for loss of enjoyment of life, if proven. Moreover, this court has clearly defined general damages to include loss of enjoyment of life. Consequently, loss of enjoyment of life is a compensable component of general damages under both La. C.C. art. 2315 and this court's existing definition of general damages. Therefore, the only remaining issue is whether loss of enjoyment of life may be separated from other elements of general damages, such as mental and physical pain and suffering, and whether that separation may be reflected by having a line for loss of enjoyment of life on a jury verdict form. [Cc]

As established above, loss of enjoyment of life is a component of general damages and therefore loss of enjoyment of life is not separate and distinct from general damages. Nevertheless, general damages in Louisiana are routinely dissected. Courts commonly list different elements of general damages, including mental anguish and physical pain and suffering, both past and future, separately. In addition, general damages for permanent scarring and/or disfigurement are often listed separately. [C] Thus, allowing a separate award for loss of enjoyment of life would not offend the existing concept of general damages and would reflect the accepted method of listing elements of general damages separately.

Moreover, loss of enjoyment of life is conceptually distinct from other components of general damages, including pain and suffering. Pain and suffering, both physical and mental, refers to the pain, discomfort, inconvenience, anguish, and emotional trauma that accompanies an injury. Loss of enjoyment of life, in comparison, refers to detrimental alterations of the person's life or lifestyle or the person's inability to participate in the activities or pleasures of life that were formerly enjoyed prior to the injury. In contrast to pain and suffering, whether or not a plaintiff experiences a detrimental lifestyle change depends on both the nature and severity of the injury and the lifestyle of the plaintiff prior to the injury.

The First Circuit Court of Appeal, in *Matos v. Clarendon Nat'l Ins. Co.,* 00-2814, p. 9 (La App. 1 Cir. 2/15/02), 808 So.2d 841, 848, described the difference between pain and suffering and loss of enjoyment of life as follows:

....

Consider, for example, two boys, one athletic and the other artistic, who are both involved in an accident and suffer similar injuries. Presumably, each boy should be awarded a similar quantum of damages for pain and suffering. However, the same injury may affect the boys very differently. The artist's lifestyle was not drastically altered by the accident, as he was able to resume his artistic activities after the accident, whereas the athlete's lifestyle is altered significantly, as he has to resign from his team and can no longer participate in athletics. Arguably, the athlete may be entitled to a greater pain and suffering award if he can demonstrate his mental anguish occasioned by the accident and its consequences. The athlete is damaged, however, well beyond his mental anguish over not being able to participate in athletics because now the athlete is forced to drastically alter his lifestyle as a result of his accident. The athlete is no longer able to participate in athletics, in competition or at practice, and has to find another avocation to fill his leisure time. Moreover, he no longer spends a significant amount of time with his teammates and is forced to seek out new friends. These detrimental changes in lifestyle go uncompensated in an award for pain and suffering. Under these circumstances, the drastic lifestyle change required of the athlete, as compared with the artist, warrants an additional award for the athlete's loss of enjoyment of life. To ignore the athlete's change in lifestyle and to award each boy roughly the same quantum of damages because each experienced similar pain and suffering would fail to compensate the athlete for all of his damage.

Given the conceptual difference between pain and suffering and loss of enjoyment of life, a separate award for loss of enjoyment of life is warranted and is not duplicative of the award for pain and suffering, if the damages resulting from loss of enjoyment of life are sufficiently proven. When given the proper jury instructions, jurors can comprehend the difference between the pain and suffering of being in a hospital, undergoing treatment, etc. and the loss of enjoyment of life that occurs because the injured party can no longer participate in a vocation or avocation that the party enjoys.

....

... Although we are mindful that there is a conflict among the state and federal courts nationwide on this issue,[3] we agree with the courts ... that have held loss of enjoyment of life to be a separate compensable element of general damages. We conclude that loss of enjoyment of life constitutes damage that is compensable under La. C.C. art. 2315 and accordingly that the jury may be allowed to give a separate award for loss of enjoyment of life. Nevertheless, whether or not loss of enjoyment of life is recoverable depends on the particular facts of the case, and should be left to the district court's discretion on a case-by-case analysis.

---

3 Courts across the country have taken varied approaches, and as many states' highest courts have yet to consider the issue of loss of enjoyment of life, the trend nationwide remains unclear. Nevertheless, states that have weighed in are sometimes either constrained or empowered to disallow or to allow a separate recovery for loss of enjoyment of life by their specific statutory scheme for tort, wrongful death, and survival actions. For instance, the Supreme Court of New Hampshire found that its wrongful death statute, allowing recovery for "the probable duration of his life but for his injury," authorized a separate award for decedent's loss of enjoyment of life, i.e. decedent's inability to carry on and enjoy life as if he would have lived. *Marcotte v. Timberlane/Hampstead Sch. Dist.,* 143 N.H. 331, 733 A.2d 394, 399 (1999). Similarly, the Supreme Court of Connecticut has "long held that loss of life's enjoyments is compensable in personal injury and wrongful death cases," *Mather v. Griffin Hosp.,* 207 Conn. 125, 540 A.2d 666, 678 (1988), while the Supreme Court of South Carolina has held that loss of enjoyment of life and pain and suffering are separately compensable elements of damage. *Boan v. Blackwell,* 343 S.C. 498, 541 S.E.2d 242, 244 (2001). In contrast, the Supreme Court of Nebraska has held that loss of enjoyment of life is not a separate category of damages but may be considered as an element of pain and suffering and/or disability. *Anderson v. Nebraska Dep't of Soc. Serv.,* 248 Neb. 651, 538 N.W.2d 732, 739 (1995). The Supreme Court of Washington, however, has upheld a jury instruction regarding plaintiff's loss of opportunity to become a professional dancer only because the court found that it did not mislead the jury or foster a double recovery in that particular case. *Kirk v. WSU,* 109 Wash.2d 448, 746 P.2d 285, 293 (1987).

Furthermore, although a separate award for loss of enjoyment of life may be recoverable by the primary tort victim for the loss of enjoyment of life sustained during the victim's lifetime, it is not recoverable by the primary tort victim's family members who are eligible to recover for loss of **consortium**, service and society under La. C.C. art. 2315(B). Loss of consortium is a harm to relational interest which occurs when the other party to the relationship suffers physical harm (invasion of an interest or personality). [C] Thus, under La. C.C. art. 2315(B), family members of the primary tort victim have an action, loss of consortium, that will compensate them for their diminished relationship with the primary tort victim. A family member's detrimental alteration in lifestyle, i.e. loss of enjoyment of life, results from the diminished relationship with the primary tort victim and therefore is already compensated with an award for loss of consortium. Hence, a wife's claim that she is unable to engage in activities that she formerly enjoyed prior to her husband's injury, such as taking vacations, attending sporting events, or dancing, is compensated under loss of consortium and need not be compensated again under loss of enjoyment of life. Allowing family members to recover for both their loss of consortium and their loss of enjoyment of life would be duplicative …

. . . .

Accordingly, we conclude that the court of appeal erred in holding that loss of enjoyment of life is erroneous as a matter of law. Instead, we find that loss of enjoyment of life is a separate compensable element of general damages that the jury may award separately from pain and suffering. However, plaintiffs may only assert a claim for the loss of enjoyment of life sustained by James Edward McGee, the primary tort victim, during his lifetime.

DECREE

For all the above reasons, we find that loss of enjoyment of life may be recoverable as a separate element of general damages that may be included on a jury verdict form. Therefore, we reverse the court of appeal's ruling granting the motion *in limine* and reinstate the district court's ruling denying the motion *in limine* to preclude plaintiffs from asserting a claim for loss of enjoyment of life.

REVERSED.

VICTORY, J., dissenting.

I respectfully dissent from the majority's opinion for the same reasons given by Justice, then Judge, Knoll when she gave her view of hedonic damages, while sitting on the Third Circuit in 1987:

> ... in my view the jury verdict form contained a duplicitous item, namely, "Loss of enjoyment of life, past and future" and awarded plaintiff $75,000. For physical pain and suffering, past and future, the jury awarded plaintiff $250,000, and for mental pain and suffering, past and future, the jury awarded $75,000. After making awards for physical and mental pain and suffering, the award for loss of enjoyment of life is duplicitous. Therefore, I respectfully dissent, finding the damage award excessive and duplicitous.

Andrews v. Mosley Well Service, 514 So.2d 491, 501-2 (La.App. 3 Cir.1987), (Knoll, J., dissenting) [subsequent history omitted].

Across the nation, the term "hedonic damages" did not make its debut until the 1980s, when economists began using the term to refer to certain aspects of an injured party's non-pecuniary losses. [C] In Louisiana, courts had *not* traditionally recognized "loss of enjoyment of life" as a separate element of damages and, in fact, such "hedonic damages" were not treated as a separate element of damages by *any* Louisiana appellate court before 1987, when the Third Circuit, over the dissent of then Judge Knoll, opined that "loss of enjoyment of life" damages could be awarded separate and apart from a general damages award. [C] Instead, the traditional Louisiana approach was to include such "hedonic damages" within the broader scope of a unified general damages award, which extends to such non-pecuniary issues as "pain and suffering" and "loss of gratification." ...

Moreover, a nationwide survey of cases shows that while state courts are split on this issue, the majority of state courts have held that hedonic damages are included in general damages such as pain and suffering, mental anguish, and physical impairment, and may not be considered as a separate element of general damages.[2]

---

2 See Loth v. Truck-A-Way Corporation, et al., 60 Cal.App.4th 757, 763, 70 Cal.Rptr.2d 571 (1998), (holding that in California, a pain and suffering award may include compensation for the plaintiff's loss of enjoyment of life but it may not be calculated as a separate award; however a plaintiff's attorney is not restricted from arguing this element to a jury); Frito-Lay, Inc., v. Cloud, 569 N.E.2d 983, 989 (Ind.Ct.App.1991), (holding it "is error to instruct the jury on the loss of quality and enjoyment of life as an element of damages separate from other elements of damage, such as pain and suffering or permanency of injury"); Poyzer v. McGraw, 360 N.W.2d 748 (Iowa 1985) (holding that loss of enjoyment of life is a factor to be considered as a part of future pain and suffering and that it would be plainly duplicative to allow a separate award for loss of enjoyment of life); Gregory v. Carey, 246 Kan. 504, 791 P.2d 1329 (1990) (finding that evidence regarding loss of enjoyment of life was admissible, but allowing the jury to consider it as a separate element of general damages was in error); Leonard v. Parrish, 420 N.W.2d 629 (Minn.App.1988) (holding that the trial court did not abuse its broad discretion in rejecting plaintiff's request for a specific instruction on loss of her enjoyment of life damages to her sense of smell and taste, instead submitting that loss as a general element of damages); Banks ex rel. Banks v. Sunrise Hospital, 120 Nev. 822, 102 P.3d 52 (2004) (acknowledging the differences in opinion among jurisdictions regarding hedonic damages, and agreeing with California and those jurisdictions permitting plaintiffs to seek compensation for hedonic loss as an element of the general award for pain and suffering, but not separately in order to reduce the possibility of confusion or duplication of awards by the jury); Nussbaum v. Gibstein, 73 N.Y.2d 912, 914, 539 N.Y.S.2d 289, 536 N.E.2d 618 (1989), and McDougald v. Garber, 73 N.Y.2d 246, 538 N.Y.S.2d 937, 536 N.E.2d 372 (1989) (each holding that "loss of enjoyment of life is not a separate element of damages deserving a distinct award but is, instead, only a factor to be considered by the jury in assessing damages for conscious pain and suffering"); First Trust Company of North Dakota v. Scheels Hardware & Sports Shop, Inc., 429 N.W.2d 5, 13-14 (N.D.1988) (holding that the trial court did not err in refusing the plaintiff's request to instruct on the loss of enjoyment of life as a separate element of damages as "[i]t would have been appropriate for the plaintiffs to have argued loss of enjoyment of life as a component of pain, discomfort, mental anguish, and impairment of health, mind, or person, all of which were set forth in the trial court's instructions as recoverable elements of damage in this case"); Willinger v. Mercy Catholic Medical Center of Southeastern Pennsylvania, Fitzgerald Mercy Division, et al., 482 Pa. 441, 447, 393 A.2d 1188 (1978) (stating "[e]ven where the victim survives a compensable injury, this Court has never held that loss of life's pleasures could be compensated other than as a component of pain and suffering. Indeed, the two types of loss are interrelated"); Corcoran v. McNeal, 400 Pa. 14, 23, 161 A.2d 367, 372-73 (Pa.1960) (holding that "[t]he loss of well-being is as much a loss as an amputation. The inability to enjoy what one has heretofore keenly appreciated as a pain which can be equated with the infliction of a positive hurt. The conscious loss of a benefit to which one is entitled hurts as much as a festering wound"); Judd v. Rowley's Cherry Hill Orchards, Inc., 611 P.2d 1216, 1221 (Utah 1980) (ruling that "[t]he pain and suffering for which damages are recoverable in a personal injury action include not only physical pain but also mental pain or anguish, that is, the mental reaction to that pain and to the possible consequences of the physical injury. Included in mental pain and suffering is the diminished enjoyment of life, as well as the humiliation and embarrassment resulting from permanent scars and disability"); Bulala, M.D. v. Boyd, et al., 239 Va. 218, 232, 389 S.E.2d 670 (1990), (holding that they have not recognized "loss of enjoyment of life" as a separately compensable element of damages in personal injury cases because the term is duplicative of other elements contained in the damage instruction); Wooldridge v. Woolett, 96 Wash.2d 659, 638 P.2d 566 (1981), (rejecting plaintiff's assertion that a qualitative loss of life's pleasures is a separate element of damages apart from pain and suffering, as well as declining to follow plaintiff's argument that such a recognition of qualitative loss of life's pleasures should give rise to a separate element of damages for a quantitative loss of those same pleasures); Wilt v. Buracker, 191 W.Va. 39, 443 S.E.2d 196 (1993), cert. denied, 511 U.S. 1129, 114 S.Ct. 2137, 128 L.Ed.2d 867 (1994), (holding that the loss of enjoyment of life resulting from permanent injury is part of the general measure of damages flowing from the permanent injury and is not subject to an economic calculation).

Louisiana's unified concept of general damages serves to balance the potentially competing public policies of making the victim whole … along with avoiding the inequitable outcome of the injured party securing a "double recovery" for a single element of harm-a recovery that would be more in the nature of **exemplary** or **punitive** damages that are not allowed under Louisiana law unless expressly provided for by statute. [C] Allowing hedonic damages as a separate item upsets this delicate balance and gives rise to multiple recovery, as "loss of enjoyment of life" fits squarely within the traditional scope of general damages, usually mental pain and suffering, for purposes of Louisiana law. This view was expressed in a recent article wherein the author stated:

> As an analytical matter, "pleasure" and "pain" are related words of opposite meaning. Awarding damages both for "lost pleasure" and "pain and suffering" appears entirely redundant. Furthermore, to the extent that hedonic damages compensate a victim for the lost ability to undertake a physical activity, those damages are already provided for as disability.
>
> …
>
> In sum, hedonic damages pose the risk of double counting for two major reasons. First, the standard is quite conceptually similar to both pain and suffering and disability, especially when one considers that pain and suffering may continue after its physical dimension passes, and that disability necessarily must continue into the future. But even if there is an analytical distinction, the problem of application remains. Given that hedonic damages, like pain and suffering, cannot be measured against a concrete economic baseline, there is no way for a jury to keep the categories distinct in their calculations.

[C]

The inability to enjoy certain things that were once enjoyed is almost always part of mental pain and suffering, which is already routinely awarded by judges and juries as a separate item of general damages.[3] Just as there is no need to separate "pain" and "suffering" from each other, there is no need to distinguish a lost enjoyment of life that is already included within the definition of general damages. …

Contrary to the majority's opinion, allowing a separate award for loss of enjoyment of life allows a plaintiff to recover more than once for the same damage

---

3 Certainly, every reason one would not "enjoy life" would fall into one of the three categories of general damages already allowed-physical pain and suffering, mental pain and suffering, or disability.

and gives rise to an endless array of potential subcategories for these losses. ... [A]ccording to the majority's rationale, in addition to adding a line for loss of enjoyment of life, perhaps the Court should add separate lines for the following: depression, sadness, moodiness, inability to attend a football game, inability to attend a baseball game, inability to go fishing, and so on *ad infinitum*. The result is nonsensical and substantially duplicative.

Further, when the Louisiana legislature has found a need for separate and distinct elements of compensation to victims, it has provided for such by statute. [For example], in 1982, the Legislature amended La. Civil Code art. 2315 by Act 202 to add the second paragraph, which reads, in pertinent part: "[d]amages may include loss of consortium, services and society, and shall be recoverable by the same respective categories of persons who would have had a cause of action for wrongful death of an injured person." This amendment allows recovery for loss of consortium. Conversely, it is apparent that the Legislature sees no reason to create "loss of enjoyment of life" as a separate element of damages, as it is already covered by the categories of general damages routinely allowed.

I agree with the Fourth Circuit and the majority view of the other states' courts and find that allowing a separate award for hedonic damages is a duplication of what is already provided for in a general damages award, specifically mental pain and suffering, and sets a dangerous stage for double recovery of damages.

For all of the above reasons, I respectfully dissent.

WEIMER, J., dissenting.

....

... Depending on the facts of the case, the jury verdict form should have a line for loss of enjoyment of life or a line for mental pain and suffering, but not both. In the alternative, the jury verdict form could include a single line for loss of enjoyment of life and mental pain and suffering, which would serve the purpose of allowing the jury to consider both components of general damages without having to draw a fine line distinguishing between the two. This resolution would serve the goal of making the plaintiff whole and would avoid duplication.

....

... To avoid duplication, the trial court should allow an itemization of mental pain and suffering or an itemization of loss of enjoyment of life, but not both, on the jury verdict form. Alternatively, the jury verdict form could include a single line for loss of enjoyment of life and mental pain and suffering.

KNOLL, Justice, additionally concurring.

Although I agree with the majority that loss of enjoyment of life may be recoverable as a separate element of general damages that may be included on a jury verdict form, I write separately to address my dissent in *Andrews v. Mosley Well Service*, 514 So.2d 491(La. App. 3 Cir.1987), *writ denied*, 515 So.2d 807 (La.1987). In my dissent, I opined that because there was no distinction between mental pain and suffering and the losses associated with enjoyment of life's activities, hedonic damages could not legally or equitably be awarded separately from mental pain and suffering damages.

Take Note

The court here distinguishes between legal and equitable remedies. **Legal remedies** are remedies historically available in a court of law, such as monetary damages. **Equitable remedies** are typically nonmonetary remedies that are awarded when the available legal remedies cannot adequately redress the plaintiff's injury. Although now permitted, equitable remedies were historically not available in courts of law.

However, I do not now believe this issue is so simplistic. Jurisprudence on hedonic damages was in its early stages when I authored my dissent, and although I recognize that writ denials do not make law, this Court did deny writs in that matter. The subsequent developments in our jurisprudence on this issue have convinced me that my dissent was not completely developed. Today I would be more cautious and rule on a case-by-case basis as with any damage award and let the courts judge this issue.

Points for Discussion

1. What is the purpose of compensatory damages? What are the differences between general damages and special damages? How does the court define general damages?

2. What are pecuniary losses?

3. How does the majority distinguish between damages for enjoyment of life and damages for pain and suffering?

4. Which of the four opinions persuades you the most on the issue of loss of enjoyment of life as a component of general damages? Why? Why does Justice Knoll write separately, additionally concurring?

5. Is not the award of damages a matter of common law rather than statutory law? Why then does the court rely on a statute in determining whether damages for loss of enjoyment of life are recoverable in Louisiana?

6. **Consortium Damages** – A loss of consortium claim is an action that the plaintiff or injured person's spouse, child, or parent is typically entitled to bring based on injuries to him or her and deriving from the injuries to the spouse or parent. "[C]onsortium claims, by their very nature, are a means of compensating for imprecise, intangible losses. Who can quantify the effect of the loss of a spouse, a child or a parent? Nonetheless, juries are called upon to exercise their collective experience, consider the evidence, and place a value on such claims." *Embry v. GEO Transportation of Indiana, Inc.*, 478 F.Supp.2d 914, 918 (E.D. Ky. 2007). **Spousal consortium** damages typically include recovery for loss of sexual relations, society, companionship, affection, and financial support. **Parental consortium** damages typically include recovery for loss of society, affection, and companionship. Consortium damages recoverable by a child for the loss of a parent, or **filial consortium** damages, typically include the child's society, affection, and companionship given to a parent. Most consortium claims must be brought along with the injured party's cause of action, as the claim is **derivative** – it arises by virtue of the injury to the plaintiff or injured person.

7. What did the *McGee* court rule concerning the appropriateness of one recovering loss of enjoyment of life damages as well as consortium damages? Are both recoverable as general damages in Louisiana? Why or why not?

8. What is the majority rule regarding a plaintiff's ability to recover for loss of enjoyment of life as a component of compensatory damages? What is your opinion regarding whether one should be able to recover for "loss of enjoyment of life?" Does money ever make one whole again?

> **FYI**
>
> For further exploration on this issue, *see* BARRY WERTH, DAMAGES (1998). DAMAGES tells the story of a family who brought a medical malpractice action against a doctor and a hospital after the mother gave birth to a profoundly disabled son and his stillborn twin.

9. For what period of time does the court say that the plaintiff is entitled to recover for loss of enjoyment of life?

10. Because compensatory damages restore a plaintiff to her pre-accident status, compensatory damages are excluded from gross income and therefore are not subject to federal (and most state) income tax. Does the exclusion of

compensatory damages from federal taxation provide a windfall to plaintiffs, particularly if part of the compensatory damage award is to compensate the plaintiff for lost wages or future earning capacity?

11. How should a plaintiff be required to prove general damages at trial? For example, should a plaintiff be permitted to break his or her mental and physical suffering down into units, such as days, hours, or minutes and have the jury assign a dollar value to each unit? Such a per-diem technique is quite controversial as it suggests mathematical precision to an element of damages for which there is no mathematical precision. Morover, such a technique does not take into account the fact that, over time, the body may adjust its threshold of pain.

12. Should a plaintiff be able to recover for a reduced life expectancy due to tortiously-caused injury? Most jurisdictions do not allow as part of general damages a separate recovery for the reduction in the plaintiff's life expectancy. What do you think?

Richardson v. Chapman

676 N.E.2d 621 (Ill. 1997)

Justice MILLER delivered the opinion of the court:

The plaintiffs, Keva Richardson and Ann E. McGregor, were injured when the car in which they were riding was hit from behind by a truck driven by defendant Jeffrey Chapman in Highland Park. ... A divided appellate court affirmed all the judgments against the defendants. ...

The accident at issue here occurred in the early morning hours of November 26, 1987, at the intersection of Interstate 94 and Clavey Road in Highland Park. Plaintiff Keva Richardson was the driver of the car, and plaintiff Ann McGregor was a passenger in the vehicle. While stopped at a traffic light, their car was struck from behind by a semitrailer being driven by defendant Chapman. Richardson suffered extensive injuries as a result of the accident and was rendered quadriplegic. McGregor sustained only slight injuries in the accident and has returned to her normal activities. At trial, Richardson introduced extensive testimony concerning her injuries and the expenses she will likely incur in the future as a consequence of the accident. ...

The plaintiffs brought the present action against Chapman, Tandem/Carrier, and Rollins. ... The case proceeded to trial on [the negligence count] alone.

....

In that portion of the appeal still remaining, Chapman and Tandem/Carrier (defendants) first challenge the amounts of damages awarded to the plaintiffs. The defendants contend that certain errors in the testimony of the economist who appeared at trial in behalf of Keva Richardson inflated the verdict returned in her favor and, further, that the damages awarded by the jury to Richardson and McGregor are excessive.

....

The defendants ... contend that the damages awarded to the plaintiffs are excessive. Before resolving this question, we will briefly summarize the evidence presented at trial regarding the two women's injuries.

Keva Richardson was 23 years old at the time of the accident. She grew up in Pampa, Texas, and received a bachelor's degree in elementary education in May 1987 from Texas Tech University. While in college, she participated in a number of athletic activities and was, by all accounts, a popular, happy person. After graduating from college, Keva obtained a position as a flight attendant with American Airlines. She planned to work in that capacity for several years before returning to school to gain a post-graduate degree in education; her ultimate goal was to teach. Keva met Ann McGregor in the flight attendant training program, and the two decided to room together upon completion of their training. At the conclusion of the program, they were assigned to the Chicago area, and they had moved there just several days before the accident occurred.

Following the accident, Keva was initially taken to Highland Park Hospital for treatment. Because of the seriousness of her injuries, however, Keva was transferred that morning to Northwestern Memorial Hospital. Dr. Giri Gereesan, an orthopedic surgeon specializing in spinal surgery, determined that Keva had incurred a fracture of the fifth cervical vertebra, which severely damaged her spinal cord and resulted in incomplete quadriplegia. Dr. Gereesan performed surgery on Keva on December 1, 1987, to stabilize her spine so that she would be able to support her head; the surgery did not repair the damage to her spinal cord, and no treatment exists that could do so.

Keva was transferred to the Rehabilitation Institute of Chicago in December 1987, where she came under the care of Dr. Gary Yarkony. Keva was initially dependent on others in all aspects of her daily life. At the Rehabilitation Institute she learned how to perform a number of basic tasks, such as sitting in a wheelchair, transferring from a bed to a wheelchair, brushing her teeth, washing her face, and putting on loose-fitting tops. Keva's initial stay at the Rehabilitation Institute lasted until April 1988, when she moved to her parents' home in Texas. Keva returned to the Rehabilitation Institute in 1988 and in 1989 for follow-up visits. Keva also required hospitalization in Texas on three subsequent occasions for treatment of conditions arising from the accident.

Testifying in Keva's behalf at trial, Dr. Gary Yarkony, who had served as her primary physician at the Rehabilitation Institute, described Keva's current condition. He explained that she cannot use her legs and that she has only limited functioning in her arms, with loss of control of her fingers and fine muscles in her hands. She suffers pain in her legs and shoulders. Her chest and abdomen are paralyzed, and she has restrictive pulmonary disease. In addition, she has no control over her bladder or bowel functions and requires assistance in emptying them. As a consequence of her physical condition, she is at risk for bladder infections, pneumonia, and pressure ulcers. Keva also suffered a number of facial injuries in the accident. Some of these scars were later repaired through plastic surgery, but others remain.

At trial, Keva's mother, Dixie Richardson, described her daughter's current activities and the level of care necessary to assist her in her daily routine. Keva requires help in taking a shower and getting dressed. She cannot put on underwear, socks, or pants by herself but is able to put on pullover shirts and sweaters. With assistance, she can brush her teeth, apply makeup, and put in her contact lenses. She is unable to cut food or button a sweater. She can push her wheelchair on a smooth, level surface but otherwise needs assistance. In her own testimony, Keva said that she is self-conscious about her appearance now and the impression she makes on others. She said that the thing she misses most is just being able to get up in the morning and begin her day; now she requires the assistance of others, throughout the day.

The jury awarded Richardson a total of $22,358,814 in damages, divided among the following six elements: $258,814 for past medical care; $11,000,000 for future medical care; $900,000 for past and future lost earnings; $3,500,000 for disability; $2,100,000 for disfigurement; and $4,600,000 for pain and suffering. In challenging Richardson's award of damages, the defendants first argue that the sum of the future medical costs found by the jury -- $11,000,000 -- is not supported by the evidence, for it exceeds even the larger of the two figures supplied by Professor Linke, $9,570,034. The defendants contend that the decision to award Richardson nearly $1.5 million more illustrates the jury's failure to properly determine damages in this case.

In response, Richardson argues that the larger award may simply be attributable to the jury's decision to make an award of expenses that she is likely to incur in the future but that were not specifically included in the calculations performed by Professor Linke. Richardson notes that Dr. Yarkony, in compiling for Linke's use the list of likely future medical costs, did not assign specific values to certain items, such as the expenses of future hospitalizations and the costs of wheelchairs and a specially equipped van. Richardson thus argues that the jury's decision to award an amount for future medical costs greater than Professor Linke's higher estimate might simply reflect the jury's desire to compensate her for those unspecified but likely expenses. We agree with Richardson that the trier of fact enjoys a certain degree of leeway in awarding compensation for medical costs that, as shown by the evidence, are likely to arise in the future but are not specifically itemized in the testimony. [C] In the present case, however, the amount awarded by the jury for future medical costs is nearly $1.5 million more than the higher of the two figures claimed at trial by Richardson. Notably, Professor Linke did not rely on the projections by the General Accounting Office (GAO) of the growth of future medical care costs, mentioned in the partial concurrence. Professor Linke explained that the GAO's study included a large number of technology-based items, while the main expense to be incurred by Richardson will be wages for attendant care. Given the disparity between the trial testimony and the jury's eventual award, we will not attribute the entire difference between those sums simply to miscellaneous costs Richardson is likely to incur in the future. For these reasons, we conclude that it is appropriate, by way of **remittitur**, to reduce by $1 million the nearly $1.5 million differential between the award for Richardson's future medical expenses and the higher figure presented in the testimony. This adjustment allows Richardson recovery for expected future medical costs for which no specific estimates were introduced, yet is not so large that it represents a departure from the trial testimony.

We do not agree with the defendants, however, that the remainder of the award of damages to Richardson, including the sums for pain and suffering, disability, and disfigurement, is duplicative or excessive or lacks support in the record. The determination of damages is a question reserved to the trier of fact, and a reviewing court will not lightly substitute its opinion for the judgment rendered in the trial court. [Cc] An award of damages will be deemed excessive if it falls outside the range of fair and reasonable compensation or results from passion or prejudice, or if it is so large that it shocks the judicial conscience. [C] When reviewing an award of compensatory damages for a nonfatal injury, a court may consider, among other things, the permanency of the plaintiff's condition, the possibility of future deterioration, the extent of the plaintiff's medical expenses, and the restrictions imposed on the plaintiff by the injuries. [C]

Here, it was the jury's function to consider the credibility of the witnesses and to determine an appropriate award of damages. We cannot say that the present award to Richardson is the result of passion or prejudice, "**shocks the conscience**," or lacks support in the evidence. The record shows that Richardson suffered devastating, disabling injuries as a consequence of the accident. The defendants urge us to compare Richardson's damages with amounts awarded in other cases. Courts in this state, however, have traditionally declined to make such comparisons in determining whether a particular award is excessive [cc], and we do not believe that such comparisons would be helpful here.

The defendants also contend that the jury's award of damages to Ann McGregor is excessive. McGregor was 22 years old at the time of the accident. She grew up in Houston, Texas, and graduated from Southern Methodist University in May 1987 with a degree in psychology. Like Keva Richardson, McGregor was accepted after graduation for a position as a flight attendant with American Airlines. As mentioned earlier, the two women met while enrolled in the flight attendant training program and were sharing an apartment in the Chicago area at the time of the accident. Following the accident, McGregor was taken to Highland Park Hospital, where she was treated and released that day; she was then off work for about two weeks. A laceration she suffered on her forehead eventually healed, with only minimal scarring. At trial McGregor testified that she continues to suffer from nightmares about the accident. The jury awarded McGregor a total of $102,215 in damages, divided among the following components: $1,615 for past medical expenses, $600 for lost earnings, and $100,000 for pain and suffering.

Like the dissenting justice below, we believe that the award of $100,000 for pain and suffering is, in these circumstances, excessive. McGregor was not seriously injured in the accident, incurring a laceration on her forehead, which left only a slight scar. The jury declined to award McGregor any compensation for disfigurement; rather, the bulk of her recovery consisted of compensation for pain and suffering. We conclude that a more appropriate figure for pain and suffering would be $50,000, which would reduce her total damages to $52,215. By way of remittitur, we accordingly reduce the judgment entered in favor of McGregor and against Tandem/Carrier and Chapman to that amount.

For the reasons stated, the judgment of the appellate court is affirmed in part, reversed in part, and vacated in part, and the judgment of the circuit court of Cook County is affirmed in part, reversed in part, and vacated in part. [W]e affirm the judgments entered in favor of plaintiffs and against Tandem/Carrier and Chapman in their reduced amounts. ... [T]his cause is remanded to the circuit court of Cook County for entry of judgment on Rollins' claim for **indemnity** in an amount consistent with this opinion and the settlement between plaintiffs and Rollins.

Judgments affirmed in part, reversed in part, and vacated in part; cause remanded.

Justice McMORROW, concurring in part and dissenting in part:

I concur in the opinion of my colleagues in all but one respect: I do not agree with the majority that it is proper to order a remittitur of the jury's award of damages to Keva Richardson for present cash value of future medical expenses or the jury's award to Ann McGregor for pain and suffering.

In determining the total verdict awarded to Richardson, the jury considered extensive evidence relating to six separate components of damages. As noted by the majority, Richardson "suffered devastating, disabling injuries." The appellate court majority's unpublished opinion describes her condition:

> "After the collision, doctors determined that the communication connection between Richardson's brain and the rest of her body had become severed and she was rendered a quadriplegic. Richardson was soon placed in traction with tongs affixed to her skull by driving screws into the side of her head. She was also placed in a roto-rest bed with 25 pound weights attached to her body for traction. Eventually, Richardson underwent surgery to stabilize her spine so it could support the weight of her head which hung like a rag doll's head. In that operation, bone from her hips was grafted to her cervical spine with the use of metal plates and screws. The surgery did not repair the injury to Richardson's spinal cord, nor does medical technology yet exist to rectify the injury."

Other evidence related Richardson's need for assistance every six hours to empty her bladder by catheterization and daily assistance to empty her bowel, over which she permanently lacks control. She has lost the use of her legs, fingers, and the fine muscles of her hand. Her chest and abdomen are paralyzed. She is subject to risk of serious infections and other conditions and, according to the evidence, having a child would be life-threatening. The appellate court opinion further stated that Richardson "may expect to be hospitalized on a regular basis for the balance of her life."

The jury awarded $11 million to compensate Richardson for her future medical needs. To this sum the majority applies a remittitur of $1 million, based on the majority's observation that the jury's award for this element of damages exceeded by $1.5 million the testimony of economist Charles Linke regarding the "upper bound" of the present cash value of Richardson's future medical needs. Linke explained that he calculated a "lower bound present value ($7.4 million) and an upper bound present value ($9.5 million)." His figures were derived from different assumptions regarding the relationship of the rate of interest to the rate of growth. In explaining his economic assumptions and methods, Linke also noted that there were different accounting methods that could be used to calculate Richardson's future medical needs. The one he employed yielded a more conservative figure for medical care than that used by the General Accounting Office, which, according to Linke, would yield the conclusion that "the present value of Keva Richardson's care needs would be approximately 12.1 million dollars."

In assuming that the $9.5 million "upper bound" figure represents the maximum amount that is sustained by the evidence with respect to Richardson's future medical expenses, the majority opinion fails to acknowledge that the information upon which Linke based his calculation of present cash value of future medical expenses represented Richardson's *minimum* care needs for the rest of her life. Dr. Yarkony, upon whose testimony Linke's economic analysis was based, detailed the specific types of medical expenses that Richardson would be expected to need in the coming years. Dr. Yarkony testified, "[T]his is the basic minimum care not covering any hospital admissions for emergencies, complications, and the like." He further testified that in his opinion Richardson would continue to require hospitalizations in the future caused by complications related to her spinal cord injury, including infections, pressure sores, pneumonia, and blood clots.

Notwithstanding the above testimony of Linke and Dr. Yarkony, the majority determines that the jury improperly affixed damages for future medical costs in an amount exceeding the experts' estimates by $1.5 million. The majority concedes that the jury could properly compensate Richardson for medical costs not otherwise included in the experts' calculations. The majority permits one third of the excess award to stand, and concludes that $500,000, rather than $1.5 million, represents the appropriate additional sum the jury could award in excess of Linke's upper bound estimate of $9.5 million. In so holding, the majority usurps the jury's function and substitutes its own judgment regarding what is reasonable and fairly supported by the expert economic and medical evidence with respect to the present value of Richardson's future medical costs. The majority's application of remittitur in the case at bar thereby operates as an arbitrary limitation on the jury's ability to assess the evidence. [Cc].

In *Riley,* 228 Ill.App.3d at 887-88, 170 Ill.Dec. 899, 593 N.E.2d 788, the appellate court summarized the applicable law of remittitur:

"Damages are a question of fact to be decided by the jury, and courts are reluctant to interfere with the jury's exercise of discretion in this area. ... A reviewing court will not disturb a jury's award of damages unless it is obviously the result of passion or prejudice.... Furthermore, an award is not excessive unless it falls outside the necessary limits of fair and reasonable compensation or it shocks the judicial conscience. ... A jury's award will not be subject to remittitur where it falls within the flexible range of conclusions which can be reasonably supported by the facts. ..."

....

Nothing in the record or the itemized jury verdict indicates that the jury departed from its customary duty to weigh the evidence and assess damages that would fairly compensate Richardson for her permanent and disabling injuries. The jury's award for future medical expenses, which arguably exceeded certain testimony, does not warrant the conclusion that the jury's determination was a departure from the flexible range of damages that was reasonably supported by the facts. There is no indication that the jury's award was the product of passion or prejudice. In fact, with respect to a different component of damages, *i.e.,* Richardson's past and future lost earnings, the jury awarded a sum that was $1.265 million *less* than the higher of the testimonial estimates presented for that item of damages. If experts' estimates of a person's future income losses or medical expenses were an exact science capable of mathematical precision, there would be no need to have a jury make the final determination of proven damages.

In the case at bar the jury heard all of the evidence, including the basis for the expert testimony. It appears uncontested that the evidence of Richardson's future medical expenses did not include every anticipated item, such as special equipment and repeated hospitalizations that are likely to occur in the future because of the serious conditions Richardson suffers as a result of her quadriplegia. The testimonial estimate of the present cash value of Richardson's future medical needs is only that-an estimate. This estimate was elicited as a minimum projection of Richardson's medical needs in the years to come. In light of these considerations, I would affirm the appellate court's holding that the variance between the jury's award for future medical needs and the experts' projection is "certainly not so great a variance that we must reject the verdict of people whom we have instructed to use their own observation and experience in the affairs of life during their deliberations."

Similarly, I depart from the majority's holding that Ann McGregor's damages award of $100,000 for pain and suffering was excessive. The majority orders a remittitur of $50,000 as a "more appropriate figure for pain and suffering." [C] The majority appears to base its conclusion on the relatively minor injury McGregor sustained, noting that she suffered a laceration on her forehead that healed with only minimal scarring. Although the majority views the award of $100,000 as overly generous for a facial laceration that did not result in permanent disfigurement, the majority substitutes its own subjective judgment for the jury's evaluation of the evidence. The record indicates that McGregor's lacerated forehead took six months to heal. The record further indicates that she suffered ongoing trauma, including recurrent nightmares resulting from the rear-end collision that left the other occupant of the car a quadriplegic. The jury, as finder of fact, had the superior ability to assess the evidence, including McGregor's testimony relating to her traumatic and painful experience. I am aware of no sound reason to nullify the function of the jury and arbitrarily reduce McGregor's award for pain and suffering to $50,000. Therefore, I cannot concur in the reasoning or result of the majority with respect to the reduction by remittitur of both plaintiffs' verdicts.

For the reasons stated, I concur in part and dissent in part from the judgment of the majority.

Justice FREEMAN joins in this partial concurrence and partial dissent.

Points for Discussion

1. Is appellate court review of a jury's damage calculation a question of law or a question of fact?

2. The *Richardson* court orders a **remittitur**, a means by which a court can control an excessive jury award. A remittitur is an order providing a plaintiff with an option – either accept a damages award smaller than that awarded by the jury or a new trial will be ordered. A remittitur is a common technique that courts employ in order to control excessive jury awards. Contrasted with a remittitur is an **additur** or increscitur, a trial court's order increasing the jury's award in order to avoid a new trial on grounds of inadequate damages. Federal courts, as well as many state courts, have deemed orders of additur unconstitutional as they provide for an award beyond the jury's verdict, thereby violating the guaranty of a jury trial. Can you see why the same cannot be said of a remittitur?

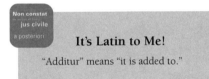

It's Latin to Me!

"Additur" means "it is added to."

3. States have also sought to control excessive jury awards by legislative enactments. Statutory tort reform measures have been adopted in many states in an effort to place limits on personal injury recovery, especially the general damages and punitive damage components of personal injury awards.

For More Information

Innumerable law review articles have been written on recent tort reform measures. *See, e.g.,* Jason M. Solomon, *Equal Accountability Through Tort Law,* 103 Nw. U. L. 1765 (2009); Lee Harris, *Tort Reform as Carrot-and-Stick,* 46 Harv. J. on Legis. 163 (2009); Julie Davies, *Reforming the Tort Reform Agenda,* 25 Wash. U. J. L.. & Pol'y 119 (2007); John C. P. Goldberg, *What Are We Reforming? Tort Theory's Place In Debates Over Malpractice Reform,* 59 Vand. L. Rev. 1075 (2006).

In re September 11th Litigation

590 F.Supp.2d 535 (S.D. N.Y. 2008)

ALVIN K. HELLERSTEIN, District Judge:

In April 2001, the Port Authority of New York and New Jersey, Inc. accepted the bid of a New York real estate developer, Larry Silverstein, to purchase 99-year **net leases** to four of the World Trade Center towers. In July 2001, the

What's That?

A "net lease" is a lease requiring the tenant to pay, in addition to the rent, all the expenses of the leased property, such as taxes, insurance, etc.

Port Authority executed net leases and related agreements, and conveyed the four net leaseholds to Towers One, Two, Four and Five to corporations formed by Silverstein to hold the net leases. Silverstein paid, and the Port Authority accepted, consideration valued at $2.805 billion.

Two months after Silverstein took possession, the towers became rubble, destroyed by the terrorist-related aircraft crashes of September 11, 2001. Towers One and Two were turned into raging infernos and collapsed, bringing down and destroying Tower Four, Tower Five, and additional buildings and properties in and around the World Trade Center. Silverstein's company, World Trade Center Properties LLC, and his several holding companies ... (collectively, "WTCP"), filed suit against American Airlines and United Airlines alleging that, but for the airlines' negligence, the terrorists would not have gained entrance into the aircrafts they hijacked and flew into Towers One and Two. WTCP also sued other aviation defendants [collectively, the "Aviation Defendants"], alleging that, because of their negligence and causation, they too are **jointly and severally liable** for WTCP's damages. WTCP's lawsuit seeks recovery of $16.2 billion, the alleged replacement value of Towers One, Two, Four and Five.

The Aviation Defendants deny liability, and allege defenses. This motion for summary judgment seeks a ruling on one defense: whether liability, if found, can exceed the market value of the leaseholds. I am asked to decide whether the lesser of the market value on September 11, 2001 of the four 99-year leaseholds, or the four towers' replacement value, is the proper measure of recoverable damages in this case.

I hold that market value as of September 11, 2001 is the limit of permissible recovery .... Thus, I grant the substantive ruling that the Aviation Defendants seek, and deny the balance of the motion. Additional proceedings consistent with my rulings are required.

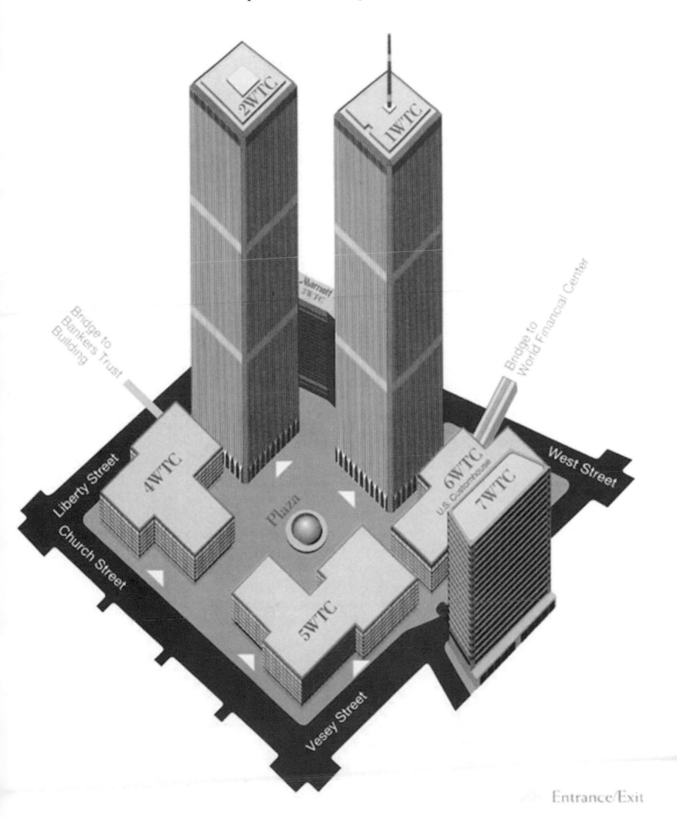

FACTUAL BACKGROUND

I. *The Sale of World Trade Center Buildings One, Two, Four and Five*

On July 16, 2001, fifty-five days before September 11, 2001, WTCP and the Port Authority executed the four 99-year net leases for World Trade Center Towers One, Two, Four and Five. The lease executions culminated a worldwide competitive bidding process that the Port Authority had initiated to implement a decision, reached several years earlier, to privatize the World Trade Center. Four finalists emerged from the bidding process. When Vornado Realty Trust, the high bidder, was not able to complete its negotiations with the Port Authority, WTCP, the second finalist, entered the negotiations and, in April 2001, executed an agreement with the Port Authority to net lease the four towers. The net leases were priced at $3.211 billion, of which $395 million was allocated to a commercial space ("Retail Mall") that was leased by The Westfield Group, and $2.805 billion was allocated to the towers. WTCP was to pay $491 million, and Westfield, $125 million, at the closings; the balance of the consideration was in the form of a 99-year stream of fixed future rental payments from the four towers, having a present value of $2.419 billion, a 99-year stream of participating future rental payments, having a present value of approximately $65 million, and a stream of additional base rental payments valued at $111 million. J.P. Morgan, engaged by the Port Authority as a consultant, found the consideration fair. WTCP valued its net leaseholds to Towers One, Two, Four and Five at $2.84 billion on its books and records.

II. *A Brief History of the World Trade Center*

....

The Port Authority of New York and New Jersey, Inc., a nonprofit, bi-state agency, had been created in 1921 to carry out a public trust "benefiting the nation, as well as the States of New York and New Jersey." [C] The Port Authority was formed "by agreement of the two states as their joint agent for the development of the transportation and terminal facilities and other facilities of commerce of the port district and for the promotion and protection of the commerce of their port." [C] The two states granted the Port Authority control of the World Trade Center's construction and operation. Construction commenced in 1965 and cost approximately one billion dollars.

It took time before the World Trade Center brought about substantial changes to the downtown business area. During the 1970s, the World Trade Center struggled to fill its space, relying heavily on government tenants. By the early 1980s, the towers began to enjoy commercial success, replacing government tenants with a variety of higher paying commercial tenants, among them premier law, accounting and financial services firms.

By September 11, 2001, the World Trade Center had become a profit center. Forty thousand workers, and many more tourists, came into the towers daily. Shopping arcades beneath the towers served tenants and visitors, and were themselves profit centers. The towers were a symbol of the city and an integral part of its skyline. New York City's downtown area flourished. If it was not the equal of the city's midtown, the downtown area was nevertheless profitable and full of businesses and residents.

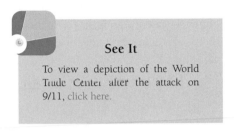

See It

To view a depiction of the World Trade Center after the attack on 9/11, click here.

WTCP argues that the World Trade Center buildings were built and used for a special and specific purpose. That may have been so, but clearly a market had developed for the buildings by the 1990s, and buyers were ready, willing, and able to pay full and fair prices. The ... bids Port Authority received [reflected] the towers' full and fair price, including their symbolic value.

....

IV. *September 11 Litigation and the Instant Motion*

Congress provided that all claims arising from, or in connection with, the terrorist-related aircraft crashes into the World Trade Center were to be brought exclusively in the United States District Court for the Southern District of New York. *See* Air Transportation Safety and System Stabilization Act ("ATSSSA"), 49 U.S.C. § 40101. The law governing such suits was to be the law of the state where the crash occurred, that is, New York State law, unless preempted by, or inconsistent with, federal law. *Id.* The Aviation Defendants' insurance limited their potential liability. *Id.*

The great bulk of wrongful death and personal injury claims against the airlines was paid and discharged without affecting these liability policies. ...

Ninety-six **wrongful death** and personal injury claimants filed suits in this court, seeking recovery of substantial but unquantifiable damages. Seventeen other claimants filed suits against the Aviation Defendants alleging property damages aggregating to approximately $6.8 billion. In addition, WTCP filed a claim for $12.3 billion ($8.4 billion of replacement cost and $3.9 billion of lost rental income). ...

....

The Aviation Defendants' pending motions for summary judgment seek rulings that would limit WTCP's potential recovery on the following issues: (1) whether WTCP is entitled only to the fair market value of the destroyed towers, rather than the higher replacement value; (2) whether WTCP is entitled to recover, in addition to market value or replacement value, its lost rental income, plus expenses in relation to preserving such rental income; (3) whether the fair market value of WTCP's leaseholds to Towers One, Two, Four and Five, as of September 11, 2001, was $2.8 billion, the amount WTCP agreed to pay in April, 2001 or some different value yet to be determined..... The discussion that follows, essentially granting the motion of the Aviation Defendants but finding issues of fact, amplifies and explains the rulings I expressed at the argument of the motion on September 24, 2008.

DISCUSSION

I. *Summary Judgment Standard*

Summary judgment may be granted if there are "no genuine issues as to any material fact and ... the moving party is entitled to judgment as a matter of law." FED. R. CIV. P. 56(c). ...

....

II. *Fair Market Value Is the Proper Measure of Damages.*

The Aviation Defendants argue that, under New York law, WTCP cannot recover $8.4 billion in replacement costs, because the diminution of the properties' market value limits recovery.

....

[In New York,] a plaintiff whose property has been injured may recover the lesser of the diminution of the property's market value or its replacement cost. [C] This rule applies even when the property in question has been completely destroyed. [C]

The New York Court of Appeals recently affirmed [this] rule in *Fisher v. Qualico Contracting Corp.*, 98 N.Y.2d 534, 749 N.Y.S.2d 467, 779 N.E.2d 178 (2002). In *Fisher,* plaintiff's Long Island home, an 8,000 square foot Victorian residence on 1.5 acres of land, was destroyed in a fire negligently started by defendant, a contractor hired by plaintiff to do work on the home. The plaintiff filed a homeowner's insurance claim and received $1,050,000 from his insurers. The subrogated insurer, as plaintiff, then sued defendant for negligence and prevailed. In the damages phase of the trial, the parties proved that the replacement cost was $1,033,000, but that the diminution in the property's market value was $480,000. The jury was instructed to award $480,000, the lesser of the two amounts. On appeal, the Court of Appeals affirmed, holding that "[r]eplacement cost and diminution in market value are simply two sides of the same coin." *Id.,* 749 N.Y.S.2d 467, 779 N.E.2d at 181-82. "Each is a proper way to measure lost property value, the lower of the two figures affording full compensation to the owner" yet "avoiding uneconomical efforts." *Id.*

....

Clearly, the price WTCP paid for the 99-year leases it acquired from the Port Authority reflected a full and fair market price for the property. If WTCP is entitled to recover, recovery of the properties' market value would fully compensate it. WTCP is not entitled to recover the larger value of replacement cost.

...

WTCP argues that it is entitled to recover the costs of its contractual obligations to "rebuild, restore, repair and replace" the destroyed World Trade Center buildings. The Aviation Defendants argue, in opposition, that they cannot be held responsible in tort for WTCP's contractual undertakings, and that, even if they could be held responsible, the new buildings that are envisioned as replacements for the destroyed buildings represent radical improvements and differences and cannot be considered replacement structures within the meaning of the contract.

When a party commits a tort that results in damage to property, the wronged party may recover damages for injuries which flow directly from that tort and are its natural and probable consequences. The tortfeasor is not responsible for damages which are remote from the wrong or indirectly related to it. [C] Stated differently, the tortfeasor is responsible only for injuries that are the direct, natural and proximate result of the tortfeasor's actions, and that the parties would have foreseen, contemplated or expected. *Palsgraf v. Long Island R. Co.,* 248 N.Y. 339, 352-53, 162 N.E. 99 (1928); [c].

If proved at trial, the direct, natural and proximate cause of the Aviation Defendants' alleged negligence in allowing the terrorists to enter and hijack the Boeing 767 airplanes and fly them into Towers One and Two of the World Trade Center would be the destruction of the two towers, and the related destruction of Towers Four and Five. The market value of the towers is the measure of recovery for their destruction. If WTCP bears a special or different burden, it flows directly from WTCP's contract clauses, not the Aviation Defendants' negligence. [C] The particular features of WTCP's contracts cannot be made the special responsibility of the Aviation Defendants, nor the natural and probable result of their negligence, nor the foreseeable consequence of their acts and omissions. [C]

Accordingly, for the reasons discussed, the Aviation Defendants are entitled to summary judgment that WTCP's potential recovery against them is limited to the September 11, 2001 market value of the destroyed net leases for Towers One, Two, Four and Five.

. . . .

There is another, important reason for enforcing the traditional New York law limiting property damage recoveries to the lesser of market value or replacement value. ATSSSA limits the liability of each Aviation Defendant to its insurance coverage. § 408(a)(1), 49 U.S.C. §§ 40101. The limit applies to all claims, whether wrongful death, personal injury or property damage.

> Notwithstanding any other provision of law, liability for all claims, whether for compensatory or punitive damages or for contribution or indemnity, arising from the terrorist-related aircraft crashes of September 11, 2001, against an air carrier, aircraft manufacturer, airport sponsor or person with a property interest in the World Trade Center, on September 11, 2001, whether fee simple, leasehold or easement, direct or indirect, their directors, officers, employees or agents, shall not be in an amount greater than the limits of liability insurance coverage maintained by that air carrier, aircraft manufacturer, airport sponsor, or person.

Id.

ATSSSA provided for liability caps to preserve the United States' aviation industry, to protect the airlines and aircraft manufacturers from the potential of crushing liability, and to ensure that plaintiffs would be able to recover damages without bankrupting the airlines. *See* 147 Cong. Rec. S9589-01, S9594 (Sept. 21, 2001) (Senator McCain) ("In addition to removing the specter of devastating potential liability from the airlines, and guaranteeing that the victims and their families will receive compensation regardless of the outcomes of the tangle of lawsuits that will ensue, the bill attempts to provide some sense to the litigation by consolidating all civil litigation arising from the terrorist attacks of September 11 in one court.").

As it turned out, 97% of eligible wrongful death claimants and an overwhelming number of personal injury claims came before the Special Master of the Victim Compensation Fund. Litigation challenging the legality of such a Fund was heard and dismissed by this Court. ...

The Victim Compensation Fund paid $7.0494 billion of congressionally appropriated funds in full settlement and discharge of claimants' wrongful death and personal injuries. Only ninety-five wrongful death and personal injury lawsuits were filed in this court by claimants killed in the hijacked aircraft or killed or injured in or around the World Trade Center or the Pentagon. The three remaining suits are now consolidated with all the property damage suits. ...

The limitation on recovery (measured at the date ATSSSA was enacted, September 22, 2001) creates a federal interest, over and above any New York State interest, to protect against unreasonable and excessive claims by particular claimants. ... A limited pool of funds should not be dissipated by liberality to a few at many others' expense.

....

CONCLUSION

For the reasons stated in this opinion, I grant the Aviation Defendants' motion in part and deny it in part.

SO ORDERED.

Points for Discussion

1. What happens to this case following this court order? Have the plaintiffs lost their causes of action against these defendants? Are the plaintiffs now entitled to recovery for their damages based on the defendants' negligence?

2. What is the appropriate measure of compensatory damages for property damage in tort according to the court order in *In re September 11th Litigation*? Why is the value of the contract not the appropriate measure of compensatory damages?

3. Why did this court not permit the plaintiffs the ability to recover for their lost future rent?

Montgomery Ward & Co., Inc. v. Anderson

976 S.W.2d 382 (Ark. 1998)

NEWBERN, Justice.

This is a tort case in which the issue concerns application of the collateral-source rule. The Trial Court held that the rule required exclusion of evidence of the partial forgiveness of a debt for medical services rendered to the plaintiff. The defendant moved for a new trial …. The Trial Court denied the motion, and we affirm.

On November 14, 1994, appellee Shirley Anderson was badly injured in a fall while shopping in appellant's Montgomery Ward store in Little Rock. Montgomery Ward personnel sent her to the hospital at the University of Arkansas for Medical Sciences ("UAMS") to be treated. Ms. Anderson had surgical and other medical-services expenses at UAMS totaling $24,512.45. Montgomery Ward moved *in limine* to prohibit Ms. Anderson from presenting the total amount billed by UAMS as proof of her medical expenses and asked that her evidence be limited to the actual amount for which she would be responsible to pay. In response, Ms. Anderson stated that, through her attorney, she had reached an agreement with UAMS that UAMS would discount the bill by fifty per cent. Ms. Anderson asserted that the collateral-source rule would prohibit Montgomery Ward from introducing evidence of the discount.

The Trial Court denied the motion *in limine,* ruling that the negotiated discount with UAMS was a collateral source, and allowed evidence of the entire amount billed by UAMS. Montgomery Ward urges that the ruling and the denial of the motion for new trial made on the same basis were erroneous.

    ….

We have held that the collateral-source rule applies unless the evidence of the benefits from the collateral source is relevant for a purpose other than the mitigation of damages. [C] The issue, then, is whether the forgiveness of a debt for medical services is a collateral source to be sheltered by the rule. …

    ….

…A trial court must "exclude evidence of payments received by an injured party from sources 'collateral' to … the wrongdoer, such as private insurance or government benefits…." [Cc] Recoveries from collateral sources "do not redound to the benefit of a tortfeasor, even though double recovery for the same damage by the injured party may result." [Cc]

In [a previous] case, we recognized that commentators had criticized the rule as being "incongruous with the compensatory goal of the tort system" and that some jurisdictions had modified or abrogated the rule. *Bell,* 318 Ark. at 490, 885 S.W.2d at 880. To refute that criticism, we quoted in the *Bell* case from F. HARPER, ET AL., THE LAW OF TORTS § 25.22, at p. 651 (2d ed.1986) as follows:

> But in these cases the courts measure "compensation" by the total amount of the harm done, even though some of it has been repaired by the collateral source, not by what it would take to make the plaintiff whole. It is "compensation" in a purely Pickwickian sense that only half conceals an emphasis on what defendant should pay rather than on what plaintiff should get.

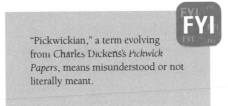

"Pickwickian," a term evolving from Charles Dickens's *Pickwick Papers,* means misunderstood or not literally meant.

We also noted that the rule had been extended to cases in other areas of the law, such as unemployment compensation received during a period later held to have resulted from a wrongful discharge ... [We have explained] the policy behind the rule as follows:

> Whether [plaintiff] received the money from her employer or from an insurance policy, she, rather than the alleged tortfeasor, is entitled to the benefit of the collateral source, even though in one sense a double recovery occurs. [C] The law rationalizes that the claimant should benefit from the collateral source recovery rather than the tortfeasor, since the claimant has usually paid an insurance premium or lost sick leave, whereas to the tortfeasor it would be a total windfall.

[C] That statement of policy ... favor[s] including discounted and gratuitous medical services within the shelter of the collateral-source rule. There is no evidence of record showing that Montgomery Ward had anything to do with procuring the discount of Ms. Anderson's bill by UAMS. The rationale of the rule favors her, just as it would had she been compensated by insurance for which she had arranged.

....

We recognize four situations in which the rule does not apply.... [A] collateral source of recovery may be introduced (1) to rebut the plaintiff's testimony that he or she was compelled by financial necessity to return to work prematurely or to forego additional medical care; (2) to show that the plaintiff had attributed his condition to some other cause, such as sickness; (3) to impeach the plaintiff's testimony that he or she had paid his medical expenses himself; (4) to show that the plaintiff had actually continued to work instead of being out of work, as claimed. [Cc] This Court has also allowed evidence of collateral sources when the plaintiff opens the door to his or her financial condition. [Cc] The Trial Court ruled that none of the exceptions applied to the facts at hand, and an examination of the abstract indicates that ruling was correct. There is no testimony by the plaintiff that arguably invokes any of the exceptions.

The RESTATEMENT (SECOND) OF TORTS § 920A(2) provides guidance on this issue and explains that the general rule is that "[p]ayments made to or benefits conferred on the injured party from other sources are not credited against the tortfeasor's liability, although they cover all or a part of the harm for which the tortfeasor is liable." Comment *b* to that Restatement section explains that, if the plaintiff is responsible for the benefit received, the law allows the plaintiff to keep it. Further, if the benefit was a gift to the plaintiff from a third party or established for the plaintiff by law, the plaintiff should not be deprived of the advantage that it confers. Another way to state the rule is to say that "it is the tortfeasor's responsibility to compensate for all harm that he [or she] causes, not confined to the net loss that the injured party receives." RESTATEMENT (SECOND) OF TORTS § 920A cmt. *b*. Comment *c* (3) indicates that gratuities of cash or services are collateral sources that are not subtracted from a plaintiff's recovery. The comment gives the example of a doctor who does not charge for medical services.

[A] substantial number of jurisdictions addressing the issue have held that the plaintiff may recover the reasonable value of nursing care or services rendered gratuitously for the plaintiff's benefit. [C] The primary issue remaining today is how to value the services, [C], but that issue is determined in this case by the total medical bill submitted to Ms. Anderson by UAMS.

. . . .

We choose to adopt the rule that gratuitous or discounted medical services are a collateral source not to be considered in assessing the damages due a personal-injury plaintiff. It is the rule recommended by the RESTATEMENT (SECOND) OF TORTS, and it is consistent with our oft-stated policy of allowing the innocent plaintiff, instead of the tortfeasor defendant, to receive any windfall associated with the cause of action. Accordingly, we hold that the Trial Court did not err by excluding evidence of the UAMS discount as a collateral source.

Affirmed.

———————

Points for Discussion

1. The **collateral-source rule** prevents a tortfeasor from benefiting from payments made to the plaintiff for injuries by sources independent of the tortfeasor. The collateral-source rule reflects the policy decision that a wrongdoer should not be permitted to benefit from a reduction in damages because of the good fortune or prudence of the plaintiff or one independent of the defendant. The most common type of collateral source is insurance proceeds, but collateral sources may take various forms, including (but not limited to) continued wages, disability payments, pension payments, and even gratuitous services. The collateral-source rule has long been criticized as allowing a plaintiff double recovery or permitting a plaintiff to be made more than whole. Do you agree with this criticism?

2. In response to the criticism in opposition of the collateral-source rule, it has been legislatively modified in many jurisdictions. *See, e.g.,* MONT. CODE ANN. § 27-1-308 (providing that any award exceeding $50,000 must be reduced by any amount paid from collateral sources); OKLA. STAT. tit. 63, § 1-1708.1D (providing for admission of payments of medical bills in medical malpractice actions unless payments are subject to subrogation or other right of recovery).

See It

To view a chart showing collateral source rule reform by state, click here.

Zimmerman v. Ausland

513 P.2d 1167 (Or. 1973)

TONGUE, Justice.

This is an action for damages for personal injuries sustained in an automobile accident. Defendant admitted liability. The issue of damages was submitted to a jury, which returned a verdict of $7,500 in favor of plaintiff. Defendant appeals. We affirm.

Defendant contends that the trial court erred in submitting to the jury the issue whether plaintiff sustained a permanent injury, as alleged in her complaint, and in instructing the jury on plaintiff's life expectancy, after taking judicial notice of the Standard Mortality Tables. ...

In support of that contention defendant says that those instructions and the submission of those issues to the jury constituted error because there was no evidence from which the jury could properly find that plaintiff's injuries were permanent; that in this case the evidence established that plaintiff's condition, involving an injury to her knee, 'is curable by routine surgery'; that all injured persons have a duty to mitigate damages by submitting to surgery 'where the risk is small and a favorable result reasonably probable'; and that this 'precludes any instruction on permanency.'

....

Plaintiff testified that her right knee was injured in the automobile accident. She said that as of the time of trial she still suffered swelling and pain in the knee after walking, as in shopping, and that as a substitute teacher she was no longer able to participate in physical education activities involving 'physical games' or to play volleyball and tennis, as in the past.

Her doctor testified that plaintiff suffered from a torn semi-lunar cartilage in her knee; that 'the probable future of this knee' was 'one of gradual deterioration'; that her injury was 'permanent'; and that it was 'very probable' that she would 'require a surgical procedure' to remove the torn cartilage. He also testified that after such an operation 'the recover (sic) is fairly good' and that 'the outlook for good recovery would be very optimistic.'

In addition, plaintiff's doctor testified on cross-examination by defendant's attorney that he had not prescribed any 'treatment' for plaintiff; that surgery is 'not always' required in cases like this; and that '* * * (t)here are two indications for immediate surgery. One, if the knee is locked. The other is if it is catching and allowing a person to fall. Otherwise, it's pretty much a matter of how much it is bothering a patient.'

Defendant's doctor, although disagreeing with the diagnosis that plaintiff suffered from a torn semi-lunar cartilage, testified that if she did have such an injury, as a 'a very frequent injury seen in athletes,' the torn cartilage should be 'surgically excised,' i.e., 'removed in total,' and that after such an operation 'the patient should recover completely' and be able 'to return to all normal and usual activities.'

He also testified that 'If the meniscal injury is of a fairly major significance and there's a major type tear, the patient will have acute symptoms from which he will never recover without surgery of the meniscus,' but that if the symptoms are not 'clear cut and they still seem to have symptoms,' a 'diagnosis by an arthrogram should be done' prior to such surgery.

There was sufficient evidence of permanent injury, in the absence of evidence sufficient to establish as a matter of law that plaintiff unreasonably failed or refused to submit to surgery.

This court has previously recognized the almost universal rule that the admissibility of evidence of mortality tables in a personal injury case is dependent upon evidence that the injury is permanent. [Cc] [T]he same is true of the submission to a jury of allegations of permanent injury and of instructions to the jury on that subject.

It is equally well established that the plaintiff in a personal injury case cannot claim damages for what would otherwise be a permanent injury if the permanency of the injury could have been avoided by submitting to treatment by a physician, including possible surgery, when a reasonable person would do so under the same circumstances. [Cc]

In considering whether plaintiff is required to mitigate her damages by submitting to surgery we must bear in mind that while plaintiff has the burden of proof that her injury is a permanent injury, defendant has the burden of proving that plaintiff unreasonably failed to mitigate her damages by submission to surgery. [Cc] However, evidence that plaintiff could reasonably have avoided all or part of the damages is admissible under a general denial. [Cc]

Ordinarily, of course, the questions whether an injury is permanent and whether a reasonable person under the same circumstances would submit to surgery are questions of fact for the jury, assuming that substantial evidence is offered. Also, in the ordinary case, both issues would be submitted to the jury under appropriate instructions.

In this case defendant did not request an instruction on mitigation of damages, with the result that this question was not submitted to the jury. Nevertheless, if the facts are such that the court must hold, as a matter of law, that the plaintiff failed to mitigate her damages by submission to surgery when a reasonable person would have done so, the plaintiff would not be entitled to claim damages for what might otherwise be a permanent injury. It would also follow, in such an event, that defendant would be correct in contending that it was error to submit the issue of permanent injury to the jury, including consideration of the mortality tables.

This result would not follow, however, unless the evidence in this case is clear and conclusive to the effect that a reasonable person under the same circumstances would have submitted to surgery. Otherwise, plaintiff would be entitled to have the jury decide both the question whether plaintiff's injury is a permanent injury and also the question whether, under the circumstances, a reasonable person would have submitted to surgery. If, in such an event, the jury found that plaintiff did not unreasonably fail or refuse to submit to surgery and if there was evidence that plaintiff's injury would otherwise be permanent, the jury could then properly award damages for permanent injury and its verdict in this case must be affirmed.

In general, as previously stated, the test to be applied in determining whether a plaintiff has unreasonably failed or refused to mitigate his damages by submitting to a surgical operation is whether, under the circumstances of the particular case, an ordinarily prudent person would do so, i.e., the duty to exercise reasonable care under the circumstances. [Cc] Conversely, if under the circumstances, a reasonable person might well decline to undergo a surgical operation, a failure to do so imposes no disability against recovering full damages. [Cc]

The factors to be considered for this purpose ordinarily include the risk involved (i.e., the hazardous nature of the operation), the probability of success, and the expenditure of money or effort required. [C] Some courts also consider the pain involved as a factor, but no such question is presented for decision in this case. [C]

....

...[T]here must be evidence relating to the extent of the risk involved in a particular type of surgical operation before a jury may properly consider the contention that a plaintiff acted unreasonably in declining to submit to a surgical operation. [Cc] The same must be true, **A fortiori**, when, as in this case, defendant contends that a court should hold as a matter of law that plaintiff unreasonably failed or refused to submit to a surgical operation. No such evidence was offered in this case.

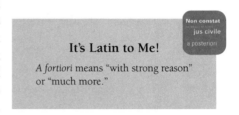

It's Latin to Me!

A fortiori means "with strong reason" or "much more."

Neither is there any evidence that plaintiff had been advised by any doctor that she should submit to a surgical operation on her knee and that she then failed or refused to do so. Indeed, both plaintiff's and defendant's doctors agreed that surgery was not indicated at the time of their examination. ...

....

We hold, however, that under the facts and circumstances of this case the evidence supporting defendant's contention that plaintiff was required to submit to surgery upon her knee and the related contention that, for failure to do so, she is barred from claiming damages for a permanent injury to her knee, were not so clear and conclusive as to make it proper for the court to decide those questions in this case as a matter of law. ...

After examining the record in this case we also hold that testimony was offered by plaintiff from which, if believed by the jury, it could properly find that plaintiff has suffered a permanent injury, and one which interferes with her normal and usual activities, including those relating to her work as a substitute teacher. It follows that the trial court did not err in submitting that issue to the jury or in instructing it on life expectancy tables. The verdict of the jury was supported by substantial evidence and the judgment of the trial court is affirmed.

Points for Discussion

1. The doctrine of avoidable consequences, also known as the **mitigation of damages doctrine**, prevents a plaintiff from claiming damages for a permanent injury if the permanency of the injury could have been avoided by submitting to treatment when a reasonable person would have done so. A plaintiff is required to take reasonable measures to alleviate the effects of an injury and may not recover from the defendant for damages that could have been avoided by submitting to proper treatment. A defendant does not have to pay for the plaintiff's refusal to act reasonably to mitigate against the permanency of the injury.

2. How can the doctrine of avoidable consequences be reconciled with the law of battery, for example, which recognizes an individual's right to control one's physical bodily integrity?

3. Contrast the doctrine of avoidable consequences with the principles of contributory or comparative negligence set forth in Chapter 6 -- Defenses (and Partial Defenses) to Negligence Actions.

Hypo 9-1

Bruno is hit by a negligently operated truck driven by Truck Driver and is gravely injured. Bruno had failed to fasten the available seatbelt before beginning to drive. Because of the accident, he accumulates many hospital bills, and his cousin quits work to care for him. Once an avid marathon runner, Bruno is now confined to a wheelchair and his life span has been reduced by twenty years. His working life has been reduced by ten years, and he lost two years of wages prior to the case against Truck Driver making it to trial. Truck Driver's attorney has learned of an available surgery that would permit Bruno to regain his ability to walk and care for himself. If Bruno were to undergo the surgery, his lost wages and loss of future life expectancy would remain the same, but he would be able to return to work within three weeks and could work as he would have and as long as he could have prior to the accident. Discuss in detail the damages issues that attorneys for both sides should consider.

B. Punitive Damages

There are three types of damages available in personal injury cases: (1) nominal damages, (2) compensatory damages, and (3) punitive or "exemplary," damages. As considered at length in the previous section, the purpose of compensatory damages is to compensate the injured party for any out-of-pocket expenses incurred as a result of the injury, as well as any resulting pain and suffering. Punitive damages, on the other hand, represent a sum in excess of any compensatory damages and are awarded to punish or deter the defendant or others from repeating the tortious conduct. Because punitive damages are awarded for the purpose of punishment and because the U.S. Constitution and some state constitutions place limitations on the imposition of punishment, punitive damage awards are subject to federal (and state) constitutional limitations. Consider the following cases.

BMW of North America, Inc. v. Gore

517 U.S. 559 (1996)

STEVENS, J., delivered the opinion of the Court, in which O'CONNOR, KENNEDY, SOUTER, and BREYER, JJ. joined. BREYER, J., filed a concurring opinion, in which O'CONNOR and SOUTER, JJ., joined. SCALIA, J., filed a dissenting opinion, in which THOMAS, J., joined. GINSBURG, J., filed a dissenting opinion, in which REHNQUIST, C.J., joined.

Justice STEVENS delivered the opinion of the Court.

The Due Process Clause of the Fourteenth Amendment prohibits a State from imposing a " 'grossly excessive' " punishment on a tortfeasor. *TXO Production Corp. v. Alliance Resources Corp.,* 509 U.S. 443, 454, 113 S.Ct. 2711, 2718, 125 L.Ed.2d 366 (1993) (and cases cited). The wrongdoing involved in this case was the decision by a national distributor of automobiles not to advise its dealers, and hence their customers, of predelivery damage to new cars when the cost of repair amounted to less than 3 percent of the car's suggested retail price. The question presented is whether a $2 million punitive damages award to the purchaser of one of these cars exceeds the constitutional limit.

I

In January 1990, Dr. Ira Gore, Jr. (respondent), purchased a black BMW sports sedan for $40,750.88 from an authorized BMW dealer in Birmingham, Alabama. After driving the car for approximately nine months, and without noticing any flaws in its appearance, Dr. Gore took the car to "Slick Finish," an independent detailer, to make it look " 'snazzier than it normally would appear.' " [C] Mr. Slick, the proprietor, detected evidence that the car had been repainted.[1] Convinced that he had been cheated, Dr. Gore brought suit against petitioner BMW of North America (BMW), the American distributor of BMW automobiles. ... The complaint prayed for $500,000 in compensatory and punitive damages, and costs.

What's That?

To "pray" for relief refers simply to that portion of the plaintiff's complaint that demands the relief or damages requested.

At trial, BMW acknowledged that it had adopted a nationwide policy in 1983 concerning cars that were damaged in the course of manufacture or transportation. If the cost of repairing the damage exceeded 3 percent of the car's suggested retail price, the car was placed in company service for a period of time and then sold as used. If the repair cost did not exceed 3 percent of the suggested retail price, however, the car was sold as new without advising the dealer that any repairs had been made. Because the $601.37 cost of repainting Dr. Gore's car was only about 1.5 percent of its suggested retail price, BMW did not disclose the damage or repair to the Birmingham dealer.

Dr. Gore asserted that his repainted car was worth less than a car that had not been refinished. To prove his actual damages of $4,000, he relied on the testimony of a former BMW dealer, who estimated that the value of a repainted BMW was approximately 10 percent less than the value of a new car that had not been damaged and repaired. To support his claim for punitive damages, Dr. Gore introduced evidence that since 1983 BMW had sold 983 refinished cars as new, including 14 in Alabama, without disclosing that the cars had been repainted before sale at a cost of more than $300 per vehicle. Using the actual damage estimate of $4,000 per vehicle, Dr. Gore argued that a punitive award of $4 million would provide an appropriate penalty for selling approximately 1,000 cars for more than they were worth.

In defense of its disclosure policy, BMW argued that it was under no obligation to disclose repairs of minor damage to new cars and that Dr. Gore's car was as

---

1 The top, hood, trunk, and quarter panels of Dr. Gore's car were repainted at BMW's vehicle preparation center in Brunswick, Georgia. The parties presumed that the damage was caused by exposure to acid rain during transit between the manufacturing plant in Germany and the preparation center.

good as a car with the original factory finish. It disputed Dr. Gore's assertion that the value of the car was impaired by the repainting and argued that this good-faith belief made a punitive award inappropriate. BMW also maintained that transactions in jurisdictions other than Alabama had no relevance to Dr. Gore's claim.

The jury returned a verdict finding BMW liable for compensatory damages of $4,000. In addition, the jury assessed $4 million in punitive damages, based on a determination that the nondisclosure policy constituted "gross, oppressive or malicious" fraud [in violation of an applicable Alabama statute governing punitive damages]. See Ala.Code §§ 6-11-20, 6-11-21 (1993).

BMW filed a post-trial motion to set aside the punitive damages award. The company introduced evidence to establish that its nondisclosure policy was consistent with the laws of roughly 25 States defining the disclosure obligations of automobile manufacturers, distributors, and dealers. The most stringent of these statutes required disclosure of repairs costing more than 3 percent of the suggested retail price; none mandated disclosure of less costly repairs. Relying on these statutes, BMW contended that its conduct was lawful in these States and therefore could not provide the basis for an award of punitive damages.

BMW also drew the court's attention to the fact that its nondisclosure policy had never been adjudged unlawful before this action was filed. Just months before Dr. Gore's case went to trial, the jury in a similar lawsuit filed by another Alabama BMW purchaser found that BMW's failure to disclose paint repair constituted fraud. [C] Before the judgment in this case, BMW changed its policy by taking steps to avoid the sale of any refinished vehicles in Alabama and two other States. When the $4 million verdict was returned in this case, BMW promptly instituted a nationwide policy of full disclosure of all repairs, no matter how minor.

In response to BMW's arguments, Dr. Gore asserted that the policy change demonstrated the efficacy of the punitive damages award. He noted that while no jury had held the policy unlawful, BMW had received a number of customer complaints relating to undisclosed repairs and had settled some lawsuits. Finally, he maintained that the disclosure statutes of other States were irrelevant because BMW had failed to offer any evidence that the disclosure statutes supplanted, rather than supplemented, existing causes of action for common-law fraud.

The trial judge denied BMW's post-trial motion, holding, *inter alia,* that the award was not excessive. On appeal, the Alabama Supreme Court also rejected BMW's claim that the award exceeded the constitutionally permissible amount. [C] The court's excessiveness inquiry applied the factors articulated in *Green Oil Co. v. Hornsby,* 539 So.2d 218, 223-224 (Ala.1989), and approved in *Pacific Mut. Life Ins. Co. v. Haslip,* 499 U.S. 1, 21-22, 111 S.Ct. 1032, 1045-1046, 113 L.Ed.2d 1 (1991). [C] Based on its analysis, the court concluded that BMW's conduct was "reprehensible"; the nondisclosure was profitable for the company; the judgment "would not have a substantial impact upon [BMW's] financial position"; the litigation had been expensive; no criminal sanctions had been imposed on BMW for the same conduct; the award of *no* punitive damages in *Yates* reflected "the inherent uncertainty of the trial process"; and the punitive award bore a "reasonable relationship" to "the harm that was likely to occur from [BMW's] conduct as well as ... the harm that actually occurred." [C]

The Alabama Supreme Court did, however, rule in BMW's favor on one critical point: The court found that the jury improperly computed the amount of punitive damages by multiplying Dr. Gore's compensatory damages by the number of similar sales in other jurisdictions. [C] Having found the verdict tainted, the court held that "a constitutionally reasonable punitive damages award in this case is $2,000,000 [C] and therefore ordered a remittitur in that amount.[10] The court's discussion of the amount of its remitted award expressly disclaimed any reliance on "acts that occurred in other jurisdictions"; instead, the court explained that it had used a "comparative analysis" that considered Alabama cases, "along with cases from other jurisdictions, involving the sale of an automobile where the seller misrepresented the condition of the vehicle and the jury awarded punitive damages to the purchaser." [Cc]

Because we believed that a review of this case would help to illuminate "the character of the standard that will identify unconstitutionally excessive awards" of punitive damages, see *Honda Motor Co. v. Oberg,* 512 U.S. 415, 420, 114 S.Ct. 2331, 2335, 129 L.Ed.2d 336 (1994), we granted certiorari, 513 U.S. 1125, 115 S.Ct. 932, 130 L.Ed.2d 879 (1995).

II

Punitive damages may properly be imposed to further a State's legitimate interests in punishing unlawful conduct and deterring its repetition. *Gertz v. Robert Welch, Inc.,* 418 U.S. 323, 350, 94 S.Ct. 2997, 3012, 41 L.Ed.2d 789 (1974); *Newport v. Fact Concerts, Inc.,* 453 U.S. 247, 266-267, 101 S.Ct. 2748, 2759-2760, 69 L.Ed.2d 616 (1981); *Haslip,* 499 U.S., at 22, 111 S.Ct., at 1045-1046. In our federal system, States necessarily have considerable flexibility in determining the level of punitive damages that they will allow in different classes of cases and in any particular case. Most States that authorize exemplary damages afford the jury similar latitude, requiring only that the damages awarded be reasonably necessary to vindicate the State's legitimate interests in punishment and deterrence. [Cc] Only when an award can fairly be categorized as "grossly excessive" in relation to these interests does it enter the zone of arbitrariness that violates the Due Process

10 The Alabama Supreme Court did not indicate whether the $2 million figure represented the court's independent assessment of the appropriate level of punitive damages, or its determination of the maximum amount that the jury could have awarded consistent with the Due Process Clause.

Clause of the Fourteenth Amendment. [C] For that reason, the federal excessiveness inquiry appropriately begins with an identification of the state interests that a punitive award is designed to serve. We therefore focus our attention first on the scope of Alabama's legitimate interests in punishing BMW and deterring it from future misconduct.

No one doubts that a State may protect its citizens by prohibiting deceptive trade practices and by requiring automobile distributors to disclose presale repairs that affect the value of a new car. But the States need not, and in fact do not, provide such protection in a uniform manner. Some States rely on the judicial process to formulate and enforce an appropriate disclosure requirement by applying principles of contract and tort law. [Cc] Other States have enacted various forms of legislation that define the disclosure obligations of automobile manufacturers, distributors, and dealers. [Cc] The result is a patchwork of rules representing the diverse policy judgments of lawmakers in 50 States.

. . . .

We may assume, *arguendo,* that it would be wise for every State to adopt Dr. Gore's preferred rule, requiring full disclosure of every presale repair to a car, no matter how trivial and regardless of its actual impact on the value of the car. But while we do not doubt that Congress has ample authority to enact such a policy for the entire Nation, it is clear that no single State could do so, or even impose its own policy choice on neighboring States. [Cc] Similarly, one State's power to impose burdens on the interstate market for automobiles is not only subordinate to the federal power over interstate commerce, [C], but is also constrained by the need to respect the interests of other States [C].

We think it follows from these principles of state sovereignty and comity that a State may not impose economic sanctions on violators of its laws with the intent of changing the tortfeasors' lawful conduct in other States. Before this Court Dr. Gore argued that the large punitive damages award was necessary to induce BMW to change the nationwide policy that it adopted in 1983. But by attempting to alter BMW's nationwide policy, Alabama would be infringing on the policy choices of other States. To avoid such encroachment, the economic penalties that a State such as Alabama inflicts on those who transgress its laws, whether the penalties take the form of legislatively authorized fines or judicially imposed punitive damages, must be supported by the State's interest in protecting its own consumers and its own economy. Alabama may insist that BMW adhere to a particular disclosure policy in that State. Alabama does not have the power, however, to punish BMW for conduct that was lawful where it occurred and that had no impact on Alabama or its residents. Nor may Alabama impose sanctions on BMW in order to deter conduct that is lawful in other jurisdictions.

In this case, we accept the Alabama Supreme Court's interpretation of the jury verdict as reflecting a computation of the amount of punitive damages "based in large part on conduct that happened in other jurisdictions." [C] As the Alabama Supreme Court noted, neither the jury nor the trial court was presented with evidence that any of BMW's out-of-state conduct was unlawful. "The only testimony touching the issue showed that approximately 60% of the vehicles that were refinished were sold in states where failure to disclose the repair was not an unfair trade practice." [C]   The Alabama Supreme Court therefore properly eschewed reliance on BMW's out-of-state conduct, [C] and based its remitted award solely on conduct that occurred within Alabama.[21] The award must be analyzed in the light of the same conduct, with consideration given only to the interests of Alabama consumers, rather than those of the entire Nation.   When the scope of the interest in punishment and deterrence that an Alabama court may appropriately consider is properly limited, it is apparent – for reasons that we shall now address – that this award is grossly excessive.

III

Elementary notions of fairness enshrined in our constitutional jurisprudence dictate that a person receive fair notice not only of the conduct that will subject him to punishment, but also of the severity of the penalty that a State may impose. [Cc] Three guideposts, each of which indicates that BMW did not receive adequate notice of the magnitude of the sanction that Alabama might impose for adhering to the nondisclosure policy adopted in 1983, lead us to the conclusion that the $2 million award against BMW is grossly excessive: the degree of reprehensibility of the nondisclosure; the disparity between the harm or potential harm suffered by Dr. Gore and his punitive damages award; and the difference between this remedy and the civil penalties authorized or imposed in comparable cases. We discuss these considerations in turn.

[A.] *Degree of Reprehensibility*

Perhaps the most important indicium of the reasonableness of a punitive damages award is the degree of reprehensibility of the defendant's conduct. [C] As the Court stated nearly 150 years ago, exemplary damages imposed on a defendant should reflect "the enormity of his offense." [Cc] This principle reflects the accepted view that some wrongs are more blameworthy than others. ...

---

21 Of course, the fact that the Alabama Supreme Court correctly concluded that it was error for the jury to use the number of sales in other States as a multiplier in computing the amount of its punitive sanction does not mean that evidence describing out-of-state transactions is irrelevant in a case of this kind. To the contrary, as we stated in TXO Production Corp. v. Alliance Resources Corp., 509 U.S. 443, 462, n. 28, 113 S.Ct. 2711, 2722, n. 28, 125 L.Ed.2d 366 (1993), such evidence may be relevant to the determination of the degree of reprehensibility of the defendant's conduct.

In this case, none of the aggravating factors associated with particularly reprehensible conduct is present. The harm BMW inflicted on Dr. Gore was purely economic in nature. The presale refinishing of the car had no effect on its performance or safety features, or even its appearance for at least nine months after his purchase. BMW's conduct evinced no indifference to or reckless disregard for the health and safety of others. To be sure, infliction of economic injury, especially when done intentionally through affirmative acts of misconduct, [C] or when the target is financially vulnerable, can warrant a substantial penalty. But this observation does not convert all acts that cause economic harm into torts that are sufficiently reprehensible to justify a significant sanction in addition to compensatory damages.

Dr. Gore contends that BMW's conduct was particularly reprehensible because nondisclosure of the repairs to his car formed part of a nationwide pattern of tortious conduct. Certainly, evidence that a defendant has repeatedly engaged in prohibited conduct while knowing or suspecting that it was unlawful would provide relevant

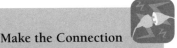

Make the Connection

Pure economic harm was historically not recoverable in tort. *See* Chapter 7, Advanced Topics in Duty of Care, *supra.*

support for an argument that strong medicine is required to cure the defendant's disrespect for the law. [C] Our holdings that a recidivist may be punished more severely than a first offender recognize that repeated misconduct is more reprehensible than an individual instance of malfeasance. [C]

....

Dr. Gore[argues] for treating BMW as a recidivist i[n] that the company should have anticipated that its actions would be considered fraudulent in some, if not all, jurisdictions. This contention overlooks the fact that actionable fraud requires a *material* misrepresentation or omission.[29] This qualifier invites line-drawing of just the sort engaged in by States with disclosure statutes and by BMW. We do not think it can be disputed that there may exist minor imperfections in the finish of a new car that can be repaired (or indeed, left unrepaired) without materially affecting the car's value.[30] There is no evidence that BMW acted in bad faith when it sought to establish the appropriate line between presumptively minor damage and damage requiring disclosure to purchasers. For this purpose, BMW could reasonably rely

29 RESTATEMENT (SECOND) OF TORTS § 538 (1977); W. Keeton, D. Dobbs, R. Keeton, & D. Owen, Prosser and Keeton on Law of Torts § 108 (5th ed. 1984).

30 The Alabama Supreme Court has held that a car may be considered "new" as a matter of law even if its finish contains minor cosmetic flaws. Wilburn v. Larry Savage Chevrolet, Inc., 477 So.2d 384 (1985). We note also that at trial respondent only introduced evidence of undisclosed paint damage to new cars repaired at a cost of $300 or more. This decision suggests that respondent believed that the jury might consider some repairs too de minimis to warrant disclosure.

on state disclosure statutes for guidance. In this regard, it is also significant that there is no evidence that BMW persisted in a course of conduct after it had been adjudged unlawful on even one occasion, let alone repeated occasions.

Finally, the record in this case discloses no deliberate false statements, acts of affirmative misconduct, or concealment of evidence of improper motive, such as were present in *Haslip* and *TXO*. *Haslip*, 499 U.S., at 5, 111 S.Ct., at 1036; *TXO*, 509 U.S., at 453, 113 S.Ct., at 2717-2718. We accept, of course, the jury's finding that BMW suppressed a material fact which Alabama law obligated it to communicate to prospective purchasers of repainted cars in that State. But the omission of a material fact may be less reprehensible than a deliberate false statement, particularly when there is a good-faith basis for believing that no duty to disclose exists.

That conduct is sufficiently reprehensible to give rise to tort liability, and even a modest award of exemplary damages does not establish the high degree of culpability that warrants a substantial punitive damages award. Because this case exhibits none of the circumstances ordinarily associated with egregiously improper conduct, we are persuaded that BMW's conduct was not sufficiently reprehensible to warrant imposition of a $2 million exemplary damages award.

[B.] *Ratio*

The second and perhaps most commonly cited indicium of an unreasonable or excessive punitive damages award is its ratio to the actual harm inflicted on the plaintiff. See *TXO*, 509 U.S., at 459, 113 S.Ct., at 2721; *Haslip*, 499 U.S., at 23, 111 S.Ct., at 1046. The principle that exemplary damages must bear a "reasonable relationship" to compensatory damages has a long pedigree. ... Our decisions in both *Haslip* and *TXO* endorsed the proposition that a comparison between the compensatory award and the punitive award is significant.

In *Haslip* we concluded that even though a punitive damages award of "more than 4 times the amount of compensatory damages" might be "close to the line," it did not "cross the line into the area of constitutional impropriety." [C] *TXO*, following dicta in *Haslip*, refined this analysis by confirming that the proper inquiry is " 'whether there is a reasonable relationship between the punitive damages award and *the harm likely to result* from the defendant's conduct as well as the harm that actually has occurred.' " *TXO*, 509 U.S., at 460, 113 S.Ct., at 2721 (emphasis in original), quoting *Haslip*, 499 U.S., at 21, 111 S.Ct., at 1045. Thus, in upholding the $10 million award in *TXO*, we relied on the difference between that figure and the harm to the victim that would have ensued if the tortious plan had succeeded. That difference suggested that the relevant ratio was not more than 10 to 1.

The $2 million in punitive damages awarded to Dr. Gore by the Alabama Supreme Court is 500 times the amount of his actual harm as determined by the jury.[35] Moreover, there is no suggestion that Dr. Gore or any other BMW purchaser was threatened with any additional potential harm by BMW's nondisclosure policy. The disparity in this case is thus dramatically greater than those considered in *Haslip* and *TXO.*

Of course, we have consistently rejected the notion that the constitutional line is marked by a simple mathematical formula, even one that compares actual *and potential* damages to the punitive award. [C] Indeed, low awards of compensatory damages may properly support a higher ratio than high compensatory awards, if, for example, a particularly egregious act has resulted in only a small amount of economic damages. A higher ratio may also be justified in cases in which the injury is hard to detect or the monetary value of noneconomic harm might have been difficult to determine. It is appropriate, therefore, to reiterate our rejection of a categorical approach. Once again, "we return to what we said ... in *Haslip:* 'We need not, and indeed we cannot, draw a mathematical bright line between the constitutionally acceptable and the constitutionally unacceptable that would fit every case. We can say, however, that [a] general concer[n] of reasonableness ... properly enter[s] into the constitutional calculus.' [C] In most cases, the ratio will be within a constitutionally acceptable range, and remittitur will not be justified on this basis. When the ratio is a breathtaking 500 to 1, however, the award must surely "raise a suspicious judicial eyebrow." *TXO,* 509 U.S., at 481, 113 S.Ct., at 2732 (O'CONNOR, J., dissenting).

[C.] *Sanctions for Comparable Misconduct*

Comparing the punitive damages award and the civil or criminal penalties that could be imposed for comparable misconduct provides a third indicium of excessiveness. As Justice O'CONNOR has correctly observed, a reviewing court engaged in determining whether an award of punitive damages is excessive should "accord 'substantial deference' to legislative judgments concerning appropriate sanctions for the conduct at issue." *Browning-Ferris Industries of Vt., Inc. v. Kelco Disposal, Inc.,* 492 U.S., at 301, 109 S.Ct., at 2934 (opinion concurring in part and dissenting in part). In *Haslip,* 499 U.S., at 23, 111 S.Ct., at 1046, the Court noted that although the exemplary award was "much in excess of the fine that could be imposed," imprisonment was also authorized in the criminal context. In this case the $2 million economic sanction imposed on BMW is substantially greater than the statutory fines available in Alabama and elsewhere for similar malfeasance.

The maximum civil penalty authorized by the Alabama Legislature for a violation of its Deceptive Trade Practices Act is $2,000; [C] other States authorize more severe sanctions, with the maxima ranging from $5,000 to $10,000. [Cc] Sig-

---

35 Even assuming each repainted BMW suffers a diminution in value of approximately $4,000, the award is 35 times greater than the total damages of all 14 Alabama consumers who purchased repainted BMW's

nificantly, some statutes draw a distinction between first offenders and recidivists; thus, in New York the penalty is $50 for a first offense and $250 for subsequent offenses. None of these statutes would provide an out-of-state distributor with fair notice that the first violation – or, indeed the first 14 violations – of its provisions might subject an offender to a multimillion dollar penalty. Moreover, at the time BMW's policy was first challenged, there does not appear to have been any judicial decision in Alabama or elsewhere indicating that application of that policy might give rise to such severe punishment.

. . . .

IV

We assume, as the juries in this case and in the *Yates* case found, that the undisclosed damage to the new BMW's affected their actual value. Notwithstanding the evidence adduced by BMW in an effort to prove that the repainted cars conformed to the same quality standards as its other cars, we also assume that it knew, or should have known, that as time passed the repainted cars would lose their attractive appearance more rapidly than other BMW's. Moreover, we of course accept the Alabama courts' view that the state interest in protecting its citizens from deceptive trade practices justifies a sanction in addition to the recovery of compensatory damages. We cannot, however, accept the conclusion of the Alabama Supreme Court that BMW's conduct was sufficiently egregious to justify a punitive sanction that is tantamount to a severe criminal penalty.

The fact that BMW is a large corporation rather than an impecunious individual does not diminish its entitlement to fair notice of the demands that the several States impose on the conduct of its business. Indeed, its status as an active participant in the national economy implicates the federal interest in preventing individual States from imposing undue burdens on interstate commerce. While each State has ample power to protect its own consumers, none may use the punitive damages deterrent as a means of imposing its regulatory policies on the entire Nation.

As in *Haslip,* we are not prepared to draw a bright line marking the limits of a constitutionally acceptable punitive damages award. Unlike that case, however, we are fully convinced that the grossly excessive award imposed in this case transcends the constitutional limit. Whether the appropriate remedy requires a new trial or merely an independent determination by the Alabama Supreme Court of the award necessary to vindicate the economic interests of Alabama consumers is a matter that should be addressed by the state court in the first instance.

The judgment is reversed, and the case is remanded for further proceedings not inconsistent with this opinion.

It is so ordered.

Justice BREYER, with whom Justice O'CONNOR and Justice SOUTER join, concurring.

The Alabama state courts have assessed the defendant $2 million in "punitive damages" for having knowingly failed to tell a BMW automobile buyer that, at a cost of $600, it had repainted portions of his new $40,000 car, thereby lowering its potential resale value by about 10%. The Court's opinion, which I join, explains why we have concluded that this award, in this case, was "grossly excessive" in relation to legitimate punitive damages objectives, and hence an arbitrary deprivation of life, liberty, or property in violation of the Due Process Clause. [C] Members of this Court have generally thought, however, that if "fair procedures were followed, a judgment that is a product of that process is entitled to a strong presumption of validity." [Cc] And the Court also has found that punitive damages procedures very similar to those followed here were not, by themselves, fundamentally unfair. [C] Thus, I believe it important to explain why this presumption of validity is overcome in this instance.

The reason flows from the Court's emphasis in *Haslip* upon the constitutional importance of legal standards that provide "reasonable constraints" within which "discretion is exercised," that assure "meaningful and adequate review by the trial court whenever a jury has fixed the punitive damages," and permit "appellate review [that] makes certain that the punitive damages are reasonable in their amount and rational in light of their purpose to punish what has occurred and to deter its repetition." [Cc]

This constitutional concern … arises out of the basic unfairness of depriving citizens of life, liberty, or property, through the application, not of law and legal processes, but of arbitrary coercion. …

Legal standards need not be precise in order to satisfy this constitutional concern. [C] But they must offer some kind of constraint upon a jury or court's discretion, and thus protection against purely arbitrary behavior. The standards the Alabama courts applied here are vague and open ended to the point where they risk arbitrary results. … This is because the standards, as the Alabama Supreme Court authoritatively interpreted them here, provided no significant constraints or protection against arbitrary results.

First, the Alabama statute that permits punitive damages does not itself contain a standard that readily distinguishes between conduct warranting very small, and conduct warranting very large, punitive damages awards. That statute permits punitive damages in cases of "oppression, fraud, wantonness, or malice." Ala. Code § 6-11-20(a) (1993). But the statute goes on to define those terms broadly, to encompass far more than the egregious conduct that those terms, at first reading, might seem to imply. ... The statute thereby authorizes punitive damages for the most serious kinds of misrepresentations, say, tricking the elderly out of their life savings, for much less serious conduct, such as the failure to disclose repainting a car, at issue here, and for a vast range of conduct in between.

Second, the Alabama courts, in this case, have applied the "factors" intended to constrain punitive damages awards in a way that belies that purpose. *Green Oil Co. v. Hornsby*, 539 So.2d 218 (Ala.1989), sets forth seven factors that appellate courts use to determine whether or not a jury award was "grossly excessive" and which, in principle, might make up for the lack of significant constraint in the statute. But, as the Alabama courts have authoritatively interpreted them, and as their application in this case illustrates, they impose little actual constraint. [The seven factors require consideration of (1) a reasonable relationship between the harm likely to occur and the harm that has actually occurred; (2) the degree of reprehensibility of the defendant's conduct; (3) removing the profit from the illegal activity; (4) the defendant's financial position; (5) the costs of litigation and the State's interest in encouraging plaintiffs to bring wrongdoers to court; (6) whether criminal sanctions have been imposed against this defendant; (7) and other civil actions brought against this defendant based on the same conduct.]

....

[T]he rules that purport to channel discretion in this kind of case, here did not do so in fact. That means that the award in this case was both (a) the product of a system of standards that did not significantly constrain a court's, and hence a jury's, discretion in making that award; and (b) grossly excessive in light of the State's legitimate punitive damages objectives.

....

I conclude that the award in this unusual case violates the basic guarantee of nonarbitrary governmental behavior that the Due Process Clause provides.

[Appendix to Justice Breyer's opinion, examining the effect of inflation on judgments issued in the 18th and 19th centuries, omitted.]

Justice SCALIA, with whom Justice THOMAS joins, dissenting.

Today we see the latest manifestation of this Court's recent and increasingly insistent "concern about punitive damages that 'run wild.'" *Pacific Mut. Life Ins. Co. v. Haslip*, 499 U.S. 1, 18, 111 S.Ct. 1032, 1043, 113 L.Ed.2d 1 (1991). Since the Constitution does not make that concern any of our business, the Court's activities in this area are an unjustified incursion into the province of state governments.

In earlier cases that were the prelude to this decision, I set forth my view that a state trial procedure that commits the decision whether to impose punitive damages, and the amount, to the discretion of the jury, subject to some judicial review for "reasonableness," furnishes a defendant with all the process that is "due." [Cc]. I do not regard the Fourteenth Amendment's Due Process Clause as a secret repository of substantive guarantees against "unfairness" – neither the unfairness of an excessive civil compensatory award, nor the unfairness of an "unreasonable" punitive award. What the Fourteenth Amendment's procedural guarantee assures is an opportunity to contest the reasonableness of a damages judgment in state court; but there is no federal guarantee a damages award actually *be* reasonable. [C]

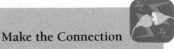

Make the Connection

The Due Process Clause of the Fourteenth Amendment will likely be a topic of considerable discussion in your Constitutional Law course.

This view, which adheres to the text of the Due *Process* Clause, has not prevailed in our punitive damages cases. [Cc] When, however, a constitutional doctrine adopted by the Court is not only mistaken but also insusceptible of principled application, I do not feel bound to give it **stare decisis** effect – indeed, I do not feel justified in doing so. [Cc] Our punitive damages jurisprudence compels such a response. The Constitution provides no warrant for federalizing yet another aspect of our Nation's legal culture (no matter how much in need of correction it may be), and the application of the Court's new rule of constitutional law is constrained by no principle other than the Justices' subjective assessment of the "reasonableness" of the award in relation to the conduct for which it was assessed.

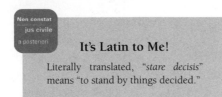

It's Latin to Me!

Literally translated, "*stare decisis*" means "to stand by things decided."

....

I

The most significant aspects of today's decision – the identification of a "substantive due process" right against a "grossly excessive" award, and the concomitant assumption of ultimate authority to decide anew a matter of "reasonableness" resolved in lower court proceedings – are of course not new. *Haslip* and *TXO* revived the notion, moribund since its appearance in the first years of this century, that the measure of civil punishment poses a question of constitutional dimension to be answered by this Court. Neither of those cases, however, nor any of the precedents upon which they relied, actually took the step of declaring a punitive award unconstitutional simply because it was "too big."

At the time of adoption of the Fourteenth Amendment, it was well understood that punitive damages represent the assessment by the jury, as the voice of the community, of the measure of punishment the defendant deserved. [Cc] Today's decision, though dressed up as a legal opinion, is really no more than a disagreement with the community's sense of indignation or outrage expressed in the punitive award of the Alabama jury, as reduced by the State Supreme Court. It reflects not merely, as the concurrence candidly acknowledges, "a judgment about a matter of degree," [C] but a judgment about the appropriate degree of indignation or outrage, which is hardly an analytical determination.

There is no precedential warrant for giving our judgment priority over the judgment of state courts and juries on this matter. ... The only case relied upon in which the Court actually invalidated a civil sanction does not even support constitutional review for excessiveness, since it really concerned the validity, as a matter of *procedural* due process, of state legislation that imposed a significant penalty on a common carrier which lacked the means of determining the legality of its actions before the penalty was imposed. See *Southwestern Telegraph & Telephone Co. v. Danaher,* 238 U.S. 482, 489-491, 35 S.Ct. 886, 887-888, 59 L.Ed. 1419 (1915). The *amount* of the penalty was not a subject of independent scrutiny. ...

....

II

One might understand the Court's eagerness to enter this field, rather than leave it with the state legislatures, if it had something useful to say. In fact, however, its opinion provides virtually no guidance to legislatures, and to state and federal courts, as to what a "constitutionally proper" level of punitive damages might be.

....

III

In Part III of its opinion, the Court identifies "[t]hree guideposts" that lead it to the conclusion that the award in this case is excessive: degree of reprehensibility, ratio between punitive award and plaintiff's actual harm, and legislative sanctions provided for comparable misconduct. [C] The legal significance of these "guideposts" is nowhere explored, but their necessary effect is to establish federal standards governing the hitherto exclusively state law of damages. ... By effectively requiring state reviewing courts to concoct rationalizations – whether within the "guideposts" or through the loophole – to justify the intuitive punitive reactions of state juries, the Court accords neither category of institution the respect it deserves.

Of course it will not be easy for the States to comply with this new federal law of damages, no matter how willing they are to do so. In truth, the "guideposts" mark a road to nowhere; they provide no real guidance at all. ...

[I]t must be noted that the Court nowhere says that these three "guideposts" are the *only* guideposts; indeed, it makes very clear that they are not – explaining away the earlier opinions that do not really follow these "guideposts" on the basis of *additional* factors, thereby "reiterat[ing] our rejection of a categorical approach." [C] In other words, ... [t]he Court has constructed a framework that does not genuinely constrain, that does not inform state legislatures and lower courts—that does nothing at all except confer an artificial air of doctrinal analysis upon its essentially ad hoc determination that this particular award of punitive damages was not "fair." [¶ ...] The elevation of "fairness" in punishment to a principle of "substantive due process" means that every punitive award unreasonably imposed is unconstitutional; such an award is by definition excessive, since it attaches a penalty to conduct undeserving of punishment. Indeed, if the Court is correct, it must be that every claim that a state jury's award of *compensatory* damages is "unreasonable" (because not supported by the evidence) amounts to an assertion of constitutional injury. [C]. And the same would be true for determinations of liability. By today's logic, *every* dispute as to evidentiary sufficiency in a state civil suit poses a question of constitutional moment, subject to review in this Court. That is a stupefying proposition.

For the foregoing reasons, I respectfully dissent.

Justice GINSBURG, with whom THE CHIEF JUSTICE [REHNQUIST] joins, dissenting.

The Court, I am convinced, unnecessarily and unwisely ventures into territory traditionally within the States' domain, and does so in the face of reform measures recently adopted or currently under consideration in legislative arenas. The Alabama Supreme Court, in this case, endeavored to follow this Court's prior instructions; and, more recently, Alabama's highest court has installed further controls on awards of punitive damages [C]. I would therefore leave the state court's judgment undisturbed, and resist unnecessary intrusion into an area dominantly of state concern.

Alabama's Supreme Court reports that it "thoroughly and painstakingly" reviewed the jury's award, [C] according to principles set out in its own pathmarking decisions and in this Court's opinions in *TXO* and *Haslip*. The Alabama court said it gave weight to several factors, including BMW's deliberate ("reprehensible") presentation of refinished cars as new and undamaged, without disclosing that the value of those cars had been reduced by an estimated 10%, the financial position of the defendant, and the costs of litigation. [C] These standards, we previously held, "impos[e] a sufficiently definite and meaningful constraint on the discretion of Alabama factfinders in awarding punitive damages." [Cc] ...

We accept, of course, that Alabama's Supreme Court applied the State's own law correctly. ...

....

The Court finds Alabama's $2 million award not simply excessive, but grossly so, and therefore unconstitutional. The decision leads us further into territory traditionally within the States' domain, and commits the Court, now and again, to correct "misapplication of a properly stated rule of law." ... The Court is not well equipped for this mission. Tellingly, the Court repeats that it brings to the task no "mathematical formula," [C] no "categorical approach," [C] no "bright line [C]". It has only a vague concept of substantive due process, a "raised eyebrow" test, [C] as its ultimate guide.

....

For the reasons stated, I dissent from this Court's disturbance of the judgment the Alabama Supreme Court has made.

[Appendix to dissenting opinion of Justice Ginsburg, setting forth details of state legislation regarding punitive damages, is omitted. *See* Points of Discussion, *infra*.]

———————

Points for Discussion

1. What is the purpose of imposing of punitive damages?

2. What guidelines does the Court provide to lower courts in assessing the appropriateness of a particular punitive damage award?

3. According to the Court, what is the relevance of the ratio, if any, between a jury's punitive damage award and its compensatory damage award?

4. If a plaintiff has been awarded compensatory damages for injuries sustained, is not the award of punitive damages a windfall to the plaintiff?

5. Upon what basis does the Court rule that the defendant's conduct in other states was immaterial to the punitive damage award in this case?

6. The *Gore* Court was presented with a state statute providing for the award of punitive damages. When a ruling of the United States Supreme Court and a state statute are in conflict, which law prevails?

7. Trial courts must provide guidance to juries in determining the appropriate amount to assess. A state's system cannot allow for unlimited jury discretion in assessing punitive damages. *See* Pacific Mut. Life Ins. Co. v. Haslip, 499 U.S. 1 (1991). The jury's award must also be subject to state review in order to ensure the reasonableness of the award. *See, e.g.,* Honda Motor Co. v. Oberg, 512 U.S. 415 (1994). States may limit or modify one's ability to receive punitive damages. *See* Cooper Industries, Inc. v. Leatherman Tool Group, Inc., 532 U.S. 424, 433 (2001).

Food for Thought

In *Biomet Inc. v. Finnegan Henderson L.L.P.,* 967 A.2d 662 (D.C. Ct. App. 2009), the jury awarded $7,134,000 in compensatory damages and $20 million in punitive damages against defendant Biomet for patent infringement, fraud, and the violation of a confidential relationship, a punitive-to-compensatory damages award ratio of 3 to 1. The firm representing Biomet appealed the jury verdict, but did not include as part of its appeal a challenge to the award of $20 million in punitive damages because the 3:1 ratio was well within constitutional standards. On appeal, the court reversed the lower court's finding of infringement against Biomet and remanded the case for recalculation. On remand, the district court determined that Biomet was only liable for $520 in compensatory damages. Following the reduction in compensatory damages, the firm moved for a reduction of the original $20 million in punitive damages, arguing that the new ratio of 38,000 to 1 was now constitutionally impermissible. The district court agreed with Biomet and reduced the amount of punitive damages from $20 million to $52,000. Nonetheless, on subsequent appeal, the court reinstated the original award of $20 million because Biomet had not challenged the amount of punitive damages in its initial appeal and therefore had waived that issue. Following the reinstatement of the original $20 million in punitive damages, Biomet brought a malpractice action against the firm, claiming that the firm had failed to perform as the reasonably prudent attorney under the circumstances because it had not challenged the punitive damage award during the first appeal. The D.C. Court of Appeals ultimately held that, in light of Supreme Court precedent, it was "reasonable for the firm to believe that, because of the original, low 3 to 1 ratio of punitive to compensatory damages, Biomet did not have a viable constitutional challenge to the punitive damage award at the time of the initial appeal" and therefore did not commit malpractice.

8. What does the Court identify as the state's interest in this case? Why is the state's interest important to an evaluation of the appropriateness of a punitive damage award?

9. Lower courts continue to rely upon the *Gore* guideposts in determining whether an award of punitive damages is excessive. In *Snyder v. Phelps*, 533 F.Supp.2d 567 (Md. Dist. Ct. 2008), the court held that an award of $8 million in punitive damages was constitutionally excessive. In *Snyder*, the father of a deceased soldier brought suit against members of a fundamentalist church for picketing the funeral of the deceased soldier. The soldier's father brought suit against the church, alleging intentional infliction of emotional distress, invasion of privacy, and conspiracy. Following a jury trial, the father was awarded $2.9 million in compensatory damages and $8 million in punitive damages. The defendants appealed on multiple grounds, but specifically argued that the jury's verdict was unconstitutionally excessive. In its review of the damage award, the court found that compensatory damages were appropriate under state law and that the award of punitive damages was appropriate in light of the defendant "utilizing [the deceased soldier's] death as a vehicle for hateful expression." While the court found the ratio between the compensatory and punitive damage award to be constitutionally permissible and the possibility for civil or criminal sanctions inapplicable in this case, the court also held that the reprehensibility of the defendant's conduct was significant. The court ultimately reasoned that a reduction in the award of punitive damages was warranted. *Id.* at 592.

On appeal, the United States Court of Appeals for the Fourth Circuit reversed, holding that "the defendant's conduct was protected by the First Amendment." *Snyder v. Phelps*, 580 F.3d 206 (4th Cir. 2009), *aff'd*, 131 S.Ct. 1207 (2011).

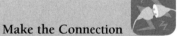

Make the Connection

An excerpt of the Supreme Court's opinion in *Snyder* appears in Chapter 17, Privacy, *infra*.

10. As an appendix to her dissent in *BMW v. Gore,* Justice Ginsburg noted state legislative activity pertaining to the availability of punitive damage awards:

See It

Click here to view the current availability of punitive damage awards by jurisdiction.

"State legislatures have in the hopper or have enacted a variety of measures to curtail awards of punitive damages. At least one state legislature has prohibited punitive damages altogether, unless explicitly provided by statute. See N.H. Rev.Stat. Ann. § 507:16 (1994)."

Hypo 9-2

Doris and Michael divorced several years ago. Without Doris's knowledge, Michael kept several photographs that he had taken of her in the nude as well as several other photos of Doris and Michael engaged in a consensual sexual act. A year after their divorce, Michael copied the photos and placed Doris's new married name, her work address and phone number, her new husband's name, and her attorney's name on each of the photos. He then distributed at least sixty copies around the small community where both he and Doris still lived and worked. Not pleased, Doris sued Michael, alleging the torts of invasion of privacy and intentional infliction of emotional distress. The jury awarded her $100,000 in compensatory damages and $100,000 in punitive damages.

A statute in the jurisdiction requires that any punitive award to a plaintiff is to be paid by the defendant to the clerk of the court, with the clerk directed to pay seventy-five percent of the punitive damage award to the State's Violent Crime Victims' Compensation Fund, set up to benefit victims of violent crimes in that state. As a result, Doris was only entitled to receive twenty-five percent of her punitive damage award.

Discuss. Why might a state set up such a fund?

State Farm Mutual Automobile Ins. Co. v. Campbell

538 U.S. 408 (2003)

Justice KENNEDY delivered the opinion of the Court.

We address once again the measure of punishment, by means of punitive damages, a State may impose upon a defendant in a civil case. The question is whether, in the circumstances we shall recount, an award of $145 million in punitive damages, where full compensatory damages are $1 million, is excessive and in violation of the Due Process Clause of the Fourteenth Amendment to the Constitution of the United States.

I

In 1981, Curtis Campbell (Campbell) was driving with his wife, Inez Preece Campbell, in Cache County, Utah. He decided to pass six vans traveling ahead of them on a two-lane highway. Todd Ospital was driving a small car approaching from the opposite direction. To avoid a head-on collision with Campbell, who by then was driving on the wrong side of the highway and toward oncoming traffic, Ospital swerved onto the shoulder, lost control of his automobile, and collided with a vehicle driven by Robert G. Slusher. Ospital was killed, and Slusher was rendered permanently disabled. The Campbells escaped unscathed.

In the ensuing wrongful death and tort action, Campbell insisted he was not at fault. Early investigations did support differing conclusions as to who caused the accident, but "a consensus was reached early on by the investigators and witnesses that Mr. Campbell's unsafe pass had indeed caused the crash." [C] Campbell's insurance company, petitioner State Farm Mutual Automobile Insurance Company (State Farm), nonetheless decided to contest liability and declined offers by Slusher and Ospital's estate (Ospital) to settle the claims for the policy limit of $50,000 ($25,000 per claimant). State Farm also ignored the advice of one of its own investigators and took the case to trial, assuring the Campbells that "their assets were safe, that they had no liability for the accident, that [State Farm] would represent their interests, and that they did not need to procure separate counsel." [C] To the contrary, a jury determined that Campbell was 100 percent at fault, and a judgment was returned for $185,849, far more than the amount offered in settlement.

What's That?

A *supersedeas bond* is an appellant's bond to stay execution on a judgment during the appeal.

At first State Farm refused to cover the $135,849 in excess liability. Its counsel made this clear to the Campbells: "'You may want to put for sale signs on your property to get things moving.'" [C] Nor was State Farm willing to post a **supersedeas bond** to allow Campbell to appeal the judgment against him. Campbell obtained his own counsel to appeal the verdict. During the pendency of the appeal, in late 1984, Slusher, Ospital, and the Campbells reached an agreement whereby Slusher and Ospital agreed not to seek satisfaction of their claims against the Campbells. In exchange the Campbells agreed to pursue a bad faith action against State Farm and to be represented by Slusher's and Ospital's attorneys. The Campbells also agreed that Slusher and Ospital would have a right to play a part in all major decisions concerning the bad-faith action. No settlement could be concluded without Slusher's and Ospital's approval, and Slusher and Ospital would receive 90 percent of any verdict against State Farm.

In 1989, the Utah Supreme Court denied Campbell's appeal in the wrongful-death and tort actions. [C] State Farm then paid the entire judgment, including the amounts in excess of the policy limits. The Campbells nonetheless filed a complaint against State Farm alleging bad faith, fraud, and intentional infliction of emotional distress. The trial court initially granted State Farm's motion for summary judgment because State Farm had paid the excess verdict, but that ruling was reversed on appeal. [C] On remand State Farm moved *in limine* to exclude evidence of alleged conduct that occurred in unrelated cases outside of Utah, but the trial court denied the motion. At State Farm's request the trial court bifurcated the trial into two phases conducted before different juries. In the first phase the jury determined that State Farm's decision not to settle was unreasonable because there was a substantial likelihood of an excess verdict.

Before the second phase of the action against State Farm we decided *BMW v. Gore,* and refused to sustain a $2 million punitive damages award which accompanied a verdict of only $4,000 in compensatory damages. Based on that decision, State Farm again moved for the exclusion of evidence of dissimilar out-of-state conduct. [C] The trial court denied State Farm's motion. [C]

Practice Pointer

A bifurcated trial is one that is conducted in two separate parts. For example, the liability phase may be conducted first. Only when liability against a defendant is imposed is there a second part to the trial where the jury fixes the amount of damages against that liable party.

The second phase addressed State Farm's liability for fraud and intentional infliction of emotional distress, as well as compensatory and punitive damages. The Utah Supreme Court aptly characterized this phase of the trial:

"State Farm argued during phase II that its decision to take the case to trial was an 'honest mistake' that did not warrant punitive damages. In contrast, the Campbells introduced evidence that State Farm's decision to take the case to trial was a result of a national scheme to meet corporate fiscal goals by capping payouts on claims company wide. This scheme was referred to as State Farm's 'Performance, Planning and Review,' or PP & R, policy. To prove the existence of this scheme, the trial court allowed the Campbells to introduce extensive expert testimony regarding fraudulent practices by State Farm in its nation-wide operations. Although State Farm moved prior to phase II of the trial for the exclusion of such evidence and continued to object to it at trial, the trial court ruled that such evidence was admissible to determine whether State Farm's conduct in the Campbell case was indeed intentional and sufficiently egregious to warrant punitive damages." [C]

Evidence pertaining to the PP & R policy concerned State Farm's business practices for over 20 years in numerous States. Most of these practices bore no relation to third-party automobile insurance claims, the type of claim underlying the Campbells' complaint against the company. The jury awarded the Campbells $2.6 million in compensatory damages and $145 million in punitive damages, which the trial court reduced to $1 million and $25 million respectively. Both parties appealed.

The Utah Supreme Court sought to apply the three guideposts we identified in *Gore, supra,* and it reinstated the $145 million punitive damages award. Relying in large part on the extensive evidence concerning the PP & R policy, the court concluded State Farm's conduct was reprehensible. The court also relied upon State Farm's "massive wealth" and on testimony indicating that "State Farm's actions, because of their clandestine nature, will be punished at most in one out of every 50,000 cases as a matter of statistical probability," [C] and concluded that the ratio between punitive and compensatory damages was not unwarranted. Finally, the court noted that the punitive damages award was not excessive when compared to various civil and criminal penalties State Farm could have faced, including $10,000 for each act of fraud, the suspension of its license to conduct business in Utah, the disgorgement of profits, and imprisonment. [C] We granted certiorari. [C]

II

We recognized in *Cooper Industries, Inc. v. Leatherman Tool Group, Inc.,* 532 U.S. 424, 121 S.Ct. 1678, 149 L.Ed.2d 674 (2001), that in our judicial system compensatory and punitive damages, although usually awarded at the same time by the same decisionmaker, serve different purposes. [C] Compensatory damages "are intended to redress the concrete loss that the plaintiff has suffered by reason of the defendant's wrongful conduct." *Ibid.* (citing RESTATEMENT (SECOND) OF TORTS § 903, pp. 453-454 (1979)). By contrast, punitive damages serve a broader function; they are aimed at deterrence and retribution. [Cc]

While States possess discretion over the imposition of punitive damages, it is well established that there are procedural and substantive constitutional limitations on these awards. [Cc] The Due Process Clause of the Fourteenth Amendment prohibits the imposition of grossly excessive or arbitrary punishments on a tortfeasor. [Cc] The reason is that "[e]lementary notions of fairness enshrined in our constitutional juris-prudence dictate that a person receive fair notice not only of the conduct that will subject him to punishment, but also of the severity of the penalty that a State may impose." [C] To the extent an award is grossly excessive, it furthers no legitimate purpose and constitutes an arbitrary deprivation of property. [C]

> **FYI**
>
> The text of the Due Process Clause of the Fourteenth Amendment provides "... nor shall any State deprive any person of life, liberty, or property, without due process of law...".

Although these awards serve the same purposes as criminal penalties, defendants subjected to punitive damages in civil cases have not been accorded the protections applicable in a criminal proceeding. This increases our concerns over the imprecise manner in which punitive damages systems are administered. We have admonished that "[p]unitive damages pose an acute danger of arbitrary deprivation of property. Jury instructions typically leave the jury with wide discretion in choosing amounts, and the presentation of evidence of a defendant's net worth creates the potential that juries will use their verdicts to express biases against big businesses, particularly those without strong local presences." *Honda Motor, supra,* at 432, 114 S.Ct. 2331; see also *Haslip, supra,* at 59, 111 S.Ct. 1032 (O'CONNOR, J., dissenting) ("[T]he Due Process Clause does not permit a State to classify arbitrariness as a virtue. Indeed, the point of due process-of the law in general-is to allow citizens to order their behavior. A State can have no legitimate interest in deliberately making the law so arbitrary that citizens will be unable to avoid punishment based solely upon bias or whim"). Our concerns are heightened when the decisionmaker is presented, as we shall discuss, with evidence that has little bearing as to the amount of punitive damages that should be awarded. Vague instructions, or those that merely inform the jury to avoid "passion or prejudice," [c] do little to aid the decisionmaker in its task of assigning appropriate weight to evidence that is relevant and evidence that is tangential or only inflammatory.

In light of these concerns, in *Gore, supra,* we instructed courts reviewing punitive damages to consider three guideposts: (1) the degree of reprehensibility of the defendant's misconduct; (2) the disparity between the actual or potential harm suffered by the plaintiff and the punitive damages award; and (3) the difference between the punitive damages awarded by the jury and the civil penalties authorized or imposed in comparable cases. [C] We reiterated the importance of these three guideposts in *Cooper Industries* and mandated appellate courts to conduct *de novo* review of a trial court's application of them to the jury's award. [C] Exacting appellate review ensures that an award of punitive damages is based upon an " 'application of law, rather than a decisionmaker's caprice.' " [C]

III

Under the principles outlined in *BMW of North America, Inc. v. Gore,* this case is neither close nor difficult. It was error to reinstate the jury's $145 million punitive damages award. We address each guidepost of *Gore* in some detail.

A

"[T]he most important indicium of the reasonableness of a punitive damages award is the degree of reprehensibility of the defendant's conduct." [C] We have instructed courts to determine the reprehensibility of a defendant by considering whether: the harm caused was physical as opposed to economic; the tortious conduct evinced an indifference to or a reckless disregard of the health or safety of others; the target of the conduct had financial vulnerability; the conduct involved repeated actions or was an isolated incident; and the harm was the result of intentional malice, trickery, or deceit, or mere accident. [C] The existence of any one of these factors weighing in favor of a plaintiff may not be sufficient to sustain a punitive damages award; and the absence of all of them renders any award suspect. It should be presumed a plaintiff has been made whole for his injuries by compensatory damages, so punitive damages should only be awarded if the defendant's culpability, after having paid compensatory damages, is so reprehensible as to warrant the imposition of further sanctions to achieve punishment or deterrence. [C]

Applying these factors in the instant case, we must acknowledge that State Farm's handling of the claims against the Campbells merits no praise. The trial court found that State Farm's employees altered the company's records to make Campbell appear less culpable. State Farm disregarded the overwhelming likelihood of liability and the near-certain probability that, by taking the case to trial, a judgment in excess of the policy limits would be awarded. State Farm amplified the harm by at first assuring the Campbells their assets would be safe from any verdict and by later telling them, postjudgment, to put a for-sale sign on their house. While we do not suggest there was error in awarding punitive damages based upon State Farm's conduct toward the Campbells, a more modest punishment for this reprehensible conduct could have satisfied the State's legitimate objectives, and the Utah courts should have gone no further.

This case, instead, was used as a platform to expose, and punish, the perceived deficiencies of State Farm's operations throughout the country. The Utah Supreme Court's opinion makes explicit that State Farm was being condemned for its nationwide policies rather than for the conduct directed toward the Campbells. [C] This was, as well, an explicit rationale of the trial court's decision in approving the award, though reduced from $145 million to $25 million. [C]

. . . .

A State cannot punish a defendant for conduct that may have been lawful where it occurred. *Gore, supra,* at 572, 116 S.Ct. 1589; [Cc]. Nor, as a general rule, does a State have a legitimate concern in imposing punitive damages to punish a defendant for unlawful acts committed outside of the State's jurisdiction. Any proper adjudication of conduct that occurred outside Utah to other persons would require their inclusion, and, to those parties, the Utah courts, in the usual case, would need to apply the laws of their relevant jurisdiction. [C]

. . . .

B

Turning to the second *Gore* guidepost, we have been reluctant to identify concrete constitutional limits on the ratio between harm, or potential harm, to the plaintiff and the punitive damages award. [Cc] We decline again to impose a bright-line ratio which a punitive damages award cannot exceed. Our jurisprudence and the principles it has now established demonstrate, however, that, in practice, few awards exceeding a single-digit ratio between punitive and compensatory damages, to a significant degree, will satisfy due process. In *Haslip,* in upholding a punitive damages award, we concluded that an award of more than four times the amount of compensatory damages might be close to the line of constitutional impropriety. We cited that 4-to-1 ratio again in *Gore.* 517 U.S., at 581, 116 S.Ct. 1589. The Court further referenced a long legislative history, dating back over 700 years and going forward to today, providing for sanctions of double, treble, or quadruple damages to deter and punish. While these ratios are not binding, they are instructive. They demonstrate what should be obvious: Single-digit multipliers are more likely to comport with due process, while still achieving the State's goals of deterrence and retribution, than awards with ratios in range of 500 to 1, *id.,* at 582, 116 S.Ct. 1589, or, in this case, of 145 to 1.

. . . .

In sum, courts must ensure that the measure of punishment is both reasonable and proportionate to the amount of harm to the plaintiff and to the general damages recovered. In the context of this case, we have no doubt that there is a presumption against an award that has a 145-to-1 ratio. The compensatory award in this case was substantial; the Campbells were awarded $1 million for a year and a half of emotional distress. This was complete compensation. The harm arose from a transaction in the economic realm, not from some physical assault or trauma; there were no physical injuries; and State Farm paid the excess verdict before the complaint was filed, so the Campbells suffered only minor economic injuries for the 18-month period in which State Farm refused to resolve the claim against them. The compensatory damages for the injury suffered here, moreover, likely were based on a component which was duplicated in the punitive award. Much of the distress was caused by the outrage and humiliation the Campbells suffered at the actions of their insurer; and it is a major role of punitive damages to condemn such conduct. Compensatory damages, however, already contain this punitive element. See Restatement (Second) of Torts § 908, Comment *c* (1977) ("In many cases in which compensatory damages include an amount for emotional distress, such as humiliation or indignation aroused by the defendant's act, there is no clear line of demarcation between punishment and compensation and a verdict for a specified amount frequently includes elements of both").

The Utah Supreme Court sought to justify the massive award by pointing to State Farm's purported failure to report a prior $100 million punitive damages award in Texas to its corporate headquarters; the fact that State Farm's policies have affected numerous Utah consumers; the fact that State Farm will only be punished in one out of every 50,000 cases as a matter of statistical probability; and State Farm's enormous wealth. [C]

While States enjoy considerable discretion in deducing when punitive damages are warranted, each award must comport with the principles set forth in *Gore*. Here the argument that State Farm will be punished in only the rare case, coupled with reference to its assets (which, of course, are what other insured parties in Utah and other States must rely upon for payment of claims) had little to do with the actual harm sustained by the Campbells. The wealth of a defendant cannot justify an otherwise unconstitutional punitive damages award. [Cc] The principles set forth in *Gore* must be implemented with care, to ensure both reasonableness and proportionality.

C

The third guidepost in *Gore* is the disparity between the punitive damages award and the "civil penalties authorized or imposed in comparable cases." [C] We note that, in the past, we have also looked to criminal penalties that could be imposed. [C] The existence of a criminal penalty does have bearing on the seriousness with which a State views the wrongful action. When used to determine the dollar amount of the award, however, the criminal penalty has less utility. Great care must be taken to avoid use of the civil process to assess criminal penalties that can be imposed only after the heightened protections of a criminal trial have been observed, including, of course, its higher standards of proof. Punitive damages are not a substitute for the criminal process, and the remote possibility of a criminal sanction does not automatically sustain a punitive damages award.

Here, we need not dwell long on this guidepost. The most relevant civil sanction under Utah state law for the wrong done to the Campbells appears to be a $10,000 fine for an act of fraud, 65 P.3d, at 1154, an amount dwarfed by the $145 million punitive damages award. The Supreme Court of Utah speculated about the loss of State Farm's business license, the disgorgement of profits, and possible imprisonment, but here again its references were to the broad fraudulent scheme drawn from evidence of out-of-state and dissimilar conduct. This analysis was insufficient to justify the award.

IV

An application of the *Gore* guideposts to the facts of this case, especially in light of the substantial compensatory damages awarded (a portion of which contained a punitive element), likely would justify a punitive damages award at or near the amount of compensatory damages. The punitive award of $145 million, therefore, was neither reasonable nor proportionate to the wrong committed, and it was an irrational and arbitrary deprivation of the property of the defendant. The proper calculation of punitive damages under the principles we have discussed should be resolved, in the first instance, by the Utah courts.

The judgment of the Utah Supreme Court is reversed, and the case is remanded for further proceedings not inconsistent with this opinion.

It is so ordered.

Justice SCALIA, dissenting.

I adhere to the view expressed in my dissenting opinion in *BMW of North America, Inc. v. Gore,* that the Due Process Clause provides no substantive protections against "excessive" or "'unreasonable'" awards of punitive damages. I am also of the view that the punitive damages jurisprudence which has sprung forth from *BMW v. Gore* is insusceptible of principled application; accordingly, I do not feel justified in giving the case **stare decisis** effect. [C] I would affirm the judgment of the Utah Supreme Court.

Justice THOMAS, dissenting.

I would affirm the judgment below because "I continue to believe that the Constitution does not constrain the size of punitive damages awards." *Cooper Industries, Inc. v. Leatherman Tool Group, Inc.,* 532 U.S. 424, 443, 121 S.Ct. 1678, 149 L.Ed.2d 674 (2001) (THOMAS, J., concurring) (citing *BMW of North America, Inc. v. Gore,* (SCALIA, J., joined by THOMAS, J., dissenting)). Accordingly, I respectfully dissent.

Justice GINSBURG, dissenting.

Not long ago, this Court was hesitant to impose a federal check on state-court judgments awarding punitive damages. In *Browning-Ferris Industries of Vt., Inc. v. Kelco Disposal, Inc.,* 492 U.S. 257, 109 S.Ct. 2909, 106 L.Ed.2d 219 (1989), the Court held that neither the Excessive Fines Clause of the Eighth Amendment nor federal common law circumscribed awards of punitive damages in civil cases between private parties. [C] Two years later, in *Pacific Mut. Life Ins. Co. v. Haslip,* [c], the Court observed that "unlimited jury [or judicial] discretion ... in the fixing of punitive damages may invite extreme results that jar one's constitutional sensibilities[.]" [c] The Due Process Clause, the Court suggested, would attend to those sensibilities and guard against unreasonable awards. [C] Nevertheless, the Court upheld a punitive damages award in *Haslip* "more than 4 times the amount of compensatory damages, ... more than 200 times [the plaintiff's] out-of-pocket expenses," and "much in excess of the fine that could be imposed." [C] And in *TXO Production Corp. v. Alliance Resources Corp.,* [c] the Court affirmed a state-court award "526 times greater than the actual damages awarded by the jury." [Cc]

It was not until 1996, in *BMW of North America, Inc. v. Gore,* [c] that the Court, for the first time, invalidated a state-court punitive damages assessment as unreasonably large. [C] If our activity in this domain is now "well established," [c] it takes place on ground not long held.

In *Gore,* I stated why I resisted the Court's foray into punitive damages "territory traditionally within the States' domain." [C] I adhere to those views, and note again that, unlike federal habeas corpus review of state-court convictions under 28 U.S.C. § 2254, the Court "work[s] at this business [of checking state courts] alone," unaided by the participation of federal district courts and courts of appeals. 517 U.S., at 613, 116 S.Ct. 1589. ...

Take Note

Habeas corpus literally means "that you have the body." It is a civil action that is typically used to demand the release from prison or jail a person who is claimed to be illegally held. The procedures and rules governing habeas corpus actions are complex and subject to rigorous federal court review.

I

The large size of the award upheld by the Utah Supreme Court in this case indicates why damages-capping legislation may be altogether fitting and proper. Neither the amount of the award nor the trial record, however, justifies this Court's substitution of its judgment for that of Utah's competent decisionmakers. In this regard, I count it significant that, on the key criterion "reprehensibility," there is a good deal more to the story than the Court's abbreviated account tells.

Ample evidence allowed the jury to find that State Farm's treatment of the Campbells typified its "Performance, Planning and Review" (PP & R) program; implemented by top management in 1979, the program had "the explicit objective of using the claims-adjustment process as a profit center." [C] "[T]he Campbells presented considerable evidence," the trial court noted, documenting "that the PP & R program ... has functioned, and continues to function, as an unlawful scheme ... to deny benefits owed consumers by paying out less than fair value in order to meet preset, arbitrary payout targets designed to enhance corporate profits." [C] That policy, the trial court observed, was encompassing in scope; it "applied equally to the handling of both third-party and first-party claims." [C]

Evidence the jury could credit demonstrated that the PP & R program regularly and adversely affected Utah residents. ...

....

The trial court further determined that the jury could find State Farm's policy "deliberately crafted" to prey on consumers who would be unlikely to defend themselves. [C] In this regard, the trial court noted the testimony of several former State Farm employees affirming that they were trained to target "the weakest of the herd" -- "the elderly, the poor, and other consumers who are least knowledgeable about their rights and thus most vulnerable to trickery or deceit, or who have little money and hence have no real alternative but to accept an inadequate offer to settle a claim at much less than fair value." [C]

The Campbells themselves could be placed within the "weakest of the herd" category. The couple appeared economically vulnerable and emotionally fragile. [C] At the time of State Farm's wrongful conduct, "Mr. Campbell had residuary effects from a stroke and Parkinson's disease." [C]

To further insulate itself from liability, trial evidence indicated, State Farm made "systematic" efforts to destroy internal company documents that might reveal its scheme, [C] efforts that directly affected the Campbell. [C] For example, State Farm had "a special historical department that contained a copy of all past manuals on claim-handling practices and the dates on which each section of each manual was changed." *Ibid.* Yet in discovery proceedings, State Farm failed to produce any claim-handling practice manuals for the years relevant to the Campbells' bad-faith case. [C]

State Farm's inability to produce the manuals, it appeared from the evidence, was not accidental. Documents retained by former State Farm employee Samantha Bird, as well as Bird's testimony, showed that while the Campbells' case was pending, Janet Cammack, "an in-house attorney sent by top State Farm management, conducted a meeting ... in Utah during which she instructed Utah claims management to search their offices and destroy a wide range of material of the sort that had proved damaging in bad-faith litigation in the past – in particular, old claim-handling manuals, memos, claim school notes, procedure guides and other similar documents." [C] "These orders were followed even though at least one meeting participant, Paul Short, was personally aware that these kinds of materials had been requested by the Campbells in this very case." [C]

Practice Pointer

Whether this mandate by State Farm's in-house counsel to destroy corporate documents was prudent (or even perhaps illegal) is a topic of considerable importance. You will likely cover this topic in a Professional Responsibility or Legal Ethics course. Suffice it to say that practicing law is not a defense to imposition of criminal or civil penalties against attorneys, even if they are acting at the direction of or on behalf of their clients.

....

"As a final, related tactic," the trial court stated, the jury could reasonably find that "in recent years State Farm has gone to extraordinary lengths to stop damaging documents from being created in the first place." [C] ...

....

State Farm's "policies and practices," the trial evidence thus bore out, were "responsible for the injuries suffered by the Campbells," and the means used to implement those policies could be found "callous, clandestine, fraudulent, and dishonest." [Cc] The Utah Supreme Court, relying on the trial court's record-based recitations, understandably characterized State Farm's behavior as "egregious and malicious." [C]

II

The Court dismisses the evidence describing and documenting State Farm's PP & R policy and practices as essentially irrelevant, bearing "no relation to the Campbells' harm." [C] It is hardly apparent why that should be so. What is infirm about the Campbells' theory that their experience with State Farm exemplifies and reflects an overarching underpayment scheme, one that caused "repeated misconduct of the sort that injured them…"? The Court's silence on that score is revealing: Once one recognizes that the Campbells did show "conduct by State Farm similar to that which harmed them," [C] it becomes impossible to shrink the reprehensibility analysis to this sole case, or to maintain, at odds with the determination of the trial court [C] that "the adverse effect on the State's general population was in fact minor." [C]

Evidence of out-of-state conduct, the Court acknowledges, may be "probative [even if the conduct is lawful in the State where it occurred] when it demonstrates the deliberateness and culpability of the defendant's action in the State where it is tortious...." [Cc] "Other acts" evidence concerning practices both in and out of State was introduced in this case to show just such "deliberateness" and "culpability." The evidence was admissible, the trial court ruled: (1) to document State Farm's "reprehensible" PP & R program; and (2) to "rebut [State Farm's] assertion that [its] actions toward the Campbells were inadvertent errors or mistakes in judgment." [C] Viewed in this light, there surely was "a nexus" between much of the "other acts" evidence and "the specific harm suffered by [the Campbells]." [C]

III

When the Court first ventured to override state-court punitive damages awards, it did so moderately. The Court recalled that "[i]n our federal system, States necessarily have considerable flexibility in determining the level of punitive damages that they will allow in different classes of cases and in any particular case." [C] Today's decision exhibits no such respect and restraint. No longer content to accord state-court judgments "a strong presumption of validity," [C] the Court announces that "few awards exceeding a single-digit ratio between punitive and compensatory damages, to a significant degree, will satisfy due process." [C] Moreover, the Court adds, when compensatory damages are substantial, doubling those damages "can reach the outermost limit of the due process guarantee." [Cc] In a legislative scheme or a state high court's design to cap punitive damages, the handiwork in setting single-digit and 1-to-1 benchmarks could hardly be questioned; in a judicial decree imposed on the States by this Court under the banner of substantive due process, the numerical controls today's decision installs seem to me boldly out of order.

. . . .

I remain of the view that this Court has no warrant to reform state law governing awards of punitive damages. [C] Even if I were prepared to accept the flexible guides prescribed in *Gore,* I would not join the Court's swift conversion of those guides into instructions that begin to resemble marching orders. For the reasons stated, I would leave the judgment of the Utah Supreme Court undisturbed.

Points for Discussion

1. May a defendant be subject to punitive damages for engaging in merely negligent conduct?

2. What standard of review is a reviewing court to apply in considering the appropriateness of a punitive damage award?

3. Should a punitive damage award be available to a plaintiff in a case where only nominal damages are awarded?

4. The United States Supreme Court has ruled multiple times that there are due process limitations on an award of punitive damages. In addition to *Gore* and *State Farm Mut. Auto. Ins. Co. v. Campbell*, consider *Philip Morris USA v. Williams*, 549 U.S. 346 (2007). In *Philip Morris*, the Court was asked to review an original award of $821,485.50 in compensatory damages and $79.5 million in punitive damages awarded to the personal representative of Williams's estate. Williams died of lung cancer after a lifetime of smoking three packs of cigarettes a day. The attorney representing the estate introduced evidence of "injury inflicted on strangers to the litigation" to demonstrate the reprehensibility of the defendant's conduct. The Court held that while "evidence of actual harm to nonparties" could be considered by a jury in determining the reprehensibility of the defendant's conduct, a state cannot use a punitive damages award to punish a defendant for harms allegedly visited on nonparties.

5. As punitive damages are intended to punish and deter reprehensible conduct, a court is likely to affirm an award of punitive damages where sufficient evidence of "an unjustifiable failure to avoid a known risk" is demonstrated and the ratio of punitive to compensatory damages does not "raise a suspicious judicial eyebrow." *BMW of North America v. Gore*, 517 U.S. 559, 583 (1996) (quoting *TXO Prod. Corp.*, 509 U.S. at 481 (1993)). For instance, in *Mathias v. Accor Econ. Lodging, Inc.*, the defendants, who owned and operated several hotel and motel chains, refused to exterminate one of their motels despite a recommendation by the motel's provider of extermination services, the recommendation of a manager to fumigate the motel, and an influx of complaints and refunds associated with a growing infestation of bed bugs. *See* 347 F.3d 672, 673-75 (7th Cir. 2003). Two of the motel guests who were bitten by bed bugs brought suit against the defendants arguing that the defendants were guilty of "willful and wanton conduct and thus [...] liable for punitive as well as compensatory damages." Following a jury trial, the plaintiffs were awarded $186,000 in punitive damages. The defendants appealed arguing that they were at worst guilty of **simple negligence** and that

the award of punitive damages was excessive. While the ratio of punitive to compensatory damages was 37.2 to 1, the court found the award permissible because "the defendant's behavior was outrageous [...] and at the same time difficult to quantify because a large element of it was emotional." The court explained that the imposition of the punitive damage award would also limit the "defendant's ability to profit from its fraud." The *Mathias* court explained the tort history of punitive damages:

> "England's common law courts first confirmed their authority to award punitive damages in the eighteenth century ... at a time when the institutional structure of criminal law enforcement was primitive and it made sense to leave certain minor crimes to be dealt with by the civil law. And still today one function of punitive-damages awards is to relieve the pressures on an overloaded system of criminal justice by providing a civil alternative to criminal prosecution of minor crimes. An example is deliberately spitting in a person's face, a criminal assault but[,] because minor[,] readily deterrable by levying of what amounts to a civil fine through a suit for damages for the tort of battery. Compensatory damages would not do the trick in such a case ...."

6. Unlike the conduct of the defendants in *Mathias, supra,* the defendant's actions in *Estate of Embry* did not rise to the level of gross negligence, and therefore the imposition of punitive damages was ruled improper. In *Embry,* a truck driver collided with the driver of a minivan after drinking coffee, choking, and subsequently losing consciousness, veering into an oncoming lane of traffic, injuring and killing several passengers. *Estate of Embry,* 478 F.Supp.2d 914, 916 (E. D. Ky. 2007). Because it was undisputed that the defendant was not speeding, intoxicated, or fatigued, the court found that the defendant was at best negligent. Because the actions of the defendant did not rise to the level of gross negligence, the court ruled that the imposition of punitive damages could not be justified.

7. *See also* Exxon Shipping Co. v. Baker, 554 U.S. 471 (2008) (holding that maximum award of punitive damages allowed under maritime law was equal to jury's award of $507.5 million in compensatory damages).

————————————

CHAPTER 10

Wrongful Death and Survival

A. Wrongful Death Actions

Moragne v. States Marine Lines, Inc.

398 U.S. 375 (1970)

Mr. Justice HARLAN delivered the opinion of the Court.

We brought this case here to consider whether _The Harrisburg,_ 119 U.S. 199, 7 S.Ct. 140, 30 L.Ed. 358, in which this Court held in 1886 that **maritime law** does not afford a cause of action for wrongful death, should any longer be regarded as acceptable law.

The complaint sets forth that Edward Moragne, a longshoreman, was killed while working aboard the vessel Palmetto State in navigable waters within the State of Florida. Petitioner, as his widow and representative of his estate, brought this suit in a state court against respondent States Marine Lines, Inc., the owner of the Vessel, to recover damages for wrongful death and for the pain and suffering experienced by the decedent prior to his death. The claims were predicated upon both negligence and the unseaworthiness of the vessel.

States Marine removed the case to the Federal District Court for the Middle District of Florida on the basis of **diversity of citizenship,** see 28 U.S.C. §§ 1332, 1441, and there filed a **third-party complaint** against respondent Gulf Florida Terminal Company, the decedent's employer, asserting that Gulf had contracted to perform **stevedoring** services on the vessel in a workmanlike manner and that any negligence or unseaworthiness causing the accident resulted from Gulf's operations.

Both States Marine and Gulf sought dismissal of the portion of petitioner's complaint that requested damages for wrongful death on the basis of unseaworthiness. They contended that maritime law provided no recovery for wrongful death within a State's territorial waters, and that the statutory right of action for death under Florida law, Fla.Stat. § 768.01 (1965), F.S.A., did not encompass unseaworthiness as a basis of liability. The District Court dismissed the challenged portion of the complaint on this ground, citing this Court's decision in *The Tungus v. Skovgaard*, 358 U.S. 588, 79 S.Ct. 503, 3 L.Ed.2d 524 (1959), and cases construing the state statute, but made the certification necessary under 28 U.S.C. § 1292(b) to allow petitioner an **interlocutory appeal** to the Court of Appeals for the Fifth Circuit.

The Court of Appeals took advantage of a procedure furnished by state law, Fla.Stat. § 25.031 (1965), ... to certify to the Florida Supreme Court the question whether the state wrongful-death statute allowed recovery for unseaworthiness as that concept is understood in maritime law. After reviewing the history of the Florida Act, the state court answered this question in the negative. 211 So.2d 161 (1968). On return of the case to the Court of Appeals, that court affirmed the District Court's order, rejecting petitioner's argument that she was entitled to reversal under federal maritime law without regard to the scope of the state statute. 409 F.2d 32 (1969). The court stated that its disposition was compelled by our decision in *The Tungus*. We granted **certiorari**, 396 U.S. 900, 90 S.Ct. 212, 24 L.Ed.2d 176 (1969), and invited the United States to participate as **amicus curiae** ... to reconsider the important question of remedies under federal maritime law for tortious deaths on state territorial waters.

In *The Tungus* this Court divided on the consequences that should flow from the rule of maritime law that 'in the absence of a statute there is no action for wrongful death,' first announced in *The Harrisburg*. All members of the Court agreed that where a death on state territorial waters is left remediless by the general maritime law and by federal statutes, a remedy may be provided under any applicable state law giving a right of action for death by wrongful act. However, four Justices dissented from the Court's further holding that 'when admiralty adopts a State's right of action for wrongful death, it must enforce the right as an integrated whole, with whatever conditions and limitations the creating State has attached.' 358 U.S., at 592, 79 S.Ct. at 506. The dissenters would have held that federal maritime law could utilize the state law to 'supply a remedy' for breaches of federally imposed duties, without regard to any substantive limitations contained in the state law. Id., at 597, 599, 79 S.Ct., at 509, 510.

The extent of the role to be played by state law under *The Tungus* has been the subject of substantial debate and uncertainty in this Court, [Cc] with opinions on both sides of the question acknowledging the shortcomings in the present law. [C] On fresh consideration of the entire subject, we have concluded that the primary source of the confusion is not to be found in *The Tungus*, but in *The Harrisburg*, and that the latter decision, somewhat dubious even when rendered, is such an unjustifiable anomaly in the present maritime law that it should no longer be followed. We therefore reverse the judgment of the Court of Appeals.

I

The Court's opinion in *The Harrisburg* acknowledged that the result reached had little justification except in primitive English legal history--a history far removed from the American law of remedies for maritime deaths. That case, like this, was a suit on behalf of the family of a maritime worker for his death on the navigable waters of a State. Following several precedents in the lower federal courts, the trial court awarded damages against the ship causing the death, and the circuit court affirmed, ruling that death by maritime tort 'may be complained of as an injury, and the wrong redressed under the general maritime law.' 15 F. 610, 614 (1883). This Court, in reversing, relied primarily on its then-recent decision in *Insurance Co. v. Brame*, 95 U.S. 754, 24 L.Ed. 580 (1878), in which it had held that in American common law, as in English, 'no civil action lies for an injury which results in * * * death.' Id., at 756.[2] In *The Harrisburg*, as in *Brame*, the Court did not examine the justifications for this common-law rule; rather, it simply noted that 'we know of no country that has adopted a different rule on this subject for the sea from that which it maintains on the land,' and concluded, despite contrary decisions of the lower federal courts both before and after *Brame*, that the rule of *Brame* should apply equally to maritime deaths. 119 U.S., at 213, 7 S.Ct., at 146.[3]

Behind the Scenes

Prior to the Supreme Court's decision in *Erie R. Co. v. Tompkins*, 304 U.S. 64 (1938), federal courts recognized and developed general federal common law in deciding federal questions and diversity of citizenship cases. Of course, since *Erie*, there no longer exists a general federal common law, as federal courts are required to apply substantive state law in diversity of citizenship cases, a topic you will likely study in a course on federal civil procedure.

Our analysis of the history of the common-law rule indicates that it was based on a particular set of factors that had, when *The Harrisburg* was decided, long

---

2 *Brame* was decided, of course, at a time when the federal courts under Swift v. Tyson, 16 Pet. 1, 10 L.Ed. 865 (1842), expounded a **general federal common law**.

3 The Court stated:

'The argument everywhere in support of such suits in admiralty has been, not that the maritime law, as actually administered in common law countries, is different from the common law in this particular, but that the common law is not founded on good reason, and is contrary to 'natural equity and the general principles of law.' Since, however, it is now established that in the courts of the United States no action at law can be maintained for such a wrong in the absence of a statute giving the right, and it has not been shown that the maritime law, as accepted and received by maritime nations generally, has established a different rule for the government of the courts of admiralty from those which govern courts of law in matters of this kind, we are forced to the conclusion that no such action will lie in the courts of the United States under the general maritime law.' 119 U.S., at 213, 7 S.Ct., at 146.

since been thrown into discard even in England, and that had never existed in this country at all. ...

One would expect, upon an inquiry into the sources of the common-law rule, to find a clear and compelling justification for what seems a striking departure from the result dictated by elementary principles in the law of remedies. Where existing law imposes a primary duty, violations of which are compensable if they cause injury, nothing in ordinary notions of justice suggests that a violation should be nonactionable simply because it was serious enough to cause death. On the contrary, that rule has been criticized ever since its inception.... Because the primary duty already exists, the decision whether to allow recovery for violations causing death is entirely a remedial matter. It is true that the harms to be assuaged are not identical in the two cases: in the case of mere injury, the person physically harmed is made whole for his harm, while in the case of death, those closest to him--usually spouse and children--seek to recover for their total loss of one on whom they depended. This difference, however, even when coupled with the practical difficulties of defining the class of beneficiaries who may recover for death, does not seem to account for the law's refusal to recognize a wrongful killing as an actionable tort. One expects, therefore, to find a persuasive, independent justification for this apparent legal anomaly.

Legal historians have concluded that the sole substantial basis for the rule at common law is a feature of the early English law that did not survive into this century—the **felony-merger doctrine**. [Cc] According to this doctrine, the common law did not allow civil recovery for an act that constituted both a tort and a felony. The tort was treated as less important than the offense against the Crown, and was merged into, or pre-empted by, the felony. [Cc] The doctrine found practical justification in the fact that the punishment for the felony was the death of the felon and the forfeiture of his property to the Crown; thus, after the crime had been punished, nothing remained of the felon or his property on which to base a civil action. Since all intentional or negligent homicide was felonious, there could be no civil suit for wrongful death.

The first explicit statement of the common-law rule against recovery for wrongful death came in the opinion of Lord Ellenborough, sitting at **nisi prius**, in Baker v. Bolton, 1 Camp. 493, 170 Eng.Rep. 1033 (1808). That opinion did not cite authority, or give supporting reasoning, or refer to the felony-merger doctrine in announcing that '(i)n a Civil court, the death of a human being could not be complained of as an injury.' [C] Nor had the felony-merger doctrine seemingly been cited as the basis for the denial of recovery in any of the other

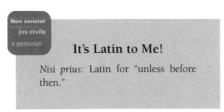

It's Latin to Me!

Nisi prius: Latin for "unless before then."

reported wrongful-death cases since the earliest ones, in the 17th century. [Cc] However, it seems clear from those first cases that the rule of *Baker v. Bolton* did derive from the felony-merger doctrine, and that there was no other ground on which it might be supported even at the time of its inception. The House of Lords in 1916 confirmed this historical derivation, and held that although the felony-merger doctrine was no longer part of the law, the rule against recovery for wrongful death should continue except as modified by statute. [C] Lord Parker's opinion acknowledged that the rule was 'anomalous * * * to the scientific jurist,' but concluded that because it had once found justification in the doctrine that 'the trespass was drowned in the felony,' it should continue as a rule 'explicable on historical grounds' even after the disappearance of that justification. [Cc] …

The historical justification marshaled for the rule in England never existed in this country. In limited instances American law did adopt a vestige of the felony-merger doctrine, to the effect that a civil action was delayed until after the criminal trial. However, in this country the felony punishment did not include forfeiture of property; therefore, there was nothing, even in those limited instances, to bar a subsequent civil suit. [Cc] Nevertheless, despite some early cases in which the rule was rejected as 'incapable of vindication,' [cc], American courts generally adopted the English rule as the common law of this country as well. Throughout the period of this adoption … the courts failed to produce any satisfactory justification for applying the rule in this country.

Some courts explained that their holdings were prompted by an asserted difficulty in computation of damages for wrongful death or by a 'repugnance * * * to setting a price upon human life.' [Cc] However, other courts have recognized that calculation of the loss sustained by dependents or by the estate of the deceased, which is required under most present wrongful-death statutes … does not present difficulties more insurmountable than assessment of damages for many nonfatal personal injuries. [Cc]

Major Themes

Note that the Court here is discussing a recurrent topic of debate in tort law, namely whether a jury can adequately assess damages for injuries, a topic covered extensively in Chapter 8 on Damages, *supra*.

….

The most likely reason that the English rule was adopted in this country without much question is simply that it had the blessing of age. … The American courts never made the inquiry whether this particular English rule, bitterly criticized in England, 'was applicable to their situation,' and it is difficult to imagine on what basis they might have concluded that it was.

Further, even after the decision in *Brame*, it is not apparent why the Court in *The Harrisburg* concluded that there should not be a different rule for admiralty from that applied at common law. Maritime law had always, in this country as in England, been a thing apart from the common law. ...

[T]he Court in *The Harrisburg* concluded that 'the admiralty judges in the United States did not rely for their jurisdiction on any rule of the maritime law different from that of the common law, but (only) on their opinion that the rule of the English common law was not founded in reason, and had not become firmly established in the jurisprudence of this country.' [C] Without discussing any considerations that might support a different rule for admiralty, the Court held that maritime law must be identical in this respect to the common law.

II

We need not, however, pronounce a verdict on whether *The Harrisburg*, when decided, was a correct extrapolation of the principles of decisional law then in existence. A development of major significance has intervened, making clear that the rule against recovery for wrongful death is sharply out of keeping with the policies of modern American maritime law. This development is the wholesale abandonment of the rule in most of the area where it once held sway, quite evidently prompted by the same sense of the rule's injustice that generated so much criticism of its original promulgation.

To some extent this rejection has been judicial. The English House of Lords in 1937 emasculated the rule without expressly overruling it. Rose v. Ford, (1937) A.C. 826. Lord Atkin remarked about the decision in *S. S. Amerika* that '(t)he reasons given, whether historical or otherwise, may seem unsatisfactory,' and that 'if the rule is really based on the relevant death being due to felony, it should long ago have been relegated to a museum.' At any rate, he saw 'no reason for extending the illogical doctrine * * * to any case where it does not clearly apply.' Id., A.C., at 833, 834. Lord Atkin concluded that, while the doctrine barred recognition of a claim in the dependents for the wrongful death of a person, it did not bar recognition of a common-law claim in the decedent himself for 'loss of expectation of life'--a claim that vested in the person in the interval between the injury and death, and thereupon passed, with the aid of a **survival statute**, to the representative of his estate. He expressed no doubt that the claim was 'capable of being estimated in terms of money: and that the calculation should be made.' Id., at 834.[6] Thus, except that the measure of damages might differ, the representative was allowed to recover on behalf of the heirs what they could not recover in their own names.

---

6 Lord Wright, concurring, stated: 'In one sense it is true that no money can be compensation for life or the enjoyment of life, and in that sense it is impossible to fix compensation for the shortening of life. But it is the best the law can do. It would be paradoxical if the law refused to give any compensation at all because none could be adequate.' (1937) A.C., at 848.

Much earlier, however, the legislatures both here and in England began to evidence unanimous disapproval of the rule against recovery for wrongful death. The first statute partially abrogating the rule was Lord Campbell's Act, 9 & 10 Vict., c. 93 (1846), which granted recovery to the families of persons killed by tortious conduct, 'although the Death shall have been caused under such Circumstances as amount in Law to **Felony**.'[7]

In the United States, every State today has enacted a wrongful-death statute. [C] The Congress has created actions for wrongful deaths of railroad employees, Federal Employers' Liability Act, 45 U.S.C. §§ 51-59; of merchant seamen, Jones Act, 46 U.S.C. § 688; and of persons on the high seas, Death on the High Seas Act, 46 U.S.C. §§ 761, 762. Congress has also, in the Federal Tort Claims Act, 28 U.S.C. § 1346(b), made the United States subject to liability in certain circumstances for negligently caused wrongful death to the same extent as a private person. [C]

Make the Connection

The Federal Torts Claim Act is legislation by which the federal government grants permission to be sued in tort under certain circumstances. *See* Immunities, Chapter 11.

These numerous and broadly applicable statutes, taken as a whole, make it clear that there is no present public policy against allowing recovery for wrongful death. The statutes evidence a wide rejection by the legislatures of whatever justifications may once have existed for a general refusal to allow such recovery. This legislative establishment of policy carries significance beyond the particular scope of each of the statutes involved. The policy thus established has become itself a part of our law, to be given its appropriate weight not only in matters of statutory construction but also in those of decisional law. [C] Mr. Justice Holmes, speaking also for Chief Justice Taft and Justices Brandeis and McKenna, stated on the very topic of remedies for wrongful death:

'(I)t seems to me that courts in dealing with statutes sometimes have been too slow to recognize that statutes even when in terms covering only particular cases may imply a policy different from that of the common law, and therefore may exclude a reference to the common law for the purpose of limiting their scope. Johnson v. United States, 163 F. 30, 32. Without going into the reasons for the notion that an action (other than

---

7 It has been suggested that one reason the common-law rule was tolerated in England as long as it was may have been that the relatives of persons killed by wrongful acts often were able to exact compensation from the wrongdoer by threatening to bring a 'criminal appeal.' The criminal appeal was a criminal proceeding brought by a private person, and was for many years more common than indictment as a means of punishing homicide. Though a successful appeal would not produce a monetary recovery, the threat of one served as an informal substitute for a civil suit for damages. Over the years, indictment became more common, and the criminal appeal was abolished by statute in 1819. [Cc]

an appeal) does not lie for causing the death of a human being, it is enough to say that they have disappeared. The policy that forbade such an action, if it was more profound than the absence of a remedy when a man's body was hanged and his goods confiscated for the felony, has been shown not to be the policy of present law by statutes of the United States and of most if not all of the States.'

Panama R. Co. v. Rock, 266 U.S. 209, 216, 45 S.Ct. 58, 60, 69 L.Ed. 250 (1924) (dissenting opinion). ...

This appreciation of the broader role played by legislation in the development of the law reflects the practices of common-law courts from the most ancient times. ... It has always been the duty of the common-law court to perceive the impact of major legislative innovations and to interweave the new legislative policies with the inherited body of common-law principles-many of them deriving from earlier legislative exertions.

[I]t is sufficient at this point to conclude, as Mr. Justice Holmes did 45 years ago, that the work of the legislatures has made the allowance of recovery for wrongful death the general rule of American law, and its denial the exception. Where death is caused by the breach of a duty imposed by federal maritime law, Congress has established a policy favoring recovery in the absence of a legislative direction to except a particular class of cases.

III

Our undertaking, therefore, is to determine whether Congress has given such a direction in its legislation granting remedies for wrongful deaths in portions of the maritime domain. We find that Congress has given no affirmative indication of an intent to preclude the judicial allowance of a remedy for wrongful death to persons in the situation of this petitioner.

    ....

Read in light of the state of maritime law in 1920, ... Congress intended to ensure the continued availability of a remedy, historically provided by the States, for deaths in territorial waters; its failure to extend the Act to cover such deaths primarily reflected the lack of necessity for coverage by a federal statute, rather than an affirmative desire to insulate such deaths from the benefits of any federal remedy that might be available independently of the Act. The void that existed in maritime law up until 1920 was the absence of any remedy for wrongful death on the high seas. Congress, in acting to fill that void, legislated only to the three-mile limit because that was the extent of the problem. ...

    ....

Since that time the equation has changed drastically … The resulting discrepancy between the remedies for deaths covered by the Death on the High Seas Act and for deaths that happen to fall within a state wrongful-death statute not encompassing unseaworthiness could not have been foreseen by Congress. Congress merely declined to disturb state remedies at a time when they appeared adequate to effectuate the substantive duties imposed by general maritime law. That action cannot be read as an instruction to the federal courts that deaths in territorial waters, caused by breaches of the evolving duty of seaworthiness, must be **damnum absque injuria** unless the States expand their remedies to match the scope of the federal duty.

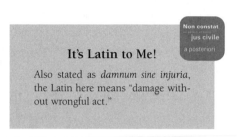

It's Latin to Me!

Also stated as *damnum sine injuria*, the Latin here means "damage without wrongful act."

To put it another way, the message of the Act is that it does not by its own force **abrogate** available state remedies; no intention appears that the Act have the effect of foreclosing any nonstatutory federal remedies that might be found appropriate to effectuate the policies of general maritime law.

… Our recognition of a right to recover for wrongful death under general maritime law will assure uniform vindication of federal policies, removing the tensions and discrepancies that have resulted from the necessity to accommodate state remedial statutes to exclusively maritime substantive concepts. [Cc][15] Such uniformity not only will further the concerns of both of the 1920 Acts but also will give effect to the constitutionally based principle that federal admiralty law should be 'a system of law coextensive with, and operating uniformly in, the whole country.' The Lottawanna, 21 Wall. 558, 575, 22 L.Ed. 654 (1875).

….

We conclude that the Death on the High Seas Act was not intended to preclude the availability of a remedy for wrongful death under general maritime law in situations not covered by the Act. Because the refusal of maritime law to provide such a remedy appears to be jurisprudentially unsound and to have produced serious confusion and hardship, that refusal should cease unless there are substantial countervailing factors that dictate adherence to *The Harrisburg* simply as a matter of **stare decisis**. We now turn to a consideration of those factors.

---

15 The incongruity of forcing the States to provide the sole remedy to effectuate duties that have no basis in state policy is highlighted in this case. The Florida Supreme Court ruled that the state wrongful-death act was concerned only with 'traditional common-law concepts,' and not with 'concepts peculiar to maritime law such as 'unseaworthiness' and the 'comparative negligence rule.' It found no reason to believe that the Florida Legislature intended to cover, or even considered, the 'completely foreign' maritime duty of seaworthiness. 211 So.2d, at 164, 166. Federal law, rather than state, is the more appropriate source of a remedy for violation of the federally imposed duties of maritime law. [C]

IV

Very weighty considerations underlie the principle that courts should not lightly overrule past decisions. Among these are the desirability that the law furnish a clear guide for the conduct of individuals, to enable them to plan their affairs with assurance against untoward surprise; the importance of furthering fair and expeditious adjudication by eliminating the need to relitigate every relevant proposition in every case; and the necessity of maintaining public faith in the judiciary as a source of impersonal and reasoned judgments. The reasons for rejecting any established rule must always be weighed against these factors.

The first factor, often considered the mainstay of stare decisis, is singularly absent in this case. ... There is no question in this case of any change in the duties owed by shipowners to those who work aboard their vessels. Shipowners well understand that breach of the duty to provide a seaworthy ship may subject them to liability for injury regardless of where it occurs, and for death occurring on the high seas or in the territorial waters of most States. ...

Nor do either of the other relevant strands of stare decisis counsel persuasively against the overruling of *The Harrisburg*. ... We do not regard the rule of *The Harrisburg* as a closely arguable proposition--it rested on a most dubious foundation when announced, has become an increasingly unjustifiable anomaly as the law over the years has left it behind, and ... has produced litigation-spawning confusion in an area that should be easily susceptible of more workable solutions. The rule has had a long opportunity to prove its acceptability, and instead has suffered universal criticism and wide repudiation. To supplant the present disarray in this area with a rule both simpler and more just will further, not impede, efficiency in adjudication. Finally, a judicious reconsideration of precedent cannot be as threatening to public faith in the judiciary as continued adherence to a rule unjustified in reason, which produces different results for breaches of duty in situations that cannot be differentiated in policy. Respect for the process of adjudication should be enhanced, not diminished, by our ruling today.

....

V

[O]ur decision does not require the fashioning of a whole new body of federal law, but merely removes a bar to access to the existing general maritime law. In most respects the law applied in personal-injury cases will answer all questions that arise in death cases.

....

The one aspect of a claim for wrongful death that has no precise counterpart in the established law governing nonfatal injuries is the determination of the beneficiaries who are entitled to recover. General maritime law, which denied any recovery for wrongful death, found no need to specify which dependents should receive such recovery. ...

. . . .

We do not determine this issue now, for we think its final resolution should await further sifting through the lower courts in future litigation. For present purposes we conclude only that its existence affords no sufficient reason for not coming to grips with *The Harrisburg*. If still other subsidiary issues should require resolution, such as particular questions of the measure of damages, the courts will not be without persuasive analogy for guidance. Both the Death on the High Seas Act and the numerous state wrongful-death acts have been implemented with success for decades. The experience thus built up counsels that a suit for wrongful death raises no problems unlike those that have long been grist for the judicial mill.

. . . .

We accordingly overrule *The Harrisburg* [and] hold that an action does lie under general maritime law for death caused by violation of maritime duties. The judgment of the Court of Appeals is reversed, and the case is remanded to that court for further proceedings consistent with this opinion. It is so ordered.

Reversed and remanded.

Points for Discussion

1. What is the felony-merger doctrine? Why was discussion of the felony-merger doctrine relevant to the Court's discussion of the wisdom of recognizing a wrongful death action in some aspects of maritime law?

2. What was the rationale justifying the rule at common law denying recognition of a wrongful death action? How important should history be to determining the current contours of the law? Do the justifications for the English rule exist in the United States? Do there remain any public policy concerns in favor of not permitting wrongful death actions?

3. As discussed in the *Moragne* case, at common law the death of either the plaintiff or the defendant extinguished any causes of action for personal injury existing between the parties. This principle led to the strange result that it was more profitable for a defendant to kill a man than it was merely to scratch him, for if the plaintiff died, any causes of action he may have had against the defendant in tort died with him. In England, this anomaly in the law changed with passage of Lord Campbell's Act in 1846.

4. In the United States, two types of legislation were enacted to change the consequences of the common law rule – (1) **wrongful death statutes** were enacted so that defined beneficiaries of one tortiously killed could bring a tort action for injuries caused by that death and (2) **survival statutes** were enacted to permit a decedent's estate to bring any actions that were extinguished by the decedent's death. *See* Section 2, *infra,* for further exploration of survival statutes.

5. **Wrongful Death Statutes –** Inasmuch as *Moragne* recognizes a common law wrongful death action, it is unusual as most wrongful death actions are statutorily created. Today, by statute, every jurisdiction permits recovery for the tortiously caused death of another. A wrongful death action is a new, independent statutory cause of action that inures to the benefit of statutorily defined plaintiffs. Although statutes vary from jurisdiction to jurisdiction, wrongful death statutes typically allow for specifically defined family members of the deceased to recover for injuries caused by the death.

6. Typically, the jury allocates the damage award among, and the award goes directly to, the beneficiaries. As a wrongful death action does not belong to the decedent's estate, the award itself does not become property of the estate and is not subject to estate creditors. If none of the statutorily defined beneficiaries are available to bring the action, no wrongful death action exists. Recoverable damages are typically defined in the statute permitting the cause of action. Consider the following case.

———————————

Selders v. Armentrout

207 N.W.2d 686 (Neb. 1973)

McCOWN, Justice.

This is an action by Earl and Ila Selders to recover damages for the wrongful deaths of three of their minor children. The children were killed in an automobile accident. The jury found the defendants Charles and William Armentrout negligent and returned a verdict against them for the exact amount of the medical and funeral expenses of the three children. The parents have appealed.

The sole issue on this appeal involves the proper elements and measure of damages in a tort action in Nebraska for the wrongful death of a minor child. The court essentially instructed the jury that except for medical and funeral expenses, the damages should be the monetary value of the contributions and services which the parents could reasonably have expected to receive from the children less the reasonable cost to the parents of supporting the children.

The defendants contend that the measure of damages is limited to **pecuniary** loss and that the instructions to the jury correctly reflect the measure and elements of damage. The plaintiffs assert that the loss of the society, comfort, and companionship of the children are proper and compensable elements of damage, and that evidence of amounts invested or expended for the nurture, education, and maintenance of the children before death is proper.

An analysis of the history of our wrongful death statutes is appropriate. The statutory provision creating a cause of action for wrongful death has never contained the word 'pecuniary' but only referred to an action for 'damages.' That statute was section 1428, Rev.St. 1913, and is now section 30-809, R.R.S.1943. The statute is still identical, word for word. What might be referred to as the procedural and limitation provisions were originally contained in section 1429, Rev. St.1913, now section 30-810, R.S.Supp., 1972. In 1913, that section provided in part: '* * * the jury may give such damages as they shall deem a fair and just compensation with reference to the pecuniary injuries resulting from such death * * *.' In 1919, that provision was changed to read: 'The verdict or judgment should be for the amount of damages which the persons in whose behalf the action is brought have sustained.' Laws 1919, c. 92, § 1, p. 235. This language and the preceding portions of the statute still remain unchanged today. In 1919, that particular language was followed by the words 'and the avails thereof shall be paid to and distributed among such persons in the same proportions as the personal property of an intestate under the inheritance laws.' From 1919 to 1945, the word 'pecuniary' did not appear in section 30-810, R.S.1943, nor any amendments to it.

In 1945, the language of section 30-810, R.S.1943, providing that 'the avails' of a wrongful death action should be distributed as personal property of an estate under inheritance laws was changed to the present language that: 'The avails thereof shall be paid to and distributed among the widow or widower and next of kin in the proportion that the pecuniary loss suffered by each bears to the total pecuniary loss suffered by all such persons.' The statutory reference to 'damages * * * sustained' remains unqualified and unrestricted.

It would seem clear that the word 'pecuniary' as it now appears in the statute does not refer to the 'damages' recoverable but only to the method of apportioning 'the avails' or the amount recovered as damages in a wrongful death action.

....

... [A] broadening concept of the measure and elements of damages for the wrongful death of a minor child has been in the development stage for many years. [C] Following a discussion of the rigid common law rules limiting recovery for wrongful death to the loss of pecuniary benefits, Prosser states: 'Recent years, however, have brought considerable modification of the rigid common law rules. It has been recognized that even pecuniary loss may extend beyond mere contributions of food, shelter, money or property; and there is now a decided tendency to find that the society, care and attention of the deceased are 'services' to the survivor with a financial value, which may be compensated. This has been true, for example, not only where a child has been deprived of a parent, * * * but also where the parent has lost a child * * *.' Prosser, Law of Torts (4th Ed.), § 127, p. 908.

The original pecuniary loss concept and its restrictions arose in a day when children during minority were generally regarded as an economic asset to parents. Children went to work on farms and in factories at age 10 and even earlier. This was before the day of child labor laws and long before the day of extended higher education for the general population. A child's earnings and services could be generally established and the financial or pecuniary loss which could be proved became the measure of damages for the wrongful death of a child. Virtually all other damages were disallowed as speculative or as sentimental.

The damages involved in a wrongful death case even today must of necessity deal primarily with a fictitious or speculative future life, as it might have been had the wrongful death not occurred. For that reason, virtually all evidence of future damage is necessarily speculative to a degree. The measure and elements of damage involved in a wrongful death case, however, have been excessively restrictive as applied to a minor child in contrast to an adult. Modern economic reality emphasizes the gulf between the old concepts of a child's economic value and the new facts of modern family life. To limit damages for the death of a child to the monetary value of the services which the next of kin could reasonably have expected to receive during his minority less the reasonable expense of maintaining and educating him stamps almost all modern children as worthless in the eyes of the law. In fact, if the rule was literally followed, the average child would have a negative worth. This court has already held that contributions reasonably to be expected from a minor, not only during his minority but afterwards, may be allowed on evidence justifying a reasonable expectation of pecuniary benefit. [Cc] Even with that modification, the wrongful death of a child results in no monetary loss, except in the rare case, and the assumption that the traditional measure of damages is compensatory is a pure legal fiction.

Particularly in the last decade, a growing number of courts have extended the measure of damages to include the loss of society and companionship of the minor child, even under statutes limiting recovery to pecuniary loss or pecuniary value of services less the cost of support and maintenance, or similar limitations. [Cc]

In this state, the statute has not limited damages for wrongful death to pecuniary loss but this court has imposed that restriction. For an injury to the marital relationship, the law allows recovery for the loss of the society, comfort, and companionship of a spouse. This court has allowed such a recovery for the wrongful death of a wife. [C] There is no logical reason for treating an injury to the family relationship resulting from the wrongful death of a child more restrictively. It is no more difficult for juries and courts to measure damages for the loss of the life of a child than many other abstract concepts with which they are required to deal. We hold that the measure of damages for the wrongful death of a minor child should be extended to include the loss of the society, comfort, and companionship of the child. To the extent this holding is in conflict with prior decisions of this court, they are overruled.

...The plaintiffs having raised the issue of the measure of damages for the wrongful death of a minor child both in the trial court and on this appeal are entitled to the benefit of the new rule announced in this case and should be afforded a new trial on the issue of damages only.

For the guidance of the court on retrial, we believe that evidence of expenses of birth, food, clothing, instruction, nurture, and shelter which have been incurred or were reasonably necessary to rear the child to the age he or she had attained on the date of death are not properly admissible. We conclude that the investment theory of measuring damages by the amounts expended in raising the child is inappropriate and improper.

The judgment of the trial court as to liability is affirmed, the judgment as to damages is reversed and the cause remanded for trial on the issue of damages only, consistent with our holding in this opinion.

Affirmed in part, and in part reversed and remanded with directions.

WHITE, Chief Justice (dissenting).

I dissent strongly to both the conclusion and the rationale of the majority opinion in this case. The opinion, in one arbitrary action, now states that: 'The measure of damages for the wrongful death of a minor child should be extended to include the loss of the society, comfort, and companionship of the child.'

There is nothing 'limited' about the range of the new measure of damages adopted by the majority opinion.

Admittedly the new rule has an emotional appeal, and from the beginning of the basic concepts of the law, legislatures and the courts have had to deal with the emotional appeals and demands that *money* be awarded as compensation for a purely emotional loss. A wrongful death action does not arise out of the common law and out of the principles of stare decisis. Our wrongful death statute is purely a legislative creation, and this court, for over a period of 50 years of decisions, has followed its judicial duty in setting out precisely how the measure of damages is to be compensated. After a long line of judicial decisions, without legislative interference, and without dissent, the Legislature enacted the 1945 statute which provides: 'The avails thereof (from a wrongful death action) shall be paid * * * in the proportion that the pecuniary loss suffered by each (heir) bears *to the total pecuniary loss suffered by all such persons.*' (Emphasis supplied.) Section 30-810, R.S.Supp., 1972. I submit that the majority opinion adopted by this court, in one arbitrary action, despite its previous pronouncement of the measure of damages in this case itself, and despite the 1945 statute and the 50 years of settled and precise determinations and decisions of this court, both before the 1945 statute and afterwards, and despite any interference by the Legislature or without action by the Legislature since the 1945 statute, by judicial **fiat** is creating a class action on behalf of the next of kin or **heirs** to recover monetary damages for 'society, comfort, and companionship,' and permit a jury to translate emotional, conjectural, and speculative sentimental values incapable of having any objective standards applied to them, into an award of money.

With the common assumption by the public and jurors of the presence of liability insurance in damage cases, and with the natural and human elements of sympathy present in the courtroom, it takes no imagination to see the amounts of verdicts that will be returned. In the hands of an imaginative lawyer, marshaling family albums and the testimony of sympathetic friends, and demonstratively organized and staged by a histrionic-minded lawyer, this court will undoubtedly be faced in the future with the almost impossible job of attempting to apply the generalized principles of excessiveness of a verdict to these judgments, which by their nature are an attempt to award money for a purely emotional loss conjectural, speculative in nature, and incapable of measurement or proof by any objective standard or related criteria.

I call attention to the following specific problems:

(1) The outright repeal by judicial fiat of the 1945 statute, which confirmed the court's continued, consistent, and unrepealed interpretation of the measure of damages in a wrongful death case. I allude to the statute again and particularly to the language 'to the total pecuniary loss suffered by all such persons.' The majority opinion skips with a light fantastic toe over this language and this statute. We must remember that we are dealing with a legislative creation here, and not a right that is sourced in judicial decision flowing from the common law. It is absolutely indisputable that this was a corrective statute, enacted in 1945, the purpose of which was to conform the distribution of the avails in a wrongful death action to the established law as to the nature of the damages. ... It is inconceivable to me that any other conclusion could be drawn except that the 1945 statute affirmed and enforced the statutory interpretation that the court had placed upon the wrongful death statute for a period of 25 years. The query arises: What authority is there is the court for repealing by judicial fiat section 30-810, R.S.Supp., 1972? And what now, may I ask, is the method or the rule devised to determine the proper distribution of the loss or award?

I submit further that under any application of the rules of statutory interpretation, the statutes must be construed **pari materia**, that it is assumed that the Legislature was familiar with the law when it enacted the statute, and it is the duty of the court to harmonize the statutes enacted on the same subject, thus this 1945 conforming statute reaffirmed and declared the legislative intent to approve and to follow what had been the settled law in Nebraska for over 25 years at the time of the 1945 statute. I suggest further that it is now 50 years since the court's original interpretation in 1923, and that the 1945 statute, and the applicable case law, has been followed continuously over the period of the last 28 years, and has existed without dissent or a discoverable attempt to legislate, repeal, or amend the two statutes.

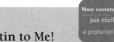

It's Latin to Me!

Pari materia literally translated means "in the same matter." This is a canon of statutory construction encouraging the interpretation of statutes on the same subject to be construed together so that inconsistencies in one statute may be resolved by looking at another statute on the same subject matter.

(2) The measure of damages. In the majority opinion, in the last few paragraphs, it is now forbidden to introduce any evidence or to instruct upon the pecuniary nature of the child's services, parent's expenses, etc. The majority opinion states: 'For the guidance of the court on retrial, we believe that evidence of expenses of birth, food, clothing, instruction, nurture, and shelter which have been incurred or were reasonably necessary to rear the child to the age he or she had attained on the date of death *are not properly admissible.* We conclude that the investment theory of measuring damages by the amounts expended in raising the child is *inappropriate and improper.*' (Emphasis supplied.) Thus the majority opinion seizes upon these pecuniary-related items and says that they shall not be considered. What, then, may I ask is the measure of damages? …

(3) The magnitude of the impact of the majority opinion and its reversal and overruling of both case and statutory law can be grasped by reading the following succinct summary of Nebraska law in the case of Wright v. Hoover, 329 F.2d 72, in which it was stated:

> …Generally, in a wrongful death action, the measure of damages is limited to the *pecuniary* loss sustained by the statutory beneficiaries. [Cc] … Where the deceased is an unemancipated child, such pecuniary loss is that which--measured by the present value of a dollar--will be sustained by the parent by reason of being deprived of the child's services during his minority, *and the loss of contributions, if any, having monetary value that might reasonably be expected to be made by the child after reaching his majority.* [Cc] In calculating the pecuniary loss to the parent, the amounts which would have been expended for the child's maintenance and support are deducted from the monetary value of the child's services and contributions. [Cc] … *Pain, anguish, loss of society and companionship are not ordinarily proper elements of pecuniary loss.* [Cc] (Emphasis supplied.)

(4) The rights created under Lord Campbell's Act in our death statute are statutory in creation and are governed solely by statute. There is a **non sequitur** inference in the majority opinion that because the 1919 statute simply mentioned damages, that therefore the statute itself is authority for a non pecuniary measure of damages such as loss of comfort, society, and companionship. Quite the contrary is true. I do not think I need to recite the elementary fact that in the event a general statute is enacted giving the right to recover damages, it then becomes a part of the judicial power and the duty of the court to lay down the measure of the damages, to be followed by a jury or a court in making its award. I point out that this court has

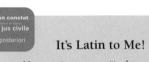

It's Latin to Me!

Non sequitur means "it does not follow."

consistently and clearly followed its duty in this respect, and more importantly, its interpretation and application of the measure of damages has been affirmed and enacted into law by the Legislature itself in the 1945 statute. Courts, generally, and this court, have universally condemned, in all contexts, attempts by trial courts to submit the issue of damages generally to a jury and have spoken quite firmly that it is the duty of the court to set out for the guidance of the jury the measuring standards for its evaluation of the *money* damages that are awarded in a tort action. The majority opinion dodges this issue completely without any indication of any nature whatsoever as to how the damages are measured except that a jury may award any and all damages that it wants to as long as they are related to comfort, society, and companionship. I submit that such a position is nothing more than a permission to take money out of one man's pocket and put it into another's on the basis of sympathy and sentimental reasons. And in this connection, I call attention to the very material distinction that this court has made, and courts generally, between awards for pain and suffering accompanied by physical injury and loss, as distinguished from speculative awards for sentimental value, such as bereavement, comfort, society, and companionship.

The majority opinion is not consistent with and is a denial of the general principles that this court and other courts have stated with reference to the allowance of compensatory damages. We have stated many times that compensatory damages are the only ones recoverable under our law (with certain exceptions not pertinent here). In general terms, we have stated many times that the law awards damages to a party injured from the negligence of another, not as a punishment of the negligent party, but as compensation for the pecuniary loss sustained by the injured party. And correlated to this we have denied and continually and consistently stated that damages which are uncertain, contingent, sentimental, conjectural, or speculative cannot be made the basis of a recovery in an action for damages. We have also stated that proof of damages must be made with a reasonable degree of certainty and even though the damages may be real, they are not recoverable if they are too remote or are speculative in nature. I call attention to these basic principles in light of the super charged emotional atmosphere that a competent and zealous trial attorney can create in the trial of a death-damage action for the loss of a minor child.

In conclusion I reiterate what seems to me must be perfectly obvious. This is a statutorily created class action, completely under the control and jurisdiction of the Legislature. It enacted the statute and over a period of 50 years has adopted and categorically confirmed our determination of the measure of damages, which measure of damages consistently follows the basic principles of damage law under Anglo-Saxon jurisprudence. I submit that whatever the majority's desire may be to change and reform the law of damages to accommodate to the emotional loss of a death of a minor child, that it is our duty as a court to abide by the legislative policy and action in this area. Besides all the other considerations mentioned the effect of such a change on insurance premiums, the matter of the distribution of the avails which question has not been answered in the majority opinion, the acceptance of any principle that the amount of the loss may be extended because the distribution of loss is covered by insurance, and many other considerations are purely for legislative policy consideration. I submit that the majority opinion, which arbitrarily and in one stroke, after 50 years of settled law and without public hearing or consideration of the different interests and policies involved, and in violation of the 1945 legislative policy clearly announced in the statute, and unrepealed, simply throws open a death claim for a minor child to a sympathy and sentiment contest in the award of money, and is a serious mistake for us to make.

[Opinions of NEWTON, J., joining in the dissent and CLINTON, Justice, dissenting, are omitted.]

———————

Points for Discussion

1. Who were the plaintiffs in *Selders*? For what losses were they seeking to recover?

2. What are pecuniary losses? What are loss of consortium damages?

3. Regarding damages for loss of minor children, are you most persuaded by the majority or dissenting opinion? What does the majority include as recoverable for a wrongful death action for loss of a minor child? Do you agree such damages should be recoverable? Why or why not? How might one go about proving such losses?

4. Do you agree with the majority opinion that a state permitting recovery for loss of consortium for loss of a spouse should also permit loss of consortium damages for loss of a minor child?

5. Does allowance for damages for wrongful death amount to a windfall to the plaintiff?

6. The dissenting judge mentions the assumption of the public and juries regarding the availability of insurance proceeds and the impact of the majority's opinion on insurance premiums. Should such insurance considerations be relevant in determining the availability of damages in a wrongful death action?

7. The dissenting judge also mentions that the only damages recoverable are compensatory damages. Is the plaintiff here seeking to recover something other than compensatory damages? Does the majority permit the plaintiff to recover in excess of compensatory damages?

Hypo 10-1

Wife's husband is killed in an accident caused by Defendant, whom she sues for wrongful death. Before the action comes to trial, she remarries and takes the name of her new husband. Her marriage to her new husband is a very happy one. When the wrongful death action for the death of her first husband comes to trial, Wife legally changes her name back to her first husband's name for purposes of the trial itself. Her attorney files a **motion in limine** with the trial court to prevent opposing counsel from mentioning the name change. Keeping in mind that only relevant evidence is admissible at a trial, should the judge grant or deny Wife's motion? Explain your position.

B. Survival Statutes

At common law, any cause(s) of action that a party may have had while she was alive was extinguished with the death of that party. Today, legislation has been enacted in every jurisdiction abrogating this common law rule. Survival statutes now permit specified causes of action, which either may have been brought by a plaintiff prior to her death or against a defendant prior to his death, to survive the death of either. Consider the following case.

Murphy v. Martin Oil Co.

308 N.E.2d 583 (Ill. 1974)

WARD, Justice:

The plaintiff, Charryl Murphy, as **administratrix** of her late husband, Jack Raymond Murphy, and individually, and as **next friend** of Debbie Ann Murphy, Jack Kenneth Murphy and Carrie Lynn Murphy, their children, filed a complaint in the circuit court of Cook County against the defendants, Martin Oil Company and James Hocker. Count I of the complaint claimed damages for wrongful death under the Illinois Wrongful Death Act and count II sought damages for conscious pain and suffering, loss of wages and property damage. The circuit court allowed the defendants' motion to strike the second count of the complaint on the ground that it failed to state a cause of action. When the court further ordered that there was no just reason for delaying enforcement or appeal from this order the plaintiffs then appealed the dismissal under Rule 304 (50 Ill.2d R. 304) to the appellate court. That court affirmed the dismissal of count II of the complaint as to its allegations of pain and suffering and reversed the judgment as to its allegations of loss of wages and property damage. The cause was remanded with directions to reinstate as much of count II as related to loss of wages and property damage. [C] We granted the plaintiff's petition for leave to appeal.

The first count set out the factual background for the complaint. It alleged that on June 11, 1968, the defendants owned and operated a gasoline station in Oak Lawn, Cook County, and that on that date the plaintiff's decedent, Jack Raymond Murphy, while having his truck filled with gasoline, was injured through the defendants' negligence in a fire on the defendants' premises. Nine days later he died from the injuries. Damages for wrongful death were claimed under the Illinois Wrongful Death Act. (Ill.Rev.Stat.1971, ch. 70, pars. 1 and 2.) The language of section 1 of the statute is:

> 'Whenever the death of a person shall be caused by wrongful act, neglect or default, and the act, neglect or default is such as would, if death had not ensued, have entitled the party injured to maintain an action and recover damages in respect thereof, then and in every such case the person who or company or corporation which would have been liable if death had not ensued, shall be liable to an action for damages, notwithstanding the death of the person injured, and although the death shall have been caused under such circumstances as amount in law to felony.'

The second count of the complaint asked for damages for the decedent's physical and mental suffering, for loss of wages for the nine-day period following his injury and for the loss of his clothing worn at the time of injury. These damages were claimed under the common law and under our survival statute, which provides that certain rights of action survive the death of the person with the right of action. (Ill.Rev.Stat.1971, ch. 3, par. 339.) The statute states:

> 'In addition to the actions which survive by the common law, the following also survive: actions of **replevin**, actions to recover damages for an injury to the person (except slander and libel), actions to recover damages for an injury to real or personal property or for the detention or conversion of personal property, actions against officers for misfeasance, malfeasance, or nonfeasance of themselves or their deputies, actions for

fraud or deceit, and actions provided in Section 14 of Article VI of 'An Act relating to alcoholic liquors', approved January 31, 1934, as amended.'

On this appeal we shall consider: (1) whether the plaintiff can recover for the loss of wages which her decedent would have earned during the interval between his injury and death; (2) whether the plaintiff can recover for the destruction of the decedent's personal property (clothing) at the time of the injury; (3) whether the plaintiff can recover damages for conscious pain and suffering of the decedent from the time of his injuries to the time of death.

This State in 1853 enacted the Wrongful Death Act and in 1872 enacted the so-called Survival Act (now section 339 of the Probate Act). This court first had occasion to consider the statutes in combination in 1882 in Holton v. Daly, 106 Ill. 131. The court declared that the effect of the Wrongful Death Act was that a cause of action for personal injuries, which would have abated under the common law upon the death of the injured party from those injuries, would continue on behalf of the spouse or the next of kin and would be 'enlarged to embrace the injury resulting from the death.' (106 Ill. 131, 140.) In other words, it was held that the Wrongful Death Act provided the exclusive remedy available when death came as a result of given tortious conduct. In considering the Survival Act the court stated that it was intended to allow for the survival of a cause of action only when the injured party died from a cause other than that which caused the injuries which created the cause of action. Thus, the court said, an action for personal injury would not survive death if death resulted from the tortious conduct which caused the injury.

This construction of the two statutes persisted for over 70 years. [Cc] Damages, therefore, under the Wrongful Death Act were limited to pecuniary losses, as from loss of support, to the surviving spouse and next of kin as a result of the death. [Cc] Under the survival statute damages recoverable in a personal injury action, as for conscious pain and suffering, loss of earnings, medical expenses and physical disability, could be had only if death resulted from a cause other than the one which gave rise to the personal injury action.

This court was asked in 1941 to depart from its decision in *Holton v. Daly* and to permit, in addition to a wrongful death action, an action for personal injuries to be brought, though the injuries had resulted in the death of the injured person. This court acknowledged that there had been other jurisdictions which held contrary to *Holton v. Daly* and permitted the bringing of both actions, but the court said that any change in the rule in Holton must come from the legislature. [Cc] In 1960, however, in Saunders v. Schultz, 20 Ill.2d 301, 170 N.E.2d 163, this court noted the absence of legislative action and permitted a widow to recover for funeral and medical expenses in an action which was independent of and in addition to an action brought by her for damages under the Wrongful Death Act. It was said:

'Viewing the situation realistically, this liability of the surviving spouse for such expenses constitutes very real damages. Since that liability results from defendant's tortious conduct, it is only legally sound, and in accordance with basic negligence principles, that the burden of such damages should fall, not on the innocent victim, but upon the tortfeasor.

The estate or the spouse, either or both as the circumstances indicate, are entitled to recover for pecuniary losses suffered by either or both which are not recoverable under the Wrongful Death Act, and all cases holding the contrary are overruled.' [C]

....

... [I]n McDaniel v. Bullard (1966), 34 Ill.2d 487, 216 N.E.2d 140, ... the parents and sister of an infant, Yvonne McDaniel, Daniel, had been killed in an automobile collision. An action was begun on behalf of Yvonne under the Wrongful Death Act and shortly after the filing of the action Yvonne died from causes which were unrelated to the collision. This court rejected the defendant's contention that the pending action under the Wrongful Death Act was abated or extinguished upon Yvonne's death. In holding that an action under the Wrongful Death Act survived under the terms of the Survival Act upon the death of the victim's next of kin, this court said, at pages 493-494, 216 N.E.2d at page 144: 'Today damages from most torts are recognized as compensatory rather than punitive, and there is no reason why an estate that has been injured or depleted by the wrong of another should not be compensated whether the injured party is living or not. ... The rule of abatement has its roots in archaic conceptions of remedy which have long since lost their validity. The reason having ceased the rule is out of place and ought not to be perpetuated.' We concluded that under the Survival Act the action for wrongful death did not abate but might be maintained for the benefit of Yvonne's estate.

This disfavoring of abatement and enlarging of survival statutes has been general. In Prosser, HANDBOOK OF THE LAW OF TORTS (4th ed. 1971), at page 901, it is said: '(T)he modern trend is definitely toward the view that tort causes of action and liabilities are as fairly a part of the estate of either plaintiff or defendant as contract debts, and that the question is rather one of why a fortuitous event such as death should extinguish a valid action. Accordingly, survival statutes gradually are being extended; and it may be expected that ultimately all tort actions will survive to the same extent as those founded on contract.' ...[W]here there have been wrongful death and survival statutes the usual holding has been that actions may be concurrently maintained under those statutes. The usual method of dealing with the two causes of action, he notes, is to allocate conscious pain and suffering, expenses and loss of earnings of the decedent up to the date of death to the survival statute, and to allocate the loss of benefits of the survivors to the action for wrongful death.

As the cited comments of Prosser indicate, the majority of jurisdictions which have considered the question allow an action for personal injuries in addition to an action under the wrongful death statute, though death is attributable to the injuries. Recovery for conscious pain and suffering is permitted in most of these jurisdictions. [C] ...

....

The holding in *Holton* was not compelled, we judge, by the language or the nature of the statutes examined. The statutes were conceptually separable and different. The one related to an action arising upon wrongful death; the other related to a right of action for personal injury arising during the life of the injured person.

The remedy available under *Holton* will often be grievously incomplete. There may be a substantial loss of earnings, medical expenses, prolonged pain and suffering, as well as property damage sustained, before an injured person may succumb to his injuries. To say that there can be recovery only for his wrongful death is to provide an obviously inadequate justice. Too, the result in such a case is that the wrongdoer will have to answer for only a portion of the damages he caused. Incongruously, if the injury caused is so severe that death results, the wrongdoer's liability for the damages before death will be extinguished. It is obvious that in order to have a full liability and a full recovery there must be an action allowed for damages up to the time of death, as well as thereafter. Considering '[i]t is more important that the court should be right upon later and more elaborate consideration of the cases than consistent with previous declarations' [c], we declare *Holton* and the cases which have followed it overruled. ...

For the reasons given, the judgment of the appellate court is affirmed insofar as it held that an action may be maintained by the plaintiff for loss of property and loss of wages during the interval between injury and death, and that judgment is reversed insofar as it held that the plaintiff cannot maintain an action for her decedent's pain and suffering.

Affirmed in part; reversed in part.

Points for Discussion

1. What is the basis of the plaintiff's claim that, without recovery for both a wrongful death action and a survival action, her recovery will be "grievously incomplete"?

2. A survival statute reverses the common law and permits select causes of action to survive the death of a party. Survival statutes do not recognize a new cause of action, but rather merely allow for a previously existing cause of action to survive the death of a party. Any actions that survive the death of the party thus belong to the deceased party's **estate**. As part of the estate, unlike a wrongful death action, it is subject to the estate's **creditors**.

3. Pursuant to the statute in *Murphy*, what causes of action survive the death of a person? What causes of action do not?

4. Do you agree with the policy that drives enactment of survival statutes? Why or why not? Should an estate be entitled to pursue punitive damages in a survival action? Should punitive damages be imposed against a deceased defendant's estate? Should all available defenses, if the plaintiff had lived, be available if the plaintiff is now deceased? Should a deceased's conduct, such as comparative negligence, still provide a defense to the defendant? What about defenses such as immunity or statutes of limitation?

5. Recall that compensatory damages typically allow recovery, for example, for a plaintiff's loss of future earnings. *See* Chapter 8, Damages. Recall further that typical wrongful death statutes permit statutory beneficiaries to recover for loss of support. Do not loss of future earnings and loss of support compensate for the same injury? If statutory beneficiaries for the wrongful death action and the heirs of the estate for the survival action are not identical, double liability issues may arise. Explain how that might be the case. To avoid issues with double liability, many jurisdictions statutorily provide for a **setoff** when the risk of double liability presents itself. Without a setoff provision, double liability may be a concern, although some courts have controlled imposition of double liability by recognizing other principles such as, for example, **collateral estoppel**. *See, e.g.,* Alfone v. Sarno, 432 A.2d 857 (N.J. 1981); Pezzulli v. D'Ambrosia, 26 A.2d 659 (Pa. 1942).

6. In the principal case, the survival statute provides for the survival of actions for "injury to the person (except **slander** and **libel**)." Slander and libel are tort actions that generally provide a remedy for injury to one's reputation. In excluding these actions from survival, such a survival statute is not unusual. Contrast with a statute providing otherwise:

(a) A cause of action for personal injury to the health, reputation, or person of an injured person does not abate because of the death of the injured person or because of the death of a person liable for the injury.

(b) A personal injury action survives to and in favor of the heirs, legal representatives, and estate of the injured person. The action survives against the liable person and the person's legal representatives.

(c) The suit may be instituted and prosecuted as if the liable person were alive.

Tex. Civ. Prac. & Rem. Code § 71.021 (2008).

Why might a jurisdiction allow all tort actions to survive the death of either party *except* for those for reputational injuries? Do you agree with such a policy?.

Hypo 10-2

Pedro and Wilma are carefully crossing a busy street on foot at the very moment that Driver carelessly enters the intersection in his car, hitting both Wilma and Pedro. Wilma is killed instantly. Pedro is critically injured as well, but is hospitalized for one week before succumbing to his injuries. Wilma is an only child who is survived by her husband and his mother. Pedro's only surviving relatives are his father and Nephie, the son of his previously deceased sister. Prior to the accident, Pedro had executed a will in which he had named Nephie as the sole beneficiary of his estate. Before any lawsuit is filed on behalf of the victims, Driver dies of natural causes. His son, Sonny, is named as the administrator of his estate. Following are statutes enacted in this jurisdiction:

"**(i)** Whenever the death of a person shall be caused by the wrongful act, neglect, or default of another, and the act, neglect, or default is such as would, if death had not ensued, have entitled the party injured to maintain an action and recover damages in respect thereof, the person who would have been liable, if death had not ensued, shall be liable to an action for damages, notwithstanding the death of the person injured.

"**(ii)** In the event of the death of the wrongdoer, such cause of action shall survive against his personal representative.

"**(iii)** Every such action shall be for the benefit of the wife or husband and child or children of the person whose death shall have been so caused, and, if there be no such wife, husband, child or children then for the benefit of the parent or parents."

(a) Identify the wrongful death language of this legislation, if any. Who may bring the wrongful death action for the death of Wilma? Who may bring the wrongful death action for the death of Pedro? For what damages?

(b) Identify the survival language of this legislation, if any. Who may bring a survival action on behalf of Wilma? Who may bring a survival action on behalf of Pedro? For what damages?

CHAPTER 11

Joint Tortfeasors

A. Joinder and Liability of Defendants

Bierczynski v. Rogers

239 A.2d 218 (Del. 1968)

HERRMANN, Justice:

This appeal involves an automobile accident in which the plaintiffs claim that the defendant motorists were racing on the public highway, as the result of which the accident occurred.

The plaintiffs Cecil B. Rogers and Susan D. Rogers brought this action against Robert C. Race and Ronald Bierczynski, ages 18 and 17 respectively, alleging **concurrent negligences** in that they violated various speed statutes and various other statutory rules of the road, and in that they failed to keep a proper lookout and failed to keep their vehicles under proper control. The jury, by answer to interrogatories in its special verdict, expressly found that Race and Bierczynski were each negligent and that the negligence of each was a **proximate cause** of the accident. Substantial verdicts were entered in favor of the plaintiffs against both defendants jointly. The defendant Bierczynski appeals therefrom. The defendant Race does not appeal; rather, he joins with the plaintiffs in upholding the judgment below.

. . . .

There was sufficient evidence of proximate causation as to Bierczynski, in our opinion, to warrant the submission of that issue to the jury. The Trial Court had before it the following evidence:

Bierczynski and Race worked at the same place, located a short distance east of Governor Printz Boulevard near Lore Avenue. They lived near each other in the southerly part of Wilmington. On the day before the accident, Bierczynski drove Race to work. On the day of the accident, Bierczynski intended to pick

Race up again; but, upon meeting, Race told Bierczynski he would take his own automobile too, because he intended to leave work early. Thereupon, one following the other, they drove toward their place of employment northerly across Wilmington to Lore Avenue in a suburban area of Brandywine Hundred. The accident occurred on Lore Avenue about 300 feet east of its intersection with River Road. Lore Avenue runs east and west and River Road north and south. Lore Avenue was 18 feet wide, macadam surfaces, without a marked center line, and was lined by guard rails at various places. For a distance of about 1,000 feet west of its intersection with River Road, Lore Avenue is a moderately steep hill; after crossing River Road, it levels off. The speed limit at the scene was 25 m.p.h.

Cecil Rogers testified as follows: He was returning from a Girl Scout trip with his daughter, headed for their home located about three blocks from the scene of the accident. He entered Lore Avenue from Governor Printz Boulevard, thus driving in a westerly direction on Lore Avenue. At a point about 300 feet east of River Road, Rogers' car was struck by Race's car which approached him sideways, moving in an easterly direction on the westbound lane. Rogers saw Race's car coming at him; he stopped in the westbound lane; but he was unable to move out of the way because there was a guard rail along that part of the road and no shoulder. Rogers first saw the Race vehicle when it was about 550 feet up Lore Avenue-or about 250 feet west of River Road. At that point, the Race car was being driven easterly on Lore Avenue in the westbound lane, almost along-side the Bierczynski car which was moving easterly in the eastbound lane. The front bumper of the Race car was opposite the back bumper of the Bierczynski car. Both cars were moving at about 55 or 60 m.p.h. down the hill. Before reaching River Road, Race swerved back into the eastbound lane behind Bierczynski, who was about a car length in front. As it crossed River Road, the Race automobile 'bottomed on the road'; and it 'careened down against the pavement and gave an impression of an explosion'; dust 'flew everywhere' sufficiently to obscure the Race car momentarily from Rogers' view. At that point, the Race and Bierczynski automobiles were only 'inches apart'. The Race car then emerged from behind the Bierczynski car and careened sideways, at about 70 m.p.h., a distance of about 300 feet to the Rogers car standing in the westbound lane. The left side of the Race car struck the front of the Rogers car. Meanwhile, the Bierczynski car was brought to a stop in the eastbound lane, about 35 feet from the area of impact. The Bierczynski car did not come into contact with the Rogers vehicle.

. . . .

In many States, automobile racing on a public highway is prohibited by statute, the violation of which is **negligence per se**. [Cc] Delaware has no such statute. Nevertheless, speed competition in automobiles on the public highway is **negligence** in this State, for the reason that a reasonably prudent person would not engage in such conduct. This conclusion is in accord with the general rule, prevailing in other jurisdictions which lack statutes on the subject, that racing motor vehicles on a public highway is negligence. [Cc]

It is also generally held that all who engage in a race on the highway do so at their peril, and are liable for injury or **damage** sustained by a third person as a result thereof, regardless of which of the racing cars directly inflicted the injury or damage. The authorities reflect generally accepted rules of **causation** that all parties engaged in a motor vehicle race on the highway are wrongdoers acting in concert, and that each participant is liable for harm to a third person arising from the tortious conduct of the other, because he has induced and encouraged the tort. See Restatement of the Law of Torts, § 876; [cc].

We subscribe to those rules; and hold that, as a general rule, participation in a motor vehicle race on a public highway is an act of concurrent negligence imposing **liability** on each participant for any injury to a non-participant resulting from the race. If, therefore, Race and Bierczynski were engaged in a speed competition, each was liable for the **damages** and injuries to the plaintiffs herein, even though Bierczynski was not directly involved in the collision itself. Bierczynski apparently concedes liability if a race had, in fact, been in progress. Clearly there was ample evidence to carry to the jury the issue of a race—and with it, implicit therein, the issue of proximate cause as to Bierczynski.

. . . .

We find no error as asserted by the appellant. The judgments below are affirmed.

Points for Discussion

1. Bierczynski's car did not strike or in any way come into contact with Rogers' car. On what theory is Bierczynski held liable to Rogers?

2. Consider and critique the court's "wrongdoers acting in concert" rule. What policies are promoted by this rule?

3. "When persons are liable because they acted in concert, all persons are jointly and severally liable for the share of comparative responsibility assigned to each person engaged in concerted activity." RESTATEMENT (THIRD) OF TORTS: APPORTIONMENT OF LIABILITY § 15 (2000).

Coney v. J.L.G. Industries, Inc.

97 Ill.2d 104, 454 N.E.2d 197, 73 Ill.Dec. 337 (1983)

THOMAS J. MORAN, Justice:

Clifford M. Jasper died as a result of injuries sustained on January 24, 1978, while operating a hydraulic aerial work platform manufactured by defendant, J.L.G. Industries, Inc. Plaintiff, Jack A. Coney, administrator of Jasper's estate, filed a two-count complaint in

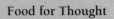

Food for Thought

Why is the plaintiff's employer not a party to this lawsuit?

the circuit court of Peoria County under the wrongful death and survival acts (Ill. Rev.Stat.1977, ch. 70, par. 1 *et seq.,* ch. 110 1/2, par. 27-6) based on a strict **products liability** theory. Defendant filed two **affirmative defenses**. The first asserted

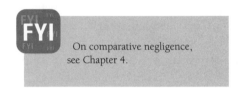

On comparative negligence, see Chapter 4.

that Jasper was guilty of **comparative negligence** or fault in his operation of the platform. The second contended that Jasper's employer, V. Jobst & Sons, Inc., was also guilty of comparative negligence in failing to instruct and train Jasper on the operation of the

platform and by failing to provide a "groundman." In these defenses, defendant requested that its fault, if any, be compared to the total fault of all parties and any judgment against defendant reflect only its percentage of the overall liability, *i.e.,* that defendant not be held jointly and severally liable.

On plaintiff's motion, the trial court struck the defenses, but it certified three questions for appeal pursuant to Supreme Court Rule 308 (73 Ill.2d R. 308) . . .

The three certified questions are:

"Whether the **doctrine** of comparative negligence or fault is applicable to actions or claims seeking recovery under products liability or strict liability in tort theories?

Whether the doctrine of comparative negligence or fault eliminates **joint and several liability**?

Whether the retention of joint and several liability in a system of comparative negligence or fault denies defendants equal protection of the laws in violation of U.S. Const. Amend. XIV, § 1 and Ill. Const.1970, § 2 as to causes of action arising on or after [*sic*] March 1, 1978. (Ill.Rev.Stat.1979, ch. 70, § 301 *et seq.*)?"

. . . .

The common law doctrine of joint and several liability holds **joint tortfeasors** responsible for the plaintiff's entire injury, allowing plaintiff to pursue all, some, or one of the tortfeasors responsible for his injury for the full amount of the damages. [Cc]

Defendant asserts joint and several liability is a corollary of the **contributory negligence** doctrine. Prior to [Alvis v. Ribar, 85 Ill.2d 1, 421 N.E.2d 886 (1981)] a plaintiff who was guilty of even slight contributory negligence was barred from recovery. Defendant maintains that joint and several liability balanced this inequity by permitting a faultless plaintiff to collect his entire judgment from any defendant who was guilty of even **slight negligence**. With the adoption of comparative negligence where damages are apportioned according to each party's fault, defendant argues it is no longer rational to hold a defendant liable beyond his share of the total damages. Defendant relies primarily on a line of cases where joint and several liability was abolished or limited in the course of construing a statutory scheme of liability. [Cc]

The vast majority of jurisdictions, however, which have adopted comparative negligence have retained joint and several liability as a part of their comparative negligence doctrine:

Alaska *Arctic Structures, Inc. v. Wedmore* (Alaska 1979), 605 P.2d 426.

Arkansas Ark.Stat.Ann. secs. 34-1001 to 34-1009 (1981).

California *American Motorcycle Association v. Superior Court* (1978), 20 Cal.3d 578, 578 P.2d 899, 146 Cal.Rptr. 182.

Colorado Colo.Rev.Stat. sec. 13-50.5-103 (1977).

Connecticut Conn.Gen.Stat.Ann. sec. 52-572o (Supp.1982).

Florida *Lincenberg v. Issen* (Fla.1975), 318 So.2d 386.

Georgia *Gazaway v. Nicholson* (1940), 190 Ga. 345, 9 S.E.2d 154.

Idaho *Tucker v. Union Oil Co.* (1979), 100 Idaho 590, 603 P.2d 156.

Maine Me.Rev.Stat. tit. 14, sec. 156 (1965).

Michigan *Conkright v. Ballantyne of Omaha, Inc.* (W.D.Mich.1980), 496 F.Supp. 147.

Minnesota *Maday v. Yellow Taxi Co.* (Minn.1981), 311 N.W.2d 849.

Nebraska *Royal Indemnity Co. v. Aetna Casualty & Surety Co.* (1975), 193 Neb. 752, 229 N.W.2d 183.

New Jersey N.J.Stat.Ann. sec. 2A:15-5.1 (Supp.1982).

New York *Kelly v. Long Island Lighting Co.* (1972), 31 N.Y.2d 25, 334 N.Y.S.2d 851, 286 N.E.2d 241.

North Dakota N.D.Cent.Code sec. 9-10-07 (1973).

Washington Wash.Rev.Code Ann. sec. 4.22.030 (Supp.1982).

Wisconsin *Wisconsin Natural Gas Co. v. Ford, Bacon & Davis Construction Corp.* (1980), 96 Wis.2d 314, 291 N.W.2d 825.

Generally, four reasons have been advanced for retaining joint and several liability:

(1) The feasibility of apportioning fault on a comparative basis does not render an indivisible injury "divisible" for purposes of the joint and several liability rule. A **concurrent tortfeasor** is liable for the whole of an indivisible injury when his negligence is a proximate cause of that damage. In many instances, the negligence of a concurrent tortfeasor may be sufficient by itself to cause the entire loss. The mere fact that it may be possible to assign some percentage figure to the relative culpability of one negligent defendant as compared to another does not in any way suggest that each defendant's negligence is not a proximate cause of the entire indivisible injury.

(2) In those instances where the plaintiff is not guilty of negligence, he would be forced to bear a portion of the loss should one of the tortfeasors prove financially unable to satisfy his share of the damages.

(3) Even in cases where a plaintiff is partially at fault, his culpability is not equivalent to that of a defendant. The plaintiff's negligence relates only to a lack of due care for his own safety while the defendant's negligence relates to a lack of due care for the safety of others; the latter is tortious, but the former is not.

(4) Elimination of joint and several liability would work a serious and unwarranted deleterious effect on the ability of an injured plaintiff to obtain adequate compensation for his injuries. [Cc]

In adopting comparative negligence, this court eliminated the total bar to recovery which a plaintiff had faced under contributory negligence. In return for allowing a negligent plaintiff to recover, this court said fairness requires that a plaintiff's damages be "reduced by the percentage of fault *attributable to him.*" (Emphasis added.) (*Alvis v. Ribar* (1981), 85 Ill.2d 1, 25, 52 Ill.Dec. 23, 421 N.E.2d

886.) Were we to eliminate joint and several liability as the defendant advocates, the burden of the insolvent or immune defendant would fall on the plaintiff; in that circumstance, plaintiff's damages would be reduced beyond the percentage of fault *attributable to him.* We do not believe the doctrine of comparative negligence requires this further reduction. Nor do we believe this burden is the price plaintiffs must pay for being relieved of the contributory negligence bar. The *quid pro quo* is the reduction of plaintiff's damages. What was said in *American Motorcycle Association v. Superior Court* (1978), 20 Cal.3d 578, 590, 578 P.2d 899, 906, 146 Cal. Rptr. 182, 189, is applicable here: "[F]airness dictates that the 'wronged party should not be deprived of his right to redress,' * * * '[t]he wrongdoers should be left to work out between themselves any apportionment.' "

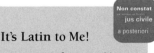

It's Latin to Me!

Quid pro quo is Latin for "something for something," as in the exchange of an item or action for something of equal of lesser value.

Non constat
jus civile
a posteriori

. . . .

We find nothing in *Alvis* which mandates either a shift in who shall bear the risk of the insolvent defendant or the elimination of joint and several liability. Defendant has not cited nor have we found persuasive judicial authority for the proposition that comparative negligence compels the abolition of joint and several liability. On the contrary, most jurisdictions which have adopted comparative negligence have retained the doctrine. Therefore, we hold that our adoption of comparative negligence in *Alvis* does not change the long-standing doctrine of joint and several liability.

. . . .

Therefore, . . . we conclude that (1) comparative fault is applicable to strict products liability actions; (2) comparative fault does not eliminate joint and several liability; and (3) retention of joint and several liability does not deny defendants equal protection of the laws. . . .

Affirmed and remanded, with directions.

Banks v. Elks Club Pride of Tennessee

301 S.W.3d 214 (Tenn. 2010)

OPINION

WILLIAM C. KOCH, JR., J.

This appeal involves the continuing viability in Tennessee of the common-law principle that imputes liability to an original tortfeasor for enhanced physical harm caused by the normal efforts of third persons to render aid which an injured party reasonably requires. A guest at a private club was injured on the club's premises. The injuries to the guest's back were compounded first by the conduct of her surgeon and second by the actions or inactions of a nursing home where the guest was a patient following her surgery. The guest filed separate lawsuits against the private club and her surgeon in the Circuit Court for Davidson County. After the cases were **consolidated**, the club and the surgeon moved to amend their answers to assert comparative fault claims against the nursing home. The trial court denied their motions but granted them permission to pursue an **interlocutory appeal**. After the Court of Appeals declined to consider the interlocutory appeal, the club and the surgeon sought this Court's permission for an interlocutory appeal. We granted their application. We now hold that an original tortfeasor is not jointly and severally liable for the further aggravation of an original injury caused by a subsequent tortfeasor's medically negligent treatment of the injury caused by the original tortfeasor's negligence. Therefore, we have determined that the trial court erred by denying the motions of the club and the surgeon to amend their complaints to assert comparative fault claims against the nursing home.

. . . .

Eighteen years ago, this Court produced a sea-change in Tennessee's tort law by replacing the common-law concept of contributory negligence with the concept of contributory fault. *McIntyre v. Balentine,* [833 S.W.2d 52 (Tenn. 1992)]. We expressly recognized at that time that many of the issues arising from the transition to a comparative fault regime would be addressed in later cases. [C]. Accordingly, it has come to pass that this Court has been presented with many opportunities since 1992 to revisit, refine, and clarify many of the central tenets of *McIntyre v. Balentine* and to address their impact on Tennessee tort law.

One of the central tenets of *McIntyre v. Balentine* is that the doctrine of joint and several liability was "obsolete" because it was inconsistent with the doctrine of comparative fault. [C] We explained that the doctrine of comparative fault, which would more closely link liability and fault, could not be reconciled with joint and several liability which could "fortuitously impose a degree of liability that is out of all proportion to fault." [C]

The announcement that the doctrine of joint and several liability was obsolete, while later characterized as dictum, was not met with universal acceptance. Mr. McIntyre and one of the parties who filed an **amicus curiae** brief requested a rehearing to address "the advisability of retaining joint and several liability in certain limited circumstances." This Court declined to grant the petition for rehearing, stating that "such further guidance should await an appropriate controversy." [C]

Thus, the *McIntyre v. Balentine* decision left behind some ambiguity regarding the continuing viability of any application of the doctrine of joint and several liability. On one hand, the Court had declared the doctrine "obsolete." On the other hand, the Court had left open the possibility that it might retain the doctrine "in certain limited circumstances" in future cases. As a result, the practicing bar set out to create opportunities for the Court to decide in what circumstances, if any, the doctrine of joint and several liability could rise from the ashes of obsolescence.

. . . .

During the past fourteen years, this Court has reaffirmed its holding that the doctrine of joint and several liability, as it existed prior to 1992, is obsolete. [Cc] At the same time, however, we have determined that the doctrine remains viable in several well-defined circumstances. We approved joint and several liability for defendants in the chain of distribution of a product in a products liability action. [C] We determined that the doctrine of joint and several liability was not obsolete in cases involving injury caused by multiple defendants who have breached a common duty. [C] We have likewise approved the application of the doctrine in cases wherein the plaintiff's injury was caused by the concerted actions of the defendants. [C]

To the extent that the doctrine of vicarious liability can be considered a species of joint and several liability, we have held that the adoption of comparative fault in *McIntyre v. Balentine* did not undermine the continuing viability of various **vicarious liability** doctrines, including the **family purpose doctrine**, [c], "respondeat superior, or similar circumstance where liability is vicarious due to an agency-type relationship between the active, or actual wrongdoer and the one who is vicari-

> **What's That?**
>
> The family purpose doctrine is the principle that a car's owner is liable for injuries caused by a family member's negligence in operating the vehicle.

ously responsible." [C] Finally, we determined that tortfeasors who have a duty to

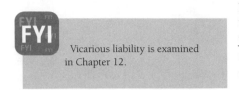

protect others from the foreseeable intentional acts of third persons are jointly and severally liable with the third person for the injuries caused by the third person's intentional acts. [Cc]

Ever since we handed down our decision in *McIntyre v. Balentine,* this Court's goal has been to assure that Tennessee's comparative fault regime strikes the proper balance between the plaintiff's interest in being made whole with the defendant's interest in paying only those damages for which the defendant is responsible. [C] We have found this balance in proceedings that link liability to fault. [Cc] Thus, we have embraced an approach in which a tortfeasor may seek to reduce its proportional share of the damages by successfully asserting as an affirmative defense that a portion of the fault for the plaintiff's damages should be allocated to another tortfeasor.

Throughout this period, we have repeatedly emphasized four core principles of the comparative fault regime that we ushered in when we decided *McIntyre v. Balentine.* These principles are: (1) that when "the separate, independent negligent acts of more than one tortfeasor combine to cause a single, indivisible injury, all tortfeasors must be joined in the same action, unless **joinder** is specifically prohibited by law"; (2) that when "the separate, independent negligent acts of more than one tortfeasor combine to cause a single, indivisible injury, each tortfeasor will be liable only for that proportion of the damages attributed to its fault"; (3) that the goal of linking liability with fault is not furthered by a rule that allows a

defendant's liability to be determined by the happenstance of the financial wherewithall of the other defendants; and (4) that the purpose of the comparative fault regime is to prevent fortuitously imposing a degree of liability that is out of all proportion to fault.

Make the Connection

Joinder is covered in the Civil Procedure course.

. . . .

Today, we state unequivocally that our decision regarding joint and several liability in *McIntyre v. Balentine* did not alter Tennessee's common-law rules with regard to liability of tortfeasors for injuries caused by subsequent medical treatment for the injuries they cause. That rule is a rule that determines "when defendants are liable for the harm they caused." Restatement (Third) of Torts: Liability for Physical Injury § 35, cmt. d, at 696-97. Thus, the rule in Tennessee is now, as it was before *McIntyre v. Balentine* was decided, that an actor whose tortious conduct causes physical harm to another is liable for any enhanced harm the other suffers due to the efforts of third persons to render aid reasonably required by the other's injury, as long as the enhanced harm arises from a risk that inheres in the effort to render aid. *See* Restatement (Third) of Torts: Liability for Physical Injury § 35, at 693.

However, at the same time, we again reaffirm our earlier decisions holding that following *McIntyre v. Balentine,* the doctrine of joint and several liability no longer applies to circumstances in which separate, independent negligent acts of more than one tortfeasor combine to cause a single, indivisible injury. [Cc] This decision is not inconsistent with our decision to retain the rule imposing liability on tortfeasors for subsequent negligent medical care for the injuries caused by the original tortfeasor. . . .

. . . .

Most of the states that have adopted the principles of comparative fault or comparative responsibility have done so by statute rather than by judicial decision. The substance of these statutes differs because states have balanced the rights and interests of the parties in different ways. Accordingly, decisions from other state courts construing their own comparative fault statute provide only limited guidance to us. However, we note that a significant number of state courts that have addressed the same question we address in this case have, like this Court, concluded that comparative fault does not prevent the continuing imposition of liability on an original tortfeasor for subsequent negligent medical care for the injuries caused by the original tortfeasor. *See, e.g ., Henry v. Superior Court,* 160 Cal.App.4th 440, 72 Cal.Rptr.3d 808, 820 (Cal.Ct.App.2008); *Ass'n for Retarded Citizens-Volusia, Inc. v. Fletcher,* 741 So.2d 520, 524-25 (Fla.Dist.Ct.App.1999); *Cramer v. Slater,* 146 Idaho 868, 204 P.3d 508, 514 (Idaho 2009); *Edwards v. Sisler,* 691 N.E.2d 1252, 1254-55 (Ind.Ct.App.1998); *Payne v. Hall,* 139 N.M. 659, 137 P.3d 599, 610 (N.M.2006).

. . . .

Ever since the advent of comparative fault in 1992, we have emphasized that the doctrine of joint and several liability no longer applies to circumstances in which separate, independent negligent acts of more than one tortfeasor combine to cause a single, indivisible injury. [Cc] Today, we have explicitly held that the doctrine of joint and several liability does not apply in cases where the injuries caused by the negligence of the original tortfeasor are enhanced by the subsequent negligence of physicians and other healthcare providers. . . .

. . . .

We reiterate that the doctrine of joint and several liability no longer applies to circumstances in which separate, independent negligent acts of more than one tortfeasor combine to cause a single, indivisible injury. We hold that an actor whose tortious conduct causes physical harm to another is liable for any enhanced harm the other suffers due to the efforts of third persons to render aid reasonably required by the other's injury, as long as the enhanced harm arises from a risk that inheres in the effort to render aid. In light of our consistent holding that the doctrine of joint and several liability no longer applies to circumstances in which separate, independent negligent acts of more than one tortfeasor combine to cause a single, indivisible injury, it is improper to maintain joint and several liability in cases involving subsequent medical negligence where there is even less cause. We find that the trial court erred by refusing to permit the Elks Lodge defendants and Dr. Boyce to amend their answers to assert a comparative fault defense against Cumberland Manor. We remand the case to the trial court for further proceedings consistent with this opinion, and we tax the costs in three equal shares to Alice J. Banks, the Elks Lodge defendants, and Robert H. Boyce and Premier Orthopaedics & Sports Medicine, P.C. for which execution, if necessary, may issue.

Points for Discussion

1. Describe (a) the operational differences between comparative liability and joint-and-several liability regimes and (b) the circumstances in which the latter regime does and does not apply.

2. If you were fashioning the applicable rule of law in a comparative negligence jurisdiction, would you abolish or retain the common law joint and several liability rule?

3. Plaintiff has been awarded a $1 million judgment against Defendants A, B, and C, and each defendant is jointly and severally liable to Plaintiff. Plaintiff can pursue and collect that judgment from which defendant or defendants?

4. Section 2(c) of the Uniform Comparative Fault Act provides that courts should determine and award damages and "enter judgment against each party liable on the basis of rules of joint-and-several liability," and should also "determine and state in the judgment each party's equitable

> **FYI**
>
> The Uniform Comparative Fault Act was drafted by the National Conference of Commissioners on Uniform State Laws and approved by that organization in 1979.

share of the obligation to each claimant in accordance with the respective percentages of fault." UCFA § 2(d) further provides that, upon motion made not later than one year following the entry of a judgment, "the court shall determine whether all or part of a party's equitable share of the obligation is uncollectible from that party, and shall reallocate any uncollectible amount among the other parties, including a claimant at fault, according to their respective percentages of fault."

5. Tortfeasors A and B are negligent and jointly and severally liable for conduct causing injury to C. The jury apportioned liability as follows: A: 1 percent, B: 99 percent. Can C recover the entire amount of damages owed from A? If so, should the jury be informed of the legal consequence and operation of the joint-and-several liability doctrine prior to its deliberations? *Compare* Kaeo v. Davis, 68 Haw. 447, 719 P.2d 387 (1986) with McGowan v. Story, 70 Wis.2d 189, 234 N.W.2d 325 (1975).

Hypo 11-1

A, B, and C decided to fire guns at a farm belonging to A's grand-mother and drove together to the farm in A's pickup truck. While driving to the farm, C fell asleep. Seeing that their friend was not awake, A and B came up with a plan to frighten C. According to the plan, A and B would prepare their guns so that each of their weapons would only fire one bullet. A and B would then awaken C by simultaneously firing the single shots in their guns into the ground; they would then point their weapons at C and click the triggers on the guns' empty chambers.

Upon arriving at the farm, A drove the pickup truck inside a barn, and A and B got out of the truck, leaving C asleep on the front seat. A and B fired their weapons into the ground near the truck, waking C. A and B then pointed their guns at C, stating in unison, "It's time to die." A and B pulled the triggers on their weapons. The pulling of the trigger on B's gun produced a click as B had planned. However, when A pulled the trigger on her gun, the gun discharged and a bullet struck and killed C.

Is B jointly and severally liable to C's estate for the negligent conduct resulting in the death of C? Discuss.

Hypo 11-2

Plaintiff was entering Convenience Store as another patron, Robber, was exiting the store. Robber grabbed Plaintiff's arm and asked Plaintiff to hand over his wallet. When Plaintiff refused, Robber pulled a gun from his coat pocket, shot Plaintiff in the abdomen, and grabbed Plaintiff's wallet. He then fled the scene. Robber was never seen again and has not been apprehended by law enforcement authorities.

Plaintiff sued Convenience Store, alleging that the store was liable for his injuries because the store failed to maintain safe premises for its customers. Convenience Store denied that it had acted negligently and pleaded, as an affirmative defense, that it was entitled to apportion any liability for Plaintiff's injuries to Robber, the assailant who intentionally shot Plaintiff.

State's apportionment of liability statute provides, in pertinent part, that "in all actions involving fault of more than one person or entity, the trier of fact shall determine the percentage of the total fault which is attributable to every person or entity causing the claimant's damages. The liability of each defendant shall be several only and shall not be joint" with the following exception: "If the trier of fact determines that the claimant or party suffering bodily injury was not at fault, the defendants against whom judgment is entered shall be jointly and severally liable for the sum of their proportionate shares of the claimant's total damages." In addition, the statute defines "fault" as "acts or omissions that are in any measure negligent or reckless toward the person or property of the actor or others."

Plaintiff has moved for partial summary judgment to strike Convenience Store's affirmative defense, arguing that Robber's intentional action in shooting Plaintiff was not "fault" under and within the meaning of State's apportionment law. You are the judge hearing the motion. Grant or deny Plaintiff's motion.

B. Satisfaction and Release

Bundt v. Embro

48 Misc.2d 802, 265 N.Y.S.2d 872 (N.Y. Sup. Ct. 1965)

WILLIAM B. GROAT, Justice.

In this consolidated action defendants Peckham Road Corporation, Edward Embro, Jr., Wallachs Auto Rental Inc., Aldo Di Belardino and GBI, Inc. (hereinafter: moving defendants) move for leave to amend their answer to interpose the affirmative defense of **discharge** and **satisfaction**.

What's That?

A legal duty or obligation is discharged or satisfied upon extinguishment (for example, the payment of an amount owed to another).

This is an action for personal injuries sustained by plaintiffs when an automobile owned and operated by defendant Embro collided with another automobile operated by defendant Aldo Di Belardino, owned by defendant Wallachs and leased to defendant GBI, Inc. Plaintiff Bundt was a passenger in the automobile operated by Embro and plaintiffs Mondini were passengers in the automobile operated by Aldo Di Belardino at the time of the accident. In their separate complaints Bundt and the Mondinis allege that both automobiles were operated in a negligent manner and that defendant Peckham, which was repairing the highway near the scene of the accident, negligently obstructed the view of the stop sign which Embro's automobile passed just before the collision occurred. Plaintiffs also allege that Peckham's negligence combined with the negligence of the other defendants to cause the accident.

The moving defendants state that plaintiffs Bundt and Mondini instituted an action against the state in the Court of Claims and that a decision rendered by that court granted judgment in the following amounts:

Hans Henning Bundt	$ 9,731.38
Guilia Mondini	47,223.69
Graziella Mondini	1,000.00
Gino Mondini	11,765.61
Enrica Ferrario	3,261.21

The moving defendants also state that the aforesaid judgment has been satisfied.

In support of their motion to amend, the moving defendants argue that, since they were joint tort feasors with the state, the satisfaction of the judgment against the state discharges them through the application of the settled rule that the satisfaction of a judgment against one joint tort feasor discharges the others.

. . . .

The rule is well settled that:

"[I]t is elementary law that one who has been injured by the joint wrong of several parties may recover his damages against either or all; but, although there may be several suits and recoveries, there can be but one satisfaction. [Cc] The reason of the rule is that while there may be many perpetrators of a wrongful act, each of whom is separately liable, yet the act and its consequences are **indivisible**, and the injured person is, therefore, limited to a single satisfaction." [C]

. . . .

Nor does this court agree with plaintiffs' argument that the rule that the satisfaction of the judgment against one joint tort feasor discharges the others has no application to a Court of Claims judgment. Section 8 of the Court of Claims Act states:

"The state hereby waives its immunity from liability and action and hereby assumes liability and consents to have the same determined in accordance with the same rules of law as applied to actions in the supreme court against individuals or corporations, provided the claimant complies with the limitations of this article."

'By the adoption of such section the State places itself, as to those making claims against the State, in the same position as a private individual or a corporation would be for his or its negligence.' (Robison v. State of New York, 263 App. Div. 240, 243, 32 N.Y.S.2d 388, 391).

The Court of Claims determined that the state was negligent and the plaintiffs were awarded judgments for the injuries sustained. If defendants are joint tort feasors with the state, the fact that the judgment satisfied is a Court of Claims judgment should not prevent application of a rule which prevents double recovery for a single injury.

The state may also be a joint tort feasor [c]. While the sovereign has

Take Note

The court notes the general rule that a government enjoys immunity from being sued in its own courts in the absence of the government's consent to the lawsuit. On this form of immunity from suit, see Chapter 11, *infra*.

always been immune from suit at common law. "When, however, the state confers upon a court jurisdiction to hear and determine all claims against it, or all claims of a particular class, the situation in that court is the same as if the claim were against a private individual or corporation." [Cc]

Therefore, if the trial court shall determine that the defendants were in fact joint tort feasors with the state, the satisfaction of a judgment against the state would operate as a discharge of the defendants.

Accordingly, leave to amend is granted to the defendants.

Points for Discussion

1. What is an "indivisible injury"?

2. The court notes that one injured by the joint wrongful conduct of others may have a number of lawsuits and recoveries but can only have one satisfaction. Explain the satisfaction doctrine and the rationale(s) supporting this approach.

3. When and under what circumstances can a state be sued for acts or omissions making the state a joint tortfeasor?

4. For more on the satisfaction of claims, see RESTATEMENT (THIRD) OF TORTS: APPORTIONMENT OF LIABILITY § 25 (2000); RESTATEMENT (SECOND) OF TORTS § 886 (1979).

Cox v. Pearl Investment Company

168 Colo. 67, 450 P.2d 60 (1969)

HODGES, Justice.

This is a negligence case which terminated in the trial court with a summary judgment in favor of the defendant on a showing that a purported **release** had been executed by the plaintiffs in favor of a joint tortfeasor. The common law rule of law

What's That?

A *release* relinquishes and gives up a right or claim against an individual or entity. For example, A, an employee, can release and give up her right to any and all tort claims and liability against B, her employer, arising out of or related to her employment with and by B.

that the release of one tort-feasor releases all others who may have liability was applied by the trial court.

As plaintiffs in the trial court, Mr. and Mrs. Cox sought recovery of damages for injuries which Mrs. Cox sustained when she fell on property owned by the defendant Pearl Investment Company. The plaintiffs' complaint acknowledges that Goodwill Industries was a tenant of the defendant. . . . When the summary judgment motion was considered by the trial court, it was shown that the tenant, Goodwill Industries, had previously paid the plaintiffs $2500 in consideration of the plaintiffs' execution of a document entitled "Covenant Not to Proceed with Suit."

. . . .

The plaintiffs' . . . assignment of error . . . does bring into focus another important issue concerning the legal effect to be given to the 'Covenant Not to Proceed with Suit' involved here. The trial court denominated it a release and, without ascribing any dignity to the expressed words that the plaintiffs reserved "the right to sue any other person or persons against whom they may have or assert any claim on account of damages arising out of the above described accident," ruled that it therefore barred any action against the defendant as a joint tort-feasor.

Although Price v. Baker, 143 Colo. 264, 352 P.2d 90 supports the trial court, we no longer deem it advisable to further impose on our body of law the harshness and rigidity of the rule and rationale of Price . . . In our present analysis of this issue, we are drawn toward only one conclusion. We can no longer countenance the continuation of a rule of law which is not only harsh and illogical, but which gives refuge and absolution to wrongdoers by depriving a litigant under these circumstances of probable just and full compensation for his injuries caused by wrongdoers. It is not possible to visualize any reasonable or compelling justification for persisting in the application of this harsh and unrealistic rule except on the basis of ancient formalisms, the reasons for which no longer prevail. . . .

. . . .

In Price, we declared "this state has long followed the universal rule that the release of one joint tort-feasor is a release of all." We hereby confirm this to be still the rule in Colorado. Also, we agree with the proposition that a joint tort-feasor is not ***ipso facto*** released by a **covenant not to sue**. We do, however, now state that the instru-

What's That?

As defined in *Black's Law Dictionary*, in a covenant (or contract) not to sue "a party having a right of action agrees not to assert that right in litigation."

ment involved in Price v. Baker, which is substantially identical to the writing involved in the case at bar, was improvidently interpreted to be an absolute and full release of all joint tort-feasors.

The manifest intent of the parties to a contract should always be given effect unless it be in violation of law or **public policy**. This is fundamental in contract law. Where a contract has the effect of releasing one joint tort-feasor but expressly reserves the right to sue others who may be liable, it should not in law be treated otherwise. The expressed reservation in this instrument of the right to sue other joint tort-feasors evinces a clear-cut manifestation that the plaintiffs were not receiving full compensation; and if this is borne out, their right to bring an action against others who were the cause of their damages should not be foreclosed. The danger of over compensation or double compensation is no excuse for barring a claim against joint tort-feasors. Obviously, no court would permit the accomplishment of this possible contingency. And certainly, the non-settling joint tort-feasor is not prejudiced, but rather, he is benefited for he would be entitled to have the amount of the judgment reduced by the amount paid by his co-tortfeasor.

The rule that the reservation of right shows the intention of the parties not to release the non-settling defendant and that such a document should be considered a covenant not to sue rather than an absolute release are numerous. . . . To be particularly noted is the early case of Matheson v. O'Kane, 211 Mass. 91, 97 N.E. 638, 39 L.R.A., N.S., 475. The facts therein are quite similar to the facts of the instant case in that the released parties were authorized to plead the instrument in bar to any action filed by the plaintiffs. It was held that this did not constitute a release of other defendants and further stated:

> "* * * But where it is evidence that the consideration paid to the plaintiff was not intended to be full compensation for his injuries, and the agreement signed by him although in form a release was clearly intended to preserve the liability of those who were not parties to it, many of the courts have sought to give effect to that intention by construing the agreement as in legal effect a covenant not to sue and not a technical release."

4 Restatement, Torts § 885 which is modeled after numerous cases like Matheson, supra, provides that a release will be construed as a covenant not to sue where the right to proceed against the remaining tort-feasors is expressly reserved. This section emphasizes the importance of the expressed intent of the contracting parties.

In the supplemental brief of the defendant, it is urged that Price, supra, establishes the rule in Colorado that the document involved there which is essentially identical to the instrument here is an absolute release of all joint tort-feasors and therefore, should not now be repudiated under the doctrine of stare decisis. This doctrine is assiduously followed by this court. However, when, as here, a prior decision is adverse to the rules of fundamental and initiates a harsh and unrealistic rule, we believe it becomes incumbent upon us at the first opportunity presented to make a necessary change.

It's Latin to Me!

Stare decisis is Latin for "to stand by things decided." Under this doctrine, courts are governed and can be bound by prior judicial rulings when deciding subsequent issues and cases.

Accordingly, the judgment is reversed and the cause remanded to the trial court for further proceedings not inconsistent with the views expressed herein.

Points for Discussion

1. Did the trial court correctly understand and apply the Colorado Supreme Court's 1969 *Price v. Baker* decision?

2. Distinguish: (a) judgment and satisfaction of judgment; (b) satisfaction and release; (c) release and covenant not to sue.

3. The court reaffirmed the rule in Colorado that the universal release of one joint tortfeasor releases all joint tortfeasors. Because this rule has been changed by both statutory and judicial developments, practitioners must research to determine a particular jurisdiction's current rule and approach.

Maloney v. Valley Medical Facilities, Inc.

984 A.2d 478 (Pa. 2009)

Justice SAYLOR.

Appeal was allowed to consider whether a plaintiff's release of principals whose potential liability was **vicarious** also discharges the plaintiff's claims against the **agent**, regardless of an express reservation of rights.

Appellee commenced the present **medical malpractice** action grounded on an asserted failure to timely diagnose and treat osteosarcoma in his wife,

Linda Maloney. He alleged, among other things, medical negligence on the part of Appellant Maurice Prendergast, M.D. (an internist) and Richard E. Brennan, M.D. (a radiologist), as well as vicarious liability on the part of institutional defendants associated with these physicians.

Following **settlement** discussions, Appellee entered into a settlement with Dr. Brennan, funded by such physician's primary liability insurer and the Medical Care Availability and Reduction of Error Fund in its capacity, effectively, as an excess insurer. [C] Appellee executed a joint tortfeasor release surrendering all claims "in any way connected with all medical professional health care services rendered by the above named Health Care Providers." Joint Tortfeasor Release, Oct. 24, 2006, ¶ 1. Notably, the "above named Health Care Providers" included the institutional defendants associated with Dr. Prendergast, namely, Appellants Beaver Internal Medicine Association and Tri-State Medical Group, Inc. (hereinafter "Employers"), but not Dr. Prendergast himself. . . . Further, a second paragraph of the release was included to expressly reflect a reservation of rights against Dr. Prendergast. *See Id.* at ¶ 2 ("It is understood that I, Max C. Maloney, am not hereby releasing any claims or demands that I have against Maurice D. Prendergast, M.D. However, I am agreeing to limit my potential recovery against Maurice D. Prendergast, M.D. . . .). The intent was also expressed in the release that it was to comply with and be interpreted in accordance with the Uniform Contribution Among Tortfeasors Act.[3]

Thereafter, Dr. Prendergast and Employers filed motions for summary judgment, each asserting that the language of the release discharged all direct and derivative claims arising from Dr. Prendergast's conduct, based on the common-law rule governing releases. [Cc] Employers also contended that the express language of the release foreclosed all claims against them.

The common pleas court granted the respective motions, initially crediting the argument that the release encompassed all claims against all of the institutional defendants, including Employers. As to Dr. Prendergast himself, the court determined that the common-law release rule applied . . .

On appeal, the Superior Court agreed that the release encompassed all claims against Employers. [C] However, the intermediate appellate court differed with the common pleas court's reasoning and holding concerning Dr. Prendergast. In this regard, the Superior Court initially stressed the application of traditional contract principles to releases, including the policy of effectuating the intention of the parties via enforcement of the ordinary meaning of release terms. . . . Based on this reasoning, the Superior Court vacated the judgment as to Dr. Prendergast and remanded for further proceedings consistent with its opinion. . . .

. . . .

3 Act of July 9, 1976, P.L. 586, No. 142 § 2 (codified at 42 Pa.C.S. §§ 8321-8327) (the "UCATA").

As noted, we accepted review to determine whether the common-law rule requiring release of a principal upon release of an agent applies in the reverse scenario. This question is one of law, and, thus, our review is plenary. Upon our review of the parties' respective positions, we find Appellee's to be persuasive.

. . . .

As Appellee develops, particularly in the medical malpractice arena, the landscape of claims and defendants can be very complex, given the potential involvement of multiple caregivers, an insurance scheme incorporating private and governmental elements, and oftentimes the high stakes attendant to claims of serious bodily injury or death. It is evident that the interests of justice are not advanced by the extension of an inflexible common-law rule to such scenarios, at least where a number of the policy considerations underlying them (for example, the absence of alleged fault on the part of the party subject to release as a matter of law) are not present. [C] As Appellee persuasively argues, there is a substantial likelihood that such an extension would impede settlements, undermining the strong public policy favoring the voluntary compromise of claims. [Cc]

. . . .

In the scenario entailing a plaintiff's surrender of vicarious liability claims only and express preservation of claims against an agent, we hold that the parties to a settlement should be afforded latitude to effectuate their express intentions. . . .

. . . .

The order of the Superior Court is affirmed.

———————

Points for Discussion

1. Do you agree with the *Maloney* court's decision and analysis?

2. Should the *Maloney* court's approach be limited to or extend beyond medical malpractice cases?

3. "A settlement is a legally enforceable agreement in which a claimant agrees not to seek recovery outside the agreement for specified injuries or claims from some or all the persons who might be liable for those injuries or claims." RESTATEMENT (THIRD) OF TORTS: APPORTIONMENT OF LIABILITY § 24a (2000). Persons or entities "released from liability by the terms of a settlement are

relieved of further liability to the claimant for the injuries or claims covered by the agreement, but the agreement does not discharge any other person from liability." *Id.*, § 24(b).

4. Should the release of an agent who has engaged in actionable negligence also release the principal who is vicariously liable for the agent's misconduct? For discussion of this issue, *see* Woodrum v. Johnson, 210 W.Va. 762, 559 S.E.2d 908 (2001).

Hypo 11-3

At the age of two, Omar, a child not suffering from asthma, was improperly prescribed and ingested an asthma medication. After he suffered seizures and severe brain damage, his parents sued Omar's doctors for malpractice. Thereafter, the suit was settled. In exchange for $900,000, Omar's mother and father signed a document releasing Omar's doctors "and all other persons, firms, corporations, or entities who are or might be liable from any and all actions, causes of action, claims, demands, and damages of every kind, character, or description, including, but not limited to, such allegedly on account of, or in any way growing out of, personal injuries and property damage resulting, or to result, from the alleged negligence and malpractice of Defendants or others."

Fourteen years after the settlement and the execution of the aforementioned release, Omar's father brought an action on Omar's behalf against two manufacturers of the asthma medication ingested by the then two-year old Omar, alleging, among other things, products liability, fraud, and misrepresentation. Moving for summary judgment, both manufacturers rely on the release signed by Omar's mother and father as part of the earlier settlement.

Is the father's suit barred by the release?

Elbaor v. Smith

845 S.W.2d 240 (Tex. 1992)

OPINION

GONZALEZ, Justice.

In this medical malpractice case we consider . . . whether **Mary Carter agreements** are void as contrary to public policy. The trial court rendered judgment in favor of the plaintiff, and the court of appeals affirmed. 845 S.W.2d 282. We hold that Mary Carter agreements are void as against public policy. We thus reverse the judgment of the court of appeals and remand this cause to the trial court for a new trial.

. . . .

At 2:00 a.m. on May 8, 1985, Carole Smith was seriously injured in a single-vehicle accident when the Corvette she was driving left the highway and collided with a tree. She received emergency treatment at the Dallas/Fort Worth Medical Center-Grand Prairie ("D/FW Medical Center") from Dr. Abraham Syrquin for multiple injuries including a compound fracture of her left ankle. In an effort to stop the bleeding, Dr. Syrquin performed emergency surgery closing the ankle wound. Ms. Smith remained under Dr. Syrquin's treatment for eight days at D/FW Medical Center after which time she was transferred to the care of Dr. James Elbaor, an orthopedic surgeon, at Arlington Community Hospital ("ACH").

While Ms. Smith was at ACH, she was treated by a team of physicians including Dr. Elbaor, Dr. Joseph Stephens, a plastic surgeon, and Dr. Bienvenido Gatmaitan, an infectious disease specialist. Upon admission to ACH, Ms. Smith was evaluated by Dr. Gatmaitan and placed on intravenous antibiotics. During the course of her stay, Dr. Stephens performed two debridements of the ankle wound. . . . On June 3, Ms. Smith was transferred to the care of Dr. Wayne Burkhead at Baylor University Medical Center ("Baylor"). Four days after admission, Dr. Burkhead removed a two inch section of bone from Ms. Smith's ankle. Ms. Smith received treatment from several orthopedic specialists over the next three years which ultimately led to the fusion of her ankle joint.

. . . .

Ms. Smith filed suit against D/FW Medical Center, ACH, Drs. Syrquin, Elbaor, Stephens, and Gatmaitan. Sometime before trial, Ms. Smith entered into

Mary Carter agreements with Dr. Syrquin, Dr. Stephens, and ACH.[3] The Mary Carter agreements provided for payments to Ms. Smith of $350,000 from Dr. Syrquin, $75,000 from ACH, and $10 from Dr. Stephens. Under the terms of each agreement, the settling defendants were required to participate in the trial of the case. The agreements also contained pay-back provisions whereby Dr. Syrquin and ACH would be reimbursed all or part of the settlement money paid to Ms. Smith out of the recovery against Dr. Elbaor.

Ms. Smith nonsuited her claim against Dr. Gatmaitan and settled and dismissed her claim against D/FW Medical Center. Dr. Elbaor filed a **cross claim** against Dr. Stephens, Dr. Gatmaitan, Dr. Syrquin, and ACH. He alleged that in the event he was found liable to Ms. Smith, that he was entitled to **contribution** from these defendants. Furthermore, Dr. Elbaor requested that the trial court hold the Mary Carter agreements void as against public policy, and alternatively, to dismiss the settling defendants from the suit. The trial court denied this request. . . .

At trial, the jury found that Ms. Smith's damages totaled $2,253,237.07, of which Dr. Elbaor was responsible for eighty-eight percent, and Dr. Syrquin for twelve percent. After deducting all credits for Dr. Syrquin's percentage of causation and settlements with other defendants, the trial court rendered judgment against Dr. Elbaor for $1,872,848.62.

. . . .

Although the Mary Carter agreements were not entered into evidence, the trial judge was troubled by them and he took remedial measures to mitigate their harmful effects by reapportioning the **peremptory challenges**, changing the order of proceedings to favor Dr. Elbaor, allowing counsel to explain the agreements to the jury, and instructing the jury regarding the agreements.

What's That?

A party exercising a *peremptory challenge* has the right to dismiss a potential juror during jury selection without having to state a reason for the challenge. Each party to a lawsuit is typically given the same number of such challenges.

During the trial, the settling defendants' attorneys, who sat at the table with Dr. Elbaor's attorneys, vigorously assisted Ms. Smith in pointing the finger of culpability at Dr. Elbaor. This created some odd conflicts of interest and some questionable representations of fact. For example, although Ms. Smith's own experts testified

---

3 These agreements acquired their name from a case out of Florida styled *Booth v. Mary Carter Paint Co.*, 202 So.2d 8, 10-11 (Fla.App.1967). When the Florida Supreme Court finally addressed Mary Carter agreements, it noted their potential to skew the trial process and thus established supervisory guidelines to limit their ill effects. *See Ward v. Ochoa*, 284 So.2d 385 (Fla.1973).

that Dr. Syrquin committed malpractice, her attorney stated during **voir dire** and in her opening statement that Dr. Syrquin's conduct was "heroic" and that Dr.

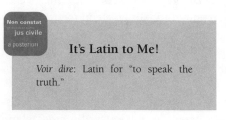

It's Latin to Me!

Voir dire: Latin for "to speak the truth."

Elbaor's negligence caused Ms. Smith's damages. And during her closing argument, Ms. Smith's attorney urged the jury to find that Dr. Syrquin had not caused Ms. Smith's damages. This is hardly the kind of statement expected from a plaintiff's lawyer regarding a named defendant. ACH and Drs. Syrquin and Stephens had remained defendants of record, but their attorneys asserted during voir dire that Ms. Smith's damages were "devastating," "astoundingly high," and "astronomical." Furthermore, on cross examination they elicited testimony from Ms. Smith favorable to her and requested recovery for pain and mental anguish. The settling defendants' attorneys also abandoned their pleadings on Ms. Smith's contributory negligence, argued that Ms. Smith should be awarded all of her alleged damages, and urged that Dr. Elbaor was 100 percent liable.

. . . .

The term "Mary Carter agreement" has been defined in different ways by various courts and commentators.[13] This Court has yet to definitively define the requisite elements of a Mary Carter agreement-our prior pronouncements utilized different definitions of the term. [Cc] Today we clarify what we mean by the term "Mary Carter agreement." A Mary Carter agreement exists when the settling defendant retains a financial stake in the plaintiff's recovery *and* remains a party

---

13 The majority of cases and commentators define "Mary Carter agreement" as one in which the settling defendant possesses a financial stake in the outcome of the case and the settling defendant remains a party to the litigation. *See Ward v. Ochoa,* 284 So.2d 385, 387 (Fla.1973); *General Motors Corp. v. Lahocki,* 286 Md. 714, 410 A.2d 1039, 1042 (1980); *Johnson v. Moberg,* 334 N.W.2d 411, 415 (Minn.1983); *Bedford School Dist. v. Caron Constr. Co.,* 116 N.H. 800, 367 A.2d 1051, 1053 (1976); *Cox v. Kelsey-Hayes Co.,* 594 P.2d 354, 357 (Okla.1978); *General Motors Corp. v. Simmons,* 558 S.W.2d 855, 858 (Tex.1977); *Vermont Union School Dist. v. H.P. Cummings Constr. Co.,* 143 Vt. 416, 469 A.2d 742, 748 (1983); John E. Benedict, Note, *It's a Mistake to Tolerate the Mary Carter Agreement,* 87 COLUMBIA L.REV. 368, 369-70 (1987); David R. Miller, Comment, *Mary Carter Agreements: Unfair and Unnecessary,* 32 SW.L.J. 779, 783-84 (1978). Many cases also describe other requisite elements of a Mary Carter agreement, such as secrecy. *See, e.g., Ward,* 284 So.2d at 387. Other cases and commentators argue that a Mary Carter agreement exists any time the settling defendant possesses a financial interest in the plaintiff's recovery. *See Bristol-Myers Co. v. Gonzales,* 561 S.W.2d 801, 805 (Tex.1978); Robin Renee Green, Comment, *Mary Carter Agreements: The Unsolved Evidentiary Problems in Texas,* 40 BAYLOR L.REV. 449, 451 (1988).

at the trial of the case.[14] This definition comports with both the present majority view and the original understanding of the term.

A Mary Carter agreement exists, under our definition, when the plaintiff enters into a settlement agreement with one defendant and goes to trial against the remaining defendant(s). The settling defendant, who remains a party, guarantees the plaintiff a minimum payment, which may be **offset** in whole or in part by an excess judgment recovered at trial. [Cc] This creates a tremendous incentive for the settling defendant to ensure that the plaintiff succeeds in obtaining a sizable recovery, and thus motivates the defendant to assist greatly in the plaintiff's presentation of the case (as occurred here). Indeed, Mary Carter agreements generally, but not always, contain a clause requiring the settling defendant to participate in the trial on the plaintiff's behalf.

Given this Mary Carter scenario, it is difficult to surmise how these agreements promote settlement. Although the agreements do secure the partial settlement of a lawsuit, they nevertheless nearly always ensure a trial against the non-settling defendant. [Cc] Mary Carter agreements frequently make litigation inevitable, because they grant the settling defendant veto power over any proposed settlement between the plaintiff and any remaining defendant. [C] Thus, "[o]nly a mechanical jurisprudence could characterize Mary Carter arrangements as promoting compromise and discouraging litigation-they plainly do just the opposite." [C]

. . . .

Many jurisdictions have decided to tolerate the ill effects of Mary Carter agreements, presumably because they believe that the agreements promote settlement. Some have sought to mitigate the agreements' harmful skewing of the trial process by imposing prophylactic protections. Indeed, Texas previously has taken such an approach. [C]; *Smithwick,* 724 S.W.2d at 8-12 (Spears, J., concurring).[19] These protective measures generally seek to remove the secrecy within which

---

14 A Mary Carter agreement does not have to expressly state that the settling defendant must participate in the trial. The participation requirement is satisfied by the mere presence of the settling defendant as a party in the case. Obviously, a Mary Carter agreement would not exist if a settling defendant acquires a financial interest in the outcome of the trial and then testifies at trial as a non-party witness. However, Rule 3.04(b) of the Texas Disciplinary Rules of Professional Conduct prohibits a lawyer from paying or offering to pay a witness contingent upon the content of the testimony of the witness or the outcome of the case. Certainly Rule 3.04(b) mandates that an attorney has an ethical duty to refrain from making a settlement contingent, in any way, on the testimony of a witness who was also a settling party.

19 The guidelines provided in the *Smithwick* concurrence require that Mary Carter agreements: (1) are discoverable; (2) should be fully disclosed "to the trial court before trial or immediately after the agreement is formed;" (3) should be considered by the trial court in allowing jury strikes and ruling on witness examination; and (4) should be fully disclosed to the jury at the start of the trial. *Smithwick,* 724 S.W.2d at 8-11.

Mary Carter agreements traditionally have been shrouded. *See Slusher v. Ospital,* 777 P.2d 437, 440 (Utah 1989) (secrecy is the essence of a Mary Carter agreement).

Justice Spears rightly noted in *Smithwick* the falsity of the premise upon which the prophylactic protection approach is founded, namely, the promotion of equitable settlements. [C] Mary Carter agreements instead:

> present to the jury a sham of adversity between the plaintiff and one co-defendant, while these parties are actually allied for the purpose of securing a substantial judgment for the plaintiff and, in some cases, exoneration for the settling defendant.

June F. Entman, *Mary Carter Agreements: An Assessment of Attempted Solutions,* 38 U.FLA. L. REV. 521, 574 (1986); [c]. The agreements pressure the "settling" defendant to alter the character of the suit by contributing discovery material, peremptory challenges, trial tactics, supportive witness examination, and jury influence to the plaintiff's cause. [C] These procedural advantages distort the case presented before a jury that came "to court expecting to see a contest between the plaintiff and the defendants [and] instead see[s] one of the defendants cooperating with the plaintiff." *Smithwick,* 724 S.W.2d at 9 (Spears, J., concurring).

Mary Carter agreements not only allow plaintiffs to buy support for their case,[20] they also motivate more culpable defendants to "make a 'good deal' [and thus] end up paying little or nothing in damages." [Cc] Remedial measures cannot overcome nor sufficiently alleviate the malignant effects that Mary Carter agreements inflict upon our adversarial system. No persuasive public policy justifies them, and they are not legitimized simply because this practice may continue in the absence of these agreements. The Mary Carter agreement is simply an unwise and **champertous** device that has failed to achieve its intended purpose. [Cc]

. . . .

The case before us reveals yet another jury trial and verdict distorted by a Mary Carter agreement. The trial judge, who fully grasped the detrimental effect these agreements could have on the outcome, attempted to monitor the lawsuit by assiduously applying the guidelines suggested in the *Smithwick* concurrence. The conduct of this trial, however, confirms the apprehension expressed by Justice Spears in *Smithwick:* that these remedial measures would only mitigate and not eliminate the unjust influences exerted on a trial by Mary Carter agreements. Equalizing peremptory strikes, reordering proceedings, thoroughly disclos-

---

20 We previously condemned the practice of buying a witness' testimony in order to silence testimony. *Tom L. Scott, Inc. v. McIlhany,* 798 S.W.2d 556, 560 (Tex.1990).

ing the true alignment of the parties, and revealing the agreement's substance cannot overcome **collusion** between the plaintiff and settling defendants who retain a financial interest in the plaintiff's success. In fact, Mary Carter agreements may force attorneys into questionable ethical situations under Rule 3.05 of the Texas Disciplinary Rules of Professional Conduct, which is titled "Maintaining the Impartiality of the Tribunal." Comment 2 to that rule notes, regarding alternate methods of dispute resolution (like Mary Carter agreements), that "a lawyer should avoid any conduct that is or could reasonably be construed as being intended to corrupt or to unfairly influence the decisionmaker." *See* SUPREME COURT OF TEXAS, TEXAS DISCIPLINARY RULES OF PROFESSIONAL CONDUCT art. X, § 9 (1990); *cf.* MODEL CODE OF PROFESSIONAL RESPONSIBILITY EC-720 (1979) (attorneys responsible for upholding adversarial system). The dissent acknowledges that Mary Carter agreements skew the trial process. This effect reasonably could be construed as unfairly influencing the decisionmaker.

As a matter of public policy, this Court favors settlements, but we do not favor partial settlements that promote rather than discourage further litigation. And we do not favor settlement arrangements that skew the trial process, mislead the jury, promote unethical collusion among nominal adversaries, and create the likelihood that a less culpable defendant will be hit with the full judgment. The bottom line is that our public policy favoring fair trials outweighs our public policy favoring partial settlements.

This case typifies the kind of procedural and substantive damage Mary Carter agreements can inflict upon our adversarial system. Thus, we declare them void as violative of sound public policy.

. . . .

. . . Accordingly, we reverse the judgment of the court of appeals and remand this cause to the trial court for further proceedings consistent with this opinion.

DOGGETT, J., dissents and files opinion joined by MAUZY and GAMMAGE, JJ.

DOGGETT, Justice, dissenting.

Today a medical doctor is prohibited from participating in the trial of a lawsuit in which he is a defendant. This extraordinary and unprecedented maneuver is rooted in the majority's growing distrust of our jury system-its unfounded belief that twelve ordinary citizens are incapable of assessing facts after full disclosure of all the surrounding circumstances. Plunging helter-skelter into uncharted territory to save another medical doctor that a jury found to have committed malpractice, the majority writes without regard to the chaotic effect of its ruling on both the retrial of this action and other complex litigation pending across

Texas. Because today's decision only serves to inject uncertainty and unfairness into trials, I dissent.

. . . .

The chief problem associated with a Mary Carter agreement is that a hidden alteration of the relationship of some of the parties will give the jury a misleading and incomplete basis for evaluating the evidence. As is true in so many areas of jurisprudence, secrecy is the first enemy of justice. To address this concern, trial judges have appropriately implemented several procedural safeguards that remove the veil of secrecy from such settlements. Accordingly, we have emphasized the importance of complete disclosure of these arrangements. [Cc] A concurrence to *Smithwick* suggested a number of specific protections regarding such agreements: discovery of them by the non-settling parties; their pretrial disclosure to the court; thorough explanation of the nature of their terms to the jury at the beginning of the trial; and restriction of a settling defendant's leading questions of the plaintiff's witnesses. 724 S.W.2d at 9-11 (Spears and Gonzalez, JJ., concurring).

In the instant case the trial court took great care to safeguard procedurally the adversarial nature and fairness of its proceedings. Nothing about the agreements now under attack was hidden from anyone. The court appropriately solicited and welcomed suggestions from Elbaor and the other parties as to what and when to tell the jury about the Mary Carter agreements. At voir dire, the court informed prospective jury members that ACH and Syrquin, by participating in the trial, could recover all or a portion of the amounts paid in settlement to Smith, depending on the size of the verdict. An additional warning was extended regarding the possibility of witness bias arising from the agreements. The implications of the agreements were also explored by various counsel during voir dire.

To offset any disadvantage to Elbaor resulting from the agreements, the trial court gave him the same number of peremptory challenges as those of Smith and the three settling defendants together. Recognizing that these settling parties effectively were no longer aligned against one another, the trial court denied them the customary right of an opponent to lead each other's witnesses. Finally, the order of presentation was changed to guarantee that Elbaor always had the final opportunity to present evidence and examine witnesses. While Elbaor specifically complains of a lack of forcefulness in Smith's assertion of her claim against Syrquin, her counsel criticized Syrquin beginning in voir dire, though crediting his efforts to save Smith's life. Since in

Take Note

Only lawyers questioning witnesses on cross-examination at a trial or a hearing are typically permitted to ask leading questions, *e.g.*, questions suggesting the answer to the person being questioned.

some multi-party suits co-defendants become aligned against one another, Elbaor might have found Syrquin and Stephens blaming him for Smith's injury even in the absence of the Mary Carter agreements. Despite Elbaor's concession that "[t]he trial court [correctly] followed Texas law when it disclosed the Mary Carter agreements and implemented the other procedures to protect [him]," the majority rejects these procedures as "miss[ing] the point," [c] thereby renewing its commitment to limit the role of the jury in the truth-seeking process. [C] Simply because jurors may initially expect the plaintiff to have interests adverse to all defendants does not mean that they are incapable of understanding that certain defendants have an incentive for the plaintiff to succeed. Indeed the same may occur in some multiparty litigation where no Mary Carter agreement is involved. The trial cannot be a "sham of adversity," [c] when the jury, as here, is fully aware of this shift in alliances. Nor does the trial become less adversarial merely because some of the parties have switched sides-the names may have changed but the struggle is left intact. So long as at least two parties with antagonistic interests remain, the likelihood that the truth will emerge is not diminished.

Accordingly, most jurisdictions allow Mary Carter agreements when trial courts implement similar procedural safeguards to those adopted here. [Cc] Indeed, the majority cannot point to a single case in any jurisdiction that has ever approved today's prohibition of a named party from participating at trial because of a disclosed pretrial agreement.

. . . .

Texas has today become the first state in the nation to lock the courthouse door on a party solely because of a pretrial contract involving a partial settlement which the majority dislikes. The elitist view that ordinary people acting as jurors are incapable of determining the facts after full disclosure has once again prevailed. While protecting the litigation process from deleterious agreements, this court should avoid precipitous action with uncertain consequences for so many litigants, particularly when, as here, the parties have exercised considerable care and the trial court has conscientiously monitored the proceedings.

Points for Discussion

1. Compare and contrast Justice Gonzalez's majority opinion and Justice Doggett's dissent. Which opinion is most persuasive in your view?

2. Do you agree with the majority that Mary Carter agreements inflict malignant effects on the adversarial system and are not justified by any persuasive public policy?

3. Justice Doggett argues: "The elitist view that ordinary people acting as jurors are incapable of determining the facts after full disclosure has once again prevailed." Is the majority's opinion "elitist"? Do you have a view or opinion as to a juror's competence and ability to assess and find facts after full disclosure of Mary Carter agreements?

4. "The most common version of" a Mary Carter agreement "is typically accomplished by the settling tortfeasor guaranteeing the plaintiff a minimum recovery, regardless of the outcome of the suit against the nonsettling defendants. The settlement then provides that the more that is recovered by the plaintiff from the nonsettling tortfeasors, the less that the settling tortfeasor is required to pay. RESTATEMENT (THIRD) OF TORTS: APPORTIONMENT OF LIABILITY § 24 comment i (2000). A variation of a Mary Carter agreement is the "loan-receipt" agreement wherein "the settling tortfeasor agrees to 'lend' a sum of money to the plaintiff, with the loan to be repaid from any recovery by the plaintiff from the nonsettling tortfeasors." *Id.*

5. Consider *Carter v. Tom's Truck Repair, Inc.*, 857 S.W.2d 172 (Mo. 1993): "There is a strong public policy against allowing secret agreements to work a fraud on either the nonsettling defendant(s), the jury, or the trial court. However, there are also strong public policy considerations in favor of allowing plaintiffs to control their own cases and settle with defendants as they choose. This court finds no reasons that these policies cannot coexist, even in the presence of a Mary Carter agreement, so long as the other defendant is not deceived. . . . [W]e are convinced that the appropriate solution is to examine these troublesome agreements on a case-by-case basis rather than brand them all as outcasts."

6. Florida, the state in which the Mary Carter agreement acquired its name, no longer recognizes the validity of such agreements. *See* Dosdourian v. Carsten, 624 So.2d 241 (Fla. 1993).

———————————

C. Contribution and Indemnity

RESTATEMENT (THIRD) OF TORTS: APPORTIONMENT OF LIABILITY (2000)

§ 22. Indemnity

(a) When two or more persons are or may be liable for the same harm and one of them discharges the liability of another in whole or in part by settlement or discharge of judgment, the person discharging the liability is entitled to recover indemnity in the amount paid to the plaintiff, plus reasonable legal expenses, if:

  (1) the indemnitor has agreed by contract to indemnify the indemnitee, or

  (2) the indemnitee

    (i) was not liable except vicariously for the tort of the indemnitor, or

    (ii) was not liable except as a seller of a product supplied to the indemnitee by the indemnitor and the indemnitee was not independently culpable.

(b) A person who is otherwise entitled to recover indemnity pursuant to contract may do so even if the party against whom indemnity is sought would not be liable to the plaintiff.

§ 23. Contribution

(a) When two or more persons are or may be liable for the same harm and one of them discharges the liability of another by settlement or discharge of judgment, the person discharging the liability is entitled to recover contribution from the other, unless the other previously had a valid settlement and release from the plaintiff.

(b) A person entitled to recover contribution may recover no more than the amount paid to the plaintiff in excess of the person's comparative share of responsibility.

(c) A person who has a right of indemnity against another person under § 22 does not have a right of contribution against that person and is not subject to liability for contribution to that person.

Yellow Cab Co. of D.C., Inc. v. Dreslin

181 F.2d 626 (D.C. Cir. 1950)

PROCTOR, Circuit Judge.

The question here concerns **contribution** between tort-feasors where the **judgment creditor** is the wife of the tort-feasor against whom contribution is sought.

A taxicab of appellant (hereinafter called "Cab Co."), driven by its agent, and an automobile, driven by appellee (hereafter called "Dreslin"), collided. Dreslin's wife and others in his car were injured. They sued the Cab Co. for damages. Dreslin joined with them, claiming for **loss of consortium, medical expenses** for Mrs. Dreslin and damages to his automobile. Among its defenses, the Cab Co. pleaded contributory negligence of Dreslin. It also cross-claimed against him for damages to the taxicab and for contribution for any sums recovered by the other plaintiffs against it. The jury's verdict established the collision to have been caused by concurrent negligent operation of the two cars. Accordingly judgments for varying amounts were entered in favor of all plaintiffs except Dreslin. In addition a declaratory judgment was entered allowing the Cab Co. contribution against Dreslin upon the several judgments except that of Mrs. Dreslin. This was disallowed because, as the Court held, "the right to contribution arises from a joint liability", and as Dreslin was not liable in tort to his wife, there was no joint liability between him and the Cab Co. as to her. This appeal is confined to that single question.

We agree with the conclusion of the trial court. Neither husband nor wife is liable for tortious acts by one against the other. That is the common law rule. It prevails today in the District of Columbia . . .

The right of contribution arises out of a common liability. The rule "hinges on the doctrine that general principles of justice require that in the case of a common obligation, the discharge of it by one of the obligors without proportionate payment from the other, gives the latter an advantage to which he is not equitably entitled". [C] Contribution, then, depends upon joint liability. An injured party plaintiff in the suit from which a right of contribution develops must have had a cause of action against the party from whom contribution is sought. Here there was no liability by Dreslin to his wife,- no right to action against him and the Cab Co., hence nothing to which a right of contribution could attach.

The argument that it would be inequitable to allow Mrs. Dreslin to be "enriched" at the sole expense of the Cab Co., permitting her husband, equally at fault, to escape any of the burden, overlooks the fact that preservation of domestic peace and felicity is the policy upon which the rule of immunity between husband and wife is based. [Cc] The judgment is

Affirmed.

Points for Discussion

1. The court notes the common-law rule that neither a husband nor a wife is liable for the tortious acts of one spouse against the other. *See* Chapter 11 for further exploration of immunity issues.

2. As stated by the court, writing in 1950: "the preservation of domestic peace and felicity is the policy upon which the rule of immunity between husband and wife is based." Does and should that policy animate contemporary approaches to wife-husband immunity issues?

3. The court's opinion sets out the majority rule. "The contribution defendant must be a tortfeasor, and originally liable to the plaintiff. If there was never any such liability, as where the contribution defendant has the defense of family immunity, assumption of risk, or the application of an **automobile guest statute**, or the substitution of **workers' compensation** for common law liability, then there is no liability for contribution." PROSSER AND KEETON ON TORTS 339-40 (5th ed. 1984) (footnotes omitted).

Sakellariadis v. Campbell

391 Ill.App.3d 795, 909 N.E.2d 353, 330 Ill.Dec. 640 (2009)

Justice CAHILL delivered the opinion of the court:

Plaintiff Gloria Sakellariadis appeals the amount of a money judgment awarded in her action against two defendants. Plaintiff's complaint alleged she was injured in two separate car accidents that occurred three months apart. The jury found both defendants responsible for an amount totaling approximately $518,000 in damages. Before the jury returned the verdict, one of the defendants settled for $150,000. Later, the trial court entered a judgment of one half the total verdict against the remaining defendant.

Plaintiff argues on appeal that the trial court erred in awarding plaintiff only 50% of the $518,000 verdict from the nonsettling defendant. Rather, the nonsettling defendant-based on a theory of joint and several liability-should have been responsible for the entire verdict, less only the $150,000 received from the settling defendant. For the reasons that follow, based primarily on the reasoning in *Burke v. 12 Rothschild's Liquor Mart, Inc.,* 148 Ill.2d 429, 170 Ill.Dec. 633, 593 N.E.2d 522 (1992); *Yanan v. Ewing,* 205 Ill.App.3d 96, 150 Ill.Dec. 440, 562 N.E.2d 1243 (1990); and section 433A of the Restatement (Second) of Torts (Restatement) (Restatement (Second) of Torts § 433A (1965)), we reject plaintiff's theory of recovery and affirm the ruling of the trial court in all respects.

Plaintiff and defendant Steven W. Campbell had a car collision in July 2001. Plaintiff and defendant Bruce E. Walters had a car collision three months later in October 2001. Plaintiff and her husband Peter Sakellariadis filed a complaint against both defendants, alleging negligence in counts I and III and loss of consortium in counts II and IV. Plaintiff's husband later voluntarily dismissed the loss-of-consortium counts and is not a party to this appeal. Plaintiff alleged in the remaining counts I and III that each defendant's negligence proximately caused her severe and permanent injuries. She alleged defendants were jointly and severally liable for the entire judgment. The trial court determined both defendants were negligent and held a jury trial solely on the question of damages.

. . . .

The trial court tendered to the jury the verdict form proposed by plaintiff. The form required jurors to assign monetary amounts and percentages of responsibility to each defendant in 14 categories of past or future injuries. . . . . The trial court . . . instructed the jury: "If you find that both defendants proximately caused the damages in a particular category, you must place a percentage for each defendant, the sum of which must total 100 percent."

While the jury deliberated but before it reached a verdict, plaintiff entered into a settlement agreement with Campbell for $150,000. On plaintiffs' motion, the trial court found the settlement to be in good faith. The court noted that despite plaintiffs' settlement with Campbell, plaintiffs claims against Walters remained pending.

The jury returned an itemized verdict of approximately $518,000, attributing 50% of the liability to each defendant. The jury award included $200,000 for past and future pain and suffering, $102,000 for the reasonable expense of future medical care and $100,000 for future disability. The jury awarded lesser amounts for past and future back surgery, future neck surgery and other past medical care.

The trial court then entered its judgment against Walters for 50% of the jury verdict. The court concluded that plaintiff had consolidated two separate, distinct torts into a single complaint "for purposes of judicial expediency." The court further concluded that the jury had determined which accident caused which injuries and had apportioned the damages accordingly.

. . . .

We first consider whether the evidence supports plaintiff's contention that defendants were joint tortfeasors who were jointly and severally liable for the entire amount of the verdict. "The common law doctrine of joint and several liability holds joint tortfeasors responsible for the plaintiffs entire injury, allowing plaintiff to pursue all, some, or one of the tortfeasors responsible for his injury for the full amount of the damages." *Coney v. J.L.G. Industries, Inc.,* 97 Ill.2d 104, 119-120, 73 Ill Dec. 337, 451 N.E.2d 197 (1983). "Where two or more persons, under circumstances creating primary accountability, directly produce a single, indivisible injury by their concurrent negligence, they are jointly and severally liable, even though there is no common duty, common design or concerted action." [C]

The existence of a single, indivisible injury is necessary to establish that multiple defendants are jointly and severally liable. [Cc]

. . . .

If a plaintiff's injuries can be apportioned among multiple tortfeasors, then the tortfeasors are not jointly and severally liable. [Cc]

A plaintiff's allegation that she was injured twice in the same part of her body will not transform two injuries into one. [C] "Where a party negligently aggravates a preexisting injury caused by another's negligence, he has committed a tort that is separate and distinct from the tort committed by the first wrongdoer [citation], and the injuries inflicted by each are separate and distinct injuries [citation]." [C] "[I]t is the aggravation, the change in the nature of the injury or the increase in the pain, as distinguished from the original injury, for which [the second driver] is liable." [C]

. . . .

. . . Plaintiff alleged she suffered injuries in each accident. The testimony of Drs. Fournier and Stamelos supported the conclusion that the injuries in the first accident were aggravated by the second accident. The jury chose to believe these doctors rather than Drs. Walsh and Perros, who opined that plaintiff did not receive lasting injuries from the accidents. . . . [T]he fact that plaintiff was injured twice in the same parts of her body does not make the injuries indivisible. The jury here was able to reach at least a "rough estimate" to fairly apportion the damages. See Restatement (Second) of Torts § 433A(1), Explanatory Notes, Comment *b*, at 435 (1965). The jury's verdict attributing 50% of the liability for plaintiff's injuries to each defendant was not against the manifest weight of the evidence.

. . . .

Finally, plaintiff argues that the Joint Tortfeasor Contribution Act (Contribution Act) (740 ILCS 100/3 (West 2006)) supports her claim that Walters should pay the difference between Campbell's settlement and the full jury verdict. But plaintiff has failed to comply with the requirements of Supreme Court Rule 341(h)(7) (210 Ill.2d R. 341(h)(7)) in that she did not elaborate on this argument in her brief or cite relevant, persuasive authority to support her theory that the Contribution Act is outcome determinative. The failure to assert a well-reasoned argument supported by legal authority is a violation of Supreme Court Rule 341(h)(7) (210 Ill.2d R. 341(h)(7)), resulting in waiver. [C]

Practice Pointer

The court's finding of a waiver of the plaintiff's argument serves as an important reminder that the failure to comply with an appellate court's rules can result in that court's refusal to address issues not addressed or argued in briefs submitted by the parties.

Waiver aside, the Contribution Act generally does not come into play if the plaintiff collects from the defendants in accordance with the jury's assessment of their respective culpabilities. [Cc] "[I]t is only when the plaintiff collects the judgment in a manner inconsistent with the jury's determination of responsibility under the Contribution Act that any action under it is necessary." [Cc] "[The Contribution Act] provides a remedy for an entity that has paid more than its ***pro rata*** share of the common liability by allowing it to seek contribution from a fellow joint tortfeasor who has not paid his *pro rata* share of the common liability." [C]

Here, Walters paid 50% of the jury verdict which was his *pro rata* share. The Contribution Act does not come into play.

. . . .

Affirmed.

————————

Points for Discussion

1. What was plaintiff's theory of recovery?

2. Did the plaintiff suffer and seek to recover for a single, indivisible injury? What was the analytical significance of the court's answer to this question?

3. The court concluded that the Illinois Joint Tortfeasor Contribution Act did not support the plaintiff's claim. Why did the court reach this conclusion?

————————

Slocum v. Donahue

44 Mass.App.Ct. 937, 693 N.E.2d 179 (1998)

After Robert Donahue pleaded guilty to motor vehicle homicide in the death of their eighteen month old son, the Slocums filed a civil action against the Donahues alleging negligence and gross negligence. The Donahues then filed a **third-party complaint** against Ford Motor Company (Ford), denying negligence and alleging that Ford was negligent and was in breach of warranties of merchantability and fitness for a particular use. The Donahues claim that, when Robert Donahue was in the car prior to the accident, he inadvertently pushed the floor mat on the driver's side, under the throttle. When he later started to back the car down his driveway, the engine began to race and, although he repeatedly stepped on the brakes, his car continued to accelerate. The car's rear wheels hit the curb across the street from his house, became airborne, turned, and then hit a fence. When he got out of the car, he saw Todd Slocum lying on the lawn. The Donahues' expert would testify at trial that the floor mat was defective, permitting it to interfere with the operation of the vacuum booster which caused the power brakes to fail to function.[4]

Prior to trial, the Slocums and Ford signed a settlement agreement providing that Ford would pay $150,000 to the Slocums in exchange for a release of any claim. Ford then moved for summary judgment as to the Donahues' claims and on the grounds that the settlement was made in good faith and, pursuant to G.L. c. 231B, § 4, that all claims for contribution were thereby extinguished, and that there was no basis for the Donahues' claims for indemnity. . . . The Donahues appeal from the final judgment dismissing their third-party complaint against Ford.[5] We affirm.

1. *Right to contribution.* Under G.L. c. 231B, § 4, as inserted by St.1962, c. 730, § 1, "When a release ... is given in good faith to one of two or more persons liable in tort for the same injury: ... (b) It shall discharge the tortfeasor to whom it is given from all liability for contribution to any other tortfeasor." The Donahues argue on appeal that the settlement between Ford and the Slocums was not made in good faith and was collusive both because the amount of the settlement was for less than the value of the case and because Ford allegedly told the Slocums that Ford would allow them to use its experts so that the Donahues' attempt to attribute liability to Ford at trial would be unsuccessful.

The seminal Massachusetts case construing this statute in this context, *Noyes v. Raymond,* 28 Mass.App.Ct. 186, 548 N.E.2d 196 (1990), controls the instant case in material respects. The issue before the court in *Noyes* was the same as that

---

4 Robert Donahue claims that he pleaded guilty in the criminal case because he feared receiving the maximum sentence if he proceeded to trial.

5 After the entry of judgment in the third-party action in the lower court, the case of the Slocums against Robert Donahue proceeded to trial. The jury returned a verdict against Donahue.

before the court here: "whether, on the basis of the limited facts about the settlement which were before the judge in advance of trial, Joseph [Noyes] was entitled to be discharged from all liability for contribution to Raymond." [C] The basis for an exception requiring an extended hearing on the issue of good faith had not been made to appear in *Noyes* and has not been presented here.

As in *Noyes*, there were facts before the judge showing that the settlement between Ford and the Slocums was fair and reasonable. It was reasonably predictable that damages would be high and that a jury would find liability on the part of Robert Donahue, in view of the fact that he pleaded guilty in the criminal case and on the basis of his admission in his deposition that, prior to the accident, he was drinking from a bottle of vodka that he kept under the driver's seat in a brown bag. Given these facts, it was not unreasonable to think that a jury might not find any liability on the part of Ford.

According to the Donahues' attorney, in February of 1995, counsel for Ford notified the Donahues' attorney that Ford was proposing a settlement offer totaling $300,000 with $150,000 to be contributed by Ford, $125,000 by Liberty Mutual Insurance Company (the policy limits of the Donahues' insurance carrier), and $25,000 by the Donahues personally.[6] The Donahues' attorney responded that she would discuss the matter with her clients, but that $25,000 was not an amount that her clients would be financially able to contribute to the settlement. Apparently the subsequent negotiations between the Slocums and Ford occurred without the Donahues' participation. In May, 1995, the Slocums settled with Ford for $150,000. *Noyes* instructs that the purpose of the contribution statute is to promote settlement, that a low settlement figure *alone* is not evidence of "bad faith," and that settlements should be routinely approved without extended hearings if the purpose of the statute is to be served. Further, the court in *Noyes* observed that lack of good faith was evidenced by "collusion, fraud, dishonesty, and other wrongful conduct." [C] In these circumstances Ford's settlement with the Slocums for an amount contemplated as its contribution to a total settlement package does not indicate **bad faith** or collusion.

As to the Donahues' contention that the Slocums' use of experts originally retained by Ford is evidence of collusion, we disagree. In *Commercial Union Ins. Co. v. Ford Motor Co.,* 640 F.2d 210 (9th Cir.), cert. denied, 454 U.S. 858, 102 S.Ct. 310, 70 L.Ed.2d 154 (1981), cited by the Donahues, the court found that the settlement was collusive because, to some extent, it was "dictated by the tactical advantage of removing a deep-pocket defendant because of the experts it could produce" and, therefore, "[was] not made in 'good faith' consideration of the relevant liability of all parties." [C] The Donahues' argument suggests that

---

6 Counsel for the Slocums had earlier indicated to Ford's counsel that they would consider settling this matter with all parties for a total settlement package of $400,000.

there was bad faith here because the Slocums were not interested in the deep pocket of Ford, but settled with Ford because they believed that Ford was not responsible for the death of their son. Such a speculation does not trigger the necessity for a more extensive hearing on the issue of good faith. [C] The motion for summary judgment was properly allowed.

2. *Right to indemnity.* "Under G.L. c. 231B, contribution is allowed between joint tortfeasors who cause another, by reason of their wrongdoing, to incur injury or damage. In addition, ... the statute permits a plaintiff to settle with one joint tortfeasor and still have recourse against remaining tortfeasors (subject to the limitations stated in the statute). The right to contribution, unlike the right to **indemnity**, is based on the shared fault of the joint tortfeasors. Indemnity, on the other hand, allows someone who is without fault, compelled by operation of law to defend himself against the wrongful act of another, to recover from the wrongdoer the entire amount of his loss, including reasonable attorney's fees." [C] "[I]ndemnity is permitted only when the would-be indemnitee does not join in the negligent act." [C] "This right to indemnity is limited to those cases in which the would-be indemnitee is held derivatively or vicariously liable for the wrongful act of another." [C]

If the claim against Ford had gone to trial and Ford had been found liable to the Donahues,[9] it would have been as a result of its negligence or breach of warranty. "Such liability will not be derivative or vicarious in nature, nor will it be constructive rather than actual. Accordingly, the third-party plaintiffs are not entitled to indemnification...." [C]

Once Ford settled with the Slocums, the sole question for the fact finder was whether Todd Slocum's death was caused by defendant Robert Donahue's negligence. Robert Donahue was free to claim that he was not negligent and that Todd Slocum's death was caused by Ford's negligence in selling a defective product. Under no set of circumstances could the jury properly have held the Donahues liable to the Slocums for the conduct of Ford. Further, in holding Robert Donahue negligent (as they did; see note 5, *supra*) the jury concluded that he was solely negligent (or was a joint tortfeasor with Ford). His liability is not vicarious and he is not entitled to indemnification from Ford. If Ford had remained in the case, any liability on its part would have been as a joint tortfeasor, and contribution would have been required. Indemnity would not have been appropriate. "Contribution and indemnity are mutually exclusive remedies." [C] Summary judgment on the issue of indemnification was appropriate.

. . . .

Judgment affirmed.

---

9 The Slocums never made a direct claim against Ford.

Points for Discussion

1. Do you agree with the court's reading and application of Massachusetts' contribution and indemnity statutes?

2. "[I]t is important to distinguish between principles of contribution and indemnification. Contribution is defined as a sharing of the cost of an injury as opposed to a complete shifting of the cost from one to another, which is indemnification. Common liability is required between a party seeking contribution and the party from whom it is sought. . . . [P]rinciples of indemnification and contribution are not interchangeable. Indemnification is distinguishable from the closely related remedy of contribution in that the latter involves a sharing of the loss between parties jointly liable." Kuhn v. Wells Fargo Bank of Nebraska, 278 Neb. 428, 771 N.W.2d 103 (2009) (footnotes omitted).

3. Where a plaintiff does not sue and join all tortfeasors as defendants in a single lawsuit, in most states a defendant can join (i.e., **implead**) another alleged tortfeasor as a third-party defendant, or can bring a separate contribution action against a tortfeasor not made a party to the original suit.

Hypo 11-4

"A sues B and C. The factfinder finds that B and C are liable, finds that A's damages are $100,000, and assigns 40 percent responsibility to B and 60 percent responsibility to C. B pays A $40,000, either because the jurisdiction does not use joint and several liability . . . or because A chooses to recover only $40,000 from B." AMERICAN LAW INSTITUTE, A CONCISE RESTATEMENT OF TORTS 256 (2000). Can B recover contribution from C?

D. Apportioning Damages Among Tortfeasors

Dillon v. Twin State Gas & Electric Co.

85 N.H. 449, 163 A. 111 (1932)

Action for negligently causing the death of the plaintiff's **intestate**, a boy of 14. A jury trial resulted in a disagreement.

The defendant maintained wires to carry electric current over a public bridge in Berlin. In the construction of the bridge there were two spans of girders on each side between the roadway and footway. In each span the girders at each end sloped upwards towards each other from the floor of the bridge until connected by horizontal girders about nineteen feet above the floor.

The wires were carried above the framework of the bridge between the two rows of girders. To light the footway of the bridge at its center a lamp was hung from a bracket just outside of one of the horizontal girders and crossing over the end of the girder near its connection with a sloping girder. Wires ran from a post obliquely downward to the lamp and crossed the horizontal girder a foot or more above it. The construction of the wire lines over and upon the bridge is termed aerial. The wires were insulated for weather protection but not against contact.

The decedent and other boys had been accustomed for a number of years to play on the bridge in the daytime, habitually climbing the sloping girders to the horizontal ones, on which they walked and sat and from which they sometimes dived into the river. No current passed through the wires in the daytime except by chance.

The decedent, while sitting on a horizontal girder at a point where the wires from the post to the lamp were in front of him or at his side, and while facing outwards from the side of the bridge, leaned over, lost his balance, instinctively threw out his arm, and took hold of one of the wires with his right hand to save himself from falling. The wires happened to be charged with a high voltage current at the time and he was electrocuted.

. . . .

ALLEN, J.

. . . .

The circumstances of the decedent's death give rise to an unusual issue of its cause. In leaning over from the girder and losing his balance he was entitled to no protection from the defendant to keep from falling. Its only liability was in exposing him to the danger of charged wires. If but for the current in the wires he would have fallen down on the floor of the bridge or into the river, he would without doubt have been either killed or seriously injured. Although he died from electrocution, yet, if by reason of his preceding loss of balance he was bound to fall except for the intervention of the current, he either did not have long to live or was to be maimed. In such an outcome of his loss of balance, the defendant deprived him, not of a life of normal expectancy, but of one too short to be given **pecuniary** allowance, in one alternative, and not of normal, but of limited, earning capacity, in the other.

If it were found that he would have thus fallen with death probably resulting, the defendant would not be liable, unless for conscious suffering found to have been sustained from the shock. In that situation his life or earning capacity had no value. To constitute actionable negligence there must be damage, and damage is limited to those elements the statute prescribes.

If it should be found that but for the current he would have fallen with serious injury, then the loss of life or earning capacity resulting from the electrocution would be measured by its value in such injured condition. Evidence that he would be crippled would be taken into account in the same manner as though he had already been crippled.

His probable future but for the current thus bears on liability as well as damages. Whether the shock from the current threw him back on the girder or whether he would have recovered his balance, with or without the aid of the wire he took hold of, if it had not been charged, are issues of fact, as to which the evidence as it stands may lead to different conclusions.

Exception overruled.

————————

Michie v. Great Lakes Steel Division, National Steel Corporation

495 F.2d 213 (6th Cir. 1974)

EDWARDS, Circuit Judge.

This is an **interlocutory appeal** from a District Judge's denial of a motion to dismiss filed by three corporations which are defendants-appellants herein. . . .

Appellants' motion to dismiss was based upon the contention that each plaintiff individually had failed to meet the requirement of a $10,000 amount in controversy for diversity jurisdiction set forth in 28 U.S.C. § 1332 (1970).

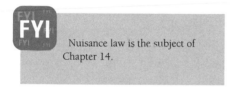

Nuisance law is the subject of Chapter 14.

The facts in this matter, as alleged in the pleadings, are somewhat unique. Thirty-seven persons, members of thirteen families residing near LaSalle, Ontario, Canada, have filed a complaint against three corporations which operate seven plants in the United States immediately across the Detroit River from Canada. Plaintiffs claim that pollutants emitted by plants of defendants are noxious in character and that their discharge in the ambient air violates various municipal and state ordinances and laws. They assert that the discharges represent a **nuisance** and that the pollutants are carried by air currents onto their premises in Canada, thereby damaging their persons and property. Each plaintiff individually claims damages ranging from $11,000 to $35,000 from all three corporate defendants jointly and severally. There is, however, no assertion of joint action or **conspiracy** on the part of defendants.

Make the Connection

Conspiracy, an agreement by two or more persons to commit a crime, is covered in a Criminal Law course.

. . . .

We believe the principal question presented by this appeal may be phrased thus: Under the law of the State of Michigan, may multiple defendants, whose independent actions of allegedly discharging pollutants into the ambient air thereby allegedly create a nuisance be jointly and severally liable to multiple plaintiffs for numerous individual injuries which plaintiffs claim to have sustained as a result of said actions, where said pollutants mix in the air so that their separate effects in creating the individual injuries are impossible to analyze.

. . . .

In Maddux v. Donaldson, 362 Mich. 425 (108 N.W.2d 33) the Michigan Supreme Court cites Landers v. East Texas Salt Water Disposal Company, 151 Tex. 251, 248 S.W.2d 731, a pollution case, in support of the above stated proposition. The court indicated that

"... it is clear that there is a manifest unfairness in 'putting on the injured party the impossible burden of proving the specific shares of harm done by each .... Such results are simply the law's callous dullness to innocent sufferers. One would think that the obvious meanness [sic] of letting wrongdoers go scot free in such cases would cause the courts to think twice and to suspect some fallacy in their rule of law'."

. . . .

It is the opinion of this court that the rule of Maddux, supra, and Landers, supra, cited therein is the better, and applicable rule in this air pollution case.

On this point we affirm the decision of the District Judge. This complaint appears to have been filed under the diversity jurisdiction of the federal courts. All parties have agreed that Michigan law alone controls.

Like most jurisdictions, Michigan has had great difficulty with the problems posed in tort cases by multiple causes for single or indivisible injuries. [Cc]

. . . .

We believe that the issue was decided in the lengthy consideration given by the Michigan court in the Maddux case. There Justice Talbot Smith (now Senior Judge, United States District court for the Eastern District of Michigan, Southern Division) in an opinion for the court majority (joined by the writer of this opinion) held:

"It is our conclusion that if there is competent testimony, adduced either by plaintiff or defendant, that the injuries are factually and medically separable, and that the liability for all such injuries and damages, or parts thereof, may be allocated with reasonable certainty to the impacts in turn, the jury will be instructed accordingly and mere difficulty in so doing will not relieve the triers of the facts of this responsibility. This merely follows the general rule that 'where the independent concurring acts have caused distinct and separate injuries to the plaintiff, or where some reasonable means of apportioning the damages is evident, the courts generally will not hold the tort-feasors jointly and severally liable.'

"But if, on the other hand, the triers of the facts conclude that they cannot reasonably make the division of liability between the tort-feasors, this is the point where the road of authority divides. Much ancient authority, not in truth precedent, would say that the case is now over, and that plaintiff shall take nothing. Some modern courts, as well, hold that his is merely the case of the marauding dogs and the helpless sheep relitigated in the setting of a modern highway. The conclusion is erroneous. Such precedents are not apt. When the triers of the facts decide that they cannot make a division of injuries we have, by their own finding, nothing more or less than an indivisible injury, and the precedents as to indivisible injuries will control. They were well summarized in Cooley on Torts in these words: 'Where the negligence of two or more persons concur in producing a single, indivisible injury, then such persons are jointly and severally liable, although there was no common duty, common design, or concert action." Maddux v. Donaldson, 362 Mich. 425, 432-433, 108 N.W.2d 33, 36 (1961). . . .

. . . .

We recognize, of course, that the *Maddux* and *Watts* cases both involve multiple collisions causing allegedly indivisible injuries. Hence, appellants are free to argue that the rule stated does not necessarily apply to the nuisance category of torts with which we deal here. Indeed, appellants call our attention to what appears to be a contrary rule applicable to nuisance cases referred to in the *Maddux* opinion. Restatement of Torts (First) § 881.

In the latest Restatement, however, both the old and the newer rule are recognized and as the Michigan court held in *Maddux*, the question of whether liability of alleged polluters is joint or several is left to the trier of the facts. Where the injury itself is indivisible, the judge or jury must determine whether or not it is practicable to apportion the harm among the tortfeasors. If not, the entire liability may be imposed upon one (or several) tortfeasors subject, of course, to subsequent right of contribution among the joint offenders.

Perhaps the best summary of the rationale for such a rule is found in Harper and James:

> In the earlier discussion of the substantive liability of joint tort-feasors and independent concurring wrongdoers who have produced indivisible harm it was indicated that there were four categories into which these parties may be placed: situations in which (1) the actors knowingly join in the performance of the tortious act or acts; (2) the actors fail to perform a common duty owed to the plaintiff; (3) there is a special relationship between the parties (e.g., master and servant or joint entrepreneurs); (4) although there is no concerted action nevertheless the independent acts of several actors concur to produce indivisible harmful consequences.

While the Restatement of Torts contains a short and apparently simple statement of the rule in category four, this type of situation has caused a great deal of disagreement in the courts. Here joint and several liability is sometimes imposed for the harm caused by the independent concurring acts of a number of persons. In all the situations in which such recovery is permitted the court must find first that the harm for which the plaintiff seeks damages is "indivisible." This can mean that the harm is not even theoretically divisible (as death or total destruction of a building) or that the harm, while theoretically divisible, is single in a practical sense so far as the plaintiff's ability to apportion it among the wrongdoers is concerned (as where a stream is polluted as a result of refuse from several factories). In the first type of case almost uniformly courts will permit entire recovery from any or all defendants. There is conflict, however, in the second situation, with some well-reasoned recent cases recognizing that the plaintiff's right to recover for his harm should not depend on his ability to apportion the damage but that this is a problem which is properly left with the defendants themselves. 1 F. Harper & F. James, The Law of Torts § 10.1 at 697-98, 701-02 (1956) (Footnotes omitted.)

. . . .

Assuming plaintiffs in this case prove injury and liability as to several tort-feasors, the net effect of Michigan's new rule is to shift the **burden of proof** as to which one was responsible and to what degree from the injured party to the wrongdoers. The injustice of the old rule is vividly illustrated in an early Michigan case, Frye v. City of Detroit, 256 Mich. 466, 239 N.W. 886 (1932). There a pedestrian was struck by an automobile, thrown in the path of a street car and struck again. Since his widow could not establish which impact killed him, a verdict was directed against her case.

. . . .

Make the Connection

The Supreme Court's *Erie* decision and a federal judge's role and function in a diversity case is addressed in a Civil Procedure course.

In this diversity case Michigan law is not finally and conclusively declared. The District Judge, under Erie R. Co. v. Tompkins, 304 U.S. 64, 58 S.Ct. 817, 82 L.Ed. 1188 (1938), had to seek to establish what the Supreme Court of Michigan would do with this case on the basis of what it has already decided. Like the District Judge, we believe that the Michigan courts would apply the Maddux principles to the case at bar. Under Maddux, each plaintiff's complaint should be read as alleging $11,000 or more in damages against each defendant. Therefore, the principle of Zahn v. International Paper Co., 414 U.S. 291, 94 S.Ct. 505, 38 L.Ed.2d 511 (1973), which would disallow aggregation of plaintiffs' claims for the purpose of establishing diversity jurisdiction, does not apply to this case.

. . . .

As modified, the judgment of the District Court is affirmed.

Points for Discussion

1. "It is the general rule that one injured by the negligence of another is entitled to recover the damages proximately caused by the act of the tortfeasor, and the burden of proof is upon the plaintiff to establish that the damages he seeks were proximately caused by the negligence of the defendant." Bruckman v. Pena, 29 Colo. App. 357, 487 P.2d 566 (1971).

2. Commenting on *Dillon*, one analyst stated: "This case does not deal with an instance of strictly concurrent causation. The loss of balance and incipient fall were accomplished facts, the serious consequences of which were certain, before the defendant's wrong became an operative cause. Within the decision are the broad propositions that in the absence of a concurrent wrong a negligent party is not liable beyond the damages shown to have been caused by his negligence, and that in actions for injury to the person, the injured person's danger from other factors, at the time of harm, must be considered." Robert J. Peaslee, *Multiple Causation and Damage*, 47 Harv. L. Rev. 1127 (1934).

3. Proposition: Courts should adopt the following rule in multiple-defendant pollution cases: Polluters should not be held jointly and severally liable where plaintiffs cannot demonstrate the specific monetary damage caused by each defendant. Agree or disagree?

RESTATEMENT (THIRD) OF TORTS:
APPORTIONMENT OF LIABILITY (2000)

§ 26. Apportionment of Liability When Damages Can Be Divided by Causation

(a) When damages for an injury can be divided by causation, the factfinder first divides them into their individual component parts and separately apportions liability for each indivisible component part . . .

(b) Damages can be divided by causation when the evidence provides a reasonable basis for the factfinder to determine:

(1) that any legally culpable conduct of a party or other relevant person to whom the factfinder assigns a percentage of responsibility was a legal cause of less than the entire damages for which the plaintiff seeks recovery and

(2) the amount of damages separately caused by that conduct.

Otherwise, the damages are indivisible and thus the injury is indivisible. . . .

Bondy v. Allen

635 N.W.2d 244 (Minn. App. 2001)

LINDBERG, Judge.

Appellant Kathryn Bondy and her husband, John, sued an ambulance service that transported her to a Rochester hospital after she was struck by a car. The district court granted summary judgment in favor of the ambulance service. Appellants argue that their expert testimony established a genuine issue of material fact as to causation. We affirm.

. . . .

Appellant Kathryn Bondy (Bondy) was a pedestrian in a designated crosswalk when a vehicle traveling 30 to 40 miles per hour struck her in November 1994. The vehicle was owned by respondent Jeffrey Allen and driven by respondent Carey Allen. Bondy sustained multiple injuries, particularly to her left hip and pelvis.

Respondent Gold Cross Ambulance Service, Inc., was called to the accident scene to transport Bondy to the emergency room. At the accident scene, Gold Cross paramedic Kenneth Schweim assessed Bondy's physical condition and concluded she was alert and oriented to her surroundings. Schweim checked her airway, breathing, and circulation and did not observe any distortion of her limbs. He then palpated her lower torso because he knew that was a fragile area, which may have been injured. Bondy did not indicate that she experienced pain during the palpations. Bondy was rolled onto her side, placed on a backboard, and secured with safety straps. The backboard was then secured to a gurney with additional safety straps across Bondy and placed in the ambulance. Bondy's husband, John, traveled in the front of the ambulance.

In the ambulance during transport, Schweim continued to assess and treat Bondy . . . He unfastened one or two safety straps around Bondy's leg and torso to remove a coat placed on her at the accident scene. Two or three straps remained fastened. At some point thereafter, the movement of the ambulance caused Bondy's left leg to slide off the backboard, allowing her foot to touch the floor below the gurney. Bondy, who had been moaning in the ambulance, screamed at this point.

Schweim immediately returned Bondy's leg to the backboard and gurney, refastened the lower straps he had previously removed, and continued the examination and treatment. When the ambulance arrived at the hospital, Bondy was turned over to the hospital's care.

The Bondys sued (1) Carey and Jeffrey Allen; (2) the City of Rochester; and (3) Gold Cross Ambulance Service. The Bondys settled with the city before the scheduled trial date. Their claims against Gold Cross for negligent training and driving were also dismissed. Gold Cross moved for summary judgment on the negligence claim for allowing Bondy's leg to slide off the gurney, arguing there was inadequate proof that the "gurney incident" caused any compensable damage. The district court initially denied summary judgment.

. . . .

The case was set for trial in November 2000. After the jury was selected and opening statements were given, the Bondys and the Allens settled. The Allens agreed to pay their insurance policy limits and Carey Allen admitted liability for striking Bondy. Gold Cross then moved to exclude all evidence relating to damage caused by Carey Allen, arguing that evidence should be limited to damage allegedly caused by Gold Cross. The district court did not rule on this motion. Instead, the court . . . granted summary judgment against the Bondys. This appeal follows.

. . . .

The Bondys . . . argue that the Allens and Gold Cross are joint tortfeasors and that the district court erred in determining that they are not subject to the single-indivisible-injury rule. They contend that because the injuries Bondy suffered are not clearly susceptible to apportionment between the initial accident and the gurney incident, they should be subject to the single-indivisible-injury rule. The Bondys assert that Gold Cross and the Allens are jointly and severally liable, unless Gold Cross and the Allens can clearly establish which damages resulted solely from their respective actions. The Bondys argue that the district court improperly placed the burden of apportioning the injuries on them.

FYI

The court's discussion of appellate court examination of the district court's decision sets out the differing standards applicable to review questions of law and mixed questions of law and fact.

Whether parties are subject to the single-indivisible-injury rule (SII rule) is a question of law. [C] An appellate court is not bound by, and need not give deference to, the district court's decision on a question of law. [C] Also, court rulings on mixed questions of law and fact are not binding on an appellate court and are subject to independent review. [C]

Joint and several liability is imposed under the SII rule when "two or more persons acting independently cause harm to a third person through consecutive acts of negligence closely related in point of time." [C] The harm must be incapable of division. [C]

. . . .

No Minnesota case has applied the SII rule to hold a medical defendant jointly and severally liable with the tortfeasor who caused the original injury for which treatment was provided. Restatement (Second) of Torts § 433A cmt. c (1965) states that an original tortfeasor may be liable not only for harm he inflicted, but also for "additional damages resulting from the negligent treatment of the injury by a physician." But a physician providing treatment may be liable only for *additional harm* caused by negligent treatment. *Id.* The Restatement groups physicians and other medical personnel together when addressing the distinct liability of the original tortfeasor for additional harm resulting from efforts of third parties rendering aid to an injured person. [C]

Minnesota and other jurisdictions have held that a negligent medical defendant in a situation similar to this one is a subsequent tortfeasor who can be held liable only for aggravating the original injury. *See Couillard v. Charles T. Miller Hosp., Inc.,* 253 Minn. 418, 427, 92 N.W.2d 96, 102 (1958) (finding doctor was subsequent tortfeasor, rather than joint tortfeasor, where doctor misdiagnosed a fractured vertebra after a fall on public bus); *see also U.S. Lines, Inc. v. United States,* 470 F.2d 487, 491 (5th Cir.1972) (stating tortfeasor and physician subsequently aggravating injury are not joint tortfeasors and physician not liable to original tortfeasor under any theory of contribution); *Stuart v. Hertz Corp.,* 351 So.2d 703, 705 (Fla.1977) (stating original tortfeasor and doctor aggravating injury not joint tortfeasors, but distinct and independent tortfeasors).

In effect, Bondy's injuries from the accident constituted a pre-existing condition when the ambulance was called to the scene. The Allens and Gold Cross were, at best, successive tortfeasors. To hold Gold Cross liable for injuries that occurred before the ambulance arrived on the scene would have a chilling effect on the provision of emergency care and is simply inconsistent with existing caselaw.

. . . .

Affirmed.

Points for Discussion

1. Did the court determine that the Allens and Gold Cross were joint or successive tortfeasors? Do you agree with the court's position?

2. Consider and critique the court's "chilling effect" rationale.

Chapter 12

Immunities

An **immunity** is an absolution from tort liability based on a defendant's status in society or with the plaintiff. Immunities recognize that there are certain individuals, entities, and activities in which some members of our society engage that are so important to society as a whole that the benefit of insulation from suit outweighs the injury caused by any tortious conduct. Historically, tort law recognized immunities of defendants in tort actions between spouses, parents, and children as well as suits brought by employees against their employers. The law also recognized immunity status for charitable entities and governmental entities at the state, local, and federal levels. However, immunity protections have eroded over the years. The cases in this chapter provide an overview of traditional immunity doctrines as applied to families, charities, employers, governmental entities, and public officials. As you consider the following cases, take careful note of the public policy concerns at play in the courts' decisions.

Make the Connection

Unlike immunities, privileges – discussed in Chapter 3 (Defenses to Intentional Torts) and Chapter 6 (Defenses (and Partial Defenses) to Negligence Actions) – depend on the *facts* of the particular case, not on the *status* of the defendant.

A. Families

Heino v. Harper

759 P.2d 253 (Or. 1988)

GILLETTE, Justice.

We are asked in this case to reconsider the rule of law in Oregon that a person is immune from liability for negligent torts committed against his or her spouse. This court first announced the rule for this state as a matter of common law in

Smith v. Smith, 205 Or. 286, 287 P.2d 572 (1955); *See also Apitz v. Dames*, 205 Or. 242, 287 P.2d 585 (1955); [cc]. Upon further consideration, however, we now agree with the overwhelming number of jurisdictions which have concluded that the public policy rationale traditionally asserted in favor of a doctrine of interspousal immunity for negligent torts does not support the rule.[1] Accordingly, we hold that the common-law rule of interspousal immunity is no longer available in this state to bar negligence actions between spouses.

---

1 Our research shows that the rule of interspousal immunity for negligent torts enjoys the following status in the United States:

A. *Doctrine fully abrogated:*

1. Alabama: Penton v. Penton, 223 Ala. 282, 135 So. 481 (1931).
2. Alaska: Cramer v. Cramer, 379 P.2d 95 (Alaska 1963).
3. Arkansas: Leach v. Leach, 227 Ark. 599, 300 S.W.2d 15 (1957).
4. California: Klein v. Klein, 58 Cal.2d 692, 26 Cal.Rptr. 102, 376 P.2d 70 (1962).
5. Colorado: Rains v. Rains, 97 Colo. 19, 46 P.2d 740 (1935).
6. Connecticut: Brown v. Brown, 88 Conn. 42, 89 A. 889 (1914) (intentional tort); Bushnell v. Bushnell, 103 Conn. 583, 131 A. 432 (1925) (negligence).
7. Indiana: Brooks v. Robinson, 259 Ind. 16, 284 N.E.2d 794 (1972).
8. Iowa: Shook v. Crabb, 281 N.W.2d 616 (Iowa 1979).
9. Kansas: Flagg v. Loy, 241 Kan. 216, 734 P.2d 1183 (1987).
10. Kentucky: Brown v. Gosser, 262 S.W.2d 480 (Ky.1953).
11. Maine: MacDonald v. MacDonald, 412 A.2d 71 (Me.1980).
12. Maryland: Boblitz v. Boblitz, 296 Md. 242, 462 A.2d 506 (1983).
13. Massachusetts: Brown v. Brown, 381 Mass. 231, 409 N.E.2d 717 (1980).
14. Michigan: Hosko v. Hosko, 385 Mich. 39, 187 N.W.2d 236 (1971).
15. Minnesota: Beaudette v. Frana, 285 Minn. 366, 173 N.W.2d 416 (1969).
16. Mississippi: Burns v. Burns, 518 So.2d 1205 (Miss.1988).
17. Missouri: S.A.V. v. K.G.V., 708 S.W.2d 651 (Mo.1986).
18. Montana: Miller v. Fallon County, 222 Mont. 214, 721 P.2d 342 (1986).
19. Nebraska: Imig v. March, 203 Neb. 537, 279 N.W.2d 382 (1979).
20. New Hampshire: Gilman v. Gilman, 78 N.H. 4, 95 A. 657 (1915).
21. New Jersey: Merenoff v. Merenoff, 76 N.J. 535, 388 A.2d 951 (1978).
22. New Mexico: Maestas v. Overton, 87 N.M. 213, 531 P.2d 947 (1975).
23. New York: State Farm Mut. Auto Ins. Co. v. Westlake, 35 N.Y.2d 587, 364 N.Y.S.2d 482, 324 N.E.2d 137 (1974).
24. North Carolina: Crowell v. Crowell, 180 N.C. 516, 105 S.E. 206 (1920).
25. North Dakota: Fitzmaurice v. Fitzmaurice, 62 N.D. 191, 242 N.W. 526 (1932).
26. Ohio: Shearer v. Shearer, 18 Ohio St. 3rd 94,480 N.E.2d 388 (1985).
27. Oklahoma: Courtney v. Courtney, 184 Okl. 395, 87 P.2d 660 (1938).
28. Pennsylvania: Hack v. Hack, 495 Pa. 300, 433 A.2d 859 (1981).
29. South Carolina: Pardue v. Pardue, 167 S.C. 129, 166 S.E. 101 (1932).
30. South Dakota: Scotvold v. Scotvold, 68 S.D. 53, 298 N.W. 266 (1941).
31. Tennessee: Davis v. Davis, 657 S.W.2d 753 (Tenn.1983).
32. Texas: Price v. Price, 732 S.W.2d 316 (Tex.1987).
33. Utah: Stoker v. Stoker, 616 P.2d 590 (Utah 1980).
34. Washington: Freehe v. Freehe, 81 Wash.2d 183, 500 P.2d 771 (1972).
35. West Virginia: Coffindaffer v. Coffindaffer, 161 W.Va. 557, 244 S.E.2d 338 (1978).
36. Wisconsin: Wait v. Pierce, 191 Wis. 202, 209 N.W. 475 (1926).
37. Wyoming: Tader v. Tader, 737 P.2d 1065 (Wyo.1987).
38. District of Columbia: D.C.Code Ann. § 30-201 (1981); Turner v. Taylor, 471 A.2d 1010 (D.C.App.1984).

The facts, as alleged in plaintiff's complaint, present a typical case of interspousal negligence. On May 5, 1982, plaintiff Dorothy Heino (wife) was riding as a passenger in an automobile driven by her husband, defendant Arno Heino (husband). At an intersection in north Portland, husband turned left into the path of an oncoming automobile driven by defendant Harper. The resulting collision injured wife. Wife filed a complaint alleging, *inter alia,* that husband was negligent in failing to keep a proper lookout, in failing to keep his automobile under proper control, and in failing to yield the right-of-way.[3] In his answer, husband asserted the defense of interspousal immunity. Based on that defense, he filed a motion for summary judgment. The trial court allowed the motion and entered final judgment in husband's favor. The Court of Appeals affirmed, citing *Moser v. Hampton, supra. Heino v. Harper,* 81 Or.App. 106, 723 P.2d 1082 (1986) (per curiam). We reverse.

. . . .

HISTORY OF COMMON-LAW INTERSPOUSAL IMMUNITY FROM TORT

This court first was called upon to declare whether the rule of interspousal immunity for negligent torts existed in Oregon in *Smith v. Smith, supra.* In approaching the problem, the court said little about the English common-law antecedents of the doctrine, stating only:

B. *Doctrine abrogated in specific circumstances:*
    1. Arizona: Fernandez v. Romo, 132 Ariz. 447, 646 P.2d 878 (1982) (automobile accidents).
    2. Georgia: Harris v. Harris, 252 Ga. 387, 313 S.E.2d 88 (1984) (husband and wife separated).
    3. Idaho: Rogers v. Yellowstone Park, 97 Idaho 14, 539 P.2d 566 (1974) (automobile accident).
    4. Nevada: Rupert v. Stienne, 90 Nev. 397, 528 P.2d 1013 (1974) (automobile accident).
    5. Rhode Island: Digby v. Digby, 120 R.I. 299, 388 A.2d 1 (1978) (automobile accident); Asplin v. Amica Mut. Ins. Co., 121 R.I. 51, 394 A.2d 1353 (1978) (doctrine inapplicable where one spouse dies as a result of the other's negligence).
    6. Vermont: Richard v. Richard, 131 Vt. 98, 300 A.2d 637 (1973) (automobile accident).
    7. Virginia: Korman v. Carpenter, 216 Va. 86, 216 S.E.2d 195 (1975) (wrongful death); Surratt v. Thompson, 212 Va. 191, 183 S.E.2d 200 (1971) (automobile accident). But see Counts v. Counts, 221 Va. 151, 266 S.E.2d 895 (1980) (interspousal immunity barred former husband's recovery against former wife for personal injuries intentionally inflicted on him at her direction).
C. *Doctrine retained for negligent torts:*
    1. Delaware: Alfree v. Alfree, 410 A.2d 161 (Del.1979).
    2. Florida: Raisen v. Raisen, 379 So.2d 352 (Fla.1979).
    3. Hawaii: Peters v. Peters, 63 Hawaii 653, 634 P.2d 586 (1981).
    4. Illinois: Ill.Ann.Stat. Ch. 40 ¶ 1001 (Smith-Hurd Supp.1986).
    5. Louisiana: L.Rev.Stat.Ann. § 9:291 (West Supp.1988). Under this section, a divorced spouse may sue the ex-spouse for personal injuries inflicted during the marriage. Duplechin v. Toce, 497 So.2d 763 (La.App.1986). Also, spouses who are judicially separated may sue each other for torts committed after the separation. Bondurant v. Bondurant, 386 So.2d 705 (La.App.1980).
    6. Oregon: Moser v. Hampton, 67 Or.App. 716, 679 P.2d 1379,aff'd by an equally divided court, 298 Or. 171, 690 P.2d 505 (1984).
3 Wife later amended her complaint to allege that she and her husband were separated and had lived apart since 1978. Our disposition of this case does not depend on the fact that the parties are alleged to be separated.

"No judicial decisions need be cited for the proposition that at early common law neither spouse could maintain [an] action against the other for either a personal or a property tort, whether it was committed before or during marriage. The common-law rule of non-liability has been universally recognized. ...."

[C] While this statement was accurate as far as it went, it failed fully to acknowledge how utterly different were the times and circumstances that saw the creation of the rule from those that prevailed when the *Smith* court chose to recognize the rule in Oregon.

The most comprehensive study of the doctrine of interspousal immunity in tort is found in Professor McCurdy's article cited by the court in *Smith: Torts Between Persons in Domestic Relation,* 43 Harv L Rev 1030 (1930). We turn to that article for a brief overview of the origins of the doctrine in England.

"[At common law a] husband was entitled to his wife's services and earnings whether performed in the home or elsewhere, for himself or another; and the husband was under a duty to support. A married woman had no capacity to sue or be sued alone in her own name, but wherever she had a substantive capacity, or was substantively the holder of a right, or subject to a duty, suit must be brought in the name of husband and wife, and judgment was enforced in favor of the husband or against both husband and wife. In the case of torts committed against a married woman, her legal personality was substantively recognized, and insofar as the tortious act caused injury to a legally recognized interest of the woman herself, it was a chose in action of the woman's [although, as already noted, the husband was entitled to its use and any action for its enforcement had to be brought in his name as well.] * * * [I]nsofar as the injury was to the husband alone, either by depriving him of some interest, such as services and earnings, or by increasing the burden of his duties, such as support, it was a chose in action of the husband's. And the converse is likewise true. A married woman substantively had capacity to commit most torts, but her liability was in a sense suspended during **coverture**, and the husband subjected. If she committed a tort during marriage, or committed a tort or contracted a debt before marriage, although the duty was substantively hers, suit must be brought against husband and wife, and judgment could be enforced against property of either * * *."

> **What's That?**
>
> "Coverture" is an archaic term meaning the condition of being a married woman.

Id. at 1032-33 (footnotes omitted).

The effect of these and related disabilities and reciprocal obligations with respect to the property of either spouse had the cumulative effect at common law of making it impossible for one spouse to be civilly liable to the other for an act that, but for the relationship, would have been an actionable tort. *Id.* at 1033. As McCurdy explained it,

> "[w]here the [tortious] act occurred before marriage, a cause of action arose. If the man was the tortfeasor, the woman's right would be a chose in action, which upon marriage the man would have the right to reduce to possession [in himself]. This union in one person of the right-duty relation discharges the duty as a matter of substance, and there is besides the procedural difficulty that the husband would be both plaintiff and defendant. If the woman was the tortfeasor, the man's right would be a chose in action against the woman, whose duty upon marriage would devolve upon the husband as a derivative duty, which would be discharged by union of the right and duty in the same person; and there is the same procedural difficulty. Where the act occurs during coverture, the matter is complicated by other factors[, but the same procedural difficulties would exist throughout, *i.e.,* any such action would feature the husband as both plaintiff and defendant-an unacceptable anomaly] * * *."

[C] As the foregoing suggests, it is difficult to state with absolute certainty whether the real impediment to interspousal tort actions at common law was substantive, procedural, or both. It nevertheless is clear that, whatever label is affixed to it, the rule arose out of views of the rights and duties of the parties to a marriage as that institution existed several hundred years ago in a society that viewed the relationship far differently than it is viewed today. ...

[T]o refer to this state of the law, as did the court in *Smith v. Smith, supra,* as the "common-law rule of non-liability" is an inaccurate oversimplification. The rule did not deny the responsibility of one spouse to make reparation for harm done to the other; it merely regarded the incidents of the relationship of marriage as the answer to the wrong. Where the husband was the wrongdoer, his duty to support the wife already existed; where the wrongdoer was the wife, any action against her had to include her husband as a defendant, and so the claim merged. It remained for the enactment of various Married Women's Property Acts in the nineteenth century to provide the impetus for doing away with the bars to most kinds of litigation between spouses. [C] . . . [I]n spite of those changes..., the old rule of interspousal immunity for negligent torts was found still to be alive when, in 1955, this court first faced the issue. We turn now to a specific discussion of the Oregon experience.

OREGON CASES DEALING WITH INTERSPOUSAL IMMUNITY FROM TORT

As noted, the question of the existence of interspousal immunity as a part of the common law of Oregon came relatively late to this court. When it came, in 1955, it came in tandem with a case involving an intentional tort committed by one spouse against another. The two cases gave this court an opportunity to announce both the existence of the rule of interspousal immunity for tort and the limitations on the scope of that rule.

The negligence case was *Smith v. Smith, supra.* ...

....

We have examined the court's reasoning in *Smith* ... in order to identify fully all the rationales the court found to lead ... to its conclusion that the common-law rule should be judicially recognized in Oregon. From this examination, we glean the following rationales: (1) No right of action for negligence has been granted between spouses by the Oregon Constitution or legislative enactment; (2) allowance of such actions would be contrary to the policy of the law to foster tranquility in the marital relationship; (3) allowance of such actions would lead to collusive actions designed to defraud insurance carriers; (4) allowance of such actions would lead to a great number of cases being brought, far too many of which would involve circumstances so trivial that they should not permit recovery although they technically do involve negligent torts. To these we think there may fairly be added a fifth rationale, never specifically advanced by the court but implicit in its entire examination of the issue: the legislature, which over the years has vastly overhauled the legal relationship of spouses in a number of different ways, has sufficiently occupied this field of the law so that it is appropriate to leave to that body any further adjustments, including adjustments in the capacity of spouses to sue each other.

On the same day that it announced *Smith,* the court also made clear that the common-law incapacity of spouses to sue each other in tort extended only to negligent torts; intentional torts between spouses were actionable. The case announcing this principle was *Apitz v. Dames, supra.*

In *Apitz v. Dames, supra,* the executor of a deceased wife brought an action against the estate of the deceased husband for wrongful death. Husband had intentionally shot and killed his wife and then killed himself. The trial court dismissed the case on the ground of interspousal immunity from tort. The Supreme Court reversed.

....

The court had two questions to dispose of in *Apitz*. First, it had to determine whether the fact that one or both of the parties to the alleged tort was dead made a difference, *i.e.,* whether the death of either spouse, without more, created a situation to which the common-law rule did not apply. Second, assuming the death of either or both spouses was not relevant, it had to decide whether the rationale for interspousal immunity for negligent torts extended also to intentional torts.

The court [first] concluded that the death of either or both parties was irrelevant. ...

....

[T]he court [next] turned to the issue that also concerns us-could the wife have sued the husband for intentionally shooting her if the result had not been fatal? As to this question, the court found the better reasoned authorities to allow such actions.

The court began by reviewing decisions from other jurisdictions holding that the infliction of an intentional tort on one spouse by the other spouse was actionable. Perhaps the most vivid material the court cited came from *Crowell v. Crowell,* 180 N.C. 516, 105 S.E. 206 (1920), a case in which a wife sued her husband for assault and battery by infecting her with a venereal disease:

> "Whether a man has laid open his wife's head with a bludgeon, put out her eye, broken her arm, or poisoned her body, he is no longer exempt from liability to her on the ground that he vowed at the altar to 'love, cherish and protect' her. Civilization and justice have progressed thus far with us, and never again will 'the sun go back ten degrees on the dial of Ahaz.' Isaiah, 38:8."

Crowell v. Crowell, supra, 180 N.C. at 524, 105 S.E. 206, *cited in Apitz v. Dames, supra,* 205 Or. at 259, 287 P.2d 585.

....

Turning from the case law to the treatises and other writings, the court, somewhat surprisingly, found support and solace in the following now-familiar statement from Dean Prosser:

> "'The chief reason relied upon by all these courts, however, is that personal tort actions between husband and wife would disrupt and destroy the peace and harmony of the home, which is against the policy of the law. This is on the bald theory that after a husband has beaten his wife, there is a state of peace and harmony left to be disturbed; and

that if she is sufficiently injured or angry to sue him for it, she will be soothed and deterred from reprisals by denying her the legal remedy-and this even though she has left him or divorced him for that very ground, and though the same courts refuse to find any disruption of domestic tranquillity if she sues him for a tort to her property, or brings a criminal prosecution against him. * * * '"

Id. at 264, 287 P.2d 585 (quoting Prosser, Law of Torts 903-04, § 99 (1941)). ... The court went on to consider various other writings and found them generally accommodating of the idea of making intentional interspousal torts actionable.

....

Thus, after *Apitz* and *Smith,* the state of the common law in Oregon was that a husband or wife was responsible to the other for intentional, but not negligent, torts.

....

IDENTIFICATION AND ANALYSIS OF KEY ELEMENTS FAVORING AND OPPOSING INTERSPOUSAL IMMUNITY FOR NEGLIGENT TORTS

From the foregoing discussion of the Oregon cases, it is possible to set forth the principal competing theoretical arguments advanced for and against retention of the doctrine of interspousal immunity for negligent torts. We do so here in outline form in order to facilitate further discussion and analysis:

A. Factors Favoring Retention of the Immunity Doctrine:

1. Maintenance of peace in the marital relationship;

2. Prevention of collusion between parties in litigation;

3. Practical difficulties in applying fully tort principles to a relationship as close and intimate as the marital relationship.

4. The doctrine should be abolished by the legislature, if at all.

B. Factors Favoring Abolition of the Immunity Doctrine:

1. Where the tort is intentional, marital harmony is already lost; the same is probably true whenever one spouse is prepared to sue the other;

2.   Litigation between spouses on every other kind of legal theory presently is permissible; saving out only negligent torts is neither symmetrical nor otherwise rational;

3.   Almost every other jurisdiction has abolished the doctrine.

The foregoing outline of the competing arguments assumes one thing—that the disability at common law was substantive; *i.e.,* that the negligent infliction of harm by a spouse on the person of the other spouse was not a tort. As already indicated, the *Apitz* court seemed to assume as much, although it never got around to explaining itself. The question is important because, if the disability were only a procedural one imposed by the common-law courts as an incident of those courts' understanding of the consequences of marriage for the separate existence of husband or wife, we could now simply declare—as the *Smith* court ought to have done, in those circumstances—the disability abolished because the reasons for it are no longer present. We turn to that question.

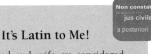

It's Latin to Me!

"Husband and wife are considered one person in law." To sue one is to sue both.

"Vir et uxor sunt quasi unica persona, quia caro una et sanguis unus." [c] ...

....

ANALYSIS

....

... As things now stand, the only kind of legal action not permitted between spouses is one for negligent injury to the person. Every other kind of action, whether that brought by a spouse as a partner seeking an accounting, as an injured party seeking damages for an intentional tort, or even as an injured party seeking damages for negligent injury to property (as opposed to the person), is available. Cohabitation and other circumstances assumed to accompany the marital relationship may call for different standards of care than that required among strangers, and may require that any action for negligent personal injury be subject to such defenses as privilege, but there is nothing in the relationship that calls for absolute immunity.

Moreover, as was also true in *Winn v. Gilroy, supra,* the Restatement (Second) Torts speaks to the issue. The Restatement rule regarding interspousal torts parallels the rule recognized by this court in the case of parent-child torts. Restatement (Second) Torts § 895F (1979) provides:

> "(1) A husband or wife is not immune from tort liability to the other solely by reason of that relationship.

> "(2) Repudiation of general tort immunity does not establish liability for an act or omission that, because of the marital relationship, is otherwise privileged or is not tortious."

§ 895F does not affirmatively create any claim. It simply denies that a status -- that of spouse -- *bars* any otherwise permissible action. [C] The Restatement rule postulates that, because of the nature of the marital relationship, conduct that might be tortious as against a stranger would not be tortious as against one's spouse; considerations similar to such doctrines as consent and privilege may render conduct between spouses nontortious.

B. The Policy (Smith) Analysis

… We turn now to a brief analysis of the policy arguments advanced in support of retention of the *Smith* rule.

1. The rule fosters marital harmony

This argument assumes that abolition of the *Smith* doctrine would encourage enmity between spouses. Would the abolition of common-law interspousal immunity for negligent torts have that effect? There are no studies or other sources or authorities that provide us with a definitive answer to this question, and its answer is one that this court is ill-equipped to posit on its own. [C]

2. Prevention of collusion

The fear of collusion is entirely a product of the relatively recent phenomenon of widely available insurance. But, as this court already has held, the presence or absence of insurance has nothing to do with the substantive obligations one party may have toward another apart from the contract of insurance itself. [C] This factor is not relevant.

3. Practical difficulties

Much is made of the fact that husband and wife live in a relationship so close and so intimate that it guarantees that there will be incidents of negligence by the spouses on a scale unparalleled in any other relationship of life. …

...Because of the nature of the marital relationship, conduct that would be tortious as against a stranger might not be tortious as against one's spouse; considerations similar to such doctrines as consent and privilege may render conduct between spouses nontortious. We think that resort to these doctrines sufficiently alleviates any practical difficulties.

4. Other reasons

It also can be argued ... that, if the doctrine of interspousal immunity for negligent torts is to be abolished, that action should be taken by the legislature. We reject this argument ....

Of course, the legislature could abolish interspousal immunity, or change it, or reenact it if changed. Common law decisions do not preclude legislative reaction; they often invite it. Moreover, the legislature has entered the field in a significant way--the statutes contain comprehensive laws relating to marriage, divorce, children and related matters. [C] But this is not a matter in which the legislature has purported to pre-empt the field. Both the legislative and judicial branches remain competent to act.

And, while we have competence, we should not hide from our responsibilities on the ground that someone else shares them. The rule we consider today is judge-made. If it is no longer valid or appropriate, it is our responsibility to say so. It must be remembered that any answer we give has substantive effect—deferring to the legislature leaves the present rule in place just as fully as if we had affirmatively declared it for the first time.

[W]e now conclude that the rule of interspousal immunity for negligent personal injury to a spouse also should be abolished. Restatement (Second) Torts § 895F correctly states the law of Oregon.

The decision of the Court of Appeals is reversed; the judgment of the trial court is reversed and the case is remanded to the trial court for further proceedings consistent with this opinion.

Points for Discussion

1. Spousal immunity to tort liability has been abolished in the majority of jurisdictions, although a respectable number of jurisdictions still recognize it as a viable doctrine. What were the policy considerations favoring spousal immunity? What are the policy considerations disfavoring it?

2. Do you agree or disagree with recognition of spousal immunity? Why?

3. Was the *Heino* court correct to take into consideration the availability of insurance in making its decision?

4. Is the abolition of the spousal immunity doctrine more appropriately addressed by courts or by legislatures?

5. Husband and Wife are married. During their marriage, Husband assaults Wife, breaking her arm. Should application of the spousal immunity doctrine prevent Wife from recovering from Husband? *See* Self v. Self, 58 Cal.2d 683 (Ca. 1962) (abolishing spousal immunity doctrine for intentional torts). What if Wife was injured while cleaning her husband's negligently maintained boat? *See* Klein v. Klein, 58 Cal.2d 692 (Ca. 1962) (abolishing spousal immunity for negligent torts).

———————————

Zellmer v. Zellmer

188 P.3d 497 (Wash. 2008)

MADSEN, J.

Three-year-old Ashley McLellan drowned in a backyard swimming pool while under the supervision of her stepfather, Joel Zellmer. The trial court ruled the parental immunity doctrine shields Zellmer from liability for negligence in connection with her death. Petitioners Stacey Ferguson[1] and Bruce McLellan, Ashley's biological parents, challenge that ruling. They contend the parental immunity doctrine should be abolished in favor of a reasonable parent standard. Alternatively, they argue the doctrine does not apply under the facts of this case.

We reaffirm that the doctrine of parental immunity precludes liability for negligent parental supervision, but not for a parent's wanton or willful failure to supervise a child. [C] We decline to recognize an exception for wrongful death actions. We further hold the parental immunity doctrine

> **It's Latin to Me!**
>
> Non constat jus civile a posteriori
>
> *In loco parentis* means "in the place of a parent."

———————————

1 Following the commencement of this action, Ashley's mother changed her surname from "Zellmer" to "Ferguson." ... To avoid confusion, we address her as Stacey Ferguson.

shields a stepparent to the same extent as a biological or adoptive parent, so long as the stepparent stands **in loco parentis** to the child. However, we agree with petitioners that summary judgment was improper because Zellmer's loco parentis status is a question of fact that may not be decided as a matter of law on this record. Thus, we reverse the summary judgment order.

FACTS

About four months after they met, Ferguson and Zellmer got married. ... Ferguson had a three-year-old daughter, Ashley, from a previous marriage. They moved to Zellmer's house on the day of the marriage, September 6, 2003. Ordinarily, Ashley went to day care while Ferguson worked. On December 3, 2003, however, Ashley stayed home sick. ... Zellmer agreed to take care of her.

According to Zellmer, at about 5:00 p.m. he started a video for Ashley in her bedroom and then went downstairs to build a fire. About an hour later, he realized she was no longer in her room. He noticed the sliding glass door leading to the backyard was open. He went outside and found Ashley floating in the swimming pool. He pulled her out and called 911. The paramedics resuscitated Ashley, but she died in the hospital two days later.

Ferguson and McLellan sued Zellmer for **wrongful death**, alleging several causes of action including negligence, negligent supervision, willful and wanton misconduct, breach of contract, negligent infliction of emotional distress, and outrage. ...

Zellmer moved for **summary judgment**. He claimed the parental immunity doctrine shielded him from liability for negligence in connection with Ashley's death. ... He asserted he stood in loco parentis to Ashley because he provided her financial and emotional support, including housing, meals, and day care. According to Zellmer, Ashley referred to him as "Daddy," and he treated her as his own daughter.

In opposition to the summary judgment motion, Ferguson disputed Zellmer's characterization of his relationship with Ashley. She denied Zellmer supported Ashley financially. She said he was unemployed throughout their marriage and she and McLellan provided for Ashley's needs. According to Ferguson, Ashley spent little time with Zellmer and was still uncomfortable around him on the day she drowned. She said "Joel and Ashley were not even close and Joel did not stand in place of a parent for Ashley." ... She said Zellmer was "impatient and short with Ashley and acted in an intimidating manner to her." Ferguson did not allow him to discipline Ashley because she did not think he knew her well enough to do so. ...

....

Ferguson described the 88 days she and Ashley lived with Zellmer as "marked by turmoil." ... She claimed Zellmer assaulted her twice, causing her to take Ashley and go stay with her parents. On the day Ashley drowned, Ferguson moved out of Zellmer's house permanently.

McLellan stated he paid child support for Ashley and exercised his visitation rights regularly following the dissolution of his marriage to Ferguson. ... According to McLellan, he paid half of Ashley's day care and medical insurance and continued to provide financial and emotional support. Ashley always referred to him as "Dad," and referred to Zellmer as "Joel." ... [McLellan] was actively involved in Ashley's life as her father since the day she was born and intended to do so until he died. [McLellan stated that, "b]ased on my observations it would be inaccurate to say that Ashley ever hoped that Joel Zellmer would play a parental role in her life." ...

     ....

The trial court granted summary judgment in favor of Zellmer. The trial court criticized the parental immunity doctrine but reasoned so long as the doctrine remains viable in Washington, it should apply to stepparents as well as to natural parents. The trial court concluded Zellmer necessarily stood in loco parentis to Ashley by virtue of assuming the status of stepparent: "when there is a marriage ceremony and there is a blended family and someone becomes a stepparent that the doctrine of parental immunity applies, and there does not have to be a finding of in loco parentis." ...

On appeal, the Court of Appeals recognized stepparents "do not earn the benefit of immunity simply by virtue of marriage to a legal parent." *Zellmer v. Zellmer,* 132 Wash.App. 674, 681, 133 P.3d 948 (2006). Reasoning that parental immunity is a "reciprocal benefit arising from a legally enforceable financial responsibility," *id.,* the Court of Appeals held a stepparent who is obligated to financially support a stepchild under the family support statute, RCW 26.16.205, is shielded by parental immunity from liability for negligent supervision of the child. *Zellmer,* 132 Wash.App. at 682, 133 P.3d 948. Because such an obligation generally arises when a stepparent is married to the child's primary residential parent and lives in the same household with the child, the Court of Appeals concluded such a stepparent would be protected by parental immunity, except in "rare circumstances." Finding no such exceptional circumstances here, the Court of Appeals affirmed the trial court.

We accepted review of the Court of Appeals decision. ...

ANALYSIS

Petitioners urge us to abolish the parental immunity doctrine. They assert the rule of parental immunity lacks modern justification and should be discarded in favor of a "reasonable parent" standard in cases of negligent supervision.

In its original form, the parental immunity doctrine operated as a nearly absolute bar to suit by a child for personal injuries caused by a parent, no matter how wrongful the parent's conduct. *See, e.g., Roller v. Roller,* 37 Wash. 242, 79 P. 788 (1905) (father raped daughter); *McKelvey v. McKelvey,* 111 Tenn. 388, 77 S.W. 664 (1903) (stepmother inflicted cruel and inhumane treatment on stepson); *Hewellette v. George,* 68 Miss. 703, 9 So. 885 (1891) (mother falsely imprisoned child in insane asylum). The parental immunity doctrine originated in three decisions near the turn of the last century and was quickly adopted by most states. [C] From its inception, however, the doctrine has been subject to extensive critical commentary. [C] Like other courts, this court has disavowed several of the original rationales underlying the doctrine, while sharply limiting its scope. Today, no jurisdiction recognizes the original formulation of the common law parental immunity doctrine, and we need not repeat our reasons for retreating from it. [Cc]

The evolution of the parental immunity doctrine in Washington is consistent with the national trend. Washington was one of the first states to recognize the parental immunity doctrine. [C] However, this court has exercised its continuing duty to determine whether the doctrine remains supported by reason and common sense in view of changing social realities, and to modify it as necessary. [C] Like other jurisdictions, this court has substantially limited the scope of parental immunity in accordance with changing views of public policy on the family relation. A parent is not immune when acting outside his or her parental capacity. [Cc] For example, when operating a business or driving a car, a parent owes a child the same duty of reasonable care applicable to the world at large, and may be held liable notwithstanding the parent/child relationship. Even when acting in a parental capacity, a parent who abdicates his or her parental responsibilities by engaging in willful or wanton misconduct is not immune from suit.[2] *See Hoffman v. Tracy,* 67 Wash.2d 31, 406 P.2d 323 (1965) (driving while intoxicated); *Livingston v. City of Everett,* 50 Wash.App. 655, 660, 751 P.2d 1199 (1988) (parent left four-year-old child unattended in a small room with two Doberman pinschers).

But this court has consistently held a parent is not liable for ordinary negligence in the performance of parental responsibilities. *Jenkins,* 105 Wash.2d 99, 713 P.2d 79 (disallowing contribution claim where parents allowed child to wander free in neighborhood; child electrocuted at utility power station); *Talarico v.*

---

2 "Willful" requires a showing of actual intent to harm, while "wanton" infers such intent from reckless conduct. [C]

Foremost Ins. Co., 105 Wash.2d 114, 712 P.2d 294 (1986) (disallowing negligent supervision claim where parent started backyard fire then left three-year-old son unattended, resulting in severe burns); *Baughn v. Honda Motor Co.,* 105 Wash.2d 118, 119, 712 P.2d 293 (1986) (disallowing contribution claim where parents allowed sight-impaired child to ride motorbike, resulting in fatal crash); *Stevens v. Murphy,* 69 Wash.2d 939, 421 P.2d 668 (1966) (disallowing suit against divorced parent who negligently injured children while transporting them home from a scheduled visitation), *overruled in part by Merrick,* 93 Wash.2d at 413, 610 P.2d 891;*DeLay v. DeLay,* 54 Wash.2d 63, 337 P.2d 1057 (1959) (disallowing negligence action against parent who instructed son to siphon gas, resulting in burn injuries); *Cox v. Hugo,* 52 Wash.2d 815, 329 P.2d 467 (1958) (disallowing contribution claim against parent who failed to prevent child from wandering into neighbor's yard where she was burned by trash fire).

There are two principal routes by which courts have concluded that children may not sue their parents for negligent supervision. Under the approach first … courts recognize a limited form of parental immunity for personal injuries resulting from the negligent exercise of parental authority and ordinary parental discretion. [C] The American Law Institute subsequently approved[,] although the approach codified in the *Restatement* is grounded in a concept of parental privilege rather than immunity. *See* RESTATEMENT (SECOND) OF TORTS § 895G (1979). Under the *Restatement,* "the proper inquiry concerns the tortious or privileged nature of a parent's act that causes injury to the child, not a special parental immunity from a child's action for personal torts as distinct from other kinds of claims." *Winn v. Gilroy,* 296 Or. 718, 681 P.2d 776, 784 (1984). Parents are not immune from suit by virtue of the parent/child relationship. The *Restatement* recognizes that in the course of exercising parental discipline and parental discretion, parents may be privileged to act in a manner that would be deemed tortious if directed at a stranger. RESTATEMENT, *supra,* § 895G (repudiation of general tort immunity does not create new liabilities for parents for conduct otherwise privileged or not tortious based on the parent/child relationship); [c].

> **FYI**
>
> The RESTATEMENT (SECOND) OF TORTS § 895G(1), Parent and Child, provides, "A parent or child is not immune from tort liability to the other solely by reason of that relationship."

States that either abolished the parental immunity doctrine or declined to adopt it in the first instance nonetheless have followed the *Restatement,* disallowing negligent supervision claims based on the concept of a parental privilege. *See Brunner v. Hutchinson Div.,* 770 F.Supp. 517, 525 (D.S.D.1991) (parental privilege must be construed broadly enough to respect the sphere of parental discretion and avoid judicial second-guessing of parental judgment); [c].

There now appears to be nearly universal consensus that children may sue their parents for personal injuries caused by intentionally wrongful conduct.[3] However, the overwhelming majority of jurisdictions hold parents are not liable for negligent supervision of their child, whether stated in terms of a limited parental immunity (among jurisdictions that have partially abrogated the parental immunity doctrine), parental privilege (among those that either abolished the immunity doctrine outright or declined to adopt it in the first instance), or lack of an actionable parental duty to supervise. [Cc]

A minority of states have followed the lead of the California Supreme Court, allowing children to sue parents for negligent supervision under a "reasonable parent" standard. [Cc].

In a trio of cases decided in 1986, we "reaffirmed the vitality of the doctrine of parental immunity with respect to assertions of negligent supervision." [Cc] We expressly rejected the "reasonable parent" standard and concluded the better approach was to continue to recognize a limited form of parental immunity in cases of ordinary negligence when a parent is acting in a parental capacity. In explaining our decision, we stated:

> Parents should be free to determine how the physical, moral, emotional, and intellectual growth of their children can best be promoted. [C] Parents should not routinely have to defend their child-rearing practices where their behavior does not rise to the level of wanton misconduct. There is no correct formula for how much supervision a child should receive at a given age.

Jenkins, 105 Wash.2d at 105, 713 P.2d 79 [internal quotation marks omitted].

The petitioners offer no persuasive arguments for overruling [our precedent]. Instead, they direct much of their criticism at long-discarded rationales underlying the original form of the parental immunity doctrine. Following *Jenkins,* the primary objective of the modern parental immunity doctrine is to avoid undue judicial interference with the exercise of parental discipline and parental discretion. This rationale remains as vital today as it was in 1986. Parents have a right to raise their children without undue state interference. [Cc] In exercising that right, parents are in need of a "wide sphere of discretion." *Borst,* 41 Wash.2d at 656, 251 P.2d 149.

---

3 However, the legislature of one state has enacted a strict form of parental immunity. *See* La.Rev.Stat. Ann. 9:571 (barring suit by unemancipated child against custodial parent or legal custodian). In a few states, courts have declined to abrogate the judicially created parental immunity doctrine on the grounds such a change should come from the legislature. *See Warren v. Warren,* 336 Md. 618, 650 A.2d 252 (1994) (declining to abrogate parental immunity in the case of motor vehicle torts, while refusing to extend it to stepparents); *Hurst v. Capitell,* 539 So.2d 264 (Ala.1989) (retaining parental immunity with limited exception in cases of sexual abuse); *Richards v. Richards,* 599 So.2d 135 (Fla.Dist.Ct.App.) (disallowing intentional tort claim by child), *review dismissed,*604 So.2d 487 (Fla.1992).

The petitioners argue the parental immunity doctrine is inconsistent with our abolition of interspousal tort immunity. [Cc] The concurrence/dissent similarly points to the erosion of judicial support for tort immunity as a basis for declining to extend the parental immunity doctrine to stepparents. [C] Unlike in the case of interspousal tort immunity, however, an important public policy interest continues to justify a limited form of parental immunity. The parental immunity doctrine is similar to the "discretionary functions" exception applicable under the federal tort claims act and the "business judgment rule," which protects the discretionary decision-making of business executives. [Cc] In each instance, the purpose of immunity is to provide sufficient breathing space for making discretionary decisions, by preventing judicial second-guessing of such decisions through the medium of a tort action. [Cc]

Even those states that have adopted the "reasonable parent" standard recognize that holding parents liable for ordinary negligence in connection with the discharge of parental duties threatens to unduly interfere with the parent/child relationship. [Cc]

The reasonable parent standard does not adequately protect against undue judicial interference in the parent/child relationship. First, it should be noted that substituting "parent" for "person" is of little consequence, as a judge or jury always is required to consider the status of the actor in applying the reasonable person standard in a negligence case. Thus, the "reasonable parent" standard is, in fact, the ordinary negligence standard. Subjecting parents to liability for negligent supervision inevitably allows judges and juries to supplant their own views for the parent's individual child-rearing philosophy.

Thus, we continue to agree with those jurisdictions that have declined to permit an action for negligent parental supervision, as it accords too little respect for family autonomy and parental discretion. [Cc]

We adhere to the parental immunity doctrine as it relates to claims of negligent parental supervision. We reaffirm our holding in *Jenkins* that parents are immune from suit for negligent parental supervision, but not for willful or wanton misconduct in supervising a child. [C]

The petitioners ask us to adopt an exception in cases where the alleged negligence results in a child's death. They argue the parental immunity doctrine lacks justification when the parent/child relationship no longer exists. We find the argument unpersuasive. The primary purpose of the doctrine is to avoid the chilling effect tort liability would have on a parent's exercise of parental discipline and parental discretion. *See Borst,* 41 Wash.2d at 656, 251 P.2d 149 ("If such suits were common-place, or even possible, the freedom and willingness of the father and mother to provide for the needs, comforts and pleasures of the family would be seriously impaired. Public policy therefore demands that parents be given immunity from such suits while in the discharge of parental duties."). In view of that purpose, whether the conduct complained of results in death rather than some lesser injury affords no reasonable basis for distinction.

Courts that have held to the contrary based their decision on the "family harmony" rationale, which this court has renounced. [C] As stated by the Court of Appeals, Division Three: "Since the underlying reasons for granting parental immunity are unaffected by the demise of a family member, the mere fact the cause of action is for wrongful death will not abrogate the parental immunity doctrine." *Chhuth v. George,* 43 Wash.App. 640, 647, 719 P.2d 562 (1986) (denying contribution claim against parent for negligent supervision of child who was fatally injured while crossing the street).

Next, petitioners argue it would be inappropriate to extend the parental immunity doctrine to stepparents in view of the modern trend to limit or abolish it.

Notwithstanding the limitations courts have placed on the scope of conduct shielded by the parental immunity doctrine, a majority of states addressing the issue hold it applies to stepparents who stand in loco parentis to the same extent as to legal parents. [Cc]

Authority to the contrary exists only in jurisdictions where stepparents either have no legal obligation to support a child, [c] or where parental immunity otherwise bars suit in the case of motor vehicle torts,[4] [Cc]. In recognition of the waning support for a broad rule of parental immunity, these jurisdictions have restricted its application to biological or adoptive parents, thus limiting the scope of persons to whom it applies rather than the range of conduct it protects.

This court has, more appropriately, limited the *scope of conduct* protected by the parental immunity doctrine to conform to changing societal views about the appropriate boundaries of parental discretion. State interference in the parent/child relationship is deemed justified under a broader range of circumstances than formerly recognized. Our legislature has narrowed the range of unfettered parental discretion through the enactment of statutes designed to protect children from abuse and exploitation. Because this court already has placed appropriate limitations on the scope of the parental immunity doctrine to accord with its modern rationale, restricting the scope of parental immunity to biological and adoptive parents is unwarranted.[5]

---

4 Most jurisdictions abrogated parental immunity in the case of motor vehicle torts, reasoning that mandatory automobile liability insurance renders it unnecessary to bar suit in order to preserve family finances or family harmony. *See Warren,* 336 Md. at 622 n. 1, 650 A.2d 252 (noting only eight states continue to apply the parental immunity doctrine in cases of motor vehicle torts).

5 The concurrence/dissent refers to the parental immunity doctrine's "weak rationale" to explain its

No court has allowed a stepparent to claim parental immunity solely by virtue of his or her marriage to the injured child's biological parent. [C] This is consistent with the common law rule that a stepparent gains no parental rights and assumes no obligations merely by reason of the relationship. [Cc] On the other hand, a stepparent standing in loco parentis has a common law duty to support and educate a child to the same extent as does a natural parent. [Cc]

The term "in loco parentis" … refers to a person who has put himself or herself in the situation of a lawful parent by assuming all obligations incident to the parental relation without going through the formalities of legal adoption and embodies the two ideas of assuming the status and discharging the duties of parenthood.

We agree with those courts that find no principled distinction between a legal parent and a stepparent who assumes all the obligations and exercises all the responsibilities of parenthood, as the public policy reasons supporting immunity for a biological or adoptive parent apply equally to one standing in loco parentis. As the Court of Appeals stated, stepparents need the same "wide sphere of discretion as legal parents" when they have assumed the responsibility to discipline and educate a child. [Cc]

A stepparent may or may not act as a parent with respect to a given child. Whether a stepparent stands in loco parentis is primarily a question of intent to be determined in view of the facts of each case. [Cc] The intention required to create an in loco parentis relationship "should not lightly or hastily be inferred." [C] The relevant focus is the stepparent's overall relationship with the child, rather than with the particular conduct upon which the child's complaint is based. [Cc]

The Court of Appeals held "stepparents who are obligated to support stepchildren under the family support statute are protected by the immunity doctrine to the same extent as legal parents." [C] We agree with the rule adopted by the Court of Appeals, but disagree with its application to the facts of this case. [A] stepparent is not subject to the family support statute unless he or she has established a loco parentis relationship with a child, which requires more than merely taking a child into one's home or exercising temporary custody and control. [Cc]

....

[A] factual inquiry into the stepparent/child relationship is necessary to ensure the application of parental immunity. [Such an inquiry] does not unjustly

unwillingness to extend protection to stepparents. Concurrence/dissent at 509. The modern parental immunity doctrine is solidly rooted in the public policy to protect the exercise of parental discretion. Moreover, as discussed above, there has been a remarkable convergence of opinion that allowing negligent parental supervision claims is bad public policy, even among those jurisdictions that either abolished the parental immunity doctrine or declined to adopt it in the first instance. The concurrence/dissent addresses an obsolete form of the parental immunity doctrine.

deprive a child of the right to seek legal redress. The parent immunity doctrine represents a balance between the child's right to be fairly compensated for personal injuries resulting from another's wrongful conduct and the parents' right to raise a child free from undue judicial interference. The infringement of the child's right is deemed justified in view of several premises, including: the natural bond of affection between a parent and child renders the deterrent purpose of civil liability unnecessary; civil liability is unnecessary to make an injured child whole as a parent already is financially responsible for the child; the intimacy of the parent/child bond makes a parent uniquely situated to judge what is best for a child; and the parent actually has the right to exercise parental discipline and parental discretion on behalf of the child. The loco parentis requirement serves the purpose of ensuring the validity of these premises as applied to a stepparent who claims the protection of parental immunity.

    ....

The loco parentis relationship should be found to exist only if the facts and circumstances show the stepparent intends to assume the responsibilities of a legal parent not only in providing financial support but also with respect to educating, instructing, and caring for the child's general welfare. [C] This is generally a question of fact that should not be resolved as a matter of law when the issue is in conflict and different inferences may reasonably be drawn from the evidence.

We agree with the petitioners that a genuine issue of fact exists as to whether Zellmer stood in loco parentis to Ashley. It is undisputed Zellmer had been married to Ashley's primary residential parent for 88 days, he provided Ashley with housing for a majority of that time, and Ashley's mother at least occasionally entrusted her to his care.

If this case involved a controversy as to Zellmer's liability under the family support statute, his declaration of intent to assume the status of parent, in conjunction with his marriage to Ashley's residential parent, would constitute an admission that could support summary judgment on the issue of his loco parentis status. In this case, however, his declaration is self-serving and subject to dispute.

    ....

The undisputed facts do not establish as a matter of law that Zellmer stood in loco parentis to Ashley. ...

    ....

Taking into account the short duration of the relationship, and viewing the facts in the light most favorable to the nonmoving party, a genuine issue of material fact exists as to whether Zellmer stood in loco parentis to Ashley. Thus, summary judgment was improper.

CONCLUSION

We confirm the viability of the parental immunity doctrine and hold it applies to a stepparent who genuinely stands in loco parentis to an injured child to the same extent as to a legal parent. We decline to recognize an exception where the alleged negligence resulted in a child's death. However, a genuine issue of material fact exists as to whether Zellmer established a loco parentis relationship with Ashley. Thus, we reverse the summary judgment order and remand for further proceedings consistent with this opinion.

WE CONCUR: RICHARD B. SANDERS, SUSAN OWENS, MARY E. FAIRHURST, JAMES M. JOHNSON, JJ., and BOBBE J. BRIDGE, **J. Pro Tem.**

ALEXANDER, C.J., (concurring/dissenting).

What's That?

A judge pro tempore is a judge appointed to occupy a position temporarily or for the time being.

I agree with the majority that the trial court erred in granting summary judgment in favor of Ashley McLellan's stepfather, Joel Zellmer, on the basis that Zellmer's loco parentis status is a question of fact that may not be decided as a matter of law on this record. Therefore, I concur in the majority's decision to the extent that it reverses the trial court's summary judgment order. However, for reasons set forth hereafter, I dissent from the majority's determination that parental immunity should be extended to a stepparent. Consequently, I favor reversing the summary judgment order on grounds that, as a stepparent, Joel Zellmer has no immunity from a suit against him for the wrongful death of Ashley McLellan. That being the case, it is, in my view, unnecessary for us to resolve the question of whether Zellmer was in loco parentis to his stepchild.

The parental immunity doctrine … has heretofore applied only to a birth or adoptive parent (hereinafter parent). [Cc] This doctrine should not be extended to stepparents for several reasons. The first is that support for the general concept of parental immunity has been steadily eroding over the last several decades in jurisdictions around the nation. We noted this very point over 25 years ago in *Merrick v. Sutterlin,* 93 Wash.2d 411, 414, 610 P.2d 891 (1980), saying: "The trend of many modern cases is to limit or entirely abolish parental immunity."[2]

---

2 Judicial support for the general concept of immunity from tort liability has been waning in this state for some time. In that regard, this court has consigned two common law immunity doctrines to the legal dustbin, notably interspousal immunity in *Freehe v. Freehe,* 81 Wash.2d 183, 500 P.2d 771 (1972), *overruled in part on other grounds by Brown v. Brown,* 100 Wash.2d 729, 675 P.2d 1207 (1984)

Indeed, the highest courts in six jurisdictions, Hawaii, Nevada, North Dakota, Utah, Vermont, and the District of Columbia, declined to adopt the doctrine in the first place.[3] Furthermore, courts of last resort in 11 states that once recognized the doctrine have subsequently abolished it. Of the remaining states where parental immunity is still recognized, many have limited the circumstances under which the doctrine can be applied by creating exceptions to its application.[5] Finally, courts in four jurisdictions that recognize the parental immunity doctrine have explicitly refused to extend the same immunity to stepparents.[6]

This court has followed the trend of limiting the circumstances where parental immunity is recognized. ...

....

While I am not presently advocating that we overrule the ... case in which we first adopted the doctrine of parental immunity, I heartily assert that we should decline to extend the doctrine to stepparents. Declining to extend the doctrine to stepparents would not interfere with any discretion that a stepparent possesses. It would simply preclude them from establishing immunity for tortious conduct that results in injuries to their stepchild.

Furthermore, the majority is precisely right--I make reference to the above-mentioned obsolete forms of the parental immunity doctrine because it is evidence of the shrinking value of this antiquated doctrine of parental immunity. We should recognize the weak rationale underlying the doctrine and the trend here and in other jurisdictions to limit its application.

The second reason I have for concluding that we are ill advised to extend the doctrine to stepparents is that there is a substantial difference between the legal

---

and charitable immunity in *Friend v. Cove Methodist Church, Inc.,* 65 Wash.2d 174, 396 P.2d 546 (1964). Governmental immunity, which existed in this state for many years by statute, was rendered extinct in the 1960s by the legislature's adoption of RCW 4.92.090 and RCW 4.96.010.

3 *Broadbent v. Broadbent,* 184 Ariz. 74, 907 P.2d 43 (1995); *Gibson v. Gibson,* 3 Cal.3d 914, 92 Cal.Rptr. 288, 479 P.2d 648 (1971); *Anderson v. Stream,* 295 N.W.2d 595 (Minn.1980); *Hartman v. Hartman,* 821 S.W.2d 852 (Mo.1991); *Briere v. Briere,* 107 N.H. 432, 224 A.2d 588 (1966); *Guess v. Gulf Ins. Co.,* 96 N.M. 27, 627 P.2d 869 (1981); *Gelbman v. Gelbman,* 23 N.Y.2d 434, 245 N.E.2d 192, 297 N.Y.S.2d 529 (1969); *Shearer v. Shearer,* 18 Ohio St.3d 94, 480 N.E.2d 388 (1985); *Winn v. Gilroy,* 296 Or. 718, 681 P.2d 776 (1984); *Falco v. Pados,* 444 Pa. 372, 376, 282 A.2d 351 (1971); *Elam v. Elam,* 275 S.C. 132, 268 S.E.2d 109 (1980).

5 *See Hebel v. Hebel,* 435 P.2d 8 (Alaska 1967); *Streenz v. Streenz,* 106 Ariz. 86, 471 P.2d 282 (1970); *Williams v. Williams,* 369 A.2d 669 (Del.1976); *Ard v. Ard,* 414 So.2d 1066 (Fla.1982); *Nocktonick v. Nocktonick,* 227 Kan. 758, 611 P.2d 135 (1980); *Sorensen v. Sorensen,* 369 Mass. 350, 339 N.E.2d 907 (1975); *Transamerica Ins. Co. v. Royle,* 202 Mont. 173, 656 P.2d 820 (1983); *Unah v. Martin,* 676 P.2d 1366 (Okla.1984); *Silva v. Silva,* 446 A.2d 1013 (R.I.1982); *Smith v. Kauffman,* 212 Va. 181, 183 S.E.2d 190 (1971); *Lee v. Comer,* 159 W.Va. 585, 224 S.E.2d 721 (1976).

6 *See Burdick v. Nawrocki,* 21 Conn.Supp. 272, 274, 154 A.2d 242 (1959); *C.M.L. v. Republic Servs., Inc.,* 800 N.E.2d 200, 209 (Ind.Ct.App.2003); *Warren v. Warren,* 336 Md. 618, 628, 650 A.2d 252 (1994); *Rayburn v. Moore,* 241 So.2d 675, 676 (Miss.1970).

duties of a parent and those of a stepparent. It is, of course, universally recognized that parents have a statutory and common law duty to support and maintain their minor children. ... In contrast, this court has held that noncustodial parents do not have responsibility equal to that of the parents for the support of stepchildren. [C] For stepparents, unlike parents, the obligation to support a stepchild terminates as a matter of law on decree of dissolution, legal separation, or death. [C] In extending parental immunity to stepparents, the majority provides them with the blanket protections afforded to a parent despite the absence of reciprocal obligations. In sum, the policy reasons underlying the parental immunity doctrine do not warrant extending the doctrine to stepparents.

For the aforementioned reasons, I dissent from the majority's determination to extend the parental immunity doctrine to stepparents who stand in loco parentis to a stepchild. At the same time, I concur with the judgment of the majority that the trial court's summary judgment order should be reversed.

WE CONCUR: CHARLES W. JOHNSON and TOM CHAMBERS, JJ.

———————————

Points for Discussion

1. Should the parental immunity doctrine shield parents from liability for torts committed against their children? What are the public policy arguments in favor of the parental immunity doctrine? Against?

2. Are the same public policy considerations at play in a lawsuit brought by a parent against his or her child for injuries caused by the child's tortious conduct? What about siblings or other kin suing one another in tort? *See, e.g.,* RESTATEMENT (SECOND) OF TORTS § 895H (providing that "[b]rothers and sisters or other kin are not immune from tort liability to one another by reason of that relationship").

3. About what do the majority and concurring/dissenting judges agree and disagree? By which opinion are you most persuaded? Why?

4. What legal relevance, if any, should be placed on the fact that the mother changed her name following the commencement of this lawsuit?

5. Should any parental immunity doctrine be equally applicable to step-parents?

6. Child was seriously injured by a riding lawnmower operated by his father. At the time of the injury, the father was working for his employer. Child sued

the employer under the doctrine of *respondeat superior* for the negligence of its employee, the father. The law in the jurisdiction is clear that Child could not sue his father due to the parental immunity doctrine. But can Child sue his father's employer for the negligence of its employee? *See* Riordan v. Corporation of the Presiding Bishop of the Church of Jesus Christ of Latter-Day Saints, 242 F.Supp.2d 635 (W.D. Mo. 2003) (permitting Child's lawsuit against employer, even though employee father is immune from liability).

B. Charities

Picher v. Roman Catholic Bishop of Portland et al.

974 A.2d 286 (Me. 2009)

SILVER, J.

William Picher appeals from a judgment of the Superior Court (Kennebec County, *Marden, J.*) granting a summary judgment to the Roman Catholic Bishop of Portland on its affirmative defense of charitable immunity. Picher argues that we should abrogate the doctrine of charitable immunity for acts of negligence associated with the sexual abuse of a minor, and that we should not extend the doctrine to intentional torts. We hold that the doctrine should not be abrogated as to Picher's negligence claims because we see no basis for permitting charitable immunity as a defense to some types of negligence claims but not others. However, we also decline to interpret the relevant statute, 14 M.R.S. § 158 (2008),[1] to extend the reach of charitable immunity to intentional torts. We therefore vacate the judgment as to the intentional tort claim of fraudulent concealment but affirm the judgment as to the remaining claims.

---

1 Title 14 M.R.S. § 158 (2008) states:

> A charitable organization shall be considered to have waived its immunity from liability for negligence or any other tort during the period a policy of insurance is effective covering the liability of the charitable organization for negligence or any other tort. Each policy issued to a charitable organization shall contain a provision to the effect that the insurer shall be estopped from asserting, as a defense to any claim covered by said policy, that such organization is immune from liability on the ground that it is a charitable organization. The amount of damages in any such case shall not exceed the limits of coverage specified in the policy, and the courts shall abate any verdict in any such action to the extent that it exceeds such policy limit.

I. BACKGROUND

Picher brought this suit against a former priest, Raymond Melville, and the Bishop, based on sexual abuse of Picher by Melville when Picher was a minor in the late 1980s. Picher asserted claims against Melville for negligence, sexual assault and battery, invasion of privacy, intentional infliction of emotional distress, clergy malpractice, and breach of fiduciary duty. Melville defaulted. Picher asserts claims against the Bishop for negligent supervision, breach of fiduciary duty, canonical agency, and fraudulent concealment of facts.

Picher alleges that the Bishop was on notice that Melville had abused a child before he was ordained as a priest and before he was assigned to the parish where the abuse of Picher occurred. Picher further alleges that the Bishop failed to report Melville to law enforcement officials and concealed Melville's propensities from parishioners and the public. The Bishop denies these allegations.

The Bishop is a **corporation sole**.[2] [C] It operates as a non-profit organization and owns, maintains, and operates multiple churches, schools, and other properties. It has no capital stock and no provision for making dividends or profits, and it derives most of its revenues from charitable sources, although parochial school tuition and fees are not considered one of its charitable sources of revenue.

From July 1, 1986, to July 1, 1988, during the period when the alleged acts occurred, the Bishop was insured by Lloyd's of London pursuant to two consecutive policies, each of which contained an endorsement entitled "Sexual Misconduct Exclusion." This endorsement provides that "[s]exual or physical abuse or molestation of any person by the Assured, any employee of the Assured or any volunteer worker does not constitute personal injury within the terms of this policy and as such any claim arising, directly or indirectly, from the aforementioned is excluded."

The Bishop moved for summary judgment based on its affirmative defense of charitable immunity. The court granted the Bishop's motion, holding that the

---

2 The Bishop was formed as a corporation sole pursuant to P. & S.L. 1887, ch. 151, which states:

> Sect. 1. The present Roman Catholic Bishop of the Diocese of Portland, and his successors in office, be and is hereby created a body politic and a corporation sole, under the name and style of the Roman Catholic Bishop of Portland, and by that name the said bishop and his successors in office, shall be known and shall hereafter have succession, with all the powers, rights and privileges prescribed, and subject to all the liabilities imposed by the general statutes of the state.

> Sect. 2. The said corporation shall be empowered to receive, take and hold by sale, gift, lease, devise or otherwise, real and personal estate of every description for charitable, educational, burial, religious and church purposes, and to manage and dispose of the same by any form of legal conveyance or transfer according to the discipline and government of the Roman Catholic church, with full power and authority to borrow money and to convey by mortgage deed.

Bishop qualifies as a charitable organization and has not waived its charitable immunity pursuant to 14 M.R.S. § 158 because it has no insurance coverage for the claims made by Picher. The court also held that the doctrine of charitable immunity covers both intentional and negligent torts. After a damages hearing, a final judgment was entered against Melville in the amount of $4,227,875. Picher appealed the grant of a summary judgment in favor of the Bishop.

II. DISCUSSION

A. Standard of Review

We review a grant of a summary judgment **de novo**, considering "the evidence in the light most favorable to the party against whom judgment has been granted to decide whether the parties' statements of material facts and the referenced record material reveal a genuine issue of material fact." [C] "We will affirm a grant of summary judgment if the record reflects that there is no genuine issue of material fact and the movant is entitled to a judgment as a matter of law." [C] "A genuine issue of material fact exists when there is sufficient evidence to require a fact-finder to choose between competing versions of the truth at trial." [Cc].

The Bishop asserts a charitable immunity defense as to Picher's claims for negligent supervision, breach of fiduciary duty, and fraudulent concealment. Because we treat the intentional tort claim of fraudulent concealment differently from the negligence claims, we discuss them separately, after we explain the history of the doctrine of charitable immunity.

B. History and Current Status of Charitable Immunity

Picher does not explicitly argue that charitable immunity should be abrogated for all acts of negligence, but he does contend that it should be abrogated for acts of negligence in cases, such as this, involving the sexual abuse of a minor. The policy rationale supporting charitable immunity is the protection of charitable funds. [C] Although the rationale itself may be challenged as outdated, as we discuss below, we would need persuasive grounds to hold that charitable funds should be protected against certain types of negligence claims but not others. Without any such grounds, we decline Picher's invitation and do not address the issue further.

Picher has, however, directly challenged the application of charitable immunity to all intentional torts, an issue we have not previously had occasion to consider. Our decision not to extend the doctrine to intentional torts is based on three aspects of its history: (1) charitable immunity is discredited and has been abandoned in the majority of jurisdictions; (2) the Legislature did not intend to expand the scope of the common law doctrine of charitable immunity when it enacted section 158; and (3) we have previously held that we would maintain, but not expand, the doctrine, and we would leave it to the Legislature to decide whether to abolish it. We address each of these in turn.

1. Charitable Immunity Is a Discredited Doctrine

This Court introduced charitable immunity as a judicial doctrine almost one hundred years ago and adopted it as an affirmative defense available to non-profit organizations to bar negligence claims. [C] [W]e acknowledged, for historical purposes, the two policy justifications for charitable immunity…. These were "(1) that funds donated for charitable purposes are held in trust to be used exclusively for those purposes, and (2) that to permit the invasion of these funds to satisfy tort claims would destroy the sources of charitable support upon which the enterprise depends." [C] We upheld charitable immunity …, not because we concluded that these policy reasons were sound, but rather because non-profit organizations had relied upon charitable immunity for so long that abrogation of the doctrine would be far-reaching and should be undertaken by the Legislature. [C]

[T]he rationale for charitable immunity has been severely criticized. [Cc] This criticism has been explained in the Restatement (Second) of Torts:

> [T]here has been resort to ideas of "public policy" for the encouragement of charities and mention of the fear that they may be stifled if donors are discouraged from making gifts because their money may go to pay tort claims. The development of liability insurance has made it quite unlikely that donors would fail to recognize it as a legitimate expense of operation. In fact, all of the supposed reasons for the immunity fail when the charity can insure against liability.

Restatement (Second) of Torts § 895E cmt. c (1979).

> **FYI**
>
> The Restatement (Second) of Torts § 895E provides, "[o]ne engaged in a charitable, educational, religious or benevolent enterprise or activity is not for that reason immune from tort liability."

A review of the history of charitable immunity and its widespread rejection in other jurisdictions confirms that it remains a doctrine in general disrepute. Charitable immunity had a precarious start in this country after it had been tried and rejected in Great Britain. It was first adopted in the United States in *McDonald v. Massachusetts General Hospital,* 120 Mass. 432 (1876). The court relied on a line of English cases, originating in 1846 from *The Feoffes of Heriot's Hospital v. Ross,* (1846) 8 Eng. Rep. 1508 (H.L.). *See* Restatement (Second) of Torts § 895E cmt. b (1979) (discussing the history of charitable immunity). ... Eventually, however, most states recognized the doctrine. [Cc]

Despite its widespread adoption in the late nineteenth century and the first half of the twentieth century, charitable immunity began to erode quickly by the 1960s. [C] The Pennsylvania Supreme Court noted that the doctrine of charitable immunity "was built on a foundation of sand." [C] By 1984, "virtually all states with decisions on the subject at all ha[d] rejected the complete immunity of charities" with only two or three states having retained "full immunity in the absence of legislation to the contrary." [C]

With respect to our neighboring states, charitable immunity has either never been adopted or has long been abolished. New Hampshire and Vermont have never adopted the doctrine. ...

In 1971, after the Massachusetts Supreme Judicial Court threatened to abolish charitable immunity, the state legislature took note and abolished it, but limited the liability of charitable institutions to $20,000 for torts committed in the course of carrying out the charitable purpose. [C] An intentional tort, such as the one being alleged in this case, would likely fall outside of Massachusetts' statutory immunity, as it would not be considered to have been committed in the course of carrying out the charitable purpose. [C] In addition, even when Massachusetts first brought the doctrine of charitable immunity to America (before later abolishing it), the state's highest court implied that an exception existed for charities that did not hire their employees with due care. [C].

A review of the remaining jurisdictions shows that only a minority of them still recognize charitable immunity, and no state has applied the doctrine to intentional torts. According to the Restatement (Second) of Torts § 895E, ... twenty-eight states, in addition to those mentioned above, and the District of Columbia have abolished the doctrine of charitable immunity by either supporting or adopting section 895E, which provides: "One engaged in a charitable, educational, religious or benevolent enterprise or activity is not for that reason immune from tort liability."[4] [C] Ohio, Louisiana, and Nebraska have also abrogated the common law doctrine of charitable immunity. [Cc]

South Carolina initially recognized the doctrine of charitable immunity, but, in 1973, the South Carolina Supreme Court explicitly declined to extend it to intentional torts. [T]he court noted the absence of a public policy rationale for extending charitable immunity to intentional torts, stating,

---

4 Those jurisdictions include: Alaska, Arizona, California, Delaware, District of Columbia, Florida, Idaho, Illinois, Indiana, Iowa, Kansas, Kentucky, Michigan, Minnesota, Mississippi, Missouri, Montana, Nevada, New York, North Carolina, North Dakota, Oklahoma, Oregon, Pennsylvania, Texas, Utah, Washington, West Virginia, and Wisconsin. Restatement § 895E, Reporter's Notes.

Regardless of the public policy support, if there now be such, for a rule exempting a charity from liability for simple negligence, we know of no public policy, and none has been suggested, which would require the exemption of the charity from liability for an *intentional tort;* and we refuse to so extend the charitable immunity doctrine.

[C] South Carolina has since abolished the doctrine of charitable immunity as to all torts, although it limits the amount of damages one can recover from a charitable institution. [C]

New Jersey still recognizes charitable immunity, but does not grant immunity for intentional torts. [C] In New Jersey, charitable immunity is provided by statute, immunizing charities from liability for negligence. [C] [T]he New Jersey Supreme Court [recently] held that the state statute granting charitable immunity did not grant immunity for intentional torts. [C] Therefore, notwithstanding the New Jersey Legislature's codification of charitable immunity, the court declined to interpret the statute to provide immunity for intentional torts. [C]

Of the remaining states that retain some form of charitable immunity, no state has explicitly applied the doctrine to intentional torts. Virginia recognizes charitable immunity, but provides an exception for the negligent hiring of an employee who commits an intentional tort. [C] …

Alabama has not directly addressed whether charitable institutions should be liable for intentional torts, but the Alabama Supreme Court has otherwise limited the doctrine of charitable immunity, and in **dicta** implied that charities could be liable for the failure to use ordinary care in the selection of employees. [C] In addition, an Alabama statute granting immunity to the unpaid directors and officers of non-profit organizations does so only when individuals have not acted with willful or wanton misconduct. [C]

In Maryland and Wyoming, the highest courts have not addressed whether the doctrine applies to intentional torts, but both have created intentional tort exceptions to other doctrines of immunity. [Cc] Arkansas and Colorado retain some form of charitable immunity, [Cc], but have never expressly applied it to intentional torts. The highest courts in Georgia and Tennessee have not addressed charitable immunity for intentional torts, but charitable immunity in both states only protects the property of charitable trusts. [Cc] Therefore, charitable institutions in those jurisdictions could potentially be liable for any tort, as long as the judgment is applied to non-charitable trust property. In Georgia, however, charitable trust funds can be used to satisfy a judgment against a charity that has failed to use ordinary care in the selection of its employees.

Hawaii and South Dakota appear not to have addressed the doctrine of charitable immunity. Finally, New Mexico has not addressed the existence of charitable immunity. [C]

2. The Legislature Did Not Intend to Expand the Scope of Charitable Immunity

In 1965, the Legislature enacted 14 M.R.S. § 158, which limits the extent of the charitable immunity defense available to a non-profit organization that is covered by liability insurance. [C] The Bishop argues that 14 M.R.S. § 158 should be interpreted to apply charitable immunity to intentional torts. This interpretation would require a determination that the Legislature intended to modify the common law because, at the time section 158 was enacted in 1965, the doctrine of charitable immunity had been applied to negligence actions, [C], but we had not had occasion to consider whether to apply the doctrine to intentional torts. When the Legislature modifies the common law by statute, it must do so with clear and unambiguous language:

> [W]e have long embraced the well-established rule of statutory construction that the common law is not to be changed by doubtful implication, be overturned except by clear and unambiguous language, and that a statute in derogation of it will not effect a change thereof beyond that clearly indicated either by express terms or by necessary implication.

Batchelder v. Realty Res. Hospitality, LLC, 2007 ME 17, ¶ 23, 914 A.2d 1116, 1124 (quotation marks omitted).

Section 158 does not clearly and unambiguously express legislative intent to expand the scope of the common law doctrine of charitable immunity. Section 158 states: "A charitable organization shall be considered to have waived its immunity from liability for negligence or any other tort during the period a policy of insurance is effective...." This language is ambiguous; the words "or any other tort," plausibly suggest that section 158 was meant to expand the applicability of charitable immunity beyond its historical bounds, to cover any tort, including intentional torts. The other interpretation is that the statute has only one purpose, which is to deny charitable immunity, to the extent it would otherwise be available under the charitable immunity doctrine, when the non-profit organization is covered by insurance.

When a statute is ambiguous, we review its legislative history to discern legislative intent. [C] The purpose of section 158 was to limit charitable immunity. [C] There is nothing in the legislative history to indicate that section 158 was intended to do anything other than that, nor is there any indication of an intent to confer immunity for intentional torts. The 1965 floor debates for section 158 reflect several facts. As originally introduced, the bill would have completely abolished charitable immunity. [C] There are repeated references in the floor debates to this

Court's decisions recognizing charitable immunity for negligence. [C] The final bill was a compromise, abolishing immunity only when the non-profit organization has insurance. [Cc] There is no evidence that the Legislature intended the bill to expand the scope of charitable immunity, nor is there any discussion in the floor debates of immunity for intentional torts. The floor debates contain several references to the discredited status of charitable immunity and to the fact that most other states had abandoned it. [C]. Section 158 is therefore properly interpreted solely as a limitation on charitable immunity, not an expansion of it.

3. The Court Has Maintained Charitable Immunity but Declined to Either Expand or Abrogate It

Charitable immunity remains a judicial doctrine, subject to our interpretation, notwithstanding that the Legislature created an exception to the doctrine with the enactment of section 158. [C]; *Thompson,* 483 A.2d at 707 & n. 3. In *Thompson,* we noted that "[t]he doctrine of charitable immunity is a creation of our common law. Except for one significant restriction imposed by statute, its applicability in Maine is controlled entirely by the precedents of this Court." 483 A.2d at 707 (footnotes omitted). It is therefore appropriate for this Court to continue to determine the scope of charitable immunity.

We have previously held that we would maintain, but neither expand nor eliminate, the doctrine of charitable immunity. We [previously] noted ... that the adoption of section 158 provides a basis "for our continued adherence to the charitable immunity doctrine." [C] Although we have maintained the doctrine to date, we have declined either to expand it beyond its traditional bounds or to contract it. [Cc].

C. Charitable Immunity and Picher's Fraudulent Concealment Claim

For three reasons, we do not recognize the defense of charitable immunity in claims involving intentional torts. First, applying charitable immunity to intentional torts would set Maine so far outside the mainstream that it would put this State in a class by itself. We do not believe it advisable to expand so profoundly a doctrine that has generally been acknowledged as bankrupt. Second, nothing in the legislative history of section 158 indicates any legislative intent to so interpret the doctrine of charitable immunity. Third, there are no convincing policy reasons to apply charitable immunity to intentional torts. We therefore hold that charitable immunity is not available as a defense to intentional torts.

[The court then concludes that Picher has stated a claim for the intentional tort of fraudulent concealment and remands his claim to the lower court to determine whether the Bishop may be held vicariously liable under the theory of *respondeat superior* for Melville's fraudulent concealment.]

D. Charitable Immunity and Picher's Negligence Claims

Having addressed Picher's intentional tort claim, we turn to his negligence claims. Because we reject Picher's argument that charitable immunity should be abrogated as a defense as to some types of negligence claims but not others, we must address two additional issues relevant to the Bishop's assertion of this defense: (1) whether the Bishop, as a corporation sole and a non-profit institution, is entitled to assert charitable immunity, and (2) whether the Bishop waived immunity through the purchase of insurance.

Principles of tort law and charitable immunity apply to the Bishop as they do to any corporation. ...

A party seeking charitable immunity bears the burden of establishing both that it is entitled to charitable immunity and that it has not waived immunity. [C] The Bishop meets the requirements for non-profit status. We have held that an organization is entitled to charitable immunity if it "has no capital stock and no provision for making dividends or profits and ... derive [s] its funds mainly from public and private charity, ... hold[ing] them in trust for the object of the institution." [C] The parties do not dispute that the Bishop meets these requirements.

The parties dispute whether the Bishop has waived charitable immunity, pursuant to 14 M.R.S. § 158, through the purchase of insurance. We have held that a charitable organization with insurance coverage is deemed to have waived its tort immunity to the extent of its insurance coverage. [C] We have previously noted that the Legislature modified charitable immunity "to the extent of permitting recovery of damages to an amount not exceeding the limits of insurance coverage which the charity might be carrying at the time of the negligent or tortious act." [C]

Picher makes both a procedural and a substantive argument about the Bishop's insurance coverage. We interpret Picher's procedural argument to be essentially that the Bishop, as the moving party on summary judgment, has the burden to demonstrate that there is no genuine issue of material fact regarding insurance coverage, and because the Bishop did not produce evidence that it submitted a claim to Lloyd's of London and that Lloyd's of London denied the claim, the Bishop has not met this burden. ... The language of the policies held by the Bishop is not in dispute, and we may interpret it as a matter of law. ...

....

Picher's claims against the Bishop are unambiguously excluded from the insurance policy.

....

...As a matter of law, Picher's claims against the Bishop are excluded from coverage, and therefore the Bishop has not waived charitable immunity.

The entry is:

Judgment affirmed as to all claims against the Bishop except fraudulent concealment. Judgment vacated as to the claim of fraudulent concealment. Remanded for further action consistent with this opinion.

ALEXANDER, J., with whom CLIFFORD, J., joins, dissenting.

The Court's opinion provides an extensively documented policy discussion of the history of charitable immunity. That discussion begins with the observation that we recognized charitable immunity "as an affirmative defense available to non-profit organizations to bar *negligence* claims." (Emphasis added.) In fact, we have emphasized the importance of charitable immunity to protect charitable resources from "invasion of these funds to satisfy *tort* claims." [Cc]

The Court employs this policy discussion to support the Court's view that Maine's common law of charitable immunity is an anachronism and that the Maine Legislature's enactment of charitable immunity into law must be amended by judicial opinion to limit its application to torts involving only negligence. The result of the Court's action today is that any charitable institution may be hauled into court and forced to expend its resources to defend a suit through trial any time a plaintiff pleads some intentional act or failure to act as part of its cause of action.

The Court's opinion, holding that charitable immunity protection may be avoided simply by pleading some intentional act or failure to act, effectively ends charitable immunity in Maine. I respectfully dissent from the Court's opinion. The articulate policy arguments expressed by the Court should be addressed to the Legislature to support legislative action to amend the law that, without ambiguity, protects charities from suit "for negligence or any other tort." 14 M.R.S. § 158 (2008).

By invading the province of the Legislature and effectively striking "or any other tort" from our statute books, the Court fails to respect the separation of powers provision, article III, section 2, of the Maine Constitution and makes a policy judgment exposing all Maine charities to a wide range of lawsuits from which, until today, they have been protected by more than a century of legislative and judicial action.

As the Court's opinion amply demonstrates, charitable immunity has been an important fixture of our law affecting the planning, funding, operation, and governance of charitable institutions in Maine for more than a century. ...

....

Today's opinion has great significance beyond this case. The existence of charitable immunity and the protection it creates is important to the planning and continued existence of many community-based organizations including local granges, arts organizations, fraternal groups, youth programs, churches, and some schools and health care providers. [S]uch protection is important because funds donated for charitable purposes are held in trust to be used exclusively for those purposes and, without charitable immunity, resources could be sacrificed "to feed the hungry maw of litigation, and charitable institutions of all kinds would ultimately cease or become greatly impaired in their usefulness." [C]

Just seven years ago, we [observed] that, "to permit the invasion of these funds to satisfy tort claims would destroy the sources of charitable support upon which the enterprise depends." [Cc].

[T]he Legislature enacted 14 M.R.S. § 158, placing into Maine statutory law a broad-based charitable immunity protection, subject to an exception only for claims covered by insurance procured by the charity. [C]. That law, unchanged until today, recognizes charitable immunity from liability "for negligence or any other tort," that is subject to waiver only by purchase of insurance. [C]

[In a previous case,] we recognized that while the Legislature could have abolished common law charitable immunity, it had instead enacted broad-based charitable immunity into statutory law, subject only to the purchase of insurance exception. [In that case, we] emphasized the importance of deference to legislative, policy-based decision-making on this subject because "[w]hat the public policy of this State in such an important area of life and action should be may necessitate the conduct of a general investigation which this Court in litigated cases is ill-equipped to undertake." [C]

Legislative enactment of broad-based charitable immunity, now more than forty years in the past, allows many poorly funded organizations to provide important community services using facilities such as grange halls, art museums, Little League ball fields, or houses of worship. These organizations serve their communities without facing the Hobson's choice of shutting down because they cannot afford the cost of insurance or remaining open to face the risk of lawsuits which, even if successfully defended, may cost more than the organization can afford.

> **FYI**
>
> A "Hobson's choice" is a choice between one thing or nothing at all. The phrase originates from Thomas Hobson, a livery stable owner in England who offered his customers the option of either taking the horse from the nearest stall or taking no horse at all.

Today the Court sweeps away the protection enacted by the Legislature. In so doing, the Court invades the province of the Legislature in an area where... we [have previously] acknowledged that the Legislature had primary authority to act to adopt, reject, expand, or modify the doctrine of charitable immunity. ...

To justify its invasion of the Legislature's province to amend 14 M.R.S. § 158, the Court appears to conduct a referendum of actions by other state supreme courts to conclude that since those courts appear to be cutting back on charitable immunity, we should follow suit. The Court's referendum, however, lacks citations to other state statutes similar to section 158.[6] It is that statute, and our obligation to respect it until amended by the Legislature, that necessarily separates Maine from other states in our approach to charitable immunity.

....

The Court concludes that section 158, recognizing immunity from liability for "negligence or any other tort," does not include intentional torts. This view violates our basic rule of statutory construction that a statute, if it is not ambiguous, must be given its common, ordinary meaning, without resort to rules of construction. [C] The protection from liability for "negligence *or any other tort*" must mean protection from suit for torts in addition to negligence, including intentional torts. Limiting application of section 158 to negligence torts, as the Court does, renders the "or any other tort" phrase superfluous. Such a limiting interpretation violates another basic rule of statutory construction that no language in a statute may be viewed as superfluous if a construction supplying meaning to a phrase is possible. [Cc]

A claim of fraud, fraudulent misrepresentation, or fraudulent concealment is a tort like any other, although one that must be proved by clear and convincing evidence. [C] It is a tort easily pled, but difficult to prove. Nothing in legislation or our prior precedents creates a charitable immunity exception to blow open the courthouse door for those who employ the tactic of adding a fraud or intentional inaction claim to a negligence claim to force charities to defend against tort actions and confront all of the attendant costs and risks to the trust resources that we have stated must be protected from such actions.

---

6 The Court's opinion also may overstate the extent to which charitable immunity has been limited in other states. It correctly quotes Prosser's observation that "virtually all states" have "rejected the complete immunity of charities," and that only two or three states have retained "full immunity in the absence of legislation to the contrary." W. Page Keeton et al., *Prosser and Keeton on the Law of Torts* § 133 at 1070 (W. Page Keeton ed., 5th ed.1984). But the Court's authority for these observations, Prosser, qualifies those broad observations, noting that some states, like Maine, "permit a recovery against a charity's non-trust fund assets-usually insurance-but not otherwise," and that in some states "immunity has been retained or reinstituted by statute, but only for certain particular cases," *id.,* including protection for religious institutions, *id.* at 1070 n. 15. The Court also counts Massachusetts among the states to have abolished charitable immunity. But with today's costs of litigation, Massachusetts' "abolition" of immunity that imposes a $20,000 limit on damages seems more like a qualified acceptance of charitable immunity than an abolition of it.

Forty-six years ago, in *Mendall,* we stated that changes in the doctrine of charitable immunity have far-reaching policy implications that should be initiated in the Legislature and receive careful legislative consideration. 159 Me. at 290, 191 A.2d at 636. That is as true today as it was then. The Court should leave amendment or abolition of the doctrine of charitable immunity and section 158 to the Maine Legislature. I would affirm the judgment of the Superior Court.

SAUFLEY, C.J., with whom LEVY, J., joins, concurring.

This case presents a classic jurisprudential problem: how to interpret legislative intent when a particular phrase within a statutory sentence plainly leads to one conclusion, but the context of the sentence within which the phrase falls leads, after consideration of the legislative history, to a flatly contrary conclusion. The question is this: Did the Maine Legislature, when it used the phrase "any other tort" in enacting 14 M.R.S. § 158 (2008), intend to expand the existing common law doctrine of charitable immunity to such an extent that it immunizes a charity from liability when the charity, whether it is a local grange or an international religious organization, engages in the intentional and surreptitious placement of a known pedophile in a position of power over vulnerable children.

In the end, I join the Court and concur in the Court's conclusion that the Legislature did not intend that result. Because, however, I agree with the dissent that the phrase "any other tort" would in a different context be understood to include intentional torts, I write separately to address the reasons I do not join the dissent.

We have emphasized that Maine statutes "must be construed as a whole in order to effectuate the legislative intent." [C] Considered in its entirety, section 158 does not purport to define or expand the charitable immunity doctrine, and the expansive phrase "any other tort," contained within the first sentence of otherwise *limiting* language, creates an ambiguity requiring resort to legislative history. That history does not contain any indication of an intent to expand charitable immunity. If the Legislature had, in fact, engaged in weighing the risks posed by *intentional torts,* including the potential sexual assault of children, against the possibility of destructive litigation costs incurred by Maine's long tradition of charitable organizations, one would have expected much more robust debate and much clearer language.

Thus, despite the dissent's understandable reliance on the plain language of the phrase "any other tort," I conclude that the context of the phrase cannot support the expansive intent that the words would otherwise convey. This is a close and difficult question for any court. If the Court has read that legislative intent incorrectly, the Legislature can remedy the Court's interpretation through clarifying language that expands charitable immunity to encompass intentional torts.

Points for Discussion

1. What is the policy rationale in support of the doctrine of charitable immunity?

2. What relevance, if any, should a charity's ability to insure against losses play in the recognition of charitable immunity? See Doctor v. Pardue, 186 S.W.3d 4 (Tex. Civ. App.—Houston, 2006) (plaintiff, who was rendered a quadriplegic after aircraft he was piloting at air show collided on runway with another aircraft piloted by a not-for-profit entity, was permitted to recover based on statute limiting liability to extent of insurance coverage).

3. What is the *Picher* court's process by which it determines whether the charitable immunity statute at issue is applicable? What is the relevance of the legislative history of the statute?

4. Should the abolition of immunity for charities be consistent with the tax exempt status of charities? Why or why not?

5. A health care services provider employed physicians who were also employed at a state-run medical school. Patients and their families brought tort actions against the providers, alleging negligence in the provision of medical care. The defendant health care services provider defended, claiming that it qualified as a charitable institution as it was formed for charitable purposes. After evaluating, *inter alia,* the health service provider's ratio of revenue to the cost of its charitable work as well as its incentive profit-based payment structure, the court concluded that the health care services provider was not entitled to charitable immunity status. *See* University of Va. Health Servs. Found. v. Morris, 275 Va. 319 (2008); *see also* Flagiello v. Pennsylvania Hospital, 417 Pa. 486 (1965) (in case where patient slipped and fell in hospital breaking her arm, court abolished charitable immunity doctrine, explaining that any justification for charitable immunity doctrine no longer exists).

C. Employers

Workers' compensation statutes, enacted in all jurisdictions, provide a no-fault remedy to employees suffering work-related and occupational injuries. These statutes make available an alternative to the tort system and can provide an employer with immunity from a worker's lawsuit alleging that her injury was caused by the employer's negligence. This section provides an introduction to and a sampling of key issues addressed in workers' compensation law and litigation, subjects addressed more extensively in Workers' Compensation and Employment Law courses.

Eckis v. Sea World Corp.

64 Cal.App.3d 1, 134 Cal.Rptr. 183 (1976)

AULT, Presiding Justice.

Defendants Sea World and Kent Burgess have appealed from a judgment entered on a jury verdict awarding Anne E. Eckis $75,000 in **compensatory damages**. Plaintiff had sought both compensatory and **punitive damages** for personal injuries she sustained while riding "Shamu the Whale," framing her complaint on three theories: **fraud**, **negligence**, and **liability** for an animal with vicious or dangerous propensities. Before the case was submitted to the jury, the trial court denied Sea World's motion for a nonsuit on the fraud cause of action. Later its motions for judgment notwithstanding the verdict and for a new trial were also denied.

. . . .

The major issue raised on appeal is the contention there was no substantial evidence to support the jury's finding that plaintiff's injuries did not occur in the course of her employment by Sea World. The facts which govern this issue are not in dispute.

When injured on April 19, 1971, plaintiff Anne E. Eckis, then 22 years old, was a full-time employee of Sea World. First hired by Sea World in 1967, she had worked variously as ticket sales girl, receptionist, in the accounting department, and in 1970 became the secretary for Kent Burgess, the director of Sea World's animal training department. From then on her job title was secretary, and that is what she considered herself to be, although from time to time she did other tasks at Burgess' request, such as taking the water temperature, doing research, and running errands. She worked five days a week, for which she was paid a salary of $450 per month. When first hired plaintiff, like all other Sea World employees, had signed an authorization for reproduction of her physical likeness. Plaintiff was also an excellent swimmer, with some scuba diving experience, and had occasionally worked as a model, sometimes for pay.

In April 1971 Gail MacLaughlin, Sea World's public relations director, and Kent Burgess asked plaintiff if she would like to ride Shamu, the killer whale, in a bikini for some publicity pictures for Sea World. Although the ride was not made a condition of her keeping her job, plaintiff eagerly agreed, thinking it would be exciting. Although warned in general terms that the ride involved dangers and aware that she might fall off, plaintiff was confident of her swimming ability and anxious to do it. She had never heard of whales pushing riders around.

Burgess had been responsible for training Shamu ever since Sea World first acquired the animal. He knew Shamu was conditioned to being ridden only by persons wearing wetsuits, and that Shamu had in the past attacked persons who attempted to ride her in an ordinary bathing suit: first a Catalina swimsuit model and then Jim Richards, one of the trainers at Sea World. In addition, Burgess had read training records which showed Shamu had been behaving erratically since early March 1971. This information he did not disclose to plaintiff.

Plaintiff was trained for the ride by Sea World trainers in the tank at Sea World during normal office working hours. First she practiced riding Kilroy, a smaller, more docile whale, while wearing a bathing suit. During her one practice session on Shamu, she wore a wetsuit, fell off, but swam to the edge of the tank without incident.

On April 19 plaintiff became apprehensive for the first time when one of Sea World's trainers said he was not going to watch her ride Shamu because it was 'really dangerous.' Plaintiff then went to Burgess and told him of her concern. He told her not to worry, said there was nothing to be concerned about, and that the ride was "as safe as it could be." He still did not tell her about the problems they had been having with Shamu or about the earlier incidents involving Richards and the swimsuit model. Thus reassured, plaintiff, wearing a bikini Sea World had paid for, then took three rides on Shamu. During the second ride one of the trainers noticed Shamu's tail was fluttering, a sign the animal was upset. During the third ride plaintiff fell off when Shamu refused to obey a signal. Shamu then bit her on her legs and hips and held her in the tank until she could be rescued.

Plaintiff suffered 18 to 20 wounds which required from 100 to 200 stitches and left permanent scars. She was hospitalized five days and out of work several weeks. She also suffered some psychological disturbance. Sea World paid all her medical expenses and continued to pay her salary as usual during this period. On advice of her counsel, she filed this civil action and a workers' compensation claim.

When an employee's injuries are compensable under the Workers' Compensation Act, the right of the employee to recover the benefits provided by the Act is his exclusive remedy against the employer (Lab.Code ss 3600, 3601;http://www.westlaw.com/Find/Default.wl?rs=dfa1.0&vr=2.0&DB=661&FindType=Y&SerialNum=1968129862 [cc].

Under section 3600, with exceptions not applicable here, liability of the employer to pay compensation under the Act, "in lieu of any other inability whatsoever," attaches:

"(b) Where, at the time of the injury, the employee is performing service growing out of and incidental to his employment and is acting within the course of his employment," and

"(c) Where the injury is proximately caused by the employment, either with or without negligence."

The provisions of the Act must be '. . . liberally construed by the courts with the purpose of extending their benefits for the protection of persons injured in the course of their employment.' (s 3202)

. . . .

Where a reasonable doubt exists as to whether an act of an employee is contemplated by the employment, or as to whether an injury occurred in the course of the employment, section 3202 requires courts to resolve the doubt against the right of the employee to sue for civil damages and in favor of the applicability of the Compensation Act. The importance of adhering to the rule requiring a liberal construction of the Act in favor of its applicability in civil litigation was emphasized by the court in Scott:

"Though it may be more opportunistic for a particular plaintiff to seek to circumscribe the purview of compensation coverage because of his immediate interest and advantage, the courts must be vigilant to preserve the spirit of the act and to prevent a distortion of its purposes. That the question before us in this case arises out of litigation prosecuted in the superior court is all the more reason for care lest rules of doubtful validity, out of harmony with the objectives of the Act, be formulated." (Scott v. Pacific Coast Borax Co., supra, 140 Cal.App.2d 173, 178, 294 P.2d 1039, 1043.)

Whether an employee's injury arose out of and in the course of his employment is generally a question of fact to be determined in the light of the circumstances of the particular case [cc]. Like other issues relating to causation, however, when the facts are undisputed and all point in the same direction, resolution of the question becomes a matter of law. [Cc]

Governed by these legal principles, we examine the evidence to determine whether it supports the finding plaintiff was not acting within the course and scope of her employment at Sea World when she sustained her injuries.

The undisputed evidence shows: at the time she was injured plaintiff was an employee of Sea World; she was injured on the employer's premises during what were her regular working hours; she was injured while engaging in an activity which her employer had requested her to perform and for which it had provided her with the training and the means to perform; in riding Shamu the Whale for publicity pictures, plaintiff was not engaged in an activity which was personal to her, but rather one which was related to, furthered, and benefited the business of her employer.

Despite this formidable array of factors which indicate her injuries did arise out of and occurred in the course and scope of her employment [cc], plaintiff maintains substantial evidence supports the special finding to the contrary. She premises her position on the claim she was hired to be a secretary, not to ride a whale. Since her injuries were unrelated to the secretarial duties she was originally hired to perform, she argues her employment 'had nothing whatsoever to do with her injury' and that her case does not come within the purview of the Compensation Act. Because of the highly unusual circumstances under which she was injured, she maintains the rules and formulas traditionally used to determine whether injuries have arisen out of or occurred in the course of employment are neither applicable nor helpful.

These arguments are without merit. The right to compensation is not limited to those cases where the injury occurs while the employee is performing the classical duties for which he was originally hired. [C] Far less than a direct request by the employer operates to bring an injury-causing activity within the provisions of the Compensation Act. For example, in Lizama v. Workmen's Comp. Appeals Bd., 40 Cal.App.3d 363, 115 Cal.Rptr. 267, the employee was injured on the employer's premises after he had clocked out from work while using a table saw to construct a bench to sit on at lunch time. Although his assigned duties did not include use of the saw and he had never used it before, the injury was held compensable because the employer had expressly or impliedly permitted such use of equipment. At page 370, 115 Cal.Rptr. at page 271, the court stated:

> "Textwriters have long proposed and California courts have applied a 'quantum theory of work-connection' that seems peculiarly appropriate for application here. [Cc] The theory merges the 'course of employment' and 'arising out of employment' tests, but does not dispense with a minimum 'quantum of work-connection.' There were at least these connections between petitioner's injury and his employment: the accident occurred on the employer's premises when petitioner was using the employer's equipment while constructing a bench for his personal comfort to be used on the employer's premises; and the employer expressly or impliedly permitted petitioner to use its equipment. . . .'"
> [C]

Where, as here, an employee is injured on the employer's premises during regular working hours, when the injury occurs while the employee is engaged in an activity which the employer has requested her to undertake, and when the injury-causing activity is of service to the employer and benefits the employer's business, the conditions imposing liability for compensation under Labor Code section 3600 are met as a matter of law, and it is immaterial that the activity causing the injury was not related to the employee's normal duties or that the circumstances surrounding the injury were unusual or unique.

It would be wholly incongruous and completely at variance with the long declared purposes and policies of the Workers' Compensation Law to say that an employee who sustained injuries under the circumstances of this case is not entitled to the benefits of the Workers' Compensation Act. Since her injuries fall within the scope of the Act, a proceeding under it constitutes plaintiff's exclusive remedy. [Cc].

. . . .

The judgment is reversed; the trial court is directed to enter a judgment in favor of Sea World.

Points for Discussion

1. Do you agree with the *Eckis* court's determination that the plaintiff was an "employee," and that her injuries arose out of and in the course of her employment with Sea World?

2. Why did the plaintiff argue that she was not an "employee" for purposes of California's Workers' Compensation Act? **Workers' compensation** laws typically provide that claimants will receive, not tort damages, but a certain percentage of their income lost as a result of work-related injuries and medical expenses. Because the *Eckis* court determined that the Act was her exclusive remedy against her employer, the plaintiff did not receive the $75,000 in compensatory damages awarded to her by the jury.

3. Texas law uniquely provides that employers and employees may opt out of that state's workers' compensation system. *See* TEX. LAB. CODE §§ 406.002, 406.034. The employer who does so, referred to as a "nonsubscriber," is subject to negligence suits and liability where an injured employee establishes that an injury suffered in the course and scope of employment was caused by the employer's negligence. Employees who wish to retain their common-law right of action to recover damages for personal injury or death must notify the employer in writing that the employees waives workers' compensation

coverage and retains all common-law rights. In an action against an employer or brought by an employee who is not covered by the workers' compensation law it is not a defense that the employee was guilty of contributory negligence, or that the employee assumed the risk of injury or death, or that the injury or death was caused by the negligence of a fellow employee. *See* TEX. LAB. CODE § 406.033.

Sisk v. Tar Heel Capital Corp.

166 N.C.App. 631, 603 S.E.2d 564 (2004)

TYSON, Judge.

Christina Sisk ("plaintiff") appeals an Opinion and Award filed by the Full Commission of North Carolina Industrial Commission ("Commission") finding plaintiff sustained an injury by accident occurring in the course of, but did not arise out of her employment. . . .

. . . .

Plaintiff began work for defendant-employer in July 1992. Defendant-employer operates a Wendy's Restaurant in Forest City, North Carolina. Plaintiff started as a crew employee and was promoted to shift supervisor in 1998. At both her initial hiring and subsequent promotion, defendant-employer presented plaintiff with documentation of defendant-employer's anti-harassment policy (the "policy"). The policy provided a procedure that employees should follow if they became victims of any form of harassment. Plaintiff signed acknowledgments of receipt of the policy on both occasions and took several quizzes testing her knowledge of the policy.

In March 2001, James Johnson ("Johnson") became general manager of the restaurant where plaintiff worked as a shift supervisor. Johnson filed disciplinary notices against plaintiff on two separate occasions in May 2001. Plaintiff testified that around that time, Johnson began making sexually suggestive comments to her, touching her in inappropriate places, pulling her onto his lap, and placing his hand down her shirt. She testified Johnson's actions left bruises where he grabbed her.

On 17 July 2001, plaintiff gave notice of her resignation to Doug Kropelnicki ("Kropelnicki"), the district manager, and Wanda Farmer ("Farmer"), director of human resources. Her notice included, "I can no longer work with harassment at the hands of James Johnson." This was the first notice by plaintiff to defendant-employer of Johnson's behavior. Plaintiff acknowledged she had not followed defendant-employer's anti-harassment procedures.

Plaintiff visited a family practice physician complaining of panic attacks on 18 July 2001. The physician prescribed medication to help with anxiety and wrote plaintiff a note to remain out of work until 23 July 2001.

Defendant-employer conducted an investigation of Johnson's behavior and immediately suspended and eventually terminated his employment on 19 July 2001. That day, Tad Dolbier ("Dolbier"), director of operations, called plaintiff and told her Johnson had been fired, and that he appreciated plaintiff as a valued employee. He asked why she did not follow the anti-harassment procedures. Plaintiff responded, "I did not want to call and create a big stink," and "if I acted like it wasn't happening, maybe it would stop." Dolbier concluded by informing plaintiff that due to her doctor's note, she was entitled paid leave until 23 July 2001. Plaintiff did not return to work.

Farmer sent plaintiff a letter dated 30 July 2001 inquiring of her employment status. Farmer indicated plaintiff's job would remain open until 6 August 2001, but that her absences since 23 July 2001 would be unpaid. Farmer requested a phone call for an update. Plaintiff's attorney responded to Farmer's letter.

Plaintiff contacted her family physician on 6 August 2001. She requested, but was denied, another note saying she could not return to work until 8 August 2001. Plaintiff next sought medical attention from Dr. Michael Knoelke ("Dr. Knoelke"), a psychiatrist on 16 August 2001. Dr. Knoelke testified plaintiff complained of memories of Johnson's behavior that affected her ability to work and drive. Dr. Knoelke diagnosed plaintiff with post traumatic stress disorder including panic attacks and major depressive disorder. Plaintiff visited Dr. Knoelke on three occasions between September 2001 and May 2002. Each visit resulted in modifying her medication due to her varying levels of stress and depression.

Plaintiff filed a Form 18 with the Commission on 20 August 2001 alleging she was "continuously assaulted and harassed by her general manager, James Johnson, [and] she began having panic attacks ... sought medical treatment ... [and] has been unable to work." Plaintiff sought compensation from 16 July 2001 forward. Defendants denied plaintiff's claim on 10 September 2001. Plaintiff filed a Form 33 requesting her claim be assigned for hearing.

The deputy commissioner filed an Opinion and Award on 30 November 2002, which found that Johnson made sexually suggestive remarks, touched plaintiff inappropriately, pulled plaintiff onto his lap, placed his hand down her shirt, and had used his supervisory position to place plaintiff at risk. The deputy commissioner found plaintiff became emotionally upset, was diagnosed with post traumatic stress disorder including panic attacks and major depressive disorder, and currently received treatment from Dr. Knoelke. The deputy commissioner concluded as a matter of law that plaintiff suffered "an injury by accident" and was "entitled to total disability [and] medical expenses incurred" from 18 July 2001 until she returned to work, or by further order of the Commission. Defendants appealed to the Full Commission.

The Full Commission reviewed the case on 22 May 2003 and found the same facts as the deputy commissioner. The Full Commission added that "based on prior appellate decisions, the Full Commission must find as fact that plaintiff's injury did not arise out of the nature of her employment [and] [p]laintiff has also failed to show that she contracted an occupational disease...." [Cc]

The Commission's conclusions of law determined plaintiff "established that she sustained an injury by accident occurring in the course of her employment with [defendant], but she failed to establish that her injury arose out of the employment." Specifically, the Commission stated, "sexual assaults are not deemed to be incident to or a natural and probable consequence of the employment under current law." Plaintiff's claim under the Worker's Compensation Act was denied. Plaintiff appeals.

. . . .

The issues on appeal are whether: (1) an injury caused by **sexual harassment** properly falls within the jurisdiction of the Workers' Compensation Act (the "Act"); and (2) the Act covers injuries resulting from intentional **assaults** by co-employees.

. . . .

Plaintiff argues sexual harassment and her resulting mental injury are compensable under the Act. We disagree.

The Act covers injuries sustained from risks incidentally and directly connected to that particular employment. [C]. The injury is compensable if it arises out of and occurs in the course of employment. [C]. The employee must be performing duties authorized by the employer in furtherance of the employer's business. [C]

"Arises out of" refers to an injury that is a "natural and probable consequence" of the employment. [C] There must be some *causal connection* between the employment and the injury. [Cc] An injury occurring "in the course of" employment happens when an employee is injured doing something reasonably expected of him or her at the time, place, and under the circumstances of the employment. [C] The injury must be peculiar to the job and not a common threat to the public generally. [C].

A similar issue arose in *Hogan v. Forsyth Country Club Co.*, 79 N.C.App. 483, 340 S.E.2d 116. An employee "made sexually suggestive remarks to [the plaintiff] while she was working, coaxing her to have sex with him[,] ... telling her that he wanted to 'take' her, ... brush[ed] up against her, rub[bed] [himself] against her buttocks, and touch[ed] her buttocks with his hands." [C] This Court determined emotional injuries resulting from sexual harassment were not a "natural and probable consequence or incident of the employment." [C] We held that sexual harassment is a risk the public generally is exposed to and is "neither covered nor barred by the Act." [C]

Here, plaintiff testified that Johnson made sexually suggestive remarks, pulled her onto his lap, placed his hand down her shirt, grabbed her buttocks, and pushed her against a wall and a table. Plaintiff attempts to distinguish *Hogan* as controlling precedent by contending her emotional injuries resulted from physical assaults not present in *Hogan*. We disagree. The facts in *Hogan* are clear that the plaintiff endured similar verbal and physical assaults as plaintiff at bar.

. . . .

We are bound by prior decisions of this Court. *In re Appeal from Civil Penalty*, 324 N.C. 373, 379 S.E.2d 30 (1989). This assignment of error is overruled.

. . . .

Plaintiff asserts her emotional injuries caused by Johnson's intentional assaults are covered under the Act. We disagree.

The Act provides compensation for injuries resulting only from **accidents**. [Cc] Our Supreme Court recognized that an assault may be classified as an accident if it is not expected or instigated by the employee. *Withers v. Black*, 230 N.C. 428, 433-34, 53 S.E.2d 668, 672-73 (1949). The assault must derive from dangers particular to the job and not common in everyday life. [Cc] If the **motive** surrounding the assault is personal in nature and unrelated to the employment, resulting injuries are not covered by the Act. [C]

Evidence shows Johnson verbally and physically assaulted plaintiff with inappropriate conversation and uninvited touching while at work. Plaintiff, a shift supervisor, worked directly under Johnson, the general manager. Plaintiff suggests the danger leading to the assaults resulted from Johnson's position as plaintiff's superior. However, plaintiff fails to offer and the record is devoid of evidence indicating the assaults resulted from dangers particular to this job and should be imputed to the employer. There is no indication Johnson's conduct resulted from a dispute over employment issues or differed from harassment experienced in everyday life. Instead, the evidence suggests his motive and actions were entirely personal in nature. Johnson's actions were foul behavior against plaintiff, but it was separate from their common employment interests. This assignment of error is overruled.

. . . .

Emotional injuries resulting from sexual harassment are not compensable under the Act. [C] Plaintiff failed to prove the intentional assaults resulted from dangers particular to her position as shift supervisor of a restaurant. We affirm the Commission's denial of compensation to plaintiff. . . .

Affirmed.

Points for Discussion

1. How does the *Sisk* court define an injury that (a) "arises out of" employment and (b) occurs "in the course" of employment? Do you agree with the court's treatment of the plaintiff's claim that her supervisor's intentional assaults were covered by and compensable under the workers' compensation statute?

2. For additional cases addressing the issue of whether claims for sexual harassment and sexual assault are compensable under workers' compensation laws and subject to the exclusivity provisions thereof, *see* Ferris v. Bakery, Confectionary and Tobacco Union, Local 26, 867 P.2d 38 (Colo. App. 1993), and Knox v. Combined Insurance Company of America, 542 A.2d 363 (Me. 1988).

D. Local and State Government

Ayala v. Philadelphia Board of Public Education

453 Pa. 584, 305 A.2d 877 (Pa. 1973)

Before JONES, C.J., and EAGEN, O'BRIEN, ROBERTS, POMEROY, NIX and MANDERINO, JJ.

OPINION OF THE COURT

ROBERTS, Justice.

Appellants, William Ayala and William Ayala, Jr., instituted this action to recover damages for injuries suffered by William, Jr., when his arm was caught in a shredding machine in the upholstery class of the Carrol School in Philadelphia. As a result of these injuries, the 15 year old student's arm was amputated.

Appellants alleged that appellee school district, through its employees, was negligent in failing to supervise the upholstery class, in supplying the machine for the without a proper safety device, in maintaining the machine in a dangerous and defective condition, and in failing to warn the children of the dangerous condition. Appellee, the Philadelphia Board of Public Education, interposed preliminary objections asserting the defense of governmental immunity. These objections were sustained and the Superior Court affirmed in a **per curiam** order. [C][1] We granted **allocatur**.

What's That?

"Allocatur" means "it is allowed." Although the use of this term formerly indicated that a writ, bill, or other pleading was permitted, it is used today in Pennsylvania as indicating permission to appeal.

We now hold that the doctrine of governmental immunity[2] --long since devoid of any valid justification--is abolished in this Commonwealth. In so doing, we join the ever-increasing number of jurisdictions which have judicially abandoned this antiquated doctrine. [Cc]

I.

It is generally agreed that the historical roots of the governmental immunity doctrine are found in the English case of Russell v. Men of Devon, 2 T.R. 667, 100 Eng.Rep. 359 (1788). [The *Russell* court,] expressing the eighteenth century societal evaluation of the individual and local governmental interests, observed that 'it is better that an individual should sustain an injury than that the public should suffer an inconvenience.' [C]

While some attribute the immunity of municipal corporations and quasi-corporations to an extension of the theory that 'the King can do no wrong', it has been noted that in Russell v. Men of Devon there is no mention of that phrase. [C] Rather,

'(e)very reason assigned by the court (in Russell) is born of expediency. The wrong to plaintiff is submerged in the convenience of the public. No moral, ethical, or rational reason for the decision is advanced by the court except the practical problem of assessing damages against individual defendants.'

[C]

....

1 Judge Hoffman filed a concurring opinion in which Judge Spaulding joined. [C] Judge Packel also filed a concurring opinion. [C] These opinions expressed discontent with the governmental immunity doctrine but stated that 'it is for the highest court of the Commonwealth to act to abrogate the inequities of the doctrine of sovereign immunity.' Id. (Hoffman, J., concurring).
2 We are not, here, confronted with the sovereign immunity of the Commonwealth.

Pennsylvania joined the numerous states adopting the immunity doctrine and, in Ford v. School District, 121 Pa. 543, 15 A. 812 (1888), held that school districts, as quasi-corporations, are not liable for the tortious conduct of employees. ...[T]he Court was reluctant to impose liability because 'the act of assembly provides no fund out of which the directors can pay damages resulting from their own misconduct or that of their officers.' [C] The Court further stated that 'individual advantage must give way to the public welfare.' [C]

....

II.

Today we conclude that no reasons whatsoever exist for continuing to adhere to the doctrine of governmental immunity. Whatever may have been the basis for the inception of the doctrine, it is clear that no public policy considerations presently justify its retention.

Governmental immunity can no longer be justified on 'an amorphous mass of cumbrous language about sovereignty. . . .' [C] As one court has stated:

'. . . it is almost incredible that in this modern age of comparative sociological enlightenment, and in a republic, the medieval absolutism supposed to be implicit in the maxim, 'the King can do no wrong,' should exempt the various branches of the government from liability for their torts, and that the entire burden of damage resulting from the wrongful acts of the government should be imposed upon the single individual who suffers the injury, rather than distributed among the entire community constituting the government, where it could be borne without hardship upon any individual, and where it justly belongs.' [C] ...

Moreover, we are unwilling to perpetuate the notion that 'it is better that an individual should sustain an injury than that the public should suffer an inconvenience.' [C] This social philosophy of nonliability is 'an anachronism in the law of today.' [C] ...

....

Recently, this Court reiterated the prevailing philosophy that liability follows tortious conduct. [W]e said:

"It is fundamental to our common law system that one may seek redress for every substantial wrong. 'The best statement of the rule is that a wrongdoer is responsible for the natural and proximate consequences of his misconduct. . . ." Battalla v. State, 10 N.Y.2d 237, 240, 219 N.Y.S.2d 34, 36, 176 N.E.2d 729, 730 (1961).'

[Cc] Appellee offers no reason-and we are unable to discern one-for permitting governmental units to escape the effect of this fundamental principle.

> 'As we have stated many times before, today cities and states are active and virile creatures capable of inflicting great harm, and their civil liability should be co-extensive. Even though a governmental entity does not profit from its projects, the taxpaying public nevertheless does, and it is the taxpaying public which should pay for governmental maladministration. If the city operates or maintains injury-inducing activities or conditions, the harm thus caused should be viewed as a part of the normal and proper costs of public administration and not as a diversion of public funds. The city is a far better loss-distributing agency than the innocent and injured victim. ...'

[C]

We must also reject the fear of excessive litigation as a justification for the immunity doctrine. Empirically, there is little support for the concern that the courts will be flooded with litigation if the doctrine is abandoned. [Cc] So, too, what this Court said in Niederman v. Brodsky, supra, 436 Pa. at 412, 261 A.2d at 89, is applicable here:

> '. . . more compelling than an academic debate over the apparent or real increases in the amount of litigation, is the fundamental concept of our judicial system that any such increase should not be determinative or relevant to the availability of a judicial forum for the adjudication of impartial individual rights. 'It is the business of the law to remedy wrongs that deserve it, even at the expense of a 'flood of litigation'; and it is a pitiful confession of incompetence on the part of any court of justice to deny relief upon the ground that it will give the courts too much work to do.' [C] We obviously do not accept the 'too much work to do' rationale. We place the responsibility exactly where it should be: not in denying relief to those who have been injured, But on the judicial machinery of the Commonwealth to fulfill its obligation to make itself available to litigants. Who is to say which class of aggrieved plaintiffs should be denied access to our courts because of speculation that the workload will be a burden? Certainly this Court is unwilling to allow such considerations to influence a determination whether a class of litigants will be denied or permitted to seek adjudication of its claims.' (Emphasis in original.)

Equally unpersuasive is the argument ... that immunity is required because governmental units lack funds from which claims could be paid. It is argued that funds would be diverted to the payment of claims and the performance of proper governmental functions would be obstructed. Initially, we note our disagreement with the assumption that the payment of claims is not a proper governmental function. 'As many writers have pointed out, the fallacy in (the no-fund theory) is that it assumes the very point which is sought to be proved i.e., that payment of damage claims is not a proper purpose.' [C]

Additionally, the empirical data does not support the fear that governmental functions would be curtailed as a result of liability for tortious conduct. ...

....

Finally, this Court addressed the financial burden argument in Flagiello v. Pennsylvania Hospital, supra. There, in rejecting the argument as it applied to the immunity of charitable institutions, we said:

> 'The voluminous arguments advanced by the defendant hospital and the amicus curiae, on the subject of the financial problems of hospitals today, are, while interesting and enlightening, wholly irrelevant to the issue before us. We have a duty to perform and that is to see that justice, within the framework of law, is done. Our function is to decide cases as they come before us on the pertinent facts and law. What could happen in the event the plaintiff obtains a verdict is not an issue here. The pleadings in this litigation require that we decide whether the defendant hospital should answer the charges brought against it by the plaintiff.'

Id. 417 Pa. at 503-504, 208 A.2d at 202.[7]

Thus, we must agree with Chief Justice Traynor of the California Supreme Court that 'the rule of governmental immunity for tort is an anachronism, without rational basis, and has existed only by the force of inertia.' Muskopf v. Corning Hospital District, supra 55 Cal.2d at 216,11 Cal. Rptr. at 92, 359 P.2d at 460. Moreover, the distinction between governmental and proprietary functions 'is probably one of the most unsatisfactory known to the law, for it has caused confusion not only among the various jurisdictions but almost always within each jurisdiction.' [C]

....

Imposition of tort liability will... be more responsive to current concepts of justice. Claims will be treated as a cost of administration and losses will be spread among all those benefited by governmental action. [Cc]

---

7 It is interesting to note that [previously this] Court, in concluding that school districts are immune, analogized to the immunity of charities. However, we [have since] abolished the doctrine of charitable immunity.

Moreover, 'where governmental immunity has had the effect of encouraging laxness and a disregard of potential harm, exposure of the government to liability for its torts will have the effect of increasing governmental care and concern for the welfare of those who might be injured by its actions.' [C]. As Dean Prosser has written:

> 'The **'prophylactic'** factor of preventing future harm has been quite important in the field of torts. The courts are concerned not only with compensation of the victim, but with admonition of the wrongdoer. When the decisions of the courts become known, and defendants realize that they may be held liable, there is of course a strong incentive to prevent the occurrence of the harm. Not infrequently one reason for imposing liability is the deliberate purpose of providing that incentive.'

Prosser, supra at 23.

III.

Appellee seems to recognize that significant public policy considerations demand abolition of the governmental immunity doctrine. Indeed, appellee does not attempt to justify retention of immunity on policy grounds. Rather, it contends that abrogation, if it is to be achieved, should be accomplished by legislative direction rather than by judicial determination.

. . . .

[H]ere, the doctrine of governmental immunity-judicially imposed -may be judicially terminated. 'Having found that doctrine to be unsound and unjust under present conditions, we consider that we have not only the power, but the duty, to abolish that immunity. ' We closed our courtroom doors without legislative help, and we can likewise open them.' ...

. . . .

On prior occasions, we recognized that errors of 'history, logic and policy' were responsible for the development of the governmental immunity doctrine. [C] Nevertheless, we suggested that the Legislature should undertake the abrogation of governmental immunity. [C] These suggestions do not preclude our Court from now abolishing this judicially created doctrine. In so doing, we join numerous other jurisdictions which similarly, by judicial decision, have abandoned governmental immunity notwithstanding prior deference to legislative action. [Cc]

. . . .

IV.

Appellee urges that abrogation of the immunity doctrine disturbs the principle of [s]tare decisis. It seems obvious, however, that appellee not only misconceives the mission of the Stare decisis principle, but also ignores the admonition of Chief Justice Cardozo:

'We tend sometimes, in determining the growth of a principle or a precedent, to treat it as if it represented the outcome of a quest for certainty. That is to mistake its origin. Only in the rarest instances, if ever, was certainty either possible or expected. The principle or the precedent was the outcome of a quest for probabilities. Principles and precedents, thus generated, carry throughout their lives the birthmarks of their origin. They are in truth provisional hypotheses, born in doubt and travail, expressing the adjustment which commended itself at the moment between competing possibilities.'

Id. at 69-70 (footnote omitted).

The doctrine of governmental immunity, created centuries ago, is, like most other principles, 'a provisional hypothesis.' As stated in Smith v. State, supra, 93 Idaho at 801, 473 P.2d at 943:

'When precedent is examined in the light of modern reality and it is evident that the reason for the precedent no longer exists, the abandonment of the precedent is not a destruction of stare decisis but rather a fulfillment of its proper function.

'Stare decisis is not a confining phenomenon but rather a principle of law. And when the application of this principle will not result in justice, it is evident that the doctrine is not properly applicable.'

This Court has repeatedly recognized that the principle of Stare decisis is not a 'confining phenomenon.' We are mindful of the observation of Mr. Justice Schaefer of the Supreme Court of Illinois:

'Precedent speaks for the past; policy for the present and the future. The goal which we seek is a blend which takes into account in due proportion the wisdom of the past and the needs of the present.'

Schaefer, Precedent and Policy, 34 U.Chi.L.Rev. 3, 24 (1966).

. . . .

The cases are numerous in which this Court has rejected principles which were 'out of accord with modern conditions of life.' [Cc].

The controlling principle which emerges from these and other decisions is clear-the doctrine of Stare decisis is not a vehicle for perpetuating error, but rather a legal concept which responds to the demands of justice and, thus, permits the orderly growth processes of the law to flourish.

V.

Finally, it is suggested that if we abolish governmental immunity, our decision to do so should not apply to the instant case. ...[A]ppellee's argument that we do not apply our newly adopted rule to the facts of this case must be rejected.

Having concluded that local governmental units-municipal corporations and quasi-corporations-are no longer immune from tort liability, the order sustaining appellee's preliminary objections is reversed and the record remanded for proceedings consistent with this opinion.

MANDERINO, J., joins in this opinion and filed a concurring opinion.

JONES, C.J., and EAGEN and O'BRIEN, JJ., dissent.

[concurring opinion of J. Manderino is omitted.]

Points for Discussion

1. Historically, the doctrine of governmental immunity provided a valid defense against tort liability for all local, state, and federal governments. In order to be sued in tort, the government had to give permission to be sued, with that permission granted by statute. However, as discussed in *Ayala,* this notion of governmental immunity has eroded over the years.

2. The *Ayala* court specifically announced that it was not considering the issue of the immunity of the Commonwealth of Pennsylvania, or the state's sovereign immunity. Rather, the issue in *Ayala* concerned governmental immunity, the immunity of the public school district. What is the difference between sovereign immunity and governmental immunity?

3. What are the policy considerations in favor of governmental immunity? Against? Which considerations do you find to be most persuasive?

4. The *Ayala* court speaks frequently of *stare decisis*. What is *stare decisis*? How is it at issue in the *Ayala* case?

RESTATEMENT (SECOND) OF TORTS § 895C (1979)
Local Government Entities

(1) Except as stated in Subsection (2), a local government entity is not immune from tort liability.

(2) A local governmental entity is immune from tort liability for acts and omissions constituting

    (a) the exercise of a legislative or judicial function, and

    (b) the exercise of an administrative function involving the determination of fundamental governmental policy.

(3) Repudiation of general tort immunity does not establish liability for an act or omission that is otherwise privileged or is not tortious.

---

5. Today, most states have some mechanism by which a government entity may be held liable for tortious injuries. Nonetheless, liability of governmental entities may be limited on grounds distinct from immunity. Consider the next two cases.

Riss v. New York

240 N.E.2d 860 (N.Y. 1968)

BREITEL, Judge.

This appeal presents, in a very sympathetic framework, the issue of the liability of a municipality for failure to provide special protection to a member of the public who was repeatedly threatened with personal harm and eventually suffered dire personal injuries for lack of such protection. The facts are amply described in the dissenting opinion and no useful purpose would be served by repetition. The issue arises upon the affirmance by a divided Appellate Division of a dismissal of the complaint, after both sides had rested but before submission to the jury.

It is necessary immediately to distinguish those liabilities attendant upon governmental activities which have displaced or supplemented traditionally private enterprises, such as are involved in the operation of rapid transit systems, hospitals, and places of public assembly. Once sovereign immunity was abolished by statute the extension of liability on ordinary principles of tort law logically followed. To be equally distinguished are certain activities of government which provide services and facilities for the use of the public, such as highways, public buildings and the like, in the performance of which the municipality or the State may be liable under ordinary principles of tort law. The ground for liability is the provision of the services or facilities for the direct use by members of the public.

In contrast, this case involves the provision of a governmental service to protect the public generally from external hazards and particularly to control the activities of criminal wrongdoers. [Cc] The amount of protection that may be provided is limited by the resources of the community and by a considered legislative-executive decision as to how those resources may be deployed. For the courts to proclaim a new and general duty of protection in the law of tort, even to those who may be the particular seekers of protection based on specific hazards, could and would inevitably determine how the limited police resources of the community should be allocated and without predictable limits. This is quite different from the predictable allocation of resources and liabilities when public hospitals, rapid transit systems, or even highways are provided.

Before such extension of responsibilities should be dictated by the indirect imposition of tort liabilities, there should be a legislative determination that that should be the scope of public responsibility [C]

It is notable that the removal of sovereign immunity for tort liability was accomplished after legislative enactment and not by any judicial arrogation of power [C]. It is equally notable that for many years, since as far back as 1909 in this State, there was by statute municipal liability for losses sustained as a result of riot [C]. Yet even this class of liability has for some years been suspended by legislative action [C], a factor of considerable significance.

When one considers the greatly increased amount of crime committed throughout the cities, but especially in certain portions of them, with a repetitive and predictable pattern, it is easy to see the consequences of fixing municipal liability upon a showing of probable need for and request for protection. To be sure these are grave problems at the present time, exciting high priority activity on the part of the national, State and local governments, to which the answers are neither simple, known, or presently within reasonable controls. To foist a presumed cure for these problems by judicial innovation of a new kind of liability in tort would be foolhardy indeed and an assumption of judicial wisdom and power not possessed by the courts.

....

[T]here is no warrant in judicial tradition or in the proper allocation of the powers of government for the courts, in the absence of legislation, to carve out an area of tort liability for police protection to members of the public. Quite distinguishable, of course, is the situation where the police authorities undertake responsibilities to particular members of the public and expose them, without adequate protection, to the risks which then materialize into actual losses [C].

Accordingly, the order of the Appellate Division affirming the judgment of dismissal should be affirmed.

KEATING, Judge (dissenting).

Certainly, the record in this case, sound legal analysis, relevant policy considerations and even precedent cannot account for or sustain the result which the majority have here reached. For the result is premised upon a legal rule which long ago should have been abandoned, having lost any justification it might once have had. Despite almost universal condemnation by legal scholars, the rule survives, finding its continuing strength, not in its power to persuade, but in its ability to arouse unwarranted judicial fears of the consequences of overturning it.

Linda Riss, an attractive young woman, was for more than six months terrorized by a rejected suitor well known to the courts of this State, one Burton Pugach. This miscreant, masquerading as a respectable attorney, repeatedly threatened to have Linda killed or maimed if she did not yield to him: 'If I can't have you, no one else will have you, and when I get through with you, no one else will want you'. In fear for her life, she went to those charged by law with the duty of preserving and safeguarding the lives of the citizens and residents of this State. Linda's repeated and almost pathetic pleas for aid were received with little more than indifference. Whatever help she was given was not commensurate with the identifiable danger. On June 14, 1959 Linda became engaged to another man. At a party held to celebrate the event, she received a phone call warning her that it was her 'last chance'. Completely distraught, she called the police, begging for help, but was refused. The next day Pugach carried out his dire threats in the very manner he had foretold by having a hired thug throw lye in Linda's face. Linda was blinded in one eye, lost a good portion of her vision in the other, and her face was permanently scarred. After the assault the authorities concluded that there was some basis for Linda's fears, and for the next three and one-half years, she was given around-the-clock protection.

No one questions the proposition that the first duty of government is to assure its citizens the opportunity to live in personal security. And no one who reads the record of Linda's ordeal can reach a conclusion other than that the City of New York, acting through its agents, completely and negligently failed to fulfill this obligation to Linda.

Linda has turned to the courts of this State for redress, asking that the city be held liable in damages for its negligent failure to protect her from harm.   With compelling logic, she can point out that, if a stranger, who had absolutely no obligation to aid her, had offered her assistance, and thereafter Burton Pugach was able to injure her as a result of the negligence of the volunteer, the courts would certainly require him to pay damages. [C] Why then should the city … not be responsible? If a private detective acts carelessly, no one would deny that a jury could find such conduct unacceptable. Why then is the city not required to live up to at least the same minimal standards of professional competence which would be demanded of a private detective?

>
>
> **FYI**
>
> The argument here refers to a well-accepted tort principle, set forth in RESTATEMENT (SECOND) OF TORTS § 323: "One who undertakes … to render services to another … is subject to liability … for physical harm resulting from his failure to exercise reasonable care to perform his undertaking if (a) his failure to exercise such care increases the risk of … harm or (b) the harm is suffered because of the other's reliance upon the undertaking."

Linda's reasoning seems so eminently sensible that surely it must come as a shock to her and to every citizen to hear the city argue and to learn that this court decides that the city has no duty to provide police protection to any given individual. What makes the city's position particularly difficult to understand is that, in conformity, to the dictates of the law, Linda did not carry any weapon for self-defense [C]. Thus, by a rather bitter irony she was required to rely for protection on the City of New York which now denies all responsibility to her.

> **See It**
>
> More bizarre than the facts described in the dissenting opinion in *Riss* are the post-case developments between the victim, Linda Riss, and the man who orchestrated her attack, Burton Pugach. Incredibly, the two eventually married. Their strange story is the subject of the 2007 documentary CRAZY LOVE.

It is not a distortion to summarize the essence of the city's case here in the following language: 'Because we owe a duty to everybody, we owe it to nobody.' Were it not for the fact that this position has been hallowed by much ancient and revered precedent, we would surely dismiss it as preposterous. To say that there is no duty is, of course, to start with the conclusion. The question is whether or not there should be liability for the negligent failure to provide adequate police protection.

The foremost justification repeatedly urged for the existing rule is the claim that the State and the municipalities will be exposed to limitless liability. ...

The fear of financial disaster is a myth. The same argument was made a generation ago in opposition to proposals that the State waive its defense of 'sovereign immunity'. The prophecy proved false then, and it would now. The supposed astronomical financial burden does not and would not exist. No municipality has gone bankrupt because it has had to respond in damages when a policeman causes injury through carelessly driving a police car or in the thousands of other situations where, by judicial fiat or legislative enactment, the State and its subdivisions have been held liable for the tortious conduct of their employees. ... That Linda Riss should be asked to bear the loss, which should properly fall on the city if we assume, as we must, in the present posture of the case, that her injuries resulted from the city's failure to provide sufficient police to protect Linda is contrary to the most elementary notions of justice.

The statement in the majority opinion that there are no predictable limits to the potential liability for failure to provide adequate police protection as compared to other areas of municipal liability is, of course, untenable. When immunity in other areas of governmental activity was removed, the same lack of predictable limits existed. Yet, disaster did not ensue.

Another variation of the 'crushing burden' argument is the contention that, every time a crime is committed, the city will be sued and the claim will be made that it resulted from inadequate police protection. Here, again, is an attempt to arouse the 'anxiety of the courts about new theories of liability which may have a far-reaching effect'. [Cc] And here too the underlying assumption of the argument is fallacious because it assumes that a strict liability standard is to be imposed and that the courts would prove completely unable to apply general principles of tort liability in a reasonable fashion in the context of actions arising from the negligent acts of police and fire personnel. The argument is also made as if there were no such legal principles as fault, proximate cause or foreseeability, all of which operate to keep liability within reasonable bounds. No one is contending that the police must be at the scene of every potential crime or must provide a personal bodyguard to every person who walks into a police station and claims to have been threatened. They need only act as a reasonable man would under the circumstances. At first there would be a duty to inquire. If the inquiry indicates nothing to substantiate the alleged threat, the matter may be put aside and other matters attended to. If, however, the claims prove to have some basis, appropriate steps would be necessary.

The instant case provides an excellent illustration of the limits which the courts can draw. No one would claim that, under the facts here, the police were negligent when they did not give Linda protection after her first calls or visits to the police station in February of 1959. The preliminary investigation was sufficient. If Linda had been attacked at this point, clearly there would be no liability here. When, however, as time went on and it was established that Linda was a reputable person, that other verifiable attempts to injure her or intimidate her had taken place, that other witnesses were available to support her claim that her life was being threatened, something more was required-either by way of further investigation or protection-than the statement that was made by one detective to Linda that she would have to be hurt before the police could do anything for her.

In dismissing the complaint, the trial court noted that there are many crimes being committed daily and the police force is inadequate to deal with its 'tremendous responsibilities'. The point is not addressed to the facts of this case. Even if it were, however, a distinction must be made. It may be quite reasonable to say that the City of New York is not required to hire sufficient police to protect every piece of property threatened during mass riots. The possibility of riots may even be foreseeable, but the occurrence is sufficiently uncommon that the city should not be required to bear the cost of having a redundancy of men for normal operations. But it is going beyond the bounds of required judicial moderation if the city is permitted to escape liability in a situation such as the one at bar. If the police force of the City of New York is so understaffed that it is unable to cope with the everyday problem posed by the relatively few cases where single, known individuals threaten the lives of other persons, then indeed we have reached the danger line and the lives of all of us are in peril. If the police department is in such a deplorable state that the city, because of insufficient manpower, is truly unable to protect persons in Linda Riss' position, then liability not only should, but must be imposed. It will act as an effective inducement for public officials to provide at least a minimally adequate number of police. If local officials are not willing to meet even such a low standard, I see no reason for the courts to abet such irresponsibility.

It is also contended that liability for inadequate police protection will make the courts the arbiters of decisions taken by the Police Commissioner in allocating his manpower and his resources. We are not dealing here with a situation where the injury or loss occurred as a result of a conscious choice of policy made by those exercising high administrative responsibility after a complete and thorough deliberation of various alternatives. There was no major policy decision taken by the Police Commissioner to disregard Linda Riss' appeal for help because there was absolutely no manpower available to deal with Pugach. This 'garden variety' negligence case arose in the course of 'day-by-day operations of government' [C]. Linda Riss' tragedy resulted not from high policy or inadequate manpower, but plain negligence on the part of persons with whom Linda dealt. [Cc]

More significant, however, is the fundamental flaw in the reasoning behind the argument alleging judicial interference. It is a complete oversimplification of the problem of municipal tort liability. What it ignores is the fact that indirectly courts are reviewing administrative practices in almost every tort case against the State or a municipality, including even decisions of the Police Commissioner. Every time a municipal hospital is held liable for malpractice resulting from inadequate record-keeping, the courts are in effect making a determination that the municipality should have hired or assigned more clerical help or more competent help to medical records or should have done something to improve its record-keeping procedures so that the particular injury would not have occurred. Every time a municipality is held liable for a defective sidewalk, it is as if the courts are saying that more money and resources should have been allocated to sidewalk repair, instead of to other public services.

The situation is nowise different in the case of police protection. Whatever effects there may be on police administration will be one of degree, not kind. ...

The truth of the matter ... is that the courts are not making policy decisions for public officials. In all these municipal negligence cases, the courts are doing two things. First, they apply the principles of **vicarious liability** to the operations of government. Courts would not insulate the city from liability for the ordinary negligence of members of the highway department. There is no basis for treating the members of the police department differently.

Second, and most important, to the extent that the injury results from the failure to allocate sufficient funds and resources to meet a minimum standard of public administration, public officials are presented with two alternatives: either improve public administration or accept the cost of compensating injured persons. Thus, if we were to hold the city liable here for the negligence of the police, courts would no more be interfering with the operations of the police department than they 'meddle' in the affairs of the highway department when they hold the municipality liable for personal injuries resulting from defective sidewalks, or a private employer for the negligence of his employees. In other words, all the courts do in these municipal negligence cases is require officials to weigh the consequences of their decisions. If Linda Riss' injury resulted from the failure of the city to pay sufficient salaries to attract qualified and sufficient personnel, the full cost of that choice should become acknowledged in the same way as it has in other areas of municipal tort liability. Perhaps officials will find it less costly to choose the alternative of paying damages than changing their existing practices. That may be well and good, but the price for the refusal to provide for an adequate police force should not be borne by Linda Riss and all the other innocent victims of such decisions.

What has existed until now is that the City of New York and other municipalities have been able to engage in a sort of false bookkeeping in which the real costs of inadequate or incompetent police protection have been hidden by charging the expenditures to the individuals who have sustained often catastrophic losses rather than to the community where it belongs, because the latter had the power to prevent the losses.

Although in modern times the compensatory nature of tort law has generally been the one most emphasized, one of its most important functions has been and is its **normative** aspect. It sets forth standards of conduct which ought to be followed. The penalty for failing to do so is to pay pecuniary damages. At one time the government was completely immunized from this salutary control. This is much less so now, and the imposition of liability has had healthy side effects. In many areas, it has resulted in the adoption of better and more considered procedures just as workmen's compensation resulted in improved industrial safety practices. To visit liability upon the city here will no doubt have similar constructive effects. No 'presumed cure' for the problem of crime is being 'foisted' upon the city as the majority opinion charges. The methods of dealing with the problem of crime are left completely to the city's discretion. All that the courts can do is make sure that the costs of the city's and its employees' mistakes are placed where they properly belong. Thus, every reason used to sustain the rule that there is no duty to offer police protection to any individual turns out on close analysis to be of little substance.

...[W]hat is of greater interest about the case is that it premised liability on pure common-law negligence. But although 'sovereign immunity', by that name, supposedly died ..., it has been revived in a new form. It now goes by the name 'public duty'.

....

Some indication of the movement of the law against the existing rule can be extracted from the fact that, whereas a few decades ago, the rule that there is no duty to provide adequate police and fire protection was attacked only intermittently, in recent years more and more insistently we have been asked to reject the rule. An assault can be found now in almost every recent volume of the New York Reports....

The rule is Judge made and can be judicially modified. By statute, the judicially created doctrine of 'sovereign immunity' was destroyed. It was an unrighteous doctrine, carrying as it did the connotation that the government is above the law. Likewise, the law should be purged of all new evasions, which seek to avoid the full implications of the repeal of sovereign immunity.

No doubt in the future we shall have to draw limitations just as we have done in the area of private litigation, and no doubt some of these limitations will be unique to municipal liability because the problems will not have any counterpart in private tort law. But if the lines are to be drawn, let them be delineated on candid considerations of policy and fairness and not on the fictions or relics of the doctrine of 'sovereign immunity'. Before reaching such questions, however, we must resolve the fundamental issue raised here and recognize that, having undertaken to provide professional police and fire protection, municipalities cannot escape liability for damages caused by their failure to do even a minimally adequate job of it.

.....

[S]ince this is an appeal from a dismissal of the complaint, we must give the plaintiff the benefit of every favorable inference. The Appellate Division's conclusion could only have been reached by ignoring the thrust of the plaintiff's claim and the evidence in the record. A few examples of the actions of the police should suffice to show the true state of the record. Linda Riss received a telephone call from a person who warned Linda that Pugach was arranging to have her beaten up. A detective learned the identity of the caller. He offered to arrest the caller, but plaintiff rejected that suggestion for the obvious reason that the informant was trying to help Linda. When Linda requested that Pugach be arrested, the detective said he could not do that because she had not yet been hurt. The statement was not so. It was and is a crime to conspire to injure someone. True there was no basis to arrest Pugach then, but that was only because the necessary leg work had not been done. No one went to speak to the informant, who might have furnished additional leads. Linda claimed to be receiving telephone calls almost every day. These calls could have been monitored for a few days to obtain evidence against Pugach. Any number of reasonable alternatives presented themselves. A case against Pugach could have been developed which would have at least put him away for a while or altered the situation entirely. But, if necessary, some police protection should have been afforded.

Perhaps, on a fuller record after a true trial on the merits, the city's position will not appear so damaging as it does now. But with actual notice of danger and ample opportunity to confirm and take reasonable remedial steps, a jury could find that the persons involved acted unreasonably and negligently. Linda Riss is entitled to have a jury determine the issue of the city's liability. This right should not be terminated by the adoption of a question-begging conclusion that there is no duty owed to her. The order of the Appellate Division should be reversed and a new trial granted.

FULD, C.J., and BURKE, SCILEPPI, BERGAN and JASEN, JJ., concur with BREITEL, JJ.

KEATING, J., dissents and votes to reverse in a separate opinion.

Order affirmed, without costs.

Points for Discussion

1. What is the holding in this case?

2. What is the plaintiff's theory of recovery? What is the applicable standard of care?

3. Do you agree with the dissenting judge taking the position that "[b]ecause we owe a duty to everybody, we owe it to nobody" is problematic?

4. What does the dissenting judge mean when he states that "one of the most important functions [of tort law] has been and is its normative aspects"? What other functions of tort law does the dissenting judge consider?

5. Which opinion, majority or dissent, is most persuasive to you? Why?

6. The *Riss* case articulates the **public duty doctrine**. A recent court distinguished the doctrines of **sovereign immunity**, **official immunity**, and the public duty doctrine:

   > The public duty doctrine states that a public employee is not civilly liable for the breach of a duty owed to the general public, rather than a particular individual. …This public duty rule is based on the absence of a duty to the particular individual as contrasted to the duty owed to the general public. …
   >
   > …Whether an individual has such a private interest depends on the facts of each case, not on broad pronouncements about the usual status of relevant functions.

   > The public duty doctrine is not an **affirmative defense**, but rather delineates the legal duty the defendant public employee owes the plaintiff … The applicability of the public duty doctrine negates the duty element required to prove negligence, such that there can be no cause of action for injuries sustained as the result of an alleged breach of

Make the Connection

The court here is pointing out an important distinction – whether the plaintiff will be able to prove the *prima facie* case for a negligence action (*see* Chapter 4) or whether the defendant will be able to defend on immunity grounds. If the public duty doctrine applies, there is no tort at all; if an immunity applies, there is a tort for which the defendant may not be held responsible.

public duty to the community as a whole. … In this way, the public duty doctrine's impact is distinguishable from the doctrine of official immunity. Application of the public duty doctrine leaves the plaintiff unable to prove all the elements of his claim for negligence, whereas application of the doctrine of official immunity merely impacts liability, but does not destroy the underlying tort.

Southers v. City of Farmington, 263 S.W.3d 603, 611-12 (Mo. 2008). In accord is § 895D(3) of the RESTATEMENT (SECOND) OF TORTS:

"A public officer acting within the general scope of his authority is not subject to tort liability for an administrative act or omission if

(a) he is immune because engaged in the exercise of a discretionary function,

(b) he is privileged and does not exceed or abuse the privilege, or

(c) his conduct was not tortious because he was not negligent in the performance of his responsibility."

7. In *Town of Castle Rock v. Gonzales,* 545 U.S. 748 (2005), the Supreme Court considered a lawsuit alleging that the municipality and its police officers violated the plaintiff's constitutional rights by failing to respond to the plaintiff's repeated reports that her estranged husband had taken their three children in violation of a restraining order issued against the husband. The husband ultimately murdered the children. The Court held that the plaintiff did not have a property interest in police enforcement of the restraining order protected by the Due Process Clause of the Fourteenth Amendment to the United States Constitution. The Court reasoned that "it is by no means clear that an individual entitlement to enforcement of a restraining order could constitute a 'property' interest for purposes of the Due Process Clause. Such a right would not, of course, resemble any traditional conception of property. Although that alone does not disqualify it from due process protection . . . the right to have a restraining order enforced does not 'have some ascertainable monetary value' . . ." Do you agree with the Court's holding? Do you agree or disagree with its conclusion that the enforcement of a restraining order has no ascertainable monetary value to a plaintiff?

8. Contrast *Riss's* application of the public duty doctrine with the next case.

————————————

DeLong v. Erie County

455 N.Y.S.2d 887 (N.Y. Sup. Ct. 1982)

Before DILLON, P.J., and HANCOCK, DENMAN, MOULE and SCHNEPP, JJ.

HANCOCK, Justice:

A municipality cannot be cast in damages for mere failure to provide adequate police protection (*Riss v. City of New York,* 22 N.Y.2d 579, 293 N.Y.S.2d 897, 240 N.E.2d 860). But "where a municipality assumes a duty to a particular person or class of persons, it must perform that duty in a nonnegligent manner * * *. As Chief Judge Cardozo succinctly stated: 'The hand once set to a task may not always be withdrawn with impunity though liability would fail if it had never been applied at all.' (*Moch Co. v. Rensselaer Water Co.,* 247 N.Y. [160], at p. 167 [159 N.E. 896])" [Cc] Applying these accepted rules to the record before us, we affirm the jury finding of co-equal liability on the part of the County of Erie and the City of Buffalo. Together, they assumed a special duty to provide emergency police assistance to Amalia DeLong, and, acting in concert in carrying out the undertaking, they were negligent. As a result of their negligence, Amalia DeLong was stabbed to death in her home by an intruder.

In its verdict the jury awarded to her administrator $200,000 for her conscious pain and suffering and $600,000 for wrongful death, finding each defendant 50% responsible. We are all of the opinion that the verdict for conscious pain and suffering should be affirmed. As for the verdict for wrongful death, a majority of the court conclude that it also should be affirmed, but two of our number would reverse and grant a new trial on damages only for that cause of action. On appeal defendants raise several questions both as to liability and damages. To discuss their contentions as to liability, a recital of the events leading to Amalia DeLong's death is necessary.

Before her death, Amalia DeLong, her husband, and their three young children resided at 319 Victoria Boulevard in the Village of Kenmore, a suburb of Buffalo located in Erie County. In October, 1976, the Village of Kenmore was one of the four communities outside of Buffalo fully served by the 911 emergency telephone system operated by the Central Police Services, an agency of Erie County, with the active assistance and cooperation of the Buffalo Police Department. The system was located in the 911 room in Buffalo Police Headquarters in downtown Buffalo. At 9:29:29 in the morning of October 25, 1976 Amalia DeLong dialed 911 on her telephone and was immediately connected to the 911 room. The transcript of her call is as follows:

9:29:29 -	Caller:	"Police?"
	Complaint Writer:	"911."
	Caller:	"Police, please come, 319 Victoria right away."
	Complaint Writer:	"What's wrong?"
	Caller:	"There's a burglar."
9:29:34 -	Complaint Writer:	"In there now?"
	Caller:	"I heard a burglar; I saw his face in the back; he was trying to break in the house; please come right away."
	Complaint Writer:	"Okay , right away."
9:29:43 -	Caller:	"Okay."

The complaint writer recorded the address on the complaint card as "219 Victoria"- not "319 Victoria". The call had lasted 14 seconds. The complaint writer had not ascertained the caller's name, that she was calling from the Village of Kenmore, or that the complete name of the street was "Victoria *Boulevard*". Aware that there was a Victoria *Avenue* in the City of Buffalo and assuming that he was dealing with a Buffalo emergency, the complaint writer stamped the word "flash" on the complaint card and routed it on the high priority conveyor to the Buffalo police dispatcher stationed on the other side of a glass partition. At 9:30:48, the dispatcher broadcast to the cars on duty in the 16th precinct (where Victoria Avenue was located) the following: "Car 16 at 219 Victoria. A burglary in progress." At 9:33:46 one of the cars radioed back: "Address of 219 Victoria does not exist - highest number 195." The dispatcher responded: "Okay. You're clear on that. No such address as 219 Victoria or burglary in progress." Thus, at 9:34, the 16th precinct cars were released from the call and no further action was taken. Less than four and one-half minutes had elapsed from the end of Amalia DeLong's call. If the call had been identified as 319 Victoria Boulevard in the Village of Kenmore, the complaint writer could, by pressing two buttons, have made instant and direct contact with the Village of Kenmore Police Department.

At approximately 9:42, neighbors observed Amalia DeLong run from the front door of her house. She was naked, covered with blood and bleeding profusely. She fell to the sidewalk. Before her collape, she uttered her only words: "The baby. The baby." Her infant child could be seen standing inside the open door.

The Village of Kenmore Police Department responded immediately to a call for assistance with a car which arrived within one minute—at 9:43. The Kenmore Police Chief testified that the police station was approximately 1375 feet from the DeLong house and that if the police car had been responding to the report of a burglary of an occupied house, it would have used the siren in approaching to scare the burglar away. The paramedics arrived at 9:47. Their records indicated that at 9:53 Amalia DeLong had no vital signs.

Amalia DeLong had received seven knife wounds: to the left side of the neck, the left side of the head, the second finger of the right hand, the nail of the third finger on the left hand, the thumb of the left hand, and a wound to the left shoulder. The laceration on the neck was fatal. It was deep and had severed the jugular vein and carotid artery on the left. The cuts on the fingers were described as being of a "defensive type".

The police in searching the house found evidence of a savage attack. A housecoat, feminine undergarments, and a brassiere with a broken clasp were found on the living room floor, and pillows, papers and other items were strewn about. There were spatterings of blood on the walls and floor in the kitchen, in the hallway and on the rug in the living room and several large stains on the front door, on the rug inside the door and on the porch.

The time of Amalia DeLong's death could not be precisely fixed, but it occurred between 9:42, the time when she spoke her last words, and 9:53, when she showed no signs of life. A pathologist testified that a person of her size could have lived from two minutes and 25 seconds to four minutes and 49 seconds after severance of the jugular vein and carotid artery. He opined that the fatal blow was inflicted at 9:38, four minutes after the dispatcher had "cleared" the call.

The purpose of the 911 emergency or "hot line" system is to assist in the delivery of police services to the people in the communities served (determined by whether the telephone exchanges in the communities are such that dialing 911 will give an automatic connection with the 911 room at Buffalo police headquarters). The public was made aware of the 911 emergency system by, among other things, a listing on the page in the telephone book for the Erie County metropolitan area headed "Emergency Numbers". The first caption appearing on the page in large type is "Police", opposite which appears in slightly smaller type a subheading "Local Police". For both police and local police the number given is "911".

The system has two components: complaint writing and dispatching. The Buffalo Police Department performed both functions until March, 1975 when the city and county entered into a contract transferring the 911 complaint writing function to the county, to be performed by county civil service employees. Under the contract, the city agreed to furnish the facilities for the 911 operation at the Buffalo Police headquarters including switchboard services, parking places, locker space and other necessaries for the county employees. The contract also provided that: "For one year from the date of this agreement, the City shall keep assigned to the complaint writing function sufficient police officers per shift experienced in complaint writing, at the City's expense, to provide training, supervision and guidance to County personnel engaged in the complaint writing function." And that "[a]fter one year, it shall be mutually agreed by the Commissioner of Central Police Services and the Commissioner of the Buffalo Police Department whether this arrangement for training and supervision shall be continued, for what period it shall be continued, or whether particular situations may at various periods require such an arrangement." And that "[t]he City of Buffalo, specifically the Buffalo Police Department '911' Emergency Control Center, expects to maintain its own dispatching personnel and supervisory Lieutenants"; and further that no substantial changes in procedures which might require changes in the complaint writing function shall be "instituted without the concurrence of the Commissioner of Central Police Services and the Commissioner of the Buffalo Police Department."

Pursuant to the contract, the Buffalo Police Department continued to train the complaint writers and were still doing so on October 25, 1976. Moreover, a lieutenant of the Buffalo Police Department or an acting lieutenant was always present in the 911 room. Although not directly in the chain of command, his function was to supervise, train and give assistance to the complaint writers and to coordinate the activities of the complaint writers and the Buffalo Police dispatchers. He was considered to be a figure of authority.

The County Commissioner of the Department of Central Police Services described the system as "a joint venture in the operations of the 911 center between the City of Buffalo and the County of Erie" with the city police performing the dispatching function and the county employees performing the complaint writing function. The Buffalo police lieutenant is there, he testified, "to supervise any * * * type of incident that the complaint writer or, I assume, the other party may have questions about."

Many pages of testimony concern the instructions for taking and recording complaints as given in the training sessions and set forth in the "Manual for 911 Services". Complaint writers were directed to obtain exact information as to the location of the call and always to repeat the address of the call for verification. The "Manual for 911 Services" contained, among others, the following instructions for taking complaints: "It is very important that the information recorded on the card be accurate and adequate to eliminate needless call backs from the dispatcher to the complaint desk and 'standby' to units. To facilitate receiving the *exact* location of calls, you *must* determine and so indicate on the card, if address is an apartment, rear house, apartment number, etc. (*Always* repeat the address to the caller for verification.) If necessary, ask the caller for the spelling of the street name or the name of the nearest cross street." And: "Sufficient time must be taken on each call to avoid confusion or incorrect addresses due to duplicate or similar sounding street names * * *."

....

On the morning of October 25, the complaint writer, in addition to mistakenly recording the address on the complaint card as 219 instead of 319 Victoria, failed to follow the instructions in four respects: (1) he did not ask the name of the caller; (2) he did not determine the exact location of the call; (3) he did not address the caller by name; (4) he did not repeat the address.

The operating procedures in effect on October 25, 1976 also called for followup action if, as with the DeLong call, the report came back to the dispatcher: "No such address." In such event, the dispatcher was required to notify the complaint writer or the 911 lieutenant (the Buffalo police lieutenant on duty in the 911 room) so that the tape recording of the call could be replayed, the Haines Directory and the street guides consulted, and other communities having street names identical or similar to the street name given by the caller immediately notified. On Amalia DeLong's call, no follow-up of any kind took place. The call was treated as a fake.

I

Our discussion of the questions raised concerning liability must start with *Riss v. City of New York,* 22 N.Y.2d 579, 293 N.Y.S.2d 897, 240 N.E.2d 860, supra in which the court found no legal responsibility for the tragic consequences of the city's failure to furnish police protection despite proof of Linda Riss' repeated and agonized pleas for assistance. ... Quite distinguishable, of course, is the situation where the police authorities undertake responsibilities to particular members of the public and expose them, without adequate protection, to the risks which then materialize into actual losses ....

Whether Amalia DeLong was a person to whom the municipalities owed a special duty so as to be accountable for negligence in the performance of that duty is the question. Defendants argue that the county and city, in maintaining the 911 emergency call system for the public generally, assumed no special obligation to protect Amalia DeLong, and that, therefore, the case is governed by the holding of no liability in *Riss.* ...

The defendants' argument misses the mark. It is not the establishment of the emergency call system to serve the Village of Kenmore, standing alone, which creates the duty. It is the holding out of the 911 number as one to be called by someone in need of assistance, Amalia DeLong's placing of the call in reliance on that holding out, and her further reliance on the response to her plea for immediate help: "Okay, right away." This is not a mere failure to furnish police protection owed to the public generally but a case where the municipality has assumed a duty to a particular person which it must perform "in a nonnegligent manner, [although without the] voluntary assumption of that duty, none would have otherwise existed" [C] The complaint writer's acceptance of the call, his transmittal of the complaint card to the dispatcher and the dispatcher's radio calls to the police cars were affirmative actions setting the emergency machinery in motion. This voluntary assumption of a duty to act carried with it the obligation to act with reasonable care [Cc].

....

While there could in this case be no direct evidence that Amalia DeLong relied to her ultimate detriment on the assurance of police assistance, the circumstantial evidence strongly suggests that she did so. Instead of summoning help from the Village police or from her neighbors (one of whom was a captain in the Kenmore Police Department), she waited for the response to her 911 call. Instead of taking her baby and going out the front door where she would have been safe, she remained defenseless in the house.

Nor can we agree that the proof was insufficient to establish proximate cause. Where different inferences may reasonably be drawn from the evidence, the question is one for the jury. [Cc] Here, the jury could have concluded that, without the critical mistakes in handling the initial transmission and the subsequent failure to conduct a follow-up, a Village of Kenmore police car would have arrived in time to prevent the attack or to stop the intruder before he could inflict the final fatal wound to the neck.

Finally, contrary to the city's contentions, we view the evidence as supporting the jury's conclusion that the city and county were equally at fault. We find no merit in defendants' other arguments on the liability issue.

II

Although, as defendants have emphasized, the period during which Amalia DeLong could have suffered from her wounds was brief (from approximately 9:30, when she completed her call, to shortly after 9:42, when she collapsed on the sidewalk), we cannot find the verdict of $200,000 for conscious pain and suffering "so disproportionate to the injur[ies] as to not be within reasonable bounds" [C] The jury could properly have considered in its award the terror Amalia DeLong must have experienced during her ultimate struggle to save herself and her child from a murderous assailant [C]. The court properly and without exception charged the jury that it should consider Amalia DeLong's fear and apprehension in their assessment of the damages.

Accordingly, the judgment insofar as it awards damages for conscious pain and suffering, should be affirmed.

Judgment affirmed with costs.

[Concurring and dissenting opinions regarding the award of $600,000 for the wrongful death action are omitted.]

Points for Discussion

1. How are *Riss* and *DeLong* distinguishable, if at all? On what basis does a majority of the *DeLong* court reach a different conclusion on the issue of the city's liability than the *Riss* court? Do you agree with the differing outcomes?

2. Is the decision in *DeLong* essentially an application of the rescue doctrine, discussed in Chapter 7 (Advanced Topics in Negligence Actions)?

Hypo 12-1

While responding to an emergency call, the car of a government-owned airport police officer collided with plaintiff. Plaintiff sues the officer for negligence. The officer moves for summary judgment based on official immunity, claiming that he was acting in a discretionary manner in responding to an emergency call. For example, he explains that he exercised his own judgment in determining which route to take based on the amount of traffic in the area at the time. How should the court rule on the summary judgment motion?

E. United States Government

Deuser v. Vecera

139 F.3d 1190 (8th Cir. 1998)

Before BOWMAN and MORRIS SHEPPARD ARNOLD, Circuit Judges, and JONES, District Judge.

BOWMAN, Circuit Judge.

Tina Marie Sellers, by and through her mother Joann Sellers; Albert Deuser; and Phyllis Menke appeal from the order of the District Court dismissing for lack of **subject matter jurisdiction** their claims brought under the Federal Tort Claims Act (FTCA). We affirm.

I.

The District Court dismissed appellants' claims under Federal Rule of Civil Procedure 12(b)(1) for lack of subject matter jurisdiction, holding that the government was protected from suit by the discretionary function exception of the FTCA. We review de novo. [C] "[W]e accept all of the factual allegations in [the] complaint as true and ask whether, in these circumstances, dismissal of the complaint was appropriate."[C] …

Tina Sellers is the daughter of, and Albert Deuser and Menke are the parents of, Larry Deuser, who is deceased. On July 3-6, 1986, the event known as the Veiled Prophet (or VP) Fair was held on the grounds of the Jefferson National Expansion Memorial in St. Louis, Missouri (the site of the Gateway Arch). Because the Expansion Memorial is a national park (a special use permit was issued to the city of St. Louis for the Fair), the Secretary of the Interior is responsible for maintaining the park and its facilities and for providing services to visitors, functions generally carried out by the National Park Service. [C] The park is within the jurisdiction of the National Park Rangers. On the evening of July 4, 1986, many thousands of people were in attendance at the Fair, including Larry Deuser. Rangers David Vecera and Edward Bridges observed Deuser grabbing women on the buttocks, to the obvious outrage of the victims and others. The rangers warned Deuser, and continued to keep an eye on him. When he urinated in public, the rangers arrested him. As the rangers made their way to their tent with Deuser, he was argumentative with them and continued making rude comments to female visitors.

After conferring with chief ranger Dennis Burnett, the rangers elected to turn Deuser over to St. Louis police. But the police department was overwhelmed with the additional workload created by the Fair, and officers were unable or unwilling to process Deuser's arrest. At this point, the rangers, together with St. Louis police officer Lawrence King, decided to release Deuser, but away from the park so that he would not return to the Fair that evening.

There is some dispute between the parties about where Deuser was released, and also some question of the timing of the events that occurred that night. It is sufficient for our purposes to know the undisputed facts: Deuser was freed in a parking lot somewhere in St. Louis, alone and with no money and no transportation. At some time after that, he wandered onto an interstate highway and was struck and killed by a motorist. Deuser's blood alcohol level was 0.214 at the time of his death, well above the legal limit for intoxication.

The appellants brought a variety of state and federal claims against a number of municipal and federal actors. ... As we noted above, the District Court now has dismissed the FTCA claim for lack of subject matter jurisdiction. In addition, the court declined to exercise supplemental jurisdiction over the state law claim against King (a decision that has not been appealed).

II.

By enacting the FTCA, Congress opted to waive the sovereign immunity to civil suit enjoyed by the United States, and to give consent to be sued "for money damages ... for injury or loss of property, or personal injury or death caused by the negligent or wrongful act or omission of any employee" of the United States acting within the scope of his employment. 28 U.S.C.A. § 1346(b)(1) (Supp.1997). The federal courts have subject matter jurisdiction over such claims "under circumstances where the United States, if a private person, would be liable to the claimant in accordance with the law of the place where the act or omission occurred." *Id.* But, as is true in other cases where Congress on behalf of the United States has waived sovereign immunity, amenability to suit is not without exception. The exception relevant here is commonly known as the discretionary function exception. It is statutory and shields the government from civil liability for claims "based upon the exercise or performance ... [of] a discretionary function or duty on the part of a federal agency or an employee of the Government, whether or not the discretion involved be abused." 28 U.S.C. § 2680(a) (1994). The exception "marks the boundary between Congress' willingness to impose tort liability upon the United States and its desire to protect certain governmental activities from exposure to suit by private individuals." [C]

To determine whether the discretionary function exception applies here to protect the rangers and the United States from suit, we engage in a two-step inquiry.

A.

First, we must consider whether the actions taken by the rangers as regards Deuser were discretionary, that is, "a matter of choice." [C] "[C]onduct cannot be discretionary unless it involves an element of judgment or choice." [C] It is axiomatic that a government employee has no such discretion "when a federal statute, regulation, or policy specifically prescribes a course of action for an employee to follow." [C] If the rangers had a policy they were to follow in releasing Deuser, as the appellants contend, "then there is no discretion in the conduct for the discretionary function exception to protect." [C]

There are two written policies that the parties contend are of relevance here. The first is the Jefferson National Expansion Memorial Standard Operating Procedure for arrests (SOP) …. The opening declaration of the SOP suggests there is little room for discretionary decisionmaking on the part of the rangers in an arrest situation: "When an arrest is made by National Park Rangers within the jurisdiction of Jefferson National Expansion Memorial, the following procedures *will always be followed:* …" Standard Operating Procedure-Arrests at 1 (emphasis added). The arrestee is to be searched, and if possible fingerprinted and photographed, before transport. The prisoner, handcuffed behind his back, is to be transported by two rangers. During business hours, the arrestee "will continue to be taken directly to the U.S. Marshall's [sic] Office." *Id.* at 2. At others times (or so we, and apparently the parties, infer from the SOP, although it is not clearly stated), "[t]he arresting Ranger plus a Shift Supervisor will transport the prisoner to the Fourth District Holdover Facility at 1200 Clark Avenue (Clark and Tucker) using the division vehilce [sic]," *id.* at 1, unless the facility is full, in which case prisoners are to be taken to one of the alternative locations noted in the SOP. There are very detailed instructions for gaining access to the Fourth District facility. Once inside, the rangers are to proceed to the booking area with the prisoner, complete the necessary paperwork, and remove all personal property from the prisoner. "The prisoner will then be turned over to the Holdover personnel and taken up to the cell block." *Id.* at 2. Except for some additional paperwork and later transport of the suspect for court appearances, the rangers' job is done once the prisoner is taken to the proper holding facility. This, appellants contend, is the procedure the rangers were compelled to follow with Deuser after they arrested him.

The rangers argue (and the District Court concluded) that the SOP arrest policy was abrogated temporarily by the VP Fair 1986 Operations Handbook. The Handbook emphasizes the "primary role" of the rangers during the Fair: "resource protection followed by the things we do best, visitor services and visitor care." VP Fair 1986 Operations Handbook-Overview and Hindsight para. 6. The opening paragraph of the Handbook's General Enforcement Guidelines makes it clear that the guidelines are in fact quite general and are for use by the rangers "in enforcement contacts[,] but in no way should [they] be construed as a substitute for sound judgement [sic] and discretionary action on the part of the Ranger." The guidelines then cover the areas of concern for enforcement by rangers during the Fair: traffic control; liquor law violations; city ordinances in effect for the duration of the Fair concerning alcoholic beverages, glass containers, and pets; access to the Arch; and a variety of crimes against persons from simple assault to murder. The Enforcement section of the Handbook then wraps up with a paragraph that makes it clear the rangers have wide latitude in making enforcement decisions:

> This will be a busy weekend and our holdover facilities at the 4th District may or may not be available per our existing agreement. Transport of federal prisoners to either St. Clair in Illinois or Cape Giraudeau [sic] in Missouri will tie up rangers that we can ill afford and create an extreme workload on the 7th of July [the first business day after the Fair] when we can least afford it. That does not mean we will not take appropriate action, only that our actions will be tempered with reality and arrests will only be on a "last resort" basis.

The rangers' argument--that the Handbook superseded the SOP for arrests on the grounds of the Expansion Memorial during the Fair--misapprehends the Handbook guidelines. The Handbook was intended to provide guidance to the rangers on the extent to which certain laws should be enforced during the Fair. Read as a whole, the Handbook suggests that enforcement in many circumstances might be relaxed during the event, so that arrests would be kept to a minimum. The rangers' "sound judgement and discretionary action" was to be exercised in the context of making decisions on *whether to make an arrest at all;* the Handbook never touches on the procedure to be followed in the event an arrest is made (except to note that holding facilities and rangers will be busy during the Fair). The Handbook did not override the standard operating procedures. Based on the record before us, it appears the SOP for processing arrestees remained unchanged during the Fair. Still, that conclusion does not mean that the rangers were required to complete an arrest, that is, to charge and incarcerate a suspect, once he was in custody.

Appellants also claim that the paragraph from the Handbook we have quoted above gave rangers discretion to act only on July 7, not July 4. That argument is absurd. The Fair ran from Thursday, July 3 to Sunday, July 6 and the paragraph opens by referring to the "busy weekend." July 7 was a Monday and the Fair was over. Why would the Handbook refer to enforcement decisions to be made during the Fair, and then make the guidelines applicable only after the Fair was over? It is clear that the reference to July 7 concerned matters that would be pending because of the Fair but that could not be handled until the first business day after the Fair.

We know that Deuser was arrested by the rangers. The SOP to be followed when a person is arrested by a ranger at the Expansion Memorial is precise and, as to the salient points, mandatory. Appellants are correct that there was very little discretion to be exercised, at least for as long as Deuser was under arrest. And it seems that the rangers initially followed the prescribed procedure: they searched Deuser and handcuffed him before transporting him. After that, it is true that the SOP was not followed-but when Deuser was released in the parking lot, the arrest was terminated. He was free to go, and further arrest procedures-booking the prisoner and so forth-were irrelevant. Deuser was not charged with a crime, so there was no reason to follow the procedures for incarceration.

The question remains whether a ranger's decision to *terminate* an arrest made at the park during the Fair would require the same sort of judgment and choice as would the initial decision to *make* the arrest. We think that it would. There is nothing in either the SOP or the Handbook that sets forth a policy-whether discretionary or otherwise-for terminating an arrest. But we conclude that this is because the decision to terminate an arrest is closely akin to the decision to make the arrest in the first place. Law enforcement decisions of the kind involved in making or terminating an arrest must be within the discretion and judgment of enforcing officers. [C]. It would be impossible to put into a manual every possible scenario a ranger might encounter, and then to decide in advance for the ranger whether an arrest should be made and, once made, under what circumstances an arrest could be terminated. Just as the rangers had discretion to decide (within constitutional limits, of course) when and whether to make an arrest, so they had-and here exercised-discretion to terminate an arrest without charging the suspect. Under the terms of the Handbook, that discretion became even broader during the Fair.

We hold that terminating Deuser's arrest, that is, releasing him without charging him with a crime, was a discretionary function reserved to the judgment of the rangers.

B.

We move now to the second part of our inquiry. Notwithstanding the judgment involved in terminating Deuser's arrest, we must ask "whether that judgment is of the kind that the discretionary function exception was designed to shield." [C] To be protected, the rangers' conduct must be "grounded in the social, economic, or political goals" of the Handbook's discretionary enforcement guidelines. [C] Because those published guidelines are clear and give officers wide discretion in making enforcement decisions during the Fair, the rangers at the outset enjoy the presumption that their conduct in releasing Deuser meets the second part of the test: that their actions were "grounded in policy." [C] That is, if a provision of the Handbook "allows the employee discretion, the very existence of the [provision] creates a strong presumption that a discretionary act authorized by the [provision] involves consideration of the same policies which led to the promulgation of the" Handbook. [C] Appellants have alleged no facts to rebut that presumption, no facts that "would support a finding that the challenged actions are not the kind of conduct that can be said to be grounded in the policy" of the Handbook. [C] In fact, they do not even address this step of the discretionary function analysis in their brief.

We think the conduct of the rangers here is the classic example of a "permissible exercise of policy judgment." [C] Social, economic, and political goals-all three-were the basis for the actions taken by the rangers.

An important function of the rangers during the Fair, according to the Handbook, was to serve and protect visitors to the park. Clearly, the decision to remove Deuser from the park served the social goals of protecting innumerable other fairgoers and ensuring that their enjoyment of the festivities was not diminished by the obnoxious and offensive behavior of a fellow attendee. Further, the decision to release Deuser, rather than to charge him for the offenses he committed, may have prevented a night of revelry that obviously was out of control from becoming a criminal conviction. And the rangers who otherwise would have spent considerable time booking Deuser were free to return to the Fair, possibly to prevent more serious or more dangerous crimes from being committed, or to apprehend the perpetrators of graver offenses, thereby continuing to further the goal of visitor protection.

The economic goals of the guidelines are clear, and are spelled out in some detail in the Handbook. Law enforcement manpower was expected to be stretched thin, both during the Fair and on the first business day following the Fair, when arrestees would have to be transported for court appearances. (In fact, the SOP tells rangers to expect the process to take all day, even under ordinary circumstances.) There were simply not enough officers to arrest and to charge all persons who might commit a crime at the park during the four-day Fair. The rangers' colleagues, St. Louis police department officers, were expected to be equally taxed with their own enforcement duties. Moreover, it was anticipated that the nearest holdover facility would be overcrowded with arrestees, meaning more miles and more manpower to transport suspects to alternative holdover facilities and to see to their arraignments. Releasing Deuser without charging him preserved already scarce law enforcement resources.

The political goals to be served by the guidelines concern law enforcement "territories." The Fair was not a National Park Service event. The Handbook acknowledges that "[t]he St. Louis Police Department is the lead agency for law enforcement." VP Fair 1986 Operations Handbook-Overview and Hindsight para. 6. As the chief ranger stated in the Handbook, the federal park rangers' "primary role is defined as resource protection followed by the things we do best, visitor services and visitor care." *Id.* When the police opted not to process Deuser's arrest, the rangers appropriately decided not to override the decision of "the lead agency for law enforcement." The Fair's success depended in part on all enforcement agencies involved working together toward a common goal, and the rangers acted properly to preserve that cooperation by releasing Deuser in this situation. Further, the Fair was designed to be an enjoyable event for the city, and it would have been unfortunate if overzealous federal law enforcement had dampened the festivities.

The language of the Handbook itself summarizes the social, economic, and political policies at work here: "This level of enforcement [necessary to achieve the rangers' primary responsibilities] is determined by Park Management and is deliberately kept flexible enough to maximize utilization of our available resources and minimize resource damage without becoming a 'roadblock' to the fair and the fair-goer." *Id.* para. 7. We hold that the conduct of the officers here was grounded in the social, economic, and political policies of the Handbook.

III.

To sum up, the rangers' decision to release Deuser away from the park, without charging him with a crime (1) required the exercise of judgment as noted in the Handbook and (2) implicated consideration of the social, economic, and political policies behind the Handbook's enforcement guidelines. Thus the rangers' conduct falls within the discretionary function exception of the FTCA, and there is no federal subject matter jurisdiction for appellants' FTCA wrongful death claims.

The judgment of the District Court is affirmed.

———————————

Points for Discussion

1. What are the consequences of this decision on the plaintiff's ability to bring this action against these defendants?

2. As discussed in *Deuser,* the Federal Tort Claims Act (the "FTCA") waives the sovereign immunity of the United States under limited circumstances. *Deuser* concerned one of the exceptions to the waiver of immunity recognized by the FTCA, the discretionary function exception. According to the *Deuser*

opinion, how is a court to determine whether a defendant's actions fall within the discretionary function exception of the FTCA?

3. What are the policy reasons in support of the discretionary function exception?

4. The RESTATEMENT (SECOND) OF TORTS § 895D(2) (1979)—Public Officers provides that a "public officer acting within the general scope of his authority is immune from tort liability for an act or omission involving the exercise of a judicial or legislative function." *See, e.g.,* Van de Kamp v. Goldstein, 129 S.Ct. 855 (2009) (Section 1983 case in which Supreme Court holds that former district attorneys were entitled to absolute immunity for conduct associated with prosecutors' basic trial advocacy responsibilities); Mireles v. Waco, 502 U.S. 9 (1991) (section 1983 action in which Supreme Court ruled defendant judge was immune from liability because actions were taken in his official capacity as judge); B.K. v. Cox, 116 S.W.3d 351 (Tex. App.—Houston [14th Dist.] 2003) (holding judge absolutely immune from tort liability for failing to report child abuse as conduct occurred while functioning in official capacity).

Chapter 13

Vicarious Liability

A. *Respondeat Superior*

Papa John's International, Inc. v. McCoy

244 S.W.3d 44 (Ky. 2008)

Opinion of the Court by Justice MINTON.

I. *INTRODUCTION.*

This is a case involving the issue of **franchisor** vicarious liability, an issue of **first impression** in Kentucky. It arises in the context of a **malicious prosecution** and **defamation** lawsuit filed by a customer as a result of a Papa John's pizza delivery gone wrong.

It's Latin to Me!

Respondeat superior is Latin for "let the superior make answer." Under this doctrine an employer can be held liable for the wrongful acts of its agents or employees when those acts are committed within the scope of the agency or employment.

The customer originally sued the delivery driver and Papa John's International, Inc., alleging that Papa John's was vicariously liable as the driver's employer. The driver's employer, however, was RWT, Inc., a Papa John's **franchisee**. Consequently, the customer filed another lawsuit against RWT; and the circuit court consolidated the cases. The circuit court granted summary judgment in favor of RWT and Papa John's for various reasons, which we will discuss in the following sections of this opinion. The Court of Appeals, however, affirmed in part and reversed in part as to both RWT and Papa John's, concluding that genuine issues of material fact precluded summary judgment.

What's That?

Generally, the scope of an employee's employment extends to and covers the reasonable and foreseeable actions engaged in by the employee in carrying out and furthering the employer's business.

As is well-settled in our case law, the driver's employer, RWT, is subject to vicarious liability for a tort committed by its employee acting within the **scope of employment**. We conclude that the acts complained of here occurred within an independent course of conduct that could not have been intended by the driver to serve any purpose of the employer. So, although for different reasons that we will discuss below, we conclude that the circuit court properly granted summary judgment dismissing the malicious prosecution claim against RWT. Accordingly, we reverse the Court of Appeals as to RWT.

The circuit court and the Court of Appeals addressed the vicarious liability of Papa John's using a mixed bag of respondeat superior and ostensible agency principles. Upon review, we conclude that we must take a more precise approach given the ubiquity of the franchise method of doing business in Kentucky. To that end, we adopt a rule in which the franchisor is vicariously liable for the tortious conduct of the franchisee when it, in fact, has control or right of control over the daily operation of the specific aspect of the franchisee's business that is alleged to have caused the harm. Papa John's had no control over the pizza delivery driver's intentional, tortious conduct in this case. So Papa John's cannot be held vicariously liable. Although for different reasons that we will discuss below, we conclude that the circuit court properly granted summary judgment dismissing the malicious prosecution and defamation claims against Papa John's. Accordingly, we reverse the Court of Appeals as to Papa John's.

II. *FACTS AND PROCEDURAL HISTORY IN THE CIRCUIT COURT.*

Gary McCoy is a resident of Prestonsburg, Kentucky. He owns two businesses, a scrap metal recycling company and a mining equipment leasing company. On the evening of February 18, 2000, he was working late at the scrap metal business. While he was working, his wife called him about dinner and told him that she would like to have Papa John's pizza, which they had never tried. His wife asked him to order one pizza for them for delivery to their home and another pizza for their housekeeper for delivery to her home. He ordered the pizzas from a Papa John's store, taking some time to inquire about how the store placed the pepperoni on the pizza, and set up the two deliveries. And he asked if the delivery driver could stop off at his business for payment because his wife did not have any money with her. The store stated that it could comply with his various requests.

The delivery driver that night was Wendell Burke. Burke delivered the two pizzas and then stopped at McCoy's business for payment. Burke and McCoy tell two stories of what occurred next, although their versions are not entirely different.

According to McCoy, after McCoy paid him, Burke remained at McCoy's business in McCoy's office and inquired about employment. McCoy was preoccupied with other matters, and it became obvious to him that Burke had no intention of leaving. So McCoy placed a hunting video in his VCR and told Burke to watch it. McCoy admitted that he had a beer can on his desk while Burke was in his office and a rifle in one corner of his office. The tape lasted about fifteen minutes. When the tape concluded, Burke left. After Burke left, McCoy received a call from the Papa John's store during which they inquired as to Burke's whereabouts.

According to Burke, when he arrived at McCoy's business, McCoy asked him to come in, which Burke did. McCoy took Burke back to his office where he paid him for the two pizzas. McCoy asked Burke to sit and talk awhile. McCoy expressed to Burke that he had been having suicidal and homicidal thoughts and had visions. While talking to him, Burke alleges that McCoy was drinking liquor and chasing it with beer. And at one point when Burke attempted to leave, McCoy stood up, picked up a rifle, showed it to Burke, and then laid it on his desk. While Burke was there, McCoy took several phone calls. After hanging up from one of the phone calls, McCoy informed Burke that that call had been from the Papa John's store; and they were inquiring as to Burke's whereabouts. Eventually, the subject of deer hunting came up; and McCoy asked Burke to watch a videotape of one of his deer hunting trips with him. When the tape ended, McCoy got up to take the tape out; and Burke slipped out. He returned to Papa John's about an hour and a half to two hours after he first left the store to deliver the pizzas.

Upon hearing Burke's version of the story and observing that Burke was quite upset, another employee of the Papa John's store felt that he should tell the police what had occurred and contacted them for him. Two officers responded to the call and took Burke's statement. The officers also took statements from two female employees who had spoken by telephone with McCoy that evening to take the pizza order. One employee described McCoy on the telephone as "extremely rude" and either "disoriented or highly irritated." The other described him as "difficult." A few hours later, the officers obtained a warrant and arrested McCoy at his home on the charge of unlawful imprisonment in the first degree. The local newspaper ran a story about the arrest a few days later.

A little over two months after the arrest, the district court, on McCoy's motion and with no opposition by the county attorney, dismissed the charge against McCoy. Although the record of the proceedings indicates that the county attorney agreed to the dismissal only with the stipulation of probable cause, McCoy was later successful—over two years later and in the midst of this civil lawsuit when confronted with a motion for summary judgment on the malicious prosecution claim on the ground that he could not establish that the criminal proceedings terminated in his favor—in having the final judgment set aside and an amended final judgment entered. The amended final judgment reflected that the district court dismissed the charges against Gary McCoy **with prejudice** and with no stipulations.

The Papa John's store where Burke worked on the night of the McCoy delivery was a Papa John's franchise that was owned and operated by RWT. Unaware that the store was not company-owned, McCoy filed an action on February 16, 2001, against Papa John's and Wendell Burke in which he alleged (1) wrongful arrest, (2) malicious prosecution, and (3) defamation. In its answer to McCoy's complaint, Papa John's represented that it was the franchisor of the Papa John's store and that RWT was the owner/operator.

McCoy, in response to Papa John's representation, filed a separate complaint against RWT on March 29, 2001, alleging (1) wrongful arrest, (2) malicious prosecution, (3) defamation, and (4) outrageous conduct. The circuit court consolidated the two civil actions.

On motions for summary judgment filed by Papa John's, RWT, and Burke, the trial court dismissed the **false arrest** claims against all three defendants because there was no question that the officers arrested McCoy according to a valid warrant. As to

> **Make the Connection**
>
> On false arrest claims and issues, see Chapter 2 and the false imprisonment materials.

Papa John's and RWT's claim that Burke was not acting within the course and scope of his employment when he gave a statement to the officers, the circuit court found as a matter of law that Burke was acting within the course and scope of his employment. Consequently for RWT, the circuit court concluded that it would be responsible under the doctrine of respondeat superior if the jury found Burke liable. But the trial court reserved ruling on summary judgment on the specific claims of malicious prosecution, defamation, and outrageous conduct.

RWT and Papa John's filed a joint motion to alter, amend, or vacate the circuit court's conclusion that Burke was acting within the course and scope of his employment. In the motion, they also renewed their previous motion for summary judgment. The trial court granted summary judgment to RWT and Papa John's on all of McCoy's claims against these two defendants. But the trial court did not dismiss the proceedings against Burke.

. . . .

IV. RESOLUTION AND DISCUSSION OF THE ISSUES.

A.   *The Malicious Prosecution Claim Against RWT Fails as a Matter of Law Because There is No Genuine Issue of Material Fact that Burke's Act in Making an Allegedly False Statement to the Officers Occurred Within an Independent Course of Conduct that Could Not Have Been Intended by Burke to Serve Any Purpose of the Employer.*

. . . .

McCoy sued RWT, Burke's employer, under a vicarious liability/respondeat superior theory. Under the doctrine of **respondeat superior**, RWT can be held vicariously liable for Burke's actions if he committed the tortious acts in the scope of his employment.

As the procedural history of this case illustrates, the concept of scope of employment is complex. And it is even more complex when the alleged tort in question is intentional, as is malicious prosecution, as opposed to the result of employee negligence. In the area of intentional torts, however, the focus is consistently on the purpose or motive of the employee in determining whether he or she was acting within the scope of employment.

For example, our predecessor court has held that an employee bus driver did not act within his **scope of employment** when he stopped the employer's bus in the middle of the street, left the bus, and assaulted another driver in a fit of road rage. In that case, the employee's motive was to settle a personal controversy; there being no issue of fact, the case stood dismissed for failure to state a cause of action. But an employee store clerk acted within the scope of his employment when he shot and killed a person in a grocery store during what he believed was a robbery. In that case, the employee's purpose was to protect the premises; scope of employment was not a jury question. And this Court has held that an automobile dealership employee acted within the scope of his employment when he sought to repossess a vehicle by intercepting a person at a stoplight, demanding that he get out of the car, and shooting the tires out on the vehicle when the person refused to get out. In that case, the trial court was correct in allowing the jury to impute liability to the employer for the employee's actions because he was acting at all times within the scope of his employment.

In this Court's most recent case addressing the scope of employment issue, in a unanimous opinion, we considered with approval the Tentative Draft of the Third Restatement of Agency, which rejected scope of employment formulations based on assessments of foreseeability, instead focusing on the employee's purpose. Since the *Patterson* opinion, the American Law Institute has written the Restatement (Third) of Agency § 7.07 (2006), entitled "Employee Acting Within Scope of Employment." It is as follows:

Take Note

Agency law and principles, including those contained in Restatements of agency, are relevant to and can influence or determine the outcome in the litigation of tort claims.

(1) An employer is subject to vicarious liability for a tort committed by its employee acting within the scope of employment.

(2) An employee acts within the scope of employment when performing work assigned by the employer or engaging in a course of conduct subject to the employer's control. An employee's act is not within the scope of employment when it occurs within an independent course of conduct not intended by the employee to serve any purpose of the employer.

(3) For purposes of this section,

(a) an employee is an agent whose principal controls or has the right to control the manner and means of the agent's performance of work, and

(b) the fact that work is performed gratuitously does not relieve a principal of liability.

This general rule is consistent with the standard advanced by Prosser and Keeton . . . in their treatise on tort law: "[I]n general, ... the master is held liable for any intentional tort committed by the servant where its purpose, however misguided, is wholly or in part to further the master's business." Thus, if the servant "acts from purely personal motives ... which [are] in no way connected with the employer's interests, he is considered in the ordinary case to have departed from his employment, and the master is not liable." This approach "conforms to the economic theory of vicarious liability ... because when the employee acts for solely personal reasons, the employer's ability to prevent the tort is limited."

Turning to the facts of this case, RWT's business was pizza and pizza delivery. Burke was supposed to deliver the two pizzas, collect payment, and return to the store to pick up more pizzas for delivery. Making a false statement to the police about a customer is no way connected to RWT's business. Indeed, there seems no more certain way to send customers to another pizza place than to accuse them falsely of imprisoning delivery drivers when they are delivering pizza. The motive alleged by McCoy is that Burke was trying to account for the inordinate amount of time that he loitered at McCoy's business. Another theory of McCoy's is that Burke's purpose was to accuse McCoy falsely of committing a crime so that he could later sue him in a civil lawsuit and obtain a judgment against him, a man who owned two businesses. But under either theory, Burke's actions did not serve any purpose of RWT; the motives advanced for Burke's conduct are purely personal. His actions, as alleged, are totally independent of RWT's purpose of pizza delivery.

If, for whatever reason, Burke did not intentionally make a false statement to the officers-either he was simply confused about what had occurred or told the truth about what had occurred-then there is no tort; and no one is liable. But if he did lie, as discussed at length above, then he was acting outside the scope of his employment; and RWT is not subject to vicarious liability for a tort committed by its employee acting outside the scope of employment. . . .

McCoy argues that RWT is liable for Burke's conduct under two different theories: (1) he was acting within the scope of his employment at the time, which theory we rejected in the preceding discussion; and (2) RWT ratified the act. However, McCoy cannot demonstrate **ratification** in this case. So we reject this argument, as well.

In order to have ratified Burke's alleged malicious prosecution of McCoy, RWT had to have both (1) knowledge that Burke's statement was false and (2) the intention to ratify it. But McCoy can point to no facts that support his contention that RWT had knowledge that Burke's statement was false. The only two persons who know what happened that night between Burke and McCoy are Burke and McCoy. Burke has never renounced his allegation against McCoy. McCoy's malicious prosecution claim against Burke will not be resolved until a jury decides the case. And for that reason, McCoy's vicarious liability claim against RWT under a ratification theory fails as a matter of law.

McCoy contends that RWT cannot insulate itself from liability by claiming ignorance. In support, he cites the following general rule:

> However, under one view, where ignorance of the facts arises from the principal's own failure to investigate and the circumstances are such as to put a reasonable person upon inquiry, the principal may be held to have ratified despite lack of full knowledge. Thus, the general rule, that in order for ratification to bind the principal he or she must have been shown to have had full knowledge of the material facts relating to the unauthorized transaction, does not apply if the principal intentionally assumed the responsibility without inquiring, or deliberately ratified, having all the knowledge with respect to the act which he or she cared to have.[20]

But McCoy fails to cite the rest of the rule, which continues as follows: "Even then, however, for this exception to apply, the principal must have had actual knowledge of the facts relied upon to put him or her on inquiry."[21] McCoy points to no evidence that RWT had actual knowledge that night that Burke was fabricating his version of the events. Even McCoy did not testify in his deposition that he told RWT when he spoke to them that night-before Burke returned to the store-that Burke had loitered on his property for over thirty minutes and watched

---

20. 3 Am. Jur. 2d *Agency* § 185 (2007).

21. *Id.; see also* Restatement (Third) Of Agency § 4.06 (2006) ("A person is not bound by a ratification made without knowledge of material facts involved in the original act when the person was unaware of such lack of knowledge.").

a hunting video. The evidence discussed by McCoy in his brief regarding RWT management having knowledge of prior incidents questioning Burke's credibility concerned information gained by law enforcement officers (and attributed by them to RWT) after the fact when Burke had already made his statement to the police officers.

. . . .

V. *CONCLUSION.*

Under the doctrine of respondeat superior, an employer can be held vicariously liable for an employee's tortious actions if committed in the scope of his or her employment. In the area of intentional torts, the focus is consistently on the purpose or motive of the employee in determining whether he or she was acting within the scope of employment. Here, we conclude that the acts complained of occurred within an independent course of conduct that could not have been intended by the employee to serve any purpose of the employer. A franchisor is vicariously liable for the tortious conduct of the franchisee when it, in fact, has control or right of control over the daily operation of the specific aspect of the franchisee's business that is alleged to have caused the harm. We conclude that Papa John's had no control over the employee's intentional, tortious conduct in this case. So Papa John's cannot be held vicariously liable. We reverse the opinion of the Court of Appeals and reinstate the judgment of the trial court for RWT and Papa John's on all claims.

———————————

Points for Discussion

1. Do you agree with the result reached in *McCoy*?

2. "Under the doctrine of *respondeat superior*, an employer is ordinarily liable for the injuries its employees cause in the course of their work. *Respondeat superior* imposes liability whether or not the employer was itself negligent, and whether or not the employer had control of the employee. The doctrine's animating principle is that a business should absorb the costs its undertakings impose on others." Bussard v. Minimed, Inc., 129 Cal.Rptr. 675, 105 Cal. App.4th 798 (2003).

3. An employer is vicariously liable only where an employee is acting within the scope of his employment. How is that scope determined? What conduct or activity falls within or outside of the liability-creating scope?

4. Note that the *respondeat superior* doctrine applies to negligence as well as intentional tort cases.

5. "While a servant need not be paid in order to expose the master to liability for the servant's torts, it is well-settled that except under certain limited circumstances, a master will only be liable for the torts of the servant committed within the scope of the servant's employment. . . . A deviation or stepping away from the master's business—a 'frolic and detour' in the language of the early common law—may preclude vicarious liability. The question whether a tortfeasor was acting within the scope of employment at the time the injury was inflicted is normally for the jury to determine." Kerl v. Rasmussen, 273 Wis.2d 106, 682 N.W.2d 328 (2004).

6. **Punitive damages** can be awarded against a master or a principal where "the principal or managerial agent authorized the doing of the act," or "the agent was unfit and the principal or a managerial agent was reckless in employing or retaining him," or "the agent was employed in a managerial capacity and was acting in the scope of the employment," or "the principal or a managerial agent of the principal ratified or approved the act." RESTATEMENT (SECOND) OF TORTS § 909 (1979).

Hypo 13-1

Law firm's annual Christmas party was, in the words of the firm's managing partner, "the best ever" with food and drink, including alcoholic beverages, provided by the firm. One of the firm's mailroom employees consumed seven or eight apple martinis and was visibly intoxicated (according to coworkers at the party, he was "wasted"). After the party ended well past midnight, the employee jumped into his car and headed home. After traveling less than two miles from the firm's offices and running through two red stop lights, the employee failed to stop at a stop sign and hit and killed a pedestrian as she stood in a crosswalk. A post-incident breathalyzer confirmed that the employee's blood alcohol content was well above the legal limit.

The estate of the deceased pedestrian has filed a lawsuit alleging, among other things, that the law firm is vicariously liable for the mailroom employee's wrongful acts. The firm has retained you as its legal counsel and seeks your provisional views and advice on its vicarious liability exposure. Discuss.

B. Independent Contractors

Bell v. VPSI, Inc.

205 S.W.3d 706 (Tex. App. 2006)

ANNE GARDNER, Justice.

I. Introduction

Appellant Linda C. Bell sued Appellees VPSI, Inc. and the Fort Worth Transportation Authority ("Transportation Authority"), asserting vicarious liability for alleged injuries she suffered in a vehicular accident while a passenger in a van driven by her husband, Homer Bell. She appeals from a summary judgment in favor of VPSI and the Transportation Authority and from the denial of her own motion for partial summary judgment, all on the issue of vicarious liability. We affirm the judgment of the trial court.

II. Background

A. The Vanpool Program

The Transportation Authority, also known as the "T," is a regional political subdivision of the State that provides public transportation services in and around Tarrant County. VPSI is a wholly-owned subsidiary of The Budget Group, Inc., a general-use car rental business. VPSI is a for-profit corporation, the business of which is providing and operating commuter vanpool programs. In conjunction with local transportation authorities, VPSI operates vanpool transportation programs in over forty urban areas across the United States.

The Transportation Authority's Rideshare Department began a vanpool program in Tarrant County in 1974 with six city-owned vans. In 1984, the Transportation Authority decided to use VPSI as a provider of vehicles and maintenance for its vanpool program. In cooperation with VPSI, the vanpool program grew to 125 vans by 1995. The program served a number of corporate employers in Tarrant County, including Lockheed, Bell Helicopter, and Burlington Northern.

In 1998, anticipating continued increase in vanpools with federal funding, the Transportation Authority contracted directly with VPSI to lease a fleet of 9-, 12-, and 15-passenger Dodge vans from VPSI for the vanpool program, and to provide management, maintenance, and insurance. The stated purposes of the vanpool program were to reduce the number of single occupancy vehicles on the road by encouraging vanpools as a viable alternative, thus reducing air pollution to meet federal environmental directives, to provide cost-effective transportation services to commuters not in a traditional bus service area, to offer a selection of vehicle sizes in order to allow smaller groups of commuters to take advantage of vanpooling as an option to driving alone; and to assist in general in providing regional transportation to commuters originating or terminating in Tarrant County.

B. Vanpool Drivers

Under the vanpool program, drivers, passengers, and their employers are solicited by the Transportation Authority and VPSI to participate in the vanpool program for commutes between their places of employment and homes. Passenger groups are formed by the Transportation Authority based upon origin and destination points; passengers pay a monthly charge to the Transportation Authority for commutes to and from work. Volunteer drivers who want to be a part of a vanpool agree to transport passengers to and from their employment in vans provided by VPSI. Each driver is assigned a van and agrees to drive and maintain the van, including scheduled and unscheduled maintenance at VPSI's cost, recruit additional passengers to keep the vanpool at optimal occupancy, and collect the vanpool passenger charges. Drivers receive coupon books to present to approved maintenance dealerships, service vendors, and repair facilities, with charges billed directly to VPSI. In exchange, the drivers receive daily commutes to and from their employment without charge and are also allowed personal use of the assigned vans on evenings and weekends for up to 250 miles per month. The Transportation Authority bills the driver for fuel consumed during the 250 personal-usage miles.

The relationship between VPSI, the Transportation Authority, and the driver is governed by a contract called the "Three-Party Volunteer Driver Agreement." The three-party agreement specifies that an Authorized Driver must have a valid driver's license; have at least five years' licensed driving experience; be at least twenty-five years of age; and be approved, in writing, by VPSI to operate vehicles provided by VPSI. The agreement further provides that the Authorized Driver "is not an agent, servant or employee of VPSI. The Authorized Driver is an independent party participating, with others, in a voluntary, not for profit, ridesharing agreement."

C. The Accident

Linda Bell's husband, Homer Bell, was regularly employed by Lockheed in Fort Worth. In March 1999, Homer entered into a three-party volunteer driver agreement with the Transportation Authority and VPSI to be an Authorized Driver under the vanpool program for daily commutes of employees to Lockheed.

On a rainy Saturday in December 1999, Homer drove the van he had been assigned, with Linda as a passenger, some twenty-eight miles from their home in

Forestburg to Decatur. From Forestburg, they traveled down the Alvord highway, turned onto Highway 287, and continued on that highway into Decatur. After stopping for about thirty minutes to service and change the van's oil at the Kwik Lube in Decatur, Homer and Linda shopped at the local Wal-Mart for about an hour, lunched at Taco Bell for approximately another half hour, and then returned to the Wal-Mart parking lot where they waited nearly another hour for their daughter to deliver their two grandchildren to them for an overnight stay.

After picking up their grandchildren, Homer and Linda left Decatur and proceeded thirteen to fifteen miles up a different road to see a display of a lighted Santa Claus figure loading his reindeer into an eighteen-wheeler. From the Wal-Mart, they drove up FM 51 to Highway 455, where they made a short detour at Slidell to see the display. After stopping to see Santa, they started driving back to Forestburg. They were on Farm Road 455 headed toward the Alvord highway, which would have taken them back to Forestburg, when the van hydroplaned on the wet roadway and crashed into a tree. Linda alleged that she sustained injuries in the accident.

D. The Suit

Linda sued Homer, VPSI, and the Transportation Authority, alleging that Homer's negligence, in exceeding a safe speed under the wet road conditions, proximately caused her injuries, and that VPSI and the Transportation Authority were vicariously liable for Homer's negligence under the doctrine[] of respondeat superior . . .

. . . .

IV. Vicarious liability

. . . Linda argues that VPSI and the Transportation Authority had a right of control over the details of Homer's activity that caused the accident, thus exposing them to vicarious liability; that Homer was in the course and scope of his employment at the time of the accident; and that Homer's mingling of personal business with vanpool business did not take him outside the course and scope of his employment or contractual duties.

What's That?

A master-servant relationship is an association between a principal and the principal's agent or subordinate. As used here, the term refers to an employer-employee relationship.

We read Linda's fourth amended petition as specifically pleading [the theory of] respondeat superior based on a master-servant relationship . . .

A. Respondeat Superior

Under the doctrine of respondeat superior, an employer is vicariously liable for the negligence of an employee acting within the scope of his employment, although the employer has not personally committed a wrong. *St. Joseph Hosp. v. Wolff,* 94 S.W.3d 513, 541-42 (Tex.2002). "The most frequently proffered justification for imposing such liability is that the principal or employer has the right to control the means and methods of the agent or employee's work." [C] This right to control distinguishes **independent contractors**, who have sole control over the means and methods of the work to be accomplished, from employees. [C] The right of control is the "supreme test" for whether a master-servant relationship, rather than an independent contractor relationship, exists. [C]

. . . .

1. *Right of control*

VPSI and the Transportation Authority contended in their motions for summary judgment that the express terms of the three-party agreement, providing that the drivers are not their employees, servants, or agents but are independent parties operating as volunteers, conclusively establishes Homer's status as a volunteer or independent contractor. A contract between the parties that establishes an independent contractor relationship is determinative of the parties' relationship in absence of extrinsic evidence indicating that the contract was a "sham or cloak" designed to conceal the true legal relationship of the parties or that despite the contract terms, the true agreement vested the right of control in the principal. [Cc][1]

Linda does not rely on extrinsic evidence to show that the contract was a sham or subterfuge; nor does she point to any summary judgment evidence of actual exercise of control to show that the true operating agreement vested the right of control in VPSI and the Transportation Authority. Rather, she relies upon other terms of the contract specifying the duties of the parties as evidence that VPSI and the Transportation Authority retained the right of control over the details of Homer's work as a driver, such that the true agreement created a master-servant relationship. She points to the list of duties that an authorized driver assumed under the contract, including the responsibility to keep the exterior and interior of the van clean; to purchase gas at major name-brand service stations; comply with recommended or required maintenance service at approved service stations; obtain VPSI's advance authorization prior to any other maintenance or repair

---

1 None of the parties separately argues that the terms "agent" or "volunteer" in the three-party agreement are determinative. Indeed, a party may be an agent without subjecting his principal to vicarious liability. To impose vicarious liability on the principal, the proper inquiry for agency is whether the agent was acting within the scope of the agency relationship at the time of the wrongful act. *See Celtic Life Ins. Co. v. Coats,* 885 S.W.2d 96, 100 (Tex.1994). Likewise, that one is working as a "volunteer" does not preclude respondeat superior liability, at least as to private parties, if the employer had a right to direct the duties of the volunteer and an interest in the work to be accomplished, accepted direct or indirect benefit from the work, and had a right to fire or replace the volunteer. *Doe v. Boys Clubs of Greater Dallas, Inc.,* 868 S.W.2d 942, 950 (Tex.App.-Amarillo 1994), *aff'd,* 907 S.W.2d 472 (Tex.1995); *see* RESTATMENT (SECOND) OF AGENCY § 225 (1958).

over a certain dollar amount; not drive outside a 200-mile radius of the driver's home; and operate the vehicle in accordance with "all applicable laws, ordinances, rules and regulations." She also emphasizes that he was required to drive the van according to a preset schedule and to participate in a basic driver safety training program, and that his decision-making was limited to choosing where to pick up passengers and whether eating or smoking would be allowed. Linda argues that the agreement's provision giving VPSI the right to terminate the agreement on thirty days' notice without cause or on twenty-four hours' notice with cause demonstrates that VPSI retained a right to control the details of Homer's compliance with the contract because it could terminate him at any time.

The right to terminate an agreement as to a worker is not evidence that details of the work are subject to the principal's control. *See Mary Kay Inc. v. Woolf,* 146 S.W.3d 813, 819 (Tex.App.-Dallas 2004, pet. denied) (citing *Cont'l Ins. Co. v. Wolford,* 526 S.W.2d 539, 541-42 (Tex.1975) (holding right to discharge worker not evidence worker was employee; worker was independent contractor as matter of law)). Similarly, requirements that a worker comply with applicable laws, regulations and safety requirements that relate to performance of the contract likewise do not constitute evidence that the employer controls the details of how the worker performs his job. *See, e.g., Hoechst Celanese Corp. v. Compton,* 899 S.W.2d 215, 221 (Tex.App.-Houston [14th Dist.] 1994, writ denied); *Granger v. Tealstone Contractors, L.P.,* No. 05-04-00636-CV, 2005 WL 565098, at *1 (Tex.App.-Dallas 2005, pet. denied) (mem.op.). Linda does not explain how the other provisions of the contract requiring Homer to assume responsibility for keeping the van clean or for maintenance, service, and repairs constitute anything more than would be required for an ordinary lease or bailment or are inconsistent with the express provision that he is not an agent, servant, employee or co-employee of VPSI and the Transportation Authority.

Considering the summary judgment evidence before us, we hold that VPSI and the Transportation Authority conclusively established by the express terms of the contract that Homer was an independent contractor. Conversely, Linda failed to conclusively establish that he was not.

———————————

Points for Discussion

1. This case illustrates and highlights the significance of the employee *or* independent contractor finding in the litigation of a tort action. A determination that an individual falls into the latter category negates a plaintiff's resort to the *respondeat superior* doctrine.

2. "The line of demarcation between an independent contractor and a servant is not clearly drawn. An **independent contractor** is one who engages to perform a certain service for another according to his own methods and manner, free from control and direction of his employer in all matters connected with the performance of the service except as to the result thereof. . . . [T]he decisive test for determining whether a person is an employee or an independent contractor is the right to control the physical details of the work." Murrell v. Goertz, 597 P.2d 1223 (Okla.App. 1979).

3. In *Nationwide Mutual Insurance Company v. Darden,* 503 U.S. 318 (1992), the United States Supreme Court adopted a common-law test for determining who qualifies as an "employee" for purposes of section 3(6) of the Employee Retirement Income Security Act of 1974, 29 U.S.C. § 1002(6). "[W]e consider the hiring party's right to control the manner and means by which the product is accomplished" and several other factors, including "the source of the instrumentalities and

    FYI
    The Employee Retirement Income Security Act is often referred to as "ERISA."

    tools; the location of the work; the duration of the relationship between the parties; . . . the extent of the hired party's discretion over when and how long to work; . . . and the tax treatment of the hired party." The Court cited the Internal Revenue Service's ruling setting forth 20 factors guiding the determination of whether an individual qualifies as a common-law "employee." Rev. Rul. 87-41, 1987 WL 419174 (1987).

RESTATEMENT (SECOND) OF TORTS § 423 (1965)

Making or Repair of Instrumentalities Used in Highly Dangerous Activities

One who carries on an activity which threatens a grave risk of serious bodily harm or death unless the instrumentalities used are carefully constructed and maintained, and who employs an independent contractor to construct or maintain such instrumentalities, is subject to the same liability for physical harm caused by the negligence of the contractor in constructing or maintaining such instrumentalities as though the employer had himself done the work of construction or maintenance.

> ## Hypo 13-2
>
> A took her car to B, a mechanic, and asked her to examine the squeaking brakes on the vehicle. B decided to overhaul the brakes. Two months later A's automobile collided with a car driven by C; the accident was caused by a brake failure in A's car. C sued A, alleging negligence. The trial court, sitting without a jury, concluded that B's negligent overhaul of the brakes was the cause of the accident and entered judgment for A. C has appealed.
>
> You are a justice on State Supreme Court. Would you affirm or reverse the trial court on the issue of A's liability to C?

C. Joint Enterprise

Erickson v. Irving

16 So.3d 868 (Fla. App. 2009)

LAGOA, Judge.

The plaintiff, Diane Erickson ("Erickson"), as personal representative of the Estate of Joseph A. Sindoni, Jr., appeals from multiple final judgments entered in this **wrongful death** case. Defendants, Community Asphalt and Abelardo Pupo ("Pupo"), cross-appeal. Because we conclude that the trial court erred in allowing the defense of **joint enterprise** to be submitted to the jury, we reverse and remand for a new trial.

I. *Factual and Procedural History*

On February 2, 2000, three friends, Robert Irving ("Irving"), David Long ("Long"), and the decedent, Joseph Sindoni, Jr. ("Sindoni"), attended a scotch-tasting event at the Loews Hotel on Miami Beach. While Irving drove the three men to the event, he decided to leave the event with someone else. As a result, Irving gave his car keys to Long, who agreed to return the car to Irving's home in Coconut Grove. Long asked Sindoni if he would like to drive, but Sindoni refused. Long and Sindoni subsequently left the event with Long driving. Although Long originally intended to drop Sindoni off at Sindoni's home before returning the car to Irving's home, Sindoni suggested that the two stop at a bar in Coral Gables. After stopping at the bar for about forty-five minutes, Long and Sindoni left with Long again driving. On the way home, the car collided with a dump truck operated by Pupo in the course of his employment with Community Asphalt. Sindoni was killed in the accident, and Long subsequently plead guilty to DUI manslaughter.

In August 2001, Erickson filed suit against, among others, Long, Irving, Pupo, and Community Asphalt. In their answer, Long and Irving plead various affirmative defenses, including Sindoni's comparative negligence, and a joint enterprise defense based on their allegation that Sindoni and Long had joint control of the car. Prior to trial, Erickson twice moved to strike the joint enterprise defense. The trial court, however, denied both motions.

The jury found Irving, Pupo, and Community Asphalt negligent. The trial court had previously determined Long's negligence as a matter of law because of his guilty plea in the criminal case. The jury also found that Long and Sindoni were involved in a joint enterprise at the time of the accident. In apportioning degrees of negligence, the jury assigned 35% to Long, 20% to Irving, 5% to Community Asphalt, 5% to Pupo, and 35% comparative negligence to Sindoni-that is, the jury found the driver and the passenger *equally* at fault. The jury awarded Sindoni's mother and father $50,000 each for past pain and suffering but no damages for future pain and suffering.

Make the Connection

The court points out the trial court's determination that an individual's guilty plea in a criminal case establishes, as a matter of law, that individual's negligence in a civil torts case involving the same criminal conduct. For more on using a non-tort statute to establish tort liability, see Chapter 4, *supra*.

Erickson filed a motion for a new trial arguing the inadequacy of the damage awards for future pain and suffering, as well as the legal insufficiency of Long and Irving's joint enterprise defense. The trial court denied the motion.

In light of the verdict on joint enterprise, Irving and Long filed a motion to enter final judgment. Long and Irving argued that because the jury found that Long and Sindoni were engaged in a joint enterprise, Long's percentage of fault had to be imputed to Sindoni, leaving Sindoni 70% at fault. Long and Irving, additionally, argued that because Sindoni should be apportioned 70% of the fault, none of the defendants were jointly and severally liable for the damages, pursuant to section 768.81(3)

For more on joint and several liability, see Chapter 9.

(c), Florida Statutes (1999). The trial court granted Long and Irving's motion, and ultimately entered a final judgment against Long in the amount of zero dollars, against Irving in the amount of $27,751.50, against Pupo in the amount of $6,937.87, and against Community Asphalt in the amount of $6,937.87.

This appeal and cross-appeal ensued.

II. *Analysis*

In order to establish the existence of a joint enterprise concerning the operation of a motor vehicle, the defendant must prove the following elements: 1) an agreement, express or implied, to enter into an undertaking, 2) a community of interest in the objects and purposes to be accomplished in the undertaking, and 3) equal authority to control the undertaking. *Kane v. Portwood,* 573 So.2d 980, 985 (Fla. 2d DCA 1991). An agreement to go to a social gathering is usually not sufficient to create a "community of interest," nor is the fact that the passenger gives the driver directions. [C] Even situations such as carpools, in which the driver and passengers agree to drive to the same workplace and the passengers have the authority to demand that the driver correct his faults, are insufficient to create a joint enterprise. *Conner v. Southland Corp.,* 240 So.2d 822 (Fla. 4th DCA 1970). The fact that a passenger pays for the expenses of a trip also does not necessarily establish a joint enterprise. *Yokom v. Rodriguez,* 41 So.2d 446 (Fla.1949). As the Supreme Court explained in *Yokom,* 41 So.2d at 448:

> It is not sufficient that the passenger indicates the route or that both parties have certain plans in common, such as a 'joy ride'; the community of interest must be such that the passenger is entitled to be heard in the control and management of the vehicle-such as practically to amount to joint or common possession thereof.

The relationship between the driver and passenger must be "in effect that of partnership, principal and agent, or master and servant, or when the circumstances are such that the vehicle, though manually operated by one person, is in the actual control of another." *Potter v. Fla. Motor Lines, Inc.,* 57 F.2d 313, 315 (S.D.Fla.1932).

The evidence in this case fails to establish that a joint enterprise existed between Long and Sindoni. As stated above, a mere "joy ride," or decision that persons will travel together to a social engagement or have plans in common is generally insufficient to establish a joint enterprise. Additionally, the fact that Sindoni purchased Long's drinks at the Coral Gables bar is also not evidence of a community of interest in the object and purpose of the evening. Moreover, the fact that one person pays the attendant expenses for a drive, the purpose of which is social, does not necessarily amount to a joint enterprise and certainly in this case is evidence of no more than a gift. As such, we conclude that the first two required elements for a joint enterprise defense-agreement and a community of interest-were not established.

Second, even if Long and Irving had been able to establish the first two elements of a joint enterprise, there was insufficient evidence to establish the third element-that Long and Sindoni had equal authority to control the car. In order for there to be a joint enterprise, the control must be "such as practically to amount to joint or common possession thereof." *Kane,* 573 So.2d at 986. No evidence exists that Sindoni was anything more than a passive passenger in the vehicle. Indeed, when he had the opportunity to drive the car, Sindoni expressly refused.

This case is, therefore, distinguishable from *Florida Power & Light Co. v. Polackwich,* 677 So.2d 880, 882 (Fla. 2d DCA 1996), in which a father and stepson were found to be engaged in a joint enterprise where together they agreed to undertake a "sailing adventure" on a catamaran, which they both had authority to control, because "[u]nlike an automobile, the catamaran was being operated by a team of men." Accordingly, the third element of equal authority to control the vehicle or undertaking was also not established. As such, we find that it was error for the trial court to allow the defense of joint enterprise to have been presented to and considered by the jury.

Finally, although it is not necessary to do so because of our conclusion that the facts in this case do not establish a joint enterprise defense, we note that it is unlikely the doctrine of joint enterprise would ever apply here. We can think of no basis-at least none that would apply to this case-upon which to reach a conclusion that the joint enterprise doctrine may be applied to absolve a driver of all civil liability for the death of his passenger when he later pleads guilty to a DUI manslaughter for that death. The judgment in this case does not further any of the established purposes of the joint enterprise doctrine. *See generally Kane,* 573 So.2d at 982-986 (discussing historical uses of joint enterprise doctrine and doubting its continued validity in modern tort actions).

Long and Irving, however, argue that any error constituted harmless error that could be remedied simply by entering judgment in accordance with the percentages of fault assessed by the jury. We find Long and Irving's contention without merit. The trial court specifically instructed the jury that each member of a joint enterprise is responsible for the negligence of another member, and indeed, the jury assigned Long and Sindoni **equal** percentages of fault even though Sindoni did not drive the vehicle and specifically refused to drive the vehicle. Given this, we cannot say that the error did not affect the jury's verdict. [C] Accordingly, because we find that it was reversible error for the trial court to allow such a defense to be submitted to the jury, we reverse and remand for a new trial.

Reversed and remanded.

Points for Discussion

1. "A 'joint enterprise' is something like a partnership . . . It is an undertaking to carry out a small number of acts or objectives, which is entered into by associates under such circumstances that all have an equal voice in directing the conduct of the enterprise." Prosser and Keeton on Torts 516-17 (5th ed. 1984).

2. The *Erickson* court concluded that a "mere 'joy ride,' or decision that persons will travel together to a social engagement," is generally insufficient to establish a joint enterprise. Can you imagine any scenarios or circumstances in which a joint decision to travel to a social arrangement could establish the joint enterprise elements listed in the court's decision? Can any such arrangement for the purpose of social travel fall with the conception of "joint enterprise" discussed in the preceding note?

3. Restatement (Second) of Torts § 491, comment *c* (1965):

    > "The elements which are essential to a joint enterprise are commonly stated to be four: (1) an agreement, express or implied, among the members of the group; (2) a common purpose to be carried out by the group; (3) a community of pecuniary interest in that purpose, among the members; and (4) an equal right to a voice in the direction of the enterprise, which gives an equal right of control. Whether these elements exist is frequently a question for the jury, under proper direction from the court."

———————

D. Bailments

Ziva Jewelry, Inc. v. Car Wash Headquarters, Inc.

897 So.2d 1011 (Ala. 2004)

STUART, Justice.

Ziva Jewelry, Inc., appeals from a summary judgment in favor of Car Wash Headquarters, Inc. ("CWH"). We affirm.

Background

Ziva Jewelry, Inc., is a jewelry wholesaler. Stewart Smith was employed by Ziva Jewelry as a traveling sales representative. In connection with that employment, Smith drove his own vehicle to meet with potential customers and traveled with samples of expensive jewelry furnished to him by Ziva Jewelry. Smith testified by deposition that he knew that sales representatives in the jewelry business constantly faced the risk of robbery. Smith stated in his deposition that he was aware that a gang of thieves preyed upon traveling jewelry sales representatives. According to Smith, these thieves are aware of where and when jewelry trade shows are held, and they will follow a jewelry sales representative to and from a jewelry trade show, waiting for an opportunity to steal the jewelry. He testified that he knew that thieves were most likely to strike when the jewelry or the sales representative's car was left unattended.[2]

Smith's practice was to keep the jewelry in the trunk of his vehicle while he was traveling on business. He kept the trunk padlocked, and he kept the only key to the padlock on the key ring with his ignition key.

On August 10, 2000, Smith was returning from a jewelry trade show; his wife had accompanied him to the trade show. He and his wife stopped at a restaurant in Cullman to eat. While they were in the restaurant, they noticed an unidentified person peeking in the window of the restaurant. After eating, the Smiths returned to their vehicle and drove to Vestavia. While in Vestavia, Smith's wife went into a store to shop and Smith went to get his car washed at Rain Tunnel Car Wash. CWH owns and operates Rain Tunnel. At Rain Tunnel, the driver leaves his vehicle with employees of the car wash, and the vehicle is sent through a wash "tunnel." Upon completion of the wash cycle, an employee drives the vehicle to another area of the car-wash premises to be hand-dried. Once the vehicle is dried, the driver is signaled to retrieve his vehicle.

Smith left his car and his keys with a car-wash employee. The jewelry was locked in the trunk. He did not advise any of the employees of the car wash of the presence of the jewelry. Smith testified that he watched the car as it went through the car-wash tunnel. He watched as the employees dried the vehicle. As he was standing at the counter waiting to pay the cashier, he saw the employee wave a flag, indicating that his car was ready for Smith. Smith then saw the employee walk away from his vehicle. While Smith was standing at the cashier counter waiting to pay, someone jumped into Smith's vehicle and sped off the car-wash premises. The police were telephoned and Smith's car was recovered 15 minutes

---

2 In fact, Smith testified that he had been robbed while working for a previous employer. On that occasion, he had left the jewelry unattended in his car while he ate in a restaurant. He testified that a traveling jewelry sales representative was "petrified constantly."

later; it was undamaged. However, the jewelry was missing from the trunk. The value of the missing jewelry was $851,935; it was never recovered.

Ziva Jewelry sued CWH, alleging that CWH, as bailee, took possession of Smith's vehicle and of the jewelry in the vehicle, but failed to exercise due care to safeguard and to return the bailed vehicle and its contents to Smith. . . .

The trial court rejected those arguments and entered a summary judgment for CWH. The trial court concluded that no bailment of the jewelry had been created. . . . Ziva Jewelry appeals.

. . . .

Discussion

"A **bailment** is defined as the delivery of personal property by one person to another for a specific purpose, with a contract, express or implied, that the trust shall be faithfully executed, and the property returned or duly accounted for when the special purpose is accomplished, or kept until the **bailor** reclaims it. In order for a bailment to exist the **bailee** must have voluntarily assumed the custody and possession of the property for another."

S/M Indus., Inc. v. Hapag-Lloyd A.G., 586 So.2d 876, 881-82 (Ala.1991).

We agree with the trial court that Smith's vehicle was the subject of a bailment. Smith delivered his vehicle to CWH for the specific purpose of having the car washed. He paid a fee for that service. As a result, CWH owed Smith a duty to use reasonable or ordinary care with regard to Smith's vehicle.

However, the above-quoted statement of the law on bailment does not answer the question whether a bailment was created as to the contents of the trunk of Smith's vehicle. The trial court correctly noted that no Alabama cases have directly addressed the issue whether a bailee is liable for the loss of contents hidden inside a bailed item. . . .

The facts of this case are strikingly similar to those of *Jack Boles Services*[, Inc. v. Stavely,* 906 S.W.2d 185 (Tex. App. 1995).] In *Jack Boles Services,* the Texas Court of Appeals addressed whether a valet-parking service was liable for a valuable painting taken when the vehicle it was in was stolen from the parking lot of a country club. The painting was hidden in the trunk of the stolen vehicle. The Texas Court of Appeals held that the valet service had no duty of care in regard to the undisclosed painting in the vehicle. That court stated:

"The general rule in other jurisdictions is that a bailee is liable for lost property of which it has actual knowledge as well as property it could reasonably expect to find contained inside a bailed item of which it has express knowledge.... In Texas, similarly, a bailee is liable for the contents of a bailed vehicle if the contents were (1) in plain view when the vehicle was bailed or (2) constitute the usual, ordinary equipment of a car, such as articles contained in a trunk, which are reasonably anticipated to be there."

Jack Boles Servs., 906 S.W.2d at 188. . . .

In *Jack Boles,* when the parking-service employees accepted responsibility for the vehicle, they had no knowledge that a valuable painting was in the trunk. The court noted that the parking-service employees had no reason to expect that an expensive painting would be in the trunk of the vehicle. For those reasons, the court concluded that the valet-parking service could not be charged with accepting responsibility for the painting merely by accepting responsibility for the vehicle.

We agree with and adopt the reasoning of *Jack Boles.* In this case, Ziva Jewelry cannot establish that CWH expressly or impliedly agreed to take responsibility for the jewelry hidden inside Smith's trunk. Ziva Jewelry acknowledges that the jewelry was not plainly visible; that its presence was not made known to the car-wash employees; and that there was no reason that the employees should have expected expensive jewelry to be in the trunk of Smith's vehicle. Thus, Ziva Jewelry cannot claim that CWH knew or that it should have reasonably foreseen or expected that it was taking responsibility for over $850,000 worth of jewelry when it accepted Smith's vehicle for the purpose of washing it.

Thus, there is no evidence indicating that CWH expressly or impliedly accepted responsibility for the jewelry in the trunk of Smith's vehicle. Without express or implied acceptance by the purported bailee, a bailment cannot arise. We agree with the trial court that the breach-of-contract claims asserted by Ziva Jewelry fail as a matter of law.

. . . .

AFFIRMED.

Points for Discussion

1. Does the court's decision stand for the proposition that the bailee will never be responsible for the loss of the contents of a bailed vehicle where the bailor does not inform the bailee of its contents?

2. Do you have any sympathy for the plaintiff? Why do you think that the plaintiff did not inform the employees of the car wash of the jewelry in the trunk of the vehicle?

3. The court states that it cannot be claimed that the car wash knew or should have reasonably foreseen or expected that it was assuming responsibility for the hundreds of thousands of dollars of jewelry in the vehicle's trunk. Do you agree? Does that mean or suggest that the car wash should not have reasonably foreseen that a customer could have had something of value in the vehicle (say, golf clubs or a laptop computer) requiring it to take precautions against the theft of any and all customer cars? Could the court have been influenced by the consequences of holding the car wash liable and ordering it to pay damages in excess of $850,000?

Hypo 13-3

Plaintiff has filed a bailment lawsuit to recover damages for the alleged theft of his motorcycle, which he claims was stolen from a parking garage owned and operated by Defendant. Plaintiff's and Defendant's relationship was governed by a written "Garage Agreement" which provided that Plaintiff (like all customers of the garage) parked at his "own risk." Plaintiff has parked his motorcycle at Defendant's garage for two years, always retaining his keys, and pays Defendant a monthly rate.

Assess the strengths or weaknesses or both of Plaintiff's claim.

E. Imputed Contributory Negligence

Watson v. Regional Transportation District

762 P.2d 133 (Colo. 1988)

LOHR, Justice.

Jayma Watson (Watson) suffered severe injuries to her right leg and foot when the motorcycle on which she was riding as a passenger collided with a bus owned and operated by the Regional Transportation District (RTD). The motorcycle was operated by Watson's husband, Randy. Watson brought a negligence action against RTD. A jury determined that she had suffered damages in the amount of $100,000 and that fifty-one percent of the damages were caused by the negligence of RTD and forty-nine percent by the negligence of Randy Watson. The trial court ruled that the negligence of Watson's husband must be imputed to her and entered judgment in favor of Watson and against RTD in the sum of $51,000. Watson appealed and RTD cross-appealed. The Colorado Court of Appeals upheld the imputation of the negligence of Randy Watson to his wife but reversed the judgment and remanded for a new trial on the basis of RTD's cross-appeal because of defects in the jury instructions. [C] We granted Watson's petition for certiorari to review the imputation of negligence issue, and granted RTD's cross-petition for certiorari to resolve a work product question not addressed by the court of appeals. We conclude that the negligence of Watson's husband should not have been imputed to her and that the trial court properly resolved the work product issue. We therefore remand the case to the court of appeals with directions to return it to the trial court for a new trial.

I.

This case arose out of a traffic accident that occurred on April 23, 1982, in Boulder, Colorado. Watson and her husband were traveling west on their motorcycle on Arapahoe Avenue at a distance behind an RTD bus. The bus stopped for a stoplight at 33rd Street and began a right turn after the light changed. Before completing the turn, the bus stopped again. Watson's husband applied the brakes on the motorcycle when he saw the bus stop. The motorcycle skidded sixty-three feet and struck the rear of the bus.

At the time of the accident, the Watsons were running errands prior to traveling to Longmont with friends. Although Jayma Watson owned the motorcycle jointly with her husband, she did not have an operator's license and did not know how to operate the motorcycle.

Watson brought an action against RTD in Boulder County District Court for the injuries she suffered in the accident, alleging that the RTD bus driver was negligent, that RTD was negligent in choosing the bus route, and that these acts of negligence were the causes of her injuries. RTD denied the allegations of negligence and affirmatively alleged that Watson's negligence or the negligence of her husband caused or contributed to the accident. RTD further asserted that any negligence of Watson's husband must be **imputed** to her.

Prior to trial, RTD moved for summary judgment. In the motion, RTD argued that the accident was caused solely by the negligence of Watson's husband. RTD further argued that Randy Watson's negligence must be imputed to Jayma Watson as a matter of law, "since Jayma Watson is the joint owner of the motorcycle, was a passenger on the motorcycle at the time of the rear-end collision, and Mr. and Mrs. Watson were proceeding to an agreed upon destination for a common purpose." RTD also argued that "[t]here is no evidence or facts which demonstrate any negligence on the part of [RTD] at the time the rear-end collision occurred."

The trial court granted RTD's motion in part, holding that Randy Watson was negligent as a matter of law and that his negligence must be imputed to Jayma Watson. The court denied the motion with respect to RTD's negligence, finding that a **genuine issue of material fact** existed as to whether RTD was negligent. Watson subsequently filed a motion to reconsider the granting of partial summary judgment. Following a hearing, the trial court rescinded its ruling that Watson's husband was negligent as a matter of law. However, the court refused to alter its ruling that any negligence on the part of Watson's husband would be imputed to Watson.

. . . .

The case proceeded to a trial before a jury. . . . At the conclusion of the evidence, the trial court directed a verdict in favor of RTD on the issue of the negligence of Watson's husband. The court instructed the jury that

[t]he Court has determined as a matter of law that Randy Watson was negligent at the time of the accident because he did not drive his motorcycle in such a manner as to avoid hitting the bus that was in front of him. This negligence is chargeable to Jayma Watson because she was a co-owner riding the motorcycle which was being used for a purpose in common with the driver and had a right to control his vehicle. Therefore, the Court has determined as a matter of law that the plaintiff, Jayma L. Watson, was negligent.

. . . .

The jury returned a verdict finding RTD fifty-one percent negligent and Jayma Watson forty-nine percent negligent and set damages at $100,000. Following the trial, RTD filed a motion for judgment notwithstanding the verdict, or in the alternative, for a new trial. RTD argued, among other things, that the trial court erred as a matter of law in failing to give the four jury instructions on Randy Watson's standard of care and **negligence per se**, and that the trial court erred in permitting Watson's counsel access to the videotape of RTD's experiment and further erred in permitting the jury to view the tape. Watson also sought relief, pursuant to C.R.C.P. 59. In her motion, Watson argued that the trial court erred as a matter of law by imputing Randy Watson's negligence to her. The trial court denied the motions.

Watson appealed to the court of appeals, contending that the trial court erred in imputing Randy Watson's negligence to her. The court of appeals affirmed the trial court's ruling. RTD cross-appealed, arguing that the trial court erred in refusing to give the three instructions regarding the duty of care owed by Watson's husband. RTD did not appeal the trial court's refusal to give the negligence per se instruction. The court held that "[t]he failure to give these instructions prejudiced RTD to the extent that the jury had access to the applicable law to determine RTD's comparative negligence, but lacked access to the specific law applicable for the determination of plaintiff's comparative negligence." [C] The court accordingly reversed the judgment and remanded for a new trial. . . . Watson petitioned for certiorari and RTD cross-petitioned. We granted certiorari to consider whether the negligence of Randy Watson was properly imputed to Jayma Watson . . .

II.

A.

This case presents an issue concerning the circumstances under which the negligence of the operator of a motor vehicle should be imputed to a passenger in a negligence action brought by the passenger against a third party to recover damages for personal injuries. The seminal Colorado case regarding this issue is *Moore v. Skiles,* 130 Colo. 191, 274 P.2d 311 (1954).[5] In *Moore v. Skiles,* the plaintiff was injured when the truck driven by her husband in which she was riding as a passenger was involved in an accident with another vehicle. The couple owned the truck jointly. The plaintiff subsequently brought an action in negligence against the driver of the other vehicle. The trial court instructed the jury that the con-

---

5 Colorado, by statute, replaced the doctrine of contributory negligence with a statutory system of comparative negligence. § 13-21-111, 6A C.R.S. (1987). Courts continued to employ the doctrine of imputed negligence after the advent of comparative negligence. *See, e.g., Hover v. Clamp,* 40 Colo.App. 410, 579 P.2d 1181 (1978). Our decision today concerns the continued viability of the rule of imputed comparative negligence. For analytical purposes, however, we conclude that cases involving imputed contributory negligence are equally applicable to the issue of imputed comparative negligence.

tributory negligence of the plaintiff's husband must be imputed to the plaintiff. In assessing the correctness of the instruction, we stated the following rule:

> [T]he owner or joint owner, riding as an occupant in his own car, using the car for a purpose in common with the driver is presumed to have a right to control the driver and a right to manage and direct the movements of the car.

[C] We held that:

> Where, as here, joint ownership of the car is shown; where joint occupancy and possession of the vehicle is admitted, and where the occupant-owners of the car use it upon a joint mission, the driver will be presumed to be driving for himself and as an agent for the other present joint owner.

[C] We therefore held that the trial court acted properly in submitting the instruction on imputed contributory negligence to the jury. *Moore v. Skiles* requires for the imputation of contributory negligence the co-existence of a number of factors, which together give rise to the presumption of a "right to control" based loosely on agency notions. The case requires not only joint ownership but also "joint occupancy and possession," and a "joint mission." The presumption of a right to control engendered by such factors, however, is rebuttable. [C].

Moore v. Skiles is somewhat typical of those cases in which contributory or comparative negligence is imputed because of the existence of a "joint enterprise" between the parties. Generally speaking, a joint enterprise

> is an undertaking to carry out a small number of acts or objectives, which is entered into by associates under such circumstances that all have an equal voice in directing the conduct of the enterprise. The law then considers that each is the agent or servant of the others, and that the act of any one within the scope of the enterprise is to be charged vicariously against the rest.

W. Keeton, D. Dobbs, R. Keeton & D. Owen, *Prosser and Keeton on the Law of Torts* § 72, at 517 (5th ed. 1984) (cited herein as "Prosser and Keeton").[6]

---

6 The theory of joint enterprise as applied to automobile cases differs from the theory of "joint venture" applied in other contexts.

> Where the enterprise is for some commercial or business purpose, and particularly where the parties have agreed to share profits and losses, it usually is called a joint venture. It is then governed, as to tort liability, by the law applicable to partnerships.... The extension of a 'joint enterprise' beyond such business ventures is almost entirely a creature of American courts.

Prosser and Keeton § 72, at 517 (footnote omitted). [C]

. . . .

Watson urges us to reconsider the rule of *Moore v. Skiles*. She argues that an owner who is a passenger in a motor vehicle has no practical ability to exercise control over the driver and that there is no basis in logic or in policy for imputing the driver's negligence to the passenger under such circumstances. This issue has occupied the attention of many courts and commentators, and we now revisit the rule of *Moore v. Skiles* with the guidance provided by those authorities.

B.

Imputed negligence is a form of vicarious liability and represents one exception to the rule in our system of tort liability that individuals are responsible for their own negligence, but not that of another. *See* 4 F. Harper, F. James, Jr., & O. Gray, *The Law of Torts* § 23.1 (2d ed. 1986) (cited herein as "Harper, James and Gray"). The rule, as applied in the present context, undoubtedly rests on the legal fiction "that an owner-passenger reserves a right to control over the physical details of driving or that the driver consents to submit himself to the control of a 'back-seat driver.' " *Smalich v. Westfall,* 440 Pa. 409, 269 A.2d 476, 482 (1970). This fiction perhaps bore some resemblance to reality before the advent of the automobile, when a passenger on a wagon pulled by a team of horses could assume control of the team from the driver. *See Bauer v. Johnson,* 79 Ill.2d 324, 38 Ill.Dec. 149, 151,

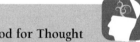

Food for Thought

What does the court's reference to a "legal fiction" mean or suggest? What role does or should a legal fiction play in the development and application of legal rules?

403 N.E.2d 237, 239 (1980); *Kalechman v. Drew Auto Rental, Inc.,* 33 N.Y.2d 397, 353 N.Y.S.2d 414, 417, 308 N.E.2d 886, 889 (1973). Today, however, "there is no longer any basis for assuming that the passenger, no matter what his relationship to the driver may be, has the capacity to assert control over or direct the operation of a moving automobile." *Kalechman,* 353 N.Y.S.2d at 418, 308 N.E.2d at 889.

The rule of imputed negligence in motor vehicle cases, and the fictional right to control upon which it is based, arose as a result of and still find their primary justifications in considerations of public policy. Earlier in the twentieth century the growing injury toll from traffic accidents prompted a search for financially responsible defendants. *Bauer v. Johnson,* 38 Ill.Dec. at 151, 403 N.E.2d at 239; Harper, James and Gray § 23.6. The search ultimately led to the employment of the doctrine of imputed negligence in motor vehicle cases, whereby liability was imposed on the defendant owner-passenger of a vehicle based upon the negligence of the driver, even though the owner-passenger was free from negligence.

Prosser and Keeton § 73. The salient rationale underlying the doctrine, as it relates to defendant owner-passengers, is that

> since automobiles are expensive, the owner is more likely to be able to pay any damages than the driver, who may be entirely impecunious; and that the owner is the obvious person to carry the necessary insurance to cover the risk, and so to distribute any losses among motorists as a class.

Prosser and Keeton § 73, at 522. Thus, the negligence of a driver was imputed to the defendant owner-passenger to provide the injured party with a financially responsible source of recovery. *See Reed v. Hinderland,* 135 Ariz. 213, 660 P.2d 464, 469 (1983); *Weber v. Stokely-Van Camp, Inc.,* 274 Minn. 482, 144 N.W.2d 540, 542 (1966). Courts justified the doctrine either by reference to the parties' legal relationship (*e.g.,* master-servant, principal-agent or joint enterprise) or simply in terms of the all-encompassing "right to control." Harper, James and Gray § 23.1; Prosser and Keeton §§ 72, 73.

The imputation of a driver's negligence to an owner-passenger, however, was later recognized in circumstances in which the owner-passenger sought recovery from a third party for injuries suffered. *Reed v. Hinderland,* 660 P.2d at 469. Absent a basis in policy or logic, but in order to provide symmetry between cases involving defendants' and plaintiffs' negligence, courts employed the rule of imputed negligence "both ways." *Johnson v. Los Angeles-Seattle Motor Express, Inc.,* 222 Or. 377, 352 P.2d 1091, 1094-95 (1960); Harper, James and Gray § 23.1. Paradoxically, the "both-ways" rationale led courts to take a rule that departed from the common law in response to a call for wider liability and to employ that rule to curtail liability by expanding the scope of the defense of contributory negligence. Harper, James and Gray § 23.6.

The "both-ways" rule of imputed contributory negligence has attracted criticism from courts and commentators pointing out its logical infirmities and questionable policy consequences. As a result, although many courts have adopted a rule similar to that of *Moore v. Skiles* and have adhered to it,[8] others have either declined in the first instance to impute contributory negligence of a driver to an

---

8 *See, e.g., Smith v. Johnson,* 283 Ala. 151, 214 So.2d 846 (1968); *Greyhound Lines, Inc. v. Caster,* 9 Storey 220, 59 Del. 220, 216 A.2d 689 (1966); *Central of Ga. Rwy. v. Luther,* 128 Ga.App. 178, 196 S.E.2d 149 (1973); *Slutter v. Homer,* 244 Md. 131, 223 A.2d 141 (1966); *Menzigian v. La Riviere,* 334 Mass. 610, 137 N.E.2d 925 (1956); *Harper v. Harper,* 225 N.C. 260, 34 S.E.2d 185 (1945); *Freeman v. Scahill,* 92 N.H. 471, 32 A.2d 817 (1943); *Fisch v. Waters,* 136 N.J.L. 651, 57 A.2d 471 (1948); *Parrish v. Walsh,* 69 Ohio St.2d 11, 429 N.E.2d 1176 (1982); *Schweidler v. Caruso,* 269 Wis. 438, 69 N.W.2d 611 (1955).

owner-passenger seeking recovery from a third party for negligent infliction of injuries, or have retreated from the doctrine after initially adopting it.[9]

We conclude that the rule of imputed comparative negligence, as expressed in *Moore v. Skiles,* is based upon a legal fiction unsupported by, and in direct opposition to, valid policy considerations. We are persuaded that the better rule is that an owner-passenger's recovery for injuries negligently inflicted by a third party should be limited only if the owner-passenger herself is negligent and if that negligence is a proximate cause of her injury. As one commentator has stated:

> The whole doctrine of vicarious liability stems from considerations other than the defendant's personal fault, for it assumes his innocence.... If the principle of liability or disability for individualized fault is taken as the norm, and vicarious liability or disability is regarded as an exceptional solution (to be justified only for reasons of policy sufficient in each case to warrant the exception), then there would be little justification indeed for imputing negligence to an innocent plaintiff in most cases.

9 *See, e.g., Reed v. Hinderland,* 135 Ariz. 213, 660 P.2d 464 (1983); *Everhard v. Thompson,* 202 N.W.2d 58 (Iowa 1972); *Gaspard v. LeMaire,* 245 La. 239, 158 So.2d 149 (1963); *Stover v. Patrick,* 459 S.W.2d 393 (Mo.1970); *Smalich v. Westfall,* 440 Pa. 409, 269 A.2d 476 (1970); *Sumner v. Amacher,* 150 Mont. 544, 437 P.2d 630 (1968); *Cole v. Woods,* 548 S.W.2d 640 (Tenn.1977). *See also* Restatement (Second) of Torts § 485 (1965).

A number of courts, while refusing to impute contributory negligence based solely on ownership or pursuant to a presumption of a "right to control," nevertheless allow the imputation of a driver's negligence to an owner-passenger pursuant to certain legal relationships between the parties. Such relationships are not presumed based on the passenger's ownership, but must be proved on a case-by-case basis. Under these cases, negligence may be imputed upon a showing of agency, *see, e.g., LaMonte v. De Diego,* 274 So.2d 254 (Fla.App.1973); *Grinter v. Haag,* 168 Ind.App. 595, 344 N.E.2d 320 (1976); *Gaspard v. LeMaire,* 245 La. 239, 158 So.2d 149 (1963); *Wilkinson v. Stevison,* 514 S.W.2d 895 (Tex.1974); *Wardell v. Jerman,* 18 Utah 2d 359, 423 P.2d 485 (1967); on a showing of a master-servant relationship, *see, e.g., Reed v. Hinderland,* 135 Ariz. 213, 660 P.2d 464 (1983); *Nowak v. Nowak,* 175 Conn. 112, 394 A.2d 716 (1978); *Grinter v. Haag,* 168 Ind.App. 595, 344 N.E.2d 320 (1976); *Smalich v. Westfall,* 440 Pa. 409, 269 A.2d 476 (1970); *Cole v. Woods,* 548 S.W.2d 640 (Tenn.1977); *see also* Restatement (Second) of Torts § 486 (1965); *but see Weber v. Stokely-Van Camp, Inc.,* 274 Minn. 482, 144 N.W.2d 540 (1966) (abandons rule of imputed negligence in master-servant relationship); or on a showing of a joint enterprise; *Reed v. Hinderland,* 135 Ariz. 213, 660 P.2d 464 (1983); *Nowak v. Nowak,* 175 Conn. 112, 394 A.2d 716 (1978); *Sumner v. Amacher,* 150 Mont. 544, 437 P.2d 630 (1968); *Kremlacek v. Sedlacek,* 190 Neb. 460, 209 N.W.2d 149 (1973); *Cole v. Woods,* 548 S.W.2d 640 (Tenn.1977); *Wilkinson v. Stevison,* 514 S.W.2d 895 (Tex.1974); *Palmeno v. Cashen,* 627 P.2d 163 (Wyo.1981). *See also* Restatement (Second) of Torts § 491 (1965). *But see Pierson v. Edstrom,* 286 Minn. 164, 174 N.W.2d 712 (1970) (abandons rule imputing negligence of one joint venturer to another so as to bar his right of recovery against a negligent third party).

Some jurisdictions reject the rule that ownership creates a rebuttable presumption of a right to control, and go further to hold that an owner-passenger is liable only for his or her own negligence. *See, e.g., Universal Underwriters Ins. Co. v. Hoxie,* 375 Mich. 102, 133 N.W.2d 167 (1965); *Kalechman v. Drew Auto Rental, Inc.,* 33 N.Y.2d 397, 353 N.Y.S.2d 414, 308 N.E.2d 886 (1973). Other jurisdictions phrase the test differently and bar recovery if the owner-passenger actually had a reasonable opportunity to control the negligent driver. *See, e.g., Bauer v. Johnson,* 79 Ill.2d 324, 38 Ill.Dec. 149, 403 N.E.2d 237 (1980); *Rocky Mountain Produce Trucking Co. v. Johnson,* 78 Nev. 44, 369 P.2d 198 (1962); *Jasper v. Freitag,* 145 N.W.2d 879 (N.D.1966); *Dickson v. Hollinger,* 257 Or. 89, 476 P.2d 557 (1970); *Johnson v. Los Angeles-Seattle Motor Express, Inc.,* 222 Or. 377, 352 P.2d 1091 (1960).

Harper, James and Gray § 23.6, at 441-42. The very considerations upon which the doctrine of imputed negligence rests are absent in the case of imputed comparative negligence where the owner is an injured passenger in his own car. [C] The sole virtue of the both ways test "is that it is logical and symmetrical. Important legal rights ought to have better footing than mere architectural symmetry." [Cc] In fact, the rule of imputed comparative negligence if applied to defeat or reduce recovery by an injured owner-passenger, only serves to frustrate the goal of broadened liability upon which the doctrine was originally based. [C] A "rule which so incongruously shields conceded wrongdoing bears a heavy burden of justification."[C] In short, symmetry is an insufficient justification for continued adherence to a rule of law that is at odds with logic and policy.

C.

The logical and practical shortcomings of the rule of imputed comparative negligence are apparent when applied to the facts of this case. The fictional "joint enterprise" upon which the Watsons embarked was simply the decision to run a couple of errands and then ride to Longmont. From this "joint enterprise" and Watson's co-ownership of the motorcycle arises a second fiction: that Jayma Watson had a "right to control" Randy Watson's actions. Jayma Watson's "right to control" leads to the third fiction: that Randy Watson was her agent. "This top heavy structure tends to fall of its own weight." Prosser and Keeton § 72, at 522. Moreover, as a practical matter any attempt on Jayma Watson's part to interfere with Randy Watson's driving at the time of the accident likely would have constituted negligence on her part as well. [C].

. . . .

E.

We therefore hold that the driver's negligence may not be imputed to an owner-passenger so as to limit the owner-passenger's recovery in an action in negligence. The owner-passenger's recovery shall be affected only if she is personally negligent, and if that negligence is a proximate cause of her injuries. In so holding, we overrule *Moore v. Skiles* and the cases that have followed it.

. . . .

The judgment of the court of appeals is affirmed in part and reversed in part and the case is returned to that court with instructions to remand the case to the trial court for a new trial in accordance with the views expressed in this opinion.

Points for Discussion

1. What is, and what is the provenance of, the "both ways" rule? What rule does the court adopt in *Watson*?

2. The Restatement (Third) of Torts: Apportionment of Liability § 5 (2000) announces the following approach applicable to the imputed contributory/comparative negligence issue: "The negligence of another person is imputed to a plaintiff whenever the negligence of the other person would have been imputed had the plaintiff been a defendant, except the negligence of another person is not imputed to a plaintiff solely because of the plaintiff's ownership of a motor vehicle or permission for its use by the other person." This section adopts the "both ways" rule, *see* comment *a* to § 5, while noting recent decisions in which that rule was not applied so as to impute the negligence of the operator of a vehicle to the owner of that vehicle. *See* comment *c* to § 5.

Chapter 14

Nuisance

The law of **nuisance** addresses and defines **private nuisances** (a plaintiff's right to be free from certain interferences with the use and enjoyment of her land

Make the Connection

Nuisance law is covered in Property Law and Land Use courses.

resulting from nontrespassory invasions) and **public nuisances** (a substantial and unreasonable interference with community interests or the general public's convenience or comfort). Examples of private nuisances include interferences with the public health ("a hogpen, the keeping of diseased animals, or a malarial pond"), public safety ("the storage of explosives" or "harboring a vicious dog"), public peace ("loud and disturbing noises"), and public comfort ("bad odors, smoke, dust and vibration"). PROSSER AND KEETON ON TORTS 643-44 (5th ed. 1984). Examples of public nuisances include defendants' activities causing "pollution of air, water, or land by dust or smoke, odors, chemicals, or noise" or "[h]eavy traffic in a neighborhood or an intense light shone directly into the plaintiff's bedroom . . ." DAN B. DODDS, THE LAW OF TORTS 1322 (2000).

THE RESTATEMENT (SECOND) OF TORTS (1979)
§ 821B. Public Nuisance

(1) A public nuisance is an unreasonable interference with a right common to the general public.

(2) Circumstances that may sustain a holding that an interference with a public right is unreasonable include the following:

    (a) Whether the conduct involves a significant interference with the public health, the public safety, the public peace, the public comfort or the public convenience, or

    (b) whether the conduct is proscribed by a statute, ordinance or administrative regulation, or

(c) whether the conduct is of a continuing nature or has produced a permanent or long-lasting effect, and, as the actor knows or has reason to know, has a significant effect upon the public right.

§ 821D. Private Nuisance

A private nuisance is a nontrespassory invasion of another's interest in the private use and enjoyment of land.

§ 821F. Significant Harm

There is liability for a nuisance only to those to whom it causes significant harm, of a kind that would be suffered by a normal person in the community or by property in normal condition and used for a normal purpose.

§ 822. General Rule

One is subject to liability for a private nuisance if, but only if, his conduct is a legal cause of an invasion of another's interest in the private use and enjoyment of land, and the invasion is either

(a) intentional and unreasonable, or

(b) unintentional and otherwise actionable under the rules controlling liability for negligent or reckless conduct, or for abnormally dangerous conditions or activities.

Carpenter v. Double R Cattle Company, Inc.

108 Idaho 602, 701 P.2d 222 (1985)

BAKES, Justice.

Plaintiffs appealed a district court judgment based upon a court and jury finding that defendant's feedlot did not constitute a nuisance. The Court of Appeals, 105 Idaho 320, 669 P.2d 643, reversed and remanded for a new trial. On petition for review, we **vacate** the decision of the Court of Appeals and affirm the judgment of the district court.

Plaintiff appellants are homeowners who live near a cattle feedlot owned and operated by respondents. Appellants filed a complaint in March, 1978, alleging that the feedlot had been expanded in 1977 to accommodate the feeding of approximately 9,000 cattle. Appellants further alleged that "the spread and accumulation of manure, pollution of river and ground water, odor, insect infestation, increased concentration of birds, ... dust and noise" allegedly caused by the feedlot constituted a nuisance. After a trial on the merits a jury found that the feedlot did not constitute a nuisance. The trial court then also made findings and conclusions that the feedlot did not constitute a nuisance.

Appellants assigned as error the jury instructions which instructed the jury that in the determination of whether a nuisance exists consideration should be given to such factors as community interest, utility of conduct, business standards and practices, gravity of harm caused, and the circumstances surrounding the parties' movement to their locations. On appeal, appellants chose not to provide an evidentiary record, but merely claimed that the instructions misstated the law in Idaho.

The case was assigned to the Court of Appeals which reversed and remanded for a new trial. The basis for this reversal was that the trial court did not give a jury instruction based upon subsection (b) of Section 826 of the Restatement (Second) of Torts. That subsection allows for a finding of a nuisance even though the gravity of harm is outweighed by the utility of the conduct if the harm is "serious" and the payment of **damages** is "feasible" without forcing the business to discontinue.

This Court granted defendant's petition for review. We hold that the instructions which the trial court gave were not erroneous, being consistent with our prior case law and other **persuasive authority**. We further hold that the trial court did not err in not giving an instruction based on subsection (b) of Section 826 of the Second Restatement, which does not represent the law in the State of Idaho. . . . Accordingly, the decision of the Court of Appeals is vacated, and the judgment of the district court is affirmed.

Take Note

The court does not adopt the approach taken in the Restatement and adopts a different position and view consistent with its view of Idaho law.

. . . .

The Court of Appeals adopted subsection (b) of Section 826 of the Restatement Second, that a defendant can be held liable for a nuisance regardless of the utility of the conduct if the harm is "serious" and the payment of damages is "feasible" without jeopardizing the continuance of the conduct. We disagree that this is the law in Idaho.

. . . .

The Court of Appeals, without being requested by appellant, adopted the new subsection (b) of Section 826 of the Second Restatement partially because of language in *Koseris* [v. J.R. Simplot Co., 82 Idaho 263, 352 P.2d 235 (1960)] which reads:

> "We are constrained to hold that the trial court erred in sustaining objections to those offers of proof [evidencing utility of conduct], since they were relevant as bearing upon the issue whether respondents, in seeking injunctive relief, were pursuing the proper remedy; nevertheless, on the theory of damages which respondents had waived, the ruling was correct."[C]

The last phrase of the quote, relied on by the Court of Appeals, is clearly **dictum**, since the question of utility of conduct in a nuisance action for damages was not at issue in *Koseris*. It is very doubtful that this Court's *dictum* in *Koseris* was intended to make such a substantial change in the nuisance law. When the isolated statement of *dictum* was made in 1960, there was no persuasive authority for such a proposition. Indeed, no citation of authority was given. The three cases from other jurisdictions which the Court of Appeals relied on for authority did not exist until 1970. *See Boomer v. Atlantic Cement Co.,* 26 N.Y.2d 219, 309 N.Y.S.2d 312, 257 N.E.2d 870 (1970); *Jost v. Dairyland Power Co-op.,* 45 Wis.2d 164, 172 N.W.2d 647 (1970). The third case from Oregon, *Furrer v. Talent Irr. Dist.,* 258 Or. 494, 466 P.2d 605 (1970), was not even a nuisance case. Rather, it was an action in "**negligence**." The Second Restatement, which proposed the change in the law by adding subsection (b) to Section 826, was also not in existence until 1970. Therefore, we greatly discount this Court's *dictum* in the 1960 *Koseris* opinion as authority for such a substantial change in the nuisance law. The case of *McNichols v. J.R. Simplot Co.,* 74 Idaho 321, 262 P.2d 1012 (1953) should be viewed as the law in Idaho that in a nuisance action seeking damages the interests of the community, which would include the utility of the conduct, should be considered in the determination of the existence of a nuisance. The trial court's instructions in the present case were entirely consistent with *McNichols*. A plethora of other modern cases are in accord. *E.g., Nissan Motor Corp. v. Maryland Shipbuilding & Drydock Co.,* 544 F.Supp. 1104 (D.Md.1982) (utility of defendant's conduct is factor to be considered in determining existence of nuisance in damages action); *Little Joseph Realty, Inc. v. Town of Babylon,* 41 N.Y.2d 738, 395 N.Y.S.2d 428, 363 N.E.2d 1163 (N.Y.Ct.App.1977) (indicating that New York still adheres to balancing of risk and utility, requiring that harm to plaintiff must outweigh social usefulness of defendant's activity); *Pendergrast v. Aiken,* 293 N.C. 201, 236 S.E.2d 787 (1977) (balancing of harm versus utility retained, despite change of section 826 Restatement (Second) of Torts); *Pate v. City of Martin,* 614 S.W.2d 46 (Tenn.1981) (determination of existence of nuisance in action for damages and injunction cannot be determined by exact rules, but depends on circumstances of each case, including locality and character of surroundings, as well as utility and social value of defendant's conduct).

The State of Idaho is sparsely populated and its economy depends largely upon the benefits of agriculture, lumber, mining and industrial development. To eliminate the utility of conduct and other factors listed by the trial court from the criteria to be considered in determining whether a nuisance exists, as the appellant has argued throughout this appeal, would place an unreasonable burden upon these industries. We see no policy reasons which should compel this Court to accept appellant's argument and depart from our present law. Accordingly, the judgment of the district court is affirmed and the Court of Appeals decision is set aside.

Costs to respondents. No attorney fees.

BISTLINE, Justice, dissenting.

We have before us today a most remarkable event: two appellate courts, each obviously unaware of its true appellate function. The Court of Appeals, in reviewing the instant case, acted as a court of law, while the Idaho Supreme Court functioned as a court of error correction. In my mind, the roles have been reversed—I always understood that the Court of Appeals was a court of error correction, and it was our function to act as a court of law. I applaud the efforts of the Court of Appeals to modernize the law of nuisance in this state. I am not in the least persuaded to join the majority with its narrow view of nuisance law as expressed in the majority opinion.

The majority today continues to adhere to ideas on the law of nuisance that should have gone out with the use of buffalo chips as fuel. We have before us today homeowners complaining of a nearby feedlot--not a small operation, but rather a feedlot which accommodates 9,000 cattle. The homeowners advanced the theory that after the expansion of the feedlot in 1977, the odor, manure, dust, insect infestation and increased concentration of birds which accompanied all of the foregoing, constituted a nuisance. If the odoriferous quagmire created by 9,000 head of cattle is *not* a nuisance, it is difficult for me to imagine what is. However, the real question for us today is the legal basis on which a finding of nuisance can be made.

The Court of Appeals adopted subsection (b) of § 826 of the Restatement (Second) of Torts.[1] The majority today rejects this Restatement section, reasoning that

---

1 § 826. **Unreasonableness of Intentional Invasion.** An intentional invasion of another's interest in the use and enjoyment of land is unreasonable if

    (a) the gravity of the harm outweighs the utility of the actor's conduct, or

    (b) the harm caused by the conduct is serious and the financial burden of compensating for this and similar harm to others would not make the continuation of the conduct not feasible.

the Court of Appeals improperly relied upon dictum in *Koseris v. J.R. Simplot Co.,* 82 Idaho 263, 352 P.2d 235 (1960). *See infra,* at 227. Instead, the majority holds that the 1953 case of *McNichols v. J.R. Simplot Co.,* 74 Idaho 321, 262 P.2d 1012 (1953) espoused the correct rule of law for Idaho: in a nuisance action seeking damages, the interests of the community, which includes the utility of the conduct, should be considered in determining the existence of a nuisance. I find nothing immediately wrong with this statement of the law and agree wholeheartedly that the interests of the community should be considered in determining the existence of a nuisance. However, where this primitive rule of law fails is in recognizing that in our society, while it may be desirable to have a serious nuisance continue because the utility of the operation causing the nuisance is great, at the same time, those directly impacted by the serious nuisance deserve some compensation for the invasion they suffer as a result of the continuation of the nuisance. This is exactly what the more progressive provisions of § 826(b) of the Restatement (Second) of Torts addresses. Clearly, § 826(b) recognizes that the continuation of the serious harm must remain feasible. *See especially* comment on clause (b), subpart f of § 826 of the Restatement. What § 826(b) adds is a method of compensating those who must suffer the invasion without putting out of business the source or cause of the invasion. This does not strike me as a particularly adventuresome or far-reaching rule of law. In fact, the fairness of it is overwhelming.

> **FYI**
>
> The referenced subpart f states that "[i]t may sometimes be reasonable to operate an important activity if payment is made for the harm that it is causing, but unreasonable to continue it without paying. The process of weighing the gravity of the harm against the utility of the conduct assesses the social value of the actor's activity in general."

The majority's rule today overlooks the option of compensating those who suffer a nuisance because the interests of the community outweigh the interests of those afflicted by the nuisance. This unsophisticated balancing overlooks the possibility that it is not necessary that one interest be ignored when the community interest is strong. We should not be adopting a rule of preference which suggests that if the community interest is preferred any other interest must be disregarded. Instead, § 826(b) accommodates adverse interests by contemplating continuation of the facility which creates the nuisance while compensating those who suffer the direct impact of the nuisance-in the instant case the homeowners who live in the vicinity of the feedlot.

The majority's rule today suggests that part of the cost of industry, agriculture or development must be borne by those unfortunate few who have the fortuitous luck to live in the immediate vicinity of a nuisance producing facility. Frankly, I think this naive economic view is ridiculous in both its simplicity and its outdated view of modern economic society. The "cost" of a product includes not only the amount it takes to produce such a product but also includes the external costs: the damage done to the environment through pollution of air or water is an example of an external cost. In the instant case, the nuisance suffered by the homeowners should be considered an external cost of operating a feedlot and producing beef for public consumption. I do not believe that a few should be required to pay this extra cost of doing business by going uncompensated for a nuisance of this sort. If a feedlot wants to continue, I say fine, providing compensation is paid for the serious invasion (the odors, flies, dust, etc.) of the homeowner's interest. My only qualification is that the financial burden of compensating for this harm should not be such as to force the feedlot (or any other industry) out of business. The true cost can then be shifted to the consumer who rightfully should pay for the *entire* cost of producing the product he desires to obtain.

The majority today blithely suggests that because the State of Idaho is sparsely populated and because our economy is largely dependent on agriculture, lumber, mining and industrial development, we should forego compensating those who suffer a serious invasion. If humans are such a rare item in this state, maybe there is all the more reason to protect them from the discharge of industry. At a minimum, we should compensate those who suffer a nuisance at the hands of industry and agriculture. What the majority overlooks is that the cost of development should not be absorbed by [a] few, but rather should be spread out and paid by all. I am not convinced that agriculture or industry will be put out of business by requiring compensation for the nuisance they generate. Let us look at the case before us. The owners of the feedlot will not find themselves looking for new jobs if they are required to compensate the homeowners for the stench and dust and flies attendant with 9,000 head of cattle. Rather, meat prices at the grocery store will undoubtedly go up. But, in my view it is far better that the cost of the nuisance be carried by the consumer of a product than by the unfortunate homeowners currently suffering under adverse conditions. Some compensation should be paid the homeowners for suffering the burden from which we all benefit.

. . . .

Points for Discussion

1. Which is the most persuasive: the majority opinion authored by Justice Bakes or Justice Bistline's dissent?

2. Note the majority's and the dissent's differing approaches to the application of section 826 of the Second Restatement.

3. Are courts better suited than legislatures to balance the utility of agricultural, lumber, mining and industrial developments and the costs of such development? How should costs be defined and measured? Who should bear the costs of industrial, agricultural, and other processes?

4. On liability rules and approaches in the context of competing uses of property, see Ronald Coase, *The Problem of Social Cost*, 3 J.L. & ECON. 1 (1960).

5. State right-to-farm statutes can provide agricultural operations with immunity from nuisance liability where the operations existed prior to the plaintiff's acquisition or use of land. *See, e.g.,* MISS. CODE ANN. § 95-3-29. For court decisions addressing such immunity provisions, *see* Bormann v. Board of Supervisors, 584 N.W.2d 309 (Iowa 1998) (state right to farm law condemned property of neighbors without just compensation and therefore violated Iowa and United States constitutions); Buchanan v. Simplot Feeders, Ltd., 134 Wash.2d 673, 952 P.2d 610 (1998) (state law upheld where urban development encroached into agricultural area). For more on this subject, *see* Alexander A. Reinert, Note, *The Right to Farm: Hog-Tied and Nuisance-Bound*, 73 N.Y.U. L. REV. 1694 (1998).

—————————————

Mills v. Kimbley

909 N.E.2d 1068 (Ind. App. 2009)

BRADFORD, Judge.

Appellant/Plaintiff/Counterclaim Defendant Gregory Mills appeals the trial court's award of summary judgment against him in his action against Appellee/Defendant/**Counterclaimant** Dean Kimbley for nuisance . . .

Mills and Kimbley are next-door neighbors. Mills lives at 310 West Edgewood Avenue in Indianapolis, where he has lived since March of 2004. Kimbley lives at

302 West Edgewood Avenue, which is the property adjacent to Mills's property on the east side, where he has lived since 1984.

Within approximately two months of his move to 310 West Edgewood Avenue, Mills began keeping a journal of what in his view were Kimbley's disruptive activities. This journal, subsequently submitted as designated evidence in the instant action, covers Kimbley's activities from May 21, 2004 through September 11, 2006, and is eighty-three pages long. On April 25, 2005, Mills began videotaping Kimbley's and his guests' activities without their permission. Due to Mills's videotaping activities, Kimbley claims to have been deprived the full use and enjoyment of certain portions of his property.

On May 8, 2006, Mills sent Kimbley a letter, in which he demanded that Kimbley not play loud music, permit loud and/or foul language, set off the house alarm, move his trash to Mills's property, enter any part of his property for any reason, contact him or his guests, nor tamper with his fence. In addition, Mills demanded that within seven days of receipt of the letter, Kimbley was to trim certain trees along the fence line and keep the property line clear of any obstructions such as "cinder blocks, mulch, and growth barriers." . . . Mills also demanded that within seven days Kimbley remove his sprinkler system, which Mills claimed was on his property, and repair a bare area of his yard, which Mills believed was caused by Kimbley's mulch pile. An inspection report issued by the City of Indianapolis found no violation in the placement of the sprinkler system.

. . . .

On October 24, 2006, Mills filed the instant action alleging nuisance . . .

On July 25, 2008, Kimbley moved for summary judgment on both Mills's claim and his own counterclaim. . . . Following an October 20, 2008 hearing, the trial court granted summary judgment against Mills . . . This appeal follows.

. . . .

In Indiana, nuisances are defined by statute. *Wernke v. Halas,* 600 N.E.2d 117, 120 (Ind.Ct.App.1992). Indiana Code section 32-30-6-6 (2006) defines an actionable nuisance as follows: "Whatever is: (1) injurious to health; (2) indecent; (3) offensive to the senses; or (4) an obstruction to the free use of property; so as essentially to interfere with the comfortable enjoyment of life or property, is a nuisance, and the subject of an action." This court has traditionally distinguished between two types of nuisance: a public nuisance, which affects an entire neighborhood or community; and a private nuisance, which affects only one individual or a determinate number of people. *See Hopper v. Colonial Motel Props., Inc.,* 762 N.E.2d 181, 186 (Ind.Ct.App.2002), *trans. denied.* A private nuisance arises when it is demonstrated that one party uses his property to the detriment of the use and enjoyment of the property of another. [C]

Both public and private nuisances are further subdivided into **nuisances** *per se,* or nuisances at law, and **nuisances** *per accidens,* or nuisances in fact. *Wernke,* 600 N.E.2d at 120. "A nuisance *per se,* as the term implies, is that which is a nuisance in itself, and which, therefore, cannot be so conducted or maintained as to be lawfully carried on or permitted to exist." [C] A house of prostitution and an obstruction that encroaches on the right-of-way of a public highway, for example, are nuisances *per se.* [C] On the other hand, an otherwise lawful use may become a nuisance *per accidens* by virtue of the circumstances surrounding the use. [C]

It is logical, therefore, that the determination that something is a nuisance *per se* is a question of law, and the determination of a nuisance *per accidens,* a question "for the jury or the judge as trier of fact." [C] This latter determination is to be made by the trier of fact in light of all the surrounding facts and circumstances, with the dispositive question being "'whether the thing complained of produces such a condition as in the judgment of reasonable persons is naturally productive of actual physical discomfort to persons of ordinary sensibility, tastes, and habits.'" [C] Summary judgment, which by definition resolves only those cases lacking material factual disputes, is rarely appropriate in *per accidens* nuisance cases. [C]

Take Note

The designation of nuisances as "at law" or "in fact" determines whether the matter is a question of law for the court or a question of fact for the jury or the judge-as-factfinder.

Here, Mills does not allege that Kimbley's use of his land is illegal or that it affects persons other than himself and his household. Accordingly, he is alleging a private, *per accidens* nuisance. Mills's nuisance claim during the summary judgment proceedings was based upon Kimbley's alleged loud music. Yet the record on appeal does not contain Mills's apparent "declaration" regarding this alleged loud music, and none of the specified portions of Exhibit A reference such loud music. Although Mills's designated Exhibits C and D indicate that he told Kimbley not to play loud music and that he and Kimbley agreed during the June 22, 2006 mediation proceeding that Kimbley's music should not be heard in Mills's home, Mills points to no specifically

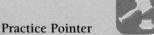

Practice Pointer

As illustrated by this case, the failure to include evidentiary materials in the record submitted to an appellate court can extinguish a claim. Counsel must insure that the record is complete and contains any and all evidence, declarations, affidavits, and other items presented to the trial court and supporting the specific arguments to be made to the appellate court.

designated evidence contained in the record on appeal supporting his allegation that loud music was played. Mills's failure to provide adequate record support for his challenge to the trial court's summary judgment waives his claim on this ground. *See* Ind. Appellate R. 46(A)(8)(a) (providing that the appellant's argument must be supported by cogent reasoning and citations to authorities and parts of the appendix relied on).

To the extent Mills's nuisance claim was based upon allegations other than those regarding loud music, his nonspecific catchall references to "those facts as explicitly identified *supra*," most of which are not part of the record on appeal, and "all of those nuisance-related facts and instances set forth in extreme detail as contained in Appellant's 88-page, single-spaced, 10-point font Journal" are not adequately specific to support his claim that a genuine issue of material fact remains on his nuisance claims. . . . Accordingly, we deem any additional allegations of nuisance by Mills waived. [C]

. . . .

The judgment of the trial court is affirmed in part and reversed in part, and the cause is remanded with instructions.

Hot Rod Hill Motor Park v. Triolo

293 S.W.3d 788 (Tex. App. 2009)

FELIPE REYNA, Justice.

Hot Rod Hill Motor Park is a race track located on Roger Deewayne Brown's property. Donmichael Lucas Triolo sued Brown and Hot Rod Hill (hereinafter "Brown"), alleging that the track constitutes a nuisance. A jury found that the track constitutes a nuisance, and the trial court entered a final judgment permanently **enjoining** Brown from conducting any races of motorized vehicles for either competition or practice. Brown appealed the **permanent injunction**, which we affirmed. *See Hot Rod Hill Motor Park v. Triolo,* 276 S.W.3d 565 (Tex.App.-Waco 2008, no pet.).

> **What's That?**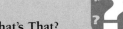
>
> A *permanent* injunction is granted by a court following a final hearing on the merits. This type of injunction should be distinguished from a *preliminary* injunction which is temporary and is issued by a court to prevent the occurrence of an irreparable injury prior to the court's decision on the merits of the claim.

Brown subsequently filed a motion to vacate, amend, or alter the permanent injunction on grounds that Triolo had sold his home located near the track. At the conclusion of a hearing on the motion, the trial court found that a change in circumstances had occurred, but that it was not sufficient to warrant dissolution or modification of the injunction. The trial court did not file findings of fact and conclusions of law as requested by Brown. On appeal, Brown maintains that the trial court erred by: (1) refusing to vacate the permanent injunction; (2) refusing to modify the permanent injunction; and (3) failing to file findings of fact and conclusions of law. We reverse and render.

PERMANENT INJUNCTION

A trial court may modify or vacate a permanent injunction because of changed conditions. *See City of Tyler v. St. Louis Sw. Ry. Co. of Tex.,* 405 S.W.2d 330, 333 (Tex.1966); *see also Kubala Pub. Adjusters, Inc. v. Unauthorized Practice of Law Comm.,* 133 S.W.3d 790, 794 (Tex.App.-Texarkana 2004, no pet.). "Changed conditions" include a change in the "factual situation or the controlling law." *Kubala,* 133 S.W.3d at 795. We review a trial court's ruling on a motion to modify or vacate a permanent injunction for **abuse of discretion**. *See Chase Manhattan Bank & Bank One, N.A. v. Bowles,* 52 S.W.3d 871, 879 (Tex.App.-Waco 2001, no pet.).

Analysis

In issue one, Brown argues that the permanent injunction should be vacated because Triolo no longer has a property interest in any land surrounding the track, thus, he can no longer raise a nuisance claim and is no longer entitled to injunctive relief. Triolo responds that an enforceable legal right to the affected property is not a prerequisite for asserting a nuisance claim, as a person's "interests" need only be affected.

Triolo testified that he has sold his home near the track. During the week, he resides at a home in Calvert, Texas. On approximately half the weekends each year, however, he and his family stay at his parents' residence near the track. Triolo sometimes visits during the week when his parents want to see his children. The Triolos also keep some items, such as a baby bed, at the house. Although his father pays the bills and taxes, Triolo testified that his parents' home is his permanent residence. He receives mail at this address, including his cellular telephone bill, and has listed this address on his driver's license, voter registration, vehicle registration, most recent income tax return, and his wife's voter registration.

Actionable nuisance involves an invasion of another's interests. *See City of Tyler v. Likes,* 962 S.W.2d 489, 503 (Tex.1997). A private nuisance may be asserted by those with "property rights and privileges in respect to the use and enjoyment of the land affected, including possessors of the land." RESTATEMENT (SEC-

OND) OF TORTS § 821E (1979). A **possessor** is one who is (1) in occupation of the land with intent to control it; (2) in occupation of the land with intent to control it, if no other person has subsequently occupied it with intent to control it; or (3) entitled to immediate occupation of the land, if no other person is in possession. RESTATEMENT (SECOND) OF TORTS § 328E (1965).

> "**Possession**" is not limited to **occupancy** under a claim of some other interest in the land, but occupancy is a sufficient interest in itself to permit recovery for invasions of the interest in the use and enjoyment of the land. Thus members of the family of the possessor of a dwelling who occupy it along with him may properly be regarded as sharing **occupancy** with intent to control the land and hence as possessors, as defined in § 328E. When there is interference with their use and enjoyment of the dwelling they can therefore maintain an action for private nuisance."

RESTATEMENT (SECOND) OF TORTS § 821E cmt. *d* (1979); *see Ft. Worth & Rio Grande Ry. Co. v. Glenn*, 97 Tex. 586, 80 S.W. 992, 994 (1904) ("If the damage be to the right of those occupying the property at the time, he must prove title, or at least a right of occupancy."); *see also New v. Khojal*, No. 04-98-00768-CV, 1999 WL 675448, at *2, 1999 Tex.App. LEXIS 6575, at *5 (Tex.App.-San Antonio Aug. 31, 1999, no pet.) (not designated for publication) ("[L]egal title is not a prerequisite for bringing trespass and nuisance claims;" "a plaintiff need only be a possessor of the property to have standing.").

Accordingly, an occupancy interest in land is sufficient to vest a person with the right to assert a nuisance claim. *See* RESTATEMENT (SECOND) OF TORTS § 821E cmt. *d*; *see also Glenn*, 80 S.W. at 994; *New*, 1999 WL 675448, at *2, 1999 Tex.App. LEXIS 6575, at *5. We do not, however, construe this rule to include part-time occupants. The Restatement contemplates a situation where a person occupies land with intent to *control* it, such as where family members regularly occupy a home along with the actual owner of the home. *See* RESTATEMENT (SECOND) OF TORTS § 328E; *see also* RESTATEMENT (SECOND) OF TORTS § 821E cmt. *d*; *Glenn*, 80 S.W. at 994. For example, in *New*, the San Antonio Court found that a man residing in his deceased mother's home could assert a nuisance claim for damage to the property. *See New*, 1999 WL 675448, at *3, 1999 Tex. App. LEXIS 6575, at *7. New had occupied the home for several years, lived in the home with his girlfriend, her two children, and his grandson, paid for taxes and repairs, and believed himself to be the owner of the house after his mother died. [C]

Triolo's occupancy does not rise to the level of that contemplated by the Restatement. He does not live at his parents' home, but merely visits on some weekends. He does not pay taxes or bills associated with the property. The record does not suggest that he believes himself to be an owner of the property. Unlike

New, Triolo is not a regular occupant of the home, but is at best a frequent visitor and; thus, fails to meet the definition of an occupant with intent to control the land. For this reason, Triolo cannot assert a nuisance claim and is no longer entitled to **injunctive** relief.

The trial court abused its discretion by failing to vacate the permanent injunction. . . . We reverse the court's judgment and render judgment that the permanent injunction is vacated.

Hypo 14-1

Plaintiff owns five acres of land upon which he has his home, a small restaurant, and room and accommodations for twenty trailers and recreational vehicles. On an adjoining tract of property, and approximately 1,500 feet from Plaintiff's home, Defendant operates an oil refinery. (According to Defendant, the refinery is a modern plant and is of the type typically used to renovate used lubricating oil.)

Plaintiff contends that for several hours on four to five days per week Defendant's refinery emits, in great quantity, nauseous gases and odors which invade Plaintiff's land and other properties located within a three-mile radius. According to Plaintiff, on those days the gases and odors are of great density and render persons of ordinary sensitivities uncomfortable and ill, thus substantially impairing Plaintiff's use and enjoyment of her land. Plaintiff has repeatedly notified Defendant of and demanded abatement of the problem; Defendant has done nothing in response to the notices and demands.

Is the refinery a private nuisance? Discuss.

Hypo 14-2

Defendants own and operate a nursery and day care center at their private home and residence. On Monday through Friday, from 7:00 a.m. to 6:00 p.m., twenty to twenty-five children from 2 to 6 years of age are at the center. Most begin to arrive at about 7:30 a.m. and leave at 5:30 p.m. and take a nap during the day after being served lunch. Weather permitting, children play outside under the supervision of Defendants who try to ensure (sometimes successfully, sometimes not) that any noise made by the playing tots is minimized.

Plaintiffs, an elderly married couple who admit that they "hate and are allergic to young, noisemaking children," own and operate a bed and breakfast next door to Defendants' day care center. On the same block (an unrestricted area not regulated by any zoning ordinance) are two gas stations, a doctor's office, an insurance and real estate agency, and several private homes. Plaintiffs' property and the day care center are located on four-lane State Highway 1, two blocks south of an intersection with U.S. Highway 42.

Over the past year, Plaintiffs have routinely complained that the noise from the day care center constitutes a private nuisance as it interferes with their and their customers' use and enjoyment of the bed and breakfast. The neighbor on the opposite side of Defendants' day care has no problem with the center or the presence of the children.

Plaintiffs have filed an action seeking a court order enjoining Defendants from operating the day care center. You are the trial court judge assigned to the case. Would you rule in favor of Plaintiffs? Do you have sufficient facts? If not, what other factual inquiries would you make?

Philadelphia Electric Company v. Hercules, Inc.

762 F.2d 303 (3d Cir. 1985)

A. LEON HIGGINBOTHAM, Jr., Circuit Judge.

This is an appeal from a final judgment of the district court in favor of Philadelphia Electric Company ("PECO") and against Hercules, Inc. ("Hercules") in the amount of $394,910.14, and further ordering Hercules to take all appropriate action to eliminate pollution on a property owned by PECO in Chester, Pennsylvania. The case was tried to a jury on theories of public and private nuisance. For the reasons set forth in the opinion that follows, we will reverse the judgment against Hercules on PECO's claims, and vacate the injunction.

I.

Prior to October of 1971, the Pennsylvania Industrial Chemical Corporation ("PICCO") owned a tract of land abutting the Delaware River in Chester, Pennsylvania where it operated a hydrocarbon resin manufacturing plant. At the time

PICCO acquired the property ("the Chester site") there was an inlet located at the southern end that opened into the Delaware River. Sometime later PICCO filled in the shoreline at the inlet and thereby created a lake ("the PICCO pond"). During the period it conducted operations on the Chester site, the evidence tended to show, PICCO deposited or buried various resins and their by-products in the PICCO pond and possibly other locations.

In 1971 PICCO ceased operations on the Chester site and sold the facility to Gould, Inc. ("Gould"). Gould did not conduct any operations on the Chester site, other than leasing certain tanks to ABM Disposal Services Company ("ABM"), which used them to store large quantities of various waste materials, though apparently not resins or resinous by-products.

In mid-1973, PECO-which operated a plant on an adjoining piece of land-obtained an option to purchase the Chester site from Gould. Prior to exercising its option, a PECO representative inspected the site on more than one occasion, including walking tours along the banks of the Delaware River and the banks of the PICCO pond. PECO learned that Gould's tenant, ABM, had caused a number of spills on the site, including oil spills in the pond area, and was informed that ABM was a "sloppy tenant." ABM was unable to clean up the Chester site in time to meet Gould's original deadline for vacating the premises, a condition of the PECO purchase agreement. PECO exercised its option and acquired the property in March of 1974. PECO has conducted no operations on the Chester site, but has leased a portion of the land to American Refining Group, Inc.

In response, PECO developed a plan whereby the remaining pond resin would be removed to a landfill, and the PICCO pond area would be backfilled and regraded. [The State Department of Environmental Resources (DER)] approved this plan on November 21, 1980. PECO produced evidence indicating that it incurred expenses of $338,328.69 in implementing the clean-up, and an additional $7,578 in collecting and carting away resinous material that continued to leach to the surface at various places around the Chester site during the summers of 1981-1983. PECO also introduced evidence of $67,500 in lost rentals from American Refining due to the continuing leaching.

In a letter dated March 10, 1981, DER expressed satisfaction with the clean-up of the pond area, but reported that a February 27, 1981 inspection revealed resins still on the Delaware River bank and continued leaching of resins into the River. PECO was asked to "submit in writing ... Philadelphia Electric's position on the control or clean-up of the resin material remaining on the bank." After PECO expressed reluctance to spend any additional money on clean-up of the Chester site, DER wrote PECO again, on May 28, 1981:

> Leachate analysis of the resin on the river bank indicates that there is a leaching problem from the resin. Such discharge constitutes an

unpermitted discharge to the waters of the Commonwealth and is a violation of the Clean Streams Law, subject to the penalties provided therein. It is therefore required that the resin material on the river bank be removed.

The record does not reveal that DER or PECO has taken any further action regarding the resinous material on the river bank, and PECO's witness testified at trial that the condition still existed.

On February 16, 1982, PECO instituted suit against Gould and Hercules, which had acquired the remaining assets of PICCO in 1973, in exchange for Hercules stock. (PICCO was dissolved on January 9, 1976.) Hercules **cross-claimed** against Gould. On cross-motions for summary judgment the district court ruled that Hercules was liable as PICCO's corporate successor under the express terms of the Agreement and Plan of Reorganization ("the Agreement") it entered into with PICCO, and because the transaction was a *de facto* merger. A jury trial was held in July of 1983. PECO, stating that discovery had shown no wrongdoing on the part of Gould, offered no evidence against Gould. At trial Hercules attempted to show that the pollution was not consistent with PICCO's operations on the Chester site, but was consistent with the operations of ABM and other industrial plants in the area. At the close of evidence, the jury was instructed on principles of public and private nuisance. The jury's verdict was rendered in the form of answers to **special interrogatories**:

1. Do you find by a preponderance of the evidence that PICCO caused the contamination of the property now owned by Philadelphia Electric Company? YES.

2. Do you find by a preponderance of the evidence that the contamination on the property now owned by Philadelphia Electric Company continues to pollute the groundwater or the Delaware River? YES.

3. In what amount do you award damages? $345,906.69.

4. Do you find by a preponderance of the evidence that ABM's activities contributed to the contamination of the Philadelphia Electric Company property? YES.

5. Was Gould aware of ABM's activities and permitted them to continue? NO.

Based on these answers, the district court moulded a verdict and entered judgment for PECO against Hercules in the amount of $394,910.14, which included delay damages of $49,003.45 pursuant to Pennsylvania Rule of Civil

Procedure 238, entered judgment for Gould on Hercules' cross-claim, and issued an injunction as follows:

> IT IS FURTHER ORDERED and DECREED that Hercules, Inc. shall forthwith take all appropriate action to abate and eliminate the contamination on the property of the Philadelphia Electric Company located at the Chester site and abate the further pollution of the groundwater and the Delaware River adjacent to the property by collecting and removing all pollutants in accordance with all applicable rules and regulations of the Pennsylvania Department of Environmental Resources, the United States Environmental Protection Agency, and any other appropriate state or federal regulatory agency.

In this appeal Hercules contends, *inter alia,* that . . . PECO had no cause of action against it for public or private nuisance. The parties are agreed that the substantive law of Pennsylvania governs this **diversity** case.

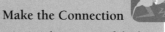

Make the Connection

Diversity jurisdiction, *i.e.,* a federal court's authority to adjudicate a case involving parties who are citizens of different states and an amount in controversy at or above the requisite statutory minimum, is addressed in a Civil Procedure course.

. . . .

Restatement (Second) of Torts § 821D defines a "private nuisance" as "a nontrespassory invasion of another's interest in the private use and enjoyment of land." The briefs and arguments, as well as the district court's opinion, [c] give much attention to the questions of whether the condition created by Hercules on the Chester site amounted to a nuisance, and whether Hercules remains liable for the nuisance even after vacating the land. For the purposes of our decision, we may assume that Hercules created a nuisance, and that it remains liable for this condition. See *Restatement (Second) of Torts* § 840A. The crucial and difficult question for us is *to whom* Hercules may be liable.

The parties have cited no case from Pennsylvania or any other jurisdiction, and we have found none, that permits a purchaser of **real property** to recover from the seller on a private nuisance theory for conditions existing on the very land transferred, and thereby to circumvent limitations on vendor liability inherent in the rule of *caveat emptor*. In a somewhat analogous circumstance, courts have not permitted **tenants** to circumvent traditional limitations on the liability of **lessors** by the expedient of casting their cause of

Non constat
jus civile
a posteriori

It's Latin to Me!

Caveat emptor is Latin for "let the buyer aware." Under this doctrine, purchasers buy at their own risk.

action for defective conditions existing on premises (over which they have assumed control) as one for private nuisance. *See Collette v. Piela,* 141 Conn. 382, 106 A.2d 473 (1954); *Clerken v. Cohen,* 315 Ill.App. 222, 42 N.E.2d 846 (1942). In *Harris v. Lewistown Trust Co.,* 326 Pa. 145, 191 A. 34 (1937), *overruled in part on other grounds, Reitmeyer v. Sprecher,* 431 Pa. 284, 243 A.2d 395 (1968), the Supreme Court of Pennsylvania held that the doctrine that a **landlord** not in possession may be liable for injuries resulting from a "condition amounting to a nuisance" is confined to "the owners or occupants of near-by property, persons temporarily on such property, or persons on a neighboring highway or other places." [C] Recovery on this theory was not available to **tenants** or their **invitees**: "A breach of duty owed to one class of persons cannot create a cause of action in favor of a person not within the class. A plaintiff must show that as to him there was a breach of duty." [C] Similarly, under the doctrine of *caveat emptor* Hercules owed only a limited duty to Gould and, in turn, to PECO. PECO concedes that this duty was not violated. PECO cannot recover in private nuisance for the violation of a duty Hercules may have owed to others-namely, its neighbors.

We believe that this result is consonant with the historical role of private nuisance law as a means of efficiently resolving conflicts between *neighboring,* contemporaneous land uses. [C] All of the very useful and sophisticated economic analyses of private nuisance remedies published in recent years proceed on the basis that the goal of nuisance law is to achieve efficient and **equitable** solutions to problems created by *discordant* land uses. In this light nuisance law can be seen as a complement to zoning regulations, [c] and not as an additional type of consumer protection for purchasers of realty. Neighbors, unlike the purchasers of the land upon which a nuisance exists, have no opportunity to protect themselves through inspection and negotiation. The record shows that PECO acted as a sophisticated and responsible purchaser-inquiring into the past use of the Chester site, and inspecting it carefully. We find it inconceivable that the price it offered Gould did not reflect the possibility of environmental risks, even if the exact condition giving rise to this suit was not discovered.

Take Note

The court makes the important point that an offered price does and should include and reflect a buyer's concerns as to the risks and other potential liabilities of the purchase. One would expect that the greater the risk and liability, the lower the buyer's offer.

Where, as here, the rule of *caveat emptor* applies, allowing a **vendee** a cause of action for private nuisance for conditions existing on the land transferred-where there has been no fraudulent concealment-would in effect negate the market's allocations of resources and risks, and subject **vendors** who may have originally sold their land at appropriately discounted prices to unbargained-for liability to remote vendees. To so extend private nuisance beyond its historical role would render it little more than an epithet, "and an epithet does not make out a cause of action."[C] . Such an extension of common law doctrine is particularly hazardous in an area, such as environmental pollution, where Congress and the state legislatures are actively seeking to achieve a socially acceptable definition of rights and liabilities. We conclude that PECO did not have a cause of action against Hercules sounding in private nuisance.

. . . .

The doctrine of public nuisance protects interests quite different from those implicated in actions for private nuisance, and PECO's claim for public nuisance requires separate consideration. Whereas private nuisance requires an invasion of another's interest in the private use and enjoyment of land, a public nuisance is "an unreasonable interference with a right common to the general public." *Restatement (Second) of Torts* § 821B(1). An action for public nuisance may lie even though neither the plaintiff nor the defendant acts in the exercise of private property rights. As William Prosser once wrote:

> There are, then, two and only two kinds of nuisance, which are quite unrelated except in the vague general way that each of them causes inconvenience to someone, and in the common name, which naturally has led the courts to apply to the two some of the same substantive rules of law. A private nuisance is narrowly restricted to the invasion of interests in the use and enjoyment of land. It is only a tort, and the remedy for it lies exclusively with the individual whose rights have been disturbed. A public nuisance is a species of catch-all low-grade criminal offense, consisting of an interference with the rights of the community at large, which may include anything from the blocking of a highway to a gaming-house or indecent exposure. Although as in the case of other crimes, the normal remedy is in the hands of the state, a public nuisance may also be a private one, when it interferes with private land. The seeds of confusion were sown when courts began to hold that a tort action would lie even for a purely public nuisance if the plaintiff had suffered "particular damage."

Prosser, *Private Action for Public Nuisance,* 52 Va.L.Rev. 997, 999 (1966) (footnotes omitted).

In analyzing the public nuisance claim, we are not concerned with the happenstance that PECO now occupies the very land PICCO occupied when it allegedly created the condition that has polluted the Delaware River waters, or that the continuing source of that pollution is located on that land. The question before us is whether PECO has **standing** to bring an individual action for damages or injunctive relief for interference with a public right.

Make the Connection

The issue of a plaintiff's standing to bring a lawsuit refers to the plaintiff's right to make a legal claim in court and to seek judicial enforcement of a claimed right or duty or a remedy for a deprivation of same. Standing is addressed in Civil Procedure and Constitutional Law courses.

Restatement (Second) of Torts § 821C(1) provides:

In order to recover damages in an individual action for a public nuisance, one must have suffered harm of a kind different from that suffered by other members of the public exercising the right common to the general public that was the subject of interference.

The same requirements apply to individual plaintiffs seeking injunctive relief. *Restatement (Second) of Torts* § 821C(2); [c]. PECO argues that the expense it incurred in cleaning up the offending condition constituted the harm requisite for standing to sue for public nuisance. We disagree. Though **pecuniary** harm certainly may be harm of a different kind from that suffered by the general public, *see Restatement (Second) of Torts* § 821C comment h, we find in this case no allegation or evidence that PECO suffered this harm "exercising the right common to the general public that was the subject of interference." The public right that was interfered with was the right to "pure water". [Cc] PECO does not allege that it used the waters of the Delaware River itself, or that it was directly harmed in any way by the pollution of those waters. Thus, this is not a case "where an established business made commercial use of the public right with which the defendant interfered." [C] If PECO-as a **riparian landowner**-had suffered damage to its land or its operations as a result of the pollution of the Delaware, it would possibly have a claim for public nuisance. But the condition of the Chester site was not the *result* of the pollution, it was the *cause* of it. DER required PECO, as owner of the Chester site, to remove the sources of the pollution. PECO has been specially harmed only

What's That?

A riparian landowner's property borders a river or stream.

in the exercise of its private property rights over the Chester site. PECO has suffered no "particular damage" in the exercise of a right common to the general public, and it lacks standing to sue for public nuisance.

. . . .

We emphasize that our decision today should not be interpreted as standing for the general proposition that a party that contaminates land, or the successors to its assets, can escape liability by the expedient of selling the land. To the contrary, it would seem that there are many avenues by which such a party may be held accountable.[20] We hold only that in this case the purchaser of that land, PECO-though we recognize that it acted as a responsible corporate citizen-had no cause of action against the vendor's successor, Hercules, for private nuisance, public nuisance, or common law **indemnity**.

For the foregoing reasons, the injunction requiring Hercules to clean up the Chester site will be vacated, and the judgment of the district court on PECO's claims against Hercules will be reversed.

Points for Discussion

1. How does the court define "private nuisance" and "public nuisance"? What is the difference between the two categories of nuisance?

2. The court declined to extend the common law private nuisance doctrine in the context of environmental pollution "where Congress and the state legislatures are actively seeking to achieve a socially acceptable definition of rights and liabilities." Do you agree with this aspect of the court's decision?

3. How did the court respond to PECO's argument that the clean-up expenses it incurred constituted the harm required for standing to sue for a public nuisance?

Boomer v. Atlantic Cement Co.

26 N.Y.2d 219, 309 N.Y.S.2d 312 (1970)

Bergan, J.

Defendant operates a large cement plant near Albany. These are actions for injunction and damages by neighboring land owners alleging injury to property from dirt, smoke and vibration emanating from the plant. A nuisance has been found after trial, **temporary damages** have been allowed; but an injunction has been denied.

20 For example, Hercules could be liable to neighboring landowners in private nuisance, or to users of Delaware River waters in public nuisance. DER or the federal Environmental Protection Agency may be able to proceed directly against Hercules on statutory or public nuisance theories.

The public concern with air pollution arising from many sources in industry and in transportation is currently accorded ever wider recognition accompanied by a growing sense of responsibility in State and Federal Governments to control it. Cement plants are obvious sources of air pollution in the neighborhoods where they operate.

But there is now before the court private litigation in which individual property owners have sought specific relief from a single plant operation. The threshold question raised by the division of view on this appeal is whether the court should resolve the litigation between the parties now before it as equitably as seems possible; or whether, seeking promotion of the general public welfare, it should channel private litigation into broad public objectives.

A court performs its essential function when it decides the rights of parties before it. Its decision of private controversies may sometimes greatly affect public issues. Large questions of law are often resolved by the manner in which private litigation is decided. But this is normally an incident to the court's main function to settle controversy. It is a rare exercise of judicial power to use a decision in private litigation as a purposeful mechanism to achieve direct public objectives greatly beyond the rights and interests before the court.

Effective control of air pollution is a problem presently far from solution even with the full public and financial powers of government. In large measure adequate technical procedures are yet to be developed and some that appear possible may be economically impracticable.

It seems apparent that the amelioration of air pollution will depend on technical research in great depth; on a carefully balanced consideration of the economic impact of close regulation; and of the actual effect on public health. It is likely to require massive public expenditure and to demand more than any local community can accomplish and to depend on regional and interstate controls.

A court should not try to do this on its own as a by-product of private litigation and it seems manifest that the judicial establishment is neither equipped in the limited nature of any judgment it can pronounce nor prepared to lay down and implement an effective policy for the elimination of air pollution. This is an area beyond the circumference of one private lawsuit. It is a direct responsibility for government and should not thus be undertaken as an incident to solving a dispute between property owners and a single cement plant — one of many — in the Hudson River valley.

The cement making operations of defendant have been found by the court at Special Term to have damaged the nearby properties of plaintiffs in these two actions. That court, as it has been noted, accordingly found defendant maintained a nuisance and this has been affirmed at the Appellate Division. The total damage to plaintiffs' properties is, however, relatively small in comparison with the value of defendant's operation and with the consequences of the injunction which plaintiffs seek.

The ground for the denial of injunction, notwithstanding the finding both that there is a nuisance and that plaintiffs have been damaged substantially, is the large disparity in economic consequences of the nuisance and of the injunction. This theory cannot, however, be sustained without overruling a doctrine which has been consistently reaffirmed in several leading cases in this court and which has never been disavowed here, namely that where a nuisance has been found and where there has been any substantial damage shown by the party complaining an injunction will be granted.

The rule in New York has been that such a nuisance will be enjoined although marked disparity be shown in economic consequence between the effect of the injunction and the effect of the nuisance.

The problem of disparity in economic consequence was sharply in focus in *Whalen v. Union Bag & Paper Co.* (208 N. Y. 1). A pulp mill entailing an investment of more than a million dollars polluted a stream in which plaintiff, who owned a farm, was "a lower riparian owner". The economic loss to plaintiff from this pollution was small. This court, reversing the Appellate Division, reinstated the injunction granted by the Special Term against the argument of the mill owner that in view of "the slight advantage to plaintiff and the great loss that will be inflicted on defendant" an injunction should not be granted (p. 2). "Such a balancing of injuries cannot be justified by the circumstances of this case", Judge Werner noted (p. 4). He continued: "Although the damage to the plaintiff may be slight as compared with the defendant's expense of abating the condition, that is not a good reason for refusing an injunction" (p. 5).

Thus the unconditional injunction granted at Special Term was reinstated. The rule laid down in that case, then, is that whenever the damage resulting from a nuisance is found not "unsubstantial", viz., $100 a year, injunction would follow. This states a rule that had been followed in this court with marked consistency (*McCarty v. Natural Carbonic Gas Co.*, 189 N. Y. 40;*Strobel v. Kerr Salt Co.*, 164 N. Y. 303;*Campbell v. Seaman*, 63 N. Y. 568).

. . . .

Although the court at Special Term and the Appellate Division held that [the] injunction should be denied, it was found that plaintiffs had been damaged in various specific amounts up to the time of the trial and damages to the respective plaintiffs were awarded for those amounts. The effect of this was, injunction having been denied, plaintiffs could maintain successive actions at law for damages thereafter as further damage was incurred.

The court at Special Term also found the amount of **permanent damage** attributable to each plaintiff, for the guidance of the parties in the event both sides stipulated to the payment and acceptance of such permanent damage as a settlement of all the controversies among the parties. The total of permanent damages to all plaintiffs thus found was $185,000. This basis of adjustment has not resulted in any stipulation by the parties.

This result at Special Term and at the Appellate Division is a departure from a rule that has become settled; but to follow the rule literally in these cases would be to close down the plant at once. This court is fully agreed to avoid that immediately drastic remedy; the difference in view is how best to avoid it.

One alternative is to grant the injunction but postpone its effect to a specified future date to give opportunity for technical advances to permit defendant to eliminate the nuisance; another is to grant the injunction conditioned on the payment of permanent damages to plaintiffs which would compensate them for the total economic loss to their property present and future caused by defendant's operations. For reasons which will be developed the court chooses the latter alternative.

If the injunction were to be granted unless within a short period -- e.g., 18 months -- the nuisance be abated by improved methods, there would be no assurance that any significant technical improvement would occur.

The parties could settle this private litigation at any time if defendant paid enough money and the imminent threat of closing the plant would build up the pressure on defendant. If there were no improved techniques found, there would inevitably be applications to the court at Special Term for extensions of time to perform on showing of good faith efforts to find such techniques.

Moreover, techniques to eliminate dust and other annoying by-products of cement making are unlikely to be developed by any research the defendant can undertake within any short period, but will depend on the total resources of the cement industry Nationwide and throughout the world. The problem is universal wherever cement is made.

For obvious reasons the rate of the research is beyond control of defendant. If at the end of 18 months the whole industry has not found a technical solution a court would be hard put to close down this one cement plant if due regard be given to equitable principles.

On the other hand, to grant the injunction unless defendant pays plaintiffs such permanent damages as may be fixed by the court seems to do justice between the contending parties. All of the attributions of economic loss to the properties on which plaintiffs' complaints are based will have been redressed.

The nuisance complained of by these plaintiffs may have other public or private consequences, but these particular parties are the only ones who have sought remedies and the judgment proposed will fully redress them. The limitation of relief granted is a limitation only within the four corners of these actions and does not foreclose public health or other public agencies from seeking proper relief in a proper court.

It seems reasonable to think that the risk of being required to pay permanent damages to injured property owners by cement plant owners would itself be a reasonable effective spur to research for improved techniques to minimize nuisance.

The power of the court to condition on equitable grounds the continuance of an injunction on the payment of permanent damages seems undoubted. (See, e.g., the alternatives considered in *McCarty v. Natural Carbonic Gas Co.*, supra.;, as well as *Strobel v. Kerr Salt Co.*, supra.;.)

The damage base here suggested is consistent with the general rule in those nuisance cases where damages are allowed. "Where a nuisance is of such a permanent and unabatable character that a single recovery can be had, including the whole damage past and future resulting therefrom, there can be but one recovery" (66 C. J. S., Nuisances, § 140, p. 947). It has been said that permanent damages are allowed where the loss recoverable would obviously be small as compared with the cost of removal of the nuisance (*Kentucky-Ohio Gas Co. v. Bowling*, 264 Ky. 470, 477).

. . . .

Thus it seems fair to both sides to grant permanent damages to plaintiffs which will terminate this private litigation. The theory of damage is the "**servitude** on land" of plaintiffs imposed by defendant's nuisance. (See *United States v. Causby*, 328 U. S. 256, 261, 262, 267, where the term "servitude" addressed to the land was used by Justice Douglas relating to the effect of airplane noise on property near an airport.)

The judgment, by allowance of permanent damages imposing a servitude on land, which is the basis of the actions, would preclude future recovery by plaintiffs or their grantees. [C]

This should be placed beyond debate by a provision of the judgment that the payment by defendant and the acceptance by plaintiffs of permanent damages found by the court shall be in compensation for a servitude on the land.

Although the Trial Term has found permanent damages as a possible basis of settlement of the litigation, on remission the court should be entirely free to re-examine this subject. It may again find the permanent damage already found; or make new findings.

The orders should be reversed, without costs, and the cases remitted to Supreme Court, Albany County to grant an injunction which shall be vacated upon payment by defendant of such amounts of permanent damage to the respective plaintiffs as shall for this purpose be determined by the court.

Jasen, J. (Dissenting).

I agree with the majority that a reversal is required here, but I do not subscribe to the newly enunciated doctrine of assessment of permanent damages, in lieu of an injunction, where substantial property rights have been impaired by the creation of a nuisance.

It has long been the rule in this State, as the majority acknowledges, that a nuisance which results in substantial continuing damage to neighbors must be enjoined. (*Whalen v. Union Bag & Paper Co.*, 208 N. Y. 1; *Campbell v. Seaman*, 63 N. Y. 568; see, also, *Kennedy v. Moog Servocontrols*, 21 N Y 2d 966.) To now change the rule to permit the cement company to continue polluting the air indefinitely upon the payment of permanent damages is, in my opinion, compounding the magnitude of a very serious problem in our State and Nation today.

. . . .

The harmful nature and widespread occurrence of air pollution have been extensively documented. Congressional hearings have revealed that air pollution causes substantial property damage, as well as being a contributing factor to a rising incidence of lung cancer, emphysema, bronchitis and asthma.

The specific problem faced here is known as particulate contamination because of the fine dust particles emanating from defendant's cement plant. The particular type of nuisance is not new, having appeared in many cases for at least the past 60 years. (See *Hulbert v. California Portland Cement Co.*, 161 Cal. 239 [1911].) It is interesting to note that cement production has recently been identified as a significant source of particulate contamination in the Hudson Valley. This type of pollution, wherein very small particles escape and stay in the atmosphere, has been denominated as the type of air pollution which produces the greatest hazard to human health. We have thus a nuisance which not only is damaging to the plaintiffs, but also is decidedly harmful to the general public.

I see grave dangers in overruling our long-established rule of granting an injunction where a nuisance results in substantial continuing damage. In permitting the injunction to become inoperative upon the payment of permanent damages, the majority is, in effect, licensing a continuing wrong. It is the same as saying to the cement company, you may continue to do harm to your neighbors so long as you pay a fee for it. Furthermore, once such permanent damages are assessed and paid, the incentive to alleviate the wrong would be eliminated, thereby continuing air pollution of an area without abatement.

It is true that some courts have sanctioned the remedy here proposed by the majority in a number of cases,[6] but none of the authorities relied upon by the majority are analogous to the situation before us. In those cases, the courts, in denying an injunction and awarding money damages, grounded their decision on a showing that the use to which the property was intended to be put was primarily for the public benefit. Here, on the other hand, it is clearly established that the cement company is creating a continuing air pollution nuisance primarily for its own private interest with no public benefit.

This kind of **inverse condemnation** [c] may not be invoked by a private person or corporation for private gain or advantage. Inverse condemnation should only be permitted when the public is primarily served in the taking or impairment of property. [Cc] The promotion of the interests of the polluting cement company has, in my opinion, no public use or benefit.

Nor is it constitutionally permissible to impose servitude on land, without consent of the owner, by payment of permanent damages where the continuing impairment of the land is for a private use. [Cc] This is made clear by the State Constitution (art. I, § 7, subd. [a]) which provides that "[p]rivate property shall not be taken for *public use* without just compensation" (emphasis added). It is, of course, significant that the section makes no mention of taking for a *private* use.

> **FYI**
>
> The takings prohibition under this state's constitution is also found in the Fifth Amendment to the United States Constitution.

In sum, then, by constitutional mandate as well as by judicial pronouncement, the permanent impairment of private property for private purposes is not authorized in the absence of clearly demonstrated public benefit and use.

I would enjoin the defendant cement company from continuing the discharge of dust particles upon its neighbors' properties unless, within 18 months, the cement company abated this nuisance.

---

6 See *United States v. Causby* (328 U. S. 256); *Kentucky-Ohio Gas Co. v. Bowling* (264 Ky. 470, 477); *Northern Indiana Public Serv. Co. v. Vesey* (210 Ind. 338); *City of Amarillo v. Ware* (120 Tex. 456); *Pappenheim v. Metropolitan El. Ry. Co.* (128 N. Y. 436); *Ferguson v. Village of Hamburg* (272 N. Y. 234).

It is not my intention to cause the removal of the cement plant from the Albany area, but to recognize the urgency of the problem stemming from this stationary source of air pollution, and to allow the company a specified period of time to develop a means to alleviate this nuisance.

I am aware that the trial court found that the most modern dust control devices available have been installed in defendant's plant, but, I submit, this does not mean that *better* and more effective dust control devices could not be developed within the time allowed to abate the pollution.

Moreover, I believe it is incumbent upon the defendant to develop such devices, since the cement company, at the time the plant commenced production (1962), was well aware of the plaintiffs' presence in the area, as well as the probable consequences of its contemplated operation. Yet, it still chose to build and operate the plant at this site.

In a day when there is a growing concern for clean air, highly developed industry should not expect acquiescence by the courts, but should, instead, plan its operations to eliminate contamination of our air and damage to its neighbors.

Points for Discussion

1. What did the *Boomer* court hold, and on what rationale? What are permanent damages, and how should such damages be calculated? See RESTATEMENT (SECOND) OF TORTS § 929 (1979).

2. What role did the court state that it was performing in deciding the case? Given legislative enactments and the comprehensive regulation of environmental pollution in the decades following the *Boomer* decision, should courts proceed cautiously when deciding whether to enjoin the operations of a company or other enterprise under the common law of nuisance?

3. Faced with fashioning a remedy for a nuisance, when should courts issue injunctions or instead award damages? For an influential discussion of this question, see Guido Calabresi & A. Douglas Melamed, *Property Rules, Liability Rules, and Inalienability: One View of the Cathedral*, 85 HARV. L. REV. 1089 (1972).

4. The dissent complains that the court's decision allows the company to indefinitely pollute the air so long as permanent damages are paid. Is that a correct characterization of the court's opinion? What incentive would a company have to address its pollution-causing conduct after the assessment and payment of such damages?

5. Consider a later New York case, Little Joseph Realty, Inc. v. Babylon, 41 N.Y.2d 738, 363 N.E.2d 1163, 395 N.Y.S.2d 428 (1977): Where "a continuing use flies in the face of a valid zoning restriction it must, subject to the existence of any appropriate equitable defenses, be enjoined unconditionally."

6. *Boomer* involved intentional activity by the defendant cement company. When is an intentional invasion of another's interest in the use and enjoyment of land unreasonable? Consider the following provisions of the Second Restatement of Torts.

RESTATEMENT (SECOND) OF TORTS (1979)
§ 826. Unreasonableness of Intentional Invasion

An intentional invasion of another's interest in the use and enjoyment of land is unreasonable if

(a) the gravity of the harm outweighs the utility of the actor's conduct, or

(b) the harm caused by the conduct is serious and the financial burden of compensating for this and similar harm to others would not make the continuation of the conduct not feasible.

§ 827. Gravity of Harm—Factors Involved

In determining the gravity of the harm from an intentional invasion of another's interest in the use and enjoyment of land, the following factors are important:

(a) the extent of the harm involved;

(b) the character of the harm involved;

(c) the social value that the law attaches to the type of use or enjoyment invaded;

(d) the suitability of the particular use or enjoyment invaded to the character of the locality; and

(e) the burden on the person harmed of avoiding the harm.

§ 828. Utility of Conduct—Factors Involved

In determining the utility of conduct that causes an intentional invasion of another's interest in the use and enjoyment of land, the following factors are important:

    (a) the social value that the law attaches to the primary purpose of the conduct;

    (b) the suitability of the conduct to the character of the locality; and

    (c) the impracticability of preventing or avoiding the invasion.

§ 829. Gravity vs. Utility—Conduct Malicious or Indecent

An intentional invasion of another's interest in the use and enjoyment of land is unreasonable if the harm is significant and the actor's conduct is

    (a) for the sole purpose of causing harm to the other; or

    (b) contrary to common standards of decency.

§ 829A. Gravity vs. Utility—Severe Harm

An intentional invasion of another's interest in the use and enjoyment of land is unreasonable if the harm resulting from the invasion is severe and greater than the other should be required to bear without compensation.

§ 830. Gravity vs. Utility—Invasion Avoidable

An intentional invasion of another's interest in the use and enjoyment of land is unreasonable if the harm is significant and it would be practicable for the actor to avoid the harm in whole or in part without undue hardship.

§ 831. Gravity vs. Utility—Conduct Unsuited to Locality

An intentional invasion of another's interest in the use and enjoyment of land is unreasonable if the harm is significant, and

    (a) the particular use or enjoyment interfered with is well suited to the character of the locality; and

(b) the actor's conduct is unsuited to the character of that locality.

Spur Industries, Inc. v. Del E. Webb Development Co.

108 Ariz. 178, 494 P.2d 700 (1972)

CAMERON, Vice Chief Justice.

From a judgment permanently enjoining the defendant, Spur Industries, Inc., from operating a cattle feedlot near the plaintiff Del E. Webb Development Company's Sun City, Spur appeals. Webb **cross-appeals**. Although numerous issues are raised, we feel that it is necessary to answer only two questions. They are:

1. Where the operation of a business, such as a cattle feedlot is lawful in the first instance, but becomes a nuisance by reason of a nearby residential area, may the feedlot operation be enjoined in an action brought by the developer of the residential area?

2. Assuming that the nuisance may be enjoined, may the developer of a completely new town or urban area in a previously agricultural area be required to indemnify the operator of the feedlot who must move or cease operation because of the presence of the residential area created by the developer?

The facts necessary for a determination of this matter on appeal are as follows. The area in question is located in Maricopa County, Arizona, some 14 to 15 miles west of the urban area of Phoenix, on the Phoenix-Wickenburg Highway, also known as Grand Avenue. About two miles south of Grand Avenue is Olive Avenue which runs east and west. 111th Avenue runs north and south as does the Agua Fria River immediately to the west. . . .

Farming started in this area about 1911. In 1929, with the completion of the Carl Pleasant Dam, gravity flow water became available to the property located to the west of the Agua Fria River, though land to the east remained dependent upon well water for irrigation. By 1950, the only urban areas in the vicinity were the agriculturally related communities of Peoria, El Mirage, and Surprise located along Grand Avenue. Along 111th Avenue, approximately one mile south of Grand Avenue and 1 1/2 miles north of Olive Avenue, the community of Youngtown was commenced in 1954. Youngtown is a retirement community appealing primarily to senior citizens.

In 1956, Spur's predecessors in interest, H. Marion Welborn and the Northside Hay Mill and Trading Company, developed feed-lots, about 1/2 mile south of Olive Avenue, in an area between the confluence of the usually dry Agua Fria and New Rivers. The area is well suited for cattle feeding and in 1959, there were 25 cattle feeding pens or dairy operations within a 7 mile radius of the location developed by Spur's predecessors. In April and May of 1959, the Northside Hay Mill was feeding between 6,000 and 7,000 head of cattle and Welborn approximately 1,500 head on a combined area of 35 acres.

In May of 1959, Del Webb began to plan the development of an urban area to be known as Sun City. For this purpose, the Marinette and the Santa Fe Ranches, some 20,000 acres of farmland, were purchased for $15,000,000 or $750.00 per acre. This price was considerably less than the price of land located near the urban area of Phoenix, and along with the success of Youngtown was a factor influencing the decision to purchase the property in question.

By September 1959, Del Webb had started construction of a golf course south of Grand Avenue and Spur's predecessors had started to level ground for more feedlot area. In 1960, Spur purchased the property in question and began a rebuilding and expansion program extending both to the north and south of the original facilities. By 1962, Spur's expansion program was completed and had expanded from approximately 35 acres to 114 acres. . . .

Accompanied by an extensive advertising campaign, homes were first offered by Del Webb in January 1960 and the first unit to be completed was south of Grand Avenue and approximately 2 1/2 miles north of Spur. By 2 May 1960, there were 450 to 500 houses completed or under construction. At this time, Del Webb did not consider odors from the Spur feed pens a problem and Del Webb continued to develop in a southerly direction, until sales resistance became so great that the parcels were difficult if not impossible to sell. Thomas E. Breen, Vice President and General Manager of the housing division of Del Webb, testified at deposition as follows:

> "Q Did you ever have any discussions with Tony Cole at or about the time the sales office was opened south of Peoria concerning the problem in sales as the development came closer towards the feed lots?

> "A Not at the time that that facility was opened. That was subsequent to that.

"Q All right, what is it that you recall about conversations with Cole on that subject?

"A Well, when the feed lot problem became a bigger problem, which, really, to the best of my recollection, commenced to become a serious problem in 1963, and there was some talk about not developing that area because of sales resistance, and to my recollection we shifted-we had planned at that time to the eastern portion of the property, and it was a consideration.

"Q Was any specific suggestion made by Mr. Cole as to the line of demarcation that should be drawn or anything of that type exactly where the development should cease?

"A I don't recall anything specific as far as the definite line would be, other than, you know, that it would be advisable to stay out of the southwestern portion there because of sales resistance.

"Q And to the best of your recollection, this was in about 1963?

"A That would be my recollection, yes.

"Q As you recall it, what was the reason that the suggestion was not adopted to stop developing towards the southwest of the development?

"A Well, as far as I know, that decision was made subsequent to that time.

"Q Right. But I mean at that time?

"A Well, at that time what I am really referring to is more of a long-range planning than immediate planning, and I think it was the case of just trying to figure out how far you could go with it before you really ran into a lot of sales resistance and found a necessity to shift the direction.

"Q So that plan was to go as far as you could until the resistance got to the point where you couldn't go any further?

"A I would say that is reasonable, yes."

By December 1967, Del Webb's property had extended south to Olive Avenue and Spur was within 500 feet of Olive Avenue to the north. . . . Del Webb filed its original complaint alleging that in excess of 1,300 lots in the southwest portion were unfit for development for sale as residential lots because of the operation of the Spur feedlot.

Del Webb's suit complained that the Spur feeding operation was a public nuisance because of the flies and the odor which were drifting or being blown by the prevailing south to north wind over the southern portion of Sun City. At the time of the suit, Spur was feeding between 20,000 and 30,000 head of cattle, and the facts amply support the finding of the trial court that the feed pens had become a nuisance to the people who resided in the southern part of Del Webb's development. The testimony indicated that cattle in a commercial feedlot will produce 35 to 40 pounds of wet manure per day, per head, or over a million pounds of wet manure per day for 30,000 head of cattle, and that despite the admittedly good feedlot management and good housekeeping practices by Spur, the resulting odor and flies produced an annoying if not unhealthy situation as far as the senior citizens of southern Sun City were concerned. There is no doubt that some of the citizens of Sun City were unable to enjoy the outdoor living which Del Webb had advertised and that Del Webb was faced with sales resistance from prospective purchasers as well as strong and persistent complaints from the people who had purchased homes in that area.

Trial was commenced before the court with an **advisory jury**. The advisory jury was later discharged and the trial was continued before the court alone. Findings of fact and conclusions of law were requested and given. The case was vigorously contested, including special actions in this court on some of the matters. In one of the special actions before this court, Spur agreed to, and did, shut down its operation without prejudice to a determination of the matter on appeal. On appeal the many questions raised were extensively briefed.

It is noted, however, that neither the citizens of Sun City nor Youngtown are represented in this lawsuit and the suit is solely between Del E. Webb Development Company and Spur Industries, Inc.

MAY SPUR BE ENJOINED?

The difference between a private nuisance and a public nuisance is generally one of degree. A private nuisance is one affecting a single individual or a definite small number of persons in the enjoyment of private rights not common to the public, while a public nuisance is one affecting the rights enjoyed by citizens as a part of the public. To constitute a public nuisance, the nuisance must affect a considerable number of people or an entire community or neighborhood. City of Phoenix v. Johnson, 51 Ariz. 115, 75 P.2d 30 (1938).

Where the injury is slight, the remedy for minor inconveniences lies in an action for damages rather than in one for an injunction. Kubby v. Hammond, 68

Ariz. 17, 198 P.2d 134 (1948). Moreover, some courts have held, in the "balancing of conveniences" cases, that damages may be the sole remedy. See Boomer v. Atlantic Cement Co., 26 N.Y.2d 219, 309 N.Y.S.2d 312, 257 N.E.2d 870, 40 A.L.R.3d 590 (1970), and annotation comments, 40 A.L.R.3d 601.

Thus, it would appear from the admittedly incomplete record as developed in the trial court, that, at most, residents of Youngtown would be entitled to damages rather than injunctive relief.

We have no difficulty, however, in agreeing with the conclusion of the trial court that Spur's operation was an enjoinable public nuisance as far as the people in the southern portion of Del Webb's Sun City were concerned.

. . . .

It is clear that as to the citizens of Sun City, the operation of Spur's feedlot was both a public and a private nuisance. They could have successfully maintained an action to **abate** the nuisance. Del Webb, having shown a special injury in the loss of sales, had a standing to bring suit to enjoin the nuisance. [Cc] The judgment of the trial court permanently enjoining the operation of the feedlot is affirmed.

MUST DEL WEBB INDEMNIFY SPUR?

> **FYI**
> A court of equity, also known as a chancery court, seeks to do justice in cases in which there is no adequate remedy at law.

A suit to enjoin a nuisance sounds in equity and the courts have long recognized a special responsibility to the public when acting as a **court of equity**. . . .

In addition to protecting the public interest, however, courts of equity are concerned with protecting the operator of a lawfully, albeit noxious, business from the result of a knowing and willful encroachment by others near his business.

In the so-called "coming to the nuisance" cases, the courts have held that the residential landowner may not have relief if he knowingly came into a neighborhood reserved for industrial or agricultural endeavors and has been damaged thereby:

> "Plaintiffs chose to live in an area uncontrolled by zoning laws or restrictive covenants and remote from urban development. In such an area plaintiffs cannot complain that legitimate agricultural pursuits are being carried on in the vicinity, nor can plaintiffs, having chosen to build in an agricultural area, complain that the agricultural pursuits carried on in the area depreciate the value of their homes. The area being [p]rimarily agricultural, and opinion reflecting the value of such property must take

this factor into account. The standards affecting the value of residence property in an urban setting, subject to zoning controls and controlled planning techniques, cannot be the standards by which agricultural properties are judged.

"People employed in a city who build their homes in suburban areas of the county beyond the limits of a city and zoning regulations do so for a reason. Some do so to avoid the high taxation rate imposed by cities, or to avoid special assessments for street, sewer and water projects. They usually build on improved or hard surface highways, which have been built either at state or county expense and thereby avoid special assessments for these improvements. It may be that they desire to get away from the congestion of traffic, smoke, noise, foul air and the many other annoyances of city life. But with all these advantages in going beyond the area which is zoned and restricted to protect them in their homes, they must be prepared to take the disadvantages." Dill v. Excel Packing Company, 183 Kan. 513, 525, 526, 331 P.2d 539, 548, 549 (1958). See also East St. Johns Shingle Co. v. City of Portland, 195 Or. 505, 246 P.2d 554, 560-562 (1952).

. . . .

Were Webb the only party injured, we would feel justified in holding that the doctrine of "coming to the nuisance" would have been a bar to the relief asked by Webb, and, on the other hand, had Spur located the feedlot near the outskirts of a city and had the city grown toward the feedlot, Spur would have to suffer the cost of abating the nuisance as to those people locating within the growth pattern of the expanding city . . .

We agree, however, with the Massachusetts court that:

"The law of nuisance affords no rigid rule to be applied in all instances. It is elastic. It undertakes to require only that which is fair and reasonable under all the circumstances. In a commonwealth like this, which depends for its material prosperity so largely on the continued growth and enlargement of manufacturing of diverse varieties, 'extreme rights' cannot be enforced. * * *." Stevens v. Rockport Granite Co., 216 Mass. 486, 488, 104 N.E. 371, 373 (1914).

There was no indication in the instant case at the time Spur and its predecessors located in western Maricopa County that a new city would spring up, full-blown, alongside the feeding operation and that the developer of that city would ask the court to order Spur to move because of the new city. Spur is required to move not because of any wrongdoing on the part of Spur, but because of a proper and legitimate regard of the courts for the rights and interests of the public.

Del Webb, on the other hand, is entitled to the relief prayed for (a permanent injunction), not because Webb is blameless, but because of the damage to the people who have been encouraged to purchase homes in Sun City. It does not equitably or legally follow, however, that Webb, being entitled to the injunction, is then free of any liability to Spur if Webb has in fact been the cause of the damage Spur has sustained. It does not seem harsh to require a developer, who has taken advantage of the lesser land values in a rural area as well as the availability of large tracts of land on which to build and develop a new town or city in the area, to **indemnify** those who are forced to leave as a result.

Having brought people to the nuisance to the foreseeable detriment of Spur, Webb must indemnify Spur for a reasonable amount of the cost of moving or shutting down. It should be noted that this relief to Spur is limited to a case wherein a developer has, with foreseeability, brought into a previously agricultural or industrial area the population which makes necessary the granting of an injunction against a lawful business and for which the business has no adequate relief.

It is therefore the decision of this court that the matter be remanded to the trial court for a hearing upon the damages sustained by the defendant Spur as a reasonable and direct result of the granting of the permanent injunction. Since the result of the appeal may appear novel and both sides have obtained a measure of relief, it is ordered that each side will bear its own costs.

Affirmed in part, reversed in part, and remanded for further proceedings consistent with this opinion.

———————

Points for Discussion

1. Do you agree with the *Spur Industries* court's ruling?

2. What have courts generally held, and what is the rule in "coming to the nuisance" cases?

3. "The fact that the plaintiff has acquired or improved his land after a nuisance interfering with it has come into existence is not in itself sufficient to bar his action, but it is a factor to be considered in determining whether the nuisance is actionable." RESTATEMENT (SECOND) OF TORTS § 840D (1979).

4. Do you favor an absolute rule barring a finding of nuisance in any case where the plaintiff came to the nuisance, or the approach taken in Restatement § 840D? If the latter, how should a court determine how much weight should be given to the fact that a plaintiff came to the nuisance?

5. The court concludes that Webb must indemnify Spur for a reasonable amount of the costs of moving or closing its facility. Does indemnification provide for fairer and more just outcomes in cases like *Spur Industries*? Could indemnification complicate the litigation and settlement of such cases and have other adverse effects and consequences on developmental activity?

City of Claremont v. Kruse

177 Cal.App.4th 1153, 100 Cal.Rptr.3d 1 (2009)

CHAVEZ, J.

Defendants and appellants Darrell Kruse (Kruse) and Claremont All Natural Nutrition Aids Buyers Information Service (also known as CANNABIS) appeal from the judgment entered in favor of plaintiff and respondent City of Claremont (the City) after the trial court issued a permanent injunction preventing defendants from operating a medical marijuana dispensary anywhere within the City. We affirm the judgment.

. . . .

On January 19, 2007, the City filed this action against Kruse for a **temporary restraining order** and a **preliminary** and **permanent injunction** to abate a public nuisance. The City's complaint alleged, among other things, that the Claremont Municipal Code requires a person to obtain a business license and business permit, and to procure a tax certificate by paying the appropriate business tax before operating a business within the City and that Kruse's operation of CANNABIS without a business license was a public nuisance as a matter of law. On February 2, 2007, the City obtained a temporary restraining order and order to **show cause** why a preliminary injunction should not issue

What's That?

A temporary restraining order, or TRO, is issued by a court for the purpose of preserving the status quo until the court can hear and decide an application for a preliminary or a permanent injunction. TROs can be granted *ex parte*, i.e., without advance notice to the person or entity who will be subject to the order.

to prevent Kruse from operating CANNABIS for the duration of the action. After a hearing on the order to show cause, the trial court issued a preliminary injunction order on April 4, 2007.

. . . .

Civil Code section 3479 defines a nuisance as: "Anything which is injurious to health, including, but not limited to, the illegal sale of controlled substances, or is indecent or offensive to the senses, or an obstruction to the free use of property, so as to interfere with the comfortable enjoyment of life or property...." "A nuisance may be a public nuisance, a private nuisance, or both. [Citation.]" (*Newhall Land & Farming Co. v. Superior Court* (1993) 19 Cal.App.4th 334, 341, 23 Cal.Rptr.2d 377.) "A public nuisance is one which affects at the same time an entire community or neighborhood, or any considerable number of persons, although the extent of the annoyance or damage inflicted upon individuals may be unequal." (Civ.Code, § 3480.)

"[A] nuisance per se arises when a legislative body with appropriate jurisdiction, in the exercise of the police power, expressly declares a particular object or substance, activity, or circumstance, to be a nuisance.... [T]o rephrase the rule, to be considered a nuisance per se the object, substance, activity or circumstance at issue must be expressly declared to be a nuisance by its very existence by some applicable law." (*Beck Development Co. v. Southern Pacific Transportation Co.* (1996) 44 Cal.App.4th 1160, 1206-1207, 52 Cal.Rptr.2d 518.) "[W]here the law expressly declares something to be a nuisance, then no inquiry beyond its existence need be made." (*Id.* at p. 1207, 52 Cal.Rptr.2d 518.) " 'Nuisances *per se* are so regarded because no proof is required, beyond the actual fact of their existence, to establish the nuisance.' [Citations.]" (*City of Costa Mesa v. Soffer* (1992) 11 Cal. App.4th 378, 382, 13 Cal.Rptr.2d 735, fn. omitted.)

We review factual issues underlying the trial court's issuance of the injunction to abate a public nuisance under the substantial evidence standard. Issues of pure law are subject to de novo review. (*People ex rel. Gallo v. Acuna* (1997) 14 Cal.4th 1090, 1136-1137, 60 Cal.Rptr.2d 277, 929 P.2d 596.)

Defendants contend their operation of CANNABIS cannot be enjoined as a nuisance under Civil Code section 3479 because the only portion of the statute that could possibly apply is the "illegal sale of controlled substances" and there was no such illegal activity in this case. They maintain that all sales of marijuana in this case complied with California's medical marijuana laws and that pursuant to the parties' **stipulation**, "[t]here is no issue in this case whether or not Defendants sold marijuana in violation of California state law."

The trial court's determination that defendants' operation of a medical marijuana dispensary constituted a nuisance per se was based not on violations of state law, however, but on violations of the City's municipal code. Section 4.06.020 of the Claremont Municipal Code states that it is unlawful to transact business without first procuring a tax certificate from the City to do so. It is undisputed that defendants operated CANNABIS without first obtaining a business license or tax certificate.

. . . .

Defendants contend their operation of a medical marijuana dispensary could have been categorized under any of the following existing permitted uses enumerated in the City's Land Use and Development Code: "cigar/cigarette/smoke shops," "food/drug and kindred products," "health, herbal, botanical stores," "pharmacies," "counseling," and "offices for philanthropic, charitable and service organizations." They maintain that the City improperly denied their applications for a business license and permit for this reason. Defendants cannot challenge the denial of their applications for a business license and permit in this appeal, however, because they chose to commence operating without obtaining the requisite approvals to do so, in violation of applicable city laws. Moreover, after the City dismissed defendants' administrative appeal from the denial of their applications for a business license and permit, defendants' proper recourse was to file a petition for **writ of mandate**. (Code Civ. Proc., § 1085; *American Federation of State, County & Municipal Employees v. Metropolitan Water Dist.* (2005) 126 Cal.App.4th 247, 261, 24 Cal.Rptr.3d 285.) They did not do so. Instead, they continued to operate illegally, despite the City's repeated directives to cease and desist from doing so. The City's discretionary decision to deny defendants' applications is not at issue in this action to enjoin defendants from operating in violation of the City's municipal code.

Section 1.12.010 of the Claremont Municipal Code expressly states that a condition caused or permitted to exist in violation of the municipal code provisions may be abated as a public nuisance: "In addition to the penalties provided in this chapter, any condition caused or permitted to exist in violation of any of the provisions ... of this code is declared a public nuisance, and may be abated by civil proceedings such as restraining orders, civil injunctions, abatement proceedings or the like." Defendants' operation of a nonenumerated and therefore expressly prohibited use, without obtaining a business license and tax certificate, created a nuisance per se under section 1.12.010.

The facts presented here are materially indistinguishable from those in *City of Corona v. Naulls* (2008) 166 Cal.App.4th 418, 83 Cal.Rptr.3d 1(*Naulls*). The defendant in *Naulls,* like Kruse, opened a medical marijuana dispensary without the approval of the City of Corona. The business license application signed by the defendant in *Naulls* contained an acknowledgment similar to that in Kruse's application, stating that all businesses must comply with municipal code requirements and that the approval of the planning department was required prior to opening. [C] Corona's municipal code, like Claremont's municipal code, listed all of the permitted uses within each zoning district, but did not include selling or distributing marijuana among the classified uses. [C] Persons seeking to use their property for a nonclassified use in Corona were required to follow procedures for obtaining the planning commission's approval of such use. The defendant in *Naulls,* like Kruse, failed to follow those procedures. [C] Corona's municipal code, like section 1.12.010 of Claremont's municipal code, expressly stated that any condition caused or permitted to exist in violation of its provisions constituted a public nuisance. [C] The court in *Naulls* found that substantial evidence supported the trial court's conclusion that the defendant's failure to comply with the city's procedural requirements before operating a medical marijuana dispensary "created a nuisance per se" pursuant to Corona's municipal code, and upheld the issuance of a preliminary injunction. [C]

We find *Naulls* persuasive here. Kruse's operation of a medical marijuana dispensary without the City's approval constituted a nuisance per se under section 1.12.010 of the City's municipal code and could properly be enjoined. [C]

Defendants contend the City failed to establish a public nuisance because it made no showing that CANNABIS's operations caused any actual harm and such showing is a necessary element of a nuisance cause of action. No such showing is required, however, for a cause of action for nuisance per se. For nuisances per se, "no proof is required, beyond the actual fact of their existence, to establish the nuisance. No ill effects need be proved." (*McClatchy v. Laguna Lands, Ltd.* (1917) 32 Cal.App. 718, 725, 164 P. 41.) *In re Firearm Cases* (2005) 126 Cal.App.4th 959, 24 Cal.Rptr.3d 659, on which defendants rely, contradicts rather than supports their position. The court in that case stated that in order to establish a public nuisance, "it is not necessary to show that harm actually occurred." [C]

. . . .

The trial court did not err by concluding that defendants' operation of a medical marijuana dispensary, without obtaining a business license and permit, constituted a nuisance per se under section 1.12.010 of the City's municipal code. [C]

. . . .

The judgment is affirmed. The City is awarded its costs on appeal.

———————————

Points for Discussion

1. Did the *Kruse* court correctly decide that the defendants' operation of a medical marijuana dispensary constituted a nuisance *per se*?

2. Is the *Kruse* court's finding of a nuisance *per se* consistent with § 3479 of the California civil code? What illegal activity was engaged in by the defendants?

3. Could the nuisance *per se* doctrine result in governmental regulation and termination of any lawful activity the government deems objectionable? Is that what happened in this case?

4. Proposition: No public nuisance may be found or established in the absence of a showing of actual harm. Do you agree or disagree?

Hypo 14-3

City has filed a lawsuit against certain manufacturers and distributors of handguns (the named defendants are 10 manufacturers, two wholesalers, and seven retailers).

City alleges that the manufacturers typically sell to "distributors" who resell to "dealers" who in turn sell handguns at retail to the general public. According to City, some persons are prohibited by law from buying guns, and all dealers are alleged to have knowingly sold guns to illegal buyers through intermediaries in "straw purchases" as revealed by a City police department sting operation against suspected violators of City's gun distribution laws. For example, an undercover police officer first told a dealer's clerk that the undercover officer could not lawfully purchase a gun because she had been convicted of a felony, and a second undercover officer then purchased the gun with the clerk's knowledge that the weapon would be given to the person who claimed to be a felon.

City alleges that the manufacturers knew of these illegal retail sales of handguns; that a small percentage of dealers accounted for a large portion of unlawfully obtained handguns; and that the manufacturers and distributors had the ability to change the distribution system to prevent illegal handgun sales, but intentionally failed to do so. In addition, City alleges that the challenged practices have generated substantial costs to the public in general and City in particular. The possession of unlawfully purchased guns is claimed to contribute to crime. City alleges that 125 murders with handguns took place in City in 2008 and that, from 2005 to 2008, 2,412 handguns used in crimes were recovered by City's police department; of that number, 722 handguns were sold through dealers named as defendants in City's suit.

City alleges a claim for public nuisance against the defendants and seeks injunctive relief and money damages for the harms caused by the unlawful marketing and distribution of handguns. Has City stated a public nuisance claim?

Chapter 15

Products Liability

Products liability is a modern, ever-evolving area of tort law that could easily be the subject of an entire course in law school. Our goal in providing the following materials to you is to introduce you to the law of products liability and pique your interest in exploring this subject further.

A. Development of Theories of Recovery

As presented in the previous pages of this text, for many years plaintiffs were unable to bring a tort claim against a defendant with whom they were not in **privity**. As this country evolved into a more industrialized society, the unfortunate consequence of the privity rule meant that persons injured

Make the Connection

Refer to the materials in Chapter 7, *supra*, discussing the common law requirement of privity of contract.

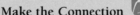

by a product manufactured by one with whom they were not in privity were unable to recover for their injuries from those who may have been most responsible – the manufacturers. As the privity rule eroded as a prerequisite to imposition of tort liability, products liability actions were made available to plaintiffs injured by manufacturers' products without regard to privity.

Over the years, courts have recognized negligence, breach of warranty, and strict liability as theories of recovery available in tort to plaintiffs suing defendants for injuries caused by defective products. The development of the various theories of recovery are the focus of the materials that follow.

1. Negligence

MacPherson v. Buick Motor Co.

111 N.E. 1050 (N.Y. 1916)

[The court's opinions in *MacPherson* are excerpted in large part beginning at p. 511. Of particular note is the majority's discussion regarding the defendant manufacturer's liability based upon *negligence* as the theory of recovery:]

[T]here is nothing inconsistent with the theory of liability on which the case was tried. It is true that the court told the jury that 'an automobile is not an inherently dangerous vehicle.' The meaning, however, is made plain by the context. The meaning is that danger is not to be expected when the vehicle is well constructed. The court left it to the jury to say whether the defendant ought to have foreseen that the car, if negligently constructed, would become 'imminently dangerous.' Subtle distinctions are drawn by the defendant between things inherently dangerous and things imminently dangerous, but the case does not turn upon these verbal niceties. If danger was to be expected as reasonably certain, there was a duty of vigilance, and this whether you call the danger inherent or imminent. ...

We think the defendant was not absolved from a duty of inspection because it bought the wheels from a reputable manufacturer. It was not merely a dealer in automobiles. It was a manufacturer of automobiles. It was responsible for the finished product. It was not at liberty to put the finished product on the market without subjecting the component parts to ordinary and simple tests. [c] Under the charge of the trial judge nothing more was required of it. The obligation to inspect must vary with the nature of the thing to be inspected. The more probable the danger, the greater the need of caution. ...

[In dissent, Chief Judge Bartlett countered, in part:]

The theory upon which the case was submitted to the jury by the learned judge who presided at the trial was that, although an automobile is not an inherently dangerous vehicle, it may become such if equipped with a weak wheel; and that if the motor car in question, when it was put upon the market was in itself inherently dangerous by reason of its being equipped with a weak wheel, the defendant was chargeable with a knowledge of the defect so far as it might be discovered by a reasonable inspection and the application of reasonable tests. This liability, it was further held, was not limited to the original **vendee**, but extended to a subvendee like the plaintiff, who was not a party to the original contract of sale.

... It has heretofore been held in this state that the liability of the vendor of a manufactured article for negligence arising out of the existence of defects therein does not extend to strangers injured in consequence of such defects but is confined to the immediate vendee. The exceptions to this general rule which have thus far been recognized in New York are cases in which the article sold was of such a character that danger to life or limb was involved in the ordinary use thereof; in other words, where the article sold was inherently dangerous. As has already been pointed out, the learned trial judge instructed the jury that an automobile is not an inherently dangerous vehicle.

The late Chief Justice Cooley of Michigan, one of the most learned and accurate of American law writers, states the general rule thus: 'The general rule is that a contractor, manufacturer, vendor, or furnisher of an article is not liable to third parties who have no contractual relations with him for negligence in the construction, manufacture, or sale of such article.' (2 Cooley on Torts (3d ed.), 1486.)

The leading English authority in support of this rule, to which all the later cases on the same subject refer, is Winterbottom v. Wright (10 Meeson & Welsby,

Make the Connection

See Chapter 7, Section A, *supra*, discussing *Winterbottom v. Wright* in the materials introducing privity of contract in negligence law.

109), which was an action by the driver of a stage coach against a contractor who had agreed with the post-master-general to provide and keep the vehicle in repair for the purpose of conveying the royal mail over a prescribed route. The coach broke down and upset, injuring the driver, who sought to recover against the contractor on account of its defective construction. The Court of Exchequer denied him any right of recovery on the ground that there was no privity of contract between the parties, the agreement having been made with the postmaster-general alone. If the plaintiff can sue,' said Lord Abinger, the chief baron, 'every passenger or even any person passing along the road, who, was, injured by the upsetting of the coach, might bring a similar action. Unless we confine the operation of such contracts as this to the parties who enter into them, the most absurd and outrageous consequences, to which I can see no limit, would ensue.'

. . . .

I do not see how we can uphold the judgment in the present case without overruling what has been so often said by this court and other courts of like authority in reference to the absence of any liability for negligence on the part of the original vendor of an ordinary carriage to any one except his immediate vendee. The absence of such liability was the very point actually decided in the English case of Winterbottom v. Wright (supra), and the illustration quoted from the opinion of Chief Judge Ruggles in Thomas v. Winchester (supra) assumes that the law on the subject was so plain that the statement would be accepted almost as a matter of course. In the case at bar the defective wheel on an automobile moving only eight miles an hour was not any more dangerous to the occupants of the car than a similarly defective wheel would be to the occupants of a carriage drawn by a horse at the same speed; and yet unless the courts have been all wrong on this question up to the present time there would be no liability to strangers to the original sale in the case of the horse-drawn carriage.

. . . .

... [This court and courts] throughout this country have adhered to the rule and [have] consistently ... refused to broaden the scope of the exceptions. I think we should adhere to it in the case at bar and, therefore, I vote for a reversal of this judgment.

————————————

Points for Discussion

1. What is "privity"? How does privity relate, if at all, to the legal issue with which the court was presented in *MacPherson*?

2. In *MacPherson,* the plaintiff sought to hold the defendant manufacturer liable in negligence. To succeed, what elements will the plaintiff have to establish to hold the defendant liable?

3. What was the basis of Chief Judge Bartlett's dissent?

4. Which decision is more persuasive to you – the majority or the dissent?

5. What are the policy considerations, if any, in support of the majority's position? The dissent?

6. The majority's opinion in *MacPherson* was revolutionary inasmuch as it permitted a plaintiff to hold a defendant liable in negligence despite the absence of privity between the parties. It was likewise important inasmuch as manufacturers of products could now be subject to liability in negligence for injuries caused by their defective products.

FYI
The consideration of what constitutes a "defective" product will be explored in materials, *infra.*

7. As illustrated by *MacPherson*, negligence was one of the earliest recognized theories of recovery for injuries caused by defective products. Today, negligence still remains a powerful and important tool for plaintiffs seeking to prove the blameworthiness of manufacturers of injury-producing products. Negligence as a theory of recovery in products cases is still quite viable, despite what may be a widely-held misperception that products liability sounds solely in strict liability.

8. As explored in the following materials, courts developed alternatives to negligence as a theory of recovery for injuries caused by defective products. Consider the next few cases and think about which theory, in your opinion, is most suitable based on the various tort policy concerns considered throughout this course.

2. Warranty

a. Express Warranties

Baxter v. Ford Motor Co.

12 P.2d 409 (Wash. 1932)

HERMAN, J.

During the month of May, 1930, plaintiff purchased a model A Ford town sedan from defendant St. John Motors, a Ford dealer, who had acquired the automobile in question by purchase from defendant Ford Motor Company. Plaintiff claims that representations were made to him by both defendants that the windshield of the automobile was made of nonshatterable glass which would not break, fly, or shatter. October 12, 1930, while plaintiff was driving the automobile through Snoqualmie pass, a pebble from a passing car struck the windshield of the car in question, causing small pieces of glass to fly into plaintiff's left eye, resulting in the loss thereof. Plaintiff brought this action for damages for the loss of his left eye and for injuries to the sight of his right eye. The case came on for trial, and, at the conclusion of plaintiff's testimony, the court took the case from the jury and entered judgment for both defendants. From that judgment, plaintiff appeals.

. . . .

The principal question in this case is whether the trial court erred in refusing to admit in evidence, as against respondent Ford Motor Company, the catalogues and printed matter furnished by that respondent to respondent St. John Motors to be distributed for sales assistance. Contained in such printed matter were statements which appellant maintains constituted representations or **warranties** with reference to the nature of the glass used in the windshield of the car purchased by appellant. A typical statement, as it appears in appellant's exhibit for identification No. 1, is here set forth:

> 'Triplex Shatter-Proof Glass Windshield. All of the new Ford cars have a Triplex shatter-proof glass windshield–so made that it will not fly or shatter under the hardest impact. This is an important safety factor because it eliminates the dangers of flying glass–the cause of most of the injuries in automobile accidents. In these days of crowded, heavy traffic, the use of this Triplex glass is an absolute necessity. Its extra margin of safety is something that every motorist should look for in the purchase of a car-especially where there are women and children.'

Respondent Ford Motor Company contends that there can be no implied or express warranty without privity of contract, and warranties as to personal property do not attach themselves to, and run with, the article sold.

. . . .

In the case at bar the automobile was represented by the manufacturer as having a windshield of nonshatterable glass 'so made that it will not fly or shatter under the hardest impact.' An ordinary person would be unable to discover by the usual and customary examination of the automobile whether glass which would not fly or shatter was used in the windshield. In that respect the purchaser was in a position similar to that of the consumer of a wrongly labeled drug, who has bought the same from a retailer, and who has relied upon the manufacturer's representation that the label correctly set forth the contents of the container. For many years it has been held that, under such circumstances, the manufacturer is liable to the consumer, even though the consumer purchased from a third person the commodity causing the damage. [C] The rule in such cases does not rest upon contractual obligations, but rather on the principle that the original act of delivering an article is wrong, when, because of the lack of those qualities which the manufacturer represented it as having, the absence of which could not be readily detected by the consumer, the article is not safe for the purposes for which the consumer would ordinarily use it.

. . . .

Since the rule of **caveat emptor** was first formulated, vast changes have taken place in the economic structures of the English speaking peoples. Methods of doing business have undergone a great transition. Radio, billboards, and the products of the printing press have become the means of creating a large part of the demand that causes goods to depart from factories to the ultimate consumer. It would be unjust to recognize a rule that would permit manufacturers of goods to create a demand for their products by representing that they possess qualities which they, in fact, do not possess, and then, because there is no privity of contract existing between the consumer and the manufacturer, deny the consumer the right to recover if damages result from the absence of those qualities, when such absence is not readily noticeable.

'An exception to a rule will be declared by courts when the case is not an isolated instance, but general in its character, and the existing rule does not square with justice. Under such circumstances a court will, if free from the restraint of some statute, declare a rule that will meet the full intendment of the law.' Mazetti v. Armour & Co., [75 Wash. 622, 135 P. 633].

We hold that the catalogues and printed matter furnished by respondent Ford Motor Company for distribution and assistance in sales ... were improperly excluded from evidence, because they set forth representations by the manufacturer that the windshield of the car which appellant bought contained Triplex nonshatterable glass which would not fly or shatter. The nature of nonshatterable glass is such that the falsity of the representations with reference to the glass would not be readily detected by a person of ordinary experience and reasonable prudence. Appellant, under the circumstances shown in this case, had the right to rely upon the representations made by respondent Ford Motor Company relative to qualities possessed by its products, even though there was no privity of contract between appellant and respondent Ford Motor Company.

Appellant assigns as error rejection of the following offer to prove: 'We now offer to prove by the witness on the stand that he didn't know anything about shatter-proof glass or any other kind of glass; that he had never been engaged in any occupation which would familiarize him with glass and know at all the difference between shatter-proof glass and any other kind of glass, and didn't know anything different at that time; that he didn't know anything about the composition or otherwise of Triplex shatter-proof windshields or Triplex shatter-proof glass; that he relied solely and wholly upon the representations made by St. John and Johnnie Delaney and what he read and saw in the catalogues from them, which have been offered in evidence; that he believed these representations to be true and by reason of his belief in these representations and by reason of these representations he purchased on or about the 13th day of May, a Model A Ford town sedan.'

With the exception of so much of the offer as related to the representations of Mr. St. John and Johnnie Delaney (a salesman for respondent St. John Motors), the testimony contemplated by the offer to prove was relevant and should have been received. While it is a matter of common knowledge that the difference between glass which will not fly or shatter and ordinary glass is not readily noticeable to a person of ordinary experience, nevertheless appellant was entitled to show an absence of familiarity with nonshatterable glass. His testimony would have tended to show that he had no experience which should have enabled him to recognize the glass in the windshield as other than what it was represented to be.

The trial court erred in taking the case from the jury and entering judgment for respondent Ford Motor Company. It was for the jury to determine, under proper instructions, whether the failure of respondent Ford Motor Company to equip the windshield with glass which did not fly or shatter was the proximate cause of appellant's injury.

We have considered the other assignments of error, and find them to be without merit.

Reversed, with directions to grant a new trial with reference to respondent Ford Motor Company; affirmed as to respondent St. John Motors.

———————————

Points for Discussion

1. What was the plaintiff's theory of recovery? What was defendant Ford Motor Company's defense? What did the court conclude regarding whether the plaintiff had a cause of action against Ford Motor Company?

2. Did the court recognize a theory of recovery against Ford Motor Company that was grounded in contract or tort? What are the court's policy justification(s) for permitting recovery against defendant Ford Motor Company?

3. Why did the plaintiffs in *Baxter* not bring a cause of action against the defendants based on negligence, where a privity requirement had already been eliminated as a bar to recovery?

4. Section 9 of the RESTATEMENT (THIRD) OF TORTS: PRODUCTS LIABILITY, provides that "[o]ne engaged in the business of selling or otherwise distributing products who, in connection with the sale of a product, makes a fraudulent, negligent, or innocent misrepresentation of material fact concerning the

product is subject to liability for harm to persons or property caused by the misrepresentation." Interestingly, recovery pursuant to this section does not require the plaintiff to prove that the product was defective, as is required under all other sections of the Third Restatement. *See* Restatement (Third) of Torts: Products Liability § 9 cmt. *d* (1997). What are the policy reasons in support of a plaintiff being permitted to recover in tort from a manufacturer for injury caused by a non-defective product based on breach of express warranty?

5. As set forth in *Baxter*, a cause of action for breach of express warranty may be established by proving that the defendant made a specific promise upon which the plaintiff relied and that breach of that promise caused in fact the plaintiff's personal or property injury. However, as reflected by section 9 of the Third Restatement, most courts today do not require the plaintiff to show subjective reliance upon the promise. Rather, proof that the defendant made promises that created an objectively justifiable reliance is sufficient. *Baxter* was an action based on a manufacterer's express statements about its product. In contrast, consider the next case.

---

b. Implied Warranties

Henningsen v. Bloomfield Motors, Inc.

161 A.2d 69 (N.J. 1960)

FRANCIS, J.

Plaintiff Clause H. Henningsen purchased a Plymouth automobile, manufactured by defendant Chrysler Corporation, from defendant Bloomfield Motors, Inc. His wife, plaintiff Helen Henningsen, was injured while driving it and instituted suit against both defendants to recover damages on account of her injuries. Her husband joined in the action seeking compensation for his **consequential losses**. The complaint was predicated upon breach of express and implied warranties and upon negligence. At the trial the negligence counts were dismissed by the court and the cause was submitted to the jury for determination solely on the issues of **implied warranty of merchantability**. Verdicts were returned against both defendants and in favor of the plaintiffs. Defendants appealed and plaintiffs cross-appealed from the dismissal of their negligence claim. The matter was certified by this court prior to consideration in the Appellate Division.

The facts are not complicated, but a general outline of them is necessary to an understanding of the case.

On May 7, 1955 Mr. and Mrs. Henningsen visited the place of business of Bloomfield Motors, Inc., an authorized De Soto and Plymouth dealer, to look at a Plymouth. They wanted to buy a car and were considering a Ford or a Chevrolet as well as a Plymouth. They were shown a Plymouth which appealed to them and the purchase followed. The record indicates that Mr. Henningsen intended the car as a Mother's Day gift to his wife. He said the intention was communicated to the dealer. When the purchase order or contract was prepared and presented, the husband executed it alone. His wife did not join as a party.

The purchase order was a printed form of one page. … The type used in the printed parts of the form became smaller in size, different in style, and less readable toward the bottom …. The smallest type on the page appears in the two paragraphs, one of two and one-quarter lines and the second of one and one-half lines, on which great stress is laid by the defense in the case. These two paragraphs are the least legible and the most difficult to read in the instrument, but they are most important in the evaluation of the rights of the contesting parties. They do not attract attention and there is nothing about the format which would draw the reader's eye to them. … De-emphasis seems the motive rather than emphasis. …

. . . .

The testimony of Claus Henningsen justifies the conclusion that he did not read the two fine print paragraphs referring to the back of the purchase contract. And it is uncontradicted that no one made any reference to them, or called them to his attention. With respect to the matter appearing on the back, it is likewise uncontradicted that he did not read it and that no one called it to his attention.

The reverse side of the contract contains 8 1/2 inches of fine print. … The page is headed 'Conditions' and contains ten separate paragraphs consisting of 65 lines in all. … In the seventh paragraph, about two-thirds of the way down the page, the warranty, which is the focal point of the case, is set forth. It is as follows:

'7. It is expressly agreed that there are no warranties, express or implied, Made by either the dealer or the manufacturer on the motor vehicle, chassis, of parts furnished hereunder except as follows.

"The manufacturer warrants each new motor vehicle (including original equipment placed thereon by the manufacturer except tires), chassis or parts manufactured by it to be free from defects in material or workmanship under normal use and service. Its obligation under this warranty being limited to making good at its factory any part or parts thereof which shall, within ninety (90) days after delivery of such vehicle To the original purchaser or before such vehicle has been driven 4,000 miles, whichever event shall first occur, be returned to it with transportation charges prepaid and which its examination shall disclose to its satisfaction to have been thus defective; *This warranty being expressly in lieu of all other warranties expressed or implied, and all other obligations or liabilities on its part,* and it neither assumes nor authorizes any other person to assume for it any other liability in connection with the sale of its vehicles. * * *." (Emphasis ours.)

... The testimony shows that Chrysler Corporation sends from the factory to the dealer a 'New Car Preparation Service Guide' with each new automobile. ... The guide ... calls for delivery of the Owner Service Certificate with the car.

This certificate, which at least by inference is authorized by Chrysler, was in the car when released to Claus Henningsen on May 9, 1955. It was not made part of the purchase contract, nor was it shown to him prior to the consummation of that agreement. The only reference to it therein is that the dealer 'agrees to promptly perform and fulfill and terms and conditions of the owner service policy.' The Certificate contains a warranty entitled 'Automobile Manufacturers Association Uniform Warranty.' The provisions thereof are the same as those set forth on the reverse side of the purchase order, except that an additional paragraph is added by which the dealer extends that warranty to the purchaser in the same manner as if the word 'Dealer' appeared instead of the word 'Manufacturer.'

The new Plymouth was turned over to the Henningsens on May 9, 1955. ... Mr. Henningsen drove it from the dealer's place of business in Bloomfield to their home in Keansburg. On the trip nothing unusual appeared in the way in which it operated. Thereafter, it was used for short trips on paved streets about the town. It had no servicing and no mishaps of any kind before the event of May 19. That day, Mrs. Henningsen drove to Asbury Park. On the way down and in returning the car performed in normal fashion until the accident occurred. She was proceeding north on Route 36 in Highlands, New Jersey, at 20-22 miles per hour. The highway was paved and smooth, and contained two lanes for northbound travel. She was riding in the right-hand lane. Suddenly she heard a loud noise 'from the bottom, by the hood.' It 'felt as if something cracked.' The steering wheel spun in her hands; the car veered sharply to the right and crashed into a highway sign and a brick wall. No other vehicle was in any way involved. A bus operator driving in the left-hand lane testified that he observed plaintiffs' car approaching in normal fashion in the opposite direction; 'all of a sudden (it) veered at 90 degrees * * * and right into this wall.' As a result of the impact, the front of the car was so badly damaged that it was impossible to determine if any of the parts of the steering wheel mechanism or workmanship or assembly were defective or improper prior to the accident. The condition was such that the collision insurance carrier, after inspection, declared the vehicle a total loss. It had 468 miles on the speedometer at the time.

The insurance carrier's inspector and appraiser of damaged cars, with 11 years of experience, advanced the opinion, based on the history and his examination, that something definitely went 'wrong from the steering wheel down to the front wheels' and that the untoward happening must have been due to mechanical defect or failure; 'something down there had to drop off or break loose to cause the car' to act in the manner described.

As has been indicated, the trial court felt that the proof was not sufficient to make out a Prima facie case as to the negligence of either the manufacturer or the dealer. The case was given to the jury, therefore, solely on the warranty theory, with results favorable to the plaintiffs against both defendants.

I.

The Claim of Implied Warranty against the Manufacturer.

In the ordinary case of sale of goods by description an implied warranty of merchantability is an integral part of the transaction. [c] If the buyer, expressly or by implication, makes known to the seller the particular purpose for which the article is required and it appears that he has relied on the seller's skill or judgment, an implied warranty arises of reasonable fitness for that purpose. [c] The former type of warranty simply means that the thing sold is reasonably fit for the general purpose for which it is manufactured and sold. [cc] As Judge (later Justice) Cardozo remarked in Ryan, supra, the distinction between a warranty of fitness for a particular purpose and of merchantability in many instances is practically meaningless. ...

. . . .

Of course such sales, whether oral of written, may be accompanied by an express warranty. Under the broad terms of the Uniform Sale of Goods Law any affirmation of fact relating to the goods is an express warranty if the natural tendency of the statement is to induce the buyer to make the purchase. [c]. And over the years since the almost universal adoption of the act, a growing awareness of the tremendous development of modern business methods has prompted the courts to administer that provision with a liberal hand. [c] ...

The uniform act codified, extended and liberalized the common law of sales. The motivation in part was to ameliorate the harsh doctrine of Caveat emptor, and in some measure to impose a reciprocal obligation on the seller to beware. The transcendent value of the legislation, particularly with respect to implied warranties, rests in the fact that obligations on the part of the seller were imposed by operation of law, and did not depend for their existence upon express agreement of the parties. And of tremendous significance in a rapidly expanding commercial society was the recognition of the right to recover damages on account of personal injuries arising from a breach of warranty. [Cc] The particular importance of this advance resides in the fact that under such circumstances strict liability is imposed upon the maker or seller of the product. Recovery of damages does not depend upon proof of negligence or knowledge of the defect. [CC]

As the Sales Act and its liberal interpretation by the courts threw this protective cloak about the buyer, the decisions in various jurisdictions revealed beyond doubt that many manufacturers took steps to avoid these ever increasing warranty obligations. Realizing that the act governed the relationship of buyer and seller, they undertook to withdraw from actual and direct contractual contact with the buyer. They ceased selling products to the consuming public through their own employees and making contracts of sale in their own names. Instead, a system of independent dealers was established; their products were sold to dealers who in turn dealt with the buying public, ostensibly solely in their own personal capacity as sellers. In the past in many instances, manufacturers were able to transfer to the dealers burdens imposed by the act and thus achieved a large measure of immunity for themselves. But, as will be noted in more detail hereafter, such marketing practices, coupled with the advent of large scale advertising by manufacturers to promote the purchase of these goods from dealers by members of the public, provided a basis upon which the existence of express or implied warranties was predicated, even though the manufacturer was not a party to the contract of sale.

. . . .

With these considerations in mind, we come to a study of the express warranty on the reverse side of the purchase order signed by Claus Henningsen. At the outset we take notice that it was made only by the manufacturer and that by its terms it runs directly to Claus Henningsen. On the facts detailed above, it was to be extended to him by the dealer as the agent of Chrysler Corporation. The consideration for this warranty is the purchase of the manufacturer's product from the dealer by the ultimate buyer. [c]

[T]he language of this warranty is that of the uniform warranty of the Automobile Manufacturers Association, of which Chrysler is a member. ...

The terms of the warranty are a sad commentary upon the automobile manufacturers' marketing practices. Warranties developed in the law in the interest of and to protect the ordinary consumer who cannot be expected to have the knowledge or capacity or even the opportunity to make adequate inspection of mechanical instrumentalities, like automobiles, and to decide for himself whether they are reasonably fit for the designed purpose. [Cc] But the ingenuity of the Automobile Manufacturers Association, by means of its standardized form, has metamorphosed the warranty into a device to limit the maker's liability. ...

The manufacturer agrees to replace defective parts for 90 days after the sale or until the car has been driven 4,000 miles, whichever is first to occur, [i]f the part is sent to the factory, transportation charges prepaid, and if examination discloses to its satisfaction that the part is defective. It is difficult to imagine a greater burden on the consumer, or less satisfactory remedy. Aside from imposing on the buyer the trouble of removing and shipping the part, the maker has sought to retain the uncontrolled discretion to decide the issue of defectiveness. ...

Also suppose, as in this case, a defective part or parts caused an accident and that the car was so damaged as to render it impossible to discover the precise part or parts responsible, although the circumstances clearly pointed to such fact as the cause of the mishap. Can it be said that the impossibility of performance deprived the buyer of the benefit of the warranty?

Moreover, the guaranty is against defective workmanship. That condition may arise from good parts improperly assembled. There being no defective parts to return to the maker, is all remedy to be denied? ...

The matters referred to represent only a small part of the illusory character of the security presented by the warranty. Thus far the analysis has dealt only with the remedy provided in the case of a defective part. What relief is provided when the breach of the warranty results in personal injury to the buyer? (Injury to third persons using the car in the purchaser's right will be treated hereafter.) As we have said above, the law is clear that such damages are recoverable under an ordinary warranty. The right exists whether the warranty sued on is express or implied. [c] And, of course, it has long since been settled that where the buyer or a member of his family driving with his permission suffers injuries because of negligent manufacture or construction of the manufacturer's liability exists. [c] But in this instance, after reciting that defective parts will be replaced at the factory, the alleged agreement relied upon by Chrysler provides that the manufacturer's 'obligation under this warranty' is limited to that undertaking; further, that such remedy is 'in lieu of all other warranties, express or implied, and all other obligations or liabilities on its part.' The contention has been raised that such language bars any claim for personal injuries which may emanate from a breach of the warranty. ...

Putting aside for the time being the problem of the efficacy of the disclaimer provisions contained in the express warranty, a question of first importance to be decided is whether an implied warranty of merchantability by Chrysler Corporation accompanied the sale of the automobile to Claus Henningsen.

. . . .

Chrysler points out that an implied warranty of merchantability is an incident of a contract of sale. It concedes, of course, the making of the original sale to Bloomfield Motors, Inc., but maintains that this transaction marked the terminal point of its contractual connection with the car. Then Chrysler urges that since it was not a party to the sale by the dealer to Henningsen, there is no privity of contract between it and the plaintiffs, and the absence of this privity eliminates any such implied warranty.

There is no doubt that under early common-law concepts of contractual liability only those persons who were parties to the bargain could sue for a breach of it. In more recent times a noticeable disposition has appeared in a number of jurisdictions to break through the narrow barrier of privity when dealing with sales of goods in order to give realistic recognition to a universally accepted fact. The fact is that the dealer and the ordinary buyer do not, and are not expected to, buy goods, whether they be foodstuffs or automobiles, exclusively for their own consumption or use. Makers and manufacturers know this and advertise and market their products on that assumption; witness, the 'family' car, the baby foods, etc. The limitations of privity in contracts for the sale of goods developed their place in the law when marketing conditions were simple, when maker and buyer frequently met face to face on an equal bargaining plane and when many of the products were relatively uncomplicated and conducive to inspection by a buyer competent to evaluate their quality. [C] With the advent of mass marketing, the manufacturer became remote from the purchaser, sales were accomplished through intermediaries, and the demand for the product was created by advertising media. ... As far back as 1932, in the well known case of *Baxter v. Ford Motor Co.*, 168 Wash. 456, 12 P.2d 409 (Sup.Ct.1932), affirmed 15 P.2d 1118, 88 A.L.R. 521 (Sup.Ct.1932), the Supreme Court of Washington gave recognition to the impact of then existing commercial practices on the strait jacket of privity, saying:

> 'It would be unjust to recognize a rule that would permit manufacturers of goods to create a demand for their products by representing that they possess qualities which they, in fact, do not possess, and then, because there is no privity of contract existing between the consumer and the manufacturer, deny the consumer the right to recover if damages result from the absence of those qualities, when such absence is not readily noticeable.' [c]

. . . .

Although only a minority of jurisdictions have thus far departed from the requirement of privity, the movement in that direction is most certainly gathering momentum. Liability to the ultimate consumer in the absence of direct contractual connection has been predicated upon a variety of theories. Some courts hold that the warranty runs with the article like a covenant running with land; others recognize a third-party beneficiary thesis; still others rest their decision on the ground that public policy requires recognition of a warranty made directly to the consumer. [Cc]

Further reference to *Decker*, supra, is enlightening:

'There certainly is justification for indulging a presumption of a warranty that runs with the article in the sale of food products. A party who processes a product and gives it the appearance of being suitable for human consumption, and places it in the channels of commerce, expects some one to consume the food in reliance on its appearance that it is suitable for human consumption. He expects the appearance of suitableness to continue with the product until some one is induced to consume it as food. But a modern manufacturer or vendor does even more than this under modern practices. He not only processes the food and dresses it up so as to make it appear appetizing, but he uses the newspapers, magazines, billboards, and the radio to build up the psychology to buy and consume his products. The invitation extended by him is not only to the house wife to buy and serve his product, but to the members of the family and guest to eat it. * * * The mere fact that a manufacturer or other vendor may thus induce the public to consume unwholesome food evidences the soundness of the rule which imposes a warranty, As a matter of public policy on the sale of food or other products intended for human consumption.' 164 S.W.2d at pages 832, 833. (Emphasis added.)

. . . .

We see no rational doctrinal basis for differentiating between a fly in a bottle of beverage and a defective automobile. The unwholesome beverage may bring illness to one person, the defective car, with its great potentiality for harm to the driver, occupants, and others, demands even less adherence to the narrow barrier of privity. ...

. . . .

Under modern conditions the ordinary layman, on responding to the importuning of colorful advertising, has neither the opportunity nor the capacity to inspect or to determine the fitness of an automobile for use; he must rely on the manufacturer who has control of its construction, and to some degree on the dealer who, to the limited extent called for by the manufacturer's instructions, inspects and services it before delivery. In such a marketing milieu his remedies and those of persons who properly claim through him should not depend upon the intricacies of the law of sales. The obligation of the manufacturer should not be based alone on privity of contract. It should rest, as was once said, upon 'the demands of social justice.'[C] ...

Accordingly, we hold that under modern marketing conditions, when a manufacturer puts a new automobile in the stream of trade and promotes its purchase by the public, an implied warranty that it is reasonably suitable for use as such accompanies it into the hands of the ultimate purchaser. Absence of agency between the manufacturer and the dealer who makes the ultimate sale is immaterial.

II.

The Effect of the Disclaimer and Limitation of Liability Clauses on the Implied Warranty of Merchantability.

Judicial notice may be taken of the fact that automobile manufacturers, including Chrysler Corporation, undertake large scale advertising programs over television, radio, in newspapers, magazines and all media of communication in order to persuade the public to buy their products. As has been observed above, a number of jurisdictions, conscious of modern marketing practices, have declared that when a manufacturer engages in advertising in order to bring his goods and their quality to the attention of the public and thus to create consumer demand, the representations made constitute an express warranty running directly to a buyer who purchases in reliance thereon. ...

In view of the cases in various jurisdictions suggesting the conclusion which we have now reached with respect to the implied warranty of merchantability, it becomes apparent that manufacturers who enter into promotional activities to stimulate consumer buying may incur warranty obligations of either or both the express or implied character. These developments in the law inevitably suggest the inference that the form of express warranty made part of the Henningsen purchase contract was devised for general use in the automobile industry as a possible means of avoiding the consequences of the growing judicial acceptance of the thesis that the described express or implied warranties run directly to the consumer.

In the light of these matters, what effect should be given to the express warranty in question which seeks to limit the manufacturer's liability to replacement of defective parts, and which disclaims all other warranties, express or implied? ...

In these times, an automobile is almost as much a servant of convenience for the ordinary person as a household utensil. For a multitude of other persons it is a necessity. Crowded highways and filled parking lots are a commonplace of our existence. There is no need to look any farther than the daily newspaper to be convinced that when an automobile is defective, it has great potentiality for harm.

. . . .

… As we have said, warranties originated in the law to safeguard the buyer and not to limit the liability of the seller or manufacturer. It seems obvious in this instance that the motive was to avoid the warranty obligations which are normally incidental to such sales. The language gave little and withdrew much. In return for the delusive remedy of replacement of defective parts at the factory, the buyer is said to have accepted the exclusion of the maker's liability for personal injuries arising from the breach of the warranty, and to have agreed to the elimination of any other express or implied warranty. An instinctively felt sense of justice cries out against such a sharp bargain. But does the doctrine that a person is bound by his signed agreement, in the absence of fraud, stand in the way of any relief?

. . . .

The warranty before us is a standardized form designed for mass use. It is imposed upon the automobile consumer. He takes it or leaves it, and he must take it to buy an automobile. No bargaining is engaged in with respect to it. In fact, the dealer through whom it comes to the buyer is without authority to alter it; his function is ministerial-simply to deliver it. The form warranty is not only standard with Chrysler but, as mentioned above, it is the uniform warranty of the Automobile Manufacturers Association. …

. . . .

… In the area of sale of goods, the legislative will has imposed an implied warranty of merchantability as a general incident of sale of an automobile by description. The warranty does not depend upon the affirmative intention of the parties. It is a child of the law; it annexes itself to the contract because of the very nature of the transaction. [C] The judicial process has recognized a right to recover damages for personal injuries arising from a breach of that warranty. The disclaimer of the implied warranty and exclusion of all obligations except those specifically assumed by the express warranty signify a studied effort to frustrate that protection. True, the Sales Act authorizes agreements between buyer and seller qualifying the warranty obligations. But quite obviously the Legislature contemplated lawful stipulations (which are determined by the circumstances of a particular case) arrived at freely by parties of relatively equal bargaining strength. The lawmakers did not authorize the automobile manufacturer to use its grossly disproportionate bargaining power to relieve itself from liability and to impose on the ordinary buyer, who in effect has no real freedom of choice, the grave danger of injury to himself and others that attends the sale of such a dangerous instrumentality as a defectively made automobile. In the framework of this case, illuminated as it is by the facts and the many decisions noted, we are of the opinion that Chrysler's attempted disclaimer of an implied warranty of merchantability and of the obligations arising therefrom is so inimical to the public good as to compel an adjudication of its invalidity. [cc]

. . . .

III.

The Dealer's Implied Warranty.

The principles that have been expounded as to the obligation of the manufacturer apply with equal force to the separate express warranty of the dealer. This is so, irrespective of the absence of the relationship of principal and agent between these defendants, because the manufacturer and the Association establish the warranty policy for the industry. The bargaining position of the dealer is inextricably bound by practice to that of the maker and the purchaser must take or leave the automobile, accompanied and encumbered as it is by the uniform warranty.

. . . .

For the reasons set forth in Part I hereof, we conclude that the disclaimer of an implied warranty of merchantability by the dealer, as well as the attempted elimination of all obligations other than replacement of defective parts, are violative of public policy and void.

. . . .

IV.

Proof of Breach of the Implied Warranty of Merchantability.

Both defendants argue that the proof adduced by plaintiffs as to the happening of the accident was not sufficient to demonstrate a breach of warranty. Consequently, they claim that their motion for judgment should have been granted by the trial court. We cannot agree. In our view, the total effect of the circumstances shown from purchase to accident is adequate to raise an inference that the car was defective and that such condition was causally related to the mishap. [Cc] Thus, determination by the jury was required.

. . . .

All other ground of appeal raised by both parties have been examined and we find no reversible error in any of them.

VII.

Under all of the circumstances outlined above, the judgments in favor of the plaintiffs and against the defendants are affirmed.

————

Points for Discussion

1. Distinguish between express warranty and implied warranty.

2. Distinguish between warranty of merchantability and warranty of fitness for a particular purpose.

3. What was the issue in *Henningsen*?

Take Note

A breach of warranty action pursuant to the Uniform Commercial Code (UCC) is based in contract, not tort. Therefore, the requirements of the UCC, such as requiring notice and the remedies available, do not govern the tort action.

4. According to *Henningsen*, what must a plaintiff prove to prevail against a defendant in tort for breach of implied warranty? Keep in mind that products liability law provides a remedy solely for personal or property injury caused by a product defect, which is a *tort* action, not a contract action. *See* RESTATEMENT (THIRD) OF TORTS: PRODUCTS LIABILITY § 2 cmt. r (1997).

3. Strict Liability

Greenman v. Yuba Power Products, Inc.

377 P.2d 897 (Ca. 1963)

TRAYNOR, Justice.

Plaintiff brought this action for damages against the retailer and the manufacturer of a Shopsmith, a combination power tool that could be used as a saw, drill, and wood lathe. He saw a Shopsmith demonstrated by the retailer and studied a brochure prepared by the manufacturer. He decided he wanted a Shopsmith for his home workshop, and his wife bought and gave him one for Christmas in 1955. In 1957 he bought the necessary attachments to use the Shopsmith as a lathe for turning a large piece of wood he wished to make into a chalice. After he had worked on the piece of wood several times without difficulty, it suddenly flew out of the machine and struck him on the forehead, inflicting serious injuries. About ten and a half months later, he gave the retailer and the manufacturer written notice of claimed breaches of warranties and filed a complaint against them alleging such breaches and negligence.

After a trial before a jury, the court ruled that there was no evidence that the retailer was negligent or had breached any express warranty and that the manufacturer was not liable for the breach of any implied warranty. Accordingly, it submitted to the jury only the cause of action alleging breach of implied warranties against the retailer and the causes of action alleging negligence and breach of express warranties against the manufacturer. The jury returned a verdict for the retailer against plaintiff and for plaintiff against the manufacturer in the amount of $65,000. The trial court denied the manufacturer's motion for a new trial and entered judgment on the verdict. The manufacturer and plaintiff appeal. Plaintiff seeks a reversal of the part of the judgment in favor of the retailer, however, only in the event that the part of the judgment against the manufacturer is reversed.

Plaintiff introduced substantial evidence that his injuries were caused by defective design and construction of the Shopsmith. His expert witnesses testified that inadequate set screws were used to hold parts of the machine together so that normal vibration caused the tailstock of the lathe to move away from the piece of wood being turned permitting it to fly out of the lathe. They also testified that there were other more positive ways of fastening the parts of the machine together, the use of which would have prevented the accident. The jury could therefore reasonably have concluded that the manufacturer negligently constructed the Shopsmith. The jury could also reasonably have concluded that statements in the manufacturer's brochure were untrue, that they constituted express warranties, and that plaintiff's injuries were caused by their breach.

The manufacturer contends, however, that plaintiff did not give it notice of breach of warranty within a reasonable time and that therefore his cause of action for breach of warranty is barred by section 1769 of the Civil Code. Since it cannot be determined whether the verdict against it was based on the negligence or warranty cause of action or both, the manufacturer concludes that the error in presenting the warranty cause of action to the jury was prejudicial.

Section 1769 of the Civil Code provides: 'In the absence of express or implied agreement of the parties, acceptance of the goods by the buyer shall not discharge the seller from liability in damages or other legal remedy for breach of any promise or warranty in the contract to sell or the sale. But, if, after acceptance of the goods, the buyer fails to give notice to the seller of the breach of any promise or warranty within a reasonable time after the buyer knows, or ought to know of such breach, the seller shall not be liable therefor.'

Like other provisions of the uniform sales act [c], section 1769 deals with the rights of the parties to a contract of sale or a sale. It does not provide that notice must be given of the breach of a warranty that arises independently of a contract of sale between the parties. Such warranties are not imposed by the sales act, but are the product of common-law decisions that have recognized them in a variety of situations. [Cc] It is true that in many of these situations the court has invoked the sales act definitions of warranties [c] in defining the defendant's liability, but it has done so, not because the statutes so required, but because they provided appropriate standards for the court to adopt under the circumstances presented. [Cc]

The notice requirement of section 1769, however, is not an appropriate one for the court to adopt in actions by injured consumers against manufacturers with whom they have not dealt. [Cc] 'As between the immediate parties to the sale (the notice requirement) is a sound commercial rule, designed to protect the seller against unduly delayed claims for damages. As applied to personal injuries, and notice to a remote seller, it becomes a booby-trap for the unwary. The injured consumer is seldom 'steeped in the business practice which justifies the rule,' [c] and at least until he has had legal advice it will not occur to him to give notice to one with whom he has had no dealings.' [c] … We conclude, therefore, the even if plaintiff did not give timely notice of breach of warranty to the manufacturer, his cause of action based on the representations contained in the brochure was not barred.

Moreover, to impose strict liability on the manufacturer under the circumstances of this case, it was not necessary for plaintiff to establish an express warranty as defined in section 1732 of the Civil Code.   A manufacturer is strictly liable in tort when an article he places on the market, knowing that it is to be used without inspection for defects, proves to have a defect that causes injury to a human being.   Recognized first in the case of unwholesome food products, such liability has now been extended to a variety of other products that create as great or greater hazards if defective. (*Peterson v. Lamb Rubber Co.,* 54 Cal.2d 339, 347, 5 Cal.Rptr. 863, 353 P.2d 575 (grinding wheel); *Vallis v. Canada Dry Ginger Ale, Inc.,* 190 Cal.App.2d 35, 42-44, 11 Cal Rptr. 823 (bottle); *Jones v. Burgermeister Brewing Corp.,* 198 Cal.App.2d 198, 204, 18 Cal.Rptr. 311 (bottle); *Gottsdanker v. Cutter Laboratories,* 182 Cal.App.2d App.2d 602, 607, 6 Cal.Rptr. 320, 79 A.L.R.2d 290 (vaccine); *McQuaide v. Bridgport Brass Co.,* D.C., 190 F.Supp. 252, 254 (insect spray); *Bowles v. Zimmer Manufacturing Co.,* 7 Cir., 277 F.2d 868, 875, 76 A.L.R.2d 120 (surgical pin); *Thompson v. Reedman,* D.C., 199 F.Supp. 120, 121 (automobile); *Chapman v. Brown,* D.C., 198 F.Supp. 78, 118, 119, affd. *Brown v. Chapman,* 9 Cir., 304 F.2d 149 (skirt); *B. F. Goodrich Co. v. Hammond,* 10 Cir., 269 F.2d 501, 504 (automobile tire); *Markovich v. McKesson and Robbins, Inc.,* 106 Ohio App. 265, 149 N.E.2d 181, 186-188 (home permanent); *Graham v. Bottenfield's Inc.,* 176 Kan. 68, 269 P.2d 413, 418 (hair dye); *General Motors Corp. v. Dodson,* 47 Tenn.App. 438, 338 S.W.2d 655, 661 (automobile); *Henningsen v. Bloomfield Motors, Inc.,* 32 N.J. 358, 161 A.2d 69, 76-84, 75 A.L.R.2d 1 (automobile); *Hinton v. Republic Aviation Corporation,* D.C., 180 F.Supp. 31, 33 (airplane).)

Although in these cases strict liability has usually been based on the theory of an express or implied warranty running from the manufacturer to the plaintiff, the abandonment of the requirement of a contract between them, the recognition that the liability is not assumed by agreement but imposed by law [cc], and the refusal to permit the manufacturer to define the scope of its own responsibility for defective products *Henningsen v. Bloomfield Motors, Inc.,* 32 N.J. 358, 161 A.2d 69, 84-96;[cc] make clear that the liability is not one governed by the law of contract warranties but by the law of strict liability in tort.   Accordingly, rules defining and governing warranties that were developed to meet the needs of commercial transactions cannot properly be invoked to govern the manufacturer's liability to those injured by their defective products unless those rules also serve the purposes for which such liability is imposed.

We need not recanvass the reasons for imposing strict liability on the manufacturer.   They have been fully articulated in the cases cited above. [cc] The purpose of such liability is to insure that the costs of injuries resulting from defective products are borne by the manufacturers that put such products on the market rather than by the injured persons who are powerless to protect themselves. Sales warranties serve this purpose fitfully at best. [c] In the present case, for example, plaintiff was able to plead and prove an express warranty only because he read and relied on the representations of the Shopsmith's ruggedness contained in the manufacturer's brochure. Implicit in the machine's presence on the market, however, was a representation that it would safely do the jobs for which it was built. Under these circumstances, it should not be controlling whether plaintiff selected the machine because of the statements in the brochure, or because of the machine's own appearance of excellence that belied the defect lurking beneath the surface, or because he merely assumed that it would safely do the jobs it was built to do. It should not be controlling whether the details of the sales from manufacturer to retailer and from retailer to plaintiff's wife were such that one or more of the implied warranties of the sales act arose. [c] 'The remedies of injured consumers ought not to be made to depend upon the intricacies of the law of sales.' [c] To establish the manufacturer's liability it was sufficient that plaintiff proved that he was injured while using the Shopsmith in a way it was intended to be used as a result of a defect in design and manufacture of which plaintiff was not aware that made the Shopsmith unsafe for its intended use.

. . . .

The judgment is affirmed.

———————————

Points for Discussion

1. What were the plaintiff's theories of recovery in *Greenman*?

2. What were the defendant manufacturer's defenses to the plaintiff's claims on appeal?

3. What is the ruling of the *Greenman* court?

4. How does the court distinguish, if at all, between a contract action for breach of implied warranty and the tort action for breach of implied warranty? What does the court say about whether or how the Sales Act affects the plaintiff's strict liability action?

5. What was the alleged product defect in *Greenman*?

6. According to the *Greenman* decision, when can a manufacturer be strictly liable in tort for an injury from the manufacturer's product?

7. What, if any, are the differences between a breach of implied warranty action and the ruling in *Greenman*?

8. What policy considerations influenced the court in adopting the rule applied in *Greenman*? Why might negligence as a theory of recovery be insufficient in cases such as *Greenman*?

9. RESTATEMENT (SECOND) OF TORTS § 402A (1964) was one of the most influential and widely adopted provisions of any section from any restatement. Drafted after *Greenman*, § 402A recognized strict liability as a theory of recovery in products actions:

    (1) One who sells any product in a defective condition unreasonably dangerous to the user or consumer or to his property is subject to liability for physical harm thereby caused to the ultimate user or consumer, or to his property, if

    (a) the seller is engaged in the business of selling such a product, and

    (b) it is expected to and does reach the user or consumer without substantial change in the condition in which it is sold.

    (2) The rule stated in Subsection (1) applies although

    (a) the seller has exercised all possible care in the preparation and sale of his product, and

    (b) the user or consumer has not bought the product from or entered into any contractual relation with the seller.

    How does § 402A differ from the ruling in *Greenman*?

10. Restatement (Third) of Torts: Products Liability seeks to advance the case law as it subsequently developed in response to the adoption of section 402A in several jurisdictions. *See, e.g.,* RESTATEMENT (THIRD) OF TORTS: PRODUCTS LIABILITY § 1 (1997), *infra.* Compare RESTATEMENT (SECOND) OF TORTS § 402A with RESTATEMENT (THIRD) OF TORTS: PRODUCTS LIABILITY § 1. What are the similarities? The differences?

> ### RESTATEMENT (THIRD) OF TORTS: PRODUCTS LIABILITY § 1 (1997)
> #### Liability of Commercial Seller or Distributor for Harm Caused by Defective Products
>
> One engaged in the business of selling or otherwise distributing products who sells or distributes a defective product is subject to liability for harm to persons or property caused by the defect.

B. Product Defects

With the exception of liability based on breach of express warranty, *see* section 2.a; *supra*, a plaintiff is required to establish that the injury-producing product contained a *defect* that caused the injury. There are three different types of product defects: (1) manufacturing or construction defects; (2) design defects; and (3) warnings or instructions defects.

Marie Pierre-Louis v. DeLonghi America, Inc., et al.

887 N.Y.S.2d 628 (N.Y. App. Div. 2009)

This appeal arises from a fire that occurred on January 13, 2003, at the home of Antoneen Darden-McCall, sued herein as Antoneen Darden and Antoneen McCall (hereinafter Darden), which took the life of Cassandra Pierre-Louis (hereafter the decedent). On the day of the fire, the decedent was a guest of Darden's son, the defendant Marques McCall, a/k/a Marcus McCall (hereafter Marques). According to the New York City Fire Department, a portable oil-filled space heater, manufactured by the defendant DeLonghi America, Inc. (hereafter DeLonghi), sold by the defendant Home Depot, Inc. (hereafter Home Depot), and purchased by Darden the day before the fire, caused the subject fire. Darden's other son, the defendant Matthew McCall (hereafter Matthew), had taken the heater out of the box when it was brought home, and, unintentionally, placed it upside down. It is undisputed that he was the only user of the subject heater prior to the fire.

The plaintiff commenced this action against, among others, DeLonghi and Home Depot, seeking, inter alia, to recover damages for personal injuries and wrongful death, alleging causes of action sounding in strict products liability. The plaintiff alleged that the heater was defectively manufactured and/or designed, and alleged a failure to warn regarding the use of the heater. DeLonghi and Home Depot (hereafter together the movants) moved for summary judgment dismissing the complaints and all cross claims insofar as asserted against them. The Supreme Court denied the motion.

"[A] manufacturer may be held liable for placing into the stream of commerce a defective product which causes injury" [c]. This burden is also imposed on a "wholesaler, distributor, or retailer who sells a product in a defective condition" [c].

There are three distinct claims for strict products liability: "[1] a mistake in manufacturing ... [2] an improper design ... or [3] an inadequate or absent warning for the use of the product" [cc].

Contrary to the movants' contention, they did not meet their initial burden of demonstrating prima facie entitlement to judgment as a matter of law with regard to the manufacturing defect claims [c]. "[A] defectively manufactured product is flawed because it is misconstructed without regard to whether the intended design of the manufacturer was safe or not. Such defects result from some mishap in the manufacturing process itself, improper workmanship, or because defective materials were used in construction" [c]. Here, the movants' own expert admitted that welds in the subject heater model would breech [sic] and oil would spurt out when the heater is operated in the upside down position, and DeLonghi's own president admitted that it was reasonably foreseeable that the subject heater would be operated in the upside down position, and specifically knew that the subject heater had previously been operated is such manner by users for a number of years prior to the subject fire.

The movants did, however, meet their initial burden of demonstrating prima facie entitlement to judgment as a matter of law regarding the design defect claims, through the submission of the opinion of their expert explaining that the subject heater was not defectively designed [c].

"To establish a prima facie case in a strict products liability action predicated on a design defect, a plaintiff must show that the manufacturer marketed a product which was not reasonably safe in its design, that it was feasible to design the product in a safer manner, and that the defective design was a substantial factor in causing the plaintiff's injury" [cc].

Contrary to the movants' contention, however, the plaintiff established the existence of triable issues of fact as to the design defect claims, through the opinions submitted by her two experts [c]. "Where, as here, a qualified expert opines that a particular product is defective or dangerous, describes why it is dangerous, explains how it can be made safer, and concludes that it is feasible to do so, it is usually for the jury to make the required risk-utility analysis" [cc]. Thus, considering the conflicting expert opinions concerning the reasonableness of the heater's design, the Supreme Court correctly determined that a question of fact exists concerning an alleged design defect [c].

Contrary to the movants' contention, they did not meet their initial burden of demonstrating prima facie entitlement to summary judgment dismissing the failure-to-warn claims [c]. The movants contend that the plaintiff cannot prevail on her claim based upon failure to warn because Matthew did not read the warnings contained in the instructions for the subject heater that operating it in the upside position can create a hazard. However, Matthew testified at his examination before trial that the heater unit was the only item that came out of the box when he set it up the day before the fire and that the only writing he saw on the subject heater itself were the numbers on the temperature dial, which contained no warning. Resolving all reasonable inferences in the manner most favorable to the opponents of the movants' summary judgment motion [cc], the movants did not establish, as a matter of law, that the subject heater actually came with the subject instructions and, therefore, with adequate warnings.

Accordingly, the Supreme Court properly denied the movants' summary judgment motion.

———————

Points for Discussion

1. What was the theory of recovery in the *Pierre-Louis* case?

2. Did the plaintiff allege that the product had an injury-producing defect in *Pierre-Louis*? If so, what type of defect was alleged?

3. Define and distinguish among the potential types of product defects according to the *Pierre-Louis* court.

4. The RESTATEMENT (THIRD) OF TORTS is consistent with the *Pierre-Louis*. Section 2, Categories of Product Defect, provides that "[a] product is defective when, at the time of sale or distribution, it contains a manufacturing defect, is defective in design, or is defective because of inadequate instructions or warnings. ..." The following materials consider each type of defect in turn.

———————

1. Manufacturing Defect

RESTATEMENT (THIRD) OF TORTS: PRODUCTS LIABILITY § 2(a) (1997)

A product contains a manufacturing defect when the product departs from its intended design even though all possible care was exercised in the preparation and marketing of the product.

Hypo 15-1

Driver purchased a new sports utility vehicle manufactured by ABC Cars. One day Driver starts the vehicle while the gearshift is in the "drive" position rather than in "park," despite the fact that ABC designed the car so that it would never start in drive. Driver's vehicle jolts forward, causing injuries to Driver, the car, and the garage in which it was parked. Evidence shows that Driver's vehicle failed to have the necessary part it was intended to have in order to prevent it from starting in any position other than park. Driver seeks to sue ABC Cars for a defective product. Explain whether Driver's vehicle was defective and whether ABC Cars can be held liable for the personal and property injuries.

Points for Discussion

1. Permitting recovery based on a manufacturing defect essentially demands perfection of manufacturers in producing their products. *See* RESTATEMENT (THIRD) OF TORTS: PRODUCT LIABILITY § 2 cmt. c (1997). Do you agree or disagree with this expectation of perfection from manufacturers?

2. Manufacturing defects (also sometimes referred to as construction defects) are variations from the intended design of a product that may understandably occur in a small percentage of products as a result of shortcomings in the manufacturing process, *e.g.,* when a product is somehow physically flawed, damaged, or improperly assembled. Accordingly, plaintiffs alleging a manufacturing defect must establish that the product deviated from either the manufacturer's intended design or from other products of the same design.

3. To hold the manufacturer liable, the plaintiff also has the burden of proving that the defect existed at the time that the product left the hands of the manufacturer.

———————————

2. Design Defect

> **RESTATEMENT (THIRD) OF TORTS: PRODUCTS LIABILITY § 2(b) (1997)**
>
> A product is defective in design when the foreseeable risks of harm posed by the product could have been reduced or avoided by the adoption of a reasonable alternative design by the seller or other distributor, or a predecessor in the commercial chain of distribution, and the omission of the alternative design renders the product not reasonably safe.

Timpte Indus., Inc. v. Gish

286 S.W.3d 306 (Tex. 2009)

Justice MEDINA delivered the opinion of the Court.

Robert Gish was seriously injured when he fell from the top of a trailer into which he was attempting to load fertilizer. He sued Timpte Industries, the manufacturer of the trailer, alleging, among other things, that several features of the trailer were defectively designed, rendering the trailer unreasonably dangerous. The trial court granted a no-evidence summary judgment in Timpte's favor, but the court of appeals reversed. [c] Finding no defect, we reverse the court of appeals' judgment and render judgment reinstating the trial court's summary judgment.

I

On the morning of June 19, 2002, Robert Gish, a long haul trucker for Scott Hinde Trucking, arrived at the Martin Resources plant in Plainview, Texas, to pick up a load of ammonium sulfate fertilizer. Gish was familiar with the plant, as he had picked up fertilizer there once or twice a week for approximately the past year. That morning Gish checked his trailer, weighed it, and waited for another customer to finish loading.

Gish's Peterbilt truck was hauling a forty-eight-foot Super Hopper trailer manufactured by Timpte Inc., a subsidiary of Timpte Industries.[1] The Super Hopper trailer is a standard open-top, twin hopper trailer, which is loaded from above through use of a downspout or other device and is emptied through two openings on its bottom. Once the trailer is loaded, a tarp is rolled over the top to protect its contents.[2] A ladder and an observation platform are attached to the front and rear of the trailer to allow the operator to view its contents.

After the truck ahead of him finished loading, Gish backed his trailer under the downspout attached to the fertilizer plant and yelled to a Martin employee to begin loading. In a typical delivery, an employee inside the Martin plant uses a front-end loader to drop fertilizer into a hopper. The fertilizer is then dropped onto a conveyer system that moves it to the downspout outside the plant and into the waiting trailer.

To prevent the granulated fertilizer from being blown away during the loading process, Gish attempted to lower the downspout by using a rope attached to it. The rope was attached to the downspout for that purpose, but Gish could not get it to work. He had previously complained to Martin employees about problems lowering the downspout, but he did not do so again that morning. Instead, using the ladder attached to the front of the trailer, Gish climbed atop the trailer (as he had on several other occasions when the downspout would not lower) and attempted to lower the downspout by hand while standing on the trailer's top rail. This top rail is also the top of the trailer's side wall. It is made of extruded aluminum, is between 5 and 5.66 inches wide, and is nine-and-a half feet above the ground.

While Gish was standing on the top rail working with the downspout, a gust of wind hit him from the back, causing him to fall. This fall fractured his legs, broke his ankles, and ruptured an Achilles tendon. Gish was in a wheelchair for six months, and he still has difficulty walking and standing.

Gish sued Martin and Timpte, asserting a cause of action for premises liability against Martin and causes of action for marketing, manufacturing, and design defects, misrepresentation, and breach of warranty against Timpte. Specifically, Gish asserted that the warning labels on the Super Hopper trailer were insufficient to warn him of the danger of climbing on top of the trailer, and that the trailer contained two design defects:

---

1 Because the interests of Timpte Inc. and Timpte Industries are the same throughout these proceedings, we refer to them collectively as "Timpte."

2 The tarp assembly consists of two end caps—one on the front and one on the rear of the trailer—a latch plate that runs the length of the driver's side of the trailer, and seven curved metal bars that cross the trailer at approximately even intervals. These bars curve up towards the middle of the trailer, such that they form a peak down the trailer's center line. Two other metal bars run the length of the trailer on either side of this peak. This assembly supports the tarp when it is rolled over the trailer, and the latch plate allows the operator to tighten the tarp taut over the trailer.

• The top two rungs of the ladders attached to the front and rear of the trailer allow a person to climb atop the trailer; and

• The top rail of the trailer is too narrow and slippery and contains too many tripping hazards for a person to walk safely along it.

The two ladders on the trailer are made of rectangular tubing with rungs spaced twelve inches apart. The front ladder that Gish used to climb atop the trailer has five rungs-two below the observation platform (which is 38 1/2 inches below the top of the front wall of the trailer), one approximately level with the platform, and two above the platform. The top rung of the ladder is thirteen inches below the top of the front wall of the trailer, and the rung second from the top is twelve inches below that. A metal bar approximately the length of the platform is mounted above the platform and near the top of the trailer to serve as a handhold while the operator stands on the platform.

Just below the middle rung of the ladder, Timpte has placed a rectangular warning label, which reads:

WARNING

1. EXERCISE EXTREME CAUTION WHILE CLIMBING ON ACCESS SYSTEM.

2. ALWAYS MAINTAIN 3-POINT CONTACT. (2 HANDS & 1 FOOT OR 2 FEET & 1 HAND)

3. DO NOT WEAR RINGS OR ANYTHING THAT CAN CATCH ON LADDER.

4. USE LADDER SIDE RAIL FOR HAND HOLD, NEVER USE THE RUNG.

5. NEVER CLIMB OVER THE TOP OF THE TRAILER AND ENTER THE INSIDE COMPARTMENTS FOR ANY REASON.

FAILURE TO FOLLOW THESE WARNINGS COULD RESULT IN SERIOUS INJURY OR DEATH.

As previously noted, the top rail of the trailer is made of extruded aluminum, which is extremely slippery. The seven bars that support the tarp also intersect with the top rail, presenting the alleged tripping hazards.

To remedy these alleged design defects, Dr. Gary Nelson, Gish's expert witness, proposed three design changes:

• Remove the top two rungs of the ladders attached to the trailer to make it impossible for a person to climb atop the trailer;

• Provide an adequate foothold and handhold at the top of the trailer so that a user on top of the trailer can maintain three-point contact with the trailer at all times; and

• If an adequate handhold cannot be provided, then widen the side rail to at least 12 inches to provide an adequate foothold.

Timpte moved for a no-evidence summary judgment, which the trial court granted. The trial court then severed Gish's claims against Timpte from the remainder of the case, making the summary judgment final for purposes of appeal. The court of appeals affirmed the trial court's judgment as to all of Gish's claims except his claim for design defect, concluding that there was "some evidence upon which reasonable factfinders could disagree as to whether the trailer's design was both unreasonably dangerous and a cause of Gish's fall." 2007 Tex.App. LEXIS 9411, at * 11-12, 2007 WL 4224411, at *4.

II

A no-evidence summary judgment motion under Rule 166a(i) is essentially a motion for a pretrial directed verdict; it requires the nonmoving party to present evidence raising a genuine issue of material fact supporting each element contested in the motion. ...

. . . .

We conclude that Timpte's motion gave fair notice to Gish that it was challenging both whether the alleged defect rendered the trailer unreasonably dangerous and whether the defect was the producing cause of Gish's injury. ...

III

To recover for a products liability claim alleging a design defect, a plaintiff must prove that (1) the product was defectively designed so as to render it unreasonably dangerous; (2) a safer alternative design existed; and (3) the defect was a producing cause of the injury for which the plaintiff seeks recovery. [Cc] To determine whether a product was defectively designed so as to render it unreasonably dangerous, Texas courts have long applied a risk-utility analysis that requires consideration of the following factors:

(1) the utility of the product to the user and to the public as a whole weighed against the gravity and likelihood of injury from its use; (2) the availability of a substitute product which would meet the same need and not be unsafe or unreasonably expensive; (3) the manufacturer's ability to eliminate the unsafe character of the product without seriously

impairing its usefulness or significantly increasing its costs; (4) the user's anticipated awareness of the dangers inherent in the product and their avoidability because of general public knowledge of the obvious condition of the product, or of the existence of suitable warnings or instructions; and (5) the expectations of the ordinary consumer.

American Tobacco Co. v. Grinnell, 951 S.W.2d 420, 432 (Tex.1997); *see also Hernandez,* 2 S.W.3d at 256 (citing *Turner v. Gen. Motors Corp.,* 584 S.W.2d 844, 847 (Tex.1979)).

The risk-utility analysis does not operate in a vacuum, but rather in the context of the product's intended use and its intended users. *Hernandez,* 2 S.W.3d at 259-60 (risk-utility analysis of a cigarette lighter must be conducted in light of its intended adult users); *Caterpillar Inc. v. Shears,* 911 S.W.2d 379, 383-84 (Tex.1995) (risk-utility analysis of a front-end loader with a removable canopy conducted in light of its specialized use in low-clearance areas). Although whether a product is defective is generally a question of fact, in the appropriate case, it may be determined as a matter of law. *Hernandez,* 2 S.W.3d at 260-61 ("[T]he issue of whether the product is unreasonably dangerous as designed may nevertheless be a legal one if reasonable minds cannot differ on the risk-utility analysis considerations."); *Grinnell,* 951 S.W.2d at 432.

In this regard, we have also rejected the contention that Texas should follow the "open and obvious danger rule":

> A number of courts are of the view that obvious risks are not design defects which must be remedied. [Cc] However, our Court has held that liability for a design defect may attach even if the defect is apparent. *Turner,* 584 S.W.2d at 850.

Shears, 911 S.W.2d at 383; *see also Hernandez,* 2 S.W.3d at 258 ("[I]n general, the obviousness of danger in and of itself is not an absolute bar ... to liability for a defective design.").[3] We have noted, however, that the obviousness of the claimed defect is "an important consideration in determining whether the product is unreasonably dangerous ... [and] may even be decisive in a particular case." *Hernandez,* 2 S.W.3d at 258.

Gish alleges that the Super Hopper trailer was defectively designed in two ways: (1) the top rail of the trailer was too narrow and presented tripping haz-

---

3 This is also the rule adopted by the Restatement. RESTATEMENT (THIRD) OF TORTS: PRODUCTS LIABILITY § 2 cmt. d (1998) ("Subsection (b) does not recognize the obviousness of a design-related risk as precluding a finding of defectiveness. The fact that a danger is open and obvious is relevant to the issue of defectiveness, but does not necessarily preclude a plaintiff from establishing that a reasonable alternative design should have been adopted that would have reduced or prevented injury to the plaintiff.").

ards; and (2) the top two rungs of the ladders mounted on the trailer were unnecessary and allowed the operator to climb to the top of the trailer. Essentially, Gish complains that the trailer's design failed to prevent him from climbing atop the trailer and then, once he was up there, failed to protect him from the risk of falling.

There is no evidence, however, that the top rail of the trailer is unreasonably dangerous in light of its use and purpose. As already noted, the top rail from which Gish fell is only 5 to 5.66 inches wide and made of extruded aluminum, an extremely slippery surface. Timpte's executive vice president of manufacturing and engineering, Jeffrey Thompson, testified that the top rail was designed this way for two reasons: (1) the width of the top rail is only as wide as necessary to support the front end of the trailer; and (2) the top rail is made of extruded aluminum and slants slightly towards the inside of the trailer so that any commodity that spills onto the top rail will slide into the trailer. Thompson testified that, were the top rail to be widened, it would add to the total weight of the trailer thereby reducing the weight of the commodity that the trailer would be permitted to carry. The utility of this design—maximizing the amount of commodity that the trailer can haul while keeping the structure of the trailer sound—is undeniably very high.

The corresponding risk of someone being injured the way Gish was is extremely low. The risk of falling while trying to balance on a 5 inch wide strip of extruded aluminum nearly ten feet above the ground is an obvious risk that is certainly "within the ordinary knowledge common to the community." *See Caterpillar Inc. v. Shears,* 911 S.W.2d 379, 382 (Tex.1995) (internal quotation marks omitted). Whether the risk of injury is common knowledge is a question of law, not fact. Id. at 383.[4] In *Shears,* we determined that the proper inquiry is whether an average user of the product would recognize the risks entailed by the use of the product as-is. *Id.; see also Sauder Custom Fabrication Inc. v. Boyd,* 967 S.W.2d 349, 350-51 (Tex.1998) (per curiam) ("The consumer's perspective is that of an ordinary user of the product, not necessarily the same as that of an ordinary person unfamiliar with the product."). Applying that principle, we held as a matter of law that the risks presented by the open cab of a front-end loader were obvious to the average user, such that no warning was required. [C] The risk of falling from the top of the trailer while trying to balance on a five-inch strip of extruded aluminum is equally obvious to an average user of the Super Hopper trailer.

As noted, though, the fact that the alleged defect is open and obvious, although an important consideration, is generally not determinative in Texas. [C] Timpte, however, asks that we revisit this rule, arguing that, in other contexts, the

---

4 We again recognize that in some situations, however, "there could be a fact question about whether consumers have common knowledge of risks associated with a product." *Shears,* 911 S.W.2d at 383. This is not such a situation.

open and obvious nature of a danger is decisive. *Gen. Elec. Co. v. Moritz,* 257 S.W.3d 211 (Tex.2008) (premises owner owes no duty to warn an independent contractor's employees of an open and obvious danger); *Humble Sand & Gravel, Inc. v. Gomez,* 146 S.W.3d 170, 183-84 (Tex.2004) (product seller owes no duty to warn of commonly known risks of the product's use). But we have long recognized that, in the context of an obvious risk, the duty to warn of defects is distinct from the duty to design safe products. *Compare Turner v. Gen. Motors Corp.,* 584 S.W.2d 844, 850 (Tex.1979) (recognizing design defect claim even if defect is apparent), *with Joseph E. Seagram & Sons, Inc. v. McGuire,* 814 S.W.2d 385, 387-88 (Tex.1991) (no duty to warn of risks associated with prolonged and excessive alcohol consumption because such risks are common knowledge). As the Restatement notes:

> Warning of an obvious or generally known risk in most instances will not provide an effective additional measure of safety. Furthermore, warnings that deal with obvious or generally known risks may be ignored by users and consumers and may diminish the significance of warnings about non-obvious, not-generally-known risks. Thus, requiring warnings of obvious or generally known risks could reduce the efficacy of warnings generally.

RESTATEMENT (THIRD) OF TORTS: PRODUCTS LIABILITY § 2 cmt. j (1998). The focus of a design defect claim, however, is whether there was a reasonable alternative design that, at a reasonable cost, would have reduced a foreseeable risk of harm. *Id.* § 2 cmt. d. Thus, if it is reasonable for a product's designer to incorporate a design that eliminates an open and obvious risk, the product reaches a more optimum level of safety by incorporating the safer design than by keeping the current design with the open and obvious risk. *See id.* § 2 cmt. a. We see no reason to discard the risk-utility analysis that Texas courts have long-applied to encourage manufacturers to reach an optimum level of safety in designing their products.

Nevertheless, the risk-utility factors here confirm that the design of the Super Hopper trailer was not defective as a matter of law. Timpte warned users to always maintain three-point contact with the trailer, which is impossible for a user standing on the top rail. Had Gish adhered to this warning, his accident would not have happened. Additionally, widening the side walls of the trailer so as to convert the top rail into a safe walkway, as Gish's expert proposed, would have increased the cost and weight of the trailer while decreasing its utility.[5] The Federal Highway Administration generally limits the gross vehicle weight of a commercial motor vehicle to 80,000 pounds; therefore, any increase in the unloaded weight of the trailer results in a decrease of the amount of commodity the trailer

---

5 Widening the side rail would also encourage other users of the Timpte trailer to use the side rail as a walkway, thus actually making it less safe.

can haul, thus reducing its overall utility to users. 23 C.F.R. § 658.17 (2008). The width of the top rail of the Super Hopper trailer is therefore not a design defect that renders the trailer unreasonably dangerous.

There is also no evidence that the top two rungs of the ladder are a design defect that renders the trailer unreasonably dangerous. Thompson testified that the top two rungs are necessary to maintain the structure and stability of the ladder when the side rails are under pressure; without them, the ladder could twist or bend. Additionally, even though Timpte warned users to use the side rails of the ladder as a handhold when climbing the ladder, were a user's hands to slip, the additional rungs provided additional handholds and an additional measure of safety. Thus, the utility of the ladder as constructed is high.

Conversely, the risk of injury from the use of the ladder is very slight. Gish's injury is only remotely related to the ladder's top two rungs: they allowed him to climb atop the trailer, where he was subsequently injured. Timpte warned users not to use the ladder to climb into the trailer itself, and the obvious nature of the risk of climbing onto the top rail negates the need for any additional warning. [C] Therefore, any risk from the ladder itself stems only from the risk that a user will ignore both Timpte's warnings and open and obvious dangers.

Additionally, as noted above, removal of the top two rungs, although it might have prevented Gish's injury,[6] might also increase the risk of injury to others who might need those rungs as a failsafe handhold. Removing the top two rungs could also cause the ladder to bend or become unstable under pressure, thereby increasing the risk of danger from its use. The inclusion of the top two rungs of the ladder is therefore not a design defect that renders the Super Hopper unreasonably dangerous.

Because there is no evidence that the design defects alleged by Gish rendered the trailer unreasonably dangerous, we reverse the court of appeals' judgment and render judgment reinstating the trial court's summary judgment.[7]

Points for Discussion

1. What was the legally relevant inquiry that the *Timpte* court applied in determining whether the ladder had a design defect?

---

6 As the observation platform is only 38 1/2 inches below the top rail of the trailer, Gish could have climbed atop the trailer from this perch even if the top two rungs of the ladder had been removed.

7 Before this appeal, Gish's premises liability claims against Martin Resources were severed from the claims against Timpte and left pending in the trial court.

2. What is the risk-utility analysis that the *Timpte* court employs? How, if at all, is the risk-utility analysis relevant to the court's determination of whether the product was defectively designed?

3. The Third Restatement explains that the risk-utility balancing test "is whether a reasonable alternative design would, at reasonable cost, have reduced the foreseeable risks of harm posed by the product and, if so, whether the omission of the alternative design by the seller or a predecessor in the distributive chain rendered the product not reasonably safe." RESTATEMENT (THIRD) OF TORTS: PRODUCTS LIABILITY § 2 cmt. d (1997). As part of the risk-utility analysis in most jurisdictions, a plaintiff must also establish that a reasonable, alternative design was or reasonably could have been available at the time of product's sale or distribution.

For More Information

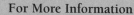

The law regarding imposition of liability based upon a defectively designed defect is vast. What is presented in these materials is an introduction to this subject matter. Be sure to take a Products Liability course or an Advanced Torts course for further exploration of this interesting and evolving area of tort law.

4. The *Timpte* court also discusses the open and obvious danger that the product presented. How should the open and obvious dangerousness of a product be assessed in determining and resolving the design defect issue?

5. Several years ago, plaintiffs sought to hold the manufacturer of Black Talon bullets liable for the death of their loved ones when a mentally unstable person went on a murderous rampage on a New York subway. Black Talon bullets are hollow-point ammunition uniquely designed to break apart at 90-degree angles, exposing sharp edges upon impact. Due to their unique design, it was alleged that the Black Talon bullets had significantly greater wounding power and caused more extensive physical injury (and deaths) than would have been caused by an ordinary bullet. Applying the risk-utility test, determine whether Black Talon bullets are defectively designed. *See* McCarthy v. Olin Corp., 119 F.3d 148 (2nd Cir. 1997) (granting defendant's motion to dismiss). *See also* RESTATEMENT (THIRD) OF TORTS: PRODUCTS LIABILITY § 2 cmt. d (1997).

6. Compare and contrast a manufacturing defect and a design defect.

———————

Hypo 15-2

Prankster Co. manufactures "gag gifts." In celebration of the birth of Logan's new baby girl, Blake purchases an exploding cigar manufactured by Prankster Co. The cigar is made to explode with a very loud noise and lots of smoke. When Logan lights the cigar, it explodes, but the heat from the explosion ignites Logan's beard, severely injuring him. Logan wishes to sue Prankster Co. for his injuries, alleging that the cigar was defectively designed. Discuss.

See RESTATEMENT (THIRD) OF TORTS: PRODUCTS LIABILITY § 2 cmt. e, illus. 5 (1997).

Hypo 15-3

"John was driving a compact automobile manufactured by ABC Auto Company when he lost control and collided with a tree. John suffered serious injuries. John brings a products-liability claim against ABC, arguing that the design of his car is defective in that it does not offer the same level of crashworthiness as does a full-size automobile. John's experts admit that reducing the size of an automobile unavoidably increases the risk of injuries to occupants in collisions. John can identify no specific feature of the ABC automobile that could have been designed differently so as to be safer without increasing its size and substantially reducing its desirable characteristics of lower cost and lower fuel economy." RESTATEMENT (THIRD) OF TORTS: PRODUCTS LIABILITY § 2 cmt. f, illus. 9 (1997). Discuss whether the ABC car has a design defect.

Malcolm v. Evenflo Co., Inc.

217 P.3d 514 (Mont. 2009)

Justice BRIAN MORRIS delivered the Opinion of the Court.

Chad and Jessica Malcolm (collectively Malcolms) sued Evenflo Company, Inc. (Evenflo) after their four-month-old son Tyler suffered fatal brain injuries in a rollover car accident. The Malcolms alleged that the Evenflo "On My Way" (OMW) child safety seat contained a design defect that caused Tyler's death. The Malcolms asserted strict liability in tort. Evenflo appeals from a judgment in the Sixth Judicial District, Park County, following a jury trial. We affirm in part, reverse in part, and remand for further proceedings.

. . . .

FACTUAL AND PROCEDURAL BACKGROUND

The "On My Way" Child Safety Seat

Evenflo manufactures child restraint systems, or child seats. Evenflo marketed the OMW as a rear-facing vehicle child safety seat intended for transporting infants weighing up to 20 pounds. Evenflo designed the OMW for use with or without its detachable base. The user routed the vehicle's seat belt through an enclosed seat belt "tunnel" on the base when they used the detachable base. The seat then latched into the base. The user also could unlatch the seat from the base and use it as a baby carrier. When used without the base, Evenflo designed the seat belt to be slipped into a U-shaped, open-ended plastic seat belt hook on one side of the seat. The user would route the seat belt over the seat's foot-end and through an open-ended plastic seat belt hook on the other side of the seat. The user then latched the seat belt into the vehicle's seat belt buckle.

The National Highway Traffic and Safety Administration (NHTSA) requires that all child restraint systems comply with the minimum requirements of Federal Motor Vehicle Safety Standard 213 (FMVSS 213). *See* 49 C.F.R. § 571.213 (2009). NHTSA required Evenflo to conduct internal testing of the OMW to determine if it complied with the FMVSS 213 standards. NHTSA and Transport Canada, the Canadian testing agency, conducted random audit FMVSS 213 tests in addition to Evenflo's internal testing.

. . . .

Evenflo first manufactured the OMW model 206 in May of 1994. By February of 1995, Evenflo's internal testing indicated that the production model 206 was prone to failure of the plastic seat belt hooks and/or the adjacent plastic shell. Internal videotapes showed the OMW seats breaking apart in the area of the vehicle seat belt path. ...

Evenflo briefly halted production of the OMW. Evenflo notified NHTSA on June 12, 1995, that it was going to conduct a "consumer corrective action/recall campaign" as the OMW did not meet the requirements of FMVSS 213. ...

Evenflo had manufactured and sold approximately 200,000 OMWs at the time of the recall. ...

. . . .

In 1997, Ruthie Gonzales of Merced, California, reported to Evenflo that her retrofitted model 207 OMW's belt hook had broken off during a rollover accident. The OMW came loose from the seatbelt and ended up on her front dashboard. Devon Orneleas of Patterson, California, reported to Evenflo on August 10, 1999, that both belt hooks had broken off her production model 207 in a rollover accident. ... Ms. Orneleas found her baby, still secured in the child seat, on the front seat floorboard after the rollover.

Ms. Orneleas testified that she had reported the incident because she wanted Evenflo to know "that they had a defective product and I wanted them to recall it." Ms. Orneleas testified that when she called Evenflo, the customer service representative said that "she was shocked and hadn't heard of that before." ...

... Three other OMW owners also called Evenflo in the years before the Malcolm accident to report that seatbelts had slipped out of the open belt hook of the OMW in rollover, side-impact, and rear-end situations. Evenflo did not test the OMW in rear-end, side impact, or rollover scenarios before the Malcolm accident.

The Malcolm Accident

The Malcolms lived south of Livingston, Montana, on a ranch near Emigrant. Chad Malcolm was the fourth generation of the family to ranch in the area. A friend gave Jessica Malcolm the OMW while Jessica was pregnant with Tyler. Jessica called Evenflo to ask if the OMW model 207 was safe to use. Evenflo assured her that the OMW was not subject to any of their recalls and that the OMW was safe to use. ...

Jessica Malcolm drove to Emigrant on the evening of July 16, 2000, in her 1996 Suburban to pick up pizza and a movie with her sister and her son Tyler. She then drove back south on Highway 89 toward the ranch. Malcolm's sister rode in the passenger seat and Tyler rode in the back in the OMW model 207 child seat. A northbound motorist swerved into Malcolm's lane and forced Malcolm off the road. The Suburban rolled three times, traveled down a steep incline, and stopped in a ditch. The accident occurred within sight of the Malcolms' ranch.

Jessica Malcolm did not suffer serious injury. Her sister sustained a severe head injury. The left belt hook of the OMW broke off during the rollover. The seat belt slipped out from the open-ended belt hook on the opposite side of the seat. The forces of the accident ejected the OMW from the Suburban. The OMW came to rest approximately 60 feet from the Suburban. Tyler remained strapped in the OMW. Tyler suffered brain injuries that resulted in his death

Pretrial

The Malcolms' case sounded exclusively in strict liability in tort, design defect theory. The Malcolms claimed that the Evenflo OMW model 207 infant child safety seat constituted a defectively designed product that failed catastrophically even though they had used the seat in a reasonably anticipated manner. The Malcolms pointed to the OMW's open-ended belt hook design and the lack of expanded polystyrene (EPS) padding. The Malcolms contended that Evenflo could have manufactured the OMW using a feasible superior alternative design that required the vehicle's seatbelt to be routed through an enclosed seat belt tunnel even when the seat was used without the base. The Malcolms also sought punitive damages. The Malcolms alleged that Evenflo "continued selling the defective product in conscious, deliberate and intentional disregard of the danger presented."

Evenflo contended that the OMW model 207 was not defective in any way. Evenflo argued that the severity of the forces involved in the accident solely caused Tyler's death. Evenflo argued that the "tremendous forces" that occurred during the rollover forced open the rear passenger door, which was immediately adjacent to Tyler's child seat. Evenflo posited that Tyler's car seat came into direct contact with the ground as the Suburban rolled. Evenflo suggested that the contact caused the seat to detach from the seat belt system and ultimately fly out the open door. Evenflo emphasized that the production model 207 passed each of the FMVSS tests conducted on the seat. Evenflo also argued that the OMW model 207 differed completely from the OMW model 206.

. . . .

Trial

. . . .

Both sides presented expert witnesses. The Malcolms contended that the OMW model 206 and model 207 were identical with respect to the faulty design of the open belt hook and the lack of padding. The Malcolms' design expert Lou D'Aulerio testified that he had analyzed [the sled test and had] determined that Evenflo had noted that the plastic shell had cracked or fractured in 157, or 27%, of the tests. D'Aulerio designated these tests "failures." The Malcolms also mentioned these test "failures" during their opening statement and closing argument.

Evenflo argued that many of the tests cited by D'Aulerio were irrelevant because they involved models other than the model 207. ... Evenflo contended that the District Court unfairly was applying its **motion in limine** regarding FMVSS 213 testing by allowing the Malcolms to introduce evidence that the OMW model 206 had "failed" during testing without allowing Evenflo to introduce evidence that the OMW model 207 had "passed" according to the minimal requirements of FMVSS 213 in each of those instances. The District Court rejected Evenflo's arguments regarding FMVSS 213.

The jury awarded the Malcolms $6,697,491 in compensatory damages. The jury also awarded the Malcolms $3,700,000 in punitive damages in a separate proceeding … .

… The District Court affirmed the jury's punitive damages award. The District Court also denied Evenflo's post-trial motions, including its motion for a new trial, motion for remittitur, motion for judgment as a matter of law. Evenflo appeals.

STANDARD OF REVIEW

We review a district court's evidentiary rulings for an abuse of discretion. …

DISCUSSION

Did the District Court abuse its discretion when it excluded Evenflo's evidence that the OMW model 207 complied with FMVSS 213 for the purposes of compensatory damages?

Section 27-1-719, MCA, governs design defect liability in Montana. A person who sells a product in a defective condition is liable for the physical harm caused by the defective product. [cc] A product is defective if it is dangerous to an extent beyond that anticipated by the ordinary user. [cc]

Strict liability recognizes that the seller is in the best position to insure product safety. [c] Design defect liability therefore places the risk of loss on the manufacturer. This imposition of risk provides "an incentive to design and produce fail-safe products which exceed reasonable standards of safety." [c] Design defect strict liability may be imposed even if the seller has "exercised all possible care," and even though the product was faultlessly manufactured. [cc].

Evenflo argues that the District Court abused its discretion when it excluded any evidence that the OMW model 207 complied with FMVSS 213. …

Evenflo urges this Court to adopt the Restatement (Third) of Torts: Products Liability § 4 (1998). Section 4 provides that compliance with an applicable regulation is admissible in connection with liability for defective design. Evenflo contends that the majority of jurisdictions hold that compliance with product safety regulation is relevant and admissible on the question of defectiveness, but is not necessarily controlling. ...

> **FYI**
>
> Section 4(B) of the Restatement (Third) of Torts provides that "[i]n connection with liability for defective design ... a product's compliance with an applicable product safety statute or administrative regulation is properly considered win determining whether the product is defect with respect to the risks sought to be reduced by the statute or regulation, but such compliance does not preclude as a matter of law a finding or product defect."

. . . .

... Montana draws "a bright line" between cases asserting strict liability in tort and those grounded in negligence theory. The court pointed to *Lutz v. National Crane Corp.,* 267 Mont. 368, 385, 884 P.2d 455, 465 (1994). ... The [*Lutz*] Court observed that "[w]hile most courts allow government regulations to be used against manufacturers in negligence cases, the same is not true where the issue is strict liability." [c] The Court emphasized that "[the] issue in products liability cases is not the *conduct* of the 'reasonable person,' but the *condition* of the product." *Lutz,* 267 Mont. at 380, 884 P.2d at 462 (emphasis in original). The Court rejected the manufacturer's attempt "to interject negligence concepts into this design defect case." [c]

This Court again distinguished strict liability from negligence when it rejected the "state of the art" defense in *Sternhagen,* 282 Mont. at 182, 935 P.2d at 1147. The Court determined that the state of the art defense "raises issues of reasonableness and foreseeability–concepts fundamental to negligence law–to determine a manufacturer's liability." [c] The attempt to inject negligence principles into strict liability law would "sever Montana's strict products liability law from the core principles for which it was adopted–maximum protection for consumers against dangerous defects in manufactured products." [c] The Court recognized that the focus in design defect cases shines on "the condition of the product," rather than "the manufacturer's conduct or knowledge." [c] The Court determined that the "strict duty mandated by the theory of strict liability is warranted even though in some situations it may result in liability being imposed upon careful manufacturers." [c]

We likewise reject Evenflo's efforts to inject negligence principles into the strict liability setting. We decline to adopt the Restatement (Third) of Torts: Products Liability, § 4. Section 4 conflicts with the core principles of Montana's strict products liability law. To recognize Section 4 improperly would inject into strict products liability analysis the manufacturer's reasonableness and level of care–

concepts that are fundamental to negligence law, but irrelevant on the issue of design defect liability. [cc] The District Court correctly relied upon Montana precedent that emphasizes the fundamental difference between strict liability and negligence law. [cc]

. . . .

We conclude that the District Court did not act arbitrarily without conscientious judgment when it denied Evenflo's evidence of compliance with FMVSS 213. ... The District Court's evidentiary rulings properly focused the jury's compensatory damages analysis on the condition of the OMW rather than on the conduct of Evenflo. [c]

Did the District Court abuse its discretion by admitting evidence regarding the recall and test failures of the OMW model 206?

Evenflo claims prejudice from the District Court's decision to allow the Malcolms to introduce evidence regarding the testing and the 1995 recall of the OMW model 206. ... Evenflo contends that the OMW model 206 and model 207 are substantially different seats and that the mode of alleged failure that led to the model 206's recall differed from the alleged defect in the model 207. ...

. . . .

Substantial Similarity

Evenflo broadly asserts that "[i]t is generally improper in a products liability case to admit evidence regarding a product model other than the one at issue." ...

. . . .

Montana law generally allows evidence of similar incidents in product liability cases when the dispute involves similar products. ...

. . . .

... The Malcolms ... introduced evidence that the model 206 and 207 were substantially similar with respect to the defects at issue. The evidence included the Malcolms' expert D'Aulerio's testimony that the OMW model 206 and 207 were "identical" with respect to the open belt hook design and the lack of EPS padding. ...

The District Court acted within its discretion when it determined that the model 206 and model 207 were substantially similar with respect to the design defects alleged by the Malcolms. [c] ... The District Court acted within its discretion when it decided that evidence regarding the model 206 constituted relevant evidence in determining Evenflo's liability for compensatory damages. [c]

. . . .

The District Court's order upholding the jury's award of punitive damages to the Malcolms …included a number of findings of fact regarding misconduct by Evenflo. The District Court found that Evenflo had known "from the outset" that it could have used the safer alternative tunnel design for the OMW. …

. . . .

… We agree that evidence of the OMW model 207's compliance with FMVSS 213 was not relevant to the issue of compensatory damages. [c] We cannot agree with the District Court that the FMVSS 213 compliance evidence would not be relevant to the issue of punitive damages. Evenflo may have been able to persuade the jury that its compliance with FMVSS 213 showed that it had not evinced "deliberate indifference" to the welfare of the occupants of the OMW. [c] …

The District Court abused its discretion by prohibiting Evenflo from introducing evidence of the OMW model 207's compliance with FMVSS 213 for the purposes of considering the appropriateness of punitive damages. [c] We vacate the jury's award of $3.7 million in punitive damages. The question of punitive damages must be put again to a jury with Evenflo being allowed to present evidence of the OMW model 207's compliance with FMVSS 213.

. . . .

We affirm in part, reverse in part, and remand for further proceedings.

We Concur: MIKE McGRATH, C.J., W. WILLIAM LEAPHART and JOHN WARNER, JJ.

[Chief Justice McGrath's special concurrence, suggesting the need for bifurcated proceedings on the punitive damages issue, is omitted. Justice Rice's concurring and dissenting opinion is also omitted.]

Justice JAMES C. NELSON, concurring in part and dissenting in part.....

I disagree with the Court's decision to vacate the Malcolms' punitive damages award and remand this case to the District Court for a retrial just so that Evenflo can present evidence of its purported "good faith" compliance with Federal Motor Vehicle Safety Standard 213 (FMVSS 213). Evenflo has failed to demonstrate that the District Court abused its discretion in excluding this evidence, and Evenflo has failed to demonstrate that it was prejudiced as a result of the court's ruling.

. . . .

Given the overwhelming and compelling evidence of fraud and malice presented at trial, it simply cannot be said that evidence of Evenflo's compliance with FMVSS 213 would have affected the jury's verdict on Evenflo's liability for punitive damages. If anything, the jury might well have punished Evenflo more harshly had it known that Evenflo was seeking to excuse its reprehensible conduct by arguing that it had complied with FMVSS 213, even though Evenflo knew all along that FMVSS 213 contained only the "minimum" requirements for safety design and even though Evenflo had been told by the National Highway Traffic Safety Administration that "mere compliance with the minimum requirements of the standard is not enough." ...

. . . .

Evenflo knew from the outset that the OMW seat could have employed a feasible alternative design: one requiring the vehicle's seatbelt to be routed through an enclosed seat-belt "tunnel" (as opposed to an open belt hook). This "bomb proof" design provides a substantial margin of safety and virtually eliminates the risk of a loss of restraint during an accident. ...

. . . .

Evenflo marketed the OMW seat with knowledge of the dangers inherent in its design. ...

. . . .

... Evenflo consciously manufactured and marketed the OMW seat as a product intended to keep infants safe and secure while traveling in a motor vehicle. ...

Evenflo manufactured the OMW seat for eight years with knowledge (much of it recorded on its own videotapes, accident reports, and sled-test records) of the risks and dangers posed by the seat's design. Worse still, Evenflo concealed this information not only from NHTSA and the general public, but also from Jessica Malcolm specifically. ...

In light of all this evidence, the District Court observed in its order reviewing the punitive damages award that Evenflo's misconduct was "neither isolated, nor accidental." In fact, Evenflo's motive was "*exclusively* profit driven." And Evenflo's reprehensible conduct—which extended over an eight-year period, involved the knowing distribution of millions of defectively designed automobile child-restraint seats, and resulted in one of the worst forms of physical harm (the death of a child)—was "among the most egregious to be encountered in a strict liability in tort, design defect case." ...

. . . .

Congress expressly cautioned, however, that "[c]ompliance with a motor vehicle safety standard prescribed under this chapter does not exempt a person from liability at common law." 49 U.S.C. § 30103(e). ...

. . . .

For the foregoing reasons, I would not vacate the Malcolms' punitive damages award. ...

. . . .

Justice PATRICIA O. COTTER joins in the Concurrence and Dissent of Justice JAMES C. NELSON.

————————

Points for Discussion

1. What was the alleged defect of the car seat in the *Malcolm* case? Was the allegation based on a manufacturing defect or a design defect or both?

2. According to the court, is the determination of a design defect a question of law or fact?

3. Note that the plaintiff's cause of action was permitted by statute in Montana rather than by common law.

4. Defendant Evenflo complained that the district court failed to admit evidence of the company's compliance with federal regulations. What was the *Malcolm* court's ruling regarding the relevance of evidence of compliance with federal regulations? The Third Restatement takes the position that while *noncompliance* with an applicable product safety statute or regulation renders a product defective, *compliance* with an applicable safety statute or regulation, while relevant, does not necessarily render a product safe. *See* RESTATEMENT (THIRD) OF TORTS: PRODUCTS LIABILITY § 4 (1997).

5. The Malcolms also sought to admit evidence of recall or testing of the defendant's product. Should evidence that a manufacturer subsequently recalled the product in question be admissible? What if a governmental directive required the product to be recalled and the manufacturer failed to do so? *See* RESTATEMENT (THIRD) OF TORTS: PRODUCTS LIABILITY § 11 (1997).

6. Defendant Evenflo complained that the district court erred in admitting evidence of a product other than the model used during the Malcolm's accident. What was the *Malcolm* court's ruling regarding the relevance of a different model? Should evidence concerning a different product typically be admissible in a products liability case?

Make the Connection

Tort damages are explored in Chapter 8, *supra*.

7. The defendant also complained about the amount of damages imposed. What damages are available to a plaintiff in a products liability action? When, if ever, is it appropriate to award punitive damages in a products liability action?

8. In determining whether a product has a design defect by applying a risk-utility analysis in a strict liability action, the focus is theoretically on the product itself and does not center on the manufacturer's conduct. Focusing on the manufacturer's conduct is more akin to a negligence determination. Do you see why this is so? Consider whether it is possible to evaluate a product's design without evaluating the manufacturer's conduct as well.

———————

3. Warnings Defect

Anderson v. Owens-Corning Fiberglas Corp.

810 P.2d 549 (Ca. 1991)

PANELLI, Associate Justice.

In this case we consider the issue "whether a defendant in a products liability action based upon an alleged failure to warn of a risk of harm may present evidence of the state of the art, i.e., evidence that the particular risk was neither known nor knowable by the application of scientific knowledge available at the time of manufacture and/or distribution." ... As will appear, resolution of this evidentiary issue requires an examination of the failure-to-warn theory as an alternate and independent basis for imposing strict liability and a determination of whether knowledge, actual or constructive, is a component of strict liability on the failure-to-warn theory. It is manifest that, if knowledge or knowability is a component, state-of-the-art evidence is relevant and, subject to the normal rules of evidence, admissible.

We granted review to resolve a conflict between decisions of the Court of Appeal. The Second District held that state-of-the-art evidence is not admissible in this case, a strict liability case based on the manufacturer's failure to warn. The First District, in *Vermeulen v. Superior Court* (1988) 204 Cal.App.3d 1192, 251 Cal.Rptr. 805, reached a contrary result. The court in each case recognized that resolution of the issue was dependent on the nature of the failure-to-warn theory and that a conflict existed among the jurisdictions as to whether knowledge or knowability was a necessary factor in the imposition of liability.

We conclude that *Vermeulen v. Superior Court, supra,* 204 Cal.App.3d 1192, 251 Cal.Rptr. 805, states the correct rule. The California courts, either expressly or by implication, have to date required knowledge, actual or constructive, of potential risk or danger before imposing strict liability for a failure to warn. The state of the art may be relevant to the question of knowability and, for that reason, should be admissible in that context. Exclusion of state-of-the-art evidence, *when the basis of liability is a failure to warn,* would make a manufacturer the virtual insurer of its product's safe use, a result that is not consonant with established principles underlying strict liability.

BACKGROUND

Defendants are or were manufacturers of products containing asbestos. Plaintiff Carl Anderson filed suit in 1984, alleging that he contracted asbestosis and

What's That?

Asbestosis is a breathing disorder caused by inhaling asbestos fibers. The effects of asbestos exposure typically do not show up for at least 20 to 30 years after the initial exposure.

other lung ailments through exposure to asbestos and asbestos products (i.e., preformed blocks, cloth and cloth tape, cement, and floor tiles) while working as an electrician at the Long Beach Naval Shipyard from 1941 to 1976. Plaintiff allegedly encountered asbestos while working in the vicinity of others who were removing and installing insulation products aboard ships. The complaint stated causes of action for negligence, breach of warranty, and strict liability and, inter alia, prayed for punitive damages. Pursuant to stipulation entered at the time of trial, plaintiff proceeded only on his cause of action for strict liability and did not seek punitive damages.

Plaintiff's amended complaint alleged a cause of action in strict liability for the manufacture and distribution of "asbestos, and other products containing said substance, which substance contained design and manufacturing defects" which caused injury to users and consumers, including plaintiff, while being used in a reasonably foreseeable manner. A fourth cause of action, entitled "Strict Liability

Punitive Damages," focused on punitive damages but also included allegations of failure to warn: Plaintiff alleged that defendants marketed their products with specific prior knowledge, from scientific studies and medical data, that there was a high risk of injury and death from exposure to asbestos or asbestos-containing products; that defendants knew consumers and members of the general public had no knowledge of the potentially injurious nature of asbestos; and that defendants failed to warn users of the risk of danger. Defendants' pleadings raised the state-of-the-art defense, i.e., that even those at the vanguard of scientific knowledge at the time the products were sold could not have known that asbestos was dangerous to users in the concentrations associated with defendants' products.

Plaintiff moved before trial to prevent defendants from presenting state-of-the-art evidence. By that time, plaintiff had indicated that he was proceeding, as to defective design, only on the "consumer expectation" prong of the design defect test set out in *Barker v. Lull Engineering Co.* (1978) 20 Cal.3d 413, 426, 143 Cal. Rptr. 225, 573 P.2d 443 (hereafter *Barker*). Accordingly, the argument on plaintiff's motion was directed primarily to the applicability of the state-of-the-art defense to that theory of strict liability. The trial court granted the motion [holding] that state-of-the-art evidence is irrelevant to any theory of strict liability. The defendants then moved to prevent plaintiff from proceeding on the failure-to-warn theory on grounds of waiver[8] and fairness. In response to the court's request for an offer of proof on the alleged failure to warn, plaintiff referred to catalogs and other literature depicting workers without respirators or protective devices and offered to prove that, until the mid-1960's, defendants had given no warnings of the dangers associated with asbestos, that various warnings given by some of the defendants after 1965 were inadequate, and, finally, that defendants removed the products from the market entirely in the early 1970's. Defendants argued in turn that the state of the art, i.e., what was scientifically knowable in the period 1943-1974, was their obvious and only defense to any cause of action for failure to warn, and that, in view of the court's decision to exclude state-of-the-art evidence, fairness dictated that plaintiff be precluded from proceeding on that theory. With no statement of reasons, the trial court granted defendants' motion and, at trial, refused plaintiff's request that the jury be instructed pursuant to BAJI No. 9.00.7.[9] After a four-week trial, the jury returned a verdict for defendants, finding in a special verdict that defendants' products had no design defects.

---

8 Defendants asserted that when plaintiff struck his cause of action for punitive damages, he necessarily struck the allegations of failure to warn.

9 In relevant part, the instruction provides: "A product is defective if the use of the product in a manner that is reasonably foreseeable by the defendant involves a substantial danger that would not be readily recognized by the ordinary user of the product and the manufacturer fails to give adequate warning of such danger.... [¶] A manufacturer has a duty to provide an adequate warning to the consumer of a product of potential risks or side effects which are known, or [in the exercise of reasonable care] should have been known, which may follow the foreseeable use of the product." The use note accompanying the instruction questions the propriety of the bracketed phrase ... and leaves it to the trial judge to determine whether the phrase should be used.

Plaintiff moved for a new trial, asserting that the court erred in precluding proof of liability on a failure-to-warn theory. Plaintiff also claimed that substantial evidence did not support the jury's special finding or the defense verdict. The court granted the motion on both grounds. As to the first ground, the parties reargued the issue of waiver. Plaintiff also urged that knowledge or knowability, and thus state-of-the-art evidence, was irrelevant in strict liability for failure to warn. Plaintiff's main concern, however, was his right to proceed on the theory: "The fact of the matter is, with or without state of the art of the medical literature, I was entitled to put on [failure to warn]." The trial court agreed.

The Court of Appeal, in a two-to-one decision, upheld the order granting a new trial on both grounds. The appellate court added that, "in strict liability asbestos cases, including those prosecuted on a failure to warn theory, state of the art evidence is not admissible since it focuses on the reasonableness of the defendant's conduct, which is irrelevant in strict liability." The dissenting justice urged that the majority had imposed "absolute liability," contrary to the tenets of the strict liability doctrine, and that the manufacturers' right to a fair trial included the right to litigate all relevant issues, including the state of the art of scientific knowledge at the relevant time. We granted review.

The parties repeat the claims made before the Court of Appeal. Defendants contend that, if knowledge or knowability is irrelevant in a failure-to-warn case, then a manufacturer's potential liability is absolute, rendering it the virtual insurer of the product's safe use. Plaintiff, on the other hand, argues that to impose the requirement of knowledge or knowability improperly infuses a negligence standard into strict liability in contravention of the principles set out in our decisions from *Greenman v. Yuba Power Products, Inc.* (1963) 59 Cal.2d 57, 27 Cal.Rptr. 697, 377 P.2d 897 to *Brown v. Superior Court* (1988) 44 Cal.3d 1049, 245 Cal.Rptr. 412, 751 P.2d 470. Plaintiff also urges that, although some courts have assumed that knowledge or knowability is a condition of strict liability for failure to warn, the issue has not been definitively resolved in this court.

DISCUSSION

General Principles of Strict Liability.

Greenman v. Yuba Power Products, Inc., supra,[c], established the doctrine of strict liability in California: "[a] manufacturer is strictly liable in tort when an article he places on the market, knowing that it is to be used without inspection for defects, proves to have a defect that causes injury to a human being." [c] "The purpose of such liability is to insure that the costs of injuries resulting from defective products are borne by the manufacturers that put such products on the market rather than by the injured persons who are powerless to protect themselves." [cc] The strict liability doctrine achieves its goals by "reliev[ing] an injured plaintiff of many of the onerous evidentiary burdens inherent in a negligence cause of action." [cc] In *Vandermark v. Ford Motor Co.* (1964) 61 Cal.2d 256, 37 Cal.Rptr. 896, 391 P.2d 168, we extended the doctrine to distributors of defective products.

Strict liability, however, was never intended to make the manufacturer or distributor of a product its insurer. "From its inception, ... strict liability has never been, and is not now, *absolute* liability.... [U]nder strict liability the manufacturer does not thereby become the insurer of the safety of the product's use. [Citations.]" *(Daly v. General Motors Corp.* (1978) 20 Cal.3d 725, 733, 144 Cal. Rptr. 380, 575 P.2d 1162, emphasis in original.) ....

Strict liability has been invoked for three types of defects-manufacturing defects, design defects, and "warning defects," i.e., inadequate warnings or failures to warn....

We recently reviewed and further refined the principles of strict liability in *Brown v. Superior Court, supra,*[c], where we concluded that a manufacturer of prescription drugs is exempt from strict liability for defects in design and is not strictly liable for injuries caused by scientifically unknowable dangerous propensities in prescription drugs.

Our cases to date have focused principally on the concept of "design defect," concededly one of the most difficult areas for precise definition. [Cc] In California, as elsewhere, when not compelled by statute, the doctrine's acceptance and the terms of its applicability have been determined to a large extent by the fundamental policies which underlie it, as set out in *Greenman v. Yuba Power Products, Inc., supra,* [c], and its progeny. Our task in the case before us is to shape the doctrine insofar as it is applicable to a product whose *only* defect may be that the manufacturer or distributor failed to warn of inherent dangers.[10]

Failure to Warn Theory of Strict Liability.

Though not without some history in this court, the theory of strict liability for failure to warn has been forged principally in the lower courts. ... Drawing on the RESTATEMENT SECOND OF TORTS SECTION 402A, comment j,[11] [we have] held that "a

---

10 In most instances, as here, the plaintiff alleges both design and warning defects. The jury in this case found no design defect. Pursuant to the new trial order, however, that issue may be retried.

11 Comment j of section 402A of the Restatement Second of Torts, provides in pertinent part: "j. *Directions or warning.* In order to prevent the product from being unreasonably dangerous, the seller may be required to give directions or warning, on the container, as to its use.... Where ... the product contains an ingredient to which a substantial number of the population are allergic, and the ingredient is one whose danger is not generally known, or if known is one which the consumer would reasonably not expect to find in the product, the seller is required to give warning against it, if [the seller] has knowledge, or by the application of reasonable, developed human skill and foresight should have knowledge, of the presence of the ingredient and the danger...."

product, although faultlessly made, may nevertheless be deemed 'defective' under the rule and subject the supplier thereof to strict liability if it is unreasonably dangerous to place the product in the hands of a user without a suitable warning and the product is supplied and no warning is given." [c] …

. . . .

Only a small minority of jurisdictions have rejected the proposal of the Restatement Second of Torts that knowledge or knowability is a condition of strict liability. The minority hold that the reason for failing to warn is irrelevant to imposition of strict liability. [Cc]

Only when the danger to be warned against was "unknowable" did the knowledge component of the failure-to-warn theory come into focus. Such cases made it apparent that eliminating the knowledge component had the effect of turning strict liability into absolute liability. The first California case to discuss knowledge or knowability as a condition of strict liability in the failure to warn context was *Oakes v. E.I. Du Pont de Nemours & Co., Inc., supra,* 272 Cal.App.2d 645, 77 Cal.Rptr. 709. Du Pont had distributed weed-killing spray products containing ingredients that proved dangerous to some human beings. Accepting the premise that knowledge or knowability was a factor in the obligation to warn under the Restatement Second of Torts (§ 402A, com. j.), the court stated: "The rationale of the strict liability rule is that the injured person is helpless to protect himself from the *actually defective product*. It is only reasonable therefore that as between the injured user and the one who places the product on the market the latter should bear the loss. The same rationale would apply to the marketing of a product which contains an ingredient which the manufacturer knows or should know 'by the application of reasonable developed human skill and foresight' is dangerous. But, in the view of this court, that is where the reason for the rule ceases and the rule of 'strict' liability itself should stop. To exact an obligation to warn the user of unknown and unknowable allergies, sensitivities and idiosyncrasies would be for the courts to recast the manufacturer in the role of an insurer beyond any reasonable application of the rationale expressed above." (272 Cal. App.2d at pp. 650-651, 77 Cal.Rptr. 709.)

. . . .

In sum, … California is well settled into the majority view that knowledge, actual or constructive, is a requisite for strict liability for failure to warn … .

However, even if we are implying too much from the language in *Brown* [c] the fact remains that we are now squarely faced with the issue of knowledge and knowability in strict liability for failure to warn in other than the drug context. Whatever the ambiguity of *Brown,* we hereby adopt the requirement, as propounded by the Restatement Second of Torts and acknowledged by the lower courts of this state and the majority of jurisdictions, that knowledge or knowability is a component of strict liability for failure to warn.

One of the guiding principles of the strict liability doctrine was to relieve a plaintiff of the evidentiary burdens inherent in a negligence cause of action. [C] Indeed, it was the limitations of negligence theories that prompted the development and expansion of the doctrine. The proponents of the minority rule, including the Court of Appeal in this case, argue that the knowability requirement, and admission of state-of-the-art evidence, improperly infuse negligence concepts into strict liability cases by directing the trier of fact's attention to the conduct of the manufacturer or distributor rather than to the condition of the product. Similar claims have been made as to other aspects of strict liability, sometimes resulting in limitations on the doctrine and sometimes not. ...

Make the Connection

You will recall that at common law contributory negligence was not a defense to strict liability actions, whereas assumption of the risk was. *See* Chapter 13, Strict Liability, *supra*.

However, the claim that a particular component "rings of" or "sounds in" negligence has not precluded its acceptance in the context of strict liability. ... [F]or example, we also held that, while ordinary contributory negligence does not bar recovery in strict liability, the plaintiff's negligence is a defense when it consists of assumption of the risk. [C]; Rest. 2d Torts, supra, § 402A, com. b. ... We had also concluded, in *Daly v. General Motors Corp., supra,* [c] that the principles of comparative negligence apply to actions founded on strict products liability. We recognized that the doctrine of strict liability was a judicial creation and, in reaching our conclusion, we blended or accommodated the "theoretical and semantic distinctions between the twin principles of strict products liability and traditional negligence." [c]

Finally, in *Barker, supra,* 20 Cal.3d 413, 143 Cal.Rptr. 225, 573 P.2d 443, this court rejected the claim that the risk/benefit test was unacceptable because it introduced an element which "rings of negligence" into the determination of design defect. ... The risk/benefit test directs the jury to weigh or balance a number of factors and sets out a list of competing considerations for the jury to evaluate in determining the existence of a design defect. ... Furthermore, we added that an instruction advising the jury to weigh benefits and risks "is not simply the equivalent of an instruction which requires the jury to determine whether the manufacturer was negligent in designing the product [citation]. It is true, of course, that in many cases proof that a product is defective in design may also demonstrate that the manufacturer was negligent in choosing such a design. As we have indicated, however, in a strict liability case, as contrasted with a negligent design action, the jury's focus is properly directed to the condition of the product itself, and not to the reasonableness of the manufacturer's conduct." [c]

As these cases illustrate, the strict liability doctrine has incorporated some well-settled rules from the law of negligence and has survived judicial challenges asserting that such incorporation violates the fundamental principles of the doctrine. It may also be true that the "warning defect" theory is "rooted in negligence" to a greater extent than are the manufacturing- or design-defect theories. The "warning defect" relates to a failure extraneous to the product itself. Thus, while a manufacturing or design defect *can be* evaluated without reference to the conduct of the manufacturer [c], the giving of a warning cannot. The latter necessarily requires the communicating of something to someone. How can one warn of something that is unknowable? If every product that has no warning were defective per se and for that reason subject to strict liability, the mere fact of injury by an unlabelled product would automatically permit recovery. That is not, and has never been, the purpose and goal of the failure-to-warn theory of strict liability. Further, if a warning automatically precluded liability in every case, a manufacturer or distributor could easily escape liability with overly broad, and thus practically useless, warnings. [c]

We therefore reject the contention that every reference to a feature shared with theories of negligence can serve to defeat limitations on the doctrine of strict liability. Furthermore, despite its roots in negligence, failure to warn in strict liability differs markedly from failure to warn in the negligence context. Negligence law in a failure-to-warn case requires a plaintiff to prove that a manufacturer or distributor did not warn of a particular risk for reasons which fell below the acceptable standard of care, i.e., what a reasonably prudent manufacturer would have known and warned about. Strict liability is not concerned with the standard of due care or the reasonableness of a manufacturer's conduct. The rules of strict liability require a plaintiff to prove only that the defendant did not adequately warn of a particular risk that was known or knowable in light of the generally recognized and prevailing best scientific and medical knowledge available at the time of manufacture and distribution.[12] Thus, in strict liability, as opposed to negligence, the reasonableness of the defendant's failure to warn is immaterial.

Stated another way, a reasonably prudent manufacturer might reasonably decide that the risk of harm was such as not to require a warning as, for example, if the manufacturer's own testing showed a result contrary to that of others in the scientific community. Such a manufacturer might escape liability under negli-

---

12 The parties do not dispute the accepted definition of scienter in the failure to warn context, namely, actual or constructive knowledge. As noted in comment j of section 402A of the Restatement Second of Torts (see *ante*, p. 532, fn. 8 of 281 Cal.Rptr., p. 553, fn. 8 of 810 P.2d), constructive knowledge is knowledge which is obtainable "by the application of reasonable, developed human skill and foresight." As we have explained, however, the element of scienter is not necessarily determinative of the duty to warn or of the liability that flows from the failure to warn. Thus, a manufacturer with knowledge, actual or constructive, might have acted reasonably in failing to warn and might escape liability for negligence; the manufacturer's reasonable conduct, however, would not relieve the manufacturer of liability on a strict liability theory.

gence principles. In contrast, under strict liability principles the manufacturer has no such leeway; the manufacturer is liable if it failed to give warning of dangers that were known to the scientific community at the time it manufactured or distributed the product. Whatever may be reasonable from the point of view of the manufacturer, the user of the product must be given the option either to refrain from using the product at all or to use it in such a way as to minimize the degree of danger. *Davis v. Wyeth Laboratories, Inc.* (9th Cir. 1968) 399 F.2d 121, 129-130, described the need to warn in order to provide "true choice": "When, in a particular case, the risk qualitatively (e.g., of death or major disability) as well as quantitatively, on balance with the end sought to be achieved, is such as to call for a true choice judgment, medical or personal, the warning must be given. [Fn. omitted.]" [c] Thus, the fact that a manufacturer acted as a reasonably prudent manufacturer in deciding not to warn, while perhaps absolving the manufacturer of liability under the negligence theory, will not preclude liability under strict liability principles if the trier of fact concludes that, based on the information scientifically available to the manufacturer, the manufacturer's failure to warn rendered the product unsafe to its users.

The foregoing examination of the failure-to-warn theory of strict liability in California compels the conclusion that knowability is relevant to imposition of liability under that theory. Our conclusion not only accords with precedent but also with the considerations of policy that underlie the doctrine of strict liability.

We recognize that an important goal of strict liability is to spread the risks and costs of injury to those most able to bear them.[13] However, it was never the intention of the drafters of the doctrine to make the manufacturer or distributor the insurer of the safety of their products. It was never their intention to impose absolute liability.

CONCLUSION

Therefore, in answer to the question raised in our order granting review, a defendant in a strict products liability action based upon an alleged failure to warn of a risk of harm may present evidence of the state of the art, i.e., evidence that the particular risk was neither known nor knowable by the application of scientific

---

13 The suggestion that losses arising from unknowable risks and hazards should be spread among all users to the product, as are losses from predictable injuries or negligent conduct, is generally regarded as not feasible. Not the least of the problems is insurability. (See Henderson, *Coping with Time Dimension in Products Liability* (1981) 69 Cal.L.Rev. 919, 948-949; Wade, *On the Effect in Product Liability of Knowledge Unavailable Prior to Marketing* (1983) 58 N.Y.U.L.Rev. 734.) Dean Wade stated the dilemma, but provided no solution: "How does one spread the potential loss of an unknowable hazard? How can insurance premiums be figured for this purpose? Indeed, will insurance be available at all? Spreading the loss is essentially a compensation device rather than a tort concept. Providing compensation should not be the sole basis for imposing tort liability, and this seems more emphatically so in the situation where the defendant is no more able to insure against unknown risks than is the plaintiff." (58 N.Y.U.L.Rev. at p. 755.)

knowledge available at the time of manufacture and/or distribution. The judgment of the Court of Appeal is affirmed with directions that the matter be remanded to the trial court for proceedings in accord with our decision herein.

LUCAS, C.J., and KENNARD, ARABIAN and BAXTER, JJ., concur.

BROUSSARD, Associate Justice, concurring.

I concur in the majority opinion, but write separately simply to emphasize the narrow scope of the opinion's holding. As the majority opinion properly recognizes, the issue presented by this case is whether so-called "state-of-the-art" evidence is admissible in a strict products liability action *when the plaintiff contends that a product is defective because it failed to contain an adequate warning of the risk that caused the injury*. I agree with the majority that when the plaintiff proceeds *on an absence-of-warning theory*, the defendant is entitled to present evidence that the risk in question was scientifically unknown at the time the product was manufactured and distributed. A warning, by its nature, presupposes that the risk to be warned against is capable of being known, and a rule which permits the trier of fact to find a product defective simply because it lacked a warning of a scientifically unknown risk would go a long way to making a manufacturer an insurer of any injuries caused by its product.

The majority's holding in this case, however, does not mean that state-of-the-art evidence is admissible in all strict products liability cases. Although the majority finds no need to reach the issue here [c], in my view it is both prudent and appropriate to make it clear that state-of-the-art evidence would not necessarily be relevant when, for example, a plaintiff in a strict products liability action relies solely on the so-called "consumer expectation" prong of the design defect standard. [c]

As Barker explained, the consumer expectation prong is "somewhat analogous to the Uniform Commercial Code's warranty of fitness and merchantability ... [and] reflects the warranty heritage upon which California product liability doctrine in part rests. As we noted in Greenman [c] 'implicit in [a product's] presence on the market ... [is] a representation that it [will] safely do the jobs for which it was built.' [c] *When a product fails to satisfy such ordinary consumer expectations as to safety in its intended or reasonably foreseeable operation, a manufacturer is strictly liable for resulting injuries*." (*Barker v. Lull Engineering Co., supra*, 20 Cal.3d 413, 429-430, 143 Cal.Rptr. 225, 573 P.2d 443, italics added.)

Under the consumer expectation standard, when a product proves to be unexpectedly unsafe when used as intended by the manufacturer, an injured plaintiff is entitled to recover for the resulting injuries, as he or she would recover in a warranty action, without regard to whether the manufacturer knew or could have known at the time of manufacture or distribution of the specific safety problem that was inherent in its product. [cc] Thus, when the plaintiff in a strict products liability action relies solely on a consumer expectation theory, state-of-the-art evidence may not be relevant or admissible.

In this case, however, plaintiff sought to rely, inter alia, on the absence of a warning to prove that the product was defective. Under these circumstances, I agree with the majority that state-of-the-art evidence was admissible.

MOSK, Associate Justice, concurring and dissenting.

In my view the trial court properly granted a new trial and the Court of Appeal, in a thoughtful analysis of the law, correctly affirmed the order. I thus concur in the result.

I must express my apprehension, however, that we are once again retreating from "[t]he pure concepts of products liability so pridefully fashioned and nurtured by this court." (*Daly v. General Motors Corp.* (1978) 20 Cal.3d 725, 757, 144 Cal.Rptr. 380, 575 P.2d 1162 (dis. opn. by Mosk, J.).)

In *Greenman v. Yuba Power Products, Inc.,* [c] this court "heroically took the lead in originating the doctrine of products liability." [c] We did so in the belief that such liability was essential to ensure that the costs of injuries caused by defective products are borne by the manufacturers that put such products on the market and profit therefrom rather than by the victims of those injuries, who are largely powerless to protect themselves. [c] The basic principle underlying products liability actions is that "the trier of fact must focus on the *product*, not on the *manufacturer's conduct*, and that the plaintiff need not prove that the manufacturer acted unreasonably or negligently in order to prevail in such an action." [c]

This focus, however, has become blurred through the years. As the majority observe, this court has incorporated a number of principles of the law of negligence into strict liability doctrine. [cc] Nevertheless, our past acquiescence in this muddled state of affairs does not justify making matters worse. Misconception compounded cannot result in authenticity.

In no area of strict products liability has the impact of principles of negligence become more pronounced than in failure-to-warn cases. From the inception of the cause of action for strict liability on the theory of failure to warn, courts have impliedly or explicitly held that there can be no liability unless the plaintiff establishes that the defendant knew or should have known of the risk. ...

The courts of some of our sister states, too, have permitted the infusion of negligence concepts into failure-to-warn strict liability actions. ...

It may be contended, with arguable merit, that in failure-to-warn cases the line between strict liability and negligence is somewhat thin. Th[is] court [has reached] this conclusion: "the characteristic that distinguishes strict liability from negligence is proof of actual or constructive knowledge of risk: In a negligence action we focus on the defendant's conduct and require plaintiff to show defendant acted unreasonably in light of a known or constructively known risk. In strict liability actions, on the other hand, we focus not on the reasonableness of a defendant's conduct but on the product, and we either ignore the question of a manufacturer's actual or constructive knowledge of risk (as in a 'consumer expectations' design defect case) or we in effect impute to the manufacturer defendant current scientific knowledge of the risk caused by his product (as in a risk/benefit design defect balancing case). [Citations.] But in all warning cases–even if the plaintiff or the court claims to analyze failure to warn or inadequacy of warning in the context of a strict products liability claim–the tests actually applied condition imposition of liability on the defendant's having actually or constructively known of the risk that triggers the warning."

The majority distinguish failure-to-warn strict liability claims from negligence claims on the ground that strict liability is not concerned with a standard of due care or the reasonableness of a manufacturer's conduct. This is generally accurate. However in practice this is often a distinction without a substantial difference. Under either theory, imposition of liability is conditioned on the defendant's actual or constructive knowledge of the risk. Recovery will be allowed only if the defendant has such knowledge yet fails to warn.

The majority rely extensively on *Brown v. Superior Court, supra,* [c]. They obviously fail to comprehend that *Brown* was based on a narrow public policy exception to strict products liability for prescription drugs, and for such drugs alone. We emphatically declared in *Brown* [c] that "there is an important distinction between prescription drugs and other products," and we elaborated on the reason for the distinction: "Public policy favors the development and marketing of beneficial new drugs, even though some risks, perhaps serious ones, might accompany their introduction, because drugs can save lives and reduce pain and suffering." [c] We added that "the broader public interest in the availability of drugs at an affordable price must be considered in deciding the appropriate standard of liability for injuries resulting from their use." [c] The majority stretch the holding and the analysis in *Brown* beyond all recognition when they rely on that case in litigation involving products other than prescription drugs. They make the narrow exception swallow up fundamental law.

We should consider the possibility of holding that failure-to-warn actions lie solely on a negligence theory. "[A]lthough mixing negligence and strict liability concepts is often a game of semantics, the game has more than semantic impact–it breeds confusion and inevitably, bad law." (Henderson & Twerski, *Doctrinal Collapse in Products Liability: The Empty Shell of Failure to Warn, supra,* 65 N.Y.U.L.Rev. at p. 278.) If, however, the majority are not ready to take that step, I would still use this opportunity to enunciate a bright-line rule to apply in failure-to-warn strict liability actions.

Here plaintiff alleged, among other claims, that defendants marketed their products "with specific prior knowledge" of the high risks of injury and death from their use. If plaintiff can establish at the new trial that defendants had *actual knowledge*, then state of the art evidence–or what everyone else was doing at the time–would be irrelevant and the trial court could properly exclude it. Actual knowledge may often be difficult to prove, but it is not impossible with adequately probing discovery. Defendants, of course, can produce evidence that they had no such prior actual knowledge.

On the other hand, if plaintiff is only able to show, by medical and scientific data or other means, that defendants *should have known* of the risks inherent in their products, then contrary medical and scientific data and state of the art evidence would be admissible if offered by defendants.

Thus I would draw a clear distinction in failure-to-warn cases between evidence that the defendants had actual knowledge of the dangers and evidence that the defendants should have known of the dangers.

With the foregoing rule in mind, the parties should proceed to the new trial ordered by the trial court and upheld by the Court of Appeal. Thus I would affirm the judgment of the Court of Appeal.

────────

RESTATEMENT (THIRD) OF TORTS: PRODUCTS LIABILITY § 2(c) (1997)

A product is defective because of inadequate instructions or warnings when the foreseeable risks of harm posed by the product could have been reduced or avoided by the provision of reasonable instructions or warnings ... and the omission of the instructions or warnings renders the product not reasonably safe.

Points for Discussion

1. What was the plaintiff's theory of recovery in *Anderson*?

2. What is state-of-the-art evidence? How is state-of-the-art evidence relevant to a strict liability warnings defect claim? Is state-of-the-art evidence relevant to a manufacturing defect claim? To a claim alleging design defect?

3. The *Anderson* majority concludes that knowledge or knowability is a component of a strict liability failure to warn products action. How does it distinguish between the knowledge or knowability component relevant to a negligence analysis and the knowledge or knowability component relevant to a strict liability analysis?

4. Explain the majority's statement that "failure to warn in strict liability differs markedly from failure to warn in the negligence context." What is the distinction that the court seeks to draw? Are you persuaded that there is a "marked" distinction?

5. Should manufacturers have a continuing duty to warn?

6. What is the consumer expectation design defect standard?

7. Why does Justice Mosk write separately?

8. Should an adequate warning ever be able to negate a product that is defectively designed?

Make the Connection

Consider whether warnings defects law has lead to instructions or warnings that border on the ridiculous. The following are just some examples found on actual labels from consumer goods:

- On a package of peanuts: "Warning: contains nuts"
- On a chainsaw: "Do not attempt to stop chain with your hands"
- On a shower cap: "Fits one head"
- On a sleep aid medication: "Warning: may cause drowsiness"
- On a bar of soap: "Directions: Use like regular soap"
- On a beer label: "Liquor ruins country, family & life"

9. Note the *Anderson* court's discussion regarding whether a product is defective as a distinct inquiry separate from evaluating the manufacturer's conduct. Before launching into its analysis, the majority begins by quoting *Barker*: "'[i]n a strict liability case ... the jury's focus is properly directed to the condition of the product itself, and not to the reasonableness of the manufacturer's conduct.'" Are you persuaded that it is possible to divorce the qualities and characteristics of the product itself from the conduct of the manufacturer in developing the product, as the majority suggests?

10. What type of defect – manufacturing, design, or inadequate instructions or warnings – might it be easier for a plaintiff to prove? Why?

11. Should a defendant be liable for failing to warn of an open and obvious danger?

Hypo 15-4

Pool Co. manufacturers above-ground swimming pools that are four feet deep. Each pool has a clearly embossed warning on the outside of the pool in large letters stating "DANGER!!—DO NOT DIVE!! SERIOUS INJURIES MAY RESULT." In disregard of the warnings, Jack, age 21, dives head first into a Pool Co. pool, suffering serious injuries. At trial, all experts agree that when Jack dove into the pool his hands hit the pool's slippery vinyl pool bottom, causing them to slide apart, allowing his head to strike the bottom of the pool. All experts also testify that the vinyl pool liner that Pool Co. utilized was the best and safest liner available and that no alternative, less slippery liner was feasible. Jack wants to sue XYZ Co. for his injuries based on a defectively designed product. Discuss.

See RESTATEMENT (THIRD) OF TORTS: PRODUCTS LIABILITY § 2 cmt. *d*, illus. 4 (1997).

Points for Discussion

1. Almost every case alleging a manufacturing defect also gives rise to a claim for design defect as well. Can you explain why that might be the case?

2. Strict liability for design defects or failure to warn does not apply to prescription drugs. *See* RESTATEMENT (THIRD) OF TORTS: PRODUCTS LIABILITY § 6(c) (1997) (defining prescriptive drug as defectively designed when foreseeable risks of harm posed by the drug are sufficiently great in relation to foreseeable therapeutic benefits such that reasonable health care provider would not prescribe it for any class of patients). What is the public policy supporting such an exception to strict liability for prescriptive drugs?

3. **Proof**—In proving and defending against a products claim, the parties may introduce and rely on direct evidence as well as circumstantial evidence. However, understanding and appreciating the theories and applicable law can prove substantially easier than proving one's case in court. For example, how does one prove that a product contained a manufacturing defect if the product was destroyed by the accident that is the basis of the lawsuit? Alternatively, how might one prove a defective design or a defective warning?

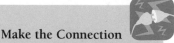

Make the Connection

Cf. Chapter 4, *supra*, for exploration of direct and circumstantial evidence in negligence actions.

Freidman v. General Motors Corp.

331 N.E.2d 702 (1975)

PAUL W. BROWN, Justice.

The single issue presented by this appeal is whether the evidence introduced by the plaintiffs was of sufficient quality to overcome the defendant's motion for a directed verdict. The Court of Appeals, having thoroughly examined the entire record, concluded that reasonable minds could differ upon the evidence presented, and reversed the judgment directing a verdict for the defendant. We affirm.

To sustain their allegation against General Motors, the plaintiffs were required to prove that the Oldsmobile Toronado, manufactured and sold by the defendant, was defective; that the defect existed at the time the product left the factory; and that the defect was the direct and proximate cause of the accident and injuries. [Cc] A defect may be proven by circumstantial evidence, where a preponderance of that evidence establishes that the accident was caused by a defect and not other possibilities, although not all other possibilities need be eliminated. [Cc]

In our judgment, the evidence presented by the plaintiffs established a prima facie case of defect for which defendant General Motors would be liable.

From the testimony of Pelunis and Morton Friedman, the jury could have found that the linkages and adjustments existing at the time of the accident were the original, factory set, adjustments, and that the defective condition, if the evidence established defect, was a defect created by the manufacturer and not by some third person after delivery.

Based upon the testimony of Morton Friedman, his wife, and his son, the jury might have concluded that the Toronado had always been started in Park, thus affording no opportunity for discovery of the alleged defect. Further, because the gear shift indicator and transmission had always operated properly, the jury might have inferred that when the gear shift indicator registered in Drive after the accident, it accurately reflected the position of the transmission.

From the testimony of eye witnesses to, and participants in, the accident, the jury might have concluded that, when Friedman started the Toronado at the Sohio station, it accelerated immediately upon ignition; that the automobile's transmission was therefore in a forward position; and that the transmission jammed, upon impact, in that same forward position.

From the testimony of English and Isenhath, the jury could have found that, subsequent to the accident, the Toronado started with the gear shift indicator in Drive position. Based upon English's testimony, the jury might have concluded further than, upon ignition, the front wheels accelerated to a speed of 30 miles per hour in five seconds.

Finally, the record clearly established that the Toronado could not have started unless the contacts in the neutral start switch were in Neutral or Park position. Even though the transmission gears and gear shift indicator were in Drive, if the contacts in the neutral start switch were in Neutral or Park, the ignition key would start the automobile, and the front wheels would immediately rotate. In light of other facts presented, this possibility approaches probability.

Because the trial court granted the defendant's motion for a directed verdict, we must construe the evidence most strongly in favor of the plaintiffs, so as to determine if reasonable minds could differ. From the evidence heretofore summarized, we believe the jury might reasonably have concluded that the defendant was guilty of manufacturing a defective automobile, which directly and proximately caused the accident. For that reason, the judgment of the Court of Appeals is affirmed.

Judgment affirmed.

C. WILLIAM O'NEILL, C. J., and HERBERT, CORRIGAN, CELEBREZZE and WILLIAM B. BROWN, JJ., concur.

STERN, Justice (dissenting).

The essential questions in this case are whether plaintiffs introduced sufficient credible evidence from which it could be inferred that a defect existed in the alignment of the transmission and the neutral safety switch, and whether that defect existed at the time the automobile left the hands of the defendant. The plaintiffs' evidence, simplified, is basically that the 17-month-old car, which had previously exhibited no malfunction, behaved in an unusual manner which contributed to an accident; that no servicing had apparently been done on the transmission or the ignition before the accident; and that after the accident the car behaved in an unusual manner, in that it could be started, and perhaps run, when the transmission was jammed and the pointer indicated that it was in Drive. No direct physical evidence was presented that any part was defective, and, in fact, there was evidence that the safety switch itself was properly aligned and that the transmission worked properly as indicated. The plaintiffs' case is that from this evidence one can infer a defect in the car, in that the car could be started in Drive, and that this defect existed at the time of manufacture.

In products liability cases, proof that a defect existed is often difficult and complex. Frequently the product in dispute will have been destroyed, beyond any possibility of analysis, or be so complex that a plaintiff would have a greater difficulty in determining the presence of a defect than would the manufacturer. In most cases, proof of the defect must necessarily be by circumstantial evidence and inference. No general rule can adequately apply to the wide range of such cases, each involving a different mixture of fact and inference, but fundamental to any such case is that some defect must be proved. As Prosser states, in Strict Liability to the Consumer in California, 18 Hastings L.J. 9, 52-54:

> 'The mere fact of an accident, as where an automobile goes into the ditch, does not make out a case that the product was defective; nor does the fact that it is found in a defective condition after the event, when it appears equally likely that it was caused by the accident itself. The addition of other facts, tending to show that the defect existed before the accident, may make out a case, and so may expert testimony. So likewise may proof that other similar products made by the defendant met with similar misfortunes, or the elimination of other causes by satisfactory evidence. In addition, there are some accidents, as where a beverage bottle explodes or even breaks while it is being handled narmally, as to which there is human experience that they do not ordinarily occur without a defect. As in cases of res ipsa loquitur, the experience will give rise to the inference, and it may be sufficient to sustain the plaintiff's burden of proof.'

Although plaintiff's evidence may be sufficient to permit an inference that something was wrong with the car, that alone is not sufficient to establish a defect, except perhaps in cases, analogous to res ipsa loquitur, in which ordinary human experience tells us that the event could not happen without a defect. The instant case is not such a case, for driver error, failure of some part, accidental or unwitting damage to the car, and other possibilities do provide other explanations. [c] In this case, the fact that something went wrong is not sufficient to support an inference that a defect caused the accident.

Make the Connection

The doctrine of *res ipsa loquitur* was explored in the negligence materials covered in Chapter 4, *supra*.

The particular defect that plaintiff alleges is that the indicator and the transmission gear linkages were both malaligned in a similar fashion, relative to the neutral start switch, so that the car as manufactured could start in Drive rather than, as intended, only in Park and Neutral. There are various ways in which that particular fact could be proved, by means of several types of evidence. [Cc]

(1) Plaintiff might introduce evidence by an expert based upon an examination of the product in question following the happening of the damaging event. Expert evidence would be direct evidence of an identifiable defect. In the instant case, two expert witnesses testified, and neither was able to point out an identifiable defect.[14] Both testified that the car could be started in an indicated Drive position, but neither identified a cause for that based upon their examination. The only explanation, offered by one of the experts, was that the pointer was probably damaged.

(2) There may simply be evidence of a damaging event occurring in the course of or following use of a product, whether by the testimony of the user or otherwise. This may be sufficient in the case where, as a matter of common knowledge, a defect is the probable cause. As already indicated, the instant case is not one involving such common knowledge.

(3) A plaintiff may produce both evidence of a damaging event occurring in the course of or following the use of a product and expert evidence that the most likely probable cause was attributable to a defect in the product being used at the time.

In the instant case, the only expert who was qualified to state such an opinion, the company expert called as a witness by the plaintiff, was not asked to state whether a defect was the probable cause, and in fact made clear in his testimony that he believed it probable that there was no defect and that the apparent starting of the car in Drive was probably caused by damage from the accident to the indicator. He stated only that it was possible for various components to be malaligned as plaintiffs' theory required.

---

14 One expert was the company witness called by the plaintiffs. The second was a metallurgist called by plaintiffs, who was not, however, qualified as an expert in automotive mechanics.

(4) In addition to evidence of an accident and the probable cause of such accident, evidence could be introduced to negate the existence of 'probable causes' not attributable to the maker.

This type of evidence was not introduced in the instant case, except with respect to the issue of maintenance on the car in the 17 months after delivery.

(5) In some cases, the physical evidence of the actual condition of the product after the accident would be such that a layman could infer that it was defective.

No such physical evidence was introduced in the instant case.

All of these forms of proof relate to whether, after something has gone wrong, that event can properly be attributed to a defect. The facts of the individual case will be crucial in determining whether such an influence is permissible. In *State Auto Mutual Ins. Co. v. Chrysler Corp. (1973),* 36 Ohio St.2d 151, 304 N.E.2d 891, for example, a new one-half ton pickup truck had been used for 77 days; the brakes failed because of a loss of brake fluid from a hold, with fibers blown outward, in a brake line which was original equipment and had not been tampered with; and the actual brake hose was unavailable, due to no fault of the plaintiff. The issue in that case was specifically whether the hole was caused by a defect or by an accidental impact of some kind, and the circumstances of that case were held sufficient to raise a jury issue. As the court stated [c]:

> 'Obviously, the most exact method of ascertaining a defect in the hose would be to subject the hose to scientific tests, under pressures applicable in an ordinary braking situation. In the absence of any direct evidence that the hose introduced by appellee Chrysler Corporation is the hose in question, this cannot be done.'

In the instant case, the most exact method of determining whether there was in fact a malalignment of the transmission parts would have been actual examination of those parts, which were under the control of plaintiffs for several months after the accident. The examination actually made was incomplete. No identifiable defect was found; nor was the testimony of the mechanics who repaired the automobile offered. Failing such examination, even by a nonexpert, plaintiffs could have introduced expert testimony that the probable cause of the accident was a defect. This was not done, and the expert testimony was only to the effect that a malalignment was possible, but, according to one expert, was not probable. The sum of the evidence is thus only that something unusual happened in the car, and that a possible explanation of that happening is a defect. I believe plaintiffs could have and should have done more in order to make a case for the jury, for the essential link of actual proof, between the accident and any possible explanation, is missing.

The same difficulty arises with regard to the issue of whether the claimed defect existed at the time the car left the hands of the defendant. Plaintiffs introduced evidence that the transmission had not been serviced or tampered with, and that the family's method of starting the car could have permitted a defect to remain undiscovered. But this, again, is only evidence of the possibility of a defect. Here, the car was 17 months old, there was no expert testimony that the claimed defect was one which would probably have existed at the time the car was manufactured, and common experience does not permit any such inference. In tracing the defect in the product into the hands of the defendant, '* * * (t)here is first of all the question of lapse of time and long continued use. This in itself will never prevent recovery where there is satisfactory proof of an original defect; but where there is no such definite evidence, and it is only a matter of inference from the fact that something broke or gave way, the continued use usually prevents the inference that more probably than not the product was defective when it was sold. The seller certainly does not undertake to provide a product that will never wear out.' Prosser, supra, at 54. In the instant case, plaintiffs' negative evidence indicates the possibility that the claimed defect could have existed at the time of manufacture; but this possibility remains only a theory, for there is a lack of any positive evidence which would overcome the inference arising from the long-continued use of the car.

At the center of plaintiffs' case, which is made up of evidence of an unusual event and a possible explanation thereof, there should be some positive proof that the possible malalignment was something more than a theory. Such proof was not presented and remains a matter of speculation. For that reason, I agree with the trial judge that plaintiffs failed to submit sufficient evidence from which it could be inferred that a defect existed in the Friedman car at the time if left the hands of the defendant.

———————

Points for Discussion

1. What was the theory of recovery in *Friedman*?

2. What was the alleged defect?

3. Describe the evidence that the plaintiffs introduced to prove that the product was defective.

4. What was the majority's ruling in *Friedman*? Describe the dissent's position. Are you most persuaded by the majority or dissent? Explain.

5. What policy considerations support the majority's and the dissent's respective positions?

6. Compare and contrast the *Friedman* majority's ruling on the proof required with the doctrine of *res ipsa loquitur* studied in the negligence materials. Is the ruling in this case analogous to application of *res ipsa loquitur*?

7. In *Friedman*, the allegedly defective product was destroyed by the accident. Keep in mind that a products liability plaintiff is only permitted to recover in tort for personal injury and damage to property other than damage to the product itself. *See* RESTATEMENT (THIRD) OF TORTS: PRODUCTS LIABILITY § 21 cmt. d (1997). Recovery for the product itself is allowable pursuant to the law governing commercial transactions rather than tort law.

———————

RESTATEMENT (THIRD) OF TORTS § 3 (1997)
Circumstantial Evidence Supporting Inference of Product Defect

It may be inferred that the harm sustained by the plaintiff was caused by a product defect existing at the time of sale or distribution, without proof of a specific defect, when the incident that harmed the plaintiff:

(a) was of a kind that ordinarily occurs as a result of product defect; and

(b) was not, in the particular case, solely the result of causes other than product defect existing at the time of sale or distribution.

C. Defenses

1. Plaintiff's Conduct

Daly v. General Motors Corp.

575 P.2d 1162 (Ca. 1978)

RICHARDSON, Justice.

The most important of several problems which we consider is whether the principles of comparative negligence expressed by us in *Li v. Yellow Cab Co. (1975)* 13 Cal.3d 804, 119 Cal.Rptr. 858, 532 P.2d 1226, apply to actions founded on strict products liability. We will conclude that they do. We also inquire whether evidence of "compensating" safety devices installed in a motor vehicle by its manufacturer is admissible to offset alleged design deficiencies, and whether, under the particular facts herein, evidence of a driver's claimed intoxication or of his asserted failure to use his vehicle's safety equipment may be considered. While agreeing that evidence of compensating design characteristics is admissible, we will further determine that under the circumstances herein prejudicial error requiring reversal occurred upon the admission of evidence of the decedent's alleged intoxication and failure to use safety devices in his vehicle.

THE FACTS AND THE TRIAL

Although there were no eyewitnesses, the parties agree, generally, on the reconstruction of the accident in question. In the early hours of October 31, 1970, decedent Kirk Daly, a 36-year-old attorney, was driving his Opel southbound on the Harbor Freeway in Los Angeles. The vehicle, while travelling at a speed of 50-70 miles per hour, collided with and damaged 50 feet of metal divider fence. After the initial impact between the left side of the vehicle and the fence the Opel spun counterclockwise, the driver's door was thrown open, and Daly was forcibly ejected from the car and sustained fatal head injuries. It was equally undisputed that had the deceased remained in the Opel his injuries, in all probability, would have been relatively minor.

Plaintiffs, who are decedent's widow and three surviving minor children, sued General Motors Corporation, Boulevard Buick, Underwriter's Auto Leasing, and Alco Leasing Company, the successive links in the Opel's manufacturing and distribution chain. The sole theory of plaintiffs' complaint was strict liability for damages allegedly caused by a defective product, namely, an improperly designed door latch claimed to have been activated by the impact. It was further asserted that, but for the faulty latch, decedent would have been restrained in the vehicle and, although perhaps injured, would not have been killed. Thus, the case involves a so-called "second collision" in which the "defect" did not contribute to the original impact, but only to the "enhancement" of injury.

At trial the jury heard conflicting expert versions as to the functioning of the latch mechanism during the accident. Plaintiffs' principal witness testified that the Opel's door was caused to open when the latch button on the exterior handle of the driver's door was forcibly depressed by some protruding portion of the divider fence. It was his opinion that the exposed push button on the door constituted a design "defect" which caused injuries greatly in excess of those which Daly would otherwise have sustained. Plaintiffs also introduced evidence that other vehicular door latch designs used in production models of the same and prior years afforded substantially greater protection. Defendants' experts countered with their opinions that the force of the impact was sufficiently strong that it would have caused the door to open resulting in Daly's death even if the Opel had been equipped with door latches of the alternative designs suggested by plaintiffs.

Over plaintiffs' objections, defendants were permitted to introduce evidence indicating that: (1) the Opel was equipped with a seat belt-shoulder harness system, and a door lock, either of which if used, it was contended, would have prevented Daly's ejection from the vehicle; (2) Daly used neither the harness system nor the lock; (3) the 1970 Opel owner's manual contained warnings that seat belts should be worn and doors locked when the car was in motion for "accident security"; and (4) Daly was intoxicated at the time of collision, which evidence the jury was advised was admitted for the limited purpose of determining whether decedent had used the vehicle's safety equipment. After relatively brief deliberations the jury returned a verdict favoring all defendants, and plaintiffs appeal from the ensuing adverse judgment.

STRICT PRODUCTS LIABILITY AND COMPARATIVE FAULT

In response to plaintiffs' assertion that the "intoxication-nonuse" evidence was improperly admitted, defendants contend that the deceased's own conduct contributed to his death. Because plaintiffs' case rests upon strict products liability based on improper design of the door latch and because defendants assert a failure in decedent's conduct, namely, his alleged intoxication and nonuse of safety equipment, without which the accident and ensuing death would not have occurred, there is thereby posed the overriding issue in the case, should comparative principles apply in strict products liability actions?

It may be useful to refer briefly to certain highlights in the historical development of the two principles strict and comparative liability. Tort law has evolved from a legal obligation initially imposed without "fault," to recovery which, generally, was based on blameworthiness in a moral sense. For reasons of social policy and because of the unusual nature of defendants' acts, liability without fault continued to be prescribed in a certain restricted area, for example, upon keepers of wild animals, or those who handled explosives or other dangerous substances, or who engaged in ultrahazardous activities. Simultaneously, and more particularly, those who were injured in the use of personal property were permitted recovery on a contract theory if they were the purchasers of the chattel or were in privity. Subsequently, liability was imposed in negligence upon the manufacturer of personalty in favor of the general consumer. ... Evolving social policies designed to protect the ultimate consumer soon prompted the extension of legal responsibility beyond negligence to express or implied warranty. Thus, in the area of food and drink a form of strict liability predicated upon warranty found wide acceptance. Warranty actions, however, contained their own inherent limitations requiring a precedent notice to the vendor of a breach of the warranty, and absolving him from loss if he had issued an adequate disclaimer.

General dissatisfaction continued with the conceptual limitations which traditional tort and contract doctrines placed upon the consumers and users of manufactured products, this at a time when mass production of an almost infinite variety of goods and products was responding to a myriad of ever-changing societal demands stimulated by wide-spread commercial advertising. From an historic combination of economic and sociological forces was born the doctrine of strict liability in tort.

We, ourselves, were perhaps the first court to give the new principle judicial sanction. In *Greenman v. Yuba Power Products, Inc. (1963),* 59 Cal.2d 57, 27 Cal. Rptr. 697, 377 P.2d 897, confronted with injury to an ultimate consumer caused by a defective power tool, we fastened strict liability on a manufacturer who placed on the market a defective product even though both privity and notice of breach of warranty were lacking. We rejected both contract and warranty theories, express or implied, as the basis for liability. Strict liability, we said, did not rest on a consensual foundation but, rather, on one created by law. The liability was created judicially because of the economic and social need for the protection of consumers in an increasingly complex and mechanized society, and because of the limitations in the negligence and warranty remedies. Our avowed purpose was "to insure that the costs of injuries resulting from defective products are borne by the manufacturer that put such products on the market rather than by the injured persons who are powerless to protect themselves." [c] Subsequently, the Greenman principle was incorporated in section 402A of the Restatement Second of Torts, and adopted by a majority of American jurisdictions. (Prosser, supra, at pp. 657-658.)

From its inception, however, strict liability has never been, and is not now, absolute liability. As has been repeatedly expressed, under strict liability the manufacturer does not thereby become the insurer of the safety of the product's user. [Cc] On the contrary, the plaintiff's injury must have been caused by a "defect" in the product. Thus the manufacturer is not deemed responsible when injury results from an unforeseeable use of its product. [Cc] Furthermore, we have recognized that though most forms of contributory negligence do not constitute a defense to a strict products liability action, plaintiff's negligence is a complete defense when it comprises assumption of risk. [Cc] As will thus be seen, the concept of strict products liability was created and shaped judicially. In its evolution, the doctrinal encumbrances of contract and warranty, and the traditional elements of negligence, were stripped from the remedy, and a new tort emerged which extended liability for defective product design and manufacture beyond negligence but short of absolute liability.

In Li v. Yellow Cab Co., supra, [c], we introduced the other doctrine with which we are concerned, comparative negligence. We examined the history of contributory negligence, the massive criticism directed at it because its presence in the slightest degree completely barred plaintiff's recovery, and the increasing defection from the doctrine. We then weighed the two principal arguments against its removal from California law, namely, that such a sharp change in direction required legislative action, and that there existed a cluster of asserted practical obstacles relating to multiple parties, the apportionment burdens on a jury and the uncertain effect on the defenses of last clear chance, assumption of risk, and wilful misconduct. Concluding that none of the obstacles was insurmountable, we announced in Li the adoption of a "pure" form of comparative negligence which, when present, reduced but did not prevent plaintiff's recovery. [C] We held that the defense of assumption of risk, insofar as it is no more than a variant of contributory negligence, was merged into the assessment of liability in proportion to fault. [C] Within the broad guidelines therein announced, we left to trial courts discretion in the particular implementation of the new doctrine. [C]

We stand now at the point of confluence of these two conceptual streams, having been greatly assisted by the thoughtful analysis of the parties and the valuable assistance of numerous amici curiae. We are by no means the first to consider the interaction of these two developing principles. As with the litigants before us, responsible and respected authorities have reached opposing conclusions stressing in various degrees the different considerations which we now examine.

Those counseling against the recognition of comparative fault principles in strict products liability cases vigorously stress, perhaps equally, not only the conceptual, but also the semantic difficulties incident to such a course. The task of merging the two concepts is said to be impossible, that "apples and oranges" cannot be compared, that "oil and water" do not mix, and that strict liability, which is not founded on negligence or fault, is inhospitable to comparative principles. The syllogism runs, contributory negligence was only a defense to negligence, comparative negligence only affects contributory negligence, therefore comparative negligence cannot be a defense to strict liability. [C] While fully recognizing the theoretical and semantic distinctions between the twin principles of strict products liability and traditional negligence, we think they can be blended or accommodated.

The inherent difficulty in the "apples and oranges" argument is its insistence on fixed and precise definitional treatment of legal concepts. In the evolving areas of both products liability and tort defenses, however, there has developed much conceptual overlapping and interweaving in order to attain substantial justice. The concept of strict liability itself, as we have noted, arose from dissatisfaction with the wooden formalisms of traditional tort and contract principles in order to protect the consumer of manufactured goods. Similarly, increasing social awareness of its harsh "all or nothing" consequences led us in Li to moderate the impact of traditional contributory negligence in order to accomplish a fairer and more balanced result. We acknowledged an intermixing of defenses of contributory negligence and assumption of risk and formally effected a type of merger. "As for assumption of risk, we have recognized in this state that this defense overlaps that of contributory negligence to some extent . . . ." (*Li, supra, [c]*) In Li, we further reaffirmed our observation in *Grey v. Fibreboard Paper Products Co. (1966),* 65 Cal.2d 240, 245, 53 Cal.Rptr. 545, 418 P.2d 153. " '(T)hat in one kind of situation, to wit, where a plaintiff unreasonably undertakes to encounter a specific known risk imposed by a defendant's negligence, plaintiff's conduct, although he may encounter that risk in a prudent manner, is in reality a form of contributory negligence. . . .' We think it clear that the adoption of a system of comparative negligence should entail the merger of the defense of assumption of risk into the general scheme of assessment of liability in proportion to fault in those particular cases in which the form of assumption of risk involved is no more than a variant of contributory negligence." [c]

Furthermore, the "apples and oranges" argument may be conceptually suspect. It has been suggested that the term "contributory negligence," one of the vital building blocks upon which much of the argument is based, may indeed itself be a misnomer since it lacks the first element of the classical negligence formula, namely, a duty of care owing to another. A highly respected torts authority, Dean William Prosser, has noted this fact by observing, "It is perhaps unfortunate that contributory negligence is called negligence at all. 'Contributory fault' would be a more descriptive term. Negligence as it is commonly understood is conduct which creates an undue risk of harm to others. Contributory negligence is conduct which involves an undue risk of harm to the actor himself. Negligence requires a duty, an obligation of conduct to another person. Contributory negligence involves no duty, unless we are to be so ingenious as to say that the plaintiff is under an obligation to protect the defendant against liability for the consequences of his own negligence." (Prosser, Law of Torts, *supra,* § 65, p. 418.)

We think, accordingly, the conclusion may fairly be drawn that the terms "comparative negligence," "contributory negligence" and "assumption of risk" do not, standing alone, lend themselves to the exact measurements of a micrometer-caliper, or to such precise definition as to divert us from otherwise strong and consistent countervailing policy considerations. Fixed semantic consistency at this point is less important than the attainment of a just and equitable result. The interweaving of concept and terminology in this area suggests a judicial posture that is flexible rather than doctrinaire.

We pause at this point to observe that where, as here, a consumer or user sues the manufacturer or designer alone, technically, neither fault nor conduct is really compared functionally. The conduct of one party in combination with the product of another, or perhaps the placing of a defective article in the stream of projected and anticipated use, may produce the ultimate injury. In such a case, as in the situation before us, we think the term "equitable apportionment or allocation of loss" may be more descriptive than "comparative fault."

Given all of the foregoing, we are, in the wake of Li, disinclined to resolve the important issue before us by the simple expedient of matching linguistic labels which have evolved either for convenience or by custom. Rather, we consider it more useful to examine the foundational reasons underlying the creation of strict products liability in California to ascertain whether the purposes of the doctrine would be defeated or diluted by adoption of comparative principles. We imposed strict liability against the manufacturer and in favor of the user or consumer in order to relieve injured consumers "from problems of proof inherent in pursuing negligence . . . and warranty . . . remedies, . . ." [cc] As we have noted, we sought to place the burden of loss on manufacturers rather than ". . . injured persons who are powerless to protect themselves . . . ." [cc]

The foregoing goals, we think, will not be frustrated by the adoption of comparative principles. Plaintiffs will continue to be relieved of proving that the manufacturer or distributor was negligent in the production, design, or dissemination of the article in question. Defendant's liability for injuries caused by a defective product remains strict. The principle of protecting the defenseless is likewise preserved, for plaintiff's recovery will be reduced only to the extent that his own lack of reasonable care contributed to his injury. The cost of compensating the victim of a defective product, albeit proportionately reduced, remains on defendant manufacturer, and will, through him, be "spread among society." However, we do not permit plaintiff's own conduct relative to the product to escape unexamined, and as to that share of plaintiff's damages which flows from his own fault we discern no reason of policy why it should, following Li, be borne by others. Such a result would directly contravene the principle announced in Li, that loss should be assessed equitably in proportion to fault.

We conclude, accordingly, that the expressed purposes which persuaded us in the first instance to adopt strict liability in California would not be thwarted were we to apply comparative principles. What would be forfeit is a degree of semantic symmetry. However, in this evolving area of tort law in which new remedies are judicially created, and old defenses judicially merged, impelled by strong considerations of equity and fairness we seek a larger synthesis. If a more just result follows from the expansion of comparative principles, we have no hesitancy in seeking it, mindful always that the fundamental and underlying purpose of Li was to promote the equitable allocation of loss among all parties legally responsible in proportion to their fault.

A second objection to the application of comparative principles in strict products liability cases is that a manufacturer's incentive to produce safe products will thereby be reduced or removed. While we fully recognize this concern we think, for several reasons, that the problem is more shadow than substance. First, of course, the manufacturer cannot avoid its continuing liability for a defective product even when the plaintiff's own conduct has contributed to his injury. The manufacturer's liability, and therefore its incentive to avoid and correct product defects, remains; its exposure will be lessened only to the extent that the trier finds that the victim's conduct contributed to his injury. Second, as a practical matter a manufacturer, in a particular case, cannot assume that the user of a defective product upon whom an injury is visited will be blameworthy. Doubtless, many users are free of fault, and a defect is at least as likely as not to be exposed by an entirely innocent plaintiff who will obtain full recovery. In such cases the manufacturer's incentive toward safety both in design and production is wholly unaffected. Finally, we must observe that under the present law, which recognizes assumption of risk as a complete defense to products liability, the curious and cynical message is that it profits the manufacturer to make his product so defective that in the event of injury he can argue that the user had to be aware of its patent defects. To that extent the incentives are inverted. We conclude, accordingly, that no substantial or significant impairment of the safety incentives of defendants will occur by the adoption of comparative principles.

In passing, we note one important and felicitous result if we apply comparative principles to strict products liability. This arises from the fact that under present law when plaintiff sues in negligence his own contributory negligence, however denominated, may diminish but cannot wholly defeat his recovery. When he sues in strict products liability, however, his "assumption of risk" completely bars his recovery. Under Li, as we have noted, "assumption of risk" is merged into comparative principles. [c] The consequence is that after Li in a negligence action, plaintiff's conduct which amounts to "negligent" assumption of risk no longer defeats plaintiff's recovery. Identical conduct, however, in a strict liability case acts as a complete bar under rules heretofore applicable. Thus, strict products liability, which was developed to free injured consumers from the constraints imposed by traditional negligence and warranty theories, places a consumer plaintiff in a worse position than would be the case were his claim founded on simple negligence. This, in turn, rewards adroit pleading and selection of theories. The application of comparative principles to strict liability obviates this bizarre anomaly by treating alike the defenses to both negligence and strict products liability actions. In each instance the defense, if established, will reduce but not bar plaintiff's claim.

A third objection to the merger of strict liability and comparative fault focuses on the claim that, as a practical matter, triers of fact, particularly jurors, cannot assess, measure, or compare plaintiff's negligence with defendant's strict liability. We are unpersuaded by the argument and are convinced that jurors are able to undertake a fair apportionment of liability.

. . . .

We find equally unpersuasive a final objection that the merger of the two principles somehow will abolish or adversely affect the liability of such intermediate entities in the chain of distribution as retailers. [cc] We foresee no such consequence. Regardless of the identity of a particular defendant or of his position in the commercial chain the basis for his liability remains that he has marketed or distributed a defective product. If, as we believe, jurors are capable of assessing fully and fairly the legal responsibility of a manufacturer on a strict liability basis, no reason appears why they cannot do likewise with respect to subsequent distributors and vendors of the product.

We note that the majority of our sister states which have addressed the problem, either by statute or judicial decree, have extended comparative principles to strict products liability.

Our research discloses that of the more than 30 states which have adopted some form of comparative negligence, three (including California) have done so judicially. The two other states, Alaska (*Butaud v. Suburban Marine & Sport. Goods, Inc., supra,* 555 P.2d 42, 46) and Florida (*West v. Caterpillar Tractor Company, Inc., supra,* 336 So.2d 80, 89-90) have likewise, judicially, extended comparative principles to strict liability actions. At least five states have adopted comparative fault statutes which are not limited in their language to negligence actions: Arkansas

(Ark.Rev.Stat. §§ 27-1763-65 (1975)); Maine (M.S.A., tit. 14, § 156 (1965)); Mississippi (3 Miss.Code Ann. § 11-7-15 (1917)); New York (CPLR, art. 14A, s 1411 (1975)); and Rhode Island (2A R.I.Gen.Laws, § 9-20-4 (1971)). The New York statute expressly applies to strict liability actions. (See CPLR, supra, art. 14A, s 1411, Practice Commentaries, C 1411:1.) The Mississippi statute has been judicially construed as extending to suits founded on strict products liability. (*Edwards v. Sears, Roebuck and Company* (5th Cir. 1975) 512 F.2d 276, 290.) On the other hand one state, Connecticut, has statutorily prohibited the use of comparative fault as a defense in strict liability actions. (Pub.L. 77-335, eff. July 1, 1977.)

Of the three decisions which have declined to apply comparative negligence to strict liability, two have noted their reliance on state comparative negligence statutes which are expressly confined to "negligence" actions. (*Melia v. Ford Motor Co.* (8th Cir. 1976) 534 F.2d 795, 802 (Nebraska "slight-gross" comparative negligence statute); *Kirkland v. General Motors Corporation* (Okla.1974) 521 P.2d 1353, 1367-1368 (noting the limiting statutory language but holding that driving while intoxicated was product misuse barring recovery); see also *Kinard v. The Coats Company, Inc.* (Colo.App.1976) 553 P.2d 835, 837.) At least three jurisdictions have applied comparative negligence statutes to strict liability actions, despite language arguably limiting the statute application to negligence. (*Dippel v. Sciano, supra,* 37 Wis.2d 443, 155 N.W.2d 55, 64; *Sun Val. Airlines, Inc. v. Avco-Lycoming Corp.* (D.Idaho 1976) 411 F.Supp. 598, 602-603; *Hagenbuch v. Snap-On Tools Corp.* (D.N.H.1972) 339 F.Supp. 676, 681-683.) Finally, one court has judicially extended a "pure" form of comparative fault to the traditional strict liability defense of "product misuse," despite the existence of a statutory scheme of "modified" comparative negligence. (*General Motors Corp. v. Hopkins* (Tex.1977) 548 S.W.2d 344, 351-352.)

Moreover, we are further encouraged in our decision herein by noting that the apparent majority of scholarly commentators has urged adoption of the rule which we announce herein. ...

. . . .

Having examined the principal objections and finding them not insurmountable, and persuaded by logic, justice, and fundamental fairness, we conclude that a system of comparative fault should be and it is hereby extended to actions founded on strict products liability. In such cases the separate defense of "assumption of risk," to the extent that it is a form of contributory negligence, is abolished. While, as we have suggested, on the particular facts before us, the term "equitable apportionment of loss" is more accurately descriptive of the process, nonetheless, the term "comparative fault" has gained such wide acceptance by courts and in the literature that we adopt its use herein.

...We reiterate that our reason for extending a full system of comparative fault to strict products liability is because it is fair to do so. The law consistently seeks to elevate justice and equity above the exact contours of a mathematical equation. We are convinced that in merging the two principles what may be lost in symmetry is more than gained in fundamental fairness.

. . . .

RETROACTIVITY

It remains for us to decide the extent to which comparative principles are to be applied to strict liability actions other than those hereafter filed. We conclude that, for reasons of public policy and the reasonable expectations of the parties to this action and litigants generally, the principles herein expressed shall apply to all cases in which trial has not begun before the date this opinion becomes final in this court. ...

. . . .

We further conclude that, under the particular circumstances, comparative principles cannot be applied retroactively to the instant case in order to justify admission of the intoxication and "nonuse" evidence here challenged. The issue of comparative fault was raised for the first time on appeal, and was never placed in issue by any party at trial herein. No jury instructions on the issue were requested or given. The jury therefore had no basis for evaluating the evidence under correct principles of comparative fault. In the event of retrial, however, the principles herein announced will, of course, apply.

We turn to an explanation of the reasons which prompt us to reverse the judgment of the trial court, and then examine, for the benefit of court and counsel one of the remaining contentions of the parties.

THE SAFETY EQUIPMENT AND INTOXICATION EVIDENCE

We must determine whether admission of evidence of decedent's failure to use available safety devices and of his intoxication constituted prejudicial error under rules heretofore applicable to strict liability cases. We conclude that it did.

While initially evidence bearing on decedent's intoxication was excluded, other evidence pertaining to the decedent's alleged failure to employ seat belts and door locks was admitted, apparently on the ground that nonuse of safety devices bore on the issues of proximate cause and mitigation of damages. Plaintiffs contended that evidence of Daly's intoxication, or of his failure to use available safety devices, was wholly inadmissible since contributory negligence was not a defense to an action founded in strict liability for a defective product. [c] The trial court ultimately admitted the intoxication evidence, ruling that such evidence related to decedent's failure to use the Opel's safety devices, which failure, the court reasoned, would bar recovery on the theory of product misuse "aside from any question of contributory negligence." (In fairness to the very able trial judge, it must be noted that the trial herein preceded rendition of our opinions in both Li and Horn.)

As we [have previously] observed ..., to accept a "nonuse" of safety equipment as a complete defense to a products liability action would constitute but a thinly disguised subversion of the rule that contributory negligence does not prevent recovery. Horn expressly rejected arguments that such "nonuse" could defeat recovery on theories of "assumption of risk," "product misuse," "proximate cause," or "mitigation of damages." [c]

Substantial time was spent on the nonuse and intoxication issues, reasonably suggesting to the jury their central importance to the defense case. There can be little doubt that the evidence of Daly's intoxication was inflammatory. The only restrictions placed on the jury's consideration of the intoxication evidence was that it bore on the "nonuse" of safety devices in general. No limitation was placed on the conclusions which the jury could draw either from a finding of "nonuse" itself, or as to the effect on its deliberations of a finding of "nonuse." In the absence of any such restrictions, we think the jury could well have concluded that decedent's negligent failure, induced by intoxication, to use the belts and locks constituted negligent conduct which completely barred recovery for his death. We do not think it reasonable to conclude that plaintiffs waived their objection by failing to request limiting instructions.

[O]ur review of the record convinces us that, notwithstanding that plaintiffs' case was founded on strict products liability, evidence of decedent's failure to use available seat belts and door locks, and of his intoxication at the time of the fatal collision, may have been improperly regarded by the jury as authorizing a defense verdict. ... Reversal is therefore required. [cc]

DEFECT COMPONENT OR PRODUCT AS A WHOLE?

We examine for the benefit of court and counsel, in the event of retrial, a single remaining contention of plaintiffs.

Plaintiffs challenge a jury instruction which directed that "(i)n determining whether or not the vehicle was defective you should consider all of the equipment on the vehicle including any features intended for the safety of the driver." They urge that only the precise malfunctioning component itself, and alone, may be considered in determining whether injury was caused by a defectively designed product. We disagree, concluding that the issue of defective design is to be determined with respect to the product as a whole, and that the trial court's instruction was correct.

The jury could properly determine whether the Opel's overall design, including safety features provided in the vehicle, made it "crashworthy," thus rendering the vehicle nondefective. Product designs do not evolve in a vacuum, but must reflect the realities of the market place, kitchen, highway, and shop. Similarly, a product's components are not developed in isolation, but as part of an integrated and interrelated whole. Recognizing that finished products must incorporate and balance safety, utility, competitive merit, and practicality under a multitude of intended and foreseeable uses, courts have struggled to evolve realistic tests for defective design which give weight to this necessary balancing. Thus, a number of California cases have recognized the need to "weigh" competing considerations in an overall product design, in order to determine whether the design was "defective." ...

The danger of piecemeal consideration of isolated components has been expressly recognized. [Cc] Specifically, it has been observed that a design rendered safe in one situation may become more dangerous in others. [C] However phrased, these decisions emphasize the need to consider the product as an integrated whole.

We find that plaintiffs' other contentions lack merit.

CONCLUSION

It is readily apparent that the foregoing broad expressions of principle do not establish the duties of the jury with that fixed precision which appeals to minds trained in law and logic. Nonetheless, rather than attempt to anticipate every variant and nuance of circumstance and party that may invoke comparative principles in a strict products liability context, we deem it wiser to await a case-by-case evolution in the application of the broad principles herein expressed.

By extending and tailoring the comparative principles announced in Li, supra, to the doctrine of strict products liability, we believe that we move closer to the goal of the equitable allocation of legal responsibility for personal injuries. ...

The judgment is reversed.

TOBRINER, CLARK and MANUEL, JJ., concur.

[Justice Clark's concurrence, joined by Justice Jefferson, is omitted.]

MOSK, Justice, dissenting.

I dissent.

This will be remembered as the dark day when this court, which heroically took the lead in originating the doctrine of products liability (*Greenman v. Yuba Power Products, Inc.* (1963) 59 Cal.2d 57, 27 Cal.Rptr. 697, 377 P.2d 897) and steadfastly resisted efforts to inject concepts of negligence into the newly designed tort [c] inexplicably turned 180 degrees and beat a hasty retreat almost back to square one. The pure concept of products liability so pridefully fashioned and nurtured by this court for the past decade and a half is reduced to a shambles.

The majority inject a foreign object the tort of negligence into the tort of products liability by the simple expedient of calling negligence something else: on some pages their opinion speaks of "comparative fault," on others reference is to "comparative principles," and elsewhere the term "equitable apportionment" is employed, although this is clearly not a proceeding in equity. But a rose is a rose and negligence is negligence; thus the majority find that despite semantic camouflage they must rely on *Li v. Yellow Cab Co.* (1975) 13 Cal.3d 804, 119 Cal.Rptr. 858, 532 P.2d 1226, even though Li is purely and simply a negligence case which merely rejects contributory negligence and substitutes therefor comparative negligence.

. . . .

This court has emphasized over and over again that strict products liability is an independent tort species wholly distinct from contract warranties (*Greenman v. Yuba Power Products, Inc., supra,* 59 Cal.2d at p. 63, 27 Cal.Rptr. 697, 377 P.2d 897)....

The bench and bar have abided by this elementary rule. They have learned to avoid injecting negligence whether of the defendant or the plaintiff into a products liability case. And they have understood the reason behind the distinction between negligence of any party and products liability. It was expressed over three decades ago by Justice Traynor in his concurring opinion in *Escola v. Coca Cola Bottling Co.* (1944) 24 Cal.2d 453, 467, 150 P.2d 436, 443: "As handicrafts have been replaced by mass production with its great markets and transportation facilities, the close relationship between the producer and consumer of a product has been altered. Manufacturing processes, frequently valuable secrets, are ordinarily either inaccessible to or beyond the ken of the general public. The consumer no longer has means or skill enough to investigate for himself the soundness of a product, even when it is not contained in a sealed package, and his erstwhile vigilance has been lulled by the steady efforts of manufacturers to build up confidence by advertising and marketing devices such as trade-marks. (Citations.) Consumers no longer approach products warily but accept them on faith, relying on the reputation of the manufacturer or the trade mark. . . . The manufacturer's obligation to the consumer must keep pace with the changing relationship between them; . . ." And again in Greenman, Justice Traynor declared the "purpose of such liability is to insure that the costs of injuries resulting from defective products are borne by the manufacturers that put such products on the market rather than by the injured persons who are powerless to protect themselves." [c]

In *Price v. Shell Oil Co. (1970)* 2 Cal.3d 245, 258, 85 Cal.Rptr. 178, 187, 466 P.2d 722, 731, this court warned that "it would do violence to the doctrine of strict liability and thwart its basic purpose, if we were to interpret (an indemnity) clause as transferring the liability for a defective article from the party putting the article in the stream of commerce, to the user or consumer of the article who is within the class the doctrine was designed to protect."

Transferring the liability, or part of the liability, from the party responsible for putting the article in the stream of commerce to the consumer is precisely what the majority propose to do. They do this by employing a euphemism: the victim's recovery is to be "proportionately reduced." The result, however delicately described, is to dilute the defect of the article by elevating the conduct of the wounded consumer to an issue of equal significance. We can be as certain as tomorrow's daylight that every defendant charged with marketing a defective product will hereafter assert that the injured plaintiff did something, anything, that conceivably could be deemed contributorily negligent: he drove the vehicle with a defective steering mechanism 56 miles an hour instead of 54; or he should have discovered a latent defect hidden in the machinery; or perhaps he should not have succumbed to the salesman's persuasion and purchased the defective object in the first instance. I need no crystal ball to foresee that the pleading of affirmative defenses alleging contributory negligence or the currently approved substitute terminology will now become boilerplate.

The majority see no problem in assessing the liability of intermediate entities in the commercial chain. I do. Consider, for example, the not uncommon situation in which, pursuant to a faulty design, a manufacturer produces widgets without negligence and precisely as designed. He turns the widgets over to a distributor who sells them to a wholesaler who in turn consigns them to a retailer, none of whom commits any active act of negligence. After a defective widget finally reaches and injures the consumer, it would be consummate supererogation for a trier of fact to attempt to measure some consumer negligence against either the faulty design of the product or the responsibility of the congeries of nonnegligent persons who placed the defective product in the stream of commerce, or their responsibility vis-a-vis each other. We have retained joint and several liability in comparative negligence [c] partly because of that very problem. In any event if the consumer used the product as intended or as foreseeable [c] it is inconsequential that he committed some extraneous act of negligence, since the injury occurs whether or not there was an act of omission or commission by the user; it results from the commercial exploitation of a defective product.

The defective product is comparable to a time bomb ready to explode; it maims its victims indiscriminately, the righteous and the evil, the careful and the careless. Thus when a faulty design or otherwise defective product is involved, the litigation should not be diverted to consideration of the negligence of the plaintiff. The liability issues are simple: was the product or its design faulty, did the defendant inject the defective product into the stream of commerce, and did the defect cause the injury? The conduct of the ultimate consumer-victim who used the product in the contemplated or foreseeable manner is wholly irrelevant to those issues.

The majority devote considerable effort to rationalizing what has been described as a mixture of apples and oranges. Their point might be persuasive if there were some authority recognizing a defense of contributory products liability, for which they are now substituting comparative products liability. However, all our research to discover such apples and oranges has been fruitless. The conclusion is inescapable that the majority, in avoiding approval of comparative negligence in name as a defense to products liability, are thereby originating a new defense that can only be described as comparative products liability. We may now anticipate similar defenses in the vast number of other tort actions. Can comparative libel, comparative slander of title, comparative wrongful litigation, comparative nuisance, comparative fraud, be far behind? By whatever name, negligence, heretofore just one subtopic in the elaborate spectrum of torts which require six volumes and appendices of the Restatement Second of Torts to cover now seems destined to envelop the entire tort field.

. . . .

[T]he majority create an impossible dilemma for trial courts. If comparative negligence is to be applied, how can the trier of fact rationally weigh the conduct of the plaintiff against the defective product? I know of no other instance in American jurisprudence in which the antagonists are the conduct of a human being versus an inanimate object.

. . . .

The majority note one "felicitous result" of adopting comparative negligence to products liability: the merger of assumption of risk which they term a "bizarre anomaly" into their innovative defense. I find that result neither felicitous nor tenable. In *Barker v. Lull Engineering Co., supra,* 20 Cal.3d at page 429, 143 Cal.

Rptr. 225, 573 P.2d 443, we defined a defective product as one which failed to perform safely when used in an intended or foreseeable manner. If a consumer elects to use a product patently defective when other alternatives are available, or to use a product in a manner clearly not intended or foreseeable, he assumes the risks inherent in his improper utilization and should not be heard to complain about the condition of the object. One who employs a power saw to trim his fingernails and thereafter finds the number of his fingers reduced should not prevail to any extent whatever against the manufacturer even if the saw had a defective blade. I would retain assumption of risk as a total defense to products liability, as it always has been.

The majority deny their opinion diminishes the therapeutic effect of products liability upon producers of defective products. It seems self-evident that procedures which evaluate the injured consumer's conduct in each instance, and thus eliminate or reduce the award against the producer or distributor of a defective product, are not designed as an effective incentive to maximum responsibility to consumers. The converse is more accurate: the motivation to avoid polluting the stream of commerce with defective products increases in direct relation to the size of potential damage awards.

In sum, I am convinced that since the negligence of the defendant is irrelevant in products liability cases, the negligence call it contributory or comparative of the plaintiff is also irrelevant. The majority, by considering the comparative negligence of a plaintiff in an action in which defendant's negligence is not an issue, apply an untenable double standard. Their error is grievously unsettling to the law of torts. More significantly, this decision seriously erodes the pattern of the law which up to now reflected a healthy concern for consumers victimized by defective products placed on the market in this mechanized age through the dynamics of mass production, national and international distribution, and psychologically subtle marketing.

. . . .

I would affirm the judgment.

Rehearing denied; BIRD, C. J., and MOSK, J., dissenting.

———————————

Points for Discussion

1. What was the plaintiff's alleged negligence in *Daly*? What is the court's ruling regarding the question whether the plaintiff's conduct may operate as a defense in this products liability action?

2. Note that the majority of the *Daly* court adopts equitable apportionment of fault (or comparative fault) as a defense to a strict liability products claim. Do you agree that comparative fault principles should apply in a strict liability products claim to reduce or eliminate a defendant's liability?

3. What type of defect was alleged in *Daly*? Should equitable apportionment of fault reduce or eliminate a defendant manufacturer's liability for other (or all) types of product defects?

4. In applying the majority's equitable apportionment of fault defense, explain whether all types of plaintiff's fault should be treated the same. Should there be recognition of plaintiff's fault that is so egregious as to amount to a superceding event, effectively shielding the manufacturer of a proven defective product from liability? *See, e.g., Ford Motor Co. v. Matthews,* 291 So.2d 169 (Miss. 1974).

5. What is the "bizarre anomaly" of the law to which the majority refers that is eliminated by adoption of apportionment of fault principles to strict liability products claims?

6. Should a plaintiff's misuse of the product be a defense (or partial defense) to plaintiff's products liability action? What if the misuse was foreseeable?

7. Nonmanufacturing commercial sellers in the chain of distribution – such as wholesalers and retailers – may be subject to liability for defective products that cause injury as well, regardless of whether those nonmanufacturers were in a position to prevent the defects from occurring. *See* RESTATEMENT (THIRD) OF TORTS § 1 cmt e (1997). Some jurisdictions have enacted legislation protecting nonmanufacturers in the chain of distribution from liability for injuries caused by a defective product. *See* RESTATEMENT (THIRD) OF TORTS § 1 cmt. e (1997). What are the justifications in favor of imposing products liability on those other than principal manufacturers? What are the arguments against? With which position regarding nonmanufacturer liability do you most agree?

8. How should the rules regarding joint and several liability apply in the nonmanufacturer products liability context?

9. In his article *Strict Products Liability and Comparative Negligence: The Collision of Fault and No-Fault,* 14 SAN DIEGO L. REV. 337 (1977), Professor Harvey R. Levine explains:

"[C]omparative fault cannot logically and consistently be applied to the strict liability cause of action. Prejudice to a plaintiff would result if the injury was required to determine the plaintiff's fault and to *compare it to the defendant's* conduct in a cause of action not requiring that a jury consider the existence, nature, or extent of defendant's culpability. How can comparative fault exist in a cause of action which proceeds irrespective of fault? What can a jury compare the plaintiff's fault with if the defendant's fault is not at issue? If the jury has not determined the nature, extent, or degree of the defendant's fault but has merely concluded the product is defective, how can it reduce the plaintiff's damages in *proportion* to respective fault?

The application of 'comparative' fault to the strict products liability cause of action would prejudice a plaintiff because of the unusual and impossible demand placed upon a jury. In essence we would ask a jury that if they find the defendant's product was defective, irrespective of fault, they should reduce the plaintiff's damage by considering the plaintiff's culpability *in proportion* to the defendant's non-culpability. This requirement may be a feat which is beyond the prowess of an American jury."

Do you agree or disagree with Professor Levine? Explain.

————————————

Hypo 15-5

"The ABC Chair Co. manufacturers and sells oak chairs. The back of the chairs have five horizontal wooden bars shaped to the contour of the human back. John, a college student, climbed up to the top bar of an ABC chair to reach the top shelf of a bookcase. The chair tipped and John fell, suffering serious harm. John brings an action against ABC, alleging that the chair should either have had the stability to support him when standing on the top bar or have had a differently designed back so that he could not use the bars for that purpose." RESTATEMENT (THIRD) OF TORTS: PRODUCTS LIABILITY § 2 cmt p. illus. 20 (1997). Discuss whether (1) the chair is defective and (2) whether ABC Chair Co. has a viable defense based on John's conduct.

Hypo 15-6

Toilet Seat Co. ("TSC") produces and manufactures toilet seats for businesses and homes. TSC has been in the toilet seat business exclusively for nearly 60 years. Its motto is "We do toilet seats and nothing else! This means we have a solid ground upon which to stand."

Although nowadays most toilet seat manufacturers use a type of thermoplastic called polystyrene, TSC is proud to use a unique material that, unlike polystyrene, requires an assembly line method of production. The first step in TSC's manufacturing process requires a TSC employee to mix wood fiber pulp with melamine (a compound used in making plastics) and pack the wood pulp/melamine mixture tightly and evenly into a toilet seat mold. After the wood and melamine have fused together and hardened, the next worker places the new seat on a conveyor rack. The seat is moved along the conveyor to the finish area. At the finish area, another worker coats each seat with glass fiber reinforced polyester, a necessary part of the process which ensures that the seat can withstand the weight of a 250-pound person. The seats then move along the assembly line to be drilled, sanded, and painted with two coats of primer and enamel paint to produce a smooth, hard, plastic-like surface.

Ernest, an employee of TSC, is assigned to work in the finish area. Sadly, recently he and his wife have had marital problems, and as a result, Ernest has been distracted at work. One day, Ernest was particularly distracted and failed to coat several seats with the glass fiber reinforced polyester before sending them along the assembly line to be drilled, sanded, and painted.

One of the uncoated toilet seats ends up in Susie Sickley's home. Susie, the single-mother of three young boys, has been ill for several weeks, and Susie's sister Mary has brought dinner by for Susie and her family. When Mary arrives at Susie's home, she finds the place a mess. Having to use the restroom very badly, Mary enters the only bathroom in the house and finds the toilet seat in a disgusting condition. Seeing only a couple of squares of toilet paper, no cleaning supplies in sight, and in dire need of relieving herself, Mary decides to stand on the toilet seat in order to empty her bladder. Soon after she manages to perch herself atop the TSC toilet seat, the seat breaks and Mary falls, breaking her hip and an arm. It is later determined that the toilet seat was not coated with the glass fiber reinforced polyester.

Mary (all 5'4", 125 pounds of her) visits you, a local attorney, to ascertain whether she might be able to sue TSC in tort. This jurisdiction has adopted the following statute:

Contributory fault does not bar recovery in an action by any person to recover damages for death or injury to person or property unless the fault was as great as the combined fault of all other persons who contribute to the injury, but any damages allowed must be diminished in proportion to the amount of contributing fault attributable to the person recovering.

Please advise Mary whether she might be able to bring a viable tort action against TSC.

2. Preemption and Other Government Actions

Medtronic, Inc. v. Lohr

518 U.S. 470 (1996)

Justice STEVENS announced the judgment of the Court and delivered the opinion of the Court with respect to Parts I, II, III, V, and VII, and an opinion with respect to Parts IV and VI, in which Justice KENNEDY, Justice SOUTER, and Justice GINSBURG join.

Congress enacted the Medical Device Amendments of 1976, in the words of the statute's preamble, "to provide for the safety and effectiveness of medical devices intended for human use." 90 Stat. 539. The question presented is whether that statute pre-empts a state common-law negligence action against the manufacturer of an allegedly defective medical device. Specifically, we must consider whether Lora Lohr, who was injured when her pacemaker failed, may rely on Florida common law to recover damages from Medtronic, Inc., the manufacturer of the device.

I

Throughout our history the several States have exercised their police powers to protect the health and safety of their citizens. Because these are "primarily, and historically, ... matter[s] of local concern," [cc], the "States traditionally have had great latitude under their police powers to legislate as to the protection of the lives, limbs, health, comfort, and quiet of all persons," *Metropolitan Life Ins. Co. v. Massachusetts,* 471 U.S. 724, 756, 105 S.Ct. 2380, 2398, 85 L.Ed.2d 728 (1985) (internal quotation marks omitted).

Despite the prominence of the States in matters of public health and safety, in recent decades the Federal Government has played an increasingly significant role in the protection of the health of our people. Congress' first significant enactment in the field of public health was the Food and Drug Act of 1906, a broad prohibition against the manufacture or shipment in interstate commerce of any adulterated or misbranded food or drug. [cc] Partly in response to an ongoing concern about radio and newspaper advertising making false therapeutic claims for both "quack machines" and legitimate devices such as surgical instruments and orthopedic shoes, in 1938 Congress broadened the coverage of the 1906 Act to include misbranded or adulterated medical devices and cosmetics. [cc]

While the FDCA provided for premarket approval of new drugs, [c] it did not authorize any control over the introduction of new medical devices, [c]. As technologies advanced and medicine relied to an increasing degree on a vast array of medical equipment "[f]rom bedpans to brainscans," including kidney dialysis units, artificial heart valves, and heart pacemakers, policymakers and the public became concerned about the increasingly severe injuries that resulted from the failure of such devices. [cc]

In 1970, for example, the Dalkon Shield, an intrauterine contraceptive device, was introduced to the American public and throughout the world. Touted as a safe and effective contraceptive, the Dalkon Shield resulted in a disturbingly high percentage of inadvertent pregnancies, serious infections, and even, in a few cases, death. [cc] In the early 1970's, several other devices, including catheters, artificial heart valves, defibrillators, and pacemakers (including pacemakers manufactured by petitioner Medtronic), attracted the attention of consumers, the Food and Drug Administration (FDA), and Congress as possible health risks. [c]

In response to the mounting consumer and regulatory concern, Congress enacted the statute at issue here: the Medical Device Amendments of 1976 (MDA or Act), 90 Stat. 539. The Act classifies medical devices in three categories based on the risk that they pose to the public. Devices that present no unreasonable risk of illness or injury are designated Class I and are subject only to minimal regulation by "general controls." 21 U.S.C. § 360c(a)(1)(A). Devices that are potentially more harmful are designated Class II; although they may be marketed without advance approval, manufacturers of such devices must comply with federal performance regulations known as "special controls." § 360c(a)(1)(B). Finally, devices that either "presen[t] a potential unreasonable risk of illness or injury," or which are "purported or represented to be for a use in supporting or sustaining human life or for a use which is of substantial importance in preventing impairment of human health," are designated Class III. § 360c(a)(1)(C). Pacemakers are Class III devices. [c]

Before a new Class III device may be introduced to the market, the manufacturer must provide the FDA with a "reasonable assurance" that the device is both safe and effective. [c] Despite its relatively innocuous phrasing, the process of establishing this "reasonable assurance," which is known as the "premarket approval," or "PMA" process, is a rigorous one. Manufacturers must submit detailed information regarding the safety and efficacy of their devices, which the FDA then reviews, spending an average of 1,200 hours on each submission. [cc]

Not all, nor even most, Class III devices on the market today have received premarket approval because of two important exceptions to the PMA requirement. First, Congress realized that existing medical devices could not be withdrawn from the market while the FDA completed its PMA analysis for those devices. The statute therefore includes a "grandfathering" provision which allows pre-1976 devices to remain on the market without FDA approval until such time as the FDA initiates and completes the requisite PMA. [c] Second, to prevent manufacturers of grandfathered devices from monopolizing the market while new devices clear the PMA hurdle, and to ensure that improvements to existing devices can be rapidly introduced into the market, the Act also permits devices that are "substantially equivalent" to pre-existing devices to avoid the PMA process. [c]

Although "substantially equivalent" Class III devices may be marketed without the rigorous PMA review, such new devices, as well as all new Class I and Class II devices, are subject to the requirements of § 360(k). That section imposes a limited form of review on every manufacturer intending to market a new device by requiring it to submit a "premarket notification" to the FDA (the process is also known as a " § 510(k) process," after the number of the section in the original Act). If the FDA concludes on the basis of the § 510(k) notification that the device is "substantially equivalent" to a pre-existing device, it can be marketed without further regulatory analysis (at least until the FDA initiates the PMA process for the underlying pre-1976 device to which the new device is "substantially equivalent"). The § 510(k) notification process is by no means comparable to the PMA process; in contrast to the 1,200 hours necessary to complete a PMA review, the § 510(k) review is completed in an average of only 20 hours. [c] As one commentator noted: "The attraction of substantial equivalence to manufacturers is clear. [Section] 510(k) notification requires little information, rarely elicits a negative response from the FDA, and gets processed very quickly." Adler, The 1976 Medical Device Amendments: A Step in the Right Direction Needs Another Step in the Right Direction, 43 Food Drug Cosm. L.J. 511, 516 (1988); [c].

Congress anticipated that the FDA would complete the PMA process for Class III devices relatively swiftly. But because of the substantial investment of time and energy necessary for the resolution of each PMA application, the ever-increasing numbers of medical devices, and internal administrative and resource difficulties, the FDA simply could not keep up with the rigorous PMA process. As a result, the § 510(k) premarket notification process became the means by which most new medical devices-including Class III devices-were approved for the market. …

II

As have so many other medical device manufacturers, petitioner Medtronic took advantage of § 510(k)'s expedited process in October 1982, when it notified the FDA that it intended to market its Model 4011 pacemaker lead as a device that was "substantially equivalent" to devices already on the market. (The lead is the portion of a pacemaker that transmits the heartbeat-steadying electrical signal from the "pulse generator" to the heart itself.) On November 30, 1982, the FDA found that the model was "substantially equivalent to devices introduced into interstate commerce" prior to the effective date of the Act, and advised Medtronic that it could therefore market its device subject only to the general control provisions of the Act …. The agency emphasized, however, that this determination should not be construed as an endorsement of the pacemaker lead's safety. *Ibid.*

Cross-petitioner Lora Lohr is dependent on pacemaker technology for the proper functioning of her heart. In 1987 she was implanted with a Medtronic pacemaker equipped with one of the company's Model 4011 pacemaker leads. On December 30, 1990, the pacemaker failed, allegedly resulting in a "complete heart block" that required emergency surgery. According to her physician, a defect in the lead was the likely cause of the failure.

In 1993 Lohr and her husband filed this action in a Florida state court. Their complaint contained both a negligence count and a strict-liability count. The negligence count alleged a breach of Medtronic's "duty to use reasonable care in the design, manufacture, assembly, and sale of the subject pacemaker" in several respects, including the use of defective materials in the lead and a failure to warn or properly instruct the plaintiff or her physicians of the tendency of the pacemaker to fail, despite knowledge of other earlier failures. [c]The strict-liability count alleged that the device was in a defective condition and unreasonably dangerous to foreseeable users at the time of its sale. [c] (A third count alleging breach of warranty was dismissed for failure to state a claim under Florida law.)

Medtronic removed the case to Federal District Court, where it filed a motion for summary judgment arguing that both the negligence and strict-liability claims were pre-empted by 21 U.S.C. § 360k(a). That section, which is at the core of the dispute between the parties in this suit, provides:

"§ 360k. State and local requirements respecting devices

"(a) General rule

"Except as provided in subsection (b) of this section, no State or political subdivision of a State may establish or continue in effect with respect to a device intended for human use any requirement-

"(1) which is different from, or in addition to, any requirement applicable under this chapter to the device, and

"(2) which relates to the safety or effectiveness of the device or to any other matter included in a requirement applicable to the device under this chapter."[15]

To carry out this grant of authority, the FDA has issued regulations under the statute which both construe the scope of *§ 360k(a)* and address the instances in which the FDA will grant exemptions to its pre-emptive effect. [c]

. . . .

The District Court initially denied Medtronic's motion, finding nothing in the statute to support the company's argument that the MDA entirely exempted from liability a manufacturer who had allegedly violated the FDA's regulations. [c] Not long after that decision, however, the United States Court of Appeals for the Eleventh Circuit concluded that *§ 360k* required pre-emption of at least some common-law claims brought against the manufacturer of a medical device. [c] After reconsidering its ruling in light of *Duncan,* the District Court reversed its earlier decision and dismissed the Lohrs' entire complaint.

The Court of Appeals reversed in part and affirmed in part. [c] Rejecting the Lohrs' broadest submission, it first decided that "common law actions are state

---

15 Subsection (b) of the statute authorizes the FDA to grant exemptions to state requirements that would otherwise be pre-empted by subsection (a). Section 360k(b) provides:

"(b) Exempt requirements

"Upon application of a State or a political subdivision thereof, the Secretary may, by regulation promulgated after notice and opportunity for an oral hearing, exempt from subsection (a) of this section, under such conditions as may be prescribed in such regulation, a requirement of such State or political subdivision applicable to a device intended for human use if-

"(1) the requirement is more stringent than a requirement under this chapter which would be applicable to the device if an exemption were not in effect under this subsection; or

"(2) the requirement-

"(A) is required by compelling local conditions, and

"(B) compliance with the requirement would not cause the device to be in violation of any applicable requirement under this chapter."

requirements within the meaning of § 360k(a)." [c] It next held that pre-emption could not be avoided by merely alleging that the negligence flowed from a violation of federal standards. [c] Then, after concluding that the term "requirements" in § 360k(a) was unclear, it sought guidance from FDA's regulations regarding pre-emption. Those regulations provide that a state requirement is not preempted unless the FDA has established " 'specific requirements applicable to a particular device.' " [c] Under these regulations, the court concluded, it was not necessary that the federal regulation specifically deal with pacemakers, but only that the federal requirement "should, in some way, be 'restricted by nature' to a particular process, procedure, or device and should not be completely openended," 56 F.3d, at 1346 (footnote omitted), and that the specific device at issue should be subject to its requirements.

Under this approach, the court concluded that the Lohrs' negligent design claims were not pre-empted. It rejected Medtronic's argument that the FDA's finding of "substantial equivalence" had any significance with respect to the pacemaker's safety, or that the FDA's continued surveillance of the device constituted a federal "requirement" that its design be maintained. [c] On the other hand, it concluded that the negligent manufacturing and failure to warn claims were pre-empted by FDA's general "good manufacturing practices" regulations, which establish general requirements for most steps in every device's manufacture, [cc], and by the FDA labeling regulations, which require devices to bear various warnings, see 56 F.3d, at 1350-1351, 21 CFR § 801.109 (1995). The court made a parallel disposition of the strict-liability claims, holding that there was no pre-emption insofar as plaintiffs alleged an unreasonably dangerous design, but they could not revive the negligent manufacturing or failure to warn claims under a strict-liability theory. [c]

Medtronic filed a petition for certiorari seeking review of the Court of Appeals' decision insofar as it affirmed the District Court and the Lohrs filed a cross-petition seeking review of the judgment insofar as it upheld the pre-emption defense. Because the Courts of Appeals are divided over the extent to which state common-law claims are pre-empted by the MDA, we granted both petitions. [c]

III

[W]e are presented with the task of interpreting a statutory provision that expressly pre-empts state law. While the pre-emptive language of § 360k(a) means that we need not go beyond that language to determine whether Congress intended the MDA to pre-empt at least some state law, [c], we must nonetheless "identify the domain expressly pre-empted" by that language, [c]. Although our analysis of the scope of the pre-emption statute must begin with its text, [c] our interpretation of that language does not occur in a contextual vacuum. Rather, that interpretation is informed by two presumptions about the nature of pre-emption. [c]

First, because the States are independent sovereigns in our federal system, we have long presumed that Congress does not cavalierly pre-empt state-law causes of action. In all pre-emption cases, and particularly in those in which Congress has "legislated ... in a field which the States have traditionally occupied," [c] we "start with the assumption that the historic police powers of the States were not to be superseded by the Federal Act unless that was the clear and manifest purpose of Congress." [cc] ...

Second, our analysis of the scope of the statute's pre-emption is guided by our oft-repeated comment, ... that "[t]he purpose of Congress is the ultimate touchstone" in every pre-emption case. [cc] As a result, any understanding of the scope of a pre-emption statute must rest primarily on "a fair understanding of *congressional purpose.* " [c] Congress' intent, of course, primarily is discerned from the language of the pre-emption statute and the "statutory framework" surrounding it. [c] Also relevant, however, is the "structure and purpose of the statute as a whole," [c] as revealed not only in the text, but through the reviewing court's reasoned understanding of the way in which Congress intended the statute and its surrounding regulatory scheme to affect business, consumers, and the law.

With these considerations in mind, we turn first to a consideration of petitioner Medtronic's claim that the Court of Appeals should have found the entire action pre-empted and then to the merits of the Lohrs' cross-petition.

IV

In its petition, Medtronic argues that the Court of Appeals erred by concluding that the Lohrs' claims alleging negligent design were not pre-empted by *21 U.S.C. § 360k(a)*. That section provides that "no State or political subdivision of a State may establish or continue in effect with respect to a device intended for human use any requirement (1) which is different from, or in addition to, any requirement applicable under this chapter to the device, and (2) which relates to the safety or effectiveness of the device or to any other matter included in a requirement applicable to the device under this chapter." Medtronic suggests that any common-law cause of action is a "requirement" which alters incentives and imposes duties "different from, or in addition to," the generic federal standards that the FDA has promulgated in response to mandates under the MDA. In essence, the company argues that the plain language of the statute pre-empts any and all common-law claims brought by an injured plaintiff against a manufacturer of medical devices.

Medtronic's argument is not only unpersuasive, it is implausible. Under Medtronic's view of the statute, Congress effectively precluded state courts from affording state consumers any protection from injuries resulting from a defective medical device. Moreover, because there is no explicit private cause of action against manufacturers contained in the MDA, and no suggestion that the Act created an implied private right of action, Congress would have barred most, if not all, relief for persons injured by defective medical devices.[16] Medtronic's construction of § 360k would therefore have the perverse effect of granting complete immunity from design defect liability to an entire industry that, in the judgment of Congress, needed more stringent regulation in order "to provide for the safety and effectiveness of medical devices intended for human use," 90 Stat. 539 (preamble to Act). It is, to say the least, "difficult to believe that Congress would, without comment, remove all means of judicial recourse for those injured by illegal conduct," [c] and it would take language much plainer than the text of § 360k to convince us that Congress intended that result.

Furthermore, if Congress intended to preclude all common-law causes of action, it chose a singularly odd word with which to do it. The statute would have achieved an identical result, for instance, if it had precluded any "remedy" under state law relating to medical devices. "Requirement" appears to presume that the State is imposing a specific duty upon the manufacturer, and although we have on prior occasions concluded that a statute pre-empting certain state "requirements" could also pre-empt common-law damages claims, [c] that statute did not sweep nearly as broadly as Medtronic would have us believe that this statute does.

… Medtronic's sweeping interpretation of the statute would require far greater interference with state legal remedies, producing a serious intrusion into state sovereignty while simultaneously wiping out the possibility of remedy for the Lohrs' alleged injuries. Given the ambiguities in the statute and the scope of the preclusion that would occur otherwise, we cannot accept Medtronic's argument that by using the term "requirement," Congress clearly signaled its intent to deprive States of any role in protecting consumers from the dangers inherent in many medical devices.

[W]hen Congress enacted § 360k, it was primarily concerned with the problem of specific, conflicting state statutes and regulations rather than the general duties enforced by common-law actions. …[Section] 360k refers to "requirements" many times throughout its text. In each instance, the word is linked with language suggesting that its focus is device-specific enactments of positive law by legislative or administrative bodies, not the application of general rules of com-

---

16 The FDA's authority to require manufacturers to recall, replace, or refund defective devices is of little use to injured plaintiffs, since there is no indication that the right is available to private parties, the remedy would not extend to recovery for compensatory damages, and the authority is rarely invoked, if at all. [c]

mon law by judges and juries. ... Of the limited number of "exemptions" from pre-emption that the FDA has granted, none even remotely resemble common-law claims.

An examination of the basic purpose of the legislation as well as its history entirely supports our rejection of Medtronic's extreme position. The MDA was enacted "to provide for the safety and effectiveness of medical devices intended for human use." [c] Medtronic asserts that the Act was also intended, however, to "protect innovations in device technology from being 'stifled by unnecessary restrictions,' " [c] and that this interest extended to the pre-emption of common-law claims. While the Act certainly reflects some of these concerns,[17] the legislative history indicates that any fears regarding regulatory burdens were related more to the risk of additional federal and state regulation rather than the danger of pre-existing duties under common law. [cc] Indeed, nowhere in the materials relating to the Act's history have we discovered a reference to a fear that product liability actions would hamper the development of medical devices. To the extent that Congress was concerned about protecting the industry, that intent was manifested primarily through fewer substantive requirements under the Act, not the pre-emption provision; furthermore, any such concern was far outweighed by concerns about the primary issue motivating the MDA's enactment: the safety of those who use medical devices.

The legislative history also confirms our understanding that § 360(k) simply was not intended to pre-empt most, let alone all, general common-law duties enforced by damages actions. There is, to the best of our knowledge, nothing in the hearings, the Committee Reports, or the debates suggesting that any proponent of the legislation intended a sweeping pre-emption of traditional common-law remedies against manufacturers and distributors of defective devices. If Congress intended such a result, its failure even to hint at it is spectacularly odd, particularly since Members of both Houses were acutely aware of ongoing product liability litigation.[18]Along with the less-than-precise language of § 360k(a), that silence surely indicates that at least some common-law claims against medical device manufacturers may be maintained after the enactment of the MDA.

---

17 Special statutory exemptions, for example, permit the FDA (with various oversight provisions) to allow investigative, experimental devices to be used in commerce without either PMA review or "substantial equivalence." See 21 U.S.C. § 360j(g); 21 CFR pt. 813 (1995). Moreover, the very existence of the pre-emption statute demonstrates some concern that competing state requirements may unduly interfere with the market for medical devices.
18 Furthermore, if Congress had intended the MDA to work this dramatic change in the availability of state-law remedies, one would expect some reference to that change in the extensive contemporary reviews of the legislation. We have been able to find no such reference. ...

V

Medtronic asserts several specific reasons why, even if § 360k does not pre-empt all common-law claims, it at least pre-empts the Lohrs' claims in this suit. In contrast, the Lohrs argue that their entire complaint should survive a reasonable evaluation of the pre-emptive scope of § 360k(a). First, the Lohrs claim that the Court of Appeals correctly held that their negligent design claims were not pre-empted because the § 510(k) premarket notification process imposes no "requirement" on the design of Medtronic's pacemaker. Second, they suggest that even if the FDA's general rules regulating manufacturing practices and labeling are "requirements" that pre-empt different state requirements, § 360k(a) does not pre-empt state rules that merely duplicate some or all of those federal requirements. Finally, they argue that because the State's general rules imposing common-law duties upon Medtronic do not impose a requirement "with respect to a device," they do not conflict with the FDA's general rules relating to manufacturing and labeling and are therefore not pre-empted.

Design Claim

The Court of Appeals concluded that the Lohrs' defective design claims were not pre-empted because the requirements with which the company had to comply were not sufficiently concrete to constitute a pre-empting federal requirement. Medtronic counters by pointing to the FDA's determination that Model 4011 is "substantially equivalent" to an earlier device as well as the agency's continuing authority to exclude the device from the market if its design is changed. These factors, Medtronic argues, amount to a specific, federally enforceable design requirement that cannot be affected by state-law pressures such as those imposed on manufacturers subject to product liability suits.

The company's defense exaggerates the importance of the § 510(k) process and the FDA letter to the company regarding the pacemaker's substantial equivalence to a grandfathered device. As the court below noted, "[t]he 510(k) process is focused on equivalence, not safety." [c] As a result, "substantial equivalence determinations provide little protection to the public. These determinations simply compare a post-1976 device to a pre-1976 device to ascertain whether the later device is no more dangerous and no less effective than the earlier device. If the earlier device poses a severe risk or is ineffective, then the later device may also be risky or ineffective." [c] The design of the Model 4011, as with the design of pre-1976 and other "substantially equivalent" devices, has never been formally reviewed under the MDA for safety or efficacy.

The FDA stressed this basic conclusion in its letter to Medtronic finding the 4011 lead "substantially equivalent" to devices already on the market. That letter only required Medtronic to comply with "general standards"-the lowest level of protection "applicable to all medical devices," and including "listing of devices, good manufacturing practices, labeling, and the misbranding and adulteration provisions of the Act." It explicitly warned Medtronic that the letter did "not in any way denote official FDA approval of your device," and that "[a]ny representation that creates an impression of official approval of this device because of compliance with the premarket notification regulations is misleading and constitutes misbranding." FDA Substantial Equivalence Letter.

Thus, even though the FDA may well examine § 510(k) applications for Class III devices (as it examines the entire medical device industry) with a concern for the safety and effectiveness of the device, see Brief for Petitioner in No. 95-754, at 22-26, it did not "require" Medtronics' pacemaker to take any particular form for any particular reason; the agency simply allowed the pacemaker, as a device substantially equivalent to one that existed before 1976, to be marketed without running the gauntlet of the PMA process. In providing for this exemption to PMA review, Congress intended merely to give manufacturers the freedom to compete, to a limited degree, with and on the same terms as manufacturers of medical devices that existed prior to 1976. There is no suggestion in either the statutory scheme or the legislative history that the § 510(k) exemption process was intended to do anything other than maintain the status quo with respect to the marketing of existing medical devices and their substantial equivalents. That status quo included the possibility that the manufacturer of the device would have to defend itself against state-law claims of negligent design. Given this background behind the "substantial equivalence" exemption, the fact that "[t]he purpose of Congress is the ultimate touchstone" in every pre-emption case, [c] and the presumption against pre-emption, the Court of Appeals properly concluded that the "substantial equivalence" provision did not pre-empt the Lohrs' design claims.

Identity of Requirements Claims

The Lohrs next suggest that even if "requirements" exist with respect to the manufacturing and labeling of the pacemaker, and even if we can also consider state law to impose a "requirement" under the Act, the state requirement is not pre-empted unless it is "different from, or in addition to," the federal requirement. § 360k(a)(1). Although the precise contours of their theory of recovery have not yet been defined (the pre-emption issue was decided on the basis of the pleadings), it is clear that the Lohrs' allegations may include claims that Medtronic has, to the extent that they exist, violated FDA regulations. At least these claims, they suggest, can be maintained without being pre-empted by § 360k, and we agree.

Nothing in § 360k denies Florida the right to provide a traditional damages remedy for violations of common-law duties when those duties parallel federal requirements. Even if it may be necessary as a matter of Florida law to prove that those violations were the result of negligent conduct, or that they created an unreasonable hazard for users of the product, such additional elements of the state-law cause of action would make the state requirements narrower, not broader, than the federal requirement. While such a narrower requirement might be "different from" the federal rules in a literal sense, such a difference would surely provide a strange reason for finding pre-emption of a state rule insofar as it duplicates the federal rule. The presence of a damages remedy does not amount to the additional or different "requirement" that is necessary under the statute; rather, it merely provides another reason for manufacturers to comply with identical existing "requirements" under federal law.

The FDA regulations interpreting the scope of § 360k's pre-emptive effect support the Lohrs' view, and our interpretation of the pre-emption statute is substantially informed by those regulations. The different views expressed by the Courts of Appeals regarding the appropriate scope of federal pre-emption under § 360k demonstrate that the language of that section is not entirely clear. In addition, Congress has given the FDA a unique role in determining the scope of § 360k's pre-emptive effect. Unlike the statute construed in *Cipollone*, for instance, pre-emption under the MDA does not arise directly as a result of the enactment of the statute; rather, in most cases a state law will be pre-empted only to the extent that the FDA has promulgated a relevant federal "requirement." Because the FDA is the federal agency to which Congress has delegated its authority to implement the provisions of the Act, the agency is uniquely qualified to determine whether a particular form of state law "stands as an obstacle to the accomplishment and execution of the full purposes and objectives of Congress," [c] and, therefore, whether it should be pre-empted. For example, Congress explicitly delegated to the FDA the authority to exempt state regulations from the pre-emptive effect of the MDA-an authority that necessarily requires the FDA to assess the pre-emptive effect that the Act and its own regulations will have on state laws. [c] FDA regulations implementing that grant of authority establish a process by which States or other individuals may request an advisory opinion from the FDA regarding whether a particular state requirement is pre-empted by the statute. See 21 CFR § 808.5 (1995). The ambiguity in the statute–and the congressional grant of authority to the agency on the matter contained within it–provide a "sound basis," (O'CONNOR, J., concurring in part and dissenting in part), for giving substantial weight to the agency's view of the statute. [cc]

The regulations promulgated by the FDA expressly support the conclusion that § 360k "does not preempt State or local requirements that are equal to, or substantially identical to, requirements imposed by or under the act." 21 CFR

§ 808.1(d)(2) (1995); see also § 808.5(b)(1)(i).[19] At this early stage in the litigation, there was no reason for the Court of Appeals to preclude altogether the Lohrs' manufacturing and labeling claims to the extent that they rest on claims that Medtronic negligently failed to comply with duties "equal to, or substantially identical to, requirements imposed" under federal law.

Manufacturing and Labeling Claims

Finally, the Lohrs suggest that with respect to the manufacturing and labeling claims, the Court of Appeals should have rejected Medtronic's pre-emption defense in full. The Court of Appeals believed that these claims would interfere with the consistent application of general federal regulations governing the labeling and manufacture of all medical devices, and therefore concluded that the claims were pre-empted altogether.

The requirements identified by the Court of Appeals include labeling regulations that require manufacturers of every medical device, with a few limited exceptions, to include with the device a label containing "information for use, ... and any relevant hazards, contraindications, side effects, and precautions." [c] Similarly, manufacturers are required to comply with "Good Manufacturing Practices," or "GMP's," which are set forth in 32 sections and less than 10 pages in the Code of Federal Regulations. In certain circumstances, the Court of Appeals recognized, the FDA will enforce these general requirements against manufacturers that violate them. [c]

While admitting that these requirements exist, the Lohrs suggest that their general nature simply does not pre-empt claims alleging that the manufacturer failed to comply with other duties under state common law. In support of their claim, they note that § 360k(a)(1) expressly states that a federal requirement must be "applicable to the device" in question before it has any pre-emptive effect. Because the labeling and manufacturing requirements are applicable to a host of different devices, they argue that they do not satisfy this condition. They further argue that because only state requirements "with respect to a device" may be pre-empted, and then only if the requirement "relates to the safety or effectiveness of the device or to any other matter included in a requirement applicable to the device," § 360k(a) mandates pre-emption only where there is a conflict between a specific state requirement and a federal requirement "applicable to" the same device.

---

19 We also note that the agency permits manufacturers of devices that have received PMA to make certain labeling, quality control, and manufacturing changes which would "enhance[ ] the safety of the device or the safety in the use of the device" without prior FDA approval. See 21 CFR §§ 814.39(d)(1) and (2) (1995).

The Lohrs' theory is supported by the FDA regulations, which provide that state requirements are pre-empted "only" when the FDA has established "specific counterpart regulations or ... other specific requirements applicable to a particular device." 21 CFR § 808.1(d) (1995).[20] They further note that the statute is not intended to pre-empt "State or local requirements of general applicability where the purpose of the requirement relates either to other products in addition to devices ... or to unfair trade practices in which the requirements are not limited to devices." § 808.1(d)(1). The regulations specifically provide, as examples of permissible general requirements, that general electrical codes and the Uniform Commercial Code warranty of fitness would not be pre-empted. [c] The regulations even go so far as to state that § 360k(a) generally "does not preempt a state or local requirement prohibiting the manufacture of adulterated or misbranded devices" unless "such a prohibition has the effect of establishing a substantive requirement for a specific device." § 808.1(d)(6)(ii). Furthermore, under its authority to grant exemptions to the pre-emptive effect of § 360k(a), the FDA has never granted, nor, to the best of our knowledge, even been asked to consider granting, an exemption for a state law of general applicability; all 22 existing exemptions apply to excruciatingly specific state requirements regarding the sale of hearing aids. See §§ 808.53-808.101.

Although we do not believe that this statutory and regulatory language necessarily precludes "general" federal requirements from ever pre-empting state requirements, or "general" state requirements from ever being pre-empted, see

---

20 FDA's narrow understanding of the scope of § 360k(a) is obvious from the full text of the regulation, which provides, in relevant part:

"(d) State or local requirements are preempted only when the Food and Drug Administration has established specific counterpart regulations or there are other specific requirements applicable to a particular device under the act, thereby making any existing divergent State or local requirements applicable to the device different from, or in addition to, the specific Food and Drug Administration requirements. There are other State or local requirements that affect devices that are not preempted by section 521(a) of the act because they are not 'requirements applicable to a device' within the meaning of section 521(a) of the act. The following are examples of State or local requirements that are not regarded as preempted by section 521 of the act:

"(1) Section 521(a) does not preempt State or local requirements of general applicability where the purpose of the requirement relates either to other products in addition to devices (e.g., requirements such as general electrical codes, and the Uniform Commercial Code (warranty of fitness)), or to unfair trade practices in which the requirements are not limited to devices.

"(2) Section 521(a) does not preempt State or local requirements that are equal to, or substantially identical to, requirements imposed by or under the act.

. . . . .

"(6)(i) Section 521(a) does not preempt State or local requirements respecting general enforcement, e.g., requirements that State inspection be permitted of factory records concerning all devices....

"(ii) Generally, section 521(a) does not preempt a State or local requirement prohibiting the manufacture of adulterated or misbranded devices. Where, however, such a prohibition has the effect of establishing a substantive requirement for a specific device, e.g., a specific labeling requirement, then the prohibition [may] be preempted." 21 CFR § 808.1(d) (1995).

Part VI, infra, it is impossible to ignore its overarching concern that pre-emption occur only where a particular state requirement threatens to interfere with a specific federal interest. State requirements must be "with respect to" medical devices and "different from, or in addition to," federal requirements. State requirements must also relate "to the safety or effectiveness of the device or to any other matter included in a requirement applicable to the device," and the regulations provide that state requirements of "general applicability" are not pre-empted except where they have "the effect of establishing a substantive requirement for a specific device." Moreover, federal requirements must be "applicable to the device" in question, and, according to the regulations, pre-empt state law only if they are "specific counterpart regulations" or "specific" to a "particular device." The statute and regulations, therefore, require a careful comparison between the allegedly pre-empting federal requirement and the allegedly pre-empted state requirement to determine whether they fall within the intended pre-emptive scope of the statute and regulations.

If anything, the language of the MDA's pre-emption statute and its counterpart regulations require an even more searching inquiry into the relationship between the federal requirement and the state requirement at issue than was true under the statute in *Cipollone.*

Such a comparison mandates a conclusion that the Lohrs' common-law claims are not pre-empted by the federal labeling and manufacturing requirements. The generality of those requirements make this quite unlike a case in which the Federal Government has weighed the competing interests relevant to the particular requirement in question, reached an unambiguous conclusion about how those competing considerations should be resolved in a particular case or set of cases, and implemented that conclusion via a specific mandate on manufacturers or producers. Rather, the federal requirements reflect important but entirely generic concerns about device regulation generally, not the sort of concerns regarding a specific device or field of device regulation that the statute or regulations were designed to protect from potentially contradictory state requirements.

Similarly, the general state common-law requirements in this suit were not specifically developed "with respect to" medical devices. Accordingly, they are not the kinds of requirements that Congress and the FDA feared would impede the ability of federal regulators to implement and enforce specific federal requirements. The legal duty that is the predicate for the Lohrs' negligent manufacturing claim is the general duty of every manufacturer to use due care to avoid foreseeable dangers in its products. Similarly, the predicate for the failure to warn claim is the general duty to inform users and purchasers of potentially dangerous items of the risks involved in their use. These general obligations are no more a threat to federal requirements than would be a state-law duty to comply with local fire prevention regulations and zoning codes, or to use due care in the training and supervision of a work force. These state requirements therefore escape pre-emption, not because the source of the duty is a judge-made common-law rule, but rather because their generality leaves them outside the category of requirements that § 360k envisioned to be "with respect to" specific devices such as pacemakers. As a result, none of the Lohrs' claims based on allegedly defective manufacturing or labeling are pre-empted by the MDA.

VI

In their cross-petition, the Lohrs present a final argument, suggesting that common-law duties are never "requirements" within the meaning of § 360k and that the statute therefore never pre-empts common-law actions. ... We do not think that the issue is resolved by the FDA regulation suggesting that § 360k is applicable to those requirements "having the force and effect of law" that are "established by ... court decision," 21 CFR § 808.1(b) (1995), that reference, it appears, was intended to refer to court decisions construing state statutes or regulations. [cc]

Nevertheless, we do not respond directly to this argument for two reasons. First, since none of the Lohrs' claims is pre-empted in this suit, we need not resolve hypothetical cases that may arise in the future. Second, given the critical importance of device specificity in our (and the FDA's) construction of § 360k, it is apparent that few, if any, common-law duties have been pre-empted by this statute. It will be rare indeed for a court hearing a common-law cause of action to issue a decree that has "the effect of establishing a substantive requirement for a specific device." 21 CFR § 808.1(d)(6)(ii) (1995). Until such a case arises, we see no need to determine whether the statute explicitly pre-empts such a claim. Even then, the issue may not need to be resolved if the claim would also be pre-empted under conflict pre-emption analysis, [c].

VII

Accordingly, the judgment of the Court of Appeals is reversed insofar as it held that any of the claims were pre-empted and affirmed insofar as it rejected the pre-emption defense. The cases are remanded for further proceedings.

It is so ordered.

Justice BREYER, concurring in part and concurring in the judgment.

This action raises two questions. First, do the Medical Device Amendments of 1976 (MDA) to the Federal Food, Drug, and Cosmetic Act ever pre-empt a state-law tort action? Second, if so, does the MDA pre-empt the particular state-law tort claims at issue here?

I

My answer to the first question is that the MDA will sometimes pre-empt a state-law tort suit. I basically agree with Justice O'CONNOR's discussion of this point and with her conclusion. See post, at 2262-2263. The statute's language, read literally, supports that conclusion. It says:

"[N]o State ... may establish ... with respect to a device ... any [state] *requirement* ... which is different from, or in addition to, any [federal] requirement...." 21 U.S.C. § 360k(a) (emphasis added).

One can reasonably read the word "requirement" as including the legal requirements that grow out of the application, in particular circumstances, of a State's tort law.

. . . .

[A] contrary holding would have anomalous consequences. Imagine that, in respect to a particular hearing aid component, a federal MDA regulation requires a 2-inch wire, but a state agency regulation requires a 1-inch wire. If the federal law, embodied in the "2-inch" MDA regulation, pre-empts the state "1-inch" agency regulation, why would it not similarly pre-empt a state-law tort action that premises liability upon the defendant manufacturer's failure to use a 1-inch wire (say, an award by a jury persuaded by expert testimony that use of a more than 1-inch wire is negligent)? The effects of the state agency regulation and the state tort suit are identical. To distinguish between them for pre-emption purposes would grant greater power (to set state standards "different from, or in addition to," federal standards) to a single state jury than to state officials acting through state administrative or legislative lawmaking processes. Where Congress likely did not focus specifically upon the matter, [c] I would not take it to have intended this anomalous result.

Consequently, I believe that ordinarily, insofar as the MDA pre-empts a state requirement embodied in a state statute, rule, regulation, or other administrative action, it would also pre-empt a similar requirement that takes the form of a standard of care or behavior imposed by a state-law tort action. It is possible that the plurality also agrees on this point, although it does not say so explicitly.

II

The answer to the second question turns on Congress' intent. *See, e.g., Barnett Bank of Marion Cty., N.A. v. Nelson,* 517 U.S. 25, 30, 116 S.Ct. 1103, 1107, 134 L.Ed.2d 237 (1996); *Allis-Chalmers Corp. v. Lueck,* 471 U.S. 202, 208, 105 S.Ct. 1904, 1909-1910, 85 L.Ed.2d 206 (1985); ante, at 2251. Although Congress has not stated whether the MDA does, or does not, pre-empt the tort claims here at issue, several considerations lead me to conclude that it does not.

First, the MDA's pre-emption provision is highly ambiguous. That provision makes clear that federal requirements may pre-empt state requirements, but it says next to nothing about just when, where, or how they may do so. The words "any [state] requirement" and "any [federal] requirement," for example, do not tell us which requirements are at issue, for every state requirement that is not identical to even one federal requirement is "different from, or in addition to," that single federal requirement; yet, Congress could not have intended that the existence of one single federal rule, say, about a 2-inch hearing aid wire, would pre-empt every state law hearing aid rule, even a set of rules related only to the packaging or shipping of hearing aids. Thus, Congress must have intended that courts look elsewhere for help as to just which federal requirements pre-empt just which state requirements, as well as just how they might do so.

Second, this Court has previously suggested that, in the absence of a clear congressional command as to pre-emption, courts may infer that the relevant administrative agency possesses a degree of leeway to determine which rules, regulations, or other administrative actions will have pre-emptive effect. *See Hillsborough County v. Automated Medical Laboratories, Inc.,* 471 U.S. 707, 721, 105 S.Ct. 2371, 2379, 85 L.Ed.2d 714 (1985); cf. *Smiley v. Citibank (South Dakota), N. A.,* 517 U.S. 735, 739-741, 116 S.Ct. 1730, 1732-1734, 135 L.Ed.2d 25 1996); *Lawrence County v. Lead-Deadwood School Dist. No. 40-1,* 469 U.S. 256, 261-262, 105 S.Ct. 695, 698-699, 83 L.Ed.2d 635 (1985); *Chevron U.S.A. Inc. v. Natural Resources Defense Council, Inc.,* 467 U.S. 837, 842-845, 104 S.Ct. 2778, 2781-2783, 81 L.Ed.2d 694 (1984). To draw a similar inference here makes sense, and not simply because of the statutory ambiguity. The Food and Drug Administration (FDA) is fully responsible for administering the MDA. *See.* 21 U.S.C. § 393. That responsibility means informed agency involvement and, therefore, special understanding of the likely impact of both state and federal requirements, as well as an understanding of whether (or the extent to which) state requirements may interfere with federal objectives. *See Hillsborough,* 471 U.S., at 721, 105 S.Ct., at 2379. The FDA can translate these understandings into particularized pre-emptive intentions accompanying its various rules and regulations. *See id., at 718, 105 S. Ct., at 2377-2378.* It can communicate those intentions, for example, through statements in "regulations, preambles, interpretive statements, and responses to comments," *ibid.,* as well as through the exercise of its explicitly designated power to exempt state requirements from pre-emption, *see* 21 U.S.C. § 360k(b); see also ante, at 2255-2256 (noting that FDA's authority to exempt state requirements from pre-emption necessarily requires FDA to assess federal laws' pre-emptive effect).

Third, the FDA has promulgated a specific regulation designed to help. That regulation says:

> "State ... requirements are preempted only when ... there are ... specific [federal] requirements applicable to a particular device ... thereby making any existing divergent State ... requirements applicable to the device different from, or in addition to, the specific [federal] requirements." 21 CFR § 808.1(d) (1995) (emphasis added).

The regulation does not fill all the statutory gaps, for its word "divergent" does not explain, any more than did the statute, just when different device-related federal and state requirements are closely enough related to trigger pre-emption analysis. But the regulation's word "specific" does narrow the universe of federal requirements that the agency intends to displace at least some state law.

Insofar as there are any applicable FDA requirements here, those requirements, even if numerous, are not "specific" in any relevant sense. See ante, at 2256-2257, 2258. Hence, as the FDA's above-quoted pre-emption rule tells us, the FDA does not intend these requirements to pre-empt the state requirements at issue here. At least in present circumstances, no law forces the FDA to make its requirements pre-emptive if it does not think it appropriate.

I cannot infer a contrary intent from Justice O'CONNOR's characterization of the federal standards applicable here as "comprehensive" and "extensive," *post*, at 2263-2264, both because that characterization is questionable, see *ante*, at 2256-2257, 2258, and because this Court has previously said that it would "seldom infer, solely from the comprehensiveness of federal regulations, an intent to pre-empt in its entirety a field related to health and safety." *Hillsborough, supra,* at 718, 105 S.Ct., at 2377. It therefore seems to me that the better indicator of the FDA's intent is its pre-emption-related regulation. And that regulation's word "specific" would seem a reasonable exercise of the leeway that statutory language and practical administrative circumstance suggest Congress intended to grant to the agency.

Fourth, ordinary principles of "conflict" and "field" pre-emption point in the same direction. Those principles make clear that a federal requirement pre-empts a state requirement if (1) the state requirement actually conflicts with the federal requirement-either because compliance with both is impossible, *Florida Lime & Avocado Growers, Inc. v. Paul,* 373 U.S. 132, 142-143, 83 S.Ct. 1210, 1217-1218, 10 L.Ed.2d 248 (1963), or because the state requirement "stands as an obstacle to the accomplishment and execution of the full purposes and objectives of Congress," *Hines v. Davidowitz,* 312 U.S. 52, 67, 61 S.Ct. 399, 404, 85 L.Ed. 581 (1941)-or (2) the scheme of federal regulation is "so pervasive as to make reasonable the inference that Congress left no room for the States to supplement it," *Rice v. Santa Fe Elevator Corp.,* 331 U.S. 218, 230, 67 S.Ct. 1146, 1152, 91 L.Ed. 1447 (1947). See, *e.g., Barnett Bank,* 517 U.S., at 31, 116 S.Ct., at 1107-1108; *Gade v. National Solid Wastes Management Assn.,* 505 U.S. 88, 98, 112 S.Ct. 2374, 2383, 120 L.Ed.2d 73 (1992) (opinion of O'CONNOR, J.); *Wisconsin Public Intervenor v. Mortier,* 501 U.S. 597, 604-605, 111 S.Ct. 2476, 2481-2482, 115 L.Ed.2d 532 (1991); *English v. General Elec. Co.,* 496 U.S. 72, 79, 110 S.Ct. 2270, 2275, 110 L.Ed.2d 65 (1990).

It makes sense, in the absence of any indication of a contrary congressional (or agency) intent, to read the pre-emption statute (and the pre emption regulation) in light of these basic pre-emption principles. The statutory terms "different from" and "in addition to" readily lend themselves to such a reading, for their language parallels pre-emption law's basic concerns. Without any contrary indication from the agency, one might also interpret the regulation's word "divergent" in light of these same basic pre-emption principles.

Insofar as these basic principles inform a court's interpretation of the statute and regulation, they support the conclusion that there is no pre-emption here. I can find no actual conflict between any federal requirement and any of the liability-creating premises of the plaintiffs' state-law tort suit; nor, for the reasons discussed above, can I find any indication that either Congress or the FDA intended the relevant FDA regulations to occupy entirely any relevant field.

For these reasons, I concur in the Court's judgment. I also join the Court's opinion, but for Parts IV and VI. I do not join Part IV, which emphasizes the differences between the MDA and the pre-emption statute at issue in *Cipollone,* because those differences are not, in my view, relevant in this action. I do not join Part VI, because I am not convinced that future incidents of MDA pre-emption of common-law claims will be "few" or "rare," *ante,* at 2259.

Justice O'CONNOR, with whom THE CHIEF JUSTICE, Justice SCALIA, and Justice THOMAS join, concurring in part and dissenting in part.

Section 360k(a), the pre-emption provision of the Medical Device Amendments of 1976 (MDA), provides that no State may establish or continue in effect "any requirement" "which is different from, or in addition to," any requirement applicable under the Federal Food, Drug, and Cosmetic Act of 1938 (FDCA) to the device. As the Court points out, because Congress has expressly provided a pre-emption provision, "we need not go beyond that language to determine whether Congress intended the MDA to pre-empt" state law. *Ante,* at 2250. We agree, then, on the task before us: to interpret Congress' intent by reading the statute in accordance with its terms. This, however, the Court has failed to do.

The cases require us to determine whether the Lohrs' state common-law claims survive pre-emption under § 360k. I conclude that state common-law damages actions do impose "requirements" and are therefore pre-empted where such requirements would differ from those imposed by the FDCA. The plurality acknowledges that a common-law action might impose a "requirement," but suggests that such a pre-emption would be "rare indeed." *Ante*, at 2259. To reach that determination, the opinion-without explicitly relying on Food and Drug Administration (FDA) regulations and without offering any sound basis for why deference would be warranted-imports the FDA regulations interpreting § 360k to "inform" the Court's reading. Accordingly, the principal opinion states that pre-emption occurs only "where a particular state requirement threatens to interfere with a specific federal interest," *ante*, at 2257, and for that reason, concludes that common-law claims are almost never pre-empted, *ante*, at 2258-2259, and that the Lohrs' claims here are not pre-empted. This decision is bewildering and seemingly without guiding principle.

The language of § 360k demonstrates congressional intent that the MDA pre-empt "any requirement" by a State that is "different from, or in addition to," that applicable to the device under the FDCA. The Lohrs have raised various state common-law claims in connection with Medtronic's pacemaker lead. Analysis, therefore, must begin with the question whether state common-law actions can constitute "requirements" within the meaning of § 360k(a).

We recently addressed a similar question in *Cipollone,* where we examined the meaning of the phrase "no requirement or prohibition" under the Public Health Cigarette Smoking Act of 1969. *Cipollone v. Liggett Group, Inc.,* 505 U.S. 504, 112 S.Ct. 2608, 120 L.Ed.2d 407 (1992). A majority of the Court agreed that state common-law damages actions do impose "requirements." [c] (SCALIA, J., joined by THOMAS, J., concurring in judgment in part and dissenting in part). As the plurality explained:

> "The phrase, '[n]o requirement or prohibition' sweeps broadly and suggests no distinction between positive enactments and common law; to the contrary, those words easily encompass obligations that take the form of common-law rules. As we noted in another context, '[state] regulation can be as effectively exerted through an award of damages as through some form of preventive relief. The obligation to pay compensation can be, indeed is designed to be, a potent method of governing conduct and controlling policy.' *San Diego Building Trades Council v. Garmon,* 359 U.S. 236, 247, 79 S.Ct. 773, 780-781, 3 L.Ed.2d 775 (1959)." [c]

That rationale is equally applicable in the present context. Whether relating to the labeling of cigarettes or the manufacture of medical devices, state common-law damages actions operate to require manufacturers to comply with common-law duties. As *Cipollone* declared, in answer to the same argument raised here that common-law actions do not impose requirements, "such an analysis is at odds both with the plain words" of the statute and "with the general understanding of common-law damages actions." *Ibid.* If § 360k's language is given its ordinary meaning, it clearly pre-empts any state common-law action that would impose a requirement different from, or in addition to, that applicable under the FDCA–just as it would pre-empt a state statute or regulation that had that effect. Justice BREYER reaches the same conclusion. [c]

The plurality's reasons for departing from this reading are neither clear nor persuasive. ... [T]he plurality essentially makes the case that the statute's language, purpose, and legislative history, as well as the consequences of a different interpretation, indicate that Congress did not intend "requirement" to include state common-law claims at all. The principal opinion proceeds to disclaim this position, however, in Parts V and VI and concludes, rather, that a state common-law action might constitute a requirement, but that such a case would be "rare indeed." [c] The Court holds that an FDCA "requirement" triggers pre-emption only when a conflict exists between a specific state requirement and a specific FDCA requirement applicable to the particular device. ...

To reach its particularized reading of the statute, the Court imports the interpretation put forth by the FDA's regulations. Justice BREYER similarly relies on the FDA regulations to arrive at an understanding of § *360k*. Ante, at 2260-2261. Apparently recognizing that *Chevron* deference is unwarranted here, the Court does not admit to deferring to these regulations, but merely permits them to "infor[m]" the Court's interpretation. Ante, at 2255. It is not certain that an agency regulation determining the pre-emptive effect of any federal statute is entitled to deference, [c], but one pertaining to the clear statute at issue here is surely not. "If the statute contains an express pre-emption clause, the task of statutory construction must in the first instance focus on the plain wording of the clause, which necessarily contains the best evidence of Congress' pre-emptive intent." *CSX Transp., Inc. v. Easterwood,* 507 U.S. 658, 664, 113 S.Ct. 1732, 1737, 123 L.Ed.2d 387 (1993). Where the language of the statute is clear, resort to the agency's interpretation is improper. See *Chevron U.S.A. Inc. v. Natural Resources Defense Council, Inc.,* 467 U.S. 837, 842-843, 104 S.Ct. 2778, 2781-2782, 81 L. Ed.2d 694 (1984). Title 21 U.S.C. § 360k(a)(1) directs the pre-emption of "any [state] requirement" "which is different from, or in addition to, any requirement applicable under [the FDCA] to the device." As explained above, and as Justice BREYER agrees, ante, at 2259-2260, the term "requirement" encompasses state common-law causes of action. The Court errs when it employs an agency's narrowing construction of a statute where no such deference is warranted. The statute makes no mention of a requirement of specificity, and there is no sound basis for determining that such a restriction on "any requirement" exists.

I conclude that a fair reading of § 360k indicates that state common-law claims are pre-empted, as the statute itself states, to the extent that their recognition would impose "any requirement" different from, or in addition to, FDCA requirements applicable to the device. From that premise, I proceed to the question whether FDCA requirements applicable to the device exist here to pre-empt the Lohrs' state-law claims.

I agree with the Court that the Lohrs' defective design claim is not pre-empted by the FDCA's § 510(k) "substantial equivalency" process. The § 510(k) process merely evaluates whether the Class III device at issue is substantially equivalent to a device that was on the market before 1976, the effective date of the MDA; if so, the later device may be also be marketed. Because the § 510(k) process seeks merely to establish whether a pre-1976 device and a post-1976 device are equivalent, and places no "requirements" on a device, the Lohrs' defective design claim is not pre-empted.

I also agree that the Lohrs' claims are not pre-empted by § 360k to the extent that they seek damages for Medtronic's alleged violation of federal requirements. Where a state cause of action seeks to enforce an FDCA requirement, that claim does not impose a requirement that is "different from, or in addition to," requirements under federal law. To be sure, the threat of a damages remedy will give manufacturers an additional cause to comply, but the requirements imposed on them under state and federal law do not differ. Section 360k does not preclude States from imposing different or additional remedies, but only different or additional requirements.

I disagree, however, with the Court's conclusion that the Lohrs' claims survive pre-emption insofar as they would compel Medtronic to comply with requirements different from those imposed by the FDCA. Because I do not subscribe to the Court's reading into § 360k the additional requisite of "specificity," my determination of what claims are pre-empted is broader. Some, if not all, of the Lohrs' common-law claims regarding the manufacturing and labeling of Medtronic's device would compel Medtronic to comply with requirements different from, or in addition to, those required by the FDA. The FDA's Good Manufacturing Practice (GMP) regulations impose comprehensive requirements relating to every aspect of the device-manufacturing process, including a manufacturer's organization and personnel, buildings, equipment, component controls, production and process controls, packaging and labeling controls, holding, distribution, installation, device evaluation, and recordkeeping. [c] The Lohrs' common-law claims regarding manufacture would, if successful, impose state requirements "different from, or in addition to," the GMP requirements, and are therefore pre-empted. In similar fashion, the Lohrs' failure to warn claim is pre-empted by the extensive labeling requirements imposed by the FDA. See, e.g., 21 CFR § 801.109 (1995) (requiring labels to include such information as indications, effects, routes, methods, frequency and duration of administration, relevant hazards, contraindications, side effects, and precautions). These extensive federal manufacturing and labeling requirements are certainly applicable to the device manufactured by Medtronic. Section 360k(a) requires no more specificity than that for pre-emption of state common-law claims.

To summarize, I conclude that § 360k(a)'s term "requirement" encompasses state common-law claims. Because the statutory language does not indicate that a "requirement" must be "specific," either to pre-empt or be pre-empted, I conclude that a state common-law claim is pre-empted if it would impose "any requirement" "which is different from, or in addition to," any requirement applicable to the device under the FDCA. I would affirm the judgment of the Court of Appeals that the Lohrs' design claim is not pre-empted by the MDA, and that the manufacture and failure to warn claims are pre-empted; I would reverse the judgment of the Court of Appeals that the MDA pre-empts a common-law claim alleging violation of federal requirements.

——————————

Points for Discussion

1. What does the Court hold in *Medtronic*? Did a majority of the justices agree that the Medical Device Amendments Act did not preempt the plaintiffs' common-law claims? What parts of Justice Stevens' opinion spoke for a plurality and not a majority of the Court?

2. Explain the positions of and arguments made in the concurring and dissenting opinions.

2. What is federal preemption?

3. How did the Court determine whether the state law products claims were preempted by the federal law?

4. Distinguish between preemption and compliance with governmental standards.

5. The question whether federal laws and regulations preempt state common-law claims has been posed to and answered by the United States Supreme Court in several recent cases. *See PLIVA, Inc. v. Mensing*, 131 S.Ct. 2567 (2011) (federal law preempted Louisiana Products Liability Act's imposition of duty on generic drug manufacturers to change drug label); *Williamson v. Mazda Motor of America, Inc.*, 131 S.Ct. 1131 (2011) (claims of motor vehicle accident victims brought against minivan manufacturer were not preempted by the Federal Motor Vehicle Safety Standard); *Bruesewitz v. Wyeth LLC*, 131 S.Ct. 1068 (2011) (products liability action against vaccine manufacturer preempted by the National Childhood Vaccine Injury Act); *Wyeth v. Levine*, 555 U.S. 555 (2009) (plaintiff's state law failure-to-warn claim against drug manufacturer not preempted by federal law); *Altria Group, Inc. v. Good*, 555 U.S. 70 (2008) (cigarette smokers' state law unfair trade practices suits not preempted by the Federal Cigarette Labeling and Advertising Act); *Riegel v. Medtronic*, 552 U.S. 312 (2008) (patient's New York common-law claims were preempted by federal Food and Drug Administration's premarket approval process); *Geier v. American Honda Motor Company*, 529 U.S. 861 (2000) (defective design action brought by injured motorist under District of Columbia tort law was not preempted by express preemption provision of the National Traffic and Motor Vehicle Safety Act but was preempted because of conflict with federal Department of Transportation standard).

Chapter 16

Defamation

This chapter provides an introduction to the law of **defamation**. "Defamation is made up of the twin torts of **libel** and **slander**—the one being, in general, written while the other in general is oral . . . . In either form, defamation is an invasion of the interest in **reputation** and good name. This is a 'relational' interest, since it involves the opinion which others in the community may have, or tend to have, of the plaintiff." Prosser and Keeton on the Law of Torts 771 (5th ed. 1984). The ensuing pages and materials examine defamation law, liability, and defenses thereto as developed in both the common law and constitutional law.

A. Common Law

1. Libel and Slander

> ### Restatement (Second) of Torts (1977)
> ### § 558. Elements Stated
>
> To create liability for defamation there must be:
>
> (a) a false and defamatory statement concerning another;
>
> (b) an unprivileged publication to a third party;
>
> (c) fault amounting at least to negligence on the part of the publisher; and
>
> (d) either actionability of the statement irrespective of special harm or the existence of special harm caused by the publication.

> ### § 559. Defamatory Communications Defined
>
> A communication is defamatory if it tends so to harm the reputation of another as to lower him in the estimation of the community or to deter third persons from associating or dealing with him.

Peck v. Tribune Co.

214 U.S. 185 (1909)

Mr. Justice Holmes delivered the opinion of the court:

This is an action on the case for a libel. The libel alleged is found in an advertisement printed in the defendant's newspaper, The Chicago Sunday Tribune, and, so far as is material, is as follows: 'Nurse and Patients Praise Duffy's. Mrs. A. Schuman, One of Chicago's Most Capable and Experienced Nurses, Pays an Eloquent Tribute to the Great Invigorating, Life-Giving, and Curative Properties of Duffy's Pure Malt Whisky.' Then followed a portrait of the plaintiff, with the words, 'Mrs. A. Schuman,' under it. Then, in quotation marks, 'After years of constant use of your Pure Malt Whisky, both by myself and as given to patients in my capacity as nurse, I have no hesitation in recommending it as the very best tonic and stimulant for all local and run-down conditions,' etc., etc., with the words, 'Mrs. A. Schuman, 1576 Mozart St., Chicago, Ill.,' at the end, not in quotation marks, but conveying the notion of a signature, or at least that the words were hers. The declaration alleged that the plaintiff was not Mrs. Schuman, was not a nurse, and was a total abstainer from whisky and all spirituous liquors. There was also a count for publishing the plaintiff's likeness without leave. The defendant pleaded not guilty. At the trial, subject to exceptions, the judge excluded the plaintiff's testimony in support of her allegations just stated, and directed a verdict for the defendant. His action was sustained by the circuit court of appeals, 83 C. C. A. 202, 154 Fed. 330.

Of course, the insertion of the plaintiff's picture in the place and with the concomitants that we have described imported that she was the nurse and made the statements set forth, as rightly was decided in *Wandt v. Hearst's Chicago American*, 129 Wis. 419, 421, 6 L.R.A.(N.S.) 919, 116 Am. St. Rep. 959, 109 N. W. 70, 9 A. & E. Ann, Cas. 864; *Morrison v. Smith*, 177 N. Y. 366, 69 N. E. 725. Therefore the publication was of and concerning the plaintiff, notwithstanding the presence of another fact, the name of the real signer of the certificate, if that was Mrs. Schuman, that was inconsistent, when all the facts were known, with the plaintiff's having signed or adopted it. Many might recognize the plaintiff's face without knowing her name, and those who did know it might be led to infer that she had sanctioned the publication under an alias. There was some suggestion that the defendant published the portrait by mistake, and without knowledge that it was the plaintiff's portrait, or was not what it purported to be. But the fact, if it was one, was no excuse. If the publication was **libelous**, the defendant took the risk. As was said of such matters by Lord Mansfield, 'Whenever a man publishes, he publishes at his peril.' R. v. Woodfall, Lofft, 776, 781. See further, Hearne v. Stowell, 12 Ad. & El. 719, 726; Shepheard v. Whitaker, L. R. 10 C. P. 502; *Clarke v. North American Co.,* 203 Pa. 346, 351, 352, 53 Atl. 237. The reason is plain. A libel is harmful on its face. If a man sees fit to publish manifestly hurtful statements concerning an individual, without other justification than exists for an advertisement or a piece of news, the usual principles of tort will make him liable if the statements are false, or are true only of someone else. See *Morasse v. Brochu,* 151 Mass. 567, 575, 8 L.R.A. 524, 21 Am. St. Rep. 474, 25 N. E. 74.

The question, then, is whether the publication was a libel. It was held by the circuit court of appeals not to be, or, at most, to entitle the plaintiff only to **nominal damages**, no **special damage** being alleged. It was pointed out that there was no general consensus of opinion that to drink whisky is wrong, or that to be a nurse is discreditable. It might have been added that very possibly giving a certificate and the use of one's portrait in aid of an advertisement would be regarded with irony, or a stronger feeling, only by a few. But it appears to us that such inquiries are beside the point. It may be that the action for libel is of little use, but, while it is maintained, it should be governed by the general principles of tort. If the advertisement obviously would hurt the plaintiff in the estimation of an important and respectable part of the community, liability is not a question of a majority vote.

We know of no decision in which this matter is discussed upon principle. But obviously an unprivileged falsehood need not entail universal hatred to constitute a cause of action. No falsehood is thought about or even known by all the world. No conduct is hated by all. That it will be known by a large number, and will lead an appreciable fraction of that number to regard the plaintiff with contempt, is enough to do her practical harm. Thus, if a doctor were represented as advertising, the fact that it would affect his standing with other of his profession might make the representation actionable, although advertising is not reputed dishonest, and even seems to be regarded by many with pride. See *Martin v. The Picayune (Martin v. Nicholson Pub. Co.)* 115 La. 979, 4 L.R.A. (N.S.) 861, 40 So. 376. It seems to us impossible to say that the obvious tendency of what is imputed to the plaintiff by this advertisement is not seriously to hurt her standing with a considerable and respectable class in the community. Therefore it was the plaintiff's right to prove her case and go to the jury, and the defendant would have got all that it could ask if it had been permitted to persuade them, if it could, to take a contrary view. *Culmer v. Canby*, 41 C. C. A. 302, 101 Fed. 195, 197; *Twombly v. Monroe*, 136 Mass. 464, 469. *See* *Gates v. New York Recorder Co.* 155 N. Y. 228, 49 N. E. 769.

It is unnecessary to consider the question whether the publication of the plaintiff's likeness was a tort *per se*. It is enough for the present case that the law should at least be prompt to recognize the injuries that may arise from an unauthorized use in connection with other facts, even if more subtilty is needed to state the wrong than is needed here. In this instance we feel no doubt.

Judgment reversed.

——————

Points for Discussion

1. Define libel.

2. Describe the plaintiff's claim in *Peck*. How, in her view, was she libeled by the defendant?

3. Justice Holmes notes that the at-issue publication "was of and concerning the plaintiff" and that the mistaken publication of a portrait of the plaintiff did not excuse the conduct of the defendant. Should the law recognize a defense of mistake in libel cases?

4. How has the plaintiff alleged she was damaged by the publication of the portrait? How should a court or jury assess and quantify damages on facts like those presented in *Peck*?

5. On nominal, general, and special harm damages in defamation actions, *see* Restatement (Second) of Torts §§ 620-622 (1977).

——————

RESTATEMENT (SECOND) OF TORTS (1977)
§ 568. Libel and Slander Distinguished

(1) Libel consists of the publication of defamatory matter by written or printed words, by its embodiment in physical form or by any other form of communication that has the potentially harmful qualities characteristic of written or printed words.

(2) Slander consists of the publication of defamatory matter by spoken words, transitory gestures or by any form of communication other than those stated in Subsection (1).

Belli v. Orlando Daily Newspapers, Inc.

389 F.2d 579 (5th Cir. 1967)

WISDOM, Circuit Judge.

This action for damages for libel and **slander** is based on a false statement relating to Mr. Melvin Belli. Belli, an attorney of national prominence, is well known in the legal profession for his pioneering in the development of demonstrative evidence as a trial tactic and his success in obtaining large judgments for plaintiffs in personal injury suits. He is well known to the general public because of his representation of Jack Ruby and others in the public eye.

> **FYI**
>
> Jack Ruby was convicted of the November 1963 murder of Lee Harvey Oswald after Oswald was arrested and charged with assassinating President John K. Kennedy. For more on Ruby, see GARRY WILLS & OVID DEMARIS, JACK RUBY: THE MAN WHO KILLED THE MAN WHO KILLED KENNEDY (Ishi Press 2011).

In March 1964 Mr. Leon Handley, an attorney in Orlando, Florida, in a conversation with Miss Jean Yothers, a columnist for the Orlando Evening Star, repeated a story he had heard concerning Belli. Handley told Yothers that the Florida Bar Association had invited Belli to serve as a member of one of the panels on the program of the Association at its 1955 Convention in Miami Beach. Belli agreed, with the understanding that 'since there were no funds provided in the budget for payment per se for his contribution as a lawyer to the program the Florida Bar instead would pick up the hotel tab for himself and his wife during their stay.' According to Handley, after

Mr. and Mrs. Belli left Florida, the Association discovered that the Bellis 'ran up a bunch of (clothing) bills' which they charged to their hotel room. The derogatory portion of the story was admittedly false: the Bellis had not charged any purchases to their hotel account. Unfortunately for all, Jean Yothers reported, with embellishments, this nine-year old story in her gossip column in the Orlando Evening Star for March 19, 1964. She commented, in part: '* * * Oops. * * * the plan backfired on the Florida Bar * * * (Mr. Belli and 'his well-dressed wife' had charged) clothing bills amounting to hundreds of $s * * * to their hotel rooms. * * * The Florida Bar had been taken. * * * After all, that was the plan.'[1]

On these facts, Belli brought this diversity action. The complaint alleges that (1) Yothers, the Orlando Evening Star, and its editor libeled Belli through publication of the article, (2) that Handley slandered Belli in making the false statement to Yothers, and (3) that all of these parties, with others, participated in a conspiracy to defame Belli.

The district court dismissed Belli's complaint for failure to state a claim upon which relief could be granted. The court relied on the erroneous assumption that the determination whether a statement is a libel (or slander) per se is solely for the court. We consider it a close question whether the publication is so clearly defamatory that as a matter of law the case should not be submitted to the jury.

---

1 The article appeared in the Orlando Evening Star under the title 'On the Town' by Jean Yothers and headed 'Florida Bar Got the Bill'. The full text is as follows:

> Jack Ruby's flamboyant attorney Melvin Belli of San Francisco makes an indelible impression whither he goeth.

> Consider the time he and Mrs. Belli were in Miami six or so years ago and Belli was a member of a panel at a program-meeting of the Florida Bar.

> Here's what happened:

> In making arrangements for Belli's participation it had been pointed out to him that since there were no funds provided in the budget for payment per se for his contribution as a lawyer to the program, the Florida Bar instead would pick up the hotel tab for himself and his wife during their stay. Belli agreed.

> Oops.

> A local attorney remembers, with embarrassed chagrin, how the plan backfired on the Florida Bar.

> After the well-dressed Mr. Belli and his well-dressed wife left town, the hotel where they had been staying received clothing bills amounting to hundreds of $s. The Bellis had shopped in Miami stores and charged clothing bills to their hotel rooms.

> The Florida Bar had been taken.

> It was hard to stomach but the Board of Governors of the Florida Bar picked up the Bellis' bill.

> After all, that was the plan.

We hold, however, that the publication itself, without reference to extrinsic facts, is capable of carrying a defamatory meaning. It is for a jury to determine whether it was so understood by the 'common mind'. We reverse and remand.

. . . .

Historically, libel, as generally distinguishable from slander, was actionable without the necessity of pleading or proving that the plaintiff had suffered any damages as a result of it. . . . A **libel per se** is one that is defamatory on its face, including a publication that is susceptible of several meanings, one of which is defamatory; it is actionable without proof of special harm. A **libel per quod** is one in which the defamatory meaning, or **innuendo**, is not apparent on the face of the publication, but must be established by proof of extrinsic facts. Here the district court held, correctly, that the Belli claim 'must be determined solely on the basis of whether it sufficiently alleges a publication which is libelous per se'– since, as is evident from the complaint, the plaintiff did not allege defamation by extrinsic facts or plead special damages.

. . . In its opinion below the court recognized that there are four categories of defamatory imputations which traditionally have been considered actionable without proof of harm. As set out in the Restatement of Torts, Second, Tentative Draft 12, Section 569, these are statements which impute to another '(1) a criminal offense, (2) a loathsome disease, (3) matter incompatible with his business, trade, profession or office, and (4) unchastity on the part of a woman plaintiff'. Such defamatory statements, whether the publication is in the form of libel or in the form of slander, are regarded as especially likely to cause harm to the reputation of the person defamed, although such harm is not and perhaps cannot be proved. *See* Restatement, Second, Tentative Draft 12, Sections 569-574; Prosser, Law of Torts § 107 (1963); I Harper and James, Law of Torts § 5.9 (1956). Florida law recognizes these four traditional categories of per se libel and slander. *Richard v. Gray*, Fla.S.Ct.1953, 62 So.2d 597, 598; *Layne v. Tribune*, 1933, 108 Fla. 177, 146 So. 234, 236, 86 A.L.R. 466; *Adams v. News-Journal Corp.*, Fla.S.Ct.1955, 84 So.2d 549, 551; *Miami Herald Pub. Co. v. Brautigan*, Fla.App.1961, 127 So.2d 718, 722.

Libel per se is not limited to these four categories: Courts use a stock formula to describe a general class of per se libel (but not per se slander). The Restatement's formula is:

One who publishes defamatory matter is subject to liability without proof of special harm or loss of reputation if the defamation is (a) Libel whose defamatory innuendo is apparent from the publication itself without reference to extrinsic facts by way of inducement. Restatement, Second, Tentative Draft 12, Section 569.

In Florida and in many states the rubric runs: a libel per se is 'any publication which exposes a person to distrust, hatred, contempt, ridicule, obloquy'. For example, in *Briggs v. Brown*, 55 Fla. 417, 46 So. 325, 330 (1908) the court states the formula for libels per se as follows:

> A civil action for libel will lie when there has been a false and unprivileged publication by letter or otherwise which exposes a person to distrust, hatred, contempt, ridicule, or **obloquy** * * * or which has a tendency to injure such person in his office, occupation, business, or employment. If the publication is false and not privileged, and is such that its natural and proximate consequence necessarily causes injury to a person in his personal, social, official, or business relations or life, wrong and injury are presumed and implied, and such publication is actionable per se.

. . . .

We find that the general law and Florida law are in agreement with Dean Prosser's conclusion: 'It is for the court in the first instance to determine whether the words are reasonably capable of a particular interpretation, or whether they are necessarily so; it is then for the jury to say whether they were in fact understood as defamatory. If the language used is open to two meanings * * * it is for the jury to determine whether the defamatory sense was the one conveyed.' Prosser, Law of Torts § 106, at 765 (1963). . . .

Both judge and jury play a part in determining whether language constitutes libel. The Supreme Court has delineated these roles in *Washington Post Co. v. Chaloner*, 1919, 250 U.S. 290, 39 S.Ct. 448, 63 L.Ed. 987:

> A publication claimed to be defamatory must be read and construed in the sense in which the readers to whom it is addressed would ordinarily understand it. * * * When thus read, if its meaning is so unambiguous as to reasonably bear but one interpretation, it is for the judge to say whether that signification is defamatory or not. If, upon the other hand, it is capable of two meanings, one of which would be libelous and actionable and the other not, it is for the jury to say, under all the circumstances surrounding its publication, including extraneous facts admissible in evidence, which of the two meanings would be attributed to it by those to whom it is addressed or by whom it may be read.

. . . The district court in this case completely excised the jury's role, a position it could take only on the assumption that the publication unambiguously carried no defamatory meaning. Since the court did not spell out its reasons, the defendants in their briefs have attempted to articulate the rationale for the holding below.

The defendants argue that the article did not 'hurt' Belli as an attorney, did not imply that he was 'losing his touch with demonstrative evidence', did not affect his ability to 'obtain those 'more adequate awards' for seamen and railroad workers for which he is so justly famous'. In effect, so the argument runs, the article was nothing more than caustic comment on the acuteness of the Florida Bar Association. Belli simply 'showed the Florida lawyers that their agreement was somewhat more favorable to him that they- in their naivete-contemplated'. In its harshest sense, they say, 'the article implies no more than that Mr. Belli 'put one over' on the Florida Bar', which is 'not quite the same as conning a destitute widow out of her homestead'. In short, Mr. Belli just got 'a little more out of the agreement than the Bar Association contemplated'.

The defendants make a case – just barely – for the view that the article is capable of being reasonably interpreted as non-defamatory. But since the article on its face is also capable of carrying a defamatory meaning, it is for the jury to decide whether the words were in fact so understood.

The plaintiff contends, in his brief, 'No person reading the headline and the article *sub judice* * * * could conclude other than that Melvin Belli, both as a lawyer and as a private citizen is grasping, conniving, contemptible, dishonest; a cheat, swindler, trickster, deceiver, defrauder; a person to be avoided, shunned and distrusted.' Without benefit of the defendants' cavalier reading of the article or the plaintiff's

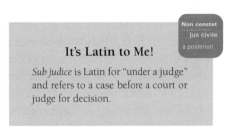

It's Latin to Me!

Sub judice is Latin for "under a judge" and refers to a case before a court or judge for decision.

retort hyperbolic, we consider that the bare bones of the article are capable of carrying the meaning that Belli tricked and deceived the Florida Bar Association out of hundreds of dollars worth of clothes.

The story alleges: (1) Belli knew that the Florida Bar Association's budget would enable him to be reimbursed only for his hotel bill; (2) subject to this limitation he agreed to participate in a panel discussion; (3) he deliberately planned to 'take' the Association for hundreds of dollars by charging clothing purchases to his hotel bill; (4) he and his well-dressed wife left Miami before the Association found out about their purchases; (5) the Association, to its embarrassment, had to pick up the tab. 'The Florida Bar had been taken. * * * After all that was the plan.'

The author's comment seems intended to insure the common reader's understanding of what purportedly happened. The common reader is likely to understand 'take', just as Miss Yothers must have understood it. A recent dictionary defines it. 'To cheat, deceive'; other dictionaries agree with this definition. The man in the street is likely to understand that hotel expenses do not include 'hundreds of dollars worth of clothing'. But any doubts the reader might have as to what purportedly happened are likely to be resolved by the reference to Belli's 'plan' to 'take' the Florida Bar. We hold that a jury might reasonably conclude that the conduct imputed to Belli was incompatible with the standards of an ethical lawyer and as such violated one of the four traditional categories of libel per se. A jury might also conclude that such conduct subjected Belli to contempt and ridicule humiliating him socially and injuring him professionally.

The Court has some doubt whether the publication in question carries a non-defamatory meaning. The Court has very little doubt that it carries a defamatory meaning. The Court has concluded however that the final determination of the issue of defamation should be made by a jury.

The story is nine years old. It was not made within the context of a discussion of an important public issue. Nevertheless, the delimiting effect of the law of libel on **First Amendment** rights and a free press impels the Court not to excise the role of the jury. 'Since one's reputation is the view which others take of him * * * whether an idea injures a person's reputation depends upon the opinions of those to whom it is published.' Developments in the Law: *Defamation,* 69 Harv.L.Rev. 875, 881-82 (1956). Thus, because it is impractical, even unreliable, to depend upon in-court testimony of recipients of the particular publication for determining whether that publication is defamatory, a logical function of the jury is to decide whether the plaintiff has been lowered in the esteem of those to whom the idea was published. As early as the seventeenth century, the court in Lord Townshend v. Dr. Hughes, 1693, 2 Mod. 150, 195, held that 'words should not be construed in a rigid or in a mild sense, but according to the general and natural meaning, and agreeable to the common understanding of all men.' Florida has adopted the common-mind test. *Loeb v. Geronemus,* Fla.1953, 66 So.2d 241. Any doubt as to the defamatory effect of a publication should be resolved by the common mind of the jury, and not by even the most carefully considered judicial pronouncement.

. . . .

We reverse the dismissal of the district court and remand the case for further proceedings consistent with this opinion.

———————

Points for Discussion

1. What did the *Belli* court hold? Do you agree or disagree with the court's holding?

2. Define and distinguish (a) libel and (b) slander.

3. Define and distinguish (a) libel *per se* and (b) libel *per quod.*

4. What adjudicative roles do judge and jury play and what functions do they perform in determining whether a communication constitutes libel?

5. Consider the following illustrations from RESTATEMENT (SECOND) OF TORTS §§ 564A, 569, and 575:

    a. "A newspaper publishes the statement that the officials of a labor organization are engaged in subversive activities. There are 162 officials. Neither the entire group nor any of them can recover for defamation." Assume that there are only four union officials. Can all four officials or any one official recover for defamation? *See* Section 564A, comment a, illustration 2.

    b. "The A newspaper publishes a statement that B . . . 'is the mistress of C.'" To whom is A liable? *See* Section 569, comment f, illustration 1.

    c. "A, a Catholic priest, says to others that B, a merchant, has been excommunicated. It is proved that in consequence of this statement B has lost Catholic customers." Has A defamed B? *See* Section 575, comment b, illustration 1.

Hypo 16-1

The year is 1945. A and B, two men who happen to be white, live in a southern state. A calls B a Negro. Should that statement constitute actionable defamation? Why or why not? *See* Charles L. Black, Jr., *The Lawfulness of the Segregation Decisions*, 69 YALE L.J. 421, 426 (1960).

Finkel v. Dauber

29 Misc.3d 325, 906 N.Y.S.2d 697 (2010)

RANDY SUE MARBER, J.

Upon the foregoing papers, the motion . . . by the Plaintiff . . . seeking partial summary judgment on the issue of liability and setting the matter down for an immediate trial on the issue of damages; the cross-motion . . . by the Defendants . . . seeking sanctions against the Plaintiff . . . are decided as provided herein.

This action arises out of prurient statements posted by the officers of a Facebook group. The group's information page shows that its name is "90 Cents Short of a Dollar", and lists five officers and six members, five of whom are the officers. The officers are Defendants Michael Dauber, Melinda Danowitz, Leah Herz and Jeff Schwartz and a non-defendant, Joe Colello. Another member, Alyssa Buono, is also not a defendant here. The listed purpose of the group is "just for fun" and "inside jokes".

Ninety Cents Short of a Dollar (hereafter referred to as "Ninety Cents") is a "secret" Facebook group, which has no public content and does not appear on a Facebook member's profile. New members must be invited by an administrator, here either of the Defendants, Michael Dauber or Melinda Danowitz. Although Ninety Cents lists only six members or "cents", ten people are listed as "cents" in the group's "recent news".

The Plaintiff alleges that she was defamed by the named Defendant members/officers, although she does not allege that the secret group's posts are accessible to anyone outside the group. Thus, it is not shown or alleged that access to Ninety Cents' content is available to Facebook users, i.e. that it is not restricted solely to the participant member/officers. The Plaintiff is silent in this regard, as are the Defendants.

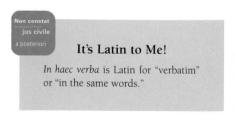

It's Latin to Me!

In haec verba is Latin for "verbatim" or "in the same words."

The Plaintiff asserts a cause of action for **defamation**, submitting a copy of posts on a Ninety Cents' thread to meet the requirement of submitting "in haec verba" statements. The Plaintiff identifies herself as the 11th cent in the posts. Her name is never used. The following explicit material is necessary for analysis (spelling, punctuation and typos are as in original):

ooooh i like this group.

BTW the 11th cent, unbeknownst to many, acquired AIDS while on a cruise to Africa (with another member of the group who shall remain nameless). While in Africa she was seen f[---]ing a horse. NICHTE NICHTE eleventh cent! I mean you know ... I kinda felt bad for the eleventh cent ... but then again I felt WORSE for the horse. ... (Leah Herz 1/29/07, 5:04pm)

In regards to the 7th cents comments,,, it was not from an African cruise... it was from sharing needles with different heroin addicts, this led to cross "mojination" which caused the HIV virus... she then persisted to screw a baboon which caused the epidemic to spread. (Jeff Schwartz 1/29/07, 7:43pm)

I heard that the 11th cent got aids when she hired a male prostitute who came dressed as a sexy fireman apparantly .. she was lonely, because her friends no longer associated with her. her sexy fireman prostitute was her only company. in addition to acquiring aids, this nameless 11th cent aquired crabs, and syphillis. (Melinda Danowitz, 1/29/07, 8:00 pm)

also i heard that the stds [sexually transmitted diseases] she got were os bad that she morfed into the devil in one of our pictures ... oops did i reviel the 11th cent?> (Michael Dauber, 1/29/07, 8:32 pm)

The Plaintiff avers that Michael Dauber's last post identifies her as the 11th cent because of the devil reference. There is an edited photograph which allegedly depicts the Plaintiff posted on Ninety Cents. The photograph, which the Plaintiff states is one of her, shows a pretty young woman smiling, edited to add an ear to the top of her head, and bearing the legend "Evil has got a new face.... It has never looked so terrifying!!!" Although not visible in the photocopy submitted to the court, there is a comment below the photo which states, "the reflection of fire in the eyes adds a nice effect." The Plaintiff submits an additional photograph which shows ten distorted masked costumed characters, none of whose identities are remotely discernible. The Plaintiff claims that she is the one with an angry faced mask, and again alleges that it marks her as the devil.

The following posts regarding Ninety Cents and its officer Defendants provide context for the group and its members:

trivia + cent fights + gh2 + aids + prostitutes + dead people + hairy chest + joe cursing + masturbation = this wall = life <33

(Melinda Danowitz 1/29/07, 10:57 pm)

... your a douche bag thats right.. and since rick james is no longer 11 can I be 11 since ... yes its one louder than 10 ...

(Jeff Schwarz 1/30/07, 11:16pm)

leah ... stop thinkin ur the sh[--] ... because ur not THE sh[--] ... u just are sh[--] ... number 2 ...

(Michael Dauber, 1/31/07, 8:51pm)

dauber that really hurt. you have left a boo boo on my heart.

I don't know if I can forgive you. ever.

especially since you didnt come to jew club

yesterday.

robots are more important to you.

so is screwing your dog ...

(Leah Herz, 1/31/07, 9:28pm)

Turning to the relevant legal analysis, the elements of a cause of action for defamation are "a false statement, published without privilege or authorization to a third party, constituting fault as judged by, at a minimum, a negligence standard, and it must either cause special harm or constitute defamation per se" (*Salvatore v. Kumar*, 45 A.D.3d 560, 563, 845 N.Y.S.2d 384 [2d Dept. 2007]); [c].

To be actionable, a statement of fact is required, and "rhetorical hyperbole" or "vigorous epithet" will not suffice [cc]. Only facts "are capable of being proven false." [C] Context is key, as assertions that a person is guilty of "**blackmail**", "**fraud**", "**bribery**" and "**corruption**" in certain contexts could be understood as hyperbole or epithet. [C] "The infinite variety of meanings conveyed by words, depending on the words themselves and their purpose, the circumstances surrounding their use, and the manner, tone and style with which they are used rules out ... a formulistic approach." [C] Determining whether a given statement expresses fact or opinion is a question of law for the court and one which must be answered "on the basis of what the average person hearing or reading the communication would take it to mean." [C]

Notwithstanding the foregoing, several guidelines have been developed to aid in such determination. The four factors are: "(1) an assessment of whether the specific language in issue has a precise meaning which is readily understood or whether it is indefinite and ambiguous; (2) a determination of whether the statement is capable of being objectively characterized as true or false; (3) an examination of the full context of the communication in which the statement appears; and (4) a consideration of the broader social context or setting surrounding the communication including the existence of any applicable customs or conventions which might signal to readers or listeners that what is being read or heard is likely to be opinion, not fact." [Cc]

In reaching a determination however, "sifting through a communication for the purpose of isolating and identifying assertions of fact" is not "the central inquiry" and the courts "should look to the over-all context in which the assertions were made and determine on that basis whether the reasonable reader would have believed that the challenged statements were conveying facts about the libel plaintiff.'" [C] The *"dispositive inquiry* ... is whether a reasonable [reader] could have concluded that [the articles were] conveying facts about the plaintiff.'" [C]

A reasonable reader, given the overall context of the posts, simply would not believe that the Plaintiff contracted AIDS by having sex with a horse or a baboon or that she contracted AIDS from a male prostitute who also gave her crabs and syphilis, or that having contracted sexually transmitted diseases in such manner she morphed into the devil. Taken together, the statements can only be read as puerile attempts by adolescents to outdo each other.

While the posts display an utter lack of taste and propriety, they do not constitute statements of fact. An ordinary reader would not take them literally to conclude that any of these teenagers are having sex with wild or domestic animals or with male prostitutes dressed as firemen. The entire context and tone of the posts constitute evidence of adolescent insecurities and indulgences, and a vulgar attempt at humor. What they do not contain are statements of fact.

. . . .

Facebook is no longer a party defendant, and as the Plaintiff has failed to state a cause of action in defamation . . . against the named individual Defendants, the

Court in searching the record . . . grants summary judgment to the Defendants and dismisses the complaint.

. . .

Points for Discussion

1. Do you agree or disagree with the court's conclusion that the plaintiff was not defamed as a matter of law? Do you agree or disagree that only a statement of fact, and not hyperbole or an epithet, is required?

2. Could the average or a reasonable reader of the Facebook postings believe that the plaintiff had contracted Acquired Immune Deficiency Syndrome (AIDS)? Who is the "average/reasonable" reader? Did the court correctly conclude that "[t]aken together, the statements can only be read as puerile attempts by adolescents to outdo each other"?

3. What kinds of statements posted on Facebook, Myspace, or other social networking sites would support an actionable claim of defamation? Would "A is a jerk" suffice? "A is a thief"? "I just heard that A was arrested for shoplifting"? "I saw A smoking weed [marijuana] at a party last night"? What about making a Facebook page in someone else's name or posting photoshopped (altered) photos?

Hypo 16-2

Bobby, a single 21-year-old man, was born and raised in Smalltown, which has a population of approximately 700 inhabitants. Since the age of seventeen he has been employed by a sprinkler business on both a full-time and part-time basis. Two years ago Bobby obtained employment with a local sprinkler business owned by his brother Neil; in that job he sold residential lawn sprinkler systems and managed installation crews.

Bobby was recently hospitalized for heat exhaustion after working long hours in the sun and summer heat on a major project for one of his brother's biggest clients. Betty, his mother's longtime next-door neighbor and a certified nurse's aide who worked at the hospital, saw Bobby in his hospital room and dropped in to talk to him. "What happened to you?" she asked Bobby. "I don't know," he responded. "I guess I passed out in the heat." Curious, Betty asked a nurse if she knew why Bobby had been admitted. The nurse indicated that a patient with AIDS had been admitted earlier that day and stated that she did not know if Bobby was that person.

On her lunch break Betty called her daughter and said: "Guess what? Bobby's in the hospital. He has AIDS!" The daughter asked, "Bobby has AIDS?" and Betty said, "Yes. Are you as shocked as I am?" Betty then informed her husband, sister, brother, and four sons that Bobby had AIDS.

Released from the hospital after a two-day stay, Bobby returned to work. He noticed that several workers he supervised no longer ate lunch with and barely spoke to him. When he mentioned this to his brother, Neil, he was informed that there was a rumor going around the town that Bobby had AIDS and that some of the workers were uncomfortable being around him and were threatening to quit their jobs. "That's crazy, Neil. I don't have AIDS. You know I don't. Who told you that lie?" "I hate to do this," Neil told Bobby," but I can't afford to lose those guys. They're great workers. I'm going to have to let you go." Unemployed, and later confronted by two Smalltown residents regarding the AIDS rumor, Bobby left Smalltown.

Bobby recently learned from Neil the rumor that he was suffering from AIDS was started by Betty and spread by her family. Bobby seeks your legal advice concerning the foregoing facts and events. Has Bobby been slandered? If so, by whom? Discuss.

Hypo 16-3

Plaintiff has filed a lawsuit alleging that an article published in the May 2010 issue of Defendant's magazine contained false and defamatory statements about her deceased father (who died in 2009). According to the complaint, the article falsely states that the plaintiff's father bribed public officials in order to obtain highway construction contracts. Is Plaintiff's lawsuit actionable? *See Gruschus v. Curtis Publishing Co.*, 342 F.2d 775 (10th Cir. 1965); RESTATEMENT (SECOND) OF TORTS § 560 (1977).

Carafano v. Metrosplash.Com, Inc.

339 F.3d 1119 (9th Cir. 2003)

THOMAS, Circuit Judge.

This is a case involving a cruel and sadistic identity theft. In this appeal, we consider to what extent a computer match making service may be legally responsible for false content in a dating profile provided by someone posing as another person. Under the circumstances presented by this case, we conclude that the service is statutorily immune pursuant to 47 U.S.C. § 230(c)(1).

I

Matchmaker.com is a commercial Internet dating service. For a fee, members of Matchmaker post anonymous profiles and may then view profiles of other members in their area, contacting them via electronic mail sent through the Matchmaker server. A typical profile contains one or more pictures of the subject, descriptive information such as age, appearance and interests, and answers to a variety of questions designed to evoke the subject's personality and reason for joining the service.

Members are required to complete a detailed questionnaire containing both multiple-choice and essay questions. In the initial portion of the questionnaire, members select answers to more than fifty questions from menus providing between four and nineteen options. Some of the potential multiple choice answers are innocuous; some are sexually suggestive. In the subsequent essay section, participants answer up to eighteen additional questions, including "anything that the questionnaire didn't cover." Matchmaker policies prohibit members from posting last names, addresses, phone numbers or e-mail addresses within a profile. Matchmaker reviews photos for impropriety before posting them but does not review the profiles themselves, relying instead upon participants to adhere to the service guidelines.

On October 23, 1999, an unknown person using a computer in Berlin posted a "trial" personal profile of Christianne Carafano in the Los Angeles section of Matchmaker. (New members were permitted to post "trial" profiles for a few weeks without paying.) The posting was without the knowledge, consent or permission of Carafano. The profile was listed under the identifier "Chase529."

Carafano is a popular actress. Under the stage name of Chase Masterson, Carafano has appeared in numerous films and television shows, such as "Star Trek: Deep Space Nine," and "General Hospital." Pictures of the actress are widely available on the Internet, and the false Matchmaker profile "Chase529" contained several of these pictures. Along with fairly innocuous responses to questions about interests and appearance, the person posting the profile selected "Playboy/Playgirl" for "main source of current events" and "looking for a one-night stand" for "why did you call." In addition, the open-ended essay responses indicated that "Chase529" was looking for a "hard and dominant" man with "a strong sexual appetite" and that she "liked sort of be[ ]ing controlled by a man, in and out of bed." The profile text did not include a last name for "Chase" or indicate Carafano's real name, but it listed two of her movies (and, as mentioned, included pictures of the actress).

In response to a question about the "part of the LA area" in which she lived, the profile provided Carafano's home address. The profile included a contact e-mail address, cmla2000@yahoo.com, which, when contacted, produced an automatic e-mail reply stating, "You think you are the right one? Proof it !!" [sic], and providing Carafano's home address and telephone number.

Unaware of the improper posting, Carafano soon began to receive messages responding to the profile. Although she was traveling at the time, she checked her voicemail on October 31 and heard two sexually explicit messages. When she returned to her home on November 4, she found a highly threatening and sexually explicit fax that also threatened her son. Alarmed, she contacted the police the following day. As a result of the profile, she also received numerous phone calls, voicemail messages, written correspondence, and e-mail from fans through her professional e-mail account. Several men expressed concern that she had given out her address and phone number (but simultaneously expressed an interest in meeting her). Carafano felt unsafe in her home, and she and her son stayed in hotels or away from Los Angeles for several months.

Sometime around Saturday, November 6, Siouxzan Perry, who handled Carafano's professional website and much of her e-mail correspondence, first learned of the false profile through a message from "Jeff." Perry exchanged e-mails with Jeff, visited the Matchmaker site, and relayed information about the profile to Carafano. Acting on Carafano's instructions, Perry contacted Matchmaker and demanded that the profile be removed immediately. The Matchmaker employee indicated that she could not remove the profile immediately because Perry herself had not posted it, but the company blocked the profile from public view on Monday morning, November 8. At 4:00 AM the following morning, Matchmaker deleted the profile.

Carafano filed a complaint in California state court against Matchmaker and its corporate successors, alleging **invasion of privacy**, **misappropriation** of the right of publicity, defamation, and **negligence**. The defendants removed the case to federal district court. The district court granted the defendants' motion for summary judgment in a published opinion. *Carafano v. Metrosplash.com, Inc.*,

207 F.Supp.2d 1055 (C.D.Cal.2002). The court rejected Matchmaker's argument for **immunity** under 47 U.S.C. § 230(c)(1) after finding that the company provided part of the profile content. [C] However, the court rejected Carafano's invasion of privacy claim on the grounds that her home address was "newsworthy" and that, in any case, Matchmaker had not disclosed her address with reckless disregard for her privacy. [C] Similarly, the court rejected Carafano's claims for **defamation**, **negligence**, and **misappropriation** because she failed to show that Matchmaker had acted with **actual malice**. [C]

. . . .

II

The dispositive question in this appeal is whether Carafano's claims are barred by 47 U.S.C. § 230(c)(1), which states that "[n]o provider or user of an interactive computer service shall be treated as the publisher or speaker of any information provided by another information content provider." Through this provision, Congress granted most Internet services immunity from liability for publishing false or defamatory material so long as the information was provided by another party. As a result, Internet publishers are treated differently from corresponding publishers in print, television and radio. *See Batzel v. Smith,* 333 F.3d 1018, 1026-27 (9th Cir.2003).

Congress enacted this provision as part of the Communications Decency Act of 1996 for two basic policy reasons: to promote the free exchange of information and ideas over the Internet and to encourage voluntary monitoring for offensive or obscene material. [C] Congress incorporated these ideas into the text of § 230 itself, expressly noting that "interactive computer services have flourished, to the benefit of all Americans, with a minimum of government regulation," and that "[i]ncreasingly Americans are relying on interactive media for a variety of political, educational, cultural, and entertainment services." 47 U.S.C. § 230(a)(4), (5). Congress declared it the "policy of the United States" to "promote the continued development of the Internet and other interactive computer services," "to preserve the vibrant and competitive free market that presently exists for the Internet and other interactive computer services," and to "remove disincentives for the development and utilization of blocking and filtering technologies." 47 U.S.C. § 230(b) (1), (2), (4).

In light of these concerns, reviewing courts have treated § 230(c) immunity as quite robust, adopting a relatively expansive definition of "interactive computer service"[2] and a relatively restrictive definition of "information content provider."[3] Under the statutory scheme, an "interactive computer service" qualifies for immunity so long as it does not also function as an "information content provider" for the portion of the statement or publication at issue.

We recently considered whether § 230(c) provided immunity to the operator of an electronic newsletter who selected and published an allegedly defamatory e-mail over the Internet. *Batzel,* 333 F.3d at 1030-32. We held that the online newsletter qualified as an "interactive computer service" under the statutory definition and that the selection for publication and editing of an e-mail did not constitute partial "creation or development" of that information within the definition of "information content provider." Although the case was ultimately remanded for determination of whether the original author intended to "provide" his e-mail for publication, [c] the *Batzel* decision joined the consensus developing across other courts of appeals that § 230(c) provides broad immunity for publishing content provided primarily by third parties. *See Green v. America Online,* 318 F.3d 465, 470-71 (3d Cir.2003) (upholding immunity for the transmission of defamatory messages and a program designed to disrupt the recipient's computer); *Ben Ezra, Weinstein, & Co. v. America Online Inc.,* 206 F.3d 980, 985-86 (10th Cir.2000) (upholding immunity for the on-line provision of stock information even though AOL communicated frequently with the stock quote providers and had occasionally deleted stock symbols and other information from its database in an effort to correct errors); *Zeran v. America Online,* 129 F.3d 327, 328-29 (4th Cir.1997) (upholding immunity for both initial publication and delay in removal of false messages connecting offensive tee-shirts to the plaintiff's name and home telephone number). . . .

The fact that some of the content was formulated in response to Matchmaker's questionnaire does not alter this conclusion. Doubtless, the questionnaire facilitated the expression of information by individual users. However, the selection of the content was left exclusively to the user. The actual profile "information" consisted of the particular options chosen and the additional essay answers provided. Matchmaker was not responsible, even in part, for associating certain multiple choice responses with a set of physical characteristics, a group of essay answers, and a photograph. Matchmaker cannot be considered an "information content provider" under the statute because no profile has any content until a user actively creates it.

---

2 "The term 'interactive computer service' means any information service, system, or access software provider that provides or enables computer access by multiple users to a computer server, including specifically a service or system that provides access to the Internet and such systems operated or services offered by libraries or educational institutions." 47 U.S.C. § 230(f)(2).

3 "The term 'information content provider' means any person or entity that is responsible, in whole or in part, for the creation or development of information provided through the Internet or any other interactive computer service." 47 U.S.C. § 230(f)(3).

As such, Matchmaker's role is similar to that of the customer rating system at issue in *Gentry v. eBay, Inc.,* 99 Cal.App.4th 816, 121 Cal.Rptr.2d 703 (2002). In that case, the plaintiffs alleged that eBay "was an information content provider in that it was responsible for the creation of information, or development of information, for the online auction it provided through the Internet." [C] Specifically, the plaintiffs noted that eBay created a highly structured Feedback Forum, which categorized each response as a "Positive Feedback," a "Negative Feedback," or a "Neutral Feedback." *Id.* In addition, eBay provided a color coded star symbol next to the user name of a seller who had achieved certain levels of "Positive Feedback" and offered a separate "Power Sellers" endorsement based on sales volume and Positive Feedback ratings. *Id.* The court concluded that § 230 barred the claims:

> Appellants' negligence claim is based on the assertion that the information is false or misleading because it has been manipulated by the individual defendants or other co-conspiring parties. Based on these allegations, enforcing appellants' negligence claim would place liability on eBay for simply compiling false and/or misleading content created by the individual defendants and other coconspirators. We do not see such activities transforming eBay into an information content provider with respect to the representations targeted by appellants as it did not create or develop the underlying misinformation.

[C] Similarly, the fact that Matchmaker classifies user characteristics into discrete categories and collects responses to specific essay questions does not transform Matchmaker into a "developer" of the "underlying misinformation."

We also note that, as with eBay, Matchmaker's decision to structure the information provided by users allows the company to offer additional features, such as "matching" profiles with similar characteristics or highly structured searches based on combinations of multiple choice questions. Without standardized, easily encoded answers, Matchmaker might not be able to offer these services and certainly not to the same degree. Arguably, this promotes the expressed Congressional policy "to promote the continued development of the Internet and other interactive computer services." 47 U.S.C. § 230(b)(1).

Carafano responds that Matchmaker contributes much more structure and content than eBay by asking 62 detailed questions and providing a menu of "pre-prepared responses." However, this is a distinction of degree rather than of kind, and Matchmaker still lacks responsibility for the "underlying misinformation."

Further, even assuming Matchmaker could be considered an information content provider, the statute precludes treatment as a publisher or speaker for "*any* information provided by *another* information content provider." 47 U.S.C. § 230(c)(1) (emphasis added). The statute would still bar Carafano's claims unless Matchmaker created or developed the particular information at issue. As the *Gentry* court noted,

> [T]he fact appellants allege eBay is an information content provider is irrelevant if eBay did not itself create or develop the content for which appellants seek to hold it liable. It is not inconsistent for eBay to be an interactive service provider and also an information content provider; the categories are not mutually exclusive. The critical issue is whether eBay acted as an information content provider with respect to the information that appellants claim is false or misleading.

[C]

In this case, critical information about Carafano's home address, movie credits, and the e-mail address that revealed her phone number were transmitted unaltered to profile viewers. Similarly, the profile directly reproduced the most sexually suggestive comments in the essay section, none of which bore more than a tenuous relationship to the actual questions asked. Thus Matchmaker did not play a significant role in creating, developing or "transforming" the relevant information.

Thus, despite the serious and utterly deplorable consequences that occurred in this case, we conclude that Congress intended that service providers such as Matchmaker be afforded immunity from suit. Thus, we affirm the judgment of the district court, albeit on other grounds.

AFFIRMED.

Points for Discussion

1. The court notes that Section 230 of the Communications Decency Act of 1996 (CDA) grants Internet services immunity from defamation liability where false or defamatory material is provided by another party and that no such immunity is enjoyed by entities in the print, television, and radio industries. What policies are promoted by this federal immunity from suits like those pursued by Christianne Carafano?

2. How does the CDA define "interactive computer service" and "information content provider"?

3. Should Congress reconsider and abolish, or at least limit, Section 230 immunity? Consider the pros and cons of any changes to the current regulatory regime.

4. The owners and operators of a cat breeding service have filed a lawsuit against an Internet service provider (ISP) after several individuals posted allegedly defamatory statements about the breeding service on an interactive website. The plaintiffs allege that they asked the ISP and the posters to remove the statements and that the statements remained posted for more than 72 hours after the request for removal. According to the suit, the plaintiffs suffered lost sales, **goodwill**, and revenue and will continue to suffer damages because of the website postings. Invoking immunity under the Section 230 of the CDA, the ISP has filed a motion to dismiss. Should that motion be granted? *See Johnson v. Arden*, 614 F.3d 785 (8th Cir. 2010).

Hypo 16-4

A lawsuit filed against a social networking company by the parents of a murder victim alleges that a paramedic posted photographs of the corpse of their daughter on the site. The paramedic, who responded to an emergency call after the parents found their strangled daughter, pleaded guilty to disorderly conduct. The parents' suit requests that the company turn over the image (which is no longer posted on the site) and seeks the identity of persons who downloaded the image as well as measures preventing the further dissemination of the image. The company has asked you, its legal counsel, for advice as to how to respond to the suit. Please advise.

2. Publication

Lewis v. Equitable Life Assurance Soc'y of the United States

389 N.W.2d 876 (Minn. 1986)

AMDAHL, Chief Justice.

Plaintiffs, Carole Lewis, Mary Smith, Michelle Rafferty, and Suzanne Loizeaux, former employees of defendant, the Equitable Life Assurance Society of the United States (company), all hired for indefinite, **at-will** terms, were discharged for the stated reason of "gross **insubordination**." They claim that they were discharged in breach of their employment contracts, as determined by an employee handbook, and that they were defamed because the company knew that they would have to repeat the reason for their discharges to prospective employers. A Ramsey county jury awarded plaintiffs **compensatory** and **punitive damages**. The Minnesota Court of Appeals affirmed the award but remanded on the issue of contract damages for future harm. We affirm in full the award of compensatory damages but reverse the award of punitive damages.

In spring 1980, the company hired plaintiffs as dental claim approvers in its St. Paul office. During the application process, a manager or supervisor of the company interviewed plaintiffs and assured them that if hired, their employment would continue as long as their production remained at a satisfactory level. Plaintiffs did not execute written contracts of employment. They were employed for an indefinite time pursuant to oral agreements, and each received a copy of the company's employee handbook. Among other topics, the handbook discussed policies regarding job security, dismissals, and severance pay.

In fall 1980, the company's Pittsburgh office requested assistance from its St. Paul office. Claim approvers from St. Paul were sent to Pittsburgh beginning in September. In October, plaintiffs, who had never traveled on company business before, were among two groups of employees sent to assist the Pittsburgh office for 2-week periods.

At the time plaintiffs departed for Pittsburgh, the company had written policies concerning travel expenses. Guidelines were set forth on the back of company expense report forms and in management manuals, and the company's St. Paul office manager was responsible for instructing prospective travelers regarding the company's policies. Because he was out of the office at the time the first group departed, the office manager delegated the responsibility to his secretary. A supervisor in the St. Paul office was given responsibility for advising the second group.

Neither the secretary nor the supervisor had performed such duties prior to instructing plaintiffs. As a result, they did not review available written guidelines, they did not give plaintiffs any written instructions, and they did not tell plaintiffs that expense reports would have to be filed. Plaintiffs were only orally given information on the company's daily allowances for meals and maid tips and they were told to keep receipts for hotel bills and airfare. In addition, each received a $1,400 travel advance which, having no instruction to the contrary, they spent in full.

When plaintiffs returned to St. Paul, each received a personal letter from management commending them on their job performance while in Pittsburgh. Upon their return, and after they had spent their travel advances, they were also informed for the first time that they would have to submit expense reports detailing their daily expenditures while in Pittsburgh. Plaintiffs complied with the company's request and prepared expense reports in which they attempted to reconstruct their expenses. Upon submission, however, they were asked to change the reports with respect to maid tips because the initial instructions had been erroneous. Plaintiffs complied with this second request. However, plaintiffs were yet again told to change their reports to reflect lower overall totals. Apparently, the company sought to recoup from each plaintiff approximately $200.[4]

Not until late November 1980 did plaintiffs receive written guidelines for completing the expense reports. The guidelines differed from the instructions given prior to their departures. At this point, the company asked plaintiffs to make additional changes in their expense reports. Plaintiffs this time refused to make further changes, maintaining that the expenses shown on their original reports had been honestly and reasonably incurred and were submitted based upon the instructions they had received prior to leaving for Pittsburgh. The company did not dispute the claims that these expenses were honestly incurred.

Nevertheless, in January 1981, plaintiffs each received a letter from the office manager requesting again that they revise their expense reports. The letter set out still another, different set of guidelines to be followed. Additionally, three plaintiffs met individually with a manager from the company's Chicago office. At the meetings they were once again asked to change their expense reports to conform to company policies. They refused and were told that they were being put on probation. They were also warned, for the first time, that termination might be considered. At trial, company managers testified that the "probation" imposed on the three plaintiffs was not given in reference to the company's dismissal policies, but was primarily for the benefit of company management, to provide time to decide whether to terminate plaintiffs.

---

4 Just prior to the expense report controversy it was discovered that another employee in the office had embezzled $10,000 from the company. Although that incident was a criminal act involving more than ten times as much money as was at stake in all plaintiffs' expense reports combined, the company chose not to prosecute the case.

A week later, the office manager received orders from Chicago to obtain from two of the plaintiffs monies they had agreed to refund to the company and then to fire all four. The office manager called the two to his office and had them refund the money, saying nothing of the fact that they were to be terminated later that day. Late in the afternoon, he called each plaintiff to his office individually and again asked them to change their reports. When they stated that they were standing by their reports, he terminated them for "gross insubordination." Another employee involved in the expense-account dispute was not terminated because she agreed to change her report and to refund $200 to the company.

Because they were fired for "gross insubordination," plaintiffs received no severance pay. Had they been fired for other reasons they would have been entitled to as much as one month's severance pay.

The company admitted that the production and performance of plaintiffs was at all times satisfactory and even commendable. Company managers acknowledged that plaintiffs should have been given more thorough instructions and that the company's written guidelines should have been reviewed prior to their departures for Pittsburgh. Management also admitted that the problems could have been avoided had plaintiffs been given proper guidelines prior to their departures.

In seeking new employment, plaintiffs were requested by prospective employers to disclose their reasons for leaving the company, and each indicated that she had been "terminated." When plaintiffs received interviews, they were asked to explain their terminations. Each stated that she had been terminated for "gross insubordination" and attempted to explain the situation. The company neither published nor stated to any prospective employer that plaintiffs had been terminated for gross insubordination. Its policy was to give only the dates of employment and the final job title of a former employee unless specifically authorized in writing to release additional information.

Only one plaintiff found employment while being completely forthright with a prospective employer about her termination by the company. A second plaintiff obtained employment after she misrepresented on the application form her reason for leaving the company. She did, however, explain the true reason in her interview. A third plaintiff obtained employment only when she left blank the question on the application form requesting her reason for leaving her last employment; the issue never arose in her interview. The fourth plaintiff has been unable to find full-time employment. All plaintiffs testified to suffering emotional and financial hardship as a result of being discharged by the company.

. . . .

[T]he company argues that the trial court's conclusion of liability on the part of the company was erroneous because: (1) the only publications of the allegedly defamatory statement were made by plaintiffs; (2) the statement in question was true; and (3) the company was qualifiedly privileged to make the statement.

1. Publication

In order for a statement to be considered defamatory, it must be communicated to someone other than the plaintiff, it must be false, and it must tend to harm the plaintiff's reputation and to lower him or her in the estimation of the community. [C] Generally, there is no publication where a defendant communicates a statement directly to a plaintiff, who then communicates it to a third person. Restatement (Second) of Torts § 577, comment m (1977). Company management told plaintiffs that they had engaged in gross insubordination, for which they were being discharged. This allegedly defamatory statement was communicated to prospective employers of each plaintiff. The company, however, never communicated the statement. Plaintiffs themselves informed prospective employers that they had been terminated for gross insubordination. They did so because prospective employers inquired why they had left their previous employment. The question raised is whether a defendant can ever be held liable for defamation when the statement in question was published to a third person only by the plaintiff.

We have not previously been presented with the question of defamation by means of "self-publication." Courts that have considered the question, however, have recognized a narrow exception to the general rule that communication of a defamatory statement to a third person by the person defamed is not actionable. *See, e.g., McKinney v. County of Santa Clara,* 110 Cal.App.3d 787, 168 Cal.Rptr. 89 (1980); *Colonial Stores, Inc. v. Barrett,* 73 Ga.App. 839, 38 S.E.2d 306 (1946); *Belcher v. Little,* 315 N.W.2d 734 (Iowa 1982); *Grist v. Upjohn Co.,* 16 Mich.App. 452, 168 N.W.2d 389 (1969); *Bretz v. Mayer,* 1 Ohio Misc. 59, 203 N.E.2d 665 (1963); *First State Bank of Corpus Christi v. Ake,* 606 S.W.2d 696 (Tex.Civ. App.1980). These courts have recognized that if a defamed person was in some way compelled to communicate the defamatory statement to a third person, and if it was foreseeable to the defendant that the defamed person would be so compelled, then the defendant could be held liable for the defamation.

Several courts have specifically recognized this exception for compelled self-publication in the context of employment discharges. In an early Georgia case an appellate court was presented with an employee discharged for alleged improper conduct toward fellow employees. *Colonial Stores, Inc. v. Barrett, supra.* At that time, the War Manpower Commission required persons seeking employment to present a certificate of availability to prospective employers. The defendant employer who discharged the employee had written the reason for discharge on the employee's certificate of availability. The employee brought suit for defamation. The court, in affirming the trial court verdict in favor of the plaintiff, held that there "may be a publication when the sender intends or has reason to suppose that the communication will reach third persons, which happens, or which result naturally flows from the sending." [C]

In a Michigan case, the plaintiff employee was discharged and subsequently brought a slander action against her former employer. *Grist v. Upjohn Co., supra.* She alleged that the defendant had given her false and defamatory reasons for her discharge and that she was forced to repeat the reasons to prospective employers in detailing her previous employment. The trial court instructed the jury that they could find a slanderous statement even though the statements by the defendant were made only to the plaintiff. Affirming the trial court's jury instruction, the Michigan appellate court held: "Where the conditions are such that the utterer of the defamatory matter intends or has reason to suppose that in the ordinary course of events the matter will come to the knowledge of some third person, a publication may be effected." [C]

Most recently, a California court considered the question of compelled self-publication in the employment discharge context. *McKinney v. County of Santa Clara, supra.* A discharged deputy sheriff brought a claim of defamation against his former employer. The California appellate court recognized that liability for defamation may arise "where the originator of the defamatory statement has reason to believe that the person defamed will be under a strong compulsion to disclose the contents of the defamatory statement to a third person *after* he has read it or been informed of its contents." [C] The court's rationale for imposing liability on a defendant for the foreseeable republication by a plaintiff of a defamatory statement was based upon the "strong causal link" between the defendant's actions and the damage caused by the republication. . . . .

. . . .

The trend of modern authority persuades us that Minnesota law should recognize the doctrine of compelled self-publication. We acknowledge that recognition of this doctrine provides a significant new basis for maintaining a cause of action for defamation and, as such, it should be cautiously applied. However, when properly applied, it need not substantially broaden the scope of liability for defamation. The concept of compelled self-publication does no more than hold the originator of the defamatory statement liable for damages caused by the statement where the originator knows, or should know, of circumstances whereby the defamed person has no reasonable means of avoiding publication of the statement or avoiding the resulting damages; in other words, in cases where the defamed person was compelled to publish the statement. In such circumstances, the damages are fairly viewed as the direct result of the originator's actions.

Properly applied, the doctrine of compelled self-publication does not unduly burden the free communication of views or unreasonably broaden the scope of defamation liability. Accordingly, we hold that in an action for defamation, the publication requirement may be satisfied where the plaintiff was compelled to publish a defamatory statement to a third person if it was foreseeable to the defendant that the plaintiff would be so compelled.

In the present action, the record indicates that plaintiffs were compelled to repeat the allegedly defamatory statement to prospective employers and that the company knew plaintiffs would be so compelled. The St. Paul office manager admitted that it was foreseeable that plaintiffs would be asked by prospective employers to identify the reason that they were discharged. Their only choice would be to tell them "gross insubordination" or to lie. Fabrication, however, is an unacceptable alternative.

2. *Issue of Truth*

Finding that there was a publication, we next turn to the issue of **truth**. True statements, however disparaging, are not actionable. [C] Since it is true that plaintiffs were fired for gross insubordination, the company argues, they cannot maintain an action for defamation. The company contends the relevant statement to consider when analyzing the defense of truth is the one that plaintiffs made to their prospective employers, that is, that they had been fired for gross insubordination. Plaintiffs counter that it is the truth or falsity of the underlying statement-that plaintiffs engaged in gross insubordination-that is relevant.

. . . .

Requiring that truth as a defense go to the underlying implication of the statement, at least where the statement involves more than a simple allegation, appears to be the better view. *See* Restatement (Second) of Torts § 581A, comment e (1977). Moreover, the truth or falsity of a statement is inherently within the province of the jury. This court will not overturn a jury finding on the issue of falsity unless the finding is manifestly and palpably contrary to the evidence. Thus, we find no error on this point because the record amply supports the jury verdict that the charge of gross insubordination was false.

3. *Qualified Privilege*

Even though an untrue defamatory statement has been published, the originator of the statement will not be held liable if the statement is published under circumstances that make it conditionally privileged and if privilege is not abused. Restatement (Second) of Torts § 593 (1977). The law in Minnesota is:

> [A] communication, to be privileged, must be made upon a proper occasion, from a proper motive, and must be based upon reasonable or probable cause. When so made in good faith, the law does not imply malice from the communication itself, as in the ordinary case of libel. Actual malice must be proved, before there can be a recovery, and in the absence of such proof the plaintiff cannot recover.

[C].

The doctrine of privileged communication rests upon public policy considerations. As other jurisdictions recognize, the existence of a privilege results from the court's determination that statements made in particular contexts or on certain occasions should be encouraged despite the risk that the statements might be defamatory. *See Calero v. Del Chemical Corp.,* 68 Wis.2d 487, 498, 228 N.W.2d 737, 744 (1975). Whether an occasion is a proper one upon which to recognize a privilege is a **question of law** for the court to determine. [Cc] In the context of employment recommendations, the law generally recognizes a qualified privilege between former and prospective employers as long as the statements are made in good faith and for a legitimate purpose. [C]

Plaintiffs argue that a self-publication case does not properly fit within the **qualified privilege** doctrine. . . . [T]he logic of imposing liability upon a former employer in a self-publication case appears to compel recognition of a qualified privilege. A former employer in a compelled self-publication case may be held liable as if it had actually published the defamatory statement directly to prospective employers. Where an employer would be entitled to a privilege if it had actually published the statement, it makes little sense to deny the privilege where the identical communication is made to identical third parties with the only difference being the mode of publication. Finally, recognition of a qualified privilege seems to be the only effective means of addressing the concern that every time an employer states the reason for discharging an employee it will subject itself to potential liability for defamation. [C] It is in the public interest that information regarding an employee's discharge be readily available to the discharged employee and to prospective employers, and we are concerned that, unless a significant privilege is recognized by the courts, employers will decline to inform employees of reasons for discharges. [C] We conclude that an employer's communication to an employee of the reason for discharge may present a proper occasion upon which to recognize a qualified privilege.

This conclusion does not necessarily determine that the company's statements were privileged. A qualified privilege may be lost if it is abused. The burden is on the plaintiff to show that the privilege has been abused. [C] While the initial determination of whether a communication is privileged is a question of law for the court to decide, the question of whether the privilege was abused is a jury question. Restatement (Second) of Torts, § 619 (1977). . . .

Affirmed in part; reversed in part.

————————

Points for Discussion

1. What is the doctrine of compelled self-publication? An essential element of a claim of defamation is that one party has made an unprivileged publication to a third party. In *Lewis* no such communication was in fact made. The employer did not communicate the reason for the termination of the employees to other employers (*i.e.*, did not publish the reasons to a third party). The "publication" was made by the plaintiffs themselves as they sought new employment. As the court notes, employers know, or should know, that an allegedly defamed former employee will be compelled to inform prospective employers of facts and reasons related to the termination of their prior employment. On that view, compelled publication is foreseeable.

2. What interests are protected and what policies are promoted by judicial recognition of the doctrine of compelled self-publication? What interests are not protected or promoted by the doctrine?

3. The court recognized and applied the doctrine of qualified or conditional privilege. What was the Minnesota law formulation of that doctrine? What are the public policy considerations supporting the privilege? Would you be in favor of or opposed to an absolute privilege for employers in compelled self-publications jurisdictions? Why?

4. What kind of conduct or actions should constitute an abuse of an employer's qualified privilege?

5. Post-*Lewis* developments in Minnesota addressed and limited employers' exposure to self-publication defamation claims. The Minnesota legislature enacted a law permitting an involuntarily terminated employee to request in writing, within fifteen working days of termination, the employer's reason(s) for the termination. Within ten working days of receipt of such request, the employer is required to inform the employee, in writing, of the truthful reason(s) for the termination. The statute further provides that "[n]o communication of the statement furnished by the employer . . . may be made

the subject of any action for libel, slander, or defamation by the employee against the employer." Minn. Stat. Ann. § 181.933. *See also* Minn. Stat. Ann. § 181.962 ("No communication by an employee of information obtained through a review of the employee's personnel record may be made the subject of any action by the employee for libel, slander, or defamation" unless the employer fails to comply with other provisions of the statute.).

B. Constitutional Law

1. Public Officials

New York Times Co. v. Sullivan

376 U.S. 254 (1964)

Mr. Justice BRENNAN delivered the opinion of the Court.

We are required in this case to determine for the first time the extent to which the constitutional protections for speech and press limit a State's power to award damages in a libel action brought by a public official against critics of his official conduct.

Respondent L. B. Sullivan is one of the three elected Commissioners of the City of Montgomery, Alabama. He testified that he was 'Commissioner of Public Affairs and the duties are supervision of the Police Department, Fire Department, Department of Cemetery and Department of Scales.' He brought this civil libel action against the four individual petitioners, who are Negroes and Alabama clergymen, and against petitioner the New York Times Company, a New York corporation which publishes the New York Times, a daily newspaper. A jury in the Circuit Court of Montgomery County awarded him damages of $500,000, the full amount claimed, against all the petitioners, and the Supreme Court of Alabama affirmed. [C]

>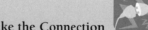
> **Make the Connection**
>
> Constitutional protections for speech and the press are addressed in Constitutional Law and First Amendment courses.

Respondent's complaint alleged that he had been libeled by statements in a full-page advertisement that was carried in the New York Times on March 29,

1960. Entitled 'Heed Their Rising Voices,' the advertisement began by stating that 'As the whole world knows by now, thousands of Southern Negro students are engaged in widespread non-violent demonstrations in positive affirmation of the right to live in human dignity as guaranteed by the U.S. Constitution and the Bill of Rights.' It went on to charge that 'in their efforts to uphold these guarantees, they are being met by an unprecedented wave of terror by those who would deny and negate that document which the whole world looks upon as setting the pattern for modern freedom. * * *' Succeeding paragraphs purported to illustrate the 'wave of terror' by describing certain alleged events. The text concluded with an appeal for funds for three purposes: support of the student movement, 'the struggle for the right-to-vote,' and the legal defense of Dr. Martin Luther King, Jr., leader of the movement, against a perjury indictment then pending in Montgomery.

The text appeared over the names of 64 persons, many widely known for their activities in public affairs, religion, trade unions, and the performing arts. Below these names, and under a line reading 'We in the south who are struggling daily for dignity and freedom warmly endorse this appeal,' appeared the names of the four individual petitioners and of 16 other persons, all but two of whom were identified as clergymen in various Southern cities. The advertisement was signed at the bottom of the page by the 'Committee to Defend Martin Luther King and the Struggle for Freedom in the South,' and the officers of the Committee were listed.

Of the 10 paragraphs of text in the advertisement, the third and a portion of the sixth were the basis of respondent's claim of libel. They read as follows:

> ¶ 3: 'In Montgomery, Alabama, after students sang 'My Country, 'Tis of Thee' on the State Capitol steps, their leaders were expelled from school, and truckloads of police armed with shotguns and tear-gas ringed the Alabama State College Campus. When the entire student body protested to state authorities by refusing to re-register, their dining hall was padlocked in an attempt to starve them into submission.'

> ¶ 6: 'Again and again the Southern violators have answered Dr. King's peaceful protests with intimidation and violence. They have bombed his home almost killing his wife and child. They have assaulted his person. They have arrested him seven times—for 'speeding,' 'loitering' and similar 'offenses.' And now they have charged him with '**perjury**'—a felony under which they could imprison him for ten years. * * *'

Although neither of these statements mentions respondent by name, he contended that the word 'police' in the third paragraph referred to him as the Montgomery Commissioner who supervised the Police Department, so that he was being accused of 'ringing' the campus with police. He further claimed that the paragraph would be read as imputing to the police, and hence to him, the padlocking of the dining hall in order to starve the students into submission. As to the sixth paragraph, he contended that since arrests are ordinarily made by the police, the statement 'They have arrested (Dr. King) seven times' would be read as referring to him; he further contended that the 'They' who did the arresting would be equated with the 'They' who committed the other described acts and with the 'Southern violators.' Thus, he argued, the paragraph would be read as accusing the Montgomery police, and hence him, of answering Dr. King's protests with 'intimidation and violence,' bombing his home, assaulting his person, and charging him with perjury. Respondent and six other Montgomery residents testified that they read some or all of the statements as referring to him in his capacity as Commissioner.

It is uncontroverted that some of the statements contained in the two paragraphs were not accurate descriptions of events which occurred in Montgomery. Although Negro students staged a demonstration on the State Capital steps, they sang the National Anthem and not 'My Country, 'Tis of Thee.' Although nine students were expelled by the State Board of Education, this was not for leading the demonstration at the Capitol, but for demanding service at a lunch counter in the Montgomery County Courthouse on another day. Not the entire student body, but most of it, had protested the expulsion, not by refusing to register, but by boycotting classes on a single day; virtually all the students did register for the ensuing semester. The campus dining hall was not padlocked on any occasion, and the only students who may have been barred from eating there were the few who had neither signed a preregistration application nor requested temporary meal tickets. Although the police were deployed near the campus in large numbers on three occasions, they did not at any time 'ring' the campus, and they were not called to the campus in connection with the demonstration on the State Capitol steps, as the third paragraph implied. Dr. King had not been arrested seven times, but only four; and although he claimed to have been assaulted some years earlier in connection with his arrest for loitering outside a courtroom, one of the officers who made the arrest denied that there was such an assault.

On the premise that the charges in the sixth paragraph could be read as referring to him, respondent was allowed to prove that he had not participated in the events described. Although Dr. King's home had in fact been bombed twice when his wife and child were there, both of these occasions antedated respondent's tenure as Commissioner, and the police were not only not implicated in the bombings, but had made every effort to apprehend those who were. Three of Dr. King's four arrests took place before respondent became Commissioner. Although Dr. King had in fact been indicted (he was subsequently acquitted) on two counts of perjury, each of which carried a possible five-year sentence, respondent had nothing to do with procuring the indictment.

. . . .

The trial judge submitted the case to the jury under instructions that the statements in the advertisement were '**libelous per se**' and were not privileged, so that petitioners might be held liable if the jury found that they had published the advertisement and that the statements were made 'of and concerning' respondent. The jury was instructed that, because the statements were libelous per se, 'the law * * * implies legal injury from the bare fact of publication itself,' '**falsity** and **malice** are presumed,' '**general damages** need not be alleged or proved but are presumed,' and '**punitive damages** may be awarded by the jury even though the amount of **actual damages** is neither found nor shown.' An award of punitive damages–as distinguished from 'general' damages, which are compensatory in nature-apparently requires proof of actual malice under Alabama law, and the judge charged that 'mere negligence or carelessness is not evidence of actual malice or malice in fact, and does not justify an award of exemplary or punitive damages.' He refused to charge, however, that the jury must be 'convinced' of malice, in the sense of 'actual **intent**' to harm or '**gross negligence** and **reckless-ness**,' to make such an award, and he also refused to require that a verdict for respondent differentiate between compensatory and punitive damages. The judge rejected petitioners' contention that his rulings abridged the freedoms of speech and of the press that are guaranteed by the **First** and **Fourteenth Amendments**.

In affirming the judgment, the Supreme Court of Alabama sustained the trial judge's rulings and instructions in all respects. 273 Ala. 656, 144 So.2d 25. . . .

Because of the importance of the constitutional issues involved, we granted the separate petitions for cer-

What's That?

The First Amendment to the United States Constitution provides that "Congress shall make no law . . . abridging the freedom of speech, or of the press . . ." This amendment was deemed incorporated into the Fourteenth Amendment, and therefore applicable to the states, in Cantwell v. Connecticut, 310 U.S. 296 (1940).

tiorari of the individual petitioners and of the Times. [C] We reverse the judgment. We hold that the rule of law applied by the Alabama courts is constitutionally deficient for failure to provide the safeguards for freedom of speech and of the press that are required by the First and Fourteenth Amendments in a libel action brought by a public official against critics of his official conduct. We further hold that under the proper safeguards the evidence presented in this case is constitutionally insufficient to support the judgment for respondent.

. . . .

Under Alabama law as applied in this case, a publication is 'libelous per se' if the words 'tend to injure a person * * * in his reputation' or to 'bring (him) into public contempt'; the trial court stated that the standard was met if the words are such as to 'injure him in his public office, or impute misconduct to him in his office, or want of official integrity, or want of fidelity to a public trust * * *.' The jury must find that the words were published 'of and concerning' the plaintiff, but where the plaintiff is a **public official** his place in the governmental hierarchy is sufficient evidence to support a finding that his reputation has been affected by statements that reflect upon the agency of which he is in charge. Once 'libel per se' has been established, the defendant has no defense as to stated facts unless he can persuade the jury that they were true in all their particulars. [Cc] His privilege of '**fair comment**' for expressions of opinion depends on the truth of the facts upon which the comment is based. [C] . . .

The question before us is whether this rule of liability, as applied to an action brought by a public official against critics of his official conduct, abridges the freedom of speech and of the press that is guaranteed by the First and Fourteenth Amendments.

. . . .

The general proposition that freedom of expression upon public questions is secured by the First Amendment has long been settled by our decisions. The constitutional safeguard, we have said, 'was fashioned to assure unfettered interchange of ideas for the bringing about of political and social changes desired by the people.' [C] 'The maintenance of the opportunity for free political discussion to the end that government may be responsive to the will of the people and that changes may be obtained by lawful means, an opportunity essential to the security of the Republic, is a fundamental principle of our constitutional system.' [C] '(I)t is a prized American privilege to speak one's mind, although not always with perfect good taste, on all public institutions,' [c] and this opportunity is to be afforded for 'vigorous advocacy' no less than 'abstract discussion.' [C] The First Amendment, said Judge Learned Hand, 'presupposes that right conclusions are more likely to be gathered out of a multitude of tongues, than through any kind of authoritative selection. To many this is, and always will be, folly; but we have staked upon it our all.' United States v. Associated Press, 52 F.Supp. 362, 372 (D.C.S.D.N.Y.1943). Mr. Justice Brandeis, in his concurring opinion in Whitney v. California, 274 U.S. 357, 375-376, 47 S.Ct. 641, 648, 71 L.Ed. 1095, gave the principle its classic formulation:

'Those who won our independence believed * * * that public discussion is a political duty; and that this should be a fundamental principle of the

American government. They recognized the risks to which all human institutions are subject. But they knew that order cannot be secured merely through fear of punishment for its infraction; that it is hazardous to discourage thought, hope and imagination; that fear breeds repression; that repression breeds hate; that hate menaces stable government; that the path of safety lies in the opportunity to discuss freely supposed grievances and proposed remedies; and that the fitting remedy for evil counsels is good ones. Believing in the power of reason as applied through public discussion, they eschewed silence coerced by law-the argument of force in its worst form. Recognizing the occasional tyrannies of governing majorities, they amended the Constitution so that free speech and assembly should be guaranteed.'

Thus we consider this case against the background of a profound national commitment to the principle that debate on public issues should be uninhibited, robust, and wide-open, and that it may well include vehement, caustic, and sometimes unpleasantly sharp attacks on government and public officials. [Cc] The present advertisement, as an expression of grievance and protest on one of the major public issues of our time, would seem clearly to qualify for the constitutional protection. The question is whether it forfeits that protection by the falsity of some of its factual statements and by its alleged defamation of respondent.

Authoritative interpretations of the First Amendment guarantees have consistently refused to recognize an exception for any test of truth-whether administered by judges, juries, or administrative officials–and especially one that puts the burden of proving truth on the speaker. [C] The constitutional protection does not turn upon 'the truth, popularity, or social utility of the ideas and beliefs which are offered.' [C] As Madison said, 'Some degree of abuse is inseparable from the proper use of every thing; and in no instance is this more true than in that of the press.' 4 Elliot's Debates on the Federal Constitution (1876), p. 571. . . .

. . . .

If neither factual error nor defamatory content suffices to remove the constitutional shield from criticism of official conduct, the combination of the two elements is no less inadequate. This is the lesson to be drawn from the great controversy over the **Sedition Act** of 1798, 1 Stat. 596, which first crystallized a national awareness of the central meaning of the First Amendment. [Cc] That statute made it a crime, punishable by a $5,000 fine and five years in prison, 'if any person shall write, print, utter or publish * * * any false, scandalous and malicious writing or writings against the government of the United States, or either house of the Congress * * *, or the President * * *, with intent to defame * * * or to bring them, or either of them, into contempt or disrepute; or to excite against them, or either or any of them, the hatred of the good people of the United States.' The Act allowed the defendant the defense of truth, and provided that the jury were to be judges both of the law and the facts. Despite these qualifications, the Act was vigorously condemned as unconstitutional in an attack joined in by Jefferson and Madison. . . .

Although the Sedition Act was never tested in this Court, the attack upon its validity has carried the day in the court of history. Fines levied in its prosecution were repaid by Act of Congress on the ground that it was unconstitutional. [C] . . . Jefferson, as President, **pardoned** those who had been convicted and sentenced under the Act and remitted their fines, stating: 'I discharged every person under punishment or prosecution under the sedition law, because I considered, and now consider, that law to be a **nullity**, as absolute and as palpable as if Congress had ordered us to fall down and worship a golden image.' [C] The invalidity of the Act has also been assumed by Justices of this Court. [Cc] These views reflect a broad consensus that the Act, because of the restraint it imposed upon criticism of government and public officials, was inconsistent with the First Amendment.

. . . .

What a State may not constitutionally bring about by means of a criminal statute is likewise beyond the reach of its civil law of libel. The fear of damage awards under a rule such as that invoked by the Alabama courts here may be markedly more inhibiting than the fear of prosecution under a criminal statute. [C] Alabama, for example, has a **criminal libel** law which subjects to prosecution 'any person who speaks, writes, or prints of and concerning another any accusation falsely and maliciously importing the commission by such person of a felony, or any other indictable offense involving moral turpitude,' and which allows as punishment upon conviction a fine not exceeding $500 and a prison sentence of six months. Alabama Code, Tit. 14, s 350. Presumably a person charged with violation of this statute enjoys ordinary criminal-law safeguards such as the requirements of an indictment and of proof beyond a reasonable doubt. These safeguards are not available to the defendant in a civil action. The judgment awarded in this case-without the need for any proof of actual pecuniary loss-was one thousand times greater than the maximum fine provided by the Alabama criminal statute, and one hundred times greater than that provided by the Sedition Act. And since there is no **double-jeopardy** limitation applicable to civil lawsuits, this is not the only judgment that may be awarded against petitioners for the same publication. Whether or not a newspaper can survive a succession of such judgments, the pall of fear and timidity imposed upon those who would give voice to public criticism is an atmosphere in which the First Amendment freedoms cannot survive. Plainly the Alabama law of civil libel is 'a form of regulation that creates hazards to protected freedoms markedly greater than those that attend reliance upon the criminal law.' [C].

The state rule of law is not saved by its allowance of the defense of truth. . . .

A rule compelling the critic of official conduct to guarantee the truth of all his factual assertions-and to do so on pain of libel judgments virtually unlimited in amount-leads to a comparable 'self-censorship.' Allowance of the defense of truth, with the burden of proving it on the defendant, does not mean that only false speech will be deterred. Even courts accepting this defense as an adequate safeguard have recognized the difficulties of adducing legal proofs that the alleged libel was true in all its factual particulars. [Cc] Under such a rule, would-be critics of official conduct may be deterred from voicing their criticism, even though it is believed to be true and even though it is in fact true, because of doubt whether it can be proved in court or fear of the expense of having to do so. They tend to make only statements which 'steer far wider of the unlawful zone.' [C] The rule thus dampens the vigor and limits the variety of public debate. It is inconsistent with the First and Fourteenth Amendments.

The constitutional guarantees require, we think, a federal rule that prohibits a public official from recovering damages for a defamatory falsehood relating to his official conduct unless he proves that the statement was made with '**actual malice**' – that is, with knowledge that it was false or with reckless disregard of whether it was false or not. . . .

. . . .

We hold today that the Constitution delimits a State's power to award damages for libel in actions brought by public officials against critics of their official conduct. Since this is such an action, the rule requiring proof of actual malice is applicable. . . .

. . . .

[W]e consider that the proof presented to show actual malice lacks the convincing clarity which the constitutional standard demands, and hence that it would not constitutionally sustain the judgment for respondent under the proper rule of law. The case of the individual petitioners requires little discussion. Even assuming that they could constitutionally be found to have authorized the use of their names on the advertisement, there was no evidence whatever that they were aware of any erroneous statements or were in any way reckless in that regard. The judgment against them is thus without constitutional support.

As to the Times, we similarly conclude that the facts do not support a finding of actual malice. The statement by the Times' Secretary that, apart from the padlocking allegation, he thought the advertisement was 'substantially correct,' affords no constitutional warrant for the Alabama Supreme Court's conclusion that it was a 'cavalier ignoring of the falsity of the advertisement (from which), the jury could not have but been impressed with the bad faith of The Times, and its maliciousness inferable therefrom.' The statement does not indicate malice at the time of the publication; even if the advertisement was not 'substantially correct'—although respondent's own proofs tend to show that it was—that opinion was at least a reasonable one, and there was no evidence to impeach the witness' good faith in holding it. The Times' failure to retract upon respondent's demand, although it later retracted upon the demand of Governor Patterson, is likewise not adequate evidence of malice for constitutional purposes. Whether or not a failure to retract may ever constitute such evidence, there are two reasons why it does not here. First, the letter written by the Times reflected a reasonable doubt on its part as to whether the advertisement could reasonably be taken to refer to respondent at all. Second, it was not a final refusal, since it asked for an explanation on this point-a request that respondent chose to ignore. Nor does the retraction upon the demand of the Governor supply the necessary proof. It may be doubted that a failure to retract which is not itself evidence of malice can retroactively become such by virtue of a retraction subsequently made to another party. But in any event that did not happen here, since the explanation given by the Times' Secretary for the distinction drawn between respondent and the Governor was a reasonable one, the good faith of which was not impeached.

Finally, there is evidence that the Times published the advertisement without checking its accuracy against the news stories in the Times' own files. The mere presence of the stories in the files does not, of course, establish that the Times 'knew' the advertisement was false, since the state of mind required for actual malice would have to be brought home to the persons in the Times' organization having responsibility for the publication of the advertisement. With respect to the failure of those persons to make the check, the record shows that they relied upon their knowledge of the good reputation of many of those whose names were listed as sponsors of the advertisement, and upon the letter from A. Philip Randolph, known to them as a responsible individual, certifying that the use of the names was authorized. There was testimony that the persons handling the advertisement saw nothing in it that would render it unacceptable under the Times' policy of rejecting advertisements containing 'attacks of a personal character'; their failure to reject it on this ground was not unreasonable. We think the evidence against the Times supports at most a finding of negligence in failing to discover the misstatements, and is constitutionally insufficient to show the recklessness that is required for a finding of actual malice. [Cc].

We also think the evidence was constitutionally defective in another respect: it was incapable of supporting the jury's finding that the allegedly libelous statements were made 'of and concerning' respondent. . . .

There was no reference to respondent in the advertisement, either by name or official position. A number of the allegedly libelous statements–the charges that the dining hall was padlocked and that Dr. King's home was bombed, his person assaulted, and a perjury prosecution instituted against him-did not even concern the police; despite the ingenuity of the arguments which would attach this significance to the word 'They,' it is plain that these statements could not reasonably be read as accusing respondent of personal involvement in the acts in question. . . . Although the statements may be taken as referring to the police, they did not on their face make even an oblique reference to respondent as an individual. . . .

. . . For good reason, 'no court of last resort in this country has ever held, or even suggested, that prosecutions for libel on government have any place in the American system of jurisprudence.' [C] The present proposition would sidestep this obstacle by transmuting criticism of government, however impersonal it may seem on its face, into personal criticism, and hence potential libel, of the officials of whom the government is composed. There is no legal alchemy by which a State may thus create the cause of action that would otherwise be denied for a publication which, as respondent himself said of the advertisement, 'reflects not only on me but on the other Commissioners and the community.' Raising as it does the possibility that a good-faith critic of government will be penalized for his criticism, the proposition relied on by the Alabama courts strikes at the very center of the constitutionally protected area of free expression. We hold that such a proposition may not constitutionally be utilized to establish that an otherwise impersonal attack on governmental operations was a libel of an official responsible for those operations. Since it was relied on exclusively here, and there was no other evidence to connect the statements with respondent, the evidence was constitutionally insufficient to support a finding that the statements referred to respondent.

The judgment of the Supreme Court of Alabama is reversed and the case is remanded to that court for further proceedings not inconsistent with this opinion.

Reversed and remanded.

———————

Points for Discussion

1. What was the applicable rule of law in Alabama concerning libelous publications of and concerning a public official?

2. The Supreme Court opines that "[t]he general proposition that freedom of expression upon public questions is secured by the First Amendment has long been settled by our decisions." What policies are promoted and what interests are served by permitting and protecting the freedom of speech and debate on public issues?

3. Is truth a defense in cases involving speech criticizing the official conduct of public officials? Does the Court's approach place certain false statements of fact beyond the reach of the law of defamation?

4. The Court stated: "Whether or not a newspaper can survive a succession of . . . judgments, the pall of fear and timidity imposed upon those who would give voice to public criticism is an atmosphere in which the First Amendment freedoms cannot survive." Do you agree or disagree with this observation?

5. Define "actual malice" and describe the Court's application of that standard to the New York Times.

6. For criticism of the Court's decision, *see* Richard A. Epstein, *Was* New York Times v. Sullivan *Wrong?*, 53 U. Chi. L. Rev. 782 (1986). While concluding that "the case was correctly decided on its facts," Professor Epstein posits that "[o]n balance, the common law rules of defamation (sensibly controlled on the question of damages) represent a better reconciliation of the dual claims of freedom of speech and the protection of individual reputation than does the *New York Times* rule that has replaced it." For additional critiques, *see* Robert F. Nagel, *How Useful is Judicial Review in Free Speech Cases?*, 69 Cornell L. Rev. 405 (1984), and Henry Paul Monaghan, *Of "Liberty" and "Property,"* 62 Cornell L. Rev. 405 (1977).

2. Public Figures

WFAA-TV, Inc. v. McLemore

978 S.W.2d 568 (Tex. 1998)

HANKINSON, Justice, delivered the opinion for a unanimous Court.

In this defamation suit arising out of the 1993 Bureau of Alcohol, Tobacco and Firearms (ATF) raid on the Branch Davidian compound at Mount Carmel, we decide whether a media plaintiff, one of only a few journalists to report live from the scene of the raid, whose reports were rebroadcast worldwide, and who willingly gave numerous interviews about his role in the failed raid, is a **public figure**. The plaintiff sued WFAA-TV Channel 8 in Dallas alleging that its news reports concerning his role in the failed raid damaged his reputation in the community. The trial court denied WFAA's motion for summary judgment, and the court of appeals affirmed. [C] Because we conclude that the plaintiff in this case became a **limited-purpose public figure** after thrusting himself to the forefront of the controversy surrounding the failed ATF assault, we reverse the court of appeals' judgment and render judgment that the plaintiff take nothing.

> **FYI**
>
> On April 19, 1993, federal agents raided the 77-acre Branch Davidian property in Waco, Texas after a 51-day standoff. The Branch Davidians' leader, David Koresh, and 79 other persons died in a fire that destroyed the compound. For more on the Branch Davidians and the raid, click here.

On February 28, 1993, ATF agents approached the Mount Carmel compound occupied by the Branch Davidians, a small religious sect that had amassed an arsenal of illegal weaponry. Two local media outlets, KWTX-TV Channel 10 in Waco and the *Waco Tribune-Herald,* learned from various sources that a major law enforcement operation would proceed at Mount Carmel that morning. KWTX-TV dispatched reporter John McLemore and cameraman Dan Mullony to report on the event.

When the ATF agents attempted to enter one of the buildings on the compound, they became involved in a gunfight with the Davidians. During the battle, four ATF agents and three Davidians were killed, and twenty ATF agents were wounded. McLemore and Mullony, the only media representatives to follow the agents onto the compound, reported live from the midst of the firefight.

Two days after the gunfight, media reports began to focus on why the ATF raid had failed and what sparked the gunfight. On March 2, 1998, Kathy Fair, a *Houston Chronicle* reporter, appeared on *Nightline,* an ABC news show anchored by Ted Koppel. During the show, Koppel and Fair discussed the media's role in the botched ATF raid. Koppel asked what went wrong with the media's coverage, and Fair initially responded that it was too early to determine. She then suggested ATF agents believed they were set up:

> I think many officers will tell you that they blame the media, particularly the local media, for the tragedy that occurred here. They think the fact that both the newspaper and the local television station, who were already at the compound, some of whom were reporters for, I believe, the TV station, allegedly were already hiding in the trees when federal agents arrived. And that was the first indication that many of them had that they had been set up, and that's a strong belief I think they have that they have not shared publicly yet, is that they think they were set up.

As soon as the *Nightline* broadcast ended, KWTX-TV began to receive calls critical of McLemore's role in the raid, even though Fair had not identified him by name.

WFAA picked up the story the next day and began to broadcast reports by Valerie Williams, a WFAA reporter, who repeated Fair's report that ATF agents saw local media hiding in trees at the compound before the attack began. WFAA then broadcast video footage of McLemore while apparently on the compound grounds. Williams then continued her report:

> The only reporters at the scene Sunday morning were Steve [sic] McLemore and a television photographer from KWTX-TV in Waco and one or two reporters from the local newspaper. McLemore's news unit was used to transport some of the wounded agents. Currently his bosses are consulting with attorneys before issuing a statement.

Later that evening, WFAA broadcast a similar piece, again repeating excerpts from *Nightline,* followed by commentary from Williams:

> [T]he only reporters at the scene Sunday morning were John McLemore and a photographer.... Wednesday night McLemore's station ... demanded a retraction from *Nightline* saying, "[T]he rumor that a Waco reporter had tipped the cult about the raid in exchange for permission to be on the compound grounds was completely false. No reporter or photographer from local media was on the compound grounds prior to the raid."

Soon after the reports aired, McLemore sued WFAA-TV, Valerie Williams, A.H. Belo Corporation, Belo Productions, Inc., the *Houston Chronicle,* and Kathy Fair for defamation, alleging that their news reports of his role in the failed raid damaged his reputation in the community. WFAA moved for summary judgment on six grounds: (1) no defamatory meaning; (2) **fair report privilege**; (3) **fair comment privilege**; (4) **truth**; (5) no **actual malice**; and (6) neutral reporting privilege. After McLemore **nonsuited** Williams and the two Belo corporations, the trial court granted summary judgment in favor of the *Chronicle* and Fair, but denied WFAA's motion for summary judgment.

Affirming the trial court's judgment, the court of appeals concluded that McLemore was a private individual, and as such, he had to prove negligence, not actual malice, in his defamation case. Because WFAA did not move for summary judgment on the grounds that it acted without negligence, the court of appeals determined that the issue was not before it and remanded the defamation action to the trial court for further proceedings consistent with its opinion. [C]

WFAA now appeals under section 22.225(d) of the Texas Government Code, which provides this Court with jurisdiction to hear a petition for review from an interlocutory order denying a media party's motion for summary judgment in a defamation case. TEX. GOV'T CODE § 22.225(d); TEX. CIV. PRAC. & REM. CODE § 51.014(6). Specifically, WFAA argues that summary judgment is proper because McLemore is a public figure, and as a matter of law, it did not broadcast its reports with actual malice.

To maintain a defamation cause of action, the plaintiff must prove that the defendant: (1) published a statement; (2) that was defamatory concerning the plaintiff; (3) while acting with either actual malice, if the plaintiff was a public official or public figure, or negligence, if the plaintiff was a private individual, regarding the truth of the statement. *See Carr v. Brasher,* 776 S.W.2d 567, 569 (Tex.1989) (citing *New York Times Co. v. Sullivan,* 376 U.S. 254, 279-80, 84 S.Ct. 710, 11 L.Ed.2d 686 (1964)). To have prevailed on its motion for summary judgment, WFAA must have disproved at least one essential element of McLemore's defamation claim. [C]

Fault is a constitutional prerequisite for defamation liability. *See Gertz v. Robert Welch, Inc.,* 418 U.S. 323, 347, 94 S.Ct. 2997, 41 L.Ed.2d 789 (1974). Private plaintiffs must prove that the defendant was at least negligent. *See Foster v. Laredo Newspapers, Inc.,* 541 S.W.2d 809, 819 (Tex.1976) (holding that "a private individual may recover damages from a publisher or broadcaster of a defamatory falsehood as compensation for actual injury upon a showing that the publisher or broadcaster knew or should have known that the defamatory statement was false"); *see also Gertz,* 418 U.S. at 347, 94 S.Ct. 2997 (holding that states may define for themselves the appropriate standard of liability for a publisher of a defamatory falsehood injurious to a private individual "so long as they do not impose liability without fault"). Public officials and public figures must establish a higher degree of fault. They must prove that the defendant published a defamatory falsehood with actual malice, that is, with "knowledge that it was false or with reckless disregard of whether it was false or not." *New York Times,* 376 U.S. at 279-80, 84 S.Ct. 710 (defining the actual malice standard and applying it to public officials); *see also Curtis Pub. Co. v. Butts,* 388 U.S. 130, 87 S.Ct. 1975, 18 L. Ed.2d 1094 (1967) (applying the *New York Times* actual malice standard to public figures).

Because a defamation plaintiff's status dictates the degree of fault he or she must prove to render the defendant liable, the principal issue in this case is whether McLemore is a public figure. The question of public-figure status is one of constitutional law for courts to decide. [Cc] Public figures fall into two categories: (1) **all-purpose**, or general-purpose, **public figures**, and (2) **limited-purpose public figures**. General-purpose public figures are those individuals who have achieved such pervasive fame or notoriety that they become public figures for all purposes and in all contexts. [C] Limited-purpose public figures, on the other hand, are only public figures for a limited range of issues surrounding a particular public controversy. [C]

To determine whether an individual is a limited-purpose public figure, the Fifth Circuit has adopted a three-part test:

(1) the controversy at issue must be public both in the sense that people are discussing it and people other than the immediate participants in the controversy are likely to feel the impact of its resolution;

(2) the plaintiff must have more than a trivial or tangential role in the controversy; and

(3) the alleged defamation must be germane to the plaintiff's participation in the controversy.

Trotter, 818 F.2d at 433 (citing *Tavoulareas v. Piro,* 817 F.2d 762, 772-73 (D.C.Cir.1987) (en banc)); *see also Waldbaum v. Fairchild Pub., Inc.* 627 F.2d 1287, 1296-98 (D.C.Cir.1980). Although the *Trotter/ Waldbaum* test does not distinguish between plaintiffs who have voluntarily injected themselves into a controversy and those who are involuntarily drawn into a controversy, some courts have held that plaintiffs who are drawn into a controversy cannot be categorized as limited-purpose public figures. Because, as we explain below, McLemore clearly voluntarily injected himself into the controversy at issue, we need not decide in this case whether "voluntariness" is a requirement under the limited-purpose public-figure test we apply. Nevertheless, the *Trotter/Waldbaum* elements provide a "generally accepted test" to determine limited-purpose public-figure status. [Cc]

Applying the *Trotter/Waldbaum* limited-purpose public-figure elements to this case, we must first determine the controversy at issue. [Cc] In *Waldbaum*, the D.C. Circuit elaborated on how to determine the existence and scope of a public controversy:

> To determine whether a controversy indeed existed and, if so, to define its contours, the judge must examine whether persons actually were discussing some specific question. A general concern or interest will not suffice. The court can see if the press was covering the debate, reporting what people were saying and uncovering facts and theories to help the public formulate some judgment.

[C] In this case, numerous commentators, analysts, journalists, and public officials were discussing the raid and the reasons why the ATF raid failed. As evidenced by Fair's comments during the *Nightline* broadcast, as well as reports by *The Dallas Morning News* and the *Fort Worth Star Telegram*, the press was actively covering the debate over why the ATF raid failed. Many such discussions focused on the role of the local media in the ATF's failure to capture the Davidian compound. The controversy surrounding the Branch Davidian raid was public, both in the sense that people were discussing it and people other than the immediate participants in the controversy were likely to feel the impact of its resolution. [Cc] While the court of appeals defined the controversy as limited to "McLemore's personal ethical standards as a journalist," we do not view it so narrowly. Based on the facts outlined above, we conclude that the public controversy at issue is the broader question of why the ATF agents failed to accomplish their mission.

To determine that an individual is a public figure for purposes of the public controversy at issue, the second *Trotter/Waldbaum* element requires the plaintiff to have had more than a trivial or tangential role in the controversy. [Cc] In considering a libel plaintiff's role in a public controversy, several inquiries are relevant and instructive: (1) whether the plaintiff actually sought publicity surrounding the controversy, [c] (2) whether the plaintiff had access to the media, [c] and (3) whether the plaintiff "voluntarily engag[ed] in activities that necessarily involve[d] the risk of increased exposure and injury to reputation." [Cc] . . .

The record reflects that McLemore acted voluntarily to invite public attention and scrutiny on several occasions and in several different ways during the course of the public debate on the failed ATF raid. For example, McLemore was the only journalist to go onto the grounds of the compound, while other reporters assigned to cover the raid did not. By reporting live from the heart of the controversial raid, McLemore assumed a risk that his involvement in the event would be subject to public debate. Following the battle, McLemore spoke to other members of the press about the attempted raid, conveying his pride in his coverage from the midst of the gunfight, and portraying himself as a hero in assisting wounded ATF agents when he remarked that his role in the raid was "at considerable personal risk" and in contrast to other journalists who "were pinned down in a ditch" outside the compound. As a journalist, McLemore had ready, continual access to the various media sources. To one group of reporters, he explained that "as a journalist, I was ... pleased to see that my coverage of this story was being broadcast to a wide audience." Thus, by choosing to engage in activities that necessarily involved increased public exposure and media scrutiny, McLemore played more than a trivial or tangential role in the controversy and, therefore, bore the risk of injury to his reputation. [C]

The third and final element we consider–that the alleged defamation is germane to the plaintiff's participation in the controversy–is also satisfied in this case. [Cc] McLemore alleges that WFAA defamed him by displaying footage of his coverage from the scene of the compound during the raid, while reporting that federal officials believed a member of the local media informed the Branch Davidians about the ATF raid. Therefore, the alleged defamation directly relates to McLemore's participation in the controversy. He was on the scene in his role as a journalist, as conveyed by the footage WFAA broadcast, and WFAA's alleged defamatory comments are indeed germane to McLemore's participation in the controversy over the media's role in the failed attack. [C] Accordingly, McLemore reached limited-purpose public-figure status through his employment-related activities when he voluntarily injected himself into the Branch Davidian raid.

We now turn to the fault standard McLemore must meet in order to sustain his defamation claim against WFAA. As a public figure, McLemore must prove that WFAA acted with actual malice in allegedly defaming him. [Cc] Actual malice is a term of art, focusing on the defamation defendant's attitude toward the truth of what it reported. [C] Actual malice is defined as the publication of a statement "with knowledge that it was false or with reckless disregard of whether it was false or not." [C] **Reckless disregard** is also a term of art. To establish constitutional recklessness, a defamation plaintiff must prove that the publisher "entertained serious doubts as to the truth of his publication." [C].

A libel defendant is entitled to summary judgment under Texas law if it can negate actual malice as a matter of law. [Cc] A libel defendant can negate actual malice by presenting evidence that shows he or she did not publish the alleged defamatory statement with actual knowledge of any falsity or with reckless disregard for the truth. [C] To negate actual malice in this case, in her affidavit, WFAA reporter Valerie Williams detailed her belief that all of the reports she made were true and set forth the basis of those reports. Specifically, she swore that "[she] believed [her] reports accurately reflected public allegations by responsible, respected and well-informed journalists and news organizations, regarding a highly newsworthy matter and concerned an official investigation by law enforcement officers of a suspected tip-off of the Branch Davidian cult." She explained in detail the foundation of her belief by providing a chronology of the actions she took and the materials she reviewed in preparing her report. This testimony as to Williams' beliefs and the basis for them was sufficient for WFAA to meet its burden of negating actual malice. [Cc] As McLemore presented no proof controverting these specific assertions, WFAA established as a matter of law that it did not act with actual malice in reporting the ATF's investigation into why the Branch Davidian raid failed, and therefore WFAA was entitled to summary judgment on McLemore's defamation claim.

Accordingly, we reverse the court of appeals' judgment and render judgment that McLemore take nothing.

———————

Points for Discussion

1. What must a public figure or public official prove in order to maintain a defamation cause of action in Texas? What must a private individual prove?

2. Define and describe (a) an "all-purpose public figure" and (b) a "limited-purpose public figure."

3. According to the court, was the plaintiff an all-purpose or limited-purpose pubic figure? What analysis did the court apply in answering that question?

4. Consider the court's discussion and analysis of the fault standard governing the plaintiff's claim. What are the plaintiff's and the defendant's respective burdens of proof? Did the defendant meet its burden?

5. The Court states that the law does "not distinguish between plaintiffs who have voluntarily injected themselves into a controversy and those who are involuntarily drawn into a controversy[. S]ome courts have held that plaintiffs who are drawn into a controversy cannot be categorized as limited-purpose public figures." Consider **Richard Jewell,** the so-called Olympic Park Bomber. How should the falsely accused Richard Jewell be characterized pursuant to defamation law? *See* http://law.jrank.org/pages/8241/Libel-Slander-Richard-Jewell-Olympic-Park-Bombing.html.

———————

3. Private Individuals

Gertz v. Robert Welch, Inc.

418 U.S. 323 (1974)

Mr. Justice POWELL delivered the opinion of the Court.

This Court has struggled for nearly a decade to define the proper accommodation between the law of defamation and the freedoms of speech and press protected by the First Amendment. With this decision we return to that effort. We granted certiorari to reconsider the extent of a publisher's constitutional privilege against liability for defamation of a private citizen. [C].

I

In 1968 a Chicago policeman named Nuccio shot and killed a youth named Nelson. The state authorities prosecuted Nuccio for the homicide and ultimately obtained a conviction for murder in the second degree. The Nelson family retained petitioner Elmer Gertz, a reputable attorney, to represent them in civil litigation against Nuccio.

Respondent publishes American Opinion, a monthly outlet for the views of the John Birch Society. Early in the 1960's the magazine began to warn of a nationwide conspiracy to discredit local law enforcement agencies and create in their stead a national police force capable of supporting a Communist dictatorship. As part of the continuing effort to alert the public to this assumed danger, the managing editor of American Opinion commissioned an article on the murder trial of Officer Nuccio. For this purpose he engaged a regular contributor to the magazine. In March 1969 respondent published the resulting article under the title 'FRAME-UP: Richard Nuccio And The War On Police.' The article purports to demonstrate that the testimony against Nuccio at his criminal trial was false and that his prosecution was part of the Communist campaign against the police.

Go Online

The John Birch Society's website can be viewed at http://www.jbs.org.

In his capacity as counsel for the Nelson family in the civil litigation, petitioner attended the coroner's inquest into the boy's death and initiated actions for damages, but he neither discussed Officer Nuccio with the press nor played any part in the criminal proceeding. Notwithstanding petitioner's remote connection with the prosecution of Nuccio, respondent's magazine portrayed him as an architect of the 'frame-up.' According to the article, the police file on petitioner took 'a big, Irish cop to lift.' The article stated that petitioner had been an official of the 'Marxist League for Industrial Democracy, originally known as the Intercollegiate Socialist Society, which has advocated the violent seizure of our government.' It labeled Gertz a 'Leninist' and a 'Communist-fronter.' It also stated that Gertz had been an officer of the National Lawyers Guild, described as a Communist organization that 'probably did more than any other outfit to plan the Communist attack on the Chicago police during the 1968 Democratic Convention.'

These statements contained serious inaccuracies. The implication that petitioner had a criminal record was false. Petitioner had been a member and officer of the National Lawyers Guild some 15 years earlier, but there was no evidence that he or that organization had taken any part in planning the 1968 demonstrations in Chicago. There was also no basis for the charge that petitioner was a 'leninist' or a 'Communist-fronter.' And he had never been a member of the 'Marxist League for Industrial Democracy' or the 'Intercollegiate Socialist Society.'

The managing editor of American Opinion made no effort to verify or substantiate the charges against petitioner. Instead, he appended an editorial introduction stating that the author had 'conducted extensive research into the Richard Nuccio Case.' And he included in the article a photograph of petitioner and wrote the caption that appeared under it: 'Elmer Gertz of Red Guild harasses Nuccio.' Respondent placed the issue of American Opinion containing the article on sale at newsstands throughout the country and distributed reprints of the article on the streets of Chicago.

Petitioner filed a **diversity action** for libel in the United States District Court for the Northern District of Illinois. He claimed that the falsehoods published by respondent injured his reputation as a lawyer and a citizen. . . .

After answering the complaint, respondent filed a pretrial motion for summary judgment, claiming a constitutional privilege against liability for defamation. It asserted that petitioner was a public official or a public figure and that the article concerned an issue of public interest and concern. For these reasons, respondent argued, it was entitled to invoke the privilege enunciated in New York Times Co. v. Sullivan, 376 U.S. 254, 84 S.Ct. 710, 11 L.Ed.2d 686 (1964). Under this rule respondent would escape liability unless petitioner could prove publication of defamatory falsehood 'with 'actual malice'—that is, with knowledge that it was false or with reckless disregard of whether it was false or not.' [C] . . .

The District Court denied respondent's motion for summary judgment in a memorandum opinion of September 16, 1970. The court did not dispute respondent's claim to the protection of the New York Times standard. Rather, it concluded that petitioner might overcome the constitutional privilege by making a factual showing sufficient to prove publication of defamatory falsehood in reckless disregard of the truth. . . . After all the evidence had been presented [at trial] but before submission of the case to the jury, the court ruled in effect that petitioner was neither a public official nor a public figure. . . . Because some statements in the article constituted libel per se under Illinois law, the court submitted the case to the jury under instructions that withdrew from its consideration all issues save the measure of damages. The jury awarded $50,000 to petitioner.

Following the jury verdict and on further reflection, the District Court concluded that the New York Times standard should govern this case even though petitioner was not a public official or public figure. It accepted respondent's contention that that privilege protected discussion of any public issue without regard to the status of a person defamed therein. Accordingly, the court entered judgment for respondent notwithstanding the jury's verdict. . . .

Petitioner appealed to contest the applicability of the New York Times standard to this case. . . . After reviewing the record, the Court of Appeals [for the Seventh Circuit affirmed].

II

The principal issue in this case is whether a newspaper or broadcaster that publishes defamatory falsehoods about an individual who is neither a public official nor a public figure may claim a constitutional privilege against liability for the injury inflicted by those statements. The Court considered this question on the rather different set of facts presented in *Rosenbloom v. Metromedia, Inc.*, 403 U.S. 29, 91 S.Ct. 1811, 29 L.Ed.2d 296 (1971).

. . . .

III

We begin with the common ground. Under the First Amendment there is no such thing as a false idea. However pernicious an opinion may seem, we depend for its correction not on the conscience of judges and juries but on the competition of other ideas. But there is no constitutional value in false statements of fact. Neither the intentional lie nor the careless error materially advances society's interest in 'uninhibited, robust, and wide-open' debate on public issues. [C] They belong to that category of utterances which 'are no essential part of any exposition of ideas, and are of such slight social value as a step to truth that any benefit that may be derived from them is clearly outweighed by the social interest in order and morality.' *Chaplinsky v. New Hampshire*, 315 U.S. 568, 572, 62 S.Ct. 766, 769, 86 L.Ed. 1031 (1942).

Although the erroneous statement of fact is not worthy of constitutional protection, it is nevertheless inevitable in free debate. As James Madison pointed out in the Report on the Virginia Resolutions of 1798: 'Some degree of abuse is inseparable from the proper use of every thing; and in no instance is this more true than in that of the press.' 4 J. Elliot, Debates on the Federal Constitution of 1787, p. 571 (1876). And punishment of error runs the risk of inducing a cautious and restrictive exercise of the constitutionally guaranteed freedoms of speech and press. Our decisions recognize that a rule of **strict liability** that compels a publisher or broadcaster to guarantee the accuracy of his factual assertions may lead to intolerable self-censorship. Allowing the media to avoid liability only by proving the truth of all injurious statements does not accord adequate protection to First Amendment liberties. As the Court stated in *New York Times Co. v. Sullivan, supra,* 376 U.S., at 279, 84 S.Ct., at 725: 'Allowance of the defense of truth, with the burden of proving it on the defendant, does not mean that only false speech will be deterred.' The First Amendment requires that we protect some falsehood in order to protect speech that matters.

The need to avoid self-censorship by the news media is, however, not the only societal value at issue. If it were, this Court would have embraced long ago the view that publishers and broadcasters enjoy an unconditional and indefeasible immunity from liability for defamation. [Cc] Such a rule would, indeed, obviate the fear that the prospect of civil liability for injurious falsehood might dissuade a timorous press from the effective exercise of First Amendment freedoms. Yet absolute protection for the communications media requires a total sacrifice of the competing value served by the law of defamation.

The legitimate state interest underlying the law of libel is the compensation of individuals for the harm inflicted on them by defamatory falsehood. . . .

Some tension necessarily exists between the need for a vigorous and uninhibited press and the legitimate interest in redressing wrongful injury. . . . In our continuing effort to define the proper accommodation between these competing concerns, we have been especially anxious to assure to the freedoms of speech and press that 'breathing space' essential to their fruitful exercise. [C] To that end this Court has extended a measure of strategic protection to defamatory falsehood.

The New York Times standard defines the level of constitutional protection appropriate to the context of defamation of a public person. Those who, by reason of the notoriety of their achievements or the vigor and success with which they seek the public's attention, are properly classed as public figures and those who hold governmental office may recover for injury to reputation only on clear and convincing proof that the defamatory falsehood was made with knowledge of its falsity or with reckless disregard for the truth. This standard administers an extremely powerful antidote to the inducement to media self-censorship of the common-law rule of strict liability for libel and slander. And it exacts a correspondingly high price from the victims of defamatory falsehood. Plainly many deserving plaintiffs, including some intentionally subjected to injury, will be unable to surmount the barrier of the New York Times test. Despite this substantial abridgment of the state law right to compensation for wrongful hurt to one's reputation, the Court has concluded that the protection of the New York Times privilege should be available to publishers and broadcasters of defamatory falsehood concerning public officials and public figures. [Cc] We think that these decisions are correct, but we do not find their holdings justified solely by reference to the interest of the press and broadcast media in immunity from liability. Rather, we believe that the New York Times rule states an accommodation between this concern and the limited state interest present in the context of libel actions brought by public persons. For the reasons stated below, we conclude that the state interest in compensating injury to the reputation of private individuals requires that a different rule should obtain with respect to them.

Theoretically, of course, the balance between the needs of the press and the individual's claim to compensation for wrongful injury might be struck on a case-by-case basis. . . . But this approach would lead to unpredictable results and uncertain expectations, and it could render our duty to supervise the lower courts unmanageable. Because an ad hoc resolution of the competing interests at stake in each particular case is not feasible, we must lay down broad rules of general application. Such rules necessarily treat alike various cases involving differences as well as similarities. Thus it is often true that not all of the considerations which justify adoption of a given rule will obtain in each particular case decided under its authority.

With that caveat we have no difficulty in distinguishing among defamation plaintiffs. The first remedy of any victim of defamation is self-help-using available opportunities to contradict the lie or correct the error and thereby to minimize its adverse impact on reputation. Public officials and public figures usually enjoy significantly greater access to the channels of effective communication and hence have a more realistic opportunity to counteract false statements then private individuals normally enjoy. Private individuals are therefore more vulnerable to injury, and the state interest in protecting them is correspondingly greater.

More important than the likelihood that private individuals will lack effective opportunities for rebuttal, there is a compelling normative consideration underlying the distinction between public and private defamation plaintiffs. An individual who decides to seek governmental office must accept certain necessary consequences of that involvement in public affairs. He runs the risk of closer public scrutiny than might otherwise be the case. . . .

Those classed as public figures stand in a similar position. Hypothetically, it may be possible for someone to become a public figure through no purposeful action of his own, but the instances of truly involuntary public figures must be exceedingly rare. For the most part those who attain this status have assumed roles of especial prominence in the affairs of society. Some occupy positions of such persuasive power and influence that they are deemed public figures for all purposes. More commonly, those classed as public figures have thrust themselves to the forefront of particular public controversies in order to influence the resolution of the issues involved. In either event, they invite attention and comment.

Even if the foregoing generalities do not obtain in every instance, the communications media are entitled to act on the assumption that public officials and public figures have voluntarily exposed themselves to increased risk of injury from defamatory falsehood concerning them. No such assumption is justified with respect to a private individual. He has not accepted public office or assumed an 'influential role in ordering society.' [C] He has relinquished no part of his interest in the protection of his own good name, and consequently he has a more compelling call on the courts for redress of injury inflicted by defamatory falsehood. Thus, private individuals are not only more vulnerable to injury than public officials and public figures; they are also more deserving of recovery.

For these reasons we conclude that the States should retain substantial latitude in their efforts to enforce a legal remedy for defamatory falsehood injurious to the reputation of a private individual. The extension of the New York Times test proposed by the Rosenbloom plurality would abridge this legitimate state interest to a degree that we find unacceptable. And it would occasion the additional difficulty of forcing state and federal judges to decide on an ad hoc basis which publications address issues of 'general or public interest' and which do not-to determine, in the words of Mr. Justice Marshall, 'what information is relevant to self-government.' *Rosenbloom v. Metromedia, Inc.*, 403 U.S., at 79, 91 S.Ct., at 1837. We doubt the wisdom of committing this task to the conscience of judges. Nor does the Constitution require us to draw so thin a line between the drastic alternatives of the New York Times privilege and the common law of strict liability for defamatory error. The 'public or general interest' test for determining the applicability of the New York Times standard to private defamation actions inadequately serves both of the competing values at stake. On the one hand, a private individual whose reputation is injured by defamatory falsehood that does concern an issue of public or general interest has no recourse unless he can meet the rigorous requirements of New York Times. This is true despite the factors that distinguish the state interest in compensating private individuals from the analogous interest involved in the context of public persons. On the other hand, a publisher or broadcaster of a defamatory error which a court deems unrelated to an issue of public or general interest may be held liable in damages even if it took every reasonable precaution to ensure the accuracy of its assertions. And liability may far exceed compensation for any actual injury to the plaintiff, for the jury may be permitted to presume damages without proof of loss and even to award punitive damages.

We hold that, so long as they do not impose liability without fault, the States may define for themselves the appropriate standard of liability for a publisher or broadcaster of defamatory falsehood injurious to a private individual.   This approach provides a more equitable boundary between the competing concerns involved here. It recognizes the strength of the legitimate state interest in compensating private individuals for wrongful injury to reputation, yet shields the press and broadcast media from the rigors of strict liability for defamation. At least this conclusion obtains where, as here, the substance of the defamatory statement 'makes substantial danger to reputation apparent.' . . .

IV

Our accommodation of the competing values at stake in defamation suits by private individuals allows the States to impose liability on the publisher or broadcaster of defamatory falsehood on a less demanding showing than that required by New York Times.   This conclusion is not based on a belief that the considerations which prompted the adoption of the New York Times privilege for defamation of public officials and its extension to public figures are wholly inapplicable to the context of private individuals.   Rather, we endorse this approach in recognition of the strong and legitimate state interest in compensating private individuals for injury to reputation.   But this countervailing state interest extends no further than compensation for actual injury.   For the reasons stated below, we hold that the States may not permit recovery of presumed or punitive damages, at least when liability is not based on a showing of knowledge of falsity or reckless disregard for the truth.

The common law of defamation is an oddity of tort law, for it allows recovery of purportedly compensatory damages without evidence of actual loss. Under the traditional rules pertaining to actions for libel, the existence of injury is presumed from the fact of publication. Juries may award substantial sums as compensation for supposed damage to reputation without any proof that such harm actually occurred. The largely uncontrolled discretion of juries to award damages where there is no loss unnecessarily compounds the potential of any system of liability for defamatory falsehood to inhibit the vigorous exercise of First Amendment freedoms. Additionally, the doctrine of presumed damages invites juries to punish unpopular opinion rather than to compensate individuals for injury sustained by the publication of a false fact. More to the point, the States have no substantial interest in securing for plaintiffs such as this petitioner gratuitous awards of money damages far in excess of any actual injury.

We would not, of course, invalidate state law simply because we doubt its wisdom, but here we are attempting to reconcile state law with a competing interest grounded in the constitutional command of the First Amendment. It is therefore appropriate to require that state remedies for defamatory falsehood reach no farther than is necessary to protect the legitimate interest involved. It is necessary to restrict defamation plaintiffs who do not prove knowledge of falsity or reckless disregard for the truth to compensation for actual injury. We need not define 'actual injury,' as trial courts have wide experience in framing appropriate jury instructions in tort actions. Suffice it to say that actual injury is not limited to out-of-pocket loss. Indeed, the more customary types of actual harm inflicted by defamatory falsehood include impairment of reputation and standing in the community, personal humiliation, and mental anguish and suffering. Of course, juries must be limited by appropriate instructions, and all awards must be supported by competent evidence concerning the injury, although there need be no evidence which assigns an actual dollar value to the injury.

We also find no justification for allowing awards of punitive damages against publishers and broadcasters held liable under state-defined standards of liability for defamation. In most jurisdictions jury discretion over the amounts awarded is limited only by the gentle rule that they not be excessive. Consequently, juries assess punitive damages in wholly unpredictable amounts bearing no necessary relation to the actual harm caused. And they remain free to use their discretion selectively to punish expressions of unpopular views. Like the doctrine of presumed damages, jury discretion to award punitive damages unnecessarily exacerbates the danger of media self-censorship, but, unlike the former rule, punitive damages are wholly irrelevant to the state interest that justifies a negligence standard for private defamation actions. They are not compensation for injury. Instead, they are private fines levied by civil juries to punish reprehensible conduct and to deter its future occurrence. In short, the private defamation plaintiff who establishes liability under a less demanding standard than that stated by New York Times may recover only such damages as are sufficient to compensate him for actual injury.

V

Notwithstanding our refusal to extend the New York Times privilege to defamation of private individuals, respondent contends that we should affirm the judgment below on the ground that petitioner is either a public official or a public figure. . . .

Respondent's characterization of petitioner as a public figure raises a different question. That designation may rest on either of two alternative bases. In some instances an individual may achieve such pervasive fame or notoriety that he becomes a public figure for all purposes and in all contexts. More commonly, an individual voluntarily injects himself or is drawn into a particular public controversy and thereby becomes a public figure for a limited range of issues. In either case such persons assume special prominence in the resolution of public questions.

Petitioner has long been active in community and professional affairs. He has served as an officer of local civic groups and of various professional organizations, and he has published several books and articles on legal subjects. Although petitioner was consequently well known in some circles, he had achieved no general fame or notoriety in the community. None of the prospective jurors called at the trial had ever heard of petitioner prior to this litigation, and respondent offered no proof that this response was atypical of the local population. We would not lightly assume that a citizen's participation in community and professional affairs rendered him a public figure for all purposes. Absent clear evidence of general fame or notoriety in the community, and pervasive involvement in the affairs of society, an individual should not be deemed a public personality for all aspects of his life. It is preferable to reduce the public-figure question to a more meaningful context by looking to the nature and extent of an individual's participation in the particular controversy giving rise to the defamation.

In this context it is plain that petitioner was not a public figure. He played a minimal role at the coroner's inquest, and his participation related solely to his representation of a private client. He took no part in the criminal prosecution of Officer Nuccio. Moreover, he never discussed either the criminal or civil litigation with the press and was never quoted as having done so. He plainly did not thrust himself into the vortex of this public issue, nor did he engage the public's attention in an attempt to influence its outcome. We are persuaded that the trial court did not err in refusing to characterize petitioner as a public figure for the purpose of this litigation.

We therefore conclude that the New York Times standard is inapplicable to this case and that the trial court erred in entering judgment for respondent. Because the jury was allowed to impose liability without fault and was permitted to presume damages without proof of injury, a new trial is necessary. We reverse and remand for further proceedings in accord with this opinion.

It is so ordered.

Reversed and remanded.

Points for Discussion

1. Justice Powell states that "[u]nder the First Amendment there is no such thing as a false idea. However pernicious an opinion may seem, we depend for its correction not on the conscience of judges and juries but on the competition of other ideas. But there is no constitutional value in false statements of fact. Neither the intentional lie nor the careless error materially advances society's interest in 'uninhibited, robust, and wide-open' debate on public issues." Do you agree?

2. The Court notes the tension "between the need for a vigorous and uninhibited press and the legitimate interest in redressing wrongful injury." Can those competing interests and concerns be accommodated?

3. The Court also notes that the *New York Times v. Sullivan* standard "exacts a ... high price from the victims of defamatory falsehood. Plainly many deserving plaintiffs, including some intentionally subjected to injury, will be unable to surmount the barrier of the *New York Times* test." What are your views on to this observation?

4. How does the Court distinguish among defamation plaintiffs, and what normative considerations underlie that distinction?

5. Was the *Gertz* plaintiff a public figure or a private individual?

6. What damages can be recovered by a private individual in a defamation lawsuit against publishers or broadcasters?

———————————

Dun & Bradstreet, Inc. v. Greenmoss Builders, Inc.

472 U.S. 749 (1985)

Justice POWELL announced the judgment of the Court . . .

In *Gertz v. Robert Welch, Inc.,* 418 U.S. 323, 94 S.Ct. 2997, 41 L.Ed.2d 789 (1974), we held that the First Amendment restricted the damages that a private individual could obtain from a publisher for a libel that involved a matter of public concern. More specifically, we held that in these circumstances the First Amendment prohibited awards of presumed and punitive damages for false and defamatory statements unless the plaintiff shows "**actual malice**," that is, knowledge of falsity or reckless disregard for the truth. The question presented in this case is whether this rule of *Gertz* applies when the false and defamatory statements do not involve matters of public concern.

. . . .

Petitioner Dun & Bradstreet, a credit reporting agency, provides subscribers with financial and related information about businesses. All the information is confidential; under the terms of the subscription agreement the subscribers may not reveal it to anyone else. On July 26, 1976, petitioner sent a report to five subscribers indicating that respondent, a construction contractor, had filed a voluntary petition for **bankruptcy**. This report was false and grossly misrepresented respondent's assets and liabilities. That same day, while discussing the possibility of future financing with its bank, respondent's president was told that the bank had received the defamatory report. He immediately called petitioner's regional office, explained the error, and asked for a correction. In addition, he requested the names of the firms that had received the false report in order to assure them that the company was solvent. Petitioner promised to look into the matter but refused to divulge the names of those who had received the report.

After determining that its report was indeed false, petitioner issued a corrective notice on or about August 3, 1976, to the five subscribers who had received the initial report. The notice stated that one of respondent's former employees, not respondent itself, had filed for bankruptcy and that respondent "continued in business as usual." Respondent told petitioner that it was dissatisfied with the notice, and it again asked for a list of subscribers who had seen the initial report. Again petitioner refused to divulge their names.

Respondent then brought this defamation action in Vermont state court. It alleged that the false report had injured its reputation and sought both compensatory and punitive damages. The trial established that the error in petitioner's report had been caused when one of its employees, a 17-year-old high school student paid to review Vermont bankruptcy pleadings, had inadvertently attributed to respondent a bankruptcy petition filed by one of respondent's former employees. Although petitioner's representative testified that it was routine practice to check the accuracy of such reports with the businesses themselves, it did not try to verify the information about respondent before reporting it.

After trial, the jury returned a verdict in favor of respondent and awarded $50,000 in compensatory or presumed damages and $300,000 in punitive damages. Petitioner moved for a new trial. It argued that in *Gertz v. Robert Welch, Inc., supra,* at 349, 94 S.Ct., at 3011, this Court had ruled broadly that "the States may not permit recovery of presumed or punitive damages, at least when liability is not based on a showing of knowledge of falsity or reckless disregard for the truth," and it argued that the judge's instructions in this case permitted the jury to award such damages on a lesser showing. The trial court indicated some doubt as to whether *Gertz* applied to "non-media cases," but granted a new trial "[b]ecause of ... dissatisfaction with its charge and ... conviction that the interests of justice require[d]" it. [C]

The Vermont Supreme Court reversed. [C] Although recognizing that "in certain instances the distinction between media and nonmedia defendants may be difficult to draw," the court stated that "no such difficulty is presented with credit reporting agencies, which are in the business of selling financial information to a limited number of subscribers who have paid substantial fees for their services." [C] Relying on this distinguishing characteristic of credit reporting firms, the court concluded that such firms are not "the type of media worthy of First Amendment protection as contemplated by *New York Times Co. v. Sullivan,* 376 U.S. 254, 84 S.Ct. 710, 11 L.Ed.2d 686 (1964),] and its progeny." [C] It held that the balance between a private plaintiff's right to recover presumed and punitive damages without a showing of special fault and the First Amendment rights of "nonmedia" speakers "must be struck in favor of the private plaintiff defamed by a nonmedia defendant." [C] Accordingly, the court held "that as a matter of federal constitutional law, the media protections outlined in *Gertz* are inapplicable to nonmedia defamation actions." [C]

Recognizing disagreement among the lower courts about when the protections of *Gertz* apply, we granted certiorari. [C] We now affirm, although for reasons different from those relied upon by the Vermont Supreme Court.

. . . .

. . . *Gertz v. Robert Welch, Inc.,* 418 U.S. 323, 94 S.Ct. 2997, 41 L.Ed.2d 789 (1974) . . . concerned a libelous article appearing in a magazine called American Opinion, the monthly outlet of the John Birch Society. The article in question discussed whether the prosecution of a policeman in Chicago was part of a Communist campaign to discredit local law enforcement agencies. The plaintiff, Gertz, neither a public official nor a public figure, was a lawyer tangentially involved in the prosecution. The magazine alleged that he was the chief architect of the "frame-up" of the police officer and linked him to Communist activity. Like every other case in which this Court has found constitutional limits to state defamation laws, *Gertz* involved expression on a matter of undoubted public concern.

In *Gertz,* we held that the fact that expression concerned a public issue did not by itself entitle the libel defendant to the constitutional protections of *New York Times.* These protections, we found, were not "justified solely by reference to the interest of the press and broadcast media in immunity from liability." [C] Rather, they represented "an accommodation between [First Amendment] concern[s] and the limited state interest present in the context of libel actions brought by public persons." [C] In libel actions brought by private persons we found the competing interests different. Largely because private persons have not voluntarily exposed themselves to increased risk of injury from defamatory statements and because they generally lack effective opportunities for rebutting such statements, [c], we found that the State possessed a "strong and legitimate ... interest in compensating private individuals for injury to reputation." [C] Balancing this stronger state interest against the same First Amendment interest at stake in *New York Times,* we held that a State could not allow recovery of presumed and punitive damages absent a showing of "actual malice." Nothing in our opinion, however, indicated that this same balance would be struck regardless of the type of speech involved.

. . . .

We have never considered whether the *Gertz* balance obtains when the defamatory statements involve no issue of public concern. To make this determination, we must employ the approach approved in *Gertz* and balance the State's interest in compensating private individuals for injury to their reputation against the First Amendment interest in protecting this type of expression. This state interest is identical to the one weighed in *Gertz.* There we found that it was "strong and legitimate." [C] A State should not lightly be required to abandon it . . .

The First Amendment interest, on the other hand, is less important than the one weighed in *Gertz.* We have long recognized that not all speech is of equal First Amendment importance. It is speech on "'matters of public concern'" that is "at the heart of the First Amendment's protection." *First National Bank of Boston v. Bellotti,* 435 U.S. 765, 776, 98 S.Ct. 1407, 1415, 55 L.Ed.2d 707 (1978), citing *Thornhill v. Alabama,* 310 U.S. 88, 101, 60 S.Ct. 736, 743, 84 L.Ed. 1093 (1940). . . .

In contrast, speech on matters of purely private concern is of less First Amendment concern. [C] As a number of state courts, including the court below, have recognized, the role of the Constitution in regulating state libel law is far more limited when the concerns that activated *New York Times* and *Gertz* are absent. In such a case,

"[t]here is no threat to the free and robust debate of public issues; there is no potential interference with a meaningful dialogue of ideas concerning self-government; and there is no threat of liability causing a reaction of self-censorship by the press. The facts of the present case are wholly without the First Amendment concerns with which the Supreme Court of the United States has been struggling." *Harley-Davidson*

Motorsports, Inc. v. Markley, 279 Or. 361, 366, 568 P.2d 1359, 1363 (1977). . . .

While such speech is not totally unprotected by the First Amendment, [c], its protections are less stringent. In *Gertz,* we found that the state interest in awarding presumed and punitive damages was not "substantial" in view of their effect on speech at the core of First Amendment concern. [C] This interest, however, *is* "substantial" relative to the incidental effect these remedies may have on speech of significantly less constitutional interest. The rationale of the common-law rules has been the experience and judgment of history that "proof of actual damage will be impossible in a great many cases where, from the character of the defamatory words and the circumstances of publication, it is all but certain that serious harm has resulted in fact." [Cc] As a result, courts for centuries have allowed juries to presume that some damage occurred from many defamatory utterances and publications. Restatement of Torts § 568, Comment *b,* p. 162 (1938) (noting that Hale announced that damages were to be presumed for libel as early as 1670). This rule furthers the state interest in providing remedies for defamation by ensuring that those remedies are effective. In light of the reduced constitutional value of speech involving no matters of public concern, we hold that the state interest adequately supports awards of presumed and punitive damages—even absent a showing of "actual malice."

. . . .

The only remaining issue is whether petitioner's credit report involved a matter of public concern. In a related context, we have held that "[w]hether … speech addresses a matter of public concern must be determined by [the expression's] content, form, and context … as revealed by the whole record." [C] These factors indicate that petitioner's credit report concerns no public issue. It was speech solely in the individual interest of the speaker and its specific business audience. [C] This particular interest warrants no special protection when-as in this case-the speech is wholly false and clearly damaging to the victim's business reputation. [Cc] Moreover, since the credit report was made available to only five subscribers, who, under the terms of the subscription agreement, could not disseminate it further, it cannot be said that the report involves any "strong interest in the free flow of commercial information." [C] There is simply no credible argument that this type of credit reporting requires special protection to ensure that "debate on public issues [will] be uninhibited, robust, and wide-open." *New York Times Co. v. Sullivan,* 376 U.S., at 270, 84 S.Ct., at 720.

In addition, the speech here, like advertising, is hardy and unlikely to be deterred by incidental state regulation. [C] It is solely motivated by the desire for profit, which, we have noted, is a force less likely to be deterred than others. *Ibid.*

Arguably, the reporting here was also more objectively verifiable than speech deserving of greater protection. See *ibid.* In any case, the market provides a powerful incentive to a credit reporting agency to be accurate, since false credit reporting is of no use to creditors. Thus, any incremental "chilling" effect of libel suits would be of decreased significance.

. . . .

We conclude that permitting recovery of presumed and punitive damages in defamation cases absent a showing of "actual malice" does not violate the First Amendment when the defamatory statements do not involve matters of public concern. Accordingly, we affirm the judgment of the Vermont Supreme Court.

It is so ordered.

Points for Discussion

1. Describe the legally relevant facts before the *Dun & Bradstreet* Court.

2. What interests are examined and balanced by Justice Powell's opinion?

3. Consider Justice Powell's declaration that "speech on matters of purely private concern is of less First Amendment concern. . . . [T]he role of the Constitution in regulating state libel law is far more limited when the concerns that activated *New York Times* and *Gertz* are absent."

4. How does a court determine whether certain speech addresses a matter of private concern or a matter of public concern? In Snyder v. Phelps, 131 S.Ct. 1207 (2011), the Supreme Court instructed that the "Free Speech Clause of the First Amendment . . . can serve as a defense in state tort suits . . ." The Court stated:

   ..."[S]peech on 'matters of public concern' ... is 'at the heart of the First Amendment's protection.'" Dun & Bradstreet, Inc. v. Greenmoss Builders, Inc., 472 U.S. 749, 758-759, 105 S.Ct. 2939, 86 L.Ed.2d 593 (1985) (opinion of Powell, J.) (quoting First Nat. Bank of Boston v. Bellotti, 435 U.S. 765, 776, 98 S.Ct. 1407, 55 L.Ed.2d 707 (1978)). The First Amendment reflects "a profound national commitment to the principle that debate on public issues should be uninhibited, robust, and wide-open." New York Times Co. v. Sullivan, 376 U.S. 254, 270, 84 S.Ct. 710, 11 L.Ed.2d 686 (1964).

That is because "speech concerning public affairs is more than self-expression; it is the essence of self-government." Garrison v. Louisiana, 379 U.S. 64, 74-75, 85 S.Ct. 209, 13 L.Ed.2d 125 (1964). Accordingly, "speech on public issues occupies the highest rung of the hierarchy of First Amendment values, and is entitled to special protection." Connick v. Myers, 461 U.S. 138, 145, 103 S.Ct. 1684, 75 L.Ed.2d 708 (1983) . . .

"'[N]ot all speech is of equal First Amendment importance,'" however, and where matters of purely private significance are at issue, First Amendment protections are often less rigorous. [Cc] That is because restricting speech on purely private matters does not implicate the same constitutional concerns as limiting speech on matters of public interest: "[T]here is no threat to the free and robust debate of public issues; there is no potential interference with a meaningful dialogue of ideas"; and the "threat of liability" does not pose the risk of "a reaction of self-censorship" on matters of public import. *Dun & Bradstreet, supra,* at 760, 105 S.Ct. 2939 (internal quotation marks omitted).

We noted a short time ago, in considering whether public employee speech addressed a matter of public concern, that "the boundaries of the public concern test are not well defined." *San Diego v. Roe,* 543 U.S. 77, 83, 125 S.Ct. 521, 160 L.Ed.2d 410 (2004) (*per curiam*). Although that remains true today, we have articulated some guiding principles, principles that accord broad protection to speech to ensure that courts themselves do not become inadvertent censors.

Speech deals with matters of public concern when it can "be fairly considered as relating to any matter of political, social, or other concern to the community," [c] or when it "is a subject of legitimate news interest; that is, a subject of general interest and of value and concern to the public," [Cc] The arguably "inappropriate or controversial character of a statement is irrelevant to the question whether it deals with a matter of public concern." *Rankin v. McPherson,* 483 U.S. 378, 387, 107 S.Ct. 2891, 97 L.Ed.2d 315 (1987).

. . . .

Deciding whether speech is of public or private concern requires us to examine the "'content, form, and context'" of that speech, "'as revealed by the whole record.'" [C] As in other First Amendment cases, the court is obligated "to 'make an independent examination of the whole record' in order to make sure that 'the judgment does not constitute a forbidden intrusion on the field of free expression.'" [C] In considering content, form, and context, no factor is dispositive, and it is necessary to evaluate all the circumstances of the speech, including what was said, where it was said, and how it was said.

Time, Inc. v. Firestone

424 U.S. 448 (1976)

Mr. Justice REHNQUIST delivered the opinion of the Court.

Petitioner is the publisher of Time, a weekly news magazine. The Supreme Court of Florida affirmed a $100,000 libel judgment against petitioner which was based on an item appearing in Time that purported to describe the result of domestic relations litigation between respondent and her husband. We granted certiorari, [c], to review petitioner's claim that the judgment violates its rights under the First and Fourteenth Amendments to the United States Constitution.

I

Respondent, Mary Alice Firestone, married Russell Firestone, the scion of one of America's wealthier industrial families, in 1961. In 1964, they separated, and respondent filed a complaint for separate maintenance in the Circuit Court of Palm Beach County, Fla. Her husband counterclaimed for divorce on grounds of **extreme cruelty** and **adultery**. After a lengthy trial the Circuit Court issued a judgment granting the divorce requested by respondent's husband. In relevant part the court's final judgment read:

"This cause came on for final hearing before the court upon the plaintiff wife's second amended complaint for separate maintenance (alimony unconnected with the causes of divorce), the defendant husband's answer and counterclaim for divorce on grounds of extreme cruelty and adultery, and the wife's answer thereto setting up certain affirmative defenses. . . .

"According to certain testimony in behalf of the defendant, extramarital escapades of the plaintiff were bizarre and of an amatory nature which would have made Dr. Freud's hair curl. Other testimony, in plaintiff's behalf, would indicate that defendant was guilty of bounding from one bedpartner to another with the erotic zest of a satyr. The court is inclined to discount much of this testimony as unreliable. Nevertheless, it is the conclusion and finding of the court that neither party is domesticated, within the meaning of that term as used by the Supreme Court of Florida . . .

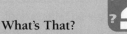

What's That?

A *satyr* has been defined as a "woodland creature depicted as having the ears, legs, and horns of a goat," or a "lecher." THE AMERICAN HERITAGE DICTIONARY 740 (4TH ED. 2001).

"In the present case, it is abundantly clear from the evidence of marital discord that neither of the parties has shown the least susceptibility to domestication, and that the marriage should be dissolved.

"The premises considered, it is thereupon

"ORDERED AND ADJUDGED as follows:

"1. That the equities in this cause are with the defendant; that defendant's counterclaim for divorce be and the same is hereby granted, and the bonds of matrimony which have heretofore existed between the parties are hereby forever dissolved. [. . .]

"4. That the defendant shall pay unto the plaintiff the sum of $3,000 per month as alimony beginning January 1, 1968, and a like sum on the first day of each and every month thereafter until the death or remarriage of the plaintiff." . . .

Time's editorial staff, headquartered in New York, was alerted by a wire service report and an account in a New York newspaper to the fact that a judgment had been rendered in the Firestone divorce proceeding. The staff subsequently received further information regarding the Florida decision from Time's Miami bureau chief and from a "stringer" working on a special assignment basis in the Palm Beach area. On the basis of these four sources, Time's staff composed the following item, which appeared in the magazine's "Milestones" section the following week:

"DIVORCED. By Russell A. Firestone Jr., 41, heir to the tire fortune: Mary Alice Sullivan Firestone, 32, his third wife; a onetime Palm Beach schoolteacher; on grounds of extreme cruelty and adultery; after six years of marriage, one son; in West Palm Beach, Fla. The 17-month intermittent trial produced enough testimony of extramarital adventures on both sides, said the judge, 'to make Dr. Freud's hair curl.' "

Within a few weeks of the publication of this article respondent demanded in writing a retraction from petitioner, alleging that a portion of the article was "false, malicious and defamatory." Petitioner declined to issue the requested retraction.[5]

Respondent then filed this libel action against petitioner in the Florida Circuit Court. Based on a jury verdict for respondent, that court entered judgment against petitioner for $100,000, and after review in both the Florida District Court of Appeal, [c] and the Supreme Court of Florida, the judgment was ultimately affirmed. [C] Petitioner advances several contentions as to why the judgment is contrary to decisions of this Court holding that the First and Fourteenth Amendments of the United States Constitution limit the authority of state courts to impose liability for damages based on defamation.

II

Petitioner initially contends that it cannot be liable for publishing any falsehood defaming respondent unless it is established that the publication was made "with actual malice," as that term is defined in *New York Times v. Sullivan,* 376 U.S. 254, 84 S.Ct. 710, 11 L.Ed.2d 686 (1964).[6] Petitioner advances two arguments in support of this contention: that respondent is a "public figure" within this Court's decisions extending New York Times to defamation suits brought by such individuals, [c], and that the Time item constituted a report of a judicial proceeding, a class of subject matter which petitioner claims deserves the protection of the "actual malice" standard even if the story is proved to be defamatorily false or inaccurate. We reject both arguments.

In *Gertz v. Robert Welch, Inc.,* 418 U.S. 323, 345, 94 S.Ct. 2997, 3009, 41 L.Ed.2d 789 (1974), we have recently further defined the meaning of "public figure" for the purposes of the First and Fourteenth Amendments:

> "For the most part those who attain this status have assumed roles of especial prominence in the affairs of society. Some occupy positions of such persuasive power and influence that they are deemed public figures for all purposes. More commonly, those classed as public figures have thrust themselves to the forefront of particular public controversies in order to influence the resolution of the issues involved."

---

5 Under Florida law the demand for retraction was a prerequisite for filing a libel action, and permits defendants to limit their potential liability to actual damages by complying with the demand. [C].
6 The "actual malice" test requires that a plaintiff prove that the defamatory statement was made "with knowledge that it was false or with reckless disregard of whether it was false or not." 376 U.S., at 280, 84 S.Ct., at 726.

Respondent did not assume any role of especial prominence in the affairs of society, other than perhaps Palm Beach society, and she did not thrust herself to the forefront of any particular public controversy in order to influence the resolution of the issues involved in it.

Petitioner contends that because the Firestone divorce was characterized by the Florida Supreme Court as a "**cause celebre**," it must have been a public controversy and respondent must be considered a public figure. But in so doing petitioner seeks to equate "**public controversy**" with all controversies of interest to the public. . . .

Dissolution of a marriage through judicial proceedings is not the sort of "public controversy" referred to in Gertz, even though the marital difficulties of extremely wealthy individuals may be of interest to some portion of the reading public. Nor did respondent freely choose to publicize issues as to the propriety of her married life. She was compelled to go to court by the State in order to obtain legal release from the bonds of matrimony. We have said that in such an instance "(r)esort to the judicial process . . . is no more voluntary in a realistic sense than that of the defendant called upon to defend his interests in court." [C] . . . She assumed no "special prominence in the resolution of public questions." [C] We hold respondent was not a "public figure" for the purpose of determining the constitutional protection afforded petitioner's report of the factual and legal basis for her divorce.

For similar reasons we likewise reject petitioner's claim for automatic extension of the New York Times privilege to all reports of judicial proceedings. It is argued that information concerning proceedings in our Nation's courts may have such importance to all citizens as to justify extending special First Amendment protection to the press when reporting on such events. We have recently accepted a significantly more confined version of this argument by holding that the Constitution precludes States from imposing civil liability based upon the publication of truthful information contained in official court records open to public inspection. *Cox Broadcasting Corp. v. Cohn*, 420 U.S. 469, 95 S.Ct. 1029, 43 L.Ed.2d 328 (1975).

Petitioner would have us extend the reasoning of Cox Broadcasting to safeguard even inaccurate and false statements, at least where "actual malice" has not been established. But its argument proves too much. It may be that all reports of judicial proceedings contain some informational value implicating the First Amendment, but recognizing this is little different from labeling all judicial proceedings matters of "public or general interest," as that phrase was used by the plurality in *Rosenbloom*. Whatever their general validity, use of such subject-matter classifications to determine the extent of constitutional protection afforded defamatory falsehoods may too often result in an improper balance between the competing interests in this area. . . . .

Presumptively erecting the New York Times barrier against all plaintiffs seeking to recover for injuries from defamatory falsehoods published in what are alleged to be reports of judicial proceedings would effect substantial depreciation of the individual's interest in protection from such harm, without any convincing assurance that such a sacrifice is required under the First Amendment. And in some instances such an undiscriminating approach might achieve results directly at odds with the constitutional balance intended. Indeed, the article upon which the Gertz libel action was based purported to be a report on the murder trial of a Chicago police officer. [C] Our decision in that case should make it clear that no such blanket privilege for reports of judicial proceedings is to be found in the Constitution.

It may be argued that there is still room for application of the New York Times protections to more narrowly focused reports of what actually transpires in the courtroom. But even so narrowed, the suggested privilege is simply too broad. Imposing upon the law of private defamation the rather drastic limitations worked by New York Times cannot be justified by generalized references to the public interest in reports of judicial proceedings. The details of many, if not most, courtroom battles would add almost nothing toward advancing the uninhibited debate on public issues thought to provide principal support for the decision in New York Times. [Cc] And while participants in some litigation may be legitimate "public figures," either generally or for the limited purpose of that litigation, the majority will more likely resemble respondent, drawn into a public forum largely against their will in order to attempt to obtain the only redress available to them or to defend themselves against actions brought by the State or by others. There appears little reason why these individuals should substantially forfeit that degree of protection which the law of defamation would otherwise afford them simply by virtue of their being drawn into a courtroom. . . .

III

Petitioner has urged throughout this litigation that it could not be held liable for publication of the "Milestones" item because its report of respondent's divorce was factually correct. In its view the Time article faithfully reproduced the precise meaning of the divorce judgment. But this issue was submitted to the jury under an instruction intended to implement Florida's limited privilege for accurate reports of judicial proceedings. [Cc] By returning a verdict for respondent the jury necessarily found that the identity of meaning which petitioner claims does not exist even for laymen. The Supreme Court of Florida upheld this finding on appeal, rejecting petitioner's contention that its report was accurate as a matter of law. Because demonstration that an article was true would seem to preclude finding the publisher at fault, [c], we have examined the predicate for petitioner's contention. We believe the Florida courts properly could have found the "Milestones" item to be false.

For petitioner's report to have been accurate, the divorce granted Russell Firestone must have been based on a finding by the divorce court that his wife had committed extreme cruelty toward him *and* that she had been guilty of adultery. This is indisputably what petitioner reported in its "Milestones" item, but it is equally indisputable that these were not the facts. Russell Firestone alleged in his counterclaim that respondent had been guilty of adultery, but the divorce court never made any such finding. Its judgment provided that Russell Firestone's "counterclaim for divorce be and the same is hereby granted," but did not specify that the basis for the judgment was either of the two grounds alleged in the counterclaim. The Supreme Court of Florida on appeal concluded that the ground actually relied upon by the divorce court was "lack of domestication of the parties," a ground not theretofore recognized by Florida law. The Supreme Court nonetheless affirmed the judgment dissolving the bonds of matrimony because the record contained sufficient evidence to establish the ground of extreme cruelty. [C]

Petitioner may well argue that the meaning of the trial court's decree was unclear, but this does not license it to choose from among several conceivable interpretations the one most damaging to respondent. Having chosen to follow this tack, petitioner must be able to establish not merely that the item reported was a conceivable or plausible interpretation of the decree, but that the item was factually correct. We believe there is ample support for the jury's conclusion, affirmed by the Supreme Court of Florida, that this was not the case. There was, therefore, sufficient basis for imposing liability upon petitioner if the constitutional limitations we announced in Gertz have been satisfied. These are a prohibition against imposing liability without fault, [c] and the requirement that compensatory awards "be supported by competent evidence concerning the injury." [C]

As to the latter requirement little difficulty appears. Petitioner has argued that because respondent withdrew her claim for damages to reputation on the eve of trial, there could be no recovery consistent with Gertz. Petitioner's theory seems to be that the only compensable injury in a defamation action is that which may be done to one's reputation, and that claims not predicated upon such injury are by definition not actions for defamation. But Florida has obviously decided to permit recovery for other injuries without regard to measuring the effect the falsehood may have had upon a plaintiff's reputation. This does not transform the action into something other than an action for defamation as that term is meant in

Gertz. In that opinion we made it clear that States could base awards on elements other than injury to reputation, specifically listing "personal humiliation, and mental anguish and suffering" as examples of injuries which might be compensated consistently with the Constitution upon a showing of fault. Because respondent has decided to forgo recovery for injury to her reputation, she is not prevented from obtaining compensation for such other damages that a defamatory falsehood may have caused her.

. . . There was competent evidence introduced to permit the jury to assess the amount of injury. Several witnesses[7] testified to the extent of respondent's anxiety and concern over Time's inaccurately reporting that she had been found guilty of adultery, and she herself took the stand to elaborate on her fears that her young son would be adversely affected by this falsehood when he grew older. The jury decided these injuries should be compensated by an award of $100,000. We have no warrant for re-examining this determination. [C.]

IV

Gertz established, however, that not only must there be evidence to support an award of compensatory damages, there must also be evidence of some fault on the part of a defendant charged with publishing defamatory material. No question of fault was submitted to the jury in this case, because under Florida law the only findings required for determination of liability were whether the article was defamatory, whether it was true, and whether the defamation, if any, caused respondent harm.

The failure to submit the question of fault to the jury does not of itself establish noncompliance with the constitutional requirements established in Gertz, however. Nothing in the Constitution requires that assessment of fault in a civil case tried in a state court be made by a jury, nor is there any prohibition against such a finding being made in the first instance by an appellate, rather than a trial, court. The First and Fourteenth Amendments do not impose upon the States any limitations as to how, within their own judicial systems, factfinding tasks shall be allocated. If we were satisfied that one of the Florida courts which considered this case had supportably ascertained petitioner was at fault, we would be required to affirm the judgment below.

But the only alternative source of such a finding, given that the issue was not submitted to the jury, is the opinion of the Supreme Court of Florida. That opinion appears to proceed generally on the assumption that a showing of fault was not required, but then in the penultimate paragraph it recites:

---

7 These included respondent's minister, her attorney in the divorce proceedings, plus several friends and neighbors, one of whom was a physician who testified to having to administer a sedative to respondent in an attempt to reduce discomfort wrought by her worrying about the article.

"Furthermore, this erroneous reporting is clear and convincing evidence of the negligence in certain segments of the news media in gathering the news. [C] Pursuant to Florida law in effect at the time of the divorce judgment (Section 61.08, Florida Statutes), a wife found guilty of adultery could not be awarded alimony. Since petitioner had been awarded alimony, she had not been found guilty of adultery nor had the divorce been granted on the ground of adultery. A careful examination of the final decree prior to publication would have clearly demonstrated that the divorce had been granted on the grounds of extreme cruelty, and thus the wife would have been saved the humiliation of being accused of adultery in a nationwide magazine. This is a flagrant example of 'journalistic negligence.'"[C].

It may be argued that this is sufficient indication the court found petitioner at fault within the meaning of Gertz. Nothing in that decision or in the First or Fourteenth Amendment requires that in a libel action an appellate court treat in detail by written opinion all contentions of the parties, and if the jury or trial judge had found fault in fact, we would be quite willing to read the quoted passage as affirming that conclusion. But without some finding of fault by the judge or jury in the Circuit Court, we would have to attribute to the Supreme Court of Florida from the quoted language not merely an intention to affirm the finding of the lower court, but an intention to find such a fact in the first instance.

. . . .

It may well be that petitioner's account in its "Milestones" section was the product of some fault on its part, and that the libel judgment against it was, therefore, entirely consistent with *Gertz*. But in the absence of a finding in some element of the state court system that there was fault, we are not inclined to canvass the record to make such a determination in the first instance. [C] Accordingly, the judgment of the Supreme Court of Florida is vacated and the case remanded for further proceedings not inconsistent with this opinion.

So ordered.

———————

Points for Discussion

1. What did *Time* magazine publish and why did Firestone demand a retraction?

2. Was Firestone a "public figure"?

3. Is there a difference between (a) a "public controversy" (as referenced in the

Court's *Gertz* decision, *supra*) and (b) a controversy of interest to the public? If so, articulate the difference.

4. The magazine argued that the "actual malice" standard applies to reports of judicial proceedings. Did the Court agree?

5. Was the magazine's report of the Firestones' divorce factually correct? How does the Court analyze and answer that query?

6. The Court remanded the case for further proceedings. Why?

---

4. Opinion

Milkovich v. Lorain Journal Co.

497 U.S. 1 (1990)

Chief Justice REHNQUIST delivered the opinion of the Court.

Respondent J. Theodore Diadiun authored an article in an Ohio newspaper implying that petitioner Michael Milkovich, a local high school wrestling coach, lied under oath in a judicial proceeding about an incident involving petitioner and his team which occurred at a wrestling match. Petitioner sued Diadiun and the newspaper for libel, and the Ohio Court of Appeals affirmed a lower court entry of summary judgment against petitioner. This judgment was based in part on the grounds that the article constituted an "opinion" protected from the reach of state defamation law by the First Amendment to the United States Constitution. We hold that the First Amendment does not prohibit the application of Ohio's libel laws to the alleged defamations contained in the article.

This lawsuit is before us for the third time in an odyssey of litigation spanning nearly 15 years. Petitioner Milkovich, now retired, was the wrestling coach at Maple Heights High School in Maple Heights, Ohio. In 1974, his team was involved in an altercation at a home wrestling match with a team from Mentor High School. Several people were injured. In response to the incident, the Ohio High School Athletic Association (OHSAA) held a hearing at which Milkovich and H. Don Scott, the Superintendent of Maple Heights Public Schools, testified. Following the hearing, OHSAA placed the Maple Heights team on probation for a year and declared the team ineligible for the 1975 state tournament. OHSAA also censured Milkovich for his actions during the altercation. Thereafter, several parents and wrestlers sued OHSAA in the Court of Common Pleas of Franklin County, Ohio, seeking a **restraining order** against OHSAA's ruling on the grounds that they had been denied **due process** in the OHSAA proceeding. Both Milkovich and Scott testified in that proceeding. The court overturned OHSAA's probation and ineligibility orders on due process grounds.

The day after the court rendered its decision, respondent Diadiun's column appeared in the News-Herald, a newspaper which circulates in Lake County, Ohio, and is owned by respondent Lorain Journal Co. The column bore the heading "Maple beat the law with the 'big lie,'" beneath which appeared Diadiun's photograph and the words "TD Says." The carryover page headline announced "... Diadiun says Maple told a lie." The column contained the following passages:

> " '... [A] lesson was learned (or relearned) yesterday by the student body of Maple Heights High School, and by anyone who attended the Maple-Mentor wrestling meet of last Feb. 8.

> " 'A lesson which, sadly, in view of the events of the past year, is well they learned early.

> " 'It is simply this: If you get in a jam, lie your way out.

> " 'If you're successful enough, and powerful enough, and can sound sincere enough, you stand an excellent chance of making the lie stand up, regardless of what really happened.

> " 'The teachers responsible were mainly head Maple wrestling coach, Mike Milkovich, and former superintendent of schools H. Donald Scott.

> . . . . .

> " 'Anyone who attended the meet, whether he be from Maple Heights, Mentor, or impartial observer, knows in his heart that Milkovich and Scott lied at the hearing after each having given his solemn oath to tell the truth.

> " 'But they got away with it.

> " 'Is that the kind of lesson we want our young people learning from their high school administrators and coaches?

> " 'I think not.'" [C]

Petitioner commenced a defamation action against respondents in the Court of Common Pleas of Lake County, Ohio, alleging that the headline of Diadiun's article and the nine passages quoted above "accused plaintiff of committing the crime of **perjury**, an indictable offense in the State of Ohio, and damaged plaintiff directly in his life-time occupation of coach and teacher, and constituted libel per se." [C] The action proceeded to trial, and the court granted a directed verdict to respondents on the ground that the evidence failed to establish the article was published with "actual malice" as required by *New York Times Co. v. Sullivan,* 376 U.S. 254, 84 S.Ct. 710, 11 L.Ed.2d 686 (1964). [C] The Ohio Court of Appeals for the Eleventh Appellate District reversed and remanded, holding that there was sufficient evidence of actual malice to go to the jury. [C] The Ohio Supreme Court dismissed the ensuing appeal for want of a substantial constitutional question, and this Court denied certiorari. [C]

On remand, relying in part on our decision in *Gertz v. Robert Welch, Inc.,* 418 U.S. 323, 94 S.Ct. 2997, 41 L.Ed.2d 789 (1974), the trial court granted summary judgment to respondents on the grounds that the article was an opinion protected from a libel action by "constitutional law," [c], and alternatively, as a public figure, petitioner had failed to make out a prima facie case of actual malice. [C] The Ohio Court of Appeals affirmed both determinations. [C] On appeal, the Supreme Court of Ohio reversed and remanded. The court first decided that petitioner was neither a public figure nor a public official under the relevant decisions of this Court. [C] The court then found that "the statements in issue are factual assertions as a matter of law, and are not constitutionally protected as the opinions of the writer.... The plain import of the author's assertions is that Milkovich, *inter alia,* committed the crime of perjury in a court of law." [C] This Court again denied certiorari. [C]

Meanwhile, Superintendent Scott had been pursuing a separate defamation action through the Ohio courts. Two years after its *Milkovich* decision, in considering Scott's appeal, the Ohio Supreme Court reversed its position on Diadiun's article, concluding that the column was "constitutionally protected opinion." [C] Consequently, the court upheld a lower court's grant of summary judgment against Scott.

The *Scott* court decided that the proper analysis for determining whether utterances are fact or opinion was set forth in the decision of the United States Court of Appeals for the District of Columbia Circuit in *Ollman v. Evans,* 242 U.S.App.D.C. 301, 750 F.2d 970 (1984), cert. denied, 471 U.S. 1127, 105 S.Ct. 2662, 86 L.Ed.2d 278 (1985). [C] Under that analysis, four factors are considered to ascertain whether, under the "totality of circumstances," a statement is fact or opinion. These factors are: (1) "the specific language used"; (2) "whether the statement is verifiable", (3) "the general context of the statement"; and (4) "the broader context in which the statement appeared." *Ibid.* The court found that application of the first two factors to the column militated in favor of deeming the challenged passages actionable assertions of fact. [C] That potential outcome was trumped, however, by the court's consideration of the third and fourth factors. With respect to the third factor, the general context, the court explained that "the large caption 'TD Says' ... would indicate to even the most gullible reader that the article was, in fact, opinion." [C] As for the fourth factor, the "broader context," the court reasoned that because the article appeared on a sports page–"a tradi- tional haven for cajoling, invective, and hyperbole"–the article would probably be construed as opinion. [C]

Subsequently, considering itself bound by the Ohio Supreme Court's decision in *Scott,* the Ohio Court of Appeals in the instant proceedings affirmed a trial court's grant of summary judgment in favor of respondents, concluding that "it has been decided, as a matter of law, that the article in question was constitution- ally protected opinion." [C] The Supreme Court of Ohio dismissed petitioner's ensuing appeal for want of a substantial constitutional question. . . . We granted certiorari, [c], to consider the important questions raised by the Ohio courts' recognition of a constitutionally required "opinion" exception to the application of its defamation laws. We now reverse.

Since the latter half of the 16th century, the common law has afforded a cause of action for damage to a person's reputation by the publication of false and defamatory statements. See L. Eldredge, Law of Defamation 5 (1978).

In Shakespeare's Othello, Iago says to Othello:

"Good name in man and woman, dear my lord,
Is the immediate jewel of their souls.
Who steals my purse steals trash;
'Tis something, nothing;
'Twas mine, 'tis his, and has been slave to thousands;
But he that filches from me my good name
Robs me of that which not enriches him,
And makes me poor indeed." Act III, scene 3.

Defamation law developed not only as a means of allowing an individual to vindicate his good name, but also for the purpose of obtaining redress for harm caused by such statements. [C] As the common law developed in this country, apart from the issue of damages, one usually needed only allege an unprivileged publication of false and defamatory matter to state a cause of action for defama- tion. See, *e.g.,* Restatement of Torts § 558 (1938); *Gertz v. Robert Welch, Inc.,* 418 U.S., at 370, 94 S.Ct., at 3022 (WHITE, J., dissenting) ("Under typical state defa- mation law, the defamed private citizen had to prove only a false publication that would subject him to hatred, contempt, or ridicule"). The common law generally did not place any additional restrictions on the type of statement that could be actionable. Indeed, defamatory communications were deemed actionable regardless of whether they were deemed to be statements of fact or opinion. See, *e.g.,* Restatement of Torts, *supra,* §§ 565-567. As noted in the 1977 Restatement (Second) of Torts § 566, Comment *a:*

> "Under the law of defamation, an expression of opinion could be defamatory if the expression was sufficiently derogatory of another as to cause harm to his reputation, so as to lower him in the estimation of the community or to deter third persons from associating or dealing with him.... The expression of opinion was also actionable in a suit for defamation, despite the normal requirement that the communication be false as well as defamatory.... This position was maintained even though the truth or falsity of an opinion-as distinguished from a statement of fact-is not a matter that can be objectively determined and truth is a complete defense to a suit for defamation."

However, due to concerns that unduly burdensome defamation laws could stifle valuable public debate, the privilege of "**fair comment**" was incorporated into the common law as an affirmative defense to an action for defamation. "The principle of 'fair comment' afford[ed] legal immunity for the honest expression of opinion on matters of legitimate public interest when based upon a true or privileged statement of fact." 1 F. Harper & F. James, Law of Torts § 5.28, p. 456 (1956) (footnote omitted). As this statement implies, comment was generally privileged when it concerned a matter of public concern, was upon true or privileged facts, represented the actual opinion of the speaker, and was not made solely for the purpose of causing harm. See Restatement of Torts, *supra,* § 606. "According to the majority rule, the privilege of fair comment applied only to an expression of opinion and not to a false statement of fact, whether it was expressly stated or implied from an expression of opinion." Restatement (Second) of Torts, *supra,* § 566, Comment *a.* Thus under the common law, the privilege of "fair comment" was the device employed to strike the appropriate balance between the need for vigorous public discourse and the need to redress injury to citizens wrought by invidious or irresponsible speech.

. . . .

Respondents would have us recognize . . . another First-Amendment-based protection for defamatory statements which are categorized as "opinion" as opposed to "fact." For this proposition they rely principally on the following dictum from our opinion in Gertz:

"Under the First Amendment there is no such thing as a false idea. However pernicious an opinion may seem, we depend for its correction not on the conscience of judges and juries but on the competition of other ideas. But there is no constitutional value in false statements of fact." [C]

Judge Friendly appropriately observed that this passage "has become the opening salvo in all arguments for protection from defamation actions on the ground of opinion, even though the case did not remotely concern the question." *Cianci v. New Times Publishing Co.*, 639 F.2d 54, 61 (CA2 1980). Read in context, though, the fair meaning of the passage is to equate the word "opinion" in the second sentence with the word "idea" in the first sentence. Under this view, the language was merely a reiteration of Justice Holmes' classic "marketplace of ideas" concept. See *Abrams v. United States,* 250 U.S. 616, 630, 40 S.Ct. 17, 22, 63 L.Ed. 1173 (1919) (dissenting opinion) ("[T]he ultimate good desired is better reached by free trade in ideas-... the best test of truth is the power of the thought to get itself accepted in the competition of the market").

Thus, we do not think this passage from *Gertz* was intended to create a wholesale defamation exemption for anything that might be labeled "opinion." [C] Not only would such an interpretation be contrary to the tenor and context of the passage, but it would also ignore the fact that expressions of "opinion" may often imply an assertion of objective fact.

If a speaker says, "In my opinion John Jones is a liar," he implies a knowledge of facts which lead to the conclusion that Jones told an untruth. Even if the speaker states the facts upon which he bases his opinion, if those facts are either incorrect or incomplete, or if his assessment of them is erroneous, the statement may still imply a false assertion of fact. Simply couching such statements in terms of opinion does not dispel these implications; and the statement, "In my opinion Jones is a liar," can cause as much damage to reputation as the statement, "Jones is a liar." As Judge Friendly aptly stated: "[It] would be destructive of the law of libel if a writer could escape liability for accusations of [defamatory conduct] simply by using, explicitly or implicitly, the words 'I think.' " [C] It is worthy of note that at common law, even the privilege of fair comment did not extend to "a false statement of fact, whether it was expressly stated or implied from an expression of opinion." Restatement (Second) of Torts, § 566, Comment *a* (1977).

Apart from their reliance on the *Gertz* dictum, respondents do not really contend that a statement such as, "In my opinion John Jones is a liar," should be protected by a separate privilege for "opinion" under the First Amendment. But they do contend that in every defamation case the First Amendment mandates an inquiry into whether a statement is "opinion" or "fact," and that only the latter statements may be actionable. They propose that a number of factors developed by the lower courts (in what we hold was a mistaken reliance on the *Gertz* dictum) be considered in deciding which is which. But we think the "'breathing space' " which " '[f]reedoms of expression require in order to survive,'" [c], is adequately secured by existing constitutional doctrine without the creation of an artificial dichotomy between "opinion" and fact.

Foremost, we think [*Philadelphia Newspapers, Inc. v. Hepps*, 475 U.S. 767 (1986)] stands for the proposition that a statement on matters of public concern must be provable as false before there can be liability under state defamation law, at least in situations, like the present, where a media defendant is involved. Thus, unlike the statement, "In my opinion Mayor Jones is a liar," the statement, "In my opinion Mayor Jones shows his abysmal ignorance by accepting the teachings of Marx and Lenin," would not be actionable. [This approach] ensures that a statement of opinion relating to matters of public concern which does not contain a provably false factual connotation will receive full constitutional protection.

[Another] line of cases provides protection for statements that cannot "reasonably [be] interpreted as stating actual facts" about an individual. [C] This provides assurance that public debate will not suffer for lack of "imaginative expression" or the "rhetorical hyperbole" which has traditionally added much to the discourse of our Nation. [C]

The *New York Times-Butts-Gertz* culpability requirements further ensure that debate on public issues remains "uninhibited, robust, and wide-open." [C] Thus, where a statement of "opinion" on a matter of public concern reasonably implies false and defamatory facts regarding public figures or officials, those individuals must show that such statements were made with knowledge of their false implications or with reckless disregard of their truth. Similarly, where such a statement involves a private figure on a matter of public concern, a plaintiff must show that the false connotations were made with some level of fault as required by *Gertz*. Finally, the enhanced appellate review required by [*Bose Corp. v. Consumers Union of United States, Inc.*, 466 U.S. 485 (1984)] provides assurance that the foregoing determinations will be made in a manner so as not to "constitute a forbidden intrusion of the field of free expression." [C]

We are not persuaded that, in addition to these protections, an additional separate constitutional privilege for "opinion" is required to ensure the freedom of expression guaranteed by the First Amendment. The dispositive question in the present case then becomes whether a reasonable factfinder could conclude that the statements in the Diadiun column imply an assertion that petitioner Milkovich perjured himself in a judicial proceeding. We think this question must be answered in the affirmative. As the Ohio Supreme Court itself observed: "[T]he clear impact in some nine sentences and a caption is that [Milkovich] 'lied at the hearing after ... having given his solemn oath to tell the truth.'" [C] This is not the sort of loose, figurative, or hyperbolic language which would negate the impression that the writer was seriously maintaining that petitioner committed the crime of perjury. Nor does the general tenor of the article negate this impression.

We also think the connotation that petitioner committed perjury is sufficiently factual to be susceptible of being proved true or false. A determination whether petitioner lied in this instance can be made on a core of objective evidence by comparing, *inter alia,* petitioner's testimony before the OHSAA board with his subsequent testimony before the trial court. As the *Scott* court noted regarding the plaintiff in that case: "[W]hether or not H. Don Scott did indeed perjure himself is certainly verifiable by a perjury action with evidence adduced from the transcripts and witnesses present at the hearing. Unlike a subjective assertion the averred defamatory language is an articulation of an objectively verifiable event." [C] So too with petitioner Milkovich.

The numerous decisions discussed above establishing First Amendment protection for defendants in defamation actions surely demonstrate the Court's recognition of the Amendment's vital guarantee of free and uninhibited discussion of public issues. But there is also another side to the equation; we have regularly acknowledged the "important social values which underlie the law of defamation," and recognized that "[s]ociety has a pervasive and strong interest in preventing and redressing attacks upon reputation." *Rosenblatt v. Baer,* 383 U.S. 75, 86, 86 S.Ct. 669, 676, 15 L.Ed.2d 597 (1966). Justice Stewart in that case put it with his customary clarity:

> "The right of a man to the protection of his own reputation from unjustified invasion and wrongful hurt reflects no more than our basic concept of the essential dignity and worth of every human being-a concept at the root of any decent system of ordered liberty.

> . . . . .

> "The destruction that defamatory falsehood can bring is, to be sure, often beyond the capacity of the law to redeem. Yet, imperfect though it is, an action for damages is the only hope for vindication or redress the law gives to a man whose reputation has been falsely dishonored." [C]

We believe our decision in the present case holds the balance true. The judgment of the Ohio Court of Appeals is reversed, and the case is remanded for further proceedings not inconsistent with this opinion.

Reversed.

Points for Discussion

1. Examine the passages of the column authored by J. Theodure Diadiun, and familiarize yourself with the procedural history of the case preceding and leading to the Supreme Court's decision in *Milkovich*. The United States Supreme Court granted *certiorari* to consider the state courts' recognition of a constitutionally-based "opinion" exception to Ohio's defamation laws.

2. Define and describe the fair comment privilege. What interests are balanced by this common law privilege?

3. Are defamatory communications of facts or opinions actionable? Under the common law, a "defamatory communication may consist of a statement of fact" and "may consist of a statement in the form of an opinion" which "is actionable only if it implies the allegation of undisclosed defamatory facts as the basis for the opinion." RESTATEMENT (SECOND) OF TORTS §§ 565, 566 (1977).

4. Is there a First Amendment-based exemption for a defamatory statement that is an "opinion" and not a "fact"?

5. Did the Diadiun column defame Milkovich?

Hypo 16-5

In 2007 A, the wife of Comedian, a world famous comic, published a cookbook promoting healthy eating entitled "Getting Your Kids To Eat Good Food." In that same year B published a cookbook entitled "Getting Your Kids To Eat Healthy Food—Without Knowing It." B subsequently filed a copyright infringement lawsuit against A, alleging that A had stolen B's idea; a federal court judge concluded that the suit was baseless and dismissed the action.

While the copyright infringement suit was pending, Comedian appeared on a nationally broadcast late night talk show. Asked by that show's host about the suit against his wife, Comedian said: "One of the fun facts of life is that wackos will appear out of nowhere and inject some adrenaline into your life. This other woman had a cookbook. My wife did not know about that book, had never seen or heard about or read it. But that didn't matter, because Miss Wacko said, 'Time for my fifteen minutes of fame,' and accused my wife of vegetable plagiarism."

After hearing about and seeing Comedian's statements on YouTube, B filed a defamation suit against Comedian. Comedian's lawyers are preparing a motion to dismiss the suit on the grounds that Comedian was only joking and had a constitutional right to express his opinion about B's copyright infringement action.

Has Comedian defamed B? Or should the defamation suit be dismissed? Why or why not?

CHAPTER 17

Privacy

The right of privacy—defined and understood as "the right to be let alone"—is protected by the common law of torts. "One who invades the right of privacy to another is subject to liability for the resulting harm to the interests of the other." RESTATEMENT (SECOND) OF TORTS § 652A (1977). The proscribed invasion "has been a complex of four distinct wrongs, whose only relation to one another is that each involves interference with the interest of the individual in leading, to some reason-able extent, a secluded and private life, free from the prying eyes, ears and pub-lications of others." Section 652A, com-ment b; PROSSER & KEETON ON TORTS 851-66 (5th ed. 1984). Four distinct types of invasion of privacy are discussed in this chapter: (1) the publi-cation of private facts, (2) intrusion upon seclusion, (3) false light, and (4) appropriation.

Make the Connection

Right to privacy claims grounded in and arising under constitutional provisions and federal and state statutes are addressed in constitu-tional law, privacy law, and other courses.

A. The Publication of Private Facts

From Samuel D. Warren & Louis D. Brandeis, *The Right to Privacy*, 4 Harvard Law Review 193, 195, 196 (1890):

> Recent inventions and business methods call attention to the . . . step which must be taken for the protection of the person, and for securing to the individual what Judge Cooley calls the right "to be left alone." . . .

> . . . The press is overstepping in every direction the obvious bounds of propriety and of decency. Gossip is no longer the resource of the idle and of the vicious, but has become a trade, which is pursued with industry as well as effrontery. To satisfy a prurient taste the details of sexual relations are spread broadcast in the columns of the daily papers. To occupy the indolent, column upon column is filled with idle gossip,

which can only be procured by intrusion upon the domestic circle. The intensity and complexity of life, attendant upon advancing civilization, have rendered necessary some retreat from the world, and man, under the refining influence of culture, has become more sensitive to publicity, so that solitude and privacy have become more essential to the individual; but modern enterprise and invention have, through invasions upon his privacy, subjected him to mental pain and distress, far greater than could be inflicted by mere bodily injury. Nor is the harm wrought by such invasions confined to the suffering of those who may be made the subjects of journalistic or other enterprise. In this, as in other branches of commerce, the supply creates the demand. Each crop of unseemly gossip, thus harvested, becomes the seed of more, and, in direct proportion to its circulation, results in a lowering of social standards and of morality. Even gossip apparently harmless, when widely and persistently circulated, is potent for evil. It both belittles and perverts. It belittles by inverting the relative importance of things, thus dwarfing the thoughts and aspirations of a people. When personal gossip attains the dignity of print, and crowds the space available for matters of real interest to the community, what wonder that the ignorant and thoughtless mistake its relative importance. Easy of comprehension, appealing to that weak side of human nature which is never wholly cast down by the misfortunes and frailties of our neighbors, no one can be surprised that it usurps the place of interest in brains capable of other things. Triviality destroys at once robustness of thought and delicacy of feeling. No enthusiasm can flourish, no generous impulse can survive under its blighting influence.

Restatement (Second) of Torts § 652D (1977)

One who gives publicity to a matter concerning the private life of another is subject to liability to the other for invasion of privacy, if the matter publicized is of a kind that

(a) would be highly offensive to a reasonable person, and

(b) is not of legitimate concern to the public.

Shulman v. Group W Productions, Inc.

18 Cal.4th 200, 74 Cal.Rptr.2d 843, 955 P.2d 469 (1998)

WERDEGAR, J.

More than 100 years ago, Louis Brandeis and Samuel Warren complained that the press, armed with the then recent invention of "instantaneous photographs" and under the influence of new "business methods," was "overstepping in every direction the obvious bounds of propriety and of decency." (Warren & Brandeis, *The Right to Privacy* (1890) 4 Harv. L. Rev. 193, 195-196.) Even more ominously, they noted the "numerous mechanical devices" that "threaten to make good the prediction that 'what is whispered in the closet shall be proclaimed from the house-tops.'" [C] Today, of course, the newspapers of 1890 have been joined by the electronic media; today, a vast number of books, journals, television and radio stations, cable channels and Internet content sources all compete to satisfy our thirst for knowledge and our need for news of political, economic and cultural events—as well as our love of gossip, our curiosity about the private lives of others, and "that weak side of human nature which is never wholly cast down by the misfortunes and frailties of our neighbors." [C] Moreover, the "devices" available for recording and transmitting what would otherwise be private have multiplied and improved in ways the 19th century could hardly imagine.

For More Information

For more on Warren's and Brandeis' *Right to Privacy* article, see MELVIN UROFSKY, LOUIS D. BRANDEIS: A LIFE (2009).

Over the same period, the United States has also seen a series of revolutions in mores and conventions that has moved, blurred and, at times, seemingly threatened to erase the line between public and private life. While even in their day Brandeis and Warren complained that "the details of sexual relations are spread broadcast in the columns of the daily papers" [c], today's public discourse is particularly notable for its detailed and graphic discussion of intimate personal and family matters—sometimes as topics of legitimate public concern, sometimes as simple titillation. More generally, the dominance of the visual image in contemporary culture and the technology that makes it possible to capture and, in an instant, universally disseminate a picture or sound allows us, and leads us to expect, to *see* and *hear* what our great-grandparents could have known only through written description.

. . . .

On June 24, 1990, plaintiffs Ruth and Wayne Shulman, mother and son, were injured when the car in which they and two other family members were riding on interstate 10 in Riverside County flew off the highway and tumbled down an embankment into a drainage ditch on state-owned property, coming to rest upside down. Ruth, the most seriously injured of the two, was pinned under the car. Ruth and Wayne both had to be cut free from the vehicle by the device known as "the jaws of life."

A rescue helicopter operated by Mercy Air was dispatched to the scene. The flight nurse, who would perform the medical care at the scene and on the way to the hospital, was Laura Carnahan. Also on board were the pilot, a medic and Joel Cooke, a video camera operator employed by defendants Group W Productions, Inc., and 4MN Productions. Cooke was recording the rescue operation for later broadcast.

Cooke roamed the accident scene, videotaping the rescue. Nurse Carnahan wore a wireless microphone that picked up her conversations with both Ruth and the other rescue personnel. Cooke's tape was edited into a piece approximately nine minutes long, which, with the addition of narrative voice-over, was broadcast on September 29, 1990, as a segment of *On Scene: Emergency Response.*

The segment begins with the Mercy Air helicopter shown on its way to the accident site. The narrator's voice is heard in the background, setting the scene and describing in general terms what has happened. The pilot can be heard speaking with rescue workers on the ground in order to prepare for his landing. As the helicopter touches down, the narrator says: "[F]our of the patients are leaving by ground ambulance. Two are still trapped inside." (The first part of this statement was wrong, since only four persons were in the car to start.) After Carnahan steps from the helicopter, she can be seen and heard speaking about the situation with various rescue workers. A firefighter assures her they will hose down the area to prevent any fire from the wrecked car.

The videotape shows only a glimpse of Wayne, and his voice is never heard. Ruth is shown several times, either by brief shots of a limb or her torso, or with her features blocked by others or obscured by an oxygen mask. She is also heard speaking several times. Carnahan calls her "Ruth," and her last name is not mentioned on the broadcast.

While Ruth is still trapped under the car, Carnahan asks Ruth's age. Ruth responds, "I'm old." On further questioning, Ruth reveals she is 47, and Carnahan observes that "it's all relative. You're not that old." During her extrication from the car, Ruth asks at least twice if she is dreaming. At one point she asks Carnahan, who has told her she will be taken to the hospital in a helicopter: "Are you teasing?" At another point she says: "This is terrible. Am I dreaming?" She also asks what happened and where the rest of her family is, repeating the questions even after being told she was in an accident and the other family members are being cared for. While being loaded into the helicopter on a stretcher, Ruth says: "I just want to die." Carnahan reassures her that she is "going to do real well," but Ruth repeats: "I just want to die. I don't want to go through this."

Ruth and Wayne are placed in the helicopter, and its door is closed. The narrator states: "Once airborne, Laura and [the flight medic] will update their patients' vital signs and establish communications with the waiting trauma teams at Loma Linda." Carnahan, speaking into what appears to be a radio microphone, transmits some of Ruth's vital signs and states that Ruth cannot move her feet and has no sensation. The video footage during the helicopter ride includes a few seconds of Ruth's face, covered by an oxygen mask. Wayne is neither shown nor heard.

The helicopter lands on the hospital roof. With the door open, Ruth states while being taken out: "My upper back hurts." Carnahan replies: "Your upper back hurts. That's what you were saying up there." Ruth states: "I don't feel that great." Carnahan responds: "You probably don't."

Finally, Ruth is shown being moved from the helicopter into the hospital. The narrator concludes by stating: "Once inside both patients will be further evaluated and moved into emergency surgery if need be. Thanks to the efforts of the crew of Mercy Air, the firefighters, medics and police who responded, patients' lives were saved." As the segment ends, a brief, written epilogue appears on the screen, stating: "Laura's patient spent months in the hospital. She suffered severe back injuries. The others were all released much sooner."

The accident left Ruth a paraplegic. When the segment was broadcast, Wayne phoned Ruth in her hospital room and told her to turn on the television because "Channel 4 is showing our accident now." Shortly afterward, several hospital workers came into the room to mention that a videotaped segment of her accident was being shown. Ruth was "shocked, so to speak, that this would be run and I would be exploited, have my privacy invaded, which is what I felt had happened." She did not know her rescue had been recorded in this manner and had never consented to the recording or broadcast. Ruth had the impression from the broadcast "that I was kind of talking nonstop, and I remember hearing some of the things I said, which were not very pleasant." Asked at deposition what part of the broadcast material she considered private, Ruth explained: "I think the whole scene was pretty private. It was pretty gruesome, the parts that I saw, my knee sticking out of the car. I certainly did not look my best, and I don't feel it's for the public to see. I was not at my best in what I was thinking and what I was saying and what was being shown, and it's not for the public to see this trauma that I was going through."

Ruth and Wayne sued the producers of *On Scene: Emergency Response*, as well as others. The first amended complaint included two causes of action for **invasion of privacy**, one based on defendants' unlawful **intrusion** by videotaping the rescue in the first instance and the other based on the **public disclosure of private facts**, i.e., the broadcast.

. . . .

The trial court granted the media defendants' summary judgment motion, basing its ruling on plaintiffs' admissions that the accident and rescue were matters of public interest and public affairs. . . .

The Court of Appeal reversed and remanded for further proceedings, but on limited grounds and as to some causes of action only. . . .

The claim that a **publication** has given unwanted publicity to allegedly private aspects of a person's life is one of the more commonly litigated and well-defined areas of privacy law. . . . [The Restatement] provides that "[o]ne who gives publicity to a matter concerning the private life of another is subject to liability to the other for invasion of his privacy, if the matter publicized is of a kind that [¶] (a) would be highly offensive to a **reasonable person**, and [¶] (b) is not of legitimate concern to the public." (Rest.2d Torts, § 652D.)

The element critical to this case is the presence or absence of legitimate public interest, i.e., newsworthiness, in the facts disclosed. After reviewing the decisional law regarding newsworthiness, we conclude, inter alia, that lack of newsworthiness is an element of the "private facts" tort, making newsworthiness a complete bar to common law liability. We further conclude that the analysis of newsworthiness inevitably involves accommodating conflicting interests in personal privacy and in press freedom as guaranteed by the **First Amendment** to the United States Constitution, and that in the circumstances of this case–where the facts disclosed about a private person involuntarily caught up in events of public interest bear a logical relationship to the newsworthy subject of the broadcast and are not intrusive in great disproportion to their relevance–the broadcast was of legitimate public concern, barring liability under the private facts tort.

. . . .

. . . [U]nder California common law the dissemination of truthful, newsworthy material is not actionable as a publication of private facts. [Cc] If the contents of a broadcast or publication are of legitimate public concern, the plaintiff cannot establish a necessary element of the tort action, the lack of newsworthiness. To so state, however, is merely to begin the necessary legal inquiry, not to end it. It is in the determination of newsworthiness–in deciding whether published or broadcast material is of legitimate public concern–that courts must struggle most directly to accommodate the conflicting interests of individual privacy and press freedom.

Although we speak of the lack of newsworthiness as an element of the private facts tort, newsworthiness is at the same time a constitutional defense to, or privilege against, liability for publication of truthful information. [Cc] Indeed, the danger of interference with constitutionally protected press freedom has been and remains an ever-present consideration for courts and commentators struggling to set the tort's parameters, and the requirements of tort law and the Constitution have generally been assumed to be congruent. (See Rest.2d Torts, § 652D, com. d, p. 388 [newsworthiness standard developed in common law but now expresses constitutional limit as well]; [cc]. Little is to be gained, therefore, in attempting to keep rigorously separate the tort and constitutional issues as regards newsworthiness, and we have not attempted to do so here. Tort liability, obviously, can extend no further than the First Amendment allows; conversely, we see no reason or authority for fashioning the newsworthiness element of the private facts tort to *preclude* liability where the Constitution would allow it.

Delineating the exact contours of the constitutional **privilege** of the press in publication of private facts is, however, particularly problematic, because this privilege has not received extensive attention from the United States Supreme Court. The high court has considered the issue in only one case involving the common law public disclosure tort, *Cox Broadcasting Corp. v. Cohn* (1975) 420 U.S. 469 [95 S.Ct. 1029, 43 L.Ed.2d 328] (Cox Broadcasting), and its holding in that case was deliberately and explicitly narrow. In *Cox Broadcasting*, a criminal court clerk, during a recess in court proceedings relating to a rape-murder case, allowed a television reporter to see the indictment, which contained the name of the victim. The television station broadcast an account of the court proceedings, using the victim's name; the victim's father alleged the broadcast to be a tortious publication of private facts. [C] The Georgia Supreme Court, relying on a Georgia statute prohibiting publication or broadcast of a rape victim's identity, held the broadcast of the victim's name was not privileged as newsworthy; the court viewed the statute as showing that the victim's identity was not a matter of legitimate public concern. The state court further held the statute did not itself infringe on the station's First Amendment rights. [C]

The federal high court reversed, but–recognizing the important interests on both sides of the newsworthiness question–proceeded cautiously and on limited grounds. "Rather than address the broader question of whether truthful publications may ever be subjected to civil or criminal liability consistently with the **First** and **Fourteenth Amendments**, or to put it another way, whether the State may ever define and protect an area of privacy free from unwanted publicity in the press, it is appropriate to focus on the narrower interface between press and privacy that this case presents, namely, whether the State may impose sanctions on the accurate publication of the name of a rape victim obtained from public records—more specifically, from judicial records which are maintained in connection with a public prosecution and which themselves are open to public inspection. We are convinced that the State may not do so." (*Cox Broadcasting,* supra, 420 U.S. at p. 491 [95 S.Ct. at p. 1044].) . . .

. . . .

Newsworthiness—constitutional or common law—is also difficult to define because it may be used as either a descriptive or a normative term. "Is the term 'newsworthy' a descriptive predicate, intended to refer to the fact there is widespread public interest? Or is it a value predicate, intended to indicate that the publication is a meritorious contribution and that the public's interest is praiseworthy?" (Comment, *The Right of Privacy: Normative-Descriptive Confusion in the Defense of Newsworthiness* (1963) 30 U. Chi. L. Rev. 722, 725.) A position at either extreme has unpalatable consequences. If "newsworthiness" is completely descriptive—if all coverage that sells papers or boosts ratings is deemed newsworthy—it would seem to swallow the publication of private facts tort, for "it would be difficult to suppose that publishers were in the habit of reporting occurrences of little interest." [C] At the other extreme, if newsworthiness is viewed as a purely normative concept, the courts could become to an unacceptable degree editors of the news and self-appointed guardians of public taste.

. . . .

Our prior decisions have not explicitly addressed the type of privacy invasion alleged in this case: the broadcast of embarrassing pictures and speech of a person who, while generally not a public figure, has become involuntarily involved in an event or activity of legitimate public concern. We nonetheless draw guidance from those decisions, in that they articulate the competing interests to be balanced. First, the analysis of newsworthiness does involve courts to some degree in a normative assessment of the "social value" of a publication. [C] All material that might attract readers or viewers is not, simply by virtue of its attractiveness, of *legitimate* public interest. Second, the evaluation of newsworthiness depends on the degree of intrusion and the extent to which the plaintiff played an important role in public events [c], and thus on a comparison between the information revealed and the nature of the activity or event that brought the plaintiff to public attention. "Some reasonable proportion is ... to be maintained between the events or activity that makes the individual a public figure and the private facts to which publicity is given. Revelations that may properly be made concerning a murderer or the President of the United States would not be privileged if they were to be made concerning one who is merely injured in an automobile accident." (Rest.2d Torts, § 652D, com. h, p. 391.)

Courts balancing these interests in cases similar to this have recognized that, when a person is involuntarily involved in a newsworthy incident, not all aspects of the person's life, and not everything the person says or does, is thereby rendered newsworthy. . . .

. . . .

. . . [N]o mode of analyzing newsworthiness can be applied mechanically or without consideration of its proper boundaries. To observe that the newsworthiness of private facts about a person involuntarily thrust into the public eye depends, in the ordinary case, on the existence of a logical nexus between the newsworthy event or activity and the facts revealed is not to deny that the balance of free press and privacy interests may require a different conclusion when the intrusiveness of the revelation is greatly disproportionate to its relevance. Intensely personal or intimate revelations might not, in a given case, be considered newsworthy, especially where they bear only slight relevance to a topic of legitimate public concern. [Cc]

. . . .

We agree at the outset with defendants that the subject matter of the broadcast as a whole was of legitimate public concern. Automobile accidents are by their nature of interest to that great portion of the public that travels frequently by automobile. The rescue and medical treatment of accident victims is also of legitimate concern to much of the public, involving as it does a critical service that any member of the public may someday need. The story of Ruth's difficult extrication from the crushed car, the medical attention given her at the scene, and her evacuation by helicopter was of particular interest because it highlighted some of the challenges facing emergency workers dealing with serious accidents.

The more difficult question is whether Ruth's appearance and words as she was extricated from the overturned car, placed in the helicopter and transported to the hospital were of legitimate public concern. Pursuant to the analysis outlined earlier, we conclude the disputed material was newsworthy as a matter of law. One of the dramatic and interesting aspects of the story as a whole is its focus on flight nurse Carnahan, who appears to be in charge of communications with other emergency workers, the hospital base and Ruth, and who leads the medical assistance to Ruth at the scene. Her work is portrayed as demanding and important and as involving a measure of personal risk (e.g., in crawling under the car to aid Ruth despite warnings that gasoline may be dripping from the car). The broadcast segment makes apparent that this type of emergency care requires not only medical knowledge, concentration and courage, but an ability to talk and listen to severely traumatized patients. One of the challenges Carnahan faces in assisting Ruth is the confusion, pain and fear that Ruth understandably feels in the aftermath of the accident. For that reason the broadcast video depicting Ruth's injured physical state (which was not luridly shown) and audio showing her disorientation and despair were substantially relevant to the segment's newsworthy subject matter.

Plaintiffs argue that showing Ruth's "intimate private, medical facts and her suffering was not *necessary* to enable the public to understand the significance of the accident or the rescue as a public event." The standard, however, is not **necessity**. That the broadcast *could* have been edited to exclude some of Ruth's words and images and still excite a minimum degree of viewer interest is not determinative. Nor is the possibility that the members of this or another court, or a jury, might find a differently edited broadcast more to their taste or even more interesting. The courts do not, and constitutionally could not, sit as superior editors of the press. [Cc]

The challenged material was thus substantially relevant to the newsworthy subject matter of the broadcast and did not constitute a "morbid and sensational prying into private lives *for its own sake*." (Rest.2d Torts, § 652D, com. h . . . italics added.) Nor can we say the broadcast material was so lurid and sensational in emotional tone, or so intensely personal in content, as to make its intrusiveness disproportionate to its relevance. Under these circumstances, the material was, as a matter of law, of legitimate public concern. Summary judgment was therefore properly entered against Ruth on her cause of action for publication of private facts. As to Wayne, he is glimpsed only fleetingly in the broadcast video and is never heard. The broadcast includes no images or information regarding him that could be offensive to a reasonable person of ordinary sensibilities. Summary judgment was therefore also proper on Wayne's cause of action for publication of private facts.

One might argue that, while the contents of the broadcast were of legitimate interest in that they reflected on the nature and quality of emergency rescue services, the images and sounds that potentially allowed identification of Ruth as the accident victim were irrelevant and of no legitimate public interest in a broadcast that aired some months after the accident and had little or no value as "hot" news. [C] We do not take that view. It is difficult to see how the subject broadcast could have been edited to avoid completely any possible identification without severely undercutting its legitimate descriptive and narrative impact. As broadcast, the segment included neither Ruth's full name nor direct display of her face. She was nonetheless arguably identifiable by her first name (used in recorded dialogue), her voice, her general appearance and the recounted circumstances of the accident (which, as noted, had previously been published, with Ruth's full name and city of residence, in a newspaper). In a video documentary of this type, however, the use of that degree of truthful detail would seem not only relevant, but essential to the narrative.

. . . .

The broadcast details of Ruth's rescue of which she complains were, as a matter of law, of legitimate public concern because they were substantially relevant to the newsworthy subject of the piece and their intrusiveness was not greatly disproportionate to their relevance. That analytical path is dictated by the danger of the contrary approach; to allow liability because this court, or a jury, believes certain details of the story as broadcast were not important or necessary to the purpose of the documentary, or were in poor taste or overly sensational in impact, would be to assert impermissible supervisory power over the press.

. . . .

. . . Summary judgment for the defense was proper as to plaintiffs' cause of action for publication of private facts . . .

Points for Discussion

1. Do you agree or disagree with the court's holding and/or analysis? Can you imagine any scenario in which a person involved in an automobile or other accident would have a reasonable expectation of privacy such that the incident should not be recorded, photographed, or broadcast?

2. How do you define "newsworthiness"?

3. Suppose that Ruth died from injuries suffered in the automobile accident prior to the broadcast of the *On Scene: Emergency Response* segment. Could an invasion of privacy lawsuit be brought? *See* RESTATEMENT (SECOND) OF TORTS § 652I (1977); *Nicholas v. Nicholas,* 277 Kan. 171, 83 P.3d 214 (2004).

4. The court opines that the "claim that a publication has given unwanted publicity to allegedly private aspects of a person's life is one of the more commonly litigated and well-defined areas of privacy law" and cites Section 652D of the Restatement (Second) of Torts. A comment accompanying that section notes that "publicity" differs from the term "publication" used in Section 577's treatment of liability for defamation. "'Publication,' in that sense, is a word of art, which includes communication by the defendant to a

third person. 'Publicity,' on the other hand, means that the matter is made public, by communicating it to the public at large, or to so many persons that the matter must be regarded as substantially certain to become one of public knowledge. The difference is not one of the means of communication, which may be oral, written or by any other means. It is one of a communication that reaches, or is sure to reach, the public." RESTATEMENT (SECOND) OF TORTS § 652D cmt. *a* (1977).

5. Note that the rules governing an absolute or conditional privilege to publish defamatory matters apply to the publication of matters invading the privacy of another. *See* RESTATEMENT (SECOND) OF TORTS §§ 652F and 652G (1977).

———————

G.D. v. Kenny

205 N.J. 275, 15 A.3d 300 (N.J. 2011)

Justice ALBIN delivered the opinion of the Court.

. . . .

During a primary contest for State Senate, opponents of candidate Brian Stack issued campaign flyers criticizing him for previously hiring a person with a criminal conviction, plaintiff G.D. One campaign flyer stated that G.D. was "a DRUG DEALER who went to JAIL for FIVE YEARS for selling coke near a public school." G.D. filed a lawsuit alleging **defamation**, violation of **privacy**, and other related torts, and named as defendants the Hudson County Democratic Organization and certain individuals, as the purported authors and distributors of the flyers.

Defendants assert **truth** as a defense. G.D. had been convicted of second-degree possession with intent to distribute cocaine and sentenced to a five-year prison term. Thirteen years later, he successfully petitioned for the **expungement** of his criminal record. Defendants reason that G.D.'s conviction was a public fact maintained as a public record long before the expungement and that the publication of that fact during a political campaign was a legitimate exercise of their free-speech rights and did not violate G.D.'s reasonable expectation of privacy.

G.D. counters that the record of his conviction was expunged and, therefore, his conviction—as a matter of law—is deemed not to have occurred. G.D. submits that, after the expungement of his record, the pronouncement that he was convicted of a crime was simply **false** and the dissemination of the expunged information violated his privacy rights.

The trial court denied the parties' cross-motions for summary judgment. The Appellate Division reversed . . .

The issue before us arises in the realm of political discourse, where speech is often harsh and caustic, but where the constitutional guarantee of free expression is given great latitude. Although our expungement statute relieves a prior offender of some civil disabilities, it does not extinguish the truth.

. . . G.D. had no reasonable expectation of privacy that information so long in the public domain before the entry of the expungement order would be erased from the public's mind or from papers already widely disseminated. We therefore affirm the Appellate Division's dismissal of G.D.'s claims on summary judgment.

. . . .

In 1991, G.D., a resident of Union City, was charged in a three-count Hudson County indictment with possession of a controlled dangerous substance (cocaine), possession with intent to distribute cocaine, and distribution of cocaine. He pled guilty to second-degree possession with intent to distribute cocaine and, on January 8, 1993, was sentenced to a five-year (flat) state-prison term. The remaining charges were dismissed. The Superior Court judge who imposed sentence noted on G.D.'s judgment of conviction that "[t]he quantity of the drugs was substantial."

From January 2000 to December 2001, G.D. worked as a part-time aide to then Hudson County Freeholder Brian Stack. He earned $6,000 per year in that position. That two-year period was the only time Stack ever employed G.D. Sometime afterward, G.D. worked at a day care center administered by Stack's estranged wife.

On June 12, 2006, a Superior Court judge granted G.D.'s petition for an order expunging any record of his 1993 drug conviction as well as any record of his arrest and the charges. The expungement order directed that certain named law enforcement and judicial agencies not release information concerning the expunged records "for any reason except as authorized by law"; that those agencies respond to requests for information "that there is no record," "except where otherwise authorized by law"; and that the "arrest ... shall be deemed not to have occurred, and [that G.D.] may answer accordingly." The Department of Corrections continued to list G.D.'s conviction on its website as late as August 21, 2008.

In 2007, Stack, who then was both the Mayor of Union City and a State Assemblyman, sought the Democratic nomination for State Senate. Stack was opposed by the Hudson County Democratic Organization, Inc. (Democratic Organization), whose chief executive officer was Bernard Kenny and whose executive director was Craig Guy. The Democratic Organization backed another candidate. G.D. supported Stack's nomination but had no involvement in the Senate campaign.

The Democratic Organization hired a political consulting and advertising firm run by Richard and CareyAnn Shaftan–Neighborhood Research Corp., d/b/a Mountaintop Media (Mountaintop Media)–to work on the campaign opposing Stack's election. During the course of his investigation, Mr. Shaftan learned of G.D.'s 1993 drug conviction, and at some point he obtained the judgment of conviction. Mr. Shaftan claims that he was "led to understand that the site of the crime was close ... to a public school." He never explained how he came to that understanding. He also claims that he had no knowledge of the expungement order during the election cycle.

Based on his research, Mr. Shaftan composed four campaign flyers attempting to discredit Stack in his bid for the State Senate nomination. The flyers were reviewed and approved by the Democratic Organization. Two of the flyers, printed in English and Spanish, disparaged Stack for his association with G.D. One flyer read as follows:

[Front]

IT'S THE COMPANY YOU KEEP and the sleazy crowd Brian Stack surrounds himself with says a lot about who Stack is.

COKE DEALERS AND EX-CONS.

THAT'S THE KIND OF "REFORM" BRIAN STACK IS ALL ABOUT.

[Back]

YOU READ ABOUT DRUG DEALER [H.M.], A STACK CRONY CURRENTLY "WORKING" AT THE COUNTY VOCATIONAL SCHOOL AFTER BEING DEPORTED FOR SELLING COCAINE NEAR A PUBLIC SCHOOL. NOW READ ABOUT STACK REFORMER # 2

[Next to photograph of G.D.:] Like [H.M.], [G.D.] is also a DRUG DEALER who went to JAIL for FIVE YEARS for selling coke near a public school. After getting out of jail, [G.D.] landed a job as a highly paid "aide" to Mayor Stack.

[Next to photograph of G.D.:] Today, [G.D.] is an aide at the controversial Union City Day Care Center–assisting the embattled Mayor's estranged wife.

DRUGS, GANGS, AND THUGS ARE NOT JUST A PROBLEM ON UNION CITY STREETS. THEY'RE A PROBLEM IN STACK'S CITY HALL TOO. AND NOW HE WANTS A PROMOTION? ? ?

The second flyer did not mention G.D.'s name but displayed his photograph. It read as follows:

[Front]

[Photographs of three men, including G.D.:] TEAM STACK:

COKE DEALERS. GUN RUNNERS. EX CONS

THE MORE PEOPLE KNOW, THE MORE QUESTIONS THEY HAVE ABOUT BRIAN STACK.

[Back]

UNION CITY MAYOR BRIAN STACK'S CLOSEST POLITICAL OPERATIVES: GUN RUNNERS, COKE DEALERS, EX-CONS.

We all know the threat that drugs and illegal guns have in our communities. But not Brian Stack. He continues to surround himself with one shady character after another–not one but two convicted drug dealers and ex-cons, whom Stack got a high paying county job and a drugged out gunrunning lowlife who was his campaign manager.

BRIAN STACK PREACHES "REFORM" AND "GOOD GOVERNMENT" BUT HIS ADMINISTRATION IS MADE UP OF SLEAZY DRUG DEALERS AND OTHERS WHO SHOULD BE NOWHERE NEAR THE PUBLIC TREASURY.

The Democratic Organization printed and paid for 17,100 copies of the first flyer and 17,100 copies of the second flyer. On May 23 and 25, 2007, 8,184 copies of each flyer were mailed to members of the public.

. . . .

The tort of **invasion of privacy** is defined as an intentional intrusion, "physically or otherwise, upon the solitude or seclusion of another or his **private** affairs or concerns" that "would be highly **offensive** to a **reasonable person**." *Bisbee v. John C. Conover Agency, Inc.,* 186 N.J.Super. 335, 339 (1982) (quoting *Restatement (Second) of Torts, supra,* § 652B). The tort of improper publication of private facts occurs "when it is shown that 'the matters revealed were actually private, that dissemination of such facts would be offensive to a reasonable person, and that there is no legitimate interest of the public in being apprised of the facts publicized.'" [C] To succeed in proving that defendants committed either of those torts, G.D. must establish that he possessed a reasonable expectation of privacy in matters and concerns that are contained in his expunged criminal-conviction record. [C] That he cannot do.

G.D. pled guilty and was sentenced in a courtroom that was open to the public. The **judgment of conviction** in G.D.'s case was a court record available to the public for thirteen years before the entry of the expungement order. During all those years, the information concerning G.D.'s conviction was available to commercial data companies as well as to newspapers and other public organizations. The reality is that criminal-conviction information is disseminated well before the entry of an expungement order. *Report of the Supreme Court Special Committee on Public Access to Court Records, supra,* at 46. Moreover, "once the Judiciary has made information available to a requester, it no longer has control of that information." [C] Indeed, in the Public-Access-to-Court-Records report, we recognized that the "expungement of criminal records could become meaningless since previously released conviction information is published in databases which the Judiciary has no power to update or correct." [Cc] Additionally, at the time of the dissemination of the campaign flyers, G.D.'s conviction data was posted on the Department of Corrections' website. G.D.'s conviction was not a hidden secret; the expungement did not expurgate his past.

A number of courts have found that an offender has no protected privacy interest in expunged criminal records. See, e.g., *Eagle v. Morgan,* 88 F.3d 620, 625-26 (8th Cir.1996); *Nilson v. Layton City,* 45 F.3d 369, 372 (10th Cir.1995); *Fraternal Order of Police, Lodge No. 5 v. City of Philadelphia,* 812 F.2d 105, 117 & n. 8 (3d Cir.1987); *White v. Thomas,* 660 F.2d 680, 686 (5th Cir.1981); *Puricelli v. Borough of Morrisville,* 820 F.Supp. 908, 918 (E.D.Pa.1993), aff'd o.b., 26 F.3d 123 (3d Cir.), *cert. denied,* 513 U.S. 930, 115 S.Ct. 321, 130 L. Ed.2d 282 (1994). With regard to New Jersey's expungement statute, the United States Court of Appeals for the Third Circuit has noted that "because expungement is available only after a minimum statutory period of ten years has elapsed, and because references to a defendant's criminal conduct may persist in public news sources after expungement, the information expunged is never truly 'private.'" *Nunez v. Pachman,* 578 F.3d 228, 229 (3d Cir.2009). The Eighth Circuit has recognized that an expungement statute cannot "permanently erase from the public record those affairs that take place in open court," and that "no governmental body holds the power to nullify [a] historical fact." *Eagle,* supra, 88 F.3d at 626-27.

This is not a case in which a defendant peered through closed curtains into a bedroom or wrongly acquired a personal diary and made highly private information available to the public. A person has a reasonable expectation of privacy in the sanctity of his or her bedroom and personal diary from **peeping toms** intent on making private facts titillating fodder for the public. This case, however, deals with public acts, a guilty plea and sentence in a public courtroom, and public facts, court records available to the public over many years.

We hold that the expungement order did not and could not create a reasonable expectation of privacy in matters so long in the public domain. Accordingly, the Appellate Division correctly entered summary judgment on those claims.

. . . .

Points for Discussion

1. How does the *Kenny* court define (a) the tort of invasion of privacy and (b) the tort of improper publication of private facts?

2. The *Kenny* court concluded that G.D. did not have a reasonable expectation of privacy in matters involving public acts, a guilty plea and sentence in a public courtroom, and court records available to the public over many years and that "the expungement did not expurgate his past." Do you agree?

3. For another case discussing public records and a claim of unreasonable publicity given to an individual's private life, see *Washington v. City of Georgetown,* 2009 WL 530782 (E.D. Ky. Mar. 3, 2009).

Hypo 17-1

A and B, boyfriend and girlfriend, had a number of intimate encounters beginning in 2009 and ending in early 2011. During one of those encounters, B photographed A (with A's knowledge and consent) while A was engaged in various sexual acts with two other people. Two weeks later A broke up with B and began dating C. An angry B e-mailed some of the explicit photographs she had taken of A to A's mother, ex-wife, and ex-in-laws, and to A's current girlfriend and boss.

A filed suit against B, contending that B's distribution of the photographs violated his right to privacy because it publicly disclosed private facts. B argues that she is entitled to summary judgment on this claim because she e-mailed the pictures to only six people; that number, she claims, is insufficient to satisfy the publicity requirement of the tort. Should the court grant or deny B's motion?

Hypo 17-2

Billy and Gina have been involved in an intimate relationship for years when, despite the use of birth control, Gina unexpectedly becomes pregnant. The couple breaks up, and Billy discovers the pregnancy several months later when Gina is no longer pregnant. Infuriated, Billy puts up several billboards in the city in which they both live, showing him holding the outline of a baby with the words "This would have been a picture of my two-month old baby if the mother had decided not to KILL our child!" Gina is completely humiliated. She claims that she had a miscarriage, not an abortion, but either way, she wants to sue Billy for invasion of privacy. Discuss.

B. Intrusion Upon Seclusion

> ### RESTATEMENT (SECOND) OF TORTS § 652B (1977)
>
> One who intentionally intrudes, physically or otherwise, upon the solitude or seclusion of another or his private affairs or concerns, is subject to liability to the other for invasion of his privacy, if the intrusion would be highly offensive to a reasonable person.

In re Marriage of Tigges

758 N.W.2d 824 (Iowa 2008)

HECHT, Justice.

A husband surreptitiously recorded on videotape his wife's activities in the marital home. The district court entered a judgment for money **damages** in favor of the wife who claimed the videotaping constituted a tortious invasion of her privacy. The court of appeals affirmed the judgment, rejecting the husband's contention the wife had no reasonable expectation of privacy in the marital home she shared with him. On further review of the decision of the court of appeals, we conclude a claim for invasion of privacy is legally viable under the circumstances of this case, and therefore affirm the judgment.

I. Factual and Procedural Background.

Upon our de novo review we make the following findings of fact. The long relationship between Jeffrey and Cathy Tigges was plagued by trust issues. Even before their marriage, Jeffrey and Cathy had recorded each other's telephone conversations without the other's knowledge and consent. Apparently undeterred by their history of discord, they were married on December 31, 1999.

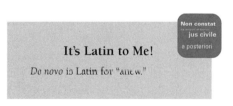

It's Latin to Me!

De novo is Latin for "anew."

Non constat
jus civile
a posteriori

Jeffrey surreptitiously installed recording equipment and recorded Cathy's activities during the marriage in the marital home. The equipment included a video cassette recorder positioned above a ceiling, a camera concealed in an alarm clock located in the bedroom regularly used by Cathy, and a motion sensing "optical eye" installed in the headboard of the bed in that room. Cathy discovered her activities in the bedroom had been recorded when she observed Jeffrey retrieving a cassette from the recorder in August 2006.

During the ensuing confrontation, Jeffrey damaged the cassette. Cathy took possession of it and restored it with the assistance of others. When she viewed the tape, Cathy discovered it revealed nothing of a graphic or demeaning nature. Although the tape was not offered in evidence, we credit Cathy's testimony that it recorded the "comings and goings" from the bedroom she regularly used. Notwithstanding the unremarkable activities recorded on the tape, Cathy suffered **damage** as a consequence of Jeffrey's actions. She felt violated, fearing Jeffrey had placed, or would place, other hidden cameras in the house.

Jeffrey filed a petition for **dissolution of marriage**. In her answer, Cathy alleged she was entitled to compensation for Jeffrey's "tortious ... violation of her privacy rights" as a consequence of his surreptitious placement of the video equipment and recording of her activities. . . . The district court found Jeffrey had invaded Cathy's privacy and entered judgment in the amount of $22,500.

. . . .

III. Discussion.

A. The Expectation of Privacy within the Marital Relationship. Although this court has never been called upon to decide whether a claim may be brought by one **spouse** against the other for an invasion of privacy resulting from **surreptitious** videotaping, the question has been confronted by courts in other jurisdictions. In *Miller v. Brooks,* 123 N.C.App. 20, 472 S.E.2d 350 (1996), a wife hired private investigators to install a hidden camera in the bedroom of her estranged husband's separate residence. [C] The husband discovered the hidden equipment and sued both his wife and her agents who assisted her in its installation. [C] The trial court granted summary judgment in favor of the defendants. [C] On appeal from that ruling, the North Carolina Court of Appeals noted the expectation of privacy "might, in some cases, be less for married persons than for single persons," but that "such is not the case ... where the spouses were estranged and living separately." [C] Finding no "evidence [the husband] authorized his wife or anyone else to install a video camera in his bedroom," the appellate court reversed the summary judgment, concluding issues of fact remained for trial in the husband's claims against his wife and her agents. [C]

As we have already noted, in the case before this court the record is unclear whether Jeffrey installed the equipment and accomplished the recording of Cathy's activities before or after the parties separated. We conclude, however, the question of whether Jeffrey and Cathy were residing in the same dwelling at the time of Jeffrey's actions is not dispositive on this issue. Whether or not Jeffrey and

Cathy were residing together in the dwelling at the time, we conclude Cathy had a reasonable expectation that her activities in the bedroom of the home were private when she was alone in that room. Cathy's expectation of privacy at such times is not rendered unreasonable by the fact Jeffrey was her spouse at the time in question, or by the fact that Jeffrey may have been living in the dwelling at that time.

Our conclusion is consistent with the decision reached by the Texas Court of Appeals in *Clayton v. Richards,* 47 S.W.3d 149 (Tex.App.2001). In that case, Mrs. Clayton hired Richards to install video equipment in the bedroom shared by Mrs. Clayton and her husband. [C] After discovering the scheme, Mr. Clayton sued his wife and Richards, alleging invasion of his privacy. The trial court denied Mrs. Clayton's motion for summary judgment, but granted the one filed by Richards. [C] On appeal, the Texas Court of Appeals concluded Richards' liability turned on whether Mrs. Clayton's acts were tortious under Texas law. [C] In its analysis of whether Mr. Clayton had a reasonable expectation of privacy in the bedroom he shared with his spouse, the court observed:

> A spouse shares equal rights in the privacy of the bedroom, and the other spouse relinquishes some of his or her rights to seclusion, solitude, and privacy by entering into marriage, by sharing a bedroom with a spouse, and by entering into ownership of the home with a spouse. *However, nothing in the ... common law suggests that the right to privacy is limited to unmarried individuals.*

> *When a person goes into the privacy of the bedroom, he or she has a right to the expectation of privacy in his or her seclusion. A video recording surreptitiously made in that place of privacy at a time when the individual believes that he or she is in a state of complete privacy could be highly offensive to the ordinary reasonable person.* The video recording of a person without consent in the privacy of his or her bedroom *even when done by the other spouse* could be found to violate his or her rights of privacy.

> As a spouse with equal rights to the use and access of the bedroom, it would not be illegal or tortious as an invasion of privacy for a spouse to open the door of the bedroom and view a spouse in bed. It could be argued that a spouse did no more than that by setting up a video camera, but that the viewing was done by means of technology rather than by being physically present. It is not generally the role of the courts to supervise privacy between spouses in a mutually shared bedroom. *However, the videotaping of a person without consent or awareness when there is an expectation of privacy goes beyond the rights of a spouse because it may record private matters, which could later be exposed to the public eye. The fact*

that no later exposure occurs does not negate that potential and permit willful intrusion by such technological means into one's personal life in one's bedroom.

[C]

Prior to catching Jeffrey in the act of removing the cassette from the concealed recorder, Cathy was unaware of his video **surveillance** scheme. . . . Jeffrey nonetheless contends his conduct is not **actionable** because Cathy was in "public view" in the home he owned jointly with her. [C] . . .

Even if we assume for purposes of our analysis that Cathy was observed by other family members including Jeffrey, who, from time to time, entered the bedroom with her knowledge and consent, she was not in "public view" and did not forfeit her right to seclusion at other times when she was alone in that room. . . . Any right of access to the bedroom held by Jeffrey did not include the right to videotape Cathy's activities without her knowledge and consent.

. . . .

B. The Elements of an Invasion of Privacy Claim. We first recognized a cause of action for violation of a privacy interest in *Bremmer v. Journal-Tribune Publishing Co.*, 247 Iowa 817, 76 N.W.2d 762 (1956). We defined the privacy interest as "the right of an individual to be left alone, to live a life of seclusion, to be free of unwarranted publicity." *Bremmer,* 247 Iowa at 821-22, 76 N.W.2d at 764-65; [c]. We have adopted the invasion of privacy principles set out in Restatement (Second) of Torts (1977). [C]

The right to privacy can be invaded by:

> (a) *unreasonable* **intrusion** *upon the seclusion of another* ...; or (b) appropriation of the other's name or likeness ...; or (c) unreasonable publicity given to the other's private life ...; or (d) publicity that unreasonably places the other in a false light before the public....

RESTATEMENT (SECOND) OF TORTS § 652A(2) (emphasis added) . . . . [W]e focus our analysis in this case on the "intrusion upon seclusion" theory. [C] Under this theory,

> [o]ne who *intentionally intrudes,* physically or otherwise, upon the solitude or seclusion of another or his private affairs or concerns, is subject to liability to the other for invasion of privacy, if the intrusion would be *highly offensive to a reasonable person.*

. . . .

1. *Intentional intrusion.* Cathy had a reasonable expectation of privacy in the bedroom when she was alone in that room. Jeffrey admitted videotaping her activities in the bedroom and various other rooms in the home. It is undisputed that he covertly installed the video recorder, recorded Cathy's bedroom activities, and attempted to retrieve a cassette from the recorder. We find this conduct clearly constituted an intentional intrusion upon Cathy's privacy.

2. *Highly offensive to a reasonable person.* Jeffrey contends the judgment in favor of Cathy must be reversed because the videotaping captured nothing that would be viewed as highly offensive to a reasonable person. He emphasizes the videotape captured nothing of a "private" or "sexual" nature in the bedroom. This contention is without merit, however, because the content of the videotape is not determinative of the question of whether Jeffrey tortiously invaded Cathy's privacy. [C] The intentional, intrusive, and wrongful nature of Jeffrey's conduct is not excused by the fact that the surreptitious taping recorded no scurrilous or compromising behavior. The wrongfulness of the conduct springs not from the specific nature of the recorded activities, but instead from the fact that Cathy's activities were recorded without her knowledge and consent at a time and place and under circumstances in which she had a reasonable expectation of privacy.

Jeffrey also contends Cathy's claim must fail because Cathy effected the only publication of the videotape by permitting her sister to view it. An intrusion upon seclusion "does *not* depend upon any publicity given to the person whose interest is invaded or to his affairs...." *See* Restatement (Second) of Torts § 652B cmt. a (emphasis added). Accordingly, Cathy had no burden to prove the videotape was published to a third party without her consent. We conclude Cathy met her burden to prove Jeffrey's intrusive videotaping would be highly offensive to a reasonable person.

. . . .

IV. Conclusion.

Cathy had a reasonable expectation of privacy when she was alone in her bedroom. Jeffrey's covert video surveillance intentionally intruded upon Cathy's expectation of privacy. The intrusion was highly offensive to a reasonable person. We therefore affirm the decision of the court of appeals.

AFFIRMED.

Points for Discussion

1. What reasonable expectation of privacy, if any, should one spouse have in a marriage? Should a spouse have a reasonable expectation of privacy in a cell phone? Mail and e-mails? A diary?

2. In *Tigges,* the husband contended that his wife's claim must fail because the only person who viewed the videotape was the wife's sister. The court was not persuaded: "An intrusion upon seclusion 'does *not* depend upon any publicity given to the person whose interest is invaded or to his affairs.'" Does this mean that a spouse's intrusion-upon-seclusion claim is actionable in a case in which no one other than the videotaping spouse knew of and watched the video?

3. A plaintiff who establishes an invasion of privacy is entitled to recover damages for (a) the harm to her "interest in privacy resulting from the invasion," (b) "mental distress proved to have been suffered if it is of a kind that normally results from such an invasion," and (c) "special damage of which the invasion is a legal cause." RESTATEMENT (SECOND) OF TORTS § 652H (1977).

Hypo 17-3

Defendant, the president of Corporation, is unhappy with a report that Plaintiff, a consumer rights advocate, has published about Corporation. Attempting to discredit Plaintiff, Defendant has an employee of Corporation call several of Plaintiff's friends in the middle of the night and ask them about Plaintiff's racial and religious views, sexual proclivities, personal habits, and political beliefs. Plaintiff sues Corporation for invasion of privacy. Does Plaintiff have a viable claim?

See Nader v. General Motors Corp., 25 N.Y.2d 560 (1970).

Snyder v. Phelps

131 S.Ct. 1207 (2011)

Chief Justice ROBERTS delivered the opinion of the Court.

A jury held members of the Westboro Baptist Church liable for millions of dollars in damages for picketing near a soldier's funeral service. The picket signs reflected the church's view that the United States is overly tolerant of sin and that God kills American soldiers as punishment. The question presented is whether the First Amendment shields the church members from tort liability for their speech in this case.

. . . .

Fred Phelps founded the Westboro Baptist Church in Topeka, Kansas, in 1955. The church's congregation believes that God hates and punishes the United States for its tolerance of homosexuality, particularly in America's military. The church frequently communicates its views by picketing, often at military funerals. In the more than 20 years that the members of Westboro Baptist have publicized their message, they have picketed nearly 600 funerals. [C]

Marine Lance Corporal Matthew Snyder was killed in Iraq in the line of duty. Lance Corporal Snyder's father selected the Catholic church in the Snyders' home-town of Westminster, Maryland, as the site for his son's funeral. Local newspapers provided notice of the time and location of the service.

Phelps became aware of Matthew Snyder's funeral and decided to travel to Maryland with six other Westboro Baptist parishioners (two of his daughters and four of his grandchildren) to picket. On the day of the memorial service, the Westboro congregation members picketed on public land adjacent to public streets near the Maryland State House, the United States Naval Academy, and Matthew Snyder's funeral. The Westboro picketers carried signs that were largely the same at all three locations. They stated, for instance: "God Hates the USA/ Thank God for 9/11," "America is Doomed," "Don't Pray for the USA," "Thank God for IEDs," "Thank God for Dead Soldiers," "Pope in Hell," "Priests Rape Boys," "God Hates Fags," "You're Going to Hell," and "God Hates You."

The church had notified the authorities in advance of its intent to picket at the time of the funeral, and the picketers complied with police instructions in staging their demonstration. The **picketing** took place within a 10-by 25-foot plot of public land adjacent to a public street, behind a temporary fence. [C] That plot was approximately 1,000 feet from the church where the funeral was held. Several buildings separated the picket site from the church. [C] The Westboro picketers displayed their signs for about 30 minutes before the funeral began and sang hymns and recited Bible verses. None of the picketers entered church property or went to the cemetery. They did not yell or use profanity, and there was no violence associated with the picketing. [C]

The funeral procession passed within 200 to 300 feet of the picket site. Although Snyder testified that he could see the tops of the picket signs as he drove to the funeral, he did not see what was written on the signs until later that night, while watching a news broadcast covering the event. [C]

. . . .

Snyder filed suit against Phelps, Phelps's daughters, and the Westboro Baptist Church (collectively Westboro or the church) in the United States District Court for the District of Maryland under that court's diversity jurisdiction. Snyder alleged . . . [an] intrusion upon seclusion [tort claim] . . .

. . . .

A jury found for Snyder . . . and held Westboro liable for $2.9 million in **compensatory damages** and $8 million in **punitive damages**. . . . The District Court **remitted** the punitive damages award to $2.1 million, but left the jury verdict otherwise intact. [C]

. . . .

Snyder argues that even assuming Westboro's speech is entitled to First Amendment protection generally, the church is not immunized from liability for intrusion upon seclusion because Snyder was a member of a captive audience at his son's funeral. [C] We do not agree. In most circumstances, "the Constitution does not permit the government to decide which types of otherwise protected speech are sufficiently offensive to require protection for the unwilling listener or viewer. Rather, ... the burden normally falls upon the viewer to avoid further bombardment of [his] sensibilities simply by averting [his] eyes." *Erznoznik v. Jacksonville,* 422 U.S. 205, 210-211, 95 S.Ct. 2268, 45 L.Ed.2d 125 (1975) . . . As a result, "[t]he ability of government, consonant with the Constitution, to shut off discourse solely to protect others from hearing it is ... dependent upon a showing that substantial privacy interests are being invaded in an essentially intolerable manner." *Cohen v. California,* 403 U.S. 15, 21, 91 S.Ct. 1780, 29 L.Ed.2d 284 (1971).

As a general matter, we have applied the **captive audience doctrine** only sparingly to protect unwilling listeners from protected speech. For example, we have upheld a statute allowing a homeowner to restrict the delivery of offensive mail to his home, [c] and an ordinance prohibiting picketing "before or about" any individual's residence. [C]

What's That?

The *Captive Audience Doctrine* is a constitutional principle allowing for speech to be restricted when the listener cannot, as a practical matter, escape from the intrusive speech.

Here, Westboro stayed well away from the memorial service. Snyder could see no more than the tops of the signs when driving to the funeral. And there is no indication that the picketing in any way interfered with the funeral service itself. We decline to expand the captive audience doctrine to the circumstances presented here.

. . . .

[W]e find that the First Amendment bars Snyder from recovery for . . . intrusion upon seclusion . . .

Justice ALITO, dissenting.

Our profound national commitment to free and open debate is not a license for the vicious verbal assault that occurred in this case.

Petitioner Albert Snyder is not a public figure. He is simply a parent whose son, Marine Lance Corporal Matthew Snyder, was killed in Iraq. Mr. Snyder wanted what is surely the right of any parent who experiences such an incalculable loss: to bury his son in peace. But respondents, members of the Westboro Baptist Church, deprived him of that elementary right. They first issued a press release and thus turned Matthew's funeral into a tumultuous media event. They then appeared at the church, approached as closely as they could without trespassing, and launched a malevolent verbal attack on Matthew and his family at a time of acute emotional vulnerability. As a result, Albert Snyder suffered severe and lasting emotional injury. . . .

Respondents and other members of their church have strong opinions on certain moral, religious, and political issues, and the First Amendment ensures that they have almost limitless opportunities to express their views. They may write and distribute books, articles, and other texts; they may create and disseminate video and audio recordings; they may circulate petitions; they may speak to individuals and groups in public forums and in any private venue that wishes to accommodate them; they may picket peacefully in countless locations; they may appear on television and speak on the radio; they may post messages on the Internet and send out e-mails. And they may express their views in terms that are "uninhibited," "vehement," and "caustic." *New York Times Co. v. Sullivan,* 376 U.S. 254, 270, 84 S.Ct. 710, 11 L.Ed.2d 686 (1964).

. . . .

On the morning of Matthew Snyder's funeral, respondents could have chosen to stage their protest at countless locations. They could have picketed the United States Capitol, the White House, the Supreme Court, the Pentagon, or any of the more than 5,600 military recruiting stations in this country. They could have returned to the Maryland State House or the United States Naval Academy, where they had been the day before. They could have selected any public road where pedestrians are allowed. (There are more than 4,000,000 miles of public roads in the United States.) They could have staged their protest in a public park. (There are more than 20,000 public parks in this country.) They could have chosen any Catholic church where no funeral was taking place. (There are nearly 19,000 Catholic churches in the United States.) But of course, a small group picketing at any of these locations would have probably gone unnoticed.

The Westboro Baptist Church, however, has devised a strategy that remedies this problem. As the Court notes, church members have protested at nearly 600 military funerals. [C] They have also picketed the funerals of police officers, firefighters, and the victims of natural disasters, accidents, and shocking crimes. And in advance of these protests, they issue press releases to ensure that their protests will attract public attention.

This strategy works because it is expected that respondents' verbal assaults will wound the family and friends of the deceased and because the media is irresistibly drawn to the sight of persons who are visibly in grief. The more outrageous the funeral protest, the more publicity the Westboro Baptist Church is able to obtain. Thus, when the church recently announced its intention to picket the funeral of a 9-year-old girl killed in the shooting spree in Tucson—proclaiming that she was "better off dead"—their announcement was national news, and the church was able to obtain free air time on the radio in exchange for canceling its protest.

> **FYI**
> The shooting of U.S. Representative Gabrielle Giffords and 18 others in Tucson, Arizona on January 8, 2011 left six people dead, including 9-year-old Christina Taylor Green.

Similarly, in 2006, the church got air time on a talk radio show in exchange for canceling its threatened protest at the funeral of five Amish girls killed by a crazed gunman.

In this case, respondents implemented the Westboro Baptist Church's publicity-seeking strategy. Their press release stated that they were going "to picket the funeral of Lance Cpl. Matthew A. Snyder" because "God Almighty killed Lance Cpl. Snyder. He died in shame, not honor–for a fag nation cursed by God .... Now in Hell-sine die." [C] This announcement guaranteed that Matthew's funeral would be transformed into a raucous media event and began the wounding process. It is well known that anticipation may heighten the effect of a painful event.

. . . .

Points for Discussion

1. Do you agree with the Supreme Court's holding? With the Court's application of the captive audience doctrine?

2. Suppose that Snyder could see the content and not just the tops of the signs carried by the Westboro picketers as he drove to his son's funeral. Same result?

3. In his dissenting opinion Justice Alito described Westboro's publicity-seeking strategy and argued that the intrusion upon seclusion claim should not have been decided and should have been remanded by the Court. Given Westboro's strategy and tactics, are you convinced that Westboro did not unreasonably intrude upon the seclusion of another in a manner that would be highly offensive to a reasonable person? That Snyder's substantial privacy interests were not invaded in an essentially intolerable manner?

Hypo 17-4

Recall the facts of Hypo 17-1. Consider further that A files an intrusion-upon-seclusion lawsuit against B. B moves for summary judgment and argues that no unlawful intrusion occurred because A knew of and consented to B's taking of the explicit photographs. Should the court grant or deny the motion?

Hypo 17-5

Plaintiff, the principal of Middle School, went on medical leave and notified Superintendent (her boss) that she would not be able to return to work until she had been cleared by her physician. Plaintiff alleges that during her leave Superintendent accessed her work computer and looked at her e-mails without her permission, and that Superintendent forwarded to his own e-mail account an e-mail with an attached letter Plaintiff had sent to her attorney; that letter (marked "Personal & Confidential") described a number of work-related problems Plaintiff was having with Superintendent. Superintendent contends that he accessed Plaintiff's e-mail account to review school-related messages that may have been sent to and not read by Plaintiff while she was on leave, and denies that he intentionally viewed any e-mails that were clearly identifiable as personal. Admitting that he forwarded to his computer Plaintiff's e-mail and attached letter to her attorney, Superintendent asserts that he thought that the e-mail concerned a school-related matter. Did Superintendent violate Plaintiff's right to privacy?

C. False Light

RESTATEMENT (SECOND) OF TORTS § 652E (1977)

One who gives publicity to a matter concerning another that places the other before the public in a false light is subject to liability to the other for invasion of his privacy, if

(a) the false light in which the other was placed would be highly offensive to a reasonable person, and

(b) the actor had knowledge of or acted in reckless disregard as to the falsity of the publicized matter and the false light in which the other would be placed.

Boese v. Paramount Pictures Corporation

952 F.Supp. 550 (N.D. Ill. 1996)

MEMORANDUM OPINION AND ORDER

ANN CLAIRE WILLIAMS, District Judge.

Plaintiff Robert A. Boese ("Boese") brought this **diversity** action against Paramount Pictures Corporation ("Paramount"), Peter Brennan, Diane Dimond, and Virginia K. Weathers n/k/a Virginia K. Johnson for **defamation per se**, statutory defamation per se, and **false light** invasion of privacy. Before the court is defendants' motion for summary judgment pursuant to Fed.R.Civ.P. 56 as to all counts. For the reasons set forth below, the court grants in part and denies in part.

Make the Connection

See Chapter 16's discussion of defamation law and doctrine.

Background

This case arises out of a Hard Copy segment that aired nationally on October 7, 1992. The segment featured a story about Virginia Weathers' experience after a fire destroyed her home in Topeka, Kansas on November 12, 1986. Plaintiff, Robert A. Boese, a forensic chemist, on behalf of American Family Insurance, conducted a chemical analysis of debris from Weathers' house. Boese concluded that one sample of the debris showed that an accelerant was present at the fire site, and forwarded a report stating that finding to the insurance company. As a result, the insurance company denied Weathers' claim.

On June 5, 1987, the State of Kansas filed two counts of **aggravated arson** against Weathers. At the preliminary hearing and the trial, Boese testified on the prosecution's behalf, relating his finding that an accelerant was present in the debris. In November 1987, the jury found Weathers not guilty of the arson charge.

On November 16, 1987, Weathers brought a civil action against American Family, B & W Consulting Forensic Chemists, Inc. ("B & W"), for which plaintiff was the president and sole shareholder, and others for alleged wrongs pertaining to the fire, the investigation, the denial of her claim, and the criminal prosecution. B & W was dismissed from the suit, but Ms. Weathers won an approximately $8 million judgment against American Family. [Cc]

On October 7, 1992, a Hard Copy segment about Weathers' experience aired nationally, including locally, in the Chicago area. The segment starts out with the story of the fire and arson investigation. [C] The Hard Copy segment contains a voiceover description of Weathers" criminal trial wherein it is stated "everyone was against [Weathers] ... the press, the town, and especially the powerful insurance company." The voiceover continues: "they brought in their big gun lawyers, their **expert witnesses**" at which point a sequence of videotaped scenes are interposed, including visuals of Weathers being sworn in, lawyers sitting at counsel's table, followed by Boese on the witness stand. [C] Then the report recounts the verdict in the criminal trial, the insurance company's continued refusal to pay her claim, and Weathers' civil suit against the insurance company and its outcome. The voiceover states that Ms. Weathers won an $8 million judgment against the insurance company. Immediately thereafter, Ms. Weathers states "Everybody lied, all the way down the line, and that came back to haunt them." [Cc] The voiceover concludes with statements about Weathers moving on with her life after this experience. In closing, the on-screen announcer states "that revenge is a dish which is most thoroughly enjoyed when it is served cold." [C]

. . . .

The court must determine whether statements attributed to defendants . . . cast plaintiff in a false light. The parties agree that plaintiff's . . . false light invasion of privacy claim [is] governed by Illinois law. *Boese v. Paramount Pictures Corp.,* 93 C 5976, 1994 WL 484622 (N.D.Ill. Sept. 2, 1994).

. . . .

The issue before the court is whether the statement cast plaintiff in a false light. Under Illinois law, there are three elements to a claim for false light invasion of privacy: "first, the allegations must show that the plaintiff was placed in a false light before the public as a result of the defendant's actions; second, the court must decide whether a trier of fact could decide that the false light in question would be 'highly offensive to a reasonable person'; and third, plaintiffs must allege and prove that the defendants acted with **actual malice**, defined ... as knowledge of falsehood or reckless disregard for whether the statements were true or false." [Cc]

Make the Connection

The Supreme Court's development and formulation of the actual malice standard is discussed in Chapter 16.

Plaintiff has set forth sufficient facts to withstand defendants' motion for summary judgment on this count for false light invasion of privacy.

As to the first element, plaintiff has set forth facts demonstrating that he was placed in a false light by the October 7, 1992 Hard Copy segment. Although not clearly obvious as plaintiff suggests, the words and pictures roughly imply that plaintiff was an expert witness for the insurance company and, in that capacity, lied on the witness stand. The implication being that plaintiff had sworn falsely on the witness stand and lacked integrity in discharging his duties. The publication prong for invasion of privacy torts means communicating the matter to the public at large or to so many persons that the matter must be regarded as one of general knowledge. [C] The Hard Copy episode aired nationally, including locally in the Chicago area, on October 7, 1992, [c], satisfying the publication prong.

The court finds that a trier of fact could decide that the charge that a person lied on the witness stand and in the discharge of his duties would be "highly offensive to a reasonable person". Finally, plaintiff has set forth several facts, considered overall, demonstrating that there is a genuine issue for trial regarding whether defendant acted with actual malice. Plaintiff highlights several facts, some of which are: (1) that defendants knew the seriousness and the potential harm to plaintiff's **reputation** and livelihood the Hard Copy segment would cause [c]; (2) that Weathers was motivated by revenge and the Paramount defendants cooperated with her [c]; (3) the defendants included Boese's picture in the segment, yet failed to contact him as a source, which was a deviation from generally accepted standards of journalism [cc]; and (4) Hard Copy's failure to investigate numerous file sources and persons is probative of **recklessness** [cc].

For the above reasons, the court finds that plaintiff has set forth sufficient facts to withstand defendants' motion for summary judgment as to this count for false light invasion of privacy.

. . . .

ANN CLAIRE WILLIAMS, District Judge.

Before the court is the Paramount Defendants' motion to **reconsider** part of the order entered by this court on October 29, 1996 . . .

Paramount defendants urge the court to reconsider its order denying their motion for summary judgment as to plaintiff's false light invasion of privacy claim. Defendants base their motion on two arguments. First, defendants argue that this court's finding that the alleged defamatory statement was not "capable of being objectively verified as true or false" requires the dismissal of plaintiff's false-light claim. Secondly, defendants argue that plaintiff has failed to establish a genuine issue of material fact regarding actual malice.

Specifically, defendants contend that a finding that a statement is a constitutionally protected expression of opinion and therefore, a non-actionable statement under the law of defamation, also applies to a false-light invasion of privacy claim. Defendants suggest that the law is very clear in this area by referring to decisions of other circuits. However, upon a closer examination, the law appears to be less settled than defendants suggest.

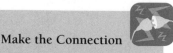

Make the Connection

Opinion as a defense to a defamation claim is discussed in Chapter 16.

While the court agrees with defendants that other circuits have found that opinion is a defense to a false-light claim;[1] the court also recognizes that courts universally have held that a statement need not be defamatory for a false-light privacy action to lie. *Silk v. City of Chicago,* No. 95 C 0143, 1996 WL 312074 *36 (N.D.Ill. June 7, 1996); *Zechman v. Merrill Lynch, Pierce, Fenner, & Smith, Inc.,* 742 F.Supp. 1359, 1373 (N.D.Ill.1990).[2] In *Silk,* the court found the alleged defamatory statement–"useless piece of s[__]t"–to be a non-actionable expression of opinion. [C] . . .

This court reaches the same conclusion the *Silk* court and *Zechman* court reached: a non-defamatory statement can still give rise to a false-light invasion of

---

1 *See Partington v. Bugliosi*, 56 F.3d 1147, 1160-61 (9th Cir.1995); *Moldea v. New York Times Co.,* 22 F.3d 310, 319 (D.C.Cir.), *cert. denied,* 513 U.S. 875, 115 S.Ct. 202, 130 L.Ed.2d 133 (1994); *White v. Fraternal Order of Police,* 909 F.2d 512, 518 (D.C.Cir.1990); *Ault v. Hustler Magazine, Inc.,* 860 F.2d 877, 880 (9th Cir.1988), *cert. denied,* 489 U.S. 1080, 109 S.Ct. 1532, 103 L.Ed.2d 837 (1989); *Rinsley v. Brandt,* 700 F.2d 1304, 1307 (10th Cir.1983); *See also* RESTATEMENT (SECOND) OF TORTS § 652E cmt. e (1977) ("When the false publicity *is also* defamatory so that either action can be maintained by the plaintiff, it is arguable that limitations of long standing that have been found desirable for the action for defamation should not be successfully evaded by proceeding upon a different theory of later origin, in the development of which the attention of the court has not been directed to the limitations. As yet there is little authority on this issue.") (emphasis added); RODNEY A. SMOLLA, LAW OF DEFAMATION § 10.02[2][a] (1995) ("To permit, via the false light tort, causes of action that would otherwise not be permitted as a matter of law because they fail to allege provably false statements of fact, is to open a wide and dangerous loophole in the fabric of defamation law").

2 *See also Douglass v. Hustler Magazine,* 769 F.2d 1128, 1134 (7th Cir.1985), *cert. denied,* 475 U.S. 1094, 106 S.Ct. 1489, 89 L.Ed.2d 892 (1986); *Cibenko v. Worth Publishers,* 510 F.Supp. 761, 766 (D.N.J.1981); *Fogel v. Forbes, Inc.,* 500 F.Supp. 1081, 1087 (E.D.Pa.1980); *Michigan United Conservation Clubs v. CBS News,* 485 F.Supp. 893, 903 (W.D.Mich.1980), *aff'd,* 665 F.2d 110 (6th Cir.1981); RESTATEMENT (SECOND) OF TORTS § 652E cmt. b ("It is not, however, necessary to the action for invasion of privacy that the plaintiff be defamed."); Rodney A. Smolla, Law of Defamation § 10.02[2][b] and [4][b] ("The single most important distinguishing characteristic of the false light tort is that the publication need not be defamatory ... [C]ourts increasingly perceive that the primary practical difference between false light and defamation is that false light claims do not need to rise to the level of being defamatory".); W. Page Keeton et al., Prosser and Keeton on the Law of Torts § 117, at 866 (5th ed. 1984) (The tort of false light invasion of privacy "is much more likely to be utilized in those cases where the false statement is not defamatory.")

privacy claim. Although, this court found the statement at issue to be an opinion and non-actionable in the defamation context, this finding does not change the court's analysis of plaintiff's false light claim.

Make the Connection

The court makes clear that the conclusion that a statement is not defamatory does not foreclose a false-light privacy claim; the latter is a separate and distinct cause of action which may be brought and litigated even though a plaintiff has not been defamed.

Points for Discussion

1. What are the elements of a claim for false light invasion of privacy under Illinois law? How does the court apply those elements?

2. How does the court answer the question whether a false light claim is extinguished by a judicial finding that a statement is not defamatory?

3. For more on the false light tort claim, see *Diane Leenheer Zimmerman, False Light Invasion of Privacy: The Light That Failed,* 64 N.Y.U. L. Rev. 364 (1989); *see also* Patricia Sanchez Abril, *Recasting Privacy Torts in a Spaceless World,* 21 Harv. J.L. & Tech. 1 (2007).

Aisenson v. American Broadcasting Company, Inc.

220 Cal.App.3d, 269 Cal.Rptr. 379 (1990)

BOREN, Associate Justice.

In 1984, appellant David Aisenson filed a lawsuit for **slander** and invasion of privacy against respondents American Broadcasting Company, Inc., its Los Angeles affiliate KABC-TV, and four KABC-TV employees (collectively, "ABC"). The lawsuit arose from ABC's broadcast of a series of television news special reports discussing the results of an opinion poll it had conducted. The poll elicited local attorneys' opinions on the performance of Los Angeles Superior Court criminal law judges. ABC reported that appellant, then a superior court judge, had received the lowest ratings of all the judges in the poll.

Appellant alleged that the comments aired on KABC-TV falsely implied that he was an incompetent judge and a "bad guy," that he refused to be interviewed, and that he attempted to suppress the broadcast of ABC's report. These comments, in their entirety, are as follows:

> Broadcast of October 25, 1983: "... The man stepping out of his home is His Honor Judge David Aisenson, the lowest ranking judge of them all. On a one to ten scale, Judge David Aisenson got an overall average score in the four's. Judge Aisenson refused to show himself to you in an interview about the survey, and refused to allow a tv camera into his courtroom. We thought you should at least see his face. Judge Aisenson, in effect, followed the lead of the judge who scored the lowest on KABC's survey six years ago...."

> Broadcast of October 27, 1983: "... Judge David Aisenson came out with the lowest score of all the judges included in the survey, an overall average score on the 10 point scale of 4.4. When lawyers were asked whether Judge Aisenson knows the law, the answer, 4.2. They gave him the lowest score overall for his sentencing habits, and the lowest score overall for his behavior on the bench. Unfortunately, we can't show you Judge David Aisenson's behavior on the bench. He won't let a television camera in his courtroom, and he won't submit to a television interview about his score as the lowest ranking judge of all those in the 1983 survey.

> "Incidentally, Judge David Aisenson is one of those few judges who wasn't put in his job by a governor. He simply ran for judge and was elected...."

> "... And please take a moment to note the names of those other judges who came out relatively low on the survey and refused to let you see and hear them on tv. Judge David Aisenson, the lowest scoring judge of them all...."

> Broadcast of November 1, 1983: "... Incidentally, the judge with the lowest score for knowing the law is the same one who has the lowest score in most categories. Judge David Aisenson...."

In addition to making the above-quoted statements about appellant, ABC also videotaped appellant as he walked from his home to his car in a manner which, appellant alleged, "[made] it appear as if [he] were a criminal or the subject of some ongoing criminal investigation." . . .

. . . .

The trial court granted ABC's motion for summary judgment and dismissed appellant's complaint. This appeal follows.

. . . .

Appellant alleges . . . that respondents placed him in a false light . . .

. . . .

A "false light" cause of action is in substance equivalent to a libel claim, and should meet the same requirements of the libel claim, including proof of malice. (*Briscoe v. Reader's Digest Association, Inc.* (1971) 4 Cal.3d 529, 543, 93 Cal.Rptr. 866, 483 P.2d 34; *Selleck v. Globe International, Inc.* (1985) 166 Cal.App.3d 1123, 1133, 212 Cal.Rptr. 838.) . . . [T]here is no evidence that ABC broadcast its statements for any reason other than those usually associated with newscasts. There is nothing here on which to base a finding of falsity or reckless disregard for the truth. Hence, there is no basis for a finding of malice.

There is, moreover, no basis for concluding that the videotape of appellant placed him in a false light.[5] Photographs are not actionable if they are fair and accurate depictions of the person and scene in question, even if they place the person in a less than flattering light, so long as the photographs do not surpass the limits of **decency** by being highly offensive to persons of ordinary sensibilities. (*Fellows v. National Enquirer, Inc.* (1986) 42 Cal.3d 234, 238, 228 Cal.Rptr. 215, 721 P.2d 97; *Gill v. Hearst Publishing Co.* (1953) 40 Cal.2d 224, 230-231, 253 P.2d 441; *Cantrell v. Forest City Publishing Co.* (1974) 419 U.S. 245, 253, fn. 5, 95 S.Ct. 465, 470, fn. 5, 42 L.Ed.2d 419: published photographs depicting plaintiffs' abject poverty, old clothing and deteriorating home were undeniably correct, therefore no verdict could be entered against photographer.) Appellant does not deny that he is in fact the person shown walking to his car in the videotape, nor does he maintain that the photographs were indecent or offensive to a person of ordinary sensibility. He simply objects that the broadcasters chose to freeze the film at the moment he appeared to spot the videocamera, and he claims that he was thereby unfairly portrayed. His disappointment that a more flattering picture was not broadcast (or that none at all was broadcast) does not rise to the level of a compensable claim for invasion of privacy. The trial court was correct in granting summary judgment on this cause of action.

. . . .

The judgment is affirmed.

---

5 The videotape not only does not falsely portray appellant, but it is also difficult to say that the videotape is unflattering to appellant in any manner. Appellant is shown walking briskly with briefcase in hand, to his automobile. The environment, appellant's physical appearance and his demeanor are wholly respectable. To some viewers, the briefcase might well indicate that appellant is an industrious judge who takes work home with him.

Hypo 17-6

While working as a staff assistant for a United States Senator, Defendant created a blog entitled "D.C. Diary" on an Internet website. Defendant wrote about his sexual activities with various women including Plaintiff, who was identified by name in a posting containing a photo of Plaintiff. Another popular website, "Voyeur," posted a link to Defendant's blog, resulting in wide circulation of Defendant's postings.

You are a lawyer and tort law specialist. Plaintiff has contacted you and related the foregoing facts and asks whether she has a viable false light claim against Defendant. Please answer Plaintiff's inquiry.

D. Appropriation

RESTATEMENT (SECOND) OF TORTS § 652C (1977)

One who appropriates to his own use or benefit the name or likeness of another is subject to liability to the other for invasion of his privacy.

Carson v. Here's Johnny Portable Toilets, Inc.

698 F.2d 831 (6th Cir. 1983)

BAILEY BROWN, Senior Circuit Judge.

. . . .

Appellant, John W. Carson (Carson), is the host and star of "The Tonight Show," a well-known television program broadcast five nights a week by the National Broadcasting Company. Carson also appears as an entertainer in night clubs and theaters around the country. From the time he began hosting "The Tonight Show" in 1962, he has been introduced on the show each night with the phrase "Here's Johnny." This method of introduction was first used for Carson in 1957 when he hosted a daily television program for the American Broadcasting Company. The phrase "Here's Johnny" is generally associated with Carson by a substantial segment of the television viewing public. In 1967, Carson first authorized use of this phrase by an outside business venture, permitting it to be used by a chain of restaurants called "Here's Johnny Restaurants."

Appellant Johnny Carson Apparel, Inc. (Apparel), formed in 1970, manufactures and markets men's clothing to retail stores. Carson, the president of Apparel and owner of 20% of its stock, has **licensed** Apparel to use his name and picture, which appear on virtually

> ### Hear It
>
> To hear Ed McMahon's famous "Here's Johnny" introduction of Johnny Carson at the Tonight Show, click here .

all of Apparel's products and promotional material. Apparel has also used, with Carson's consent, the phrase "Here's Johnny" on labels for clothing and in advertising campaigns. In 1977, Apparel granted a license to Marcy Laboratories to use "Here's Johnny" as the name of a line of men's toiletries. The phrase "Here's Johnny" has never been registered by appellants as a **trademark** or **service mark**.

Appellee, Here's Johnny Portable Toilets, Inc., is a Michigan corporation engaged in the business of renting and selling "Here's Johnny" portable toilets. Appellee's founder was aware at the time he formed the corporation that "Here's Johnny" was the introductory slogan for Carson on "The Tonight Show." He indicated that he coupled the phrase with a second one, "The World's Foremost Commodian," to make "a good play on a phrase."

Shortly after appellee went into business in 1976, appellants brought this action alleging . . . invasion of . . . publicity rights. They sought damages and an injunction prohibiting appellee's further use of the phrase "Here's Johnny" as a corporate name or in connection with the sale or rental of its portable toilets.

After a bench trial, the district court issued a memorandum opinion and order, *Carson v. Here's Johnny Portable Toilets, Inc.,* 498 F.Supp. 71 (E.D.Mich.1980), which served as its findings of fact and conclusions of law. The court ordered the dismissal of the appellants' complaint. . . .

. . . .

The appellants . . . claim that the appellee's use of the phrase "Here's Johnny" violates the common law right of privacy and right of publicity. The confusion in this area of the law requires a brief analysis of the relationship between these two rights.

In an influential article, Dean Prosser delineated four distinct types of the right of privacy: (1) intrusion upon one's seclusion or solitude, (2) public disclosure of embarrassing private facts, (3) publicity which places one in a false light, and (4) **appropriation** of one's **name** or **likeness** for the defendant's advantage. Prosser, *Privacy,* 48 Calif.L.Rev. 383, 389 (1960). This fourth type has become known as the **"right of publicity."** *Factors Etc., Inc. v. Pro Arts, Inc.,* 579 F.2d 215, 220 (2d Cir.1978), *cert. denied,* 440 U.S. 908, 99 S.Ct. 1215, 59 L.Ed.2d 455 (1979); *see Zacchini v. Scripps-Howard Broadcasting Co.,* 433 U.S. 562, 572, 97 S. Ct. 2849, 2855, 53 L.Ed.2d 965 (1977). Henceforth we will refer to Prosser's last, or fourth, category, as the "right of publicity."

Dean Prosser's analysis has been a source of some confusion in the law. His first three types of the right of privacy generally protect the right "to be let alone," while the right of publicity protects the celebrity's **pecuniary interest** in the commercial exploitation of his identity. [Cc] Thus, the right of privacy and the right of publicity protect fundamentally different interests and must be analyzed separately.

We do not believe that Carson's claim that his right of privacy has been invaded is supported by the law or the facts. Apparently, the gist of this claim is that Carson is embarrassed by and considers it odious to be associated with the appellee's product. Clearly, the association does not appeal to Carson's sense of humor. But the facts here presented do not, it appears to us, amount to an invasion of any of the interests protected by the right of privacy. In any event, our disposition of the claim of an invasion of the right of publicity makes it unnecessary for us to accept or reject the claim of an invasion of the right of privacy.

The right of publicity has developed to protect the commercial interest of celebrities in their identities. The theory of the right is that a celebrity's identity can be valuable in the promotion of products, and the celebrity has an interest that may be protected from the unauthorized commercial exploitation of that identity. In *Memphis Development Foundation v. Factors Etc., Inc.,* 616 F.2d 956 (6th Cir.), cert. denied, 449 U.S. 953, 101 S.Ct. 358, 66 L.Ed.2d 217 (1980), we stated: "The famous have an exclusive legal right during life to control and profit from the commercial use of their name and personality." [C]

The district court dismissed appellants' claim based on the right of publicity because appellee does not use Carson's name or likeness. [C] It held that it "would not be prudent to allow recovery for a right of publicity claim which does not more specifically identify Johnny Carson. [C] We believe that, on the contrary, the district court's conception of the right of publicity is too narrow. The right of publicity, as we have stated, is that a celebrity has a protected pecuniary interest in the commercial exploitation of his identity. If the celebrity's identity is commercially exploited, there has been an invasion of his right whether or not his "name or likeness" is used. Carson's identity may be exploited even if his name, John W. Carson, or his picture is not used.

In *Motschenbacher v. R.J. Reynolds Tobacco Co.,* 498 F.2d 821 (9th Cir.1974), the court held that the unauthorized use of a picture of a distinctive race car of a well known professional race car driver, whose name or likeness were not used, violated his right of publicity. In this connection, the court said:

> We turn now to the question of "identifiability." Clearly, if the district court correctly determined as a matter of law that plaintiff is not identifiable in the commercial, then in no sense has plaintiff's identity been **misappropriated** nor his interest violated.

> Having viewed a film of the commercial, we agree with the district court that the "likeness" of plaintiff is itself unrecognizable; however, the court's further conclusion of law to the effect that the driver is not identifiable as plaintiff is erroneous in that it wholly fails to attribute proper significance to the distinctive decorations appearing on the car. As pointed out earlier, these markings were not only peculiar to the plaintiff's cars but they caused some persons to think the car in question was plaintiff's and to infer that the person driving the car was the plaintiff.

[C]

In *Ali v. Playgirl, Inc.,* 447 F.Supp. 723 (S.D.N.Y.1978), Muhammad Ali, former heavyweight champion, sued Playgirl magazine under the New York "right of privacy" statute and also alleged a violation of his common law right of publicity. The magazine published a drawing of a nude, black male sitting on a stool in a corner of a boxing ring with hands taped and arms outstretched on the ropes. The district court concluded that Ali's right of publicity was invaded because the drawing sufficiently identified him in spite of the fact that the drawing was captioned "Mystery Man." The district court found that the identification of Ali was made certain because of an accompanying verse that identified the figure as "The Greatest." The district court took judicial notice of the fact that "Ali has regularly claimed that appellation for himself." [C]

Behind the Scenes

Muhammad Ali is considered by many to have been the greatest boxer of all time. For more information on his life and accomplishments, visit www.ali.com.

In *Hirsch v. S.C. Johnson & Son, Inc.,* 90 Wis.2d 379, 280 N.W.2d 129 (1979), the court held that use by defendant of the name "Crazylegs" on a shaving gel for women violated plaintiff's right of publicity. Plaintiff, Elroy Hirsch, a famous football player, had been known by this nickname. The court said:

The fact that the name, "Crazylegs," used by Johnson, was a nickname rather than Hirsch's actual name does not preclude a cause of action. All that is required is that the name clearly identify the wronged person. In the instant case, it is not disputed at this juncture of the case that the nickname identified the plaintiff Hirsch. It is argued that there were others who were known by the same name. This, however, does not vitiate the existence of a cause of action. It may, however, if sufficient proof were adduced, affect the quantum of damages should the jury impose liability or it might preclude liability altogether. Prosser points out "that a stage or other fictitious name can be so identified with the plaintiff that he is entitled to protection against its use." [C] He writes that it would be absurd to say that Samuel L. Clemens would have a cause of action if that name had been used in advertising, but he would not have one for the use of "Mark Twain." If a fictitious name is used in a context which tends to indicate that the name is that of the plaintiff, the factual case for identity is strengthened. [C]

[C].

In this case, Earl Braxton, president and owner of Here's Johnny Portable Toilets, Inc., admitted that he knew that the phrase "Here's Johnny" had been used for years to introduce Carson. Moreover, in the opening statement in the district court, appellee's counsel stated:

> Now, we've stipulated in this case that the public tends to associate the words "Johnny Carson", the words "Here's Johnny" with plaintiff, John Carson and, Mr. Braxton, in his deposition, admitted that he knew that and probably absent that identification, he would not have chosen it.

[C] That the "Here's Johnny" name was selected by Braxton because of its identification with Carson was the clear **inference** from Braxton's testimony irrespective of such **admission** in the opening statement.

We therefore conclude that, applying the correct legal standards, appellants are entitled to judgment. The proof showed without question that appellee had appropriated Carson's identity in connection with its corporate name and its product.

. . . .

The judgment of the district court is **vacated** and the case **remanded** for further proceedings consistent with this opinion.

————————————

Brill v. Walt Disney Company

246 P.3d 1099 (Okla. App. 2010)

BAY MITCHELL, Judge.

¶ 1 Oklahoma stock race car driver Mark Brill, Plaintiff/Appellant ("Brill"), seeks review of an order granting Defendants/Appellees', The Walt Disney Company, Pixar Animation Studios, Michael Wallis individually and Michael Wallis, LLC ("Defendants") respective Motions to Dismiss for failure to state a claim pursuant to 12 O.S.2001 § 2012(B)(6). Specifically, Brill claims that the fictional animated race car character "Lightning McQueen" in the movie *Cars* constitutes a misappropriation of his likeness and violates his right of publicity pursuant to common law and 12 O.S.2001 § 1449. . . .

See It

To see an image of Lightning Mc-Queen, click here.

¶ 2 Brill filed his original Petition in May 2008, with four subsequent amendments thereto. Brill asserts that since 1995, he has driven a red race car with the number 95 painted on the doors in yellow. Further, he alleges his "race car is a 2-door body style with relatively long hood, swept back windshield, a distinctive tail fin and dirt track tires made by Goodyear." The record reflects Brill's vehicle is a modified Chevrolet Monte Carlo. Brill races at the Oklahoma State Fair Speedway as well as at tracks in Oklahoma City, Enid, Clinton and Ada, Oklahoma. Brill additionally owns and operates a machine shop, an auto repair shop, and a race track in Meeker, Oklahoma. Brill has allegedly used the image of his race car to promote his racing and businesses since 1996.

¶ 3 "Lightning McQueen" is the animated fictional talking car and rookie racing sensation featured in *Cars*. Lightning McQueen has no driver. The windshield depicts his eyes and the grill of the car displays a smiling face that talks. Lightning McQueen is a red race car of a fictional make/model with a large yellow lightning bolt painted on the side and the number 95 displayed in yellow over the lightning bolt. Lightning McQueen is covered with numerous fictitious sponsor stickers such as Rust-eze Medicated Bumper Ointment, Lightyear tires and Gasprin Hood Ache Relief.

¶ 4 Defendant Michael Wallis ("Wallis") was hired by Pixar Animation Studios ("Pixar") as a consultant in 2001, and he led the animators on a tour of Route 66 to assist them in their research in development of the *Cars* movie. Wallis's sworn Declaration . . . provides that Wallis never visited a racetrack with the

Pixar team, never met Brill, nor saw his race car. Wallis had no knowledge of Mark Brill or his car until after the filing of this lawsuit.

. . . .

Invasion of Privacy: Right of Publicity

¶ 6 In *McCormack v. Oklahoma Publishing Co.*, 1980 OK 98, ¶ 8, 613 P.2d 737, 740, the Oklahoma Supreme Court recognized the tort of invasion of privacy in the four categories[5] set out in the RESTATEMENT (SECOND) OF TORTS, § 652A (1977). Specifically applicable hereto is the third category of privacy invasion: "One who appropriates to his own use or benefit the name or *likeness* of another is subject to liability to the other for invasion of privacy." § 652C (emphasis added). A person's right of publicity is additionally protected by Oklahoma statute 12 O.S.2001 § 1449(A), which provides in pertinent part:

> Any person who knowingly uses another's name, voice, signature, photograph, or *likeness*, in any manner, on or in products, merchandise, or goods, or for purposes of advertising or selling, or soliciting purchases of, products, merchandise, goods, or services, without such person's prior consent, or, in the case of a minor, the prior consent of his parent or legal guardian, shall be liable for any damages sustained by the person or persons injured as a result thereof, and any profits from the unauthorized use that are attributable to the use shall be taken into account in computing the actual damages. In establishing such profits, the injured party or parties are required to present proof only of the gross revenue attributable to such use, and the person who violated this section is required to prove his or her deductible expenses. Punitive damages may also be awarded to the injured party or parties. The prevailing party in any action under this section shall also be entitled to attorney's fees and costs.

(emphasis added).

¶ 7 Although the issue has been presented in the 10th Circuit, there is no prior reported Oklahoma state court decision addressing the right of publicity. Brill argues the common law right of publicity is broader than the statutory right in that the use of one's "identity" is actionable even if one's "likeness" or name is not used. We disagree. The common law right of publicity, as set forth in the Restatement, is limited to the appropriation of "the name or likeness of another."

---

5 These four categories of invasion of privacy include: (a) unreasonable intrusion upon the seclusion of another; (b) appropriation of the other's name or likeness; (c) unreasonable publicity given to the other's private life; and (d) publicity that unreasonably places the other in a false light before the public.

"The interest protected [in § 652C of the Restatement] is the interest of the individual in the exclusive use of his own identity, in so far as it is represented by his *name or likeness,* and insofar as the use may be of benefit to him or to others." § 652C, Comment a (emphasis added). The statutory right of publicity "protect[s] against the unauthorized use of certain features of a person's identity–such as *name, likeness, or voice*–for commercial purposes." *Cardtoons, L.C. v. Major League Baseball Players Ass'n,* 95 F.3d 959 (10th Cir.1996) (emphasis added). Thus, the issue for us is whether Lightning McQueen does not constitute a "likeness" of Brill as a matter of law. The similarities in the appearance of Brill's race car and Lightning McQueen are that they are both red race cars and have the yellow number 95 on the side. The similarities, according to Brill, are "so striking that it defies explanation as mere chance." Further, Brill argues that his red number 95 stock car is his likeness and/or identity.

¶ 8 The phrase "name or likeness" "embraces the concept of a person's character, which is legally protected against appropriation by another for his or her own use or benefit." AM. JUR.2d Privacy § 71 (2010). "The term 'likeness' does not include general incidents from a person's life, especially when fictionalized.... The term 'likeness' includes such things as pictures and the use of a singer's distinctive voice." [C]

¶ 9 In *Cardtoons,* the court held a company's use of player likenesses on its cards violated the Oklahoma right of publicity statute and infringed on the players association's property rights. The *Cardtoons* decision includes a discussion of *White v. Samsung Electronics America,* 971 F.2d 1395 (9th Cir.), *cert. denied,* 508 U.S. 951, 113 S.Ct. 2443, 124 L.Ed.2d 660 (1993), which construed California right of publicity law. In *White,* the defendant had published an advertisement featuring a costumed robot that parodied Vanna White, the letter-turner on the "Wheel of Fortune" television gameshow. The *White* court determined the robot did not constitute a "likeness" of Vanna White within the meaning of California statutory law. While a federal court decision is not binding or controlling on an Oklahoma court construing Oklahoma law, it is persuasive in the absence of authoritative state law. *See Johnson v. Ford Motor Co.,* 2002 OK 24, ¶ 26, 45 P.3d 86, 95. We find that just as a mechanical robot with a blonde wig standing in front of a game board resembling a famous game show wheel cannot be construed as a likeness to Vanna White, a fictional, talking, driver-less red race car with the number 95 on it cannot be construed as a likeness of a driver of a similarly colored/numbered race car.

¶ 10 In order to establish a ***prima facie* case** of statutory violation of the right of publicity, a plaintiff must plead facts establishing the three elements of

It's Latin to Me!

Prima facie is Latin for "at first sight" or "on first appearance."

the claim: (1) Defendants knowingly used Brill's name or likeness, (2) on products, merchandise or goods, (3) without Brill's prior consent. Just as under the Restatement, the statute only concerns the use of another *person's* name, voice, signature, photograph or likeness, not the name, photograph or likeness of another person's car. Regardless of the purported similarities of Brill's car to Lightning McQueen, those similarities without more simply do not equate to a knowing use of Brill's personal likeness. The law does not support a contrary interpretation of these facts.

¶ 11 Brill cites *Motschenbacher v. R.J. Reynolds Tobacco Co.*, 498 F.2d 821 (9th Cir.1974) in support of his proposition that a race car driver's identity extends to the likeness of his car. Brill misconstrues the holding of *Motschenbacher.* The defendant in *Motschenbacher* used a picture of the driver/plaintiff's race car in an advertisement. While the car in the advertisement had been altered from the appearance of plaintiff's actual race car, (the defendant removed the plaintiff's sponsors, changed the number, added a spoiler, and added itself to the car as a sponsor), the *plaintiff appeared to be driving the car in the advertisement* (although his features were not clearly visible). The court reversed the summary judgment for defendant, emphasizing the critical fact that the car in the advertisement clearly had a driver, which implied that the person driving the car was plaintiff. [C]

¶ 12 Unlike *Motschenbacher,* the car in this case is a fictional, animated, talking car that clearly has no driver. The image of Lightning McQueen raises no inference of a driver, and thus implicates no driver's right of publicity protected by common law or statute. The law protects people's right of publicity (as opposed to their cars). Defendants' use of the talking car character, Lightning McQueen, in no way constitutes an *unauthorized* use of Brill's likeness for commercial purposes and thus, does not violate Brill's statutory and/or common law right of publicity as a matter of law.

. . . .

Points for Discussion

1. What is the right of publicity, and what does that right protect?

2. Note, as stated by the court in *Brill*, that the right of publicity can be protected by common law and by statute. Which was at issue in *Brill*?

3. What is one's likeness? Can the right of publicity be violated when the defendant has not used the plaintiff's name or likeness? How is this question answered in *Carson* and *Brill*?

4. Brill distinguishes *Motschenbacher v. R.J. Reynolds Tobacco Co.,* 498 F.2d 821 (9th Cir. 1974). Were you persuaded?

5. Can an action alleging that a deceased person's name or likeness has been appropriated be maintained? *See* Restatement (Second) of Torts § 652I (1977).

6. Section 46 of the Restatement (Third) of Unfair Competition provides that "[o]ne who appropriates the commercial value of a person's name, likeness, or other indicia of identity for purposes of trade is subject to liability." Section 47 of that Restatement limits the scope of "for purposes of trade" as follows: the "use for 'for purposes of trade' does not ordinarily include the use of a person's identity in news reporting, commentary, entertainment, works of fiction or nonfiction, or in advertising that is incidental to such uses."

Hypo 17-7

Pop Star, widely considered one of the greatest artists of all time, recently died. After his death, Video Game Creator developed a video game in which users assume the role of a homeowner trying to repel a horde of zombies. As part of the game, one of the zombies available to users was a "dancing zombie" who bared a striking resemblance to Pop Star—it looked, dressed, and danced just like Pop Star at the height of his fame. Pop Star's family is not pleased and asks you, a tort law specialist, whether they have a claim against Video Game Creator. Please advise.

Hypo 17-8

Defendant was hired during a child custody dispute to investigate Plaintiff. Learning of inconsistencies in the manner in which Plaintiff came to possess bearer bonds during the investigation, Defendant reported the discrepancies to the authorities. Thereafter, Plaintiff was charged with and convicted of felony theft of the bonds.

Defendant publishes a newsletter which is sent, free of charge, to law enforcement authorities, financial institutions, law firms, and other organizations. The newsletter contains articles on financial fraud investigations and provides information on upcoming conferences. One article discussed the role Defendant played in uncovering and reporting Plaintiff's illegal activities. As set out in the article, Plaintiff, who worked as a secretary at a brokerage firm, stole bearer bonds from a customer of the firm, cashed the bonds, and used the money for her personal use. Detailing Defendant's investigation of Plaintiff and noting that a jury convicted her of theft, the article mentioned Plaintiff by name and included her photograph. Plaintiff learned of the publication of the article and filed a lawsuit against Defendant, contending that Defendant invaded her privacy by appropriating her name or likeness.

Defendant has moved for summary judgment on the ground that the use of Plaintiff's name and likeness in the article discussing her crime and felony conviction is a matter of public concern. Evaluate and discuss Plaintiff's claim and Defendant's argument.

Appendix of Selected Legal Terms

(the following terms are from Black's Law Dictionary)

a fortiori   *adv.* By even greater force of logic; even more so.

abatement   *n.* The act of eliminating or nullifying.

abrogate   *vb.* To abolish (a law or custom) by formal or authoritative action; to annul or repeal. *Cf.* obrogate. -- abrogation, *n.*

absolute liability   Strict liability. Liability that does not depend on actual negligence or intent to harm, but that is based on the breach of an absolute duty to make something safe. -- Also termed liability without fault. *Cf.* fault liability.

abuse of discretion   1. An adjudicator's failure to exercise sound, reasonable, and legal decision-making. 2. An appellate court's standard for reviewing a decision that is asserted to be grossly unsound, unreasonable, illegal, or unsupported by the evidence.

accrue   *vb.* To come into existence as an enforceable claim or right; to arise.

actual damages   An amount awarded to a complainant to compensate for a proven injury or loss; damages that repay actual losses. -- Also termed compensatory damages; tangible damages; real damages.

actual knowledge	Direct and clear knowledge, as distinguished from constructive knowledge.
additur	[Latin "it is added to"] A trial court's order, issued usually with the defendant's consent, that increases the jury's award of damages to avoid a new trial on grounds of inadequate damages. • The term may also refer to the increase itself, the procedure, or the court's power to make the order. -- Also termed *increscitur*. *Cf.* Remittitur.
administratrix	*Archaic.* A female administrator.
admiralty	*n.* A court that exercises jurisdiction over all maritime contracts, torts, injuries, or offenses. • The federal courts are so called when exercising their admiralty jurisdiction, which is conferred by the U.S. Constitution (art. III, § 2, cl. 1).
adverse possession	The use or enjoyment of real property with a claim of right when that use or enjoyment is continuous, exclusive, hostile, open, and notorious. Also termed adverse dominion. *Cf.* prescription.
advisory jury	A jury empaneled to hear a case when the parties have no right to a jury trial. *See* Fed. R. Civ. P. 39(c). • The judge may accept or reject the advisory jury's verdict.
affirmative defense	A defendant's assertion of facts and arguments that, if true, will defeat the plaintiff's or prosecution's claim, even if all the allegations in the complaint are true. • The defendant bears the burden of proving an affirmative defense. *Cf.* negative defense.

agency	A fiduciary relationship created by express or implied contract or by law, in which one party (the agent) may act on behalf of another party (the principal) and bind that other party by words or actions.
agent	One who is authorized to act for or in place of another; a representative. -- Also termed commissionaire. *Cf.* Principal.
aggressor doctrine	The principle precluding tort recovery for a plaintiff who acts in a way that would provoke a reasonable person to use physical force for protection, unless the defendant in turn uses excessive force to repel the plaintiff.
alcalde	[fr. Arabic al-qadi "the Cadi" or "the judge"] Spanish law. 1. Hist. A judicial officer. • The alcalde's functions typically resembled those of a justice of the peace. 2. The mayor of a Spanish or Spanish-American town, usu. with a judicial element. • This is the modern sense.
allocatur	[Law Latin] It is allowed. • This word formerly indicated that a writ, bill, or other pleading was allowed. It is still used today in Pennsylvania to denote permission to appeal. -- Also termed *allogatur.*
alternative liability	Liability arising from the tortious acts of two or more parties -- when the plaintiff proves that one of the defendants has caused harm but cannot prove which one caused it -- resulting in a shifting of the burden of proof to each defendant.
amicus curiae	[Latin "friend of the court"] A person who is not a party to a lawsuit but who petitions the court or is requested by the court to file a brief in the action because that person has a strong interest in the subject matter. -- Often shortened to *amicus.* -- Also termed friend of the court. Pl. *amici curiae.*

ancillary
administrator
A court-appointed administrator who oversees the distribution of the part of a decedent's estate located in a jurisdiction other than where the decedent was domiciled (the place of the main administration).

antecedent
adj. Earlier; preexisting; previous. -- antecedent (preceding thing), n. -- antecedence (quality or fact of going before), n.

arbitrary
adj. 1. Depending on individual discretion; specifically, determined by a judge rather than by fixed rules, procedures, or law. 2. (Of a judicial decision) founded on prejudice or preference rather than on reason or fact. • This type of decision is often termed arbitrary and capricious. *Cf.* capricious.

arbitration
n. A method of dispute resolution involving one or more neutral third parties who are usually agreed to by the disputing parties and whose decision is binding. -- Also termed (redundantly) binding arbitration. *Cf.* mediation.

arbitrator
n. A neutral person who resolves disputes between parties, esp. by means of formal arbitration. mediator; arbiter. -- Also termed (in Latin) *compromissarius*.

arguendo
[Latin "in arguing"] 1. For the sake of argument, 2. During the course of argument.

arise
vb. 1. To originate; to stem (from) <a federal claim arising under the U.S. Constitution>. 2. To result (from) <litigation routinely arises from such accidents>.

asportation
n. The act of carrying away or removing (property or a person). • Asportation is a necessary element of larceny. — Also termed carrying away. *See* larcenary.

assumption of risk The act or an instance of a prospective plaintiff's taking on the risk of loss, injury, or damage.

attorney-client relationship The formal legal representation of a person or client by a lawyer.

automobile guest statute A law that bars a nonpaying passenger in a noncommercial vehicle from suing the host-driver for damages resulting from the driver's ordinary negligence. • Though once common, guest statutes remain in force in only a few states. — Also termed automobile-guest statute.

bad faith *n.* Dishonesty of belief or purpose. — Also termed *mala fides.*

bailee A person who receives personal property from another as a bailment. *See* bailment.

bailment A delivery of personal property by one person (the bailor) to another (the bailee) who holds the property for a certain purpose under an express or implied-in-fact contract. • Unlike a sale or gift of personal property, a bailment involves a change in possession but not in title.

bailor A person who delivers personal property to another as a bailment. — Also spelled bailer.

bare licensee A licensee whose presence on the premises the occupier tolerates but does not necessarily approve, such as one who takes a shortcut across another's land. -- Also termed naked licensee; mere licensee.

beneficiary   *n.* 1. A person for whose benefit property is held in trust; especially, one designated to benefit from an appointment, disposition, or assignment (as in a will, insurance policy, etc.), or to receive something as a result of a legal arrangement or instrument. 2. A person to whom another is in a fiduciary relation, whether the relation is one of agency, guardianship, or trust. 3. A person who is initially entitled to enforce a promise, whether that person is the promisee or a third party. -- beneficiary, *adj.*

bona fide   *adj.* [Latin "in good faith"] 1. Made in good faith; without fraud or deceit. 2. Sincere; genuine. -- bona fide, *adv.*

breach   *n.* A violation or infraction of a law or obligation.

breach of trust   A trustee's violation of either the trust's terms or the trustee's general fiduciary obligations; the violation of a duty that equity imposes on a trustee, whether the violation was willful, fraudulent, negligent, or inadvertent. • A breach of trust subjects the trustee to removal and creates personal liability.

breach of warranty   A breach of an express or implied warranty relating to the title, quality, content, or condition of goods sold.

burden of proof   A party's duty to prove a disputed assertion or charge. • The burden of proof includes both the burden of persuasion and the burden of production. — Also termed *onus probandi*.

burglary   *n.* 1. The common-law offense of breaking and entering another's dwelling at night with the intent to commit a felony. 2. The modern statutory offense of breaking and entering any building -- not just a dwelling, and not only at night -- with the intent to commit a felony. • Some statutes make petit larceny an alternative to a felony for purposes of proving burglarious intent. -- Also termed (in sense 2) breaking and entering; statutory burglary. *Cf.* robbery.

business visitors   A person who is invited or permitted to enter or remain on another's land for a purpose directly or indirectly connected with the landowner's or possessor's business dealings. -- Also termed business invitee; business guest. *See* invitee.

but for cause   The cause without which the event could not have occurred. -- Also termed actual cause; cause in fact; factual cause.

bystander   One who is present when an event takes place, but who does not become directly involved in it.

case in chief   1. The evidence presented at trial by a party between the time the party calls the first witness and the time the party rests. 2. The part of a trial in which a party presents evidence to support the claim or defense. *Cf.* rebuttal.

causation   The causing or producing of an effect.

cause in fact   The cause without which the event could not have occurred. -- Also termed actual cause; cause in fact; factual cause.

certify   *vb.* 1. To authenticate or verify in writing. 2. To attest as being true or as meeting certain criteria. 3. (Of a court) to issue an order allowing a class of litigants to maintain a class action; to create (a class) for purposes of a class action.

certiorari   [Law Latin "to be more fully informed"] An extraordinary writ issued by an appellate court, at its discretion, directing a lower court to deliver the record in the case for review. • The writ evolved from one of the prerogative writs of the English Court of King's Bench, and in the United States it became a general appellate remedy. The U.S. Supreme Court uses certiorari to review most of the cases that it decides to hear. -- Abbr. *cert.* -- Also termed writ of *certiorari*. *Cf.* certification.

champertous   *adj.* Of, relating to, or characterized by champerty; constituting champerty.

champerty   *n.* An agreement between an officious intermeddler in a lawsuit and a litigant by which the intermeddler helps pursue the litigant's claim as consideration for receiving part of any judgment proceeds; specifically, an agreement to divide litigation proceeds between the owner of the litigated claim and a party unrelated to the lawsuit who supports or helps enforce the claim.

charge   *n.* A formal accusation of an offense as a preliminary step to prosecution. -- Also a jury charge. *vb.* To instruct a jury on matters of law.

charterparty   A contract by which a ship, or a principal part of it, is leased by the owner, especially to a merchant for the conveyance of goods on a predetermined voyage to one or more places or for a specified period of time; a special contract between the shipowner and charterer, especially for the carriage of goods by sea. — Also written charter-party; charter party. — Often shortened to charter. — Also termed charter agreement.

chattel   Movable or transferable property; personal property; especially, a physical object capable of manual delivery and not the subject matter of real property.

circumstantial evidence Evidence based on inference and not on personal knowledge or observation. -- Also termed indirect evidence; oblique evidence. *Cf.* direct evidence.

collateral estoppel 1. The binding effect of a judgment as to matters actually litigated and determined in one action on later controversies between the parties involving a different claim from that on which the original judgment was based. 2. A doctrine barring a party from relitigating an issue determined against that party in an earlier action, even if the second action differs significantly from the first one. -- Also termed issue preclusion; issue estoppel; direct estoppel; estoppel by judgment; estoppel by record; estoppel by verdict; cause-of-action estoppel; technical estoppel; estoppel *per rem judicatam*. *Cf. res judicata*.

collateral-source rule The doctrine that if an injured party receives compensation for the injuries from a source independent of the tortfeasor, the payment should not be deducted from the damages that the tortfeasor must pay. • Insurance proceeds are the most common collateral source. -- Also termed collateral-benefit rule.

commission *n.* 1. A warrant or authority, from the government or a court, that empowers the person named to execute official acts. 2. The authority under which a person transacts business for another. 3. A body of persons acting under lawful authority to perform certain public services.

common area 1. Landlord-tenant law. The realty that all tenants may use though the landlord retains control and responsibility over it. 2. An area owned and used in common by the residents of a condominium, subdivision, or planned-unit development. -- Also termed common elements.

common carriers   A commercial enterprise that holds itself out to the public as offering to transport freight or passengers for a fee. • A common carrier is generally required by law to transport freight or passengers or freight, without refusal, if the approved fare or charge is paid. -- Also termed public carrier.

common law   *n.* 1. The body of law derived from judicial decisions, rather than from statutes or constitutions; caselaw. *Cf.* statutory law.

comparative fault   A plaintiff's own negligence that proportionally reduces the damages recoverable from a defendant. -- Also termed comparative fault.

comparative negligence   A plaintiff's own negligence that proportionally reduces the damages recoverable from a defendant. — Also termed comparative fault.

compensatory damages   An amount awarded to a complainant to compensate for a proven injury or loss; damages that repay actual losses.

concerted action   An action that has been planned, arranged, and agreed on by parties acting together to further some scheme or cause, so that all involved are liable for the actions of one another. -- Also termed concert of action.

concurrent negligence   The negligence of two or more parties acting independently but causing the same damage.

concurrent tortfeasor   Two or more tortfeasors whose simultaneous actions cause injury to a third party. • Such tortfeasors are jointly and severally liable.

consent   *n.* 1. Agreement, approval, or permission as to some act or purpose, especially given voluntarily by a competent person; legally effective assent. • Consent is an affirmative defense to assault, battery, and related torts, as well as such torts as defamation, invasion of privacy, conversion, and trespass. Consent may be a defense to a crime if the victim has the capacity to consent and if the consent negates an element of the crime or thwarts the harm that the law seeks to prevent.

conservator   *n.* A guardian, protector, or preserver. • Conservator is the modern equivalent of the common-law guardian. Judicial appointment and supervision are still required, but a conservator has far more flexible authority than a guardian, including the same investment powers that a trustee enjoys. The Uniform Probate Code uses the term conservator, and Article 5 is representative of modern conservatorship laws. -- conservatorship, *n.*

consolidate   *vb.* 1. To combine or unify into one mass or body. 2. Civil procedure. To combine, through court order, two or more actions involving the same parties or issues into a single action ending in a single judgment or, sometimes, in separate judgments.

consortium   The benefits that one person, especially a spouse, is entitled to receive from another, including companionship, cooperation, affection, aid, financial support, and (between spouses) sexual relations.

conspiracy	*n.* An agreement by two or more persons to commit an unlawful act, coupled with an intent to achieve the agreement's objective, and (in most states) action or conduct that furthers the agreement; a combination for an unlawful purpose. • Conspiracy is a separate offense from the crime that is the object of the conspiracy. A conspiracy ends when the unlawful act has been committed or (in some states) when the agreement has been abandoned. A conspiracy does not automatically end if the conspiracy's object is defeated.
constructive fraud	Unintentional deception or misrepresentation that causes injury to another. -- Also termed legal fraud; fraud in contemplation of law; equitable fraud; fraud in equity.
constructive knowledge	Knowledge that one using reasonable care or diligence should have, and therefore that is attributed by law to a given person.
constructive notice	Notice arising by presumption of law from the existence of facts and circumstances that a party had a duty to take notice of, such as a registered deed or a pending lawsuit; notice presumed by law to have been acquired by a person and thus imputed to that person. -- Also termed legal notice.
contract	*n.* An agreement between two or more parties creating obligations that are enforceable or otherwise recognizable at law.
contribution	The right that gives one of several persons who are liable on a common debt the ability to recover proportionately from each of the others when that one person discharges the debt for the benefit of all; the right to demand that another who is jointly responsible for a third party's injury supply part of what is required to compensate the third party. — Also termed right of contribution.

contributory negligence	A plaintiff's own negligence that played a part in causing the plaintiff's injury and that is significant enough (in a few jurisdictions) to bar the plaintiff from recovering damages. • In most jurisdictions, this defense has been superseded by comparative negligence.
conversion	*n.* The act of changing from one form to another; the process of being exchanged.
corporation sole	A series of successive persons holding an office; a continuous legal personality that is attributed to successive holders of certain monarchical or ecclesiastical positions, such as kings, bishops, rectors, vicars, and the like. • This continuous personality is viewed, by legal fiction, as having the qualities of a corporation. *Cf.* corporation aggregate.
counterclaimant	*n.* A claim for relief asserted against an opposing party after an original claim has been made; especially, a defendant's claim in opposition to or as a setoff against the plaintiff's claim. -- Also termed counteraction; countersuit; cross-demand. *Cf.* cross-claim.
court of equity	A court that (1) has jurisdiction in equity, (2) administers and decides controversies in accordance with the rules, principles, and precedents of equity, and (3) follows the forms and procedures of chancery. *Cf.* court of law.
coverture	*n.* Archaic. The condition of being a married woman.
creditor	1. One to whom a debt is owed; one who gives credit for money or goods. -- Also termed debtee. 2. A person or entity with a definite claim against another, especially a claim that is capable of adjustment and liquidation. 3. Bankruptcy. A person or entity having a claim against the debtor predating the order for relief concerning the debtor.

cross claim	*n.* A claim asserted between codefendants or coplaintiffs in a case and that relates to the subject of the original claim or counterclaim. *See* FED. R. CIV. P. 13(g). -- Also termed cross-action; cross-suit. *Cf.* counterclaim.
cross-appeal	An appeal by the appellee, usually heard at the same time as the appellant's appeal.
cross-complaint	A claim asserted by a defendant against another party to the action. -- Also termed (in some jurisdictions) cross-petition.
custom	*n.* A practice that by its common adoption and long, unvarying habit has come to have the force of law.
damnum sine injuria	[Latin "damage without wrongful act"] Loss or harm that is incurred from something other than a wrongful act and occasions no legal remedy. • An example is a loss from fair trade competition. -- Also termed *damnum absque injuria*; *absque injuria damnum*; *absque injuria*. *Cf. injuria absque damno.*
de novo	*adj.* Anew.
decretal	*adj.* Of or relating to a decree.
deed of trust	A deed conveying title to real property to a trustee as security until the grantor repays a loan. • This type of deed resembles a mortgage. -- Also termed trust deed; trust indenture; indemnity mortgage; common-law mortgage.

defamation *n.* 1. The act of harming the reputation of another by making a false statement to a third person. • If the alleged defamation involves a matter of public concern, the plaintiff is constitutionally required to prove both the statement's falsity and the defendant's fault. 2. A false written or oral statement that damages another's reputation. *See* libel; slander. *Cf.* disparagement.

defective *adj.* (Of a product) containing an imperfection or short-coming in a part essential to the product's safe operation.

delict *n.* [Latin *delictum* "an offense"] Roman & civil law. A violation of the law; especially, a wrongful act or omission giving rise to a claim for compensation.

delictual actions *adj.* Of, relating to, or involving a delict; tortious. -- Also termed delictal.

delinquency *n.* 1. A failure or omission; a violation of a law or duty. *See* juvenile delinquency. 2. A debt that is overdue in payment.

demurrer [Law French *demorer* "to wait or stay"] A pleading stating that although the facts alleged in a complaint may be true, they are insufficient for the plaintiff to state a claim for relief and for the defendant to frame an answer. • In most juris-dictions, such a pleading is now termed a motion to dis-miss, but the demurrer is still used in a few states, including California, Nebraska, and Pennsylvania. *Cf.* denial.

deposition A witness's out-of-court testimony that is reduced to writing (usually by a court reporter) for later use in court or for discovery purposes.

derivative action   A lawsuit arising from an injury to another person, such as a husband's action for loss of consortium arising from a injury to his wife caused by a third person.

dictum   *n.* 1. A statement of opinion or belief considered authoritative because of the dignity of the person making it.   2.   A familiar rule; a maxim.   3.   *obiter dictum. Pl. dicta.*

dilatory exception   An exception intended to delay but not dismiss an action.

direct evidence   Evidence that is based on personal knowledge or observation and that, if true, proves a fact without inference or presumption. -- Also termed positive evidence. *Cf.* circumstantial evidence; negative evidence.

directed verdict   A ruling by a trial judge taking a case from the jury because the evidence will permit only one reasonable verdict. -- Also termed instructed verdict.

discharge   *n.* Any method by which a legal duty is extinguished; especially, the payment of a debt or satisfaction of some other obligation.

disclaimer   *n.* 1. A renunciation of one's legal right or claim. 2. A repudiation of another's legal right or claim.   3.   A writing that contains such a renunciation or repudiation.   4. renunciation. -- disclaim, *vb.*

discovery   *n.* Compulsory disclosure, at a party's request, of information that relates to the litigation <the plaintiff filed a motion to compel discovery>. See Fed. R. Civ. P. 26-37; Fed. R. Crim. P. 16. • The primary discovery devices are interrogatories, depositions, requests for admissions, and requests for production. Although discovery typically comes from parties, courts also allow limited discovery from nonparties.

discovery rule   The rule that a limitations period does not begin to run until the plaintiff discovers (or reasonably should have discovered) the injury giving rise to the claim. • The discovery rule usually applies to injuries that are inherently difficult to detect, such as those resulting from medical malpractice. *See* statute of limitations. *Cf.* Occurrence Rule.

dissolution   The termination of a previously existing partnership upon the occurrence of an event specified in the partnership agreement, such as a partner's withdrawal from the partnership, or as specified by law.

diversity   *n.* 1. Diversity of Citizenship. 2. Ethnic, socioeconomic, and gender heterogeneity within a group; the combination within a population of people with different backgrounds. • The Supreme Court has found diversity in education to be a compelling government interest that can support a narrowly tailored affirmative-action plan.

diversity of citizenship   A basis for federal-court jurisdiction that exists when (1) a case is between citizens of different states, or between a citizen of a state and an alien, and (2) the matter in controversy exceeds a specific value.

doctrine of attractive nuisance   A dangerous condition that may attract children onto land, thereby causing a risk to their safety.

doctrine of comparative negligence

A plaintiff's own negligence that proportionally reduces the damages recoverable from a defendant. -- Also termed comparative fault.

domestic animal

1. An animal that is customarily devoted to the service of humankind at the time and in the place where it is helped. 2. Any animal that is statutorily so designated.

dram shop statute

A statute allowing a plaintiff to recover damages from a commercial seller of alcoholic beverages for the plaintiff's injuries caused by a customer's intoxication. -- Also termed civil-liability act; civil-damage law.

duty

A legal obligation that is owed or due to another and that needs to be satisfied; an obligation for which somebody else has a corresponding right.

duty of loyalty

A person's duty not to engage in self-dealing or otherwise use his or her position to further personal interests rather than those of the beneficiary.

egress

1. The act of going out or leaving. 2. The right or ability to leave; a way of exit. *Cf.* ingress.

ejectment

1. The ejection of an owner or occupier from property. 2. A legal action by which a person wrongfully ejected from property seeks to recover possession, damages, and costs. 3. The writ by which such an action is begun. • The essential allegations in an action for ejectment are that (1) the plaintiff has title to the land, (2) the plaintiff has been wrongfully dispossessed or ousted, and (3) the plaintiff has suffered damages. -- Also termed action of ejectment; action for the recovery of land; ejection.

eminent domain The inherent power of a governmental entity to take privately owned property, especially land, and convert it to public use, subject to reasonable compensation for the taking.

empirical *adj.* Of, relating to, or based on experience, experiment, or observation. — Also termed empiric.

employee A person who works in the service of another person (the employer) under an express or implied contract of hire, under which the employer has the right to control the details of work performance. -- Also spelled employe. *Cf.* independent contractor.

enjoin *vb.* To legally prohibit or restrain by injunction.

enterprise liability Liability imposed on each member of an industry responsible for manufacturing a harmful or defective product, allotted by each manufacturer's market share of the industry. -- Also termed industry-wide liability. *See* market-share liability.

estate The amount, degree, nature, and quality of a person's interest in land or other property; especially, a real-estate interest that may become possessory, the ownership being measured in terms of duration.

exculpatory contracts A contractual provision relieving a party from liability resulting from a negligent or wrongful act. • A will or a trust may contain an exculpatory clause purporting to immunize a fiduciary from a breach of duty; the clause may reduce the degree of care and prudence required of the fiduciary. But courts generally find that if an exculpatory clause in a will or trust seeks to confer absolute immunity, it is void as being against public policy.

executor   *n.* 1. One who performs or carries out some act. 2. A person named by a testator to carry out the provisions in the testator's will. *Cf.* administrator.

executrix   *n.* Archaic. A female executor. -- Abbr. exrx. -- Also termed executress. *Pl.* executrixes. *See* executor.

exemplary damages   Damages awarded in addition to actual damages when the defendant acted with recklessness, malice, or deceit; specifically, damages assessed by way of penalizing the wrongdoer or making an example to others. • Punitive damages, which are intended to punish and thereby deter blameworthy conduct, are generally not recoverable for breach of contract. -- Also termed vindictive damages; punitive damages; presumptive damages; added damages; aggravated damages; speculative damages; imaginary damages; smart money; punies.

expert witness   A witness qualified by knowledge, skill, experience, training, or education to provide a scientific, technical, or other specialized opinion about the evidence or a fact issue. -- Also termed skilled witness.

false arrest   An arrest made without proper legal authority. *Cf.* false imprisonment.

family purpose doctrine   The principle that a vehicle's owner is liable for injuries or damage caused by a family member's negligent driving. • Many states have abolished this rule. -- Also termed family-purpose doctrine; family-automobile doctrine; family-car doctrine. *Cf.* guest statute.

fee simple   An interest in land that, being the broadest property interest allowed by law, endures until the current holder dies without heirs; especially, a fee simple absolute. -- Often shortened to fee. -- Also termed estate in fee simple; tenancy in fee; exclusive ownership; fee-simple title; *feudum simplex*.

felony   n. A serious crime usually punishable by imprisonment for more than one year or by death. • Examples include burglary, arson, rape, and murder. -- Also termed major crime; serious crime. *Cf.* misdemeanor.

felony-murder rule   The doctrine holding that any death resulting from the commission or attempted commission of a felony is murder. • Most states restrict this rule to inherently dangerous felonies such as rape, arson, robbery, and burglary. *Cf.* misdemeano-manslaughter rule.

fiat   n. [Latin "let it be done"] 1. An order or decree, especially an arbitrary one. 2. A court decree, especially one relating to a routine matter such as scheduling. -- Also termed fiaunt.

fiduciary duty   A duty of utmost good faith, trust, confidence, and candor owed by a fiduciary (such as a lawyer or corporate officer) to the beneficiary (such as a lawyer's client or a shareholder); a duty to act with the highest degree of honesty and loyalty toward another person and in the best interests of the other person (such as the duty that one partner owes to another).

filial consortium   A child's society, affection, and companionship given to a parent.

Fireman's Rule   A doctrine holding that a firefighter, police officer, or other emergency professional may not hold a person, usually a property owner, liable for unintentional injuries suffered by the professional in responding to the situation created or caused by the person.

first impression	Case of first impression. A case that presents the court with an issue of law that has not previously been decided by any controlling legal authority in that jurisdiction.
foreclosure	A legal proceeding to terminate a mortgagor's interest in property, instituted by the lender (the mortgagee) either to gain title or to force a sale in order to satisfy the unpaid debt secured by the property. *Cf.* repossession.
foreseeability	*n.* The quality of being reasonably anticipatable. • Foreseeability, along with actual causation, is an element of proximate cause in tort law. -- foreseeable, *adj.*
franchisee	One who is granted a franchise.
franchisor	One who grants a franchise. -- Also spelled franchiser.
fraud	*n.* A knowing misrepresentation of the truth or concealment of a material fact to induce another to act to his or her detriment. • Fraud is usually a tort, but in some cases (especially when the conduct is willful) it may be a crime. -- Also termed intentional fraud.
fraudulent concealment	The affirmative suppression or hiding, with the intent to deceive or defraud, of a material fact or circumstance that one is legally (or, sometimes, morally) bound to reveal. -- Also termed hidden fraud.
general deterrence	A goal of criminal law generally, or of a specific conviction and sentence, to discourage people from committing crimes.

general federal common law In the period before *Erie v. Tompkins* (304 U.S. 64, 58 S.Ct. 817 (1938)), the judge-made law developed by federal courts in deciding disputes in diversity-of-citizenship cases. • Since *Erie*, a federal court has been bound to apply the substantive law of the state in which it sits. So even though there is a "federal common law," there is no longer a general federal common law applicable to all disputes heard in federal court.

general intent The intent to perform an act even though the actor does not desire the consequences that result.

genuine issue of material fact In the law of summary judgments, a triable, substantial, or real question of fact supported by substantial evidence. • An issue of this kind precludes entry of summary judgment.

grantor One who conveys property to another.

gravamen The substantial point or essence of a claim, grievance, or complaint.

gross negligence 1. A lack of slight diligence or care. 2. A conscious, voluntary act or omission in reckless disregard of a legal duty and of the consequences to another party, who may typically recover exemplary damages. -- Also termed reckless negligence; wanton negligence; willful negligence; willful and wanton negligence; hazardous negligence, *magna neglegentia*.

guardian ad litem A guardian, usually a lawyer, appointed by the court to appear in a lawsuit on behalf of an incompetent or minor party. -- *Abbr*. GAL. -- Also termed special advocate; special guardian; law guardian. *Cf*. next friend; attorney ad litem.

guest
1. A person who is entertained or to whom hospitality is extended. 2. A person who pays for services at an establishment, especially a hotel or restaurant.

harm
n. Injury, loss, damage; material or tangible detriment.

hedonic damages
Damages that attempt to compensate for the loss of the pleasure of being alive. • Such damages are not allowed in most jurisdictions. -- Also termed (erroneously) hedonistic damages.

heir
A person who, under the laws of intestacy, is entitled to receive an intestate decedent's property. *Cf.* ancestor. -- Also termed legal heir; heir at law; lawful heir; heir general; legitimate heir.

hold
vb. 1. To possess by a lawful title 2. (Of a court) to adjudge or decide as a matter of law (as opposed to fact). *Cf.* find. 3. To direct and bring about officially; to conduct according to law. 4. To keep in custody or under an obligation. 5. To take or have an estate from another; to have an estate on condition of paying rent or performing service. 6. To conduct or preside at; to convoke, open, and direct the operations of. 7. To possess or occupy; to be in possession and administration of.

imminently dangerous
(Of a person, behavior, activity, or thing) reasonably certain to place life and limb in peril. • This term is relevant in several legal contexts. For example, if a mental condition renders a person imminently dangerous to self or others, he or she may be committed to a mental hospital. And the imminently dangerous behavior of pointing a gun at someone's head could subject the actor to criminal and tort liability. Further, the manufacturer of an imminently dangerous product may be held to a strict-liability standard in tort.

implead *vb.* 1. To bring (someone) into a lawsuit; especially, to bring (a new party) into the action. *Cf.* interplead. 2. Hist. To bring an action against; to accuse. -- Formerly also spelled emplead; empleet.

implied assumption of the risk An assumption based on the plaintiff's conduct that seems to consent to relieve another of liability for negligence. • For this defense to apply, the plaintiff's conduct must suggest (1) open consent to the risk, (2) voluntary participation in the activity, and (3) full understanding of the danger. *See volenti non fit injuria.*

imputation *n.* The act or an instance of imputing something, especially fault or crime, to a person; an accusation or charge.

imputed knowledge Knowledge attributed to a given person, especially because of the person's legal responsibility for another's conduct. •

in loco parentis *adv. & adj.* [Latin "in the place of a parent"] Of, relating to, or acting as a temporary guardian or caretaker of a child, taking on all or some of the responsibilities of a parent. •

in toto *adv.* [Latin "in whole"] Completely; as a whole.

incurred risk The act or an instance of a prospective plaintiff's taking on the risk of loss, injury, or damage. -- Also termed assumption of risk.

indemnification *n.* 1. The action of compensating for loss or damage sustained. 2. The compensation so made.

indemnity   *n.* 1. A duty to make good any loss, damage, or liability incurred by another. 2. The right of an injured party to claim reimbursement for its loss, damage, or liability from a person who has such a duty. 3. Reimbursement or compensation for loss, damage, or liability in tort; especially, the right of a party who is secondarily liable to recover from the party who is primarily liable for reimbursement of expenditures paid to a third party for injuries resulting from a violation of a common-law duty. *Cf.* contribution. -- indemnitory, *adj.*

independent contractor   One who is entrusted to undertake a specific project but who is left free to do the assigned work and to choose the method for accomplishing it. • It does not matter whether the work is done for pay or gratuitously. Unlike an employee, an independent contractor who commits a wrong while carrying out the work does not create liability for the one who did the hiring. -- Also termed contract labor. *Cf.* employee.

indivisible   *adj.* Not separable into parts; held by two or more people in undivided shares.

informed consent doctrine   1. A person's agreement to allow something to happen, made with full knowledge of the risks involved and the alternatives. 2. A patient's knowing choice about a medical treatment or procedure, made after a physician or other healthcare provider discloses whatever information a reasonably prudent provider in the medical community would give to a patient regarding the risks involved in the proposed treatment or procedure. — Also termed knowing consent.

infra   *adv. & adj.* [Latin "below"] Later in this text. • *Infra* is used as a citational signal to refer to a later-cited authority. In medieval Latin, *infra* also acquired the sense "within." *Cf. intra; supra.*

ingress   1. The act of entering.   2. The right or ability to enter; access. *Cf.* egress.

inherently dangerous   (Of an activity or thing) requiring special precautions at all times to avoid injury; dangerous *per se*. *See* dangerous instrumentality; inherently dangerous activity.

injury   *n.* 1. The violation of another's legal right, for which the law provides a remedy; a wrong or injustice.   *See* wrong. 2. Scots law. Anything said or done in breach of a duty not to do it, if harm results to another in person, character, or property.   3. Any harm or damage. • Some authorities distinguish harm from injury, holding that while harm denotes any personal loss or detriment, injury involves an actionable invasion of a legally protected interest.

injunctive   *adj.* That has the quality of directing or ordering; of or relating to an injunction. -- Also termed injunctional.

innkeeper   A person who, for compensation, keeps open a public house for the lodging and entertainment of travelers. • A keeper of a boarding house is usually not considered an innkeeper. -- Also termed hotelkeeper.

insane   *adj.* Mentally deranged; suffering from one or more delusions or false beliefs that (1) have no foundation in reason or reality, (2) are not credible to any reasonable person of sound mind, and (3) cannot be overcome in a sufferer's mind by any amount of evidence or argument.   *See* insanity.

insanity   Any mental disorder severe enough that it prevents a person from having legal capacity and excuses the person from criminal or civil responsibility. • Insanity is a legal, not a medical, standard. — Also termed legal insanity; lunacy. *Cf.* sanity.

insurer　One who agrees, by contract, to assume the risk of another's loss and to compensate for that loss. -- Also termed underwriter; insurance underwriter; carrier; assurer (for life insurance).

intangible　*n.* Something that lacks a physical form; an abstraction, such as responsibility; espeially, an asset that is not corporeal, such as intellectual property.

intentional infliction of emotional distress　The tort of intentionally or recklessly causing another person severe emotional distress through one's extreme or outrageous acts. • In a few jurisdictions, a physical manifestation of the mental suffering is required for the plaintiff to recover. -- Also termed (in some states) outrage. See emotional distress. *Cf.* negligent infliction of emotional distress. -- Abbr. IIED.

interlocutory appeal　An appeal that occurs before the trial court's final ruling on the entire case. • Some interlocutory appeals involve legal points necessary to the determination of the case, while others involve collateral orders that are wholly separate from the merits of the action.

interrogatories　*n.* A written question (usually in a set of questions) submitted to an opposing party in a lawsuit as part of discovery.

intervening cause
An event that comes between the initial event in a sequence and the end result, thereby altering the natural course of events that might have connected a wrongful act to an injury. • If the intervening cause is strong enough to relieve the wrongdoer of any liability, it becomes a superseding cause. A dependent intervening cause is one that is not an act and is never a superseding cause. An independent intervening cause is one that operates on a condition produced by an antecedent cause but in no way resulted from that cause. -- Also termed intervening act; intervening agency; intervening force; independent intervening cause; efficient intervening cause; supervening cause; *novus actus interveniens; nova causa interveniens. See* superseding cause.

intestate
n. One who has died without a valid will. *Cf.* testator.

inverse condemnation
An action brought by a property owner for compensation from a governmental entity that has taken the owner's property without bringing formal condemnation proceedings. -- Also termed constructive condemnation; reverse condemnation.

invitee
A person who has an express or implied invitation to enter or use another's premises, such as a business visitor or a member of the public to whom the premises are held open. • The occupier has a duty to inspect the premises and to warn the invitee of dangerous conditions. — Also termed licensee with an interest. *Cf.* licensee (2); trespasser; business visitor.

joinder
n. The uniting of parties or claims in a single lawsuit. *Cf.* consolidation.

joint enterprise
An undertaking by two or more persons with an equal right to direct and benefit from the endeavor, as a result of which one participant's negligence may be imputed to the others. -- Also termed common enterprise.

joint tortfeasors   Two or more tortfeasors who contributed to the claimant's injury and who may be joined as defendants in the same lawsuit. See joint and several liability.

joint and several liability   Liability that may be apportioned either among two or more parties or to only one or a few select members of the group, at the adversary's discretion. • Thus, each liable party is individually responsible for the entire obligation, but a paying party may have a right of contribution and indemnity from nonpaying parties.

jointly liable   Liability shared by two or more parties.

judgment   A court's final determination of the rights and obligations of the parties in a case. • The term judgment includes an equitable decree and any order from which an appeal lies.

judgment as a matter of law   A judgment rendered during a jury trial -- either before or after the jury's verdict -- against a party on a given issue when there is no legally sufficient basis for a jury to find for that party on that issue. • In federal practice, the term judgment as a matter of law has replaced both the directed verdict and the judgment notwithstanding the verdict. *Cf.* Summary judgment.

judgment creditor   A person having a legal right to enforce execution of a judgment for a specific sum of money.

judgment *non obstante veredicto*   A judgment entered for one party even though a jury verdict has been rendered for the opposing party. -- Also termed judgment *non obstante veredicto.* -- Abbr. JNOV; judgment N.O.V. *See* judgment as a matter of law.

judicial notice	A court's acceptance, for purposes of convenience and without requiring a party's proof, of a well-known and indisputable fact; the court's power to accept such a fact. -- Also termed judicial cognizance; judicial knowledge.
justification	*n.* 1. A lawful or sufficient reason for one's acts or omissions; any fact that prevents an act from being wrongful. 2. A showing, in court, of a sufficient reason why a defendant acted in a way that, in the absence of the reason, would constitute the offense with which the defendant is charged.
kangaroo court	1. A self-appointed tribunal or mock court in which the principles of law and justice are disregarded, perverted, or parodied. • Kangaroo courts may be assembled by various groups, such as prisoners in a jail (to settle disputes between inmates) and players on a baseball team (to "punish" teammates who commit fielding errors). 2. A court or tribunal characterized by unauthorized or irregular procedures, especially so as to render a fair proceeding impossible. 3. A sham legal proceeding. • The term's origin is uncertain, but it appears to be an Americanism. It has been traced to 1853 in the American West. "Kangaroo" might refer to the illogical leaps between "facts" and conclusions, or to the hapless defendant's quick bounce from court to gallows.
landlord-tenant	The familiar legal relationship existing between the lessor and lessee of real estate. -- Also termed landlord-and-tenant relationship. *See* lease.
landlord	1. At common law, the feudal lord who retained the fee of the land. -- Sometimes shortened to lord. 2. One who leases real property to another. -- Also termed (in sense 2) lessor.
landowner	One who owns land.

larceny   *n.* The unlawful taking and carrying away of someone else's personal property with the intent to deprive the possessor of it permanently. • Common-law larceny has been broadened by some statutes to include embezzlement and false pretenses, all three of which are often subsumed under the statutory crime of "theft."

last clear chance rule   The rule that a plaintiff who was contributorily negligent may nonetheless recover from the defendant if the defendant had the last opportunity to prevent the harm but failed to use reasonable care to do so (in other words, if the defendant's negligence is later in time than the plaintiff's). • This doctrine allows the plaintiff to rebut the contributory-negligence defense in the few jurisdictions where contributory negligence completely bars recovery. -- Also termed discovered-peril doctrine; humanitarian doctrine; last-opportunity doctrine; subsequent-negligence doctrine; supervening-negligence doctrine.

lessee   One who has a possessory interest in real or personal property under a lease; tenant.

lessor   One who conveys real or personal property by lease; especially, landlord.

liability insurance   Insurance that broadly covers an insured's liability exposure, including product liability, contractual liability, and premises liability.

libel   *vb.* To defame (someone) in a permanent medium, especially in writing.

licensee   1. One to whom a license is granted. 2. One who has permission to enter or use another's premises, but only for one's own purposes and not for the occupier's benefit.

licensee by invitation
One who is expressly or impliedly permitted to enter another's premises to transact business with the owner or occupant or to perform an act benefiting the owner or occupant.

life estate
An estate held only for the duration of a specified person's life, usually the possessor's. • Most life estates -- created, for example, by a grant "to Jane for life" -- are beneficial interests under trusts, the corpus often being personal property, not real property. -- Also termed estate for life; legal life estate; life tenancy.

lineal heirs
A person who is either an ancestor or a descendant of the decedent, such as a parent or a child. *Cf.* collateral heir.

locality rule
1. The doctrine that, in a professional-malpractice suit, the standard of care to be applied to the professional's conduct is the reasonable care exercised by similar professionals in the same vicinity and professional community. 2. The doctrine that, in determining the appropriate amount of attorney's fees to be awarded in a suit, the proper basis is the rate charged by similar attorneys for similar work in the vicinity.

locus in quo
[Latin "place in which"] T he place where something is alleged to have occurred.

loss of chance doctrine
A rule in some states providing a claim against a doctor who has engaged in medical malpractice that, although it does not result in a particular injury, decreases or eliminates the chance of surviving or recovering from the preexisting condition for which the doctor was consulted. -- Also termed lost-chance doctrine; increased-risk-of-harm doctrine.

loss of consortium

1. A loss of the benefits that one spouse is entitled to receive from the other, including companionship, cooperation, aid, affection, and sexual relations. 2. A similar loss of benefits that one is entitled to receive from a parent or child. *See* consortium.

lost profits

1. Contracts. A measure of damages that allows a seller to collect the profits that would have been made on the sale if the buyer had not breached. 2. Patents. A measure of damages set by estimating the net amount lost by a plaintiff-inventor because of the infringing defendant's actions.

lunatic

adj. Archaic. An insane person. *See* insane.

majority

The status of one who has attained the age (usually 18) at which one is entitled to full civic rights and considered legally capable of handling one's own affairs. *See* age of majority. *Cf.* minority.

malice

n. 1. The intent, without justification or excuse, to commit a wrongful act. 2. Reckless disregard of the law or of a person's legal rights. 3. Ill will; wickedness of heart. • This sense is most typical in nonlegal contexts.

malicious prosecution

1. The institution of a criminal or civil proceeding for an improper purpose and without probable cause. • The tort requires an adversary to prove four elements: (1) the initiation or continuation of a lawsuit; (2) lack of probable cause; (3) malice; and (4) favorable termination of the lawsuit. 2. The tort claim resulting from the institution of such a proceeding. • Once a wrongful prosecution has ended in the defendant's favor, he or she may sue for tort damages. -- Also termed (in the context of civil proceedings) malicious use of process; (archaically) malicious institution of civil proceedings. *Cf.* abuse of process; vexatious suit.

malpractice   An instance of negligence or incompetence on the part of a professional. -- Also termed professional negligence.

manifestly erroneous   An error that is plain and indisputable and that amounts to a complete disregard of the controlling law or the credible evidence in the record.

maritime law   The body of law governing marine commerce and navigation, the carriage at sea of persons and property, and marine affairs in general; the rules governing contract, tort, and workers'-compensation claims or relating to commerce on or over water. -- Also termed admiralty; admiralty law; sea law. *Cf.* general maritime law; law of the sea.

market share   The percentage of the market for a product that a firm supplies, usually calculated by dividing the firm's output by the total market output.

market share liability   Liability that is imposed, usually severally, on each member of an industry, based on each member's share of the market or respective percentage of the product that is placed on the market. • This theory of liability usually applies only in the situation in which a plaintiff cannot trace the harmful exposure to a particular product, as when several products contain a fungible substance. For example, it is sometimes applied to a claim that the plaintiff was harmed by exposure to asbestos. *See* enterprise liability.

Mary Carter agreements

A contract (usually a secret one) by which one or more, but not all, codefendants settle with the plaintiff and obtain a release, along with a provision granting them a portion of any recovery from the nonparticipating codefendants. • In a Mary Carter agreement, the participating codefendants agree to remain parties to the lawsuit and, if no recovery is awarded against the nonparticipating codefendants, to pay the plaintiff a settled amount. Such an agreement is void as against public policy in some states but is valid in others if disclosed to the jury.

master

n. One who has personal authority over another's services; specifically, a principal who employs another to perform one or more services and who controls or has the right to control the physical conduct of the other in the performance of the services; employer.

material

adj. 1. Of or relating to matter; physical. 2. Having some logical connection with the consequential facts. 3. Of such a nature that knowledge of the item would affect a person's decision-making; significant; essential. *Cf.* relevant.

medical expenses

An expense for medical treatment or healthcare, such as drug costs and health-insurance premiums. • Medical expenses are tax-deductible to the extent that the amounts (less insurance reimbursements) exceed a certain percentage of adjusted gross income.

medical malpractice

A doctor's failure to exercise the degree of care and skill that a physician or surgeon of the same medical specialty would use under similar circumstances. -- Often shortened to med. mal.

Megan's Law   A statute that requires sex offenders who are released from prison to register with a local board and that provides the means to disseminate information about the registrants to the community in which they dwell. • Although many of these statutes were enacted in the late 1980s, they took their popular name from Megan Kanka of New Jersey, a seven-year-old who in 1994 was raped and murdered by a twice-convicted sex offender who lived across the street from her house. All states have these laws, but only some require community notification (as by publishing offenders' pictures in local newspapers); in others, people must call a state hotline or submit names of persons they suspect. -- Also termed registration and community-notification law; community-notification law.

minor   *n.* A person who has not reached full legal age; a child or juvenile. — Also termed infant. *Cf.* adult.

misdirection   An erroneous jury instruction that may be grounds for reversing a verdict.

misfeasance   *n.* 1. A lawful act performed in a wrongful manner. 2. More broadly, a transgression or trespass; malfeasance. *Cf.* nonfeasance. -- misfeasant, *adj.* -- misfeasor, *n.*

mitigation of damages doctrine   The principle requiring a plaintiff, after an injury or breach of contract, to make reasonable efforts to alleviate the effects of the injury or breach. • If the defendant can show that the plaintiff failed to mitigate damages, the plaintiff's recovery may be reduced. -- Also termed avoidable-consequences doctrine.

mortgagee   One to whom property is mortgaged; the mortgage creditor, or lender. -- Also termed mortgage-holder.

mortgagor   One who mortgages property; the mortgage-debtor, or borrower. -- Also spelled mortgager; mortgageor.

motion in limine   A pretrial request that certain inadmissible evidence not be referred to or offered at trial. • Typically, a party makes this motion when it believes that mere mention of the evidence during trial would be highly prejudicial and could not be remedied by an instruction to disregard. If, after the motion is granted, the opposing party mentions or attempts to offer the evidence in the jury's presence, a mistrial may be ordered. A ruling on a motion in limine does not always preserve evidentiary error for appellate purposes. To raise such an error on appeal, a party may be required to formally object when the evidence is actually admitted or excluded during trial.

negligence   *n.* 1. The failure to exercise the standard of care that a reasonably prudent person would have exercised in a similar situation; any conduct that falls below the legal standard established to protect others against unreasonable risk of harm, except for conduct that is intentionally, wantonly, or willfully disregardful of others' rights. • The term denotes culpable carelessness. — Also termed actionable negligence; ordinary negligence; simple negligence. 2. A tort grounded in this failure, usually expressed in terms of the following elements: duty, breach of duty, causation, and damages.

negligence *per se*   Negligence established as a matter of law, so that breach of the duty is not a jury question. • Negligence *per se* usually arises from a statutory violation. -- Also termed legal negligence.

negligent infliction of emotional distress The tort of causing another severe emotional distress through one's negligent conduct. • Most courts will allow a plaintiff to recover damages for emotional distress if the defendant's conduct results in physical contact with the plaintiff or, when no contact occurs, if the plaintiff is in the zone of danger. *See* emotional distress; zone-of-danger rule. *Cf.* intentional infliction of emotional distress. -- Abbr. NIED.

net leases A lease in which the lessee pays rent plus property expenses (such as taxes and insurance).

next friend A person who appears in a lawsuit to act for the benefit of an incompetent or minor plaintiff, but who is not a party to the lawsuit and is not appointed as a guardian. -- Also termed *prochein ami*. *Cf.* guardian *ad litem*.

nisi *adj.* [Latin "unless"] (Of a court's ex parte ruling or grant of relief) having validity unless the adversely affected party appears and shows cause why it should be withdrawn. *See* decree *nisi*.

nisi prius [Latin "unless before then"] A civil trial court in which, unlike in an appellate court, issues are tried before a jury. • The term is obsolete in the United States except in New York and Oklahoma. -- Abbr. n.p. -- Also termed *nisi prius court*.

nominal damages 1. A trifling sum awarded when a legal injury is suffered but when there is no substantial loss or injury to be compensated. 2. A small amount fixed as damages for breach of contract without regard to the amount of harm. -- Also termed contemptuous damages. *Cf.* substantial damages.

nonfeasance *n.* The failure to act when a duty to act existed. *Cf.* malfeasance; misfeasance; feasance.

nonsuited   *n.* 1. A plaintiff's voluntary dismissal of a case or of a defendant, without a decision on the merits. • Under the Federal Rules of Civil Procedure, a voluntary dismissal is equivalent to a nonsuit. -- Also termed voluntary discontinuance. 2. A court's dismissal of a case or of a defendant because the plaintiff has failed to make out a legal case or to bring forward sufficient evidence. -- Also termed involuntary nonsuit; compulsory nonsuit. *See* judgment of nonsuit.

normative   *adj.* Establishing or conforming to a norm or standard.

nuisance   1. A condition, activity, or situation (such as a loud noise or foul odor) that interferes with the use or enjoyment of property; especiall, a nontransitory condition or persistent activity that either injures the physical condition of adjacent land or interferes with its use or with the enjoyment of easements on the land or of public highways. • Liability might or might not arise from the condition or situation. -- Formerly also termed annoyance.

nuisance *per accidens*   A nuisance existing because of the circumstances of the use or the particular location. • For example, a machine emitting high-frequency sound may be a nuisance only if a person's dog lives near enough to the noise to be disturbed by it. -- Also termed nuisance in fact.

nuisances *per se*   Interference so severe that it would constitute a nuisance under any circumstances; a nuisance regardless of location or circumstances of use, such as a leaky nuclear-waste storage facility. -- Also termed nuisance at law; absolute nuisance.

objective standard   A legal standard that is based on conduct and perceptions external to a particular person. • In tort law, for example, the reasonable-person standard is considered an objective standard because it does not require a determination of what the defendant was thinking.

occupant 1. One who has possessory rights in, or control over, certain property or premises. 2. One who acquires title by occupancy.

offset *n.* Something (such as an amount or claim) that balances or compensates for something else; setoff.

omission *n.* 1. A failure to do something; especially, a neglect of duty. 2. The act of leaving something out. 3. The state of having been left out or of not having been done. 4. Something that is left out, left undone, or otherwise neglected. — Formerly also termed omittance. — omit, *vb.* — omissive, omissible, *adj.*

owner One who has the right to possess, use, and convey something; a person in whom one or more interests are vested. • An owner may have complete property in the thing or may have parted with some interests in it (as by granting an easement or making a lease). *See* ownership.

pain and suffering Physical discomfort or emotional distress compensable as an element of noneconomic damages in torts. *See* damages.

parental consortium A parent's society, affection, and companionship given to a child.

pari materia [Latin "in the same matter"] *adj.* On the same subject; relating to the same matter. • It is a canon of construction that statutes that are in *pari materia* may be construed together, so that inconsistencies in one statute may be resolved by looking at another statute on the same subject.

partnership A voluntary association of two or more persons who jointly own and carry on a business for profit. *Cf.* joint venture; strategic alliance.

pecuniary damages	Damages that can be estimated and monetarily compensated. • Although this phrase appears in many old cases, it is now widely considered a redundancy -- since damages are always pecuniary.
pecuniary losses	A loss of money or of something having monetary value.
penal statute	A law that defines an offense and prescribes its corresponding fine, penalty, or punishment. -- Also termed penal law; punitive statute.
pendent	adj. 1. Not yet decided; pending. 2. Of or relating to pendent jurisdiction or pendent-party jurisdiction. 3. Contingent; dependent.
per curiam	adv. & adj. [Latin] By the court as a whole.
per se	adv. & adj. 1. Of, in, or by itself; standing alone, without reference to additional facts. 2. As a matter of law.
permanent damage	Damages for past, present, and future harm that cannot be avoided or remedied.
permanent injunction	An injunction granted after a final hearing on the merits. • Despite its name, a permanent injunction does not necessarily last forever. -- Also termed perpetual injunction; final injunction.
persuasive authority	Authority that carries some weight but is not binding on a court.

petition for declaratory judgment	A binding adjudication that establishes the rights and other legal relations of the parties without providing for or ordering enforcement. • Declaratory judgments are often sought, for example, by insurance companies in determining whether a policy covers a given insured or peril. -- Also termed declaratory decree; declaration.
possession	The fact of having or holding property in one's power; the exercise of dominion over property.
possessor	One who has possession of real or personal property; especially, a person who is in occupancy of land with the intent to control it or has been but no longer is in that position, but no one else has gained occupancy or has a right to gain it
possibility	An event that may or may not happen.
preexisting condition	A physical or mental condition evident during the period before the effective date of a medical-insurance policy.
prejudice	*n.* Damage or detriment to one's legal rights or claims.
prejudicial errors	An error that affects a party's substantive rights or the case's outcome, and thus is grounds for reversal if the party properly objected. -- Also termed harmful error; prejudicial error; fatal error.
premises	*n.* A previous statement or contention from which a conclusion is deduced.
premises liability	A landowner's or landholder's tort liability for conditions or activities on the premises.

present value
The sum of money that, with compound interest, would amount to a specified sum at a specified future date; future value discounted to its value today. -- Also termed present worth.

prescriptive easement
An easement created from an open, adverse, and continuous use over a statutory period. -- Also termed easement by prescription; adverse easement. *See* adverse possession.

prima facie
adj. Sufficient to establish a fact or raise a presumption unless disproved or rebutted.

primary assumption of the risk
A legal conclusion that the defendant was not negligent because the defendant either did not owe a duty of care to the injured party or did not breach any duty owed. • Courts decide questions of duty through policy judgments, which include the relative balance between risks and utilities.

privacy
The condition or state of being free from public attention to intrusion into or interference with one's acts or decisions.

private necessity
A necessity that involves only the defendant's personal interest and thus provides only a limited privilege.

private nuisances
A condition that interferes with a person's enjoyment of property; especially, a structure or other condition erected or put on nearby land, creating or continuing an invasion of the actor's land and amounting to a trespass to it.

privilege
A special legal right, exemption, or immunity granted to a person or class of persons; an exception to a duty.

privity   The connection or relationship between two parties, each having a legally recognized interest in the same subject matter (such as a transaction, proceeding, or piece of property); mutuality of interest.

privity of contract   The relationship between the parties to a contract, allowing them to sue each other but preventing a third party from doing so. • The requirement of privity has been relaxed under modern laws and doctrines of implied warranty and strict liability, which allow a third-party beneficiary or other foreseeable user to sue the seller of a defective product.

pro rata   *adv.* Proportionately; according to an exact rate, measure, or interest. *See* ratable. -- *pro rata, adj.*

probative   *adj.* Tending to prove or disprove. • Courts can exclude relevant evidence if its probative value is substantially outweighed by the danger of unfair prejudice.

products liability   *n.* A manufacturer's or seller's tort liability for any damages or injuries suffered by a buyer, user, or bystander as a result of a defective product. • Products liability can be based on a theory of negligence, strict liability, or breach of warranty.

prophylactic   *adj.* Formulated to prevent something.

proximate cause   1. The causing or producing of an effect. 2. Causality.

public duty doctrine   The rule that a governmental entity (such as a state or municipality) cannot be held liable for an individual plaintiff's injury resulting from a governmental officer's or employee's breach of a duty owed to the general public rather than to the individual plaintiff. -- Also termed public-duty rule. *See* special-duty doctrine.

public necessity   A necessity that involves the public interest and thus completely excuses the defendant's liability.

public nuisance   An unreasonable interference with a right common to the general public, such as a condition dangerous to health, offensive to community moral standards, or unlawfully obstructing the public in the free use of public property. • Such a nuisance may lead to a civil injunction or criminal prosecution. -- Also termed common nuisance.

public policy   Broadly, principles and standards regarded by the legislature or by the courts as being of fundamental concern to the state and the whole of society.

punitive damages   Damages awarded in addition to actual damages when the defendant acted with recklessness, malice, or deceit; specifically, damages assessed by way of penalizing the wrongdoer or making an example to others.

quash   *vb.* 1. To annul or make void; to terminate. 2. To suppress or subdue; to crush.

ratification   1. Adoption or enactment, especially where the act is the last in a series of necessary steps or consents. 2. Confirmation and acceptance of a previous act, thereby making the act valid from the moment it was done. • This sense includes action taken by the legislature to make binding a treaty negotiated by the executive.

reasonable and ordinary care   As a test of liability for negligence, the degree of care that a prudent and competent person engaged in the same line of business or endeavor would exercise under similar circumstances. -- Also termed due care; ordinary care; adequate care; proper care. *See* reasonable person.

reasonable diligence
1. A fair degree of diligence expected from someone of ordinary prudence under circumstances like those at issue. 2. *See* due diligence.

rebuttable presumption
An inference drawn from certain facts that establish a prima facie case, which may be overcome by the introduction of contrary evidence. -- Also termed *prima facie* presumption; disputable presumption; conditional presumption; *praesumptio juris. Cf.* conclusive presumption.

recklessness
n. Conduct whereby the actor does not desire harmful consequence but nonetheless foresees the possibility and consciously takes the risk. • Recklessness involves a greater degree of fault than negligence but a lesser degree of fault than intentional wrongdoing.

release
n. 1. Liberation from an obligation, duty, or demand; the act of giving up a right or claim to the person against whom it could have been enforced. -- Also termed discharge; surrender. 2. The relinquishment or concession of a right, title, or claim.

remand
n. 1. Adoption or enactment, especially where the act is the last in a series of necessary steps or consents. 2. Confirmation and acceptance of a previous act, thereby making the act valid from the moment it was done. • This sense includes action taken by the legislature to make binding a treaty negotiated by the executive.

remittitur
1. An order awarding a new trial, or a damages amount lower than that awarded by the jury, and requiring the plaintiff to choose between those alternatives. 2. The process by which a court requires either that the case be retried or that the damages awarded by the jury be reduced. *Cf.* additur.

res ipsa loquitur　[Latin "the thing speaks for itself"] The doctrine providing that, in some circumstances, the mere fact of an accident's occurrence raises an inference of negligence so as to establish a *prima facie* case. -- Often shortened to *res ipsa.*

respondeat superior　[Law Latin "let the superior make answer"] The doctrine holding an employer or principal liable for the employee's or agent's wrongful acts committed within the scope of the employment or agency. — Also termed master–servant rule. *See* scope of employment.

respondent　1. The party against whom an appeal is taken; appellee. • In some appellate courts, the parties are designated as petitioner and respondent. In most appellate courts in the United States, the parties are designated as appellant and appellee. Often the designations depend on whether the appeal is taken by writ of *certiorari* (or writ of error) or by direct appeal. 2. The party against whom a motion or petition is filed. *Cf.* Petitioner. 3. At common law, the defendant in an equity proceeding. 4. Civil law. One who answers for another or acts as another's security.

reverse　*vb.* To overturn (a judgment) on appeal. The equivalent expression in British English is to allow the appeal.

riparian land　1. Land that includes part of the bed of a watercourse or lake. 2. Land that borders on a public watercourse or public lake whose bed is owned by the public.

satisfaction　*n.* The giving of something with the intention, express or implied, that it is to extinguish some existing legal or moral obligation. • Satisfaction differs from performance because it is always something given as a substitute for or equivalent of something else, while performance is the identical thing promised to be done. -- Also termed satisfaction of debt.

scope of employment The range of reasonable and foreseeable activities that an employee engages in while carrying out the employer's business; the field of action in which a servant is authorized to act in the master-servant relationship. *See respondeat superior. Cf.* Course of Employment; zone of employment.

secondary implied assumption of the risk 1. The act or an instance of voluntarily encountering a known unreasonable risk that is out of proportion to any advantage gained. • With secondary assumption of the risk, the fact-finder considers the reasonableness of the plaintiff's conduct in the particular case, balancing the risks and utilities under the circumstances. 2. An affirmative defense to an established breach of a duty, based on a claim that the plaintiff acted unreasonably in encountering a known risk. See contributory negligence.

servitude The condition of being a servant or slave.

settlement *n.* 1. The conveyance of property — or of interests in property — to provide for one or more beneficiaries, usually members of the settlor's family, in a way that differs from what the beneficiaries would receive as heirs under the statutes of descent and distribution.

severally *adj.* Distinctly; separately.

shocks the conscience To cause intense ethical or humanitarian discomfort. • This phrase is used as an equitable standard for gauging whether (1) state action amounts to a violation of a person's substantive-due-process rights, (2) a jury's award is excessive, (3) a fine or jail term is disproportionate to the crime, or (4) a contract is unconscionable. *See* Conscience of the Court.

shoplifting *n.* Theft of merchandise from a store or business; specifically, larceny of goods from a store or other commercial establishment by willfully taking and concealing the merchandise with the intention of converting the goods to one's personal use without paying the purchase price. *See* larceny.

show cause To produce a satisfactory explanation or excuse, usually in connection with a motion or application to a court.

simple negligence Negligence in which the actor is not aware of the unreasonable risk that he or she is creating, but should have foreseen and avoided it. -- Also termed inadvertent negligence.

sine qua non *n.* [Latin "without which not"] An indispensable condition or thing; something on which something else necessarily depends. — Also termed *conditio sine qua non*

slander *n.* 1. A defamatory assertion expressed in a transitory form, esp. speech. • Damages for slander -- unlike those for libel -- are not presumed and thus must be proved by the plaintiff (unless the defamation is slander *per se*).

slight negligence The failure to exercise the great care of an extraordinarily prudent person, resulting in liability in special circumstances (especially those involving bailments or carriers) in which lack of ordinary care would not result in liability; lack of great diligence.

slip and fall A lawsuit brought by a plaintiff for injuries sustained in slipping and falling, usually on the defendant's property.

social guest A guest who is invited to enter or remain on another person's property primarily for private entertainment as opposed to entertainment open to the general public. *See* licensee.

sovereign immunity 1. A government's immunity from being sued in its own courts without its consent. • Congress has waived most of the federal government's sovereign immunity. See Federal Torts Claim Act. 2. A state's immunity from being sued in federal court by the state's own citizens. -- Also termed government immunity; governmental immunity.

special damages Damages that are alleged to have been sustained in the circumstances of a particular wrong. • To be awardable, special damages must be specifically claimed and proved. -- Often shortened to specials. -- Also termed particular damages.

special relationship A nonfiduciary relationship having an element of trust, arising especially when one person trusts another to exercise a reasonable degree of care and the other knows or ought to know about the reliance. *Cf.* fiduciary relationship.

specific deterrence A goal of a specific conviction and sentence to dissuade the offender from committing crimes in the future.

spousal consortium A spouse's society, affection, and companionship given to the other spouse.

standard of care In the law of negligence, the degree of care that a reasonable person should exercise.

standing *n.* A party's right to make a legal claim or seek judicial enforcement of a duty or right. • To have standing in federal court, a plaintiff must show (1) that the challenged conduct has caused the plaintiff actual injury, and (2) that the interest sought to be protected is within the zone of interests meant to be regulated by the statutory or constitutional guarantee in question. — Also termed standing to sue. *Cf.* Justiciability.

stare decisis   *n.* [Latin "to stand by things decided"] The doctrine of precedent, under which it is necessary for a court to follow earlier judicial decisions when the same points arise again in litigation. See precedent; *non quieta movere.* *Cf. res judicata;* law of the case.

statute of limitations   A law that bars claims after a specified period; specifically, a statute establishing a time limit for suing in a civil case, based on the date when the claim accrued (as when the injury occurred or was discovered). • The purpose of such a statute is to require diligent prosecution of known claims, thereby providing finality and predictability in legal affairs and ensuring that claims will be resolved while evidence is reasonably available and fresh. -- Also termed nonclaim statute; limitations period. *Cf.* statute of repose.

statute of repose   A statute barring any suit that is brought after a specified time since the defendant acted (such as by designing or manufacturing a product), even if this period ends before the plaintiff has suffered a resulting injury. *Cf.* statute of limitations.

statutory rape   Unlawful sexual intercourse with a person under the age of consent (as defined by statute), regardless of whether it is against that person's will. • Generally, only an adult may be convicted of this crime. A person under the age of consent cannot be convicted. -- Also termed rape under age.

stevedores   Maritime law. A person or company that hires longshore and harbor workers to load and unload ships. *Cf.* seaman.

stipulation   *n.* 1. A material condition or requirement in an agreement; especially, a factual representation that is incorporated into a contract as a term.

strict liability Liability that does not depend on actual negligence or intent to harm, but that is based on the breach of an absolute duty to make something safe. • Strict liability most often applies either to ultrahazardous activities or in products-liability cases. -- Also termed absolute liability; liability without fault. *Cf.* fault liability.

subject matter jurisdiction Jurisdiction over the nature of the case and the type of relief sought, the extent to which a court can rule on the conduct of persons or the status of things. -- Also termed jurisdiction of the subject matter; jurisdiction of the cause; jurisdiction over the action. *Cf.* personal jurisdiction.

subjective standard A legal standard that is peculiar to a particular person and based on the person's individual views and experiences.

subpoena *vb.* 1. To call before a court or other tribunal by subpoena.

subrogation *n.* The substitution of one party for another whose debt the party pays, entitling the paying party to rights, remedies, or securities that would otherwise belong to the debtor. • For example, a surety who has paid a debt is, by subrogation, entitled to any security for the debt held by the creditor and the benefit of any judgment the creditor has against the debtor, and may proceed against the debtor as the creditor would.

subrogee One who is substituted for another in having a right, duty, or claim. • An insurance company frequently becomes a subrogee after paying a policy claim, as a result of which it is then in a position to sue a tortfeasor who injured the insured or otherwise caused harm.

substantial factor *n.* An agent or cause that contributes to a particular result.

sudden emergency doctrine	A legal principle exempting a person from the ordinary standard of reasonable care if that person acted instinctively to meet a sudden and urgent need for aid.
summary judgment	A judgment granted on a claim or defense about which there is no genuine issue of material fact and upon which the movant is entitled to prevail as a matter of law. • The court considers the contents of the pleadings, the motions, and additional evidence adduced by the parties to determine whether there is a genuine issue of material fact rather than one of law. This procedural device allows the speedy disposition of a controversy without the need for trial. — Also termed summary disposition; judgment on the pleadings. *See* judgment.
supersedeas bond	An appellant's bond to stay execution on a judgment during the pendency of the appeal. -- Often shortened to *supersedeas*. *Cf.* appeal bond.
superseding cause	An intervening act or force that the law considers sufficient to override the cause for which the original tortfeasor was responsible, thereby exonerating that tortfeasor from liability. -- Also termed sole cause. *Cf.* intervening cause.
supervisory writ	A writ issued to correct an erroneous ruling made by a lower court either when there is no appeal or when an appeal cannot provide adequate relief and the ruling will result in gross injustice.
supra	[Latin "above"] Earlier in this text; used as a citational signal to refer to a previously cited authority. *Cf. infra*.

survival action   A lawsuit brought on behalf of a decedent's estate for injuries or damages incurred by the decedent immediately before dying. • A survival action derives from the claim that a decedent would have had -- such as for pain and suffering -- if he or she had survived. In contrast is a claim that the beneficiaries may have in a wrongful-death action, such as for loss of consortium or loss of support from the decedent. *Cf.* wrongful death action.

survival statute   A law that modifies the common law by allowing certain actions to continue in favor of a personal representative after the death of the party who could have originally brought the action; especially, a law that provides for the estate's recovery of damages incurred by the decedent immediately before death. *Cf.* death statute.

survivorship   1. The state or condition of being the one person out of two or more who remains alive after the others die. 2. The right of a surviving party having a joint interest with others in an estate to take the whole. *See* right of survivorship.

tangible   *adj.* 1. Having or possessing physical form; corporeal. 2. Capable of being touched and seen; perceptible to the touch; capable of being possessed or realized. 3. Capable of being understood by the mind.

temporary damages   Damages allowed for an intermittent or occasional wrong, such as a real-property injury whose cause can be removed or abated.

temporary restraining order   A court order preserving the status quo until a litigant's application for a preliminary or permanent injunction can be heard. • A temporary restraining order may sometimes be granted without notifying the opposing party in advance. *Cf.* emergency protective order under PROTECTIVE ORDER. -- Abbr. TRO. -- Often shortened to restraining order.

tenant	*n.* One who holds or possesses lands or tenements by any kind of right or title.
third party beneficiary	A person who, though not a party to a contract, stands to benefit from the contract's performance.
third party complaint	A complaint filed by the defendant against a third party, alleging that the third party may be liable for some or all of the damages that the plaintiff is trying to recover from the defendant.
tort	1. A civil wrong, other than breach of contract, for which a remedy may be obtained, usually in the form of damages; a breach of a duty that the law imposes on persons who stand in a particular relation to one another.
tortfeasor	One who commits a tort; a wrongdoer.
trespass vi et armis	[Latin "with force and arms"] 1. At common law, an action for damages resulting from an intentional injury to person or property, especially if by violent means; trespass to the plaintiff's person, as in illegal assault, battery, wounding, or imprisonment, when not under color of legal process, or when the battery, wounding, or imprisonment was in the first instance lawful, but unnecessary violence was used or the imprisonment continued after the process had ceased to be lawful. 2. *See trespass quare clausum fregit.* • In this sense, the "force" is implied by the "breaking" of the close (that is, an enclosed area), even if no real force is used.
trespasser	One who commits a trespass; one who intentionally and without consent or privilege enters another's property. • In tort law, a landholder owes no duty to unforeseeable trespassers. *Cf.* invitee; licensee.

trespass
n. 1. An unlawful act committed against the person or property of another; especially, wrongful entry on another's real property. 2. At common law, a legal action for injuries resulting from an unlawful act of this kind. 3. Archaic. misdemeanor — trespass, *vb.* — trespassory, *adj.*

trespass on the case
At common law, an action to recover damages that are not the immediate result of a wrongful act but rather a later consequence. • This action was the precursor to a variety of modern-day tort claims, including negligence, nuisance, and business torts. -- Often shortened to case. -- Also termed action on the case; *breve de transgressione super casum.*

trust
n. 1. The right, enforceable solely in equity, to the beneficial enjoyment of property to which another person holds the legal title; a property interest held by one person (the trustee) at the request of another (the settlor) for the benefit of a third party (the beneficiary). • For a trust to be valid, it must involve specific property, reflect the settlor's intent, and be created for a lawful purpose. The two primary types of trusts are private trusts and charitable trusts.

vacate
vb. 1. To nullify or cancel; make void; invalidate. *Cf.* overrule. 2. To surrender occupancy or possession; to move out or leave.

vi et armis
[Latin "with force and arms"] 1. At common law, an action for damages resulting from an intentional injury to person or property, especially if by violent means; trespass to the plaintiff's person, as in illegal assault, battery, wounding, or imprisonment, when not under color of legal process, or when the battery, wounding, or imprisonment was in the first instance lawful, but unnecessary violence was used or the imprisonment continued after the process had ceased to be lawful. 2. *See trespass quare clausum fregit.* • In this sense, the "force" is implied by the "breaking" of the close (that is, an enclosed area), even if no real force is used.

vicarious *adj.* Performed or suffered by one person as substitute for another; indirect; surrogate.

vicarious liability Liability that a supervisory party (such as an employer) bears for the actionable conduct of a subordinate or associate (such as an employee) based on the relationship between the two parties. *See respondeat superior.*

vicious propensity An animal's tendency to endanger the safety of persons or property. See vicious animal..

vis major *n.* [Latin "a superior force"] 1. A greater or superior force; an irresistible or overwhelming force of nature; force majeure. *Cf.* Act of God. 2. A loss that results immediately from a natural cause without human intervention and that could not have been prevented by the exercise of prudence, diligence, and care. -- Also termed act of nature; act of providence; superior force; irresistible force; *vis divina.*

viz. *Abbr.* [Latin *videlicet*] Namely; that is to say.

waiver *n.* 1. The voluntary relinquishment or abandonment — express or implied — of a legal right or advantage; forefeiture. • The party alleged to have waived a right must have had both knowledge of the existing right and the intention of forgoing it. *Cf.* estoppel.

wanton *adj.* Unreasonably or maliciously risking harm while being utterly indifferent to the consequences.

warranty deed A deed containing one or more covenants of title; especially, a deed that expressly guarantees the grantor's good, clear title and that contains covenants concerning the quality of title, including warranties of seisin, quiet enjoyment, right to convey, freedom from encumbrances, and defense of title against all claims. -- Also termed *general warranty deed; full-covenant-and-warranty deed. Cf.* quitclaim deed; special warranty deed.

wherein *conj.* 1. In which; where. 2. During which. 3. How; in what respect. — wherein, *adv.*

wild animal 1. An animal that, as a matter of common knowledge, is naturally untamable, unpredictable, dangerous, or mischievous. *See ferae naturae.* 2. Any animal not statutorily designated as a domestic animal. -- Also termed wild creature.

willful *adj.* Voluntary and intentional, but not necessarily malicious. — Sometimes spelled wilful. *Cf.* wanton. — willfulness, *n.*

windfall An unanticipated benefit, usually in the form of a profit and not caused by the recipient.

workers' compensation A statute by which employers are made responsible for bodily harm to their workers arising out of and in the course of their employment, regardless of the fault of either the employee or the employer.

writ of *certiorari*   [Law Latin "to be more fully informed"] An extraordinary writ issued by an appellate court, at its discretion, directing a lower court to deliver the record in the case for review. • The writ evolved from one of the prerogative writs of the English Court of King's Bench, and in the United States it became a general appellate remedy. The U.S. Supreme Court uses *certiorari* to review most of the cases that it decides to hear. -- Abbr. *cert. Cf.* certification.

writ of trespass   *n.* 1. An unlawful act committed against the person or property of another; especially, wrongful entry on another's real property. 2. At common law, a legal action for injuries resulting from an unlawful act of this kind. 3. Archaic. misdemeanor. -- trespass, *vb.* -- trespassory, *adj.*

wrongdoer   *n.* One who violates the law. — wrongdoing, *n.*

wrongful birth   A lawsuit brought by parents against a doctor for failing to advise them prospectively about the risks of their having a child with birth defects.

wrongful conception   A lawsuit brought by a parent for damages resulting from a pregnancy following a failed sterilization. -- Also termed wrongful pregnancy action.

wrongful death   A statute authorizing a decedent's personal representative to bring a wrongful-death action for the benefit of certain beneficiaries. -- Formerly also termed death-damage statute.

zone of danger   The doctrine allowing the recovery of damages for negligent infliction of emotional distress if the plaintiff was both located in the dangerous area created by the defendant's negligence and frightened by the risk of harm.

Index

†